CASES IN
STRATEGIC MANAGEMENT

SEVENTH EDITION

CASES IN STRATEGIC MANAGEMENT

SEVENTH EDITION

PAUL W. BEAMISH

Associate Dean, Research
Richard Ivey School of Business
The University of Western Ontario

McGraw-Hill Ryerson

Toronto   Montreal   Boston   Burr Ridge IL   Dubuque IA   Madison WI   New York   San Francisco
St Louis   Bangkok   Bogatá   Caracas   Kuala Lumpur   Lisbon   London   Madrid   Mexico City
Milan   New Delhi   Santiago   Seoul   Singapore   Sydney   Taipei

Cases in Strategic Management
Seventh Edition

ISBN: 0-07-088957-0

1 2 3 4 5 6 7 8 9 10 TRI 0 9 8 7 6 5

Printed and bound in Canada

Vice President, Editorial and Media Technology: Patrick Ferrier
Executive Sponsoring Editor: Nicole Lukach
Sponsoring Editor: Kim Brewster
Marketing Manager: Kelly Smyth
Developmental Editor: Darren Hick
Senior Production Coordinator: Madeleine Harrington
Supervising Editor: Anne Nellis
Copy Editor: Jim Zimmerman
Cover Design: Greg Devitt
Interior Designer: Michelle Losier
Cover Image Credit: Coneyl Jay/Getty Images
Composition: Lynda Powell
Printer: Tri-Graphic Printing

National Library of Canada Cataloguing in Publication

Beamish, Paul W., 1953-
    Cases in strategic management / Paul W. Beamish. — 7th ed.

5th ed. published under title: Strategic management : text, readings
    and cases.
ISBN 0-07-088957-0

    1. Strategic planning—Canada—Case studies. 2. Industrial management—Canada—Case studies. I. Beamish, Paul W., 1953- . Stategic managment. II. Title.

HD30.28.B42 2004   658.4'012'0971   C2004-901084-0

To the memory of two splendid teachers:

John and Catherine Beamish

about the author

Paul W. Beamish is Associate Dean of Research and Development and professor of International Strategy at the Richard Ivey School of Business, University of Western Ontario. He is the author or co-author of 40 books, over 90 articles or contributed chapters, and 85 case studies. His articles have appeared in *Strategic Management Journal*, *Journal of International Business Studies*, *Academy of Management Journal*, *Academy of Management Review* and elsewhere. His consulting and management training activities have been in both the public and the private sector for such organizations as Boeing, Labatt/Interbrew, The World Bank, the Canadian Foreign Service Institute, and the Harvard Institute for International Development. He has received case writing awards from the European Foundation for Management Development, The Management Development Centre of Hong Kong, The Academy of International Business and the Administrative Sciences Association of Canada. He worked for the Procter & Gamble Company of Canada and Wilfrid Laurier University before joining Ivey's faculty in 1987. He is the founding Director of Ivey's Asian Management Institute.

contents

The case details the history and development of the company, highlighting the evolution of the corporate concept of a "third place," and the key individuals in the organization in this development. The second part of the case details the international expansion activities of the firm, highlighting the potential cultural and economic challenges which it may increasingly face as it expands to more traditional coffee-drinking markets, and low-income emerging markets. The third and final section of the case details the increasing pressure placed on Starbucks by the anti-globalization movement. Although Starbucks has actively pursued a number of socially responsible operating policies, such as the purchase of Fair-Trade coffee, the subsidization of health care facilities in Central America, and the introduction of a number of socially responsible coffee products in its stores, it continues to be the target of anti-globalization activities. The case concludes with the question as to whether the company will be able to continue to grow as rapidly and profitably as in the recent past as it reaches saturation points in the domestic market.

The case discusses the key elements of corporate and business strategy employed by LVMH. It first develops the context of the luxury business, providing an in-depth look at the performance drivers, key players and their strategies. Set in the landscape, it then examines the specific strategies adopted by the biggest player, LVMH. The company wants to double its current sales ($10 billion in an $80 billion industry) and profits by 2005. Towards this goal LVMH has entered into multiple business lines ranging from leather goods to wines and spirits to art auctions. Many of these acquisitions have come at steep premiums, and none have turned a profit yet. Investors and analysts feel that the company should divest some of its holding and get back to its roots in leather goods and wines. However, Mr. Arnault, the CEO of the company, feels that there are significant synergies that emerge when operating a portfolio of global brands across the entire landscape of luxury businesses. This sets the stage for a good evaluation of its value chain and value-adding activities, the promised synergies, and their potential impact on revenues and profits. It also raises questions on how LVMH can grow in this business, which geographic regions it should invest in, and which product-market it should retain.

The new Sears catalogue contained a 20-page section called "Elements." This section bore a striking resemblance to the format of an IKEA catalogue, and the furniture being offered was similar to IKEA's knocked-down, self-assembly line. The head of IKEA's North American operations wondered how serious Sears was about its new initiative, and what, if anything, IKEA should do in response.

The Newell Company, a multi-billion dollar company dealing in hardware and home furnishing, office products and housewares, was contemplating a merger with Rubbermaid, a renowned manufacturer of plastic products. Newell had a remarkable record of success in growth by acquisition, and Rubbermaid would mark a quantum step in this program. However, the purchase of Rubbermaid would pose a formidable challenge to Newell's capacity to integrate and strengthen acquisitions. Issues concerning corporate strategy and advantage are studied to determine the wisdom of the proposed merger.

Part 6 Strategy and Market Diversification

The CEO of Vincor was preparing for the board meeting to discuss the possible acquisition of Goundrey Wines, Australia. Vincor had embarked upon a strategic internationalisation plan in 2000, acquiring R.H. Phillips and Hogue in the United States. Although Vincor was the largest wine company in Canada and the fourth largest in North America, to be a major player, Vincor had to look beyond the region. The acquisition of Goundrey Wines in Australia would be the first step. Convincing the board would be difficult, as the United States was a close and attractive market and one where Vincor had already spent more than U.S.$100 million on acquisitions. In contrast, Australia was very far away.

In April 2003, the Council of Forest Industries of British Columbia (COFI) kicked off a new initiative, the Dream-Home-China project, to explore the Chinese forest products market. Several of COFI's 100-plus member companies were facing a decision on whether to participate in this project, or to pursue the world's largest potential market on their own.

A proposed joint-marketing venture would introduce Neilson brand chocolate bars to Mexican consumers. Pepsico Foods' Mexican subsidiary—already servicing 450,000 retail stores—has suggested a joint-branding agreement. However, Neilson must also consider an alternative distribution arrangement which would offer them greater control over their name, but at the cost of slower market access.

Palliser is a large, successful family-owned manufacturer in Manitoba that must respond to the increasingly global nature of its business. Its current business strategy, a product of international trade liberalization, was centred on exports to the U.S. However, management perceives the inherent risks and limitations connected with such a strategy and is faced with a foreign entry mode decision in Mexico and/or China.

Part 7 Using Technology for Strategic Advantage

One of Dow Jones & Company's most respected brands, The Wall Street Journal, is threatened by Internet news providers, including their own Interactive Edition. The case focuses on changing industry boundaries, new technology, potential cannibalization, and a threat to the company's traditional business model.

Trojan Technologies Inc., a manufacturer of water disinfection equipment, was seeking new areas for growth. China in particular offered an intriguing market because it had as much water as Canada, but forty times the population. Its economic boom would further stress current water resources. Management's task was to determine if Trojan's technology was appropriate for China, whether they should enter China, and if so, when, where, and how?

Part 8   Organization Design

Part 9 Governance/Boards of Directors

Jonathon Elderslie, recently retired after running his own company for 30 years, must decide what questions he should ask before deciding whether to join the board of directors of a publicly traded company. While flattered by the invitation, he has some concerns, given the current climate of concern about corporate governance and, more specifically, the views about the role of a director expressed by one of his business acquaintances.

Canada-based CCL Industries Inc. was one of the top packagers of consumer products in the world. Over its 50-year history, the company had grown to be a multinational firm, employing 7,500 people with over $1.6 billon in sales. CCL faces an uncertain environment that had already led to a major strategic reorientation when its plan to sell its largest division was cancelled. A global economic slowdown and lower consumer confidence, coupled with extensive international operations, significantly increased the risk to CCL's sales and already slim profits. In the past, the company prospered through product diversification gained through acquisition. The economic slowdown and increased uncertainty meant that this strategy may not be appropriate in the future. The chief executive officer recognizes that the time, attention, advice, composition, and operations of the board of directors would likely have to be altered to reflect this new reality.

Western Area Youth Services is a children's mental health centre and non-profit organization. The board of directors had been discussing the implications of a significant potential liability for staff salaries. A merger was identified as a possible solution, and the executive director of the centre was instructed by the board to begin the process of seeking a possible merger partner for the agency. She wonders how she might initiate the process on behalf of the board, and what she should look for in a potential partner. She also wonders how a merger might benefit the agency at this point in time.

Part 10 Managing Strategic Change

Maple Leaf Foods is Canada's largest and most dominant food processor. The recently appointed senior marketing director discovers on her first day on the job that the hot dog business at the company is completely broken: market share is down, profits are in free-fall, the products taste bad, there is a proliferation of brands, and her team is a mess. To make matters worse, she inherits a job where there is little market data in the files and little to go by to help guide her decisions. She must prepare a short-term plan and a clear strategy for the future.

preface and acknowledgements

This book was made possible with the academic and intellectual support from colleagues at the Ivey Business School at the University of Western Ontario (UWO), and others across the country. The primary stimulus for this book was the ongoing need for new, high-quality Canadian material.

Having decided to produce a book of cases in strategic management, a number of other decisions were made: (1) to bring together primarily Canadian cases written not only at Ivey, but by faculty across North America; (2) to include only decision-oriented cases, which arguably provide the best training for future managers; and (3) to include cases dealing with international business, high-technology industries, service industries, not-for-profit industries, and business ethics.

Much useful feedback was solicited and received on the sixth edition from colleagues at dozens of institutions across Canada. This included detailed reviews from:

Anthony Atkinson, University of Waterloo

Jack Ito, University of Regina

Don Ausman, University of Alberta

Elizabeth Croft, University of Northern British Columbia

Shamsud D. Chowdhury, Dalhousie University

Michele Bowring, University of Manitoba

Theodore Peridis, York University

Allan Matadeen, Simon Fraser University

Stuart Proudfoot, University of Calgary

Bryan J. Poulin, Lakehead University

Knud Jensen, Ryerson University

Ike Hall, British Columbia Institute of Technology

This edition contains 14 new cases. New cases were written or selected not only for their ability to achieve the desired pedagogical objectives, but with an eye to retaining student interest. Some of the new cases deal with such topical issues as terrorism, the Internet, volunteerism, and the environment; and are set in industries ranging from ice hockey to hot dogs to fireworks to television.

Professors wishing to delve deeply into certain industries have the option of reorganizing the available material. The book contains three or more cases in each of the following industry groups:

- publishing
- recreation
- furniture
- entertainment
- consumer products

The cases themselves have been organized into the 10 subject areas which follow. These subject areas follow closely the current, mainstream approach to the teaching of strategic management.

1. Introduction to the Role of the General Manager
2. Environmental and Industry Analysis
3. Strategy and the General Manager's Preferences/Values
4. From Values to Ethics to Social Responsibility
5. Strategy and Resources/Capabilities
6. Strategy and Market Diversification
7. Using Technology for Strategic Advantage
8. Organization Design
9. Governance/Boards of Directors
10. Managing Strategic Change

A comprehensive Case Teaching Notes package is available to text adopters. This Case Teaching Notes manual contains detailed teaching notes for each of the cases. It also includes an overview of the cases, possible industry groupings, case sequencing and possible course outlines, follow-up cases, and Web addresses.

I am indebted to several groups of people for assisting in the preparation of this book. First, I am grateful to the case contributors from Ivey, and wish to thank Tima Bansal, Terry Deutscher, Nick Fry, Jeffrey Gandz, Mary Heisz, Amy Hillman, the late Bud Johnston, Gerry Keim, Allen Morrison, and Larry Tapp, in addition to the following doctoral and research assistants: Claude Calleja, Nikhil Celly, Chris Chung, Gayle Duncan, Scott Hill, Barbara Jenkins, Akash Kapoor, Philip Antoine Kendis, Colleen Lief, Mope Ogunsulire, Marty Ostermiller, Gail Robertson, Ian Sullivan, Jingan Tang, and Shari Ann Wortel.
Cases were also contributed by colleagues from other institutions:

Mary Brooks, Dalhousie University
Cyril Bouquet, York University
Andrew Delios, National University of Singapore
Anthony Goerzen, University of Victoria
Trevor Hunter, King's College; UWO
Ruihua Jiang, Lehigh University
Geoffrey Lewis, University of Melbourne
Michael H. Moffett, Thunderbird, AGSIM
Kent E. Neupert, Boise State University
Detlev Nitsch, Wilfrid Laurier University
Thomas Poynter, St. John's, Newfoundland

Kannan Ramaswamy, Thunderbird, AGSIM
Joachim Schwass, IMD Switzerland
Ulrich Steger, IMD Switzerland
Robert W. Sexty, Memorial University
John Ward, IMD Switzerland
C. Patrick Woodcock, University of Ottawa

In addition, I wish to thank the various executives who provided the required access to complete the cases in this book, and to recognize those students on whom the cases were tested for classroom use.

I look forward to your feedback.

Paul W. Beamish

SUPERIOR SERVICE

Service takes on a whole new meaning with McGraw-Hill Ryerson and *Cases in Strategic Management*. More than just bringing you the textbook, we have consistently raised the bar in terms of innovation and educational research–both in management and in education in general. These investments in learning and the education community have helped us to understand the needs of students and educators across the country, and allowed us to foster the growth of truly innovative, integrated learning.

i-Learning Sales Specialist

Your Integrated Learning Sales Specialist is a McGraw-Hill Ryerson representative who has the experience, product knowledge, training, and support to help you assess and integrate any of our products, technology, and services into your course for optimum teaching and learning performance. Whether it's using our test bank software, helping your students improve their grades, or putting your entire course online, your *i*-Learning Sales Specialist is there to help you do it. Contact your local *i*-Learning Sales Specialist today to learn how to maximize all of McGraw-Hill Ryerson's resources!

i-Learning Services Program

McGraw-Hill Ryerson offers a unique *i*Services package designed for Canadian faculty. Our mission is to equip providers of higher education with superior tools and resources required for excellence in teaching. For additional information, visit www.mcgrawhill.ca/highereducation/eservices.

Teaching, Technology & Learning Conference Series

The educational environment has changed tremendously in recent years, and McGraw-Hill Ryerson continues to be committed to helping you acquire the skills you need to succeed in this new milieu. Our innovative Teaching, Technology & Learning Conference Series brings faculty together from across Canada with 3M Teaching Excellence award winners to share teaching and learning best practices in a collaborative and stimulating environment. Preconference workshops on general topics, such as teaching large classes and technology integration, will also be offered. We will also work with you at your own institution to customize workshops that best suit the needs of your faculty.

case 1 mGAMES

Jeffrey Lopez hung up the phone, leaned forward and buried his face in his hands. It seemed a challenge at this particular moment to try to remember why he had been so excited about his appointment as president and chief executive officer (CEO) of mGAMES (a developer of gaming software for mobile devices) just eight months ago. Lopez stood up from his large mahogany desk, walked to the window and looked out over the horizon towards Boston. It was 9:15 a.m. on Monday, July 22, 2002, and Lopez had just finished taking two telephone calls. The first had come from Benson Marks, principal shareholder and chairman of the board of mGAMES. In their call, Marks had told Lopez that he had just gotten off the phone with an old friend at Credit Suisse First Boston in New York. Specifics could not be provided, but rumors were circulating throughout the bank that a large and well-respected personal digital assistant PDA manufacturer was in the process of arranging financing to make a play for mGAMES. During the conversation, Marks reminded Lopez that he did not believe a takeover could be achieved without his consent—since he held 44.5 per cent of mGAMES shares—but he also acknowledged that over the past year he had become increasingly concerned with the performance of mGAMES. "Now Jeff . . . you know I'm 100 per cent behind you. But we've got to do something here. I need you to put a plan together and I'd like to see something within the next week."

The second call had come from Bjorger Pedersson, senior vice-president of product development with a large Scandinavian telecommunications company (sales of US$23 billion). Lopez had not spoken to Pedersson since first meeting him six months earlier at an industry conference in Las Vegas, but he remembered clearly how the two of them had seemed to really click.

Pedersson was clearly excited and got right to the point:

Jeffrey, our people have been looking at your organization now for the past five months. We've been trying to identify potential strategic partners for game

Scott Hill prepared this case under the supervision of Professor Allen Morrison solely to provide material for class discussion. The authors do not intend to illustrate either effective or ineffective handling of a managerial situation. The authors may have disguised certain names and other identifying information to protect confidentiality.

IVEY

Richard Ivey School of Business
The University of Western Ontario

development, and mGAMES is No. 1 on our list. We want to work with you. In fact, we are thinking about an exclusive agreement that would essentially take up all of your capacity. We've got $70 million set aside for this to help set you up… and we've also already allocated some space for you in our new research facility in Menlo Park, California.

We'd like you to fly here as soon as possible to begin discussions. This could be very big. Our projections show that mobile gaming will be a $6 billion market in five years. As our exclusive partner, the upside in this deal for you guys is enormous.

I know we are jumping the gun a little. But our board wants us to move as quickly as possible, and I am looking for a partner who understands the importance of speed. I've got strict orders to have an agreement in place—with some-one—within 45 days.

When the conversation with Pedersson ended, Lopez was clearly excited. How-ever, as he looked again out the window, his ears resonated with the final words he had heard during the earlier conversation with Benson Marks: "mGAMES needs a plan that it can win with! Not only now, but for years to come."

PDAs, MOBILE PHONES AND HANDHELD GAMING DEVICES

Beginning in the mid-1990s, handheld devices—PDAs and mobile phones—had be-come the largest new consumer-based technology craze worldwide. By the end of 2001, it was estimated that over seven million mobile phones were manufactured and shipped worldwide every week. PDAs were also growing in popularity, and though at the end of 2001 only 28 million total units had been cumulatively sold, projections were that another 10 million units would be shipped during 2002.

There were some geographic differences in the adoption of various handheld units. Most Asian, European and Middle Eastern consumers had been early to adopt mobile phones and seemed reluctant to buy into the concept of the PDAs. By 2001, mobile phones had become an essential part of their lifestyle, even to the extent that the qual-ity of any given individual's mobile phone was often recognized as a status symbol. The weak adoption of PDAs in these parts of the world was partially due to the fact that early PDAs offered software in English only.

In contrast, North Americans were PDA-crazy, being particularly attracted to the potential for the power of PC-type functionality in the palm of their hands. Com-pared to Asians and Europeans, North Americans had been relatively slow to adopt mobile phones. One reason for this was because of industry restructuring following the breakup of AT&T and the repositioning of the Baby Bells. The result was not only consumer uncertainty but also a range of often confusing and expensive calling plans. Another reason for the comparatively slow adoption of cell phone technolo-gies was the bulkiness of early mobile phones. However, by 2002, the market in North America had become essentially saturated with many wireless plans offering even lower long-distance rates than wired alternatives.

With North American cellular markets maturing and growth of PDAs accelerating, there was great uncertainty as to who would win out in the future of the handheld de-vice business. Some observers predicted that rather than one format conquering the other, they would all add features and begin to look and perform similarly. Indeed, convergence between mobile phone and PDA technologies was occurring on all fronts. According to Phil Redman of The Gartner Group, "the handset (mobile phone) manufacturers are gunning to take on the PDAs and vice versa. Handsets are simply becoming wireless PDAs."[1]

By 2002, an increasing number of new mobile phones offered built-in personal planning software packages, and a greater number of new PDAs offered short message service (SMS), voice and/or e-mail communication capabilities. In an exciting yet ambiguous market environment, the only certainty was that consumers were getting tired of carrying multiple devices around.

Convergence in the industry was also occurring when gaming functionality was considered. Nintendo's portable Gameboy system had long since offered personal planning and task list cartridges, and rumors were now circulating that the new Gameboy Advance system—to be released in the fall of 2002—would also offer wireless communication capability. Telecom manufacturers like Ericsson and Nokia were also reportedly engaged in the development of handheld gaming devices that had advanced gaming controls, wireless communication capability and PDA functionality. Handspring's new model had a slot to accept cartridges for playing games and running applications, and Palm had also added card slots to its latest models. David Grasior, president of wireless platform provider Synovial, asserted that "the handheld device of the future will do the things that keep you entertained when you're away from your PC and productive when you don't have a PC handy."[2]

The ongoing convergence of gaming devices, PDA and mobile phones is shown in Figure 1 below:

Figure 1   Convergence in the Handheld Industry

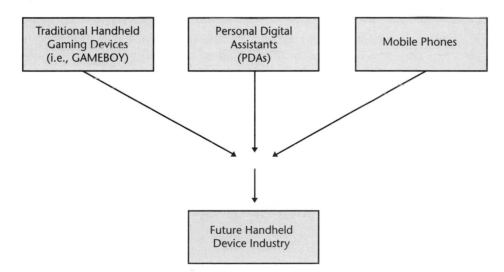

---

[1]Infoworld, November 26, 2001, p.1.

[2]Computer Games Magazine, December 6, 2001, p.2.

Competition in the emerging "handheld device industry" was fierce. Essentially, every established PC manufacturer, every telecom manufacturer, most electronics manufacturers and many others sought to become players in this multibillion-dollar segment. New technologies and new models were constantly being released. Color capability, communication capabilities, screen size, processor speed, RAM capacity, overall size of the unit and total functionality were all key criteria in the consumer's purchase decision.

Like many others, Alex Green, vice-president of business development for Motorola, believed that gaming functionality would become increasingly important in the market for handheld devices. He summarized where he saw this industry heading:

> [The future will bring us] cell phones with the power of an Xbox, PDAs on which you could play multiplayer Half-Life, with users all over the world, in real time, with real time taunting over the microphone.[3]

MOBILE GAMING

Handheld gaming devices of one variety or another had been around for several decades. Electronic gaming devices were a big hit when they first arrived on the market in the mid-1970s and were fashioned so that each device was its own game. It did not take long for the major electronics manufacturers to realize the market potential for these electronic games, and soon thereafter, handheld electronic gaming became a multimillion-dollar industry. As technology evolved, more competitors entered the market. To compete, game manufacturers rolled out ever-more complex games, leading industry sales to skyrocket. Things looked very promising for these manufacturers—until Nintendo revolutionized the market for handheld gaming devices with the launch of the cartridge-based Gameboy system in the early 1990s. The Gameboy system captivated young consumers, providing them with the new-found ability to play multiple games with advanced graphics on a single handheld gaming device. By 1995, Nintendo possessed over 85 per cent share of the handheld gaming device market.

However, like console-based gaming, the market for handheld games on the Gameboy device was somewhat fickle. Consumers constantly demanded more advanced technology including improved performance controls, greater processor speeds and better graphics. While new and exciting games were absolutely critical to the success of any handheld gaming device, the pattern was consistent: after a couple strong years with any particular hardware product, sales would flatten until something bigger and better was released.

In the late 1990s, the first wave of what some called "the gaming-generation" arrived in the workplace, in conjunction with technology advances and the increasing popularity of mobile phones and PDAs. Game designers and manufacturers soon began to realize the huge upside potential of wireless gaming on handheld devices. In fact, many believed that with the continuous influx of the gaming-generation into the working world, it would actually be wireless gaming functionality that would become the most important driver in the success of any handheld device. In 2001, Datamonitor Research projected that wireless gaming would become a $6-billion market worldwide by 2005, with four out of every five handheld device users playing wireless games. [4]

---

[3]Computer Games Magazine, "Gaming Gifts on the Go," June 12, 2001, p.2.

[4]Wireless Review; Overland Park, February 1, 2001; Betsy Harter, p.1.

Despite the longer-term promise, in 2002, games designed for mobile phones and PDAs were a far cry from the action-packed games available on Gameboy or other hand-held gaming devices. Game developers were still restricted by network and device limitations. As a result, there was some uncertainty as to which market segment would be the first to adopt the concept of wireless (interactive) gaming. When speaking about this market, the president of one mobile game development company argued:

> [The hand-held segment] is not—nor will it ever be—the 'gamer' market for people who play Quake, Ultima, Everquest and Doom. It's about games that everybody already knows how to play. People think it takes complex games to get people hooked. It doesn't. People also get hooked on very fun, simple games. Our research shows that 80 per cent of people play these familiar games.[5]

Other industry insiders disagreed. They believed technology improvements within the handheld device industry would captivate even the most hard-core gamers. The president of a major wireless airtime provider commented:

> Those guys still have to get up and go to the bathroom, and they have to get more Cheetos. You don't want to lose track of the game while you're getting a Coke and a 14-pound bag of M&M's. If you play Diablo, and someone would let you do it wirelessly from a PDA, would you pay $9.95 to do it? You better believe it![6]

In short, while there were too many variables to allow an accurate assessment of how the market for wireless gaming would play itself out, those closest to the industry considered the $6-billion projection by 2005 to be conservative. Perhaps Greg Costikyan, chief design officer for unplugged Games—the individual regarded as the pre-eminent authority in the wireless gaming industry—summed things up best: "Someone's going to make a lot of money here."

mGAMES

The mGAMES company developed, manufactured and distributed gaming software for various handheld and mobile devices. In 2001, net company sales reached $60.04 million and operating profits were $8.87 million. (See Exhibits 1, 2 and 3 for a review of mGAMES' financial performance.) In July 2002, mGAMES had 92 employees divided among software development, operations, marketing, sales and service. With the exception of five regional sales managers, all employees were based at company headquarters. Just over 70 per cent of company revenue came from sales in the United States and Canada, 20 per cent came from Europe and 10 per cent came from Japan.

The company began operating independently in 1995 as a wholly owned affiliate of BHM Inc. BHM was a video game development company that started up in 1984 in Hastings, Massachusetts, by Benson H. Marks, using inheritance money he had received from the sale of his grandfather's extensive collection of classic cars. Marks, who in 1984 was 42 years old, held a master's degree in computer engineering from the University of Waterloo in Canada and an MBA degree from the Massachusetts Institute of Technology in Boston.

With a personal interest in video games and first-hand knowledge of the spectacular financial success realized by companies such as Commodore and Atari,

---

[5]Ibid. p.2.
[6]Ibid. p.3.

Marks visualized an incredible future for the video game industry. He anticipated software would absorb the bulk of industry profits and that the greatest profits would come to firms that developed niche and game-based software. In May 1984, Marks launched BHM by hiring four graduates from MIT's combined computer science/computer engineering program. Noal Fisher, a 29-year-old computer engineer, was appointed general manager of software operations with a mandate to lead the charge in the development of video games that would, in Marks' words, "give kids something to really talk about."

From 1984 to 1994, BHM's software division experienced several ups and downs in its quest to develop hit video games. All BHM games that were deemed to have potential to become hits were sold or licensed to companies including the likes of Nintendo and Sega. These companies would then rebrand or relabel the games for distribution under their own name. In total, BHM saw 34 of its games brought to market and sold over 4.7 million copies worldwide in this nine-year period of time. Beginning in 1994, the company also began to market games under its own BHM brand. The advantage of self-marketing was that it allowed software companies to sell successful games (with some modifications) on multiple hardware platforms. Over time, the major hardware manufacturers also developed their own in-house software divisions to compete against the independent vendors. What emerged was a complex system whereby companies like Nintendo and Sega developed some proprietary games and contracted for the development of other games. In addition, independent companies like BHM developed and sold their own branded games and essentially worked as contractors to balance out their business portfolio.

Despite the early growth of BHM, Marks constantly wondered about the future of his business, specifically, the potential for new gaming applications. BHM's game development costs were rising year after year in the face of increased competition and more complex technologies. Along with increased development costs came bigger gambles on the next "great game." Failure could be devastating: successful games would gush cash for the company, particularly given the low variable costs of production (less than five per cent).

In early 1994, Marks received a call from Ichiro Hasegawa, senior vice-president with a major Japanese entertainment hardware and software company. Hasegawa expressed the organization's interest to enter into an arrangement with BHM to modify a number of its games for distribution in Japan. In addition, Hasegawa indicated his company's interest in starting a mobile gaming unit that would design and manufacture hand-held gaming devices. Marks handpicked five of his top software developers and announced the beginning of a new mobile gaming division and the acquisition of additional space for a small-cartridge manufacturing facility. Noal Fisher was assigned to be the division's director. From 1993 to 1994, the division modified and manufactured 26 game cartridges from the BHM library for the Japanese company, generating average annual sales of $12.1 million and pre-tax profits of $4.3 million

With this success, in 1995, the mobile gaming division was spun off into mGAMES, a wholly owned affiliate of BHM. Fisher was appointed president and CEO and Marks became chairman of the board. By this time, the software engineering staff had increased fivefold to 26 people. Twelve individuals were employed in manufacturing and shipping, and six more served as full-time sales and customer service representatives.

Over time, additional customers were added to mGAMES roster. In 1997, Marks took mGAMES public, selling some 55.5 per cent of his shares in the process. At the time, net sales were $33.1 million, and operating profits were $7.6 million. In looking back at the events surrounding the public offering, Marks commented:

We decided to take it public because the mobile gaming industry had such a promising future. The projections I'd seen suggested that new mobile products and associated gaming applications would cause the market to grow to the billion-dollar level in the next five years. At the time of the initial offering, the stock was trading at 40 times its earnings. My other businesses weren't coming even close to doing that well. This was a hot industry and the P/E multiple was outstanding. I also thought that with publicly traded shares, it would be easier to secure financing for our long-term growth.

In retrospect, the timing of the IPO might have been a mistake. Back then, Palm had sales of a couple million. Well look at them today! Also, no one thought games would ever be played on cell phones like they are today.

In taking mGAMES public, Marks was able to maintain effective control because no other single shareholder held more than three per cent of the stock.

Not long after the IPO, however, mGAMES' sales began to waver. Demand for its games tapered off towards the end of 1998, and management was finding it increasingly difficult to deal with customers like Nintendo and Sega. As a result, analysts had downgraded the stock to a sell rating, and Benson Marks found himself again on a quest for new gaming applications.

It was during a fall fishing trip in the Florida Keys in 1998 that Marks had the fortune of meeting Nathan Dorward, a senior executive with a major PDA manufacturer. Dorward talked about his company's forays into the development of "full-fledged computers that would rest in the palm of your hand." Dorward was also familiar with recent developments in wireless communications, and he raved to Marks about the potential for these hand-held computers to "talk to one another wirelessly through the air." Soon thereafter, Marks returned to Hastings, excited about the associated potential for new gaming applications.

In early 1998, mGAMES introduced four new PDA-based games, all downloadable over the Internet. Three of the games were designed to be used on machines that used Palm-based operating systems; the fourth game was designed for a new PDA operating system being developed by Microsoft. The games generated $4.9 million in new sales and, by the end of 1999, the stock was back on track. In the year 2000, mGAMES signed development contracts with a total of five global companies interested in tapping into the PDA gaming market.

CHANGES IN TOP MANAGEMENT

In October of 2001, Noal Fisher announced that he would be stepping down as president of mGAMES to assume a senior executive position with a major California-based technology company. The move was a surprise to his staff who believed that Fisher had seemed happier than he had been in some time. When queried at his going-away party, his response was "the time just seems right. We are coming off some important successes and I am ready for my next big challenge. Besides, I have always wanted to get closer to 'the valley.'" Benson Marks' public statements reflected his appreciation for all that Fisher had achieved, and he offered Fisher his best wishes in his new position.

One month later, Marks appointed 39-year-old Jeffrey Lopez to the vacated position of president and CEO of mGAMES. Lopez, who was at the time serving as the vice-president of sales and marketing at mGAMES, assumed his new duties on November 5, 2001.

Lopez was born in Boston and graduated from the University of Massachusetts with an undergraduate degree in computer science. After graduating, he entered the MBA program at New York University and graduated in the top 10 per cent of his 1991 class. Interested in working in the computer industry, Lopez moved to Seattle to join Microsoft. Over the next several years, Lopez took on increasingly senior positions at Microsoft, including management positions in marketing, sales and business development. Lopez was described by his friends as "very smart," "a workaholic," "driven," and "at times hot-headed."

Lopez first became acquainted with Benson Marks at a trade show in Orlando in 1993. The men kept in touch over the next three years and, in 1997, Marks asked whether Lopez would ever be interested in working for mGAMES. "He had the track record and experience to lead the company into the future of the mobile game development industry. He was my first choice for the job." One month later, Lopez joined the company in the newly created position of vice-president of sales and marketing. Lopez explained his reason for joining mGAMES:

> I guess part of what intrigued me was wanting to be a big fish in a much smaller pond. I was looking for a company where I had a lot more autonomy and could have a bigger impact. I also could see that mGAMES was in a fantastic industry segment. Another reason I took the job—on top of the $150,000 signing bonus—was that I missed living in the East. My parents were in the Boston area and were getting older. I wanted to be closer to them.

The majority of mGAMES' employees were extremely pleased with the appointment. David Salt, mGAMES' chief financial officer (CFO) reported:

> I think Marks made the right decision in picking Lopez. The president needs to be someone who will move mGAMES towards the future of the mobile gaming industry. Jeff has the experience and credibility. I think he will be the guy to initiate change and listen to the ideas, not only of customers—but employees as well.

EMERGING CHALLENGES

In assuming his new position, Lopez was aware of several challenges facing the company. One problem was the escalating costs of developing new games. The company's best selling game, Messenger of the Deep, accounted for nearly 17 per cent of mGAMES' 2001 sales, representing approximately 883,000 units at $11.40 each. (More complex variations of Messenger of the Deep were also manufactured by sister company BHM for the Sony PlayStation and Nintendo 64, with an average retail price of $45.95.) While Messenger was a solid performer, it was by no means a blockbuster. True blockbuster games generated sales of over three million cartridges and provided enormous cash flow.

NEW GAME DEVELOPMENT

Cash flow was essential for funding new games. In 2001, development costs in the industry averaged over $600,000 for each new mobile game, up almost 300 per cent since the mid-1990s. While mGAMES was able to piggyback on the full versions of some BHM games developed for Sony's Playstation or the new Nintendo Game Cube, portable games had to be much simpler, and the crossover potential was minimal. Also, as separate companies, mGAMES had to pay market-based fees to BHM to license its games. And even though mGAMES had an inside track on accessing BHM's "hits," by the time they were identified as hits and then converted to run-on mobile devices, they were usually on the downward side of customer interest. To complicate matters, hardware advances pioneered by Sony, Nintendo and more recently by Microsoft had significantly raised customer demands for faster and ever more elaborate mobile games. As the complexity of the development process increased, so too did development costs. Of mGAMES' library of 117 games, only seven had been introduced to the market in 2001, and by mid-2002, only three new games had come out.

INTERNAL ISSUES

The company was having internal problems with production and inventory control. All sales of video games were subject to extensive performance parameters, and rejected cartridges became the sole financial burden of mGAMES. In 2001, mGAMES' rejection rates were nearly twice the industry average. Some blamed cartridge labelling and packaging problems for high rejection rates. Others blamed software glitches that caused almost 30 per cent of PDA customers to have their systems lock up in downloading games from the Internet. While the Internet downloading problem had been rectified, the cartridge labelling problems continued.

In addition to quality control problems, the sales staff frequently blamed software developers for producing inferior games with weak "look and feel." Software developers, in turn, blamed the sales and marketing staff for ineffective research and for weak customer contacts. The production department was often blamed either for over-producing or for not having the right products available when needed. When Lopez met individually with managers to discuss possible solutions, he was disappointed with their responses. Shelley Coutu, vice-president of product development commented:

> Pressure from the sales staff to have new products developed or to increase production is unrealistic. I don't think they understand what goes into developing the product. This isn't like the old days when we were developing Pong-like games. These games are incredibly complex and the worse thing that could happen once the project ships is to find a software glitch.

Mike Colbert, vice-president of production, argued:

> My life would be a lot simpler if sales could just give us accurate forecasts. It is impossible to plan without knowing what the customer wants. I've lost 20 per cent of my staff over the past eight months because they are tired of putting in unplanned 16-hour days. A lot of my people are getting demoralized.

In June 2002, tensions had risen to a boiling point. The monthly meeting of the executive council (Lopez, plus the CFO and all six vice-presidents) had ended badly when Coutu and Peter Ames, vice-president of sales, got into a shouting match. For the past nine months, sales of games for Sony's Playstation had not kept up with the growth in hardware sales. When pressed for a reason, Ames and Coutu pointed the finger of blame at each other, and things quickly went from bad to worse. After the meeting, David Salt huddled with Lopez to share his observations:

> These kinds of conflicts have to end. I don't know why Noal Fisher ever promoted Colbert to the job. Quite frankly he needs to be replaced. His outburst was out of line and he really adds nothing to the team.

Lopez, who was relatively new to the company, was still trying to sort out the people and personalities. Since taking over, he and Salt had become good friends and he welcomed the private chats they seemed to have on an increasingly frequent basis. While he agreed that Colbert's reactions were inappropriate, he thought that Coutu could have been more helpful as well, and he was puzzled as to why Salt had such a one-sided interpretation of events.

Despite these problems, there was some excitement within the organization around the current ramp-up project the company had undertaken in preparation for the launch of Nintendo's new Gameboy Advance system. Preliminary reviews of that system had been spectacular. Sega was also developing a competitive system and had made it clear that it would also like mGAMES to continue to be involved in its business. Industry analysts were projecting revitalization in the market for handheld gaming devices, and market analysts projected a promising future for mGAMES. Early estimates around the market size for games developed for the new Nintendo system alone were in the $1-billion range over the next two years.

Before July 22, 2002, Lopez had intended to focus his short-term efforts on addressing the mounting internal problems facing mGAMES and by focusing on the handheld gaming device segment. However, after taking the two telephone calls he'd received that morning, this priority now seemed to fade.

OTHER CONSIDERATIONS

As part of the Gameboy Advance ramp-up project, Lopez recognized that mGAMES would require additional office and research and development space in order to support the major new initiative into wireless gaming applications anticipated for the new Nintendo system. Lopez and Salt had done some preliminary budgeting; they were projecting the need to spend $1.2 million more on research and development during the remainder of 2002 and $3.1 million in 2003. Together with increased investment in sales and manufacturing, plus factoring in added overhead costs, Lopez figured that a net new investment of about $5.6 million would be required over the next 18 months to move the company to the forefront of wireless mobile gaming. These numbers were very preliminary and were to be the focus of the next planned executive committee meeting in early August.

Related to the expansion, Lopez had just learned that the tenant in the top two floors (18,000 square feet) of the mGAMES office building had just gone bankrupt. Lopez had received confirmation from the building manager that a significant discount on mGAMES overall price per square foot was theirs for the taking if they agreed to take both floors. Lopez figured they would only need one-half of the additional square footage (9,000 square feet) now but that the additional space might be desirable in another six months. The building manager was pushing mGAMES for a three-year commitment and indicated that if he did not have a contract signed before July 30, 2002, he would turn it over to another company that had already expressed an interest in taking over both floors.

WEIGHING OPTIONS

Lopez was a believer in the future of wireless gaming. He believed in the growth projected for the industry in the next five-year period and was eager for mGAMES to become a major player in that growth. Like everyone else who worked around the industry, he was unsure how the whole technology convergence would play out. However, with the number of mobile phones that were being shipped every week, he suspected the telecom manufacturers might have the advantage in the long run. In the nearer term, however, most observers predicted that the action would most likely be focused on the new generation of gaming devices just hitting the market. Here, the market would include new cartridge-based games plus downloadable and wireless games. Several other members of the mGAMES management team, as well as two prominent members of the company's board of directors, were also extremely excited about the company's forays into wireless gaming—particularly the recent development agreements that had been signed with the PDA manufacturers.

However, Jane Parkes, mGAMES' vice-president of marketing, was far less optimistic. She was concerned about the validity of the projections for the future of wireless gaming, particularly the feasibility of wireless gaming on mobile phones. Small screen size and Internet access fees were viewed as major obstacles to mobile phone-based gaming. Lopez was aware, however, that Parkes was extremely excited about the new Gameboy Advance system and the associated new opportunities that mGAMES would expect to enjoy upon its launch. Parkes had clearly expressed her belief that mGAMES' hopes to improve upon its 7.3 per cent market share in this segment would rest on the success of this launch. Any investment in new wireless technology would not only be expensive and technically risky, but would detract from the company's current focus on cartridge and downloadable games.

As Lopez stared out the window, he reflected on the road that mGAMES had travelled. He knew that the calls he had received that morning meant that mGAMES could no longer continue to cater to all the handheld device manufacturers. It was time to make some choices. He clearly understood that the organization had Nintendo and Sega to thank for its previous success, and he tried to predict the ripple effect of breaking ties with these Japanese manufacturers. While no one could be certain what the future would hold for mobile gaming, most everyone in the industry believed that the future was bright, and Lopez wanted mGAMES to play a big part in it.

exhibit 1 Income Statement (in millions of dollars)

	1995	1996	1997	1998	1999	2000	2001
Net Sales	16.81	22.65	33.13	41.09	45.81	55.89	60.04
Cost of Goods Sold	6.40	9.33	16.84	19.74	22.96	27.50	30.12
Gross Profit	10.41	13.32	16.29	21.35	22.85	28.39	29.92
Selling & Admin Expenses	2.31	3.11	5.22	7.94	8.23	11.07	12.26
R&D Expenses	1.26	1.97	2.86	3.91	4.53	6.64	7.67
Depreciation & Amortization	0.35	0.51	0.61	0.72	0.80	1.07	1.12
Operating Profit	6.49	7.73	7.60	8.78	9.29	9.61	8.87
Total Interest	0.12	0.29	0.38	0.43	0.48	0.70	0.76
Non-Op income / Expenses	0.21	0.46	0.89	1.13	1.27	1.43	1.50
Pretax Income	6.16	6.98	6.33	7.22	7.54	7.48	6.61
After Tax Income	3.92	5.61	5.06	6.35	6.40	6.02	5.44

exhibit 2   Unit and Dollar Sales

	1995	1996	1997	1998	1999	2000	2001
Unit Sales (in millions of units)	1.42	2.12	2.79	3.55	4.2	4.16	3.89
Sales (in $ millions)	17.26	23.45	33.28	41.32	48.66	58.13	63.01

exhibit 3   2001 Balance Sheet (in millions of dollars)

Assets		Liabilities	
Cash and Equivalents	0.70	Notes Payable	1.20
Accounts Receivable	4.52	Accounts Payable	4.96
Inventories	6.12	Accrued Expenses	3.96
Other Current Assets	9.56	Taxes Payable	1.81
		Other Current Liabilities	1.21
Total Current Assets	**20.90**		
		Total Current Liabilities	**13.14**
Gross Plant	6.74		
Accumulated Depreciation	−1.75	Deferred Taxes	0.90
Net Plant	4.99	Long-term Debt	8.20
Deferred Charges	0.46	Other Long-term Liabilities	0.62
Intangible Leases	31.50		
Other Long-term Assets	0.32	**Total Liabilities**	**22.86**
Total Assets	**63.16**		
		Equity	
		Preferred Stock	27.00
		Common Stock	7.00
		Retained Earnings	5.70
		Other Liabilities	0.60
		Total Equity	**40.30**
		Total Liabilities and Equity	**63.16**

case 2 Coral Divers Resort

Jonathon Greywell locked the door on the equipment shed and began walking back along the boat dock to his office. He thought about the matters that had weighed heavily on his mind during the last few months. Over the years, Greywell had established a solid reputation for the Coral Divers Resort as a safe and knowledgeable scuba diving resort. It offered not only diving, but a beachfront location. As a small but well-regarded all-around dive resort in the Bahamas, many divers had come to prefer his resort to other crowded tourist resorts in the Caribbean.

However, over the last three years, revenues had declined and, for 1995, bookings were flat for the first half of the year. Greywell felt he needed to do something to increase business before things got worse. He wondered if he should add some specialized features to the resort that would distinguish it from others. One approach was to focus on family outings. Rascals in Paradise, a travel company that specialized in family diving vacations, had offered to help him convert his resort to one which specialized in family diving vacations. They had shown him the industry demographics that indicated that families were a growing market segment (see Exhibit 1 on the next page) and made suggestions about what changes would need to be made at the resort. They had even offered to create menus for children and to show the cook how to prepare the meals.

Another potential strategy for the Coral Divers Resort was adventure diving. Other resort operators in the Bahamas were offering adventure-oriented deep depth dives, shark dives, and night dives. The basic ingredients for adventure diving, reef sharks in the waters near New Providence and famous deep water coral walls, were already in place. However, either of these strategies, family or adventure, would require changes and additions to his current operations. He was not sure whether any of the changes was worth the time and investment or whether he should instead try to improve upon what he was already doing.

Professors Kent E. Neupert of the University of Houston and Paul W. Beamish of the University of Western Ontario prepared this case solely to provide material for class discussion. The research assistance of Tara Hanna is gratefully acknowledged. The authors do not intend to illustrate either effective or ineffective handling of a managerial situation. The authors may have disguised certain names and other identifying information to protect confidentiality.

IVEY

Richard Ivey School of Business
The University of Western Ontario

Version: (A) 2001-08-17

exhibit 1   U.S. Population Demographics and Income Distribution:
1970, 1980, and 1990

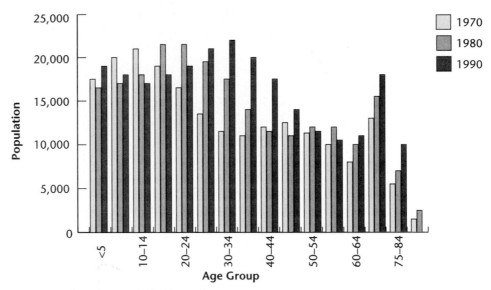

* numbers are in the thousands
* from the American Almanac, 1994-1995, from US Bureau of Census

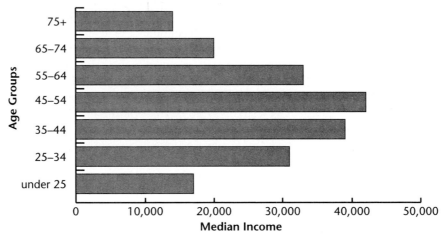

* from The Official Guide to the American Marketplace, 1992

A final option, and one which he had only recently thought about, was to leave New Providence and try to relocate. At issue here was how much he might be able to recover if he sold Coral Divers and whether better opportunities existed elsewhere in the Bahamas or around the Caribbean.

SCUBA DIVING INDUSTRY OVERVIEW

Skin diving is an underwater activity of ancient origin in which a diver swims freely, unencumbered by lines or air hoses. Modern skin divers use three pieces of basic equipment: a face mask for vision, webbed rubber fins for propulsion, and a snorkel tube for breathing just below the water's surface. The snorkel is a plastic tube shaped like a J and fitted with a mouthpiece. When the opening of the snorkel is above water, a diver will be able to breathe. For diving to greater depths, the breath must be held; otherwise, water will enter the mouth through the snorkel.

SCUBA diving provides divers with the gift of time to relax and explore the underwater world without having to surface for their next breath. "Scuba" is an acronym for "**S**elf-**C**ontained **U**nderwater **B**reathing **A**pparatus." While attempts to perfect this type of apparatus date from the early 20th century, it was not until 1943 that the most famous scuba, or Aqualung, was invented by the Frenchmen Jacques-Yves Cousteau and Emil Gagnan. The Aqualung made recreational diving possible for millions of nonprofessional divers. Scuba diving is also called free diving, because the diver has no physical connection with the surface. Although some specially trained commercial scuba divers descend below 100 metres (328 feet) for various kinds of work, recreational divers rarely go below a depth of 40 metres (130 feet) because of increased risk of nitrogen narcosis, a type of intoxication similar to drunkenness, or oxygen toxicity, which causes blackouts or convulsions.

The scuba diver wears a tank that carries a supply of pressurized breathing gas, either air or a mixture of oxygen and other gases. The heart of the breathing apparatus is the breathing regulator and the pressure-reducing mechanisms that deliver gas to the diver on each inhalation. In the common scuba used in recreational diving, the breathing medium is air. As the diver inhales, a slight negative pressure occurs in the mouthpiece, which signals the valve that delivers the air to open. The valve closes when the diver stops inhaling, and a one-way valve allows the exhaled breath to escape as bubbles into the water. When using a tank and regulator, a diver can make longer and deeper dives and still breathe comfortably.

Along with scuba gear and its tanks of compressed breathing gases, the scuba diver's essential equipment includes a soft rubber mask with a large faceplate; a soft rubber diving suit for protection from cold; long, flexible, swimming flippers for the feet; buoyancy compensator device (known as a BC or BCD); weight belt; waterproof watch; wrist compass; and diver's knife. For protection from colder water, neoprene-coated foam rubber wet suits consisting of jacket, pants, hood, and gloves are worn.

Certification Organizations[1]

There are several international and domestic organizations that train and certify scuba divers. PADI (**P**rofessional **A**ssociation of **D**iving **I**nstructors), NAUI (**N**ational **A**ssociation of **U**nderwater **I**nstructors), SSI (**S**cuba **S**chools **I**nternational), and NASDS (**N**ational **A**ssociation of **S**cuba **D**iving **S**chools) are the most well known of these organizations. Of these, PADI is the largest certifying organization.

PADI (**P**rofessional **A**ssociation of **D**iving **I**nstructors) is the largest recreational scuba diver training organization in the world. Founded in 1967, PADI has issued more than 5.5 million certifications since it began operation. Since 1985, seven of every ten American divers and an estimated 55 percent of all divers around the world are trained by PADI instructors using PADI's instructional programs. At present PADI certifies well over half-a-million divers internationally each year and has averaged a 12 percent increase in certifications each year since 1985. In 1994, PADI International issued 625,000 certifications, more than in any other single year in company history.

---

[1]Information on certifying agencies drawn from materials published by the various organizations.

PADI's main headquarters are in Santa Ana, California. Its distribution centre is in the United Kingdom and it has seven local area offices in Australia, Canada, Japan, New Zealand, Norway, Sweden, and Switzerland, with professionals and member groups in 175 countries and territories. PADI is made up of four groups: PADI Retail Association, PADI International Resort Association, Professional Members, and PADI Alumni Association. The three association groups emphasize the "three Es" of recreational diving: education, equipment, and experience. By supporting each facet, PADI provides holistic leadership to advance recreational scuba diving and snorkel swimming to equal status with other major leisure activities, while maintaining and improving the excellent safety record PADI has experienced. PADI offers seven levels of instruction and certification ranging from entry-level to instructor.

NAUI (National Association of Underwater Instructors) first began operation in 1960. The organization was formed by a nationally recognized group of instructors that was known as the National Diving Patrol. Since its beginning, NAUI has been active worldwide, certifying sport divers in various levels of proficiency from basic skin diver to instructor. In addition, NAUI regularly conducts specialty courses for cave diving, ice diving, wreck diving, underwater navigation, and search and recovery.

Industry Demographics[2]

Scuba diving has grown steadily in popularity, especially in recent years. For the period 1989-1994, increases in the number of certifications averaged over 10 percent per year. The total number of certified divers worldwide is estimated to be over 10 million. Of these newly certified scuba divers, approximately 65 percent are male and 35 percent are female. Approximately half are married. Approximately 70 percent of them are between the ages of 18 and 34, while about 25 percent are between 35 and 49 (see Exhibit 2). They are generally well educated, with 80 percent having a college education. Overwhelmingly, they are employed in professional, managerial, and technical occupations. Their average annual household income is $75,000. Forty-five percent of divers travel most often with their families. Another 40 percent travel with friends or informal groups.

exhibit 2   Diver Demographics: Age of Divers

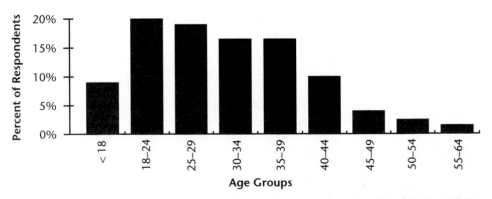

* information taken from the PADI 1991 Diver Survey Results and Analysis, Preliminary Draft

---

[2]This section draws from results of surveys conducted by scuba diving organizations and publications for the years 1991-1993.

Divers are attracted to diving for various reasons: seeking adventure and being with nature are the most often cited reasons (over 75 percent for each). Socializing, stress relief, and travel also are common motivations. Two-thirds of divers travel overseas on diving trips once every three years, while 60 percent travel domestically on dive trips each year. On average, divers spend $2,816 on dive trips annually, with an average equipment investment of $2,300. Aside from upgrades and replacements, the equipment purchase could be considered a one-time cost. Warm-water diving locations are generally chosen 2 to 1 over cold-water diving sites. Cozumel in Mexico, the Cayman Islands, and the Bahamas are the top three diving destinations outside the continental United States for Americans.

According to a consumer survey, the "strongest feelings" that divers associate with their scuba diving experiences are "excitement" and "peacefulness." In a recent survey, the two themes drew an equal number of responses. However, there seem to be very distinct differences in the two responses. One suggests a need for stimulation, while the other suggests relaxation and escape. Visual gratification ("beauty") is another strong motivation for divers. The feelings of "freedom, weightlessness, and flying" were also popular responses.

Under PADI regulations, 12 is the minimum age for certification by the majority of scuba training agencies. At age 12, the child can earn a Junior Diver certification. The Junior Diver meets the same standards as an Open Water diver but generally must be accompanied on dives by a parent or other certified adult. At age 15, the Junior Diver certification can be upgraded to Open Water status by an instructor. This upgrade may require a skills review and evaluation. Pre-dive waiver and release forms require the signature of a parent or guardian until the minor turns 18.

A cautious approach to young divers is based on the concept of readiness to dive. An individual's readiness to dive is determined by physical, mental, and emotional maturity. Physical readiness is easiest to assess: Is the child large and strong enough to handle scuba equipment? An air tank and weight belt can weigh over 40 pounds (18 kilograms), although most dive shops can provide equipment specially sized for smaller divers. Mental readiness refers to whether the child has the academic background and conceptual development to understand diving physics and perform the arithmetic required for certification. The arithmetic understanding focuses on allowable bottom time, which requires factoring in depth, number of dives, and length of dives. Emotional readiness is the greatest concern. Will the junior diver accept the responsibility of being a dive buddy? Divers never dive alone and dive buddies are supposed to look out for and rely on each other. Do they comprehend the safety rules of diving and willingly follow them? Most dive centres accept students from age twelve, but the final determination of readiness to dive rests with the scuba instructor. Instructors are trained to evaluate the readiness of all students prior to completion of the course work and will only award a certification to those who earn it, regardless of age.

DIVING IN THE BAHAMAS[3]

New Providence Island, the Bahamas

New Providence Island is best known for its major population centre, Nassau. Nassau's early development was based on its superb natural harbour. As the capital of the Bahamas, it is the seat of government, also home to 400 banks, elegant homes, ancient

---

[3]Based on information drawn from *The Islands of the Bahamas: 1994 Dive Guide*, published by the Bahamas Ministry of Tourism, Commonwealth of the Bahamas, in conjunction with the Bahama Diving Association.

forts, and a wide variety of duty-free shopping. It has the island's most developed tourist infrastructure, with elegant resort hotels, casinos, cabaret shows, and cruise ship docks. More than two-thirds of the population of the Bahamas live on New Providence and most of these 150,000 people live in or near Nassau, on the northeast corner of the island.

With thousands of vacationers taking resort courses (introductory scuba courses taught in resort pools), Nassau has become known as a destination that is as good for an exploratory first dive as it is for more advanced diving. There are many professional dive operations in the Nassau/Paradise Island area (see Exhibit 3). While all offer resort courses, many also offer a full menu of dive activities designed for the more advanced and experienced diver. Within a 30-minute boat ride of most operations are shipwrecks, beautiful shallow reefs, and huge schools of fish.

In contrast to the bustle of Nassau, the south side of New Providence Island is quieter and more laid-back. Large tracts of pine trees and rolling hills dominate the central regions, while miles of white sand beach surround the island. At the west end of the island is Lyford Cay, an exclusive residential area. Nearby, the winding canals of the Coral Harbour area offer easy access to the sea. While golf and tennis are available, the primary attraction is good scuba diving and top-quality dive operators.

The southwest side of the island has been frequently used as an underwater movie/film set. The "Bond Wrecks" are popular diving destinations for divers and operators. The Vulcan Bomber used in *Thunderball* has aged into a framework draped with colourful gorgonians and sponges. The freighter Tears of Allah, where James Bond eluded the Tiger Shark in *Never Say Never Again*, remains a popular dive attraction in just 40 feet (12 metres) of water. The photogenic appeal of this wreck has improved with age as more and more marine life congregates on this artificial reef.

exhibit 3   Names and Location of Diving Operators in the Bahamas (based on the Bahamas Diving Association membership)

Abaco	**New Providence Island/Nassau**
• Brendal's Dive Shop	• Bahama Divers
• Dive Abaco	• Coral Divers Resort
• Walker's Cay Undersea Adventures	• Custom Aquatics
	• Dive Dive Dive
Andros	• Diver's Haven
• Small Hope Bay Lodge	• Nassau Scuba Center
	• Stuart Cove's Dive South Ocean
Bimini	• Sun Divers
• Bimini Undersea Adventures	• Sunskiff Divers
Cat Island	**San Salvador**
• Cat Island Dive Center	• Riding Rock Inn
Eleuthera/Habour Island	**Live-Aboard Dive Boats**
• Romora Bay Club	• Blackbeard's Cruises
• Valentine's Dive Center	• Bottom Time Adventures
	• Nekton Diving Cruises
Exuma	• Out Island Voyages
• Exuma Fantasea	• Sea Dragon
	• Sea Fever Diving Cruises
Long Island	
• Stella Maris Resort	

There are also natural underwater attractions. Shark Wall and Shark Buoy are popular dive spots. Drop-off dives like Tunnel Wall feature a network of crevices and tunnels beginning in 30 feet of water and exiting along the vertical wall at 70 or 80 feet. Southwest Reef offers magnificent coral heads in only 15 to 30 feet of water, with schooling grunts, squirrelfish, and barracuda. A favourite of the shallow reef areas is Goulding Cay, where broad stands of Elkhorn coral reach nearly to the surface.

TYPES OF DIVING

A wide array of diving activities is available in the Bahamas. These include shark dives, wreck dives, wall dives, reef dives, drift dives, night dives, and so forth. Illustrative examples follow.

Shark Diving

The top three operators of shark dives in the Caribbean are in the Bahamas. While shark diving trips vary with the operators running them, there is at least one common factor in the Bahamas: the Caribbean Reef Shark (Carcharhinus perezi). When the dive boat reaches the site, the sound of the motor acts as a dinner bell. Even before the divers are in the water, the sharks gather for their handouts.

Long Island in the Bahamas was the first area to promote shark feed dives on a regular basis. This method began 20 years ago and has remained relatively unchanged. The feed is conducted as a feeding frenzy. Sharks circle as divers enter the water. After the divers position themselves with their backs to a coral wall, the feeder enters the water with a bucket of fish. This is placed in the sand in front of the divers and the action develops quickly. At Walker's Cay, in Abaco, the method is similar except for the number and variety of sharks in the feed. While Caribbean Reef Sharks make up the majority, Lemon Sharks, Bull Sharks, Hammerhead Sharks, and other species also appear.

The shark feed off Freeport, Grand Bahama, is a very organized event in which the sharks are fed either by hand or off the point of a polespear. The divers are arranged in a semicircle with safety divers guarding the viewers as the feeder is positioned at the middle of the group. If the sharks become unruly, the food is withheld until they calm down. The sharks then go into a regular routine of circling, taking their place in line and advancing to receive the food. Although the sharks come within touching distance, most divers resist the temptation to reach out.

Shark Wall, on the southwest side of New Providence, is a pristine dropoff decorated with masses of colourful sponges along the deep-water abyss known as the Tongue of the Ocean. Divers position themselves along sand patches among the coral heads in about 50 feet of water as Caribbean Reef Sharks and an occasional Bull or Lemon Shark cruise mid-water in anticipation of a free handout. During the feeding period, the bait is controlled and fed from a polespear by an experienced feeder. There are usually six to 12 sharks present, ranging from four to eight feet in length. Some operators make two dives to this site, allowing divers to cruise the wall with the sharks in a more natural way before the feeding dive.

The Shark Buoy, also on the southwest side of New Providence, is tethered in 6,000 feet of water. Its floating surface mass attracts a wide variety of ocean marine life such as dolphin fish, Jacks, Rainbow Runners, and Silky Sharks. The Silky Sharks are typically small, three to five feet long, but swarm in schools of 6 to 20, with the sharks swimming up to the divemasters' hands to grab the bait.

From the operator's standpoint, the only special equipment needed for shark dives is a chain mail diving suit for the feeder's protection, some type of feeding apparatus, and intestinal fortitude. The thrill of diving among sharks is the main attraction for the divers. For the most part, the dives are safe, with only the feeder taking an occasional nick from an excited shark.

Divers participating in shark dives were required to sign waivers prior to the actual dive. As the fine print in most life insurance policies noted, claims for any scuba-related accidents were not payable. However, there did exist specialty insurers such as Divers Alert Network.

Wreck Diving

Wreck diving is divided into three levels: non-penetration, limited penetration, and full penetration. Full penetration and deep wreck diving should be done only by divers who have completed rigorous training and have extensive diving experience. Non-penetration wreck diving refers to recreational diving on wrecks without entering an overhead environment that prevents direct access to the surface. Divers with open-water certification are qualified for this type of diving without further training as long as they are comfortable with the diving conditions and the wreck's depth. Limited penetration wreck diving is defined as staying within ambient light and always in sight of an exit. Full penetration wreck diving involves an overhead environment away from ambient light and beyond sight of an exit. Safely and extensively exploring the insides of a wreck involves formal training and mental strength. On this type of dive, the first mistake could be the last.

Wall Diving

In a few regions of the world, island chains, formed by volcanos and coral, have been altered by movements of the earth's crustal plates. Extending approximately due east-west across the central Caribbean Sea is the boundary between the North American and Caribbean crustal plates. The shifting of these plates has created some of the most spectacular diving environments in the world, characterized by enormous cliffs, 2,000 to 6,000 feet high. At the cliffs, known as walls, the diver experiences the overwhelming scale and dynamic forces that shape the ocean more than in any other underwater environment. It is on the walls that a diver is most likely to experience the feeling of free motion, or flying, in boundless space. Many of the dives in the Bahamas are wall dives.

Reef Diving

Reefs generally are made up of three areas: a reef flat, a lagoon or bay, and a reef crest. The depth in the reef flat averages only a few feet with an occasional deeper channel. The underwater life on a shallow reef flat may vary greatly in abundance and diversity within a short distance. The reef flat is generally a protected area, not exposed to strong winds or waves, making it ideal for novice or family snorkellers. The main feature distinguishing bay and lagoon environments from a reef flat is depth. Caribbean lagoons and bays may reach depths of 60 feet, but many provide teeming underwater ecosystems in as little as 15–20 feet. This is excellent for underwater photography and ideal for families or no-decompression-stop diving. The reef's crest is the outer boundary that shelters the bay and flats from the full force of the ocean's waves. Since the surging and pounding of the waves is too strong for all but the most advanced divers, most diving takes place in the protected bay waters.

FAMILY DIVING RESORTS

The current average age of new divers is 36. As the median age of new divers increased, families became a rapidly growing segment of the vacation travel industry. Many parents are busy and do not spend as much time with their children as they would prefer. Many parents who dive would like to have a vacation that would combine diving and spending time with their children. In response to increasing numbers of parents travelling with children, resort operators have added amenities ranging from babysitting services and kids' camps to dedicated family resorts with special facilities and rates. The resort options available have greatly expanded in recent years. At all-inclusive self-contained resorts, one price includes everything: meals, accommodations, daytime and evening activities, and water sports. Many of these facilities offer special activities and facilities for children. Diving is included or available nearby.

For many divers, the important part of the trip is the quality of the diving, not the quality of the accommodations. But for divers with families, the equation changes. Children, especially younger children, may find it difficult to do without a comfortable bed, television, or VCR, no matter how good the diving promises to be. Some resorts, while not dedicated to family vacations, do make accommodations for divers with children. Condos and villas are an economical and convenient vacation option for divers with children. The additional space of this type of accommodation allows parents to bring along a babysitter. Having a kitchen on hand makes the task of feeding children simple and economical. Most diving destinations in the Bahamas, Caribbean, and Pacific offer condo, villa, and hotel-type accommodations. Some hotels organize entertaining and educational activities for children while parents engage in their own activities.

As the number of families vacationing together has increased, some resorts and dive operators have started special promotions and programs. On Bonaire, part of the Netherlands Antilles, August has been designated Family Month. During this month, the island is devoted to families, with a special welcome kit for children and island-wide activities including "eco-walks" at a flamingo reserve, snorkelling lessons, and evening entertainment for all ages. In conjunction, individual resorts and restaurants offer family packages and discounts. Similarly, in Honduras, which has very good diving, a resort started a children's dolphin camp during summer months. While diving family members are out exploring the reefs, children between ages 8 and 14 spend their days learning about and interacting with a resident dolphin population. The program includes classroom and in-water time as well as horseback riding and paddle boating.

One travel company, Rascals in Paradise (1-800-U-RASCAL), specializes in family travel packages. The founders, Theresa Detchemendy and Deborah Baratta, are divers, mothers, and travel agents who have developed innovative packages for diving families. Theresa says, "The biggest concern for parents is their children's safety, and then what the kids will do while they're diving or enjoying an evening on the town." The Rascals people have worked with a number of family-run resorts all over the world to provide daily activities, responsible local nannies, and child-safe facilities with safe balconies, playgrounds, and children's pools.

They have also organized Family Weeks at popular dive destinations in Belize, Mexico, and the Cayman Islands. Family Week packages account for over 50 percent of Rascals' bookings each year. On these scheduled trips, groups of three to six families share a teacher/escort who brings along a fun program tailored for children and serves as activities director for the group. Rascals Special Family Weeks packages are priced on the basis of a family of four (two adults and two children, age 2–11) and include a teacher/escort, one babysitter for each family, children's activities, meals, airport transfers, taxes, services, and cancellation insurance (see Exhibit 4). For example, in 1995, a seven-night family vacation at Hotel Club Akumal, on the Yucatan coast, was US$2,080-$3,100 per family.[4] Rascals also packages independent family trips to 57 different condos, villas, resorts, or hotels which offer scuba diving. An independent family trip would not include a teacher/escort (see Exhibit 5). A seven-night independent family trip to Hotel Club Akumal ran US$624-$1,779.[5]

Rascals' approach is unique in the travel industry because they personally select the resorts with which they work. "We try to work with small properties so our groups are pampered and looked after," says Detchemendy. "The owners are often parents and their kids are sometimes on the property. They understand the characteristics of kids." Typically, Detchemendy and Baratta visit each destination, often working with the government tourist board in identifying potential properties. If the physical structure is already in place, it is easy to add the resort to the Rascals booking list. If modifications are needed, the two sit down with the management and outline what needs to be in place so that the resort can be part of the Rascals program.

Rascals evaluates resorts according to several factors: (1) Is the property friendly toward children and does it want them? (2) How does the property rate in terms of safety? (3) What are the facilities and is there a separate room to be used as a Rascals Room? (4) Does the property provide babysitting and child care by individuals who are screened and locally known? A successful example of this approach is Hotel Club Akumal, in Akumal, Mexico. Detchemendy and Baratta helped the resort expand its market reach by building a family-oriented resort that became part of the Rascals program. Baratta explained, "In that case, we were looking for a place close to home, with a multi-level range of accommodations, that offered something other than a beach, that was family-friendly, and not in Cancun. We found Hotel Club Akumal, but they didn't have many elements in place, so we had to work with them. We established a meal plan, an all-inclusive product and designated activities for kids. We went into the kitchen and created a children's menu and we asked them to install a little kids' playground that's shaded." The resort became one of their most popular family destinations.

Rascals offered two types of services to resort operators interested in creating family vacations. One was a consulting service. For a modest daily fee plus expenses, Baratta or Detchemendy, or both, would conduct an on-site assessment of the resort. This usually took one or two days. They would provide a written report to the resort regarding needed additions or modifications to the resort to make it safe and attractive for family vacations. Possible physical changes might include the addition of a Rascals room, child-safe play equipment, and modifications to existing buildings and structures, such as rooms, railings, and docks, to prevent child injuries. Rascals always tried to use existing equipment or equipment available nearby. Other non-structural changes could include the addition of educational sessions, playtimes, and other structured times for entertaining children while their parents were diving. The report

---

[4]Lunch and airport transfer not included. Prices reflect seasonal fluctuations and are subject to change. Airfares not included.

[5]Based on a family of four with two adults and two children age 2–11. Rates are to be used as a guide only. Each booking is quoted separately and will be dependent on season, type of accommodation, ages and number of children, meal and activity inclusions. All prices are subject to change. Some variations apply. Airfares not included.

exhibit 4   Rascals in Paradise Pricing Guide: Rascals Special Family Weeks

Destination	Duration	Price	Notes
Bahamas			
South Ocean Beach	7 nights	$3,120–$3,970	Lunch not included
Small Hope Bay	7 nights	$3,504	Scuba diving included; local host only
Mexico			
Hotel Buena Vista	7 nights	$2,150–$2,470	
Hotel Club Akumal	7 nights	$2,080–$3,100	Lunch and airport transfer not included

Prices are based on a family of four with two adults and two children aged 2–11. All packages include the following (except as noted): accommodations, Rascals escort, meals, babysitter, children's activities, airport transfers, taxes and services, and a $2,500 cancellation insurance per family booking. Airfares not included.

exhibit 5   Rascals in Paradise Pricing Guide: Independent Family Trips

Destination	Duration	Price	Notes
Bahamas			
South Ocean Beach	7 nights	$1,355–$1,771	
Small Hope Bay	7 nights	$2,860–$3,560	All meals, bar service, babysitter, and diving included
Hope Town Harbour Lodge	7 nights	$ 962–$1,121	
Treasure Cay	7 nights	$ 875–$1,750	
Stella Maris, Long Island	7 nights	$1,547–$2,597	
Mexico			
Hotel Buena Vista	7 nights	$1,232–$1,548	All meals included
Hotel Club Akumal	7 nights	$ 624–$1,779	
Hotel Presidente	7 nights	$1,120–$1,656	
La Concha	7 nights	$ 655–$ 963	
Plaza Las Glorias	7 nights	$ 632–$1,017	

Prices are based on a family of four with two adults and two children aged 2–11. Rates are per week (seven nights) and include accommodations and applicable taxes. These rates are to be used as a guide only. Each booking is quoted separately and will be dependent on season, type of accommodation, ages and number of children, and meal and activity inclusions. All prices are subject to change. Some variations apply. Airfares not included.

also included an implementation proposal. Then after implementation, the resort could decide whether or not to list with the Rascals for bookings.

Under the second option, Rascals provided the consulting service at no charge to the resort. However, they asked that any requests for family bookings be referred back to Rascals. Rascals would then also list and actively promote the resort through its brochures and referrals. For resorts using the Rascals booking option, Rascals would provide premiums such as hats and T-shirts, in addition to the escorted activities. This attention to the family was what differentiated a Rascals resort from other resorts. Generally, companies that promote packages receive net rates from the resorts which are from 20 percent to 50 percent lower than "rack" rates. Rascals, in turn, promoted these special packages to the travel industry in general and paid a portion of their earnings out in commissions to other travel agencies.

Rascals tried to work with its resorts to provide packaged and prepaid vacations. This approach created a win-win situation for the resort managers and the vacationer. Packages or an all-inclusive vacation was a cruise ship approach. It allowed the inclusion of many activities in the package. For example, such a package might include seven nights' lodging, all meals, babysitting, children's activities, and scuba diving. This approach allowed the vacationer to know, up front, what to expect. Moreover, the cost would be included in one set price, so that the family would not have to pay for each activity as it came along. The idea was to remove the surprises and make the stay enjoyable. It also allowed the resort operator to bundle activities together, providing more options than might otherwise be offered. As a result, the package approach was becoming popular with both resort owners and vacationers.

In its bookings, Rascals required prepayment of trips. This resulted in higher revenues for the resort since all activities were paid for in advance. Ordinarily, resorts on their own might only require a two- or three-night room deposit. Then, the family would pay for the rest of the room charge on leaving, after paying for other activities or services as they were used. While the vacationer might think they had a less expensive trip this way, in fact, prepaid activities were generally cheaper than à la carte activities. Moreover, they potentially yielded lower revenues for the resort. Rascals promoted prepaid vacations as a win-win, low-stress approach to travel. Rascals had been very successful with the resorts it listed. Fifty percent of their bookings were repeat business, and many inquiries were based on word-of-mouth referrals. All in all, Rascals provided a link to the family vacation market segment that the resort might not otherwise have. It was common for Rascals-listed resorts to average annual bookings of 90 percent.

CORAL DIVERS RESORT

Coral Divers Resort had been in operation ten years. Annual revenues had reached as high as $554,000. Profits generally had been in the 2 percent range, but for the past two years, losses had been experienced. The expected turnaround in profits in 1994 had never materialized (see Exhibit 6). While not making them rich, the business had provided an adequate income for Greywell and his wife, Margaret, and their two children, Allen, age 7, and Winifred, age 5. However, revenues had continued to decline. From talking with other operators, Greywell understood that resorts with strong identities and reputations for quality service were doing well. Greywell thought that the Coral Divers Resort had not distinguished itself in any particular aspect of diving or as a resort.

The Coral Divers Resort property was located on a deep-water channel on the southwest coast of the island of New Providence in the Bahamas. The property occupied 3 acres (1.2 hectares) and had beach access. There were six cottages on the property, each having a kitchenette, a full bath, a bedroom with two full-size beds, and a living room with two sleeper sofas. Four of the units had been renovated with new paint, tile floors, microwave, colour TV, and VCR. The two other units ranged from "adequate" to "comfortable." Greywell tried to use the renovated units primarily for families and couples, while putting groups of single divers in the other units. Also on the property was a six-unit attached motel-type structure (see Exhibit 7 on page 27 for prices). Each of these units had two full-size beds, a pullout sofa, sink, refrigerator, microwave, and TV. The resort had the space and facilities on the property for a kitchen

exhibit 6 Comparative Balance Sheets, as at June 30 (US$)

	1994	1993	1992
ASSETS			
Current assets:			
Cash	5,362	8,943	15,592
Accounts receivable	2,160	8,660	2,026
Inventories	5,519	6,861	9,013
Prepaid expenses	9,065	8,723	8,195
Total current assets	**22,106**	**33,187**	**34,826**
Fixed assets:			
Land	300,000	300,000	300,000
Building	200,000	200,000	200,000
Less: Accumulated depreciation	(70,000)	(60,000)	(50,000)
Boats	225,000	225,000	225,000
Less: Accumulated depreciation	(157,500)	(135,000)	(112,500)
Vehicles	54,000	54,000	54,000
Less: Accumulated depreciation	(32,400)	(21,600)	(10,800)
Diving equipment	150,000	150,000	150,000
Less: Accumulated depreciation	(90,000)	(60,000)	(30,000)
Total fixed assets	**579,100**	**652,400**	**725,700**
Total Assets	**601,206**	**685,587**	**760,526**
LIABILITIES			
Current liabilities:			
Accounts payable	1,689	4,724	1,504
Bank loan	20,000	0	2,263
Mortgage payable, current portion	25,892	25,892	25,892
Note payable, current portion	40,895	40,895	40,895
Total current liabilities	**88,476**	**71,511**	**70,554**
Long-term liabilities:			
Mortgage payable, due in 1996	391,710	417,602	443,494
Note payable, five-year	81,315	122,210	163,105
Total long-term liabilities	**473,025**	**539,812**	**606,599**
Total Liabilities	**561,501**	**611,323**	**677,153**
SHAREHOLDERS' EQUITY			
Jonathon Greywell, capital	44,879	44,879	44,879
Retained earnings	(5,174)	29,385	38,494
Total shareholders' equity	**39,705**	**74,264**	**83,373**
Total Liabilities and Shareholders' Equity	**601,206**	**685,587**	**760,526**

continues on the next page

exhibit 6   *(continued)*

	1994	1993	1992
Revenues:			
Diving and lodging packages	482,160	507,670	529,820
Day diving	11,680	12,360	14,980
Certifications	5,165	5,740	7,120
Lodging	2,380	1,600	1,200
Miscellaneous	1,523	1,645	1,237
Total revenues	**502,908**	**529,015**	**554,357**
Expenses:			
Advertising and promotion	15,708	15,240	13,648
Bank charges	1,326	1,015	975
Boat maintenance and fuel	29,565	31,024	29,234
Cost of goods sold	762	823	619
Depreciation	73,300	73,300	73,300
Dues and fees	3,746	4,024	3,849
Duties and taxes	11,405	18,352	17,231
Insurance	36,260	34,890	32,780
Interest, mortgage, note, and loan	40,544	40,797	41,174
Management salary	31,600	31,600	31,600
Office supplies	12,275	12,753	11,981
Professional fees	11,427	10,894	10,423
Repairs and maintenance, building	15,876	12,379	9,487
Salaries, wages, and benefits	196,386	194,458	191,624
Telephone and fax	9,926	9,846	7,689
Trade shows	14,523	14,679	14,230
Utilities	20,085	19,986	17,970
Vehicles, maintenance and fuel	12,753	12,064	11,567
Total expenses	**537,467**	**538,124**	**519,381**
Net income	**(34,559)**	**(9,109)**	**34,976**
Retained earnings, beginning	**29,385**	**38,494**	**3,518**
Retained earnings, ending	**(5,174)**	**29,385**	**38,494**

Note: Bahama$1 = US$1.

and dining room, but it had not been used. However, there was a small family-run restaurant and bar within walking distance.

Greywell had three boats, which could carry from eight to twenty passengers each. Two were 40-foot fibreglass V-hull boats powered by a single diesel inboard with a cruising speed of 18 knots and protective cabin, with dry storage space. The third was a 35-foot covered platform boat. Greywell also had facilities for air dispensing, equipment repair, rental and sale, and tank storage.

Coral Divers Resort, affiliated with PADI and NAUI, had a staff of eleven, which included four scuba diving instructors. Greywell, who worked full-time at the resort, was a certified diving instructor by both PADI and NAUI. The three other diving instructors had various backgrounds. One was a former U.S. Navy SEAL working for

***exhibit* 7**   Coral Divers Resort Pricing Guide: Family Dive Vacations

Destination	Duration	Price	Notes
Bahamas			
Coral Divers Resort	7 nights	$1,355–$1,455	Standard accommodations, continental breakfast, and daily two-tank dive included
Coral Divers Resort	7 nights	$1,800–$1,950	Deluxe accommodations, continental breakfast, and daily two-tank dive included

Prices are based on a family of four with two adults and two children aged 2–11. Rates are per week (seven nights) and include accommodations and applicable taxes. Rates will be dependent on season, type of accommodation, and ages and number of children. All prices are subject to change. Airfares not included. Prices dropped to $600–$700 per week for the standard package and $800–$900 for deluxe accommodation if diving was excluded.

Coral Divers as a way to gain resort experience. Another was a local Bahamian whom Greywell had known for many years. The third was a Canadian who had come to the Bahamas on a winter holiday and never left. There were two boat captains and two mates. Given the size of the operation, the staff was scheduled to provide overall coverage, with all of the staff rarely working at the same time. In addition, there was a housekeeper, a groundskeeper, and a person who minded the office and store. Greywell's wife, Margaret, worked at the business on a part-time basis, taking care of administrative activities such as accounting and payroll. The rest of her time was spent looking after their two children and their home.

A typical diving day at Coral Divers for Greywell began around 7:30 a.m. He would open the office and review the activities list for the day. If there were any divers that needed to be picked up at the resorts in Nassau or elsewhere on the island, the van driver would need to leave by 7:30 a.m. to be back for the 9 a.m. departure. Most resort guests began to gather around the office and dock about 8:30. By 8:45, the day's captain and mate began loading the diving gear for the passengers.

The boat left at 9 a.m. Morning dives were usually "two-tank dives," that is, two dives utilizing one tank of air each. The trip to the first dive site took about 20-30 minutes. Once there, the captain would explain the dive, the special attractions of the dive, and tell everyone when they were expected back on board. Most dives lasted 30-45 minutes, depending on depth. The deeper the dive, the faster the air consumption. A divemaster always accompanied the divers on the trip down. The divemaster's role was generally to supervise the dive. The divemaster was responsible for the safety and conduct of the divers while under water.

Once back on board, the boat would move to the next site. Greywell tried to plan dives that had sites near each other. For example, the first dive might be a wall dive in 60 feet of water, while the second would be a nearby wreck 40 feet down. The second would also last about 40 minutes. If things went well, the boat would be back at the resort by noon. This allowed for lunch and sufficient surface time for divers who might be going back out in the afternoon. Two morning dives were part of the resort package. Whether the boat went out in the afternoon depended on whether enough non-resort guest divers had contracted for afternoon dives. If they had, Greywell was happy to let resort guests ride and dive along free of charge. If there were not enough outside paying divers, there were no afternoon dive trips and the guests were on their own to swim at the beach, go sightseeing, or just relax. When space was available it was possible for non-divers (either snorkellers or bubble-watchers) to join the boat trip for a fee of $15-$25.

Greywell's Options

Greywell's bookings ran 90 percent of capacity during the high season (December through May) and 50 percent during the low season (June through November). Ideally, he wanted to increase the number of bookings for the resort and dive businesses during both seasons. Adding additional diving attractions could increase both resort and dive revenues. Focusing on family vacations could increase revenues since families would probably increase the number of paying guests per room. Breakeven costs were calculated on the basis of two adults sharing a room. Children provided an additional revenue source since the cost of the room had been covered by the adults and children under 12 incurred no diving-related costs. However, either strategy, adding adventure diving to his current general offerings or adjusting the focus of the resort to encourage family diving vacations, would require some changes and cost money. The question became whether the changes would increase revenue enough to justify the costs and effort involved.

Emphasizing family diving vacations would probably require some changes to the physical property of the resort. Four of the cottages had already been renovated. The other two also would need to be upgraded. This would run $10,000 to $20,000 each, depending on the amenities added. The Bahamas had duties up to 50 percent which caused renovation costs involving imported goods to be expensive. The attached motel-type units also would need to be refurbished at some point. He had the space and facilities for a kitchen and dining area, but had not done anything with it. The Rascals in Paradise people had offered to help set up a children's menu. He could hire a chef or cook and do it himself or offer the concession to the nearby restaurant or someone else. He would also need to build a play structure for children. There was an open area with shade trees between the office and the cottages that would be ideal for a play area. Rascals would provide the teacher/escort for the family vacation groups. It would be fairly easy to find babysitters for the children as needed. The people, particularly on this part of the island, were very family-oriented and would welcome the opportunity for additional income. In asking around, it seemed that $5 per hour was the going rate for a sitter. Toys and other play items could be added gradually. The Rascals people had said that, once the program was in place, he could expect bookings to run 90 percent capacity annually from new and return bookings. While the package prices were competitive, the attraction was in group bookings and the prospect of a returning client base.

Adding adventure diving would be a relatively easy thing to do. Shark Wall and Shark Buoy were less than an hour away by boat. Both of these sites offered sharks that were already accustomed to being fed. The cost of shark food would be $10 per dive. None of Greywell's current staff was particularly excited about the prospect of adding shark feeding to their job description. But these staff could be relatively easily replaced. Greywell could probably find an experienced divemaster who would be willing to lead the shark dives. He would also have to purchase a special chain mail suit for the feeder at a cost of about $10,000. While there were few accidents during the feeds, Greywell would rather be safe than sorry. His current boats, especially the 40-footers, would be adequate for transporting divers to the sites. The other shark dive operators might not be happy about having him at the sites, but there was little they could do about it. Shark divers were charged a premium fee. For example, a shark dive would cost $100 for a two-tank dive, compared to $25-$75 for a normal two-tank dive. He figured that he could add shark dives to the schedule on Wednesdays and Saturdays without taking away from regular business. He needed a minimum of four divers on a trip at regular rates to cover the cost of taking out the boat. Ten or twelve divers was ideal. Greywell could usually count on at least eight divers for a normal dive, but he did not know how much additional new and return business he could expect from shark diving.

A third option was for Greywell to try to improve his current operations and not add any new diving attractions. This would require him to be much more cost-efficient in his operations. Actions such as strictly adhering to the minimum required number of divers per boat policy, along with staff reductions might improve the bottom line by 5-10 percent. He would need to be very attentive to materials ordering, fuel costs, and worker productivity in order to realize any gains with this approach. However, he was concerned that by continuing as he had, Coral Divers Resort would not be distinguished as unique from other resorts in the Bahamas. He did not know what would be the long-term implications of this approach.

As Greywell reached the office, he turned to watch the sun sink into the ocean. Although it was a view he had come to love, a lingering thought was that perhaps it was time to relocate to a less crowded location.

case 3 Asiasports: Hockey Night in Hong Kong

On March 5, 1999, Tom Barnes, executive director of Asiasports Limited (Asiasports), spent several hours in a meeting with the two main shareholders of the private company, Shane Weir and Bill Gribble. In the meeting, the trio discussed the business strategy for Asiasports for the next five years. Asiasports, a sports management company, was involved in the development of ice hockey in Hong Kong. Barnes, Weir and Gribble had to make decisions about whether the company should promote hockey outside of Hong Kong and its choice of sports properties. An implementation plan also had to be developed for the chosen strategy.

TOM BARNES

Tom Barnes, 32, was born in St. Louis, Missouri, in the United States. He had been active in hockey since his high school days, where he served as captain of his high school team. After completing an undergraduate degree in organizational behavior at the University of Miami at Ohio, Barnes worked for Enterprise Leasing in St. Louis and Seattle, Washington. In February 1993, following the suggestions of relatives who were living in Hong Kong, Barnes moved there. Once he arrived in Hong Kong, Barnes began to work for the large cable programmer, Star TV. This job gave Barnes an entry back into the sports world as he worked as a program researcher for the prime sports channel of Star TV. Six months into his term at Star TV, Barnes discovered the existence of a hockey league in Hong Kong while on a hiking trip in rural Lantau Island. In the fall of 1993, he joined the fledgling ice hockey league, which was the predecessor of one of Asiasports' main properties.

Richard Ivey School of Business
The University of Western Ontario

Andrew Delios prepared this case solely to provide material for class discussion. The author does not intend to illustrate either effective or ineffective handling of a managerial situation. The author may have disguised certain names and other identifying information to protect confidentiality.

HISTORY OF HOCKEY

Ice hockey had been played for several hundred years. Forerunners to the present version of the game were played on frozen lakes and ponds in Great Britain, France and Holland in the 18th century. From these beginnings, hockey began to take more shape in the 19th century in Canada. A primitive variant of today's game emerged near Halifax, Nova Scotia, Canada in the early 1800s. Local schoolboys adopted hurley, a form of field hockey played with a stick and ball, to winter conditions. In the 1870s, students at McGill University in Montreal, Quebec, Canada assigned a set of rules to hockey and played the first exhibition game. The first formal ice hockey league was launched in Kingston, Ontario, Canada in 1885.

Ice hockey was originally played with seven players on the ice. In 1911 the seventh position, the 'rover,' was dropped. Later amendments to the rules permitted player substitutions, and the number of players on a team began to exceed ten. Various other initiatives and rule changes shaped the game into its 1990s version. These rule changes facilitated the opening-up of the game, and made hockey into a faster sport.

In the 1990s, hockey was a sport of power, speed, agility and knowledge. Players had to master the ability to skate; they had to learn to control the puck (the sport's ball) with a stick while maneuvering at high speeds; they had to interact well with teammates; and they had to have endurance and strength. Speed was one of the compelling aspects of the game. The fastest players skated at speeds of 50 kilometres per hour, and the hardest shooters propelled the puck at nearly 200 kilometres per hour. Hockey also had an aggressive aspect. Body contact between players was allowed, but not to the extent seen in rugby or American football.

INTERNATIONAL SPREAD OF HOCKEY

From its beginnings in Eastern Canada, hockey gradually spread to Western Canada and the northern states of the U.S. Hockey also spread east across the Atlantic to Scandinavian countries like Sweden, Finland, Norway, and other northern European countries like Russia, Belarus, Lithuania, Latvia and the Czech and Slovak Republics. Later, regions in Europe with warmer climates, Great Britain, Switzerland, Germany and Italy, embraced the sport.

This spread led to hockey's inclusion in the inaugural Olympic Winter Games, held in 1924 in Chamonix, France. Participating countries were drawn from Western European and North American countries. In the 1950s, Eastern Europe countries began to participate in Olympic and World Championship events. This growth continued, and in 1998, Japan and China also competed in Olympic hockey.

Women's hockey made its debut in the 1998 Winter Olympics. Prior to that, women's hockey had been recognized internationally, through sanctioned World Championships. At a national level, women's hockey leagues were prominent in the U.S., where several college leagues had operated since the mid-1970s. In the 1990s, women's hockey was played in North America, Europe and Asia. China, Japan and South Korea were the principal countries in Asia in which women's hockey was played. In Canada, close to 20,000 women were enrolled in hockey leagues in 1997. In the U.S. this number was greater as participation had grown fourfold since 1990.

When hockey spread internationally, its growth in new countries was supported by two factors. The first factor was that hockey had to be seen as an exciting and attractive sport for both viewing and participation. Hockey faced competition for the participant and viewer from a variety of other sports. In the United States, for example, hockey had to compete with team sports such as baseball, American football, basketball and soccer, as well as individual sports like tennis and golf. The second factor was that hockey had to develop at a grassroots level. Children had to have the opportunity to play hockey when young, to help develop an interest that would carry over into participation as a player, viewer, and volunteer in hockey associations when an adult.

HOCKEY ASSOCIATIONS

International Ice Hockey Federation[1]

Representatives of Bohemia, Switzerland, France, Belgium and Great Britain founded the International Ice Hockey Federation (IIHF, or Ligue Internationale de Hockey sur Glace) in 1908. The aim of the IIHF was to control the sports of ice hockey and in-line hockey and to organize international competitions.

In its first ten years, the IIHF was purely a European institution. However, in the last two decades of the 20th century, and with the growth of in-line hockey, the sport of hockey became increasingly global. The IIHF grew along with hockey. In 1999, it consisted of 55 member federations.

The IIHF was involved directly with a number of tournaments and leagues, such as the European Senior Championships, the World Senior and Junior Tournaments, the Asia/Oceania Junior Championships and the European and World Women Championships. The IIHF had indirect, but substantive involvement in other tournaments. These tournaments included the well-known Olympic Games, as well as lesser-known ones like the Continental Cup and the Super Cup. Aside from ice hockey tournaments, the IIHF helped to organize several in-line competitions and tournaments. These were organized at the grassroots level, for generating new interest in specific cities and countries, and at a national competitive level. Finally, the IIHF ran a development program for hockey. This program focused on development in four areas: coaching, officiating, playing and administration.

National Hockey Associations

A number of European, North American and Asian countries had national-level ice hockey associations. These bodies oversaw the development and promotion of the sport within the national domain, as well as in national competitions. National associations, such as the Canadian Hockey Association or USA Hockey, ran development programs for coaches, players and officials. The associations organized national championships and put together the junior and senior teams that competed in international championships.

As an example, the Canadian Hockey Association (CHA) was the sole governing body of amateur hockey in Canada. It worked in conjunction with 13 branch associations, the Canadian Hockey League, and the Canadian Inter-University Athletic Union. The CHA maintained offices in several major cities in Canada, and operated on an annual budget of Cdn$15.1 million (US$9 million, see Exhibit 1). With a relatively small budget, it relied on the co-operation of volunteers to fulfil its mandate to the approximately 500,000 registered hockey players in Canada.

---

[1]Information in this section was derived in part from the International Ice Hockey Federation's homepage: http://www.iihf.com., April 1999.

exhibit 1   Sources of Funding for Canadian Hockey Association
              (1997 to 1998)

Source	Funding (Canadian dollars)
Sponsors	4,055,000
Program/Event Revenue	4,690,000
Membership/Service Fees	1,809,000
Merchandise	1,743,000
Sport Funding Agencies	1,465,000
Government	1,110,000
Other	268,000
Total	**$ 15,140,000**

Note: Major sponsors included Nike Inc., Royal Bank of Canada, Esso (Imperial Oil) and Air Canada.

Source: Canadian Hockey Association web-page: http://www.canadianhockey.ca/e/index.html, April 1999.

National Hockey League[2]

The National Hockey League (NHL) was the premier hockey league in 1999. The league had teams based in Canada and the U.S. The players in the NHL had a variety of nationalities: American, British, Canadian, Czech, Finnish, German, Russian, Slovak and Swedish, to name a few. The largest group of players was Canadian, but in the 1990s the percentage of players from the U.S. and Europe had been increasing.

The NHL, which was not the first professional league formed in North America, commenced operations in 1917. Initially, it had four Canadian teams: the Montreal Canadiens, the Montreal Wanderers, the Ottawa Senators and the Toronto Arenas. After several decades of sporadic growth and a bout of competition from a since-disbanded rival league, the World Hockey Association, in 1999 the NHL had expanded to 27 teams.

In the 1990s, the NHL adopted an aggressive marketing stance in which promotional activities in the U.S. and elsewhere in the world were an important component. The NHL ran several programs designed to grow the game of hockey. NHL Skate was one of these. NHL Skate aided the creation of multi-purpose ice skating facilities. A related program was NHL Hockey Playground. This program had the goal of creating off-ice hockey rinks in urban environments. A third program, NHL A.S.S.I.S.T., helped youth organizations defray costs associated with playing the sport: equipment costs, costs of travel and the cost of renting an ice rink. NHL A.S.S.I.S.T. had a worldwide mandate and had financed teams in Canada, China, Hungary, Ireland, Romania and the United States.

As a further aid to the promotion of the sport, the NHL actively sought greater penetration of U.S. television markets. Despite success as a television product in Canada and several European countries, the popularity of professional hockey on U.S. television had waned in the late 1990s. To increase television viewership, the NHL had continued to increase the number of U.S.-based franchises through the 1990s. In the late 1990s, the NHL planned to add new teams in such places as Atlanta, Georgia in the U.S. The 30-team league would have teams placed throughout North America, including cities in the south and southwest portions of the U.S.

---

[2]Material in this section was drawn from material available on the National Hockey League's official web-site: www.nhl.com., April 1999.

It was in these cities, in which snow and ice were a rarity, that the NHL had faced its greatest growing pains in the 1970s and 1980s. However, in the 1990s, expansion had been successful because the game's premier player was a member of a Los Angeles-based team for the first half of the 1990s. The adoption of hockey in the south was also aided by an innovation: the creation of the in-line skate.

IN-LINE HOCKEY

In the mid-1980s, two brothers in Minnesota developed an in-line skate that could be used to play hockey. Their efforts led to the incorporation of the Rollerblade company. Subsequently, the popularity of in-line skating as a form of recreation and exercise exploded in the U.S. and elsewhere in the world. In the late 1980s and early 1990s, in-line hockey leagues began to mushroom in the U.S. In-line hockey was particularly well liked in the southern states of the U.S., in places where ice hockey had traditionally had difficulty gaining acceptance as a legitimate sport. California, where in-line skating had been adopted enthusiastically, saw the growth of several professional, semi-professional, amateur and development in-line hockey leagues. Children's participation in in-line hockey was also widespread and growing.

To deal with the rapid growth of in-line hockey, national hockey associations worked to organise the sport on a national and sub-national basis. For instance, in December 1994, USA Hockey created USA Hockey InLine to address the growth in demand for playing, coaching and officiating programs within in-line hockey in the U.S. Accordingly, the mission of USA Hockey was "to promote and facilitate the growth of in-line hockey in America and to provide the best possible experience for all participants by encouraging, advancing and administering the sport."[3]

USA Hockey InLine provided many services to its members. It offered resources and educational programs to coaches, referees and league administrators. It organised and sanctioned tournaments for players of all ages and skill levels. It co-ordinated national teams that competed in IIHF-sanctioned tournaments.

National associations were not the only ones to adopt and help in-line hockey. As part of its efforts to expand the sports fan base, the NHL created the NHL Breakout program. This program sponsored street and in-line hockey in 22 NHL North American cities in 1999. The tournaments concluded with a National Championship, which was held in January 2000. The NHL Breakout tournament was open to players of all ages and skill levels. Games were played on portable, inflatable in-line hockey rinks, which were also developed by the NHL.

Private companies also became involved in the promotion and organisation of in-line hockey. TOHRS was one such company. TOHRS was an in-line hockey tournament organisation that was sanctioned by USA Hockey. It provided 50 tournaments in the U.S. each year, drawing a total of more than 100,000 participants. Players from all ages and all levels competed in these tournaments. The majority of these tournaments were held in southern U.S. states such as Florida, California, Texas and Georgia, places where ice hockey was played infrequently at a grassroots level.

One reason for the popularity of in-line hockey in southern locations was its suitability to warm weather conditions. Unlike ice hockey, which required an outdoor ice surface (and a cold climate) or an indoor ice arena, in-line hockey could be

---

[3]The mission statement and other material on USA Hockey were sourced from USA Hockey's web-site: http://www.usahockey.com., April 1999.

played anywhere there was a hard, paved surface. Parking lots were a popular location for in-line hockey games as were indoor roller skating rinks. In-line hockey was also played on portable rinks. The NHL Breakout tournament was played on this type of rink. Other tournaments and leagues also used these rinks. California's Pro Beach Hockey Series, which was broadcast on ESPN and ESPN2, was played on a portable Pro Beach Hockey rink. This rink (50 metres by 23 metres) was three-quarters the size of an ice hockey rink. It had 1,200 seats for spectators.

ASIASPORTS

Sports Management

Asiasports was a sports management company (sometimes called a sports marketing company). Sports marketing companies generally carried out a variety of activities. Among these were the organisation of fund raisers and sport event design and development, event production and consulting, sponsorship sales and management, media advertising, direct marketing, sales promotion and public relations.

Sports marketing companies often became synonymous with a particular form of sport. For example, Ryno Sports, which was based in California, principally promoted beach volleyball and beach softball. It sold sports that typified the California lifestyle. In connection with these sports, Ryno Sports provided a variety of services ranging from complete event management to professional athletic exhibitions, instructional clinics, turnkey events, consulting and the merchandising of gifts and merchandise.

Some sports marketing companies held a variety of sports properties. Lanier Sports Marketing, which operated out of Cary, North Carolina in the U.S., created, marketed and produced several types of sports in North Carolina. The company helped to create a boxing event called "King of the Ring," and it broadcast boxing. The company's other projects included sponsoring of golf tournaments and distributing and selling tickets for the local university basketball team. Finally, aside from these promotional activities, the company had an advertising arm that created and produced commercials and provided media planning and placement services.

Structure of Asiasports

Asiasports was formally incorporated on July 1, 1996. It was a widely held private company. The main shareholders were Shane Weir and Bill Gribble, each with a 30 per cent share. Barnes possessed 10 per cent, a Hong Kong venture capital company owned 10 per cent, and the remaining 20 per cent was held by 30 other people. The company had a board of directors. Seven to eight shareholders sat on the board; however, Weir and Gribble held most of the decision-making power. While it was a widely held company, its financial resources were limited to the pockets of Weir, Gribble and Barnes, which were not exceptionally deep.

Barnes made quarterly reports to the board, and the company had an annual general meeting. The board helped to set the strategic direction of the company, while Barnes had the autonomy to make day-to-day operating decisions. To aid his tasks, Barnes had one assistant, Keith Fong, and he contracted out secretarial support. When needed, Asiasports made use of volunteers composed of hockey league members and their families. However, all of the hands-on work for the company was done by Barnes and his assistant.

Growth of Asiasports

Weir, Gribble and Barnes founded Asiasports in response to opportunities for the promotion of hockey in Hong Kong. Prior to the founding of Asiasports, hockey in Hong Kong had been played on an informal basis for many years. Following the conclusion of a hockey tournament in March 1995, Barnes spoke with Weir and Gribble about their idea to create a sports marketing company for the promotion of hockey in Hong Kong. Barnes, who was looking for a new position at that time, began working for Asiasports on a full-time basis in July 1996.

Asiasports was founded with the mandate to manage hockey and other activities. In 1999, Asiasports was still in the entrepreneurial stage and Barnes was considering adding a variety of new hockey and non-hockey-related sports properties. It was by the addition of new properties and the expansion of existing ones, that sponsorship income had increased by 50 per cent from 1996 to 1999. During the same period, player fees had grown by 20 to 25 per cent on an annual basis. With the exception of the World Ice Hockey 5's event, all sports properties were individually profitable. Even so, the company had experienced a loss on its 1998 operations.

In its first three years of operations, Asiasports had organised and managed several leagues and events. Some of these were hockey-related, while others involved other sports such as slo-pitch softball and golf. Hockey itself did not have as high a profile in Hong Kong as other sports such as horse racing, soccer and tennis. Horse racing was a popular spectator event, with nightly broadcasts of race results on Hong Kong's main TV channels. Soccer and tennis were the main participant sports. A multitude of tennis courts and soccer fields were squeezed into the tight land space in Hong Kong.

Sources of Revenues

As a sports management company, Asiasports derived its revenues from a variety of sources. Its two primary sources of revenues were player fees and sponsorship income. Player fees represented money collected from participants in the leagues and tournaments organised by Asiasports. As an example, for a player in the South China Ice Hockey League (SCIHL), the fee for the 1998-99 season was HK$1,800 (US$230) (also see Exhibit 2).

exhibit 2   Revenues and Expenses for World Ice Hockey 5's
                Tournament (1999) (HK$)

Consolidated Financial Status		
Revenue (all sources)	Gordie Howe Event	235,520
	Sponsorship	542,000
	Players' Fees	148,759
	Merchandise	40,110
	Total Revenue	**966,389**
Expenses (all sources)	Gordie Howe Event	389,826
	Tournament Costs	843,970
	Total Expenses	**1,233,796**
Net Profit		**(267,407)**

exhibit 2   *(continued)*

Tournament Costs		
Expenses	Asia Sports Management Fees	85,000
	Video Production	30,000
	Working Staff	70,000
	Ice Rental	450,000
	Program Production	43,000
	Merchandise	88,750
	Other Expenses	77,220
	Total Expenses	**843,970**

Gordie Howe Event		
Revenue	Friday Dinner and Gala	65,000
	Gala Dinner	170,520
	Total revenue	**235,520**
Expenses	Appearance Fee	78,000
	Friday Dinner	11,626
	Books	68,000
	Personnel Costs	30,000
	Hotel costs	194,000
	Miscellaneous costs	8,200
	Total Expenses	**389,826**
Net Income—Gordie Howe Event		**(154,306)**

Sponsorship		
Revenue	Title Sponsor Sunday	—
	Co-Title Sponsor Nortel	250,000
	Associate Sponsor (Yellow Pages)	80,000
	Associate Sponsor (Budweiser)	80,000
	Dragon Centre/Sky Rink Team sponsorship	30,000
	Distacom— Team sponsorship	30,000
	French restaurant—Team sponsorship	15,000
	Cap. Z—Team sponsorship	15,000
	Ski at Whistler—Team sponsorship	15,000
	Lan Kwai Fong Holdings	10,000
	Drink Sponsors	—
	HK Land	7,000
	Dresdner Bank	5,000
	Kan and Co.	5,000
	Total Sponsorship Revenue	**542,000**

Player Fees and Merchandise Sales		
Player Entrance Fees	Foreign	83,359
	Local	65,400
	Total Player Fees	**148,759**
Merchandise Sales	**Total**	**40,110**
	Total Player Fees and	
	Merchandise Revenues	**730,869**

Source: Company documents.

exhibit 3   Sponsors for World Ice Hockey 5's (1999)

Main Sponsors	Other Sponsors
SUNDAY	Hong Kong Land
Nortel Networks	Distacom
Budweiser	Ski AT Whistler
Yellow Pages	Fred Kan & Co.
Swire Coca Cola	The Hong Kong Tourist Association
Air Canada	Hong Kong St. John's Ambulance
The Festival Walk	Texon Media
The Empire Hotel	Empire Brew
	Hong Kong Club
	Conrad International Hotel
	Dresdner RCM Global Investors
	API Prism
	Comforce Advertising and Promotion
	Asia Business Group
	Can-Am Ice Hockey Association

Source: Company documents.

For most of Asiasports' activities conducted in Hong Kong, player fees represented 50 per cent of its income. The other 50 per cent came from sponsorship income. Asiasports had engaged a number of sponsors for the SCIHL, and for its annual ice hockey tournament, the World Ice Hockey 5's. The main sponsors for the SCIHL were Budweiser, the SUNDAY network, Nortel Networks, the Hong Kong Yellow Pages, Caltex and Jack-in-the-Box. The number of sponsors for the World Ice Hockey 5's was the greatest, as shown in Exhibit 3.

In return for sponsorship, Asiasports gave sponsoring companies exposure. The principal sponsor for the ice hockey tournament was identified in the tournament's title—SUNDAY World Ice Hockey 5's. Tournament and league sponsors also had their names placed on the sweaters of competing teams, a practice similar to European hockey and football leagues, and auto-racing circuits in the U.S. and Europe. Sponsors were likewise identified in programs developed for tournaments. Sponsors also received name exposure through print and electronic media coverage of Asiasports-sponsored events. The two primary events, or sports properties, were the South China Ice Hockey League and the World Ice Hockey 5's.

ASIASPORTS PROPERTIES

South China Ice Hockey League

The South China Ice Hockey League (SCIHL) stimulated much interest in hockey in Hong Kong. The league began in the fall of 1995 with four teams and about 60 players. In the 1996-97 season, six teams competed in the league which involved about 100 players. In the fourth and most recent season (1998–99), six teams and more than 100 players competed in the first division, and another six teams competed in the second division. The first division was the competitive league. The second division was a developmental league. Both men and women who were new to hockey, and children, were members of second division teams.

The SCIHL was originally founded in response to Hong Kong expatriates' desire to play hockey while living in Hong Kong. However, the current coverage of SCIHL extended beyond that original objective. The players came from many of the expatriates who lived in Hong Kong: Canada, China, Finland, France, Japan, Sweden, Switzerland and the United States, among other countries (see Exhibit 4). The majority of the players in the second division were from Hong Kong.

The growth of participation of players from Hong Kong echoed the mushrooming popularity of hockey throughout Asia. Barnes believed Asia's fascination with ice skating owed much to the exposure to figure skating in the Winter Olympics and the success of Asian figure skating champions, like Michelle Kwan, Chen Lu and Kristi Yamaguchi. This interest, he said, often leads skaters to turn to ice hockey. Barnes noted, "Once you master skating around in circles, you'll eventually get bored and want to try something else like ice hockey."

In the SCIHL, as in other areas of Southeast Asia, games were played in ice rinks located in shopping malls. There were five ice rinks in Hong Kong in 1999, with the most recent built in 1998. The venue for the SCIHL was the Skyrink, which was located in the Dragon Centre Shopping Mall, Kowloon. The size of a shopping mall rink was two-thirds that of a standard rink. Consequently, five players—two forwards, two defence and one goaltender—played on a team, rather than the six used in a standard ice hockey game (see the Appendix on page 31). Fewer players meant that the game was faster and higher scoring than the six-player version. It was more entertaining for the casual spectators that watched the game while shopping in the mall.

exhibit 4   Population and Nationality of Hong Kong Residents (1996)

Place of Birth / Nationality	Number of People	Per cent of Population
Place of Birth		
Hong Kong	3,749,332	60.30
China and Macau	2,096,511	33.72
Elsewhere	371,713	5.98
Nationality for Elsewhere category		
Filipino	118,449	1.91
Chinese	57,393	0.92
British	44,703	0.72
United States American	18,502	0.30
Japanese	17,999	0.29
Indian, Pakistani, Bangladeshi	17,379	0.28
Thai	15,494	0.25
Canadian	10,816	0.17
Australian	7,777	0.13
Portuguese	323	0.01
Others	62,878	1.01
Total	**6,217,556**	**100.00**

Note: People born in Hong Kong, China and Macau held a variety of nationalities.
Source: 1996 Population By-census. Census and Statistics Department, Hong Kong.

World Ice Hockey 5's

The World Ice Hockey 5's was an annual event that had been held since the early 1990s. The idea for the tournament had sprung from a group of American and Canadian hockey players who played hockey at the City Plaza Rink, in Tai Koo Shing, Hong Kong. Four teams competed in this tournament, in which five games were played over a weekend. It was named Hockey 5's because five, rather than six players, played for each team (see the Appendix on page 31 for a summary of rules for this game).

The first World Ice Hockey 5's tournament was held in 1994. The Swedish company Ericsson sponsored this tournament which saw three local teams and three overseas teams (Beijing, Bangkok and Bahrain) compete for the title. The number of teams grew to nine in 1995, with Moosehead as the lead sponsor.

The event continued to grow through the next three years. In 1996, ten teams competed, with overseas teams from Tokyo, South Korea, Dubai, Bangkok, Singapore and Beijing. In 1997, the number of teams grew by 50 per cent and the name, World Ice Hockey 5's—Hong Kong, was coined. This tournament also marked the introduction of women's teams, from Hong Kong, Japan and Harbin, China, to the tournament. With the continued expansion of the tournament, two venues were used to stage the tournament.

The 1998 tournament saw the introduction of a Kids Division and an All-Asia Men's Division. The number of teams in this tournament more than doubled to 34. Sixty-four games were played over four days at the Skyrink and the City Plaza rink. The 1999 tournament was billed as Asia's largest ice hockey tournament and the world's largest ice hockey 5's tournament. It had more than 40 teams competing in four divisions: Kid's Division, Women's Division, Men's Division 1 and Men's Division 2 (see Exhibit 5). Because of the growth in the tournament, it was held over a period of 10 to 11 days, rather than one weekend.

The growth in the number of teams in the tournament sparked wider media coverage of the event. The tournament had 49 clippings and stories written about it in Chinese and English language print media in Hong Kong, and in print media in Japan and Canada. In the electronic media, ATV, a Hong Kong broadcaster, covered the tournament's final two days. A special five-minute feature was also carried on TVB Pearl. Other coverage was received from CNN and the Asia Sports show.

exhibit 5   Participation in World Ice Hockey 5's Tournament (1999)

Kid's Division	Women's Division	Men's Division 1	Men's Division 2
Number of Teams:			
11 Teams	6 Teams	15 Teams	10 Teams
Sources of Teams:			
Hong Kong	Canada	Canada	Hong Kong
Philippines	Hong Kong	Bangkok	Macao
Singapore	Japan	Hong Kong	Philippines
Taiwan	Philippines	Japan	Singapore
	Singapore	Singapore	United Arab Emirates
		Taiwan	
		United States	
		United Arab Emirates	

Source: Company documents.

Asiasports' special guest for the 1999 tournament, Gordie Howe, enhanced media coverage because Howe was widely regarded as one of the greatest players in the sport of hockey. Both local and international media mentioned Howe's attendance at the tournament in their coverage of the 7th annual World Ice Hockey 5's.

In observing the tournament, Howe noticed parallels between the present situation for hockey in Hong Kong, and that in the southern United States in the 1970s. Howe said, "When I heard they played hockey in Hong Kong, I had the same reaction as when they started playing hockey in Florida" (reported in Hong Kong Standard, 12/03/1999). In 1999, Florida had two professional teams competing in the NHL.

Other Properties/Events

Asiasports organised a number of other hockey tournaments in different parts of Asia and Southeast Asia. In 1997, Asiasports ran tournaments in Macao, Bangkok, Thailand and Jakarta, Indonesia. In 1998 and 1999, the company continued to be active in Asian tournament hockey. Manila in the Philippines, Dubai, and Bangkok were each the site of an Asiasports hockey tournament. Asiasports also assisted with signing up teams for a tournament in 1998 in Ulaan Baatar, Mongolia.

Aside from running hockey tournaments, Asiasports supported the development of hockey. It ran programs for coaches and training programs for children who wanted to play ice hockey or in-line hockey. Occasionally, Asiasports promoted non-hockey sporting events, such as softball or golf, but when it did this, it competed directly with other sports management companies in Hong Kong. When Asiasports concentrated on hockey it had no direct competition in Hong Kong, and little across the rest of Southeast Asia. Even rink operators were not competitors because ice skating rinks were concerned with attracting a figure skating audience.

FUTURE GROWTH

Setting for Expansion

By the spring of 1999, Asiasports had been successful in developing the SCIHL and the World Ice Hockey 5's tournament. However, these properties alone were not enough to meet the company's mandate, and Barnes' goal of bringing hockey to prominence in Southeast Asia. In 1999, hockey still existed as a fringe sport in Hong Kong and other Southeast Asian countries like the Philippines, Taiwan, Thailand, Malaysia and Singapore. No national bodies organised the sport in these countries.

The growth of hockey in these countries had been sporadic and slow, especially compared to the more northerly Asian countries, China, Japan and South Korea. In Japan, for example, hockey was played at many levels. Developmental leagues existed for children, many universities had their own teams, a variety of people played in informal leagues, and a semi-professional (semi-pro) league, similar to what could be seen in Europe, China and South Korea, also existed. Women's hockey in all three countries was strong. China's women's national team was the third best in the world in the latter half of the 1990s.

The growth in the popularity of hockey in China, Japan and South Korea had attracted the attention of the IIHF. It was involved in linking ice hockey in these countries to the hockey world at large. However, ice hockey in Hong Kong and other Southeast Asian countries had yet to draw any serious attention from the IIHF. Even so, the IIHF was aware of Asiasport's activities in Hong Kong. Unlike the IIHF, the NHL had expressed some interest in hockey in Southeast Asia. It had offices in Japan and Australia. It played two league games in Japan each year. Further, the NHL had provided Asiasports with merchandise and logos for Asiasports' events.

Options

Several options existed for Asiasports. These options included both geographic and product diversification, as well as an increased focus on existing products. Barnes wanted to bring hockey to Asia, but in considering these options, he thought "he would take Asiasports where the money was, to keep the company alive."

1. **Set up Hockey Leagues in Southeast Asia.** In 1999, the only established hockey league in Southeast Asia was SCIHL in Hong Kong. The opportunity existed to set up similar leagues in Bangkok, Manila, Taipei, Singapore and Ho Chi Minh City. The state of hockey in these cities was similar to that in Hong Kong in the early 1990s, and each city possessed a viable rink on which hockey could be played. Further, Bill Gribble was located in Taiwan, and he had done some groundwork on establishing hockey in Taipei.

2. **Develop and Expand Existing Tournaments.** Asiasports organized four to five tournaments each year across several cities in Southeast Asia. One option was to deepen its involvement in these tournaments. It could do this by committing more time to developing sponsors for the various events, by seeking a wider coverage of cities for the tournaments, and by giving tournament partners in various cities access to players who competed in the SCIHL.

3. **Develop In-line Hockey.** In 1999, in-line hockey did not enjoy as good a penetration in Hong Kong as ice hockey because it was still new. Furthermore, in-line skating was difficult to do as a recreation in Hong Kong because of the danger caused by the crowded roads, and steep inclines found on many roads. Even so, in-line hockey had begun to sprout in Hong Kong and was played at two locations: Discovery Bay on Hong Kong Island, and Diamond Hill in Kowloon. An advantage to developing in-line hockey was that the NHL had expressed an interest in promoting in-line hockey in Hong Kong. If this option was pursued, there was the chance for Asiasports to develop a tie-in with the NHL for the promotion of the sport and the sale of NHL-branded merchandise.

4. **Develop Other Properties.** This option included the development of a series of golf and softball tournaments. While this activity would bring Asiasports into more direct competition with other sports management companies in Hong Kong, it would broaden the base of Asiasports' properties and increase the number of potential participants and sponsors.

5. **Develop a Semi-Pro League in Hong Kong.** This option represented a shift in the way Asiasports did business. Developing a semi-pro league meant that players would receive a salary for playing, rather than paying a fee. The loss of user revenues and the higher cost structure would have to be offset by increases in sponsorship revenues. A semi-pro league would have a higher profile, as did the World Hockey 5's tournament, than the SCIHL. As well, the league could be an avenue by which hockey in Hong Kong could be linked to that in China, Japan, South Korea and perhaps elsewhere in the world.

As Barnes considered these options, he could not divorce himself from the context of Asiasports. It was a young, entrepreneurial company that had the financial and human resource constraints typically faced by such companies. It could not pursue all options, and its biggest challenge might be to solidify its current activities in Hong Kong before expanding. Even so, whichever option was selected, it had to be selected soon because the 1999–2000 season was approaching rapidly.

The Richard Ivey School of Business gratefully acknowledges the generous support of The Richard and Jean Ivey Fund in the development of this case as part of the *Richard and Jean Ivey Fund Asian Case Series*

appendix   Understanding the Game of Ice Hockey 5's

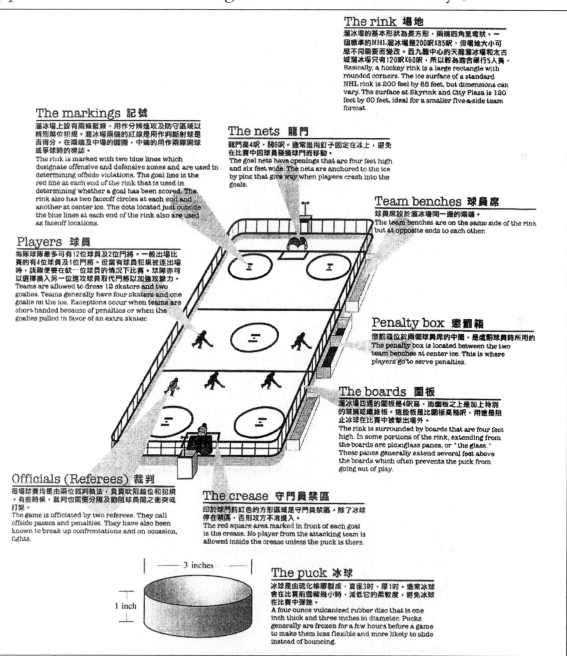

Source: Company documents.

case 4 A Note on the Cuban Cigar Industry

The air was thick with anticipation. The tension was palpable. In 2002, Cuba was preparing to receive former U.S. president Jimmy Carter, the first U.S. president to visit Cuba following the embargo. Business leaders in the Northern Hemisphere were very attentive, as the possibility of a softening in U.S.-Cuban relations could lead to an easing of the embargo's restrictions, and the resumption of trade with the largest trading block in the Northern Hemisphere. John Hernandez, a recent MBA graduate from a prestigious institution in Canada and an avid cigar smoker, viewed this scenario and wondered what effect the visit could have on the current environment, and if there was potential to enter the Cuban cigar industry. With an inheritance of $1 million coming available in the next month, he thought back to his strategy sessions and looked to evaluate this industry.

HISTORY

The history of Cuba and tobacco are interwoven. When Columbus arrived in Cuba, little did he know that the medicinal herb enjoyed by the natives would become the scourge of society to some and a multibillion-dollar industry worldwide. Although the origin of tobacco is still disputed, as is the derivation of the name tobacco, its introduction to Western civilization is well documented and accepted as owing to the expedition to the "New World" of Christopher Columbus.

Columbus sailed to the Americas in 1492. In his quest for the riches of the Orient, he came across a race of native people, called the Taino, who were smoking tobacco leaves roughly rolled into a shape which they called "cohiba." It is written by Batholomeu de las Casa of the first expedition into Cuba,

Akash Kapoor prepared this case under the supervision of Professor Paul W. Beamish solely to provide material for class discussion. The authors do not intend to illustrate either effective or ineffective handling of a managerial situation. The authors may have disguised certain names and other identifying information to protect confidentiality.

Copyright © 2003, Ivey Management Services   Version: (A) 2003-02-04

These two Christians met many people on the road . . . men always with a fire-brand in their hands, and certain herbs to take their smokes, which are some dried herbs put in a certain leaf . . . after the fashion of a musket . . . such as boys make at the feast of the Holy Ghost. These are lit at one end and the other end they chew or suck, and take it in with their breath the smoke. These were claimed to drive away all weariness, and were called Tobago.[1]

Tobacco was brought to the Western world after this expedition, and the Spaniards held a monopoly over the tobacco trade for many years. Cuba was considered to be Spain's lifeline between the Old and New Worlds. However, in 1762, Britain invaded and briefly dominated the island. During this brief period, Cuba was opened to world-wide trade and a new-found prosperity. When Spain retook control one year later, trade restrictions were imposed; however, the seeds of prosperity had been planted in the community. In 1817, Spain removed trade restrictions and began a period of renewed prosperity. World demand for Cuban products was so high that in 1845, tobacco replaced coffee as the second most important agricultural product, and demand for Cuban tobacco continued to increase.[2] In the 1850s, paper bands were introduced in Cuba to distinguish the many prestigious brands of cigars. The powerful and wealthy members of high society soon wanted custom-designed bands as symbols of their importance and taste. Hence, the Cuban cigar established a reputation as an "accoutrement of wealth, power and prestige."[3]

In 1868, the first of two upheavals in the Cuban cigar industry took place. The Ten Years' War saw a number of growers flee the country for America, taking with them prized Cuban seed. Key West and Tampa were major beneficiaries of this migration.

The second upheaval came at the time of the revolution between 1959 and 1962. When Fidel Castro overthrew then-President Batista and nationalized approximately $1 billion of U.S.-owned property, the U.S. government subsequently imposed an economic blockade on Cuba. This action was a shock to the island's economy, as the United States was one of its largest trading partners. The revolution was a major and unexpected catalyst for worldwide competition, as Cuba saw a major departure of its key players in the industry. Not only did they bring seed, but they brought their knowledge, skill and expertise, keys to cigar making and production.

The first exodus gave the U.S. cigar industry a major boost, the ability to produce a cigar of similar quality sold at a much lower price. The revolution had a far greater impact on the Cuban cigar industry exodus of many key players and workers to other countries. This essentially opened the doors of the cigar industry to competition, as growers, manufacturers, rollers and actual Cuban seed and knowledge found their way to the United States, Dominican Republic and Honduras, to name but a few. In 1997, 250 million cigars were exported from the Dominican Republic, an example of the market which United States cigar consumers represent.

The Cuban revolution also brought with it a command economy, and the cigar industry in Cuba was not spared. The entire industry was placed under state control, and the celebrated brands of Cuban cigars were disbanded in favor of nameless cigars.

---

[1] Tabago, published by H.F. & Ph. F. Reemstra, Cigarette Makers, Germany, 1960.

[2] L. Glenn Westfall, "Don Vicente Martinez Ybor, The Man and His Empire: Development of the Clear Havana Industry in Cuba and Florida in the Nineteenth Century," Garland Publishing, Inc., New York and London, c. 1987.

[3] Nathanial Lande and Andrew Lande, "The Havanas: Past, Present, and Future," Smoke Magazine, Summer 1998, Volume III, Issue 3.

However, after the disastrous response to these cigars and their horrendous quality, the state reinstituted the brands and allowed 'private farming' for tobacco plantations. It would take until the 1970s before they fully re-established the reputation that Cuban cigars had enjoyed for centuries.

In 1975, the World Court ruled that exiled Cuban cigar makers had the right to use their former brand names. Many great cigar families who had left their homeland, such as the Cifuentes family (Partagas) and the Menendez family (Montecristo), wished to continue production of their brand name cigars, and the ruling gave them the opportunity. This is why, in many cases, there are two versions of many Cuban brands: those produced with Cuban tobacco and those produced with non-Cuban tobacco. The families produced their own tobacco, and developed new packaging and cigar bands for their new versions of cigars. Partagas, Montecristo, Upmann, Hoyo de Monterrey, and Romeo y Julieta are some of the examples of Cuban brands that have dual versions.

Originally, Cuban tobacco leaves were shipped to Spain for rolling in the factories; however, when the shipments arrived and it was found that the fabricated cigars survived the journey in much better condition than the actual leaf, the cigar factories in Cuba were established. It is from these humble beginnings that the myth of the Havana cigar was born and continues to be pervasive today.

THE PRODUCT

The cigar has remained much the same over hundreds of years. There are three basic types of cigar produced in Cuba: handmade, hand-finished and machine-made. Structurally, the difference among the three is that handmade cigars use long filler and are bunched and rolled entirely by hand, whereas hand-finished cigars are bunched by machine and only the wrapper is put on by hand. Machine-made cigars are fully automated and generally use short filler and a composite binder. Long filler refers to a full tobacco leaf, short filler to cut up or leftover tobacco. The finished product, the cigar itself, comes in many different shapes and sizes. The distinction between brands comes from the blend used in the filler, the type of binder and the wrapper used to finish the product. These "recipes" are closely guarded secrets. The product itself however does not complete the package. It is at this point that the marketing and the mystique of the Havana cigar begin to take the product from the workers' bench to the consumer. The bands, the boxes and the traditions were all elements of the Havana cigar.

THE PLANTS

The cigar is constructed from the leaves of two different tobacco plants. One plant yields the filler (tripa) and the binder (capote) of the cigar, and the other yields the wrapper (capa).

The Havana cigar contains leaves from two different types of tobacco plants, the criollo plant and the corojo plant. The criollo plant produces the tobacco to be blended and the binder that holds the tobacco together. The corojo plant produces the wrapper that finishes the cigar and dictates its final appearance. Recently, the Cubans have been experimenting with new strains of tobacco that are more resistant to the elements and pests, scourges of the tobacco industry. The criollo plant is grown in the sun; the corojo, or other strain for the wrapper, is grown under muslin cloth to protect it and to maintain a uniform leaf color and texture. This tending and careful harvesting of the wrapper leaves adds to the cost of the production.

Growing tobacco is a nine-month to 10-month process, beginning in the summer months with tilling and ground preparation, and ending with the harvesting of the leaves from January through March. Harvesting is a very large undertaking that takes time, patience and much labor. Therefore, the fields are planted a few weeks apart so harvesting is also staggered.

The various leaves on each tobacco plant are harvested on different days. A typical tobacco plant has 16 to 18 leaves. Pickers start from the bottom and work to the top, or coronas, because the leaves at the bottom of the plant ripen earlier. As such, harvesting occurs over a staggered period. The leaves at different levels are given different classifications, and their uses differ based on their characteristics. There are only five major categories: capa, capote, and those used for the filler, volado, seco and ligero. The picking of the leaves requires a great deal of judgment and experience on the part of the growers, as explained by one of Cuba's most revered tobacco growers, Don Alejandro Robaina.

> Too early or too late, the cigar will not be good. You have to take the leaf at the precise moment.[4]

When the leaves are picked they are green. They are loaded into carts and taken to curing barns, or casas del tabaco. The drying process usually takes 50 days. Inside the barns, the leaves are strung with needles and threaded onto long poles. During the curing process, the leaves turn to a light brown. Once this occurs, they are removed from the barns and prepared for the first fermentation. This process allows the tobacco to undergo chemical changes, enhancing the flavor and aroma, while reducing the bitterness and the impurities within the tobacco. This first fermentation takes about 30 days. Depending upon the leaves, they are then classified and perhaps stripped of their stems. A second fermentation follows and lasts up to 60 days. The tobacco is then aired and packed in large square bales called tercios. These bales weigh about 150 pounds (68 kilograms) and are covered with royal palm leaves and burlap. The bales may be stored in the warehouse for up to two years before being shipped to the factories for cigar production.

PUTTING THE CIGAR TOGETHER

The long-held legend of the Havana being rolled on the thighs of virgins is a fanciful myth. A journalist in the 1940s observed female workers sorting leaves and placing the piles in their laps, and the legend was born. The actual construction of the cigar is less fantastical, yet requires a great deal of skill and experience from the torcedores, or rollers. A cigar is put together by taking different leaves from the criollo plant and blending them according to the recipes that the master blender carefully guards and prepares. Many blends have been passed down from generation to generation, while others are newly conceived for new brands. Generally there will be up to three leaves in the blend, a combination of the ligero, seco and volado leaves. These leaves are placed on top of each other in the correct blend and formed carefully to ensure proper tightness and construction. The binder is then used to bunch the blended tobacco. After a process of shaping the bunches in pressed moulds, the wrapper is stretched over the bunched, formed leaves. The torcedores shape the wrapper to the correct size with a chaveta, or semi-circular knife. A piece is then taken from the excess wrapper

---

[4]Jonathan Futrell and Lisa Linder, "Up in Smoke," Conran Octopus Limited, London, c. 1998.

to make the head of the cigar, which holds the cigar together. This is put on with an odorless, tasteless vegetable gum. The cigar is then inspected for girth and length and is then taken through a rigorous process of fumigation and aging, and then through to quality control for inspection, grading and presentation. The drying and aging of the cigars is necessary to remove excess moisture from the cigars, and to remove the harshness from the new cigar. A good roller in Cuba can produce 100 to 150 cigars a day. Machine-made cigars can be produced in quantity of 10,000 cigars a day. It is the premium cigars, however, that Cuba has been focused on to this point.

TOBACCO GROWING REGIONS

The five main tobacco growing regions in Cuba are: Oriente (Eastern Provinces), Remedios (Villa Clara Province), Partidos (Eastern la Habano Province), Semi Vuelta and the famed Vuelta Abajo (in Pinar del Rio Province) (see Exhibit 1). The average temperature is 25°C (75°F) and the average relative humidity is around 80 per cent. The pinnacle of these regions is the Vuelta and Semi-Vuelta areas in the Pinar del Rio region. It is believed that this region is the cradle of the Havanas, producing the finest tobacco in the world. It is from this region that the tobacco and wrappers for the super premium cigars come. Approximately 70 per cent of all tobacco grown in Cuba is harvested here.[5] The distinction here is the soil and the microclimate that keeps the humidity ideal for growing and cultivating tobacco. The private (run by families) farm system in Cuba also allows family traditions and secrets to remain and be passed on, in spite of the constant demand and pressure to increase yields. The Cuban government has been the only buyer of the output from these farms since the revolution. The other regions are not as famous as the Vuelta Abajo region, which is the only region that produces all the components used in the cigar; however, they do also produce some cigar-quality tobacco. Generally speaking, the tobaccos from the other regions are used as follows: from the Partido region, the tobacco is used for wrappers; from the Semi-Vuelta, tobacco is used for filler and cigarettes; from the Oriente and Remedios regions, the tobacco is used for filler, cigarettes and for export to overseas markets. Thus, the very best tobacco of the Vuleta Abajo is in finite supply, and should the industry need to expand, these other regions may become a significant part of the future industry.

PESTS AND DISASTERS

In all the regions, the farmers and growers are most concerned with the conditions of the plantations and the climate. A major crop can be decimated and yields can be affected within days should the climate become too extreme or disease become introduced into the crop. A major concern for growers is a disease called blue mould. It is a mildew that thrives in adverse climatic conditions and can destroy entire crops within days. It has affected all the major tobacco growing regions in the Caribbean at one time, and was more of a threat in Cuba when the economic crisis prevented the purchase of sufficient pesticides to combat the mould. New strains of tobacco seed are being engineered and tested that may have a resistance to this scourge; however, this is always a significant variable which the industry examines every year, since

---

[5]Business Tips on Cuba, July 1998, "The Cigar Market." Printed in La Habana, Cuba.

without sufficient quality raw material, the system will be stretched to meet demand in the marketplace.

OTHER REGIONS

As noted earlier, members of the tobacco labor force fled Cuba in great numbers and in two waves, taking Cuban tobacco seed with them. They found their way into many Central American and Carribean countries, where they planted the seeds and tried to replicate the Cuban tobacco. Other countries, such as Cameroon and the United States (Connecticut and Virginia in particular), have been producing quality tobacco for many years also. Whether or not the quality has attained that of the Cuban tobacco is a matter of great debate; however, the threat to the Cuban cigar is more intense now, as the market begins to slow down.

> Just as wine drinkers have adapted to new world blends, so the cigar lover is learning to embrace a different—and invariably cheaper—kind of smoke.[6]

> See Exhibit 2 for more detailed information on the various tobacco growing regions and the characteristics of the tobacco in those regions.

THE CUBAN ENVIRONMENT

The United States is one of the largest markets for cigars in the world. Thus a brief recount of the U.S. relationship with the Cuban environment is necessary.

Prior to the revolution, with then-President Batista in power, it was perceived that U.S. interests in Cuba moulded the direction of the country. Seventy per cent of the land was controlled by less then 10 per cent of landowners, with U.S. owners controlling 25 per cent of Cuban land. The sugar trade with the United States was enormous, accounting for fully one-third of U.S. sugar imports. The deterioration of relations between the two countries began with the revolution and culminated in the early 1960s with the Cuban missile crisis and imposition of the trade and financial embargo in 1962. The loss of U.S. trade and investment, particularly in the sugar industry, was devastating to the Cuban economy. It was at this point that the Russians stepped in and essentially subsidized the economy by picking up the sugar quotas the United States had cut off. Cuba's economy became heavily dependent on Soviet support, and it also adopted the command type of economy. Cuba's economy was heavily reliant on sugar, and thus became heavily dependent on the former USSR. Essentially, the Soviets bartered crude oil and refined products at below-market prices in exchange for Cuban sugar at relatively high price levels (51 cents per pound in 1986, compared with a world market price of six cents). The Russians thus counteracted most of the effects of the U.S. blockade and accounted for as much as one-fourth of Cuba's national income in some years.[7]

However, the effects of the embargo could still be felt. The Russian assistance hid the fact that Cuba was reliant on suppliers and markets as far away as Europe and Asia. Ships that traded with Cuba were unable to enter U.S. ports and thus incurred higher

---

[6]Up in Smoke, by Jonathan Futrell and Lisa Linder, c1998, Contran Octopus Limited, London.

[7]"Cuba's Agriculture: Collapse & Economic Reform," Agricultural Outlook 1998, Economic Research Service/USDA, pp. 26-31.

import costs as ships had to go to non-U.S. ports with empty ships. The higher transport are costs paid by the Cubans.

Between 1989 and 1991, the economies in Eastern Europe collapsed and the Soviet Union dissolved. This proved to be disastrous to the Cuban economy, as they lost their major source of foreign assistance, as well as their major markets. An ancillary event was the loss of Soviet subsidized oil, which plunged Cuba into an energy crisis. Cuban foreign trade fell 75 per cent, and economic output fell 50 per cent. By 1994, agricultural production had fallen 54 per cent from 1989 levels.[8]

The response from the Cuban government was to implement an austerity program geared to steer through the crisis and begin rebuilding the Cuban economy. This "Special Period in Peacetime" program clamped down on rations, including food, fuel and electricity. Cuban leaders began to reform the economy by looking to the future of their country and studying activities that would develop and bring in hard currency. Industries such as tourism and biotechnology were encouraged, as was domestic food production.

Another major initiative was the encouragement of foreign economic associations in areas such as mining, tourism and telecommunications, among others, as well as tobacco. The initiatives taken, including legalizing the use of American dollars, produced signs of economic recovery. While Cuba's economic recovery has started, there are still serious shortcomings and problems to be faced. For example, the Cuban trade deficit continues, foreign exchange problems persist and energy is still in short supply. Agricultural production has not completely returned to pre-crisis levels. Industry infrastructure remains in poor condition, and investment resources are still in short supply.

The situation amplifies the effect of the embargo on the Cuban economy. Denied access to the largest trading entity in the Northern Hemisphere makes the needs of the country more expensive. Measures taken in the 1990s have added to the pressure on Cuba to maintain its health and viability. The Helms-Burton Act, officially known as the Cuban Liberty and Democratic Solidarity Act of 1996, added to this burden in several ways. First, it limited the trade that subsidiaries of U.S. companies in other countries could conduct with Cuba. Second, it allowed the United States to impose sanctions on countries trading with Cuba. Third, it barred officials of corporations doing business in Cuba from entering the United States. Essentially, the United States is trying to extend its embargo to other trading partners of Cuba, in an effort to further alienate and pressure the Cuban regime. Exhibit 3 details the purposes of the Helms-Burton Act from the text of the agreement.

PRESENT DAY

Cuba has entered a pivotal point in its existence. With a population in 2002 of 11,224,321 and per capita gross national product (GNP) of only $1,700, Cuba was a poor country. In December 1999, the first commercial transaction took place between the United States and Cuba since the Kennedy administration imposed the embargo 40 years earlier. The restrictions of the embargo were eased slightly to allow foodstuffs to be bought, but only on a cash-and-carry basis. No credit could be granted to buy the goods. And despite the vehemence of the rhetoric against the Cuban government, Cuban-Americans send home between US$600 to US$950 million every year. In every year in the past decade, the United Nations has overwhelmingly condemned the

---

[8]Ibid.

embargo. On November 27, 2001, the vote was a 167-to-three renunciation of the embargo. As farm prices decline in the United States, pressure builds to open up a market 90 miles from U.S. shores. All this comes at a time when the Cuban-American population holds a great deal of political sway in the elections of Florida and in the United States. Some have even argued that George Bush owed his presidency to the State of Florida and its Hispanic voters.

> The Cuban national nightmare, the thing that keeps good revolutionaries awake at night in cold sweats, is the example of Puerto Rico—a Spanish Caribbean island whose independence and culture has been largely swallowed up by the giant to the north. There is an acute Cuban fear that American investment, American tourism, American cultural influence and an American political system (fuelled, of course, by good old American campaign contributions) will someday swamp Cuban society and turn it into a cross between Cancun and Las Vegas.[9]

All of this was occurring at a time when there was increased investment and assistance into Cuba from countries other than the United States.

The debate on whether the embargo will be lifted or not is wide-ranging, with opinions and speculation across all spectrums of thought. Yet, whether or not the embargo will be lifted, the effect on the Cuban cigar industry is significant and affects the way the business operates. The industry has survived and even prospered without the U.S. market over the past 40 years. In today's marketplace, can Cuba sustain that?

THE MAJOR COMPANIES

The worldwide cigar industry has two major corporations: Altadis and Swedish Match (see Exhibit 4). These two entities control, through ownership or interest in other companies, the distribution of Havana cigars and Cuban brand names worldwide. There are other smaller companies; however, we will focus on the major players that affect the Cuban cigar industry.

ALTADIS S.A.

Altadis is the result of a 1999 merger, valued at US$3.3 billion, between two giants in the industry: Spanish Tabacalera S.A. and the French SEITA S.A (see Exhibits 5 and 6). In 2000, Altadis also completed a joint venture agreement with Habanos S.A., the company that holds the monopoly on Cuban cigar exports out of Cuba, and the company that owns all Cuban brands outside of the United States. Altadis purchased 50 per cent of Habanos for US$477 million, giving it access to most of the major Cuban brands in all markets. As a result, Altadis is the largest cigar company in the world, selling 3.3 billion cigars in 2000. It had sales of over US$10 billion in 2001 and a market capitalization of US$7.2 billion.

When the two companies merged, the management of Tabacalera became responsible for the worldwide cigar and distribution businesses. Worldwide market share in the major markets was as follows in the year 2000: United States 37 per cent, Spain 42 per cent, and France 33 per cent.

The history of Tabacalera and Cuba is very strong and is in direct contrast to the relationship that competitors in the United States share with Cuba. Tabacalera, the

---

[9] "End the Cuba Embargo Now," Esquire, New York, September 2001, by Walter Russell Mead.

Spanish catalyst behind the merger to form Altadis, was and is Cuba's biggest and most revered cigar partner. It is this former government-controlled entity that annually invests upwards of US$25 million in Cuba's industry, thereby serving the dual purpose of aiding the financially strapped industry and ensuring Tabacalera the largest access to Cuban tobacco and finished cigars. According to a cigar analyst, this relationship means that Altadis will have better and stronger relationships with the Cubans than any American company.

To give perspective on what the merger means, consider that prior to the merger:

1. Tabacalera and Seita were the largest purchasers of Cuban-produced cigars, accounting for almost 40 per cent of the 1998 exports;
2. They were the two largest sources of financing for Cuban-produced tobacco at almost US$50 million for the 1998 tobacco harvest; and
3. They were the two largest purchasers of Cuban-produced tobacco leaf, accounting for almost all of the 13,000 tonnes exported in 1998.

These two companies that separately dominated the Cuban export market are now the largest cigar company in the world.

HABANOS S.A.

Habanos S.A. was formed in 1994 as the export, distribution and marketing arm of the state tobacco firm. They are the official owners of all of the Cuban brand names. As mentioned above, Habanos S.A. entered into a joint venture agreement with Altadis that has brought increased investment into the Cuban industry, as well as stability and increased production capacity. Also, the joint venture brought greater exposure for the Cuban cigars worldwide. In 2001, Habanos S.A. revenues were US$150 million, US$129 million of which was from exports and tourist sales of approximately 118 million cigars. The export of tobacco leaf brought in US$17 million. One of the major initiatives of the joint venture is to enter the machine-made cigar industry with Cuban-produced tobacco, gaining leverage from the country's existing reputation for tobacco. The machine-made cigar market is US$10 billion worldwide.

ALTADIS U.S.A. (FORMERLY HAV-A-TAMPA AND CONSOLIDATED CIGAR)

In August 2000, Hav-A-Tampa and Consolidated Cigar were legally merged to form Altadis U.S.A. This created a powerful entity in the U.S. market as the new entity now controlled more than a third of the U.S. cigar market, including many of the non-Cuban produced Cuban brands. Altadis sells close to two billion cigars per year, and through their equity position in the company, Cuban Cigar Brands, Altadis U.S.A. has sole ownership of their rights to these non-Cuban produced Cuban brand names, including Montecristo and H.Upmann.

SWEDISH MATCH AND GENERAL CIGAR

Swedish Match is the second largest cigar company in the world. With the acquisitions of El Credito Cigars Inc. and the machine-made cigar division of U.S. cigar company General Cigar Holdings Inc. in 1999, and the acquisition of 64 per cent of General

Cigar Holdings Inc.'s remaining business in 2000, Swedish Match purchased a significant role in the premium cigar market. General Cigar has the rights to market many of the non-Cuban-produced Cuban brand names in the United States, and has the best selling premium cigar in the United States, the Macunado (produced in Jamaica). Swedish Match is highly diversified in tobacco products and accessories, and through General Cigar has a well-established presence in the huge U.S. cigar market.

CIGAR INDUSTRY

Since the collapse of the Eastern European economies, Cuba's need for hard currency has been paramount to supply the country with the basic essentials. As such, the cigar industry in Cuba provided a much-needed lift to the economy at a pivotal point.

The cigar industry is a study in Cuban history and in the Cuban people. It is a part of the culture and folklore. Domestically, 300 million cigars are smoked in Cuba annually; however, the domestic market is not often considered or focused on in analysis, as it is the foreign premium cigar exports that bring in the hard currency. The farms are small, and the communities lend help and support during harvest times. Communities work together and form traditions that have passed down for centuries. Notwithstanding, the workers in the cigar factories are paid per piece, often making more than the average salary. Farmers can buy tracts of land and they are responsible for that land, even though they must produce to meet the state quota. There is a sense of ownership once again, and this has lead directly to the resurgence of the industry after the post-revolution regime had nationalized the industry. Foreign ownership of land, however, is currently not permitted under the socialist regime.

The production in the premium cigar factories is under the direct control of Cuba's Union of Tobacco Enterprises and is completely separate from the Altadis-Habanos joint venture. However, the expertise of Altadis in various functions within the factories will surely be felt at some point, particularly in quality control. As the joint venture is responsible for the export and marketing of the products from these factories, Habanos has appointed exclusive dealers throughout the world to distribute the Havana cigars. Only these dealers have access to the cigar supply. Jurisdictions not covered by these dealers have sale and purchase agreements directly with Habanos S.A. From there, the dealers sell to wholesalers and retailers in their jurisdictions.

The production and export of cigars have undergone radical changes during and since the 1990s. The emergence of Cigar Aficionado, a magazine devoted to lovers of cigars and celebrity endorsement of cigar smoking, touched off a boom in the cigar market in the mid-1990s. The graphs in Exhibits 7 and 8 clearly show the increase in the 1990s of consumption in the U.S. market. Exhibit 9 shows the increased exports of Cuban cigars in this same period, none of which was to the United States. The boom in the industry touched off a period of growth and expansion, both worldwide and domestically. Tobacco acreage expanded, the number of farmers increased and factories were constructed. For example, in 1995, there were 25,000 small farmers in Cuba producing tobacco. This increased to 37,000 by 1998. During the same period, the number of factories increased to 33 from 17, and thousands of new rollers were being trained. The industry ramped up, expecting the surge in demand to continue through to the new millennium. Through the 1990s, Habanos S.A. consistently set its target production of cigars at 200 million by the year 2000.

New reforms broke up large, state-owned, co-operative plantations and allowed growers to buy land through governmental loans, and then pay in kind through tobacco harvests. These same reforms helped to increase the quality and yields of tobacco, as an incentive was introduced in the form of ownership. In the early 1990s, yields of the precious wrapper tobacco were very low, sometimes below 10 per cent. Initiatives such as this, as well as foreign investment in the industry, have gone a long way to improving quality and yields, although there is still room for major improvement. For example, yields of 25 per cent to 30 per cent for the wrapper tobacco are not uncommon in Cuba, although some in the premium regions have near-perfect yields. Contrast this with Connecticut, where it is common to average yields of 80 per cent to 90 per cent.

As tobacco firms increased production and worked on improving quality, the perception began to shift towards the thought that too much production would mean a decrease in quality, and cigar buyers worldwide began to question the astronomical production goals set by Habanos. They questioned whether the quality of the Havana cigars could be maintained with new rollers, and ramped up production. After all, they had tripled production in a five-year time frame (see Exhibit 9).

The present day has seen those production goals scaled back since, by all accounts, the boom of the 1990s has tapered off. The Cuban industry has experienced bouts with blue mould, tobacco theft and drought, all affecting the supply of tobacco necessary for production. In response, Habanos S.A. has changed its focus. Ana Lopez, the head of marketing for Habanos S.A. is clear on the direction of the Havana cigar: "We are not concerned with figures anymore . . . We are only interested in quality. Quality is the key for Cuban cigars at the moment."[10]

The shift in focus towards an emphasis on quality also affects the production numbers, as there will be more diligence in the entire process to ensure a superior product. In an industry often dominated by perception, the Cubans have recognized the importance of their product and their actions in bringing that product to the export market. The worldwide cigar companies have been consolidating through the late 1990s and early 2000, and as other producers in the world become more adept at the art of cigar making, the Cuban cigar will face serious challenges in the future. Yet, in the opinion of many, when the Havana is right, there is absolutely no substitute. The question is, Can they continue to get it right?

BRANDING

COHIBA, Montecristo, Romeo y Julieta. These names evoke reverence among cigar smokers. More than the actual cigar itself, the persona behind these brands extends throughout the world. It is this type of presence that gives the Havana cigar unparalleled acceptance the world over. The brands themselves differ in the size and the blend of the tobacco.[11] Given the importance of the brand to the Cuban mystique, the most serious threats to the Havana cigars are brand pirating and forgeries. Fake cigars bearing the name of these famous brands have the potential effect of damaging the prestige of the brand name, as the cigar may have some of the attributes of the real thing, but the smoke itself would fail to satisfy the smoker. Products identifying themselves as Havana cigars, or using the name Havana or Cuba or even Vuelta Abajo in their title, have the effect of giving consumers the perception that the origin of the smoke is Cuban, when that may not be the case.

---

[10] "The Rebirth of Habanos," by James Suckling, Cigar Aficionado, posted on Web site July 1, 2002, www.cigaraficiando.com.

[11] For a list of popular vitolas, or sizes, visit the Web site:http://habanossa.com/galeras.asp.

The most current example and case of brand infringement, as the Cubans would call it, is with the COHIBA brand. General Cigar registered the brand name COHIBA in 1978 and then put out a limited number of cigars in order to protect the copyright. COHIBA was created post revolution by the Cuban government, and is often considered the pinnacle of cigars. The General Cigar COHIBAs are manufactured in the Dominican Republic with non-Cuban materials. This is a point of great contention with the Cubans, as they contend that the COHIBA name is synonymous with Cuban cigars worldwide, and General Cigar is unrightfully using their brand name. The case was set to go to trial in late 2002.

However, this case exemplifies the importance of the brand and the image of the cigar. The General Cigar Company COHIBA is made from different materials in a different blend. It is, however, the name that consumers recognize and associate with the pinnacle of cigars. The Cubans do not want their flagship cigar to be diluted by another company using the name, and it is their stated ambition to protect their brand identities worldwide.

THE FUTURE

The Cuban cigar industry is in a state of transformation. The demand for cigars has leveled off, and has even begun to drop somewhat in the worldwide market. The importance of the export business to the Cuban economy is inescapable. In order to move forward, the Cubans have begun to look closely at their industry and at the marketplace, and with the relationships and support they have built with foreign ventures, they are trying to improve. They are investigating new agricultural methods to improve yields and quality, and looking at methods and tobacco strains that will help stave off disease while maintaining the legendary appearance and flavor of the original plants. All these initiatives are geared towards bringing a better, more consistent product to the customer. The joint venture with Altadis has given them the avenue to pursue the US$10 billion machine-made cigar industry, with the introduction of mini versions of their popular brands. The distribution networks and experience that Altadis has in the machine-made market, combined with the branding of the Cuban product, have created considerable potential in this industry. However, they also pose many challenges.

THE TASK

Armed with all this information, Hernandez must analyse the industry and the environment surrounding it in order to decide whether the potential of this industry is significant enough to warrant investment in it. He wondered if his studies in the MBA program had given him the tools to assess a possible start.

exhibit 1   Map of Cuba

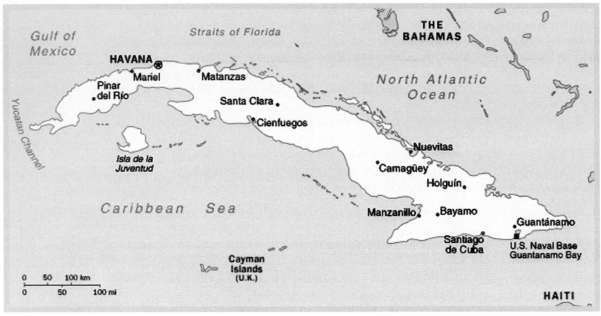

Source: CIA World Factbook 1998.

Map of Tobacco-Growing Regions in Cuba

- ■ VUELTA ABAJO
- ▦ SEMI-VUELTA
- ▨ REMEDIOS
- ▩ PARTIDO
- ☐ ORIENTE

exhibit 2   Cigar Tobacco-Growing Regions

Dominican Republic (DR)—The last 20 years have seen a surge in the quality and variety of cigar tobacco from the DR, and as such, it is now a major producer of top quality tobacco. The primary growing region is the Cibao River Valley, near the city of Santiago in the northern half of the country. Most of the Dominican cigar makers are located close to this city. Most Dominican tobacco is derived from Cuban seed varieties. Although not as strong, it is quite full-flavored.

United States—North of Hartford, the Connecticut River Valley produces some of the finest wrapper leaf tobacco in the world—Connecticut Shade. The fine brown to brownish-yellow leaf has a high degree of elasticity, and it creates a mild- to medium-bodied smoke; it is widely used on premium cigars. Another variety, Connecticut Broadleaf, produces a dark, almost black leaf that is used on maduro-style cigars. It is heavier and veinier than shade-grown tobacco.

Honduras/Nicaragua—These Central American countries produce high-quality Cuban-seed and Connecticut-seed tobaccos, including shade-grown wrapper. Honduras has suffered from periodic blue mould infestations in recent years; Nicaragua's tobacco region is still recovering from a 10-year civil war. Both countries produce a full-bodied tobacco with strong, spicy flavors and heady aromas.

Indonesia—Sumatra-variety tobacco comes from this series of islands that make up Indonesia. The tobacco may be referred to as Java or Sumatra. Sumatra wrapper leaves are often dark brown and have neutral flavors. The majority of wrapper leaf grown there is used in the manufacture of small cigars.

Ecuador—Ecuador produces quantities of high-quality tobacco, both filler and wrapper, shade- and sun-grown. Growers there have been using both Connecticut- and Sumatra-seed varieties. In each case, the tobacco usually seems milder and less robust in strength and flavor than the originals.

Mexico—The San Andres Valley is world famous for a sun-grown variant of Sumatra-seed tobacco. Mexican leaves are used widely as binder and filler in cigars. The variety also serves widely as a maduro wrapper because it can stand up to the cooking and sweating process that creates the darker leaf colors. Cigars manufactured in Mexico are usually made with 100 per cent local tobacco.

Cameroon/Central African Republic—This area of West Africa is known for a high-quality wrapper leaf. In recent years, production has suffered from management changes and bad weather. The Cameroon leaf is prized for its neutral characteristics, which make it an ideal wrapper for full-flavored filler tobaccos.

Source: Compiled from Altadis U.S.A. and Cigar Aficionado Web sites.

exhibit 3   Helms-Burton Act Excerpts H.R. 927

Cuban Liberty and Democratic Solidarity (LIBERTAD) Act of 1996 (Enrolled as Agreed to or Passed by Both House and Senate)

—H.R.927—

One Hundred Fourth Congress
of the
United States of America
AT THE SECOND SESSION
Begun and held at the City of Washington on Wednesday, the third day of January,
one thousand nine hundred and ninety-six

An Act

To seek international sanctions against the Castro government in Cuba, to plan for support of a transition government leading to a democratically elected government in Cuba, and for other purposes.

SEC. 3. PURPOSES.

The purposes of this Act are—

(1) to assist the Cuban people in regaining their freedom and prosperity, as well as in joining the community of democratic countries that are flourishing in the Western Hemisphere;

(2) to strengthen international sanctions against the Castro government;

(3) to provide for the continued national security of the United States in the face of continuing threats from the Castro government of terrorism, theft of property from United States nationals by the Castro government, and the political manipulation by the Castro government of the desire of Cubans to escape that results in mass migration to the United States;

(4) to encourage the holding of free and fair democratic elections in Cuba, conducted under the supervision of internationally recognized observers;

(5) to provide a policy framework for United States support to the Cuban people in response to the formation of a transition government or a democratically elected government in Cuba; and

(6) to protect United States nationals against confiscatory takings and the wrongful trafficking in property confiscated by the Castro regime.

Source: Thomas, Legislative Information on the Internet: http://thomas.loc.gov.

exhibit 4   The Structure of Two Major Companies in Cigar Industry

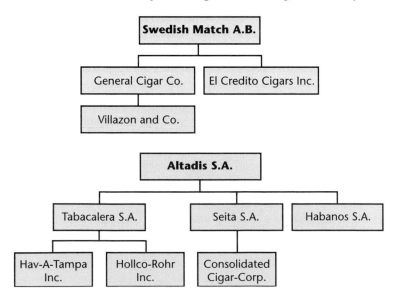

exhibit 5   History of Tabacalera S.A.

1501	Rodrigo de Jerez, a Spanish sailor who traveled with Columbus, is persecuted by the Inquisition for smoking in public, a deep-rooted custom among sailors, merchants and soldiers.
1530	The pipe begins to be used and, among the lower classes, the "roll of leaves," predecessor of the cigar, is popular.
1571	The Sevillian doctor Nicolas Monardes writes "De Hierba Panacea," the first book on tobacco, in which he disseminates the great virtues and medicinal effects of the plant.
1620	The first tobacco processing plant was constructed in Seville.
1758	Inauguration of the Royal Factory of Seville, which was the world's largest tobacco processing factory until the middle of the twentieth century.
1817	The growing, processing and selling of tobacco are deregulated.
1828	The cigarette emerges as the new way of smoking. Cigarettes are sold in "rolls" and individually.
1904	The manufacture of "Elegantes" brand cigarettes begins in packs of 18 cigarettes.
1933	The "Ideales" brand of cigarettes is launched. Manufactured by a partially mechanized process using a mixture of select Cuban tobaccos, they become the most popular and most heavily consumed smoking items in Spain, and remain so until the 1960s.
1941	The Use and Consumption tax, a tobacco levy, is created.
1945	Incorporation of TABACALERA, S.A., the Spanish government tobacco monopoly. Commercial launch of 'BUBI,' the first brand of Virginia tobacco cigarettes manufactured by Tabacalera.
1958	Manufacture of filter cigarettes began in response to new market trends.
1974	In June, Tabacalera brought 'Fortuna,' a Virginia tobacco cigarette, onto the market. By the end of the year, this brand occupied the number-one slot in sales of Virginia tobacco cigarettes.
1979	The manufacture of cigarettes low in nicotine and tar began.
1983	It becomes obligatory to print the regulation health warning on packs of cigarettes.
1986	Spain enters the European Economic Community (EEC). The tax regulation affecting tobacco products changed with the advent of the VAT and a special levy on tobacco.
1997	The Tabacalera Cigars International (TCI) subsidiary is created as a vehicle for expansion into the USA, Central America and the Caribbean. TCI purchases Havatampa, the distributor Max Rohr, Tabacalera San Cristobal de Honduras and Tabacalera San Cristobal de Nicaragua. Tabacalera thus assumes world leadership in the cigar market.
1999	On February 1st, Logista began operating as an independent company. In December Tabacalera and Seita merge, creating ALTADIS.

Source: http://www.altadis.com/en/quienes/nuestrahistoria.html#Spain.

exhibit 6   History of Sieta S.A.

1560	Jean Nicot introduced tobacco into France.
1674	Under Louis XIV's reign, a tax farm was established for managing tobacco sales.
1681	Louis XIV's controller-general of finances, Jean-Baptiste Colbert, extended the farm's monopoly to include the manufacturing of tobacco products. A decree regulated a limited cultivation of tobacco.
1791	Abolition of the farm's monopoly.
1810	Napoleon Bonaparte reinstated the tobacco monopoly (cultivation, production and sale). A state agency was set up to operate the monopoly.
1926	French Prime Minister Raymond Poincaré created an organization responsible for reimbursing public debt, including a service to manage the tobacco monopoly called the Service d'Exploitation Industrielle des Tabacs (SEIT).
1935	Seit became Seita when it was given responsibility for managing production of matches (Allumettes).
1959	Seita became a French public industrial/commercial entity, an Etablissement Public à Caractère Industriel et Commercial (EPIC).
1961	Seita began direct distribution of tobacco products to tobacconists, taking over from the French tax authority.
1962	Seita's staff, comprised of civil servants or state employees, assumed an autonomous legal status.
1970	The EEC abolished customs barriers among member states.
1980	Under the law of July 2nd, Seita became a corporation, the capital of which could be partially divested by the French State.
1984	Gauloises Blondes were launched. Under the law of July 13th, the French State became Seita´s sole shareholder.
1993	Jean-Dominique Comolli was appointed Seita´s Chairman and Chief Executive Officer.
1995	Privatization of Seita. December 22nd: acquisition of Poland-based ZPT Radom.
1998	Strategic alliance between Seita and Tabacalera S.A. Acquisition of Reynolds in Finland. Creation of Seita Tupakka, renamed Altadis Finland. Acquisition of the leading American Cigar manufacturer, Consolidated Cigar Holdings Inc, renamed Altadis USA: The Seita Group becomes a world leader in cigars.
1999	Announcement of the merger of Tabacalera and Seita, giving rise to the creation of Altadis.

Source: http://www.altadis.com/en/quienes/nuestrahistoria.html#France

exhibit 7   U.S. Large Cigar Consumption 1920 to 2000

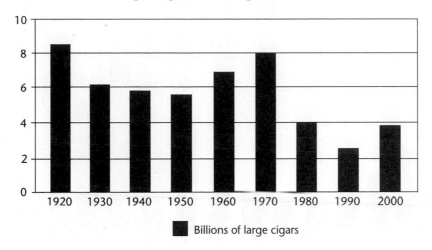

Source: Perelman's Pocket Cyclopedia of Cigars, 2002 Edition.

exhibit 8   The Premium Boom
Annual Imports of Premium Cigars into the United States
1990 to 2001

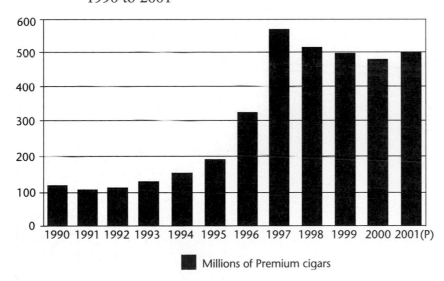

Source: Perelman's Pocket Cyclopedia of Cigars, 2002 Edition.

exhibit 9   Cuba's Cigar Exports

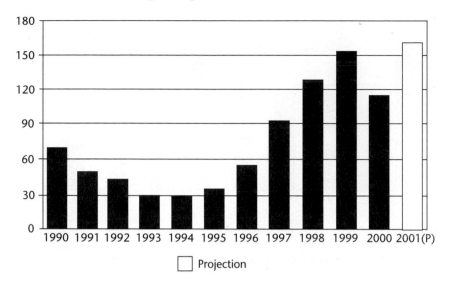

  Projection

Source: "Increased Production, Decreased Quality: by Marvin R. Shanken. Weekly Wrapper, posted March 21, 2001.

case 5 The Chinese Fireworks Industry

In February 1999, Jerry Yu was spending the Chinese New Year holidays in Liuyang (lee-ou-yang), a city known as "the home of firecrackers and fireworks," located in Hunan Province in China. Jerry was an ABC (America-Born-Chinese). With an MBA, he was running a small family-owned chain of gift stores in Brooklyn, New York. Liuyang was his mother's hometown. During his visit, his relatives invited him to invest in a fireworks factory that was owned by a village. Mr. Yu had been impressed by the extravagant fireworks shows he had seen during the festival; however, he wanted to assess how attractive the Chinese fireworks industry was before he even looked at the financial details of the factory.

HISTORY OF FIREWORKS AND FIRECRACKERS

Fireworks referred to any devices designed to produce visual or audible effects through combustion or explosion. The art of making fireworks was formally known as pyrotechnics. Firecrackers were a specific kind of fireworks, usually in the form of a noisemaking cylinder. Firecrackers were often strung together and fused consecutively, a staple of Chinese New Year celebrations, weddings, grand openings, births, deaths and other ceremonial occasions.

The main ingredients of fireworks had remained almost the same over the past 1,000 years: 75 parts-by-weight potassium nitrate, 15 parts charcoal and 10 parts sulfur. It burned briskly when lighted, but did not erupt or make any noise. When it was found that a projectile could be thrust out of a barrel by keeping the powder at one end

Ruihua Jiang prepared this case under the supervision of Professor Paul Beamish solely to provide material for class discussion. The authors do not intend to illustrate either effective or ineffective handling of a managerial situation. The authors may have disguised certain names and other identifying information to protect confidentiality.

IVEY

Richard Ivey School of Business
The University of Western Ontario

and igniting it, black powder became known as gunpowder. Today, smokeless powder has replaced black powder as the propellant in modern weaponry, but black powder remains a main ingredient in fireworks, both as a propellant and as a bursting charge.

It was generally believed that the Chinese were the first makers of fireworks. The Chinese made war rockets and explosives as early as the sixth century. One legend said that a Chinese cook, while toiling in a field kitchen, happened to mix together sulfur, charcoal and saltpetre, and noticed that the pile burned with a combustible force when ignited. He further discovered that when these ingredients were enclosed in a length of bamboo sealed at both ends, it would explode rather than burn, producing a loud crack. This was the origin of firecrackers. In fact, the Chinese word for firecrackers—bao-zhu—literally means "exploded bamboo."

The loud reports and burning fires of firecrackers and fireworks were found to be perfect for frightening off evil spirits and celebrating good news at various occasions. For more than a thousand years, the Chinese had been seeing off past years and welcoming in new ones by firing firecrackers.

Fireworks made their way first to Arabia in the seventh century, then to Europe sometime in the middle of the 13th century. By the 15th century, fireworks were widely used for religious festivals and public entertainment. Most of the early pyrotechnicians in Europe were Italians. Even today, the best-known names in the European and American fireworks industry were Italian in origin. From the 16th to the 18th century, Italy and Germany were the two best-known areas in the European continent for fireworks displays.

In 1777, the United States used fireworks in its first Independence Day celebration, and fireworks have became closely associated with July Fourth celebrations ever since.

Up until the 1830s, the colors of the early fireworks were limited, but by 1999, there were six basic colors used in fireworks.

LIUYANG—THE HOMETOWN OF FIRECRACKERS AND FIREWORKS

According to historical records in China, firecrackers and fireworks "emerged during the Tang dynasty (618-907 AD), flourished during the Song Dynasty (960-1279 AD), and originated in Liuyang." For more than 1,000 years, Liuyang had been known as the "hometown of firecrackers and fireworks of China," a title that was officially conferred to Liuyang by the State Council of China in 1995. As early as 1723, Liuyang fireworks were chosen as official tributes to the imperial family and were sold all over the country. Exports started early: by 1875, firecrackers and fireworks were being shipped to Japan, Korea, India, Iran, Russia, Australia, England, U.S., and other countries. In China, the name Liuyang had become almost synonymous with firecrackers and fireworks. Liuyang-made firecrackers and fireworks won numerous awards over its long history of fireworks making.

The long history and tradition had made fireworks more than just a livelihood for the Liuyang people. Almost every native person in the area knew something about fireworks making, or had actually made firecrackers or fireworks in their lifetime. As a result, Liuyang claimed an impressive pool of skilled labor. Firecrackers and fireworks had become the pillar industry of Liuyang. In peak seasons more than 400,000 people, or about one-third of the total population in the Liuyang District (including Liuyang City and the surrounding counties) would work in fireworks or related industries. Liuyang claimed more than 500 fireworks manufacturers. Among them, only one was a state-owned enterprise (SOE) with more than 1,000 workers. The rest were owned either by villages or families. Among them, about a dozen or so were medium-to-large factories with employment between 100 to 500 workers. The rest were small workshops employing anywhere from 10 to 50 people, depending on market demand.

Liuyang was the top fireworks exporter in the world, making up 80 per cent of fireworks export sales of Hunan Province, and 60 per cent of that of China (see Exhibit 1 for information on revenue and export sales of Liuyang fireworks). The trademarked brand "Red Lantern" had become well known to fireworks-lovers around the world.

The Product

Fireworks could be classified into two categories: display fireworks and consumer fireworks. The display fireworks, such as aerial shells, maroons, and large Roman candles, were meant for professional (usually licensed) pyrotechnicians to fire during large public display shows. They were devices that were designed to produce certain visual or audio effects at a greater height above the ground than the consumer fireworks, which the general public could purchase in convenience stores and enjoy in their own backyards. Display fireworks were known as Explosives 1.3 (Class B prior to 1991) in the U.S. The consumer fireworks belonged to Explosives 1.4 (Class C prior to 1991). The difference lay mainly in the amount of explosive components contained in the product. Canada had a similar classification system. In the U.K., it was more carefully divided into four categories: indoor fireworks; garden fireworks; display fireworks; and display fireworks for professionals only.

There were many varieties of fireworks. Liuyang made 13 different types with more than 3,000 varieties. The major types included fountains, rockets, hand-held novelties, nail and hanging wheels, ground-spinning novelties, jumping novelties, floral shells, parachutes and firecrackers.

Historically, firecrackers made up 90 per cent of the total production and sales. Over the past 50 years or so, however, there had been a shift away from firecrackers to fireworks. In 1999, firecrackers made up only about 20 per cent of the total sales. The skill levels of fireworks-making had been greatly improved. For instance, the old-day fireworks could reach no more than 20 metres into the sky, while the new ones could go as high as 400 metres.

Not much had changed in fireworks-making. Over the last few decades, numerous novelties were added to the fireworks family. However, innovation had never reached beyond product variations. The ingredients had remained more or less the same. The process technology had not changed much either, although some manual processes, such as cutting the paper, rolling the cylinders, mixing powder, and stringing the cylinders could now be done by machines.

exhibit 1 Liuyang Firecrackers and Fireworks: Total Revenue and Export Sales (US$000)

	1992	1993	1994	1995	1996
Total Revenue	49,639	55,542	86,747	126,506	134,940
Tax Revenue	5,099	7,010	11,829	15,422	18,434
Export Sales	15,100	30,200	51,240	84,030	85,560

Source: Liuyang Firecrackers and Fireworks Exhibition, 1998.

Safety Issues

The fact that fireworks were made with gunpowder and listed under explosives brought about the issue of safety. Numerous accidents related to fireworks had resulted in tragic human injuries and considerable property damage. As a result, fireworks had become heavily regulated in most countries.

According to the manufacturers, fireworks were the most dangerous during the production process. Powder mixing and powder filling, in turn, were the two most dangerous procedures. The workers had to abide by strict safety measures. Even a tiny spark caused by the dropping of a tool on the floor or the dragging of a chair could start a major explosion. The quality of the ingredients was also of significant importance. Impure ingredients could greatly increase the possibility of accidents. In Liuyang, almost every year, there would be one or more accidents that resulted in deaths and damages.

Once the fireworks were made, they were relatively safe to transport and store. Even in firing, good quality fireworks rarely caused any problems if everything was done properly. Most of the fireworks-related accidents occurred during private parties or street displays, and quite often involved children playing with fireworks that needed to be handled by adults, or adults firing shells that required professional expertise. Most accidents were linked to consumer backyard events rather than to public displays.

According to the United States Consumer Products Safety Commission's (CPSC) data, injuries related to fireworks had declined by 44 per cent, even though their use had increased (see Exhibit 2). For 1997, there were an estimated 8,300 fireworks-related injuries, 32 per cent of which were caused by firecrackers. Of all the injuries related to firecrackers, 42 per cent involved illegal firecrackers.

Children from ages five to 14 were the most frequently involved in fireworks-related injuries. However, fireworks were not the only consumer product that might cause injuries to this age group. According to a 1997 CPSC Injury Surveillance Report, fireworks were actually safer than some much more benign-looking products, like baseballs, pens and pencils. However, fireworks-related injuries were usually the most dramatic and the most widely publicized accidents, which partly explained the fact that fireworks was the only category among the products listed in Exhibit 3 (on the next page), for which prohibition, instead of education and adult supervision, was often urged.

In the United States, multiple government agencies were involved in regulating fireworks. The Bureau of Alcohol, Tobacco and Firearms (BATF) controlled the manufacture, storage, sales and distribution of explosives, i.e., Class B fireworks. The

exhibit 2   Total Fireworks Consumption and Estimated Fireworks-Related Injuries In U.S.: 1994 to 1998

Year	Fireworks Consumption, Millions of Pounds	Estimated Fireworks-Related Injuries	Injuries per 100,000 Pounds
1994	117.0	12,500	10.7
1995	115.0	10,900	9.4
1996	118.0	7,800	6.2
1997	132.8	8,300	6.2
1998	112.6	7,000	6.2

Source: American Pyrotechnics Association.

exhibit 3   Estimated Emergency Room Treatment per 100,000 Youths (Ages 5 to 14)

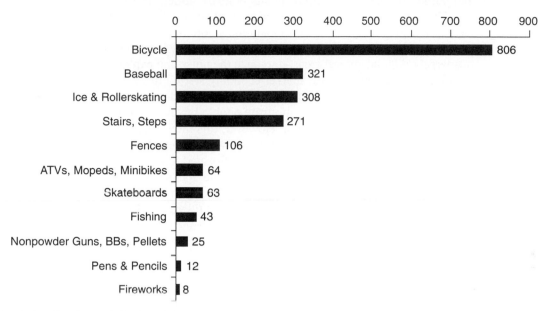

Source: American Pyrotechnics Association.

CPSC regulated Class C consumer fireworks, and the Department of Transportation dealt with the transportation of fireworks. Although at the federal level, fireworks and firecrackers were allowed as long as the safety features were up to the standard, local governments would have their own different regulations regarding fireworks consumption. Out of the 50 states, 10 would not allow any fireworks, five would allow novelty fireworks, 18 would allow "safe and sane" fireworks, while the remaining 17 would allow essentially all consumer fireworks. For display fireworks, permits would have to be obtained from federal and local authorities and fire departments.

All legal consumer fireworks offered for sale in the United States had been tested for stability by the Bureau of Explosives and approved for transportation by the U.S. Department of Transportation. Because of the limited amount of pyrotechnic composition permitted in each individual unit, consumer fireworks would not ignite spontaneously during storage, nor would they mass-explode during a fire. Therefore, no special storage was required.

In most of Europe, similar regulations were in place for safety considerations, only the requirements were regarded as less stringent. In Canada, however, regulations were extremely restrictive. On the list of fireworks companies that were allowed to sell fireworks to Canada, no Chinese companies were found.

THE FIRECRACKERS AND FIREWORKS INDUSTRY IN CHINA

The firecrackers and fireworks industry in China was dominated by small family-owned-and-operated workshops. It was essentially a low-tech, highly labor-intensive industry. After 1949, government-run factories replaced the family-owned workshops. The increased scale and government funds made possible the automation of some processes. However, the key processes like installing powder, mixing color ingredients and putting in fuses, were still manually done by skilled workers.

The factories themselves were made up of small workshops that stood away from each other, so that in case of an accident the whole factory would not explode. For the same safety consideration, the workshops were usually located near a water source and in sparsely populated rural areas, to reduce the noise and explosion hazard.

After the reform towards market economy started in 1979, most of the factories were broken up and became family-run units of production again. It was hoped that this privatization might help to motivate people better, to increase their productivity and consequently raise the output. However, this move also served to restrict further technological innovations. There were hardly any research and development (R & D) facilities, nor human and capital resources allocated to R & D in most fireworks companies. The few resources that were available were all spent on product varieties. Even in Liuyang, out of the 400,000 or so people working in the industry, only four were engineers with advanced professional training and titles. The 40-some research facilities scattered in the Liuyang area were poorly funded and equipped.

In fact, the majority of the workers were regular farmers who had learned how to make fireworks just by watching and following their elders. They would come to work in fireworks workshops when there were jobs to be done, and return to till their fields if there were none. In Liuyang, for instance, only four to five factories were operating year-round. The rest of the 500-plus workshops would operate as orders came in. Since the fireworks-making communities were very concentrated geographically and had lasted for generations, only a few places (like Liuyang) came to claim a large pool of skilled fireworks-makers.

Although Liuyang was by far the most well-known place for making fireworks in China, it faced increasing competition within the country. Also located in Hunan Province, Liling was another major manufacturing community of fireworks. Liling fireworks might not enjoy the same reputation and variety as Liuyang products, but they were fierce in price competition. In the neighboring Jiangxi Province, Pingxiang and Wanzai fireworks had become strong competitors both in price and quality, especially on the low- and medium-priced market. In the high-end product market, especially in large-type display fireworks and export market, Dongguan in Guangdong Province, had taken advantage of its closeness to Hong Kong and more sophisticated management and marketing practices, and snatched market share from Liuyang.

The initial capital requirement for starting a fireworks-manufacturing facility was relatively low. To set up a factory with the necessary equipment for making large display shells would require RMB1,000,000.[1] However, setting up a small family workshop making consumer firecrackers and fireworks would require less than RMB100,000. Consequently, the number of small manufacturers mushroomed after the government started to encourage private business ventures.

The labor cost was low in the area. Skilled workers engaged in major processes would earn an average of RMB800 to RMB1,000 per month. A non-skilled worker would be paid only RMB300 to RMB400 every month. Therefore, the labor cost took no more than 20 per cent of the total cost. For the small private workshops, the percentage would be around 10 per cent.

The main raw materials for fireworks were gunpowder, color ingredients, paper, fuse and clay soil. None would be difficult to procure. The prices and supply were both

---

[1] In 1999, the exchange rate was around 8.30 yuan per US$1.00.

quite stable. The one possible problem in supply was quality. Major manufacturers would usually establish long-term relationships with their suppliers to guarantee the quality of the materials. The small workshops would often go with the lowest prices, sometimes at the cost of quality, which could lead to fatal results.

The emergence of the small companies intensified competition. The private workshops were flexible and quick in responding to market demand. They did not entail much administrative cost. Compared to government-owned or some collectively owned factories, they did not have the social responsibilities of health care, retirement benefits and housing. They usually did not do any product research or design. Oblivious to intellectual property protection, they would copy any popular product design and sell it for much less. The resulting price drop had become a serious problem for the whole industry. As the profit margin kept shrinking, some workshops would hire cheap, unskilled workers, use cheap equipment and raw materials to cut down on cost. The results could be disastrous. Fireworks-related damages and injuries and factory accidents were reported every year, pushing the authorities to impose stricter regulations.

THE DOMESTIC MARKET

Firecrackers and fireworks had long been an integral part of any ceremonies held in China. Until recently, demand had been stable, but had risen in the past two decades because of increased economic development and living standards. Economically, market reform and unprecedented growth had given rise to the daily appearance of multitudes of new companies and new stores. As people's income level and living standards kept rising, fancier and pricier fireworks and firecrackers were desired over the cheap simple firecrackers, thereby creating more profit opportunities for fireworks manufacturers. Almost every household would spend at least a couple hundred yuan on firecrackers and fireworks during the Spring Festival.

However, since the beginning of the 1990s, increased concerns over environmental pollution and safety of human life and property led more and more cities to regulate the consumption of fireworks and firecrackers. Every year, high profile fireworks-related accidents were reported and emphasized on mass media before and after the traditional Spring Festival. Some articles even condemned firecrackers and fireworks as an old, uncivilized convention that created only noise, pollution and accidents. In a wave of regulations, city after city passed administrative laws regarding the use of fireworks. By 1998, one-third of the cities in China had completely banned the use of firecrackers and fireworks. Another one-third only allowed fireworks in designated places. This led to a decline in domestic market demand.

In the meantime, domestic competition grew intensely. The reform towards a market economy made it possible for numerous family-run workshops to appear. They competed mainly on price. Almost every province had some fireworks-making workshops or factories, many set up and run with the help of skilled workers who had migrated from Liuyang. These small establishments usually were located in rural, underdeveloped areas where labor cost was minimal. The manufacturing was done manually, sometimes without safety measures, using cheap raw materials and simplified techniques. The products were sold locally at low prices, making it difficult for Liuyang fireworks to sell in those areas. To make things worse, these products would often copy any new or popular product designs coming out of Liuyang or other traditional fireworks communities, even using their very brand names.

In the past, fireworks were sold through the government-run general merchandise companies. Eventually, private dealers took over a large part of the business. Overall, the distribution system was rather fragmented. The old government-run channels were not very effective, especially for general merchandise. In the new distribution channels, wholesale dealers would get shipments directly from the manufacturers, and then re-sell to street peddlers and convenience stores.

In the countryside, wholesale markets would appear in local townships, with wholesale dealers and agents of the manufacturers setting up booths promoting their products. Small peddlers in the surrounding areas would get supplies from the market and then sell them in small towns or villages. The wholesale markets in China were important outlets for distributing general merchandise like fireworks.

In the display fireworks market, the buyers were often central and local governments, who would purchase the product for public shows on national holidays or special celebrations. Obviously, a local company would have advantages in supplying to local government in its area. Large fireworks shows usually would use invited bidding to decide on suppliers. The amount of fireworks used could range from RMB100,000 to several million yuan, depending on the scale of a fireworks show.

Account receivables and bad debt control were a problem not just for fireworks manufacturers, but for all businesses in China. Bad debts and lack of respect for business contracts had created a credit crisis in China. The bad debt problem greatly increased transaction costs, slowed down the cash turnover, and had become a headache for fireworks manufacturers. Some had chosen to withdraw from selling in the domestic market, although the profit margin was higher than in the export market.

Legal restrictions, local protectionism, cutthroat price competition, hard-to-penetrate distribution channels and bad debt were impacting negatively on the domestic sales of Liuyang fireworks. In 1997, seeing the decline of its fireworks sales, Liuyang Firecrackers and Fireworks Industry Department, the government agency in charge of the overall development of the pillar industry, decided to start an offensive strategy. First, it opened local offices in most of the 29 provinces, major cities and regions to promote Liuyang fireworks. Second, it regulated the prices that Liuyang fireworks companies could quote and sell in export sales. Third, it resorted to a government-to-government relationship in order to secure contracts for large public fireworks displays in each province. One year after introducing the offensive strategy, Liuyang fireworks sales had increased.

THE EXPORT MARKET

Since the opening of the Chinese economy in 1979, exporting had become a major market for the Chinese fireworks industry. As one of the most celebrated products out of China, export sales of fireworks had risen between 1978 and 1998. According to government statistics, the recorded export sales of firecrackers and fireworks reached US$143 million and US$172 million in 1994 and 1995 respectively. The estimate for 1998 was about US$200 million.

The general belief was that China-made fireworks actually made up about 80 per cent to 90 per cent of the world's fireworks market. The products from China were rich in variety and low in price, but also had a lower reputation in quality control, packaging and timing control, compared to the products made in Japan and Korea. China-made fireworks also would wholesale for much lower prices, usually 80 per cent lower than similar products made in Japan or Korea.

There was little overall co-ordination of export sales. As more and more companies were allowed to export directly, competition kept intensifying and the profit margins on export sales kept slipping. Some manufacturers would even sell at or below cost, just to get the tax refund that the government set aside to encourage export, which could sometimes reach 20 per cent. As a result, underpricing each other became a common practice. Therefore, despite its dominant share of the world market, the Chinese fireworks export industry enjoyed limited profitability. Exhibit 4 provides a comparison of the free on board (FOB) prices quoted by the Chinese companies to U.S. markets versus the prices quoted by the U.S. importers and wholesalers to the retailers and end users on some consumer and display fireworks items. The importers enjoyed a high markup even after paying the 12.5 per cent U.S. import duty. Of course, the importers had to absorb the cost of getting permits, shipping, storing and carrying the inventory for three to four months before making the sales.

Besides suffering from low profit margin, the Chinese fireworks makers were also risking losing their brand identities. Given the low cost and reasonably good quality of the Chinese fireworks, many large fireworks manufacturers and dealers in the West started to outsource the making of their brand-name fireworks. Failing to see the importance of brand equity, the Chinese fireworks manufacturers were sometimes reduced to mere manufacturing outfits for foreign companies, gradually losing their own brands. There were also fireworks merchants in Korea, Japan or Spain, who would buy

exhibit 4   Comparison of FOB Import Prices from China and
Wholesale Prices of Chinese Fireworks in U.S.

Product Type	Packing	FOB China[1] US$	Wholesale in U.S.[2] US$
Thunderbombs	12/80/16	12.40	42.00
Tri-Rotating Wheel	24/12	15.50	48.50
Changing Color Wheel	72/1	20.70	57.60
Jumping Jack	20/48/12	16.70	60.00
Cuckoo	24/6	14.50	50.40
Ground Bloom Flower	20/12/6	16.40	62.40
Color Sparkler	24/12/8	16.60	66.74
Moon Traveller	25/12/12	9.20	40.00
Crackling Whips	72/12	16.99	50.40
Aerial Display	4/1	19.40	68.00
Evening Party	12/1	12.60	60.00
Assorted Fountain	18/4	10.30	64.20
Assorted Rockets	36/12	24.20	68.00
4" Display Shell w/ Tail	36/1	52.65	165.00
6" display	10/1	41.82	160.00
8" display	6/1	54.53	190.00
12" display	2/1	60.95	190.00

[1]FOB major ports in South China. Cost, Insurance, Freight to major ports in U.S. would be $3.00 to $4.00 more per carton.

[2]U.S. import duty rate for fireworks from China was 12.5 per cent.

Source: China Sunsong Fireworks Corp. and Web sites of various fireworks wholesalers in U.S.

the products from China, and then repackage them, or replace the fuses with better quality ones, then resell them for much higher prices.

The export market was usually divided into five blocks: Southeast Asia, North America, Europe, South America and the rest of the world. The most popular market had been Europe, where the regulations on fireworks were less stringent, and orders were of larger quantities and better prices. The United States was considered a tough market because of complex regulations and high competition, nevertheless a necessary one if a company wanted to remain a viable world-player. The Canadian market was virtually closed to the Chinese fireworks due to its regulations, although most of the fireworks consumed in Canada were imported, and had probably originated in China before being repackaged in other countries. The result of the stricter regulations in Canada was higher prices for consumers. It was estimated that a fireworks display that cost less than $3,500 in the U.S. would cost Canadians $8,000.

The foreign importers were powerful buyers for several reasons. First, they were very well informed, both through past dealings with China and the Internet. Second, they were able to hire agents who were very familiar with the industry in China. Third, they could deal directly with the factories that were willing to take lower prices. Fourth, there were basically no switching costs, so they could play the suppliers against each other.

The diversity of the cultures in the destination countries greatly reduced the seasonality of the fireworks production and sales. As a result, orders evened out throughout the year. However, the peak season was still towards the end of the year. For the U.S., it was before July 4. Usually, the importers would receive the shipment two or three months beforehand.

The Internet was gradually becoming a marketing outlet for Chinese fireworks. According to a fireworks company's office in Shenzhen, 20 per cent to 30 per cent of the business inquiries they got were through the Internet. However, export sales were still made mainly through foreign trade companies or agents.

In recent years, foreign investments were also funneled into the fireworks industry. In Liuyang, four of the large fireworks factories had foreign investments, made mainly by the fireworks trading companies in Hong Kong.

In 1999, about four-fifths of the 5,000 or so containers of fireworks exported from China annually, were consumer fireworks. However, demand for display fireworks was growing at a faster pace. It was predicted that the demand for display fireworks would increase as organized public shows grew more popular; at the same time, demand for consumer fireworks was expected to decline as regulations were getting stricter. Fireworks shows were increasingly being used in promotional campaigns, and were finding customers among amusement parks, sports teams and retailers for store openings, anniversaries and holiday celebrations.

The Future of the Fireworks Industry in China

The managers of the Chinese fireworks companies that Jerry talked to expressed mixed feelings towards the future outlook of their industry. One pessimistic view was that this was a sunset industry and held that regulations were killing the industry. Moreover, as people became more environmentally conscious and more distracted by the endless diversities of modern entertainment, traditional celebrations using firecrackers and fireworks would die a gradual death. As to the function of attracting public attention for promotional purposes, fireworks also faced challenges from new technologies, such as laser beams combined with sound effects.

In fact, "make-believe firecrackers" already appeared as substitutes in China. These were made of red plastic tubes strung together like firecrackers with electric bulbs installed inside the tubes. When the power was turned on, the lights would emit sparks, accompanied by crackling reports that sounded like firecrackers. These were being used at weddings and grand openings in cities where firecrackers and fireworks were banned. More interesting substitutes were spotted at some weddings in Beijing, where people paved the road with little red balloons, and made the limousine carrying the bride and groom run over the balloons to make explosive cracking sounds as well as leave behind red bits and pieces of debris. Also, more and more young couples were getting married in Western styles, in a church or a scenic green meadow outdoors, where serene and quiet happiness prevailed over the traditional noisy way of celebrating. Therefore, some managers believed that firecrackers and fireworks were doomed to fade off into history.

The more optimistic view, however, was that the industry would not die at all. If the right moves were made by the industry, it could even grow. Some said that tradition would not die so easily. It was in their national character for the Chinese to celebrate with an atmosphere of noisy happiness. Moreover, even in the West, the popularity of fireworks was not suffering from all the regulations. No real substitutes could replace fireworks, which combined the sensual pleasures of visual, audio and emotional stimuli. For instance, the U.S. Congressional resolution in 1963 to use bells to replace fireworks in celebrating Independence Day never really caught on.

Fireworks were also being combined with modern technologies like laser beams, computerized firing and musical accompaniment to make the appeal of fireworks more irresistible. The safety problem was not really as serious as people were made to believe, and would only improve with new technological innovations like smokeless fireworks.

However, both sides agreed that the Chinese fireworks industry would have to change its strategy, especially in international competition, to stay a viable and profitable player.

THE DECISION

Meanwhile, Jerry had to decide whether it was worthwhile to invest in the fireworks industry. He wondered whether he could apply the industry analysis framework he had studied in his MBA program.

The Richard Ivey School of Business gratefully acknowledges the generous support of The Richard and Jean Ivey Fund in the development of this case as part of the *Richard and Jean Ivey Fund Asian Case Series.*

case 6 Halterm

INTRODUCTION

It was mid-November 1996 and Patrick Morin, President of Halterm, was making his way towards Gate 24 Terminal 3 at Heathrow airport. There was still plenty of time to make the noon flight to Halifax. He was on his way home after touring a number of European container terminals and visiting with customers. The trip had been well worthwhile in helping him develop his ideas about the business plan he would present to his Board in December.

He'd been at Halterm a half year. It was an exciting time to work in this business but the stakes were high. The day before the previous Board meeting, P&O Containers had announced its merger with Nedlloyd, creating one of the world's largest container lines. Any rationalization could result in lost business. P&O, a customer of Halterm, was a member of the Grand Alliance while Nedlloyd was a member of the Global Alliance; assuming the European Commission approved the merger, which alliance would the new company choose? That approval was expected mid-December.

However, it was more complicated than that. P&O was a participant in the Grand Alliance's Asia East Coast Express (AEX) service calling at Halterm and its Pacific Atlantic Express (PAX) service that called Ceres, Halifax's other container terminal. The alliance members had decided to consolidate terminals within ports of call. Therefore, even if P&O remained within the Grand Alliance, it was possible that Halterm would lose its P&O business to Ceres. In addition, this proposed merger was probably only the beginning; the industry was entering a period of consolidation and restructuring, as technology challenged traditional approaches. The Board was looking for concrete plans in the face of these uncertainties.

ABOUT THE COMPANY

Halterm operates a 70-acre ship-to-shore cargo transfer and storage facility in Halifax, Nova Scotia. As Canada's largest Atlantic coast container terminal operation, it services the needs of domestic and international shipping lines that call at the Port of

This case has been prepared by Dr. Mary R. Brooks, Dalhousie University, as a basis for classroom discussion rather than to illustrate effective or ineffective handling of an administrative situation.

Richard Ivey School of Business
The University of Western Ontario

Halifax by providing the logistical link between the ocean-going vessels and the inland transportation system. Although specializing in handling container cargo, the facility is a full-service operation and provides stevedoring services for ro-ro and break-bulk cargo[1] as well. Halterm's other competitive advantages are its deep-water berths, its link to the Canadian National (CN) inland rail network and its ability to provide efficient, low cost container handling services to most container vessels. The terminal operates at the mouth of Halifax harbour on premises leased from the Halifax Port Corporation (HPC). (See Appendix A on page 87.)

Located within one hour of the Great Circle Route,[2] the Port of Halifax is well situated to service the needs of major international shipping lines that carry cargo between North America and Europe, the Mediterranean, and Southeast Asia and services diverse geographic locations. (See Appendix B on page 88.) Halifax is the first port-of-call inbound and the last port-of-call out for North America-Europe trade; this means that import cargo discharged in Halifax can be delivered to inland customers more quickly than from other east coast ports. Conversely, inland shippers have more time to get export cargo ready for shipment through Halifax as compared to other east coast ports. Finally, the Port of Halifax is ice-free on a year-round basis.

The Port's principal disadvantage is its lack of a local market. Halifax depends largely (80%) on its ability to service inland markets that are located 1,300-2,500 km (800-1,500 miles) from the port. This makes the cost of inland transport more expensive relative to other major east coast ports.

History

Halterm started operations in 1969 as a joint venture company owned by Clarke Transport Canada Inc. (Clarke), CN and Halifax International Containers (Halicon), itself a partnership of the Province of Nova Scotia and the City of Halifax. Halterm was initially established to service the needs of Dart Container Line, a shipping consortium that included Clarke.

In 1968, Brian Doherty, Halterm's first terminal manager and an employee of Clarke, was assigned by Clarke to set up a new container facility. National Harbours Board (NHB), the predecessor of HPC, was building a new pier (Pier C) south of Pier B for Clarke as a private facility. Dart wanted to establish a North Atlantic container service with a Canadian call and was exploring possibilities in Montreal, Saint John and Halifax. Port characteristics at the time favoured Halifax. In return for making the private terminal at Pier C a common user facility, Clarke acquired a long-term management contract. In return for a small investment, each partner (Clarke, CN and Halicon) took one-third ownership. For its part, Dart promised to make Halifax its Canadian port of call as long as it called at Canada. Halterm, the first common user container terminal in North America with on-dock rail facilities, was born.

By 1972 Halterm was in full operation with two ship-to-shore gantry cranes, two ship berths and the required support equipment. In 1974 a third ship-to-shore gantry crane was added and steady growth followed throughout the 1970s. However, the

---

[1] Ro-ro (roll on/roll off) cargo is that which moves on wheeled trailers or flatbeds and includes cars. Breakbulk cargo is packaged in some format, most commonly pallets.

[2] The shortest shipping route between north Europe and the east coast of the US.

1980s brought more than a worldwide recession. Brian Doherty describes the events that almost destroyed Halterm ten years after its founding:

> By the late 1970s there was a perception that the terminal didn't have the capacity to handle future volumes. The Chairman of Halterm, lawyer Bill Mingo, was keen to expand capacity and began to look at the development of a second facility with the intention that Halterm would operate both facilities. Despite what Halterm management believed was the best proposal to operate the facility, NHB chose to seek another operator [Ceres]. What this did was encourage a price war with disastrous financial results for both terminal operators. Prices dropped by a third. Although ZIM [ZIM Israel Navigation Company] and Dart remained with Halterm, both ACL and Hapag Lloyd moved to the new terminal.

Brian Doherty continues:

> Then Dart was acquired by OOCL [Orient Overseas Container Limited]. Dart was in financial difficulty. OOCL moved Dart operations to Montreal. This was Halterm's lowest point; it had gone from a financially well-off company to a loss position. A lawsuit was launched against Dart because it breached its promise to stay in Halifax. About this time, Stanley Clarke sold his business to NCC [Newfoundland Capital Corporation Limited].

In 1984, Halicon terminated its participation in Halterm as the government could not be seen as a partner in only one of two competing facilities. Halterm purchased Halicon's shares and put them in trust, hoping to find a new partner to buy them. Brian Doherty continues:

> As the managing partner of the joint venture, NCC was not interested in absorbing the potential losses. We went to New York and convinced an alliance of K-Line, NOL [Neptune Orient Lines] and OOCL to relocate their Pacific service from Saint John to Halifax in return for dropping the lawsuit against Dart and giving Furness Withy Terminals, an OOCL subsidiary, the opportunity to take up Halicon's shares. This put us back on a recovery track.

Since then, the facility has undergone two significant capital expansions. In 1984 the operating system of Halterm was renewed at a cost of approximately $10 million; the yard cargo-handling system was changed from a maintenance-intensive straddle carrier system to one that employed rubber-tire yard gantries, yard tractors and chassis. In 1991, a fourth conventional ship-to-shore gantry crane and additional support equipment were added at a total cost of approximately $15 million. Brian Doherty, then president of Halterm, recalls the thinking of the day:

> At the end of the 1980s we started to do studies. The first post-Panamax[3] ships were being built and we got quotes on the price of a post-Panamax crane. It didn't make sense to buy just one but one was all we needed for our existing business. We weren't prepared to make the infrastructure investment to support only one post-Panamax crane so we added a traditional one. This way we could guarantee service.

The terminal was simultaneously expanded with the addition of a new 12-acre working pier at Pier B, increasing the total area to its present size and adding a third deep-water berth. The company needed Pier B for feeder operators and smaller vessels

---

[3]The classic distinction in the ship size is between Panamax ships (those that carry up to 4,000 TEUs no more than 13 across and can pass through the Panama Canal) and post-Panamax (those that generally carry in excess of 5,000 TEUs, with 16 or 17 containers in width and are too wide to pass through the Panama Canal). The Suez Canal can handle post-Panamax vessels. Conventional cranes cannot service post-Panamax vessels efficiently because of container stack height and the limitations of crane reach. While the reach issue can be dealt with by stowing all cargo for a particular port on one side of the vessel, this may result in stability problems for the vessel, particularly during loading/unloading operations.

in order to keep the main berth at Pier C free for the larger vessels that had berth guarantees in their contracts.

Patrick Morin became President of Halterm in March of 1996. Born in Northern Ontario, he grew up in Sept Isles on the north shore of the St. Lawrence River, where his parents worked for the Quebec North Shore and Labrador Railway. In 1973, armed with a degree in electrical engineering from the University of Ottawa, he returned to Sept Isles to work for the Iron Ore Company of Canada (IOC) for the next 17 years. During that time he wore many hats, including managing the IOC's in-house consulting group that had a mandate to optimize the train system for the handling of IOC's logistical needs. In 1989 he joined St. Lawrence Stevedoring, one of the Cast group of companies; its primary business was to transfer iron ore coming in from Brazil to the smaller vessels that would take the ore into the Great Lakes system. When the company was sold in 1991, he stayed with Cast, working as Vice-President, Cast Terminal Inc. in Montreal.

In 1993 Morin moved to Zeebrugge, Belgium to take over the European end of the Cast operation as Vice-President Customer Service. By this time, Cast was one of two large container operators on the Montreal-North Europe route. However, Cast's major creditor, the Royal Bank of Canada, was keen to extricate itself from the company whose shares it had acquired in a 1983 restructuring. When CP's proposal to acquire Cast passed the scrutiny of the Competition Bureau and the National Transportation Agency in early 1995, it was clear to Morin that CP would move in its own management. He returned to North America and worked for a small company he hoped to acquire. However, the Halterm opportunity came up and, in March 1996, Morin arrived at Halterm.

Halterm was not an unknown company to Morin. On behalf of Cast, he had explored Halterm as an alternative to Montreal several years earlier. He believed the company was a good business, fairly efficient but very expensive. Morin described his early days at the company:

> On arrival, my first order of business had to be visiting customers; 80% of our stevedoring contracts with the lines were up. Within the first six months, we concluded contracts with Melfi (a new call), renewed our contracts with SPM, Maersk and ZIM with changes, and worked towards the setting up of the Halifax Employers' Association [to negotiate with the unions].
>
> In getting to know our customers, I found that Halterm was not viewed as the most expensive of terminals. However, it was only working at 60% capacity. Its labour reputation was good but not progressive. Labour [in Halifax] is quite entrenched in its thinking. They still insist on a lunch hour when all work stops. The current situation works best for underperforming lines but is not optimized for those who run on a tight schedule.
>
> At my first Board meeting I was asked to produce a mission and a strategic plan for the business. We had previously developed strategies but something new was needed. The next meeting, we presented the mission and were given the go-ahead to develop the strategy.

It is that strategy that Morin will present at the December board meeting.

Halterm Facilities and Operations Today

Halterm's primary business is the efficient loading and unloading of container ships that range in size from small coastal feeder vessels (having the capacity to carry 275 TEUs[4]) to large, fourth-generation container ships (capacity up to 4,000 TEUs). The

---

[4]A TEU is a Twenty-foot Equivalent Unit, a standard measure for container cargoes. A container measuring 40' x 8' x 8' would be 2 TEU in size.

overall length of the berths is 990 metres (3,250 feet.) The terminal's main berth at Pier C can accommodate ships with a maximum draft (depth of the ship beneath the water line) of 14 metres (45 feet), more than any other North American east coast port. (See Appendices A and C on pages 87 and 89.)

Ships are loaded or unloaded at a rate of 22-25 containers per crane working hour. The number of container moves achieved per crane hour is the single most important measure of terminal efficiency used by the shipping lines, and crane productivity is generally higher on larger container ships. As such, it is a major criterion used by shipping lines when selecting a terminal operator.

The majority of import containers discharged in Halifax are destined for the inland markets of Montreal, Toronto, and Chicago via CN's double-stack rail service to these centres. Halterm's operating system is designed to transfer containers directly from the ship to rail. Import containers destined for local markets by truck are delivered from the ship to a pre-determined terminal storage area where they are held until picked up by a local trucking firm (contracted by the shipping line).

Containers to be loaded onto a ship (export containers) arrive at Halterm either by truck or by rail, with the majority arriving by rail. CN delivers these containers directly to the on-dock rail facility, where they are off-loaded and stored awaiting the arrival of the ship. Halterm has the capacity to store 12,500 TEUs. Halterm has a total of 2,800 metres of rail track, sufficient to hold an entire unit train that can be assembled and discharged directly from the terminal to its final inland destination. In addition, a 1,525 metre loop track, following the perimeter of the terminal, provides for buffer rail storage capacity.

To facilitate the efficient movement of truck traffic to and from the terminal, Halterm and the HPC invested $700,000 in a new, automated truck-handling facility in 1994. This increased the truck-handling capacity from an average of 130 container moves per day to 300 per day. As a result, truck turnaround times improved substantially.

Halterm also established an Electronic Data Interchange (EDI) system in partnership with CN and several of its larger customers. EDI allows Halterm to electronically receive and send cargo information on all rail movements as well as that concerning cargo to be loaded or discharged from ships. On the trucking side, hand-held computer units automatically update the yard control system in real-time and eliminate the need for multiple data entry at various stages of the operation. This technology will be extended to rail, terminal and ship operations in the near future. At its present volume, Halterm is operating at 60% of its capacity.

Finances

Halterm receives container handling revenue from its customers based on the volume of containers handled and the ancillary services provided. Container handling rates charged to Halterm's customers are established by contract and are unregulated. Contracts that continue to the end of 1998 or longer account for over 95% of Halterm's forecasted volume. Approximately 70% of Halterm's costs are variable based on throughput. The largest single cost is salaries and wages, which represent 56% of total costs. The next single largest expense is wharfage and berthage assessments (13%); these assessments are a "pass-through" expenditure collected from Halterm's customers and paid to HPC. Other costs include equipment repairs and maintenance, land and building rental, fuel, and general administration.

The single largest capital item for Halterm is a ship-to-shore gantry crane (replacement cost approximates $7 million). These cranes, given proper repair and preventive maintenance, have a useful life of 30-40 years. Halterm has an aggressive repair and maintenance program, and estimates that, for other than cranes, annual capital expenditures required to maintain throughput capacity over the next 10 years will average $850,000. Halterm's financial data are in Appendix D on pages 89–90.

Employees and Labour Relations

The Port of Halifax has enjoyed a stable relationship between its employers and unionized workers for the past 20 years. Halterm employs a full-time staff of 30 non-unionized personnel who are responsible for the co-ordination of Halterm's operations and the administration of Halterm's business. Many of these personnel are long-term employees. Three groups of unionized employees form a basic work force of 165. Halterm and its unions operate under the terms of a collective agreement negotiated by the Halifax Employers' Association that represents all employers of unionized labour in the Port of Halifax. Five-year collective agreements with all union locals expired on December 31, 1995, and the parties are now engaged in negotiations for a new contract. Until these negotiations are completed, the existing agreement will prevail. The last major work interruption occurred in 1976. Morin commented:

> Contract negotiations have been continuing since my arrival. There are three unions and we've completed none of the labour contracts to date. If we are seriously going to attract the lines of the next century, we need to have greater flexibility in the union contracts.

Customers and Requirements

Halterm services 13 domestic and international shipping lines that call at the Port of Halifax. The terminal's three largest customers are ZIM, Maersk Canada Inc., and NOL. Combined, these three carriers account for 70% of Halterm's current total container volume. ZIM is Halterm's largest single customer and has been using Halterm for over 25 years. NOL began its service relationship in 1986 and Maersk in 1989. A list of customers is in Appendix E on page 90.

Customers use Halterm under service contracts that are generally reopened for rate negotiations at the end of each three-year period. The contracts set out the services to be provided and the corresponding rates of compensation. Services may include the loading or discharge of containers to and from container ships, intra-terminal movement of containers, the receipt and delivery of containers to and from rail cars and trucks, the stuffing and stripping of cargo, the provision of power and storage space for temperature-controlled containers, and so on. Each rate is calculated on the basis of the cost of labour plus an appropriate mark-up for overhead services. Contracts with major customers may contain volume rebate allowances to encourage greater use of Halterm. The typical contract with customers contains performance guarantees (in the form of the number of lifts per hour), cranes to be made available, and so on.

Because of lines' requirements for service guarantees and their unwillingness to wait for a berth, asset utilization in the industry is mediocre. Morin is particularly concerned that Halterm is not getting the lifts per crane or lifts per hour offered by other terminals. It has become quite clear during this trip that Canadian terminals have not kept pace with their European counterparts, particularly in investing in new technology. The productivity improvements Morin had seen at European terminals were impressive. (See Table 1 on the next page.)

table 1 Ports and Performance Benchmarks

Terminal	TEU (000)	Average Lifts/hr	Annual Lifts/crane	Operation*
Cast (Montreal)	200	25	67,000	RTG
Racine (Montreal)	280	22	70,000	RTG
Halterm (Halifax)	155	22	39,000	RTG
FCT (Zeebrugge)	170	39	57,000	Straddle
ECT (Rotterdam)	580	25	72,500	Auto
Felixstowe	1,400	21	70,000	RTG
Hessenatie (Antwerp)	600	35	75,000	Straddle

Note: * RTG=rubber tired yard gantries; straddle = straddle carriers; auto=robotized
Source: Halterm.

The terminal must understand the lines' requirements more broadly that just providing a list of services. With the massive capital investment required to be a player in the container market, shipowners will avoid calling at any port where berth space is not available on demand. Berth availability is only a minimum condition for consideration as part of the carrier's network; port choice hinges on services, landside connections, door-to-door costs and transit time. The line essentially buys the port's services with an eye to selling its own. Therefore, they are looking for additional services, electronic data interchange (EDI), on-dock transfer, and distribution and warehousing facilities to make the port an integral part of the just-in-time concept. In addition, the first port-of-call status on inbound cargo and last port-of-call status on outbound is the most desirable position as it enhances a port's ability to attract time-sensitive cargoes. If shippers are buying container services on transit time, such a status will very often give a port the edge in seeking to match shippers and carriers. Once the port is chosen, there remains the choice of terminal.

Although the list of customers for any terminal tends to be short, marketing a terminal is not easy. Visiting customers is a key role for the president. Customer relations tend to become personal but, in the end, terminal choice by the shipping line is a serious commercial decision based on the terminal's operating performance and berth availability. For Morin, the relationships have been carefully tended, but operations must deliver the desired service.

Morin believed that understanding the lines' requirements was insufficient; the terminal must discern the requirements of the customer's customers. Shippers tend to be port-blind. They buy the services of a carrier and pay very little attention to the route. They expect the carrier to deliver what it has promised in terms of any special equipment, services, and delivery time at an agreed time and price. It is up to the carrier to ensure that the quoted price delivers profit. Once the carrier has booked the cargo, it is a matter of ensuring that its choice of port delivers what has been promised the customer. This includes choosing a terminal that will minimize labour costs for a given standard of productivity; calls with time and a half or double time labour charges erode the profit margin on the sale. The carrier's schedule must work to attract the shipper's booking and still earn the carrier an acceptable profit.

Customers have the right to cancel their terminal contracts on 90 days written notice. (While being re-negotiated, the terms of the existing agreements prevail.) Of Halterm's volume, 72% is from shipping lines whose contracts expire on December 31,

1998. An additional 25% of volume is covered by service contracts due to expire December 31, 1996 and which are presently under re-negotiation. To win the business long term, Halterm must at least match, if not exceed, the productivity achieved by the best terminals in the business while keeping prices to the lines low enough to allow them to offer their customers a competitively priced door-to-door package.

Business Development

As a result of internal discussions, the company developed its mission statement:

> Halterm's mission is to become the container terminal of choice for shipping lines serving Canada and midwest US by providing superior, cost-effective performance.

To support this objective, the terminal launched a number of initiatives aimed at improving customer service and reducing terminal operating costs. Customer service initiatives focused on improved ship productivity, faster truck turnaround times, and embedding a service quality culture throughout the operation. Higher ship and terminal productivity also resulted in reduced operating costs and improved margins. With respect to new business development, Halterm maintains an active marketing program that concentrates on developing relationships with those carriers known to be considering a North Atlantic east coast port-of-call. Halterm is targeting customers with a particular interest in serving midwest US markets through Chicago, in order to maximize the potential of investments made by CN.

In 1995, CN opened its new $200 million St. Clair tunnel, linking Sarnia, Ontario to Port Huron, Michigan. Prior to the opening of the tunnel, Halifax was neither price- nor time-competitive into Chicago. The tunnel reduced the transit time from Halifax to Chicago to 54 hours, a full 24 hours less than before the tunnel opened. CN now has the capacity to carry double-stack containers from Halifax to Chicago; double-stack systems reduce unit costs and allow for more competitive inland transportation pricing. In addition, in May 1996, CN broke ground on a new 67-acre intermodal rail transfer facility in Chicago developed in conjunction with the Illinois Central. The facility has a capacity to handle up to 225,000 container or trailer units, a dramatic increase from the previous capacity of 75,000 units. The facility also permits more efficient connections with the Illinois Central. These two investments by CN have meant that Halifax is now service-competitive for traffic to Chicago and the mid-south, destinations like Memphis, Kansas City and St. Louis. Halifax's US midwest business has grown from "abysmally low," to quote Craig Littzen, Vice-President Intermodal of CN, to 40,000 TEUs. The service to the US midwest via the North American east coast has a total potential market of 1.5 million TEUs (see Appendix F on page 91). CN's investments and a new business plan for Halterm should ensure a larger share of midwest traffic for Halifax.

Management of Halterm

Halterm shares are owned equally by Newfoundland Capital Corporation and Canadian National, the Furness Withy shares held by OOCL having been acquired by the other two in October of 1996. The management contract is held by NCC.

Newfoundland Capital Corporation is a publicly traded management company engaged in the transportation and communications sectors. Through the Clarke Transport Group, NCC has joint venture interests in a shipping firm and positioned itself as an integrated, full-service provider of transportation services and logistical solutions.

Through its communications group, NCC owns 30 newspapers and specialty magazine publications and operates 13 radio stations across Canada. NCC has managed Halterm since 1981 when it acquired Clarke.

According to Morin, Halterm's relationship with NCC is fairly autonomous; it operates as a distinct responsible entity. Roy Rideout, president and chief operating officer of NCC, concurs:

> The most important roles I have in relation to Halterm are the selection of the president and providing the necessary coaching. Newfoundland Capital is there to assist the president where on-site resources may be thin. I try not to get involved in the day-to-day business.

Morin believes that NCC brings financial and human resources expertise to assist the company, while Clarke has significant transport expertise of use to the company. In addition, there is a strong relationship between Clarke and CN through the Pool Car Division of Clarke. However, the future of NCC is somewhat uncertain. Patrick Morin:

> Right now Newfoundland Capital is under significant pressure to increase shareholder value. It has been trading at $3-4 a share over the past few years and is considerably undervalued. The communications analysts don't understand transportation and so they undervalue it. The transportation analysts don't understand communications and so they undervalue it. Both discount it because its dual focus is perceived as a lack of focus.

Canadian National is the sixth largest freight railroad in North America. It operates the larger of Canada's two principal railroads, serving the major cities, ports and natural resource regions in Canada with connections to most major United States railroads. The government-owned company was privatized in Canada's largest initial public offering on November 17, 1995.

Canadian National's interest in Halterm was one of the files Craig Littzen acquired when he arrived at CN in the summer of 1995 as CN was being readied for privatization. Early on he pushed for the removal of OOCL's interest through Furness Withy, feeling:

> I was unhappy with the ownership structure. We were a passive owner, as was OOCL. Why should a company [OOCL] that gained its interest through call guarantees be entitled to a share of the profits when it no longer calls at Halifax? As a publicly owned company, we couldn't be seen to be active in the management of the terminal. Now that CN is a private company, it can take a more active role, given the strategic importance of the Halifax gateway to CN.

Both Littzen and Rideout pushed for the acquisition of OOCL's interest in the terminal. They are keen to pursue a new vision for Halterm and eager to see Morin's strategy and business plan.

THE GLOBAL CONTAINER SHIPPING AND PORT INDUSTRIES

The concept of containerized shipping services was first developed in 1956 for relatively high value and volume cargo that required special protection. It was not until the late 1960s, however, that containerization was adopted widely by the shipping industry. The use of containers had benefits both portside and inland. Operating efficiencies led to a dramatic growth in business. Containerization permitted shipping lines to offer their customers a fully integrated water- and land-based transportation system. Container shipping is faster, less costly and offers better cargo protection. As a result, it has become the dominant means of transporting manufactured and semi-finished goods to markets around the world.

Worldwide container terminal throughput has grown at an average annual rate of 9.5% over the past 15 years and is forecast to grow at 7.2% annually until 2010, according to *The Greater Halifax Multi-Modal Transportation Study* prepared by Booz-Allen & Hamilton Inc. Throughput volumes at the Port of Halifax have grown at an average annual rate of 3.8% over the past 15 years and an average annual rate of 5.0% over the past 5 years, and are forecast to grow by 5% per year until 2005. Over the period 1980-1995, container throughput over North American ports increased from 9.9 million TEUs to 21.8 million TEUs, an annual growth rate of 5.4%.

Container traffic growth has been highest in East Asia where container terminal throughput increased annually by 13.6% over the 1980-95 period. The greatest future growth is expected to occur in Southeast Asia, particularly Thailand, Korea, and Singapore. Markets in China and India are also anticipated to provide significant growth opportunities, with China expected to be the market growth leader over the next decade. Goods shipped from Southeast Asia and India to markets such as Montreal, Toronto, and the US midwest can be cost-effectively delivered to the east coast of North America via the Suez Canal. The route has prospects for a very high growth rate. Macrsk already provides a direct shipping link to these markets through its Suez services.

In addition to the increasing containerization of trade and rising trade volumes, there are a number of important structural and operational changes happening in the international container shipping industry.

First among these is the trend toward industry rationalization. Many carriers, rather than operating their own ships on select trade routes, have joined major global alliances where several lines combine ships in an operating consortium and expand their market reach. Four global alliances have been announced over the past year: (1) Maersk and Sea-Land; (2) The Grand Alliance of NYK, P&O, Hapag-Lloyd and NOL; (3) The Global Alliance of APL, Mitsui O.S.K., Nedlloyd and OOCL; and (4) the alliance of Hanjin, DSR-Senator and Cho Yang. Two of these major alliances call on the Port of Halifax: the Maersk/Sea-Land alliance with its North Atlantic and Suez services, and the Grand Alliance with its AEX service calling Halterm and its PAX calling Ceres.

The second major trend is the growth in ship size. The largest containership in 1980 was 3,055 TEU; by 1996 the largest ship was rated to carry 6,250 TEU. As ships became larger, the depth advantages offered by Halifax over New York translated into more cargo as vessels sought to lighten their load before calling New York westbound or to add cargo before heading east.

Furthermore, *Containerisation International* recently noted that 60% of the new vessels on order were post-Panamax size. This is a dramatic change from the industry's original reticence to adopt the technology. After American President Lines' (APL) delivery of 5 in 1988, it was another four years before Hyundai Merchant Marine followed APL's lead. Since then, shipping lines have continued to order ever-larger container ships in an effort to further reduce per-TEU ocean cargo costs; ship-related cost savings are projected to be as high as 20%. (The Top 20 container shipping companies are presented in Appendix G on page 91, while those ordering post-Panamax ships are noted in Appendix H on page 92.) Because of their larger size, post-Panamax ships require deeper harbour entrance channels and terminal berths. The minimum depth requirement is between 13 and 14 metres (42-45 feet). This will present a problem for many east coast North American ports, as evident from Appendix C on page 89. Post-Panamax ships have been deployed on the largest, fastest growing trade routes to service the Europe/Far East, Asia/West Coast North America and intra-Asian trade routes. They are not expected to be in service on the North Atlantic for another five years as there are no facilities currently capable of servicing these vessels. The Port of Halifax is the east coast North Atlantic container port that could best handle the latest generation of post-Panamax ships on order.

With new post-Panamax vessels costing in excess of US$100 million, and many lines ordering sufficient numbers to optimize network schedules, the decision about ports served becomes more critical. How do consortia view terminal choice? A recent article in *Container Management* summed it up: apart from terminal costs, other criteria that are important in terminal choice include crane performance and turnaround time, berthing windows, port deviation times and the advantages of being able to develop a hub-and-spoke network. To compete, the article noted, many have lowered their prices and added performance guarantees (in terms of moves per crane hour). Some ports have also offered volume discounts to attract certain types of cargoes.

The *Multi-Modal Transportation Study* concluded that "international container trade is the platform of port-related economic growth." It also noted that the two container terminals in Halifax have the capacity at the berth of handling in excess of 1 million TEUs, but land storage at both terminals limits Halifax to serving only 500,000 TEUs. Furthermore, the study noted that New York, Baltimore, Hampton Roads and Montreal have all announced infrastructure investments. These range from $7 million being spent in Montreal to expand Racine Terminal by 6 acres to the $675 million allocated by New York for redesign of the terminals and deepening of the channels. (Appendix I on page 92 provides more data from this study.)

The dilemma of port development is that private terminals like Halterm must often compete with heavily subsidized public facilities. (Some ports are disadvantaged by their competitors' access to public funds as local municipalities subsidize economic development with various tax concessions; it is also common for governments to allow ports to issue low grade bonds to raise capital.) For example, the Port of New York's dredging program, once authorized, will be provided by the US Army Corps of Engineers and not reflected in New York's financial statements or its charges to its customers. The port industry is undergoing a dramatic shift worldwide as governments privatize or corporatize their facilities, and port management companies like Hutchison Ports, P&O Ports and PSA Corporation spread their operations globally.

COMPETITORS

Halterm's competitive position must be considered in two distinct contexts. The first is the overall competitive position of the Port of Halifax compared to alternative east coast North American ports. The second is Halterm's direct competitive position with the competing container terminal in the Port of Halifax, the Ceres terminal at Fairview Cove. Morin:

> Marketing a container terminal is really marketing Halifax as a port of call. If a line chooses Halifax, we have a 50% chance of getting the business. Capacity limits how many lines will call one terminal.
>
> What's important to our customers, the shipping lines, is the productivity of the port call. Quick turnaround is the key. What is the point of them working hard to make gains on the water side if we waste it at the terminal? The lines also force us to compete on price. The shipper weighs the service he gets from the line against the price he is charged. If he chooses Maersk, he doesn't care if the box is loaded at New York or at Halifax. This means that the carrier's going to look to cost to make the decision and productivity is part of that cost.

The Port of Halifax is served on a direct-call basis by many of the world's larger container carriers. It has established a relatively strong position on the North Atlantic, Mediterranean and Far East trade routes that serve markets in Atlantic Canada, Quebec and Ontario. Over the past two years, the Port of Halifax has begun to make inroads into the midwest US market and participate in the growth represented by trade with Southeast Asia via the Suez Canal.

Volume growth in the Port of Halifax tends to parallel that of the North American east coast port system as a whole, which includes, in addition to the Port of Halifax, the Ports of Montreal, Hampton Roads, New York/New Jersey, Baltimore, Boston, and Philadelphia. Geographically, Halifax does not compete with Charleston, Savannah, Jacksonville or Miami.

Over the long term, the Port of Halifax is well positioned for the trend towards large ships; its water depth and ease of access make it a natural selection. One distinct future possibility is that the Port of Halifax will be used to lighten post-Panamax ships to reduce their draft to a level where they can enter shallower east coast United States ports such as New York. This would require the discharge of substantial additional cargo in Halifax to reduce ship draft from 14 metres (45 feet) to 11.6 metres (38 feet).

As for the competing terminal operation in Halifax, it is owned and operated by Ceres Terminals Inc., a US-based company that also operates container terminals in Europe and on the east coast of the United States. The two compete for customers on the basis of price, service and capacity availability. (See Appendix A on page 87 for more information on the Ceres terminal at Fairview Cove.) Morin explained:

> They [Ceres] are a very traditional well-run company. They've been in business a long time and they have one key advantage over us. Because they are part of a network of terminals [over 30 in Canada and the US], they can move equipment in from other locations and the best of what they learn elsewhere can be applied here. In addition, they can spread their base costs over many operations. As an independent operator we don't have that.

Halterm has maintained a dominant position in the local market since 1989-1990 and its current market share is 63% based on the most recent estimate of total port throughput for 1996 (see Appendix B on page 88). The largest single customer calling Halifax, ACL, calls at Ceres.

THE FUTURE

Looking forward, Morin could see three issues he needed to consider in developing his business plan for the Board meeting on December 11 and the proposal for the AEX/PAX service, due on December 12: (1) the potential approval of the P&O merger with Nedlloyd by the European Commission and the uncertainty about which alliance the merged company would choose; (2) the imminent consolidation of the AEX/PAX service at one of the terminals; and (3) long term, the likelihood of investment in post-Panamax facilities by one of the Halifax terminals within the next five years.

As for the first, Morin expected that the P&O Nedlloyd merger would be approved and that the merged company would join the Grand Alliance (offering the AEX/PAX service) rather than Nedlloyd's current alliance (the Global Alliance).

Less certain and of considerable concern was the terminal choice to be made by the AEX/PAX service. The service represented a new Suez routing and accounted for close to 20% of Halterm's business. More important, the alliance was likely to be very successful on the route. In addition, Halterm was not able to guarantee the crane times requested as they conflicted with those already offered to existing customers; he had heard that Ceres faced the same problem in developing their proposal for the service. Furthermore, relations with Hapag Lloyd, the lead negotiator for the AEX/PAX service, were strained. P&O was indifferent and support from NYK was unknown but not likely positive. The only one of the four lines in the service clearly in favour of Halterm appeared to be NOL. The SPM contract would be up the end of December and, as a feeder to Hapag Lloyd, it was likely that SPM would follow whatever decision was made by Hapag Lloyd. The odds were clearly in favour of Ceres winning the AEX/PAX business.

As for the longer term, it was only a matter of time before Halifax needed to make a post-Panamax facility investment decision. With an investment of $22 million for two post-Panamax cranes and yard support equipment coupled with a further investment of $4 million by the Halifax Port Corporation to change the rail gauge for the cranes on the berth, Halterm could convert its existing facility to service post-Panamax ships. However, this would only be a short-term investment because it would not increase the capacity landside to handle larger volumes through the terminal. There is not really any adjacent land available for expansion.

Although none of Halifax's competitor ports on the US east coast have made the complete investment (cranes, dredging, berth strengthening, additional rail facilities, etc.) necessary to seize this business opportunity, it was only a matter of time. Just a few days ago the Greater Halifax Partnership released its *Multi-Modal Transportation Study* (see Appendix I on page 92 for key details) including details on proposed investments at competing ports. With plenty of media present at its release, the high profile report argued that Halifax needed to do something about serving post-Panamax shipping or the port would be relegated to a feeder role in the new restructured global networks. Public pressure was mounting to do something. Even taxi drivers had added the post-Panamax word to their vocabulary. Morin did not want to move sooner than might be financially advisable. If Halterm built a post-Panamax facility, would the business materialize or would it be a "field of dreams"?

As the plane prepared to land in Halifax, Morin recalled the points made by Brian Doherty in a recent conversation:

> Today we face three problems in this port. First, there is the labour problem; labour doesn't want to change. We need the right people with the right skills and the right agreement. If we don't have a contract with labour that makes sense, the lines will leave.
>
> Second, we must resolve the matter of the two terminals. There are days when ships are waiting for one to become free and there is berth space available at the other. We need to maximize the utilization of Halifax's assets. No one will invest until this is resolved. We must get beyond this mistaken belief that we need [local] competition.
>
> Third, the rail line needs to deal with only one terminal [operator]. They are getting poor utilization of their doublestack equipment. They are ready to come to the table if this is resolved.

The plane touched down and Morin knew he must now begin to put his ideas on paper and prepare his presentation to the Board.

appendix A   Halifax's Container Terminals

	Halterm	Ceres
Ship Berths	3	2
Length	C = 600 m (1,968 feet)	660 m (2,165 feet)
	B = 381 m (1,250 feet)	
Ship-to-shore cranes	4	3
Acreage (Open)	71.6	61.5
Rail capacity	450 TEUs	250 TEUs
Storage	12,500 TEUs	7,000 TEUs

Map of Halifax

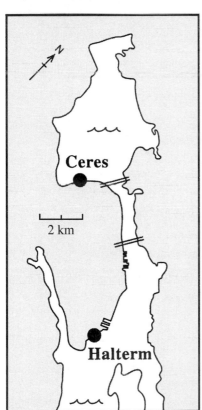

Map of Halterm

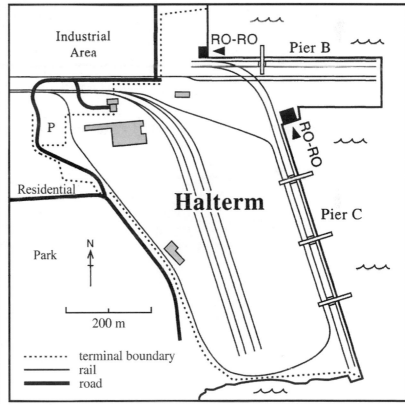

appendix B   Halifax Container Business and Halterm's Share

Year	Port of Halifax Total Volume (containers)	Halterm Volume (containers)	Halterm Percentage of Total Volume
1985	165,190	49,947	30.2
1986	174,352	65,288	37.4
1987	211,925	98,889	46.7
1988	261,925	128,310	49.0
1989	287,503	143,026	49.7
1990	278,313	135,613	48.7
1991	219,286	122,914	56.1
1992	181,391	124,183	68.5
1993	184,002	124,642	67.7
1994	187,682	135,508	72.2
1995	229,948	148,234	64.5
1996 Forecast	236,000	148,500	63.0

Source: Halterm.

Container Cargo Handled by the Port of Halifax by Geographic Region

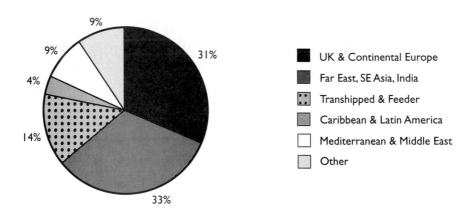

- ■ UK & Continental Europe
- ◼ Far East, SE Asia, India
- ⬚ Transhipped & Feeder
- ▨ Caribbean & Latin America
- ☐ Mediterranean & Middle East
- ▨ Other

Source: Port of Halifax Directory.

appendix C East Coast North America Ports

Rank	Ports	TEU (000) volumes	Labour (Lifts/hr)	Depth * Restrictions (Feet)**	Terminal Utilization (percent)
1	New York/New Jersey	2,276	25	36	56
2	Hampton Roads	1,078	24	42	62
3	Charleston	1,031			
4	Jacksonville	911			
5	Montreal	726	24	36	89
6	Miami*	656			
7	Savannah*	627			
8	Baltimore	535	23	39	32
9	Halifax	383	25	45	75
10	Palm Beach	162			

Note: * The only post-Panamax cranes in the Top 10 ports are at Miami and Savannah.
    ** Channel or berth, whichever is shallower.

Source: Port rank and volumes come from *Containerisation International Yearbook*; depth restrictions, labour productivity and terminal utilization from Greater Halifax Partnership (1996), *The Greater Halifax Multi-Modal Transportation Study* by Booz Allen & Hamilton Inc.

appendix D Selected Historical Financial and Operating Data

	Years ended December 31 (in $000)				
	1996 (F)	1995	1994	1993	1992
Revenue	36,118	35,161	31,747	28,847	28,476
Operating and administrative costs	30,393	29,610	26,515	24,111	23,869
Earnings before interest, marketing fee, depreciation and amortization	5,725	5,551	5,232	4,736	4,607
Interest	719	824	780	851	944
Marketing fee	406	657	539	394	470
Depreciation and amortization	1,736	1,798	1,958	2,049	1,947
Net income	2,864	2,272	1,955	1,442	1,246

Note: (1) Marketing fee paid to a third party, which obligation was terminated in September 1996.

appendix D *(continued)*

Balance Sheet (as at December 31 in $000)	1996 Forecast	1995 Actual
ASSETS		
Current Assets		
Accounts receivable	5,529	4,123
Prepaid expenses and supplies	765	971
Total current assets	6,294	5,094
Long-term Assets		
Due from related company	1,997	1,064
Property and equipment less accumulated depreciation	10,388	11,802
Deferred charges, net of accumulated amortization	2,716	—
Total Assets	21,395	17,960
LIABILITIES AND SHAREHOLDERS' EQUITY		
Current Liabilities		
Bank indebtedness	1,528	1,529
Accounts payable and accrued liabilities	3,274	3,184
Due to related party	282	252
Current portion of long-term debt	1,600	1,100
Total Current Liabilities	6,684	6,065
Long-term Debt	8,250	6,100
Shareholders' Equity	6,461	5,795
Total Liabilities and Shareholders' Equity	21,395	17,960

appendix E   Halterm's Current Customers

Line	Routes	Routes (incl. Halifax)	Owner (Headquarters in North America)
Hapag-Lloyd	Global	AEX and PAX	Germany (New Jersey)
Maersk Canada	Global	Europe-N. America; east coast-Suez	Denmark (New Jersey)
Melfi Marine Corp.	Niche	Halifax-Cuba	Cuba
NYK Line (Canada) Inc.	Global	AEX and PAX	Japan (New Jersey)
National Shipping Co. of Saudi Arabia	Niche	N. America east coast-Med.-Gulf	Saudi Arabia (New Jersey)
Navis Shipping Inc.	Niche	Halifax-Cuba	Canada (Nova Scotia)
Neptune Orient Lines	Global	AEX and PAX	Singapore (New Jersey)
Oceanex Limited Partnership	Regional	Halifax-Newfoundland	Canada (Quebec)
P&O Containers	Global	AEX and PAX	UK (New Jersey)
Sea-Land Services Inc.	Global	Global with Maersk	US (New Jersey)
St. Pierre RoRo Services and SPM Containerline	Regional	St. Pierre-Halifax-Portland/Boston	France (St. Pierre)
Transatlantic Agencies	Transatlantic	Germany-Halifax	Germany (Maryland)
ZIM Israel Navigation Company (Canada) Ltd.	Global	Asia-N. America-Med.	Israel (New York)

appendix F   North American Traffic through East Coast Ports (share of TEUs)

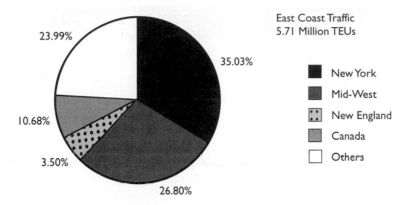

Note: Halterm's traffic is 78% to Canada and 22% to New England and the Mid-West.
Source: Halterm data.

appendix G   Leading Container Service Operators (as of September 1, 1995)

Rank	Company	Vessels	Total TEU	% Vessels Over 3500 TEU
1	Sea-Land	109	196,708	12
2	Maersk	97	186,040	19
3	Evergreen/Uniglory Marine	90	181,982	10
4	Cosco	148	169,795	6
5	NYK/TSK	73	137,018	12
6	Nedlloyd	60	119,599	13
7	MOL	66	118,208	14
8	P&O	46	98,893	20
9	Hanjin	35	92,332	23
10	Mediterranean Shipping	71	88,955	0
11	APL	38	81,547	18
12	ZIM	60	79,738	0
13	K Line	43	75,528	0
14	DSR-Senator	39	75,497	0
15	Hapag-Lloyd	28	71,688	29
16	Neptune Orient Lines/PUL	35	63,469	23
17	Yangming	27	60,034	11
18	Hyundai	23	59,195	26
19	OOCL	23	55,811	4
20	CMA	26	46,026	15

Source: Data are from John Fossey "Top Shots," *Containerisation International* (November 1995): 55-59 at 56.

appendix H Leading Operators of Post-Panamax Tonnage (as of November 1, 1996)

Carrier	TEU (Ships) in Service	TEU (Ships) on Order	Projected Fleet Size
Hyundai Merchant Marine	59,772 (12)	11,102 (2)	70,874 (14)
APL	50,692 (11)		50,692 (11)
Maersk Line	24,000 (4)	48,000 (8)	72,000 (12)
OOCL	29,760 (6)	9,936 (2)	39,696 (8)
Mitsui OSK Lines	23,606 (5)		23,606 (5)
Evergreen Line	16,092 (3)	53,640 (10)	69,732 (13)
P&O Nedlloyd (if merged)	12,613 (3)	28,750 (5)	42,940 (8)
Hanjin	10,604 (2)	26,696 (4)	39,309 (7)
MISC	8,938 (2)		8,938 (2)
Cosco		31,500 (6)	31,500 (6)
Neptune Orient Lines		39,272 (8)	39,272 (8)
Yang Ming Marine Transport		23,500 (5)	23,500 (5)
Total	250,267 (51)	288,302 (53)	538,569 (104)

Source: Containerisation International Yearbook.

appendix I Data from the Multi-Modal Transportation Study

Port Shares

Port	1980		1995	
	Volume	Share	Volume	Share
New York/New Jersey	1,947	55.6%	2,263	45.5%
Hampton Roads	391	11.1%	1,078	21.6%
Montreal	301	8.7%	726	14.6%
Baltimore	663	18.9%	535	10.7%
Halifax	201	5.7%	383	7.7%
Total (5 ports)	3,503	100.0%	4,985	100.0%

Cost of Planned Port Construction

Port	Investment ($M)	Acreage	$000 per Acre
Charleston	$137	65	$2,100
Hampton Roads	$548	238	$2,300
Seattle	$367	105	$3,500
Long Beach	$411	170	$2,400
Vancouver	$224	92	$3,400

Source: Greater Halifax Partnership (1996), *The Greater Halifax Multi-Modal Transportation Study* by Booz-Allen & Hamilton Inc.

case 7 TVOntario

INTRODUCTION

In the fall of 2000, Bob Baker was appointed managing director of revenue and development at TVOntario (TVO), a Crown corporation of the province of Ontario. He was responsible for development (i.e., fundraising and membership services) and for the Sales and Licensing Department. During Baker's first few months on the job, it had become clear that the Sales and Licensing Department was continuing to experience rapidly declining revenues. Questions as to the true profitability of the department had been raised with management and with the board of directors.

Some members of TVO management and some members of the board of directors believed that the Sales and Licensing Department had outlived its usefulness and should be shut down. However, they wanted Baker to analyse the situation and propose any viable alternatives before they made a final decision.

It was spring of 2001, and Baker had been given only a few months to determine the future, if indeed there was to be one, for the TVOntario Sales and Licensing Department. He was under pressure from the board of directors and from the Sales and Licensing Department (where morale was at an all-time low) to make a decision as soon as possible. While Baker understood the need to act quickly, he wanted to be sure the decision would be in the best long-term interests of TVO, and had targeted late June for making his recommendations.

Gail Robertson prepared this case under the supervision of Professor Paul Beamish solely to provide material for class discussion. The authors do not intend to illustrate either effective or ineffective handling of a managerial situation. The authors may have disguised certain names and other identifying information to protect confidentiality.

Version: (A) 2001-07-05

Ivey

Richard Ivey School of Business
The University of Western Ontario

THE NORTH AMERICAN BROADCAST INDUSTRY[1,2]

The television broadcast industry was changing rapidly worldwide. The current industry configuration was dramatically different from what it had been 10 years ago and was likely to look completely different again a few years from now. It was a major challenge for any network and for TVO to thrive in this changing environment.

In 2000, the television market in the United States continued to be the largest in the world and was served by three key distribution channels: the national commercial television networks, the independent local commercial television stations and cable television services (including pay cable). Commercial broadcast television (TV) stations in the United States could be affiliated with one of the four national commercial television networks (ABC, CBS, NBC or Fox), with one of the two new networks (WB or UPN), or these stations could have no network affiliation at all. Commercial TV stations were required to broadcast at least 28 hours per week and at least two hours per day of educational programming to maintain a network license under Federal Communications Commission (FCC) regulations.

All the U.S. networks were divisions of larger corporations. ABC was owned by Walt Disney Co., CBS Corp. by Viacom Inc., Fox by News Corp. and NBC by General Electric Co. WB was 75 per cent owned by Time Warner Inc. and 25 per cent owned by Tribune Co. UPN was a 50-50 joint venture between Chris-Craft Industries Inc. and Viacom Inc. The U.S.-based Public Broadcasting System (PBS) was the station most closely aligned with the mandate of Canada's TVOntario. As of 1999, there were 1,616 full-power television stations in the United States. Of these, 1,243 were commercial stations and 373 were educational stations. In addition, 2,194 low-power television stations were licensed to operate.

The Canadian television market was dominated by Canada's major, government-funded network, Canadian Broadcasting Corporation (CBC), and by CanWest Global Broadcasting Corporation and CTV. In addition, there were numerous cable television specialty networks in Canada, as was the case in the United States. One difference between the Canadian and U.S. television markets was that while low-powered television stations in the United States served community channels and college markets, in Canada the networks used low-powered television stations as "repeaters" to carry programming signals to rural parts of the country.

CBC was made up largely of radio and television properties and its mandate was to:

- Tell Canadians stories reflecting the reality and the diversity of the country;
- Inform Canadians about news and issues of relevance and interest;
- Support Canadian arts and culture; and
- Build bridges among Canadians, between regions and two linguistic communities.[3]

In keeping with this mandate, CBC services were available to the vast majority of Canadians. However, with recent government cutbacks, CBC had some challenges

[1]Year 2000 Outlook Upbeat for Cable, Radio, and TV. Broadcasting & Cable Industry Survey, January 27, 2000. Broadcasting & Cable Magazine. pp. 1-23.
[2]Broadcasting & Cable Industry Survey, January 27, 2000.
[3]www.cbc.ca, June 1, 2001.

ahead. An organization called Friends of CBC had been lobbying actively to preserve the CBC for Canadians.

Global Television, a private corporation, had expanded its broadcast reach to include 94 per cent of English-speaking Canada by 2000. CanWest Global also boasted a leading film and TV production and distribution operation (CanWest Entertainment), a growing new media business (CanWest Interactive) and significant international broadcasting presence in New Zealand, Australia and Ireland, as well as being Canada's largest newspaper publisher, with many major papers under the CanWest umbrella.[4]

CTV was owned by Bell Globemedia, a premier multimedia company, which was in turn 70 per cent owned by BCE Inc., 20 per cent owned by Thomson Corporation and 10 per cent owned by The Woodbridge Company Ltd. CTV's conventional broadcast signals were able to reach 99 per cent of English-speaking Canadians. CTV offered a wide range of programming, and it owned a number of network stations, an independent station in Vancouver, six CBC affiliate stations along with ASN, a satellite television service in the Maritimes. CTV had a strong showing in the specialty and pay TV arena. Included in its offerings were TSN, The Comedy Network and the award-winning Discovery Channel. CTV also owned a 50–per-cent interest in Landscape Entertainment Corp., a new Canadian production and content venture, which was expected to become a premier producer of worldwide content for film, television and the Internet, and which complemented CTV's ownership in production houses and music publishers. Included under the Bell Globemedia umbrella were also *The Globe and Mail* newspaper, and the Sympatico/Lycos Internet portal.[5]

Viewing trends showed that many Canadians preferred American content in programming. Thus, Canadian broadcasters regularly paid to rebroadcast syndicated American programs. As a result, polls repeatedly showed that as many as 19 of the top 20 television programs in Canada originated from the United States. To enable continued production of Canadian-made programs, Canadian networks were mandated by the CRTC to purchase and air domestic content.

Cable Television Systems

Cable system operators received signals from program providers through special antennas, microwave relay systems, earth stations and fibre-optic cables. The system amplified the signals, combined them with locally originated programs and ancillary services, and distributed them to subscribers. David Spencer, an associate professor of film and media studies at The University of Western Ontario, stated, "Cable providers have retransmitted network broadcasts for years without having a contract or having to pay them any royalties. This is because the networks realized that the cable providers were extending their audience reach for them."[6]

By May of 1999, the top 25 cable operators in the United States served approximately 91 per cent of that market's subscribers, up from 85 per cent in 1998. The 10 largest operators had signed up 71 per cent of the 68 million cable subscribers in the United States, up from 45 per cent in 1994. In Canada, Rogers Cablesystems was the major player, with similar cable penetration into the marketplace.

---

[4]www.canwestglobal.com, June 1, 2001.

[5]www.ctv.ca, June 1, 2001.

[6]David Spencer – Interview, September 28, 2000.

Cable revenues were primarily obtained from subscriber fees, as well as from installation charges, pay-per-view sales, set-top converter rentals, remote control sales and rentals, advertising, carriage fees from home shopping channels and fees from infomercial presenters. Other sources of revenue in the recent past had come from digital video services, high-speed Internet access, local and long-distance telephone services, commercial competitive local exchange carrier operation, high-definition television (HDTV), video on demand and e-commerce. Total revenues in the cable industry were increasing by 15 per cent annually, increases which were projected to continue through 2004.

The growth of cable had both helped (by increasing the audience reach) and hurt (in the battle for advertising dollars) the networks.

Broadcast Industry Regulation

In the United States, the broadcast industry was regulated primarily through the Federal Communications Commission (FCC). In Canada, the Canadian Radio-Television and Telecommunications Commission (CRTC) had evolved from a series of commissions and hearings into an agency responsible for regulating broadcasting and telecommunications in Canada. The CRTC operated as an independent public authority, serving the public interest and governed by the Broadcasting Act of 1991 and the Telecommunications Act of 1993. The Broadcasting Act had been put in place to ensure that all Canadians would have access to a wide variety of high-quality, Canadian programming.

Fifty-five per cent of prime-time radio and television content was required to be Canadian. This content requirement was calculated on a rolling average basis so that the quotas were typically not difficult to meet. The CRTC regulated over 5,900 broadcasters in television, cable distribution, AM and FM radio, pay and specialty television, direct-to-home satellite systems, multipoint distribution systems, subscription television and pay audio. As was the case in the United States, the Canadian broadcast industry was becoming saturated and highly competitive.

Revenue Generation in the Broadcast Industry

The North American broadcast industry revenues came primarily from three sources: national spot advertising sold to national and regional advertisers, advertising time sold to local advertisers and network compensation payments (payments to affiliates for broadcast network commercials and programming). Thus, television stations had traditionally relied largely on advertising revenues to fund operations. Cable system operators were less dependent on advertising, obtaining 65 per cent to 70 per cent of revenues from subscriber fees paid by consumers. TVO and the U.S.-based networks like PBS received no traditional advertising funding, but instead received money from government grants and public donations in the form of membership and/or sponsorship. Fifteen per cent of the PBS budget came from government funding, while TVO received 70 per cent of its funding from government sources. Many TVO viewers also had access to PBS through their signal providers, and PBS had a high membership penetration in southern Ontario. PBS was thus a key competitor to TVO, especially in the children's program arena, where they often aired the same programs, and in the area of membership solicitation.

In North America, there were tens of thousands of individual broadcast and cable companies, but the larger networks commanded the lion's share of the advertising business. In the United States, ABC, CBS and NBC accounted for more than 40 per cent of total industry advertising revenues, and even more in Olympic years. Because of this revenue base, these networks were able to purchase and provide first-run programming for prime-time hours (8 p.m. to 11 p.m. Eastern and Pacific time) and thus attract a larger share of the television audience.

Part of the negotiation process that ensued upon sale of a program to a station or network was the determination of who would obtain and/or keep the advertising revenues.

Program Syndication

Content producers were free to sell and syndicate their programs to competing and international stations.

Regardless of their network affiliation, all broadcast stations obtained some programs from independent sources, mainly syndicated TV shows or syndicated feature films which were either made for TV or had been previously shown in theatres and on cable television.

Broadcast stations (both local stations and network affiliates) could purchase a license to air a syndicated program, which gave them the ability to sell the advertising slots and keep the revenues to offset the cost of the program. The cash price for a program varied, based on its desirability and the number of times it was to be aired. The competitive environment for a particular type of programming also influenced the going rate for that program.

Thus, networks could also earn revenues through the sale of in-house productions. TVO had additionally done this through its Sales and Licensing Department. However, due to the increasingly competitive nature of the industry, TVO was unable to command higher prices for its products, prices that had been commonplace only a decade ago.

HISTORY OF TVONTARIO

TVOntario was established in 1970 as the Ontario Educational Communications Authority (OECA) by William (Bill) Davis, who was the minister of education for Ontario at that time. The mandate of OECA was to provide commercial-free television programming and interactive media resources that would educate, inform and entertain. The educational properties of OECA were to be closely linked to the province's education curriculum as well as to the skill and learning needs of the people of Ontario, from birth until long after retirement. The name of the English-language network was later changed to TVOntario (TVO). TVOntario was the corporate body which encompassed both the English-language network, TVO, and the French-language *tfo* network, which had been established in 1987.

To date, TVO had remained true to its original mandate and had been responsive to changes in education and technology. Over three million viewers watched TVO/*tfo* each week, with TVO available in 98.5 per cent of Ontario households and *tfo* to 77 per cent of all Ontario households. Outside Ontario, *tfo* was also available to over 400,000 French-speaking households in Atlantic Canada and Quebec through cable distribution, multimicrowave distribution systems and direct-to-home services. Throughout TVO's tenure, no other broadcaster had been linked as closely as TVO to the provincial education curriculum or to the lifelong learning needs of the people of Ontario.

TVO's children's programming had always been and continued to be non-violent, unbiased and uninterrupted by commercials. Research had shown a growing demand for quality programming for children under 12 years of age, and TVO had not only met that need, but had been recognized as a world leader in educational broadcasting for all ages, with more than 850 international awards to its credit. The children's shows *Polka Dot Door* and *Polka Dot Shorts*, both produced at TVO, had been widely acclaimed for their educational and entertainment value. TVO had been well recognized in the area of children's program broadcasting over the past few years. Of particular note was the success of its live, hosted children's programming, made available seven days a week. Through *TVO Kids*, it met preschooler needs in the morning and those of school-aged children in the afternoon and on weekends, with *TVO Kids Crawlspace* and *The Nook*. For French viewers, tfo's acclaimed *Mega* program met those same needs. While most networks in the business of broadcasting children's programming had some kind of hosted concept, not all were as successful as the TVO offerings.

TVO's adult programming had always explored important issues in the province of Ontario through debate, discussion and documentaries. TVO's *Studio 2* and tfo's *Panorama* focused on reflecting Ontario ideas and issues back to Ontario citizens. *Saturday Night at the Movies*, hosted for years by Elwy Yost, not only broadcast movies but set the artistic and historic context for viewers through artist, actor and behind-the-scenes interviews. A tribute to the quality of this programming was that *Saturday Night at the Movies* was often a required or recommended component of film studies courses. The Elwy Yost interviews were placed in the permanent archives of the Academy of Motion Picture Arts and Sciences in Los Angeles.

TVO had prided itself in meeting the needs of all of its consumer groups by offering a wide range of programming for all ages. Some of this programming was produced in-house, some was purchased for rebroadcast and some was co-produced.

TVO had recently created a new media division to implement a strategy of linking on-air educational broadcasting and Internet programming in the delivery of formal, curriculum-based education and lifelong learning skills development training. The direction and impact of this department had yet to be determined, though there was some optimism among those at TVO that revenue generation would be a part of the mix.

REVENUE GENERATION AND REVENUE SOURCES AT TVONTARIO

Revenues in the broadcast industry traditionally came largely from advertising. From its inception, TVO had chosen to rely on sources of revenue other than advertising.

In 2000-01, TVO's total operating budget was $63.2 million. Government funding accounted for $51.5 million in revenues, with $3.5 million coming from project and federal grants, and $48 million coming from the Ontario government. Earned revenues and development were $8.4 million, and other earned revenue was $3.3 million for that year.

There were six key sources of earned revenue for TVO:

Membership and Fundraising

TVO had approximately 79,000 members in 2001. Donations from memberships were becoming more important to the success of TVO over time. One could become a TVO member with any donation and receive *Signal* magazine with a donation of $40 or more. *Signal* was TVO's membership magazine, which included a program schedule and 'behind the scenes' stories on TVO/*tfo*. TVO membership campaigns had raised $5.1 million in 2000-01, down from previous years. TVO had traditionally accomplished its goals with the help of staff and a large contingent of volunteers. With this in mind, Baker had been working to rebuild this department to position it for future success.

Sponsorships

Corporate sponsorship for TVO programming had raised approximately $600,000 in 2000-01, with five major sponsors contributing to major initiatives:

- Dairy Farmers of Ontario—*TVO's Open House* and *TVO Kids "Bod Squad"*
- Alcan Aluminum Ltd—*TVO Teachers' Awards*
- Kodak Professional Motion Imaging—*TVO Telefest*
- Via Rail—*Saturday Night at the Movies* and *Cinema*
- The Globe and Mail—*Gregg and Company* and *Allan Gregg in Conversation with....*

Sponsorship revenues were down considerably from previous years, and the first half of the year found the department without staff. Baker had recently rebuilt this department and was confident that the new team would do great things in sponsorship in the future.

Sales and Licensing

The Sales and Licensing Department sold TVO programs primarily to other public broadcasters, educational networks, commercial cable and satellite networks and directly to educators for negotiated license fees. These license fees were generally based on usage rights and the volume of viewers in the geographical area. Thus, one broadcaster could pay $500 for a program while another broadcaster would pay $50,000 for the same program. Sales were primarily to other parts of Canada and the United States, but there had been sales to Europe, China and Latin America as well (close to 150 countries in total). At one time, revenues from this department had been in excess of $5 million, but there had been steady declines over the past few years, and net revenues of only $2.8 million were expected for the upcoming fiscal year end.

Through International Telefilm of Canada, TVO's Sales and Licensing Department sold video cassettes of curriculum resources to schools and school boards throughout Canada. Other distributors had been retained to handle international sales.

The Sales and Licensing Department had contracted Viewer Services, a private company, to handle all merchandise sales arising from the broadcast schedule, as well as offering TVO merchandise for sale at open houses and *TVO Kids* external events and live public broadcasts. Historically, merchandise sales had been low. At one time, TVO had attempted a partnership with Irwin Toys to sell the *Polka Dot Door* toy products, but it had not been profitable for either party, and the partnership was dissolved. Since 1994, there had been in excess of $2 million in retail sales of trademark licensing for *Polka Dot Door*. However, in light of declining sales, consumer product sales were terminated in March 2001.

New Business Ventures

TVO was developing partnerships with private sector businesses, earning over $600,000 in 1998-99 for contracts to maintain transmitters for OnTV, Global and Rogers in Ontario. Bell Sympatico carried *tfo* co-produced educational multimedia projects with major Canadian firms such as Enzyme and Micro-Intel (Quebecor) and their online games.

All of these revenue sources were considered important to TVO, and initiatives were in place to develop strategies for all areas. However, Baker's major concern at this time was with the future of the Sales and Licensing Department.

SALES AND LICENSING AT TVONTARIO

The Sales and Licensing Department at TVO had grown, as many departments of this type do, out of unsolicited consumer demand. As TVO developed its educational programs, broadcasters, educators and others began to approach TVO with requests to purchase programs, broadcast rights, video cassettes, etc. The demand continued to grow, and TVO management, recognizing a potentially important source of revenue, appointed one person to manage the sale of TVO products in the early 1970s. Over time, the Sales and Licensing Department was formed.

The Sales and Licensing Department had sold TVO products in 148 countries around the world; *Inquiring Minds* had been sold in 46 countries and *Polka Dot Short*s in 43 countries, including the sale for broadcast through the BBC in England. TVO was the largest foreign supplier of curriculum materials to the U.S. Instructional television (ITV) market, and TVO materials had been sold into all 50 states.

The two most successful products for the Sales and Licensing Department had been the children's educational programs, *Concepts in Science* and *Concepts in Math*. However, with the decline of in-house production over the past 10 years, and most noticeably, the past five years, revenues from the Sales and Licensing Department had dropped dramatically, even for these programs. As well, the prices that the department could command for sale of programs had diminished over time. Prices in the United States, however, were not diminishing as drastically as prices in Canada and other parts of the world.

Cindy Galbraith, the manager of the Sales and Licensing Department, believed that things could be turned around for Sales and Licensing if TVO's Programming Department would produce some salable products. A salable product was that which had no marketing restrictions, i.e., no rights, content or technical restrictions; there could still be some geographical set-ups required, but they were typically manageable.

In 1996, TVO had produced 44.9 hours of new, salable product. That year, sales and licensing had earned $5.2 million in revenues. By 2000-01, TVO was producing only 8.1 hours of salable product with year-end revenues projected at $2.8 million. Galbraith felt strongly that with an 81 per cent decline in salable product, the Sales and Licensing Department staff should be commended for experiencing only a 46 per cent reduction in revenues. (See Exhibit 1 on the next page for an Analysis of Salable Product Decline.)

DECLINING REVENUES AT TVONTARIO

Other changes in the marketplace had contributed to the declining revenues in the Sales and Licensing Department and were of concern for the future.

Sixty per cent of sales and licensing revenues had typically come from the U.S. education market, these sales being totally dependent on curriculum correlations. The sales decline in this area over the past five years had been 20 per cent. *Third-party distribution rights* were responsible for minimizing the sales decline. However, an analysis of third-party distribution costs was not conclusive in determining whether or not it

exhibit 1   Declining Product Analysis
            Ontario Educational Communications Authority Sales and Licensing Department

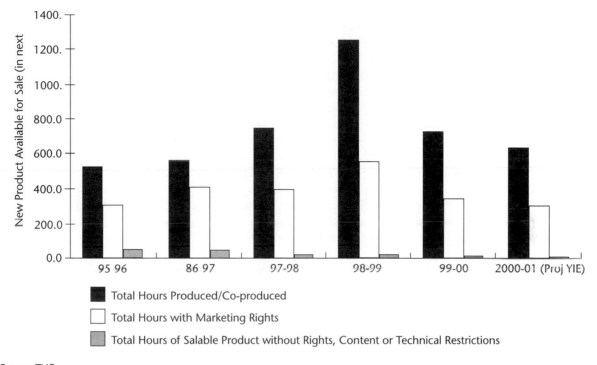

■ Total Hours Produced/Co-produced

□ Total Hours with Marketing Rights

▨ Total Hours of Salable Product without Rights, Content or Technical Restrictions

Source: TVO

would be cost-effective to continue with these sales. As of November 2000, third-party product had generated $374,000 in gross revenues. After hard costs were applied (i.e., repurposing of tape, direct sales fulfilment, guide development, producer royalties), the net revenue was $92,000. Once the cost of labor and promotion, as well as the cost of the manager of product development (whose full-time job had been sourcing the product) was added, it was questionable whether the venture would be profitable over time. Thus, U.S. sales would be dependent on program inventory. The production year that was best in terms of production of TVO's top-10 U.S. sellers was 1988. No top-10 sellers had been produced in the last three years.

Programming had provided sales and licensing with interstitial material or mini clips that would fit within the confines of a full-length program in lieu of commercials, etc. (the shows *Video Clips*, *The Bod Squad*, *What's My Sign*, etc.). The curriculum was not sold for some of the interstitials produced so far. Sales and Licensing had tried to fit these mini-programs into the curriculum requirements of educational clients, but the short segments were ahead of their time and problematic for 99 per cent of the market which did not have access to computer delivery methods. While boards of education were asking for more Internet–based programming, the majority of teachers delivering the programs did not yet have the necessary computer access to utilize this type of programming.

Broadcast license fees were on the decline with the advent of new cable, satellite, and digital channels worldwide. While pricing rates could be as low as $400 per hour, they could still go as high as $10,000 to $15,000 per hour. At the lower rates, fees were at times insufficient to cover the cost of tape conversion for interstitial materials. It was becoming more and more difficult to find customers who would make it possible for TVO to sell programs at a profit.

The Programming Department at TVO had been developing more two-minute *interstitial segments* to replace 15-minute segments. Given that educational license fees were charged on a per-minute basis, significant potential revenue had been lost.

Programming at TVO, with the assistance of the Business Development Group, had over the past few years engaged in *pre-selling properties* that were to be produced in-house. These sales were not managed through the Sales and Licensing Department, and thus, 100 per cent of the resulting revenues were credited directly to the Programming Department. The Sales and Licensing Department had not traditionally devoted a great deal of energy to pre-sales, given the system that was in place for crediting revenue.

Copyright fees had always been an issue, and had become a more significant one. The step-up fees (i.e., the additional fees payable once a program was to be aired outside of the originally intended market area) to talent collectives upon sale of a program often made it unprofitable and, thus, impossible to make the sale where there were low license fees. Some one-off exception agreements had been struck with the talent collectives to make sales, but these were time-consuming to negotiate and hardly worth the effort.

Programming was no longer renewing Ontario broadcast rights, so Sales and Licensing now had to cover that cost, as well as the cost of step-ups for inventory. The renewal cost was typically 50 per cent of the original fee paid to the talent collectives.

Management and the board of directors at TVO did not want programming sold to their key competitor, CBC, in the interest of preserving the TVO brand. At one time, Galbraith had been confident she could sell *Polka Dot Shorts* and a number of other programs to CBC, given discussions she had had with CBC staff. *Polka Dot Shorts* would have been sold to CBC at a fee of $15,000 an hour. This window of opportunity appeared to have passed TVO by, and without the CBC sale, Galbraith was faced with her only market in Canada being British Columbia's Knowledge Network, where the fee paid would be $2,000 an hour.

Galbraith had made recommendations for the revitalization and growth of the TVO Sales and Licensing Department. She had recommended that each of the proposed steps be taken annually for the next five years to return Sales and Licensing to the $4-million-plus revenue level.

Galbraith's suggestions were:

- Produce, at TVO, a broadcast television series modelled after *Inquiring Minds* (13 × 30-minute segments), with two or three stand-alone segments that could be cut for curriculum use. Produce with on-screen hosts in link segments, so that international customers could replace hosts with their own; make music and effects, scripts and cue sheets standard deliverables.

- Produce, at TVO, a broadcast television series for children aged six to nine years of age, either 13 × 30-minute segments or 26 × 15-minute segments. The series could be either animated or live action with high production values.

- Produce, at TVO, three 60-minute documentaries similar to the former *Vista* documentaries.

- Produce, at TVO, a minimum of 15 hours of core curriculum programming in math, science or language arts for kindergarten to Grade 12 as a video series. Each series would be a minimum of 100 minutes with 10 × 15 minutes series being optimal.

- Produce, at TVO, English as a Second Language (ESL) programs, a high-demand product with limited worldwide supply.

- Produce, at TVO, an updated core curriculum series by doing some minor reshooting of current material.

- Set a more realistic contribution margin target for the Sales and Licensing Department. Anecdotal evidence indicated a realistic margin was 20 per cent to 35 per cent; TVO's target had been 50 per cent.

- Build meaningful communication between Programming and Sales and Licensing—given that Programming did not directly benefit from the Sales and Licensing revenues, communication and co-operation has been minimal.

The Sales and Licensing Department had devoted considerable energy over the past few years to securing distribution rights to third-party product and selling that product in Canada and internationally. Their greatest third-party success had come from the distribution of the *Pingu* series, which had been produced by a Dutch independent. However, the venture was not without problems. TVO's management and board of directors objected to selling the product to CBC, whom they believed to be TVO's key competitor in Ontario. CBC refused to purchase product for broadcast outside of Ontario only, as Ontario was its largest market and it was not reasonable or cost-effective to offer separate programming for the Ontario market. Without the CBC sale, Sales and Licensing was not able to forecast sufficient sales to interest the producers of the program. It remained to be seen whether third-party product distribution could still work in some form for TVO.

Galbraith recognized that it was virtually impossible to recoup total production costs through outside sale of product, but she believed that partial cost recovery had been and should continue to be the goal for in-house production. Galbraith believed that more than 70 per cent of the in-house production costs could be recovered through the efforts of Sales and Licensing with a well-researched and targeted program, but noted that any new programming would first have to meet the needs and mandate of the Programming Department. She had suggested to the senior administration that a portion of the Sales and Licensing revenue be funnelled into Programming to produce salable product, but the proposal had been declined repeatedly.

Sales and Licensing had also been fighting to have in-house product produced with a music and effects (M & E) version complete at the time of production. An M & E version of a program would allow international customers to dub in their own voice in their language of choice. Seldom was programming produced with an M & E version. The cost of adding M & E's post-production was three times the cost of doing it at the time of production and often made the sale impossible. Programming had not typically produced programs with M & E's at the time of production, as it was an added cost for programming with no guarantee that product would be sold by Sales and Licensing and with no return of the Sales and Licensing revenues directly to Programming. Senior management had issued a directive to Programming to produce with M & E's, but had not enforced the directive as of yet.

Distribution Alternatives

Galbraith had spent considerable time investigating the possibility of changing the method of distributing product under the umbrella of Sales and Licensing.

Currently Sales and Licensing had on staff, in addition to Galbraith, a sales executive in Canada, one international sales executive and three support staff, along with two sales executives based in the U.S. office in North Carolina (see Exhibit 2). In addition to the TVO staff, Sales and Licensing used the services of one educational non-broadcast distributor in Canada, five educational non-broadcast distributors in the United States and 10 to 12 international broadcast distributors on average. The non-broadcast distributors took 70 per cent to 75 per cent commission on sales, and the international broadcast distributors took 25 per cent to 30 per cent commission on sales.

A number of years ago, TVO had tried to sell products directly in the United States to save on distributor commissions, but between the cost of catalogues and the cost of managing sales from TVO, it had lost money over a five-year period.

Galbraith had looked closely at three alternative distribution models for Sales and Licensing:

● Contracting Canadian and international sales to an outside distributor;

● Contracting Canadian, international and U.S. sales to an outside distributor; and

● Contracting Canadian, and international sales to an outside distributor and handling U.S. sales out of Toronto.

Galbraith had concluded that net revenues would either decrease or would be minimal, making it impossible to justify the change (see Exhibit 3 on the next page for budget estimates for distribution alternatives).

Everyone in the Sales and Licensing department was fiercely loyal to TVO and wanted to do what was best for the organization as a whole. Galbraith summed up the feelings of those in the department when she said, "The painful death we're going through is so demoralizing . . ." Staff were at the point where they just wanted a decision made, regardless of which way it went. Meanwhile, they continued to work their hardest to bring in what revenues they could and to look for new solutions.

exhibit 2   Sales and Licensing Staff (April 2000)

Manager
Sales & Licensing
Cindy Galbraith

Sales Executive Canada
Debra Bennett

Sales Executive International
Smilika Baiiozovic

Sales Executive U.S. ITV
Beth Stafford

Supervisor U.S. Sales
Vicky Etheridae

Sales Assistant
Kathy Marchese

Sales Fulfilment Co-ordinator
Carmela Nunes

Sales Analyst
Mari Cromb

Source: TVO

exhibit 3   Distribution Alternatives – Financial Summary Sales and Licensing (all amounts in CDN$000)

	2000-01 Year End Forecast	Prop. Budget	2001-02		
			Alt A	Alt B	Alt C
Gross Revenue	**2,785.5**	**2,569.9**	**2,569.9**	**2,569.9**	**2,569.9**
Full-time salaries	444.9	448.7	346.7	202.0	302.0
Benefits	73.5	74.0	57.2	33.3	35.0
Overtime	8.0	8.0	8.0	8.0	8.0
Freelance	7.0	10.0	10.0	10.0	10.0
Sub-total Labor	**533.4**	**540.7**	**421.9**	**253.3**	**355.0**
Travel	34.0	48.0	37.0	17.0	37.0
Consulting		10.0	10.0	10.0	10.0
Telephone	18.0	18.0	18.0		
Office Supplies	6.0	9.0	9.0	5.0	5.0
Memberships	1.5	1.5	0.6	0.6	0.6
Periodicals	1.0	1.0	1.0	1.0	1.0
Translations		2.0	2.0	2.0	2.0
Subtotal Dept Oper'ns	**60.5**	**89.5**	**77.6**	**35.6**	**55.6**
Advertising	12.0	15.0	5.0	5.0	5.0
Promotion	80.0	120.0	70.0	30.0	70.0
Bldg. rental	17.0	23.0	23.0		
Equip. rental	5.0	6.0	6.0		
Mailing	10.0	12.0	12.0		
Tape	68.3	54.4	45.1	38.1	45.1
Publications	26.0	30.0	30.0	30.0	30.0
Dev't. fund	17.0	20.0	20.0	10.0	20.0
Cost of Sales	31.0	30.0	30.0	30.0	30.0
Bad Deb/WHolding Tax	174.8	22.4	22.4	162.4	162.4
Commission	250.0	212.4	375.0	1,075.1	375.1
Copyright	385.0	329.6	329.6	329.6	329.6
Subtotal Dep't. Specific	**1,076.1**	**874.8**	**968.1**	**1,710.2**	**1,067.2**
Project/Program costs	10.0				
Total Expenditures	**1,680.0**	**1,505.0**	**1,467.6**	**1,999.1**	**1,477.8**
Net Revenue	**1,105.5**	**1,064.9**	**1,102.3**	**570.8**	**1,092.2**
Contribution Margin	**40%**	**41%**	**43%**	**22%**	**42%**

Source: TVO

PROGRAMMING CHALLENGES

The programming departments at TVO were charged with filling their broadcast hours with programming that met the mandate of TVO, while staying within a modest budget. Programs for TVO came from three sources: in-house production, co-production and acquisition.

In-house production at TVO had become very costly over the past few years. On the surface, outsourcing production had seemed to be the most economical method of producing programming. TVO's production budget was $20 million per year; t*f*o's production budget was $10 million per year. Production costs ranged anywhere from $30,000 to $200,000 per hour for in-house production versus TVO's $2,000 to $5,000 per hour contribution for co-production. Outside producers had access to Telefilm funding, which was not available to TVO, though there were rumors in the industry that a change in funding criteria may be forthcoming. If TVO were to have access to this funding, it could change the programming decisions dramatically.

Given the current climate, TVO, which had in the past produced more properties in-house, was now producing only one-third of its programming in-house. Most of the in-house production money was going to the hosting shows for children's programming such as *The Crawlspace*, *The Nook* and *Mega* and for Ontario-based interview programs like *Studio 2* and *Panorama*.

TVO broadcasted an average of 8,647 hours per year, with a minimum of 70 per cent Canadian content. T*f*o broadcasted an average of 7,530 hours per year with a minimum of 60 per cent Canadian content.

In 1997-98, TVO delivered 255 hours of Canadian co-produced and independently produced programming, 604 hours of foreign co-productions and acquisitions and 719 hours of in-house production for airing. TVO, when co-producing a program, would negotiate for TVO's usage, based on the percentage of budget that TVO was putting up for the production. For a small percentage of the production cost, TVO was likely to have usage rights for Ontario only; for a larger share of the total cost, TVO could gain some exclusivity across Canada. The outside producer could ultimately sell the program to any and all broadcasters except where TVO had obtained exclusivity. Typically, TVO's creative head would make a pre-buy (usually more expensive than a standard license fee) in order to get a credit, and to get a first window or first airing for the productions. TVO would also look for sole broadcasting rights in Ontario, and the independent producer would have the right to sell the product anywhere else in the world. This arrangement made it economical for TVO to produce programs, but impossible for Sales and Licensing to resell the properties. Alternatively, TVO could purchase programming for rebroadcast, which they did for many of their children's programs, such as *Arthur* and *Magic School Bus*.

The programming managers did not typically communicate their plans to the Sales and Licensing Department, and were somewhat frustrated by the inability of Sales and Licensing to continue to sell their programs. Programming managers had suggested selling the formats of the interstitial programs, but had been told by Sales and Licensing staff that this was not as easy as it sounded, given that customers could easily develop their own formats without paying for them. Programming managers had also wondered whether there was a market for product spin-off sales from TVO properties. The characters associated with *TVO Kids Crawlspace* and *The Nook* were very popular in Ontario. Children lined up for hours for an autograph whenever the show hosts went out into the Ontario community, and the TVO membership was always receptive to *TVO Kids* memorabilia. However, Cindy Galbraith had pointed out that while interest seemed high, not much TVO product had actually been purchased by these potential customers.

The programming managers were open to seeing the development of a business model for internal production of children's programs in particular, versus the current move to outsourcing. They also felt there might be some money to be made from cable flow-through and possibly from advertising, though advertising had not previously been considered at TVO. They wondered why *Polka Dot Shorts*, which had sold in 64 countries, was not selling in the United States, as it seemed to be a natural spin-off market. Sales and Licensing had said they could sell the program to CBC, but programming did not want to dilute their brand by selling to the competition. However, the United States was a totally different matter.

Programming managers stated they would be more than happy to have Sales and Licensing sell as much of their product as possible, given that their objective was exposure, both inside and outside of Ontario. With their current budgets, programming managers did not see how they could increase production of salable product. They wondered whether a more economical distribution system might be the answer.

FINANCIAL IMPLICATIONS

Sales and Licensing had been reasonably profitable throughout its existence at TVO, but not as profitable as membership or sponsorship activities. On the Sales and Licensing profit and loss statements, the department appeared to be earning 50 per cent margins. In reality, it was earning considerably less than that amount. Approximately 12 per cent of the Sales and Licensing revenues were required for administrative support. The Accounting Department argued that another 15 per cent to 20 per cent of the sales revenues was used for tape dubbing/reformatting, phone, mail, office space, warehousing, etc., making the actual profit margins much lower than they first appeared (see Exhibit 4 for Sales and Licensing financial statements).

Looking at the cost of other revenue-generating activities, Baker noted that the Membership Department spent 44 cents for every one dollar raised. However, he wasn't certain that Membership could make up for the revenue shortfall should Sales and Licensing shut down; nor did he believe TVO could make up the shortfall through sponsorships, at least not in the short term.

Baker had an expense budget of $5.5 million, which he was expected to use to generate $12 million in revenues. At present, there were 23 staff in his departments, including the Sales and Licensing staff. This was half of the staffing level prior to his arrival at TVO, and they were producing the same revenue.

Galbraith's wish list for salable programming was going to require considerable seed funding, and there were no guarantees that the programming would be picked up by broadcasters outside Ontario. Galbraith maintained that while Sales and Licensing would never recover total cost of production, new salable programming with solid production values would not only be an asset to the Programming Department, but would allow Sales and Licensing to make sales that would offset some of the costs of in-house production. No production cost estimates or sales estimates had been developed to date, though Baker wanted to see some solid projections before backing this option. However, there wasn't much time in which to develop them.

THE PROBLEM

Baker believed that the Sales and Licensing Department could be resuscitated, but not in its present form. He needed to come up with a plan before the board of directors decided to shut the department down. He saw early June as his deadline for development of a proposal for the board. One major concern was that Baker wasn't certain he would be able to implement anything substantial in time to salvage what was left of Sales and Licensing, even if he did come up with a viable proposal.

exhibit 4   Sales and Licensing Revenue History (all amounts in CDN$000)

Manager of Sales' Revenues by Market Segment

Year	Licensing	Consumer Sales	Co-revenue
2001-02 Budget	5.0	25.0	300.0
2000-01 Proj.	10.0	30.0	300.0
1999-00 Actual	43.1	39.3	347.5
1998-99 Actual	39.8	34.1	266.8
1997-98 Actual	61.2	70.1	402.5

Licensing: U.K. license continuing for Polkaroo; no active Canadian licensees.
Consumer Sales: New partner Viewer Plus.
Co-Revenue: Targets set by past practice; all receivables from co-producing partners and royalty payments from copyright collectives.

Canadian Sales:

Year	Revenue
2001-02 Budget	242.3
2000-01 Projected	280.9
1999-00 Actual	360.1
1998-99 Actual	838.4
1997-98 Actual	1,001.9

International Sales:

Year	Revenue
2001-02 Budget	300.0
2000-01 Projected	200.0
1999-00 Actual	558.2
1998-99 Actual	1,075.8
1997-98 Actual	722.7

U.S. Sales by Segment:

Year	ITV	Cassettes	Publications
2001-02 Budget	1,409.0	360.2	28.0
2000-01 Projected	1,427.0	396.9	35.0
1999-00 Actual	1,340.6	563.7	26.0
1998-99 Actual	1,547.1	626.7	37.5
1997-98 Actual	1,496.4	729.5	37.2

Source: TVO

OPTIONS

Baker had been exploring his options and had come up with the following alternatives:

- Spin off an arm's-length production company from TVO. This production company would have access to the Telefilm grants and TVO would have first rights to the programs, which could also be sold through Sales and Licensing. Baker was in the early stages of looking at the feasibility of this option.

- Find a donor who would contribute the funds to produce a special program series, which would be of interest to the TVO audience, but would also be a salable commodity for Sales and Licensing.

- Find a more economical distribution system for Sales and Licensing.

- Develop a plan to gradually phase out the Sales and Licensing Department at TVO; put the Sales and Licensing budget dollars into Membership or Sponsorship activities to generate additional income from these activities.

case 8 Mainstreet Equity Corp. (A)

It was March 23, 2001, and the board of directors of Mainstreet Equity Corp. was nearing the end of a two-hour meeting.

Bob Dhillon, president and chief executive officer (CEO) of the firm summarized:

> The issue boils down to this: Is now the time that Mainstreet should rapidly expand its holdings in the market in order to become the leading brand and largest, most profitable owner of multifamily apartment properties in Canada? If so, where and how fast should we grow? If not, what do we need to do first, before we can go into a phase of very rapid growth?

THE CORPORATION

The Founding of Mainstreet

Mainstreet Equity Corp. was incorporated as a numbered company in Alberta on May 21, 1997. It began trading on the Alberta Stock Exchange a year later, and on the Toronto Stock Exchange (under the stock symbol MEQ) on May 31, 2000. The firm commenced active operation as a real estate company involved in the acquisition, management and divestiture of multifamily residential rental properties with its first major real estate transaction on December 7, 1998. At that time, Mainstreet acquired 10 buildings consisting of 271 units in Calgary, Alberta.

Bob Dhillon

The key person responsible for developing and executing Mainstreet's strategy was Bob Dhillon, president and CEO of the corporation. With more than 20 years of

Professor Terry H. Deutscher prepared this case solely to provide material for class discussion. The author does not intend to illustrate either effective or ineffective handling of a managerial situation. The author may have disguised certain names and other identifying information to protect confidentiality.

experience in the real estate industry, Dhillon had bought and sold more than $150 million in real estate (80 per cent of it in Calgary) before he founded Mainstreet. Besides his extensive dealings in the Calgary real estate market, Dhillon had wide-ranging interests and experience. He had owned a travel consolidation business, was currently the exclusive distributor of TabascoTM products in South Asia, and served as the Honorary Consul of Belize for Alberta.

These features have characterized Dhillon's ventures:

- They were very profitable, enabling Dhillon to maintain a comfortable lifestyle without the need for any compensation from Mainstreet. (His earnings from the corporation came from appreciation of the shares—he owned 38.7 per cent of the approximately nine million outstanding shares of Mainstreet, as well as share options of the company.)

- They required expert skills in developing and maintaining a business network, an aspect that Dhillon greatly enjoyed.

- Success in the ventures required considerable expertise in negotiation.

Currently, Dhillon divided his time among Mainstreet (his main interest, consuming 80 per cent of his normal 65-hour workweek), his work for McIlhenny Company as their distributor of Tabasco products in South Asia (which consumed 10 per cent of his time, mostly in three or four trips annually to Asia or to the firm's headquarters in Louisiana), and his activities in Belize, where he was spearheading a 2,300-acre island resort development (five per cent of his time), and numerous other ventures (five per cent).

In 1998, Dhillon graduated with an MBA degree from the Richard Ivey School of Business at The University of Western Ontario. As one of his classmates in the program described it:

> Before the Executive MBA Program, Bob was a "flipper," very successful at buying and selling apartment buildings in the Calgary market. Starting from a very small base, he did larger and larger deals, eventually earning the respect of the major players in the market. It was in the EMBA program that Bob conceived the initial Mainstreet concept. Instead of simply buying and selling properties, Mainstreet would upgrade and manage them, thereby enhancing their value.

Dhillon was aggressive, ambitious and entrepreneurial. He was known among his classmates for his stated goal of becoming the world's first Sikh billionaire.

Managing Mainstreet

Dhillon gratefully acknowledged the role of the EMBA program in the launch of Mainstreet, and the strategic contribution of David Mitchell, who preceded him by one year in the Calgary section of the program.

> I used every single course at Ivey to build the strategy for Mainstreet. Whether it was building a brand, running an efficient operation, financing growth or making a speech, I thought about the lessons from the courses in terms of what they meant for Mainstreet. Every major decision about our strategy was discussed, debated, and tested with Dave (Mitchell).

Mitchell became a major shareholder in Mainstreet. Although he did not have a formal role in the corporation, his discussions with Dhillon continued throughout the initial years of operation of the company—in the same penetrating, no-holds-barred, politically incorrect tone as always. He continued to be Dhillon's principal sounding board outside the organization.

"Mainstreet has always been a very lean organization," Mitchell commented. "In the early days, it operated out of the trunk of Dhillon's car, then subsequently out of the studio apartment in Mainstreet's first building that was also used by contractors for storing building materials." Dhillon definitely intended to keep Mainstreet lean and agile as the firm grew. "For every dollar we spend we ask ourselves: is that the best way to spend money on the business, or could that dollar be more efficiently used elsewhere?"

In 1999, Mainstreet built itself an office on the ground floor of one if its apartment buildings, just outside the Calgary downtown area. Late in 2000, the office was remodelled and expanded. From it, eight people ran Mainstreet's corporate office and its Calgary operations; two others ran a satellite operation in Edmonton. Brief descriptions of their areas of responsibility are presented with the organization chart in Exhibit 1.

Besides Dhillon, there were two senior internal managers in the corporation, Johnny Lam (chief financial officer) and Don Murray (operations manager). Lam held a certified accounting designation, and more than 20 years of financial management experience in Europe, Asia and North America. He worked for Coopers & Lybrand and HBM Holdings in Singapore before joining Mainstreet in 1999. As CFO, his major responsibilities were financial strategy and reporting. He supported Dhillon in evaluating property purchases and sales, and in negotiations with lenders.

Before joining Mainstreet in April 2000, Murray had consulted with the company for the previous year. Through most of the 1990s, he held positions of increasing responsibility in the operations area of Boardwalk Equities, one of the largest multifamily companies in Canada today. Boardwalk was a Calgary-based firm that grew rapidly in the 1990s and, by 2001, owned more than 25,000 multifamily units, the largest portfolio of residential property in Canada. Like Lam, Murray was attracted to Mainstreet by Dhillon's vision of rapidly growing a major Canadian real estate business while preserving the values of a small entrepreneurial firm. Operating clean, efficient and profitable buildings was a major part of that vision, and that was Murray's focus.

Dhillon also relied heavily on Mainstreet's board of directors for advice on major strategic decisions like the one he faced in March 2001. Brief biographical sketches of the five board members are presented in Exhibit 2.

Dhillon, his advisors and the Mainstreet management team shared the view that it was imperative for the success of the company that it stay non-bureaucratic and quick to react as it grew. Murray explained the difference between Mainstreet's culture and the industry's:

> The multifamily rental sector in Canada is comprised mainly of property management companies that manage the apartments for owners who do not want the headaches of the daily operations. These fee management companies become somewhat bureaucratic and are not quick decision-makers. To make a decision to do any major work or improvements requires the approval of the owner of the individual apartment building.
>
> Fee managers typically work for several different properties whose owners have differing levels of capital available to them. Therefore, the consistency of product, the co-ordination of the staff, and the affordability of supplies change building by building, making the property manager's job a difficult one.

In contrast, Mainstreet owns all its properties; therefore, decisions are made on a global basis. Quality control, consistent service levels, bulk buying, and staffing efficiencies are all possible. Mainstreet can change direction to fix a problem very quickly without having to consult a large number of individual owners.

THE MULTIFAMILY REAL ESTATE SECTOR IN CANADA

There were five main sectors in the Canadian Real Estate industry: commercial, retail, industrial, residential housing, and multifamily. Each had its own distinctive financing, operating and valuation methods. The multifamily sector consisted of apartment buildings and row housing (also called townhouses). In Canadian urban centres with populations over 50,000 it was estimated that there were 1.44 million multifamily residential units available for rent in 2000. Table 1 shows how these units were distributed according to size of the property.

table 1 Multifamily Units by Building Size, Canada 2000

Building Size	Number of Units	Proportion of all Units
6–19	437,316	30.4%
20–49	346,125	24.0%
50–199	471,996	32.8%
200+	184,329	12.8%

The Canadian multifamily sector in early 2001 had some distinctive characteristics:

Vacancy Rates

As of October 2000, the overall apartment vacancy rate in Canada was at 1.6 per cent, down from 2.6 per cent the previous year, and at its lowest level since 1987. Furthermore, these low vacancy rates characterized the whole country, with 22 of Canada's 26 major urban centres recording lower vacancy rates in Fall 2000 than in 1999. Exhibit 3 shows vacancy rates for 1998-2000 in 15 major metropolitan areas across Canada (part A) and a 10-year history and projection of vacancy rates in Calgary and Edmonton (part B). In the 10-year period from 1991 to 2001, which was a period of high gains in employment in Alberta's two major cities, the number of rental units per capita in Calgary and Edmonton had actually declined by more than 20 per cent.

Future Supply of Residential Rental Units

It did not appear that new construction in the short run was likely to address the need for apartments in Canada. Why not? Costs of development (including land and construction costs, development charges, building permit fees and taxes) were so high that developers would have to charge rents far beyond what the market would support.[1] As Dhillon described it, "I can buy a building in Calgary today for $60,000 a door (i.e., a unit) that

---

[1]"New Ottawa high rise ends drought," *Toronto Globe and Mail*, March 27, 2001, p. B17.

would cost $100,000 a door to build. Therefore, there will be no new supply on the market until rents go up significantly." The reasons for this disparity, which Dhillon estimated to be from 40 per cent to 100 per cent of current property values in Canadian cities, can be traced back to the late 1970s. Dhillon explained:

> At that time, there was a building boom in the multifamily sector because the federal government provided significant tax incentives for construction of new units. The resulting oversupply, and then the recession of the early 1980s, resulted in high vacancy rates and low rents. Consequently, there has been very little new construction in the multifamily sector in the last 15 years, and the rent structure in the Canadian marketplace is still significantly below what would be required to make new building economically feasible.

Another factor affecting the supply of multifamily rental units was the trend to convert rental properties into condominiums, effectively removing them from the rental market. For example, in Edmonton, throughout most of the 1990s, the supply of rental units declined by about one per cent per year, largely due to condominium conversion. By the turn of the century, however, the pace of conversion had slowed somewhat because most of the properties that were deemed to be "ownership quality" had already been changed over to condominiums.[2]

In summary, according to Dhillon:

> What would it take for us to see substantial increases in the supply of multifamily rental units in Canada? A lot! Rents would have to increase by 50 per cent or more in most cities. Interest rates would have to stay low—because interest is the biggest single cost factor in these properties. And, finally, construction costs and localized economics (land availability and prices, and development fees) would have to be reasonable.

Canadian Demographic Trends

Between 1981 and 2001, a period during which the increase in stock of multifamily residential rental units was virtually zero, the Canadian population grew by almost 25 per cent. Exhibit 4 shows projected population growth by age group in Canada for 2001 to 2021. It is noteworthy that the young adult population (aged 20 to 29), who are primarily renters, was expected to grow by 9.5 per cent during this period, although this is slightly under the overall growth in the country of 11 per cent. The other demographic factor affecting the rental market was immigration, which was expected to stay at high levels for the foreseeable future. Immigration was a key driver of the rental market, because immigrants were much more likely than Canadians of similar demographic profiles to rent apartments.

Property Ownership and Management

Ownership of multifamily properties in Canada was highly fragmented. The largest portfolios of these properties were held by the aforementioned Boardwalk Equities (approximately 25,000 units, primarily in Alberta) and Minto Management (approximately 10,000 units in Ottawa and 8,000 more in Southern Ontario). With its 1,600 units, Mainstreet was one of 10 largest owners of multifamily units in the country.

---

[2]Canada Mortgage and Housing Corporation Rental Market Report for Edmonton, 2001.

Private investors, whose principal careers were not in real estate, held the great majority of apartments and row housing properties.

The major multifamily rental firms managed their properties themselves. However, most private investors had careers and busy lives aside from their real estate holdings. "The last thing these people want," according to Dhillon, "is a phone call at midnight about a toilet that isn't working. Therefore, most private investors outsource the actual management of their properties to Property Management companies." For a fee that was typically three to five per cent of the rent, plus a modest percentage of outside maintenance and capital improvement charges, these firms managed a building. They hired a resident manager, contracted for maintenance and repairs, advertised for new tenants, etc. In Dhillon's opinion, the preponderance of private ownership of smaller properties and reliance on so-called "fee managers" created a real opportunity for consolidation and professional management.

> In theory, a 'mom and pop' owner of a small property with 20 to 50 units thinks the fee manager will take over all the headaches, and they will just be able to cash a nice cheque every month. But reality can be very different. First, the fee manager isn't paid particularly well, and can be fortunate to clear 0.5 per cent from the management fees. Second, the owners aren't eager to spend money on the building for regular maintenance, let alone improvements such as energy-efficient devices. They'd rather go to Hawaii, or buy a new Cadillac than replace the carpets or upgrade the appliances. What has to get done is done; what isn't critical is deferred. Over time, what results is a building with a lot of deferred maintenance (carpets, paint, appliances, common areas) that starts to be uncompetitive at the rental rates for its market segment. It gets more difficult to rent vacant units because the building looks "tired." In order to keep the building full, the fee manager doesn't want rents to be increased with the market, and so the building slips into a lower market segment with a lower class of tenant. The net effect of these inefficiencies and the downward economic cycle that appears to be under way in March 2001 is an opportunity for Mainstreet to acquire property and make the necessary investments to unlock its true potential.

Don Murray, Mainstreet's operational manager, listed several reasons for Mainstreet to have a competitive advantage over property management companies:

1. Economies of scale, for example, through bulk purchases.
2. Proprietary software, including accounting programs for financial control and property management programs for control of everyday operations.
3. A computer network system that was online in all Mainstreet properties, eliminating paperwork and providing immediate information updates at any location.
4. Branding to give consistent quality, level of service and recognition across the board:
   a. Common color scheme at entrances of buildings
   b. Intercom system and security
   c. Uniforms for Mainstreet managers and maintenance staff
   d. Common signage
5. Web site: in the past six months, the percentage of inquiries and subsequent rentals through www.mainstreetequities.com had grown from zero to 15 per cent.
6. Operational synergies among properties located in the same vicinity.
7. Potential for internal tenant transfers between properties.
8. Ability to provide "24-7" service to tenants.

THE MAINSTREET STRATEGY

As Dhillon described:

> Mainstreet is focused solely on the multifamily segment of the Canadian real estate sector, and we aim to be the best in the industry. "Apartments are us." We are reinventing a dinosaur business by investing in capital improvements, re-engineering operations and branding the properties. It's a great opportunity for a well-managed company to create shareholder value. Where else are government-guaranteed loans at interest rates of six per cent[3] available for investments with significant potential for capital appreciation?

Mainstreet's financial objective was to deliver consistent returns that were well above the average for a real estate company. There were six linked components of the company's strategy.

Step One: Acquisitions

A key element of Mainstreet's strategy was to buy properties that were under-performing but had a high potential for appreciation under the Mainstreet brand. Unlike residential properties, where the vast majority of homes were sold through the local MLS (Multiple Listing Services) real estate board, the market for multifamily units was not efficient. Trades were done exclusively, and it was difficult to get information on transactions. Consequently, it was very difficult to put a price on an apartment building. Value depended on a host of variables, such as location, construction type, condition, presence of assumable financing, suite sizes, curb appeal and taxation.

Typically, the buildings Mainstreet targeted were apartment or townhouse developments in the middle to lower sector of the multifamily segment, in good locations. Dhillon knew the Calgary market so well that when he received a call from a broker (or a bank receiver) about a given property, he knew instinctively whether or not it was worth further investigation. If so, operations manager Murray would do a workup on what investments would have to be made to bring the property under the Mainstreet brand, and CFO Lam would run the financial analysis. The final call on whether to proceed with an offer was made by Dhillon.

Of course, as Dhillon moved further afield from Calgary, he was not able to rely on local knowledge and instinct about the available deals. However, he believed the multi-family residential segment in Canada was controlled by a tight network of about 100 people (10 big landlords and 90 key real estate players, of which he was one). He was well acquainted with many of these major players, and they would be the primary sources of deals if Mainstreet were to decide to expand outside Alberta.

Step 2: Capital Improvements

Once Mainstreet had purchased a new property, a "swat team" of Mainstreet employees and contractors moved immediately to bring the building under the Mainstreet brand. Murray co-ordinated the effort, which rapidly upgraded the property by renovating the common areas of the development in the characteristic Mainstreet manner. A distinctive Mainstreet sign was placed in front of the building, initially labelled

---

[3]In March 2001, the Bank of Canada overnight rate (for funds loaned to Canadian chartered banks) was five per cent and the banks' prime rate was 5.75 per cent.

"Under New Management." A uniquely designed canopy was immediately placed over the front entrance to the building, and the common areas (front lobby and hallways) were renovated using a combination of Mainstreet's signature colors, a vibrant forest green and a deep shade of purple. Typically, the floor in the front lobby was replaced with ceramic tile, and lighting in the lobby and hallways was upgraded. Vacant units were also completely renovated before they were rented again. This typically included a new energy-efficient refrigerator and dishwasher, new kitchen cupboards, countertops, paint and carpets. Generally, Mainstreet spent about $4000 inside each unit in upgrading a newly purchased property. As a high-volume purchaser, Mainstreet obtained both significant price concessions from suppliers and reliable supply on a just-in-time basis so that Mainstreet did not require a high inventory investment.

Step 3: Operational Efficiency

Next, in a program that was organized and managed by Murray, Mainstreet installed energy-efficient devices in the building, such as:

- Replacing incandescent light fixtures with fluorescent (for example, installing a $20 fluorescent fixture cut electricity consumption from $30 per year for a 60-watt light bulb to $8);
- Installing aerators on shower heads and water faucets that cut water flow rates by more than half;
- Replacing toilets with modern, low-volume fixtures that reduced water consumption from six gallons per flush to 1.6.

Murray had data on costs and savings for each of the upgrades, and paybacks were usually less than one year.

As well as the physical changes in the buildings, Mainstreet changed the manner in which the property operated. A new resident manager was installed, consistent with the targeted group of tenants, and the property was moved to an efficient management system with a dedicated maintenance team, an automatic debit rent collection system, and integrated accounting and property management software. The net effect of these changes was to cut annual operating costs, which were typically about $2,400 per unit in a purchased property, by 20 to 25 per cent.

Exhibit 5 portrays Mainstreet's operational procedures diagrammatically. Each apartment building was set up as a separate business unit. A computer, Internet connection and proprietary software were installed at the property. These devices allowed just-in-time information to reach the head office. All deposits, work orders for problems, and tenant information were input directly at the site level. Double entry was eliminated, and information about the project was available at the head office at the touch of a button.

Rent collection at Mainstreet was simplified with automatic debit from tenant bank accounts on the first of the month, unlike mom-and-pop operations where it might well be the 10th or 15th before the entire rent was deposited. This system required no manpower except for inputting of data into the system.

Step 4: Value Enhancement

Along with the significant improvements in the property came an increase in rents, typically in the order of 25 per cent to 50 per cent, but sometimes even more. Alberta was not subject to legislated rent controls, an issue which could become a factor should

Mainstreet decide to expand beyond the province. However, Dhillon believed, even if a protesting tenant brought Mainstreet to court, the corporation could easily justify the rent increase by the improvements in the property.

Rental increases were not always perceived negatively. Typically, 70 per cent of tenants moved out and 30 per cent accepted the increase, feeling that it was worthwhile because of the value-enhancing improvements. Mainstreet would transfer a current tenant into a renovated suite as well as do some renovations in an occupied suite. In one recent instance, Mainstreet had implemented a 40 per cent rent increase in one of its Edmonton properties but had no net increase in the vacancy rate because the higher rents were justified by renovations and enhancements. As well as the immediate cash flow effects, the rent increases had one other significant benefit for Mainstreet: the least desirable renters moved out, and they were easily replaced by a better class of tenant.

Step 5: Financing

Based on the increased value of the property, Mainstreet could obtain long-term, government-insured mortgages at favorable interest rates. This freed up capital for acquisition of new high-potential properties. Mainstreet's account manager at People's Trust described how this worked:

> Bob is an astute buyer. Mainstreet typically buys properties that have high deferred maintenance, but good upside potential. It can obtain a first mortgage for 75 per cent of the purchase price from us at a favorable rate of interest, say prime plus 1.25 per cent. Furthermore, Mainstreet could obtain a second mortgage for 15 per cent of the purchase price, at a higher interest rate—say 13 per cent—and sometimes a third mortgage at an even higher rate. Sometimes, a highly motivated vendor provides some financing for the transaction with a vendor take-back mortgage.
>
> Next, Bob invests a significant amount, say 30 per cent of the cost of the building, in a complete renovation of the property, which justifies a substantial rent increase, of 30 per cent to 50 per cent. But because the investment has also produced energy savings and Mainstreet has scale economies in operations, operating income for the building has actually increased by more than the dollar amount of the rent increase. This improved cash flow makes the property now worth substantially more; it could easily be appraised at 75 per cent to 100 per cent over the purchase price, based on the improved operating income alone. Now Bob can refinance the property with a CMHC (Central Mortgage and Housing Corporation) guaranteed loan, at 6.1 per cent interest,[4] for 75 per cent of the new market value. Mainstreet pays off the original mortgages, recovers its investment for improvements, and owns an asset with substantial cash flow. The surplus cash goes into the next round of building purchases and capital improvements.

See Exhibit 6 for an actual example of what Mainstreet calls the value creation process.

Step 6: Divestitures

Most mature assets are held for cash flow purposes, but Mainstreet does selectively sell some properties that do not offer sufficient potential value.

---

[4]Interest rates on CMHC guaranteed loans were typically 0.75 per cent above Canadian long-term bond rates.

RESULTS

Exhibit 7 portrays the financial results of Mainstreet's first years of operation, while Table 2 below shows Mainstreet's growth in units. The results were generated through internal growth alone, with no new equity issues.

table 2   Growth in Mainstreet Holdings 1998-2001

	Dec. 31, 1998	Sept. 30, 1999	Sept. 30, 2000	Jan. 1, 2001
Number of Units				
Calgary	271	548	816	874
Edmonton	0	356	554	670
Total	271	904	1,370	1,544
Market Value	$17 million	$50 million	$90 million	$100 million

THE GROWTH OPPORTUNITY IN MARCH 2001

At the March 23, 2001, board meeting, Dhillon wanted to get feedback from his directors on what he felt was the critical choice that Mainstreet faced: how rapidly to expand. Should Mainstreet be satisfied with steady growth in Alberta, and plan to add 300 to 400 units in the next year? Or, he thought, was this the time to "bet the farm," extend the Mainstreet brand outside Alberta, and double the size of the company in the next year?

Dhillon was aggressively pro-expansion, and he opened the discussion by making the case for it. He summarized arguments on both the supply (low vacancy rates, low property values compared with replacement costs, and low and falling interest rates) and demand (population growth in the renter segment, and increasing immigration) sides. Furthermore, he believed,

> The end result of a slowdown in the economy or even a full-fledged recession, is that liquidity dries up and the volume of buy-and-sell transactions for rental properties slows down as well. However, that is also a time of opportunity for Mainstreet. As the old saying goes, 'Cash is king in a recession.'

However, Dhillon also listened carefully to the comments of his board members who, for the most part, were more cautious:

- The U.S. economy seems to be going into a deep freeze. My instincts tell me that this might be the time to go slowly rather than expand rapidly.
- We need more data. Let's take the time to digest the numbers from the economy before we move precipitately, and plan carefully before shooting from the hip in an immediate aggressive expansion.
- There's still room to expand right here in Alberta, in your own back yard. Going into other markets is a lot riskier. And these markets are much more regulated than Alberta. I know that in the Vancouver area, development costs are 20 per cent higher than Calgary, just because of the additional bureaucracy—permits, local regulations, etc.

On the other hand, there were also arguments in favor of aggressive expansion. As one board member expressed:

> Go for it! The fundamentals in this market—vacancy rates, new construction costs, interest rates—have never been better. We're cyclical players in the market. When

the economy turns down, it's a great time for us to buy. Furthermore, we benefit from lower interest rates, since our major expense is interest on our debt. In fact, if interest rates go where we expect, in the next year we will refinance two-thirds of our mortgage portfolio, at interest rates averaging two per cent less than we are currently paying. Now is the time to move.

As CEO of Mainstreet and by far its largest shareholder, Dhillon had to make the call on the biggest decision in Mainstreet's short but successful history.

exhibit 1   Organizational Chart

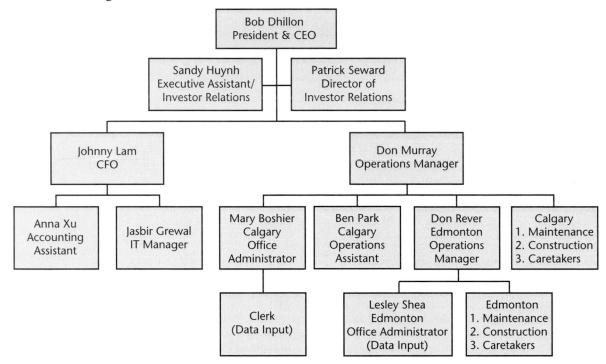

*Please note that the operations managers in each city are supervisors for all caretakers in their city. For example, Don Murray is responsible for 40 caretakers, a large construction crew and a three-man maintenance engineering team. (To be a member of the maintenance team, members must maintain boiler/mechanical certificates.)

Mary Boshier, office administrator: Computer input, handling tenant and resident manager problems and inquiries, monthly autodebit for rent collection.

Sandy Huynh, executive assistant to Bob Dhillon: Duties included management of Tabasco distribution, pro forma analysis, investor relations at an administrative level (quarterly reports, annual filings, annual general meeting, press releases, compiling mail-outs).

Ben Park, operations assistant: Renovation scheduling, inspection of units, communicating with contractors, co-ordinated with Don Murray and Mary Boshier.

Patrick Seward, director of Investor Relations, based in Toronto: Background in investment banking (CIBC Wood Gundy, Deloitte & Touche), specializing in real estate. Relationships with financial analysts and media. Sourcing large real estate and financing deals.

Anna Xu, accounting assistant to Johnny Lam: Payroll, payables, receivables, maintaining and organizing accounting records with accounting and property management software.

Don Rever, Edmonton operations manager: Co-ordinates Edmonton operations.

Lesley Shea, Edmonton office administrator.

exhibit 2   Board of Directors

Joe Amantea is senior partner at the law firm Warren Tettensor in Calgary. He acts as corporate counsel on behalf of Mainstreet.

Frank Boyd is chairman of The Apex Corporation, a real estate development company based in Calgary and operating in Canada and the United States. Apex, which is the largest land development company in Western Canada, has recorded 39 consecutive quarters of earnings increases. Its major businesses are in single-family residential homes and land development.

Darrell Cook is president of Gibraltar Mortgage Ltd. A Fellow of the Certified General Accountants' Association of Canada with an MBA from University of Calgary, he has more than 25 years of experience in real estate acquisition and development. He is a substantial investor in Mainstreet, owning 25.6 per cent of the outstanding common shares.

Bob Dhillon is president and CEO of Mainstreet Equity Corp.

Rowland Fleming is the former president and CEO of the Toronto Stock Exchange (1994 to 1999). He has more than 30 years of experience in the financial services industry in Canada, including terms as vice-president of the Bank of Nova Scotia, president and CEO of National Trust Company, and president and CEO of the Dominion of Canada General Insurance Company.

Larry Tapp is dean of the Richard Ivey School of Business at the University of Western Ontario. In 1985, he initiated what was then the largest leveraged buy-out outside of the United States, a $552 million deal that created Lawson Mardon Group, one of the world's largest packaging conglomerates. As CEO of the group, he took it public in one of the largest international share offerings ever by a Canadian company.

exhibit 3A   Apartment Vacancy Rates—By Census Metropolitan Area
1998-2000

Census Metro Area	1998	1999	2000
Calgary Alberta	0.6	2.8	1.3
Edmonton Alberta	1.9	2.4	1.4
Halifax Nova Scotia	5.5	3.6	3.6
Hamilton Ontario	3.2	1.9	1.7
Kitchener Ontario	1.5	1.0	0.7
London Ontario	4.5	3.5	2.2
Montreal Quebec	4.7	3.0	1.5
Ottawa Ontario	2.1	0.7	0.2
Quebec Quebec	5.2	3.3	1.6
Regina Saskatchewan	1.7	1.4	1.4
St. John's Newfoundland	15.4	9.2	3.8
Toronto Ontario	0.8	0.9	0.6
Vancouver British Columbia	2.7	2.7	1.4
Victoria British Columbia	3.8	3.6	1.8
Winnipeg Manitoba	4.0	3.0	1.5
Canada	3.5	2.6	1.6

Source: Canada Mortgage and Housing Corporation Rental Market Report for Edmonton, 2001.

exhibit 3B Apartment Vacancy Rates—Ten-Year History for Edmonton and Calgary

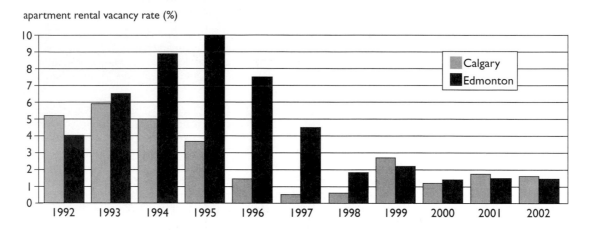

apartment rental vacancy rate (%)

exhibit 4 Canadian Population (thousands)

Age	2001	2006	2011	2016
0-4	1,715.9	1,640.2	1,666.4	1,708.7
5–9	2,026.6	1,790.4	1,715.8	1,741.8
10–14	2,076.6	2,096.4	1,863.6	1,790.1
15–19	2,081.0	2,155.3	2,175.0	1,945.5
20–24	2,097.0	2,167.6	2,241.4	2,261.2
25–29	2,100.3	2,194.1	2,263.5	2,336.4
30–34	2,252.5	2,201.6	2,293.0	2,360.0
35–39	2,641.7	2,326.8	2,278.1	2,367.1
40–44	2,659.1	2,675.7	2,370.3	2,324.0
45–49	2,384.9	2,663.7	2,681.7	2,385.2
50–54	2,114.7	2,362.9	2,637.4	2,657.5
55–59	1,625.9	2,073.7	2,318.3	2,588.5
60–64	1,291.1	1,578.1	2,011.3	2,251.4
65–69	1,137.8	1,222.4	1,495.8	1,907.4
70–74	1,012.0	1,030.5	1,112.7	1,365.7
75–79	815.2	858.7	879.7	957.2
80–84	525.7	627.5	666.2	688.1
85–89	295.2	351.3	422.5	452.9
90 and over	149.2	211.8	269.0	331.0
Total	31,002.40	32,228.70	33361.7	34419.8

Source: Statistics Canada

exhibit 5   Operational Procedure

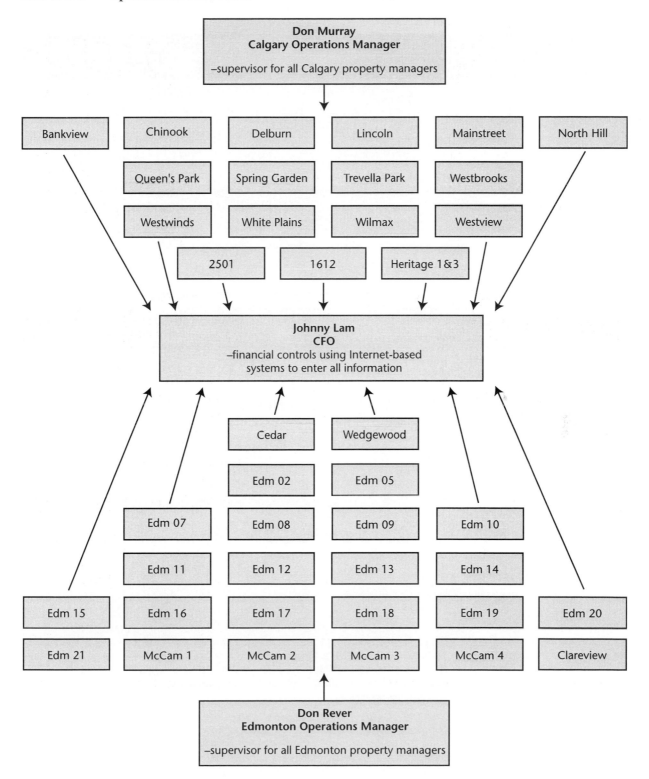

exhibit 6   Example of Value Creation

West Wind, a 31-unit apartment in Calgary

Stage 1 — Acquisition

	Amount	Per unit
Purchase price	$1,080,000	$34,839
1st Mortgage loan 75% @ 7%/yr.	810,000	
2nd & 3rd Mortgage 25% @ 12.5%/yr.	270,000	
Equity	—	
Rent	163,000	5,258
Vacancy and bad debt allowance (3%)	4,890	158
Operating expenses	77,500	2,500
Operating income	80,610	2,600
Mortgage interest	90,450	
Depreciation	7,709	
Income before income taxes	$ (17,549)	

Stage 2 — Value enhancement through capital improvement. Actual annualized income after capital expenditure of $315,000, increased rents and operational efficiency improvements.

	Amount	Per unit
Capital expenditure	$ 315,000	$10,161
Rent	255,708	8,249
Vacancy & bad debt allowance (3%)	7,671	247
Operating expenses	71,484	2,306
Operating income	176,553	
Mortgage interest	90,450	
Depreciation	10,324	
Income before income taxes	$ 75,779	

Stage 3 — Consolidate mortgage loans

	Amount	Per unit
Appraised market value of the property with operating income of $176,553	$2,046,000	$66,000
CMHC insured mortgage @ 6.1%/yr. on 75% of appraised value	$1,534,500	

These funds will pay off the original mortgages of $1.08 million and leave $454,500 for further purchases and capital improvements. With an investment of $315,000, Mainstreet has acquired an asset that provides positive cash flow and is worth $2 million; furthermore, by refinancing with a low interest CMHC guaranteed loan, it has generated $454.5 thousand in cash for further investments.

Source: Adapted from Mainstreet Equity Corp. internal documents.

exhibit 7   Financial Statements

CONSOLIDATED BALANCE SHEETS (Thousands of dollars)

As at	September 30, 1998	September 30, 1999	September 30, 2000
ASSETS			
Real estate properties	$10,789	$37,152	$66,034
Cash	1,506	1,415	898
Other current assets	34	526	569
Deferred charges	152	359	1,178
	$12,482	$39,452	$68,679
LIABILITIES			
Mortgages payable	$10,219	$34,127	$63,122
Bank indebtedness	80	—	396
Accounts payable	161	286	532
Refundable security deposits	145	366	—
Income taxes payable	—	426	931
Deferred income taxes	7	264	
	10,613	36,469	64,981
SHAREHOLDERS' EQUIITY			
Share capital	1,859	1,869	1,869
Retained earnings	9	1,114	1,829
	1,869	2,983	3,698
	12,482	39,452	68,679

CONSOLIDATED STATEMENTS OF INCOME AND RETAINED EARNINGS
For the year ended September 30, 2000 and the nine months ended September 30, 1999 and 1998
(Thousands of dollars, except per share amounts)

As at	September 30, 1998 (12 months)	September 30, 1999 (9 months)	September 30, 2000 (12 months)
REVENUE			
Rental income	$1,778	$2,971	$7,740
Sale of real estate properties	—	3,223	2,609
Interest income	71	84	41
	1,849	6,277	10,390
EXPENSES			
Property operating expenses	643	904	2,077
Cost of sales, real estate properties	—	1,778	2,002
General and administrative expenses	230	327	858
Financing cost	773	1,210	3,382
Depreciation and amortization	186	273	711
	1,832	4,492	9,030
Income before income taxes	16	1,786	1,360
Income taxes – Current	—	426	(23)
– Deferred	7	256	667
Net income	9	1,104	716
Retained earnings, beginning of year	—	9	1,113
Retained earnings, end of year	$9	$1,113	$1,829
Earnings per share – Basic	*	$0.12	$0.08
– Fully diluted	*	$0.12	$0.08

* Less than 1 cent per share
Source: Mainstreet Equity Corp. Annual Reports

case 9 Russki Adventures

On July 15, 1991, Guy Crevasse and Andrei Kakov, the two major partners in Russki Adventures (Russki), contemplated their next move. They had spent the last year and a half exploring the possibility of starting a helicopter skiing operation in the USSR. Their plan was to bring clients from Europe, North America, and Japan, to a remote location in the USSR to ski the vast areas of secluded mountain terrain made accessible by the use of helicopters and the recent business opportunities offered by "glasnost."

During the exploration process, Crevasse and Kakov had visited a number of potential locations in the USSR, including the Caucasus Mountains near the Black Sea, and the Tien Shen and Pamir ranges north of Pakistan in the republics of Kazakistan and Tadzhikistan, respectively. After close inspection of the three areas, and consideration of many issues, the partners had decided upon the Caucasus region.

After almost two years of planning and research, the thought of making a solid commitment weighed heavily on their minds. Their first option was to accept the partnership offer with Extreme Dreams, a French company that had started a small ski operation in the Caucasus Mountains during the 1991 season. Their second option was to enter a partnership with the USSR's Trade Union DFSO and a Russian mountaineer, and establish their own venture in a Caucasus Mountains area made available to them by a Soviet government agency. Their final option was to wait, save their money and not proceed with the venture at this time.

THE PARTNERS

Andrei Kakov, 27, was born in Russia. His family emigrated to Italy, and then to Canada when he was 17 years old. After completing an undergraduate degree in economics at the University of Toronto, he worked with Sebaco for two years before enrolling in

Ian Sullivan prepared this case under the supervision of Professor Paul Beamish solely to provide material for class discussion. The authors do not intend to illustrate either effective or ineffective handling of a managerial situation. The authors may have disguised certain names and other identifying information to protect confidentiality.

Copyright © 1992, Ivey Management Services   Version: (A) 1999-08-13

1989 in the Masters of Business Administration (MBA) program at the University of Western Ontario (Western). Sebaco was a Canadian-Soviet joint venture that, since 1980, had been facilitating business ventures in the Soviet Union by acting as a liaison between the foreign firms and the different levels of Soviet government and industry. This job gave Kakov extensive contacts in the Soviet Union and in many of the firms, such as McDonald's and Pepsico, which were doing business in the Soviet Union. Kakov was fluent in Russian, Italian, English, and Japanese.

Guy Crevasse, 28, had an extensive ski racing career which began at a young age and culminated in the World Cup with the Canadian National Ski Team. His skiing career took him to many countries in Europe, North America, and South America. During his travels he learned to speak French, Italian, and some German. After retiring from competitive ski racing in 1984, Crevasse remained active in the ski industry as a member of the Canadian Ski Coaches Federation. He led the University of Western Ontario Varsity Ski Team to four consecutive Can-Am titles as a racer/coach while pursuing an undergraduate degree at Western. Before returning to Western to complete an MBA, Crevasse worked for Motorola Inc. in its sales and marketing departments, where he worked on key accounts, set up product distribution channels, and developed product programs with original equipment manufacturers in the automobile industry. Crevasse had also worked with a ski resort planning and development firm on a number of different projects.

OVERVIEW OF THE SKIING AND HELICOPTER SKIING INDUSTRIES

Development of the Ski Resort Industry

In 1990, the worldwide ski market was estimated at 40 million skiers. The great boom period was in the 1960s and 1970s when growth ran between 10 to 20 per cent annually. However, the growth stagnation which began during the 1980s was expected to continue during the 1990s. Some of this decline was attributable to increased competition for vacationers' time, the rapidly rising real costs of skiing, and baby boom effects. The only growth segment was female skiers, who represented 65 per cent of all new skiers. The total revenue generated by ski resorts in the United States for 1990 was estimated at $1.5 billion. This figure did not include any hotel or accommodation figures.

Prior to World War II, most skiing took place in Europe. Since there were no ski lifts, most skiing was essentially unmarked wilderness skiing, requiring participants who enjoyed the thrill of a downhill run to spend most of their time climbing. There were no slope grooming machines and few slopes cut especially for skiing. The development of ski lifts revolutionized the sport, increased the accessibility to many previously inaccessible areas, and led to the development of ski resorts. After the skiing market matured, competition for skiers intensified and resort operators shifted their efforts away from the risk sport focus towards vacation and entertainment. In order to service this new market and to recover their large capital investments, the large resorts had developed mass market strategies, and modified the runs and the facilities to make them safer and easier to ski in order to serve a greater number of customers.

Introduction of Helicopter Skiing

This change in focus left the more adventurous skiing segments unsatisfied. For many, the search for new slopes and virgin snow was always a goal. The rapid rise in the popularity of skiing after World War II increased demand on existing ski facilities and thus competition for the best snow and hills became more intense. Those who wanted to experience the joys of powder skiing in virgin areas were forced to either get up earlier to ski the good snow before the masses got to it, or hike for hours from the top of ski areas to find new areas close to existing cut ski runs. Hiking to unmarked areas was tiring, time consuming, and more dangerous because of the exposure to crevasses and avalanches.

This desire to ski in unlimited powder snow and new terrain away from the crowds eventually led to the development of the helicopter skiing industry. The commonly held conception was that powder skiing was the champagne of all skiing, and helicopter skiing was the Dom Perignon. The first helicopter operations began in Canada. From the beginning of the industry in 1961, Canadian operations have been typically regarded as the premium product in the helicopter skiing industry for many reasons, including the wild, untamed mountains in the western regions. For many skiers worldwide, a trip to a Western Canadian heli-ski operation is their "mecca."

Operators used helicopters as a means of accessing vast tracts of wilderness areas which were used solely by one operator through a lease arrangement with the governments, forest services, or regional authorities. The average area leased for skiing was 2,000 to 3,000 square kilometres in size, with 100 to 150 runs. Due to the high costs in buying, operating, maintaining, and insuring a helicopter, the vast majority of operators leased their machines on an as-needed basis with rates based on hours of flight time.

In the 1970s and early 1980s, the helicopter skiing industry was concentrated among a few players. During 1990 and 1991, the number of adventure/wilderness skiing operators increased from 41 to over 77. The industry could be divided between those operations that provided day trips from existing alpine resorts (day-trippers) and those operations that offered week-long trips (destination-location).

By 1991, the entire global market for both day-trippers and destination-location was estimated to be just over 23,000 skiers per year, with the latter group representing roughly 12,000 to 15,000 skiers. Wilderness skiing represented the largest area of growth within the ski industry in the 1970s and 1980s. Market growth in the 1980s was 15 per cent per year. Only capacity limitations had restrained growth. The addictive nature of helicopter skiing was illustrated by the fact that repeat customers accounted for over 75 per cent of clients annually. The conservative estimate of total margin available to the destination-location skiing industry (before selling and administration costs) was US$12.4 million in 1990. Table 1 gives typical industry margin figures per skier for heli-skiing.

From a cost standpoint, efficient management of the helicopter operations was essential. Table 2 provides a larger list of industry key success factors.

Combination of Resort and Helicopter Skiing

The number of resorts operating day facilities doubled in 1990. Competition in the industry increased for a number of reasons. Many new competitors entered because of the low cost of entry (about $250,000), low exit barriers, the significant market growth,

table 1 Helicopter Skiing Margin per Skier Week (North America)

Price		$3,500	100%
Costs:	Helicopter*	1,260	36%
	Food & Lodging	900	26%
	Guides	100	3%
	Total Operating Costs	2,260	65%
	Total Margin	1,240	35%

* *Note:* Helicopter costs were semi-variable, but were based largely on a variable basis (in-flight hours). The fixed nature of helicopter costs arose through minimum flying hours requirements and the rate negotiations (better rates were charged to customers with higher usage). On average, a helicopter skier used seven hours of helicopter time during a one week trip. A typical all-in rate for a 12-person helicopter was $1,800 per flying hour. Hence the above figure of $1,260 was calculated assuming full capacity of the helicopter using the following: $1,800 per hour for seven hours for 10 skiers + pilot + guide.

table 2 Helicopter Skiing Industry Key Success Factors

Factors within Management Control:
- establishing a safe operation and reliable reputation
- developing great skiing operations
- attracting and keeping customers with minimal marketing costs
- obtaining repeat business through operation's excellence
- providing professional and sociable guides
- obtaining operating permits from government
- managing relationships with environmentalists

Location Factors:
- accessible destinations by air travel
- available emergency and medical support
- favourable weather conditions, i.e. annual snowfall, humidity, altitude
- appropriate daily temperature, sunshine, daylight time
- suitable terrain
- quality food and lodging

and the rewarding margin in the industry. The major growth worldwide came mainly from the day operations at existing areas, as they attempted to meet the needs for adventure and skiing from their clientele. The major concentration of helicopter operators was in Canada; however, competition was increasing internationally. Industry representatives thought that such growth was good because it would help increase the popularity of helicopter skiing and introduce more people to the sport.

In Canada, where helicopter skiing originated, the situation was somewhat different. Out of the twenty wilderness skiing operations in Canada in 1991, only two were tied to resorts. However, for the rest of the world, roughly 80 per cent of all the operations were located and tied closely to existing ski operations. Both Crevasse and Kakov realized that there were opportunities to create partnerships or agreements with existing resorts to serve as an outlet for their helicopter skiing demand.

RUSSKI'S RESEARCH OF THE HELI-SKI INDUSTRY

Profile of the Skier

The research that the Russki group had completed revealed some important facts. Most helicopter skiers were wealthy, independent, professional males of North American or European origin. Increasingly, Japanese skiers were joining the ranks. The vast majority of the skiers were in their late 30s to mid 60s in age. For them, helicopter skiing provided an escape from the high pace of their professional lives. These people, who were financially secure with lots of disposable income, were well educated and had done a great many things. Helicopter skiing was a good fit with their calculated risk-taker image. Exhibit 1 describes a typical customer. It was not unusual for the skiing "addict" to exceed 100,000 vertical feet of skiing in a week. A premium was then charged to the skier.

Buyers tended to buy in groups rather than as individuals. They typically had some form of close association, such as membership in a common profession or club. In most cases, trips were planned a year in advance.

Geographically, helicopter skiers could be grouped into three segments: Japan, North America (USA and Canada), and Europe. In 1991, they represented 10 per cent, 40 per cent (30% and 10%), and 50 per cent of the market respectively. There were unique features associated with each segment and Crevasse and Kakov knew that all marketing plans would need to be tailored specifically to each segment. In general, they felt that the European and North American customers placed more emphasis on the adventure, were less risk adverse, and had a propensity to try new things.

Analysis of the Competition

Crevasse and Kakov had thought that more detailed information on their competitors would help answer some of their questions. During the winter of 1991, they conducted a complete physical inspection of skiing and business facilities of many helicopter skiing operations. As a result of the research, Russki determined that the following companies were very significant: Rocky Mountain Helisports (RMH), Cariboo Snowtours, and Heliski India. RMH and Cariboo Snowtours were industry leaders and Heliski India was another new entrant trying to establish itself in the market. A close analysis had provided Crevasse and Kakov with some encouraging information.

Rocky Mountain Helisports, the first operation to offer helicopter skiing, was started in 1965 in Canada by Gunther Pistler, a German immigrant and the "inventor" of helicopter skiing. In 1991 his operation, servicing 6,000 skiers, represented roughly 40 to 50 per cent of the worldwide destination-location market. He followed a strategy which cloned small operating units at seven different sites in the interior of British Columbia. RMH's strategy was designed to offer a product that catered to a variety of different skier abilities and skiing experiences. The company serviced all segments that could afford the $4,000 price of admission, including introducing less able skiers to the experience of helicopter skiing. Compared with the revenue of traditional Canadian ski resorts, such as Whistler Resorts in British Columbia, RMH's gross revenue for the 1990 season was larger than any resort in Canada at over $21 million. RMH, which had developed a loyal following of customers in North America and Europe, enjoyed

exhibit 1   Description of a Typical Helicopter Skiing Addict

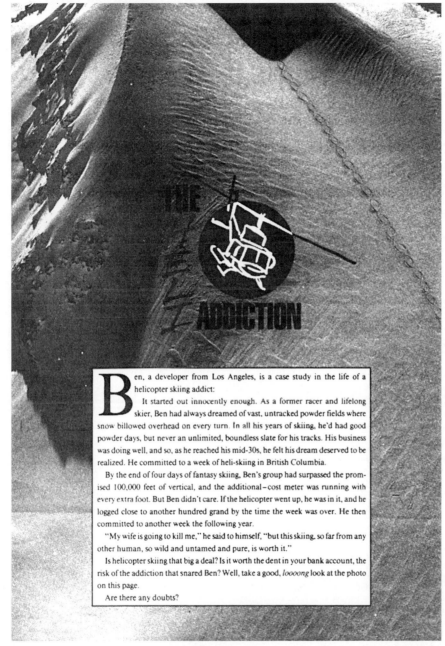

Ben, a developer from Los Angeles, is a case study in the life of a helicopter skiing addict:

It started out innocently enough. As a former racer and lifelong skier, Ben had always dreamed of vast, untracked powder fields where snow billowed overhead on every turn. In all his years of skiing, he'd had good powder days, but never an unlimited, boundless slate for his tracks. His business was doing well, and so, as he reached his mid-30s, he felt his dream deserved to be realized. He committed to a week of heli-skiing in British Columbia.

By the end of four days of fantasy skiing, Ben's group had surpassed the promised 100,000 feet of vertical, and the additional–cost meter was running with every extra foot. But Ben didn't care. If the helicopter went up, he was in it, and he logged close to another hundred grand by the time the week was over. He then committed to another week the following year.

"My wife is going to kill me," he said to himself, "but this skiing, so far from any other human, so wild and untamed and pure, is worth it."

Is helicopter skiing that big a deal? Is it worth the dent in your bank account, the risk of the addiction that snared Ben? Well, take a good, *loooong* look at the photo on this page.

Are there any doubts?

Source: Powder, The Skier's Magazine, November 1990.

significant competitive advantage because of proprietary client lists, a loyal consumer base, and economies of scale due to its large size.

Cariboo Snowtours, the second largest operation in the world, was established by another German immigrant, Fritz Mogler, at Blue River, British Columbia. In 1991, Cariboo Snowtours served over 2,000 skiers, a number which represented roughly 18 per cent of the market. Mogler developed a strategy of one mega-operation and enjoyed economies of scale in the operations area. Similar to RMH, Cariboo Snowtours had a loyal following from North America and Europe, and catered to a variety of skiing abilities and price levels.

Heliski India was a new entrant to the helicopter skiing business. In 1990, the first year of operation, the company serviced 30 skiers in a three-week period, increasing to 120 skiers during the 1991 season. Heliski India followed a more exclusive and adventurous strategy aimed at the experienced helicopter skiing enthusiast. To cover the high costs and low volume, the operation charged $5,500.

Russki estimated margins and profit dynamics for these three operations. Exhibit 2 contains the projection for RMH. These projected statements were best guess estimates based on discussions with a wide range of industry experts, managers, and investors. Cariboo Snowtour's total profit was estimated as slightly over $2 million,

exhibit 2   Russki's 1991 Projections:* Profit Dynamics of Typical RMH Operation

REVENUES					
Ski season duration	– peak	20 wks			
	– regular	0 wks			
Total season duration:	20 wks				
Revenue per skier	– peak		$ 3500		
Weekly group size: (10 skiers + 1 guide × 4)	44 people				
Total Season Regular Revenue (3,500 × 40 skiers × 20 wks)				$2,800,000	
Revenue from Skiers Exceeding 100,000 virtual feet (10%)				280,000	
TOTAL REVENUE					$3,080,000
EXPENSES					
Variable:	9 nights lodging/person/night		$ 80	$ 720	
	9 days meals/person/day		50	450	
Total variable cost/person/week				$ 1170	
Total Annual Variable Costs (20 wks × 44 × $1,170)					$1,029,600
Contribution Margin					$2,050,400
Fixed:					
Helicopter cost/weekly basis (20 week season)			$ 50,000	$1,000,000	
Guides –1 guide per 10 skiers @ $50,000 per guide/year 4 guides				$ 200,000	
Support staff –5 employees @ $20,000 per employee				$ 100,000	
Promotional				$ 250,000	
TOTAL DIRECT FIXED COSTS					$1,550,000
TOTAL MARGIN (Revenue – Dir. Variable Costs – Dir. Fixed Costs)					$ 500,400
Annual Overhead – communication			$ 20,000		
– staff travel			50,000		
– office branch			20,000		
– office North America			100,000		
– insurance @ $5/day/person			50,000		
TOTAL OVERHEAD					$ 240,000
Operating Profit					$ 249,600
Number of operations 7					
Total Operating Profit					$1,747,200

*These projected statements were best guess estimates based on discussions with a wide range of industry experts, managers, and investors.

while Heliski India was projected to turn a small profit. Crevasse and Kakov found these figures very encouraging.

LAND USAGE AND ENVIRONMENTAL CONCERNS IN THE INDUSTRY

The helicopter skiing industry was facing some land use issues which were tough on many operators, but which also created new opportunities on which Russki wanted to capitalize. Of particular concern to many helicopter skiing operations, especially European, were pressures from environmentalists who were concerned that noise from helicopters could adversely affect wildlife habitat, and start avalanches.

As a result, severe downsizing or complete shutdown of existing European operations had recently occurred, leaving only eight helicopter skiing operations in continental Europe in 1991. The one Swiss and one Austrian operation were under pressure to close, and a 1992 season for the latter was already doubtful. The six small operations in Italy, which worked in conjunction with existing ski areas, were basically the only helicopter skiing available in Western Europe. Flying for skiing in France was illegal due to environmentalists' concerns about a negative impact on the limited areas in the Alps. In Sweden, a few companies operated with a shorter season due to the high latitude, and provided less expensive daily services for visitors who skied within the existing lift systems, but week-long packages were not part of their program.

The North American industry had not been exposed to the same environmental and limited area constraints as the European, mainly because of the vast size of the mountain ranges and good relationships with all interested parties. The American operators, who were associated mostly with the large ski areas, had good working relationships with the forest services, which controlled the areas and issued the working permits.

Canadian operators received their permits from the Ministry of Lands and Forests and the provincial governments. Helicopter skiing had been encouraged because of its ability to bring money into the regions. Due to the vast size of the Canadian mountain ranges and the limited competition for the land use, pressure on the operators in any form had been minimal or nonexistent.

Crevasse and Kakov realized that the environmental and capacity constraints in Europe provided helicopter skiing operators worldwide with significant opportunities. Thus far, it had been mainly the North American operators who had capitalized on this situation, and Russki wanted to find a way to capture unsatisfied demand.

RUSSIAN ENVIRONMENT

The Political Environment

Crevasse and Kakov knew that starting a venture in the Soviet Union at this time would be complex. The political situation was very unstable in July 1991, and most expert predictions were not encouraging, including the possibility that the Soviet Union might not exist in the near future. There was a major power struggle going on: the hardliners, most of whom were from the old guard of the Communist Party, were trying to hang on to power; and others, such as Russian President Boris Yeltsin, wanted sweeping democratic changes. The new buzz word on the streets was not "glasnost" or "peristroika" but "razgosudarstvo," which refers to the breakup of the Soviet state.

Secession pressures from many of the republics, such as the Baltics, tested the mettle of the political leaders, peristroika, and the strength of the union itself.

On a regional basis, the future status of some of the regions and republics where the physical conditions met the requirements for helicopter skiing, such as Georgia and Kazakhistan, was unknown. However, Crevasse and Kakov were encouraged by the fact that experts predicted that, no matter what the state of the whole union, Russia would remain intact and continue to function as a unit. This was one of the many reasons why the Russian Republic was selected for the potential initial location.

The Economic Environment

The economy of the Soviet Union was in dire straits. Confusion, lack of focus, and compromise, were crippling the process of change from a government-controlled economy to a market-based one. Real Gross Domestic Product was projected to drop anywhere from three to 11 per cent or more in 1991. Soviet President Mikhail Gorbachev had been given authority to overhaul the economy. However, what changes he would initiate, and whether he still had the support and power to see the process through to completion, were questionable.

Therefore, developing a helicopter skiing operation in the Soviet Union presented Russki with a difficult business environment. Marshall Goldman, Director of Harvard's Russian Research Centre, summed up part of the dilemma facing any new venture in the Soviet Union at this time:

> for those entrepreneurs who think chaos is an ideal environment, this is a perfect time, but for others it is a scary time. The society is collapsing. The economy—both the marketing portion and the planning and administrative sector—is a shambles.

Russki's research indicated that only 20 per cent of the 1,300 joint ventures signed since 1987 were operational because of currency exchange problems, bureaucratic delays, and lack of legal framework to make agreements. Also, it had been very hard for the few operational ventures to realize a return on their investment. In 1991, any business in the Soviet Union had to be viewed with a long-term bias in mind. The big question for many businesses was getting hard currency out of Soviet ventures because there was no international market for the Soviet currency, the ruble. Those who were operating business ventures in the Soviet Union suggested to Russki that it was not an area for the fainthearted to tread. PlanEcon's Keith Crane advised that, "even after the agreement has been signed it can be very difficult to get down to specifics and venture into working entities. It took McDonald's 14 years to do it." Due to the political and economic realities of the Soviet environment, firms were making deals with republics, with city agencies, directly with Soviet firms or factories, and sometimes with all of them. More and more frequently, firms had to go to the enterprise level to find the right people and partners. Additionally, foreign firms found the business environment difficult because the concept of business that Westerners had was very different from the one that the Soviets had after 70 years of a controlled Marxist economy. The addition of cultural differences made for a demanding business climate. Russki thought long and hard about the fact that doing business in the Soviet Union had never been easy. In 1991, as the nation wrestled with the gargantuan task of restructuring the country, most firms were finding it more confusing than ever. No road map or blueprint for business development existed.

In addition, without the significant financial resources of a highly capitalized firm that could overlook short-term profits for long-term gains, Crevasse and Kakov realized they would be in a more exposed position if they decided to go ahead with the venture.

Political unrest or civil war in the Soviet Union, especially in Russia, could destroy their business and investment. Without a steady supply of repeat and new customers, the venture would be finished as an on-going concern. They knew that credibility from an existing operation or established name would make the task of attracting customers to an uncertain environment easier but, in a time of crisis, would guarantee nothing.

The Opportunities

Despite all the negatives, Crevasse and Kakov thought that helicopter skiing in the Soviet Union would be developed on a large scale in the next few years for a number of reasons. The sport was experiencing tremendous growth, environmental pressures were great in Europe, and capacity at all of the good locations was already stretched.

Therefore, a current opportunity existed in the industry. The partners speculated about how fast they could proceed with their business plan and whether they were exposing themselves to too much risk for the return. Would the opportunity still exist in a couple of years? Could a business of this nature function with the future of the Soviet Union being so unstable? The complete answer to these questions was unknown. Crevasse and Kakov felt as if they were doing a case back at business school where someone had left out half the case facts. Regardless, this was a real-life situation, and a decision had to be made on the knowledge available.

After looking closely at their competition and the general environment, they concluded that, despite the instability in the Soviet environment, there were a number of strong points that suggested that they might be able to make a venture of this nature work. On a positive note, the Canadian prime minister, Brian Mulroney, had recently signed the Foreign Investment Protection agreement to ensure stability of Canadian ventures in the USSR. Also encouraging to entrepreneurs wanting to enter the Soviet Union was the new law that allowed for full ownership of Soviet subsidiaries by foreign firms. Experts suggested that these agreements would be honoured by whatever form of government was in place.

The critical factor in the minds of the Russki partners was the fact that they would be taking in all revenue in hard currency. Thus, the absence of profit repatriation risk decreased this business exposure dramatically. Russki would operate all of the sales and administrative tasks outside of the Soviet Union and, as a result, all of its revenues would be collected in the West in hard currency, thereby eliminating the currency risk completely. This was a position that would be envied by any firm attempting to do business in the Soviet Union. Also, Russki was attractive to all levels of government because the venture would bring desperately needed hard currency into the country.

Mt. Elbrus, the highest peak in Europe and the Caucasus mountain region, was where Russki had options to locate. It was well known throughout Europe and its high altitudes and warm climate offered ideal skiing conditions. Because a strong allegiance already existed between the European customers and the Canadian operators, Russki's Canadian background would sit well with customers. In addition, Russki would deliver comparative cost advantage for the Europeans in a Soviet operation, as shown in Exhibit 5 on page 131, even if Russki charged similar costs for a week of skiing.

The uniqueness of the region and mystique of Russia offered an interesting alternative for tourism. Russia had a 2,000-year history and a rich culture, which was reflected in the traditions of the local people and the architecture. Furthermore, the Black Sea area which was close to the Caucasus Mountains had been used as a resort area for centuries. The dramatic changes during the early 1990s in the Soviet Union and Eastern Europe had resulted in tremendous interest in these areas.

Since Russki already had the money required for startup, the company could move quickly without having to take time to raise the capital. The low cost of leasing Soviet helicopters, pilot salaries, service, and fuel as compared with North America was a distinct advantage, and one of the original attractions of Russia. Negotiations with the Russians had shown that this cost advantage was obtainable. The high costs of helicopter operations represented the largest part of the operating costs in helicopter skiing. Lower helicopter costs in Russia would result in cost savings in the range of 50 per cent or more in this expense relative to North American competitors.

The Russki management team was strong. Both men were business school-trained individuals with international work experience, language skills, and ski industry background. Additional hard-to-copy assets, including access to the "Crazy Canucks" (a World Cup ski team) and European ski stars as guest guides, and Soviet knowledge, would be tough for anyone to match in the short term.

POSITIONING AND MARKETING OF RUSSKI ADVENTURES

Positioning and Pricing

The Russki team had considered two positioning strategies, a high and low pricing strategy. A premium pricing and service strategy like that of Heliski India at around US $6,000 would require superior service in every aspect of the operation. The lower priced strategy at $3,500 to $4,000 was $500 below the US$4,000 to US$4,500 pricing of Canadian operators like RMH for the initial season. The second positioning strategy would be designed to target a larger market and concentrate on building market share during the first few years, allowing more time and flexibility to move down the learning curve.

Even with parallel pricing of US$4,000, the "all in" (as shown in Exhibit 5 on page 131) would give a cost advantage to the European and Japanese customers. Crevasse and Kakov knew that this situation would help challenge customers' traditional allegiance to the Canadian operators.

Based on a "best guess scenario," profit models for the two pricing strategies using conservative sales levels are shown in Exhibits 3 and 4. Though the higher priced strategy was more lucrative, Crevasse and Kakov felt that they had a higher capacity to execute the lower price strategy during the first few years of operations regardless of which partner they chose. They were not sure that they could meet the sales volume for the premium strategy as shown in Exhibit 4 (on page 138), regardless of the realization of savings from use of Russian helicopters. (In the unlikely event that the projected helicopter saving could not be realized, the discounted cash flow in Exhibit 3 dropped from $526,613 to $293, and in Exhibit 4 from $597,926 to $194,484.)

These estimates were extremely conservative. One helicopter could service 44 people per week (four groups of ten skiers and one guide). All projections for the profit dynamics were made with the number of skiers per week below capacity. In addition, the first two years were estimated using 10 and 15 skiers respectively. In subsequent years, the number of skiers was increased, but never to full capacity, in order to keep estimates conservative. Russki realized that operating at or close to capacity on a weekly basis would increase its efficiency and returns dramatically.

Russki also built in an additional $250 in the variable costs per skier per week for contingent expenses such as the cost of importing all food stuffs.

exhibit 3   Profit Dynamics, Low-Price Strategy with Low Helicopter Costs

	Year 1	Year 2	Year 3	Year 4	Year 5
REVENUES					
Total season duration	10 weeks	15 weeks	15 weeks	20 weeks	20 weeks
Revenue per skier—peak	$ 4,000	$ 4,000	$ 4,000	$ 4,000	$ 4,000
Weekly group size	10	15	20	25	25
Total Season Revenue	$400,000	$900,000	$1,200,000	$2,000,000	$2,000,000
EXPENSES					
Total variable cost					
(variable cost/skier @ $1,000)	$100,000	$225,000	$ 300,000	$ 500,000	$ 500,000
Contribution Margin	$300,000	$675,000	$ 900,000	$1,500,000	$1,500,000
FIXED					
Helicopter cost (assumes Soviet costs					
of $10,000/week)	$100,000	$150,000	$ 150,000	$ 200,000	$ 200,000
Guides—1 guide per 10 skiers @					
$50,000 per guide/year	$ 50,000	$ 75,000	$ 100,000	$ 125,000	$ 125,000
Soviet staff—3 employees @					
$5,000 per employee	$ 15,000	$ 15,000	$ 15,000	$ 15,000	$ 15,000
Promotional	$100,000	$100,000	$ 100,000	$ 100,000	$ 100,000
TOTAL DIRECT FIXED COSTS	$265,000	$340,000	$ 365,000	$ 440,000	$ 440,000
TOTAL MARGIN (Revenues – Direct					
variable costs – Direct fixed costs)	$ 35,000	$335,000	$ 535,000	$1,060,000	$1,060,000
TOTAL OVERHEAD	$ 35,000	$115,000	$ 115,000	$ 115,000	$ 115,000
OPERATING PROFIT	0	$220,000	$ 420,000	$ 945,000	$ 945,000

	Year 0	Year 1	Year 2	Year 3	Year 4	Year 5
Investment	$–230,000					
Operating profit		0	$220,000	$ 420,000	$ 945,000	$ 945,000
N.A. partner's share: 100%		0	$220,000	$ 420,000	$ 945,000	$ 945,000
Taxes @ 30% Profit	$–230,000	0	$154,000	$ 294,000	$ 661,500	$ 661,500
DCF Year 1–5 PV @ 20.00%		$526,613				
IRR	71.86%					

If Russski proceeded with the lower priced approach, it would position its product just below the industry standard at $4,000 initially. The intent would be to attack the market as the Japanese automobile manufacturers had done when entering into the North American luxury car market.

Crevasse and Kakov were encouraged by the numbers because the conservative sales estimates using the low price positioning strategy would allow them to generate a profit in the second year of operations if they could realize the projected savings with Russian helicopters. However, if they didn't, the strategy would still show a profit in the third year. They thought that the return on their investment would be sufficient as far as the internal rate of return was concerned, but they wondered whether the risk of the Soviet environment would increase their demands even more.

exhibit 4   Profit Dynamics, Premium-Price Strategy with Low Helicopter Costs

	Year 1	Year 2	Year 3	Year 4	Year 5
REVENUES					
Total season duration	5 weeks	10 weeks	10 weeks	20 weeks	20 weeks
Revenue per skier—peak	$ 6,000	$ 6,000	$ 6,000	$ 6,000	$ 6,000
Weekly group size	10	10	15	15	20
Total season revenue	$300,000	$600,000	$900,000	$1,800,000	$2,400,000
EXPENSES					
Total variable cost					
(variable cost/skier @ $1,000)	$ 50,000	$100,000	$150,000	$ 300,000	$ 400,000
Contribution Margin	$250,000	$500,000	$750,000	$1,500,000	$2,000,000
FIXED					
Helicopter cost (assumes Soviet costs					
of $10,000/week)	$ 50,000	$100,000	$100,000	$ 200,000	$ 200,000
Guides—1 guide per 10 skiers @					
$50,000 per guide/year	$ 50,000	$ 50,000	$ 75,000	$ 75,000	$ 100,000
Soviet staff—3 employees @					
$5,000 per employee	$ 15,000	$ 15,000	$ 15,000	$ 15,000	$ 15,000
Promotional	$100,000	$100,000	$100,000	$ 100,000	$ 100,000
TOTAL DIRECT FIXED COSTS	$215,000	$265,000	$290,000	$ 390,000	$ 415,000
TOTAL MARGIN (Revenues – Direct					
variable costs – Direct fixed costs)	$ 35,000	$235,000	$460,000	$1,110,000	$1,585,000
TOTAL OVERHEAD	$ 35,000	$115,000	$115,000	$ 115,000	$ 115,000
OPERATING PROFIT	0	$120,000	$345,000	$ 995,000	$1,470,000

	Year 0	Year 1	Year 2	Year 3	Year 4	Year 5
Investment	$–230,000					
Operating profit		0	$120,000	$345,000	$ 995,000	$1,470,000
N.A. partner's share: 100%		0	$120,000	$345,000	$ 995,000	$1,470,000
Taxes @ 30% Profit	$–230,000	0	$ 84,000	$241,500	$ 696,500	$1,029,000
DCF Year 1–5 PV @ 20.00%		$597,926				
IRR		70.78%				

Product

Crevasse and Kakov planned to model the Russki product after the RMH operation, which was the best in the industry, by evaluating what RMH had built and improving on its processes. Although Russki wanted very much to differentiate itself from the rest of the industry, the partners were not sure how far they could go within the constraints of the Soviet environment.

Geographical Distribution

Although Russki would focus on the European and North American markets, the former segment was most important. Both Crevasse and Kakov realized that they would

exhibit 5   Cost Comparison by Geographic Location

North America:

Costs for customer to go Heli-skiing in North America from different geographic locations.

Origin of Skier	Trip	Transportation	Total
Japan	$4,000	$2,500	$6,500
Europe	$4,000	$2,000	$6,000
North America	$4,000	$ 750	$4,750

Russia:

Cost for customer to go Heli-skiing in Russia from different geographic locations.

Origin of Skier	Trip	Transportation	Total
Japan	$4,000	$2,000	$6,000
Europe	$4,000	$1,000	$5,000
North America	$4,000	$2,500	$6,500

Conclusion: This comparative analysis of all-in costs to the consumer shows that the Russian operation offers a 20 per cent cost advantage to the European customers.

need a strong European operation in marketing and sales if they were going to capitalize on the opportunity available. Developing these functions quickly, especially in Europe which was not their home turf, was a major concern. They had to decide on the best sales and marketing channels immediately and set them up as soon as possible if they decided to go ahead with the venture.

Promotion

Due to the small size of the target market and promotion budgets, the new company would have to make sure that the promotional dollars spent were directed effectively. Russki would do this by direct mail, personal selling by the owners, travel agents, and free tour incentives to trip organizers and guides. Long-term word of mouth would be the best promotional tool, but it had to be supplemented especially in the start-up phase of the business.

Additionally, Crevasse and Kakov planned to increase the value to customers by inviting business and political speakers to participate in the skiing activities with the groups in return for their speaking services. Celebrity skiers such as Canadian Olympic bronze medallist and World Cup champion, Steve Podborski, would be used as customer attractions. As outlined in Table 3 (on the next page), they budgeted $100,000 for promotional expenses.

Labour

Where possible, Russki planned to employ Russians and make sure that they received excellent training and compensation, thereby adding authenticity to the customers' experience. Providing local employment would also ensure the Canadian company's existence and create positive relations with the authorities.

table 3 Marketing Promotion Budget—Year 1

Information nights with cocktails @ $1000 /night @ 20 cities	$ 20,000
Travel Expenses	10,000
Trip Discounts (1 free trip in 10 to groups)	25,000
Direct Mail	5,000
Brochures	5,000
Commissions	15,000
Celebrity	20,000
	$100,000

Currency

Through Kakov's contacts, Russki had worked out a deal to purchase excess rubles from a couple of foreign firms which were already operating in the Soviet Union but which were experiencing profit repatriation problems. Russki would pay for as many things as possible with soft currency.

THE PARTNERSHIP DILEMMA

During the exploration period, Crevasse and Kakov had well over a dozen offers from groups and individuals to either form partnerships, or provide services and access to facilities and natural resources. They even had offers from people who wanted them to invest millions to build full-scale alpine resorts. Many of the offers were easy to dismiss because these groups did not have the ability to deliver what they promised or their skill sets did not meet the needs of Russki. Crevasse and Kakov's inspection and site evaluation helped them to determine further the best opportunities and to evaluate first hand whether the site and potential partner were realistic. This research gave Russki a couple of excellent but very distinct partnership possibilities. They knew that both options had trade-offs.

Extreme Dreams

A partnership with the Extreme Dreams group had some definite strengths. This French company, located in Chamonix, an alpine town in the French Alps, had been running the premier guiding service in and around Mont Blanc, the highest peak in the Alps, for 11 years. Chamonix was the 'avant garde' for alpinists in Europe and one of the top alpine centres in the world. Extreme Dreams had a 5,000-person client list, mostly European but with some North American names.

What Extreme Dreams had was the operational expertise Russki needed to acquire in order to run the helicopter skiing and guiding side of the business. However, they lacked experience in the key functional areas of business. During the 1991 winter season, it had run a three-week operation servicing 50 skiers in the Elbrus region in the Caucasus Mountains. The Soviet partner facilitated an arrangement with a small resort villa in the area. The facilities, which had just been upgraded during the summer, now met Western standards.

The French company had invested roughly $100,000 U.S., and although it did not have a capital shortage, the partnership agreement that was outlined would require

Russki to inject the same amount of capital into the business. The firm would be incorporated in the United States and the share split would be equal amounts of 45 per cent of the stock with 10 per cent left over for future employee purchase. The Soviet partner, a government organization that helped facilitate the land use agreements and permits, would be paid a set fee for yearly exclusive use of the land.

However, Extreme Dreams lacked experience in the key functional areas of business. Possibly, this situation could be rectified by the partnership agreement whereby the management team would consist of three members. Marc Testut, president of Extreme Dreams, would be in charge of all operations. Guy Crevasse would act as president for the first two years and his areas of expertise would be sales and marketing. Andrei Kakov would be chief financial officer and responsible for Soviet relations.

Extreme Dreams had overcome the lack of some food stuffs by importing, on a weekly basis, products not securely attainable in Russia. These additional costs were built into the variable cost in projected financial statements. Russki would do the same if it did not choose Extreme Dreams as a partner.

Trade Union DFSO

The other potential partnership had its strengths as well. The partnership would be with the All-Union Council of Trade Union DFSO, and with a mountaineer named Yuri Golodov, one of the USSR's best-known mountaineers, who had agreed to be part of the management team. Golodov, who had been bringing mountaineers from all over the world to parts of the Soviet Union for many years, possessed valuable expertise and knowledge of the Caucasus area. One of his tasks would be coordination of travel logistics for Soviet clientele. Sergei Oganezovich, chief of the mountaineering department, had made available to Russki the exclusive rights to over 4,000 square kilometres in the Caucasus mountain range about 50 kilometres from the area awarded to Extreme Dreams. A small user fee per skier would be paid to the trade organization in return for exclusive helicopter access to the area.

A profit-sharing agreement with Golodov, which would allow him to purchase shares in Russki and share in the profits, was agreed to in principle by Russki, the Trade Union DFSO, and Golodov. Under this agreement, Crevasse and Kakov would remain in control of the major portion of the shares. Capital requirements for this option would be in the $230,000 range over the first two years. The two Canadians would perform essentially the same roles as those proposed in the Extreme Dreams agreement. If Crevasse and Kakov selected this option, they would need to bring in a head guide, preferably European, to run the skiing operations. On a positive note, a small resort centre that met the standards required by Western travellers had been selected for accommodations in the area.

As far as medical care in case of accidents, both locations were within an hour of a major city and hospital. Less than an hour was well under the industry norm. In addition, all staff were required to take a comprehensive first aid course.

After discussions with many business ventures in the Soviet Union and with Extreme Dreams, Russki concluded that having the ability to pay for goods and services with hard currency would be a real asset if the situation were critical. Russki would use hard currency, where necessary, to ensure that the level of service was up to the standard required by an operation of this nature.

Crevasse and Kakov knew that selecting a compatible and productive partner would be a great benefit in this tough environment. Yet, they had to remember that a partnership would not guarantee customer support for this venture in the Soviet environment or that the USSR would remain stable enough to function as an on-going concern.

THE DECISION

Crevasse and Kakov knew that it would take some time for the business to grow to the level of full capacity. They were willing to do whatever it took to make ends meet during the early years of the business. Because helicopter skiing was a seasonal business, they realized that they would need to find a supplementary source of income during the off-season, especially in the start-up phase.

However, they also were confident that, if they could find a way to make their plan work, they could be the ones to capitalize on the growing market. The Soviet Union had the right physical conditions for helicopter skiing, but the business environment would present difficulties. Moreover, the two partners were aware that starting a venture of this nature at any time was not an easy task. Starting it in the present state of the Soviet Union during a recession would only complicate their task further. Yet the timing was right for a new venture in the industry and, in general, they were encouraged by the potential of the business.

Crevasse and Kakov had to let all parties involved know of their decision by the end of the week. If they decided to go ahead with the venture, they had to move quickly if they wanted to be operational in the 1992 season. That night they had to decide if they would proceed, whom they would select as partners if they went ahead, and how they would go. It was going to be a late night.

case 10 Prince Edward Island Preserve Co.

In August, 1991, Bruce MacNaughton, president of Prince Edward Island Preserve Co. Ltd. (P.E.I. Preserves), was contemplating future expansion. Two cities were of particular interest: Toronto and Tokyo. At issue was whether consumers in either or both markets should be pursued, and if so, how. The choices available for achieving further growth included mail order, distributors, and company-controlled stores.

BACKGROUND

Prince Edward Island Preserve Co. was a manufacturing company located in New Glasgow, P.E.I., which produced and marketed specialty food products. The company founder and majority shareholder, Bruce MacNaughton, had realized that an opportunity existed to present P.E.I. strawberries as a world class food product and to introduce the finished product to an "up-scale" specialty market. With total sales in the coming year expected to exceed $1.0 million for the first time, MacNaughton had made good on the opportunity he had perceived years earlier. It had not been easy, however.

MacNaughton arrived in P.E.I. from Moncton, New Brunswick, in 1978. Without a job, he slept on the beach for much of that first summer. Over the next few years he worked in commission sales, waited tables in restaurants, and then moved to Toronto. There he studied to become a chef at George Brown Community College. After working in the restaurant trade for several years, he found a job with "Preserves by Amelia" in Toronto. After six months, he returned to P.E.I. where he opened a restaurant. The

Professor Paul W. Beamish prepared this case solely to provide material for class discussion. The author does not intend to illustrate either effective or ineffective handling of a managerial situation. The author may have disguised certain names and other identifying information to protect confidentiality.

Ivey Management Services prohibits any form of reproduction, storage or transmittal without its written permission. This material is not covered under authorization from CanCopy or any reproduction rights organization. To order copies or request permission to reproduce materials, contact Ivey Publishing, Ivey Management Services, c/o Richard Ivey School of Business, The University of Western Ontario, London, Ontario, Canada, N6A 3K7; phone (519) 661-3208; fax (519) 661-3882; e-mail cases@ivey.uwo.ca.

Richard Ivey School of Business
The University of Western Ontario

table 1

Operation	Year Opened				
	1985	1989	1990	1991	Projected 1992
New Glasgow - Manufacturing and Retail	X	X	X	X	X
Charlottetown - Restaurant (Perfect Cup)		X	X	X	X
New Glasgow - Restaurant (Tea Room)			X	X	X
Charlottetown - Retail (CP Hotel)				X	X
Toronto or Tokyo?					X

restaurant was not successful and MacNaughton lost the $25,000 stake he had accumulated. With nothing left but 100 kg. of strawberries, Bruce decided to make these into preserves in order to have gifts for Christmas 1984. Early the following year, P.E.I. Preserves was founded.

The products produced by the company were priced and packaged for the gift/gourmet and specialty food markets. The primary purchasers of these products were conscious of quality and were seeking a product which they considered tasteful and natural. P.E.I. Preserves felt their product met this standard of quality at a price that made it attractive to all segments of the marketplace.

Over the next few years as the business grew, improvements were made to the building in New Glasgow. The sense of style which was characteristic of the company was evident from the beginning in its attractive layout and design.

In 1989 the company diversified and opened "The Perfect Cup," a small restaurant in P.E.I.'s capital city of Charlottetown. This restaurant continued the theme of quality, specializing in wholesome, homemade food featuring the products manufactured by the company. The success of this operation led to the opening in 1990 of a small tea room at the New Glasgow location. Both of these locations showcased the products manufactured by the P.E.I. Preserve Co.

In August 1991, the company opened a small (22 sq. metre) retail branch in the CP Prince Edward Hotel. MacNaughton hoped this locale would expand visibility in the local and national marketplace, and serve as an off-season sales office. P.E.I. Preserves had been given very favourable lease arrangements (well below the normal $275 per month for space this size) and the location would require minimal financial investment. As Table 1 suggests, the company had experienced steady growth in its scope of operations.

MARKETPLACE

Prince Edward Island is Canada's smallest province, both in size and population. Located in the Gulf of St. Lawrence, it is separated from Nova Scotia and New Brunswick by the Northumberland Strait. The major employer in P.E.I. was the various levels of government. Many people in P.E.I. worked seasonally, in either farming (especially potato), fishing, or tourism. During the peak tourist months of July and August, the island population would swell dramatically from its base of 125,000. P.E.I.'s half million annual visitors came "home" to enjoy the long sandy beaches, picturesque scenery, lobster dinners, arguably the best-tasting strawberries in the world, and slower pace of life. P.E.I. was best known in Canada and elsewhere for the books, movies and (current) television series about Lucy Maud Montgomery's turn-of-the-century literary creation, Anne of Green Gables.

P.E.I. Preserves felt they were competing in a worldwide market. Their visitors were from all over the world and in 1991 they expected the numbers to exceed 100,000 in the New Glasgow location alone. New Glasgow (population 200) was located in a rural setting equidistant (15 km.) from Charlottetown and P.E.I.'s best known North Shore beaches. In their mailings they planned to continue to promote Prince Edward Island as "Canada's Garden Province" and the "little jewel it was in everyone's heart"! They had benefitted, and would continue to benefit, from that image.

MARKETING

Products

The company had developed numerous products since its inception. These included many original varieties of preserves as well as honey, vinegar, mustard, and tea (repackaged). (Exhibit 1 on the next two pages contains a 1990 price list, ordering instructions, and a product picture used for mail order purposes.) The company had also added to the appeal of these products by offering gift packs composed of different products and packaging. With over 80 items, it felt that it had achieved a diverse product line and efforts in developing new product lines were expected to decrease in the future. Approximately three-quarters of total retail sales (including wholesale and mail order) came from the products the company made itself. Of these, three-quarters were jam preserves.

With the success of P.E.I. Preserves, imitation was inevitable. In recent years, several other small firms in P.E.I. had begun to retail specialty preserves. Another company which produced preserves in Ontario emphasized the Green Gables tie-in on its labels.

Price

P.E.I. Preserves were not competing with "low-end" products, and felt their price reinforced their customers' perception of quality. The 11 types of jam preserves retailed for $5.89 for a 250 ml jar, significantly more than any grocery store product. However, grocery stores did not offer jam products made with such a high fruit content and with champagne, liqueur or whisky.

In mid-1991, the company introduced a 10 per cent increase in price (to $5.89) and, to date, had not received any negative reaction from customers. The food products were not subject to the seven per cent National Goods and Services Tax or P.E.I.'s 10 per cent Provincial Sales Tax, an advantage over other gift products which the company would be stressing.

Promotion

Product promotion had been focused in two areas—personal contact with the consumer and catalogue distribution. Visitors to the New Glasgow location (approximately 80,000 in 1990) were enthusiastic upon meeting Bruce, "resplendent in the

exhibit 1   P.E.I. Preserves Mail-Order Catalogue

Mail Order
Canada

Prince Edward Island Preserve Co.
RR# 2 Hunter River
Prince Edward Island
Canada
C0A 1N0
Tel. (902) 964-2524
Fax. (902) 566-5565

PRODUCTS

Preserves
1. Strawberry & Grand Marnier 250ml 5.69
2. Raspberry & Champagne 250ml 5.69
3. Wild Blueberry & Raspberry in Champagne 250ml 5.69
4. Strawberry, Orange & Rhubarb 250ml 5.69
5. Raspberry & Peach 250ml 5.69
6. Blueberry, Lemon & Fresh Mint................250ml 5.69
7. Black Currant 250ml 5.69
8. Gooseberry & Red Currant 250ml 5.69
9. Sour Cherry Marmalade 250ml 5.69
10. Orange Marmalade with Chivas Regal 250ml 5.69
11. Lemon & Ginger Marmalade with Amaretto 250ml 5.69
12. Strawberry & Grand Marnier 125ml 3.60
13. Raspberry & Champagne 125ml 3.60
14. Wild Blueberry & Raspberry in Champagne 125ml 3.60
15. Raspberry & Peach 125ml 3.60
16. Black Currant 125ml 3.60
17. Orange Marmalade with Chivas Regal 125ml 3.60

Honeys
18. Summer Honey with Grand Marnier 250ml 5.95
19. Summer Honey with Amaretto 250ml 5.95
20. Summer Honey with Grand Marnier 125ml 3.50
21. Summer Honey with Amaretto 125ml 3.50

Mustards
22. Hot & Spicy Mustard 250ml 3.95
23. Champagne & Dill Mustard 250ml 3.95
24. Honey & Thyme Mustard 250ml 3.95
25. Hot & Spicy Mustard 125ml 2.75
26. Champagne & Dill Mustard 125ml 2.75
27. Honey & Thyme Mustard 125ml 2.75

Vinegars
28. Raspberry Vinegar 350ml 5.95
29. Black Currant Vinegar 350ml 5.95
30. Peach Vinegar 350ml 5.95
31. Raspberry Vinegar 150ml 3.50
32. Black Currant Vinegar 150ml 3.50
33. Peach Vinegar 150ml 3.50

Specials
34A. Catharines Hors d'oeuvre & Pasta Sauce . 250 ml 6.49
35. Catharines Hot Antipasto.........................250 ml 5.69
36. Catharines Antipasto................................250 ml 5.69

Spices *(recipes included)*
37A. Bloody Mary, Bloody Caesar Mix 3.95
38A. Apple Spices - for pies, butters, chutneys...............3.95
39A. Mulling Spices - for wine, cider, or ale...................4.95
40A. Hot Chocolate - rich & tasty, just add hot water 4.95

Tea - *No tea is fresher than ours*
41. a) Monks Blend b) Strawberry c) Raspberry
41. d) Earl Grey e) English Breakfast f) Blackcurrant
42. Sachets...50 g   2.95
43. Tea by the Pound, all blends ....1 lb 14.95

Maple Products
44A. Pure Maple Syrup ....100 ml   3.95
45A. Pure Maple Syrup ....250 ml   5.95
46A. Pure Maple Syrup ....500 ml 10.95
47A. Maple Syrup with Light Rum ....250 ml   5.95
48A. Maple Butter, excellent on pancakes, toast or baking
....250 ml   5.95

Coffees - *We think this is the best coffee available*
First Colony - ground coffee, available 8 oz. and 2 oz.
49A. Columbian Supremo ....8 oz.   6.49
50A. Irish Cream   50B. Swiss Chocolate Almond
                                       8 oz.   6.49
50C. Chocolate Raspberry Truffle...........8 oz.   6.49
51A. Special House Blend.........................2 oz.   2.25
52. All flavours available in 2 oz. packs
    (order coffee by # and letter, i.e. 52C is a 2 oz Chocolate Raspberry Truffle)

Teapots - If you've had tea with us, these are the ones!
56. Executive Tea set Black with Sterling Silver   49.95
57.   Sky Blue with Sterling Silver   49.95
58. *1-2 cup teapot*   Fern Green with Gold Inlay   49.95
     1 cup & saucer
59.   Rust with Gold Inlay 49.95
60. Romance Tea set Black with Sterling Silver   59.95
61.   Sky Blue with Sterling Silver   59.95
62. *1-2 cup teapot*   Fern Green with Gold Inlay   59.95
     2 cups & saucers
63.   Rust with Gold Inlay 59.95
64. Gift Packages - We pack all for long journeys!
A. P.E.I.Summer House 24.99
B. Taster's Choice Duo..............2-125 ml Preserves Crated   8.25
C. Taster's Choice Trio.2-125 ml Preserves,1-125 HoneyCrated 11.95
D. Crated vinegars ....2-150ml Vinegars Crated   7.49
E. Crated Preserves (2 jars) ....250 ml size 12.49
F. Crated Preserves (3 jars) ....250 ml size 17.95
G. Tea-for-Two ....1-125 ml Preserves, Tea, 1-125 ml Honey 11.95
75. 8" Brass Planter - filled with Swiss Chocolate, Hot Chocolate, Chocolate Coffee and more Chocolate 23.99
76. 6" Brass Planter - 1-125 ml Preserve, 1-125 ml Honey with Liqueur, Honey Dipper and Chocolate 16.50
77. 4" Brass Planter - 125 ml Honey with Liqueur and Honey Dipper 10.95
78. Wicker House - 2-250 ml Preserves with Liqueur, 1-250 ml Honey with Liqueur, 100 ml Maple Syrup, Irish Cream Coffee, Strawberry Tea 39.95
79. 14" Wicker Hamper - 1-125 ml Preserve, 1-125 ml Honey with Liqueur, 1 Raspberry Tea, 1 Irish Cream Coffee, Honey Dipper 32.95
80. Hunter Green S M L XL Sweatshirt 29.95
    87% Cotton, 13% Poly, Preshrunk
81. Deep Lavender S M L XL Sweatshirt 29.95
    87% Cotton, 13% Poly, Preshrunk

Shipping cost per Address

Value of Order	*Shipping Cost
$ 0. - $30.	5.00
$31. - $40.	6.00
$41. - $55.	7.00
$56. - $65.	8.00
$66. - $75.	9.00
$76. - $100.	10.00
$101. & over	5% of order

All packages are packed well for shipping. We use double strength corrugated boxes and finish the packages with a heavy brown paper wrap.

*Please note that if the postage cost is less than the amount charged to us, we then will charge you the least amount. That is why we prefer if you paid by credit card. Thank you, Bruce.

Gift Wrapping
$3.50 *per package*

Using the appropriate gift wrap for the season, we'll give your package that little extra. We can supply a small card with your salutation, or if you send us your card with your order, we will include it.

Gift Packaging
Friends, we have many packaging ideas, too many for our catalogue. If you wish us to do up a basket in a certain price range, or any special order for that matter just give us a call, fax or mail in your request. We are here for you!

Method of Payment   MasterCard   VISA
☐MasterCard ☐Visa
CREDIT CARD NUMBER
Cardholder Name
Please Print
We require a signature
mo./   yr.
Expiry Date

---

① **SOLD TO:**   ☐Mr. ☐Mrs. ☐Ms.
Name
Please Print
Address
City _____ Prov _____ PostalCode _____
May we have your phone number in case of a question about your order?
Home (   ) _____ Work (   ) _____

Send to me at the above address.
Ship to arrive: ☐Now ☐Christmas ☐Other...........

Prod.#	Quantity	Price Each	Gift Wrap	Total Price
			3.50☐	
			3.50☐	
			3.50☐	
			3.50☐	
			3.50☐	
			3.50☐	
			3.50☐	
		Shipping		
		Total Cost		

② **Send to:**   ☐Mr. ☐Mrs. ☐Ms. ☐Firm
Name
Please Print
Address
City _____ Prov._____ Postal _____
Greetings from:
Ship to arrive: ☐Now ☐Christmas ☐Other........

Prod.#	Quantity	Price Each	Gift Wrap	Total Price
			3.50☐	
			3.50☐	
			3.50☐	
			3.50☐	
			3.50☐	
			3.50☐	
			3.50☐	
			3.50☐	
		Shipping		
		Total Cost		

Dear Shopper,
If you have visited our store recently, and wish to purchase an item which is not on this list, please feel free to do so.
On a separate sheet of paper, write a description of the item to the best of your ability, and we will do our best to satisfy your request.

sincerely,

Bruce MacNaughton

For *FAST* delivery call:
(9:00 am to 5:00 pm A.S.T.)
(902) 964-2524
Fax **(902) 566-5565**

*Prices subject to change without notice.

exhibit 1   *(continued)*

family kilt," reciting history and generally providing live entertainment. Bruce and the other staff members realized the value of this "Island Touch" and strove to ensure that all visitors to New Glasgow left with both a positive feeling and purchased products.

Visitors were also encouraged to visit the New Glasgow location through a cooperative scheme whereby other specialty retailers provided a coupon for a free cup of coffee or tea at P.E.I. Preserves. In 1991, roughly 2,000 of these coupons were redeemed.

Approximately 5,000 people received their mail-order catalogue annually. They had experienced an order rate of 7.5 per cent with the average order being $66. They hoped to devote more time and effort to their mail-order business in an effort to extend their marketing and production period. For 1991 to 1992, the order rate was expected to increase by as much as 15 per cent because the catalogue was to be mailed two weeks earlier than in the previous year. The catalogues cost $1 each to print and mail.

In addition to mail order, the company operated with an ad hoc group of wholesale distributors. These wholesalers were divided between Nova Scotia, Ontario, and other locations. For orders as small as $150, buyers could purchase from the wholesalers' price list. Wholesale prices were on average 60 per cent of the retail/mail-order price. Total wholesale trade for the coming year was projected at $150,000, but had been higher in the past.

Danamar Imports was a Toronto-based specialty food store supplier which had previously provided P.E.I. Preserves to hundreds of specialty food stores in Ontario. Danamar had annually ordered $80,000 worth of P.E.I. Preserves at 30 per cent below the wholesale price. This arrangement was amicably discontinued in 1990 by Mac-Naughton due to uncertainty about whether he was profiting from this contract. P.E.I. Preserves had a list of the specialty stores which Danamar had previously supplied, and was planning to contact them directly in late 1991.

Over the past few years, the company had received numerous enquiries for quotations on large-scale shipments. Mitsubishi had asked for a price on a container load of preserves. Airlines and hotels were interested in obtaining preserves in 28 or 30 gram single-service bottles. One hotel chain, for example, had expressed interest in purchasing 3,000,000 bottles if the cost could be kept under $0.40 per unit. (Bruce had not proceeded due to the need to purchase $65,000 worth of bottling equipment, and uncertainty about his production costs.) This same hotel chain had more recently been assessing the ecological implications of the packaging waste which would be created with the use of so many small bottles. They were now weighing the hygiene implications of serving jam out of multi-customer-use larger containers in their restaurants. They had asked MacNaughton to quote on $300,000 worth of jam in two-litre bottles.

FINANCIAL

The company had enjoyed a remarkable rate of growth since its inception. Sales volumes had increased in each of the six years of operations, from an initial level of $30,000 to 1990's total of $785,000. These sales were made up of $478,000 from retail sales (including mail order) of what they manufactured and/or distributed, and $307,000 from the restaurants (the Tea Room in New Glasgow, and Perfect Cup Restaurant in Charlottetown.) Exhibits 2 and 3 (on the next two pages) provide Income Statements from these operations, while Exhibit 4 (on page 151) contains a consolidated balance sheet.

This growth, although indicative of the success of the product, has also created its share of problems. Typical of many small businesses which experience such rapid growth, the company had not secured financing suitable to its needs. This, coupled with the seasonal nature of the manufacturing operation, had caused numerous periods of severe cash shortage. From Bruce's perspective, the company's banker (Bank of Nova Scotia) had not been as supportive as it might have been. (The bank manager in Charlottetown had last visited the facility three years ago.) Bruce felt the solution to the problem of cash shortages was the issuance of preferred shares. "An infusion of 'long-term' working capital, at a relatively low rate of interest, will provide a stable financial base for the future," he said.

At this time, MacNaughton was attempting to provide a sound financial base for the continued operation of the company. He had decided to offer a preferred share issue in the amount of $100,000. These shares would bear interest at the rate of eight percent cumulative and would be non-voting, non-participating. He anticipated that the sale of these shares would be complete by December 31, 1991. In the interim he required a line of credit in the amount of $100,000 which he requested to be guaranteed by the Prince Edward Island Development Agency.

Projected Sales for the Year Ended January 31, 1992 were:

New Glasgow Restaurant	$ 110,000
Charlottetown Restaurant	265,000
Retail (New Glasgow)	360,000
Wholesale (New Glasgow)	150,000
Mail Order (New Glasgow)	50,000
Retail (Charlottetown)	75,000
Total	$1,010,000

exhibit 2   P.E.I. Preserve Co. Ltd. (Manufacturing and Retail) Statement of Earnings and Retained Earnings, Year Ended January 31, 1991 (Unaudited)

	1991	1990
Sales	$478,406	$425,588
Cost of sales	217,550	186,890
Gross margin	260,856	238,698
Expenses		
Advertising and promotional items	20,632	6,324
Automobile	7,832	3,540
Doubtful accounts	1,261	—
Depreciation and amortization	11,589	12,818
Dues and fees	1,246	2,025
Electricity	7,937	4,951
Heat	4,096	4,433
Insurance	2,426	1,780
Interest and bank charges	5,667	17,482
Interest on long-term debt	23,562	9,219
Management salary	29,515	32,600
Office and supplies	12,176	10,412
Professional fees	19,672	10,816
Property tax	879	621
Rent	—	975
Repairs and maintenance	6,876	9,168
Salaries and wages	70,132	96,386
Telephone and facsimile	5,284	5,549
Trade shows	18,588	12,946
	249,370	242,045
Earnings (loss) from manufacturing operation	11,486	(3,347)
Management fees	—	7,250
Loss from restaurant operations - Schedule 2	3,368	—
Earnings before income taxes	8,118	3,903
Income taxes	181	1,273
Net Earnings	7,937	2,630
Retained earnings, beginning of year	9,290	6,660
Retained earnings, end of year	$ 17,227	$ 9,290

exhibit 3   P.E.I. Preserve Co. Ltd. Schedule of Restaurant Operations (Charlottetown and New Glasgow) Year Ended January 31, 1991 (Unaudited)

	Schedule 2 1991
Sales	$306,427
Cost of Sales	
Purchases and freight	122,719
Inventory, end of year	11,864
	110,855
Salaries and wages for food preparation	42,883
	153,738
Gross Margin	152,689
Expenses	
Advertising	2,927
Depreciation	6,219
Electricity	4,897
Equipment lease	857
Insurance	389
Interest and bank charges	1,584
Interest on long-term debt	2,190
Office and supplies	2,864
Propane	2,717
Rent	22,431
Repairs and maintenance	3,930
Salaries and wages for service	90,590
Supplies	12,765
Telephone	1,697
	156,057
Loss from Restaurant Operations	$ 3,368

OPERATIONS

Preserve production took place on site, in an area visible through glass windows from the retail floor. Many visitors, in fact, would videotape operations during their visit to the New Glasgow store, or would watch the process while tasting the broad selection of sample products freely available.

Production took place on a batch basis. Ample production capacity existed for the $30,000 main kettle used to cook the preserves. Preserves were made five months a year, on a single shift, five day per week basis. Even then, the main kettle was in use only 50 per cent of the time.

Only top quality fruit was purchased. As much as possible, P.E.I. raw materials were used. For a short period the fruit could be frozen until time for processing.

The production process was labour intensive. Bruce was considering the feasibility of moving to an incentive-based salary system to increase productivity and control

exhibit 4   P.E.I. Preserve Co. Ltd. Balance Sheet, as at January 31, 1991 (Unaudited)

	1991	1990
Current Assets		
Cash	$ 5,942	$ 592
Accounts Receivable		
Trade	12,573	6,511
Investment tax credit	1,645	2,856
Other	13,349	35,816
Inventory	96,062	85,974
Prepaid expenses	2,664	6,990
	132,235	138,739
Grant Receivable	2,800	1,374
Property, Plant and Equipment	280,809	162,143
Recipes and Trade Name, at Cost	10,000	10,000
	$425,844	$312,256
Current Liabilities		
Bank indebtedness	$ 2,031	$ 9,483
Operating and other loans	54,478	79,000
Accounts Payable and accrued liabilities	64,143	32,113
Current portion of long-term debt	23,657	14,704
	144,309	135,300
Long-term Debt	97,825	99,679
Deferred Government Assistance	54,810	—
Payable to Shareholder, non-interest bearing,		
no set terms of repayment	43,373	49,687
	340,317	284,666
Shareholders' Equity		
Share capital	55,000	5,000
Contributed surplus	13,300	13,300
Retained earnings	17,227	9,290
	85,527	27,590
	$425,844	$312,256

costs. Because a decorative cloth fringe was tied over the lid of each bottle, bottling could not be completely automated. A detailed production cost analysis had recently been completed. While there were some minor differences due to ingredients, the variable costs averaged $1.25 per 250 ml bottle. This was made up of ingredients ($.56), labour ($.28) and packaging ($.20/bottle, $.11/lid, $.03/label and $.07/fabric and ribbon).

Restaurant operations were the source of many of Bruce's headaches. The New Glasgow Restaurant had evolved over time from offering 'dessert and coffee/tea' to its present status where it was also open for meals all day.

Management

During the peak summer period, P.E.I. Preserves employed 45 people among the restaurants, manufacturing area and retail locations. Of these, five were managerial positions (see Exhibit 5). The company was considered a good place to work, with high morale and limited turnover. Nonetheless, most employees (including some management) were with the company on a seasonal basis. This was a concern to MacNaughton who felt that if he could provide year-round employment, he would be able to attract and keep the best quality staff.

Carol Rombough was an effective assistant general manager and bookkeeper. Maureen Dickieson handled production with little input required from Bruce. Kathy MacPherson was in the process of providing, for the first time, accurate cost information. Natalie Leblanc was managing the new retail outlet in Charlottetown, and assisting on some of the more proactive marketing initiatives Bruce was considering.

Bruce felt that the company had survived on the basis of word-of-mouth. Few follow-up calls on mail order had ever been done. Bruce did not enjoy participating in trade shows—even though he received regular solicitations for them from across North America. In 1992, he planned to participate in four *retail* shows, all of them in or close to P.E.I. Bruce hoped to be able eventually to hire a sales/marketing manager, but could not yet afford $30,000 for the necessary salary.

The key manager continued to be MacNaughton. He described himself as "a fair person to deal with, but shrewd when it comes to purchasing. However, I like to spend enough money to ensure that what we do—we do right." Financial and managerial constraints meant that Bruce felt stretched ("I haven't had a vacation in years") and unable to pursue all of the ideas he had for developing the business.

THE JAPANESE CONSUMER

MacNaughton's interest in the possibility of reaching the Tokyo consumer had been formed from two factors: the large number of Japanese visitors to P.E.I. Preserves, and the fact that the largest export shipment the company had ever made had been to Japan. MacNaughton had never visited Japan, although he had been encouraged by Canadian federal government trade representatives to participate in food and gift shows in Japan. He was debating whether he should visit Japan during the coming year. Most of the information he had on Japan had been collected for him by a friend.

Japan was Canada's second most important source of foreign tourists. In 1990, there were 474,000 Japanese visitors to Canada, a figure which was expected to rise to 1,000,000 by 1995. Most Japanese visitors entered through the Vancouver or Toronto airports. Within Canada, the most popular destination was the Rocky Mountains (in Banff, Alberta numerous stores catered specifically to Japanese consumers). Nearly 15,000 Japanese visited P.E.I. each year. Excluding airfare, these visitors to Canada spent an estimated $314 million, the highest per-capita amount from any country.

The Japanese fascination with Prince Edward Island could be traced to the popularity of *Anne of Green Gables*. The Japanese translation of this and other books in the same series had been available for many years. However, the adoption of the book as required reading in the Japanese school system since the 1950s had resulted in widespread awareness and affection for "Anne with red hair" *and* P.E.I.

exhibit 5   Key Executives

President and General Manager - Bruce MacNaughton, Age 35

Experience:	Seventeen years of "front line" involvement with the public in various capacities;
	Seven years of managing and promoting Prince Edward Island Preserve Co. Ltd;
	Past director of the Canadian Specialty Food Association.
Responsibilities:	To develop and oversee the short-, mid-, and long-term goals of the company;
	To develop and maintain quality products for the marketplace;
	To oversee the management of personnel;
	To develop and maintain customer relations at both the wholesale and retail level;
	To develop and maintain harmonious relations with government and the banking community.

Assistant General Manager - Carol Rombough, Age 44

Experience:	Twenty years as owner/operator of a manufacturing business;
	Product marketing at both the wholesale and retail level;
	Personnel management;
	Bookkeeping in a manufacturing environment;
	Three years with the Prince Edward Island Preserve Co. Ltd.
Responsibilities:	All bookkeeping functions (i.e. Accounts Receivable, Accounts Payable, Payroll);
	Staff management—scheduling and hiring;
	Customer relations.

Production Manager - Maureen Dickieson, Age 29

Experience:	Seven years of production experience in the dairy industry;
	Three years with the Prince Edward Island Preserve Co. Ltd.
Responsibilities:	Oversee and participate in all production;
	Planning and scheduling production;
	Requisition of supplies.

Consultant - Kathy MacPherson, Certified General Accountant, Age 37

Experience:	Eight years as a small business owner/manager;
	Eight years in financial planning and management.
Responsibilities:	To implement an improved system of product costing;
	To assist in the development of internal controls;
	To compile monthly internal financial statements;
	To provide assistance and/or advice as required by management.

Store Manager - Natalie Leblanc, Age 33

Experience:	Fifteen years in retail
Responsibilities:	To manage the retail store in the CP Hotel;
	Assist with mail order business;
	Marketing duties as assigned.

The high level of spending by Japanese tourists was due to a multitude of factors: the amount of disposable income available to them, one of the world's highest per person duty-free allowances (200,000 yen), and gift-giving traditions in the country. Gift-giving and entertainment expenses at the corporate level are enormous in Japan. In 1990, corporate entertainment expenses were almost ¥5 trillion, more than triple the U.S. level of ¥1.4 trillion. Corporate gift giving, while focused at both year end (seibo) and the summer (chugen), in fact, occurred throughout the year.

Gift giving at the personal level was also widespread. The amount spent would vary depending on one's relationship with the recipient; however, one of the most common price points used by Japanese retailers for gift giving was offering choices for under ¥2000.

The Japanese Jam Market

Japanese annual consumption of jam was approximately 80,000 tons. Imports made up 6-9 per cent of consumption, with higher grade products (¥470 or more per kilo wholesale CIF) making up a third of this total. Several dozen firms imported jam, and utilized a mix of distribution channels (see Exhibit 6). Prices varied, in part, according to the type of channel structure used. Exhibit 7 provides a common structure. Import duties for jams were high—averaging about 28 per cent. Despite such a high

exhibit 6   Jam Distribution Channel in Japan

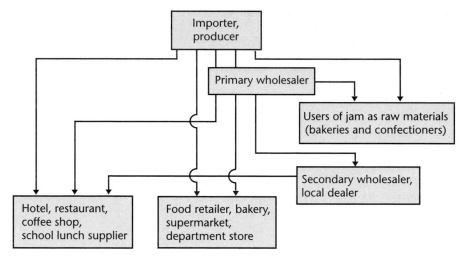

Source: Access to Japan's Import Market, Tradescope, June 1989

exhibit 7   Example of Price Markups in Japan

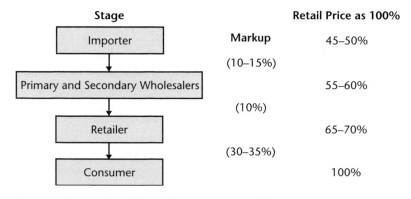

Source: Access to Japan's Import Market, Tradescope, June 1989

exhibit 8   The Japanese Jam Market

To expand sales of imported jam or to enter the Japanese market for the first time, it is necessary to develop products after precise study of the market's needs. Importers who are making efforts to tailor their products to the Japanese market have been successfully expanding their sales by 10 per cent each year. Based on the analysis of successful cases of imported jam, the following factors may be considered very important.

Diversification of consumer preferences: Strawberry jam occupies about 50 per cent of the total demand for jam and its share is continuing to rise. Simultaneously, more and more varieties of jam are being introduced.

Low sugar content: European exporters have successfully exported low sugar jam that meets the needs of the Japanese market. Jam with a sugar content of less than 65 per cent occupies a share of 65-70 per cent of the market on a volume basis.

Smaller containers: Foreign manufacturers who stick to packaging products in large-sized containers (650g, 440g, 250g), even though their products are designed for household use, have been failing to expand their sales. On the other hand, foreign manufacturers who have developed products in smaller containers (14g, 30g, 42g) specifically for the Japanese market have achieved successful results.

Fashionable items: Contents and quantity are not the only important aspects of jam. The shape and material quality of the containers and their caps, label design and product name can also influence sales. It is also important that the label not be damaged in any way.

Development of gift items: Sets of various types of imported jams are popular as gift items. For example, there are sets of 10 kinds of jam in 40g mini-jars (retail price ¥2,000) sold as gift sets.

Selection of distribution channel: Since general trading companies, specialty importers and jam manufacturers each have their own established distribution channels, the selection of the most appropriate channel is of the utmost importance.

Source: Access to Japan's Import Market, Tradescope, June 1989.

tariff barrier, some firms had been successful in exporting to Japan. Excerpts from a report on how to access Japan's jam market successfully are contained in Exhibit 8.

CANADIAN WORLD

In Spring 1990, P.E.I. Preserves received its biggest-ever export order; $50,000 worth of product was ordered (FOB New Glasgow) for ultimate shipment to Ashibetsu, on the northern Japanese island of Hokkaido. These products were to be offered for sale at Canadian World, a new theme park scheduled to open in July 1990.

In 1981, Japan's first theme park was built outside Tokyo. Called Tokyo Disneyland, in 1989 it had an annual revenue of $815 million, 14.7 million visitors, and profits of $119 million. Not surprisingly, this success has spawned a theme park industry in Japan. Over the past decade, 20 parks with wide-ranging themes have opened. Another 16 were expected to open in 1991-92.

The idea to construct a theme park about Canada was conceived by a Japanese advertising agency hired by the Ashibetsu city council to stop the city's declining economy. The city's population had decreased from 75,000 in 1958 to 26,000 in 1984 due principally to mine closures.

With capital investment of ¥750,000,000, construction started in mid 1989 on 48 of the 156 available hectares. The finished site included six restaurants, 18 souvenir stores, 16 exhibit event halls, an outdoor stage with 12,000 seats, and 20 hectares planted in herbs and lavender.

The theme of Canadian World was less a mosaic of Canada than it was a park devoted to the world of Anne of Green Gables. The entrance to the Canadian World was a replica of Kensingston Station in P.E.I. The north gateway was Brightriver Station, where Anne first met with Matthew. There was a full-scale copy of the Green Gables house, Orwell School where you could actually learn English like Anne did, and so forth. Canadian World employed 55 full-time and 330 part-time staff. This included a high school girl from P.E.I. who played Anne—complete with (dyed) red hair—dressed in Victorian period costume.

In late August 1991, Canadian World still had a lot of P.E.I. Preserves' products for sale. Lower than expected sales could be traced to a variety of problems. First, overall attendance at Canadian World had been 205,000 in the first year, significantly lower than the expected 300,000. Second, the product was priced higher than many competitive offerings. For reasons unknown to Canadian World staff, the product sold for 10 per cent more than expected (¥1200 vs ¥1086).

Wholesale price in P.E.I.	$ 3.50
Freight ($4.20/kilo, P.E.I. to Hokkaido)	.80
Duty (28% of wholesale price + freight)	1.20
Landed cost in Japan	5.50
Importer's Margin (15%)	.83
Price to Primary Wholesaler	6.33
Wholesaler Margin (10%)	.63
Price to Retailer	6.96
Canadian World mark up (30%)	2.09
Expected retail price	$ 9.05
Exchange (Cdn. $1.00 = 120 yen)	¥1086

Third, the product mix chosen by the Japanese buyers appeared to be inappropriate. While it was difficult to locate any of the company's remaining strawberry preserves in the various Canadian World outlets which carried it, other products had not moved at all. Canadian World personnel did not have a tracking system for product-by-product sales. Fourth, the company's gift packs were not always appropriately sized or priced. One suggestion had been to package the preserves in cardboard gift boxes of three large (250 ml) or five small (125 ml) bottles for eventual sale for under ¥2000.

An increasing portion of all of the gifts being sold at Canadian World were, in fact, being made in Japan. Japanese sourcing was common due to the high Japanese duties on imports, the transportation costs from Canada, and the unfamiliarity of Canadian companies with Japanese consumer preferences.

THE TOKYO MARKET

With ten million residents, Tokyo was the largest city in Japan and one of the most crowded cities anywhere. Thirty million people lived within 50 kilometres of Tokyo's Imperial Palace. As the economic centre of the nation, Tokyo also had the most expensive land in the world—U.S. $150,000 per square metre in the city centre. Retail space in one of Tokyo's major shopping districts would cost $75–$160 per square metre or

$1,600 to $3,400 per month for a shop equivalent in size to that in the CP Prince Edward Hotel. Prices in the Ginza were even higher. In addition to basic rent, all locations required a deposit (guarantee money which would be repaid when the tenant gave up the lease) of at least $25,000. Half of the locations available in a recent survey also charged administrative/maintenance fees (five to 12 per cent of rent), while in about one-third of the locations a "reward" (gift) was paid by tenants to the owner at the time the contract was signed. For a small site it might amount to $10 to $15,000.

THE TORONTO MARKET

With three million people, Toronto was Canada's largest city and economic centre. It contained the country's busiest airport (15 million people used it each year) and was a popular destination for tourists. Each year, roughly 20 million people visited Toronto for business or vacation.

MacNaughton's interest in Toronto was due to its size, the local awareness of P.E.I., and the high perceived potential volume of sales. The company did not have a sales agent in Toronto.

The Toronto market was well served by mass market and specialty jam producers at all price points. Numerous domestic and imported products were available. Prices started as low as $1.00 (or less) for a 250 ml. bottle of high sugar/low fruit product. Prices increased to $2.00 to $2.50 for higher fruit, natural brands and increased again to $3.00 to $3.50 for many of the popular branded imports. The highest-priced products, such as P.E.I. Preserves, were characterized by even higher fruit content, highest quality ingredients, and a broader selection of product offerings.

The specialty domestic producers were from various provinces and tended to have limited distribution areas. The specialty imports were frequently from France or England. The Canadian tariff on imports was 15 per cent for most countries. From the United States, it was 10.5 per cent and declining.

The cost of retail space in Toronto varied according to location but was slightly lower than that in Tokyo. The cost of renting 22 square metres would be $100 per square metre per month (plus common area charges and taxes of $15 per square metre per month) in a major suburban shopping mall, and somewhat higher in the downtown core. Retail staff salaries were similar in Toronto and Tokyo, both of which were higher than those paid in P.E.I.

FUTURE DIRECTIONS

MacNaughton was the first to acknowledge that, while the business had been "built on gut and emotion, rather than analysis," this was insufficient for the future. The challenge was to determine the direction and timing of the desired change.

case 11 Alberta Energy Company and the Ethics of Operation Kabriole*

It is September 1998. Gwyn Morgan, President and CEO of Alberta Energy Company (AEC), is quietly sitting in his Calgary office staring out the window towards the Rocky Mountains. He has a difficult decision to make that could affect his company immensely. He has been approached by the Alberta RCMP with a proposal that might finally put an end to the period of industrial sabotage that has plagued not only his company, but also the entire oil and gas industry. The terrorism had been costly and had intimidated company staff. The RCMP was proposing that AEC property be bombed to secure cover for an undercover agent. Worse yet, for this operation to work, only a select few individuals would be allowed to know the truth. The sting was to be known as the "Operation Kabriole." How will he explain his actions to company's directors and shareholders after the fact? How would they react? How would the industry react? How would the media respond? How would the nearby residents and communities feel? He wondered how things had gotten to this point.

INDUSTRY BACKGROUND

In 1998, the oil and gas industry in Alberta had grown to a $26 billion a year industry and now comprised 20% of Alberta's Gross Provincial Product. The industry is regulated by the Alberta Energy and Utilities Board (EUB), established in 1995 through the amalgamation of the Energy Resources Conservation Board and the Public Utilities Board. The EUB, an independent, quasi-judicial agency of the government of Alberta, is mandated to adjudicate issues relating to the operation of utilities in Alberta and to ensure that development, transportation, and monitoring of these resources is in the public interest. Companies wishing to explore or develop new oil and gas sites, such as, wells, plants, and pipelines, or make changes to existing sites, must apply to the EUB for approval.

Richard Ivey School of Business
The University of Western Ontario

* Note about "Kabriole": If spelt with a "c" instead of a "k," the word refers to a curved, tapered leg, often with a decorative foot, characteristic of Chippendale and Queen Anne furniture and named after its resemblance to the leg of a leaping animal.

The oil and gas industry in Alberta grew rapidly during the late 1980s and throughout the 1990s. In 1998, the EUB received approximately 25,500 applications for development and related activities for the oil and gas industry. This was up from 12,800 in 1990. The number of oil and gas companies also rose from 70 in 1970 to approximately 1,200 in 1998. During this time the EUB had 90 field surveillance staff working out of eight field centers. Surveillance staff was responsible for monitoring Alberta's growing infrastructure of 264,000 km of pipeline, 75,080 operating wells, 33,791 inactive wells, and 644 gas plants, in addition to investigating 1,354 accidental spills or releases of gas and oil and responding to public complaints. This extensive infrastructure placed severe limits on the EUB's ability to adequately perform its monitoring functions.

THE ALBERTA ENERGY COMPANY (AEC)

AEC was created by the Alberta Government, through the AEC Act in 1975, "to provide Albertans and other Canadians with a special opportunity to participate, through share ownership, in the industrial and energy-related growth in the province of Alberta."

Over the years, the company expanded into areas other than oil and gas, including forestry, pipelines, petrochemicals, coal and steel. In 1992 it began to refocus activities toward the oil and gas industry through divestiture of other divisions and expansion of its oil and gas activities. At the same time, the Alberta government was selling off its shares in the company and the company was fully privatized in 1994.

The company is traded on the Toronto Stock Exchange (Symbol "AEC") and the New York Stock Exchange (Symbol "AOG") with major institutional investors owning a large portion of AEC's shares. Financial highlights are given in Exhibit 1.

In 1998, AEC activities were focused on two aspects of the petroleum business: four upstream operations in natural gas and oil exploration and production, and two midstream operations in natural gas storage, pipelines and natural gas liquids processing. The company operates in a decentralized manner with six semi-autonomous, entrepreneurial business units outlined in Exhibit 2 (on the next page).

exhibit 1   Financial Highlights, Alberta Energy Company Ltd.

	1997	1996
Revenues, net of royalties ($ millions)	1,208.6	932.6
Cash Flow ($ millions)	544.7	411.9
Net Earnings ($ millions)	21.7	68.0
Net Earnings per Share ($, fully diluted)	0.23	0.65
Dividend ($ per Common Share)	0.40	0.40
Common Shares Outstanding (millions)	112.1	111.5
Direct Capital Investment ($ millions)	824.9	2,028.9
Long-Term Direct Debt ($ millions)	1,006.8	968.3
Debt-to-Capitalization Ratio	29:71	32:68
Interest Coverage	12.4x	8.8x

Source: Alberta Energy Company Ltd., *1998 Annual Report.*

exhibit 2   Alberta Energy Company Ltd. Summary of Operations

AEC East (Upstream)	Shallow gas and oil exploration and development in the plains area of the Western Canadian Sedimentary Basin. 1997 operating statistics include: production of 325 million cubic feet/day of natural gas and 17,389 barrels/day of conventional oil, proven and probable reserves of 1,543 billion cubic feet of natural gas and 65.8 million barrels of conventional oil, and 55 exploration and 209 development wells.
AEC West (Upstream)	Exploration and production of natural gas in the West Peace River Arch. 1997 operating statistics include: production of 263 million cubic feet/day of natural gas and 11,421 barrels/day of liquids, proven and probable reserves of 2,142 billion cubic feet of natural gas and 51.7 million barrels of oil and natural gas liquids, and 90 exploration and 123 development wells.
AEC International (Upstream)	1.8 million acres of exploration lands in large blocks of Australia and Argentina. 1997 operating statistics include: 1,683 barrels/day of conventional oil, 4.2 million barrels of proven and probable conventional oil, and 4 exploration and 7 development wells.
AEC Syncrude (Upstream)	Second-largest owner of the Syncrude Project, the single largest source of oil production in Canada, and the world's largest producer of oil sands-based light, sweet oil. Ownership interests are 13.75% interest in the joint venture and 5.0% gross overriding royalty on an additional 6.25%. In 1997, sales were 28,447 barrels/per day of oil.
AEC Storage and Hub Services (Midstream)	Operated AECO, North America's largest independent natural gas storage and trading facility. Assets included: 85-billion cubic foot gas storage reservoir in Alberta, 14-billion cubic foot Wild Goose Gas Storage in California, and contracts with terms varying from one to 15 years.
AEC Pipelines and Gas Processing (Midstream)	Alberta's largest intra-provincial oil transporter and owns natural gas liquids extraction assets. Assets include: 70% ownership of AEC Pipelines, L.P., 35% interest in EmpressStraddle Plant, and 33% interest in Alberta Ethane Gathering System.

Source: Alberta Energy Company Ltd., *1998 Annual Report*, pages 13-23.

AEC and the Community

Over the years, AEC developed a strong reputation in Alberta communities as both a socially and environmentally responsible company through its operations practices; for example, sponsorship and donation activities. AEC is a founding sponsor of the Imagine philosophy that encourages corporate support of charitable organizations across Canada. AEC supports over 300 initiatives and programs and annually contributes at least 1% of its pre-tax profits (based on a three-year rolling average), or about $1.2 million. Part of this allocation includes matching employee donations to any Canadian charity.

Contributions are made to a variety of organizations, but there is a focus on health and education. Assistance is provided to traditional and complementary health and wellness organizations consistent with a corporate value to encourage healthy and balanced lifestyles. Educational and sport programs are considered to provide skills and information that benefit the young throughout their lives. Examples of initiatives supported are:

- Assistance for the purchase of a magnetic resonance imager (MRI) for the Grande Prairie Mistahia Regional Hospital.

- Support for DARE, a province-wide drug awareness program for Grade 6 students.

- A major community partner in The National Sport Centre-Calgary and its Youth Education Through Sport (YES).

- Support for annual fundraising telethons for the Medicine Hat Public School Foundation and Medicine Hat Regional Health Foundation.

- Support for women's emergency shelters in AEC-based communities.

- Sponsorship of Junior Achievement in major areas of operation.

AEC is also involved in Aboriginal communities in Alberta through investments in the development of programs aimed at improving the capacity of local people to help themselves. These programs include awarding contracts to Aboriginal-owned companies, and providing on-the-job training and scholarships for Aboriginal students pursuing oil- and gas-related studies.

Another of AEC's basic values and most ardent commitments is to the environment. The company strives to safeguard the beauty and balance of the environment in which it operates and is pursuing initiatives to reduce emissions by improving production efficiency. It is also working with the Tree Canada Foundation on a "carbon sink" pilot tree-planting program intended to decrease the amount of carbon dioxide in the air.

The production and processing of natural gas and oil involves substantial risk for the environment. The potential for adverse impact of their operations on the environment is a major challenge for the company.

THE FLARING PROBLEM

In Alberta, most farmers own only the top six inches (15 cm) of topsoil, but what is underneath remains the property of the provincial government (with the exception of gravel deposits). The government leases this land to the oil and gas companies, who, in turn, explore and drill for oil and gas. Should an oil company find oil and/or gas beneath the topsoil owned by a farmer, they are permitted (by the EUB) to erect oil and gas wells on that site regardless of whether it is in the middle of the farmer's crops, pastures, corrals, or even front yard. Petroleum companies work with landowners to minimize any adverse impact, and they pay approximately $5,000 per year for loss of land use. This arrangement has been in place for many years, but as the number of wells increased a minority of farmers began to complain of the ill effects the wells had on their crops, cattle, and families.

The cause of the farmers' concern is the flare stacks associated with well sites. Flaring is routinely used in the energy industry throughout Alberta and the world. A typical application occurs when oil is being produced and the solution gas (gas which bubbles out of the oil as it is brought to surface pressure) is uneconomical to recover and is flared (burned) near the well site. In 1996, Alberta alone had more than 5,200 solution gas flares operating. These account for approximately 1.8 billion m^3 of flared gas per year. The theory is that through flaring, substances in the gas are converted to their safest form possible. For example, hydrogen sulfide (H_2S), a highly toxic chemical, is converted to sulfur dioxide, a less dangerous chemical. Unfortunately, the ability of flare stacks to accomplish this task is affected by conditions such as:

- Composition of the flare stream
- Flow rate of flare gases
- Wind velocity
- Ambient turbulence
- Presence of hydrocarbon droplets in the flare stream
- Presence of water droplets in the flare stream

The flaring process releases some 250 compounds. The fact that these flares are not able to convert all the chemicals to safe forms means that some toxins may be released into the environment surrounding the flare stack. Farmers believe it is these toxins that are the cause of health problems occurring in their families, livestock, and crops.

In fact, studies have supported the farmers' claims. A 1996 Finnish study comparing two communities (one with sour gas pollution, one without) found that members of the polluted community suffered from more headaches, respiratory infections and coughing than the non-polluted community. Another study found that H_2S in low doses might cause persistent neurological dysfunction; for example, memory loss. A retrospective study performed by the Alberta and federal governments, which looked at 630,000 dairy and beef cattle near 231 sour gas plants, found delays in first births and delays between births in areas of highest exposure to sour gas emissions.

Farmer Frustrations

Because of the research evidence, farmers have become increasingly vocal and active regarding the effects of pollution on their families and farms. Health problems alleged to be associated with flaring include asthma, coughing, headaches, aching muscles, shortness of breath, and memory loss. Illness in cattle and poor crops have also been attributed to the pollution. There is a growing perception among farmers that their concerns are not being taken seriously. Many reports of these problems appeared in newspapers and other media. The stories claimed that farmers could not get help from government or through the legal channels such as the EUB Environmental Appeals Board set up to deal with farmers' concerns.

Hundreds of rural dwellers claimed that the increasing oil and gas developments, poor regulations, and lack of government interest compromised their livelihoods, livestock, and health. There were some controls on the number of wells, batteries, pipelines or gas plants that could be situated in one area, yet they claimed that the government either ignored the protests or failed to enforce the regulations that did exist. The EUB received about 800 complaints annually, but its ability to respond was limited. The Alberta government reduced its funding by 28% between 1992 and 1998 despite a fourfold increase in drilled wells. The EUB lost its capacity to provide a meaningful level of auditing or inspection of petroleum industry activities. Farmers, environmentalists, and industry spokespersons felt that insufficient scientific evidence existed. The difficulty was that studies performed were not conclusive of the harm caused, especially when low doses of chemicals were involved. Many farmers did not know whether they should complain to a government department or local municipal districts about the spells, leaks, dead cattle or bad land deals. It was alleged some farmers signed compensation agreements that bound them to secrecy, while others were afraid to speak out.

The situation became volatile, with acts of terrorism occurring against the oil and gas industry. In February 1998, a particularly violent event occurred near Bowden, Alberta when a beef farmer shot and killed an oil and gas company vice-president supervising the cleanup of a well site on his farm. A petroleum company that previously operated the site had caused the pollution. The farmer had been attempting to get the well cleaned up for two and one-half years and apparently broke down over all the frustrations at getting the clean up done.

The eco-terrorism also occurred in AEC West's area of operations in northwest Alberta, especially in the Peace River area. In the mid 1990's, the vandalism of petroleum installations began and continued during 1997 and into 1998. Over one hundred acts of terrorism had occurred since mid-1996 and the major acts are listed in Exhibit 3. Property damage was running in the millions of dollars, and there was concern for the safety of field workers and neighbors. Some employees had received threats of harm. The RMCP had not charged anyone with responsibility for the acts.

exhibit 3   Chronology of Selected Terrorist Activities

Date	Event
1996	Nails thrown on remote roads on land leased by oil companies. Power lines cut down. Shots fired through offices of two gas plants near Hythe, Alta.
December, 1997	Fire at Norcen Energy well south of Hythe, Alta. Cement studded with shotgun shells is found in fire.
April 25, 1998	Three shots fired at AEC well site building.
June 16, 1998	AEC pipeline is hit with homemade projectile bomb.
July 31, 1998	AEC sweet gas well at Goodfare, Alta. bombed.
Aug. 2, 1998	Sour gas well near Demmitt, Alta. bombed.
Aug. 24, 1998	Suncor Energy oil well south of Hinton, Alta. is bombed.

The police force was experiencing a shortage of staff and limited resources to devote to the terrorism. The petroleum industry's concern for its property and for employees and neighbors plus the inability of the police to address the problem resulted in cooperative efforts between the industry and the police.

Police/Industry Cooperation

Throughout 1998, the police and industry representatives cooperated in a variety of ways in an effort to address the vandalism problem. On March 27, 1998, a meeting was held between senior police officers and officials of AEC and other petroleum companies. The companies recognized the police force's lack of resources and discussed the possibility of contributing financial and other resources.

The industry officials decided instead to support the South Peace Crime Prevention Society (SPCPS), a local organization. The SPCPS was a dormant local community organization that was revived through the combined efforts of AEC, other petroleum companies and local business people. Industry would support the Society, which in turn would provide assistance to the RCMP. Security Management Consulting Inc., a private security firm working for AEC and several other companies, suggested this approach. AEC donated $25,000 to SPCPS out of a total of $188,000 raised from industry. The industry assistance enabled the RCMP to obtain additional resources to address the vandalism; for example, to support a Rural Crime Watch program and to purchase all terrain vehicles for accessing marshy areas. AEC also donated a computer, appropriate software, and technical staff support to SPCPS, near to where much of the vandalism had occurred.

AEC offered a $50,000 reward for information resulting in the arrest of the persons responsible for the vandalism. The company approached Crime Stoppers to act as custodian of the funds with the RCMP to determine who received the reward. Crime Stoppers was limited to allocating $2,000 to the reward and AEC contacted other companies for donations bringing the total to about $125,000.

Rev. Wiebo Ludwig

Rev. Wiebo Ludwig, leader of the Church of the Shepherd King sect of the Christian Reform Church, along with his friend, Richard Boonstra, felt strongly that flaring was responsible for a range of human and animal birth deformities and stillbirths. Ludwig had become widely known as an outspoken critic of the petroleum industry and flaring in particular.

Although several companies had operations in the area, only AEC officials contacted Ludwig and his family regarding possible damage as a result of flaring near their farm, known as Trickle Creek Farm, at Hythe, Alberta. The company had offered to monitor air quality and conduct soil and water analyses. These offers were declined. Ludwig had met with AEC's president and CEO, Gwyn Morgan, in January 1998 when he railed about the damage to his family and property from flaring. He suggested that AEC should pay conciliatory compensation for the hardships imposed on his family.

From March through July 1998, AEC officials negotiated with Ludwig to purchase the Trickle Creek Farm. The farm was appraised at $438,000 to $450,000 and in negotiations with AEC Ludwig demanded as much as $1.5 million for the property.

On July 29, Ludwig was offered $800,000. AEC's rationale for purchasing the farm at an inflated price was based on a belief that Ludwig was behind much of the vandalism and the company wanted him removed from the area before someone got hurt or even killed.

A few days later, Ludwig refused the offer, as he did not agree with the clauses added at the last moment by AEC to the sale agreement. The clauses included a restrictive confidentiality clause relating to the terms of the agreement, a standard waiver clause in real estate transactions proclaiming that the land was free of environmental problems, and three variations relating to the time before the family could reside in the area.

At this time, the acts of vandalism resumed (refer to Exhibit 3 on page 163).

OPERATION "KABRIOLE" AND THE STING

The petroleum industry, the police, and the communities in the area were increasingly concerned about the vandalism. In late summer 1998, the RCMP put together a special initiative labeled "Operation Kabriole" to focus on the petroleum vandalism problem, and asked the industry for assistance. The operation was targeted at Ludwig, and he and his supporters were to be under 24-hour ground and airplane surveillance. The operation's budget was $354,750, but before it was over, the operation would cost $750,000.

Ed McGillivary, AEC's director of environment, health, and safety, received a call from Robert Wraight, a friend of Ludwig's. Wraight offered his services as an undercover agent if AEC would purchase his land for $109,000. AEC flew Wraight, at their expense, to Calgary and set up a meeting with the RCMP.

After discussions with the RCMP, Wraight agreed to become a paid agent and attempt to gather evidence for a case against Ludwig. The evidence gathering included wearing a concealed tape recorder and then visiting the Ludwig farm. As an informant, Wraight was given a $10,000 signing bonus and placed on the payroll at $475 per week. Later the police picked up $14,000 in other expenses that he incurred. AEC did not purchase Wraight's farm.

The RCMP approached AEC for their cooperation and the company agreed to provide resources if it would help solve the vandalism problem. The company offered to supply high-tech night vision equipment from its private security firm. This offer was refused, as it was not consistent with RCMP policy. The security firm was to provide tips to the RCMP on Ludwig's movements, something that many other organizations and individuals were doing.

In order to enhance Wraight's credibility, it was proposed by the RCMP that a petroleum installation be deliberately vandalized. The RCMP proposed blowing up an old vehicle that they were willing to purchase from AEC for $8,000. Gwyn Morgan objected to this as he felt that it would cause stress among employees who feared that their vehicles might be vandalized. Instead, it was agreed that an abandoned, remote petroleum site building would be bombed. No date was set for the bombing but it was agreed that the sooner the better.

In mid-September, County officials and AEC discussed and agreed to co-sponsor two town hall style meetings to help the community deal with the increasing vandalism. In an effort to increase dialogue between the company and concerned stakeholders, AEC offered to hire professional facilitators to conduct the meetings. The meetings were set for October 20 and 21. There was no attempt to coordinate the timing of the bombing and the meetings.

GWYN MORGAN'S MORAL DILEMMA

Gwyn Morgan was being asked to approve an act of vandalism, and the company would not be able to disclose its involvement in the near future. All through the planning of the sting, he expressed that he wanted a complete disclosure of the context for AEC's cooperation. He knew that this might be difficult given the process through which charges are laid and the timing of court proceedings.

Morgan was concerned that the vandalism was escalating into life-threatening sabotage. The direct and indirect costs to AEC were now over two million dollars, but there were more serious concerns. Putting explosive devices on wellheads, pipelines, and gas production facilities was dangerous to employees and potentially dangerous to surrounding residents. Employees had received anonymous death threats creating stress for them and their families.

Morgan had many thoughts floating around in his head as he considered the decision. He was concerned about how the public would react to being deceived. Although the RCMP had assured him that the explosion would be safely discharged, he still worried about the success of the clandestine operation. He agonized over the level of cooperation between AEC and the RCMP even though the RCMP assured him that such cooperation would be helpful in preventing extremely serious crimes. Only four others at AEC knew of the operation, and he wondered how shareholders, the directors, and other employees would react when the event was disclosed.

He was aware that injury or death could be avoided and thought that to do nothing by being a bystander would be the easy way out. Furthermore, the company was cooperating with an organization that society relies upon for law and order. Despite this, he anticipated that it might be viewed differently in the future as the media and the public questioned the close relationship between the company and the RCMP. The public might perceive that the line between corporate interests of the oil industry and law enforcement had become blurred. Moreover, they might not appreciate the company having been less than forthcoming about the staged bombing.

He knew that he and the company would be held accountable in any judicial process if the eco-terrorists were caught and charged. The public might not consider it appropriate for business to supply money and other resources to a police force. Thinking back over the events of the preceding months, he wondered if cooperating with the RCMP had been wise or appropriate. AEC's security firm, Ed McGillivary and himself had been in contact with the police force.

The dilemma for Morgan meant agonizing over compliance with the RCMP sting or being a bystander resisting any further involvement with police attempts to catch those responsible. He had to balance the protection of individuals from harm and the inclination to cooperate with the police against the consequent requirement to be less than forthcoming in corporate announcements. He was president and CEO and it was his decision to make. Looking out the window again, he noticed that storm clouds had moved in and that the Rocky Mountains were no longer visible.

case 12 GT's Medical Equipment Division & IMed Inc. (A)

Bob Shepard was sitting at his desk contemplating what action he should take. He had met with outside legal counsel earlier that day. During this meeting, the lawyers had outlined possible actions (see Exhibit 1 on the next page). Yet, in spite of this meeting, Bob felt frustrated and angry. His tenure as manager of the division had been nothing but a variety of unpleasant surprises.

Bob was general manager of the Medical Equipment Division within General Technologies (GT) Inc. GT was a major U.S.-based conglomerate that had approximately a dozen large divisions, all of which were major corporations unto themselves. These divisions were mostly in the telecommunications, electrical, and high-tech businesses. The Medical Equipment Division was the newest and smallest division, one that had been born out of orphan medical product lines from other divisions plus some new product development projects. GT was known for its aggressive as well as progressive management style.

Two years ago, Bob was promoted to GM of the Medical Equipment Division. This was after a very successful sojourn at the larger Telecommunications Equipment Division. He was hired into GT as a marketing representative, after having completed an MBA at a top Midwestern U.S. business school. In marketing, he initiated new approaches to customer relations and services, which gave him the fastest sales growth in the division. This success had translated into promotions, first to sales group manager and then to product group manager. During this time, he had built the group into one of the most competitive and profitable segments in the division by aggressively cutting costs, maintaining relatively low prices, and more effectively targeting customers. When he took over as head of the Medical Equipment Division his mandate was clear—*make the division profitable.*

IVEY

Richard Ivey School of Business
The University of Western Ontario

exhibit 1   The Lawyers' Briefing

The lawyers advised Bob of the following potential actions. These actions were presented to Bob in order of legal risk and cost, the first option having no legal cost and risk, while the latter options have considerable legal costs and risks.

Costs and risks were uncertain. However, the lawyers estimated the second option would probably cost less than one hundred thousand dollars (at least initially); the third option would probably cost several hundred thousand dollars to begin to proceed with (the final cost would depend on how far the charges proceeded); and the last option probably would cost in excess of several million dollars. The legal risks of the first two options would be relatively minimal, but the legal risks of the last two options could be significant because, almost certainly, countercharges would be forthcoming. The liability and costs of fighting these countercharges would be very difficult to estimate, and they would be clearly the highest if option four were selected.

The lawyers also noted that these escalating risks and costs could be similarly applied to the opposing party in the suits—that is, option four would carry more risks and costs for Keith and IMed too.

1. Do nothing.

2. Begin to investigate charges or possible charges but do not charge Keith and IMed yet. Attempt to find out what happened and whether IMed is using any of the technology that Keith worked on at GT. The action taken would be to hire both internal and external investigators to find out who is using what technology, where Keith's missing personnel documents are, and who developed what technologies.

3. Advise the lawyers to draft charges against Keith and his company. This would allow GT's lawyers and experts to cross-examine, under oath, Keith and other IMed employees. It would also give GT a peek at their technology although they had some idea of the technology through searches of the patent filings. This approach would be much more expensive than option two, but it would give GT all of the information categorically and it would possibly let GT get a peek at how their patent ideas fit into their working sensor.

4. Aggressively attempt to inflict the maximum damage to Keith and IMed. This would involve hiring an investigator to seek all damaging information on IMed and Keith (i.e., financial, legal, etc.). As many lawsuits as possible would be filed against both Keith and IMed. In addition, find out about the IPO. The lawyers advised that filing charges against Keith and IMed and getting a cease and desist court order against IMed during the IPO would be very damaging. However, they warned that GT would have to go into the cease and desist court hearings with very strong statements of misconduct against both Keith and IMed. This was because such a restraining order would constrain Keith and IMed from doing any business at all for a certain amount of time. For a judge to grant such an order, the evidence would have to be persuasive. Furthermore, such a move would tend to inflict the maximum legal damage to IMed, because it would demonstrate to the new shareholders that IMed had not provided full and accurate information in their IPO. Almost certainly shareholders would begin a class action suit against IMed.

THE MEDICAL EQUIPMENT DIVISION'S HISTORY

The Medical Equipment Division had evolved over a period of years from a variety of products and projects in the Electronic and Scientific Equipment Divisions. Initially, the division started as an intrepreneurial R&D unit. Then, when Bob was assigned as GM of the division, the distribution and marketing rights of medical equipment products made by other divisions were transferred into this division. The aim was to develop revenues and income support for new R&D projects as well as building marketing, sales, and service support resources in the division.

GT decided to put medical products into a separate division because the other divisions were clearly not providing adequate product development and marketing support. Product development initiatives and sales were being lost in other departments because the engineers and sales support staff were not knowledgeable about the diverse medical specialties and the complex purchasing decisions in medical institutions (see Exhibit 2 and Exhibit 3). Yet, the business looked attractive. The population was aging and medicine was turning more and more to technological solutions. GT felt that their technological knowledge and abilities could provide them with an important advantage in this market.

From a competitive stance, the new division faced a variety of problems. Competitors were of two types. Large competitors, such as Toshiba, Siemens, Hewlett-Packard, Beckman Instruments, and Abbot Laboratories, were all billion-dollar-plus companies having large, highly knowledgeable sales forces, huge R&D budgets, a broad product scope, and usually several critical patents. Where these companies did not have patent protection they competed on strong customer relationships. In fact, the market for some of these products had evolved to the point where the products were of similar quality, but customer relationships differentiated the better competitors in the market. In addition, after sales, service and support in the form of providing ancillary products and quick repair and replacement (i.e., within hours) was very important.

There were also numerous small companies in the medical equipment market. These generally worked through distributors and relied on patents, market focus, or specialization to protect themselves from the larger competitors.

Approximately seven years ago, executives at GT were grappling with the decision with what to do with medical products because the barriers to entry were high and increasing rapidly. Yet, they had not developed a medical business large enough or products distinctive enough to provide them with such barriers to entry. They considered divesting the business, but because it was not a business unto itself, selling it would be difficult. Another argument against selling it was that the market segment looked quite attractive, having a growth rate in excess of 20 percent annually.

exhibit 2   Partial List of Medical Specialities

• Surgery	• Immunology
• Radiology	• Neurology
• Pharmaceutical	• Oncology
• Cardiology	• Endocrinology
• Genetics	• Anesthesiology

exhibit 3   List of Medical Equipment Markets

• Cardiovascular devices	• Medical lasers
• Pacemakers and defibrillators	• Medical plastics
• Health care products and commodities	• Monitors and instrumentation
• Home testing and test kits	• Surgical instruments
• Biomaterials	• Clinical lab equipment and
• Medical imaging equipment	instrumentation

Fortunately, the decision was aided by the fact that a successful product developer in the medical sensing field, Keith Fischer, approached them with an idea. He suggested that GT fund the development of a new medical product, a blood analyzing sensor. GT was very enthusiastic about the idea, because it would potentially allow them to develop R&D capabilities, customer servicing capabilities, and sales and marketing abilities, based upon this product and its patent; then they could leverage these strengths as new products were developed.

Keith had developed the scientific basis for a sensing device while doing his Ph.D. at a California university. During these studies he realized the potential of a blood sugar sensor for diabetics. Therefore, he quit the program and began developing the device on his own. Relatives and several government business/research grants subsidized the development of the product. The resulting product gave a diabetic patient blood sugar results within seconds and without the messy chemical strips that were normally required. When the sensor was introduced it was well received and within weeks a major medical equipment distributor purchased the rights to the technology.

Keith, out of a job and still only in his late 20s, had become a relatively wealthy man due to the success of this prior sensor (estimated wealth $5 million to $10 million). Yet, since he was a scientist at heart, his inventive drive had merely been whetted. Thus, Keith began considering extensions to his previous sensor work. When the idea of a complete blood analysis sensor evolved, he approached GT, where he proceeded to convince them of the merits of his new idea. He talked avidly of how a more general blood chemical analysis device should and could be developed.

GT managers saw the enormous potential of this product. Presently, chemical blood analysis took up to two weeks; even in the case of emergencies it often took several hours. The problem with present approaches was that before every analysis a variety of fresh chemicals had to be mixed to calibrate the electronic sensing device. Then other chemicals had to be used to treat the blood prior to having the machine analyze the results. This procedure always had to be done by highly qualified lab technicians to ensure accurate results. Furthermore, many small hospitals and most doctors' clinics did not have the facilities or the technicians to perform such an analysis. Therefore, a sensor that could produce blood analysis results quickly, with no expensive calibration procedure, would be an enormous product breakthrough.

All those who listened to Keith loved his idea, and GT immediately offered him a position as manager of a new R&D unit. The research unit's initial objective would be to develop the blood sensing device. Then, when the product reached the commercial stage, a Medical Equipment Division would be formed. GT made its desires clear to Keith: they wanted to become a leading medical equipment supplier, and they saw this as a rare opportunity to build such a business.

Keith accepted the position because he felt that GT's technological resources could allow him to develop a variety of new medical sensing devices. Furthermore, the position satisfied his immediate desire to be a scientist, yet also gave him the opportunity to evolve into a variety of management roles, if he so desired in the future. Keith clearly felt that GT was offering him a future with enormous potential.

The project started with tremendous enthusiasm. Keith hired a core of top scientists. Lab and office space was established, and for three years they methodically researched and developed various components of the complex sensing device. Compared to the blood sugar sensor, this device was many times more complex because of the variety of tests that had to be performed simultaneously and the complex relationships between blood gases, solubles, and organics. The research was extremely difficult and at times the team ran into problems that initially appeared to be insurmountable. However, with time and patience, research led them to work-around solutions.

During the fourth year progress slowed dramatically. In particular, the team could not find a comprehensive solution to a sensor calibration problem. The sensor would not stay calibrated between tests. The dilemma was that it had to be very sensitive to measure the various blood chemicals, yet this sensitivity also created calibration problems. The most minute environmental changes affected the results. To use the sensor in its present state meant that a lab technician would have to recalibrate it after each test. They had tried a wide variety of solutions, most of them extremely expensive and complex, but each solution had only corrected parts of the problem and combining them had proven to be impossible—at least so far.

At this point in time, Keith was beginning to feel some pressure for progress. Clearly the problem was a major hurdle for the project and team. To this end, Keith had begun considering a wide variety of potential new avenues of research. And after much research, Keith felt a solution might lie in an ion battery technology used in a new CO2 gas analyzer for liquids. Approximately a month before he had met the inventor of the analyzer, Dr. Jim Slatery, at a conference. The two immediately struck up a scientific kinship, and after several visits and long discussions Keith began to be quite excited about the potential for this new avenue of research. However, the other researchers, all having Ph.D.s, were quite reticent about this technical approach. First, it would mean throwing out much of the prior work and starting afresh. Second, the team would have to acquire new skills in a scientific area called gas-liquid ion battery technology. This would take both time and money. And finally, the other researchers pointed out that this technology had a long research history that was littered with failures and difficulties. Even the simplest of gas-liquid ion batteries were extremely difficult to keep stable for any length of time, and manufacturing them had proven to be virtually impossible. The complex battery that would be required in this case was unheard of in such research.

In the meantime, top management in the Electrical Equipment Sector was becoming worried about the lack of progress. The project was consuming almost $4 million annually in operating costs, and the accumulated capital costs were not being amortized against any profits. To date they had sunk over $25 million into the project and it seemed to be stalled. Based on these concerns, they decided to bring a professional manager into the project. Bob Shepard volunteered for the position and he was quickly promoted into it.

Bob realized that if he were successful it would have a very positive effect on his career in the company. However, he also realized that marketing and business management was his forte, not management of R&D projects. Therefore, he accepted the position on the condition that the unit be turned into a division, and marketing, sales, and service groups that represented medical products in other divisions be rolled into the new division within three months. This would give the division a chance to build some revenue and profit streams to offset the ongoing research costs.

Upon taking the job, Bob met with research staff to try and understand the depths of the project problems. He quickly realized that the project was incurring a variety of difficulties all stemming from the calibration problem. For example, the underlying disagreement over a solution to the calibration problem was factionalizing the group into two camps, particularly because Keith, their leader, was absent most of the time, either visiting Dr. Slatery or devoting time to researching the new technology—nobody in fact knew which. Bob realized he had to provide some direction to the project or it might disintegrate. He also understood that the team could not afford to pursue both lines of research, because one line of research was expensive enough. Therefore, he decided to defuse the issue by having a democratic vote. The vote was held and the solid-state approach won over the gas-liquid ion battery.

Within the day Keith handed in his resignation. He felt not only betrayed by GT and its initial commitment to fund his research, but also slighted that they would bring in a manager who knew nothing about the technology and allow that person to make unilateral decisions without consulting him.

PUSHING FOR A COMMERCIAL PRODUCT

Bob asked the remaining team to concentrate on two objectives: develop a prototype, and then attempt to incrementally improve the calibration problem. His first objective of developing a prototype was aimed at getting a marketable product out as soon as possible. He felt that they could compete initially with the machine in its present state, because, although it had calibration problems, it was smaller than competitive machines. They could then introduce sensor upgrades as the calibration problem was solved. He saw it as largely a marketing problem.

The product came onto the market halfway through 1992. The division spent a great deal on marketing, billing it as the newest technology of its kind in modern medicine. As shown in Exhibit 4, sales increased slowly during the remainder of 1992. However, in 1993 sales responded to various marketing initiatives and promotional deals. Clearly the market had become interested in the "revolutionary solid state" device. Revenues increased by 30 percent. The downside to this was that considerable expenses were being incurred because of a higher-than-expected return rate and a high service cost associated with the product. Customers were calling service technicians because the product required a slightly different approach to calibration than previous equipment. In the meantime the research team was kept busy trying to fix the calibration problem. They had made some improvements, but medical technicians in the labs still had to calibrate it after each test to ensure accuracy.

The real surprise was in 1994 when the market, despite greater marketing and promotional efforts, was not particularly taken with the new product. The problem appeared to be that technicians were familiar with the calibration process used on the old

exhibit 4   Income Statement for Medical Equipment Division (in thousands $)

	1990*	1991*	1992*	1993	Actual 1994	Budgeted 1994
Revenue	10,238	11,671	14,006	21,008	19,958	25,210
Manufacturing costs	6,040	7,003	8,123	13,235	13,571	15,126
Gross margin	4,198	4,669	5,882	7,773	6,387	10,084
Research expenses	4,097	4,192	4,687	5,007	4,256	3,942
Administration expenses	245	269	487	483	479	490
Sales and marketing	789	907	1,815	2,722	3,539	3,362
Depreciation	788	946	1,135	1,362	1,634	1,961
Profit	(1,721)	(1,645)	(2,241)	(1,801)	(3,521)	329

*The first three years' income statements are consolidated to account for the various activities that were integrated into the Medical Equipment Division in 1992. It does not include the $25 million development costs for the sensor. This is the report that top managers in the Electrical Equipment Division were looking at when they met with Bob.

machines. The new machines, although smaller and very slightly cheaper, required a new calibration technique that required additional training and different chemicals. Thus, medical managers had a hard time justifying the cost benefits of the product, and technicians and doctors were not actively supporting the product because it did not provide them with any key advantage.

The majority of technicians appeared to be telling their managers that they would rather stick with old technology because it made the process easier and more consistent for them. However, there was also a more subtle issue, revealed to Bob when he attended a sales convention: a medical technician quite bluntly stated that "he was not about to support the decision to buy a product that was ultimately aimed at putting him out of business." Due to these problems, sales actually declined slightly in 1994 and compared to Bob's budgeted breakeven situation, the division was faced with a very large loss.

KEITH'S ENDEAVOURS DURING THIS TIME

Bob had heard that, since his departure from GT two years ago, Keith had been doing research on gas-liquid ion battery technology with Dr. Jim Slatery. Then approximately three months ago, Bob heard they had incorporated as International Medical Systems (IMcd) Inc., and were trying to get funding to build a blood chemical sensor prototype. Bob approached his boss and got the authority to talk to Keith in an attempt to investigate how the research was going, and possibly discuss GT's involvement as venture partner. Keith refused to meet with Bob. Then just last week Bob heard they had successfully developed a blood chemical sensor prototype based on the gas-liquid ion battery technology. Furthermore, they were trying to go public—that is, sell stock on the stock markets through an Initial Private Offering (IPO)—with the hopes of introducing a product in six months to a year.

At this point Bob realized he had to do something. He felt that Keith had clearly violated any anti-competition contracts that he had signed while at GT, something that all employees were asked to sign when they joined. Furthermore, IMed's new product could contain a variety of technologies that Keith had developed while at GT. Again this could be deemed as stealing GT's knowledge assets that they had paid him to work on and develop. GT also required employees to sign a proprietary knowledge and technology agreement giving them the rights to any technology developed in their labs.

Bob also understood that his business division would be in big trouble if IMed's product were successful, as rumours suggested it might be, if and when it came to market. Furthermore, what would his superiors say when they found out that the product they had been counting on had walked out from under their noses—possibly due to Bob's decision to intervene in the project?

Bob's superiors were already concerned with the financial trends in the new division. The unit was consuming valuable resources, yet it was not progressing, financially, in the way they had hoped. Furthermore, completion of the technological breakthrough that they had sought to develop in their labs was nowhere in sight.

Two days ago, Bob had felt he had to start considering some alternative actions. In particular, he felt that he had to consider the legal implications of Keith leaving the company with assets and technological secrets, and using them to IMed's benefit. Bob went back and asked for Keith's prior personnel file. He found that the confidentiality and proprietary information and technology agreements were missing from the file, as were the five-year anti-competition contract. This concerned him enormously, and the lawyers told him that this would make prosecution more difficult—although not impossible as long as the necessary evidence was there. He also talked to several of the scientists that had been involved in the research efforts during Keith's employment, but they did not know whether Keith had taken research knowledge from GT because they did not know what technologies were in IMed's product. Bob instructed one of the junior scientists to begin cataloguing the technologies and patents that had been worked on during Keith's employment.

The lawyers had indicated to Bob that a fast decision was essential if any action was to be taken. Bob decided that he had to make a decision before the end of the day.

case 13 The Saga of the Sinking and Raising of the Irving Whale

On Tuesday, September 8, 1970, the front page headline of *The Chronicle-Herald,* Halifax, Nova Scotia daily newspaper, read:

> "Oil Barge Goes Down in Gulf With Cargo"

The barge was the *Irving Whale* which had sunk in the Gulf of St. Lawrence off the coast of Prince Edward Island the night before. The cargo was 4,297 tonnes of Bunker C fuel oil. Media coverage of the accident continued for several days and was closely followed by Robert Greene, a sales representative for a food wholesaling company. He was alarmed that owners of the barge, Irving Oil Company of Saint John, New Brunswick, appeared reluctant to take responsibility for the sinking or the cargo trapped in the barge. The possibility of pollution was great and would be disasterous for fishing and other industries in the Gulf of St. Lawrence.

Robert felt that the company should take responsibility for the fuel oil and prevent a pollution problem. He was a customer of Irving gasoline stations, and the company's lack of social sensitivity troubled him. As a protest, he returned his Irving Oil credit card with a note expressing his concern. The return of the card and the note were not acknowledged. For the next twenty-seven years, Robert followed the coverage of the sinking, the pollution that occurred, and the efforts to raise the barge.

THE SINKING

The Irving Oil Company built the *Irving Whale* in 1966 as a supply barge to service coastal areas of the Atlantic Canada. The barge was 82.3 metres long, 17.7 metres wide, and 5 metres deep, about the size of a hockey rink. On Saturday, September 5, 1970, at 8:45 AM the *Irving Whale* left Halifax harbour on its way to Bathurst, New Brunswick. Witnesses stated that the barge was riding low in the water under the weight of 4,297 tonnes (4,773,967 litres) of Bunker C fuel oil. It was unmanned and being towed by the *Irving Maple*, a tug captained by John Anstey.

IVEY

Richard Ivey School of Business
The University of Western Ontario

The *Irving Whale* made good time travelling at about 8 knots and reached the Canso Causeway at approximately 1:00 PM Sunday. The remainder of its trip would take it north around the eastern edge of PEI and into an area notorious for sudden storms and rough seas. Captain Anstey reached this area in the early morning of September 7 where he reported winds gusting at 32 knots and choppy seas.

Around 7 AM that morning Anstey radioed Halifax to report a vibration on the towrope probably being caused by the rough weather. He decided to increase the length of the tow on the *Irving Whale* from 321 metres to 482 metres. This decision was made because of concern that the stormy seas might bring the barge too close to the *Irving Maple* and endanger the crew. Immediately after lengthening the tow, the *Irving Whale*'s stern submerged and the ship assumed a 45 degree angle. For almost four hours Anstey sent continuous reports to Halifax updating the Coast Guard of the slowly sinking barge. Finally, at 10:23 AM on September 7, 60 kilometres (37.5 miles) north of PEI, the *Irving Whale* sank in 67 metres of water. It was still attached to the *Irving Maple* by the towrope Captain Anstey had refused to disconnect. The seabed where the barge sank was sandy with few rocks or debris and it was believed little damage had been sustained. The sinking of the *Irving Whale* represented one more oil spill in a list of incidents in and around Canadian waters.

1970 *OPERATION OIL* REPORT

Canada's East Coast was a common location for oil spills due to its proximity to major oil shipping lanes. The *Irving Whale* sinking was not the first time an oil tanker had met with trouble in the region. Eight months earlier, the Liberian tanker *Arrow*, a ship more than twice the size of the *Irving Whale*, had run aground in Chadabucto Bay, Nova Scotia, spilling 15,960 tonnes of oil. This was one of the most devastating spills in Canada, severely affecting the surrounding wildlife and environment. Ironically, during the *Arrow* spill, the *Irving Whale* had been called in to assist in the cleanup and salvage. There were at least a dozen oil spills on the East Coast each year from both ships and land-based sources. In the oil industry spills were not uncommon. So much oil was moved annually that losses of even 1-2% would cause substantial pollution. The size and frequency of spills had increased the public's awareness and concern about oil pollution in Canada.

Internationally, the world's attention to the problems of oil pollution had peaked after the 1967 sinking of the *Torrey Canyon*. The *Torrey Canyon* was one of the world's largest oil tankers in service at the time. It ran aground off England, leaking nearly 120,000 tonnes of oil into the English Channel and onto beaches of France. This event more than any other focused global concerns on the transportation of pollutants and became a catalyst for numerous multinational agreements. These included the 1969 Bonn agreement on the "Pollution of the North Sea by Oil" and the 1969 Brussels pact on the "Civil Liability Convention" for oil pollution damage (CLC). The sinking of the *Arrow* in Canada brought home the *Torrey Canyon* episode and the dangers inherent with petroleum transportation. As a direct result of the *Arrow* spill, the federal government set up a task force to study the issue of oil pollution.

The task force, *Operation Oil*, found that worldwide nearly 600,000 tonnes of oil were spilled annually, equivalent to nearly 33 ships the size of the *Arrow*. Within Canada the report observed that federal and provincial legislation on oil pollution was nearly nonexistent. The report determined that fines present in the industry amounted to little more than a slap on the wrist of violators. Companies making millions of dollars daily were being fined, in some cases, $2,000 to $3,000 for illegal dumping and leakage. *Operation Oil* also noted that during its five-month tenure at least eleven other spills were reported on Canada's East Coast. These included a 13,650 litre spill off Newfoundland's Burin Peninsula by the *Irving Whale* in February 1970. In September of that same year *Operation Oil* submitted its first report to the federal minister of transportation, Don Jamieson, adamantly calling for a complete overhaul of regulations and practices governing the oil industry.

RESPONSE TO THE SINKING

A week after receiving the *Operation Oil* report, Transportation Minister Jamieson received the first account of the sinking of the *Irving Whale*. The seriousness of the situation prompted the Minister to immediately fly to the scene. He observed a 400 km^2 oil slick moving in the direction of the Isle-de-Madeleine, PEI and northern Nova Scotia. With the *Arrow* incident still fresh in the mind of government, Jamieson acted swiftly by calling in the Coast Guard and the military in the hopes that the spill could be contained before doing serious damage.

The cleanup crews were allowed unlimited use of government funds to combat the spill. Troops were put on standby in Canadian Forces Base Gagetown in case shifting winds aggravated the situation. An aircraft hanger in PEI was used to store tonnes of peat moss to soak up oil that reached land and beaches. As part of the main assault on the slick, numerous government-owned ships and equipment were moved to the site, including a 500 metre boom flown in from British Columbia. A submersible two-man diving bell was employed so that vents leaking oil on the sunken barge could be welded shut to prevent further contamination. The 1970 cleanup of oil from the *Irving Whale* used approximately $3,600,000 of federal funds.

At Irving Oil Limited, president and founder of the company K.C. Irving, flew back to Canada from the United States soon after receiving word of the sinking. When asked by *The Moncton Transcript* a day after the sinking who was responsible for the clean up, K.C. Irving replied "we're hoping there will be nothing to cleanup." In an interview with *The Daily Gleaner* that same day he stated that his company was "prepared to take any action to keep pollution at a minimum" and that the Irving Company was watching the situation "like a cat watching a mouse."

A spokesman for Atlantic Towing Limited, a subsidiary of Irving Oil Inc., had commented that "for the sinking to happen, there would have to be a failure of some sort." Later reports confirmed doors that should have been kept shut were open and, coupled with high seas, resulted in the *Irving Whale* being swamped. Irving Oil Limited received insurance to compensate for their loss of property. While the insurance companies paid for the *Irving Whale,* they never did claim ownership of it.

The government continued to receive updates of the oil leakage spill that had now reached the Isle-de-Madeleine and stained 80 km of shoreline essential to tourism and fishing. As the costs of the cleanup continued to rise, Transportation Minister Jamieson was under increasing pressure to recoup the expenses to the public purse. His attempts to force compensation from the Irving Company were futile. Irving claimed that the sinking had occurred outside Canada's 12-mile territorial zone and the government did not have jurisdiction over the incident or any right to effect penalties. The oil company knew that the laws regarding the leakage were on its side and the government was nearly powerless to impose sanctions. Frustrated by the magnitude of recent oil spills and the lack of accountability in the industry, the minister of transportation used the numerous spills as a basis for tabling new legislation in the House of Commons. In a press conference held five days after the *Irving Whale* sinking, Jamieson outlined the legislation aimed at improving government control over oil industry pollution.

The legislation included an attempt to reach international agreement on expanding Canada's jurisdictional zone so that more polluters could be held responsible when a spill took place near national boundaries. Limits on the use of unmanned vessels and the amount of pollutant carried aboard a ship would also be enforced to curb the occurrence of future leakage incidents. A fund was created to defray the costs of cleaning up oil pollution and would be financed through a levy on all oil shipped through Canadian waters. In a statement to *The Chronicle-Herald* Jamieson stated that the *Irving Whale* incident had been the impetus for much of the legislation. He noted the methods employed to transport the barge were "a pretty hazardous way of moving noxious cargoes of this kind around."

THE SHIP-SOURCE OIL POLLUTION FUND (SOPF)

Most of Jamieson's proposed legislation was passed and included the creation of the 1973 Maritime Pollution Claims Fund (MPCF). The MPCF was set up to compensate persons or businesses affected by oil pollution and was funded through a $0.15 per tonne levy on oil shipped through Canadian waters. Some 65 contributors including oil companies, power generating authorities, pulp and paper manufacturers, chemical plants and other heavy industries made payments to the MPCF. Although Canada was a signatory to many international funds such as the International Oil Pollution Compensation Fund (IOPC Fund), obtaining payments from these funds was difficult due to the number of countries governing them. The MPCF gave Canada its own source and control of monies for oil pollution expenses. On September 1, 1976, the Department of Transportation stopped the $0.15 per tonne levy when the MPCF had reached almost $35 million. On April 24, 1989, amendments were made to the *Canada Shipping Act* and the MPCF was renamed the Ship-source Oil Pollution Fund (SOPF).

The mandate of the SOPF (Exhibit A) was to meet the claims of any person(s) affected by oil pollution. It was to provide funds for cleanup and preventative action when necessary. In addition it would be used to cover claims exceeding the funds available under international agreements or those not meeting international fund criteria. Claims outside territorial waters but within national fishing zones also fell under SOPF payment criteria. The SOPF was designed so that the party responsible for pollution would compensate the fund for payments made allowing the Fund to replenish itself. Exceptions to this policy were made when the polluter could not be found or when the amount owed exceeded what the polluter could afford. Whether or not the SOPF could be applied to costs incurred in the *Irving Whale* disaster would depend on an interpretation of the respective legislation.

exhibit A   The Ship-Source Oil Pollution Fund

The following are highlights of the conventions governing the SOPF:

1. The SOPF is liable to pay claims for oil pollution damage or anticipated damage at any place in Canada or in Canadian waters caused by the discharge of oil from a ship.

11.0 *The classes of claims for which the Fund may be liable are:*

11.1 Claims for oil pollution damage.

11.2 Claims for costs and expenses of oil spill clean up including the cost of preventative measures.

11.3 Claims for oil pollution damage where the identity of the ship that caused the discharge cannot be established.

11.3 Claims by persons in the fishing industry of loss of income.

12.0 *Claims*

12.1 Any person may file a claim with the Administrator of the SOPF for oil pollution damage.

12.2 The Administrator has a duty to investigate and assess the claim and for these purposes, has powers to summon witnesses and to obtain documents.

12.3 The Administrator may either make an offer or decline the claim. The unsatisfied claimant may appeal the Administrator's decision to the Federal Court of Canada within 60 days.

12.4 When the Administrator pays a claim, the Fund is subrogated to the rights of the claimant and is obligated to recover the amount of compensation paid to claimants from the shipowner or any other person liable. As a consequence, the Administrator is empowered to commence an action *in rem* against the ship (or against the proceeds of sale, if the ship has been sold) to obtain security to protect the SOPF in the event that no other security is provided. The Administrator is entitled to obtain security either prior to or after receiving a claim and has been subrogated to the rights of the claimant but the action can only be continued *after* the Administrator has paid claims.

12.5 The Administrator has a duty to take reasonable measures to recover from the owner of the ship, the IOPC Fund or any other person the compensation paid to claimants from the SOPF. This includes the right to prove a claim against the Shipowners Limitation Fund set up under the 1969 Civil Liability Convention.

12.8 A Response Organization as defined in the Act has no direct claim against the SOPF but may have a claim for unsatisfied costs and expenses after exhausting its right of recovery against the shipowner, etc.

Source: Ship-Source Oil Pollution Fund, *Fact Sheet,* April 1997.

AFTER THE SINKING

Public interest in the *Irving Whale* had faded by the late 1970s as other events occupied newspaper headlines. The barge continued to sit at the bottom of the Gulf of St. Lawrence slowly leaking Bunker C oil at a rate of 80 litres a day. Continuous Coast Guard surveillance of the site along with reports from passing vessels recorded any sightings of oil in the area. All the while behind the scenes government officials sought a solution to the polluting wreck. In his book, *Above the Law*, Paul Polango states that although there were plans to raise the *Irving Whale* in the mid-seventies, none was technologically sound enough to guarantee a safe cleanup.

The *Irving Whale* remained on the St. Lawrence seabed until a combination of events rekindled public interest in the barge. In 1989 the supertanker *Kiriki* broke up north of the Canary Islands, leaking a devastating 79,800 tonnes of oil that reached as far as Morocco. In that same year the *Exxon Valdez* leaked 42,000 tonnes of Bunker C when it ran aground just off Alaska. This well-publicized event resulted in the pollution of more than 3,600 km^2 of shoreline and the deaths of thousands of seabirds and other animals. The *Kiriki* and *Exxon Valdez* incidents brought the issue of oil pollution to the forefront of public attention again.

NEW GOVERNMENT INITIATIVES

The Canadian government responded by commissioning a report on the status of oil pollution in Canada. The *1990 Public Review Panel on Tanker Safety and Marine Response Capability* authored by David Brander-Smith (Exhibit B) made 107 recommendations

exhibit B   1990 Public Review Panel on Tanker Safety and Marine Spills Response Capability

Highlights of Major Findings:

The capability to respond effectively to a spill of any significant magnitude does not presently exist anywhere in Canada.

Each year, based on current levels of tanker traffic, Canada can expect over 100 small oil spills, about 10 moderate spills and at least one major spill. A catastrophic spill (over 10,000 tonnes), for which we are wholly unprepared, can be expected once every 15 years.

The risk of spills is highest in eastern Canada, particularly Newfoundland. Placentia Bay is considered by many to be the most likely place in Canada for a major spill.

Canada's tanker fleet is old and in need of replacement. The estimated life span of a tanker is 20 years, but Canadian tankers are on average older than that.

The Coast Guard's investigative and prosecution efforts are seriously inadequate and do little to deter polluters. Indeed, the chances of polluters being caught are small; of being caught and prosecuted even smaller. If polluters are prosecuted, the chances of being found guilty are minuscule and, if found guilty, fines are paltry. In the few instances where prosecutions are attempted and prove successful, fines are unacceptably meagre: between 1979 and 1988, the average fine under the *Canada Shipping Act* was $4,700.

Industry relies inordinately upon the Coast Guard for spill response. To date, the amount it has invested in spill-related R&D and in response equipment has not been commensurate with the risks inherent in the loading, discharging and transportation of its products.

Source: David Brander-Smith, Denise Therrien and Stan Tobin. *"Protecting our water," Final Report of the Canada Public Review Panel on Tanker Safety and Marine Spills Response Capability,* September 1990, pp. i-ii.

to the government. Included was a proposal to examine the wreck of the *Irving Whale* and "a decision made as to whether or not to remove the oil and/or raise the barge." The government tendered two assessments on the status of the *Irving Whale* to private salvage firms. The reports made suggestions concerning the barge that ranged from pumping out the oil and raising the vessel to covering the barge with sand and concrete and leaving it on the ocean floor.

As the *Irving Whale* incident once again moved into the public eye, parties affected by the incident increased pressure on the government to make a decision on how the pollution from the vessel would be handled. All agreed that something had to be done to reduce the potential harm to the region's resources. Environmentalists were claiming that endangered beluga whales in the St. Lawrence would be in jeopardy if a substantial oil leak occurred. Representatives of the $300 million annual lobster and snow crab fisheries were concerned that reports about their product being tainted with Bunker C oil would effectively shut down their industry. The tourism sector of the region, worth approximately $100 million annually, survived on its ability to attract visitors to pristine shores, birds and plant life. It was concerned that all of this would be at risk if the *Irving Whale* split open, releasing the rest of its cargo. No decision was made until 1994 when the federal government announced the *Irving Whale* and its cargo would be raised during the summer of 1995.

THE SALVAGE OPTIONS

The alternatives available for salvaging the *Irving Whale* caused public debate. The lift option proposed by the government involved the placement of two ships outfitted with cranes over the wreckage. Cables attached to the cranes would be passed under the bow and stern of the *Irving Whale* and the cranes would then bring the barge to a few metres beneath the ocean surface. Once there another barge would be placed under the *Irving Whale* and then refloated, lifting the *Irving Whale* above the surface. Many people thought that attempting to raise the barge and cargo together was reckless. The effects of 26 years of seawater would have weakened the ship's hull and the stress might cause it to break, releasing the remainder of the *Irving Whale*'s cargo. The government disagreed, saying it was confident that this would not happen and cited recent ultrasound tests showing the wear on the ship's hull had been less than 5% of its thickness.

Another option for salvaging the *Irving Whale* was to first pump out the oil contained in it before it was raised. This method had been used successfully with the *Arrow* and offered the government an alternative that was safer than lifting because it decreased the riskiness of leakage from a weak hull. Pumping out the barge though would prove difficult as the cold ocean temperatures had congealed the *Irving Whale*'s cargo to a point that the oil in it now had the consistency of taffy and heating would be required. In addition the pumping option would demand a substantial time period of more than a month to complete. In an area where sudden wind gusts were common, the government did not want a prolonged operation. The extra considerations that had to be put in place for this option would double the 1994-estimated $10-million cost of the lift alternative.

Covering the barge with sand and concrete was also considered. The depth of the barge meant that any sand or concrete used would be unaffected by tidal currents and other marine conditions. The covering option also provided the lowest cost of all the options. Accepting this option though meant that the problem may come back to haunt the government in the future.

There was also the opinion that nothing should be done. Some people thought that the sea had suffered pollution accidents many times the size of the *Irving Whale* with no apparent effect on marine life or coastal areas. The *Irving Whale*'s cargo was only about one-eleventh the size of the *Exxon Valdez* and the discharge rate was a mere 80 litres per day. Attempting to salvage the barge was an unnecessary waste of money and could do more harm than good. Mother Nature had taken care of itself before and would do so again. The government's attempt at salvaging the *Irving Whale* was simply a ploy at grabbing headlines without giving thought to the consequences. The salvage and who would pay had become secondary for many to environmental concerns.

However, some groups thought the cost of the salvage was important, especially since the decision as to who would pay had yet to be determined. Greenpeace, a well-known international environmentalist group, told *The Globe and Mail* on June 12, 1996, that the Irving Oil Company should bear the total cost of the salvage effort. Greenpeace indicated their interpretation of the *Canada Fisheries Act* proved that ownership of the barge was not important for determining who was liable. This was despite a claim by Irving Oil that the company no longer owned the barge. The *Act*, in the opinion of Greenpeace, only needed the presence of fish in the water, the presence of a pollutant in that same water and the party responsible for releasing the pollutant. Greenpeace stated that its investigation showed the company responsible for fines of $300,000 daily for a maximum two-year period. Greenpeace was of the opinion it was a corporate problem and not a concern of the Canadian taxpayers. As they put it, "It's the *Irving Whale*, not the *Canada Whale*." On August 24, 1995, *The Globe and Mail* had written its own editorial stating that the Irving Company should pay for the salvage and "should not try to escape its civic and ethical (if not legal) responsibility." As attention on the *Irving Whale* incident increased, so did the focus on the Irving Oil Company.

THE IRVING COMPANY

All along, the original owners of the *Irving Whale*, Irving Oil Company Limited, had attempted to distance themselves from the issue. The events surrounding the Irving Whale were not the first controversy the company had faced in its 46-year history and would probably not be the last. The successful family-run empire had shown its ability to handle past difficulties, and this was an important reason for the growth and endurance of the $7.5 billion company. By 1990 the wealth and influence of the Irving Company and its subsidiaries had reached every corner of Atlantic Canada.

The jewel in the Irving crown was its Saint John oil refinery, capable of turning out 250,000 barrels of crude a day. Part of this product was used to supply Irving-owned bus lines and truck companies with the bulk reserved for more than 3,000 Irving gas stations. Irving Pulp and Paper had ownership or lease to more than 3.4 million acres of timberland in New Brunswick alone and its newsprint mill put out as much as 1,000 tonnes a day. The timber also supplied Kent Hardware stores and prefabricated house building projects owned by Irving.

Along with selling personal computers, life insurance, and frozen food, the Irving conglomerate owned all four of New Brunswick's English newspapers and one of the province's main television stations. To service this expanse of companies, Irving Limited acquired its own fleet of airplanes along with a fleet of ships thought to outnumber the Canadian navy. In *Citizens Irving,* John DeMont observes that a New Brunswick resident would have trouble not doing business with the Irving Company on a daily basis. The Irving Company employed one in every five New Brunswick residents, not including government workers.

K.C. Irving, the company's hardworking patriarch, started Irving Oil in his home town of Bouctouche, New Brunswick with a few gas pumps competing against huge national corporations. He was renowned for his shrewd bargaining, problem-solving skills, and keen sense of memory about every facet of the business. It was said that K.C. could remember the names of every one of his employees even when they numbered in the hundreds and he would never ask a worker to do something he would not do himself. His company paid competitive wages and expected nothing less than complete employee loyalty.

K.C. Irving was known for his aggressive business practices. It was not uncommon, for example, for the Irving Company to undercut prices or buy out businesses in order to reduce competition. When the oil company passed to K.C.'s three sons, they continued to run it using the hands-on management style of their father. They regularly entered the thousands of Irving gas stations scattered across eastern North America at infrequent intervals to quiz the franchise owner on such things as placing Irving-made items closer to the cash register or inspecting the bathrooms for cleanliness. They demanded total satisfaction for the customer. There was even a rumour that the opening of a truck stop was once delayed for a number of days until regular-sized bars of soap were put into the shower facilities because the Irvings felt that was what truckers wanted.

Despite its ability to service customers while running a sound business, the Irving Company continually found itself involved in controversies. In *The Globe and Mail*, March 22, 1994, Chris Morris reported that the company often brought these disputes on itself. On one occasion the company threatened to move a prefab home building plant from New Brunswick to Nova Scotia when the company could not get agreement from workers on wage concessions. Workers and family were appalled by the decision, especially since the plant was located in Bouctouche, K.C.'s hometown. Irving even went so far as to accept applications from 400 Nova Scotians near the proposed location of the new plant. Eventually these workers were told the move would not happen as NB plant workers had accepted the concessions. Another time the managing editor of two Irving-owned newspapers was "reassigned" when the company was dissatisfied with the slant of stories being printed. In later newspaper reports the managing editor stated that she wanted to make it clear she had not been "reassigned," but had, in fact, been fired. The Irvings were strong-willed and decisive in their business dealings.

THE IRVING COMPANY POSITION

The *Irving Whale* sinking was another controversy that had hurt the public image of the company. Some consumers had begun a boycott of Irving products in PEI over concerns about the effects the pollution from the *Irving Whale* would have on their tourism and lobster industries. Across Canada the debate over who was responsible for the *Irving Whale* continued in newspaper editorials. The Irving Company maintained that it was not legally responsible and would not pay. Irving cited at least three legal reasons for its stance:

- In an interview with *The Financial Post* in November 1993 the company had said that the ship was "the property of the Canadian government." While a court ruling has never been made on this point, it would seem that Canadian shipping laws at the time of the sinking supported this view inasmuch that when the barge sank, its charter was revoked, removing Irving's ownership of it. John O'Connor, a Quebec lawyer and expert in marine law recalled the government having purchased the ship off the Irvings for $1 in the 1970's. This has never been proven to be true or false.

- Since the barge sank in international waters, Canada did not have legal authority to hold Irving responsible. It was not until at least 1977 that Canada had drawn the line from Cape Breton, Nova Scotia to Port-au-Basque, Newfoundland to claim sovereignty over the entire Gulf of St. Lawrence. Before that time the area in which the *Irving Whale* had sunk was international and Irving was not liable to any country.

- *The Canada Shipping Act* definition of a ship had not been amended until 1987 to include "shipwreck," making owners responsible for costs of a polluting vessel. Unless the government were willing to make its laws and jurisdiction retroactive Irving saw no way it could be held responsible.

Besides the legal reasons, Irving also stated that its company's contributions to the Ship-source Oil Pollution Fund had more than covered the costs of the salvage. On July 17, 1996, Irving placed advertisements in Atlantic Canada newspapers with the heading "Raising the Whale: Oil Industry Fund Should Pay." The advertisement stated, that the fund contained over $247 million, entirely made up of contributions from the oil industry. Irving calculated that the value of its part of the Fund totalled at least $45 million dollars, more than enough to compensate any costs incurred. In its opinion the *Irving Whale* salvage was an excellent example of why the Fund was originally started, and the money from it, not unlike an insurance policy, should be used to cover the costs. The advertisement stated that despite reports that Canadian taxpayers would have to bear the costs of raising the Whale, there was no need for Canadian taxpayers to pay any costs.

In addition, the Irving Company had contributed to the salvage by agreeing to take the *Irving Whale* off the government's hands and pay for cleaning the barge. The government had resolved to hand over the ship to Irving to defray the estimated $2 million dollar cost of removing the oil and marine life build-up on the barge. The Irving Company insisted that it was not making any money off the transfer and was in fact losing. The estimated market value of the barge was about $200,000, while the cargo it contained was worth between $10,000 and $500,000 depending on the condition and amount of the Bunker C oil aboard. Irving had offered to take the barge as its group of companies owned a shipyard and oil refinery that could clean up the ship more cheaply than any other party. Irving said it would refloat the Whale and use it for hauling lumber amongst its various family-owned mills and plants. Along with the cleanup costs, Irvings also offered approximately $3 million worth of its own equipment and expertise to assist with the salvage effort.

SALVAGE DELAYS

As the date neared for the 1995 lifting of the *Irving Whale* to the surface, operational delays were increasing salvage costs. The salvage plan called for cables to be passed under the sunken barge so it could be hoisted to the surface, but divers were having difficulty tunnelling under the barge in order to place the slings. The weather was not co-operating, and the salvage team was having trouble finding an appropriate weather window in which to operate.

These obstacles were minor compared to a last-minute turn of events. On July 6, just days before the salvage, the federal government announced that two weeks prior Irving Oil had told them that in addition to the presence of Bunker C fuel the *Irving Whale* was thought to contain 7.2 tonnes of polychlorinated biphenyl (PCBs). PCBs had been banned in Canada since 1977, and the *Environmental Protection Act* (EPA) of 1988 legislated companies to immediately report any incidence of PCBs. The company had claimed that it was not sure if the PCBs were present or not, but wanted to notify the government in case they were. It was known that during routine cleaning of ships in the Irving fleet months before, PCBs from a similar barge had been removed. The government decided that with this new information it was even more important that the *Irving Whale* be lifted as soon as possible to avoid further contamination. The environmental assessments had been thoroughly supportive of a lift, and the operation should continue.

One environmental group from Quebec disagreed. Daniel Green of the Société pour Vaincre la Pollution (SVP) went to court arguing that the revelation of PCBs was reason enough to stop the salvage effort, as PCBs had not been accounted for in the original environmental assessment. The court agreed and issued an injunction halting the salvage for a three-month period. As a result the operation was denied a viable weather window for 1995 to complete its task. SVP also stated that the Irving company should be held liable for noncompliance of reporting the PCBs as dictated in the EPA of 1988, seven years before the actual revelation.

Deputy Prime Minister Sheila Copps later admitted that the government had missed a reference to the PCBs in a 1992 environmental assessment because it had been listed in the report under its trade name, Monsanto MGS 295S. Still not satisfied, Green's group stated that if the government did not act, SVP would proceed to lay charges as a private citizen. As the pressure increased to make the Irving Company responsible, Copps was being prompted to act. She announced that preliminary evidence showed there may have been a violation of the law and five months after the revelation called in the RCMP and Justice Department for a formal investigation. Questions were asked about how much the government and Irving actually knew and when they knew it. A month later the investigation was stopped due to insufficient evidence. The delays caused the loss of a full year in the salvage effort and cost nearly $17 million in operational spending during the summer of 1995.

SUMMER 1996

During the following summer the government was again faced with court challenges on the salvage. This time the government had been very thorough in its assessment, and the courts granted the Canadian Coast Guard permission to proceed. By mid-July ships had been maneuvered into position after the remnants of Hurricane Bertha had stalled the exercise. The weather forecast was for clear skies and light winds, and

Captain Bill Dancer, project supervisor with the Coast Guard, was optimistic that the *Irving Whale* would reach the surface within the next week. On July 30, 1996, the barge was successfully raised.

Who would pay for raising the barge was not resolved. Costs were estimated at $34 million, well above the 1994 assessment of $10 million. In Canada it was common practice for the SOPF to pay for the cost associated with accidents involving oil-laden tankers. This often meant compensating fishers for destroyed equipment or providing funds to the Canadian Coast Guard to clean up a spill. Payments were made to claimants after an investigation confirmed that oil had been the source of the pollution. In order to replenish its funds the SOPF used the Canadian principle of "polluter pays." This meant that the company or party responsible for the spill paid into the SOPF any money the Fund had paid to claimants. It was only when the polluter could not be identified or could not afford to pay that the Fund assumed the entire cost.

In the case of the *Irving Whale* the Canadian government had been unsuccessfully petitioning the Irving Oil Company for payment of the salvage. The Irving Company was the original owner of the *Irving Whale*, but claimed it was not responsible for the costs associated with the recovery operation. Sheila Copps, the deputy prime minister, had said that the SOPF represented a "creative way" to pay for the salvage while making Irving accountable for costs incurred.

Twenty-six years had passed since Robert Greene had read about the sinking of the *Irving Whale*. He was now the general manager of the wholesale company and was even more aware of social responsibilities being demanded of business. He wondered if the Irving Oil Company was responsible for any costs incurred in the lift. Could the company have been justified in its decision not to pay the government for the sinking? Should Irving have to pay the entire cost and was it responsible for the delay and subsequent expenses? What about the fact that the Irving Company had offered services and equipment in the lift totalling $3 million? In addition to this there was also the consideration that the company had taken responsibility for cleaning up the barge, a cost Irving now estimated to be around $20 million due to the additional costs of PCB disposal. Finally, Greene questioned the validity of Irving's claim that money it donated to the SOPF be used for the cleanup.

During the 26-year period, Robert had not purchased anything at an Irving service station. He wondered what could influence the company to become more socially responsible.

case 14 General Motors Defense

If you don't like change, you're going to like irrelevance a lot less.

General Eric K. Shinseki
Chief of Staff, U.S. Army

In October 1999, the recently appointed Chief of Staff of the U.S. Army, Eric Shinseki, held a meeting with eight leading defense industry manufacturers. During this meeting, he went into detail regarding his vision for the type of equipment he felt the U.S. Army currently lacked. Of particular importance was the need for a new, medium-weight armored vehicle. Contrary to past practice, Shinseki planned to award a multibillion-dollar contract within only 11 months. Any manufacturers wishing to be considered were asked to have a prototype ready by May 2000 for testing at Fort Knox.

Among the industry leaders present was Bill Pettipas, executive director of General Motors Defense in London, Ontario. Pettipas was convinced that an existing GM-developed platform was ideal for the army's needs. At issue however was how to pursue the contract. Should they go it alone, or joint venture (JV)? A possible JV partner was General Dynamics. General Dynamics was interested in exploring the possibility of a joint venture with GM for the contract, but made it clear that they would also submit a bid on their own. For Pettipas, the question was, which arrangement would result in the greatest likelihood of success?

GENERAL MOTORS

General Motors (GM), the world's largest vehicle manufacturer, designed, built and marketed cars and trucks worldwide. GM had been the global automotive sales leader since 1931 and employed about 355,000 people. GM cars and trucks were sold under

Richard Ivey School of Business
The University of Western Ontario

the following brands: Buick, Cadillac, Chevrolet, GMC, Pontiac, Saab, Saturn and Oldsmobile. GM also produced cars through its Holden, Opel, and Vauxhall units. Non-automotive operations included Hughes Electronics (DIRECTV), Allison Transmission (heavy-duty automatic transmissions), GM Locomotive (locomotives, diesel engines), and GM Defense (light armored vehicles). GM had a 49 per cent stake in Isuzu Motors and 20 per cent stakes in Fuji Heavy Industries (Subaru), Suzuki Motor, and Fiat Auto (Alfa Romeo, Lancia). Their GMAC subsidiary provided financing.

GENERAL MOTORS DEFENSE

In 1999, less than one per cent of GM's total annual revenues of $167 billion came from defense. General Motors (GM) had a rich history of military vehicle production, having supplied its first vehicle for the U.S. military during the First World War and continuing to supply vehicles ever since. After the Second World War, GM continued to produce armored vehicles, including the M551 Sheridan light tank.

General Motors Defense (GMD), London, Ontario, was a group of GM-owned business units engaged in the design, production and support of light armored vehicles, their supporting turret systems and a wide range of commercially based military trucks. GMD consisted of research, design and manufacturing facilities in London, Ontario; Goleta, California; Troy, Michigan; Adelaide, Australia; and Kreuzlingen, Switzerland. GMD also had offices in Washington, D.C.; Ottawa, Canada; and Canberra, Australia for government relations.

GMD was a proven manufacturer of quality armored vehicles and turrets. Its two main platforms were light armored vehicle (LAV) and Piranha. GMD supplied these platforms to numerous military forces in over 15 countries, including Australia, Canada, Saudi Arabia, Switzerland and the United States. These vehicles had been used in operations in Bosnia, Somalia, Cyprus, Panama, Haiti and as part of Operation Desert Storm. GMD was also well equipped for providing services in project/program management, subcontract management and product support. GMD's North American chassis operation had a large plant, which was composed of a manufacturing and test facility covering 34,000 square metres, a 1.2 kilometre banked test track and a 310,000 litre swim tank. GMD's advanced production technologies included computer-driven laser cutters, rectilinear robotic welders, CAD-CAM systems and flexible machining centres.

GMD's weapons and electronics operation also had proven experience in the design, manufacture and integration of turrets and fire control systems. GMD was recognized globally as the leading manufacturer in multipurpose lightweight turrets. GMD had recently acquired MOWAG of Switzerland. MOWAG was in charge of the design and development of the Piranha family of vehicles as well as the HMMWV-based Eagle 4×4. GMD greatly benefited from MOWAG's innovative design and world-class manufacturing techniques. GMD had also recently acquired Military Trucks in Detroit, Michigan. Military Trucks sold commercially based GM vehicles adapted for use by military customers. Lastly, General Motors Defense Australia (GMDA) was a centre of production for LAV-25 turret systems and was responsible for Asia-Pacific markets.

Main Platform of GM Defense

GMD's LAVs were produced in a number of different variants. These included mortar, anti-tank, ambulance, logistic, personnel carrier, recovery, air defense, command and control, electronic warfare, mobile repair, reconnaissance and assault guns with 90 millimetre and 105 millimetre main guns.

In the LAV family, the LAV III had been recently developed and was being put in production. The LAV III was a four-wheel drive, (selective eight-wheel drive) armored vehicle weighing approximately 18 tons. It was designed and manufactured with a common hull configuration and was well suited for multiple capability, joint and combined arms formations. The LAV III could attain speeds of 62 miles per hour (100 kilometres per hour) on the highway and had a maximum range of 312 miles. The basic infantry carrier vehicle (ICV) had armor that protected the two-man crew and seven on-board soldiers from machine gun bullets, mortar and artillery fragments. The LAV III ICV variant included configurations such as the reconnaissance, anti-tank guided missile and medical evacuation vehicles, as well as carriers for mortars, engineer squads, command groups, reconnaissance and fire support teams. The Mobile Gun System variant included General Dynamics Land Systems 105 millimetre cannon mounted in a low-profile turret integrated on the General Motors LAV III chassis.

Bill Pettipas

In 1982, Bill Pettipas worked at Canadian Forces headquarters in Ottawa. During his 28 years in the Canadian military, he had once served as commanding officer of the Royal Canadian Regiment in London, Ontario. When he was sent to Norway to look at a missile system in 1982, he was approached by a General Motors executive who offered him a sales position at GMD. Pettipas rejected the offer, but a year later, he changed his mind, retired from the Canadian Forces and joined GMD.

Pettipas started his new job as a domestic sales manager. His responsibility was to sell to the Canadian military. However, Pettipas struggled as he made the transition from the armed forces to business. He did not initially know much about the business, but he soon determined that people did not buy a product as much as they did the personality that sold it. He believed that sales success was based on building relationships, even in an industry in which sales revolved around a $700,000 to $2-million armored vehicle. Not only did Pettipas focus on the final customer, the soldier, but he also really believed in his products.

In the 1980s, GM Diesel (the former name of GM Defense) grew at a slow, steady pace as small contracts gave way to larger ones, including deals with Australia, New Zealand, Saudi Arabia and the U.S. marines. There were, however, hard times in the late 1980s when GM attempted to sell its Diesel division. It turned out there were no takers that were acceptable to General Motors. The division itself then made a bid for greater freedom and won, and convinced GM Corporation to allow the GM Locomotive Group, of which GM Defense was a part, to have its own strategy board, giving it more autonomy for conducting its business.

Early in 1999, Bill Kienapple, former executive director of GMD, handpicked Pettipas as his successor. Kienapple recognized the value of Pettipas's military background and charismatic leadership style. Kienapple believed that employees were very loyal to Pettipas and that Pettipas had a well-rounded understanding of the business and the customer. Pettipas could walk the GMD shop floor and call to just about everyone by name. Pettipas possessed vision and a keen ability to focus on the core of an issue. With common sense, he could get an idea of how to achieve his goals and then accomplish them through the power of personality.

THE U.S. ARMY

The U.S. Army was made up of 10 active duty divisions—six heavy divisions and four light divisions. The brigades, battalions and companies within a heavy division were organized around the conveyances—tanks or Bradley fighting vehicles—that take that unit to the fight. The brigades in a light division, such as the 82nd Airborne, were organized around infantry who parachute, march or helicopter to the fight.

The U.S. Army was well suited for the war it was designed to fight: a huge counter-strike against an invading Soviet army on the plains of Central Europe. The U.S. Army's institutional identity was reflected by its heavy pieces, especially the near-invincible Abrams tank, none of which was destroyed by the enemy in the 1991 Gulf War. The Abrams was first completed in 1980, and it had been a peerless war machine. It could kill enemy tanks at standoff range, beyond the reach of enemy fire. The Abrams could survive almost any strike because of its armor. It had a layer of metal protection so thick that the tank weighed 70 tons.

The Abrams was too big to be transported efficiently to the battlefield by air. The only means to transport the Abrams was by ship, a process that took weeks. Once the Abrams reached the battlefield, it guzzled a gallon of fuel per half mile travelled. Since a huge fuel supply followed the Abrams and other armored vehicles to war, it created a division's cumbersome logistic tail. Support units, such as those handling fuel, spare parts, and maintenance, made up more than 80 per cent of the heavy army's lift requirement, when getting itself to war. The material that had to be loaded, transported, unloaded and set up just to support the fighting was often discussed in terms of the tooth-to-tail ratio.

Among the U.S. military services, the army had 480,000 active members, compared to 375,000 in the navy, 359,000 in the air force, and 175,000 in the marines. The personnel budget allocated to the active army was 40 per cent more than the navy and the air force; the budget for the army was more than three times of that for the marines.

The U.S. Army was fragmented in terms of culture. Any plan to blend the light and heavy elements of the army would create a more common culture. The army valued its specialization. For example, a cadet at West Point chose his branch during his senior year at the academy. Each branch had a set of rituals and traditions. Thus, only a minority of those in the army saw transformation as something they needed to think about.

The U.S. Army's Equipment Need

During the 1990s, the U.S. Army faced missions that it did not welcome and found itself ill-equipped to perform. During the Cold War era, the U.S. Army knew exactly who the enemy was, how it would fight and where. Even though the U.S. Army's two main combat vehicles—the Abrams tank and the Bradley fighting vehicle—did not share a common chassis and each required its own logistics tail, the army managed to find ways to circumvent the problems. For the enormous logistic tail problem, the U.S. Army positioned fuel, spare parts and support material in the battlefield in advance. For the tank's weight problem, the U.S. Army reinforced the various European bridges the tanks would likely cross to engage the Soviet army.

However, the need for the transformation became apparent during and after the 1991 Gulf War. The desert war revealed two potentially disastrous flaws. The first was that the armored units could not quickly get to the battlefield. After the Iraqi army took

0073102849

ETAT DE LITEM A SUIVRE

MODERN COMPETITIVE STRATEGY
STATUS UPDATE TO FOLLOW
ETAT DE LITEM A SUIVRE

SUBTOTAL / TOTAL PARTIEL ---|

** Shipping charges and tax, if applicable, are not reflected on this document. **
** Please see your invoice for final pricing information. **

** Frais de transport et taxes, si applicables, ne sont pas inclus dans ce document **
** S.V.P. Veuillez vous référer à votre facture pour le montant exact. **

PRE

MESSAGES / INSTRUCTIONS SPECIALES:

THIS IS NOT AN INVOICE / CECI N'EST PAS UNE FACTURE

COMPLIMENTS OF / CE VOLUME VOUS EST OFFERT PAR VOTRE REPRESENTANT (E)
JENNIFER THORNE

for Land Power in the 21st Century," by Colonel D.A. Macgregor. Reimer believed that the drastic reorganization would make the U.S. Army leaner and more efficient. Even though Reimer distributed copies of the book to every general in the U.S. Army, he faced strong resistance from the senior officers.

In June of 1999, General Shinseki was appointed the U.S. Army's 34th Chief of Staff, and promised to reform the bulky U.S. Army, making it nimble as well as lethal. He wanted to create an army that would be flexible enough to perform peacekeeping missions or to fight an all-out war against Iraq and North Korea. Moving away from traditional, ponderous U.S. Army's tanks and armored vehicles, Shinseki proposed to bring whole new advanced systems and technologies into the army.

COMPETITORS TO GENERAL MOTORS DEFENSE

General Dynamics

General Dynamics (GD) was a leading defense company. GD operated in four areas: combat systems (tanks, amphibious assault vehicles and munitions), marine (warships and nuclear submarines), aerospace (business jets), and information systems and technology (command and control systems). It employed 43,000 people worldwide and had annual sales of $10 billion.

In 1952, GD had been established when its predecessor and current operating division, Electric Boat, had acquired the aircraft company Canadair Ltd. As a subsidiary, Electric Boat built nuclear-powered submarines (Seawolf, Ohio, Los Angeles classes). In 1982, GD added its combat systems business unit, General Dynamics Land Systems (GDLS). GDLS built the M1 tank and Abrams combat vehicle. In 1997, GD added an information systems and technology business unit, Advanced Technology Systems, and returned to the aerospace business with Gulfstream in 1999.

GD's corporate headquarters were located in Falls Church, Virginia, near Washington D.C. Government relations, international affairs, legal affairs and public relations, human resources and finance were among the functions managed by the headquarters staff. In particular, government relations served as the company's liaison with Congress and all branches and agencies of the U.S. federal government that bought or oversaw the procurement of GD's products and services. GD's international department represented the company's interests before the elements of the U.S. government responsible for defense trade policy and international arms and technology transfers. For most of the U.S. Department of Defense programs, General Dynamics had shared the market with United Defense. Representing the ground combat system of the United States, the signature product line of GD was the Abrams main battle tank; that of United Defense was the Bradley fighting vehicle.

General Dynamics Land System

General Dynamics Land System (GDLS) was a wholly owned subsidiary of General Dynamics based in Sterling Heights, Michigan. GDLS manufactured tracked and wheeled armored vehicles, as well as amphibious combat vehicles, for the U.S. Army, the U.S. Marine Corps, and international allies. In 1982, GDLS was formed after its parent company acquired and integrated Chrysler Corporation's defense operations.

GDLS's principal products were the U.S. Army's M1A2 Abrams SEP main battle tank, internationally recognized as the world's finest main battle tank, and the U.S. Marine Corps advanced amphibious assault vehicle (AAAV).

GDLS had delivered more than 8,500 Abrams main battle tanks to the U.S. Army and international allies. GDLS had been a great contributor in the U.S. Army's core programs: Abrams Tank, Future Combat System, Crusader, Future Scout and Cavalry System, Wolverine, and Fox programs. GDLS had worked in partnership with the U.S. Army on all of these programs to ensure its mission success.

GDLS employed 3,500 people in eight states and had annual sales that exceeded $1.1 billion. GDLS operated the United States' only main battle tank production facility in Lima, Ohio. In the other satellite plants, GDLS machined Abrams components. Recently, GDLS tried to develop more medium- and light-weight armored vehicle systems, using its proven record in engineering research, development and technological innovation in the defense industry. GDLS had a strong array of capabilities: precision machining, experience with steel and aluminum and special armor, product fabrication, assembly, technical training, total package fielding, manufacturing technical assistance, contract logistics support services, systems integration, combat systems development, electronic production and assembly, software development and prototype development. To enhance its capabilities, GDLS had acquired AV Technology in 1998 and Robotics Systems Technology in 1999.

United Defense

United Defense (UD) was a leader in the design, development and production of combat vehicles (the Bradley armored infantry vehicle), fire support equipment (self-propelled howitzers), combat support vehicles, weapons delivery systems (missile launchers, artillery systems) and amphibious assault vehicles. For several defense programs that represented critical elements of the U.S. military forces, UD had been a sole-source prime contractor. The U.S. government thus accounted for almost 80 per cent of sales. The board of United Defense included former Secretary of Defense Frank Carlucci and John M. Shalikashvili, former chairman of the Joint Chiefs of Staff. For the past 60 years, United Defense had produced more than 100,000 combat vehicles and 100,000 weapon systems in use by the U.S. Department of Defense and its international allies.

UD's Ground Systems Division produced the U.S. Army's primary armored infantry vehicle, the Bradley. Since United Defense had introduced its first Bradley fighting vehicle in 1981, the company had consistently improved the Bradley vehicles to meet and exceed the requirements of the changing battlefield. GD's Abrams, as a battle tank, was suited for fighting a war against an invading Soviet army on the plains of Central Europe. On the other hand, United Defense's Bradley, provided more nimble mobility, more lethal firepower and superior protection that gave it a fighting edge in the changing battlefield of the post-Cold War era.

THE CONTRACT PROPOSAL

Pettipas knew that the GMD's existing platform would be a perfect match with the transformation requirement of the U.S. Army. Nevertheless, he had to decide how to pursue the multibillion-dollar contract and do so within an incredibly short amount of time. He was contemplating whether GMD should go it alone or form a joint venture bid with another industry leader.

In anticipation of a possible program start, GMD had explored co-operating with GDLS in 1997 to pursue the Canadian Armored Combat Vehicle Program (ACV). Thus GD seemed a possible joint venture partner for the new U.S. Army contract. He had been informed that GDLS was also interested in exploring the possibility of a joint venture with GM for the contract.

The anticipated $600 million Canadian ACV Program was to develop and field a replacement for the Canadian army's nearly 200 Cougar vehicles. GMD in London, Ontario, was intended to be the prime contractor and provide the light armored vehicle chassis. GDLS would provide the 105 millimetre, two-man automated turret. Computing Devices Canada would provide the turret electronics and fire control software. GMD and GDLS implicitly agreed that GDLS would become the prime contractor if there were U.S. military programs, integrating the turret on GMD's chassis. The ACV program was considerably delayed by the Canadian Department of National Defense, and no contract was made available prior to the 1999 joint bid possibility. Pettipas realized that the previous joint effort with GDLS had created a close bond between GMD and GDLS.

Pettipas recalled that GDLS and Vickers Defense Systems (VDS) had formed another joint venture company 10 months ago. The joint venture company, Vehicle Armor and Armament Ltd (VAA Ltd), was established to progress work on the Future Scout and Cavalry System program (FSCS). Vickers Defense Systems was a subsidiary of Vickers PLC. Vickers PLC was a U.K.-based international engineering company, focusing on land defense systems and equipment, marine propulsion systems and motion control equipment, superalloys and components for the gas turbine and automotive industries.

Both GDLS and VDS were members of the SIKA International consortium. The consortium had been established to compete for the multibillion-dollar FSCS program, and it was later awarded a three-and-a-half year development contract. The consortium consisted of Lockheed Martin, British Aerospace, GDLS, Vickers Defense Systems, Computing Devices Company, Northrop Grumman, Pilkington Optronics, Shorts Missile Systems and Smiths Industries. The joint venture company was to provide the SIKA consortium with the most cost effective chassis and weapon system solutions for the FSCS requirement. By creating synergy among their engineering staffs to facilitate the best technical solution for the SIKA consortium, the joint venture, located in Newcastle, England, was responsible for the design and production of a demonstrator as well as providing other significant design and management support activities. GDLS joined with VDS to ensure that GDLS could maintain its leading positions in the design, development and manufacture of armored vehicles for the future. Recalling all these movements by GDLS, Pettipas began to wonder about the company's real (or hidden) intentions.

Perplexed, Pettipas had yet to decide which arrangement—solo or joint venture—would result in the greater likelihood of success. It wasn't helping to know that GD was planning to submit a bid on their own.

Reasons to Go Solo

In 1982, GMD made a sole bid for a vehicle program for the U.S. Marines, offering to provide nine different variants. It won the program, and was asked to provide six variants. Subsequently, GMD went into production and supplied 750 light armored vehicles. GMD won this program because it was technically capable of designing and manufacturing advanced 8×8 prototypes (with a licence from MOWAG), whereas its competitors made a bid with less advanced 6×6 prototypes. GMD's leading technologies on 8×8 light armored vehicles led to winning other programs as well. Through the U.S. Department of Defense, GMD supplied 1,117 light armored vehicles (with 10 different variants) to Saudi Arabia.

When GMD developed a teaming arrangement with GDLS for the proposed Canadian army program in 1997, the plan was for GM to share design and manufacturing responsibilities with GD. GMD would provide the light armored vehicle chassis, and GD the turret. In 1999, GMD acquired its long-time licensor, MOWAG. This greatly enhanced GMD's design and manufacturing capabilities for both light armored vehicle chassis and automated turrets.

With superior design and manufacturing capabilities, GMD focused on commonality across its product lines of light armored vehicles. GMD also emphasized its commonality with the U.S. Army support units. The U.S. Army had long suffered from logistics tail problems. The operational problems of the U.S. Army in the Gulf, Haiti, Bosnia, Somalia and Kosovo made it clear that the U.S. Army would need some commonality across its armored units. Somewhat surprisingly, the U.S. Army had not had major programs to improve commonality in the last 20 years.

Even though Pettipas believed that GMD's 8×8 light armored vehicles were technically competitive and would provide significant benefits to the U.S. Army, he was concerned about their relatively high prices. Notwithstanding this, he did not want to compete on price. He did not want to trade inferior low-priced products for soldiers' lives on the battlefield.

If GMD made a sole bid for the Brigade Combat Team (BCT) program, it would not have to worry about co-ordination problems with partners. More importantly, GMD might face even more serious problems if it formed a joint venture with GD. Since proprietary data and knowledge would have to be disseminated down to lower levels for manufacturing processes, GMD would have no other choice but to share some proprietary information with a joint venture partner.

Pettipas knew that GD would make its own bid for 6×6 prototypes. He was not very concerned about GD's bid because he saw little chance for them to win the program with what he believed to be inferior vehicles. However, a serious problem might occur if the joint venture proposal won the BCT program. Even though GD, at the time, was behind GMD in terms of technologies for 8×8 light armored vehicles, it could certainly enhance its 8×8 capabilities through learning processes in the proposed joint venture. In the worst case, GMD might breed a future competitor by forming a GMD-GD joint venture. In the longer term, it could create a potentially disastrous outcome that could never be reversed. Pettipas was concerned: What if GD caught up on GM's design and manufacturing capabilities right after the end of the proposed joint venture, and made its own bid for 8×8 light armored vehicles in future programs?

Reasons to Form a Joint Venture

If GMD and General Dynamics formed a joint venture, General Dynamics might add value through the contribution of its mobile gun systems (MGS) that would be installed on turrets of light armored vehicles. In 1997, GMD joined with General Dynamics and Computing Devices Canada (CDC) for the proposed Canadian ACV Program. At that time, CDC provided the turret electronics and fire control software. Recently, General

Dynamics had acquired CDC (renamed General Dynamics Canada) and enhanced its technologies on MGS. To save in-house development costs, the MGS for GMD's light armored vehicles was being outsourced from General Dynamics Canada.

Pettipas also considered the merits of partnering with United Defense. He felt however that General Dynamics was a better fit than United Defense, in every aspect. GMD focused on commonality across its product lines. He thus believed that General Dynamics would be a better candidate for a joint venture because GMD not only shared the manufacturing processes of Canadian combat vehicles with General Dynamics in 1997 but also it outsourced MGS from General Dynamics Canada. Besides, United Defense was not a public firm. Even though United Defense had strong connections with the U.S. government (George Bush Sr. was on the board), there were some rumors that United Defense might be sold to another competitor (possibly to General Dynamics) or it might be broken up. Considering that there was consolidation underway between the major European players, Pettipas would not hesitate in choosing General Dynamics as a partner, if he decided to form a joint venture for the BCT program.

Even though Pettipas was confident that GMD (with a sole bid) would have no problem in winning the BCT program on technical grounds, he was not quite sure about the political front. If GMD were to make a sole bid, it would have to compete against two major players. General Dynamics and United Defense were in fact the only players in the U.S. armored tanks/vehicles industry, and they thus had significant political power regarding U.S. Army programs, relative to all foreign competitors. Both General Dynamics and United Defense engaged in heavy lobbying activities through their strong Government Relations departments. Pettipas reflected on a common practice in the U.S. defense industry—'kill the program.'

'KILL THE PROGRAM'

It was a common practice in the U.S. defense industry for firms to try and kill any program in which they could not compete, or for any program in which they did compete but lost. The logic was that by seeing the cancellation of programs, the funds from the cancelled programs would be available for new programs in which they would have opportunities. Numerous existing programs could be cancelled to fund a major new program. Thus, even if a contractor won a multibillion-dollar program for delivering orders for multiple years, that party could not be sure that this contract would continue with the U.S. military due to this industry-specific practice.

Although the U.S. military sometimes cancelled programs, they did not necessarily face hefty penalties at the time of cancellation. Because of uncertain environments in the U.S. defense industry, contractors usually hedged against any possibility of cancelled programs by amortizing non-recurring expenses (or contingent penalties) into their development costs. Factoring the chance of cancellation into the price of the early-delivered vehicles was a common industry practice agreed upon both by the U.S. military and contractors. There was also a straightforward way to pay penalties for cancelled programs. However, the former was more commonly used in the industry.

Pettipas wondered whether GM might need a U.S. partner for political reasons when bidding for the BCT program, or for political assistance from the U.S. partner after winning the program, so as to keep the program rolling. He thought about winning the program with a sole bid. He envisioned GM would be against two major

U.S. competitors if it won with a sole bid, and both would presumably be lobbying heavily for the program's cancellation.

General Dynamic's Solo Bid

General Dymanics clarified that it would make a sole bid for the BCT program with its 6×6 prototypes. General Dynamics Land Systems aimed for the BCT program with a low-cost approach. Since General Dynamics licensed 6×6 technologies from an Austrian engineering company, it intended to fully exploit its resources and capabilities by bidding its prototype. Even though 6×6 light armored vehicles were technically inferior to 8×8 ones, General Dynamics felt they had a great chance of winning the program due to its price attractiveness. With a license from the Austrian company, General Dynamics Land Systems had supplied its 6×6 light armored vehicles to Kuwait, and made a bid for the Polish army program.

A few years earlier, General Dynamics and United Defense had competed head to head for the U.S. Marine program—advanced amphibious assault vehicle (AAAV). Historically, United Defense had supplied medium-sized amphibious vehicles to the U.S. military because of its superior technologies for the medium-sized armored vehicles (thanks to the Bradley family). However, for the U.S. Marine AAAV program, General Dynamics won the contract.

case 15 Planet Starbucks (A)

> You get more than the finest coffee when you visit Starbucks. You get great people, first-rate music, a comfortable and upbeat meeting place, and sound advice on brewing excellent coffee at home. At home you're part of a family. At work you're part of a company. And somewhere in between there's a place where you can sit back and be yourself. That's what a Starbucks store is to many of its customers—a kind of "third place" where they can escape, reflect, read, chat or listen.
>
> 1995 Annual Report, Starbucks Corporation

> During the World Trade Organization talks in November 1999, protesters flooded Seattle's streets; and among their targets was Starbucks, a symbol, to them, of free-market capitalism run amok, another multinational out to blanket the earth. Amid the crowds of protesters and riot police were black-masked anarchists who trashed the store, leaving its windows smashed and its tasteful green-and-white decor smelling of tear gas instead of espresso. Says an angry Schultz: "It's hurtful. I think people are ill-informed. It's very difficult to protest against a can of Coke, a bottle of Pepsi, or a can of Folgers. Starbucks is both this ubiquitous brand and a place where you can go and break a window."
>
> "Planet Starbucks," *Business Week*, September 9, 2002, p. 100.

Ubiquitous—that was the term often applied to Starbucks. It had indeed become omnipresent within the United States and Canada throughout the 1990s. Now the company—and its founder, Howard Shultz—had set its sights on the global marketplace. Howard Schultz had stepped down as Chief Executive Officer and President in 2000 and taken on the title with associated duties of Chief Global Strategist (he remained Chairman of the Board). Between 1999 and 2002, the company averaged sales growth of over 25% per annum, and despite the recession wracking the global economy, 2003 was expected to show the same rapid growth. But the North American coffee markets were quickly reaching saturation. Howard Schultz and Starbucks knew that if Starbucks was to continue to meet the market's expectations for growth, the global marketplace would have to support it. By 2003, Starbucks had become the growing target of the antiglobalist movement, and many questioned its ability to successfully expand the U.S.-based business model to the global marketplace.

Richard Ivey School of Business
The University of Western Ontario

STARBUCKS HISTORY AND ORIGINS

Starbucks was founded in Seattle by Gerald Baldwin, Gordon Bowker, and Ziev Siegl in 1971 as a gourmet coffee bean roaster and distributor. The Starbucks name was a combination of Seattle's past, the Starbo mining camp of the nineteenth century and the first mate's name in *Moby Dick*, the classic American novel of whaling on the open seas. In 1982, Howard Schultz joined the company as a member of their marketing team. After a visit to Italy, Schultz urged the partners to consider opening Espresso bars in conjunction with their coffee sales. In 1984, Starbucks opened its first Espresso bar, a small corner of the company's downtown Seattle Starbucks store, to rave reviews. Although Schultz urged the company to expand the Espresso bar line, the controlling partners, now Baldwin and Bowker, were unwilling to enter what they considered the fast-food business, wishing to focus on the coffee-roasting niche market. The company had recently purchased Peet's Coffee and Tea, a Berkeley, California, coffee roaster and distributor, straining the company's management and financial capabilities. The partners wished to focus on these two main businesses.

Howard Schultz then left Starbucks and, actually with the financial backing of his former partners, opened *Il Giornale* in 1985, an espresso bar that sold coffee and assorted coffee beverages made exclusively with Starbucks' beans. Two years later, Schultz bought the former Seattle Starbucks company, six stores and roasting plant, for $3.8 million from Baldwin (who wished to focus on managing Peet's) and Bowker (who wished to cash out of the business). Schultz now was in control of Starbucks and with new investors, began building a global business which reached sales of $3.3 billion in 2002 and was acclaimed one of the top 100 growing global brands.

The Starbucks Concept

Howard Schultz's dream was to take the concept of the Italian—specifically Milan—espresso bar to every corner of every city block in the world. By the fall of 2002, the Starbucks business was a complex three-legged stool for global development: (1) retail coffee and assorted specialty items; (2) specialty sales; and (3) Frappuccino coffee drinks and specialty coffee ice creams sold through other retailers globally.

> **What We Are About.** Starbucks purchases and roasts high-quality whole bean coffees and sells them along with fresh, rich-brewed, Italian-style espresso beverages, a variety of pastries and confections, and coffee-related accessories and equipment—primarily through its company-operated retail stores. In addition to sales through its company-operated retail stores, Starbucks sells primarily whole bean coffees through a specialty sales group, a direct response business, supermarkets, and online at Starbucks.com. Additionally, Starbucks produces and sells bottled Frappuccino® coffee drinks and a line of premium ice creams through its joint venture partnerships, and offers a line of innovative premium teas produced by its wholly owned subsidiary, Tazo Tea Company. The Company's objective is to establish Starbucks as the most recognized and respected brand in the world.
>
> To achieve this goal, the Company plans to continue to rapidly expand its retail operations, grow its specialty sales and other operations, and selectively pursue opportunities to leverage the Starbucks brand through the introduction of new products and the development of new distribution channels.
>
> starbucks.com

Starbucks' initial public offering was in 1992 (NASDAQ: SBUX). The company had, however, broken new ground the previous year when it became the first privately held company in the United States to offer its employees a stock ownership plan. The plan, termed Bean Stock, offered shares to both full-time and part-time employees.

The company had seemingly re-energized the entire coffee industry. Although Starbucks itself made up a relatively minuscule percentage of the entire North American coffee industry, it had sparked the expansion of coffee cafes like itself, rejuvenated the traditional mass market coffee sellers, and expanded all facets of the industry as distributed through the traditional supermarket distribution system. This *Starbucks Effect*, as it was termed, was based on the perceived premium product's cachet extending to all of the collateral products, both complements and substitutes. In the case of Starbucks itself, the perceived premium was both in the product's quality and in the method of its delivery.

> First, every company must stand for something. Starbucks stood not only for good coffee, but specifically for the dark-roasted flavor profile that the founders were passionate about. That's what differentiated it and made it authentic.
>
> Second, you don't just give the customers what they ask for. If you offer them something they're not accustomed to, something so far superior that it takes a while to develop their palates, you can create a sense of discovery and excitement and loyalty that will bond them to you.
>
> Howard Schultz, *Pour Your Heart Into It*, Hyperion Press, 1997, p. 35.

THE STARBUCKS EXPERIENCE

The concept of Starbucks went far beyond being a coffeehouse or coffee brand. Emerging from Howard Schultz's original idea of an Italian Espresso coffee bar, it had evolved into its own Americanized version of a specialty coffee provider of coffee shop services. As described in the introductory quote from Howard Schultz, Starbucks based its customer's retail experience on high quality coffee, *arabica* bean-based coffee, but then surrounded the delivery of the coffee with specialty services and atmosphere.[1] Special pastries and selected music provided an atmosphere of both warmth and comfort.[2] Employees were trained to not only provide a wide array of advice on coffee selection and appropriateness to potential customer needs, but to engage the customer. The customer was to feel they were not at home, not at work, but "a third place."

The People

The maintenance and development of this quality experience required a strong organizational commitment. The decade of the 1990s saw Starbucks expand its talent pool on the most influential senior levels, with key additions contributing greatly to the evolution of the company's business lines. Howard Schultz began assembling an experienced team of professionals to drive Starbucks' growth.

---

[1]The traditional coffee sold by U.S. mass market brands like Folgers and Maxwell House was the lower grade and cheaper robusta bean.

[2]The experience itself had evolved. In his early attempts to reproduce the Italian coffee bar, Schultz had provided little seating with opera music. The seating was expanded and the music replaced, as American customers complained.

In 1989, Howard Behar, with more than 20 years in retail, joined the company as the director of store operations. Behar refocused much of the Starbucks development away from the pure product itself—coffee—to the consumer's experience in a Starbucks. Behar believed the core component of the experience was in quality of service. Starbucks' employees (termed *partners* by Starbucks) needed to be highly motivated to pay continuing attention to repeat customer needs. The company invested in extensive employee training, but this investment would be lost if the company could not retain its people. One of the biggest barriers to retention was, in turn, compensation and benefits, in which the service industry was notoriously deficient.

Starbucks' solution was to offer health care benefits to all employees who worked more than 20 hours per week. Although an expensive benefit to provide by industry standards, Behar argued that if employee retention were improved and quality of service preserved, it would more than pay for itself. The company followed this first instrumental move with the introduction of the employee stock ownership plan in 1991 (Bean Stock), which was intended to increase the ownership culture of store management. Howard Behar would eventually become President of North American operations.[3]

In 1990, Orin Smith joined the company as Chief Financial Officer and quickly filled the role of the company's right-brain to Howard Behar's left-brain. Smith had extensive experience in a number of organizations and consulting, and was a strong believer in process development. Where Behar had focused on the people, Smith focused his development efforts within Starbucks on the organizational processes which would support effective execution of strategies. Smith believed in strict organizational discipline, including careful use of the Starbucks brand, and insisted for many years on company-owned and operated stores, rather than the franchising common among most American retailers. Behar became the unofficial defender of the quality of the Starbucks brand. Orin Smith would eventually become President and Chief Executive Officer of Starbucks. As illustrated by Exhibit 1, the Starbucks experience was based on people.

The Supply Chain

The pursuit of premium quality also drove Starbucks back up the coffee supply chain. Coffee, although second only to petroleum in volume of global trading, was highly fragmented. It was estimated that a full one-third of the world's coffee farms were three acres or less in size. This typically resulted in a consolidation process which handed off coffee from farmer to collector, collector to miller, miller to exporter or broker, and finally to importer. In the past, the importer and brokers then sold coffee to the large mass-market coffee roasters and producers.

Starbucks wished to improve the quality and integrity of its coffee by working back up the supply chain to the actual growers. As a result, Starbucks refined its coffee quality while effectively bypassing much of the middle market. As Starbucks developed expertise and relationships with the coffee growers themselves, the company worked tirelessly to increase the quality of the *green coffee* (unroasted beans) purchased while taking cost out of its supply chain. This would eventually prove a point of exposure for Starbucks politically, but also position the firm for opportunities in sustainable economic initiatives with these growers.

---

[3]Behar had retired in 1999, but returned to the company on a full-time basis in 2001.

Howard Schultz continued to add key leaders in the business in the early 1990s—people who would continue to fill the gaps in the organization and solidify a corporate culture which was a difficult balance between entrepreneurship and disciplined growth. These decisions proved critical, as Starbucks embarked upon a massive expansion which would test the organization's capabilities.

Expansion

At McClintock Drive and Ray Road, you can walk out of a Starbucks, built into a grocery store lobby, and gaze across the parking lot—at a brand new Starbucks. With the retailer's rapid expansion, it isn't unusual to find multiple sites within a mile or two of each other. And although having two in the same parking lot certainly isn't the norm, it's something that does happen on occasion.

"2 Starbucks, 1 Lot," *Arizona Republic*, October 21, 2002, p. B5.

As Starbucks moved into a market, it focused on location. Providing ready access to consumer foot traffic, such as commuting routes, allowed Starbucks to place its third place directly between the other two places. Stores were located in pivotal positions for consumer recognition and access. Corner locations, the hallmark of the early store growth, provided high visibility and maximum exposure. As stores expanded in North America to more and more of the automobile-based cities, plentiful parking became critical to any store's accessibility.

The company was also admired and criticized for its market-swarming expansion techniques. As stores proliferated, Starbucks broke with many retail distribution traditions by in-filling, introducing stores which could not help but cannibalize existing store sales. This also led to the characterization of Starbucks as *ubiquitous*. With stores appearing across the street from existing stores, the firm did often actually appear to be everywhere you looked. The strategy, although not acknowledged officially, prevented competitor entry in established Starbucks markets through store proliferation. It had, however, led to a disquieting downward trend in sales per store. Between 1995 and 1998, Starbucks had averaged $0.69 million per store per year. Beginning in 1999, this revenue per store value had continuously declined, falling to $0.559 million per store in 2002.

The company was widely considered ruthless in its real estate practices. Practices included paying premiums over existing rental prices to push square footage prices up, retaining closed properties to prevent competitor entry, and generally aggressive property negotiations. The refusal to franchise allowed the firm to pursue real estate and store proliferation strategies which did not conflict with corporate goals; all stores were Starbucks-owned and operated, and therefore "turf" was not an issue.

Through the later 1980s and early 1990s, Starbucks focused expansion in the Pacific Northwest and California markets. Howard Schultz's expansion strategy revolved around establishing regional beachheads which the company needed to provide logistical support for stores, while maintaining quality. In 1993, the company entered the Washington, D.C. market, followed soon after in 1994 by Boston.[4] The Boston entry was through acquisition, buying out the Coffee Connection chain in the region. Beginning in late 1994, the company expanded rapidly to the major metropolitan areas of Minneapolis, New York,

---

[4]The choice of Washington, D.C. was a surprising choice to everyone but Starbucks' management team. The company had tracked closely the catalogue sales of Starbucks products in the early 1990s, identifying the Washington, D.C. area as an extremely strong market for Starbucks mail order products, and therefore a logical first step on the East Coast.

Atlanta, Dallas, and Houston. By the mid-1990s, Starbucks had stores in more than 40 states and was starting to look to the limitations of market saturation.

There were no hard and fast rules for store growth or saturation. Starbucks itself believed that only Seattle, with one store per 9,400 people, was actually at the saturation point. The island of Manhattan, with one store per 12,000 people, was still considerably below that point.

INTERNATIONAL EXPANSION

> "We remain highly respectful of the culture and traditions of the countries in which we do business," says Howard Schultz, chairman and chief global strategist. "We recognize that our success is not an entitlement, and we must continue to earn the trust and respect of customers every day."

Although the first Starbucks store outside the United States was opened in Vancouver, British Columbia in 1988, this was essentially a regional expansion—from Seattle outwards and northward in the Pacific Northwest—rather than an intended international expansion. Beginning in the mid-1990s, the company aggressively pursued true international expansion. Starbucks used two basic structures for international expansion—company-owned and licensing agreements—to move first across Asia (1996), the Middle East (1998), and finally Europe (2001) and Latin America (Mexico, 2002).[5]

The company had defied many of its critics with the growth and success of its international stores. Market analysts and critics had argued that Starbucks' premium prices, paper cups, and smoke-free cafes would not fit within traditional cultural practices in places like Tokyo and Vienna. Once again the chain proved the naysayers wrong by seemingly creating their own market and their own third-place experience in some of the largest coffee-consuming cultures in the world.[6]

Japan. Starbucks' true international expansion had begun in Japan in October 1995 with the formation of a joint venture (JV) with Sazaby, a Japanese retailer and distributor with its own chain of Afternoon Tea stores. Sazaby proved to be an excellent partner, with expertise in both retail beverages and real estate.

The JV had opened its first store in Ginza in 1996 and had flourished. By 2002, it had more than 250 stores nationwide, and projected more than 500 stores by 2003. Although average Japanese store sizes were half that of the United States, they averaged nearly twice the sales. The JV had proven so successful that it undertook an initial public offering in October 2001, the only unit within Starbucks' international network to be listed independently of the parent.

Sazaby was also the prototype of the qualities Starbucks looked for in potential business partners. Starbucks officially listed the following characteristics as desired in its international partners:[7]

● Shared values and corporate culture

---

[5]A third structure, company ownership, had been confined to the United Kingdom, Thailand, and Australia.

[6]According to the Coffee Research Institute, the 10 largest coffee importing countries for the decade of the 1990s were the United States (25.6% of global imports), Germany (14.2%), Japan (7.7%), France (7.5%), Italy (6.3%), Spain (3.8%), Holland (3.4%), the United Kingdom (3.4%), Canada (2.8%), and Sweden (2.2%). Note that these are importation statistics, and not consumption. Source: www.coffeeresearch.org/market/importations, accessed 10/6/02.

[7]www.starbucks.com/aboutus/international.asp, accessed on 9/28/02

- Strong multi-unit retail/restaurant experience
- Dedicated human resources
- Commitment to customer service
- Quality image
- Creative ability, local knowledge, and brand-building skills
- Strong financial resources.

China. With the opening of its first store in January 1999 in the World Trade Centre in Beijing, Starbucks added the People's Republic of China to its growing list. In the next three-and-a-half years, its footprint was expanded to 35 shops, focused in and about Beijing and Shanghai. The reception to Starbucks in a culture grounded in tea was remarkably successful. Although Starbucks was heavily criticized for opening an outlet in a souvenir shop in Beijing's Forbidden City in 2001, the shop flourished.

Europe. The company's entry into continental Europe had been anticipated for years, but with much trepidation. Europe's longstanding traditions of coffee consumption and independently owned and operated coffeehouses constituted an established market which was not considered open to American entry. Starting in Switzerland and Austria in 2001, the company then expanded into Spain, Germany, and Greece in 2002. Although many critics argued—as they had in Japan before—that local customers would not be attracted to smoke-free, paper-cup coffee consumption, the lines were long.

Each country of entry was evaluated in detail, including focus groups, quantitative market assessment, and detailed identification of appropriate business partners. As part of the expansion process, Starbucks brought all foreign managers to its Seattle offices for a rigorous 13-week training course in the Starbucks experience. By the end of 2002, Starbucks had 1,312 of its total 5,886 stores outside of the United States. The current plan was to open two international stores for every one new domestic store.

CORPORATE SOCIAL RESPONSIBILITY

Starbucks defines corporate social responsibility as conducting our business in ways that produce social, environmental, and economic benefits to the communities in which we operate. In the end, it means being responsible to our stakeholders.

There is growing recognition of the need for corporate accountability. Consumers are demanding more than "product" from their favorite brands. Employees are choosing to work for companies with strong values. Shareholders are more inclined to invest in businesses with outstanding corporate reputations. Quite simply, being socially responsible is not only the right thing to do; it can distinguish a company from its industry peers.

Corporate Social Responsibility Annual Report
Starbucks Coffee, Fiscal 2001, p. 3.

Starbucks had found itself, somewhat to its surprise, an early target of the anti-globalist movement. Like McDonald's before it, it appeared to be yet another American cultural imperialist, bringing a chain-store sameness to all countries everywhere. Like McDonald's, Starbucks found that its uniquely defined brand and experience did not have to conform to local cultural norms, but could exist alongside traditional practices, creating its own market and successfully altering some consumer behaviors.

Unlike McDonald's, however, Starbucks was the purveyor of a commodity, coffee, which was priced and sold on global markets. Coffee was sourced from hundreds of thousands of small growers in Central and South America, many of whom were severely impoverished by all global income and purchasing power standards. As coffee prices plummeted in the late 1990s, companies like Starbucks were criticized for both benefiting from lower-cost sourcing and for their unwillingness to help improve the economic conditions of the coffee growers themselves.

By 2001, Starbucks had implemented a multitude of programs to pursue its program for corporate social responsibility (CSR) and pursue sustainable economic development for the people in its supply chain. Although not wishing to own the supply chain, Starbucks' strategy was a complex combination of altered business practices in procurement, direct support to the coffee growers, and the formation of brands which would provide conduits for consumers wishing to support CSR initiatives. Exhibit 2 provides a brief overview of some of these programs.

Procurement

Coffee was traditionally bought and sold using *market pricing*, buying from wholesalers at a global market price—the so-called New York "C." Since Starbucks purchased only arabica bean premium-grade green coffee, it always paid a premium above New York "C." Both New York "C" prices and the premium, however, moved up and down with global market conditions. Traditional robusta bean purchases by mass-market labels were made on the wholesale markets through brokers and buyers.

Starbucks, however, preferred to purchase using *outright pricing*, in which the price was negotiated directly with small and medium-sized farmers, cutting out the segment of the supply chain which the wholesalers usually occupied. In principle, a greater proportion of the price went directly to the producers, assuring a higher return to the small farmer. In addition to the pricing structure, Starbucks was also attempting to break from traditional market practices of always buying in the cash market. As illustrated in Exhibit 3, the company was moving aggressively to purchase more and more of its coffee under long-term contract (3 to 5 years, on average), guaranteeing prices to growers over multiple crop years.

A long-term dilemma of coffee farmers was the lack of access to affordable credit. Farmers without adequate working capital financing were often forced to accept low prices for coffee from buyers—so-called *coyotes* in Central and South America—in relative desperation. In an effort to stop this financial exploitation, Starbucks initiated a number of loan guarantee programs in 2002 to provide pre-harvest and post-harvest financing for coffee farmers. As a result, Starbucks provided financing for more than 1.2 million pounds of coffee in 2002 (205 farmers received pre-harvest financing, 691 post-harvest financing).[8]

Direct Support

Starbucks was a regular and growing giver, supporting relief organizations such as CARE, the nonprofit international relief organization, as well as providing direct

---

[8]*Corporate Social Responsibility Annual Report*, Starbucks Coffee, Fiscal 2002, p. 8.

support to farmers and farm communities around the world.[9] For example, Starbucks had contributed $43,000 in 2001 to the construction of a health clinic and school in Guatemala and a health clinic in East Timor. The company was also providing aid in a variety of ways to the improvement of coffee processing facilities in a number of the countries of origin.

Conduit Brand Development

Much of the growing pressure on all multinational companies for sustainable development and social responsibility arose directly from consumer segments. In an effort to provide a direct conduit for these consumer demands, Starbucks had initiated a company program called *Commitment to Origins*, "dedicated to creating a sustainable growing environment in coffee originating countries." Under the program, Starbucks had introduced *Shade Grown Mexico* coffee, *Fair Trade Certified* coffee, and *Serena Organic Blend* coffee.

Shade Grown Mexico coffee was introduced in 1998 in partnership with Conservation International (CI), a nonprofit environmental organization. Coffee purchased by Starbucks from CI's Conservation Coffee Program was cultivated under the canopy of shade trees in origin countries. This practice was considered ecologically sound and helped support bio-diversity. *Shade Grown Mexico* coffee purchases had grown from 304,000 pounds in 2000 to 1.8 million pounds in 2002 (see Exhibit 4).[10] The *Shade Grown Mexico* coffee had been selectively introduced in Starbucks stores in North America and through online sales at starbucks.com.

Beginning in 2000, Starbucks began working with TransFair USA, a nonprofit organization which provided independent certification for all *Fair Trade* coffee in the United States.[11]

> The concept of *Fair Trade* addressed the question of the just distribution of the burdens and benefits of trade. The *Fair Trade* movement argues that when most of the customers' purchasing dollar goes to the retailer, the marketer, the wholesaler, and the speculator and very little goes to the laborer or the farmer, something is wrong with the mutual benefits of the exchanges, particularly when those who provide the product have earnings that do not even cover subsistence costs.[12]

Although Starbucks had introduced *Fair Trade* coffee in North American stores, and promoted it through various brochures and promotions ("Coffee of the Day" monthly), it continued to be heavily criticized for not expanding the program faster. *Fair Trade* coffee purchases also expanded rapidly, rising from 190,000 pounds in 2002 to more than 1.1 million pounds in 2002.

The third category of conduit brand development was Serena Organic Blend coffee. Organic coffee was grown without the use of synthetic pesticides, herbicides or

---

[9]Starbucks was one of CARE's largest North American corporate donors. Cumulative contributions to CARE by Starbucks over time totaled more than $2 million. Starbucks' work with CARE began in 1991.

[10]Starbucks also noted that growers of *Shade Grown Mexican* coffee received price premiums of 60% over local coffee prices in fiscal 2001.

[11]TransFair USA is associated with Equal Exchange, a *Fair Trade* organization promoting socially responsible business practices with coffee growers in Central and Latin America.

[12]John Kohls and Sandra L. Christensen, "The Business Responsibility for Wealth Distribution in a Globalized Political-Economy: Merging Moral Economics and Catholic Social Teaching," *Journal of Business Ethics*, February 2002, p. 12.

chemical fertilizers. Like *Shade Grown* coffee, *Organic Blend* was an environmental-sustainable development conduit. As illustrated in Exhibit 4, Starbucks' purchases of organic coffee had more than tripled between 2000 and 2002.

These product brand programs allowed consumers wishing to support these sustainable development initiatives to express their interest through purchasing—at a price.[13] All three coffees were roughly 20-25% more expensive compared to Starbucks' traditional blends (whole bean coffee sales).

GROWING PRESSURES

By the spring of 2003, Starbucks was at what many thought the pinnacle of its prospects.

- It was operating nearly 5,700 stores in 28 countries.

- It had made more than $215 million in profit on $3.29 billion in sales in 2002, and sales and profits were both expected to grow 25% in 2003.

- It was named by *Interbrand* one of the most recognizable global brands, although the company still spent less than $20 million per year in advertising.

- The New York "C" coffee prices remained at near-record lows, decreasing sourcing costs and increasing gross operating margins.

Starbucks was one of the few companies to continue rapid sales and earnings growth through the 2001-2002 period, and the company was continuing to expand international operations at a breakneck pace. But all was not aromatic in the Starbucks marketplace.

Service quality and employee motivation and retention were continuing issues. Although *barista* (the coffee brewers in Starbucks lingo) pay was still superior to other low-end wage jobs, rapid expansion was confronting the firm with employee fatigue. Store managers and employees were overworked and underpaid. Required overtime for store managers had only been eliminated in 2000 as a result of the settlement of a class action suit brought in California by disgruntled store managers.[14]

The limits to remaining expansion opportunities in North America were now in sight. Seattle, with a Starbucks store for every 9,400 people, was considered by the company the limit.[15] Manhattan, with 124 stores, or one store per 12,000 people, was considered still open to further development. But same-store sales in the United States, Canada, and even Japan were now beginning to show declines which persisted; in the past, in-filling store entry had caused only temporary same-store sales declines for the most part.

Although very aggressive in the eyes of many, the anti-globalization movement continued to focus much of its efforts on Starbucks. Plummeting coffee prices on world markets in 2001 and 2002 had led to more and more pressure on Starbucks to increase the

---

[13]Starbucks reported that buyers paid $1.26/lb. for non-organic green and $1.41/lb. for organic green in 2001, when New York "C" prices were hovering at roughly $0.50/pound. Although production costs varied significantly across countries and regions, coffee growers associations estimated average production costs to be $0.80/pound.

[14]In a highly publicized settlement, Starbucks had settled a class action suit in 2001 brought by store managers in California who complained the company refused to pay legally mandated overtime. Prior to the case, managers were required to sign affidavits upon hiring that they agreed to work 20 hours per week overtime without additional compensation.

[15] "Planet Starbucks," *BusinessWeek*, September 9, 2002, p. 101.

prices it paid to growers. Howard Shultz himself increasingly became the target of mail, fax, and e-mail campaigns to pressure Starbucks into more proactive policies for grower income support (see Exhibit 5). Although Starbucks had actively pursued a number of corporate social responsibility initiatives, it was accused of polishing its image more than truly working to improve the lives of those its existence depended upon: the coffee growers.

Rapid international expansion seemed to only magnify the growing pressures. As Starbucks moved into more and more countries, labor and real estate practices came under increasing scrutiny, as did its image as global imperialist. Wall Street looked on with a critical eye as the firm entered the global marketplace through joint ventures which assured the firm of less profits per store than in the domestic past. Earnings growth was sure to slow. The question grew as to how far and how fast the company could still go.

exhibit 1   Starbucks Mission Statement

Establish Starbucks as the premier purveyor of the finest coffee in the world while maintaining our uncompromising principles as we grow.

The following six principles will help us measure the appropriateness of our decisions:

1. Provide a great work environment and treat each other with respect and dignity.
2. Embrace diversity as an essential component in the way we do business.
3. Apply the highest standards of excellence to the purchasing, roasting, and fresh delivery of our coffee.
4. Develop enthusiastically satisfied customers all the time.
5. Contribute positively to our communities and our environment.
6. Recognize that profitability is essential to our future success.

Source: starbucks.com

exhibit 2   Starbucks' CSR Programs Focusing on Coffee Growers

exhibit 3   Starbucks Coffee Sourcing Practices, 2001-2002

	Percentage of Total Fiscal 2001	Coffee Purchased Fiscal 2002
Price Basis		
Market pricing (New York C-basis)	88%	26%
Outright pricing (negotiated)	12%	74%
Relationships		
Direct relationships (from farms and co-ops)	9%	32%
Indirect relationships (through wholesalers)	91%	68%
Purchase Terms		
Purchased under long-term contract	3%	36%
Purchased in cash market	97%	64%
Amounts by category are not mutually exclusive.		

Source: Corporate Social Responsibility Annual Report, Starbucks Coffee, Fiscal 2002, p. 6.

exhibit 4   Conduit Brand Coffee Purchases by Starbucks, 2000-2002

Conduit Brand	Pounds of Coffee Purchased 2000	2001	2002
Fair Trade Certified Coffee	190,000	653,000	1,100,000
Certified Organic Coffee	570,000	874,000	1,700,000
Conservation (Shade-Grown) Coffee	304,000	684,000	1,800,000
Volumes are by fiscal year. Certified Organic includes Organic Fair Trade and Organic Conservation (Shade-Grown) coffee. Amounts by category are not mutually exclusive.			

Source: Corporate Social Responsibility Annual Report, Starbucks Coffee, Fiscal 2002, p. 8.

exhibit 5   The "Starbucks Campaign"

Participate in the Organic Consumers Association "Global Week of Action against Starbucks," September 21-28.

In October 2001, Starbucks made a commitment to buy 1 million more pounds of Fair Trade coffee and brew Fair Trade coffee once a month. Don't let Starbucks stop there—Send a Free Fax to demand that Starbucks brew Fair Trade Coffee of the Day EVERY WEEK!

The coffee industry is in crisis. Coffee prices are at an all time low, remaining below $.50 since August with no increase in sight. This means that farmers are becoming even more impoverished, going further into debt and losing their land. Meanwhile, coffee companies such as Starbucks have not lowered consumer prices but are pocketing the difference, even taking into account the quality premiums in the specialty industry.

The Fair Trade Labeling Organizations International recently released figures that show a total production by groups on the Fair Trade Coffee Register of 165,000,000 pounds in year 2000, whereas total sales were only 30,000,000 pounds. This leaves an additional 135,000,000 pounds of Fair Trade coffee produced by cooperatives that are not receiving a Fair Trade price.

Source: Global Exchange, Global Economy, www.globalexchange.org/economy/coffee/starbucks accessed 10/6/02.

appendix 1   Starbucks Consolidated Statement of Earnings, 1998-2002 (millions of US$)

Income items	1998	1999	2000	2001	2002
Net revenues	$1,308.7	$1,686.8	$2,177.6	$2,649.0	$3,288.9
Retail	1,102.6	1,423.4	1,823.6	2,229.6	2,792.9
Specialty	206.1	263.4	354.0	419.4	496.0
Less cost of sales & occupancy costs	(578.5)	(747.6)	(961.9)	(1,112.8)	(1,350.0)
Gross operating income	730.2	939.2	1,215.7	1,536.2	1,938.9
Less store operating expenses	(418.5)	(543.6)	(704.9)	(875.5)	(1,121.1)
Less general & admin expenses	(77.6)	(89.7)	(110.2)	(151.4)	(202.2)
Less other operating expenses	(52.4)	(54.6)	(78.4)	(93.3)	(127.2)
Income from equity investees	-	3.2	20.3	28.6	35.8
EBITDA	181.8	254.5	342.5	444.6	524.3
EBITDA margin (%)	*13.9%*	*15.1%*	*15.7%*	*16.8%*	*15.9%*
Less depreciation & amortization	(72.5)	(97.8)	(130.2)	(163.5)	(205.6)
Operating income	109.2	156.7	212.3	281.1	318.7
Net interest income (expense)	7.1	7.3	7.1	10.8	9.3
Internet investment losses & other	-	-	(58.8)	(2.9)	13.4
Earnings before tax (EBT)	116.4	164.0	160.6	288.9	341.4
Less corporate income tax	(48.0)	(62.3)	(66.0)	(107.7)	(126.3)
Net income or earnings	68.4	101.7	94.6	181.2	215.1
Return on sales (%)	*5.2%*	*6.0%*	*4.3%*	*6.8%*	*6.5%*
Effective tax rate (%)	*41.2%*	*38.0%*	*41.1%*	*37.3%*	*37.0%*
Shares outstanding	358.5	363.7	376.3	380.0	385.6
Earnings per share (EPS)	$ 0.19	$ 0.28	$ 0.25	$ 0.48	$ 0.56
EPS growth rate	*11.4%*	*46.6%*	*−10.1%*	*89.8%*	*17.0%*

Source: Starbucks Coffee Company, Annual Report, 1999, 2000, 2001, 2002. EBITDA = Earnings before interest, taxes, depreciation and amortization.

appendix 2   Starbucks Consolidated Balance Sheet, 1998-2002 (millions of US$)

	1998	1999	2000	2001	2002
Assets					
Cash & cash equivalents	$ 123.5	$ 117.8	$ 132.2	$ 220.6	$ 402.2
Accounts receivable	51.0	47.6	76.4	90.4	97.6
Inventories	143.1	180.9	201.7	221.3	263.2
Prepaid expenses & other	19.7	40.2	48.0	61.7	84.6
Total current assets	$ 337.3	$ 386.5	$ 458.2	$ 593.9	$ 847.5
Investments in unconsolidated subsidiaries	38.9	68.1	55.8	63.1	106.0
Property, plant & equipment, net	600.8	760.3	930.8	1,135.8	1,265.8
Other assets	15.8	37.7	46.7	58.2	73.5
Total fixed assets	$ 655.5	$ 866.0	$1,033.3	$1,257.1	$1,445.2
Total Assets	$ 992.8	$1,252.5	$1,491.6	$1,851.0	$2,292.7
Liabilities & Equity					
Short-term debt	$ 33.6	$ 63.8	$ 56.3	$ 62.0	$ 74.9
Accounts payable	49.9	56.1	73.7	127.9	136.0
Accrued payroll	35.9	43.9	69.7	81.5	105.9
Accrued occupancy costs	17.5	23.0	29.1	35.8	51.2
Income taxes payable	18.3	30.8	35.8	70.3	54.2
Other current liabilities	24.2	33.6	47.0	67.7	115.3
Total current liabilities	$ 179.5	$ 251.2	$ 311.7	$ 445.3	$ 537.5
Long-term debt	-	7.0	6.5	5.8	6.1
Deferred taxes & other long-term liabilities	19.0	33.3	21.4	19.1	22.5
Common equity	794.3	961.0	1,152.0	1,380.9	1,726.6
Total liabilities & equity	$ 992.8	$1,252.5	$1,491.6	$1,851.0	$2,292.7

Source: Starbucks Coffee Company, Annual Report, 1999, 2000, 2001, 2002.

appendix 3   Starbucks Statements of Cash Flow, 1998–2002 (millions of US$)

	1998	1999	2000	2001	2002
OPERATING ACTIVITIES					
Net earnings	$ 68.4	$ 101.7	$ 94.6	$ 181.2	$ 215.1
Adjustments to reconcile to net cash:					
Depreciation and amortization	80.9	107.5	142.2	177.1	221.1
Gain on sale of investment	–	–	–	–	(13.4)
Internet-related investment losses	–	–	58.8	2.9	–
Provision for impairment and asset disposals	7.2	2.5	5.8	11.0	26.6
Deferred income taxes, net	2.1	0.8	(18.3)	(6.1)	(6.1)
Equity in income of investees	0.0	(2.3)	(15.1)	(15.7)	(22.0)
Tax benefit from exercise of stock options	10.5	18.6	31.1	30.9	44.1
Cash provided/used by changes in working capital:					
Net purchases of trading securities	–	–	(1.4)	(4.0)	(5.7)
Accounts receivable	(19.8)	3.8	(25.0)	(20.4)	(6.7)
Inventories	(23.5)	(36.4)	(19.5)	(19.7)	(41.4)
Prepaid expenses and other current assets	(2.5)	(7.6)	0.9	(10.9)	(12.5)
Accounts payable	4.6	4.7	15.6	54.1	5.5
Accrued compensation and related costs	9.9	7.6	25.4	12.1	24.1
Accrued occupancy costs	5.3	5.5	6.0	6.8	15.3
Accrued taxes	7.2	12.4	5.0	34.5	(16.2)
Deferred revenue	–	–	6.8	19.6	15.3
Other accrued expenses	1.8	10.3	5.7	2.8	34.0
Net cash provided by operating activities	$ 152.2	$ 229.2	$ 318.6	$ 456.3	$ 477.3
INVESTING ACTIVITIES					
Purchase of available for sale securities	$ (51.4)	$(122.8)	$(118.5)	$(184.2)	$(340.0)
Maturity of available for sale securities	5.1	3.6	58.8	93.5	78.3
Sale of available for sale securities	112.1	85.1	49.2	46.9	144.8
Purchase of businesses, net of cash acquired	–	(15.7)	(13.5)	–	–
Additions to equity and other investments	(12.4)	(30.9)	(43.9)	(12.9)	(6.1)
Proceeds from sale of equity investment	–	–	–	–	14.8
Distributions from equity investees	2.8	9.0	14.3	16.9	22.8
Additions to property, plant and equipment	(201.9)	(257.9)	(316.5)	(384.2)	(375.5)
Additions to other assets	(3.2)	(6.9)	(3.1)	(4.6)	(24.5)
Net cash provided (used) by investing activities	$(148.8)	$(336.4)	$(373.2)	$(428.5)	$(485.3)
FINANCING ACTIVITIES					
Increase (decrease) in short-term debt	$ 4.8	$ 29.9	$ (7.5)	$ 5.7	$ 12.9
Proceeds from sale of common stock under esop*	4.6	9.4	10.3	13.0	16.2
Proceeds from exercise of stock options	20.8	33.8	58.5	46.7	91.3
Principal payments on long-term debt	(2.0)	(1.2)	(1.9)	(0.7)	(0.7)
Repurchase of common stock	–	—	–	(49.8)	(52.2)
Net cash provided by financing activities	$ 28.3	$ 71.9	$ 59.4	$ 14.8	$ 67.4

Source: Starbucks Coffee Company, Annual Report, 1999, 2000, 2001, 2002.
esop = employee stop ownership plan

appendix 4 Starbucks Corporation Store, Revenue and Profit Growth, 1992-2002

	1992	1993	1994	1995	1996	1997	1998	1999	2000	2001	2002	Average Annual Growth Rate
United States & Canada												
Company-Owned	162	261	399	627	929	1,270	1,622	2,038	2,446	2,971	3,496	36%
Licensed	3	11	26	49	75	94	133	179	530	809	1,078	80%
International												
Company-Owned	–	–	–	1	9	31	66	104	173	295	384	
Licensed	–	–	–	–	2	17	65	177	352	634	928	
Total Stores												
Company-Owned	162	261	399	628	938	1,301	1,688	2,142	2,619	3,266	3,880	37%
Licensed	3	11	26	49	77	111	198	356	882	1,443	2,006	92%
Total Stores	165	272	425	677	1,015	1,412	1,886	2,498	3,501	4,709	5,886	43%
Percent of total licensed	2%	4%	6%	7%	8%	8%	10%	14%	25%	31%	34%	
Revenues & Profits												
Revenues (millions)	$93	$164	284.9	$465	$698	$975	$1,309	$1,680	$2,169	$2,649	$3,289	43%
Change (%)		76%	74%	63%	50%	40%	34%	28%	29%	22%	24%	
Net profit (millions)	$4	$9	$10.2	$26	$42	$55	$68	$102	$95	$181	$215	49%
Change (%)		107%	20%	155%	62%	31%	24%	50%	-7%	92%	19%	
Revenue/store	$0.564	$0.601	$0.670	$0.687	$0.688	$0.691	$0.694	$0.673	$0.620	$0.563	$0.559	0%
Change (%)		7%	12%	2%	0%	0%	1%	-3%	-8%	-9%	-1%	
Net profit/store	$0.025	$0.031	$0.024	$0.038	$0.041	$0.039	$0.036	$0.041	$0.027	$0.038	$0.037	4%
Change (%)		26%	-23%	60%	8%	-6%	-7%	13%	-34%	42%	-5%	
Earnings per share (EPS)	$0.03	$0.04	$0.05	$0.09	$0.14	$0.17	$0.19	$0.27	$0.25	$0.46	$0.56	34%
Change (%)		33%	25%	80%	56%	21%	12%	42%	-7%	84%	22%	
Share Price (eoy)	$1.89	$3.42	$2.88	$4.73	$8.25	$10.45	$9.05	$12.39	$20.03	$14.84	$14.84	23%
Change (%)		81%	-16%	64%	74%	27%	-13%	37%	62%	-26%	0%	

Source: Company Reports and Thomas Weisel Partners LLC, "Starbucks Corporation," February 6, 2002, pp. 14-17.

appendix 5 Starbucks' International Operations

Asia-Pacific	Middle East	Europe
Australia	Bahrai	Austria
Guam	Israel	Germany
Hong Kong	Kuwait	Greece
Indonesia	Lebanon	Portugal
Japan	Oman	Spain
Malaysia	Qatar	Switzerland
New Zealand	Saudi Arabia	United Kingdom
P.R. of China	United Arab Emirates	
Philippines		
Singapore	**North America**	
South Korea	Canada	
Taiwan	Mexico	
Thailand	United States	

Source: Starbucks.com, 10/07/02.

appendix 6 Starbucks Corporation, Closing Share Price (weekly, adjusted for share splits)

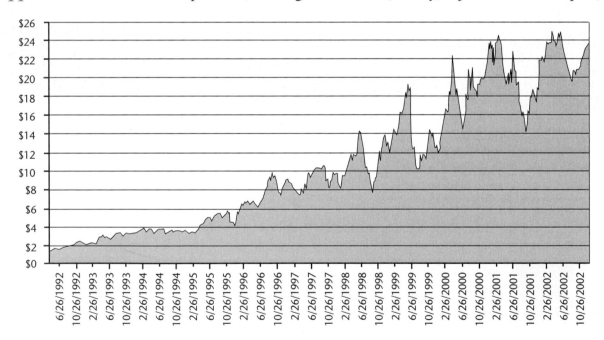

case 16 Louis Vuitton Moët Hennessy: In Search of Synergies in the Global Luxury Industry

Mr. Bernard Arnault, variously heralded as the "Emperor of Luxury," the "Pope of Fashion," and the "Lord of Logos," had settled into the plush executive suite atop the elegant headquarters of Louis Vuitton Moët Hennessey (LVMH). Situated in the fashionable eighth arrondissement, visitors had to be checked by his personal bodyguards before the bulletproof glass doors silently retracted to usher them into the inner sanctum of the global fashion empire that Mr. Arnault had built. Seated in the midst of sumptuous luxury, Mr. Arnault was perhaps the quintessential ambassador of his company's products. He had consistently been voted the *Best Dressed CEO* many times over by several of the leading journals in the business press. This was, however, a time for reflection, rethinking, and perhaps redesigning the strategies that his company would follow as it entered a very challenging period in its young life. Would LVMH be able to deliver on its promise of doubling its sales and profits over the next five years?

2001 had been a roller-coaster year for LVMH. Under Mr. Arnault's leadership, LVMH was clearly well down the road in executing a strategy that called for a diversified portfolio of luxury brands and the simultaneous expansion into multiple geographical regions where the firm was underrepresented. It had hardly been an easy endeavor. Many of the brand acquisitions and line extensions had come at a high price, and most of these businesses were yet to generate substantial profits. Much of the group's profitability was still riding on the shirttails of the established business lines; namely, wines and spirits, and leather goods. Analysts were therefore questioning the value of building a portfolio of global brands that spanned diverse product markets from wines and spirits, to leather goods, perfumes, art, and online retailing. Mr. Arnault took much pride in pointing out that, "We're the only group that has the ability to manage different activities that cover the entire range of the luxury business." He was deeply convinced that this collection of global brands was the stepping-stone

Richard Ivey School of Business
The University of Western Ontario

for realizing lucrative synergies in the fashion business, synergies that would add to the bottom line. It was obvious that these "synergies" had different meanings for the analysts than for Mr. Arnault.

Was the expansion into multiple brands and businesses justified? Did the umbrella brand LVMH add any value to the individual brands such as Givenchy, Guerlain, Chateau d'Yquem, and DKNY that were well established in their own right? Was there any compelling strategic logic in the expansion into art auction houses, Internet companies, and media ventures? What synergies could be tapped across these ventures to enhance overall shareholder value? Where should LVMH focus its efforts geographically to position itself for future growth? These were a few of the critical questions that Mr. Arnault sat down to contemplate as he looked out at the rush-hour crowds milling around the Arc de Triomphe.

THE LUXURY GOODS INDUSTRY

The luxury business encompassed a wide range of products and services. It was reported that the industry generated roughly $80 billion each year (including jewelry, watches, leather goods, wines and champagne, fragrances and apparel). Largely focused on an elite population that had sizable disposable incomes, purveyors of luxury and fashion had to deliver cutting-edge, innovative products of exceptional quality and were constantly looking for ways in which to distinguish their offerings from those of their competitors.

THE TARGET MARKET: *BON CHIC BON GENRE*

The major firms in the industry were quite unified in their pursuit of the target customers, simply defined as "high net-worth individuals." A recent survey by Cap Gemini Ernst and Young reported that in 2000 more than 7.2 million individuals worldwide held over $1 million each in financial assets, a 3% increase over the previous year. It was believed that these individuals accounted for roughly $27 trillion of the world's wealth. Membership in this group was expected to increase by an average of 8% annually for the next five years. In geographical terms, North America was home to roughly a third of these high net-worth individuals, followed closely by Europe and Asia.

The typical target customers had a keen eye for fashion and trends. They belonged to a rarefied group that did not flinch at paying $12,000 for a custom-designed Louis Vuitton suitcase, $7,500 for a bottle of Château d'Yquem premier grand cru, or $500,000 for a Silver Tourbillon wristwatch from Patek Phillipe. Most of the notable luxury goods companies maintained long waiting lists of customers who desired to buy a handbag, a wristwatch, or some other exclusive product that was in short supply. *The Wall Street Journal* had even reported a run on Louis Vuitton handbags by buyers who had flown across continents to shop in the company's stores in France.

On a global basis, Japan was perhaps the market most closely targeted by luxury goods manufacturers. The Japanese were believed to account for roughly 30% of the global market for luxury goods (including purchases by Japanese tourists overseas, which accounted for about 15%), making them the most important buyer segment. Attracted by this lucrative market, many of the industry leaders had virtually saturated

Japan with stores despite the recent economic turmoil, and there was no sign of any slowdown in expansion plans. It was precisely this reliance on the Japanese consumer that threatened the success of the leading design houses. Exhibit 2 shows luxury brand sales by geographic region for the major firms in the industry.

LUXURY RETAILING: COUNTRY-SPECIFIC COMPETITIVE ADVANTAGE

Country-specific factors were inextricably linked with brand power and heritage and, hence, gaining a foothold in the country known best for a particular line of products was of paramount importance. Access to local artisans, local raw materials, and the ability to tap into the local knowledge base were all extremely crucial aspects of building a reputation in this business. Although this meant that the costs of labor were often prohibitive given the low volumes manufactured, it was an essential element of defining brand reputation. Italy, for example, was widely believed to be the leader in the manufacture of leather goods. It was home to some of the best leather design houses, the best manufacturers of leather processing equipment, and some of the best leather retailing outlets. Complemented by the burgeoning fashion clothing business in Milan, the leather industry in Florence was able to develop synergistic advantages. Over the years, the Italian customer had developed a very sophisticated awareness of leather fashion products. Therefore, to compete successfully in this region, companies had to strive hard to attract Italian customers, who were demanding and knowledgeable. Firms such as Bottega Veneta, Salvatore Ferragamo, and Tod's were a few of the Italian companies at the forefront in leather goods. Thus, the "Made in Italy" label was considered to be an important element that discerning customers worldwide insisted upon when buying luxury leather goods.

France was widely seen as the hotbed of creativity in the ready-to-wear-fashion business. Tracing its lineage to the French court at Versailles and the pomp and circumstance that surrounded French royalty, the country had given birth to some of the most well-reputed design houses. The leading *parfumieres* and cosmetic goods companies traced similar roots. The legendary flower fields of the Provence region provided much of the critical raw materials that these industries required. France also dominated the wine business that was built on locational advantages, such as access to fertile land, and winemaking heritage. Winemaking had been part of the culture for a very long period of time and helped put regions such as Burgundy and the Loire valley on the oenophile's map. The support of the French government and the careful control of the industry through the appellation system also helped the wineries gain a foothold in world markets.

Switzerland had built a global reputation for its jewelry and watches. Many of the leading firms that competed in these segments traced their heritage to the master craftsmen and jewelers who fled religious persecution in France and settled around Geneva to establish the traditions of Swiss craftsmanship. Over time, quality and precision had become synonymous with Switzerland.

While each of the major design houses had originated through a focus on a distinct set of products that were rooted in local craftsmanship, they had since branched out through cross-border acquisitions to build empires spanning wines and champagnes, apparel, watches, and jewelry. The quintessential global luxury product company was a result of such aggressive expansion.

THE MAJOR PLAYERS

The major competitors in the luxury goods industry, LVMH, Gucci, Richemont, Bulgari, and Hermès, controlled approximately 22% of worldwide industry sales. All of these firms competed in multiple product lines and multiple geographic markets. LVMH and Bulgari dominated the Asia-Pacific region, while Richemont and Hermès were strong contenders in Europe. Gucci was a well-entrenched player in both Europe and North America and had been building a strong presence in Japan as well. Exhibit 3 provides a summary of major product lines of the key players.

Gucci

In 1923, Guccio Gucci opened a small shop selling leather goods in Florence, Italy. Originally a reseller of luggage imported from Germany, Gucci benefited from the economic expansion following World War I. Since its inception, the company had displayed an innovative streak, improvising with leather alternatives during the lean years in Italy under Benito Mussolini. After the Second World War, Gucci began to execute its global expansion strategy with a store in New York in 1953, its first outside Italy. Unfortunately, the company suffered major setbacks in the 1970s and 1980s after finding itself the subject of scandals, murder plots, and mafia murders, catapulting it to the front pages of newspapers for the wrong reasons. There was intense in-fighting within the controlling Gucci family that resulted in poor strategy and the unwitting dilution of valuable brand equity. In the late '80s, a Middle Eastern investment group, Investcorp, bought 50% of the company. At that time, the brand was already very weak, having been plastered on over 22,000 items ranging from watches to perfumes to shoes sold even in department stores. A patrician brand had become decidedly plebian. The revival of Gucci started with the appointment of Mr. Domenico De Sole as the CEO after Investcorp bought out the other 50% of the company. The new CEO hired Mr. Tom Ford, a highly acclaimed designer who thoroughly revamped Gucci's product designs. The company initiated buybacks and terminations of licenses and took firmer control of the brand, its products, and their distribution. Investcorp sold its holdings through an IPO in 1996, making a fivefold return on its original investment.

Gucci embarked on a multibrand model more recently. It acquired Yves Saint Laurent's fragrance and ready-to-wear apparel lines and added the renowned shoemaker, Sergio Rossi, to its umbrella of brands. The multibrand strategy was expected to deliver important synergies. The manufacture of leather goods and shoes sold under various labels was being centralized. Similar centralization was initiated in the multiple lines of timepieces such as YSL, Boucheron, and Bedat & C° that the company offered. The company relied on a dense network of subcontractors to manufacture most of its products. Gucci's retail stores typically carried all its product lines, allowing for some distribution synergies. The Gucci group reported consolidated sales of $2.26 billion in 2001.

Richemont

Richemont, the second largest luxury goods company in the world, was headquartered in Zug, Switzerland. It was controlled by Rembrandt, a South African company which was owned by the Rupert family. The family had originally made its fortune in tobacco. In 1988, some of the tobacco assets were spun off, and Richemont was born. Richemont still controlled the well-known Rothmans International and Dunhill brands.

Richemont was very widely diversified, with interests in companies such as Canal +, a French media company, and Vivendi, a French water and media conglomerate.

Richemont's forte had always been in jewelry and watches, where it dominated the world scene with storied brand names such as Cartier, Van Cleef & Arpels, and Piaget. Together, sales of watches and jewelry accounted for nearly 70% of total luxury product sales generated by the company in 2000. It also had staked relatively smaller positions in apparel and fashion accessories through brands such as Dunhill, Sulka, Shanghai Tang, and Chloe.

In geographic terms, the company generated 38% of its sales in the Asia-Pacific market (21% in Japan) and 39% in Europe in the year 2000. The Americas' market accounted for 21%. Unlike the Gucci or LVMH models that were built around a family of brands under one umbrella, Richemont emphasized the stand-alone nature of each brand and did not appear to be interested in any synergies across its brand portfolio. In most cases, the parent company was a behind-the-scenes player and offered full autonomy in brand management with important caveats to protect against brand dilution. Richemont operated a network of 720 exclusive stores, 452 of which were company owned.

Hermés

Thierry Hermés founded the company in 1837, focusing initially on the manufacture and sale of leather harnesses for horses. Although still largely family owned (>80%), it commanded a worldwide reputation for quality and fashion leadership. By early 2001, it generated 78% of its sales outside France, mostly through its network of over 200 exclusive stores in important luxury centers of the world. It had relied on a single-brand strategy for its multiple product lines that spanned diverse luxury products ranging from clothing to fragrances and leather accessories. Japan was clearly an important market for the company and accounted for roughly 25% of its sales in the year 2000. Hermés had positioned itself among the super premium purveyors of luxury goods, offering crocodile-skin handbags for $8,800 and cotton poplin shirts for $340. In terms of its price positioning of leather goods, it hardly faced any competition, even from the other well-known players such as Gucci and LVMH, whose prices were lower in comparison. Only Bulgari and the Richemont brand, Cartier, were probably the closest in terms of comparability of price points.

Hermés had built its sterling reputation by integrating a large proportion of its production and retail operations. Over 75% of the products it sold were manufactured in-house. The company was even willing to take over key suppliers of inputs such as fine leather and crocodile skins just to assure superior quality at the input end. It operated 23 production sites in Europe, of which 21 were in France. At the output end, the company blended both directly owned stores with selected franchise operations, often buying back franchises should strategic need dictate such moves. In 2000, Hermés acquired 31.5% of Leica Camera A.G., a company that specialized in high-end photographic equipment.

Bulgari

Bulgari traced it origins to a small village in Greece named Epirius that was well known for silversmiths. Mr. Sotirio emigrated from Epirius to Italy and opened his first jewelry shop in Rome. The company was listed on the Milan and London stock exchanges, although the family still held controlling shares and exercised both strategic and management control over the entire range of operations. Bulgari had grown in terms of both geographic reach as well as product variety through an intense phase of expansion that started in the early 1990s. It operated in seven luxury segments that included watches, jewelry, perfumes, fashion accessories, silks, tableware, and eyewear. In early 2001, it had formed a joint venture partnership with Marriott International. The joint venture was supposed to focus on leveraging the Bulgari brand name in building luxury resorts. It was known in the luxury business for its "classical chic" design sensibilities that appealed both to traditionalists as well as the trendier clientele that tended to be largely comprised of first-time buyers. The broad appeal was an essential ingredient to Bulgari's success story.

Bulgari relied on a network of franchised outlets and company-owned stores to reach its customers. It had a 99-store network, of which 72 stores were company owned. It also distributed its products through other channels such as airport duty-free shops. Although it had interests across a wide spectrum of luxury products, a substantial part of its revenue was attributed to watches (46% of company sales in 2000) and jewelry (33% of sales in 2000). In geographic terms, Japan and the United States were the leading markets, while the Asia-Pacific region as a whole accounted for 36% of total company sales. Reflecting its Italian location, the company preferred to use a network of contractors for many of its production functions. While it produced its entire range of watches and perfumes in-house, it contracted out the manufacture of other product lines such as jewelry and fashion accessories. The company had reported sales of $595 million and EBIT of $101 million in 2000.

THE ASCENT OF LOUIS VUITTON MOËT HENNESSY

"An unprecedented cocktail of talent, audacity, and thoroughness in the quest for excellence" was the way in which the company described itself in a recent annual report. Louis Vuitton Moët Hennessy was largely a reflection of its charismatic CEO, Mr. Arnault, who not only engineered the creation of the group through a series of acquisitions, but also defined the fundamental strategic direction that the company would take in its evolution to become a global player. Mr. Arnault graduated from the prestigious Polytechnique and went to the United States to run a construction company that had been founded by his father. Upon his return to France in 1984, he saw an opportunity to enter the branded textiles and clothing business by buying the bankrupt textile company Boussac for $80 million. The purchase included Christian Dior, the haute couture house that was in decline at the time. Soon thereafter, Mr. Arnault dismantled the assets of Boussac (with the exception of Dior), and netted $810 million to launch his vision of luxury fashion retailing.

In July 1988, in collaboration with British brewer Guinness, he acquired 24% of LVMH, a group that had already been formed through a merger between Louis Vuitton and Moët Hennessy. At that time, Louis Vuitton had already established alliances with Veuve Cliquot, Canard Duchêne, and Henriot, established wine and champagne labels along with Givenchy, a fragrance powerhouse. Mr. Arnault's 24% stake exceeded the individual holdings of the Louis Vuitton and Moët Chandon families, and by 1990 he became the CEO of the LVMH group. In less than a decade, he had transformed the company through a spree of acquisitions and opportunistic expansion into overseas markets (Appendix 2 shows the ownership structure and key investments of LVMH).

By early 2001, the company had been reorganized around five divisions spanning wines and spirits, fashion and leather goods, perfumes and cosmetics, watches and jewelry, and selective retailing. It reported group sales of $10.7 billion in 2001. Appendix 3 shows the major brand names held by key players in the luxury goods industry.

LVMH controlled more than 50 luxury brands across its product lines, spanning prestigious luxury names such as Louis Vuitton, a brand dating back to 1854, Chateau d'Yquem (1593), Veuve Clicquot (1772), and Guerlain (1828); sophisticated, upscale brands such as Givenchy and Kenzo; to the younger edgier names such as Urban Decay and Hard Candy. In an interview published in the *Harvard Business Review*, Mr. Arnault observed that a "star brand is timeless, modern, fast growing, and highly profitable." By those yardsticks, he had been able to gather quite a few star brands for his company. It was brand power that had propelled the company to leadership positions in almost every segment it served. LVMH was ranked number one in champagne and cognac, fashion and leather goods, and selective retailing. It was ranked number three in watches and jewelry and perfumes and cosmetics (www.lvmh.com). Appendix 4 provides financial and operating statistics for LVMH.

LVMH BUSINESSES

In the interest of transparency, LVMH was organized in a divisional format comprising five divisions, with each division functioning as an SBU (Strategic Business Unit) with its own General Manager and top management team. These divisions also managed overseas sales of their respective lines. Exhibit 4 provides a breakdown of revenues by product line and geographic region.

Wines and Spirits

LVMH was clearly the world leader in the wine and spirits business. Through Hennessy, it held 40% of the cognac market and between 20%-25% of the overall champagne market. In the premium champagne segment, LVMH had a dominant share of 50% built around exclusive brands such as Moët Chandon and Veuve Clicquot. It had also ventured outside the traditional wine belts in France and Italy to acquire high-end wine producers in Napa Valley, California (Newton Vineyards), and Australia (Mount Adam). Given the rising prominence of both California and Australia in the wine business, it was believed that these moves would allow the company to market a truly global selection of wines and champagnes. The division contributed 20% of group sales and had an operating margin of approximately 30% in 2000. In 2001, the company witnessed a 4% decline in division sales due to the poor performance of cognac labels in the traditional stronghold market, Japan. Collectively, the wines and spirits division reported sales of $1.92 billion in 2001.

Fashion and Leather Goods

LVMH had a very-well-established stable of brands in this segment accounting for 30% (€3.61 billion) of group sales in 2001. Much of the sales of this flagship division were concentrated in the Asia-Pacific region, particularly Japan. The company had made important cross-border acquisitions in this area to fortify its presence and heritage. It had acquired controlling interests in Fendi, the Italian leather designer; Donna Karan, a leading US designer; and had entered into a joint venture with Prada, another well-known Italian company in leather products and ready-to-wear apparel. Much of the sales in this segment were directly attributable to the Louis Vuitton brand that specialized in leather goods. This label had grown by leaps and bounds under the leadership of its legendary designer, Mr. Marc Jacobs. Demand for Louis Vuitton products often exceeded supply, requiring customers to go on a waiting list that often took several months to clear. A case in point was the introduction of the Graffiti line, which became an instant success, generating a waiting list that took over a year to fulfill.

The company was able to leverage synergies across its fashion brands. For example, its Kenzo production facility had been transformed into a logistics platform for men's ready-to-wear products serving other brands such as Givenchy and Christian Lacroix. Given the historically lower profit margins in the ready-to-wear market, synergies resulting in cost savings could boost profitability. The Louis Vuitton label, combined with the strength of the LVMH group, afforded opportunities for expanding into new brands and products. Using this launching pad, the company engaged in significant brand expansion efforts to reach a wider audience. These efforts were well supported by the fashion buyers. As Muriel Zingraff, Harrods' fashion and beauty director, observed, "What I will say is that we may have more patience with smaller brands if they are owned by a parent company, such as LVMH or the Gucci Group."[1]

Fragrances and Cosmetics

The fragrances and cosmetics division that generated 18% of company sales in 2000 had a powerful collection of brands that vied with the leather and fashion goods for the limelight. This division managed the blockbuster brands such as Christian Dior, Guerlain, Kenzo, and Givenchy. The company also had recently acquired popular U.S. brands such as Bliss, Hard Candy, Urban Decay, and Fresh that were geared toward a younger audience. Europe was the largest market for fragrances, perhaps due to the heritage of the brands that the company offered. The recent acquisitions in the U.S. were an integral part of the drive to internationalize LVMH's fragrance and cosmetics offerings. This division had been able to leverage R&D synergies across brands. Thus, while its R&D expenditure was in line with the industry norms, LVMH was able to generate twice the average growth rate of the industry. It was believed that these R&D skills would help boost sales of the acquired companies. As part of a larger drive to consolidate margins in this division, the company had been integrating R&D, production, distribution, sourcing, and other back-office operations across brands. These moves were quite beneficial. For example, integrating the purchasing function across brands had resulted in raw materials cost savings of 20%.[2] Analysts believed that the fragrances division was also positioned to reap the spillover benefits arising from the co-branding strategy under which many of the brands were linked directly to ready-to-wear apparel brands, a unique avenue of differentiation at LVMH.

Watches and Jewelry

The latest portfolio addition at LVMH, watches and jewelry, contributed only 5% of sales in 2000 and an operating margin of roughly 10%. In watches, the company owned prestigious brands that included Tag Heuer, Ebel, and Zenith, and Fred Joallier

[1]Sherwood, J. *Battling It Out in Style*. theage.com, March 2001.
[2]Hurley, J., & Telsey, D.L. (2001) *Luxury Goods: Value in the Magnetism of Brands*. Bear Stearns.

and Chaumet in jewelry. Unlike its constellation of brands in other divisions, many thought that the company did not have quite the same star power in watches and jewelry. Competitors such as Richemont, Hermés, and Bulgari seemed to have more recognizable brands and more upscale products in this category. However, tangible synergies appeared a distinct possibility because the division could centralize the manufacture of movements and also utilize Tag Heuer's expertise in retail distribution across all brands. The jewelry business was also extremely competitive due to the presence of leading brands such as Cartier and Van Cleef & Arpels. Despite the Place Vendôme heritage of both Chaumet and Fred Joallier, neither of them was currently profitable.

Selective Retailing

The vertical integration strategy of LVMH came to fruition when the selective retailing arm was established. This division managed LVMH investments in Sephora, DFS Galleria, and Miami Cruiseline Services. While this division contributed 28% of company sales in 2000, it had not made a profit in the previous three years. DFS Galleria with 150 duty-free and general merchandise stores was the world's largest travel retailer. Acquired in 1996, this business was a victim of poor timing, since the Asian financial crisis hit soon thereafter. LVMH had since instituted several good management practices, including the execution of a strategy that would reduce DFS's reliance on Asian airports, selective closing of underperforming stores and the creation of DFS Galleria stores in large metropolitan areas. Despite these changes, Japanese travelers were its most important and loyal customers and any macroeconomic development that hurt Japanese travel invariably found its way to DFS's bottom line.

Miami Cruiseline Services (MCS) was acquired in January 2000. It offered retail services on board cruise ships and counted 76% of the world's major cruise lines (over 100 ships) as its customers. Conceived as an extension of the DFS concept, Miami Cruiseline focused primarily (90%) on North American passengers, thus counterbalancing the reliance on Japanese tourists that has plagued DFS. It also managed duty-free operations at the Miami International Airport, the gateway to Latin America, opening possibilities of strengthening LVMH's brands in a region of the world where they were underrepresented.

In addition to these distribution assets, LVMH had recently acquired La Samaritane, the prestigious Paris department store. The company had also entered the retailing end of the made-to-order tailoring business with the acquisition of Thomas Pink, the legendary Mayfair tailoring house that had a worldwide reputation for excellence in shirts. Thomas Pink had retail outlets in the United States as well. LVMH had also taken a minority position in the 200-year-old U.K. fashion retailer, Asprey & Garrard, that had global aspirations of its own.

Auction Houses

Auction houses specializing in art and antiquities were another new line of business for LVMH. In 1999, LVMH spent between $60 and $100 million to acquire Philips, "one of the perennial also-rans of the auction world."[3] It subsequently acquired Geneva-based Gallery de Pury & Luxembourg and the Parisian auction house L'Etude Tajan. It had also recently engineered a merger with Bonham & Brooks, the top automotive

---

[3]Rohleder, Anna. *The Auction Business Waits for the Hammer to Fall.* Forbes.com. Nov. 14, 2001.

auctioneer. The auction business at the upper levels had very poor margins given the competition between the heavyweights, Christie's and Sotheby's. The LVMH acquisitions were primarily in mid-market auctions and hence considered more economically viable. It was also rumored that Mr. Arnault was taking a closer look at Sotheby's, and if he succeeded in buying the Sotheby name, he would then be able to package the auction line along with some of the other high-fashion brands to bring in new customers. Forbes noted that, "He could use the champagnes, rare wines, jewelry, and fashion, as well as the cachet of its parties and product launches, to lure new customers. In terms of synergy, it would all fit together nicely."

THE LVMH APPROACH TO COMPETITIVE STRATEGY

Innovation, differentiation, and positioning were the fundamental pillars of the competitive strategy that LVMH followed. It had mastered the art of differentiating itself in every market segment in which it operated. The company valued long-term performance and was willing to plough investments into new product brands and provide brand support for extended periods of time before expecting tangible profits. Unfortunately, although this long-term orientation and reinvestment of profits improved its market share over the long haul, it did not match the aspirations of the investing public, especially in major capital markets such as the United States. Success sometimes did take a long time to percolate to the bottom line.

MANAGING THE BUSINESS MODEL

Creativity and innovation were synonymous with success in the fashion business. As two analysts recently observed, "Luxury brands must foster an appreciation (and tolerance) for creativity that is unconstrained by commercial or production constraints."[4] At LVMH, creative autonomy was a principle that was guarded zealously. In almost all its acquisitions, LVMH had maintained the creative talent as an independent pool without attempting to generate synergies across product lines or brands. When Mr. John Galliano, the design guru at Christian Dior, came up with newspaper dresses, Mr. Arnault did not stop him from showing his creations at the fashion shows. Although the dresses were hardly intended to be commercial successes, they created sensational coverage in the fashion media. This exposure allowed LVMH to capitalize on the creations in other ways. Mr. Arnault believed that, "If you think and act like a typical manager around creative people—with rules, policies, data on customer preferences, and so forth—you will quickly kill their talent."[5] Thus, the company was decentralized by design and had a very small cadre of managers. New products contributed 15% of LVMH revenues in leather goods and 20% of sales in fragrances and cosmetics in 2000.

Integrating Production

Customers who were willing to pay substantial premiums for branded luxury products demanded very high levels of quality and craftsmanship. For example, some of the

---

[4]Ibid.

[5]Hurley, J., & Telsey, D.L. (2001) *Luxury Goods: Value in the Magnetism of Brands.* Bear Stearns.

leather accessories such as handbags made under the Louis Vuitton brand went through several hundred steps, carefully engineered by accomplished craftsmen. The extent of careful attention that the production process entailed was probably one reason why many of the Louis Vuitton products commanded astronomical price premiums in the range of 70%, widely speculated to be among the highest in the industry. LVMH believed in vertical integration, internalizing much of its production across product lines for quality control purposes. One of the benefits of this internalization approach was the boost it provided to the margins. Some analysts had estimated that the company saved 19.5% of material costs by centralizing some of the procurement activities in the fragrances business.[6] Coupled with some supply chain initiatives, these analysts believed that the company was able to boost the operating margin from 6.7% to 8.9%. However, there were others who expressed the opposite view. Analysts at Deutsche Bank, for example, had observed, "The gross margin generated by a luxury brand with in-house production does not appear to be higher than that of a brand that outsources."[7] Their analysis reported that integrated design houses were able to gain only a slender advantage (<1%) in terms of gross margins over their disaggregated competitors. They reasoned that integrating the distribution chain was far more lucrative than integrating the production process.

Distribution and Positioning

LVMH had the largest network of company-owned stores in the business (>1,275). It had recently premiered a new global store concept. These global concept stores had between 400-1000m^2 of retail space[8] and promoted all the brands under the LVMH umbrella. The company was operating 26 such stores as of 2000 and had reported a halo effect on sales at smaller LVMH stores that were in close proximity to a global store. Despite its control over distribution, LVMH faced challenges in pricing. For example, its Louis Vuitton handbags cost 40% more in Japan than they did in France. This imperfection had encouraged an arbitrage business in handbags run by groups from Japan who flew into France with the sole purpose of buying Louis Vuitton handbags for resale through parallel channels in Japan.[9] The company attempted to control this gray market by maintaining a database, identifying customers through their passport numbers, and thus making it difficult for the arbitrageurs. Counterfeit handbags and accessories were another big problem that had persisted for a very long time. In fashion centers such as Milan, Venice, and Florence, it was not uncommon to see hawkers peddling fake goods in the very same exclusive market zones where the designers had their boutiques.

In the customer-facing front-end operations, the selective retail ventures such as Sephora and DFS Galleria were thought to play a crucial role. These retail stores helped LVMH gather vital competitive intelligence and an enhanced understanding of the luxury goods customer. For example, their DFS Galleria stores carried an assortment of products from LVMH as well as its competitors, thus offering an ideal environment for understanding current customer needs and how the competition was faring

---

[6]Bernard Arnault of LVMH: The Perfect Paradox of Star Brands. *Harvard Business Review*, October 2001. pp. 116-123.

[7]Mills, E. LVMH. Credit Suisse First Boston, 9 March 2001.

[8]Deutsche Bank, A.G. Luxury Goods Sector: Traversing the Twilight Zone, October 9, 2001.

[9]*Economist*. July 14, 2001.

in meeting those needs. The acquisition of Sephora, an upscale fragrances and cosmetics retailer, opened vertical integration pathways for LVMH. Sephora had expanded to key markets in the U.K., Japan, Italy, and more recently in the U.S. Although the company felt that this retailing arm was crucial, Sephora had been losing money.

While designing and producing cutting-edge products was one side of the picture, getting the message across to potential buyers and organizing the distribution outlets were a completely different proposition. Fashion shows and fashion journals were important gatekeepers in the business, and their opinions were particularly influential in determining the success of product suites. Despite the appearance of objectivity, some fashion editors and, consequently, writers were constrained by the power of large design houses that were key to the success of the fashion magazines. As one former editor observed, "I have been coerced into featuring products. If the advertising spend of a company is massive, it will demand editorial mentions commensurate with the money it's pouring into the magazine."[10] A typical ad in a leading fashion magazine cost upwards of $50,000, and hence commanded the attention of editors. When Louis Vuitton advertised the premiere of its Graffiti line, its stores generated long waiting lists because of the demand spike that was created as a consequence of the advertising. The size of operations commanded by a designer appeared to have important benefits. The influence spread to buyers who acquired collections on behalf of the department store chains as well. These buyers did not need to be courted. They automatically migrated toward the design house that had the most clout, a beneficial fallout of the size of the design house. These buyers were more willing to take a chance on even the small brands that a design house might promote because such support had its rewards, such as preferential allotment of scarce inventory.

THE FUTURE

Mr. Arnault strode over to the window to peer at the serpentine queue outside the Louis Vuitton store. He was thrilled to see the throngs of loyal customers. It bode well for the partnership that LVMH had forged with DeBeers to market brand-name diamonds—a market that was estimated to exceed $25 billion. It was expected that De Beers would share its knowledge and supply sources for diamonds, while LVMH would bring brand name and luxury management expertise.

A few days earlier, LVMH had announced that it would sell 70% of its holdings in the auction business Phillips de Pury and Luxembourg, bringing its ownership stake to 27.5%. The analysts had interpreted this as an inglorious retreat for Mr. Arnault, who had vowed to compete successfully against Christie's, the auction house owned by Mr. Pinault, who wrested a significant piece of Gucci when LVMH mounted a hostile bid on that company. The markets were quite hopeful that this move to sell off the auction business would help boost earnings, especially since it had been a drag on earnings for quite some time. LVMH shares rose over 3% on the announcement. Was this a portent of more divestments to come? Had Mr. Arnault had a change of heart over the synergistic growth of LVMH as a fashion empire spanning multiple lines? Now that LVMH had retreated from auctions, would the specialty retailing ventures that were consistent loss-makers be spun off? Perhaps the most critical question was whether massive divestments that would refocus the group around Louis Vuitton would make strategic and economic sense in the industry environment where the company

---

[10]Sherwood, J. *Battling It Out in Style*, theage.com, March 2001.

found itself. It had indeed been a thrilling ride, and there was much to reflect upon as Mr. Arnault thumbed through the press clippings on the sale of Phillips de Pury and Luxembourg.

exhibit 1   Individuals Who Own over $1m in Financial Assets (in millions)

	1998	1999	2000
North America	2.06	2.48	2.54
Europe	1.84	2.17	2.31
Asia	1.33	1.71	1.70
Latin America	0.19	0.19	0.19
Middle East	0.22	0.22	0.22
Eastern Bloc	0.20	0.20	0.20
Africa	0.04	0.04	0.04
Worldwide Total	21.60	25.50	27.00

Source: Cap Gemini, Ernst & Young, 2001.

exhibit 2   Luxury Brand Sales by Geographic Regions in 2000

	Japan	Asia	Europe	N. America	Rest of the world
Bulgari	21.0%	17.0%	37.0%	21.0%	4.0%
Gucci	22.5%	17.9%	30.4%	26.4%	2.8%
Hermès	26.0%	12.0%	42.0%	15.0%	5.0%
LVMH	15.0%	17.0%	34.0%	26.0%	8.0%
Richemont	20.0%	19.0%	40.9%	20.1%	N/A

Source: Bear, Stearns & Co. Inc.

exhibit 3   Lines of Business of the Major Fashion Houses

	Bulgari	Gucci	Hermés	LVMH	Richemont
Leather Goods	X	X	X	X	X
Shoes		X	X	X	
Watches	X	X	X	X	X
Jewelry	X	X	X	X	X
Ready-to-Wear		X	X	X	X
Fragrances/cosmetics	X	X	X	X	
Silks	X	X	X	X	X
Tableware	X		X	X	X
Writing instruments			X	X	X
Wines and Spirits				X	
Specialty Retailing				X	
Auctions				X	

Source: Bear, Stearns & Co. Inc. and Company reports.

exhibit 4   Geographic Sales Composition of LVMH Product Lines

Line of Business	% of LVMH revenues	Americas	Japan	Asia	Europe	France	Rest of the world
Wine and Spirits	17.85	38	10	12	26	12	2
Fashion & Leather goods	33.04	24	33	15	16	10	2
Perfumes & Cosmetics	18.40	25	7	8	35	20	5
Other Selective Retail	26.29	37	N/A	23*	9	26	5
Watches & Jewelry	4.35	28	14	12	29	8	9
Other	0.07						
Total	100.00	27	15	15	20	17	6

Source: Deutsche Bank, A.G.

appendix 1   Stock Market Reactions to LVMH Acquisitions and Divestiture

Event	LVMH Stock Performance (% change)				CAC 40 Index Performance (% change)			
	3 days prior[1]	Day announced [A]	3 days after[1] [B]	Total change [A+B]	3 days prior	Day announced	3 days after	Total change after
10/29/96 Buy DFS	−0.87	−1.59	+6.25	+4.66	−0.56	−1.15	+0.77	−0.38
4/19/96 Buy Chateau d'Yquem	−6.58	+10.00	−3.59	+6.41	−	1.82	−1.97	
7/21/99 Buy Sephora	−2.16	−0.90	−1.09	−1.99	−2.35	−1.03	−1.35	−2.38
9/13/99 Buy Tag Heuer	−0.79	−1.43	−0.25	−1.68	+0.50	−0.60	−1.16	−1.76
11/21/00 Buy La Samaritane	−2.88	+2.30	−3.50	−1.20	−4.20	0.98	−0.40	+0.58
12/17/00 Buy Phillips	−9.49	+4.87	−5.62	−0.75	−3.48	+0.82	−2.00	−1.18
11/24/01 Buy Fendi	−1.85	+2.20	−8.30	−6.10	−0.41	−0.21	−2.61	−2.82
11/27/01 Buy DKNY	+0.73	−2.80	−5.50	−8.30	−0.76	−1.72	−0.89	−2.61
2/19/02 Sell Phillips stake	−1.65	−3.54	+6.21	+2.67	−1.28	−2.09	−0.41	−2.50

[1] Time period may be less than 3 days in case of intervening holidays

Source: Stock market prices from Bloomberg and Big Charts.

appendix 2   Ownership Structure of LVMH and Its Holdings

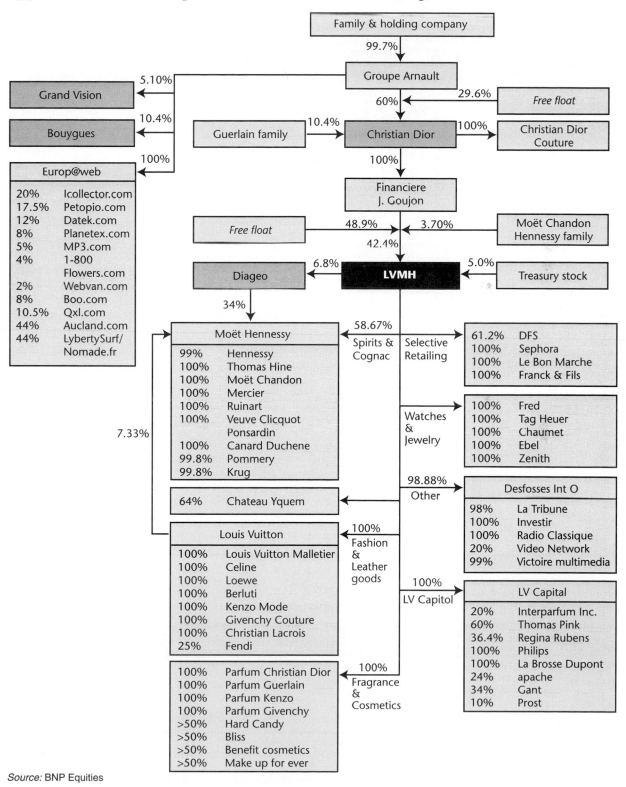

appendix 3   Leading Multibrand Luxury Goods Companies[1]

Gucci	LVMH[2]	Richemont	Bulgari
Alexander McQueen	Bulgari	Art & Auction	A. Lange & Sohne
Bedat & C°	Benefit	Alfred Dunhill	Logomania
Bottega Venetta	Bliss	Baume et Mercier	Lucea
Boucheron	Canard Duchene	Cartier	Rosenthal
Gucci	Celine	Chloe	
Sergio Rossi	Chandon Estates	Hackett	
Stella McCartney	Chateau d'Yquem	IWC	
YSL Beaute	Chaumet	Jaeger-LeCoultre	
Yves St. Laurent	Christian Lacroix	Lancel	
	DFS Group	Montblanc	
	Dom Perignon	Montegrappa	
	Donna Karan	Officine Panerai	
	Ebel	Old England	
	eLuxury.com	Piaget	
	Etude Tajan	Purdey	
	Fendi	Seeger	
	Fred Joaillier	Shanghai Tang	
	Givenchy	Sulka	
	Guerlain	Vacheron Constantin	
	Hard Candy	Van Cleef & Arpels	
	Hennessy		
	Hine		
	Kenzo		
	Krug		
	La Samaritane		
	La Tribune		
	Le Bon marche		
	Loewe		
	Louis Vuitton		
	Marc Jacobs		
	Mercier		
	Miami Cruiseline Services		
	Moët & Chandon		
	Parfums Christian Dior		
	Phillips de Pury & Luxembourg		
	Pucci		
	Sephora		
	Solistice		
	Tag Heuer		
	Thomas Pink		
	Tod's		
	Veuve Cliquot		
	Zenith		

[1] Hermés sells under a single brand name, "Hermés."
[2] Partial list of brands for LVMH

appendix 4   Operating and Financial Statistics for LVMH

METRIC ($ million)	Wines & Spirits 1999	2000	2001	2002	Fashion & Leather 1999	2000	2001	2002	Perfumes & Cosmetics 1999	2000	2001	2002	Watches & Jewelry 1999	2000	2001	2002	Selective Retailing 1999	2000	2001	2002
Net Sales	1972	2057	1965	1994	2021	2819	3180	3691	1499	1824	1964	2056	119	541	483	486	1904	2894	3060	2937
Operating Income	577	630	595	660	727	1029	1122	1141	128	162	131	142	4	52	24	(11)	(2)	(2)	(171)	18
Operating Margin	29%	31%	30%	33%	36%	37%	35%	31%	9%	9%	7%	7%	3%	10%	5%	–2%	–0.1%	–0.1%	–6%	1%

Note: Selective retailing figures for 2000 and 2001 are restated in 2002 annual report taking into account the reclassification made in 2002. LVMH partially hedges its foreign exchange exposure. In 2001, 2002, 2003, the hedge coverage was 0.92, 0.89, and 0.86 USD/Euro. Variations, if any, are due to rounding off.

Sources: LVMH Annual Report for 2000 and 2002, http://www.lvmh.com, company financials at http://www.mergentonline.com

case 17 IKEA (Canada) Ltd.

Founded as a mail order business in rural Sweden in 1943, IKEA had grown to more than US$1 billion in sales and 70 retail outlets by 1985, and was considered by many to be one of the best-run furniture operations in the world. Although only 14 per cent of IKEA's sales were outside Europe, the company's fastest growth was occurring in North America.

Success, however, brought imitators. In mid-1986, Bjorn Bayley and Anders Berglund, the senior managers of IKEA's North American operations, were examining a just-published Sears Canada catalogue, which contained a new 20-page section called "Elements." This section bore a striking resemblance to the format of an IKEA Canada catalogue (see Exhibits 1 and 2 for sample pages), and the furniture being offered was similar to IKEA's knock-down, self-assembled line in which different "Elements" could be ordered by the customer to create particular designs. Bayley and Berglund wondered how serious Sears was about its new initiative, and what, if anything, IKEA should do in response.

THE CANADIAN FURNITURE MARKET

Canadian consumption of furniture totalled more than $2 billion in 1985, an average of well over $600 per household. Imports accounted for approximately 18 per cent of this total, half of which originated in the United States. The duties on furniture imported into Canada were approximately 15 per cent.

Furniture was sold to Canadian consumers through three types of stores: independents, specialty chains and department stores. Although the independents held a 70 per cent market share, this figure was declining due to their inability to compete with the chains in terms of advertising, purchasing power, management sophistication and sales

Professor Paul W. Beamish prepared this case solely to provide material for class discussion. The authors do not intend to illustrate either effective or ineffective handling of a managerial situation. The authors may have disguised certain names and other identifying information to protect confidentiality.

Ivey Management Services prohibits any form of reproduction, storage or transmittal without its written permission. This material is not covered under authorization from CanCopy or any reproduction rights organization. To order copies or request permission to reproduce materials, contact Ivey Publishing, Ivey Management Services, c/o Richard Ivey School of Business, The University of Western Ontario, London, Ontario, Canada, N6A 3K7; phone (519) 661-3208; fax (519) 661-3882; e-mail cases@ivey.uwo.ca.

Richard Ivey School of Business
The University of Western Ontario

exhibit 1   Sample Page from IKEA Catalogue

GUTE. EIGHTEEN DIFFERENT CHESTS OF DRAWERS TO FIT IN ALMOST ANYWHERE.

GUTE chests of drawers ●möbelfakta White lacquered or pine veneered particleboard, natural or nutbrown stained. W80 cm, D40 cm. QA.
49/2. 2 drawers. H49 cm. White **$94.** Natural or nutbrown **$98.**
49/6. 6 drawers. H49 cm. White **$115.** Natural or nutbrown **$125.**
87/4. 4 drawers. H87 cm. White **$130.** Natural or nutbrown **$145.**

87/8. 8 drawers. H87 cm. White **$170.** Natural or nutbrown **$185.**
126/6. 6 drawers. H126 cm. White **$175.**
Natural or nutbrown **$195.**
126/10. 10 drawers. H126 cm. White **$215.**
Natural or nutbrown **$225.**

support. The average sales per square metre in 1985 for furniture stores of all three types was $1,666 (the figure was $2,606 for stores which also sold appliances) and the average cost of goods sold was 64.5 per cent.

While the major department stores such as Eaton's and Sears tended to carry traditional furniture lines close to the middle of the price/quality range, chains and independents operated from one end of the spectrum to the other. At the upper end of the market, specialty stores attempted to differentiate themselves by offering unique product lines, superior service and a specialized shopping atmosphere. The lower end of the

exhibit 2   Sample Page from Elements Section of Sears Catalogue

Dressers and chests whose quality and practicality are inherent—
in the colors and sizes you want. Assemble them yourself with ease.

Your choice of clear knot-free pine veneer over non-warp platewood core
or White baked-on European-quality low gloss enamel on a platewood core.

3 Drawer Units. 38 cm deep, 54 cm high (15 x 21¼").	4 Drawer Units. 38 cm deep, 69 cm high (15 x 27¼").	6 Drawer Units. 38 cm deep, 99 cm high (15 x 39")
Wide. 75 cm wide (29½").	Wide. 75 cm wide (29½").	Wide. 75 cm wide (29½").
012 065 012 DLT – *Pine* Each.139.98	012 065 011 DLT – *Pine* Each.159.98	012 065 010 DLTJ – *Pine* Each.219.98
012 065 002 DLT – *White* Each.139.98	012 065 001 DLT – *White* Each.159.98	012 065 000 DLTJ – *White* Each.219.98
Narrow. 50 cm wide (19½").	Narrow. 50 cm wide (19½").	Narrow. 50 cm wide (19½").
012 065 015 DLT – *Pine* Each.119.98	012 065 014 DLT – *Pine* Each.139.98	012 065 013 DLT – *Pine* Each.189.98
012 065 005 DLT – *White* Each.119.98	012 065 004 DLT – *White* Each.139.98	012 065 003 DLT – *White* Each.189.98

market, on the other hand, was dominated by furniture warehouses which spent heavily on advertising, and offered lower price, less service, and less emphasis on a fancy image. The warehouses usually kept a larger inventory of furniture on hand than the department stores, but expected customers to pick up their purchases. Over half the warehouse sales involved promotional financing arrangements, including delayed payments, extended terms, and so on.

The major firms in this group—both of whom sold furniture and appliances—were The Brick and Leon's. The Brick had annual sales of $240 million from 15 Canadian stores, and was rapidly expanding from its western Canada base. With 30 additional stores in California under the Furnishings 2000 name, The Brick intended to become the largest furniture retailing company in the world. Leon's had annual sales of $160 million from 14 stores, and was growing rapidly from its Ontario base. These 14 stores were operated under a variety of names. Leon's also franchised its name in smaller cities in Canada. For part of their merchandise requirements, The Brick and Leon's often negotiated with manufacturers for exclusive products, styles and fabrics and imported from the U.S., Europe and the Far East. Although both firms had had problems earlier with entry to the U.S. market, each intended to expand there.

Most furniture retailers in Canada purchased their products from Canadian manufacturers after examining new designs and models at trade shows. There were approximately 1,400 Canadian furniture manufacturers, most of whom were located in Ontario and Quebec. Typically, these firms were small (78 per cent of Canadian furniture plants employed fewer than 50 people), undercapitalized and minimally automated. One industry executive quipped that one of the most significant technological developments for the industry had been the advent of the staple gun.

Canadian-produced furniture typically followed American and European styling, and was generally of adequate to excellent quality but was often more costly to produce. The reason for high Canadian costs was attributed to a combination of short manufacturing runs and high raw material, labor and distribution costs. In an attempt to reduce costs, a few of the larger manufacturers such as Kroehler had vertically integrated—purchasing sawmills, fabric warehouses, fiberboard and wood frame plants—but such practices were very much the exception in the industry.

THE IKEA FORMULA

IKEA's approach to business was fundamentally different from that of the traditional Canadian retailers. The company focused exclusively on what it called "quick assembly" furniture, which consumers carried from the store in flat packages and assembled at home. This furniture was primarily pine, had a clean European-designed look to it, and was priced at 15 per cent below the lowest prices for traditional furniture. Its major appeal appeared to be to young families, singles and frequent movers, who were looking for well-designed items that were economically priced and created instant impact.

According to company executives, IKEA was successful because of its revolutionary approach to the most important aspects of the business: product design, procurement, store operations, marketing and management philosophy, which stressed flexibility and market orientation rather than long-range strategy. Each of these items is discussed in turn.

Product Design

IKEA's European designers, not the company's suppliers, were responsible for the design of most of the furniture and accessories in IKEA's product line, which totalled 15,000 items. The heart of the company's design capability was a 50-person Swedish workshop which produced prototypes of new items of furniture and smaller components such as "an ingenious little snap lock for table legs which makes a table stronger and cheaper at the same time" and a "clever little screw attachment which allows for the assembly of a pin back chair in five minutes." IKEA's designers were very cost conscious, and were constantly working to lower costs in ways that were not critical to the consumer.

"The quality of a work top," for example, would be superior to that of the back of a bookshelf which would never be seen. "Low price with a meaning" was the theme.

Although it was not impossible to copyright a particular design or process, IKEA's philosophy was "if somebody steals a model from us we do not bring a lawsuit, because a lawsuit is always negative. We solve the problem by making a new model that is even better."

Procurement

IKEA's early success in Sweden had so threatened traditional European furniture retailers that they had promised to boycott any major supplier that shipped products to the upstart firm. As a result, IKEA had no choice but to go to the smaller suppliers. Since these suppliers had limited resources, IKEA began assuming responsibility for the purchase of raw materials, packaging materials, storage, specialized equipment and machinery, and engineering. What began as a necessity soon became a cornerstone of IKEA's competitive strategy, and by 1986 the firm had nearly 100 production engineers working as purchasers. Together with IKEA's designers, these engineers assisted suppliers in every way they could to help them lower costs, dealing with everything from the introduction of new technology to the alteration of the dimensions of a shipping carton.

Although IKEA sometimes leased equipment and made loans to its suppliers, the firm was adamant that it would not enter the furniture manufacturing business itself. In fact, to avoid control over—and responsibility for—its suppliers, the company had a policy of limiting its purchases to 50 per cent of a supplier's capacity. Many products were obtained from multiple suppliers, and frequently suppliers produced only a single standardized component or input to the final product. Unfinished pine shelves, for example, were obtained directly from saw mills, cabinet doors were purchased from door factories, and cushions came from textile mills.

In total, IKEA purchased goods from 1,500 suppliers located in 40 countries. About 52 per cent of the company's purchases were from Scandinavia, 21 per cent from other countries of western Europe, 20 per cent from eastern Europe and seven per cent elsewhere.

Store Operations

IKEA stores were usually large one or two-storey buildings situated in relatively inexpensive stand-alone locations, neither in prime downtown sites nor as part of a shopping mall. Most stores were surrounded by a large parking lot, adorned with billboards explaining IKEA's delivery policy, product guarantee, and the existence of a coffee shop and/or restaurant.

On entering a store, the customer was immediately aware of the children's play area (a room filled with hollow multi-colored balls), a video room for older children, and a receptionist with copies of IKEA catalogues, a metric conversion guide, index cards for detailing purchases, and a store guide. The latter, supplemented by prominent signs, indicated that the store contained lockers and benches for shoppers, a first-aid area, restrooms, strollers and a baby-care area, an "As-Is" department (no returns permitted), numerous check-outs, suggestion boxes and, in many cases, a restaurant. All major credit cards were accepted.

Traffic flow in most IKEA stores was guided in order to pass by almost all of the merchandise in the store, which was displayed as it would look in the home, complete with all accessories. Throughout the store, employees could be identified by their bright red IKEA shirts. Part-time employees wore yellow shirts which read "Temporary Help—Please Don't Ask Me Any Hard Questions." The use of sales floor staff was minimal. The IKEA view was that "salesmen are expensive, and can also be irritating. IKEA leaves you to shop in peace."

While IKEA stores were all characterized by their self-serve, self-wrapping, self-transport, and self-assembly operations, the company's philosophy was that each new store would incorporate the latest ideas in use in any of its existing stores. The most recent trend in some countries was an IKEA Contract Sales section, which provided a delivery, invoicing and assembly service for commercial customers.

Marketing

IKEA's promotional activities were intended to educate the consumer public on the benefits of the IKEA concept and to build traffic by attracting new buyers and encouraging repeat visits from existing customers. The primary promotional vehicle was the annual IKEA catalogue which was selectively mailed out to prime target customers who, in the Toronto area for instance, had the following characteristics:

Income $35,000+	Primary Age Group 35-44
Owner Condominium or Townhouse	Secondary Age Group 25-34
University Degree	Husband/Wife both work
White Collar	Two Children
	Movers

With minor variations, this "upscale" profile was typical of IKEA's target customers in Europe and North America. In Canada, IKEA management acknowledged the target market, but felt that, in fact, the IKEA concept appealed to a much wider group of consumers.

IKEA also spent heavily on magazine advertisements, which were noted for their humorous, slightly off-beat approach. In Canada, IKEA spent $2.5 million to print 3.6 million catalogues, $2 million on magazine advertising, and $1.5 million on other forms of promotion in 1984.

Management Philosophy

The philosophy of Ingvar Kamprad, the founder of IKEA, was "to create a better everyday life for the majority of people." In practice, this creed meant that IKEA was dedicated to offering, and continuing to offer, the lowest prices possible on good quality furniture, so that IKEA products were available to as many people as possible. Fred Andersson, the head of IKEA's product range for the world, stated: "Unlike other companies, we are not fascinated with what we produce—we make what our customers want." Generally, IKEA management felt that no other company could match IKEA's combination of quality and price across the full width of the product line.

IKEA also made a concerted effort to stay "close to its customers," and it was not unusual for the general manager of IKEA Canada, for instance, to personally telephone customers who had made complaints or suggestions. Each week an employee newsletter detailed all customer comments, and indicated how management felt they should be dealt with.

Another guiding philosophy of the firm was that growth would be in "small bites." The growth objective in Canada, for instance, had been to increase sales and profits by 20 per cent per year, but care was given to sequence store openings so that managerial and financial resources would not be strained.

Internally, the company's philosophy was stated as "freedom, with responsibility," which meant that IKEA's managers typically operated with a good deal of autonomy. The Canadian operation, for instance, received little in the way of explicit suggestions from head office, even in the one year when the budget was not met. The Canadian management team travelled to head office as a group only once every several years. As Bjorn Bayley explained:

> We are a very informal management team, and try to have everyone who works for us believe that they have the freedom to do their job in the best way possible. It's almost impossible to push the philosophy down to the cashier level, but we try.

IKEA IN CANADA

IKEA's formula had worked well in Canada. Under the direction of a four-man management team, which included two Swedes, the company had grown from a single store in 1976 to nine stores totalling 800,000 square feet and, as shown in Exhibit 3, predicted 1986 sales of more than $140 million. The sales of IKEA Canada had exceeded budget in all but one of the past five years, and usually by a wide margin. Net profits were approximately five per cent of sales. Profit and loss statements for 1983 and 1984, the only financial statements available, are presented in Exhibit 4 (on the next page).

IKEA Canada carried just less than half of the company's total product line. Individual items were chosen on the basis of what management thought would sell in Canada, and if IKEA could not beat a competitor's price by 10 to 15 per cent on a particular item, it was dropped. Most of the goods sold in the Canadian stores were supplied from central warehouses in Sweden. To coordinate this process a five-person stock supply department in Vancouver provided Sweden with a three-year forecast of Canada's needs, and placed major orders twice a year. Actual volumes were expected to be within 10 per cent of the forecast level. As Bayley noted, "you needed a gambler in the stock supply job."

Individual stores were expected to maintain 13.5 weeks of inventory on hand (10.5 weeks in the store and three weeks in transit), and could order from the central warehouse in Montreal or, if a product was not in stock in Montreal, direct from Sweden. Shipments from Sweden took six to eight weeks to arrive, shipments from Montreal two to

exhibit 3   IKEA Canada Sales by Store (including mail order; Cdn. $000s)

	1981	1982	1983 (Actual)	1984	1985	1986 (Forecasted)	Mail[1] Order (%)
Vancouver	$12,122	$11,824	$12,885	$19,636	$19,240	$25,500	6.8
Calgary	7,379	8,550	7,420	7,848	9,220	11,500	8.6
Ottawa	5,730	6,914	8,352	9,015	10,119	12,500	1.8
Montreal			8,617	12,623	15,109	22,000[2]	2.2
Halifax	3,634	4,257	4,474	6,504	7,351	9,000	22.9
Toronto	11,231	13,191	16,249	18,318	22,673	30,500	1.8
Edmonton	6,506	7,474	8,075	8,743	9,986	16,000	15.4
Quebec City		5,057	8,284	9,027	10,037	12,000	6.1
Victoria					2,808	3,500	
Total	**$46,602**	**$57,267**	**$74,356**	**$91,714**	**$106,543**	**$142,500**	**6.7**

[1]1984 most recent data available

[2]Projected growth due to store size expansion

exhibit 4   Statement of Earnings and Retained Earnings, Year Ended
August 31, 1984 (with comparative figures for 1983)

	1984	1983
Sales	$92,185,188	$74,185,691
Cost of merchandise sold	49,836,889	38,085,173
Gross Profit	42,348,299	36,100,518
General, administrative and selling expenses	28,016,473	23,626,727
Operating profit before the undernoted	14,331,826	12,473,791
Depreciation and amortization	1,113,879	1,066,285
Franchise amortization	257,490	257,490
Franchise fee	2,765,558	2,225,571
	4,136,927	3,549,347
Earnings from operations	10,194,899	8,924,444
Rental income	769,719	815,683
Less: rental expense	245,803	258,296
	523,916	557,387
Interest expense	2,453,116	3,042,471
Less: other income	438,683	65,757
	2,014,433	2,976,714
Earnings before income taxes	8,704,382	6,505,117
Income Taxes:		
Current	3,789,773	2,716,645
Deferred	(70,400)	175,500
	3,719,373	2,892,145
Net earnings for the year	4,985,009	3,612,972
Retained earnings beginning of year	5,501,612	1,888,640
Retained earnings, end of year	$10,486,621	$ 5,501,612

Source: Consumer and Corporate Affairs, Canada

three weeks. In practice, about 50 per cent of the product arriving at a store came via each route.

IKEA's success in Canada meant that the firm was often hard pressed to keep the best selling items in stock. (Twenty per cent of the firm's present line constituted 80 per cent of sales volume.) At any given time in Canada IKEA stores might have 300 items out of stock, either because actual sales deviated significantly from forecasts or because suppliers could not meet their delivery promises. While management estimated that 75 per cent of customers were willing to wait for IKEA products in a stock-out situation, the company, nevertheless, began a deliberate policy of developing Canadian suppliers for high demand items, even if this meant paying a slight premium. In 1984, the stock control group purchased $57 million worth of goods on IKEA's behalf, $12 million of which was from 30 Canadian suppliers, up from $7 million the previous year.

As indicated in Exhibit 3, IKEA Canada sold products, rather reluctantly, by mail order to customers who preferred not to visit the stores. A senior manager explained:

To date we have engaged in defensive mail order—only when the customer really wants it and the order is large enough. The separate handling, breaking down of orders and repackaging required for mail orders would be too expensive and go against the economies-through-volume approach of IKEA. Profit margins of mail order business tend to be half that of a store operation. There are more sales returns, particularly, because of damages—maybe four per cent—incurred in shipping. It is difficult to know where to draw the market boundaries for a mail order business. We don't want to be substituting mail order customers for store visitors.

In 1986, the management team which had brought success to IKEA's Canadian operations was breaking up. Bjorn Bayley, who had come to Canada in 1978, was slotted to move to Philadelphia to spearhead IKEA's entry into the U.S. market, which had begun in June 1985 with a single store. With early sales running at a level twice as high as the company had predicted, Bayley expected to be busy, and was taking Mike McDonald, the controller, and Mike McMullen, the personnel director, with him. Anders Berglund who, like Bayley, was a long-time IKEA employee and had been in Canada since 1979, was scheduled to take over the Canadian operation. Berglund would report through Bayley to IKEA's North American Sales Director, who was located in Europe.

NEW COMPETITION

IKEA's success in Canada had not gone unnoticed. IDOMO was a well-established Toronto-based competitor, and Sears Canada was a new entrant.

IDOMO

Like IKEA, IDOMO sold knocked-down furniture which customers were required to assemble at home. IDOMO offered a somewhat narrower selection than IKEA but emphasized teak furniture to a much greater extent. With stores in Hamilton, Mississauga (across from IKEA), Toronto and Montreal, IDOMO appeared to have capitalized on the excess demand that IKEA had developed but was not able to service.

The products and prices offered in both the 96-page IDOMO and 144-page IKEA catalogues were similar, with IKEA's prices slightly lower. Prices in the IKEA catalogues were in effect for a year. IDOMO reserved the right to make adjustments to prices and specifications. A mail order telephone number in Toronto was provided in the IDOMO catalogue. Of late, IDOMO had begun to employ an increased amount of television advertising. IDOMO purchased goods from around the world and operated a number of their own Canadian factories. Their primary source of goods was Denmark.

Sears

The newest entrant in the Canadian knocked-down furniture segment was Sears Canada, a wholly owned subsidiary of Sears Roebuck of Chicago and, with $3.8 billion in annual revenues, one of Canada's largest merchandising operations. Sears operated 75 department stores in Canada, selling a wide range (700 merchandise lines comprising 100,000 stock keeping units) of medium price and quality goods. Sears Canada also ran a major catalogue operation which distributed 12 annual catalogues to approximately four million Canadian families. Customers could place catalogue orders by mail, by telephone, or in person through one of the company's 1,500 catalogue sales units, which were spread throughout the country.

A quick check by Bayley and Berglund revealed that Sears' Elements line was being sold only in Canada and only through the major Sears catalogues. Elements products were not for sale, nor could they be viewed, in Sears' stores. In the fall/winter catalogue that they examined, which was over 700 pages in length, the Elements line was given 20 pages. Although Sears appeared to offer the same "type" of products as IKEA, there was a narrower selection within each category. Prices for Elements' products seemed almost identical to IKEA prices. One distinct difference between the catalogues was the much greater emphasis that IKEA placed on presenting a large number of coordinated settings and room designs.

Further checking indicated that at least some of the suppliers of the Elements line were Swedish, although it did not appear that IKEA and Sears had any suppliers in common.

The IKEA executives knew that Sears was generally able to exert a great deal of influence over its suppliers, usually obtaining prices at least equal to and often below those of its competitors, because of the huge volumes purchased. Sears also worked closely with its suppliers in marketing, research, design and development, production standards and production planning. Many lines of merchandise were manufactured with features exclusive to Sears and were sold under its private brand names. There was a 75 per cent buying overlap for the catalogue and store and about a 90 per cent overlap between regions on store purchases.

Like any Sears' product, Elements furniture could be charged to a Sears charge card. Delivery of catalogue items generally took about two weeks and, for a small extra charge, catalogue orders would be delivered right to the consumer's home in a Sears truck. If a catalogue item was out of stock, Sears policy was either to tell the customer if and when the product would be available, or to substitute an item of equal or greater value. If goods proved defective (10 per cent of Sears Roebuck mail-order furniture purchasers had received damaged or broken furniture), Sears provided home pick-up and replacement and was willing, for a fee, to install goods, provide parts, and do repairs as products aged. Sears emphasized that it serviced what it sold, and guaranteed everything that it sold—"satisfaction guaranteed or money refunded." In its advertising, which included all forms of media, Sears stressed its "hassle-free returns" and asked customers to "take a look at the services we offered . . . they'll bring you peace of mind, long after the bill is paid."

In their assessment of Sears Canada, Bayley and Berglund recognized that the company seemed to be going through something of a revival. Using the rallying cry that a "new" Sears was being created, Sears executives (the Canadian firm had 10 vice presidents) had experimented with new store layouts, pruned the product line, and improved customer service for catalogue orders. Richard Sharpe, the chairman of Sears Canada, personally addressed as many as 12,000 employees per year, and the company received 3,000 suggestions from employees annually. Perhaps as a result of these initiatives, and a cut in workforce from 65,000 to 50,000 over several years, Sears Canada posted its best-ever results in 1985.

CONCLUSION

With the limited data they had on Sears, IKEA management recognized that their comparison of the two companies would be incomplete. Nonetheless, a decision regarding the Sears competitive threat was required. Any solution would have to reflect Kamprad's philosophy:

> Expensive solutions to problems are often signs of mediocrity. We have no interest in a solution until we know what it costs.

case 18 Newell Company: The Rubbermaid Opportunity[1]

In October 1998, the board of directors of the Newell Company was considering a proposed merger with Rubbermaid Incorporated to form a new company, Newell Rubbermaid Inc. The transaction would be accomplished through a tax-free exchange of shares under which Rubbermaid shareholders would receive Newell shares valued at approximately $5.8 billion at a ratio which represented a 49 per cent premium on Rubbermaid's current stock price. At the time of the transaction the annual revenues of Newell and Rubbermaid were, respectively, about $3.2 billion and $2.4 billion. If approved, the agreement would mark a quantum step in Newell's growth, but, equally, it would pose a formidable challenge to the company's demonstrated capacity to integrate and strengthen its acquisitions.

NEWELL: RIDING THE ACQUISITION TIGER

In 1998, the Newell Company had revenues of $3.7 billion distributed across three major product groupings: Hardware and Home Furnishings ($1.8 billion), Office Products ($1.0 billion), and Housewares ($.9 billion). Over the past ten years the company had achieved a compound sales growth rate of 13 per cent, an earnings per share growth rate of 16 per cent and an average annual return on beginning shareholder equity of 21 per cent. These results were consistent with Newell's formal goals of achieving earnings per share growth of 15 per cent per year and maintaining a return on beginning equity of 20 per cent or above. Further financial details on Newell are given in Exhibit 1 (on the next page).

IVEY

Richard Ivey School of Business
The University of Western Ontario

[1]This case has been written on the basis of published sources only. Consequently, the interpretation and perspectives presented in this case are not necessarily those of Newell Company or any of its employees.

exhibit 1   Selected Financial Information for Newell Company, 1996-1998 ($000)

	To End Q3/98	12/31/97	To End Q3/97	12/31/96
Net sales	**$2,650,263**	**$3,336,233**	**$2,395,037**	**$2,972,839**
Cost of products sold	1,786,640	2,259,551	1,631,253	2,020,116
Selling, general and administrative expenses	404,882	497,739	365,123	461,802
Goodwill amortization and other	40,502	31,882	22,872	23,554
Operating Income	418,239	547,061	375,789	467,367
Interest expense	43,966	76,413	54,363	58,541
Other, non-operating, net	(213,373)*	(14,686)	(12,862)	(19,474)
Profit before tax	587,546	485,334	334,288	428,300
Income taxes	250,740	192,187	132,373	169,258
Net Income	**$336,806**	**$293,147**	**$201,915**	**$259,042**
Current assets	1,767,370	1,433,694		1,148,464
Property, plant and equipment	834,486	711,325		567,880
Trade names, goodwill, other	2,001,862	1,559,594		1,342,086
Total Assets	**4,603,718**	**4,011,314**		**3,058,430**
Current liabilities	1,061,675	714,479		665,884
Long-term debt	912,650	786,793		685,608
Other non-current liabilities	243,862	285,241		206,916
Convertible preferred securities	500,000	500,000		
Shareholders' equity	1,885,531	1,725,221		1,500,022
Total Liabilities and Shareholders' Equity	**4,603,718**	**4,011,314**		**3,058,430**
Approximate common shares outstanding (000)	173,000	163,300		162,000
Earnings per share (fully diluted)		$1.80		$1.60
Stock price $High/Low	$54/37	$43/30		$33/25

* Primarily gain from sale of Black & Decker holdings.
Source: Company Financial Reports.

Acquisitions

Acquisitions were the foundation of Newell's growth strategy. Given the relatively slow growth of the product markets in which it chose to operate, Newell's corporate goal for internal growth was only three per cent to five per cent per annum—with internal growth being defined as the growth of businesses that Newell had owned for over two years. Actual internal growth in the past five years had averaged about five per cent per annum. This put a premium on acquisitions if Newell was to meet its aggressive growth targets. Indeed, over $2 billion of its current sales were the result of over 20 acquisitions made since 1990.

Newell's approach to acquisition was both aggressive and disciplined. Its targeted acquisition candidates were generally mature businesses with 'unrealized profit potential' which further passed a number of screening criteria, including having a:

● strategic fit with existing businesses—which implied product lines that were low in technology, fashion and seasonal content and were sold through mass distribution channels.

- number one or two position in their served markets and established shelf space with major retailers.
- long product life cycle.
- potential to reach Newell's standard of profitability, which included goals for operating margins of 15 per cent, and Sales, General and Administrative costs at a maximum of 15 per cent.

The size of the acquisitions varied. In 1996, Newell made one acquisition for $46 million cash, in 1997, three material acquisitions for $762 million cash and in 1998 to date, four material acquisitions for about $413 million cash. Once acquired, the new companies were integrated into the Newell organization by means of an established process that had come to be called "newellization."

Newellization

Newellization was the profit improvement and productivity enhancement process employed to bring a newly acquired business up to Newell's high standards of productivity and profit. The Newellization process was pursued through a number of broadly applicable steps, including the:

- transfer of experienced Newell managers into the acquired company.
- simplification and focusing of the acquired business's strategy and the implementation of Newell's established manufacturing and marketing know-how and programs.
- centralization of key administrative functions including data processing, accounting, EDI, and capital expenditure approval.
- inauguration of Newell's rigorous, multi-measure, divisional operating control system.

Newell management claimed that the process of Newellization was usually completed in two or three years.

Continuing Operations

A summary of Newell's product groups and major lines is outlined in Table 1. These products were, for the most part, sold through mass merchandisers. In 1997, Wal-Mart accounted for 15 per cent of Newell's sales; the other top ten Newell customers (each with less than 10 per cent of Newell sales) were Kmart, Home Depot, Office Depot, Target, J.C. Penney, United Stationers, Hechtinger, Office Max and Lowe's. International sales had increased from eight per cent of total sales in 1992 to an expected 22 per cent in 1998 as Newell followed customers and opportunities into Mexico, Europe and the Americas.

table 1 Newell Product Lines, 1998

Housewares	Hardware and Home Furnishings	Office Products
Aluminum Cookware and Bakeware	Window Treatments	Markers and Writing Products
Glassware	Home Storage	Office Storage
Hair Accessories	Picture Frames	
	Hardware	

Newell's fundamental competitive strategy, which applied to all of its operations, was to differentiate on the basis of superior service to its mass merchandise customers. For Newell, superior service included industry-leading quick response and on-time, in-full delivery, the ability to implement sophisticated EDI tie-ins with its customers extending to vendor-managed inventories, and the provision of marketing and merchandising programs for product categories that encompassed good, better and best lines.

Organization

Newell centralized certain key administrative functions such as data management (including order-fulfillment-invoice activities), divisional coordination and control, and financial management. Otherwise, the presidents of the company's 18 product divisions were responsible for the full scope of manufacturing, marketing and sales activities for their product lines and for the performance of their businesses.

Divisional coordination and control were facilitated by the fundamental similarities of the Newell businesses. These similarities made it possible for corporate level management to develop a common pool of managers and know-how that could be transferred relatively easily from one division to another. The business similarities also made it possible for corporate management to apply a common set of detailed operating standards and controls across the businesses, and to play a knowledgeable role in reviewing divisional progress and plans. Corporate management held monthly reviews (called brackets meetings) with divisional presidents to track multiple operating and financial measures and to ensure that appropriate attention was given to items that were off budget. As a result, divisional management operated in a goldfish bowl under high pressure, but they were paid very well for meeting their targets.

Outlook

In Newell's view, the company's adherence to a highly focused strategy had established a sustainable competitive advantage for the corporation and this, coupled with abundant acquisition opportunities and internal growth momentum, would support the continuing achievement of its financial goals.

RUBBERMAID: A FALLEN ICON

Rubbermaid was a well-known, and, for several decades, a renowned manufacturer of a wide range of plastic products ranging from children's toys through housewares to commercial items. From 1986 through 1995 Rubbermaid was ranked among the top 10 in *Fortune's* list of America's most admired companies, including the No. 1 spot in 1993 and 1994. But by March 1998 Rubbermaid had fallen to No. 100. After a wonderful run of growth and profitability, extending as far back as the 1960s, the company had clearly hit a rough patch.

Rubbermaid earned its early reputation by setting aggressive goals for 15 per cent growth in revenues and profits and then, by and large, meeting its targets. Under the intense and very personal management of Stanley Gault, an ex-senior executive at

General Electric and CEO and chairman of Rubbermaid from 1980 to 1991, the company was pressed to broaden its product line through development and acquisition and to meet demanding operating targets. From propitious beginnings Rubbermaid became an ubiquitous brand and a Wall Street darling—with sales and profits, respectively, at the end of Gault's tenure of $1.7 billion and $162 million.

Rubbermaid's earnings momentum continued into the early years of Gault's successor, Wolfgang Schmidt, but the good times were to be short-lived. In 1994 Rubbermaid was hit by a doubling of plastic resin prices.[2] The company's clumsy reactions to this shock revealed a number of accumulating problems. *Fortune* enumerated them in a 1995 article:[3]

- Customer relations: Rubbermaid angered its most important retail buyers with the heavy-handed way it has passed along its ballooning costs. Some are so angry that they have given more shelf space to competitors…

- Operations: Although it excels in creativity, product quality, and merchandising, Rubbermaid is showing itself to be a laggard in more mundane areas such as modernizing machinery, eliminating unnecessary jobs, and making deliveries on time…

- Competition: It has been slow to recognize that other housewares makers—once a bunch of no-names who peddled junk—have greatly improved over the past half dozen years. The premium prices that Rubbermaid charges over its rivals have grown too large, and customers are turning away.

- Culture: The company's extraordinary financial targets…seem unrealistic—and straining to reach them is proving increasingly troublesome. Some of the friction between Rubbermaid and its customers can be traced to Rubbermaid's voracious appetite for growth.

Rubbermaid's profits peaked in 1994 at $228 million. In 1995 sales were up eight per cent but the company took a restructuring charge of $158 million pre-tax and net earnings fell to $60 million. The restructuring charges were taken in anticipation of a two-year program designed to reduce costs, improve operating efficiencies and accelerate growth. In 1997, Rubbermaid reported[4] that the realignment activities were substantially complete and that the company "has or initiated closure of all nine locations slated for closure in the plan, completed the associated reductions, and achieved the estimated annual savings of $50 million anticipated in the 1995 program." Unfortunately, this action did not have a material effect on sales, which remained essentially flat, and operating profits, which dipped somewhat, as detailed in the financial summary given in Exhibit 2 (on the next page). Thus, early in 1998, Rubbermaid announced another restructuring charge, which it estimated would reach at least $200 million pre-tax, to fund a program that would include centralizing global procurement and consolidating manufacturing and distribution worldwide.

---

[2]Materials accounted for between 45 and 50 per cent of Rubbermaid's net sales.

[3]Lee Smith, "Rubbermaid Goes Thump," Fortune, October 2, 1995.

[4]Rubbermaid Annual Report, 1997.

exhibit 2   Selected Financial Information for Rubbermaid, 1995-1998 ($000)

	To End Q3/98	12/31/97	To End Q3/97	12/31/96	12/31/95
Net sales	**$1,936,829**	**$2,399,710**	**$1,825,416**	**$2,354,980**	**$2,344,170**
Cost of products sold	1,383,564	1,748,424	1,327,990	1,649,520	1,673,232
Selling, general and administrative expenses	353,805	416,641	314,229	432,063	402,586
Operating income	199,460	234,645	183,197	273,397	268,352
Interest expense	27,795	35,762	28,463	24,348	10,260
Restructuring costs	73,740	16,000	16,000		158,000
Other, non-operating, net	(23,749)	(51,032)	(49,729)	4,046	4,457
Income taxes	42,586	91,370	77,717	92,614	35,863
Net Income	**$79,088**	**$142,536**	**$110,746**	**$152,398**	**$59,772**
Current assets	952,841	816,204		856,720	
Other assets	445,995	399,716		475,346	
Property, plant and equipment	784,228	707,974		721,914	
Total Assets	**2,183,064**	**1,923,984**		**2,053,980**	
Current liabilities	802,231	567,084		742,841	
Long-term debt	152,556	153,163		154,467	
Other non-current liabilities	171,302	153,385		142,992	
Shareholders' equity	1,056,885	1,050,262		1,013,700	
Total Liabilities and Shareholders' Equity	**2,183,064**	**1,923,984**		**2,053,980**	
Approximate common shares outstanding (000)		149,900		151,000	158,800
Earnings per share (fully diluted)		$0.95		$1.01	$0.38
Stock price $High/Low		$30/22		$30/22	$34/25

Source: Company Financial Reports.

Rubbermaid Lines of Business

In 1998, Rubbermaid manufactured and sold over 5,000 products[5] under four key brand names:

- Rubbermaid: a wide range of household utility products encompassing five categories (Kitchen, Home Organization, Health Care, Cleaning, and Hardware/Seasonal) and 23 product lines.
- Graco: children's products in six product lines focusing on baby strollers and related items.
- Little Tikes: juvenile products, with 11 product lines focusing on toys and furniture.
- Curver: a European-based home products business with revenues of $180 million, acquired at the beginning of 1998.

Rubbermaid's international sales and operations had been growing in recent years as it followed its customers abroad. The Curver acquisition increased foreign sales,

---

[5]In 1997 Rubbermaid had sold its Office Product business to Newell for a $134 million pretax gain, which it promptly offset by a one-time charge of $81 million for asset impairment related to acquisitions.

including exports from the United States, to about 25 per cent of total revenues, helping the firm along the path to its goal of 30 per cent by 2000.

Rubbermaid Strategy

Rubbermaid's strategy reflected an uneasy balance of not necessarily consistent ambitions. The 15 per cent growth goals of the past had disappeared from public statements, but there was no question that the company remained aggressive in its goals and optimistic about its prospects. To achieve its aims Rubbermaid relied on a multi-faceted competitive strategy. It wanted, at once, to be a company with a:

- strong consumer franchise based on unique product features, quality and rapid innovation, and on brand recognition and aggressive advertising. Rubbermaid had, for example, set a goal that 10 per cent of each year's sales should come from new, high value products and it had reduced new product time to market from 20-plus months in the 1980s to six months currently, with a goal of four months by 2000.

- low-cost sourcing, production, and fulfillment base. The company was in the process, for example, of cutting product variations by 45 per cent and consolidating its supplier base from 9,000 to less than 2,000 vendors.

- reliable and efficient supplier to mass merchandisers. Rubbermaid was moving, for example, to scheduling manufacturing by customer order and to just-in-time service and continuous replenishment of its best-selling items.

There was a tension at work behind these aims. In its 1996 Annual Report Rubbermaid noted that its market was at a point of inflection, in which the control of information was shifting from mass marketers to individual consumers. In this context Rubbermaid claimed that it would strike a new balance in its strategies, to continue to lead in innovation while becoming a low-cost producer. Similarly, in its 1997 Annual Report, the company noted that in a squeeze of higher costs and lower retail prices it was making bold moves to become the low-cost producer, while retaining world-class quality and innovation. Finally, another "point of inflection": in his 1997 Letter to Shareholders, Wolfgang Schmidt promised that, "with the initiatives of the past two years and the opportunities ahead, we are at the inflection point from which we can combine our financial strength and innovation capabilities with a more favorable cost climate to generate stronger shareholder returns."

THE OUTLINE OF A DEAL

Newell's appetite for all of Rubbermaid might have been whetted with its $247 million acquisition of Rubbermaid's Office products division in 1977, adding about $160 million of annualized revenues to Newell's developing office products line of business. Whatever the stimulus, talks soon began on a total combination of the two firms.

Negotiations led to a provisional agreement under which Rubbermaid shareholders would receive 0.7883 shares of Newell common stock for each share of Rubbermaid common stock that they owned. Based on Newell's closing price of $49.07 on October 20, 1998 this represented $38.68 per Rubbermaid share or a premium on 49 per cent over Rubbermaid's closing price of $25.88. Under this arrangement Newell would issue approximately 118 million shares of common stock to Rubbermaid shareholders. Rubbermaid shareholders would end up holding approximately 40 per cent of the combined company. The transaction represented a tax-free exchange of shares and would be accounted for as a pooling of interests. A simple pro forma of the results of the transaction is given in Exhibit 3.

Newell management forecast[6] that, as soon as the transaction was completed, they would begin the "Newellization" process and improve Rubbermaid's operating efficiencies to achieve 98 per cent on-time and line-fill performance and a minimum 15 per cent pretax margin. They also expected revenue and operating synergies through the leveraging of Newell Rubbermaid's brands, innovative product development, improved service performance, stronger combined presence in dealing with common customers, broader acquisition opportunities, and an increased ability to serve European markets. They forecast that by 2000 these efforts and opportunities would produce increases over anticipated 1998 results of $300 million to $350 million in operating income for the combined company.

exhibit 3   Simple Pro Forma Financial Information for NewellRubbermaid, EndQ3-1998 ($000)

	Newell Q3/97-Q3/98	Rubbermaid Q3/97-Q3/98	Simple Pro Forma NewellRubbermaid Q3/97-Q3/98
Net sales	3,591,459	2,511,123	6,102,582
Cost of products sold	2,414,938	1,803,998	4,218,936
Selling, general and administrative expenses	537,498	456,217	993,715
Goodwill amortization and other	49,512		49,512
Operating Income	589,511	250,908	840,419
Interest expense	66,016	35,094	101,110
Other, non-operating, net	(215,197)*	48,688	(166,509)
Profit before tax	738,692	167,126	905,818
Income taxes	310,554	56,239	366,793
Net Income	428,138	110,887	539,025
Balance Sheet as of End Q3/98			
Current assets	1,767,370	952,841	2,720,211
Property, plant and equipment	834,486	784,228	1,618,714
Trade names, goodwill, other	2,001,862	445,995	2,447,857
Total Assets	4,603,718	2,183,064	6,786,782
Current liabilities	1,061,675	802,231	1,863,906
Long-term debt	912,650	152,556	1,065,206
Other non-current liabilities	243,862	171,302	415,164
Convertible preferred securities	500,000		500,000
Shareholders' Equity	1,885,531	1,056,885	2,942,416
Total Liabilities and Shareholders' Equity	4,603,718	2,183,064	6,786,782
Approximate common shares outstanding (000)	173,000	150,000	291,000
Earnings per share (fully diluted)	$2.47	$0.74	$1.85

* Primarily gain from sale of Black & Decker holdings.
Source: Estimates based on Company Financial Reports.

[6]Newell Press release, October 21, 1998.

case 19 Vincor and the New World of Wine

On September 16, 2002, Donald Triggs, chief executive officer (CEO) of Vincor International Inc. (Vincor) was preparing for the board meeting to discuss the possible acquisition of Goundrey Wines, Australia. Vincor had embarked upon a strategic internationalization plan in 2000, acquiring R.H Phillips and Hogue in the United States. Although Vincor was the largest wine company in Canada and the fourth largest in North America, Triggs felt that to be a major player, Vincor had to look beyond the region. The acquisition of Goundrey Wines in Australia would be the first step. Convincing the board would be difficult, as the United States was a close and attractive market where Vincor had already spent more than US$100 million on acquisitions. In contrast, Australia was very far away.

THE GLOBAL WINE INDUSTRY

Wine-producing countries were classified as either New World producers or Old World producers. Some of the largest New World producers were the United States, Australia, Chile and Argentina. The largest of the Old World producers were France, Italy and Spain (see Exhibit 1). The world's top 10 wine exporters accounted for more than 90 per cent of the value of international wine trade. Of those top 10, half were in western Europe, and the other half were New World suppliers, led by Australia (see Exhibit 2).

France

France had been a long-time world leader in the production of wine, due to historical and cultural factors. France was the top producer of wine in the world (see Exhibit 1). The French had developed the vins d'appellation d'origine contrôlée (AOC) system

Nikhil Celly prepared this case under the supervision of Professor Paul W. Beamish solely to provide material for class discussion. The authors do not intend to illustrate either effective or ineffective handling of a managerial situation. The authors may have disguised certain names and other identifying information to protect confidentiality.

Copyright © 2003, Ivey Management Services   Version: (A) 2003-12-05

Richard Ivey School of Business
The University of Western Ontario

centuries ago to ensure that the quality of wine stayed high. There were many regions in which quality grapes could be grown in France. Some of their better-known appellations were Bordeaux, Burgundy and Champagne. France was the second largest exporter of wine (see Exhibit 2).

Italy

Italy, like France, also had a very old and established wine industry that relied on the appellation method to control the quality. Italy was the second largest producer of wine in the world (see Exhibit 1) and the largest exporter (see Exhibit 2).

Australia

Grape vines were first introduced to Australia in 1788. The wine "industry" was born in the 1860s when European immigrants added the skilled workforce necessary to develop the commercial infrastructure. The Australian wine industry grew after 1960 with the development of innovative techniques to make higher quality wine while keeping costs down. Australia was the sixth largest producer of wine in the world (see Exhibit 1). Australia had 5.5 per cent of the total export market and was ranked fourth in the world for its export volume (see Exhibit 2).

Chile

The first vines were introduced to Chile in the 16th century. Due to political and economic instability, the wine industry was not able to develop and take on a global perspective until 1979 when Chile began to focus on the exporting of natural resources to strengthen its economy. Despite being only the 10th largest producer, Chile had 4.5 per cent of the total export market and was ranked fifth in the world (see Exhibit 2).

Argentina

Argentina had a long history of making wine. However, the quality of the wine from Argentina was never as high, due to the small area of land that was capable of producing high quality grapes. Argentina was the fifth largest producer of wine in the world (see Exhibit 1), but did not feature in the top 10 exporters of wine.

All of the countries, with the exception of Argentina, were capable of shipping brands that could compete at a wide range of price points. The French wines typically were capable of competing in the higher price classes, and could retail for more than US$100 per bottle.

MAJOR WORLD MARKETS

After a 2.2 per cent gain in 2001, the global wine market was estimated to have increased another 1.2 per cent in 2002 to 2.55 billion cases, according to The Global Drinks Market: Impact Databank Review and Forecast 2001 Report. Wine consumption was projected to expand by 120 million cases by 2010. Most of the growth was expected to come from major wine-consuming nations, such as the United States, United Kingdom, Australia and South Africa, as well as from less developed wine markets, such as China and Russia.

Wine imports were highly concentrated. The 10 top importing countries accounted for all but 14 per cent of the value of global imports in the late-1980s. In 2001, half the value of all imports was purchased by the three biggest importers: the United Kingdom (19 per cent), the United States (16 per cent) and Germany (14 per cent).

France and Italy were the number one and two countries in the world for per capita consumption (see Exhibit 3). However, the consumption rate in France was relatively stagnant, while Italy was showing a decrease. Italy, unlike France, had a very small market for imported wines. The import market sizes for France and Italy were respectively 13.4 per cent and 2.8 per cent in 2001, based on volume.

The United Kingdom's wine market was considered to be the "crucible" for the global wine market (Wine Market Report, May 2000). The United Kingdom had very small domestic wine production and good relationships with many of the wine-producing countries in the world. This coupled with the long history of wine consumption, resulted in an open and competitive market. The United Kingdom was ranked number seven for consumption in 2001 with a trend of increasing consumption. The United Kingdom wine market was dominated by Old World country imports; however New World imports had grown as Australian wines replaced French wines as the number one import (see Figure 1).

Other Countries

In 2001, Canada was ranked number 30 in the world for per capita consumption, with an increasing trend. Japan had seen a steady increase in the size of its imported wine market. Asia presented a great opportunity for wine producers around the world because it had populous markets that had yet to be tapped.

figure 1   United Kingdom Wine Market Share

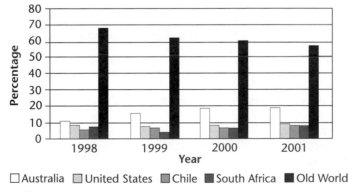

Source: Company files.

THE U.S. WINE INDUSTRY

The international image of the U.S. wine industry until the mid 1970s was that of a low-quality jug wine producer. This changed in 1976 during a blind wine-tasting contest in France where California wines from Napa Valley beat out several well-established European wines for the top honors. From that time forward, there has been a focus on developing high-quality wines that could compete in the international market from the northern California appellations, such as Napa Valley and Sonoma County. The United States was the fourth largest producer of wine (1.98 billion litres) in 2001 (see Exhibit 1), with California wines accounting for 90 per cent of production volume. There were more than 3,000 wineries in all 50 states. The nation's top wine-producing states were California, New York, Washington and Oregon.

The United States saw huge gains in the total volume and value of its wine exports, increasing from US$85 million in 1988 to US$548 million in 2002. The major markets for U.S wines included the United Kingdom, Canada and Japan. Together they represented 66 per cent of the total export market value for the United States (see Exhibit 4).

The United States was the third largest wine market in the world, consuming 2.13 billion litres a year in 2001. It was also one of the biggest untapped wine markets in the world; seven per cent of the U.S. population accounted for 86 per cent of the country's wine consumption. The total wine market in the United States in 2001 was $21.1 billion, with an average growth rate of six per cent since 1994. Of this, approximately $10 billion were sales of New World wines.

While California wines dominated the domestic market (67 per cent market share) due to the ideal growing conditions and favorable marketing and branding actions taken by some of California's larger wineries, imports were on the rise. The United States had one of the most open markets in the world for wine, with low barriers to entry for imports. Imports represented 530 million litres for a 25 per cent share of the market. By 2002, wine imports grew by 18 per cent (see Figures 2 and 3).

Wine was the most popular alcoholic beverage in the United States after beer, which accounted for 67 per cent of all alcohol consumed. The table wine category represented 90 per cent of all wine by volume, dessert wine was six per cent and sparkling wine accounted for four per cent. U.S.-produced table wine held an 83 per cent share of the volume and 78 per cent of the value. Premium wine ($7 and more per 750 ml bottle) sales increased eight per cent over 2001, accounting for 30 per cent of the volume, but a sizeable 62 per cent of winery revenues. Everyday value-priced wines selling for less than $7 per bottle grew about 1.5 per cent by volume. This segment represented 70 per cent of all California table wine shipments and 38 per cent of the value.

figure 2   United States Wine Markets 1998 to 2001

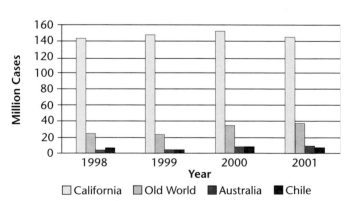

Source: Company files.

figure 3   United States Wine Market Growth Rates

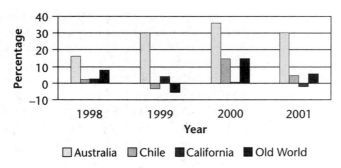

□ Australia ▨ Chile ▦ California ■ Old World

Source: Company files.

The United States wine industry was fragmented, with the largest producer, E. & J. Gallo, supplying 30 per cent and no other producer supplying more than 15 per cent by volume in 2002.

In the United States, a law mandated the implementation of a three-tier distribution system. The wine producers were required to sell to a wholesaler, who then sold to an established customer base of grocery stores, liquor stores, hotels and restaurants. Wineries were capable of using a two-tier distribution system, which allowed wineries to sell directly to the customers through gift shops located at the winery. The role of the distribution channel was growing and taking on greater strategic importance as the trend towards international and domestic consolidation grew.

THE CANADIAN WINE INDUSTRY

Canadians had been making wine for more than two centuries, but Canada's modern-day success in the production of high-quality vinifera-based wines went back only a quarter century. The signing of the North American Free Trade Agreement in 1988, together with a ruling under the General Agreement on Tariffs and Trade (GATT), required Canada to abandon the protection it offered its wine industry. While many producers felt threatened, many more responded by reaffirming their belief in their capacity to produce premium wines, and redoubled their efforts to prove it. New vineyards were planted with only the finest varieties of grapes: Chardonnay, Riesling, Sauvignon Blanc, Pinot Gris, Gewürztraminer, Pinot Noir, Cabernet Sauvignon, Merlot and others.

During 1988, the Vintners Quality Alliance (VQA) was launched in Ontario, culminating six years of voluntary initiatives by the leaders of Ontario's wine industry. This group set the standards, to which they agreed to comply, to elevate the quality of Canadian wines and provide quality assurances to the consumer. British Columbia adopted similar high standards in 1990, under the VQA mark.

The 1990s was a decade of rapid growth. The number of commercial wineries grew from about 30 in 1990 to more than 100 by the end of the decade, and consumers began to recognize the value represented by wines bearing the VQA medallion. Canadian vintners continued to demonstrate that fine grape varieties in cooler growing conditions could possess complex flavors, delicate yet persistent aromas, tightly focused structure and longer aging potential than their counterparts in warmer growing regions of the world.

In Canada, despite increasing import competition, sales of Canadian quality wines were increasing as consumers moved up the quality and price scale (see Figure 4).

Canadian quality wines began to capture both domestic and international recognition not only in sales but also by garnering an impressive list of significant wine awards, beginning in 1991 when Inniskillin won the Grand Prix d'Honneur for its 1989 icewine at the prestigious VinExpo, in Bordeaux, France. New access for Canadian wines, especially icewine, in the European market, and expanding market opportunities in the United States and Asia were giving Canadian wines greater market exposure.

figure 4   The Canadian Wine Market

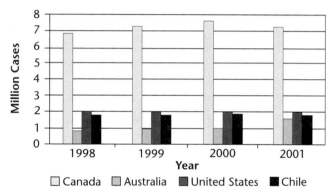

Source: Company files.

THE AUSTRALIAN WINE INDUSTRY

The Australian wine industry was structured to be able to deliver large quantities of high-quality branded wine to the world's major markets, at costs less than many of their Old World and New World competitors. Since Australia had a very limited domestic market (population of only 17 million), the wineries realized that if the industry was to continue to grow it would have to do so internationally.

As a result, Australian wineries had gained, and were expected to continue to gain, market share. Growth had been in exports as well as domestic sales (see Exhibits 5 and 6). Australia had recently overtaken France as the largest exporter to the United Kingdom, where seven of the top 10 wine brands were Australian. Exports to North America had grown at 27 per cent by volume in 2001. Consumption of Australian wine in Canada was up 24 per cent and in the United States consumption was up 35 per cent. The growth trends were expected to continue. Export growth had been driven by sales of premium red wine which accounted for 53 per cent of Australia's wine exports.

Domestic wine consumption had grown from 296 million litres in 1991 to 398 million litres in 2001, an annual growth rate of four per cent. The Australian domestic market was relatively unregulated compared to North America, although alcohol taxes were high (42 per cent). Wineries were allowed to have their own retail outlets and sell directly to retailers or on-premise customers. The 7,500 licensed liquor retail outlets, accounted for 56 per cent of wine sales while the 28,000 licensed on-premise outlets accounted for 44 per cent of wine sales.

Although there were 1,300 wineries in Australia, the industry was the most concen trated of any major wine region, with 80 per cent of production being accounted for by four players: Southcorp Wine, Beringer Blass, BRL Hardy and Orlando Wyndham. The large wineries had their own sales forces, as well as warehouses in the major markets.

Southcorp Wines was Australia's largest winery and vineyard owner, with sales of AUD$1.5 billion. Beringer Blass was owned by the Fosters Group and had wine revenues of approximately AUD$800 million (seven million cases). The purchase of Beringer (for AUD$2.6 billion) provided the company with significant growth and U.S. market access.

BRL Hardy had revenues of more than AUD$700 million. The company had several top brands and a very strong U.K. market position. A recent joint venture in the United States with Constellation brands had improved their United States market access. Orlando Wyndham was owned by Pernod Ricard, a French publicly traded spirits company.

TRENDS IN THE GLOBAL WINE INDUSTRY

Wine was unique among alcoholic beverages in that its top 25 brands represented only seven per cent of the global market. In 2002, Martini vermouth was the world's most widely distributed wine, while Gallo's E. & J. Wine Cellars was the largest-selling brand, at 25 million cases annually, with most of those sales in the United States.

Globally, vermouth and other fortified wines were projected to continue their long-term decline, but this would be more than offset by expected growth in table wines, which accounted for more than 90 per cent of total wine consumption. The hottest sales category was Australian wines, with brands such as Rosemount Estate, Jacob's Creek and Lindemans showing double-digit growth rates.

The North American market was expected to exhibit annual growth rates of three per cent. There were positive demographics, with the 20 to 39 age group having a per capita consumption at 7.9 litres and the 40+ age group having a per capita of 14.0 litres. The ongoing trends were a shift in consumer preference to red wines and premium wines (see Exhibits 7, 8).

The global wine market was consolidating in terms of its retail, wholesale and production operations. One key to success seemed to be distribution and marketing. Globalization was also altering the structure of firms both within the wine industry and among those distributing and retailing wine. Rapid growth in supermarkets and in concentration among distributors was driving wine companies into mergers and acquisitions to better meet the needs of those buyers and their customers. Since information about the various niches and the distribution networks in foreign markets was expensive to acquire, new alliances between wine companies were being explored with a view to capitalizing on their complementarities in such knowledge.

Recent examples of such alliances included the purchase by the owner of Mildara Blass (Fosters Brewing Group) of Napa Valley-based Beringer, the alliance between Southcorp/Rosemount and California's Mondavi, BRL Hardy's joint venture with the second largest U.S. wine company, Constellation Brands (to operate as Pacific West Partners) and the purchase by New Zealand's biggest wine firm (Montana) of the country's second largest winery (Corbans). See Exhibit 9 for the 10 largest wine companies worldwide.

VINCOR INTERNATIONAL INC.

Vincor International Inc. (Vincor) was formed as a combination of a number of Canadian wineries—Barnes Wines, Brights Wines, Cartier Wines, Inniskillin Wines and Dumont—over the period from 1989 to 1996. Vincor began operations in 1989 with a management buyout of Ridout Wines (Ridout) from John Labatt Ltd. The Ridout management team, led by Allan Jackson, Peter Graigner and John Hall, sought out Donald Triggs to lead the purchase and become CEO. They raised more than Cdn$2 million in equity, largely from personal finances, and borrowed $25 million to buy out Ridout. The new company was renamed Cartier Wines and Beverages.

Vincor had grown in three stages to become Canada's largest wine company in 2002. The first stage of growth had been a leveraged buyout (LBO) in turbulent times, 1989 to 1995, followed by a period of consolidation and rationalization—Building Canada's Wine Company (1990 to 2000). The third stage of growth was Building an International Wine Company (2000 onwards).

The first stage had seen the formation of Vincor and wine company acquisitions. From 1995 to 2000, Vincor acquired eight wineries, integrated its sales, marketing, production and accounting, and merged two wine-kit companies. This lead to economies of scale and a 21 per cent market share in 2000.

During this period, Vincor developed Canada's first premium wine brands: Jackson-Triggs, Inniskillin and Sawmill Creek. The Canadian wine market had seen a shift from popular (less than $7 retail price) to premium ($7 to $10 retail price), leading Vincor to start focusing on the premium and super-premium ($10 to $15 retail price) segments. They developed vineyards and re-capitalized wineries to support premium growth. Product coverage was also achieved in the growing ultra-premium ($15 to $20 retail price) and specialty (more than $20 retail price) segments. The year 2000 saw Vincor at a strategic crossroads. Triggs recalled:

> We were faced with three options. We could choose to be a cash cow by further developing our dominant Canadian position. A second option was to develop a diversified Canadian beverage conglomerate. A third option was to expand to the United States and perhaps beyond.
>
> We went for option 3. The move was driven by opportunities as well as threats. In terms of opportunities, the global trend was one of strong growth and premiumisation. There was an industry consolidation favoring global brands. The market was fragmented with the largest player only having one per cent market share. The markets for New World wine were growing. The dynamics in the U.S. market were highly profitable with very high profit margins. We were already #5 in North America and #22 globally.
>
> On the risk side, wine was an agricultural industry and as such susceptible to changing weather conditions. A diversified portfolio in terms of production and markets would only be an asset.

Triggs and Vincor decided to go international. The company's mission statement was drafted to reflect the new strategic plan:

> To become one of the world's top-10 wine companies, producing Vincor-owned New World, premium branded wines, which are marketed and sold through Vincor-controlled sales and distribution systems in all major premium wine consuming regions.

Where Were the Big Markets?

According to Triggs:

> The United States was the largest market with New World wine sales of $10 billion followed by the United Kingdom and Australia at $3.7 billion each. Canada and the rest of

Europe were next at $700 million. Japan was the sixth largest with sales of about $500 million. To be a New World market player, Vincor needed to be in five to six markets.

In 2002, the company's strategy was formulated for each region. In Canada, the aim was to build share in premium segments, to develop export capability and to generate cash and improve return on capital employed. In the United States, Vincor decided to focus on portfolio migration to high-end super-premium, enhancement of sales capability, product innovation and a shift to consumer marketing. Vincor's international strategy was to develop new geographic markets for core brands, specifically for icewine, a signature product for Canada that had attained world recognition. It was a luxury product in terms of pricing and margins and one of the top-five wine brands in select Asian duty-free stores. The U.S. launch was in F'01 in 1,850 high-end restaurants. By 2002, Inniskillin was being sold in 3,300 premium restaurants across the United States. The European launch of Inniskillin was slated for F'02.

U.S. ACQUISITIONS

R.H. Phillips

On October 5, 2000, Vincor acquired R.H. Phillips, a leading California estate winery, which produced a range of super-premium wines. The aggregate purchase price, including acquisition costs, was US$56.7 million. In addition, R.H. Phillips' debt of US$33.8 million was assumed and refinanced by the company. The Phillips acquisition and the refinancing of the assumed debt were funded entirely through borrowing from the company's senior lender.

R.H. Phillips was established in 1981 by John and Karl Giguiere. It was located in the Dunnigan Hills Viticultural Region near the wine regions of Napa and Sonoma. R.H. Phillips specialized in the production of super-premium wines, marketing its products under the brands R.H. Phillips, Toasted Head, EXP and Kempton Clark. Its wines were sold throughout the United States and in several other countries, including Canada. In 2001, its brands generated sales revenues of approximately US$25 million for Vincor. Its wines were distributed across the United States by a network of 13 sales executives, distributors and brokers.

The Phillips acquisition established a presence for Vincor in the U.S. wine market, in addition to adding strong brands, which were well-positioned in the super-premium category, one of the fastest growing segments of the wine market. With its national network of distributors and sales professionals, R.H. Phillips provided a platform for future acquisitions in the United States (such as the Hogue acquisition), while also facilitating the marketing of Vincor's products in the United States.

The Hogue Cellars

On September 1, 2001, Vincor acquired Hogue Cellars for US$36.3 million. Hogue was the second largest wine producer in Washington state, well-known for its super premium wine. Hogue was a family-controlled and family-operated winery founded in 1982 by Mike and Gary Hogue.

The Washington state wine industry had emerged as the second largest producer of premium wines in the United States, after California. Hogue produced red varietals, including Cabernet Sauvignon, Merlot and Syrah, as well as white varietals, including Chardonnay, Sauvignon Blanc, Riesling and Pinot Gris. In 2001, sales of Hogue-produced premium wine were 415,400 cases. In addition to its owned brands,

Hogue was the U.S. agent for Kim Crawford wines of New Zealand and Heritage Road wines from Brian McGuigan wines of Australia.

The Hogue acquisition added 11 sales people nationally and immediately increased Vincor's annual U.S. sales volume to more than one million cases and its annual U.S. revenues to more than US$60 million.

INTEGRATION WITH R.H. PHILLIPS

Vincor's management believed that Hogue was an excellent complement to the R.H. Phillips portfolio, as Hogue was primarily a super-premium brand, with approximately 88 per cent of its volume in the super-premium category. The strength of the Hogue product range lay in different varietals from the R.H. Phillips range. Different appellations greatly reduced portfolio overlap, as the character and taste of the wines were clearly distinct. Given the price and quality positioning of both businesses, customers were similar, and opportunity existed to improve the efficiency and effectiveness of the sales force, while simultaneously developing incremental sales for all brands in the combined portfolio. Vincor incurred expenses of US$4 million from the integration of Hogue and R.H. Phillips and from transaction costs related to the Hogue acquisition. It was management's objective that the integration of Hogue and R.H. Phillips would result in the realization of annual synergies of US$2.8 million.

VINCOR IN 2002

In 2002, Vincor was Canada's largest producer and marketer of wines, with leading brands in all segments of the market in Canada. Vincor had a 22 per cent market share and sales of Cdn$376.6 million (see Exhibit 11 for Financials). Andrés Wines Ltd., the second largest winery in Canada, had approximately an 11 per cent market share. Vincor was North America's fourth largest wine producer in terms of volume and the world's 22nd largest wine producer in terms of revenue.

The company had wineries in British Columbia, Ontario, Quebec, New Brunswick, California and Washington state, marketing wines produced from grapes grown in the Niagara Peninsula of Ontario, the Okanagan Valley of British Columbia, the Dunnigan Hills of California, the Columbia Valley of Washington state and other countries. The company's California and Washington wines were available throughout the United States and in parts of Canada (see Exhibit 10 for corporate structure).

Canada's government liquor distribution systems and the company's 165-store Wine Rack chain of retail stores sold Vincor's well-known and industry-leading brands: Inniskillin, Jackson-Triggs, Sumac Ridge, Hawthorne Mountain, R.H. Phillips, Toasted Head, Hogue, Sawmill Creek, Notre Vin Maison, Entre-Lacs, L'Ambiance, Caballero de Chile, Bellini, Spumante Bambino, President Canadian Champagne, Okanagan Vineyards, Salmon Harbor and other table, sparkling and fortified wines, Vex and the Canada Cooler brands of coolers, and the Growers and Vibe brands of cider.

In the United States, R.H. Phillips, Toasted Head, EXP, Kempton Clark and Hogue wine brands were distributed through a national network of more than 127 distributors, supported by eight brokers and 40 sales managers. The company's icewines were sold in the United States through a dedicated team of sales managers and internationally, primarily through the duty-free distribution channel. The company had seven employees outside of Canada engaged full-time in the sale of icewine.

Vincor's portfolio had evolved as per Table 1.

table 1   Evolution of Vincor's Portfolio—Table Wine

	F'95		F'02	
	% By Vol	% by $	% By Vol	% by $
Popular	83	80	47	28
Premium	17	20	53	72

Source: Company files.

The company's objectives in 2002 were to obtain a top quartile return on capital employed (ROCE) of 16 per cent to 20 per cent and to achieve sales of Cdn$1 billion and an earnings per share (EPS) of more than 15 per cent. At the time these objectives were to be met as per Table 2.

table 2   Company Sales Objectives (Cdn$ millions)

	Current	5 Years
Canada	300	400
United States	100	200
Icewine	15	50
Acquisitions	0	350
Total	415	1,000

Source: Company files.

GOUNDREY WINES PTY. LTD.

Goundrey Wines was one of the pioneer winery operations in Western Australia. The Goundrey family had established the vineyard in 1972, and the first vintage was produced in 1976. By 1995, the business had grown to approximately 17,000 cases in annual sales and was sold to Perth businessman Jack Bendat. Bendat expanded both the vineyards and the winery to reach 2002 sales levels of 250,000 cases annually and revenues of AUD$25 million. Goundrey was one of the largest wineries in Western Australia, selling under two labels, Goundrey and Fox River (see Exhibit 12 for financials).

Bendat was 77 years old, and health and family concerns had resulted in his recent decision to sell the business. Vincor believed it would be able to purchase the assets of Goundrey for AUD$46 million plus working capital at close (estimated at AUD$16.5 million) plus transaction costs of AUD$2 million for an enterprise value of AUD$64.5 million.

The majority of the Goundrey brand volume (85 per cent) was sold in the $15 to $30 super-premium segment of the Australian market. The ultra-premium segment ($30 to $50) accounted for seven per cent of sales and the premium ($10 to $15) for the remaining eight per cent. The company's sales were almost entirely in the domestic market, with three per cent export sales. When asked what was Goundrey's export strategy, Bendat said, "I answer the phone."

Goundrey employed its own sales force in Queensland and New South Wales, with a total of 13 sales reps and four sales managers in two states. In other states, Goundrey had appointed distributors. In all regions, Goundrey was the most important winery for the distributor. Goundrey had tighter control of its distribution capability in Australia than most of its competitors. Goundrey consumption was running at more than 26 per cent year-over-year growth.

Located 350 km south of Perth, the winery could process 3,500 tonnes of grapes. The winery also had its own bottling capability, enabling it to support an export business where each export market has different labeling requirements.

Triggs felt the Goundrey acquisition would be an important strategic move for Vincor. He saw several major advantages. First, the acquisition would be a significant step in achieving Vincors' strategy of converting from a North American to a global player. The Australian wine industry had captured market share in the world's new wine markets and was poised to continue to do so. Second, the Western Australia region had an established reputation for super- and ultra-premium wines. Although the grape harvest was a mere four per cent of the Australian total, more than 25 per cent of Australia's super-premium wines were sourced from that state. Third, the company had developed its own sales force in Queensland and New South Wales. Triggs wanted the proposal to go through.

exhibit 1   Top 10 Producers of Wine in the World—2001

Country	Wine Production* (million litres)	Share of World Production (%)
France	5,330	19.9
Italy	5,090	19.0
Spain	3,050	11.4
United States	1,980	7.4
Argentina	1,580	5.9
Australia	1,020	3.8
Germany	900	3.4
Portugal	770	2.9
South Africa	650	2.4
Chile	570	2.1
World	27,491	

* Does not include juice and musts (the expressed juice of fruit and especially grapes before and during fermentation; also the pulp and skins of the crushed grapes).
Note: 1 litre = 0.26 gallons; each case contains 12 × 750 ml bottles = 9 litres.
Source: G. Dutruc-Rosset, Extract of the Report on World Vitiviniculture, June 24, 2002.

exhibit 2   Top 10 Exporters of Wine in the World—2001

Country	Wine Production* (million litres)	Share of World Exports (%)
Italy	1,830	26.5
France	1,580	22.9
Spain	990	14.4
Australia	380	5.5
Chile	310	4.5
United States	300	4.3
Germany	240	3.5
Portugal	200	2.9
South Africa	180	2.6
Moldavia	160	2.3
World	6,897	

Source: G. Dutruc-Rosset, Extract of the Report on World Vitiviniculture, June 24, 2002.

exhibit 3   Top 10 Wine-Consuming Nations—2001

Country	Wine Consumption (million litres)	Share of World Consumption (%)
France	3,370	15.4
Italy	3,050	13.9
United States	2,133	9.7
Germany	1,966	9.0
Spain	1,400	6.4
Argentina	1,204	5.5
United Kingdom	1,010	4.6
China	580	2.6
Russia	550	2.5
Romania	470	2.1
World	21,892	

Source: G. Dutruc-Rosset, Extract of the Report on World Vitiviniculture, June 24, 2002.

exhibit 4   U.S. Wine Exports—Top Countries (by Dollar Value in 2002)

Country Ranking by 2002 Dollar Value	Value ($000)	Volume (litres 000)
United Kingdom	188,895	95,446
Canada	92,571	50,348
Japan	81,199	32,342
Netherlands	53,201	26,388
Belgium	18,791	10,884
France	13,326	5,943
Germany	11,818	8,634
Ireland	10,153	5,380
Switzerland	7,199	3,914
Denmark	5,710	3,933
Mexico	5,001	3,705
Taiwan	4,868	2,736
South Korea	3,865	2,439
China	3,370	2,537
Singapore	3,002	1,822
Sweden	2,782	1,145
Hong Kong	2,393	1,140

Source: Wine Institute and Ivie International using data from U.S. Dept. of Commerce, USA Trade Online. History revised. Numbers may not total exactly due to rounding.

exhibit 5   Australia Wineries

	1998 to 1999	2000 to 2001
Wineries (number)	1,150	1,318
Hectares under vine	122,915	148,275
Wine grape production	793	1,035
Wine consumption	373	398
Wine exports		
million litres	216	339
AUD$ million	$ 991	$ 1,614
Wine imports		
million litres	24	13
AUD$ million	$ 114	$ 92

Source: Company files.

exhibit 6   Australia—Top Export Markets—2001

	Million Litres	AUD$ Million
United Kingdom	183	762
United States	78	457
Canada	17	106
New Zealand	23	83
Germany	13	55
Other	61	301
All Markets	375	1,764

Source: Company files.

exhibit 7   The Wine Market—Canada—Fiscal 2002

	Retail Price	% By Volume	Trend	% By Sales
Popular	< $7	33%	−5%	20%
Premium	$7–$10	35%	5%	30%
Super-Premium	$10–$15	24%	19%	33%
Ultra-Premium	$15–$20	6%	31%	15%
Specialty	>$20	2%	45%	6%

Source: Company files.

exhibit 8 The U.S. Market for California Wine—Fiscal 2002

	Retail Price	% By Volume	F'02 Trend*	% By Sales
Jug	<$3	36%	–4%	12%
Premium	$3–$7	36%	–2%	27%
Super-Premium	$7–$15	18%	8%	28%
Ultra-Premium	>$15	10%	3%	33%

* Total U.S. table wine market +1%; imports +9%; states other than California +4%

Source: Company files.

exhibit 9 Top 10 Wine Companies and Sales in 2002 (US$)

Company	Country	Wine Sales ($ Million)
E. & J. Gallo Winery	United States	1,500
Foster's Group	Australia	818
Seagram	Canada	800
Constellation Brands	United States	712
Southcorp	Australia	662
Castel Freres	France	625
Diageo	Britain	590
Henkell & Sonlein	Germany	528
Robert Mondavi	United States	506

Note: Excludes France's LVMH, which earned more than 75 per cent of its $1.6 billion in wine sales from champagne.

Source: Direction des Etudes/Centre Français du Commerce Exterieur.

exhibit 10 Vincor's Significant Legal Subsidiaries—2001 (all wholly owned)

Subsidiary	Jurisdiction of Incorporation
Hawthorne Mountain Vineyards (2000) Ltd	Canada
The Hogue Cellars, Ltd	Washington
Inniskillin Wines Inc	Ontario
Inniskillin Okanagan Vineyards Inc	British Columbia
R.H. Phillips, Inc	California
Spagnol's Wine & Beer Making Supplies Ltd	Canada
Sumac Ridge Estate Winery (2000) Ltd.	Canada
Vincor (Quebec) Inc	Quebec

Source: Company files.

exhibit 11   Vincor Consolidated Financials (1998 to 2002) (Cdn$ millions)

						Average Annual Growth	
	F'98	F'99	F'00	F'01	F'02	F'01-02	F'98-02
Revenue	206.4	253.2	268.2	294.9	376.6	27.70%	17.70%
EBITDA	28.1	35.0	37.9	49.5	70.5	42.40%	26.10%
% Revenue	13.60%	13.80%	14.10%	16.80%	18.70%		
Net Income	10.8	11.7	13.3	14.3	26.9	40.10%	25.60%
Avg.Capital Empl'd	145.5	191.6	222.1	310.4	468.2		
ROCE (EBIT)	14.50%	13.80%	12.70%	13.10%	12.50%		
Funds Employed							
Receivables	30.4	33.3	35.7	37.4	55.1		
Inventory	65.1	83.1	70.7	125.9	175.6		
Working Capital	57.8	73.3	67.9	111.9	184.9		
Net Fixed Assets	45.2	60.0	73.3	165.9	178.8		
Other Assets	59.8	87.1	82.7	133.4	161.5		
Funds Employed	162.8	220.4	223.9	411.2	525.2		
Turnover	1.2x	1.1x	1.2x	.7x	.7x		
Financing							
Debt (net)	50.9	92.5	80.5	254.5	110.1		
Deferred Tax	9.6	12.1	14.1	11.4	18.3		
Equity	102.3	115.8	129.3	145.3	396.8		
Financing	162.8	220.4	223.9	411.2	525.2		

Note: EBITDA — Earnings Before Interest, Taxes, Depreciation and Amortization
Source: Company files.

exhibit 12   Goundrey Financials (for years ending June 30) (000s)

	1999	2000	2001
Sales (000)	16,280	21,509	20,942
EBITDA	3,102	6,014	3,548
EBITDA%Sales	19.1%	28.0%	16.9%

Source: Company files.

case 20 Council of Forest Industries

In April 2003, the Council of Forest Industries (COFI) of British Columbia launched a comprehensive market development program to create new opportunities for Canadian wood products in China. Several of COFI's 100-plus member companies were facing a decision on whether to participate in this program or to pursue the world's largest potential market on their own.

THE FOREST INDUSTRY IN CANADA AND BRITISH COLUMBIA (B.C.)

With 10 per cent of the world's land base, Canada had 417.6 million hectares of forest, of which 235 million were considered commercial forests. Canada was also the world's largest exporter of forest products. Its forest industry was a key contributor to the national economy. Canadian companies had been logging for more than 120 years, yet almost 80 per cent of the forests remained untouched. In 2002, the forest industry made up 13 per cent of all Canadian manufactured shipments.

British Columbia's (B.C.) forests accounted for 45 per cent of total Canadian softwood (coniferous tree) stock and 12 per cent of hardwood (deciduous tree) stock. Although forests covered 62 per cent of B.C., the accessible "working forest" was limited to 24 per cent of the province. Ninety-five per cent of B.C.'s forests were publicly owned, and a provincial licensing and regulatory system tightly controlled their use.

Forestry activity contributed approximately $17 billion to the province's gross domestic product (GDP). Forestry activity in B.C. generated approximately $4 billion in government revenues annually. The forest sector's contribution to government coffers was almost equivalent to the Ministry of Education's annual kindergarten to Grade 12

Jing'an Tang prepared this case under the supervision of Professor Paul W. Beamish solely to provide material for class discussion. The authors do not intend to illustrate either effective or ineffective handling of a managerial situation. The authors may have disguised certain names and other identifying information to protect confidentiality.

operating budget. More than 270,000 British Columbians—14 per cent of the total workforce—were employed directly or indirectly by the forest industry. In Metro Vancouver alone, forestry accounted for over 120,000 direct and indirect jobs. Exhibits 1, 2, 3 and 4 show details of B.C. and Canadian forest production and trade activities.

BACKGROUND OF COUNCIL OF FOREST INDUSTRIES

The Council of Forest Industries had served as the leading trade association for lumber and other forest products manufacturers in British Columbia since 1960. COFI represented more than 100 forest company operations producing lumber, engineered wood products, pulp and paper, plywood and a variety of value-added products for national and international markets. COFI was governed by a board of directors elected by its members. It engaged members through a committee structure that maintained member involvement in every aspect of COFI activities.

COFI's vision was global competitiveness for the B.C. forest industry. COFI existed, on behalf of its members, to create a climate for consistent healthy economic performance of the B.C. forest industry.

COFI was committed to providing members with service in the following areas: quality control—including grader training and certification; government and public relations—provincial and regional; market access and development on a global scale; management support, advice and advocacy related to forestry, aboriginal affairs, occupational health and safety; transportation, environment and emerging issues of concern.

Traditionally, the B.C. forest industry was composed of a multitude of small companies. In the 1950s, many associations were formed in the forest industry. The proliferation of associations resulted in redundant and underfinanced export-oriented promotional campaigns and the duplication of operational expenditures. In 1960, most of the regional or small associations banded together to form the Council of Forest Industries of B.C. (CFI). In 1966, these and other similar organizations ceased to exist as separate entities and amalgamated into a single organization, COFI, to rationalize operations and achieve best efficiency.

In 1962, the U.S. forest industry was primarily focused on domestic markets. They requested tariff restrictions on Canadian lumber, which had been capturing increasing U.S. market share. COFI, representing the unified B.C. lumber industry, was instrumental in defeating this movement both as a participant in Trade Commission hearings and in the political arena.

In 1971, the Cooperative Overseas Market Development Program (COMDP) was initiated. It was equally financed by the Canadian federal government, the provincial government of British Columbia, and COFI. In 1989, the Cooperative Industrial and Market Development Program (CIMDP) was formed. Financed in the same manner as the COMDP, its purpose was to assist the growth of secondary manufacture of wood products in B.C.

In January 2003, COFI amalgamated with three regional associations in B.C.'s interior: Cariboo Lumber Manufacturer's Association, the Northern Forest Products Association and the Interior Lumber Manufacturer's Association. It was said that the struggling forestry industry could no longer sustain multiple associations. Some industry managers had even given notice that they intended to resign if the forestry associations failed to identify and implement a more focused model. This merger of the four associations under the COFI banner was intended to result in lower fees for its members and enhanced levels of service in the areas of public affairs, community relations, forest policy and international markets and trade. Large member companies such as Slocan, Weyerhaeuser, Weldwood, West Fraser, Tembec and Pope & Talbot all supported the merger. Exhibit 5 shows top global softwood lumber producers in 2001.

COFI MEMBERSHIP FEE STRUCTURE

COFI provided members with an optional level of service, and fees were structured accordingly. Service options were described as "policy" and "quality control." These two areas operated independently within COFI, and companies could subscribe to one or both.

Policy ("Corporate") Membership

Any corporate body engaged in the manufacture of forest products could apply to be a policy/corporate member for the purpose of subscribing to COFI's "policy" service (which included all COFI activities except quality control). A particular company and its subsidiaries were considered a single policy/corporate member. If approved by the board for membership, each policy/corporate member was entitled to nominate as a director to the board, its chief executive officer (CEO). Each policy/corporate member had full voting privileges at all general meetings of the organization.

Annual dues, and special assessments approved by the board, for policy/corporate members that saw and plane lumber ("sawmill operations") or further break down, finger-join or significantly process sawn lumber ("remanufacturing operations") were calculated on total lumber shipments per Mfbm.[1] Annual dues and special assessments approved by the board for policy/corporate members with "non-lumber forest product operations" (such as plywood, OSB-oriented strand board or veneer products, poles and posts and various manufactured forest products made from other than sawn lumber) were calculated on total log consumption using a formula to convert production to a round-wood equivalent.

The COFI board of directors determined the annual dues and any special assessments for policy/corporate members. Annual dues for the first half of 2003 were as follows:

- Sawmill operations   51 cents Mfbm
- Remanufacturing operations   20 cents Mfbm
- Non-lumber forest products operations   13.5 cents/M3
- Minimum dues $1,200/year

Minimum Dues

All policy/corporate members paid minimum annual dues of $1,200 regardless of total production or log consumption. All policy/corporate members could apply to subscribe to COFI's quality control (QC) service at the same rates as quality control ("limited") members but without the same restrictions as those who subscribe to quality control only.

Quality Control ("Limited") Membership

Any corporate body engaged in the manufacture of forest products could apply to be a QC/limited member for the purpose of subscribing to COFI's quality control service only.

---

[1]Mfbm—1,000 board feet

QC/limited members were not entitled to receive notice of, attend or vote at any general meeting of the organization. An application fee of $600 had to accompany an application for QC/limited membership. This fee was non-refundable once the COFI quality control committee had approved the applicant.

It was the objective of the COFI quality control division to provide a full-service QC program at competitive rates that were appropriate for a level of inspection service that assured all COFI subscribers maintain high standards.

The COFI quality control committee determined the annual dues rate on total shipment volumes (per Mfbm). The committee also determined whether it was appropriate to provide any QC/limited member with QC service on a per diem basis, what the per diem rate would be, and what the minimum dues were for QC/limited members. In January of 2003, the quality control committee established interim rates, subject to change if needed, as follows:

- Quality Control—regular inspection program   29 cents Mfbm
- Quality Control—per diem rate $300/half day—$600 /full day
- Minimum Annual Dues $1,200

MARKET ACCESS AND TRADE DIVISION OF COFI

The mandate of the division was to help secure the right or opportunity to conduct commercial business in world markets. The major functions and responsibilities were to focus on market access to secure the right or opportunity and positive climate to conduct commercial business, including issues such as tariffs and non-tariff barriers, building codes and product standards, environment and plant health, incoming missions of international visitors with influence on market access, education of key government, academic and trade personnel on the industry and products/product uses, and advocacy of wood versus non-wood products.

Paul Newman, the director for the market access and trade division, indicated that to fulfil COFI's marketing and trade missions, the division had organized and co-ordinated different programs to promote B.C. forest products in foreign countries.

Acting upon the collective interests of the B.C. forest industry, COFI tried to remove the regulative entry barriers for B.C. forest products. COFI organized meetings between the B.C. provincial government and host country governments, and contacted various regulatory and technical standard committees to promote Canadian wood products standard and certification marks (grade stamps). COFI had worked successfully with the Japanese government to revise the building and fire safety code in Japan, which facilitated the export of Canadian wood products to that country. In China, COFI had organized several trade missions to major cities such as Beijing and Shanghai, and co-ordinated meetings between B.C. government officials with their Chinese counterparts. These missions tried to forge relationships with key policy makers in China. In 2001, at the invitation of the Chinese Ministry of Construction, COFI co-ordinated the development of a new chapter on wood frame construction, using the input of technical experts in Canada and the United States.

COFI also co-operated with other specific product associations, for instance the SPF (spruce, pine and fir) association, to develop specific products-oriented trade shows or other marketing programs to promote member companies' products to the foreign market.

Beyond these missions, the market access and trade division also published and distributed monthly newsletters to its member companies, updating the latest market and general economic information in the key foreign markets.

SOME MEMBER COMPANIES OF COFI

The 100-plus member companies included multibillion dollar companies such as Weyerhaeuser, Weldwood and Slocan, as well as smaller firms such as Atco Lumber and Kozek with fewer than 100 employees.

Weyerhaeuser Company was one of the world's largest integrated forest products companies. It had offices or operations in 18 countries, with customers worldwide. Weyerhaeuser was principally engaged in the growing and harvesting of timber; the manufacture, distribution and sale of forest products; and real estate construction, development and related activities. Its worldwide headquarters were in Federal Way, Washington, U.S.A. Currently it had 57,000 employees with annual sales of US$18.5 billion. While it owned or leased 7.3 million acres of timberland in the United States, the majority of its timberland was in Canada with 35.4 million acres. It was one of the largest members of COFI.

Weldwood of Canada Limited, incorporated in 1964 in Vancouver, British Columbia, was a wholly owned subsidiary of International Paper Company. Its products ranged from lumber, plywood, laminated veneer lumber, treated wood products to northern bleached softwood Kraft pulp. It had 3,400 employees in Canada.

Slocan, formed in Richmond, British Columbia, in 1978, was one of Canada's largest producers of dimension lumber, laminated wood beams and wood chips and a significant producer of panel products and pulp. Almost 80 per cent of the timber processed in its 10 sawmills, one plywood mill and one OSB (oriented strand board) plant were harvested from interior forestlands subject to long-term forest tenure agreements with the provincial government. Slocan had 4,000 employees, with annual sales of $932 million.

Beyond these large member companies, there were also small players. They hired fewer employees and had simple production lines and fewer categories in their product portfolios.

The larger member companies were active in pushing B.C. forest products into foreign markets. Due to the similarity of their products, some of them competed head-on in foreign markets. Some invested more in developing the market, and some placed more effort towards exporting. When it came to member firms' marketing efforts, according to Newman, COFI would step back from their business activities.

> Multinational companies compete with each other almost everywhere in the world. COFI, as an industry association, tries to promote collective interests for all members and will never favor certain members or intervene with members' specific economic transaction.

CHINESE MARKET FOR HOUSING WOOD PRODUCTS

With one of the fastest growing economies in the world and 1.26 billion citizens. China had enormous potential as a new market for B.C. wood products. Nowhere was this more evident than in China's exploding residential construction market.

The overwhelming majority of residential and commercial buildings in China were constructed using concrete or steel. Density of construction and the absence of a domestic fibre supply had led to the widespread use of these non-organic building materials, even though Chinese consumers were increasingly aware of their disadvantages. The environmental impact of the production and disposal of these non-renewable and non-organic construction materials, the poor heat insulation, as well as the expense of non-organic construction made wood frame construction an attractive alternative.

In the last decade, the Chinese central government had privatized more than 70 per cent of China's housing inventory, creating a private sector housing market that did not exist previously. Furthermore, the rapid growth of China's middle class, rising consumer expectations for housing quality and the embrace of Western lifestyles had fuelled a growing demand for high quality and comfortable single dwelling homes. In fact, China had an ambitious plan to create 5,000 new satellite cities, resettling residents out of existing cities into model communities that would provide improved standards of housing and centres for new industry. Shanghai, an emerging powerhouse in Asia, was forecast to require an addition 14 million square feet of new residential accommodation annually to house its swelling population. This need was mirrored in other centres, with total Chinese residential construction estimated at two billion square feet per year. The opportunity for Canadian wood product producers was enormous.

Despite the benefits of wood frame construction and the growing demand for single-dwelling housing, until now only 500 wood frame homes had been built in China each year. Furthermore, long-term growth was constrained by quality problems, lack of a building code and unfamiliarity with the method. Though a large pool of Chinese builders and developers wanted to build wood frame homes, they had been held back by a lack of technical guidance and practical know-how.

A COFI-led B.C. delegation visited the People's Republic of China on a mission of goodwill to raise awareness of the benefits of wood frame construction. Led by Ron MacDonald, former president and CEO of the Council of Forest Industries, the delegation travelled to Beijing and Shanghai and met with some of China's most important construction and trade policy-makers. As a result of the visit and COFI's ongoing market development initiatives, China invited Canada to develop a stand-alone wood frame building code. This code would eliminate a significant obstacle that had prevented B.C. companies from entering the Chinese market.

COFI and its funding partners in the provincial and federal governments had developed a comprehensive market development strategy that sought to lay down a solid foundation of building codes and standards that would underpin a broad-based program of training for designers, builders and developers. Moreover, COFI intended to create a quality standard for wood frame structures in China that would ensure that wood buildings met consistent levels of construction quality and would provide an assurance to consumers and key service providers such as banks and insurance companies. Delivery of program elements would be undertaken by partnerships created between competent entities located in China and Canada.

In November 2002, COFI established a Canada Wood office in Shanghai and was expected to open another office in Beijing by mid-2003. COFI encouraged members travelling to China to contact these offices to discuss issues relating to the provincial forest industry's activities in China.

THE DREAM-HOME-CHINA PROJECT

On April 17, 2003, British Columbia's forest industry was partnering with the B.C. provincial government on an aggressive five-year strategy to open up new opportunities for B.C. wood products in the fast-growing Chinese housing market. The cornerstone of the strategy was the $12-million Dream-Home-China demonstration site planned for Shanghai. To be developed over three years as a 50–50 partnership between the province's Forest Innovation Investment, along with B.C. forestry companies and industry associations, the site would showcase single-family homes, townhouses and low-rise apartments—all using wood-frame construction. An on-site presentation centre would highlight advanced wood technologies and provide B.C. forestry associations and companies with a central location to market their products, technologies and expertise to the Chinese housing market.

As members of COFI and other industry associations, any companies in the B.C. forestry industry could volunteer to donate their products or services to build this demonstration site. COFI would try to bridge member companies with the provincial government project officials in charging of this market initiative; however, it was up to the government to decide which company and what products would be selected.

exhibit 1   British Columbia Log Exports by Country of Destination
2000 to 2002 (000s of cubic metres)

Year	United States	Japan	China	South Korea	Taiwan	Other	Total
2000	1,424.1	857.9	0.3	27.3	12.1	4.1	2,325.8
2001	1,644.0	1,086.3	1.6	53.1	21.1	3.8	2,809.9
2002	1,973.1	1,735.6	19.5	218.0	12.2	6.0	3,964.4

Source: Statistics Canada.

exhibit 2   British Columbia Shipments by Markets 2002

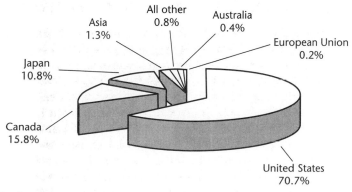

Source: Statistics Canada.

exhibit 3   Dollar Value of Exports of all Forest Products from Canada 2002
          (Cdn$ millions)

	United States	Japan	Other Pac.Rim*	United Kingdom	European Union	All Other	Total
Crude Materials							
Logs, Poles, Other Roundwood & Misc.	394.3	261.9	42.7	0.3	5.6	7.2	712.0
Wood Chips and Sawdust	128.9	60.2	1.0	0.3	11.4	0.4	202.2
Total Crude Materials	523.2	322.1	43.7	0.6	17.0	7.6	914.2
Fabricated Materials							
Wood							
Lumber, Hardwood	538.8	17.1	47.2	38.1	135.7	34.0	810.9
Lumber, Softwood	8,782.1	1,284.7	250.9	67.2	166.0	29.9	10,580.8
Total Lumber	9,320.9	1,301.8	298.1	105.3	301.7	63.9	11,391.7
Plywood, Hardwood	254.4	0.1	–	–	0.1	0.4	255.0
Plywood, Softwood	175.5	44.1	0.8	6.0	2.5	0.6	229.5
Total Plywood	429.9	44.2	0.8	6.0	2.6	1.0	484.5
Waterboard	1,720.8	40.0	6.1	–	–	0.7	1,767.6
Particleboard	303.0	–	–	–	–	–	303.0
Fiberboard	505.2	0.5	2.3	2.1	6.8	3.6	520.5
Shingles/Shakes	367.5	0.2	1.8	1.3	1.0	1.0	372.8
Veneers, Hardwood	291.5	1.0	21.8	0.6	16.8	6.1	337.8
Veneers, Softwood	191.6	0.6	0.5	–	0.1	0.1	192.9
Misc. Fabricated Wood	2,549.4	27.9	3.8	8.4	3.5	8.2	2,601.2
Total wood	15,679.9	1,416.2	335.2	123.7	332.5	84.6	17,972.1
Pulp and Paper							
Pulp, All Grades	3,081.0	532.6	1,626.1	215.1	1,296.3	152.3	6,903.4
Paper, Newsprint	4,851.1	173.1	164.4	252.7	353.5	529.2	6,324.0
Paper, All Other	10,243.3	28.6	176.3	26.0	62.8	221.2	10,758.2
Total Pulp and Paper	18,175.4	734.3	1,966.8	493.8	1,712.6	902.7	23,985.6
Total Fabricated Materials	33,855.3	2,150.5	2,302.0	617.5	2,045.1	987.3	41,957.7
Grand Total							
2002	34,378.5	2,472.6	2,345.7	618.1	2,062.1	994.9	42,871.9
2001	35,585.6	2,598.2	2,051.7	596.4	2,246.4	1,010.3	44,088.6
2000	36,245.1	2,472.6	2,345.7	618.1	2,062.1	994.9	44,738.5

*Includes East Asia and Oceania.
Source: Statistics Canada.

exhibit 4   Canada Lumber Production Softwood and Hardwood 2000 to 2002 (millions of board feet)

	2000	2001	2002
Softwood			
British Columbia			
Coast	2,850.8	2,242.5	2,450.7
Interior	10,776.0	10,535.3	11,772.5
Total	13,626.8	12,777.8	14,223.2
Alberta	2,656.7	2,646.9	2,796.6
Saskatchewan/Manitoba	576.5	493.9	629.4
Ontario	2,889.0	3,434.1	3,112.8
Quebec	7,237.2	7,751.4	7,487.0
New Brunswick	1,333.8	1,449.1	1,431.6
Nova Scotia	732.5	602.0	826.5
Total Softwood	**29,052.5**	**29155.2**	**30,507.1**
Hardwood	**458.8**	**433.4**	**441.6**
Total (soft and hard)	**29,511.3**	**29,588.6**	**30,948.7**

Source: Statistics Canada.

exhibit 5   Top Global Softwood Lumber Producers 2001

Rank	Company	Headquarters	Production (MM bf)*
1	Weyerhaeuser	USA	6,281.0
2	International Paper	USA	3,638.0
3	Stora Enso	Finland	2,415.0
4	Canfor	Canada	2,265.0
5	West Fraser	Canada	2,007.0
6	Georgia – Pacific	USA	1,882.0
7	Finnforest	Finland	1,801.0
8	Abitibi – Consolidated	Canada	1,704.0
9	Louisiana – Pacific	USA	1,420.0
10	Slocan	Canada	1,384.0
11	Sierra Pacific	USA	1,350.0
12	Tembec Canada	Canada	1,233.0
13	UPM–Kymmene	Finland	1,123.0
14	Buchanan	Canada	1,100.0
Total			29,603.0
Total World			**140,000.0**

* MM bf – a million board feet or Thousand thousand board feet.
Source: Company Reports, Wood Markets.

case 21 Neilson International in Mexico (A)

In January, 1993, Howard Bateman, vice-president of International Operations for Neilson International, a division of William Neilson Limited, was assessing a recent proposal from Sabritas, a division of Pepsico Foods in Mexico, to launch Neilson's brands in the Mexican market. Neilson, a leading producer of high-quality confectionery products, had grown to achieve a leadership position in the Canadian market and was currently producing Canada's top selling chocolate bar, "Crispy Crunch." In the world chocolate bar market, however, Neilson was dwarfed by major players such as M&M/Mars, Hershey/Lowney and Nestlé-Rowntree. Recognizing their position as a smaller player with fewer resources, in a stagnant domestic market, Neilson in 1990 formed its International Division to develop competitive strategies for their exporting efforts.

Recent attempts to expand into several foreign markets, including the United States, had taught them some valuable lessons. Although it was now evident that they had world class products to offer to global markets, their competitive performance was being constrained by limited resources. Pepsico's joint-branding proposal would allow greater market penetration than Neilson could afford. But, at what cost?

Given the decision to pursue international opportunities more aggressively, Bateman's biggest challenge was to determine the distributor relationships Neilson should pursue in order to become a global competitor.

Richard Ivey School of Business
The University of Western Ontario

Gayle Duncan and Shari Ann Wortel prepared this case under the supervision of Professors P.W. Beamish and C.B. Johnston solely to provide material for class discussion. The authors do not intend the case to illustrate either effective or ineffective handling of a managerial situation. The authors may have disguised certain names and other identifying information to protect confidentiality.

THE CHOCOLATE CONFECTIONERY INDUSTRY[1]

The "confectionery" industry consisted of the "sugar" segment, including all types of sugar confectionery, chewing gum, and the "chocolate" segment which included chocolates and other cocoa-based products. Most large chocolate operations were dedicated to two major products: boxed chocolates and bar chocolates which represented nearly 50 per cent of the confectionery industry by volume.

Competition from imports was significant, with the majority of products coming from the United States (39 per cent). European countries such as Switzerland, Germany, the United Kingdom and Belgium were also major sources of confectionery, especially for premium products such as boxed chocolates. (See Exhibit 1 for a profile of chocolate exporting countries.) In order to maintain production volumes and to relieve the burden of fixed costs on operations, Canadian manufacturers used excess capacity to produce goods for exporting. Although nearly all of these products were traditionally exported to the United States, in the early nineties, the world market had become increasingly more attractive.

Firms in the confectionery industry competed on the basis of brand name products, product quality and cost of production. Although Canadian producers had the advantage of being able to purchase sugar at the usually lower world price, savings were offset by the higher prices for dairy ingredients used in products manufactured for domestic consumption. Other commodity ingredients, often experiencing widely fluctuating prices, caused significant variations in manufacturing costs. Producers were reluctant to raise their prices due to the highly elastic demand for chocolate.

exhibit 1   World Chocolate Exports (Value as % of Total)—1990

	1987	1988	1989	1990
Africa	x1.5	x1.0	x1.1	x0.7
Americas	8.1	9.1	9.2	x9.1
LAIC[1]	2.1	1.9	1.4	x1.4
CACM[2]	0.1	x0.1	x0.1	x0.1
Asia	2.5	3.2	3.4	2.9
Middle East	x0.5	x0.5	x0.7	x0.4
Europe	86.4	85.0	84.2	85.4
EEC (12)[3]	73.3	71.8	71.3	73.5
EFTA[4]	12.5	12.7	12.1	11.5
Oceania	x1.5	1.8	x2.1	x1.8

Figures denoted with an "x" are provisional or estimated.
Adapted from: The United Nations' "International Trade Statistics Yearbook," Vol. II, 1990.
[1]LAIC = Latin American Industrialists Association.
[2]CACM = Central American Common Market.
[3]EEC (12) = The 12 nations of the European Economic Community.
[4]EFTA = European Free Trade Association.

---

[1]Some information is this section was derived from: J. C. Ellert, J. Peter Killing and Dana Hyde, "Nestlé-Rowntree (A)," in *Business Policy, A Canadian Casebook*, Joseph N. Fry et al. (Eds.), Prentice Hall Canada Inc., 1992, pp. 655-667.

Consequently, they sometimes reformatted or reformulated their products through size or ingredient changes to sustain margins. Three major product types were manufactured for domestic and export sales:

Blocks   These products are molded blocks of chocolate that are sold by weight and manufactured in a variety of flavours, with or without additional ingredients such as fruit or nuts. Block chocolate was sold primarily in grocery outlets or directly to confectionery manufacturers. (Examples: baking chocolate, Hershey's Chocolate Bar, Suchard's Toblerone.)

Boxed Chocolates   These products included a variety of bite-sized sweets and were generally regarded as "gift" or "occasion" purchases. Sales in grocery outlets tended to be more seasonal than for other chocolate products, with 80 per cent sold at Christmas and Easter. Sales in other outlets remained steady year round. (Examples: Cadbury's Milk Tray, Rowntree's Black Magic and After Eights.)

Countlines   These were chocolate-covered products sold by count rather than by weight, and were generally referred to by consumers as "chocolate bars." The products varied widely in size, shape, weight and composition, and had a wider distribution than the other two product types. Most countlines were sold through non-grocery outlets such as convenience and drug stores. (Examples: Neilson's Crispy Crunch, Nestlé-Rowntree's Coffee Crisp, M&M/Mars' Snickers, and Hershey/Lowney's Oh Henry!)

Sweet chocolate was the basic semi-finished product used in the manufacture of block, countline, and boxed chocolate products. Average costs of sweet chocolate for a representative portfolio of all three product types could be broken down as follows:

Raw material	35%
Packaging	10
Production	20
Distribution	5
Marketing/sales	20
Trading profit	10
Total (of manufacturer's selling price)	100%

For countline products, raw material costs were proportionately lower because a smaller amount of cocoa was used.

In value terms, more chocolate was consumed than any other manufactured food product in the world. In the late eighties, the world's eight major markets (representing over 60 per cent of the total world chocolate market) consumed nearly three million tonnes, with a retail value close to $20 billion. During the 1980's countline was the fastest growing segment, with close to 50 per cent of the world chocolate market by volume and an average annual rate of growth of seven per cent. An increasing trend towards indulgence in snack and "comfort" foods strongly suggested that future growth would remain strong.

COMPETITIVE ENVIRONMENT

In 1993, chocolate producers in the world included: M&M/Mars, Hershey Foods, Cadbury-Schweppes, Jacobs Suchard, Nestlé-Rowntree, United Biscuits, Ferrero, Nabisco and George Weston Ltd. (Neilson). Chocolate represented varying proportions of these manufacturers' total sales.

For the most part, it was difficult to sustain competitive advantages in manufacturing or product features due to a lack of proprietary technology. There was also limited potential for new product development since the basic ingredients in countline product manufacturing could only be blended in a limited variety of combinations. This forced an emphasis on competition through distribution and advertising.

Product promotion played a critical role in establishing brand name recognition. Demand was typified by high-impulse and discretionary purchasing behaviour. Since consumers, generally, had a selection of at least three or four favourite brands from which to choose, the biggest challenge facing producers was to create the brand awareness necessary to break into these menus. In recognition of the wide selection of competing brands and the broad range of snack food substitutes available, expenditures for media and trade promotions were considerable. For example, Canadian chocolate bar makers spent more than $30 million for advertising in Canada in 1992, mostly on television. This was often a barrier to entry for smaller producers.

MAJOR COMPETITORS

M&M/Mars

As the world leader in chocolate confectionery, M&M/Mars dominated the countline sector, particularly in North America and Europe, with such famous global brands as Snickers, M&Ms and Milky Way. However, in Canada, in 1992, M&M/Mars held fourth place, with an 18.7 per cent market share of single bars. (Exhibits 2 and 3 compare Canadian market positions with major competitors.)

M&M/Mars' strategy was to produce high-quality products which were simple to manufacture and which allowed for high volume and automated production processes. They supported their products with heavy advertising and aggressive sales, focusing marketing efforts on strengthening their global brands.

exhibit 2   Single Bars Canadian Market Share: 1991—1992

Manufacturer	1992	1991
Neilson	28.1%	29.4%
Nestlé/Rowntree	26.9%	26.2%
Hershey/Lowney	21.6%	21.9%
M&M/Mars	18.7%	19.0%
Others	4.7%	3.5%

Source: Neilson News—Issue #1, 1993

exhibit 3   Top Single Bars in Canada: 1991—1992

Top Single Bars	Manufacturer	1992	1991
Crispy Crunch	Neilson	1	1
Coffee Crisp	Nestlé/Rowntree	2	3
Kit Kat	Nestlé/Rowntree	3	2
Mars Bar	M&M/Mars	4	4
Caramilk	Cadbury Schweppes	5	6
Oh Henry!	Hershey/Lowney	6	5
Smarties	Nestlé/Rowntree	7	7
Peanut Butter Cups	Hershey/Lowney	8	8
Mr. Big	Neilson	9	11
Aero	Hershey/Lowney	10	10
Snickers	M&M/Mars	11	9
Crunchie	Cadbury Schweppes	12	12

Source: Neilson News—Issue #1, 1993

Hershey/Lowney

Hershey's strength in North America was in the block chocolate category in which it held the leading market position. Hershey also supplied export markets in Asia, Australia, Sweden, and Mexico from their chocolate production facilities in Pennsylvania. In Canada, in 1992, Hershey held third place in the countline segment with a 21.6 per cent share of the market.

Hershey's strategy was to reduce exposure to volatile cocoa prices by diversifying within the confectionery and snack businesses. By 1987, only 45 per cent of Hershey's sales came from products with 70 per cent or more chocolate content. This was down from 80 per cent in 1963.

Cadbury Schweppes

Cadbury was a major world name in chocolate, with a portfolio of brands such as Dairy Milk, Creme Eggs and Crunchie. Although its main business was in the United Kingdom, it was also a strong competitor in major markets such as Australia and South Africa.

Cadbury Schweppes diversified its product line and expanded into new geographic markets throughout the 1980s. In 1987, Cadbury International sold the Canadian distribution rights for their chocolate products to William Neilson Ltd. Only in Canada were the Cadbury brands incorporated into the Neilson confectionery division under the name Neilson/Cadbury. In 1988, Cadbury sold its U.S. operations to Hershey.

Nestlé-Rowntree

In 1991, chocolate and confectionery comprised 16 per cent of Nestlé's SFr 50.5 billion revenue, up sharply from only eight per cent in 1987. (In January 1993, 1SFr = $0.88 CAD = .69 U.S.) This was largely a result of their move into the countline sector through the acquisition in 1988 of Rowntree PLC, a leading British manufacturer with strong global brands such as Kit Kat, After Eights and Smarties. In 1990, they also added Baby Ruth and Butterfinger to their portfolio, both "Top 20" brands in the U.S. Considering these recent heavy investments to acquire global brands and expertise, it was clear that Nestlé-Rowntree intended to remain a significant player in growing global markets.

NEILSON

Company History

William Neilson Ltd. was founded in 1893, when the Neilson family began selling milk and homemade ice cream to the Toronto market. By 1905 they had erected a house and factory at 277 Gladstone Ave., from which they shipped ice cream as far west as Winnipeg and as far east as Quebec City. Chocolate bar production was initiated to offset the decreased demand for ice cream during the colder winter months and as a way of retaining the skilled labour pool. By 1914, the company was producing one million pounds of ice cream and 500,000 pounds of chocolate per year.

William Neilson died in 1915, and the business was handed down to his son Morden, who had been involved since its inception. Between 1924 and 1934, the "Jersey Milk," "Crispy Crunch" and "Malted Milk" bars were introduced. Upon the death of Morden Neilson in 1947, the company was sold to George Weston Foods for $4.5 million.

By 1974, "Crispy Crunch" was the number one selling bar in Canada. In 1977, "Mr. Big" was introduced and became the number one teen bar by 1986. By 1991, the Neilson dairy operations had been moved to a separate location and the ice cream division had been sold to Ault Foods. The Gladstone location continued to be used to manufacture Neilson chocolate and confectionery.

Bateman explained that Neilson's efforts under the direction of the new president, Arthur Soler, had become more competitive in the domestic market over the past three years, through improved customer service and retail merchandising. Significant improvements had already been made in Administration and Operations. All of these initiatives had assisted in reversing decades of consumer-share erosion. As a result, Neilson was now in a position to defend its share of the domestic market and to develop an international business that would enhance shareholder value. (Exhibit 4 outlines the Canadian chocolate confectionery market.)

Neilson's Exporting Efforts

Initial export efforts prior to 1990 were contracted to a local export broker—Grenadier International. The original company objective was to determine "what could be done in foreign markets" using only working capital resources and avoiding capital investments in equipment or new markets.

Through careful selection of markets on the basis of distributor interest, Grenadier's export manager, Scott Begg, had begun the slow process of introducing Neilson brands into the Far East. The results were impressive. Orders were secured for containers of "Mr. Big" and "Crispy Crunch" countlines from local distributors in Korea, Taiwan, and Japan. "Canadian Classics" boxed chocolates were developed for the vast Japanese gift ("Omiyagi") market. Total 1993 sales to these markets were projected to be $1.6 million.

For each of these markets, Neilson retained the responsibility for packaging design and product formulation. While distributors offered suggestions as to how products could be improved to suit local tastes, they were not formally obliged to do so. To secure distribution in Taiwan, Neilson had agreed to launch the "Mr. Big" bar under the distributor's private brand name "Bang Bang" which was expected to generate a favourable impression with consumers. Although sales were strong, Bateman realized that since consumer loyalty was linked to brand names, the brand equity being generated for "Bang Bang," ultimately, would belong to the distributor. This put the distributor in a powerful position from which it was able to place significant downward pressure on operating margins.

exhibit 4   Canadian Confectionery Market—1993

	Dollars (millions)	%
Total Confectionery Category	$1,301.4	100.0
Gum	296.5	22.8
Boxed Chocolates	159.7	12.3
Cough Drops	77.0	5.9
Rolled Candy	61.3	4.7
Bagged Chocolates	30.3	2.3
Easter Eggs	22.0	1.7
Valentines	9.4	0.7
Lunch Pack	3.6	0.3
Countline Chocolate Bars	641.6	49.3
Total Chocolate Bar Market Growth	+ 8%	

Source: Neilson Marketing Department Estimates

Market Evaluation Study

In response to these successful early exporting efforts, Bateman began exploring the possible launch of Neilson brands into the United States (discussed later). With limited working capital and numerous export opportunities, it became obvious to the International Division that some kind of formal strategy was required to evaluate and to compare these new markets.

Accordingly, a set of weighted criteria was developed during the summer of 1992 to evaluate countries that were being considered by the International Division. (See Exhibit 5 for a profile of the world's major chocolate importers.) The study was intended

exhibit 5   World Chocolate Imports (value as % of total)—1990

	1987	1988	1989	1990
Africa	x0.7	x0.7	x0.7	x0.7
Americas	x15.6	x15.0	x13.9	x13.2
LAIC[1]	0.2	0.4	1.1	x1.3
CACM[2]	x0.1	x0.1	x0.1	x0.1
Asia	11.7	x13.9	x15.6	x12.9
Middle East	x3.5	x3.3	x3.9	x2.8
Europe	70.8	68.9	67.7	71.4
EEC (12)[3]	61.1	59.5	57.7	59.3
EFTA[4]	9.3	9.0	8.9	8.4
Oceania	x1.3	x1.7	x2.1	x1.8

Figures denoted with an "x" are provisional or estimated.

Adapted from: The United Nations' "International Trade Statistics Yearbook," Vol. II, 1990.

[1]LAIC = Latin American Industrialists Association.
[2]CACM = Central American Common Market.
[3]EEC (12) = The 12 nations of the European Economic Community.
[4]EFTA = European Free Trade Association.

to provide a standard means of evaluating potential markets. Resources could then be allocated among those markets that promised long-term incremental growth and those which were strictly opportunistic. While the revenues from opportunistic markets would contribute to the fixed costs of domestic production, the long-term efforts could be pursued for more strategic reasons. By the end of the summer, the study had been applied to 13 international markets, including the United States. (See Exhibit 6 for a summary of this study.)

Meanwhile, Grenadier had added Hong Kong/China, Singapore and New Zealand to Neilson's portfolio of export markets, and Bateman had contracted a second local broker, CANCON Corp. Ltd, to initiate sales to the Middle East. By the end of 1992, the International Division comprised nine people who had achieved penetration of 11 countries for export sales (see Exhibit 7 on page 283 for a description of these markets). As of January 1993, market shares in these countries was very small.

THE U.S. EXPERIENCE

In 1991, the American chocolate confectionery market was worth US$5.1 billion wholesale. Neilson had wanted to sneak into this vast market with the intention of quietly selling off excess capacity. However, as Bateman explained, the quiet U.S. launch became a Canadian celebration:

> Next thing we knew, there were bands in the streets, Neilson t-shirts and baseball caps, and newspaper articles and T.V. specials describing our big U.S. launch!

The publicity greatly increased the pressure to succeed. After careful consideration, Pro Set, a collectible trading card manufacturer and marketer, was selected as a distributor. This relationship developed into a joint venture by which the Neilson Import Division was later appointed distributor of the Pro Set cards in Canada. With an internal sales management team, full distribution and invoicing infrastructures and a 45-broker national sales network, Pro Set seemed ideally suited to diversify into confectionery products.

Unfortunately, Pro Set quickly proved to be an inadequate partner in this venture. Although they had access to the right outlets, the confectionery selling task differed significantly from card sales. Confectionery items demanded more sensitive product handling and a greater amount of sales effort by the Pro Set representatives who were used to carrying a self-promoting line.

To compound these difficulties, Pro Set sales plummeted as the trading-card market became over-saturated. Trapped by intense cashflow problems and increasing fixed costs, Pro Set filed for Chapter 11 bankruptcy, leaving Neilson with huge inventory losses and a customer base that associated them with their defunct distributor. Although it was tempting to attribute the U.S. failure to inappropriate partner selection, the U.S. had also ranked poorly relative to other markets in the criteria study that had just been completed that summer. In addition to their distribution problems, Neilson was at a serious disadvantage due to intense competition from the major industry players in the form of advertising expenditures, trade promotions and brand proliferation. Faced with duties and a higher cost of production, Neilson was unable to maintain price competitiveness.

The International Division was now faced with the task of internalizing distribution in the U.S., including sales management, broker contact, warehousing, shipping and collections. Neilson managed to reestablish a limited presence in the American

exhibit 6   Summary of Criteria for Market Study (1992)

Criterion	Weight	Aust-ralia	China	Hong Kong	Indo-nesia	Japan	Korea	Malay-sia	New Zealand	Singa-pore	Taiwan	Mexico	EEC	U.S.A.
* U.S. countline	—	4	4	4	4	4	4	4	4	4	4	4	4	4
1 Candybar economics	30	20	20	30	20	20	28	20	15	25	15	20	10	10
2 Target market	22	12.5	14	13	15.5	19	15	10	7	9.5	12.5	21	22	22
3 Competitor dynamics	20	12	15	8	7.5	11	13.5	10	12	14.5	12	11	20	6.5
4 Distribution access	10	9	4	4	3.5	5	6	6.5	9	3.5	7.5	9.5	9	9
5 Industry economics	9	2.5	3.5	6	5.5	2	5	2.5	7	4.5	3	3.5	3.5	4.5
6 Product fit	8	7	6	6	6	3	7.5	7.5	7.5	8	4	8	5	8
7 Payback	5	4	4	1	2.5	4	5	2.5	4	2	2	5	2	1
8 Country dynamics	5	5	1	4	3	5	3.5	4.5	4.5	5	4	3	2	4
TOTAL	109	72	67.5	72	63.5	69	83.5	63.5	66	72	60	81	73.5	65

Competitor Dynamics	Score	Mexico
Financial success of other exporters	0–8	5
Nature (passivity) of competition	0–6	2.5
Brand image (vs. price) positioning	0–6	3.5
SCORE/20	/20	11

Due to Neilson/Cadbury's limited resources, it was not feasible to launch the first Western-style brands into new markets. The basic minimum criterion for a given market, therefore, was the presence of major Western industry players (e.g., Mars or Hershey). Countries were then measured on the basis of 8 criteria which were weighted by the International Group according to their perceived importance as determinants of a successful market entry. (See above table.) Each criterion was then subdivided into several elements as defined by the International Group, which allocated the total weighted score accordingly. (See table, right.)

This illustration depicts a single criterion, subdivided and scored for Mexico.

Source: Company Records

exhibit 7   Neilson Export Markets—1993

Agent (Commission)	Country	Brands
Grenadier International	Taiwan	Bang Bang
	Japan	Mr. Big, Crispy Crunch, Canadian Classics
	Korea	Mr. Big, Crispy Crunch
	Hong Kong/China	Mr. Big, Crispy Crunch, Canadian Classics
	Singapore	Mr. Big, Crispy Crunch
CANCON Corp. Ltd.	Saudi Arabia	Mr. Big, Crispy Crunch, Malted Milk
	Bahrain	Mr. Big, Crispy Crunch, Malted Milk
	U.A.E.	Mr. Big, Crispy Crunch, Malted Milk
	Kuwait	Mr. Big, Crispy Crunch, Malted Milk
Neilson International	Mexico	Mr. Big, Crispy Crunch, Malted Milk
	U.S.A.	Mr. Big, Crispy Crunch, Malted Milk

Source: Company Records

market using several local brokers to target profitable niches. For example, they placed strong emphasis on vending-machine sales to increase product trial with minimal advertising. Since consumer purchasing patterns demanded product variety in vending-machines, Neilson's presence in this segment was not considered threatening by major competitors.

In the autumn of 1992, as the International Division made the changes necessary to salvage past efforts in the U.S., several options for entering the Mexican confectionery market were also being considered.

MEXICO

Neilson made the decision to enter the Mexican market late in 1992, prompted by its parent company's, Weston Foods Ltd., own investigations into possible market opportunities which would emerge as a result of the North American Free Trade Agreement (NAFTA). Mexico was an attractive market which scored very highly in the market evaluation study. Due to their favourable demographics (50 per cent of the population was within the target age group), Mexico offered huge potential for countline sales. The rapid adoption of American tastes resulted in an increasing demand for U.S. snack foods. With only a limited number of competitors, the untapped demand afforded a window of opportunity for smaller players to enter the market.

Working through the Ontario Ministry of Agriculture and Food (OMAF), Neilson found two potential independent distributors:

Grupo Corvi   A Mexican food manufacturer, operated seven plants and had an extensive sales force reaching local wholesalers. They also had access to a convoluted infrastructure which indirectly supplied an estimated 100,000 street vendor stands or kiosks (known as "tiendas") representing nearly 70 per cent of the Mexican confectionery market. (This informal segment was usually overlooked by marketing research services and competitors alike.) Grupo Corvi currently had no American or European-style countline products.

Grupo Hajj   A Mexican distributor with some experience in confectionery, offered access to only a small number of retail stores. This limited network made Grupo Hajj relatively unattractive when compared to other distributors. Like Grupo Corvi, this local firm dealt exclusively in Mexican pesos, historically, a volatile currency. (In January 1993, 1 peso = CDN$0.41.)

While considering these distributors, Neilson was approached by Sabritas, the snack food division of Pepsico Foods in Mexico, who felt that there was a strategic fit between their organizations. Although Sabritas had no previous experience handling chocolate confectionery, they had for six years been seeking a product line to round out their portfolio. They were currently each week supplying Frito-Lay type snacks directly to 450,000 retail stores and tiendas. (The trade referred to such extensive customer networks as "numeric distribution.") After listening to the initial proposal, Neilson agreed to give Sabritas three months to conduct research into the Mexican market.

Although the research revealed strong market potential for the Neilson products, Bateman felt that pricing at 2 pesos (at parity with other American-style brands) would not provide any competitive advantage. Sabritas agreed that a one peso product, downsized to 40 grams (from a Canadian-U.S. standard of 43 to 65 grams), would provide an attractive strategy to offer "imported chocolate at Mexican prices."

Proposing a deal significantly different from the relationships offered by the two Mexican distributors, Sabritas intended to market the "Mr. Big," "Crispy Crunch" and "Malted Milk" bars as the first brands in the "Milch" product line. "Milch" was a fictitious word in Spanish, created and owned by Sabritas, and thought to denote goodness and health due to its similarity to the word "milk." Sabritas would offer Neilson 50 per cent ownership of the Milch name, in exchange for 50 per cent of Neilson's brand names, both of which would appear on each bar. As part of the joint branding agreement, Sabritas would assume all responsibility for advertising, promotion, distribution and merchandising.

The joint ownership of the brand names would provide Sabritas with brand equity in exchange for building brand awareness through heavy investments in marketing. By delegating responsibility for all marketing efforts to Sabritas, Neilson would be able to compete on a scale not affordable by Canadian standards.

Under the proposal, all "Milch" chocolate bars would be produced in Canada by Neilson. Neilson would be the exclusive supplier. Ownership of the bars would pass to Sabritas once the finished goods had been shipped. Sabritas in turn would be responsible for all sales to final consumers. Sabritas would be the exclusive distributor. Consumer prices could not be changed without the mutual agreement of Neilson and Sabritas.

ISSUES

Bateman reflected upon the decision he now faced for the Mexican market. The speed with which Sabritas could help them gain market penetration, their competitive advertising budget, and their "store door access" to nearly a half million retailers were attractive advantages offered by this joint venture proposal. But what were the implications of omitting the Neilson name from their popular chocolate bars? Would they be exposed to problems like those encountered in Taiwan with the "Bang Bang" launch, especially considering the strength and size of Pepsico Foods?

The alternative was to keep the Neilson name and to launch their brands independently, using one of the national distributors. Unfortunately, limited resources meant that Neilson would develop its presence much more slowly. With countline demand in Mexico growing at 30 per cent per year, could they afford to delay? Scott Begg had indicated that early entry was critical in burgeoning markets, since establishing market presence and gaining share were less difficult when undertaken before the major players had dominated the market and "defined the rules of play."

Bateman also questioned their traditional means of evaluating potential markets. Were the criteria considered in the market evaluation study really the key success factors, or were the competitive advantages offered through ventures with distributors more important? If partnerships were necessary, should Neilson continue to rely on independent, national distributors who were interested in adding Neilson brands to their portfolio, or should they pursue strategic partnerships similar to the Sabritas opportunity instead? No matter which distributor was chosen, product quality and handling were of paramount importance. Every chocolate bar reaching consumers, especially first-time buyers, must be of the same freshness and quality as those distributed to Canadian consumers. How could this type of control best be achieved?

case 22 Palliser Furniture Ltd.

In mid-December 1997, Arthur DeFehr, president of Palliser Furniture Ltd. of Winnipeg, Manitoba, prepared for the following week's senior management committee meeting (see Exhibit 1 on the next page for an organizational chart) during which the company's strategy for expansion would be discussed and finalized. While a number of factors appeared to recommend expansion into Latin America, there had been a recent dramatic increase in competition from Asia that had to be taken into account in their plans. As a result, it was unclear how and when Palliser should respond and what form this investment, if any, should take.

A BRIEF HISTORY OF PALLISER FURNITURE LTD.

With the proceeds from the sale of his car, A. A. DeFehr set up a woodworking shop in his basement in 1944 to produce various household items (i.e., laundry hangers, ironing boards). A major turning point was reached in 1949 when he brought his latest innovation, a three-legged end table, to T. Eaton & Co., one of Canada's largest retailers, and found a very receptive buyer. In particular the retailer appeared to be less sensitive to the price of the end table compared to his other products; as a result, the woodworking shop's focus was promptly redirected towards the production of residential furniture. By 1964, DeFehr Manufacturing Ltd. (DML) was operating in a 45,000 square foot building with 50 employees and annual sales of CDN$1 million. Four years later, DML entered the upholstered furniture market when it made its first investment outside of Winnipeg, purchasing a bankrupt upholstery plant in Calgary, Alberta.

Anthony Goerzen prepared this case under the supervision of Professor Paul Beamish solely to provide material for class discussion. The authors do not intend to illustrate either effective or ineffective handling of a managerial situation. The authors may have disguised certain names and other identifying information to protect confidentiality.

exhibit 1   Palliser Furniture Ltd. Senior Management

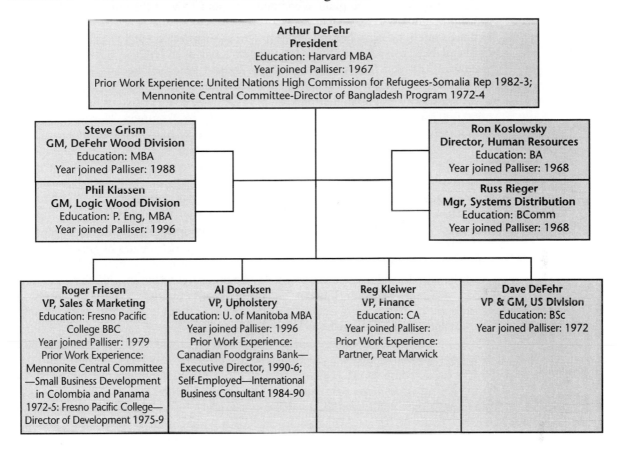

Throughout 1960-70, the firm's sales grew at an annual compounded rate of 25% as A. A. DeFehr's three sons, Frank, Arthur, and Dave, joined the family business. Art recalled when

> Frank and I made our first effort at selling in the United States. We loaded up the wagon and made our first stop in the parking lot of a store in Grand Forks. The store manager came out and said, "The colour is wrong, the style is wrong, and the price is wrong."

Nonetheless, by 1973, exports to the U.S. accounted for 20% of the firm's total sales. As the CDN$:US$ ratio continued to rise, however, exports became increasingly difficult and, in 1975, the company withdrew entirely from the export market.

In 1979, the company's founder took on the position of chairman of the board and Frank, the eldest son, became president. All the company's operations were amalgamated in 1980 under the name of Palliser Furniture Ltd. In order to maintain a presence in the US market that would not be subject to the whims of currency exchange, Palliser established a small plant in Fargo, North Dakota in 1981. This plant became a beachhead in the U.S., allowing Palliser to secure market access, as well as creating a window into the world's largest market. In 1984, Frank stepped down and Art became president. In response to increased competition from Taiwan, Palliser established a trading company in Taipei in 1986 to develop brokerage revenues by importing finished furniture from various offshore producers as well as furniture components (i.e., knobs and handles) for Palliser's own production. By 1987, U.S. sales through the Fargo plant accounted for about 15% of the company's CDN$100 million sales. In 1989, to support the firm's growing U.S. sales, a showroom was opened in High Point, North Carolina. The 1980s were good years for Palliser as it grew at 18% per year, reaching total annual sales of over CDN$135 million by the end of the decade. During this time, A. A. DeFehr gradually became less involved in the firm, leaving day-to-day management decisions to his three sons.

In order to establish a stronger U.S.-based presence, Palliser purchased an idle 400,000 square foot furniture production facility in Troutman, North Carolina for US$6 million in 1991. Dave spearheaded this initiative, moving to Troutman and taking on U.S. citizenship to manage the growth of Palliser's U.S. investments. Rising pressure for efficiency, however, led the company to close the small Fargo plant and lay off its workforce of 285 in 1994, and this production responsibility was transferred to the Canadian operations.

Between 1990 and 1995, revenue grew at 8% to 10% per year, with total annual sales surpassing CDN$200 million by 1992. During this period, however, philosophical differences within the DeFehr family arose pertaining to issues of growth, size, and the role of the third generation. While A. A. DeFehr would have preferred that all three sons take turns leading the firm over time, there was a meeting in 1995 to resolve long-term ownership and family issues. Art decided to purchase the Leather Division and Frank again became president of Palliser. However, after 18 months it was agreed that Art would purchase majority control (53%) of Palliser, merge the Leather Division back into the parent company and resume the role of president. Frank purchased two supply subsidiaries and retained a 5% ownership in Palliser. Dave retained his 34% share of the company and became chairman of the board although he remained only partially involved in regular operations, focusing instead on the U.S. Division and two retail outlets which he purchased in North Carolina. The 8% balance of the firm was owned by their sister, Irene Loewen.

With an overall total of 1.8 million square feet of production space, total annual sales reached CDN$325 million by 1997 (see Exhibits 2 and 3 on the next two pages), with CDN$25 million of that amount contributed by the U.S. Division. Sales growth was again very strong, rising to 18% per year. Although this growth came exclusively from U.S. exports, domestic sales still accounted for almost 50% of the total revenue.

THE CANADIAN FURNITURE INDUSTRY

The furniture industry in Canada had a long history as part of the country's industrial base. In 1996, there was a total of 1,406 firms in the furniture and fixture industry employing over 49,000 employees and shipping product valued at more than CDN$5.6 billion at wholesale prices. More specifically, in the household furniture segment, there were 676 firms with sales of CDN$2.3 billion annually.

The Canadian market for household furniture was estimated at CDN$2.1 billion at wholesale prices in 1997. Demand was forecast to grow at a real annual rate of 1% into the next century, compared to a projected rate of 1.5% for total consumer expenditures. The U.S. furniture market, in contrast, was expected to grow at a rate of almost 3%. Niche markets were expected to grow at significantly higher rates, especially furniture for the elderly and for home entertainment applications. Key consumer niches were expected to include high-income earners and new immigrants. All furniture was sold through retail outlets, and trade shows were an important venue

exhibit 2   Condensed Balance Sheet (CDN$000s as at December 31, 1997)

	1997	1996
ASSETS		
Current		
Accounts Receivable	53,758	44,122
Income Taxes Recoverable	0	448
Inventories	60,576	52,016
Prepaid Expenses	2,693	2,200
Total Current Assets	117,027	98,786
Property, Plant, and Equipment	67,423	58,811
Other Assets	1,605	1,193
	186,055	158,790
LIABILITIES AND SHAREHOLDERS' EQUITY		
Current		
Bank Indebtedness, with a Majority of the Assets		
Pledged as Collateral Security	43,398	41,109
Accounts Payable and Accrued Liabilities	29,846	23,994
Income Taxes Payable	4,333	0
Loans Payable	6,229	5,797
Current Portion of Long-term Debt	360	952
Total Current Liabilities	84,166	71,852
Long-term Debt, with a Majority of the Assets		
Pledged as Collateral Security	40,757	32,412
Deferred Income Taxes	2,858	2,535
	127,781	106,799
Shareholders' Equity		
Share Capital	40,264	44,764
Contributed Surplus	1,250	1,270
Retained Earnings	16,760	5,957
Total Shareholders' Equity	186,055	158,790

for sales to retailers. One of the largest international trade shows was held annually in High Point, North Carolina.

While Canada was a relatively small player on the world scene, making up only 2% of the world market for household furniture, it was located next to the world's largest market that consumed 28% of global production. Other major markets were Japan with 15% of total international consumption and Germany with 10%. Canadian manufacturers exported over CDN$1 billion of furniture, 95% of which was destined for the U.S. In total, Canadian shipments to the U.S. accounted for less than 15% of total U.S. imports. Canada also imported CDN$816 million of furniture, 60% of which originated in the U.S. Other important sources of imports into Canada were made up of lower-quality products from China and Taiwan (16% of total imports) and high-quality products from Italy (7%).

The Canadian furniture industry, located primarily in Ontario and Quebec, was characterized by a few large operations and many small ones. By comparison, the U.S.

exhibit 3   Condensed Income Statement (CDN$000s as at December 31, 1997)

	1997	1996
Sales	324,061	277,210
Deduct Freight	22,118	18,789
Net Sales	301,943	258,421
Cost of Sales	208,532	182,091
Gross Margin	93,411	76,330
Expenses		
Manufacturing, Selling and Administration	55,718	48,232
Depreciation and Amortization	6,868	6,787
Interest	4,638	4,606
	67,224	59,625
Income Before Income Allocations, Loss on Partnership Investment and Income Taxes	26,187	16,705
Income Allocations		
Employee Profit-Sharing Incentive Plans	6,379	3,509
Income Before Loss on Partnership Investment and Income Taxes	19,808	13,196
Loss on Partnership Investment	668	2,522
Income Before Income Taxes	19,140	10,674
Provision for Income Taxes	7,622	4,714
Net Income for the Year	11,478	5,960

industry had seven times as many plants, 12 times the number of employees, and 15 times the shipments of the Canadian industry. Further, the average U.S. plant was twice the size of its Canadian counterpart; in fact, the largest U.S. furniture producer was equal in size to the entire Canadian market. The two largest firms in the Canadian furniture industry in 1997 were Dorel Industries Inc. and Palliser Furniture Ltd. While both companies had become international producers, Palliser generated over 85% of its revenue from Canadian operations whereas Dorel derived less than 20% of its revenue from Canada with the balance from plants in Europe, Asia, and the U.S.

In response to favorable market conditions, the Canadian furniture industry achieved a record of solid growth behind high tariff walls until 1987. The industry then underwent extensive restructuring as a result of both growing import pressure and an economic downturn in the late 1980s and early 1990s. Competitive pressure increased following the liberalization of trade as a result of the 1987 Canada-U.S. Free Trade Agreement (FTA), later replaced by the 1994 North American Free Trade Agreement (NAFTA). Further, in the 1995 accord made during the Uruguay Round negotiations under the General Agreement on Tariffs and Trade (GATT), Canada agreed to reduce its Most Favoured Nation (MFN) tariffs on furniture, furniture parts, and raw materials. Canada's tariffs on MFN furniture ranged from 6% to 24% and were scheduled to be reduced by one-third between 1995 and 2000. The GATT agreement was favorable to producers in both Europe and Asia since both were subject to Canada's MFN tariff regime.

Restructuring in the Canadian furniture industry following trade liberalization resulted in a dramatic decline of manufacturers, more rationalized, specialized, and productive operational structures, and a reorientation of marketing efforts toward the U.S. Between 1988 and 1996 in the household furniture segment, for example, the number of manufacturers fell by 42%, the number of employees decreased by 29%, and yet (after several years of adjustment) the total value of shipments remained unchanged. Throughout this period of adjustment, exports increased each year, reaching levels in 1997 that were 330% over 1988 figures, and productivity in terms of value-added per employee increased from CDN$33,000 to CDN$49,000 over the same period.

The furniture industry was labor-intensive, employing primarily unskilled and semi-skilled workers, especially immigrants. In 1996, wage rates in the industry were CDN$10.66/hour, well below the overall average of CDN$16.83 for the manufacturing sector in Canada. Yet, Canadian manufacturers had slightly higher wage costs than their U.S. counterparts; this was an important factor since the cost of labor relative to the final cost of product for leather and wooden furniture was 20% and 25%, respectively. Labor supply had not been a critical problem for the Canadian industry, although there was an ongoing shortage of people with specialized skills. With the introduction of more computerized equipment, the demand for better-educated workers increased, although approximately 40% of the existing work force had not completed secondary school.

Barriers to entry were fairly low, although this had begun to change with the arrival of productivity-improving technologies such as computer-aided design and computer-numeric controlled machinery. State-of-the-art machinery tended to be adopted most quickly by larger firms that had the necessary managerial and financial resources. In addition to these computer technologies, a variety of management techniques had become more widely used among Canadian manufacturers. For example, in response to retailers' demands for quicker and more efficient responses to orders and also to alleviate pressure on working capital, just-in-time manufacturing systems were adopted by many firms. In addition, various quality control techniques were implemented, including material inspection processes and more sophisticated production procedures to prevent, rather than correct, error.

Due to the entrepreneurial nature of most furniture manufacturers, many operations lacked professional management, although management sophistication tended to increase with company size. In particular, there appeared to be a widespread belief that Canadian manufacturers lacked marketing skills and were generally oriented towards the production aspect of the business. The U.S. industry, in contrast, was generally credited with having a much greater marketing orientation than its Canadian counterpart. Canadian manufacturers and retailers generally agreed that the key success factors in the furniture business were (in order of importance) overall product quality, quick delivery, innovative design, customer service, and price. In contrast, U.S. manufacturers perceived their key competitive success factors to be quality of raw materials, product design, location and quality of showrooms, extent of marketing activity, and price.

PALLISER'S STRATEGY

Palliser was profoundly affected by the FTA and the NAFTA. Beginning in 1989 with the reduction of tariff barriers, there began an intense downward pressure on prices in Palliser's base domestic market. Retailers attempted to appropriate in two years the anticipated savings resulting from the reduction of import duties that were actually phased in over four. Palliser's management then realized that neither the main Winnipeg facility nor the Fargo plant was strong enough to compete head-to-head with U.S. producers. As a result, there began an intensive effort to revamp the firm's strategy in line with the internationalization of the industry. Implementation of this strategic shift took place between 1989 and 1994, when the company redefined its markets, rationalized its distribution channels, and shifted manufacturing locations.

Palliser's first priority was to protect its Canadian sales base and then to grow through exports to the U.S. The company dropped its prices as necessary in important markets and began to modify its product line in a number of ways to maximize the production efficiency of the product mix. For example, Palliser reduced the number of wood species from three to one, thus reducing the cost of raw materials inventory. In addition, Palliser decided to retain only those product lines that were the retailers' first or, at worst, second choice. As a result, the dining room line was completely eliminated, with concentration instead on bedroom and living room markets. Thus, Palliser's product line was narrowed, and was made up of products in contemporary styles that competed on value, quality, and delivery in the medium price categories. At the same time, Palliser World Trade's Taipei office was, in the view of Roger Friesen, established to encourage

> the people in Palliser to think outside of Winnipeg. Aside from developing a stream of new revenues, the trading company was intended to act as a window on new ideas and potential competitors in foreign markets.

To reduce the sensitivity to cost of Canadian labor, Palliser then introduced a line of leather furniture, since the retail prices of these products were substantially higher than wooden products as was the cost of production materials (typically 54% of the sales prices versus 36% for wood). Further, Palliser's senior management perceived that the market for leather furniture was increasing more rapidly than other lines and there appeared to be excellent opportunities for growth, particularly for those manufacturers that were early movers. In fact, between 1994 and 1997 the North American leather furniture market grew between 15% and 18% annually compared to 3% to 4% for the industry as a whole. American leather furniture producers (i.e., Klausner, Viewpoint, etc.) were noted for traditional designs, whereas Italian companies (i.e., Natuzzi, Softline, Flep, etc.) captured over 50% of the North American leather furniture market with contemporary designs and colors. Since the furniture market appeared to be heading away from traditional designs into lighter "life style" fashions, Palliser's intention was to displace Italian imports with good quality, innovative, contemporary designs in the broad middle range of the market (i.e., leather couch retail price of US$800–US$1,299). Among Palliser's selling points was that it could guarantee quick delivery, a factor that had become increasingly important because retailers were becoming more resistant to holding inventory. Palliser also had a related cost advantage in that the Italian producers had to maintain a long and expensive inventory pipeline. While Palliser was able to make significant inroads into the leather market, the Italians proved to be very aggressive in maintaining their share of the lower price market.

Motivated by the conventional wisdom that wage rates were lower and that productivity was higher in the U.S., a 400,000 square foot facility that had ceased production in Troutman, North Carolina was purchased in 1991 for US$6 million. The initial intention was that this plant would produce wooden furniture, enabling Palliser to compete on equal terms with U.S. producers in the major markets along the Eastern Seaboard. However, Palliser was not able to achieve acceptable quality of output or productivity per worker with its 256 employees at this plant. In an effort to improve the situation, the plant's product line was converted to leather furniture, given the firm's success in capturing a share of this lucrative market. A short while later, Palliser's increasing focus on cost minimization through large production runs led management to consider redundant the relatively small Fargo operation, and the facility was closed in 1994.

Prior to the FTA, Palliser attempted to maximize Canadian market share by maintaining a wide distribution base, often with several distributors competing with each other for the same sales. In an effort to strengthen relationships with its top distributors before they were lured away by new U.S. competitors, Palliser decided to rationalize its Canadian distribution system by eliminating almost half of its 800 distributors. This show of commitment to the remaining distributors reinforced Palliser's strong Canadian position, although the move immediately wiped out 10% to 12% of its Canadian sales. In the U.S. market, on the other hand, Palliser began to offer its distributors the convenience of delivered prices rather than cost plus freight which was the industry standard. Within a unified production and distribution system, Palliser hoped to capture the freight savings on shipments to U.S. customers when made from Troutman versus Winnipeg.

As the organization continued to prosper, management began to feel increasingly vulnerable, given that the vast majority of the firm's investments were in Canada and the majority of the costs were denominated in Canadian dollars, whereas its growing markets were abroad. In addition, since Palliser had become one of the largest furniture manufacturers in Canada and the second largest employer in Manitoba, with almost 2,900 employees in Winnipeg, the firm's rising profile made it a recurring target for union recruitment drives. The possibility that unionization could lead to higher labor rates was an important consideration since the cost of labor in the production of furniture was a significant component of the final cost of products.

PALLISER'S LATIN AMERICAN VISION

Palliser's initial interest in Mexico came about in an indirect way in the early 1990s. Once their children had left home, Leona and Arthur DeFehr were interested in finding a spot to get away for a few months from the cold Winnipeg winter. They gravitated towards Mexico, rather than the more popular destination of Florida, primarily because of their interest in foreign cultures. When they were in Mexico, Art often filled his free time with visits to local manufacturers and furniture retailers. As he became more familiar with the furniture industry in Mexico, he decided that a more careful review of the opportunities for Palliser was in order.

Palliser's initial effort in Mexico in the early 1990s was to prospect for export sales. After the "Tequila Crisis," the near collapse of Mexico's banks in 1994, Palliser effectively withdrew from the Mexican market, although Palliser World Trade began importing a few items (i.e., occasional tables) into the U.S. and Canada. In addition, Palliser had established a CDN$2 million per year foothold in Latin America with shipments to Guatemala, Honduras, Costa Rica, and Ecuador. Once the financial problem subsided, Palliser attempted to reinstate its exporting program to Mexico, but early success was modest.

Palliser continued to look very seriously at upgrading its involvement in Mexico as various opportunities became apparent. It was known, for example, that several major companies like Reebok, Nike, Florsheim, Rockport, and L.A. Gear had engaged in the cutting and sewing of leather products in Mexico. Palliser also knew that Arkea Salotti S.A., the leading Mexican upholstered furniture producer, who marketed the "Zarkin Leather" brand, had an annual turnover of only US$8 million. Although there were other major producers of upholstered furniture (i.e., Muebles Boal, Sabone, Mueblicentro, Monaco, Industria Mueblera Fenig, Dimher, Gestalt, Muebles Drexel, etc.), all had sales of less than US$5 million annually. While there was a clear preference on the part of retailers to buy from Mexican plants, supply was often outstripped by demand, and most retailers, frustrated with delivery delays, were looking for alternatives.

Another opportunity for Palliser was in the "Rustic" furniture segment, a line of products that looked like "antique Mexican" furniture based on Spanish colonial designs. Total production of Rustic furniture in Mexico was over US$100 million in 1997, 60% of which was exported to the U.S., with sales increasing at 15% annually. The undisputed leader of the Rustic furniture segment was Segusino S.A. Founded in 1985, Segusino employed over 1,400 people in its factory and another 2,300 in various surrounding artisans' workshops. Segusino's sales by 1997 were more than US$35 million, with shipments spread throughout North America and Europe. A junior-level team began to investigate the prospect of establishing an operation that would send finished leather covers back to Winnipeg or Troutman for final assembly into furniture. Although the resulting report made a very positive recommendation (see Exhibit 4), senior management decided to pause to look more deeply into the matter. Given the various possibilities, Art believed

exhibit 4   Estimated Costs and Revenues of Establishing a Plant in Northern Mexico (all figures in Cdn$)

Production Facility:			
Refurbished Factory Space & Land	$7,000,000 - 9,000,000		
Machinery & Equipment	$3,000,000 - 5,000,000		
Office Equipment & Computers	$200,000 - 300,000		
Annual Expenses:			
Travel & Entertainment	$23,000 ($750/month + $15,000 car)		
Factory Operation (i.e., power)	10-15% of sales		
Inventory	10% of sales		
Accounts Receivable	15% of sales		

Projected Annual Revenues:	Year 1	Year 2	Year 3
Leather Cut-and-Sew	$ 2,500,000	$ 4,800,000	$ 8,400,000
Finished Furniture			
Latin America	$ 2,300,000	$ 5,400,000	$ 9,000,000
North America	$ 6,000,000	$ 8,500,000	$14,000,000
Total	$10,800,000	$18,700,000	$31,400,000

Key Personnel Annual Wages:	Base Salary	Typical Benefits	Profitability Bonus
General Manager	$50,000	$17,500	$50,000 - 300,000
Sales Manager	$55,000	$19,250	$10,000 - 15,000
Financial Manager	$45,000	$15,750	$4,500 - 6,000
Plant Supervisor	$25,000	$ 8,750	$2,500 - 3,000
Sales Representative	$16,000	$ 5,500	1% of sales
Clerical & Hourly Employees	$ 4,800	$ 1,700	$500

Projected Number of Workers:	Year 1	Year 2	Year 3
Leather Cut-and-Sew	21	40	70
Finished Furniture			
Latin America	23	54	90
North America	60	85	140
Total	104	179	300

that whatever decision Palliser made in Mexico, it would become the platform for business growth into Latin America, a long-term and complex investment.

THE MEXICAN FURNITURE INDUSTRY

Total furniture production in Mexico amounted to US$2.9 billion at wholesale prices in 1997, an increase of 17% over 1996 levels. Over 60% of the Mexican industry produced residential furniture valued at a total of US$1.74 billion in 1997. Wooden furniture was produced by 80% of manufacturers, with others working in metal and, to a lesser extent, plastic. The production of metal furniture had remained fairly static over the previous five years, while the production of wooden furniture increased by 17%. Around 13% of the firms produced upholstered furniture, with total annual sales of US$226 million at wholesale prices. Only 7% of producers made kitchen furniture, with an annual value of US$122 million.

The Mexican market had an apparent domestic consumption of around US$4.35 billion at retail prices, of which US$3.35 billion was made up of home furniture in 1997. Bedroom and living room retail sales accounted for US$2.51 billion. There were about 16,000 retail outlets with an average annual turnover of US$270,000. Small and medium-sized outlets (fewer than five employees) served almost half of the market and 600 large outlets controlled another 25%. Large-scale non-specialist distribution, direct sales, and marginal outlets shared the remainder.

Between 1991 and 1997, exports from Mexico quadrupled, reaching US$1.7 billion, with 96% of these exports destined for the U.S. The dramatic increase in exports was linked directly to the NAFTA agreement. It encouraged exports to the U.S., primarily from maquiladoras that were responsible for over 60% of furniture exports in 1996. Residential furniture accounted for 70% of total exports, of which 18% was upholstered and 2% was kitchen furniture. Imports, on the other hand, totalled US$250 million by 1996, after having dropped by 50% following the 1994 Mexican financial crisis. By 1997, domestic demand was still only 80% of what it had been a decade earlier. The majority of imports (74%) were made up of household furniture.

There were 200,000 people employed in the Mexican furniture industry, creating an average annual production of US$20,000 per employee. In total, there were around 20,000 companies making both wooden and metal furniture, of which 321 were maquiladoras employing 44,000 people. In 1997, around 40% of the industry was located in the northern third of Mexico. Over 95% of Mexican wooden furniture manufacturers were small firms, employing fewer than 15 people. Around 800 firms employed between 16 and 250 workers, and fewer than 20 firms were relatively large, with over 250 employees. These factories typically paid their workers US$1.00-1.50/hour payable in cash on a weekly basis according to Mexican law.

THE MEXICO DECISION

In October 1997, a senior-level team made an extended trip to Mexico to become more familiar with the wide range of regions and to investigate other products and supply options. The trip led through seven Mexican states and countless factories that were potential suppliers, buyers, partners, or acquisition targets. The team's overall impression was that the opportunities were very good, although much of the potential lay in shipping product back to the U.S., at least initially. This suggested a location that had a good labor climate as well as availability and was also well located in terms of both suppliers and northern transportation routes. An obvious possibility was to locate in one of the maquiladora districts along the northern border; this location was never considered seriously, however, because Palliser did not want to become involved in these socially unstable zones. The result of this research was that Saltillo, Coahuila emerged as the strongest candidate.

Coahuila was a province located adjacent to the Texas border. It was equidistant from California and the Mid-Atlantic States and was directly south of Winnipeg. Silver mining and ranching were not part of the heritage of this region, unlike most other parts of Mexico; success had come through industrial development. There was a strong entrepreneurial and industrial mentality in this area and, as a result, an excellent infrastructure had encouraged a number of large industrial groups to locate there.

Saltillo was a city of 700,000 people about 80 km from Monterey, a major centre of three million inhabitants in the neighbouring state of Nuevo Leon. Established about 400 years ago, Saltillo had an historic city centre with a number of newer areas that included gated communities, a golf course, a tennis club, good shopping, etc. Lying at an altitude of 6,000 feet, Saltillo enjoyed a dry, temperate climate. The cost of living in Saltillo was modest compared to most other international cities and, overall, it was considered an excellent location for expatriates.

Since Saltillo had an established agricultural equipment-manufacturing sector, the city was attractive to various industries, including the automobile sector. Chrysler and GM both had assembly plants in Saltillo, and a great number of operations had also been set up nearby to supply the automotive industry, paying workers around US$1.75-2.00/hour. It was rumored that GM had made the decision to add to its production capability in Saltillo, thus assuring the continued economic development of the region.

Saltillo had also become home to a number of manufacturers whose experience was relevant to Palliser. Garden State Tanning Ltd., for example, had a leather-cutting operation to supply BMW and GM, with plans to significantly increase their throughput. Lear Seating Inc. also had two seating plants dedicated to supplying seats to the car industry. There were also a few other firms located in the Saltillo area that were potential suppliers of furniture components (i.e., the foam producers, Woodbridge Ltd. and Foamex Ltd.). Fruit of the Loom Inc., the garment company, had also decided to locate in Saltillo, constructing five plants in a very short time that employed 3,000 people. Techno Trim, a division of Johnson Controls Inc., also had plans to set up a new fabric cutting and sewing installation with 800 employees. During their trip, the Palliser team was able to tour many of these facilities. They found that, since the auto industry was very male-oriented, the industrial job opportunities for females were limited. As a result, Fruit of the Loom's employees were over 80% female who were willing to accept lower wages than the autoworkers—probably US$1.00-1.25/hour.

In summary, Arthur concluded that

> the Mexican leather furniture industry is made up of small manufacturers with low sales volumes who do not have the capability of Palliser given our experience and financial strength. If we act now, Palliser could be the controlling force in the Mexican leather industry in 10 years, precluding our competition from making a similar move.

CHINA—THE GIANT BEGINS TO RISE

Early in the 1990s, an important trend emerged in the furniture industry as China opened itself up to the world economy. Given that wage rates in Taiwan had risen steadily in step with its growing economy, large Taiwanese furniture producers increasingly looked to

China's vast and inexpensive supply of workers to reinstate their competitive cost advantage. The resulting newly established Taiwanese-owned factories in China were not truly start-up companies; rather, Taiwanese management brought their 20+ years of experience to bear on these new operations, which emerged as sophisticated competitors from the beginning.

Given the generally bulky nature of furniture, transportation costs were a significant component of the delivered cost structure. As a result, it was challenging for offshore firms to compete for North American sales. Nonetheless, Asian firms had begun to make clear inroads into the U.S. residential furniture market. By the early 1990s, imported product from China began to make a noticeable impact in the North American market. In 1992, U.S. imports of wooden residential furnishings amounted to US$970 million from Taiwan (12.3% of the total market) and US$528 million (6.7%) from other East Asian countries.

The Taiwanese-owned furniture producers in China were typically very large and highly focused operations, making a small number of products targeted for Western European and North American markets. These operations had, however, a number of important disadvantages that had to be overcome to enable them to be viable competitors outside of Asia. First, given that the Chinese had very limited sources of high quality raw wood, they were forced to source their hardwood requirements from the North Eastern U.S. The Chinese had, however, devised various ways of making do with inferior grades of wood, mostly by using people, who were more adept than machines, to do the work. While the first arrivals of furniture from China were clearly of inferior quality, quality improved dramatically in the ensuing years. By 1997, quality had risen to such an extent that, on certain pieces, it was difficult to find a difference between furniture produced in China and Canada. Second, transportation on a container of furniture from China to North America or Europe added at least 45 days onto the delivery time and about 15% onto the delivered cost of product. As a result, factory designs were based on the principle of economies of scale and on the availability of cheap labor, enabling them to offset these distance-related disadvantages. However, rising ocean freight costs (three rate hikes in the summer of 1997 alone), port congestion, and the inadequacy of inland infrastructure began to make business more difficult for those involved in Chinese exports.

The first Taiwanese firm to build a factory in China was Lacquer Craft Mfg., which set up an operation in the southern Chinese city of Dong Guang in 1992. By 1997, the monthly production of this factory's 3,000 employees included 8,000 sets of dining room tables and chairs, 4,500 sets of buffets and hutches, and 35,000 occasional tables. Construction had already begun in 1997 on a one million square foot building in the northern Chinese city of Tianjin, as the company projected a sales increase of US$30 million to a total of over US$100 million by 1998. Palliser World Trade had developed a solid import business in Chinese furniture and maintained good relationships with well over 25 large Chinese furniture manufacturers, all of whom seemed to be expanding their operations and looking for Western markets. Opportunities appeared for Palliser to become more involved in the Chinese furniture industry. Lacquer Craft's president, for example, indicated in 1997 that he "would love to put Palliser's name on one of [his] factories."

Since its establishment, Palliser World Trade had been active in the Far East, with 60% of its CDN$14 million annual revenues in 1997 derived from products purchased in Asia. In a meeting with a major North American retailer, however, Palliser was told that its assistance in dealing with the Chinese was no longer needed. The best Chinese producers were increasingly able to market without an intermediary, and the largest

North American buyers were capable of making the direct connections that would save them the 25% margin charged by a broker. Of the top 100 retailers that Palliser counted as customers, perhaps 30 had the resources to develop the capability to buy directly from the Chinese. The balance of 70 companies would still be interested in working with Palliser as an intermediary, but it was known that once a certain number of retailers purchased direct, wholesale price points would be established making it difficult for brokers to set their own pricing. In addition, Palliser found that one of its largest North American retailer customers had taken drawings of a Palliser table to Asia and was successful in finding a Chinese manufacturer who would make it more cheaply, resulting in a loss of CDN$500,000 in annual revenue for Palliser. It appeared that, not only would it become increasingly difficult for Palliser to maintain a pure trading business in China, but that Asian manufacturers were a force that had to be reckoned with. According to Roger Friesen,

> competition from China is highlighting the fact that we do not know the details of our costs of production on specific pieces of furniture. There are some types of furniture that we will be able to do better here and others where we will not be able to match the Chinese. Our knowledge of our precise costs needs to be improved and we need to focus on those products that we can do better than anyone else.

THE DECEMBER 1997 SENIOR MANAGEMENT COMMITTEE MEETING

During recent trips to Mexico, Palliser management had heard many rumors about other furniture companies that were actively considering the possibility of locating in Mexico; therefore, time was of the essence. The decision to go ahead in Mexico was, according to Art,

> a complex one that would have an obvious immediate impact on the company and, more significantly, it would probably have an impact on Palliser 20 years down the road.

At the same time, although it had been "many years since Palliser's senior management had travelled to Asia," the threats and opportunities in China had to be evaluated prior to any move.

The Richard Ivey School of Business gratefully acknowledges the generous support of The Richard and Jean Ivey Fund in the development of this case as part of the RICHARD AND JEAN IVEY FUND ASIAN CASE SERIES.

---

case 23 The Wall Street Journal: Print versus Interactive

In early January 1999, Peter Kann, chief executive officer of Dow Jones & Company, pondered the future of one of the company's most valuable brands and products, The Wall Street Journal. A meeting with Kann's top management team had been called for the following month to discuss the future of this brand, primarily focusing on the relative positioning and performance of the print and Interactive Journal.

The Wall Street Journal had enjoyed an unrivaled position as the top daily business newspaper in the United States for over 109 years. The Journal was the largest circulation newspaper in the United States, with approximately 1.8 million subscribers, reached five million worldwide readers daily, and enjoyed tremendous loyalty among readers. However, the newspaper industry was facing a future of little-to-no growth and mounting competition from other forms of news delivery, most recently and saliently, the Internet.

Internet news providers threatened the typical newspaper's core product and service of timely, current news reporting and delivery. The threat to The Wall Street Journal was felt not only from competitors on the Web, such as CNN and CBS MarketWatch who operated free sites, but from its own Interactive Journal. The Interactive Journal was introduced in 1996, and within a year became the largest paid subscription site on the Internet. But what would the rising demand for instant, Web-based news do to the company's mainstay business of the print edition? Would the Interactive Journal serve as a complement or a substitute for print? Given this, Peter Kann wondered how the two products should be positioned, priced and promoted in order to maximize revenue for both. The answers to these questions would fundamentally shift the industry as well as Dow Jones & Company.

Richard Ivey School of Business
The University of Western Ontario

DOW JONES & COMPANY

Dow Jones & Company was a global provider of business news and information. Its primary operations were in three business segments: print publishing, electronic publishing, and general-interest community newspapers.

The print publishing segment included The Wall Street Journal, Barron's, National Business and Employment Weekly, The Asian Wall Street Journal, The Wall Street Journal Europe, Far Eastern Economic Review and SmartMoney Magazine. The electronic publishing segment included The Wall Street Journal Interactive Edition, Dow Jones Newswires, Dow Jones Interactive and the Dow Jones Indexes.

The Wall Street Journal Print Edition

The Wall Street Journal (WSJ), Dow Jones' flagship publication, was long considered the most respected source of business and financial news in the United States. By 1999, The Wall Street Journal was one of the most recognized brands in the world, with a subscription renewal rate of 80 per cent. Its circulation rate of approximately 1.8 million subscribers remained relatively stable in the 1990s.

Over 600 reporters and editors—who also support other Dow Jones products—contributed to an outstanding record of journalistic excellence. In 1997, the company received its 19th Pulitzer Prize, an award also given to its chief executive officer in 1972. Each of the print editions of The Wall Street Journal drew heavily upon The Wall Street Journal's worldwide news staff. The Wall Street Journal Europe, headquartered in Brussels, had an average circulation in 1998 of 71,000, and sold on day of publication in continental Europe, the United Kingdom, the Middle East, and North Africa. The Asian Wall Street Journal, headquartered in Hong Kong, had an average circulation of 62,000 in 1998, and was printed in Hong Kong, Singapore, Japan, Thailand, Malaysia, Korea and Taiwan. In addition, the company distributed special editions of Wall Street Journal news within 30 newspapers in 26 countries, published in 10 languages, with a combined circulation of four million.

Despite its long-standing traditional front page format without full paper-width headlines, six columns, dot print photos, and the "What's News" summaries, the Journal innovated many new formats in the 1990s. Starting in 1993, the Journal expanded its business and economic trend regional coverage to select parts of the United States, including Texas, Florida, California, New England, the Northwest and the Southeast. These Journal editions consisted of a four-page weekly section included in papers distributed in those regions. Four-color advertising, introduced in 1995, saw increased revenue of 60 per cent in 1997, contributing to overall advertising linage up 13 per cent, on top of a 14 per cent growth in 1996. 1997 saw the addition of a daily page of international business news, and 1998, a two-page technology section. Weekend Journal, introduced in 1998, expanded typical content to include lifestyle issues such as personal finance, food and wine, sports, travel, and residential real estate, as well as other new editorial features appealing to new advertisers and readers.

However, these new innovations in the Journal served as supplements rather than substitutes to the three traditional sections of the five-day-a-week paper. Kann explains, "Visually, the Journal has a unique trademark quality. It's a uniquely recognizable page. But the main reason we haven't changed it is it's a very useful format." Section A included the front page and business and political news. Section B, "Marketplace," focused more on lifestyle and marketing issues, including regional editions, and the technology section. Finally, Section C, "Money & Investing," centered on financial news, daily stock and bond quotes and other financial information. Dow Jones also announced plans to spend US$230 million between 1999 and 2002 to expand the number of color pages and total page capacity. This investment would increase the color page capacity from eight to 24 and the total page capacity from 80 to 96.

Economics of Print Publishing

Within the relevant range (circulation and advertising within 15 per cent), most print WSJ expenses were fixed. Variable components (including newsprint, ink, plates, production and delivery overtime) accounted for approximately 15 per cent of costs. Print WSJ revenues came from two primary sources: sales/subscriptions and advertising. Advertising rate growth was dependent upon at least roughly preserving the circulation level. Hence, if circulation dropped 10 per cent, ad revenue could fall 10 per cent or more.

The paper was printed in 17 company-owned U.S. and 13 overseas plants, 12 of which were leased. Company employees (through the company's National Delivery Service, Inc. subsidiary) delivered 75 per cent of U.S. subscriber copies by 6:00 a.m. daily. This system provided delivery earlier and more reliably than the postal service. Company plants were unionized, operated one shift daily, six days a week, and were important to maintaining the Journal's traditional size, which was larger than typical print newspapers. This size format was believed to be more appealing to advertisers and to readers alike.

The Print Newspaper Industry

Wall Street had long found newspaper stocks appealing and therefore priced them at a premium to the rest of the market. Exhibit 1 includes stock data for Dow Jones & Company. However, newspapers faced increasing media competition in the 1990s, making advertising sales a harder pitch. Local newspapers in general turned to supplemental advertising flyers and catalogues placed between the pages of daily and Sunday papers in order to provide more dependable cash flow. In addition, growth of classified ads was strong due to the general expansion of the economy, resulting in strong real estate, automobile and job markets. Classified volume typically contributed 15 to 25 per cent of total newspaper linage sales and was the industry's most profitable ad category on a per-line basis in the 1990s. However, classified ads also faced increased competition from on-line offerings. Overall, newspapers benefited from the robust economy in 1998 by encouraging more advertisers to buy more linage at increased rates. The total advertising market in the United States for print media was US$72 billion in 1999, up from US$55 billion in 1995, and projected to exceed US$83 billion by 2001.

Despite relatively stable cash flows in the past, newspaper circulation was in a general downward trend from 1987 through late 1996, although there was some stability starting in 1997. Local distribution of newspapers, both home and newsstands, was increasingly contracted out to third parties.

The Wall Street Journal was the first national daily paper in the United States and enjoyed status as the only national daily until the advent of USA Today in 1985. In the late 1990s, the New York Times and Los Angeles Times also nominally entered into the nationally distributed sector of the industry. However, their entry into the nationally distributed sector did not indicate a shift towards nationally focused news; The New York Times and Los Angeles Times still concentrated on a fairly targeted geographic

exhibit 1   Stock Performance for Dow Jones & Company

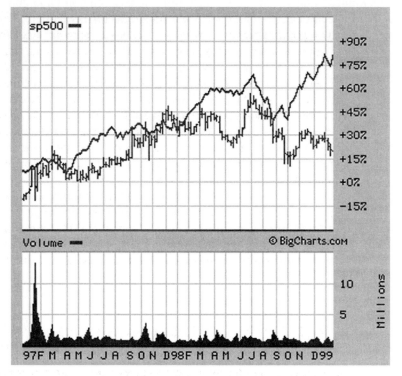

Source: Interactive Chart—dowjones.htm; October 4, 1999.

region in terms of subscribers and content. In addition, the business-versus-general-interest focus of The Wall Street Journal kept it relatively immune from direct competitors until the expansion of UK-based Financial Times in 1998. While the Financial Times's focus was primarily business news, its exposure in the U.S. market was dwarfed by that of The Wall Street Journal, with the circulation level of the Journal around 35 times that of the Financial Times.

The Wall Street Journal Interactive Edition

The Wall Street Journal Interactive Journal (http://wsj.com), introduced in April 1996, was another innovation for Dow Jones as well as for the publishing industry. While initially a free site, subscribers were first asked to pay in August of 1996. Subscribers totaled over 100,000 within the first year of launch, and reached over 266,000 by the end of 1998. While many competitors were delivering news on the Web for free, The Wall Street Journal Interactive Edition became the largest paid subscription site on the World Wide Web. Around one per cent of the content at the Web site was free access, with the remaining 99 per cent accessible only to subscribers. "Our proprietary information has value, and we have the guts to charge," said Peter Kann.

U.S. News & World Report called the Interactive Journal "the best single financial site on the Internet." The Interactive Journal offered continuously updated news and market information, access to the international editions, in-depth background reports on over 20,000 companies and pay-per-view access to the Dow Jones Publication library. In addition, the Interactive Journal included proprietary information and coverage not found in the print editions. Within each story in the Interactive Journal were links to stock quotes and other information about the companies discussed.

Careers.wsj.com was a free site, launched in 1997 and linked to the Interactive Journal, that offered a searchable database of employment listings and content from the National Business and Employment Weekly.

Advertising sales were relatively stable in 1998, coming off two relatively strong years of growth. Subscription renewal rates were approximately 75 to 80 per cent. Further comparison of subscribers, subscriber revenue and acquisition costs for both the print and Interactive editions is given in Exhibits 2 and 3.

Economics of Electronic Publishing

Typically for Web-based publishing, most costs were fixed or step-function fixed, except for subscriber acquisition and advertising selling expenses.

For free sites, primary revenue came from advertising, with the number of people visiting the site largely determining the fees charged to advertisers. For subscription sites, however, revenue came from both advertising and subscriptions, similar to print publishing. A third category of revenue also became possible in electronic publishing: transaction fees. Forrester Research predicted that on-line revenue from subscriptions, advertising and transaction fees would grow from just over US$520 million in 1997 to US$8.5 billion within five years.

The total advertising market for Internet medium was approximately US$2 billion in 1999 and was projected to exceed US$5 billion in 2001. As a quarterly comparison, the first quarter of 1996 saw total U.S. Internet advertising spending at US$29.9 million. By the first quarter of 1998, this number had grown to US$351.3 million and second quarter of 1998 to US$423.0 million. Unlike television, radio or print advertising, an almost unlimited supply of advertising and a concurrent glut of it accompanied the advent of the Internet. As a result, advertising rates plummeted in 1998 due to the lack of target viewers. However, this trend did not apply to Web sites that could offer advertisers access to more targeted demographics.

exhibit 2   Per-Subscriber Revenue and Acquisition Costs

	Print WSJ	Electronic WSJ
1 Year Subscription Non-Print Subscriber	N/A	$59
1 Year Subscription Print Subscriber	$175	$29
Advertising Revenue Per Year Per Subscriber	$500	$40
Average Acquisition Cost New Subscriber	$160	$40
Average Renewal Cost	$5	$5
Renewal Rate	80%	75%

exhibit 3   The Wall Street Journal Print/Electronic Interaction

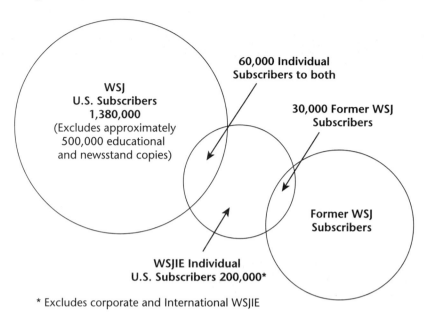

* Excludes corporate and International WSJIE

A 1998 GVU Internet survey indicated the attitudes about pay versus free sites on the Internet. Of those individuals who refused to pay for information on the Internet, 44.5 per cent did so because the information was available elsewhere for free, while 32.7 per cent would not pay for Internet information because they were already paying to gain access to the Internet itself. Other reasons given for the resistance to pay for site access included excessive cost and poor site quality. Similarly, a survey conducted by the BBDO advertising agency found that 60 per cent of respondents replied negatively when asked if they would be willing to pay for an on-line subscription edition of their favorite print publication. Of those that answered "yes," 89 per cent indicated they would not be willing to pay more than the newsstand price for an on-line version.

Unlike print publishing, editorial and news skills for a near-real time environment became necessary skills for electronic publishing. With continual news updates, reliability and quality of journalism reports became subject to increased time pressure. Accuracy, the elimination of bias, clarity and comprehensiveness in the face of a flood of information became critical for electronic publishing. In addition, new skills of technology, ease of Web site navigation, effective layout for a computer screen, etc., became necessary for Web publishing.

The Wall Street Journal Interactive Edition was expected to attain its break-even point in 1999. Forrester Research estimated the average annual operating costs of content Internet sites at US$893,000 and of transactional sites at US$2.8 million in 1998. For Income Statement information for both Print and Electronic products, see Exhibits 4 and 5 (on the next page). Company-wide financial information is provided in Exhibits 6 through 8 (see pages 306–308).

The electronic publishing division, which included Dow Jones Interactive, provided subscribers with a news library of over 5,000 publications, including a full-text archive of The Wall Street Journal and Dow Jones Newswires as well as roughly 1,200 non-U.S. news sources, and the 50 largest U.S. newspapers and business magazines.

exhibit 4   Print Publishing—Primarily The Wall Street Journal
              ($ Millions)

	1997	1998
Revenue:		
Advertising	$ 790	$ 777
Circ. & Other	$ 353	$ 360
TOTAL	$1,143	$1,137
Operating Expenses	$ 896	$ 931
Operating Income	$ 247	$ 174

exhibit 5   Electronic Products—DOW Jones Interactive, DOW Jones
              Newswires, The Wall Street Journal Interactive Edition
              ($ Millions)

	1997	1998
Revenue:		
Dow Jones Newswires/Indexes	$204	$220
Interactive Publishing	$159	$172
TOTAL	$363	$393
Operating Expenses	$302	$315
Operating Income	$ 61	$ 78

The Internet/Web Publishing Market

Growth in the use of the Internet exploded in the 1990s. It was estimated that in 1998, the number of worldwide Internet users was over 147 million, with over 57 million in the United States alone. The number of U.S. households joining the Internet was estimated at 760 per hour in 1999, with nearly 38 per cent of households being reached by the Internet. Nearly 90 per cent of Internet users gathered news and information from the Web's news, information and entertainment sites. In 1996, Pew Research Center estimated that only four per cent of Americans got their news on-line. This number jumped to nearly 20 per cent in 1999.

It was projected that by 2003, over 55 million professionals, managers and executives would be using the Internet at work. In 1999, over 17 per cent of the on-line population preferred to receive their financial news on-line.

Internet penetration by age was concentrated in younger generations by the end of 1998. Fifty-nine per cent of 12- to 17-year-olds used the Internet, with the percentage dropping with each higher age group to 27 per cent of the population aged 55 to 64, and only 14 per cent of the population over age 65. In 1996 the male-to-female ratio of Internet use was 57 to 43, but by 1998, this ratio had changed to 51 to 49.

The Interactive Journal competed with a variety of business news sources on the Internet, including sites maintained by traditional print competitors such as Business Week, Fortune, The New York Times, and The Financial Times. In addition, it faced

exhibit 6   Consolidated Statements of Income (Loss), for the Years Ended December 31, 1998, 1997, and 1996

(in thousands except per share amounts)	1998	1997	1996
REVENUES			
Advertising	$1,031,210	$1,011,864	$ 896,981
Information Services	670,441	1,101,696	1,125,625
Circulation and Other	456,455	458,958	458,986
TOTAL Revenues	2,158,106	2,572,518	2,481,592
EXPENSES			
News, Operations and Development	677,381	899,868	820,564
Selling, Administrative and General	762,803	895,707	831,270
Newsprint	163,146	152,478	164,766
Second Class Postage and Carrier Delivery	117,649	114,442	110,256
Depreciation and Amortization	142,439	250,734	217,756
Restructuring	76,115	1,001,263*	
Operating Expenses	1,939,533	3,314,492	2,144,612
Operating Income (Loss)	218,573	(714,974)	336,980
OTHER INCOME (DEDUCTIONS)			
Investment Income	12,266	3,473	4,249
Interest Expense	(7,193)	(19,367)	(18,755)
Equity in Losses of Associated Companies	(21,653)	(49,311)	(5,408)
(Loss) Gain on Disposition of Businesses & Investments	(126,085)	52,595	14,315
Other, Net	(4,250)	(9,300)	(121)
Income (Loss) Before Income Taxes & Minority Interests	71,658	(763,884)	331,260
Income Taxes	63,083	37,796	147,728
Income (Loss) Before Minority Interests	8,575	(801,680)	183,532
Minority Interests in (Earnings) Losses of Subsidiaries	(213)	(452)	6,437
NET INCOME (LOSS)	$ 8,362	$ (802,132)	$ 189,969
PER SHARE			
Net Income (Loss) Per Share:			
Basic	$ .09	$ (8.36)	$ 1.96
Diluted	.09	(8.36)	1.95
Weighted-Average Shares Outstanding:			
Basic	95,180	95,993	96,703
Diluted	96,404	95,993	97,371
Cash Dividends	$ .96	$ .96	$ .96

* This restructuring cost is associated with the divestment of Dow Jones Markets (formerly Telerate).

competition from non-print competitors such as CNNfn, Bloomberg, on-line brokerage firms, CBS MarketWatch, TheStreet.com and Yahoo and others who received their news from Reuters. Many of these competitors provided news and information on their Web site for free (for example, CNNfn, Yahoo, Bloomberg, and The New York Times). Still others provided limited free information for non-print subscribers and free on-line access to print subscribers (e.g., Fortune and Business Week). Due to the ease of entry into Web publishing, as opposed to print publishing, competition was growing and fluid. One important difference between print competitors and purely

exhibit 7   Financial Highlights

(in thousands except per share amounts)	1998	1997	% increase (decrease)
Income Statement Results			
CONSOLIDATED			
Revenues	$2,158,106	$2,572,518	(16.1)
Operating Income (Loss)	218,573	(741,974)	—
EBITDA[1]	437,127	510,023	(14.3)
Net Income (Loss)	8,362	(802,132)	—
Net Income (Loss) Per Share – Diluted	.09	(8.36)	—
EXCLUDING SPECIAL ITEMS[2]			
Revenues	1,872,204	1,776,238	5.4
Operating Income	327,915	335,955	(2.4)
EBITDA	416,456	454,071	(8.3)
Net Income	185,039	185,707	(0.4)
Net Income Per Share – Diluted	1.92	1.92	
Financial Position and Cash Flows			
Long-Term Debt, Including Current Portion	$ 149,889	$ 234,124	(36.0)
Stockholders' Equity	509,340	780,822	(34.8)
Capital Expenditures	225,834	347,797	(35.1)
Cash from Operations	306,226	459,763	(33.4)
Purchase of Treasury Stock, Net of Put Premiums	291,215		—
Revenues and Operating Income (Loss) by Segment			
REVENUES			
Print Publishing	$1,161,939	$1,143,395	1.6
Electronic Publishing[3]	393,178	363,232	8.2
Community Newspapers	317,087	300,611	5.5
Segment Revenues	1,872,204	1,807,238	3.6
Divested/Joint Ventured Operations:			
Print and Television Operations		21,091	—
Telerate	285,902	744,189	(61.6)
Consolidated Revenues	$2,158,106	$2,572,518	(16.1)
OPERATING INCOME (LOSS)[4]			
Print Publishing	$ 173,582	$ 247,191	(29.8)
Electronic Publishing	56,060	61,089	(8.2)
Community Newspapers	44,760	50,584	(11.5)
Corporate	(22,602)	(18,189)	(24.3)
Segment Operating Income	251,800	340,675	(26.1)
Divested/Joint Ventured Operations:			
Print and Televisions Operations		(18,239)	—
Telerate	(33,227)	(1,064,410)	96.9
Consolidated Operating Income (Loss)	$ 218,573	$ (741,974)	—

[1]EBITDA is computed as operating income (loss) excluding depreciation and amortization and restructuring costs.
[2]Consolidated excluding Telerate operations and loss on its sale, and other special charges/gains.
[3]1997 revenue includes $31 million of one-time index licensing fees.
[4]excluding restructuring charges, segment operating income was as follows (000's):

	1998	1997
Pring Publishing	$223,496	$251,903
Electronic Publishing	65,921	78,138
Community Newspapers	61,100	50,584
Corporate	(22,602)	(18,189)
	$327,915	$362,436

exhibit 8   Five-Year Financial Summary

(in thousands except per share amounts)	1998	1997	1996	1995	1994
REVENUES					
Advertising	$1,031,210	$1,011,864	$ 896,981	$ 771,779	$ 724,990
Information Services	670,441	1,101,696	1,125,625	1,092,002	976,800
Circulation and Other	456,455	458,958	458,986	419,980	389,187
TOTAL Revenues	2,158,106	2,572,518	2,481,592	2,283,761	2,090,977
EXPENSES					
News, Operations and Development	677,381	899,868	820,564	748,945	642,184
Selling, Administrative and General	762,803	895,707	831,270	764,161	681,244
Newsprint	163,146	152,478	164,766	157,047	107,178
Second Class Postage and Carrier Delivery	117,649	114,442	110,256	103,497	96,751
Depreciation and Amortization	142,439	250,734	217,756	206,070	205,303
Restructuring	76,115	1,001,263			
Operating Expenses	1,939,533	3,314,492	2,144,612	1,979,720	1,732,660
Operating Income (Loss)	218,573	(714,974)	336,980	304,041	358,317
OTHER INCOME (DEDUCTIONS)					
Investment Income	12,266	3,473	4,249	5,379	4,884
Interest Expense	(7,193)	(19,367)	(18,755)	(18,345)	(16,858)
Equity in Losses of Associated Companies	(21,653)	(49,311)	(5,408)	14,193	(5,434)
(Loss) Gain on Disposition of Businesses & Investments	(126,085)	52,595	14,315	13,557	3,097
Other, Net	(4,250)	(9,300)	(121)	4,075	(5,981)
Income (Loss) Before Income Taxes & Minority Interests	71,658	(763,884)	331,260	322,900	338,025
Income Taxes	63,083	37,796	147,728	139,878	157,632
Income (Loss) Before Minority Interests	8,575	(801,680)	183,532	183,022	180,393
Minority Interests in (Earnings) Losses of Subsidiaries	(213)	(452)	6,437	6,550	787
Income (Loss) Before Cumulative Effect of Accounting Changes	8,362	(802,132)	189,969	189,572	181,180
Cumulative Effect of Accounting Changes					(3,007)
NET INCOME (LOSS)	$ 8,362	$ (802,132)	$ 189,969	189,572	178,173
PER SHARE Basic					
Income (Loss) Before Cumulative Effect of Accounting Changes	$ .09	$ (8.36)	$ 1.96	$ 1.96	$ 1.83
Net Income (Loss)	.09	(8.36)	1.96	1.96	1.80
PER SHARE Diluted					
Income (Loss) Before Cumulative Effect of Accounting Changes	.09	(8.36)	1.95	1.94	1.82
Net Income (Loss)	.09	(8.36)	1.96	1.94	1.79
Weighted-Average Shares Outstanding ('000's):					
Basic	95,180	95,993	96,703	96,907	99,002
Diluted	96,404	95,993	97,371	97,675	99,662
Dividends	$ .96	$ .96	$ .96	$ .92	$ 84

exhibit 8   (continued)

(in thousands except per share amounts)	1998	1997	1996	1995	1994
OTHER DATA					
Long-term debt, including Current Portion, as a % of Total Capital	22.7%	23.1%	17.0%	13.9%	16.9%
Newsprint Consumption (Metric Tons)	278,000	270,000	252,000	224,000	221,000
Number of Full-Time Employees at Year End	8,253	12,309	11,844	11,232	10,265
Cash from Operations	306,226	459,763	405,157	371,887	403,142
Capital Expenditures	225,834	347,797	232,178	218,765	222,434
Cash Dividends	91,662	92,116	92,969	89,131	83,360
Total Assets	1,491,322	1,919,734	2,759,631	2,598,700	2,445,766
Long-term Debt, Including Current Portion	149,889	234,124	337,618	259,253	300,870
Stockholders' Equity	509,340	780,822	1,643,993	1,601,751	1,481,611

on-line competitors had to do with branding. Companies with established brand names outside of the Internet had a cost advantage over competitors that were Internet-born (e.g., Yahoo and Amazon) due to the high costs of marketing new brands.

Print versus Interactive Customers

Since its introduction, the Interactive Journal was not aggressively promoted to current print subscribers of the Wall Street Journal. Partially, this was a result of the difference in customer profiles for the two products.

Print WSJ customers had a higher average age than Interactive Journal customers and were more likely to be retired. Print customers tended to use the Internet more at work than at home, to have a higher total value of investments, were more likely to have a home office, and were more likely to live in the eastern United States. Interactive Journal customers, on the other hand, were more likely to have children at home, to use the Internet at home than at work, to have a lower total value of investments, to use on-line brokers and other on-line information, and to travel internationally for business.

Simmons Market Research Bureau reported that of WSJ print readers, 9.3 per cent had completed high school, 8.3 per cent had some college education, 33.57 per cent had graduated from a four-year college or university, and 30.68 per cent had attended graduate school. The subscription base of WSJ was characterized by an average age of 52, with an average household income of US$75,000. The majority of print readers were 35 years old or older (75.7 per cent), with only 24.3 per cent within the 18 to 34 age group. Most print subscribers were male, with a male-to-female ratio of 75 to 25. Nearly 74 per cent of WSJ print subscribers read the paper every day, spending on average 50 minutes per issue. As of 1999, 40 per cent of Interactive Journal subscribers read the edition on a daily basis, and 36 per cent reported using the edition a few times a week.

Current Pricing, Promotion and Positioning

Currently, the Interactive Journal is positioned as a supplement, not a substitute for the print edition, and is priced accordingly. Non-print subscribers pay $59 per year, while print subscribers pay $29 per year. The print edition is priced at $175 per year, with newsstand copies for seventy-five cents each. The print pricing compares with other print competitors as follows: Business Week—US$42.95 for 51 issues; Fortune—US$54.55 for 26 issues; Forbes—US$23.97 for 17 issues; USA Today—US$119/year; New York Times—US$208/year for weekly editions only; and Financial Times—US$175/year,[1] although most magazine competitors did offer discount subscription rates.

The Challenge

The challenge ahead of Peter Kann was a serious one, but he was no stranger to tensions. His Pulitzer Prize was awarded for coverage of the Indian-Pakistan war. As he looked towards the next month's meeting, which would largely shape the direction of the future for The Wall Street Journal print and interactive, Kann wondered: Would the future mean prosperous co-existence of the two formats or a battle with but one format as the victor?

---

[1]This price is the effective price after taking into consideration widespread discounting.

case 24 Trojan Technologies Inc.: The China Opportunity

In August 1999, Sarah Brown, senior market associate of Trojan Technologies of London, Ontario, reflected on the water shortages anticipated in developing countries as a result of their explosive economic growth. Trojan sold water disinfection equipment, and Sarah's job was to find new areas for growth. China was particularly intriguing because it had as much water as Canada but 40 times the population, and its economic boom would further stress current water resources. Given Trojan's high growth expectations, China offered an enormous opportunity. Sarah knew little of China: how decisions were made for water disinfection equipment, whether Trojan's patents would be protected, what level of resources would be required, etc. Her task in new market development was to determine if Trojan should enter China, and if so, when, where and how. Ralph Brady, the vice president of New Business Development, wanted to see her recommendations within the month.

TROJAN TECHNOLOGIES INC.: MORE THAN "LIGHT IN A PIPE"

An Overview of Trojan

Located in London, Ontario, Canada, Trojan Technologies Inc. started with a staff of three in 1977. Its original technology was based on a pioneering patent on an ultraviolet (UV) water disinfection system. The idea was simple—often referred to as "light in a pipe"—but its implementation embodied complex engineering, science and technology. Banks of UV light tubes were installed inside an open water channel constructed of either concrete or metal. As water flowed through the channel, the

Ruihua Jiang prepared this case under the supervision of Professors Pratima Bansal and Paul Beamish solely to provide material for class discussion. The authors do not intend to illustrate either effective or ineffective handling of a managerial situation. The authors may have disguised certain names and other identifying information to protect confidentiality.

Version: (A) 2000-06-15

Richard Ivey School of Business
The University of Western Ontario

high-intensity UV light destroyed the DNA structures of the microorganisms in the water so the risk of disease would be eliminated.

There were two major applications of UV technology. One was to disinfect the wastewater discharged into receiving waters. Applications included primary, secondary and tertiary treatment for industrial, commercial and municipal waste treatment processes. The other was to disinfect incoming clean water. Applications included household drinking water supplies, municipal drinking water treatment plants, industrial product and process water requirements, and commercial applications (See Exhibit 1).

As UV technologies became more accepted as an environmentally responsible and cost-effective replacement for the widely used chemical disinfection methods, Trojan had posted an annual compound revenue growth rate of 27 per cent since 1989, and 36

exhibit 1   Applications of Trojan's UV Systems

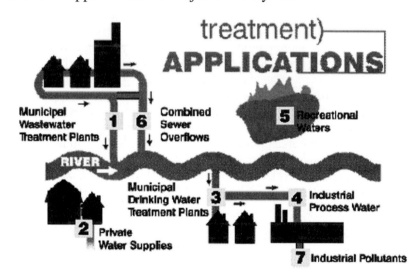

1. **Municipal Wastewater Treatment Plants**

   System UV4000 – 10 million gallons per day and up or 37,800 cubic meters per day and up
   System UV3000 – 1 million gallons per day to 30 million gallons per day or 3,780 cubic meters per day to 113,400 cubic meters per day.

2. **Private Water Supplies**

   Aqua UV Units – 2 to 12 gallons per minute or 5.5 to 45 liters per minute

3. **Municipal Drinking Water Treatment Plants**

   System UV8000 – 20 to 2000 gallons per minute or 75 to 7,500 liters per minute

4. **Industrial Process Water**

   System UV8000 – 20 to 2,000 gallons per minute or 75 to 7,500 liters per minute

5. **Recreational Waters**

6. **Combined Sewer Overflows**

   System UV4000 – 10 million gallons per day and up or 37,800 cubic meters per day and up

7. **Industrial Pollutants**

   System UV3000 PTP – up to 1 million gallons per day or up to 3,780 cubic meters per day
   System UV3000 – 1 million gallons per day to 30 million gallons per day or 3,780 cubic meters per day to 113,400 cubic meters per day   AIR2000 - for remediation of contaminated air, soil and groundwater

Source: The company website of Trojan Technologies Inc., http://www.trojanuv.com, August 1999

per cent since 1994. In 1998, Trojan was a TSE 300 company, employing about 400 employees, with annual sales reaching almost $70 million. As a world leader in ultra-violet water disinfection technology and the world's largest supplier of ultraviolet disinfection systems for municipal wastewater applications, Trojan now had some 2,000 UV systems in operation around the world, treating in excess of six billion gallons of water per day.

In 1998, the company approved a five-year strategic plan, which projected a continued growth rate of at least 30 per cent for the following five years. By 2003, the annual sales were expected to reach over $300 million and total employment more than 1,000.

To achieve the goal, Trojan was actively looking for growth opportunities. Trojan decided to increase its investment in the clean water market. Currently, 95 per cent of Trojan's business was in the wastewater market. The clean water business' five per cent contribution was marginal. However, recent research results showed that UV could destroy giardia and crytosporidium in municipal drinking water supplies, which further enhanced its competitiveness in the clean water market. Giardia and crytosporidium are responsible for waterborne outbreaks causing diarrheal infections, and are resistant against chlorine.

In the same year, Trojan obtained the exclusive worldwide licence for an innovative photocatalytic technology used in air treatment applications. The Air 2000 system using the technology won the 1998 Environmental Technology Innovator Award in the U.S., and had similar features to Trojan's UV water systems, i.e., they were both more environmentally positive and cost-effective substitutes for current treatment technologies.

Trojan was also looking to expand geographically, especially to new markets with legal regulations and standards regarding discharging water and clean water. One potential market being evaluated was Asia, especially the world's most populous country—China. Trojan made a breakthrough sale of a $4.5-million System UV4000™ water disinfection unit to Hong Kong in 1999, after a few smaller installations there. In the same year, Trojan shipped seven industrial clean water units to Mainland China through a Chinese-owned company in the U.S. Sales had also been made to Thailand, Indonesia, the Philippines, Taiwan and Korea.

The Product Market

Water disinfection was usually the last step in water treatment, following other physical, chemical or biological purification processes, killing the organisms, viruses, and bacteria in the effluents from primary and secondary treatment. Three water disinfection methods were commonly known: ozone, chlorine, and UV. Chlorine was the most commonly used in the world, accounting for over 80 per cent of the market. Chlorine offered a residual disinfection effect that lasted after treatment point, and could prevent the growth of algae and slime in pipes and tanks, a feature that was important when the water supply and sewage systems were dated and leaking. However, chlorine could combine with the residual elements in the treated water and create new environmentally harmful and potentially carcinogenic compounds which often resulted in facilities installing dechlorination equipment to reduce chlorination by-products. Also, chlorine must be handled and transported cautiously as spills are toxic. Therefore, it was under considerable scrutiny in Europe and North America.

In contrast to the traditional chlorination method, UV technology had the advantage of being environmentally positive. It did not add anything to the water or change its chemistry, nor did it use dangerous additives or leave chemical residues harmful to plant and marine life. It was also more efficient, treating water instantly. Chlorination required contact time so large contact tanks needed to be constructed. The relative capital cost of UV and chlorine depended on the cost of labor and land, the size of the facility and the need for dechlorination equipment. Generally, operating and maintenance costs were lower for UV, offering a better net present value in the life of the equipment (see Exhibit 2 on the next page). The major ongoing costs of UV units are the electric power consumption and lamp replacements. The UV units also required limited space for installation, which was important to large metropolitan areas, where land costs could be high. The Water Environment Research Foundation funded research in 1995 to compare UV and chlorination. The research confirmed the environmental and economic advantages of UV technology, and predicted that, as existing chlorine facilities concluded the end of their useful life, many would be replaced with UV systems.

For both the wastewater and clean water market, roughly four segments could be identified: (1) the municipal; (2) the industrial; (3) the commercial (dealing with the discharges from and the water supplies for office buildings, hotels, restaurants, shopping malls, etc.); (4) the residential. Trojan could supply products for all the four segments in both clean and wastewater markets. However, the municipal wastewater market was the most important revenue source for Trojan. A UV disinfection system typically accounted for about four per cent of the total cost of a municipal water treatment plant.

Trojan had about 80 per cent of the world's UV wastewater treatment market. Trojan's 1998 annual report estimated "that only 5% to 10% of municipal wastewater sites in North America use UV-based technology . . . (and) of the approximate 62,000 wastewater treatment facilities operating worldwide, only 2,500 currently utilize UV disinfection systems."

Trojan's UV units vary considerably in price. A small residential unit could range from $200 to $1,000. Commercial and industrial units could be as high as $100,000, while municipal units could cost several million dollars. The cost of the unit would depend on the volume and the quality of water (both in and out).

International Presence

Most of Trojan's sales were made through its 90-plus agents scattered around the world. The agents worked on commission. By leveraging their relationships with major project design and contractor companies in their territories, these agents could influence the type of disinfection technology that was used in the project. When the customer, such as the municipal government, made the decision, it was important that the customer be familiar with UV technology. In Hong Kong, for instance, Trojan initially sold a few small installations, which convinced the government officials to install a larger system because of the advantages of UV systems.

So far Trojan's development had been focused in North America and Europe. Because of the greater interest in and financial resources for environmental protection, this area accounted for 80 per cent of the world's total water treatment market, of which North America had about 55 per cent, and Western Europe about 24 per cent. Although industry experts estimated that the annual growth rate for these developed areas would slow down to less than five per cent in the coming years, replacement of chlorine systems would fuel growth in UV. However, as these markets matured, competition was escalating and profit margins thinning. Furthermore,

exhibit 2   Comparison of UV and Chlorination

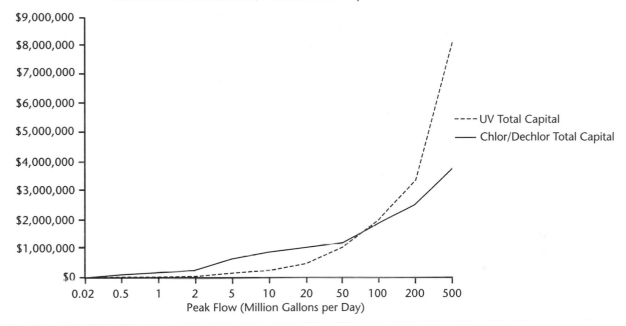

Ultraviolet vs. Chlorination/Dechlorination Capital

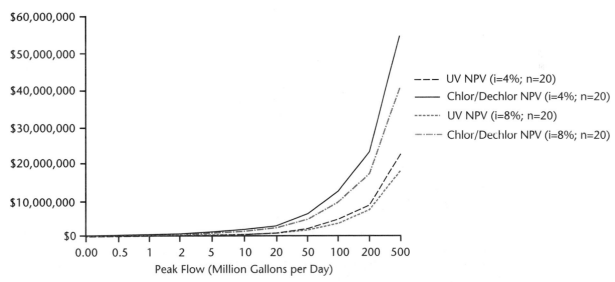

Ultraviolet vs. Gas Chlorination/Dechlorination Net Present Value of Total Costs

Source: Trojan Technologies Inc.

technology regulations and customer preferences could change rapidly in these markets. In addition to their London, Ontario head office, Trojan had branch offices in The Hague, Netherlands, California, U.S.A., Australia and UK. In 1998, out of a total of 1,975 wastewater installations worldwide, 1,526 were in the U.S., 227 in Canada, 64 in Europe, 34 in South America, 82 in Asia, and 34 in Australia and New Zealand.

Human Resources

UV systems required very little maintenance. Usually one Trojan staff person was enough to help with the installation and the training of local staff. Trojan's London staff could often assist in maintenance of the units through verbal instructions. Only occasionally would on-site repair be required.

Currently, the company did not have personnel experienced with the Chinese water disinfection market and Chinese business practices. There were five engineers working in the R & D department, however, who were originally from Mainland China. None of them had a business or marketing background and none of them was in a management position.

Competitive Pressure

As the pioneering leader in ultraviolet water treatment technologies, Trojan had been able to thrive with the growing demand for the UV technology without facing much competition. However, the market had become increasingly competitive in the past two years. On June 29, 1999, the company announced lower than expected earnings for the fiscal year, citing competitive pressures, increased product development, and patent litigation as reasons behind the earnings disappointment. The next day its share price plummeted from $38.80 to $27.10. Trojan's main competitors in UV technology were Wedeco in Germany, and Infilco Degremont and Calgon Carbon in the U.S. To Trojan's knowledge, none had entered China. However, Trojan also faced competition from manufacturers of chlorine-based disinfection systems, where numerous companies existed. The most powerful players were the full-service water treatment companies, who could provide a complete set of services from consulting, to design, to installation and maintenance.

The company had responded to the competitive challenge with a series of strategic moves. One was to accelerate the development of next-generation technologies; the other was to launch a comprehensive cost engineering program. The strategic moves, together with the patent litigation discussed in detail below, would nevertheless incur increased costs for the short term.

Trojan had also made some significant investments recently. In 1998, Trojan acquired Sunwater Limited of U.K. and spent $2.8 million in purchasing a 39-acre property for future expansion. Additional capital expenditures were expected in support of company growth. In the same year, Trojan issued 700,000 common shares for gross proceeds of $21.7 million. In 1998, the net debt-equity ratio stood at 0.53:1, compared to 0.20:1 in 1997.

Exhibits 3 and 4 (on the next two pages) provide the financial statements of Trojan Technologies Inc.

Intellectual Property Protection

Trojan was built on patented technologies. As a high-tech enterprise, Trojan spent heavily on research and development. The management believed that continued development of proprietary, state-of-the-art technologies was critical to maintaining a competitive edge in an increasingly competitive environment. However, direct and indirect imitation of its patented technologies would seriously hurt its business and damage the return on its investment in R&D.

The raw materials for the UV systems were concrete channels, metal reactors, pipes, UV lamps, and electronic components. Many of the components were made of

exhibit 3   Consolidated Balance Sheets as at August 31 1998 (in CDN$000)

	1998 $	1997 $
ASSETS		
Current Assets		
Temporary investments	21,730	—
Accounts receivable	32,266	23,294
Accrued revenue on contracts in progress	18,965	5,618
Inventory	12,117	6,105
Prepaid expenses	320	254
Income taxes receivable	393	—
Total Current Assets	85,791	35,271
Investments in other companies	2,191	2,236
Capital Assets	16,367	12,866
Patents, trademarks and licence (net of accumulated amortization of $825,117 ($650,637 in 1997))	1,512	729
Goodwill (net of accumulated amortization of $25,231)	984	—
	106,845	51,102
LIABILITIES AND SHAREHOLDERS' EQUITY		
Current Liability		
Bank indebtedness	23,296	6,308
Accounts payable and accrued charges	14,258	10,356
Income taxes payable	—	1,108
Deferred income taxes	2,224	1,300
Current portion of long-term debt	1,195	—
Total Current Liabilities	40,973	19,072
Long-term debt	6,407	
Deferred income taxes	282	338
Shareholders' Equity		
Share capital	42,108	19,070
Retained earnings	17,075	12,622
	59,183	31,692
	106,845	51,102

stainless steel and manufactured in a Trojan subsidiary in London, Ontario. These parts were all standard and easily available. The single most important input was the patented ballasts. These circuits were designed for each unit and ensured superior effectiveness and reliability of the UV lamps. As well, Trojan offered unique knowledge by custom-designing each unit to the quality and volume of water at the site.

Trojan's management was constantly on the watch for any possible loss of intellectual property. In January 1999, Trojan initiated patent infringement action in the U.S., accusing Calgon Carbon Corporation, Calgon Carbon Canada, Inc. and the City of Hinesville, Georgia of infringing Trojan's U.S. Patent for a fluid purification device based on its System UV4000™ technology. The action intended to seek damages and an injunction against further infringement and also showed Trojan's determination to defend its patent rights in the world.

exhibit 4   Consolidated Statements of Income and Retained Earnings for the Year Ended August 1, 1998 (in CDN$000)

	1998 $	1997 $
Sales	69,852	51,150
Cost of goods sold	40,586	30,156
Gross margin	29,266	20,994
EXPENSES		
Administrative and selling expenses	13,560	10,415
Research and development, net	3,318	3,184
Interest and bank charges	1,183	210
Amortization	1,807	982
	19,868	14,791
Operating income	9,398	6,203
Other income		
Interest income	51	248
Income from equity investment	935	698
Income before special charge and income taxes	10,384	7,149
Special charge	2,650	—
Income taxes	2,571	2,414
Net income	5,163	4,735
Retained earnings, beginning of year	12,623	7,888
Share issue costs, net of taxes	(712)	—
Retained earnings, end of year	17,074	12,623
Earnings per share		
Basic	0.67	0.62
Fully diluted	0.67	0.61

THE CHINA OPPORTUNITY

The Environmental Protection Market in China

China's economy had been growing at double-digit speed since its 1979 reforms. However, the development had come at the cost of the environment. By taxing environmental resources such as air, land and water, its economic growth was constrained. China's population was 1.2 billion and was expected to grow to 1.5 billion by 2020 at the current rate. Already, 60 million were without sufficient clean water for their needs. Arguably, the additional people would further tax water resources, which would mean further deterioration of coastal and inland waters so that drinking water and water needed for industrial processes would become increasingly scarce. The failure of the government to respond quickly and responsibly could lead to devastating social and economic outcomes.

Recognizing the constraints imposed by a deteriorating environment on sustainable development, the Chinese government put environmental protection onto its agenda as a key issue. By the year 2000, an aggregate investment of US$34 billion, almost one per cent of China's GNP, was anticipated in order to control national pollution. The investment in environmental protection would continue well into the next century. Exhibit 5 presents the forecasted investments in environmental protection and demand for equipment in China from 2001 to 2010. The forecasted ten-year annual growth rate of the industry would be 23 per cent, way above the annual GNP growth. Priority in environmental protection for the next few years would go to four areas: development of urban sewage treatment systems; equipment to curb air pollution; solid waste disposal; and monitoring equipment.

Even though the size of the market was growing, corporate profits were not. While the annual output for the environmental protection industry increased by 721 per cent from 1988 to 1993, the average profit margin decreased from 22 per cent to 13 per cent, and to 8.5 per cent in 1997. The environmental protection industry in China was heavily concentrated in the densely populated coastal areas, due to the higher level of industrialization and commensurate pollution in these areas. The trend would most likely continue for the next decade, because these areas would remain financially better off and better endowed, with advanced technologies and human resources in science and research. China had recently designated a few Environmental Industry Parks, encouraging foreign direct investments in the industry. Exhibit 6 identifies the output in the environmental protection industry by province for three years, i.e., 1988, 1993, 1997.

Water Resources and Water Treatment in China

The per capita water resource in China was only one-quarter of the world average. By 1997, about 400 of China's 668 cities were suffering from water shortages, of which more than 100 had serious water shortages and poor-quality water supply. Underground

exhibit 5   Ten-Year Forecast for the Chinese Environmental Market (2001 to 2010, US$ billions)

Year	2001	2002	2003	2004	2005	2006	2007	2008	2009	2010	Total
Investment Amount	58.5	63.5	68.5	74.0	79.9	86.4	93.2	100.6	108.8	117.9	851.3
Market Demand	23.4	25.4	27.4	29.6	32.0	34.6	37.3	40.2	43.5	47.2	340.6

exhibit 6   Distribution of Chinese Environmental Industry (Annual Production Output, US$ billions)

Year	Country Total	Eight Provinces, Municipalities with Highest Annual Production in Environmental Industry							
1988	3.8	Jiangsu 0.899	Liaoning 0.472	Shanghai 0.36	Shandong 0.188	Jilin 0.182	Hunan 0.155	Zhejiang 0.136	Beijing 0.130
1993	31.2	Jiangsu 4.734	Zhejiang 4.448	Liaoning 2.606	Tianjing 2.435	Guangdong 2.287	Shanghai 1.781	Anhui 1.311	Hubei 1.273
1997	52.17	Jiangsu 9.755	Zhejiang 7.263	Shandong 3.914	Tianjing 2.848	Guangdong 2.845	Shanghai 2.425	Sanxi 2.21	Henan 2.16

water resources were overexploited. Ninety per cent of the urban water resources were seriously polluted; about 50 per cent of the drinking water supplies in major cities were below the national standard.

Water pollution resulted from two major sources: industrial wastewater and sewage water. Industrial wastewater could be effectively reduced through cleaner production processes. However, municipal wastewater would increase with the rise of living standards. The average per capita water usage in China had already increased from 162 litres in 1986 to 208 litres in 1996. The average percentage of municipal wastewater in the total wastewater discharge was around 40 per cent in China. However, in rich coastal cities like Shanghai and Guangzhou, the percentage was already close to 50 per cent and still on the rise.

About 82 per cent of China's wastewater was discharged into water bodies without any treatment, seriously contaminating the water resources of the country, and resulting in epidemic diseases and deteriorating aquatic life. The National Environmental Agency had required that by 2000, 74 per cent of the industrial wastewater and 25 per cent of the sewage water be treated before being discharged into receiving waters.

Therefore, one priority in water treatment in China had been the construction of urban water treatment plants. Urban water treatment facilities were growing in number faster than industrial wastewater facilities. Yet, of the 668 cities existing in 1997, only 123 cities had a total of 307 urban water treatment plants. Moreover, the majority of the country's 17,000 towns did not have any sewage and water treatment facilities. Therefore, the potential demand of the municipal segment would be significant in the coming years.

The Water Treatment Industry in China

In 1997, there were 2,558 manufacturers of water treatment systems. More than 80 per cent of the companies were small enterprises with limited resources and low technological strength. Most of the domestic-made products were 10 to 20 years behind current world technology levels. Many were being made by village and township enterprises. Experts believed that 70 to 80 per cent of the domestic-made water treatment equipment was below acceptable international standards.

Water disinfecting equipment was among the products most in demand. However, the most widely used disinfection method was chlorination. Ultraviolet disinfection was a new idea to China. The cost of chlorination was roughly $200 per ton of water treated in China. One major cost of UV was electricity, which cost about $.10 per kilowatt hour in China.

A large proportion of the water treatment projects, especially the costly municipal water plants, received foreign funding. The environmental sector had absorbed more than US$3.3 billion in foreign funds by 1999. Foreign capital from various sources like the World Bank, the Asian Development Bank, United Nations Development Program, as well as bilateral government organizations and multi-lateral international organizations made up a substantial contribution to the environmental projects. The majority of the bilateral government loans made it clear that 60 per cent of the loan total must be used to purchase equipment from designated sources. Even when no such conditions were attached, foreign-made equipment was preferred for advanced technology and quality, or sometimes for other obscure considerations (e.g., foreign trips desired by the city officials). As a result, the municipal water treatment market was dominated by imported products, although the imports were usually three to six times more expensive than the domestic products. The U.S. Department of Commerce estimated that the percentage of imports of the total demand for wastewater treatment equipment had risen from 2.7 per cent in 1992 to 37.7 per cent in 1996. The government had, however, repeatedly called for the development of a domestic water treatment industry.

The project design market of water treatment plants was still dominated by domestic players. Since the engineering design market of China was not yet open to foreign competition, almost 98 per cent of the water treatment project design market in China was dominated by the "big eight institutes." The "big eight institutes" referred to the five institutes of civil engineering design affiliated with the Ministry of Construction and the institutes of civil engineering design in Beijing, Tianjing and Shanghai.

The Legal Environment and the Decision-Making Process

China's legal framework regarding environmental protection was quite advanced relative to other developing countries. Environmental policy had been written into the country's constitution since 1983, and the Environmental Protection Law was released in 1989. Standards for air, surface water, and noise had been established. The National Environmental Protection Agency (NEPA) was the leading government institution for developing policies, laws, and regulations related to environmental protection. Approximately 2,300 Environmental Protection Bureaus (EPBs) or Environmental Protection Offices (EPOs) existed at every level of local government, setting standards, monitoring the environment, conducting inspections, and issuing punishments for violations (usually in the form of fines). In addition, most EPBs and EPOs at the provincial level had in-house research institutes.

The legal framework for environmental protection in China was similar to that developed in the West. However, the implementation of the policies was considerably different. The levels of bureaucracy were deep and the project approval process lacked transparency. The involvement of numerous decision-makers made it difficult for firms to identify the person who had the power to make a binding decision.

The Municipal Segment

Theoretically, municipal governments had the power to determine what to do in building a water supply or treatment plant in their city. However, assistance in funding, foreign exchange, fuel, or transportation services might have to come from the central government, and therefore, approvals from higher levels were necessary. Large projects would always require feasibility studies submitted to both the Ministry of Construction and NEPA for approval. Frequently, contracts were awarded after a bidding process. However, the selection of the winning bid was not always based on business considerations. Personal contacts with the key people could influence the bidding process. The key decision-makers, however, varied from place to place.

In the coastal areas, different ways of building and maintaining water treatment facilities were being explored. Among them were long-term contracts, build-operate-transfer forms (in which a firm would build the facility, operate it and collect fees for a predetermined period before transferring it to the government), and turnkey projects (a foreign operator would build the project which would be turned over to the local authority for maintenance).

The Industrial and the Commercial Segments

The decision-making for industrial and commercial facilities was decentralized. The government environmental agencies were in charge of stipulating standards, issuing permits, and conducting inspections. Although approvals from higher level authorities were always necessary, unless they had a vested interest, usually decisions made by the managers of the businesses would be honored. Contracts would be awarded through a bidding system. Again, the bidding processes were not transparent, and the final decision could be based on many non-business factors.

The Residential Segment

More than 90 per cent of urban families had access to running water, which was purified to some extent, but never clean enough for drinking. At home, people would boil water before they drank it. The demand for small, under the sink, household water purification products was weak, largely because of the lack of penetration of this type of equipment into the Chinese household market.

Urban real estate developers often installed sewage systems for residential buildings, and sometimes also installed sewage treatment facilities. The decisions for procuring supplies lay with the developers, given the fact that all equipment was inspected and approved by environmental agencies.

Problems of the Chinese Environmental Market

The environmental protection market in China was not a well developed, orderly market with normal and healthy market competition. Problems abounded. Some issues were common to the whole Chinese market, which was in the painful process of changing from a command to a market economy.

First, there was an issue of local protectionism. Many local governments restricted products made outside their areas to protect their tax revenues. Some even required permissions for the sale of non-locally-made products. Second, corruption led to unfair competition. Bribery or abnormally high commissions were sometimes necessary to make sales. The bidding process was often not transparent, creating opportunities for corruption. Last but not least, there was a lack of respect and protection for intellectual property. Despite all the protection laws, violations of intellectual property happened with alarming frequency. It was not unusual for good products to not succeed because of competition from cheaper and inferior imitations. The water treatment market was no exception. One CEO of a Beijing water treatment company commented that one could not afford to go after all the imitators. However, he pointed out that quality, reputation and financial strength were still essential to stay in the market, especially the municipal water treatment market.

THE DECISION

There was little doubt that China offered enormous market potential and a strong need for water disinfection. Furthermore, selling environmental products in developing countries offered significant sustainable growth opportunities for Trojan. However, a number of issues complicated the decision so that Sarah was not sure if, when, how, and where Trojan should enter the Chinese market.

The contrast between the image outside of Sarah's window and her image of China was startling. As her gaze moved to the glass of crystal-clear water on her desk, she recognized the enormous value of clean water, and that China should not be without it. The question was whether Trojan would be one of the companies that provided it.

The Richard Ivey School of Business gratefully acknowledges the generous support of The Richard and Jean Ivey Fund in the development of this case as part of the RICHARD AND JEAN IVEY FUND ASIAN CASE SERIES.

case 25 Gametronics Gaming Equipment Ltd.

"Now that we've formed a strategic alliance to handle the manufacturing side of the business, we can use our distinctive competence in game design to gain a share of the exploding Internet gaming market. But is this the best way to ensure that Gametronics captures short-term revenues while establishing a dominant position in the emerging on-line segment?"

Fernando Di Carlo, CEO of Gametronics Inc., was reflecting on the direction he had set for his fledgling firm, as he talked to Nolin LeChasseur, director of marketing. The two were discussing how best to allocate responsibilities and resources between Gametronics and its sister company, Internet Gaming Software Solutions (IGSS), to take advantage of a huge opportunity in Internet-based casino games.

Gametronics had been founded by Mr. Di Carlo in 1995 with startup capital from a few private investors, including Mr. Di Carlo himself. The company designed software and hardware to compete with traditional slot machines and Video Lottery Terminals (VLTs) which were sold to commercial casinos and government-run gaming establishments. By June 1999, the investors were anxious to see a revenue stream materialize from what they believed was a very promising gaming market. There was increasing pressure on management to formulate and execute a strategy that would avoid the need for major new financing, while still positioning Gametronics to exploit future opportunities. In an environment of constrained resources, decisions needed to be made about the sequence and timing of new initiatives, and difficult choices had to be made in prioritizing action items. The risks of running afoul of regulatory bodies that supervised this often-controversial industry also had to be taken into account.

THE GAMING INDUSTRY

It was estimated that there were over 1900 licensed casinos and gaming sites operational in the world. While the largest centres were located in the US, attempts were being made in Europe, Asia and the Caribbean to bring those casinos in line with the world-class product available in major American gaming centers. The gaming industry in North America had grown rapidly in the 1960s and 1970s, beginning with early successes in Nevada (Las Vegas and Reno, for example), and later on the East Coast of the United States, primarily in Atlantic City. Large, flashy casinos offered the player traditional gaming activities such as roulette and various card games (like blackjack and poker). In addition, casinos usually had several hundred coin-operated slot machines. Slot machines offered players the opportunity to win large amounts of cash instantly simply by pulling a lever and awaiting the final positioning of the reels that were set into motion by the action of the lever. Certain alignments of the reels, when they stopped spinning, resulted in payoffs of various amounts.

To attract customers, casinos featured entertainment in the form of glitzy shows headlined by well-known show business personalities. Names like Frank Sinatra, Liberace, and Elvis Presley had, in the prime of their careers, been common sights on Las Vegas and Atlantic City marquees. The glamour, the bright lights, the all-night activity, and the lure of easy money all contributed to the mystique of these gaming destinations. Sedate suburbanites could get away for a weekend and pretend they were high rollers, enjoying an exciting, stimulating environment. Any sort of pleasure was easily available, money and other commodities flowed freely, and the everyday, tedious routines of life were temporarily suspended.

Casinos were extraordinarily profitable businesses. Surface impressions to the contrary, all the spending on drinks, expensive shows, and flashy trappings was based on shrewd cost-benefit calculations. The harsh reality, from a customer's point of view, was that casino games were set up mathematically to produce a positive return to the house. The probabilities of winning at cards, dice, roulette, or other games were not complicated to compute. It was thus not difficult to ensure that the total payouts to winners, in aggregate and over large numbers of plays, were less than the bets placed. Notwithstanding the occasional large jackpot, where a bettor might win many thousands of dollars with a relatively small wager, the more bets placed, the more certain it became that the house would eventually come out substantially ahead, thanks to the inexorable laws of statistics. One of a casino's most important marketing initiatives was a customer loyalty and "comp" program. Casinos competed on their ability to attract the "big spenders," or "high rollers," who came for the excitement, the thrills, and the entertainment, but were not overly concerned about the cost. Once a casino had identified one of these key players, they tried very hard to ensure that he or she would keep returning to their establishment, instead of visiting a competing casino. Many of these players were offered free "junkets," including air, hotel, meals and show tickets, to encourage them to return to the casino. More often, the enticements were more modest, such as a complimentary dinner, or a round of drinks. The intended result was the same, however: keep the players coming back.

The virtual certainty of a tidy gross profit, and the fact that this was largely a cash business, had led to a concern among law enforcement officials that casinos might be operated for the benefit of organized crime interests. As well, the appearance of fair dealing and being on the "up and up" had to be maintained if customers were expected to keep returning to the casinos. The ease with which games could be rigged, or outcomes fixed to unfairly deny players a legitimately won prize, was seen by criminal justice authorities as a reason to establish tight regulations around the ownership and operation of the gambling industry. Anyone with an interest in a casino, or who was a supplier to the industry, was subjected to personal investigations, including background checks, fingerprinting, and monitoring of past and present business activities. In addition, any games or slot machines had to be vetted by independent, government-controlled laboratories to ensure that players would not be cheated. Payoffs had to be fair, and be true to the advertised frequency and quantity.

The Market for Gaming Machines

The land-based, traditional, gaming industry, from the point of view of gaming equipment suppliers, consisted of two markets: Video Lottery Terminals (VLTs) and casino slot machines. VLTs, a relatively recent phenomenon, were machines placed in taverns, hotels, racetracks, and other publicly accessible locations. This market was, in most jurisdictions, directly controlled by local governments. In North America, state or provincial governments owned the machines, regulated their content, and collected the profits. Casino-based machines, on the other hand, were owned by private companies in the U.S. that not only operated the gambling floor (along with dining and beverage establishments), but often had hotel and entertainment facilities as well. VLTs were, for the most part, a secondary attraction in the locations where they were installed, while casino-based machines were placed in settings where gambling was the primary motivation for patrons to attend. Despite this difference, most machines that were sold in one market could also be successful in the other. In appearance and operation, the characteristics of a well-designed machine were very similar in both settings.

In 1999, the United States had seven states with laws permitting VLTs, with approximately 56,000 machines in operation. Growth of the market was expected from two sources: First, jurisdictions other than those that already had them were investigating the possibility of launching their own VLT programs. Second, the current installed base of machines was beginning to reach the end of its operational life. The replacement market alone was estimated at 30% of the installed machines over the next three years, for a total of 16,800 machines.

In 1999 there were about 1,700 casinos operating in the U.S., with a total of over 800,000 slot machines. Slot machines were monitored on a daily basis for productivity, in terms of revenue and profit volumes, and newer machines with greater attractiveness for players were always being sought. It was estimated that 30% of the existing machines would be due for replacement over the next three years, representing total acquisitions of 240,000 new machines by casinos.

The VLT phenomenon had also taken hold in Canada, with almost every province having implemented or planning a VLT program. Almost 40,000 terminals were in operation already, resulting in a replacement market estimated at 12,000 machines over the next three years. In addition, orders for approximately 23,000 to 28,000 additional new machines were expected as a result of expansion of existing video lottery programs, primarily from Eastern Canada.

Casino slot machines in Canada numbered 17,000, not including 4,000 machines just being planned for installation in British Columbia. Also not included in the total were an estimated 5,000 machines that would be required to meet the demand of a recently-authorized racetrack VLT program in Ontario. Gametronics had estimated that the three-year replacement market for casino slots was approximately 5,100 machines, bringing total anticipated three-year demand to 14,100 machines.

In summary, the Canadian market was estimated to represent approximately 50,000 machines over the next three years. Added to a total U.S. demand of over 260,000, this implied a forecast North American market size of well over 300,000 machines over three years.

SLOT MACHINE TECHNOLOGY

The North American gaming machine market was dominated by mechanical reel-based slot machines that had been introduced in the 1960s. These machines featured multiple (usually three) wheels that were set to spin by the player's pull on a lever. Whether a player won or lost was determined by the position of the images on the wheels when they stopped spinning. Manufacturers had developed variants on the basic theme over the years, by changing the number of reels and the images on them, developing "stepper technology" that allowed for a greater number of stops, or outcomes, on a reel, and the introduction of electronic memory on the machines to enable winnings to be paid out on a net basis instead of after each pull on the handle. This latter innovation eliminated the need for the player to reinsert coins for each pull, increasing the number of pulls per hour and therefore the amounts wagered. Since the 1980s however, little technological improvement had taken place in traditional reel/stepper slot machines.

Video graphics first appeared in casino slot machines in the 1980s. International Game Technology was the first to introduce video poker, which represented a departure from traditional slot machines in two respects. First, it was interactive, requiring the player to make decisions about which cards to discard and which to hold for each hand. This feature allowed the player some influence over the outcome of each hand, unlike the traditional slot where the result could not be affected once the lever was pulled. Second, the video screen interface allowed for more interesting and attractive graphics, making for a more entertaining gaming session. Providing some measure of entertainment for the player was seen as a way of offering greater value for the money wagered. It was thought that more entertaining machines would be played more often, and with larger bets, than dull, repetitive ones. Machines that encouraged larger, more frequent bets were attractive to the casino operators, who measured machine performance on the basis of an index called "win per unit per day."

More recently, the flexibility of the video screen approach to gaming machines had been employed to create multigame machines. Bally Gaming International Inc. introduced its GameMaker, which offered up to ten different games on a single console. The rising popularity of video poker and multi-game machines was seen as evidence that both slot machine players and video lottery customers were becoming increasingly receptive to more complex and interactive gaming experiences.

More evidence to support this conclusion came from the success of Silicon Gaming's new "Odyssey" machine. A player using this product was able to choose between video slot, video poker, and keno games using a large touch screen. These innovations, combined with the designs of the games themselves and the cabinet styling, represented a revolution in the industry. They had proved to be very successful and had produced excellent revenue in Nevada and other U.S. trials.

COMPETITORS

The major participants in the casino gaming machine industry were International Gaming Technology (IGT) and Bally Gaming. IGT, based in Reno, Nevada, shipped 80,000 to 90,000 machines per year and had an excellent reputation for product, service, and reliability. Their principal market strength, however, may also have been their major point of vulnerability. Gametronics executives believed that IGT's patent on reel/stepper technology, while providing a competitive advantage in the traditional market, had dampened their interest in actively developing the more interactive, video-based machines of the future. They increasingly relied, it was believed, on persuading casino operators that customers still preferred mechanical slot machines, an argument that was becoming more and more difficult to sustain.

Bally Gaming, of Las Vegas, Nevada, shipped approximately 45,000 machines annually, with most using IGT's reel/stepper technology under license. While they had shown signs of awareness that a market for more interactive play was emerging, their main market focus remained the traditional slot machine category.

In the VLT segment, four firms predominated: Video Lottery Consultants (VLC), Williams Industries, IGT, and Spielo. The majority of the terminals produced by these firms and currently in use in various North American VLT programs were based on relatively outdated technology; while they delivered acceptable performance in the current marketplace, they were not readily adaptable to the more interactive, entertaining gaming experiences likely to be required from future-generation video lottery devices.

The above firms (i.e., IGT, Bally Gaming, VLC, Williams Gaming, and Spielo) collectively held the dominant share of the North American gaming machine market. However, a number of smaller suppliers existed, including Aristocrat Leisure Industries, Universal Distributing, Sigma Games, Casino Data Systems, Acres Gaming Inc. and Innovative Gaming Corporation of America. These smaller firms competed in geographic or specialized product niches where the large firms' size was not as big an advantage, either in manufacturing scale economies, or in product development cost recovery.

THE INTERNET GAMING MARKET

The Internet was originally developed in 1970 by research divisions from various universities and governments to provide an effective means of maintaining communication during critical or catastrophic events such as war or natural disaster. The Internet soon began to be used by universities to transfer information and exchange data. With the 1990s came the development of the World Wide Web, along with user-friendly Web browsers that opened up access to the Internet to a broad cross-section of the general public. In recent years, Internet usage had skyrocketed, with the total number of users by the end of 1999 conservatively projected at over 200 million.

During the preceding 12 -18 months, commercial activity on the Internet had also begun to soar. Secure protocols for payment over the World Wide Web had been developed, and were constantly being improved by industry giants, including MasterCard and Visa. By offering seamless, secure payment capabilities, the Internet now provided consumers with almost unlimited choice in commercial activity, and the ability to use their credit cards online with confidence. Forrester Research, a well-respected forecasting firm based in Cambridge, Massachusetts, estimated that online shopping (or "e-commerce") activity would reach $6.6 billion by the year 2000.

Paralleling the growth in all types of electronic commerce, Internet gaming activity had also expanded quickly in the past few years. As with many aspects of Internet activity however, there were vast discrepancies in quality, integrity, and profitability among the existing gaming sites. Of the 280 gaming-related sites on the Net, only about half were capable of accepting real wagers, and of these, less than 20% (or approximately 25-30 sites) could be considered of reasonable quality. Despite this disparity across gaming sites, and the ad hoc manner in which online gaming had evolved, the potential of this burgeoning market appeared to be huge. Some industry analysts estimated that more than US$2 billion annually was currently being wagered on Internet gaming sites. This amount was projected to grow to over US$10 billion within two years.

As might be expected, the established land-based gaming interests (that is, the traditional casino operators) were beginning to pay close attention to the Internet gaming marketplace. Many of them either were planning or just beginning to execute strategies for entering this new territory. Internet-based gaming provided an opportunity for a casino to extend loyalty programs to all its customers at minimal cost. For example, if a casino could hand a CD to departing guests that enabled them to access their favorite games and receive credit for their play at the casino's Internet site, they would have a strong tool to maintain player loyalty, thus encouraging repeat visits to the casino itself. This benefit would be in addition to the incremental profit from online wagering by these customers.

In many respects, present market conditions presented an ideal opportunity for introducing a high-quality, innovative casino gaming initiative to the Internet gaming market. In the opinion of Gametronics management, few existing sites were offering high-quality, innovative, gaming experiences, and the big shooters in the land-based gaming industry had not yet staked out any territory along the new electronic frontier.

Regulatory Complications

As noted above, the gaming industry was very closely, and often inconsistently, regulated. Regulators had to be sensitive to potential criticism from some members of the public for allowing gambling at all. Objections to the whole notion of legalized gambling were often based on religious or moral convictions. There were also more secular objections, however. Many social scientists had expressed concerns about the effect of widespread gambling on society as a whole, citing the effects of compulsive gambling and gambling addiction on the families and children of those so afflicted. These critics were most vocal about what they saw as the deleterious impact of VLTs, which, some psychologists had found, were particularly alluring to those with addictive tendencies and thus exacerbated the social problems that flowed from these behaviors. It was particularly ironic, said some, that governments were not only sponsoring, but profiting from the misery caused by what were termed "insidious machines."

Many industry outsiders took issue with the ethical questions raised by making profits from human misery. It was true that the vast majority of gamblers simply saw their losses as a price that they voluntarily paid in return for entertainment value received. However, it was also difficult to deny that a notable percentage of gamblers wagered in ways (and in amounts) that were destructive, both to themselves and those close to them. To deal with these concerns, Gametronics planned to monitor players on their Websites, to identify those whose play patterns seemed to suggest they might have a problem. Triggers that would cue a warning message to the player might be repeated large losses or excessive hours spent logged on to the site. Players would be cut off completely if their unhealthy play patterns persisted. As Mr. DiCarlo put it: "I want to have a million players each betting a dollar, not a thousand people gambling away their mortgage payments. Our goal is to provide entertainment, not to profit on the backs of people who should not be gambling. We are not indifferent to where the revenue comes from."

Debate around the whole subject of gambling had, on occasion, become heated and highly polarized. As a result, regulators were forced to tread very cautiously between liberal and restrictive policies. "Hands-off' advocates noted that legislation clearly made the business a legal one in many jurisdictions, and thus one which citizens had every right to conduct. Gambling industry spokespeople described the industry as one that sold entertainment: for every dollar spent at the tables or in the slot machines, some entertainment value was returned to the customer. If the customer decided that better value could be obtained at a different slot machine, or by going to a movie, attending a sporting event, or watching television, he or she was free to make that choice. Licenses could therefore not be withheld without justification.

Regulators also had to be very careful to maintain the appearance, and the reality, of transparency and fair dealing when it came to the nature of the games they licensed. For example, the win percentage had to be approved, and randomness, or chance, had to be the basis for wins or losses. No manipulation of win parameters on the part of game manufacturers or operators could be permitted; nor could there be even a hint of corruption around the major participants in the industry, whether they were executives of supplier companies, casinos, or regulatory bodies. Because of the sensitivity of the issues, and the potential for very public embarrassments if a mistake were made, regulators were extremely deliberate and cautious. Game hardware and software makers had to secure separate licenses for each jurisdiction, a procedure that could cost up to US$250,000 per jurisdiction. Once the company was approved, each of its products also had to be submitted to the local regulators for certification. The approvals processes for game-specific software and hardware could be extremely lengthy (up to three years in Nevada, for instance), and cost up to US$25,000 for each game, plus $15,000 for electrical safety certification.

Casinos themselves were governed at the local level in North America, but the Internet, being a broadcast medium, was the domain of national governments. There had been previous attempts to regulate content on the Internet, notably in the area of pornography, but these had largely been unsuccessful. Attempts to define and regulate appropriate Internet content had proved impossible to enforce. The difficulty arose from the nature of the medium—it really existed nowhere and everywhere at once (in cyberspace), and was thus impossible to pin down long enough for any legal sanctions to be applied. A Website's physical operations need not be located in Canada to be accessible to Canadians—thus Canadian laws were not effective at the content-production end of the value chain, because "illegal" content could simply be produced offshore. At the consumer end of the chain, traditions and statutes concerning privacy, free speech, anonymity, and freedom itself made it impossible for lawmakers to control what was seen on computer users' screens.

Given the swashbuckling, laissez-faire nature of the Web, it seemed like a natural environment for computer-based gambling. No regulator could hope to control it, security and transactional integrity issues had largely been resolved, and the quality and sophistication of the software had become outstanding. Despite the market's apparent potential, however, some care had to be taken. Beyond the regulatory bureaucracies were legislative bodies which set out the basic frameworks under which regulations were developed. Legislators were sensitive to public opinion, and some came from constituencies which were strongly opposed to gambling as a matter of moral principle. For example, in 1998 Congressman Jon Kyl tabled a bill in the U.S. House of Representatives that would outlaw any gambling on the Internet, at least on sites physically located within U.S. boundaries. If the bill were to pass, Gametronics could, of course, simply proceed with existing plans to operate their Website from offshore, and be immune to prosecution. The concern was that this could be interpreted as deliberate flouting of the law, and might therefore have an adverse effect on the company's chances of being licensed for any land-based applications in U.S. territory. Formally, the company might be perceived as de facto criminals for their Internet business, thus disqualifying them from participating in any U.S.-regulated gaming activity. If this were to happen, the prospects for Gametronics selling any VLT and slot machine software were limited.

Web-Based Gaming

The principal online gaming competitors had adopted a franchise-like structure. A typical company licensed a suite of games with e-commerce software able to process credit cards and cheques. The owner of the site was required to establish a Web presence in a jurisdiction that allowed an Internet casino, and to operate the business. To be successful, a site owner had to have the ability to manage an Internet business, have knowledge of the casino market and be able to market the site effectively. But from the licensor's point of view, sales of Internet sites were more important than working on the success of each site. The approach only worked because of the immaturity of the Internet casino world. According to Fernando Di Carlo:

> "Once players are exposed to the level of game quality similar to land based casinos, we anticipate that they will convert [from existing low-quality sites] in droves. Given the fact that players are used to the land based casino experience, they are aware of the difference in services provided. As the level of players' expectations increases, better-quality sites will overcome this inferior product."

GAMETRONICS AND THE INTERNET

Gametronics' shareholders had established a sister company, Internet Gaming Software Solutions (IGSS), to operate the Internet-based side of the business. IGSS was a software company that specialized in the design, development and marketing of interactive Internet software specifically for e-commerce and gaming applications. IGSS would market two products: 1) Internet casinos for independent operators, and 2) a turnkey Internet casino intended for traditional casino operations.

Independent Internet Casinos   IGSS would jointly own and operate several Internet Casinos. These independent online casinos would be marketed by way of a "Super Brand" and would provide players with a high-quality gaming experience superior to that offered by existing Web-based competitors. IGSS casinos were to be targeted to both existing Internet casino players and to potential new players.

Turnkey Casino Software   Gametronics management anticipated that in the near future land-based casinos would add Internet extensions to their current gaming business, both as incremental revenue sources and as loyalty-building vehicles. To exploit this opportunity, Internet Gaming Software Solutions offered an Internet solution called "TICS" (Turnkey Internet Casino Software). It was to be a complete turnkey solution that included back-end, front-end, Internet and game interfaces, real-time marketing recommendation technology, and e-commerce.

IGSS would compete in the existing gaming market place on the superior characteristics of game software it would source from Gametronics. The lack of entertainment value and crude layout of existing Web gaming sites provided an opportunity for a company with a core competence in game design. In addition, IGSS would be well positioned to provide efficient services to existing land-based gaming operations. There was also a possibility for either a sale or a joint venture with a large land-based casino. Exhibit 1 (on the next page) depicts graphically how Gametronics and IGSS fit into the industry supply chain, and how the relationships were expected to evolve.

In the opinion of Gametronics managers, present market conditions represented an ideal opportunity for introducing a high-quality, innovative casino gaming initiative to the Internet gaming market. While some of the "good-quality" Internet gaming

exhibit 1   Graphic Depiction of the Gaming Industry

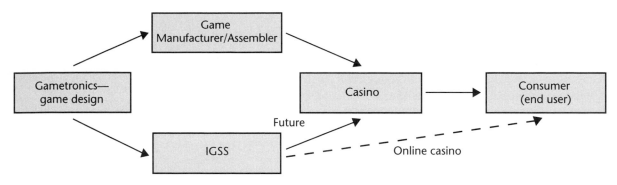

sites were posting successful financial returns, from a gaming-quality standpoint hardly any of them offered the entertainment value of existing land-based casino or video lottery games. Areas where the current market players were vulnerable included:

Game Design & Development   In many cases, Internet casino sites were developed and operated by firms with expertise in software development, e-commerce, Web design, or other Internet-related fields, but with little or no gaming expertise. Game design and development was therefore generally weak, and the games offered very little in the way of entertainment value to attract and hold players.

Poor Marketing Efforts   Many current online casinos were developed and operated under turnkey arrangements made with a few key Internet gaming companies. These firms developed the technology necessary for setting up and operating the online casinos, and then sold these turnkey packages to investors as Internet casinos. The investors actually owned the casinos, with the gaming firms providing technical services in return for a percentage of revenues generated. This structural arrangement did not inherently encourage quality in the actual gaming experiences for players however, as the gaming firm was much more motivated to sell more casino licenses than to optimize the performance of existing operations. Investors who purchased these sites were generally financially focused, having entered the market because of its potential for excellent returns, but having little or no direct gaming expertise. As a result of this vacuum created between the gaming company's focus being elsewhere once the sites were up and running, and the ownership lacking gaming expertise, many existing sites were quite inept at marketing themselves effectively.

Formally, IGSS executed an exclusive license with Gametronics for the use of their game software on the Internet. Gametronics had capabilities in the land-based casino slot machine and video gaming marketplaces with state-of-the-art technology and innovative game designs, and could transfer these skills to the Internet through IGSS. The overall approach was to make the gaming experience fun and entertaining for players, as opposed to simply providing a vehicle for online gambling. Games offered creative special effects, frequent payouts, bonus structures, multiple levels of play, and other innovative features designed to attract and retain player interest.

With its Internet gaming initiative, IGSS intended to bring this same innovative approach to the world of online gaming. The following were some of the key features in IGSS' Internet gaming approach:

Existing Suite of Proven Games   Gametronics had an existing suite of state-of-the art games that IGSS would introduce online. All of these games were designed and developed by Gametronics, and had received positive reviews in the casino and video lottery gaming markets for their features and entertainment value.

Effective Marketing Efforts   Unlike many existing online casinos whose owners had little or no gaming expertise, IGSS' management team had extensive experience in the gaming industry, not just in Canada but across North America and around the world. IGSS intended to use this gaming expertise and knowledge to develop and implement effective, aggressive marketing plans for its online casino offerings. Many of the most successful marketing tools currently used in land-based casinos would be brought to the online gaming forum.

Security & Integrity   Gametronics games were independently tested by Gaming Laboratories International (GLI), providing assurance to players as to the legitimacy and "fairness" of the games. In addition, state-of-the art encryption for all data transfers would offer secure e-commerce, using the highest standards for commercial activity available on the World Wide Web.

Ongoing Involvement & Casino Management   IGSS would retain substantial shares in its Internet casino sites. Its principal focus for maximizing returns would be on effectively promoting and managing these sites—not trying to sell "turnkey" cookie-cutter sites to as many independent investors as possible. IGSS had access to extensive expertise both in technical areas (e.g., hardware and communications experts, software designers, Web-page developers) and in the creative aspects of game development. This in-house expertise would be supplemented by an external advisory board offering ongoing advice to the firm on new markets (e.g., sports-book betting, bingo, pari-mutuel wagering) and/or new technologies as the marketplace evolved.

IGSS did not want to become just one more entry into the online gaming marketplace. The plan was to so dramatically supersede the quality, professionalism and entertainment value of anything currently available online that it would quickly attract players, build player loyalty, develop a solid player base and develop a formidable foundation for future growth.

As proposed, online casinos would be jointly owned by an investor and IGSS, which would retain a majority share. Projected minimum net revenue from each Internet casino site in the first year and second years were US$2.1 million and $7.5 million respectively. Of this, IGSS would receive a percentage corresponding to their share of ownership. IGSS would earn an additional fee of at least US$25,000 per month per site for providing management and operations expertise. One such deal, representing an investment of approximately US$6 million from one investor for three online casinos, was close to being completed. Development time, both for the IGSS infrastructure and for adapting games to the necessary specifications, was estimated at six months.

Startup costs of the IGSS operation were considerable. The table below outlines some of the key budget items that were involved. Forecasts were uncertain because the physical facility housing the computer hardware was to be located in Costa Rica, where the reliability and quality of some of IGSS' key requirements could prove a problem. Even the reliability of local electrical supply would be an issue with a computer-based, 24-hour, seven-day operation like this. In addition to these operational concerns, there was a need to have the mind and management of the company (IGSS) at the head office in Barbados. For tax and other reasons, the Barbados office had to have real, decision-making management permanently placed on the site.

Estimated Costs Associated with IGSS ($000s)	
IGSS startup and operation:	
Hardware (e.g., servers, secure power supply, etc.)	250
Operating expenses:	
Payroll (CEO, administrative staff, sales, hardware technicians)	30/mo
Facility costs (rent, Internet access, utilities, etc.)	10/mo
Costs for each online casino:	
Games software (from Gametronics)	500
E-commerce software	250
Web-page design	150
Pre-launch advertising	250

In addition to these plans for independent online casinos, IGSS was also developing a self-contained Internet solution called "TICS" (Turn-key Internet Casino Software). It would be the first complete turnkey solution to include back-end, front-end, Internet interface, game interface, real-time marketing solution, with real-time recommendation technology, and e-commerce. The TICS solution was to enable land-based casinos to quickly and easily add an Internet casino extension to their current gaming businesses.

TICS would be marketed to casino operators at a price of US$1 to $3 million plus cost of games (approx. US$500,000 to US$1.5 million) and service maintenance costs, (approx. 30% of the contract). IGSS might also share in a small percentage (2%–5%) of revenues earned by each Internet casino. Recognizing that some smaller casinos might not have the resources to establish their own exclusive Internet presence, IGSS could provide for a Commerce Service Provider site. These sites would combine several casinos into one address that still allowed each participant to maintain customer loyalty by involvement in an Internet extension of the land-based operation.

THE GAMETRONICS ORGANIZATION

Gametronics' offices were located in a renovated church in downtown Toronto's trendy Yorkville area. Upon walking in, a visitor was dazzled by the striking architectural features that had been retained when the building's original interior was subdivided into four floors and separate work/office areas. Huge diagonal beams slashed through the spaces at various, seemingly random, points. Vast stained-glass windows dominated some of the perimeter offices, while suffusing the whole with a surreal, but warm, light.

On the fourth floor, which housed the game developers, programmers, and Mr. Di Carlo's office, one encountered what appeared to be a dark warren of desks festooned with computer screens, water bottles, and bits of paper and hardware. The dress code was decidedly informal, with not a tie or even a shirt cuff anywhere in evidence. Groups gathered around different desks at various times, apparently to observe and comment on some new feature or development undergoing a trial run at the time.

The rest of Gametronics' operations were on the second floor of the building. Plans existed for eventual development and occupancy of the third floor as well, but this would take place at some point in the future, when it became necessary to expand to accommodate growth. For now, the second floor was home to the Directors of Human Resources and Sales (Janis Valentine and Deborah Ingram) and the Vice President, Operations, John Kousik. (Please refer to Exhibit 2 for a complete organization chart.) A reception desk, a product showroom, and several meeting rooms were also on this level. On this floor, the ambience was slightly more typical of a conventional "business," with some individuals dressed in a way that would not be inappropriate in a Bay Street boardroom. This was clearly the area meant to be the interface with the outside: prospective customers, investors, regulators, and others from less informal environments would not feel out of place here. Nevertheless, the atmosphere was casual, friendly, and collegial, with little evidence of strict hierarchy or positional authority.

Sales

Gametronics had, in 1999, a sales staff of one, Ms. Deborah Ingram. She described her activities as being "on hold" for the time being, while some regulatory issues were being sorted out: "I have all the customers lined up and ready to place orders. All we need to do is get the licences, and we're off to the races." Several orders had been agreed to in principle, but delivery had to be delayed when the licensing process took longer than anticipated. No substantial shipments of product had yet been made.

exhibit 2   Gametronics Organization Chart

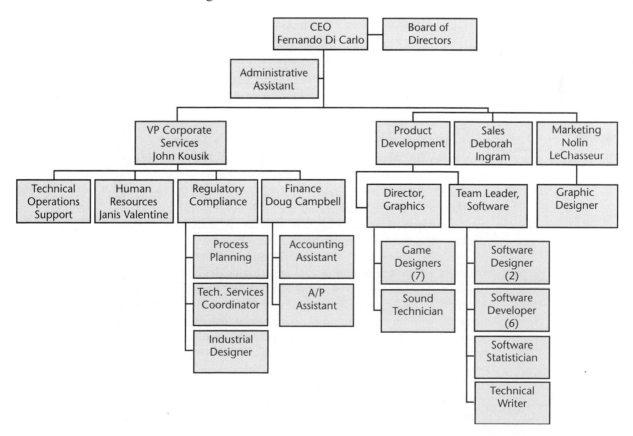

The selling cycle could be a lengthy one for gaming equipment. Gametronics, like other manufacturers, participated in various trade shows. The shows were attended by representatives of the casinos, who were always on the lookout for innovations that would generate more revenue for their establishments. With an average payout to players of 92% of the total wagers, most slot machines generated from $125 to $350 in net revenue. A casino with several hundred slot machines had a strong incentive to maximize the win-per-machine. A low-performing unit represented an opportunity cost to the casino.

Typically, a casino's slot manager (or general manager), if impressed with a particular machine, might agree to install it on a trial basis, with the intention of, perhaps, ordering several of them later if the trial proved to be successful. Manufacturers, as a rule, would not receive any money for these trials, although the casino might agree to share the net revenue ("win") from the trial machine with the manufacturer.

Ms. Ingram was anxious to begin selling machines to Native groups in the United States. She indicated that this market would be her first priority once the regulatory compliance "handcuffs" were removed and she could actually sell product.

> "Licensing is a very costly and lengthy process. Atlantic City and Las Vegas are obvious targets, but you have to be licensed in each state you want to sell in. The Native market is a little softer. There are special Native Gaming shows, where you show your products, like at any other trade show. The Native casino operators, if they like what they see, send a letter to the state gaming authority saying 'We want to buy this machine.' This starts the licensing process immediately. By contrast, a jurisdiction like Las Vegas is much more expensive, complicated and time-consuming. It can take three years to get a license in Nevada. So, if I want the shortest time-to-market, the Native market is it. There is not as much red tape, because they are treated as sovereign nations, and the line-up of applications is much shorter. I'd much rather have six months to the [casino] floor than three years."

Ms. Ingram felt that, once things started to move, she might be able to hire a salesperson for the Canadian market, while she focused on growing Gametronics' penetration in the rest of North America.

Human Resources

Janis Valentine, Director of Human Resources, was a veteran of start-up companies before joining Gametronics, so she was well aware of the special challenges this kind of firm faced. She had implemented professional Human Resource practices and policies regarding all the basic elements of administration within the company. Recruiting, selection, compensation, training, and benefits were all handled in ways that were consistent with current practice in those areas.

With the move away from establishing an in-house manufacturing operation, Valentine's role was no longer consumed with the heavy demands of hiring and administering personnel activities for an assembly plant. Her focus had shifted to creating enough systems and structure to ensure that the company could be effectively managed, without imposing so many rules and regulations that its creative spark would be stifled. In her view, "you have to have some minimum amount of rules and procedures to be able to call yourself an organization, but I would not say that we've gone too far in that respect."

Valentine's main activity at present was designing and implementing training programs. At the moment, this consisted primarily of in-service technical training for software people, who often needed to be brought up to date on new developments in existing software, or new operating platforms on which games might run more efficiently. Her task was made more difficult because of the on-again/off-again nature of the company's current cash flow. There were occasions in the past when she had had to cancel someone's attendance at a conference, for example, because of short-term budget constraints. It was currently impossible to devise any kind of long-term training plan because the lack of a formal budget made the whole exercise very much an ad hoc activity.

Operations and Regulatory Compliance

John Kousik had been hired in March of 1999 to fill the role of vice president, operations. He described his role as being responsible for everything except marketing and game design, thus making him the chief administrative officer in the firm. Kousik's background as a chief of police in Windsor, Ontario (which was the site of the first commercial casino in the province of Ontario) had given him a wealth of expertise and familiarity with the regulatory side of this business. In addition, his previous career had provided him with a great deal of management skill and experience.

Kousik felt that Gametronics' founders had seriously underestimated the complexity and lengthiness of the regulatory approval process.

> "They developed a terrific concept, and a great marketing and sales plan, but did not appreciate the timing implications of the licensing and laboratory certification aspects of the business. As a result, they were successful in creating the appetite, but were not able to deliver any product, because of a lack of the necessary approvals. You have to understand the regulators here too: they're dealing with a new, PC-based game platform, where they were used to the old mechanical ones. Like anybody else, they perceive some risk in changing and embracing new technologies, so it's understandable that the process would be more time-consuming."

Kousik's number one priority task was ensuring that this mistake was not repeated. He felt that Gametronics' credibility in the market had been dealt a serious blow when they were unable to deliver on some of the supply commitments they had made. As a result, he had put all sales activity on hold for an estimated 15 to 18 months.

> "The next round of sales calls has to be based, not on a concept or a vision or mission, but on a product that has been fully approved and is ready for delivery. To do this will mean creating a detailed budget for the deployment of human and physical resources, to ensure that all the pieces are in place. We will also need to revisit what we think it will take, in terms of structure, governance, policies and procedures, to deliver a quality product on time. In other words, we've got to restructure the company."

Despite this daunting agenda, Kousik felt that the right people were there to do the job, and that it was more a question of realigning responsibilities and working relationships than it was a house-cleaning task: "The people that are here right now are absolutely capable of doing it," he said.

Kousik saw the decision, in late 1998, to outsource manufacturing as a good move, because it enabled Gametronics to focus on what he called their "key thrusts": game design and software development. In addition, it avoided potential problems from having two distinct cultures within one organization, where the game design was the more glamorous area, while the manufacturing operations were the "meat and potatoes." The firm that had been contracted to perform the final assembly of game consoles would be paid an average of $250 per completed machine. This added a little to the cost of doing it in-house, at projected volumes, said Kousik, but it was well worth it. Maintaining Gametronics' own plant, including basic production personnel, would have run in the neighborhood of $22,000 per month.

Budgets

Exhibit 3 details the total human resources payroll needs of Gametronics' head office, at full operation. The payroll budget was approximately two-thirds of the total operating expenditures, with the other third consisting primarily of rent and communications expenses. The company had no external debt, but also had no substantial sources of revenue at the moment. It was estimated that, without a further equity injection or other major changes from the status quo, available cash could run out in approximately six months. On the other hand, more sales of online casinos could change the company's cash position virtually overnight.

Details of the costs associated with the IGSS Costa Rica operation were outlined in a previous table.

Research and Development

Silicon Gaming spent US$40 million developing its Odyssey machine, primarily on software development. When asked how Gametronics could hope to compete in this market when its total R&D spending was only a fraction of this amount ($2.8 million for its latest product, World Casino Tour™), Fernando Di Carlo described Silicon Gaming's development effort as relatively inefficient compared to Gametronics.

> "We went straight to a workable solution instead of exploring every possible path and turning over every rock like Silicon Gaming did. With our combination of gaming knowledge, gifted game developers, and talented programmers, we wasted far fewer resources and came up with a better game than they did. OK, we were a little lucky too, but I really believe we made most of our own luck by ensuring we had the right people on board to get the job done."

Silicon Gaming's terminal had been installed in several casinos and had been generating significantly enhanced revenue per terminal compared to the averages generated by other machines. The terminal had been under development since 1994, and came with a significantly higher price tag (US$16,000 approx.) than the more traditional entries in the slot/VLT marketplace, which sold for about US$5,500-7,500. Mr. Di Carlo thought that Silicon Gaming was at a disadvantage, relative to Gametronics, due to the excessive R&D costs of their product. Gametronics, with more moderate startup costs, would be able to market their product at a more competitive price.

Highlights of a Sample Product (World Casino Tour™)
According to Gametronics, their recently completed flagship product had the following characteristics which set it apart from the competition:

Expanded Player Demographics
Statistics suggested that the majority of VLT players were drawn from 10%–15% of the population. In order to capture a larger share of the population, Gametronics designed World Casino Tour™ to attract and engage a broad base of players. Due to its unique travel theme, wide variety of game choices and unique interface, Gametronics' product was expected to appeal to a broader cross-section of the population.

exhibit 3   Staffing Needs

The following table shows Gametronics' anticipated corporate and manufacturing staffing levels, including position quantities and projected pay levels.

Description	Quantity	Unit Rate	Annual Total
Head Office			
President & CEO	1	280,000	280,000
Legal Counsel	1	75,000	75,000
Exec. VP Marketing/Game Development	1	150,000	150,000
VP Manufacturing	1	150,000	150,000
Regional Sales Director	5	70,000	350,000
Project Manager (Asia)	1	150,000	150,000
Director of Finance	1	100,000	100,000
Director Human Resources	1	65,000	65,000
Sales Executive	2	45,000	90,000
Director Software Engineer	1	100,000	100,000
Director Game Design	1	70,000	70,000
Marketing Director	1	70,000	70,000
Graphics Animation Specialist	10	60,000	600,000
Software Engineer	10	60,000	600,000
Industrial Design	2	50,000	100,000
Office, Administration,/Bookkeeping	4	40,000	160,000
Sub-Total Corporate Office	42		$3,110,000
Manufacturing Operations (now outsourced)			
General Manager	1	110,000	110,000
Assembly Technician	15	35,000	525,000
Quality Control	8	40,000	320,000
Technical Support	5	40,000	200,000
Service Technician	5	40,000	200,000
Shipping/Receiving	3	40,000	120,000
Purchasing	2	70,000	
		40,000	110,000
Game-tracking coordinator	1	35,000	35,000
Stores (raw & finished goods)	2	35,000	70,000
Sub-Total Manufacturing Facility	42		$1,690,000

This table represents staffing levels at maturity, i.e., once sales reached the projected levels. It does not, however, take into account staffing requirements for the IGSS operation. Personnel to run the offshore Websites would be in addition to these estimates.

Added Entertainment Value   World Casino Tour™ rewarded players with added entertainment value for their gaming dollar, A unique travel theme allowed games to be played in a choice of six destinations: Las Vegas, Atlantic City, Paradise Island, Monte Carlo, Macau, and a Mississippi river boat. The graphics, symbols, and sound effects combined to authenticate the chosen destination. This was a new concept in video gaming.

Gametronics' World Casino Tour™ video lottery terminal was unveiled at the World Gaming Expo in Las Vegas (October 14-16, 1997) where it was met with positive reviews and approval from industry representatives, including gaming officials from various lottery jurisdictions including: Atlantic Lottery Corporation, Lotto Quebec, Western Canada Lottery Corporation, Ohio Lottery, and the Montana Gaming Commission.

Gametronics landed a contract with Fleetwood Distributing of Billings, Montana, the second largest machine operator in the state, for the purchase of a minimum 1,150, 1,750, and 2,350 Gametronics terminals per year, for 3 years respectively, at a total value over $42 million ($8,000 per machine). However, no shipments had yet been made on this order.

The World Casino Tour™ terminal was similar in design and concept to Silicon Gaming's Odyssey terminal. The Odyssey terminal had been installed as a video slot machine in casinos in Nevada and Missouri, and consistently delivered greater win-per-unit performance statistics than traditional slots or video poker machines—up to 2 times the average machine in some instances. Mr. Di Carlo believed that this outstanding performance was gained because Gametronics' machine had

- better-quality sound,
- made bonus features available on all games (as opposed to only some games with the Odyssey product), and
- provided instantaneous game selection, much faster than Odyssey's, and had multiple "themes," which gave it an attractive initial impression to a much broader base of potential players.

Machines were expected to sell for an average price of $8,000. As the table below shows, this compared favorably with pricing of competitive offerings. Additionally, once an initial critical mass of machines was installed in the marketplace, Gametronics expected to generate substantial ongoing revenues from licensing game software. Individual game upgrades would be available at a cost of $500 per game per terminal. Alternatively, customers would be allowed to purchase an annual upgrade package for $2,000 per terminal which would entitle them to a minimum of four and a maximum of six new games each year.

Competitive Price Comparisons	
Make	**Price per unit US$**
Gametronics World Casino Tour™	$7,500–$7,950
Bally Game Magic	$11,000 (projected)
IGT Vision	$12,500
Silicon Gaming	$16,000

CONCLUSION

Some complex and interesting times were ahead for Fernando Di Carlo and his team. He wondered whether launching the Internet business now would prove to be the right strategy in the long run. While the opportunity looked attractive, there were also some risks that could sink the company. Even if the IGSS move was the right one though, there remained the managerial question of how resources (human and financial) should be allocated between IGSS and the core game development business. Finally, an implementation plan, including possible structural changes, had to be developed.

case 26 Scotch-Brite (3M)

In June 1990, the 3M operating committee met in world headquarters in St. Paul, Minnesota, to consider a proposal to rationalize the North American production and distribution of Scotch-Brite hand scouring pads. Due to increased consumer demand, the decision had been made to upgrade the equipment which converted the jumbo-sized rolls into consumer and industrial-sized packages and quantities. At issue was where this upgraded processing equipment would be located.

Currently, most of the conversion took place in Alexandria, Minnesota, from jumbo rolls supplied from Perth, Ontario. The Alexandria facility then shipped finished goods to eight distribution centres around the United States. (See Exhibit 1.)

The Canadian division of 3M was now proposing that all production and distribution for Scotch-Brite hand pads take place from Perth. This would mean $4 million in new equipment would go to Perth, the current Scotch-Brite work force in Alexandria would be shifted to different responsibilities, and Perth would now ship directly to the various distribution centres. (See Exhibit 2.) This proposal to grant a regional product mandate to Perth had not gone unopposed. The Alexandria plant felt it would be preferable to place the new converting equipment in their facility, and to maintain the existing relationship with Perth.

3M BACKGROUND

3M was a multinational enterprise with 80,000 employees, subsidiaries and operations in 50 countries, and worldwide annual sales in excess of US$10 billion. During the past decade, 3M's outside-the-U.S. (OUS) sales had climbed from about one-third to nearly one-half of total sales. This growth was a result of a conscious strategy of global expansion. The company was organized into four divisions: Industrial and Consumer, Electronic and Information Technologies, Life Sciences, and Graphic Technologies.

Professor Paul W. Beamish prepared this case solely to provide material for class discussion. The author does not intend to illustrate either effective or ineffective handling of a managerial situation. The author may have disguised certain names and other identifying information to protect confidentiality.

Ivey Management Services prohibits any form of reproduction, storage or transmittal without its written permission. This material is not covered under authorization from CanCopy or any reproduction rights organization. To order copies or request permission to reproduce materials, contact Ivey Publishing, Ivey Management Services, c/o Richard Ivey School of Business, The University of Western Ontario, London, Ontario, Canada, N6A 3K7; phone (519) 661-3208, fax (519) 661-3882, e-mail cases@ivey.uwo.ca.

Richard Ivey School of Business
The University of Western Ontario

exhibit 1   Present Scotch-Brite Product Flowchart

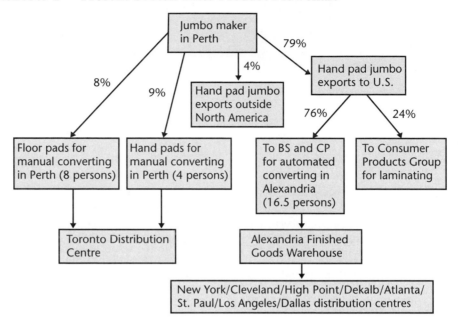

Among the more familiar products were Scotch brand transparent tapes, magnetic tapes, cassettes, and cartridges. Abrasives and adhesives were early products of the company and still formed a very important portion of the business.

Developing other technologies and applying them to make problem-solving products was the basis on which 3M had been able to grow. So many new products were produced on an ongoing basis that 25 percent of any year's sales were of products that did not exist five years before.

3M Canada Inc., like its parent company, was a highly diversified company which manufactured thousands of different products for industry, business, the professions, and the consumer. The head office and main plant were located in London, Ontario,

exhibit 2   Proposed Scotch-Brite Product Flowchart (All Hand Pad)

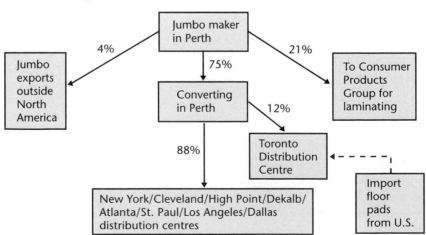

with sales and service centres across the country. 3M Canada was established as part of the newly founded International Division in 1951. Additional subsidiaries were set up at that time in Australia, Brazil, France, West Germany, Mexico, and the United Kingdom. 3M Canada employed about 2,000 people. In addition to operations in London and Perth, the company had manufacturing plants in Toronto, Havelock, Simcoe, Ontario, and Morden, Manitoba. 3M Canada was the sixth-largest of 3M's subsidiaries.

With the exception of two or three people from the worldwide organization, everyone working for 3M Canada was Canadian. The Canadian subsidiary annually lost 10 to 15 people to the worldwide organization. Although a high proportion of the professional management group in Canada had a career goal to work in the worldwide organization at some stage, this was not a requirement. For example, several managers at the plant manager level and above had indicated a preference to stay in Canada despite offers within the worldwide organization.

The Canadian subsidiary, under the direction of its president, Jeffery McCormick, was expected to generate sales growth and to produce an operating income on Canadian sales. Increasingly, emphasis was being placed on achieving certain target market share levels.

Within Canada, the 25 individual business units were split among eight groups, each of which operated as a profit centre. Variability existed in each with respect to the amount of divisional input from the United States.

The headquarters' perception of the competencies of the Canadian subsidiary varied according to the business and functional area. For example, Canadian manufacturing and engineering had a solid reputation for getting things done.

In terms of research, Canada specialized in three somewhat narrow areas. These dealt with polymer chemistry, materials science, and electromechanical telecommunications. Several dozen scientists pursued research in these areas within Canadian laboratories.

The Canadian subsidiary did not have a critical mass in R&D for all the technologies necessary to support Scotch-Brite. In addition it was not deemed feasible to move (or build) a pilot plant to Canada for Scotch-Brite testing purposes, since pilot plants tended to serve a multitude of products.

Partly as a consequence of the 1988 Canada-U.S. Free Trade Agreement, the overall level of company harmonization between the two countries had risen. Some U.S. divisions were asking for more direct control over their businesses in Canada. The Canadian president needed to deal with these issues and to develop the necessary organizational response.

The Canadian subsidiary had placed a lot of importance on building intercompany sales. Over 20 percent of its sales were of this type, and further increases were intended.

3M Canada sales in 1990 were over $500 million, while aftertax earnings were in the range of 10 percent. (See Exhibits 3 and 4 on the next two pages for financial statements.)

THE PERTH SCOTCH-BRITE PLANT

The $5 million Perth plant went into operation in 1981, employing 22 people. The plant covered 36,000 square feet (3,345 square metres) on a 78-acre (32 hectare) site, and was the first Canadian production facility for this product line. It was built to

exhibit 3   3M Canada Inc., Consolidated Statement of Earnings and
Retained Earnings, for the Year Ended October 31, 1989

	1989 (000s)	1988 (000s)
Revenue:		
Net sales*	561,406	516,663
Other income	8,823	3,536
	570,229	520,199
Costs and expenses:		
Cost of goods sold and other expenses	451,298	412,826
Depreciation and amortization	16,908	15,921
Interest	312	239
Research and development	1,876	2,010
	470,394	430,996
	99,835	89,203
Provision for income taxes	41,636	38,339
Net earnings for the year	58,199	50,864
Retained earnings—beginning of year	215,960	185,496
	274,159	236,360
Dividends	28,046	20,400
Retained Earnings—End of Year	246,113	215,960

*Includes net sales to parent and affiliated companies of 106,773 and 89,709, respectively.

supplement the jumbo output of Alexandria, which was nearing capacity. The plant was designed with sufficient capacity to produce enough hand pads and floor pads to eliminate imports, but with exports in mind. In 1981, the Canadian duty on shipments from the United States to Canada was 13.5 percent, while shipments from Canada could enter the United States duty-free.

Over the next decade, the plant was expanded several times, and employment grew to 80 people. Throughout this period, the plant exclusively produced Scotch-Brite. Scotch-Brite was a profitable, growing product line in a core business area. The total scouring pad market in which Scotch-Brite competed was estimated to be $60 million in the United States and nearly $5 million in Canada.

Scotch-Brite material was a web of nonwoven nylon or polyester fibres impregnated throughout with abrasive particles. The result was a pad, disk, or wheel used to scour, clean, polish, or finish materials such as wood, metal, plastic, and many other surfaces.

As Scotch-Brite material wears down it exposes more abrasives so that it continues to be effective all through its life. Because it is made of a synthetic fibre it does not rust or stain. Some types of Scotch-Brite have a sponge backing so that both scouring and washing can be done with the one product. Other versions of this material have integral backing pads and handles made of strong plastic to enable the user to scour and clean flat surfaces and corners with ease.

Scotch-Brite products were made in sheet, roll, and wheel shapes, and used in a wide variety of applications in the metalworking, woodworking, and plastics industries, as well as in the hotel and restaurant trade, and the home.

exhibit 4   3M Canada Inc., Consolidated Balance Sheet as at October 31, 1989

	1989 (000s)	1988 (000s)
ASSETS		
Current assets:		
Interest-bearing term deposits	66,998	52,896
Accounts receivable	73,524	69,631
Amounts due from affiliated companies	18,050	13,670
Other receivables and prepaid expenses	5,472	4,592
Inventories:		
Finished goods and work in process	67,833	63,745
Raw materials and supplies	9,321	10,601
	241,198	215,135
Fixed assets:		
Property, plant, and equipment—at cost	180,848	164,313
Less accumulated depreciation	85,764	75,676
Other assets	9,590	8,856
	345,872	312,628
LIABILITIES		
Current liabilities:		
Accounts payable—trade	21,600	18,388
Amounts due to affiliated companies	18,427	17,985
Income taxes payable	9,394	12,437
Deferred payments	1,437	1,422
Other liabilities	20,832	18,367
	71,690	68,599
Deferred income taxes	14,669	14,669
	86,359	83,268
SHAREHOLDERS' EQUITY		
Capital stock:		
Authorized—unlimited shares		
Issued and fully paid—14,600 shares	13,400	13,400
Retained earnings	246,113	215,960
	259,513	229,360
	345,872	312,628

Floor and carpet cleaning companies, schools, hospitals, and building maintenance personnel used a wide variety of Scotch-Brite disks and pads for floor maintenance. Other smaller hand-held pads were used for cleaning painted surfaces such as door frames, stairs, walls, sinks, and tiled surfaces. Scotch-Brite products were used in hotels and restaurants for griddle and grill cleaning, deep-fat fryer scouring, as well for carpet and floor maintenance. Several types of Scotch-Brite products were available for home use. These ranged from a gentle version designed for cleaning tubs, sinks, tile, and even fine china, to a rugged scouring pad with a built-in handle for scouring barbecue grills.

THE PERTH PROPOSAL

During the 1980s as the Perth plant grew in size and experience, its reputation as a workforce with a demonstrated ability to work effectively began to develop. With increased confidence came a desire to assume new challenges. An obvious area for potential development would be to take on more of the Scotch-Brite value-added function in Perth, rather than to ship semi-finished goods to the United States.

In the mid-1980s, the Perth managers advocated that they should now supply finished goods to the United States for certain mandated products. The Scotch-Brite manufacturing director during this period opposed this approach. He claimed that nothing would be saved as all the finished goods would have to be sent to Alexandria anyway, for consolidation and distribution to the customer.

The U.S.-based manufacturing director also argued that mandating products could reduce the utilization of the larger, more expensive maker at Alexandria which would increase the unit burden costs on other products there. During this period, the Perth maker operated as the swing maker, with utilization cycling in order to keep the Alexandria maker fully loaded.

With a change in management came a willingness to take a fresh look at the situation. The new manager, Andy Burns, insisted that a more complete analysis of all the delivered costs be provided. To that end, a study was initiated in December 1989 to determine the cost of converting and packaging Scotch-Brite hand pads in Perth, rather than shipping jumbo to Alexandria for converting and packaging.

The task force struck in Canada was led by Len Weston, the Perth plant manager. Procedurally, any proposal would first go to Gary Boles, manufacturing director for Canada, and Gord Prentice, executive vice president of manufacturing for Canada. Once their agreement had been obtained, the Perth plant manager would continue to champion the project through the 3M hierarchy, although people such as Prentice would facilitate the process.

The proposal would next go to the Building Service and Cleaning Products (BS + CP) Division for review and agreement. If successful, the proposal would then be sent back to Canadian engineering to develop an Authority for (Capital) Expenditure, or AFE. It would then be routed through senior Canadian management and U.S. division and group levels. The final stage was for the AFE to go to the operating committee at the sector level for assessment. See Exhibits 5 and 6 (on the next page) for partial organization charts for 3M Worldwide and International.

The Perth proposal acknowledged that Alexandria was a competently managed plant and that putting the new equipment in either location would reduce costs from their current levels. At issue was where the greater cost savings would be generated. The Perth proposal argued that these would occur in Perth (see Exhibit 7 on page 348) through a combination of reduced freight and storage costs, and faster and more efficient manufacturing. The Perth proposal's overall approach was to emphasize what was best for shareholders on the basis of total delivered costs.

Overall employment needs were expected to increase by 8 persons in Canada, yet decline by at least double that in Alexandria. (See Table 1 on page 348.) Some of the modest employment increases in Canada could be traced to the fact that the small amount of manual converting in Perth would now be automated. It had been viable to convert a small quantity of hand pads in Canada, even manually, when shipping costs and duties were factored in.

The biggest reason for the small number of proposed new hires in Canada was the plan to discontinue floor pad manual converting in Perth and to shift those operators to

exhibit 5   3M International—Partial Organization Chart

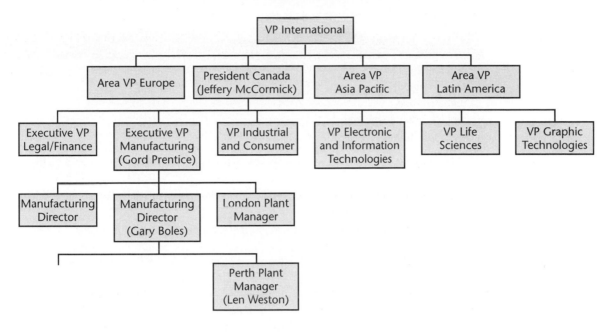

exhibit 6   3M International—Partial Organization Chart

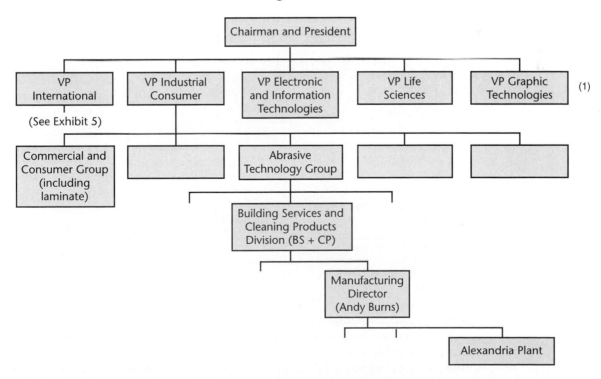

Note: (1) Operating Committee made up of the 4 sector vice-presidents, the V.P. International, and several other key executives.

exhibit 7   Sample Unit Cost Comparison (US$ per Case)

	Current Alexandria Operation	Upgraded Cutter Alexandria	Upgraded Cutter Perth
Jumbo cost ex Perth	$ 6.20	$ 6.20	$ 6.20
Jumbo freight to Alexandria	$ 0.70	$ 0.70	—
Jumbo storage	$ 0.70	$ 0.70	$ 0.05
Jumbo burden absorption	—	—	($ 0.20)[1]
Input cost to converting	**$ 7.60**	**$ 7.60**	**$ 6.05**
Converting waste	$ 0.95	$ 0.65	$ 0.45
Converting labour	$ 1.35	$ 0.30	$ 0.15[2]
Variable converting overhead	$ 0.60	$ 0.45	$ 0.30
Fixed converting overhead	$ 1.00	$ 0.55	$ 0.85[3]
Packaging supplies	$ 1.20	$ 1.20	$ 1.20
Fin. goods whse./mat. hand	$ 0.45	$ 0.45	$ 0.25
Fin. goods direct charges	$ 1.15	$ 1.15	$ 0.90
Cost including converting	**$14.30**	**$12.35**	**$10.10**
Freight to branch	$ 0.90	$ 0.90	$ 1.05
Cost delivered to branch	**$15.20**	**$13.25**	**$11.15**

[1]Volume savings through equipment usage.
[2]Lower than Alexandria due to faster equipment speed and smaller production teams.
[3]Higher than Alexandria due to larger investment in equipment.
Source: Perth proposal.

table 1   Changes in Staffing for Each Proposal

Perth Proposal	
Add in Perth	1 maintenance
	3 shippers
	4 production operators*
Total	8 persons @ labour rate US$13.18/hour
Delete in Alexandria	Maintenance?
	Shipping/receiving?
	16.5 production operators
Alexandria Proposal	
Add in Alexandria	6 operators @ 15.43

*In addition, eight persons in floor pad manual conversion and four persons in hand pad manual conversion would now be shifted to hand pad automated conversion in Perth.

the automated hand pad area. The initial response to this in Canada, in several quarters, had been less than enthusiastic.

The Canadian floor pad business manager felt that he might now have to pay a premium if purchasing from the United States. As well, he was concerned that some of his customers might notice a difference in performance. He felt the manually converted floor pads from Perth were of slightly higher quality than the automatically converted ones from Hutchinson, Minnesota. The Canadian business manager had built a higher market share for 3M floor pads in Canada than his U.S. counterparts, and he did not wish to see this jeopardized.

A shift from floor pad manual converting to hand pad automated converting would also have immediate implications for the operators. Currently most of the manual floor pad (and hand pad) jobs were on a one-shift (day) basis. A second, evening shift was sometimes required, but no one worked the midnight-to-morning shift. With automation, all operators would now need to work a three-shift rotation in order to maximize machine utilization. In a non-union plant, with a ten-year tradition of day jobs in converting, and with a no-layoff policy, this could be an emotional issue. The task of selling it to the operators would fall to Weston.

THE ALEXANDRIA RESPONSE

The Alexandria response was less a proposal, and more a reaction to the Perth initiative. A variety of concerns, some old and some new, were raised.

- First, the increased production volume in Canada and the resultant re-exports to the United States would cause an increased vulnerability to currency fluctuations.
- Second, lengthening the supply distance would make it more difficult to guarantee delivery to U.S. customers.
- Third, the Perth plant would now need to be interfaced with the 3M-USA computer-based materials management system in order to have effective transportation. This would require the Canadian information technology group to work with the logistics people in order to develop a program which would allow for cross-border integration of information.
- Fourth, the cost of shipping finished goods to the branches would increase in both Perth and Alexandria. In Perth it would be due to the smaller volumes and increased distances associated with shipping a single product line. In Alexandria it would now take longer to make up a truckload without the hand pads.
- Fifth, since Scotch-Brite converting was already well established in Alexandria, and there would be savings wherever the new equipment was located, it was safer to keep it where the manufacturing experience already existed rather than to rely on optimistic projections from Perth.

CONCLUSION

In part, due to the distances involved, regional production mandates on various products had been granted as early as the 1970s by 3M in Europe. Scotch-Brite, in fact, was already also being produced in Europe, Asia, and Mexico. However, unlike these other production mandates, the Perth proposal was to supply the core U.S. market. For the operating committee, the decision would come down to how much confidence they had in the Perth proposal.

case 27 Bata Shoe Organization (A)

Thomas G. Bata (Bata Jr.) cradled the telephone slowly and gazed down again at the figures he had been studying. The story was clear…the Millennium strategy was not working.

Bata Jr. felt compelled to convince the board and his parents to replace the CEO of Bata Shoe Organization (Bata). Though the family and the board knew things were bad, no one wanted to face another change in leadership. It was October 2000 and Bata Jr. had just spoken to the CEO, who had confirmed that he would not be changing the strategy that was centralizing many activities and implementing a global way of doing things.

Bata Jr. felt frustrated. Although he sat on the board of directors of the company, his options appeared to be limited. There seemed little he could do to dissuade the CEO from his strategy. He felt helpless to do anything more than urge change. Because of the company's ownership structure, Bata Jr. and his sisters were powerless to help save the company that bore their name and represented the culmination of their family's legacy of ten generations of shoemaking.

With the current ownership structure, the family had little direct control over the company. The majority of shares were held in a trust administered by trustees who, although well intentioned, were aged and falling short of the challenges posed by rapid and difficult changes in the industry. The absence of leadership at critical junctures had already cost the company more than half its value. Now, misguided strategy was threatening its future viability. Not only was the Bata reputation at stake but the family's financial heritage also hung precariously in the balance. The time had come for the Bata family to make a decision—walk away or roll up their sleeves and fix what was wrong.

Richard Ivey School of Business
The University of Western Ontario

Research Associate Colleen Lief prepared this case under the supervision of Professors Joachim Schwass, Ulrich Steger and John Ward as a basis for class discussion rather than to illustrate either effective or ineffective handling of a business situation. Thanks to Mope Ogunsulire for original research helpful in the preparation of this case.

Note: Some names have been disguised.

BATA: FROM FOUNDING TO THE 1950s

The Bata Shoe Organization grew from its beginnings in Zlin, Czechoslovakia, in 1894 to become one of the largest shoe companies in the world. However, the road from this humble start to finding its place among global industry giants was not without obstacles. The company faced considerable external turmoil during its long history—from the disruptive effects of World War II to the rise of Communism in key markets and the nationalization of its assets in several developing countries. Perhaps the most significant event occurred in 1945, when Communist regimes expropriated the family's holdings in Eastern and Central Europe, which had previously served as its nerve center. Having lost its entire headquarters operation, Bata was left with about 30 different operating companies scattered throughout the globe. The organization founded by Tomas Bata (Tomas) and inherited by Thomas J. Bata (Bata Sr.), though, would ultimately become a Canada-based global manufacturing and retailing empire operating in 68 countries with over 50,000 employees selling over 250 million pairs of shoes every year—primarily through company-branded retail shops.

Tomas had built a paternalistic organization that reflected the "moral testament" found among his papers at his death in 1932. Tomas believed that the Bata Shoe Organization should not be a source of private wealth for his descendants but should rather be preserved as a public trust, a means of improving living standards within its communities and providing customers with good value for money.[1] Bata was innovative for its times. One of the first companies to have profit-sharing for employees, it also provided housing, education and a short, five-day work week. This was the philosophy that guided the creation of the first family trust in the 1950s.

BATA: FROM THE 1950s TO 1984

After World War II, a severe shoe shortage resulted in a sellers' market for footwear manufacturers. Said Bata Jr., "If you could supply, you were able to sell." Bata operated successfully for years as a loose confederation of about 40 independent entrepreneurial operations. But by the 1980s, the market had begun to change—people no longer simply needed to buy shoes. Functionality was balanced with price, style and, now, brands. The emergence of brands resulted from a shift in industry emphasis from manufacturing to marketing and was underscored by the arrival of competitors like Adidas and Nike. Shoe production also shifted, first to cheaper southern European countries, then to low-cost countries like China. These trends led Bata to reduce its European production capacity (the company went from 18 European factories in the 1950s to none by 2002), while it shifted its focus from manufacturing to distribution.

During this period, too, a critical battle for control of the company took place between Bata Sr. and his uncle, Jan Bata (Jan). Tomas had died without a will. But a handwritten memorandum made out to his half-brother which appeared to sell the business to Jan at a fraction of its value was discovered. Since Bata Sr. was 17 years old when his father died, he could not yet operate this large enterprise anyway, so the issue of rightful ownership remained unresolved for many years. The trouble finally started when Jan refused to initiate an orderly transfer of the firm to Bata Sr. once his age and skills had become equal to the challenge of his inheritance. The ensuing court battle

---

[1]Bata, Thomas J., with Sonja Sinclair. Bata: Shoemaker to the World. Toronto: Stoddart, 1990.

was not settled until 1966, when Bata Sr. finally won title to the company's shares. It had been unclear in the intervening 19 years who actually owned the business. It was only as a result of the odd and sometimes controversial behavior of his uncle, along with the sheer force of personality, that Bata Sr. persuaded the operating companies to recognize him as the firm's leader. His extraordinary powers of persuasion enabled him to convince many in the organization, even those senior to him in age and experience, that he was the rightful owner, even before the court battle was settled. Once ownership ceased to be an issue, Bata Sr. established two trusts in Bermuda to hold the 80% of company shares that were not held by the charitable foundation created by Tomas long ago in furtherance of his social agenda. Domicile in Bermuda assured favorable tax treatment of company profits, which enhanced organic growth and expansion potential and drove its organizational structure (refer to Exhibit 1).

BATA JR. LEADS THE FAMILY FIRM

In 1984 the structure of the company changed when Bata Jr. became CEO of the company (refer to Exhibit 2) and the first supervisory board was established in response to Bata Sr's. retirement at age 70. Bata Jr. had been groomed to take the helm at Bata one day. Years of preparation had culminated in his moving from the deputy CEO position to the firm's chief leadership role. Up until that time, the company had had no formal oversight, and Bata Sr. counted on the counsel of three or four close advisors. When his son took over as CEO in 1984, Bata Sr. stayed on as honorary chairman of the newly created board. A non-family, non-executive chairman, two outside business executives, two trustees and a representative of the company's charitable foundation were appointed to the board in accordance with the ownership structure. The trustees, who also appointed themselves to seats on the board, appointed these directors.

Structured as a self-perpetuating entity, the trust was put in place to ensure the continuity of the business, in fulfillment of the founder's aim. The family, which in addition to Bata Sr. and his wife Sonja now included their four children (refer to Exhibit 3), did not directly own the firm's shares, but could benefit from its success through dividends paid to the trust. Because of poor company performance and a frugal family tradition, however, dividends were very modest. The first set of trustees was appointed by the senior Batas; subsequently, the trustees appointed their own successors. The trustees were under no obligation to do what the family wanted. Said Bata Jr.:

> The family, like myself, was always kept interested but we never quite understood what our role was because we didn't own any shares. We were consulted from time to time but the trustees had no requirement to do anything we requested or wanted.

However, for many years, Bata Sr. exercised some indirect control through his personality and personal relationships with the trustees, and thereby held informal influence.

As CEO of the company, Bata Jr. was accountable to the board. The directors tended to be prestigious individuals, some of whom had been chairmen of large multinational companies, albeit in unrelated industries. The board was procedurally heavy, and Bata Jr. spent much time preparing for board meetings, where the emphasis was on reporting and process. It was an uneasy relationship—and Bata Jr. questioned the wisdom of the existing structure. In an exchange with one of the trustees, Bata Jr. said, "The problem between you and me is [that] I can't sleep seeing what's going on." "I can," responded the trustee, to which Bata Jr. replied, "That's why it's wrong, you acting as an owner because you do sleep at night."

At this time, the Bata Company began to encounter financial difficulties. In September 1990 a new senior vice-president of finance and development admitted that the company's return on equity was poor. He said, "My two to three year target is a 16% return."[2]

By then, Bata was a global giant, employing 66,000 people and manufacturing and selling more footwear than anyone else in the world. Its dependency on its Canadian domestic market was marginal—3% to 4% of its revenue—and it was strong overseas. It was then, for example, the largest shoe retailer in Italy, India and Indonesia. Realizing that manufacturing shoes in the industrialized West was a dying business, Bata Jr. systematically transformed the company's operations in Western Europe and North America into "niche manufacturers" making specialty footwear for various industries.

In earlier decades, national ownership laws forced Bata to list shares of its local subsidiaries on many domestic stock exchanges in the Asia-Pacific region. Bata Jr. ultimately saw in this situation an opportunity both to consolidate the company's holdings in the region and to raise much-needed equity for Bata. With a 20% listing on the Singapore Stock Exchange, the firm could have raised $150 million. Bata would have had enough to settle all its bank loans worldwide and to strengthen its balance sheet for the challenges ahead. Bata Jr. ardently supported the deal and viewed this potential transaction as key to the firm's future. But his parents opposed the deal on the grounds that selling shares would place the company on a slippery slope, which could ultimately erode the trust's majority stake and the founder's legacy. When the board of directors bowed to their influence and vetoed the deal, Bata Jr. resigned as CEO in 1993. This lack of support was the final straw for Bata Jr.—the culmination of the frustration of a long series of differences with his parents and the board.

FROM 1994 TO 1999: THE REVOLVING DOOR YEARS

Between 1994 and 1999 Bata went through two CEOs and a period with no CEO. First came Stanley Heath,[3] the company's first non-family chief executive, who was previously head of RJR Nabisco's Latin American food operations. Heath, together with several of his senior managers, resigned in 1995—after only a year—amid growing tension with the senior family members. His efforts to implement a restructuring plan that involved closing large portions of Bata's European operations were not well received. According to the Financial Times in June 1996, Bata Sr. described Heath as "a very fine gentleman," but noted that neither he, nor his new management team, were "shoe people" and that the shoe industry "is a very, very peculiar business."

By contrast, one Bata manager, upon resignation in 1995, said:

> …You can't appoint a new chief executive and then poke your nose in all over the place. [4]

In 1996 Bata's European operations continued to encounter trouble, as retail stores in Germany, Belgium and the Netherlands, and one of four subsidiaries in France, were all losing money. Drastic action was required. At the insistence of the younger family members, a new director with retail and merchandising experience, Jack Butler, joined

---

[2] Collison, R. "How Bata Rules Its World." Canadian Business, September 1990, Vol. 63, Iss. 9: 28+.

[3] Simon, B. "Footwear Family Goes out of Fashion." Financial Times, London, June 6, 1996: 25+.

[4] Ibid.

the board in April 1996 and later became executive chairman, working about 40% of the time. He and Bata Jr., who had assumed a board seat upon his resignation as CEO, set up a committee to study the problems in the European operations and recommend corrective action. Although Butler was a valued executive chairman and member of the board, he resigned after only six months. His strong personality led to major disagreements with the family matriarch and trustees. In spite of Butler's early exit, the committee's work was successful. Bata's European operations bounced back in 1997 with a strong balance sheet and the best profit year ever, largely due to the elimination of money-losing operations and the efforts of an excellent regional manager.

After Butler left Bata, one of the trustees became interim chairman and an internal candidate was chosen to fill the newly created post of president. The company continued on without a CEO until March 1999, when Jim Pantelidis assumed the post.[5] Pantelidis' appointment, and the way it was done, proved to be controversial. When the board first formed a CEO selection committee, the four Bata siblings were excluded from the decision-making process, despite the fact that Bata Jr. sat on the board. The committee went on to appoint Pantelidis, then in his mid-50s and a 30-year veteran of the oil industry, as CEO. He lacked the support of the Bata siblings and one of the board members, who questioned the relevance of his past experience in tackling the unique but pressing problems before them.

In an interview in January 2000,[6] Pantelidis explained that his strategy aimed "to position the company in the next millennium—to re-establish it as a major force in the shoe business." The plan was to streamline operations so that each plant specialized in producing one type of footwear for a global market. At the same time, the company would update and enlarge many of its stores and introduce new styles designed to appeal more to younger and middle-income family shoppers. Pantelidis also aimed to cut 10% of the company's $400 to $600 million costs over five years. Said Pantelidis:

> What needs to happen in this organization…is for it to start thinking more globally and start taking advantage of our scale and size.

But there was little momentum behind the strategy, and efforts to explain the new operating model within the company fell short. Senior family members were becoming increasingly nervous about how the business was being run. Even the board, which struggled under the weight of age and inertia, voiced its concern about the strategy to the CEO, who remained intransigent.

Despite a lack of substantive support for the Millennium strategy and in direct contravention of the company's mandatory retirement age of 70, the CEO and the 73-year-old chairman were both reappointed at the annual meeting in October 2000. Following that meeting, it became clear to Bata Jr. that this dire situation required drastic action. The family could agree to the business being sold and not put their own effort into finding a solution. Alternatively, they could take a deep breath and jump into a sea of trouble, and fight to save their birthright. Given the constraints imposed by the current ownership structure, though, Bata Jr. wondered what he could, and should, do.

---

[5] Strauss, M. "Canada: Bata to Revamp Worldwide Operations." *Globe and Mail* (Toronto), January 17, 2000.

[6] Strauss, M. "Canada: Bata to Revamp Worldwide Operations." *Globe and Mail* (Toronto), January 17, 2000.

exhibit 1   Ownership Structure from 1950s to 1984

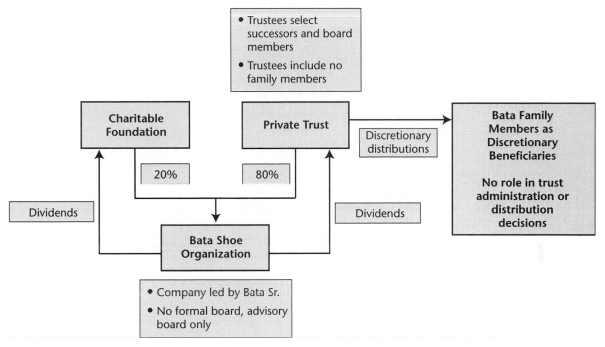

Source: Company information

exhibit 2   Ownership Structure from 1984 to 2001

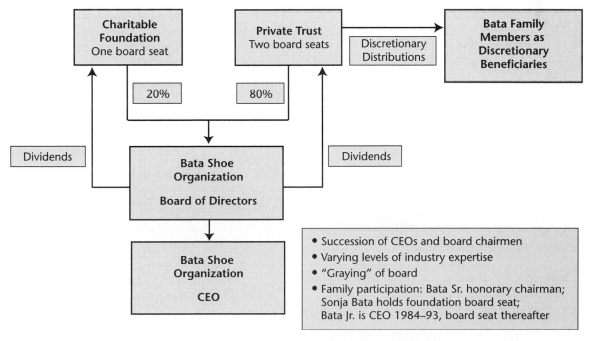

Source: Company information

exhibit 3   Bata Family Tree

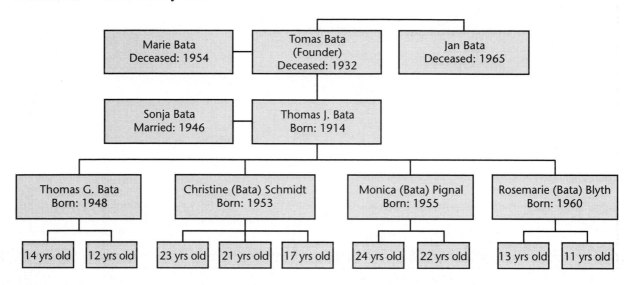

Source: Company information

case 28 Victoria Heavy Equipment Limited—2001

Brian Walters sat back in the seat of his Lear jet as it broke through the clouds en route from Squamish, a small town near Vancouver, British Columbia, to Sacramento, California. As chairman of the board, majority shareholder, and chief executive officer, the 51-year-old Walters had run Victoria Heavy Equipment Limited as a closely held company for years. During this time it had become the second-largest producer of mobile cranes in the world, with 2000 sales of $150 million and exports to more than 70 countries. But in early 2001 the problem of succession was in his thoughts. His son and daughter were not ready to run the organization, and he personally wanted to devote more time to other interests. He wondered about the kind of person he should hire to become president. There was also a nagging thought that there might be other problems with Victoria that would have to be worked out before he eased out of his present role.

COMPANY HISTORY

Victoria Heavy Equipment Limited (Victoria) was established in 1917 in Victoria, British Columbia, to produce horse-drawn log skidders for the forest industry. The young firm showed a flair for product innovation, pioneering the development of motorized skidders, and later, after diversifying into the crane business, producing the country's first commercially successful hydraulic crane controls. In spite of these innovations, the company was experiencing severe financial difficulties in 1963 when it was purchased by Brian Walters Sr., the father of the current chairman. By installing tight financial controls and paying close attention to productivity, Walters was able to turn the company around, and in 1970 he decided that Victoria would focus exclusively on cranes, and go after the international market.

Paul W. Beamish and Thomas A. Poynter prepared this case solely to provide material for class discussion. The authors do not intend to illustrate either effective or ineffective handling of a managerial situation. The authors may have disguised certain names and other identifying information to protect confidentiality.

IVEY

Richard Ivey School of Business
The University of Western Ontario

At the time of Brian Walters Sr.'s retirement in 1983, it was clear that the decision to concentrate on the crane business had been a good one. The company's sales and profits were growing, and Victoria cranes were beginning to do well in export markets. Walters Sr. was succeeded as president by his brother James, who began to exercise very close personal control over the company's operations. However, as Victoria continued to grow in size and complexity, the load on James became so great that his health began to fail. The solution was to appoint an assistant general manager, John Rivers, through whom tight supervision could be maintained while James Walters' workload was eased. This move was to no avail, however. James Walters suffered a heart attack in 1985, and Rivers became general manager. At the same time, the young Brian Walters, the current chairman and chief executive officer, became head of the U.S. operation.

When Brian Walters took responsibility for Victoria's U.S. business, the firm's American distributor was selling 30 to 40 cranes per year. Walters thought the company should be selling at least 150. Even worse, the orders that the American firm did get tended to come in large quantities, as many as 50 cranes in a single order. This played havoc with Victoria's production scheduling. Walters commented, "We would rather have 10 orders of 10 cranes each than a single order for 100." In 1990, when the U.S. distributor's agreement expired, he offered the company a five-year renewal if it would guarantee sales of 150 units per year. When the firm refused, Walters bought it, and in the first month fired 13 of the 15 employees and cancelled most existing dealerships. He then set to work to rebuild, only accepting orders for 10 cranes or less. His hope was to gain a foothold and a solid reputation in the U.S. market before the big U.S. firms noticed him.

This strategy quickly showed results, and in 1991 Walters came back to Canada. As Rivers was still general manager, there was not enough to occupy him fully, and he began travelling three or four months a year. While he was still very much a part of the company, it was not a full-time involvement.

VICTORIA IN THE MID-1990S

Victoria entered the mid-1990s with sales of approximately $75 million, and by 2000, partly as a result of opening the new plant in California, had succeeded in doubling this figure. Profits reached their highest level ever in 1998, but declined somewhat over the next two years as costs rose and the rate of sales growth slowed. Financial statements are presented in Exhibits 1 and 2. The following sections describe the company and its environment in the mid-1990s.

Product Line

The bulk of Victoria's crane sales in the 1990s came from a single product line, the LTM 1000, which was produced both in its Squamish facility (the firm had moved from Victoria to Squamish in the early 1920s) and its smaller plant in California, built in 1994. The LTM 1000 line consisted of mobile cranes of five basic sizes, averaging $750,000 in price. Numerous options were available for these cranes, which could provide uncompromised on-site performance, precision lifting capabilities, fast highway travel, and effortless city driving. Because of the numerous choices available, Victoria preferred not to build them to stock. The company guaranteed 60-day delivery and "tailor-made" cranes to customer specifications. This required a large inventory of both parts and raw material.

exhibit 1   Victoria Balance Sheet for the Years 1996-2000 ($000s)

	1996	1997	1998	1999	2000
ASSETS					
Current Assets					
Accounts receivable	$12,492	$11,940	$14,664	$15,768	$16,426
Allowance for doubtful accounts	(439)	(465)	(423)	(445)	(474)
Inventories	31,729	36,637	37,047	38,439	40,567
Prepaid expenses	178	156	234	159	193
Total current assets	43,960	48,268	51,522	53,921	56,712
Advances to shareholders	1,950	1,950	1,950	1,950	1,950
Fixed assets: property plant and equipment	10,260	10,470	10,312	11,029	11,083
Total assets	$56,170	$60,688	$63,784	$66,900	$69,745
LIABILITIES AND SHAREHOLDERS' EQUITY					
Current Liabilities					
Notes payable to bank	$11,599	$12,328	$13,887	$15,241	$16,998
Accounts payable	14,568	17,029	15,814	15,697	16,479
Accrued expenses	1,611	1,678	2,613	2,251	1,732
Deferred income tax	628	600	594	612	517
Income tax payable	817	1,038	918	780	774
Current portion of long-term debt	1,368	1,336	1,300	1,332	1,354
Total current liabilities	$30,591	$34,009	$35,126	$35,913	$37,854
Long-term debt	9,426	9,165	9,030	9,007	9,171
Total liabilities	40,017	43,174	44,156	44,920	47,025
SHAREHOLDERS' EQUITY					
Common shares	300	435	442	585	652
Retained earnings	15,853	17,079	19,186	21,395	22,068
Total shareholders' equity	16,153	17,514	19,628	21,980	22,720
Total liabilities and shareholders' equity	$56,170	$60,688	$63,784	$66,900	$69,745

exhibit 2   Victoria Income Statement for the Years 1996-2000 ($000s)

	1996	1997	1998	1999	2000
Revenue					
Net sales	$95,079	$116,566	$129,519	$142,329	$151,414
Costs and Expenses					
Cost of sales	73,857	89,755	95,994	107,727	113,712
Selling expense	11,205	13,851	16,402	17,155	19,656
Administrative expense	4,026	5,800	8,235	8,692	10,557
Engineering expense	2,013	2,533	2,748	2,923	3,163
Gross income	3,978	4,627	6,140	5,832	4,326
Income taxes	1,621	1,921	2,445	2,257	1,881
Net income	$ 2,357	$ 2,706	$ 3,695	$ 3,575	$ 2,445

Walters had used a great deal of ingenuity to keep Victoria in a competitive position. For example, in 1997, he learned that a company trying to move unusually long and heavy logs from a new tract of redwood trees in British Columbia was having serious problems with its existing cranes. A crane with a larger-than-average height and lifting capacity was required. Up to this point, for technical reasons, it had not been possible to produce a crane with the required specifications. However, Walters vowed that Victoria would develop such a crane, and six months later it had succeeded.

Although the LTM 1000 series provided almost all of Victoria's crane sales, a new crane had been introduced in 1999 after considerable expenditure on design, development and manufacture. The $975,000 A-100 had a 70-tonne capacity and could lift loads to heights of 61 metres, a combination previously unheard of in the industry. Through the use of smooth hydraulics even the heaviest loads could be picked up without jolts. In spite of these features, and an optional ram-operated tilt-back cab designed to alleviate the stiff necks which operators commonly developed from watching high loads, sales of the A-100 were disappointing. As a result, several of the six machines built were leased to customers at unattractive rates. The A-100 had, however, proven to be a very effective crowd attraction device at equipment shows.

Markets

There were two important segments in the crane market—custom-built cranes and standard cranes—and although the world mobile crane market was judged to be $945 million in 2000, no estimates were available as to the size of each segment. Victoria competed primarily in the custom segment, in the medium- and heavy-capacity end of the market. In the medium-capacity custom crane class Victoria's prices were approximately 75 per cent of those of its two main competitors. The gap closed as the cranes became heavier, with Victoria holding a 15 per cent advantage over Washington Cranes in the heavy custom crane business. In heavy standard cranes Victoria did not have a price advantage.

Victoria's two most important markets were Canada and the United States. The U.S. market was approximately $360 million in 2000, and Victoria's share was about 15 per cent. Victoria's Sacramento plant, serving both the U.S. market and export sales involving U.S. aid and financing, produced 60 to 70 cranes per year. The Canadian market was much smaller, about $66 million in 2000, but Victoria was the dominant firm in the country, with a 60 per cent share. The Squamish plant, producing 130 to 150 cranes per year, supplied both the Canadian market and all export sales not covered by the U.S. plant. There had been very little real growth in the world market since 1995.

The primary consumers in the mobile crane industry were contractors. Because the amount of equipment downtime could make the difference between showing a profit or loss on a contract, contractors were very sensitive to machine dependability, as well as parts and service availability. Price was important, but it was not everything. Independent surveys suggested that Washington Crane, Victoria's most significant competitor, offered somewhat superior service and reliability, and if Victoria attempted to sell similar equipment at prices comparable to Washington's, it would fail. As a result, Victoria tried to reduce its costs through extensive backward integration, manufacturing 85 per cent of its crane components in-house, the highest percentage in the industry. This drive to reduce costs was somewhat offset, however, by the fact that much of the equipment in the Squamish plant was very old. In recent years, some of the slower and less versatile machinery had been replaced, but by 2000 only 15 per cent of the machinery in the plant was new, efficient, numerically controlled equipment.

Victoria divided the world into eight marketing regions. The firm carried out little conventional advertising, but did participate frequently at equipment trade shows. One of the company's most effective selling tools was its ability to fly in prospective customers from all over the world in Walters' executive jet. Victoria believed that the combination of its integrated plant, worker loyalty, and the single-product concentration evident in their Canadian plant produced a convinced customer. There were over 14 such visits to the British Columbia plant in 2000, including delegations from China, Korea, France and Turkey.

Competition

As the world's second largest producer of cranes, Victoria faced competition from five major firms, all of whom were much larger and more diversified. The industry leader was the Washington Crane Company, with 2000 sales of $600 million and a world market share of 50 per cent. Washington had become a name synonymous around the world with heavy-duty equipment and had been able to maintain a sales growth-rate of over 15 per cent per annum for the past five years. It manufactured in the United States, Mexico and Australia. Key to its operations were 100 strong dealers worldwide with over 200 outlets. Washington had almost 30 per cent of Canada's crane market.

Next in size after Victoria was Texas Star, another large manufacturer whose cranes were generally smaller than Victoria's and sold through the company's extensive worldwide equipment dealerships. The next two largest competitors were both very large U.S. multinational producers whose crane lines formed a small part of their overall business. With the exception of Washington, industry observers suggested that crane sales for these latter firms had been stable (at best) for quite some time. The exception was the Japanese crane producer Toshio which had been aggressively pursuing sales worldwide and had entered the North American market recently. Sato, another Japanese firm, had started in the North American market as well. Walters commented:

> My father laid the groundwork for the success that this company has enjoyed, but it is clear that we have some major challenges ahead of us. Washington is four times our size and I know that we are at the top of their hit list. Our Japanese competitors are also going to be tough. The key to our success is to remain flexible—we must not develop the same kind of organization as the big U.S. firms.

Organization

In 1994, a number of accumulating problems had ended Brian Walters' semi-retirement and brought him back into the firm full time. Although sales were growing, Walters saw that work was piling up and things were not getting done. He believed that new cranes needed to be developed, and he wanted a profit-sharing plan put in place. One of his most serious concerns was the development of middle managers, given a perceived lack of depth. The root cause of these problems, Walters believed, was that the firm was overly centralized. Most of the functional managers reported to Rivers, and Rivers made most of the decisions. Walters concluded that action was necessary: "If we want to grow further we have to change."

Between 1994 and 1997 Walters reorganized the firm by setting up separate operating companies and a corporate staff group. In several cases, senior operating executives were placed in staff/advisory positions, while in others, executives held positions in both operating and staff groups. Exhibit 3 (on the next page) illustrates Victoria's organizational chart as of 1998.

exhibit 3   Victoria Organizational Structure, 1994-98

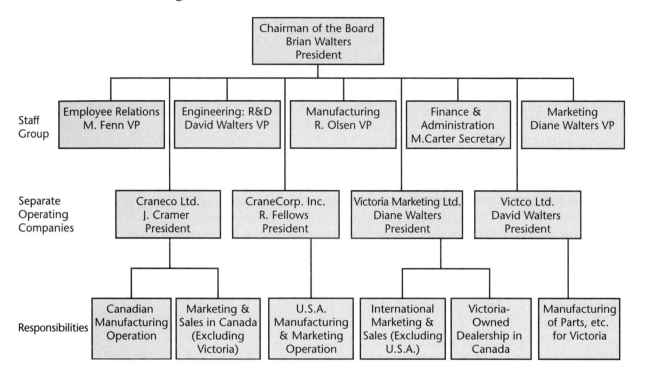

By early 1999 Walters was beginning to wonder "if I had made a very bad deci-sion." The staff groups weren't working. Rivers had been unable to accept the redistri-bution of power and had resigned. There was "civil war in the company." Politics and factional disputes were the rule rather than the exception. Line managers were upset by the intervention of the staff VPs of employee relations, manufacturing, and marketing. Staff personnel, on the other hand, were upset by "poor" line decisions.

As a result, the marketing and manufacturing staff functions were eradicated with the late-2000 organizational restructuring illustrated in Exhibit 4. The services previously supplied by the staff groups were duplicated to varying extent inside each division.

In place of most of the staff groups, an executive committee was established in 1999. Membership included the president and head of all staff groups and presidents (general managers) of the four divisions. Meeting monthly, the executive committee was intended to evaluate the performance of the firm's profit and cost problems, han-dle mutual problems such as transfer prices, and allocate capital expenditures among the four operating divisions. Subcommittees handled subjects such as research and de-velopment (R&D) and new products.

The new organization contained seven major centres for performance measure-ment purposes. The cost centres were:

1. Engineering; R&D (reporting to Victco Ltd.)
2. International Marketing (Victoria Marketing Ltd.)
3. Corporate staff

exhibit 4   Victoria Organizational Structure, late 2000

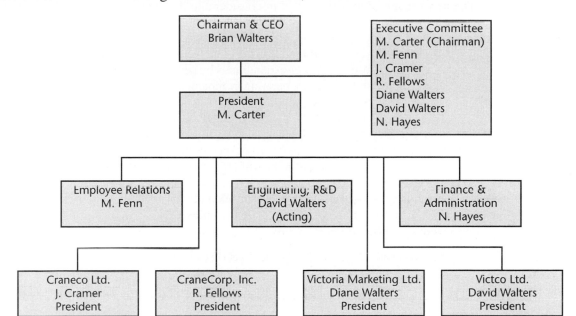

The major profit centres were:

4. CraneCorp. Inc. (U.S. production and sales)
5. Victco Ltd. (supplying Victoria with components)
6. Craneco (Canadian production and marketing)
7. Victoria-owned Canadian sales outlets (reporting to Victoria Marketing Ltd.)

The major profit centres had considerable autonomy in their day-to-day operations and were motivated to behave as if their division was a separate, independent firm.

By mid-2000, Brian Walters had moved out of his position as president, and Michael Carter, a long-time employee close to retirement, was asked to take the position of president until a new one could be found.

Walters saw his role changing.

> If I was anything, I was a bit of an entrepreneur. My job was to supply that thrust, but to let people develop on their own accord. I was not concerned about things not working, but I was concerned when nothing was being done about it.

In the new organization Walters did not sit on the executive committee. However, as chairman of the board and chief executive officer, the committee's recommendations came to him and ". . . they constantly tried me on." His intention was to monitor the firm's major activities rather than to set them. He did have to sit on the product development subcommittee, however, when "things were not working . . . there was conflict . . . the engineering group (engineering, R&D) had designed a whole new crane and nobody, including me, knew about it." Mr. McCarthy, the VP of engineering and R&D, called only five to six committee meetings. The crane his group developed was not to Walters' liking. (There had been a high turnover rate in this group, with four VPs since 1998.) Recognizing these problems, Walters brought in consultants to tackle the problems of the management information system and the definition of staff/line responsibilities.

In spite of these moves, dissatisfaction still existed within the company in 2001. The new organization had resulted in considerable dissension. Some conflict centred around the establishment of appropriately challenging budgets for each operating firm, and even more conflict had erupted over transfer pricing and allocation of capital budgets. In 2000-01, even though requested budgets were cut equally, lack of central control over spending resulted in over-expenditures by several of the profit and cost centres.

The views of staff and the operating companies' presidents varied considerably when they discussed Victoria's organizational evolution and the operation of the present structure. Diane Walters, the president of Victoria International Marketing, liked the autonomous system because it helped to identify the true performance of sections of the company. "We had separate little buckets and could easily identify results." Furthermore, she felt that there was no loss of efficiency (due to the duplication of certain staff functions within the divisions) since there was little duplication of systems between groups, and each group acted as a check and balance on the other groups so that "manufacturing won't make what marketing won't sell." Comments from other executives were as follows:

> The divisionalized system allowed me to get closer to my staff because we were a separate group.

> We ended up with sales and marketing expertise that was much better than if we had stayed under manufacturing.

> If you (run the firm) with a manufacturing-oriented organization, you could forget what people want.

> In a divisionalized system there was bound to be conflict between divisions, but that was not necessarily unhealthy.

Some executives saw the decentralized, semi-autonomous operating company structure as a means of giving each person the opportunity to grow and develop without the hindrance of other functional executives. Most, if not all, of the operating company presidents and staff VPs were aware that decentralization brought benefits, especially in terms of the autonomy it gave them to modify existing practices. One senior executive even saw the present structure as an indicator of their basic competitive stance, "Either we centralize the structure and retract, or we stay as we are and fight with the big guys." With minimal direction from Brian Walters, presidents were able to build up their staff, establish priorities and programs, and essentially, were only held responsible for the bottom line.

Other executives believed that Victoria's structure was inappropriate. As one put it, "The semi-independence of the operating companies and the lack of a real leader for the firm has resulted in poor co-ordination of problem solving and difficulty in allocating responsibility." As an example, he noted how engineering's response to manufacturing was often slow and poorly communicated. Even worse, the executive noted, was how the priorities of different units were not synchronized. "When you manufacture just one product line all your activities are inter-related. So when one group puts new products first on a priority list, while another is still working out bugs in the existing product, conflict and inefficiencies have to develop."

The opposing group argued that the present organization was more appropriate to a larger, faster growing and more complex company. As one senior executive put it, "We're too small to be as decentralized as we are now. All of this was done to accommodate the Walters' kids anyway, and it's now going to detract from profitability and growth." Another executive stated that rather than being a president of an operating company he would prefer to be a general manager at the head of a functional group, reporting to a group head. "If we had the right Victoria Heavy Equipment president," he said, "we wouldn't need all these divisional presidents." Another continued,

> Right now the players (divisional presidents and staff VPs) run the company. Brian Walters gives us a shot of adrenaline four or six times a year, but doesn't provide any active leadership. When Brian leaves, things stop. Instead, Brian now wants to monitor the game plan rather than set it up for others to run. As we still only have an interim president (Carter), it is the marketplace that leads us, not any strategic plan or goal.

THE NEW PRESIDENT

Individual views about the appropriate characteristics of a new president were determined by what each executive thought was wrong with Victoria. Everyone realized that the new president would have to accommodate Brian Walters' presence and role in the firm and the existence of his two children in the organization. They all generally saw Brian as wanting to supply ideas and major strategies, but little else.

All but one of Victoria's executives agreed that the new president should not get involved in day-to-day activities or in major decision making. Instead, he should "arbitrate" among the line general managers (subsidiary presidents) and staff VPs and become more of a "bureaucrat-cum-diplomat" than an aggressive leader. As another put it, "The company will drive itself; only once in a while he'll steer a little."

THE 2001 SITUATION

Industry analysts predicted a decline of 10 per cent in world crane sales, which totalled 1,200 units in 2000, and as much as a 30 per cent decrease in the North American market in 2001. Victoria's sales and production levels were down. Seventy-five shop floor employees had been laid off at Squamish, bringing total employment there to 850, and similar cuts were expected in Sacramento. Worker morale was suffering as a result, and the profit-sharing plan, which had been introduced in early 2000 at Walters' initiative, was not helping matters. In spite of the optimism conveyed to workers when the plan was initiated, management had announced in October that no bonus would be paid for the year. Aggravating the problem was the workforce's observation that while certain groups met their budget, others did not, and hence all were penalized. This problem arose because each bonus was based on overall as well as divisional profits.

Many of the shop-floor workers and the supervisory staff were also disgruntled with the additions to the central and divisional staff groups, which had continued even while the workforce was being reduced. They felt that the paperwork these staff functions created was time-consuming and of little benefit. They noted, for example, that there were four or five times as many people in production control in 2001 as there were in 1995 for the same volume of production. In addition, they pointed out that despite all sorts of efforts on the part of a computer-assisted production control group, inventory levels were still too high.

Brian Walters commented on the 2001 situation and his view of the company's future:

> What we are seeing in 2001 is a temporary decline in the market. This does not pose a serious problem for us, and certainly does not impact on my longer term goals for this

company, which are to achieve a 25 per cent share of the world market by 2005, and reach sales of $375 million by 2014. We can reach these goals as long as we don't turn into one of these bureaucratic, grey-suited companies that are so common in North America. There are three keys for success in this business—a quality product, professional people and the motivation for Victoria to be the standard of excellence in our business. This means that almost everything depends on the competence and motivation of our people. We will grow by being more entrepreneurial, more dedicated, and more flexible than our competitors. With our single product line we are also more focused than our competitors. They manage only by the numbers—there is no room in those companies for an emotional plea, they won't look at sustaining losses to get into a new area, they'll turn the key on a loser . . . we look at the longer term picture.

"The hazard for Victoria," Walters said as he looked out of his window toward the Sacramento airstrip, "is that we could develop the same kind of bureaucratic, quantitatively oriented, grey-suited managers that slow down the large U.S. competitors." "But that," he said, turning to his audience, "is something I'm going to watch like a hawk. We need the right people."

case 29 TV Asahi Theatrical Productions, Inc.

In April 1996, Kenji Sudo, vice-president of TV Asahi's Theatrical Productions, Inc., was in a pensive mood. He had just heard that one of their musicals had been nominated for a variety of Tony Awards.[1] This was tremendous news. It was the 50th anniversary of the Tony Awards, and this year's televised show was expected to be a spectacular event. Even in a run-of-the-mill year, getting a Tony nomination almost guaranteed that the musical would be profitable, and possibly very profitable because of the TV exposure.

Yet, there was also some unsettling news. During the past week he had been talking to several top managers in TV Asahi (pronounced ah-saw-hee), the Japanese parent company of the Theatrical Productions unit. All of the managers had voiced some doubt about the role of the Theatrical Productions subsidiary in TV Asahi. Through these conversations, Kenji realized that they didn't understand the business, and inevitably they didn't know what to do with it.

This lack of commitment was clearly a concern for Kenji. He had spent 14 years of his life building the subsidiary into a profitable musical theatre production company and the number one Asian company in the U.S. live theatre business. Last year the subsidiary had been very profitable, and Kenji thought these results would go a long way toward improving the attitude of top management toward the subsidiary, but this appeared not to be the case. He wondered what Asahi would do about the Theatrical Productions unit, and of course the ultimate question for him was: What should he do about it?

Professors Patrick Woodcock and Paul W. Beamish prepared this case solely to provide material for class discussion. The authors do not intend to illustrate either effective or ineffective handling of a managerial situation. The authors may have disguised certain names and other identifying information to protect confidentiality.

IVEY

Richard Ivey School of Business
The University of Western Ontario

---

[1]The Tony Awards are the most prestigious live theatre awards in the world, and are quite literally the Academy Awards of the theatre industry.

TV ASAHI AND THE NEWSPAPER AND BROADCASTING INDUSTRY IN JAPAN

TV Asahi Theatrical Productions, Inc., was part of TV Asahi's Special Events Division whose parent company was Asahi National Broadcasting Co., Ltd. (TV Asahi), of Japan (see Figure 1 for an organizational chart). TV Asahi was part of a small keiretsu[2] involving interlocking ownership of three other companies: Asahi Shimbun (newspapers), Toei (movies and TV production), and Obunsha (publishing). The Asahi group of companies was privately owned by the employees and three Japanese families. The largest company in this group was the Asahi Shimbun, the largest newspaper company in Japan. This newspaper company dominated the other two companies in a variety of ways, including having the largest revenues, profits, and ownership in them. The presidents of the smaller companies were appointed by the Asahi Shimbun and had always been former Asahi Shimbun managers.

THE JAPANESE NEWSPAPER INDUSTRY

The Japanese newspaper industry was tightly controlled and dominated by a few privately owned firms. There were five major players in the industry, with Asahi being the largest. Most of these companies had some degree of regional focus, while others differentiated themselves by focusing on specialized news such as business or sports. None of these companies faced any direct international competition, since foreign

figure 1   TV Asahi Organizational Chart

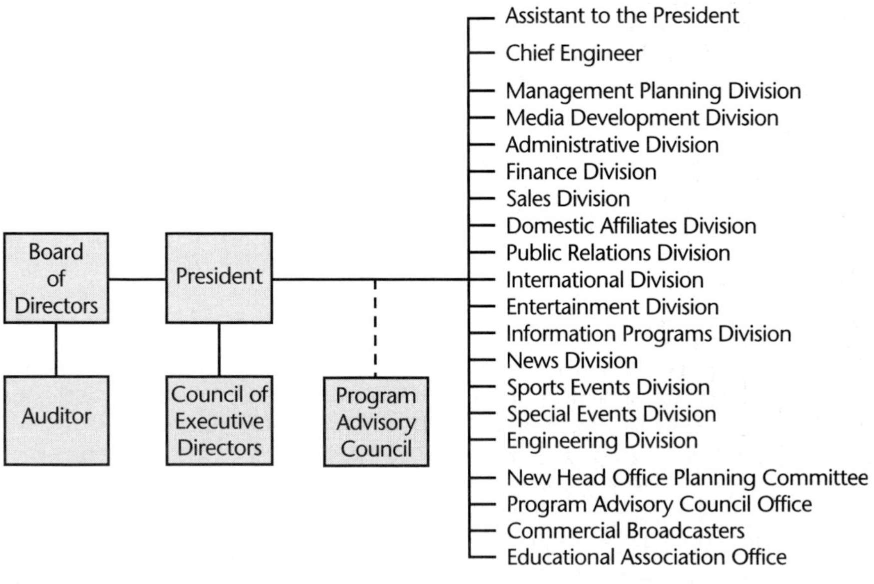

- Assistant to the President
- Chief Engineer
- Management Planning Division
- Media Development Division
- Administrative Division
- Finance Division
- Sales Division
- Domestic Affiliates Division
- Public Relations Division
- International Division
- Entertainment Division
- Information Programs Division
- News Division
- Sports Events Division
- Special Events Division
- Engineering Division
- New Head Office Planning Committee
- Program Advisory Council Office
- Commercial Broadcasters
- Educational Association Office

Board of Directors — President — Auditor — Council of Executive Directors — Program Advisory Council

Source: TV Asahi Publications, 1996

---

[2]A keiretsu is a group of Japanese firms that usually has joint ownership and operates to varying degrees as one large firm. The degree of interlocking ownership can be quite small (e.g., 5 percent). The operational linkages can include sharing of capital, exchange of technology and personnel, and joint management decision making.

firms faced enormous entry barriers related to the Japanese language, culture, and distribution, all of which were critical to the business. None of these companies had newspaper interests outside of Japan.

In general, the industry had been slow to respond to the technological changes and related shifts in economies of scale and scope which had been the rage of English-language-based newspapers around the world. The retiring competitive environment had produced organizations that were quite conservative and bureaucratic. Historically, the industry had been very profitable, but the recession of the early 1990s had affected all sectors, including this one.

THE JAPANESE TELEVISION INDUSTRY

The television broadcasting industry was also relatively concentrated. Yet, it was clearly more competitive and dynamic than the newspaper industry. This was due to a variety of factors, including the continual demand for creativity in programming, and technological developments, as well as both national and international competition. National competition was significant in comparison to the newspaper industry because the incremental costs of broadcasting nationally versus regionally were relatively small. Therefore, a company tended to broadcast in as many regions as its licence allowed. International competition was moderate, but some English TV programming was broadcast in the populated regions (e.g., CNN news), and very popular international programs were dubbed into Japanese (e.g., Dallas). The larger broadcasting companies all had international divisions which were largely unprofitable.

There were four large national TV broadcasting companies in Japan. They were, in order of size, Nippon Hoso Kyokai (NHK), Fuji Television Network, Inc. (Fuji TV), Tokyo Broadcasting System (TBS), and TV Asahi. In addition, there was a variety of smaller, regional companies (e.g., TV Tokyo and Kansai TV) and some pay television channels (e.g., Japan Satellite Broadcasting). A summary description of the top three firms is provided in Table 1 (on the next page).

TV ASAHI

TV Asahi was the smallest of the four national broadcasting companies in Japan. Despite its ranking, it was a sizable organization. Its revenues for 1995 were in excess of US$1 billion and it had over 1,300 employees worldwide.

TV Asahi started in 1959 as a small news and information educational channel. It had quite naturally evolved into its present niche, which was news and information programming, although it carried some variety, drama, animation, and sports programming. In addition, the company produced or promoted concerts, musical theatre, art exhibits, and other international cultural events. Yet, over 50 percent of TV Asahi's programming was live broadcasting, reflecting its news and information content. It was the first station to introduce prime-time evening news.

Internationally, TV Asahi had 21 international news bureaus, the two most important being Paris and New York. These 21 international offices were used to establish a balanced global coverage of international news events, to establish ties with other broadcasters around the world, to develop international co-productions, and to sell Asahi's programming to non-Japanese broadcasters.

TV Asahi had been involved in cooperative international programming and news reporting for over a decade. In 1982 it signed an exclusive agreement with CNN (U.S.),

table 1   Summary Description of Top Three Competitors

NHK is the largest national broadcasting company, and because of its size and dominance in the industry it is often referred to as the Japanese Broadcasting Corporation. NHK is focused entirely on television and radio broadcasting in Japan, although NHK does license some of its news, cultural, and business programs to broadcasters in other countries who desire some Japanese content for their local audiences. This company is very research- and development-oriented. It was the major force behind Japan's development of the high- definition television standards and broadcasting equipment. Now it is the only company in the world that broadcasts high-definition digital signals. From a programming perspective, NHK is known for its sports programming. Finally, this company has considerable technical and programming skills compared with the other competitors. The large market share and historical government support allowed it to develop these skills and consequently build market share that could support the skills.

Fuji TV is owned by a company called Jujisankei Communications Group. It is the second-largest television broadcaster in Japan and it is particularly well known for its animation, children's programming, and variety shows. This company is a largely diversified mass-media company. It has taken an aggressive approach to international development through acquisitions and joint ventures with companies such as US Today. It acquired a number of companies in Europe relating to creative software production and licensing rights. It also produced Japanese musical productions. It owns its own theatre hall for live theatre as well as an art gallery with many of Picasso's sculptures. The company is into publishing computer software and multimedia, computer magazines, and Internet shopping, and it owns a few regional newspapers, and a film business. Its core competence is its creative programming capabilities.

TBS is a national television and radio broadcasting company. TBS is a relatively aggressive company that tends to produce racy shows, at least by Japanese standards. It is in all types of production, from drama to news broadcasting. Recently, it got itself into trouble with its investigative reporting of a "Tokyo bombing cult." TBS is the third-largest broadcaster, just slightly larger than Asahi.

Source: Company Internet sites and Time Warner documents on the Japanese media industry.

centred around joint news and information programming. It had also collaborated with a number of other foreign news broadcasters, including TF1 (France), RTL (Germany), BBTV (Thailand), CTV (Taiwan), CCTV (China), RTRC (Russia), and RTM (Malaysia). In addition, Asahi offered Japanese news, culture, and entertainment to tele- vision stations that broadcast to a Japanese audience in New York, San Francisco, Los Angeles, and Hawaii, although this was a very small part of its broadcasting business.

However, Asahi was in the process of trying to broaden its scope of broadcasting skills and products into the non-news sectors of the industry. For example, it was cur- rently trying to build a reputation in children's animation shows; it had developed a very popular children's animation show in Japan, and it was selling this show, with some success, to foreign broadcasters. The managers believed that the only way Asahi would grow and challenge some of its rivals was to add non-news-related shows. In their opinion, they had as much of the news market as they were going to capture in Japan, and moving into non-Japanese news broadcasting in a foreign country would be very difficult, if not impossible. So their one avenue for growth was in the more popu- lar TV shows such as variety, drama, etc. Thus, they were slowly exploring ways of developing some of the skills that their rivals had in this aspect of broadcasting.

ORGANIZATIONAL CHARACTERISTICS

TV Asahi's organizational chart is shown in Figure 1 on page 368. The chairman was a former newspaper executive appointed from Asahi Shimbun, as were all previous chairmen. In addition, a few other top managers were from Asahi Shimbun. This gave the company a distinctive "news culture."

Organizationally, the company was relatively conservative and bureaucratic in both its systems and its structures. None of the employees, including Kenji, was paid on the basis of performance. The reporting systems tended to be quite formal, and seniority was clearly an important issue in career advancement. In fact, Asahi had all of the classical Japanese organizational attributes. Lifetime employment was the norm, and personnel got to know each other through socializing during work and the frequent (often biweekly) after-work "get togethers" for drinks. Socializing was important, because it made the cooperative Japanese decision-making and working environment function smoothly. It also provided workers with mentors and management contacts which could later prove valuable when the person moved into a management position. This system also inculcated the organizational culture (e.g., group decision-making approach) into the employees.

TV Asahi's conservative organizational style was due, in part, to its heritage in the news industry and ownership roots in Asahi Shimbun. The news programming format provided the least amount of motivation for innovation and change, simply because a news report was a news report in any language and station. News stations tended to differentiate themselves on the operational aspects of gathering and reporting news. In essence, the depth and speed of coverage differentiated a good station from an "also-ran." In this respect, TV Asahi was clearly an extension of Asahi Shimbun. Yet, such a culture had clearly gotten in the way of the move toward a more creative broadcasting format and content.

Such a classical Japanese organizational approach had proven to be very effective in producing organizational efficiency, decision-making leading to very effective implementation, and a focused organizational strategy. Yet, it had also created some concerns. The biggest worry was the lack of creativity and specialization leading to a lack of fundamental research and development in the organization. A cooperative and generalist approach tended to attenuate the ability of the organization to take risks in decision-making and to try creative ideas. In some Japanese industries, this had clearly been a problem.

NEW FORCES ACTING ON THE TV INDUSTRY

Governmental controls on the industry had also contributed to the tempered competitive environment. The Japanese government had historically controlled the industry through regulatory policies that restricted channel ownership. Channels were awarded on the basis of availability and the owners' perceived honour, reverence, and trustworthiness in Japanese society. Historically, it had been very important for the owners to be standard-bearers of cultural honour, probity, and respect because they were reporting the news. Unlike North Americans, the Japanese were very concerned about what was televised. In particular, they did not condone programming that brings shame to them or their society. To a large extent the government had used ownership as a method of self-monitoring. This had resulted in an industry that had historically been concentrated in a few hands. Such a restrictive industry structure was wonderful for the companies. They enjoyed a stable competitive environment and commensurate levels of profitability.

However, a number of forces were changing the nature of the business. The recession, which began in 1992 and still continued, had reduced profitability dramatically in the broadcasting business, due to the "shrinkage" in advertising volume and rates. TV Asahi and Fuji TV had both delayed the development of their new headquarters office buildings. TV Asahi's was to be a 50-floor office building with a large theatre and retail shopping mall at the ground level. All of the broadcasters were searching for ways to save money and reorganize to improve efficiency. Some companies had even laid off workers for the first time since their inception some 40 years ago. Bankruptcies were at an all-time high and this was expected to continue for the near term. The financial crisis had forced two banks into bankruptcy and more were expected to follow.

The government was also looking at ways to deregulate the broadcasting industry in the next two years. The change in policy was being driven by the availability of many more channels and the merging of a variety of technologies, including telecommunications, satellite dishes, computers, digital broadcasting, and international competition. If Japan did not implement this deregulation, there was the potential that a wide variety of competitors would circumvent the present regulations, creating chaos. Furthermore, the government had come to view competition as essential to the development of new technologies and innovations in this fast-changing industry.

The four national broadcasters were, however, not pleased with this movement toward deregulation. They had been fighting the deregulation movement in a number of ways, but the predominant approach was to use political suasion. Having come from such a non-competitive environment, it was about the only response that they knew and had practised over the years. It now appeared that some sort of deregulation was going to occur within the next several years, and ultimately full deregulation was viewed as a distinct possibility in the long term.

THE SPECIAL EVENTS DIVISION

The Special Events Division of TV Asahi, which the Theatrical Productions unit was part of, employed approximately 50 people. The mandate for this division was to enhance the image of TV Asahi through the sponsoring of various special events. A few of these events had been turned into TV specials and/or publications. The division had become involved in a wide and eclectic number of activities:

- It published a number of different magazines and educational videos.
- It had created The Sakura Campaign to further world peace, in which cherry trees had been planted annually for the last five years at the former site of the Berlin wall.
- It had funded and produced several art exhibitions; the latest one was an exhibition of Vincent van Gogh. A variety of publications had resulted from this show.
- It had brought a variety of musical talent, both classical and popular, to Japan. Some of the recent performers included Prince, New Kids on the Block, and Van Halen. It brought the Vienna Boys Choir to Japan annually for a series of concerts.
- In addition, it had brought Broadway musical productions to Japan through the Theatrical Productions sub-unit.

The Special Events Division was not perceived as one of the more dynamic divisions in TV Asahi. Its objective was primarily to "give back" to the community and Japanese society, and secondarily, to create unusual and different TV programming material. The primary objective, although unusual by Western standards, was considered an important aspect of Japanese business and represented the cooperative interface between business and Japanese society. Most Japanese companies accomplished this in some manner. Despite this honourable objective, the Special Events Division was not considered one of the more exciting places to work in Asahi. In fact, a transfer to the division was jokingly referred to as early retirement. A number of managers in the division were "burnt out" TV Asahi managers who had transferred to the division to get out of the hustle and bustle of the demanding TV business. An indication of the instability in this division was the turnover of its president. For as long as Kenji could remember, the president of the Special Events Division had been replaced yearly, due to either retirement or transfer.

TV ASAHI THEATRICAL PRODUCTIONS, INC.

Asahi Theatrical Productions was founded because of a fondness for music by TV Asahi's second-highest manager, Mr. Hidedata Nishimura. In particular, Hidedata loved Western-style musicals and he felt that the Japanese public would also enjoy this form of entertainment if they were exposed to it. His idea was to bring these musicals to Japan, using Asahi's Special Events Division. However, the division did not have the staff or skills to do this. Therefore, in 1982 he recruited Mr. Kenji Sudo and Mr. Yasu Kata Nishimura, his younger brother, to manage the selection and licensing of the musicals in New York and to manage the operational aspects in Japan, respectively.

Kenji Sudo was well suited to the position. He had been employed at Fuji TV in New York for the previous 20 years. During this time he had developed strong Western management skills, including an entrepreneurial bent, something that would become quite useful in his new position.

Kenji immediately went to work and was able to license the Japanese rights to the musical *Sophisticated Ladies*, which toured Japan during 1983. After that Asahi licensed *My One and Only* in 1984 and *Dreamgirls* in 1986 (see Table 2 on the next page). The first two musicals were not financial successes, but they provided Asahi with some fame, particularly with young Japanese girls who loved this form of entertainment. The third production, *Dreamgirls*, was a major hit. It ran almost double the length of the previous two productions in Japan and, with every show sold out, it more than paid for itself. From it, Asahi received considerable publicity and recognition. The top managers in TV Asahi especially got tremendous adulation, and were often asked by top managers in other large companies and institutions if they could get some tickets for them.

At this point, both Kenji and Hidedata knew they had developed an interesting business opportunity. Furthermore, Kenji was starting to develop some important contacts and musical-theatre-specific knowledge. Based on this and the success of *Dreamgirls*, Asahi formalized the Theatrical Productions Unit into TV Asahi Theatrical Productions, Inc., in 1988. Mr. Hidedata assumed the role of president, a role that was little more than a Japanese figurehead of the corporation. He left all operational details to the two vice-presidents, Kenji and Yasu Kata, who ran their separate operations in the United States and Japan, respectively.

table 2   Asahi's Theatrical History

Year	Title	Involvement	Japanese
1983	Sophisticated Ladies	Japanese Tour	32 Performances
1984	My One and Only	Japanese Tour	32 Performances
1986	Dreamgirls	Japanese Tour	53 Performances
1988	Blues in the Night	Producer	
	West Side Story	Japanese Tour	43 Performances
1989	Can-Can	Japanese Tour	35 Performances
	Blues in the Night	Japanese Tour	48 Performances
1990	South Pacific	Japanese Tour	32 Performances
1991	The Secret Garden	Producer	
1991	Grand Hotel	Japanese Tour	48 Performances
1992	Jelly's Last Jam	Producer	
	Guys and Dolls	Producer	
1993	The Secret Garden	Japanese Tour	60 Performances
	Guys and Dolls	Japanese Tour	61 Performances
	The Who's Tommy	Producer	
	Blues in the Night	Japanese Tour	46 Performances

Additionally, in 1988 Asahi began investing in musical productions rather than just buying the Japanese rights to them. As a producer,[3] Asahi would now have more favourable access to the licensing rights of top musicals, although it would have to select its investments during the inception stages of the project, prior to the knowledge of whether the musical would be a hit or not. Its first investment was in an off-Broadway production called *Blues in the Night*. It was not a financial success, and from this Kenji realized that he must concentrate on major investments and top Broadway musicals, not off-Broadway productions.

In 1991, Kenji's associate and sponsor in Japan, Hidedata, set up a company, called International Musical, Inc. (IMI), to handle secondary and amateur performance rights and licensing in Japan. Hidedata was retiring in 1994, and IMI would allow him to continue to work in a business that had been his hobby for more than ten years. IMI complemented Asahi Theatrical Production's work by focusing on secondary musical rights and licences, and it would work with Asahi whenever possible. Furthermore, IMI would leave the Broadway and West End[4] musical rights and licences to Asahi.

In 1991, Kenji managed to convince Asahi to make another investment in a musical production. This time it was a Broadway musical entitled *The Secret Garden*. This was a considerable breakthrough for Asahi Theatrical Productions. Investing in Broadway or West End theatre production was a risky business for anyone. Only two out of ten investments made money, another one out of ten would break even, and the other seven would lose money. These were very poor odds, and some top managers in Asahi were not terribly comfortable making such an investment. To become a investor, or a producer as they were called in the business, a company had to invest $250,000 to

[3]Investors are called "producers" in the musical theatre business.
[4]Broadway and West End are the theatres, in New York and London (U.K.), respectively, that produced the best plays and musicals in the world.

$500,000. The producers then had no real rights to the musical other than to the profits derived from the show. In other words, this did not give the investor the right to take the show to Japan. These rights had to be negotiated separately, and a producer had no more legal claim to the rights than a non-producer, although investing in a musical obviously gave the investor an inside track on getting the rights.

On average, about five Broadway and West End musicals were shown annually. There were almost 100 theatres on Broadway and in the West End (split about half-and-half, and only a half-dozen in each location focused on musicals). Most of these theatres searched out directors who had creative ideas, or, less often, were presented with creative ideas. Directors having successful track records, such as Andrew Lloyd Webber, were widely sought after, because they could attract talent, money, and ultimately a paying audience. While the directors looked after the creative and artistic side of the production, the theatres managed the business aspects of the show: financing, advertising, selling of tickets, etc.

Broadway theatre management was a difficult business, and many of the theatres were jointly owned because of the rarity of skills and assets necessary. A successful theatre owner was a rare commodity; the position required a unique mix of skills, including excellent communication skills, good contacts in the business, adroit intuition as to the wishes and desires of the audience, and hardcore business acumen. Needless to say, few people had such a complex mix of skills. Thus, the few successful theatre companies tended to buy up those that failed. On Broadway only about three to four owners had been successful at developing musicals with any sort of consistency. Ultimately the directors could take their talent anywhere, and Andrew Lloyd Webber, the most successful musical director in the world, often selected a theatre not on its past record, but on its willingness to pay royalties and provide financial support for the production.

Unfortunately, musicals tended to be either big hits or big busts. A show that received poor reviews on opening night might not even last a week. A big hit that had garnered Tony Awards might play for over a year on Broadway, and subsequently in different international locations. The Tony Awards were important to a show because a nomination provided four minutes of television air time for the show during prime-time viewing. Such television coverage would be unaffordable to all but the largest and most successful shows, yet it contributed enormously to the awareness and image of the musical.

BRINGING A MUSICAL TO JAPAN

Getting the rights to a musical and bringing it to Japan was a very involved process. First the rights to the music and/or story had to be purchased. Then the talent (performers) had to be "acquired." The easiest way to do this was to wait until the show ended its Broadway run and then bring the actors to Japan. Signing the performers involved dealing with their managers and unions. Star performers often required separate negotiations, while regulars had more standard contracts. Then the unions had to be satisfied that the theatre was up to standard and that the appropriate care (e.g., flight, travel, hotel, food, rest) was provided to its members. The union negotiations often represented the most frustrating part of the negotiation process because of their restrictive rules, and at times their perceived confrontational approach. In addition to all of this, theatres had to be secured (they had to be rented two years in advance of the actual show in Japan because of the lack of appropriate venues), sets had to be transported and/or built, backstage personnel had to be acquired and/or trained. Thus, getting a show to Japan was not only time-consuming but also expensive. To bring a Broadway production to Japan cost US$7 to $8 million.

Asahi had developed some skill in putting on these musical productions in Japan. Mr. Yasu Kata Nishimura, the manager of the Japanese operations, had developed excellent liaisons, and where necessary, contacts in the Japanese theatre industry. Finding an appropriate theatre was one of the most difficult obstacles to overcome in putting on live theatre in Japan. Large Broadway-type theatres were very rare in Japan, and often another type of venue had to be adapted for the situation. Yasu Kata had become quite proficient at managing the Japanese tours. He had developed relationships with the large theatre owners. He understood the needs and desires of the various Western directors, actors, and workers. He also had developed considerable knowledge in the business aspects of the production, such as advertising, promotion, ticket sales, etc. In addition, Yasu had developed a subtitling system that allowed the Japanese audience to follow the story in Japanese, and some of the stories were published using Asahi's publishing subsidiary. Clearly, Kenji and Yasu had become a very effective team.

To aid with the financing of the Japanese tours, Asahi got sponsors. These sponsors would usually contribute about US$1 million, a sum that would help defray some initial costs. Then, the remaining costs would be covered, if possible, by ticket sales. In general, because of the enormous costs of most productions that Asahi brought to Japan, it was lucky to break even, although the odd one had been profitable. It should also be noted that although Asahi had purchased the rights for a Japanese musical theatre tour, that did not give it the right to broadcast the show on television. The TV rights involved further negotiations of licensing agreements which were even more complex and costly than those of the Japanese tour rights. Usually, after a musical had been televised, the potential for live theatre runs to that audience was limited. Therefore, any royalty payments for television rights had to consider the opportunity costs of losing any subsequent live theatre royalties.

The success of the investment in *The Secret Garden* motivated Kenji and Asahi to become more involved in the investment side of the business. One of Kenji's more important associations was with Mr. Landesman, president of Jujamcyn Theatres, who was one of the top Broadway theatre owners who tended to specialize in musicals. Through Kenji's close association with Mr. Landesman, he actively sought new musical productions in which he could invest. This relationship developed into a formal agreement in the early 1990s by which Asahi agreed to invest $1 million annually in Jujamcyn Theatre productions over the next three years. This non-exclusive agreement was due to expire in the next year. In this agreement, Asahi, through Kenji, was to be offered investments in every Broadway musical that Jujamcyn Theatres developed. Kenji would decide whether to invest or not, on the basis of Landesman's recommendations. Then Kenji would submit a formal investment proposal to TV Asahi and Asahi would usually take about three to four months to officially give the okay for the investments. So far, head office had never said no to a show that Kenji had committed to, and in fact, Kenji often wondered on what basis they would turn down a project that he recommended.

From 1992 to 1996, Kenji had committed Asahi, as producer, to seven musicals. Most of them were profitable, and some were very successful. During that time, only three musicals were brought to Japan, and a fourth was scheduled to begin a Japanese tour this year (1996). All of the musicals that toured Japan were ones in which Asahi had initially been a producer. Furthermore, during this time, all of the musicals that they had invested in had received some sort of Tony Award, whether for a singer, a song, or the musical itself. The 1992 musical *Guys and Dolls* received the coveted Tony's Best Revival Musical. Clearly, the investment aspect of the business was going very well.

Asahi's success was also due to Kenji's induction as a voting member for the Tony's in 1993, the only Asian to be given such an honour. This provided Kenji with considerable fame, which allowed him to establish a broad network of relationships in this rather cliquish and exclusive business.

Asahi's managers clearly did not understand the business, but some of them were enjoying the successes of the theatre division. Presidents of other major Japanese corporations had asked them for tickets to performances. Kenji had also been able to introduce TV Asahi's top executives to several top U.S. executives. For example, the Kennedy Center had been a Jujamycn investor, and when the president of the Kennedy Center, a very well-known figure in U.S. business circles, came to Japan, Kenji arranged a dinner with him and the president of TV Asahi. All of this brought considerable honour to TV Asahi top managers. However, Kenji wondered whether this was enough to keep them interested in the business.

Kenji was the principal person behind the success of Asahi's Theatrical Productions investing. He had the contacts and the understanding of the business skills and entrepreneurial attitudes necessary in the business. He even had a good sense of humour, which stood him in good stead when he had to mix with his business peers in New York. Other than Kenji, the only employee in Asahi Theatrical Productions was Kenji's assistant, a Japanese woman who looked after office details while Kenji developed business opportunities. Kenji negotiated which musicals they would invest in and usually committed Asahi to a dollar figure for each production. Other legal and financial aspects were handled by either outside help or by TV Asahi in its head office.

THE QUESTION OF THE FUTURE

TV Asahi Theatrical Productions, Inc., had been very successful in 1995, making a profit of approximately $1.5 million on revenues of about US$15 million. Needless to say, such revenues and profits were small compared to TV Asahi's annual revenues (less than 1 percent). However, in Kenji's eyes there was considerable opportunity for further growth. This included additional investment in musicals, investments in other types of live entertainment, and attempts to move more into the theatre management and creative side of the business. There was also the considerable, yet untapped, opportunity of musicals in the West End theatres in London. Demand for Broadway musicals had exploded, particularly outside of Broadway and the West End. If Asahi could tap into this growth, it could become a significant player in the business. There was also the potential of trying to integrate the creative and artistic talent represented in this business into the TV business.

The problem was that Kenji and Yasu Kata, his Japanese counterpart, didn't actively support any growth opportunities since Hidedata had retired from TV Asahi, although they had not actively dissuaded growth in the past. Neither Kenji or Yasu Kata had actively trained others in TV Asahi, so their specialized skills were unique. Now, Yasu Kata was scheduled to retire in less than two years and Kenji had inquired about a replacement for Yasu Kata. He found out that TV Asahi had no plans in place for replacing Yasu Kata—in fact they really had not thought about it. Kenji was in his mid-50s and, as a U.S. resident, did not have to, and did not want to, retire at the mandatory Japanese retirement age of 60. He felt that he had considerable energy left to devote to this business over the next decade. Kenji was also involving some young Japanese located in New York, largely university musical and theatre students, in his business dealings and associations. He saw his role as an informal mentor and friend to these Japanese associates, none of whom was formally employed by Asahi.

Unfortunately, Kenji realized that part of the problem was that since Nishimura's retirement neither he nor Yasu Kata had developed a strong set of new relationships with TV Asahi's top managers. Prior to Nishimura's retirement, Kenji had been in constant contact with Nishimura. Each understood the business and the other's desires and attitudes about a decision. However, Kenji had not been a lifetime employee of TV Asahi, and in fact had not even been employed with TV Asahi in Japan. This was a disadvantage, because he now had few contacts with whom he could develop a relationship in TV Asahi. Not only was he not a TV Asahi person, but he had lived outside of Japan for over three decades.

While Kenji pondered his fate, he wondered what must be going through the minds of the top TV Asahi executives in Tokyo. They appeared not to understand the business. It represented a relatively small amount of their deployed assets, yet he felt strongly that it could contribute more to TV Asahi's future. Disney Corporation had just invested in a Broadway theatre, and some of the other Japanese broadcasting corporations had been actively getting involved in theatre during the last several years.

Two recent musical successes in Japan were motivating other broadcasters to consider this type of unusual and highly desirable source of entertainment as an investment and potential broadcasting opportunity. Asahi had a tremendously successful run of *The Secret Garden*, which had won a Tony Award prior to its Japanese tour. Then Japan Broadcasting (JBS) invested nearly $2 million in the Broadway show *The Will Rogers Follies*, winner of the 1991 Tony award for best musical. JBS had negotiated the rights to broadcast the show to its TV audience in late 1995, and it was expected that the show would complete a Japanese tour after its five-year stint on Broadway. JBS had accomplished this feat by hiring a New York–based media consultant and paying a lot of money. NTV, a subsidiary of NHK, had also become involved in televising Broadway musicals. They had produced and televised the musical *Annie* in Japan solely for the purpose of a television production, and they were continuing to try to work with top directors to find new shows to be televised. Suntory, Inc., Japan's largest liquor company, had also invested in musicals during the past four years. They had developed an agreement with another Broadway and off-Broadway theatre owner, Shubert Theatres. This relationship had produced eight shows, including *The Grapes of Wrath*, *The Heidi Chronicles*, and *Cities of Angels*. Suntory was expected to sign another long-term agreement with Shubert in the upcoming months. The message was quite simple that Japanese money was willing to invest in top Western musicals. It also indicated to Kenji that considerable opportunity existed for this business and his talents within a variety of Japanese companies.

Televising the shows in Japan was viewed as a tremendously risky business. But the financial risks were moderated in some decision-makers' eyes by the realization that it would provide recognition and very high advertising ratings to the channel. Financially, some felt that a musical broadcast might break even if it was combined with an Asian tour followed by an Asian-only broadcast of the show, as long as the show was a hit. However, this was a difficult thing to manage and it clearly posed a variety of risks. The key to any musical was getting the right one. Clearly, the Japanese were most interested in top Broadway and West End musicals. In this regard, the audiences were quite discerning, and they knew the difference between a first- and a second-rate show. In addition, the musicals best suited to Asian audiences were those that had little conversation and lots of music, because much of the audience did not understand English.

THE FUTURE

Every year Asahi had renewed the contract that employed Kenji. However, Kenji was now wondering what the company would do when this year's or possibly next year's contract renewal came up. Furthermore, what should he do? Kenji realized that the key to figuring out what he should do really lay in figuring out what TV Asahi would do, given its options.

Kenji realized that TV Asahi had a variety of options available to it. It could withdraw financial support now; it could do nothing; or it could get actively involved in further developing the Theatrical Production's activities. Ultimately, Asahi's decisions would affect his decision. Yet, there was also the broader question of whether he should be proactive or reactive. These were complex questions, with many cultural ambiguities. He knew that he had become partially Western and partially Japanese in his management attitudes, something that made his decision even more complex. Should he manage this situation as a Westerner or as a Japanese manager? He had worked, and he thought he always would work, for a Japanese company, yet he also realized that he would have to continue to work in this business in the United States. In this regard, his brain was telling him one thing, but his heart was telling him something quite different.

The Richard Ivey School of Business gratefully acknowledges the generous support of the Richard and Jean Ivey Fund in the development of this case as part of the RICHARD AND JEAN IVEY FUND ASIAN CASE SERIES.

case 30 Lonely Planet Publications

Steve Hibbard reflected on the irony of life. The case study he and his fellow students had written as an assignment during the final year of his MBA had led to his current job as general manager, business administration, of Lonely Planet Publications—a job that was now leading him to question much of what he had learnt during the MBA.

Since joining Lonely Planet, Steve Hibbard had implemented a number of significant changes, but he was now wondering how far he could go before, as he put it, "the introduction of 'management science' ruined the place." On the other hand, Lonely Planet was a rapidly growing, global business, and Steve sensed it would run into trouble if it did not become more formalized and systematic in the way it operated.

The immediate issue was the introduction of a mission statement, a process Steve had started over a year ago. He now saw the first draft (Figure 1) as his own attempt to come to terms with the essence of the highly successful publisher of travel guides. The second draft (Figure 2) was more specific, but did not fully capture the spirit of the company. And besides, many people in the organization questioned the point of the exercise.

In fact, Steve had run into a lot of flak in attempting to introduce a formal mission statement. The process had brought to the surface a great deal of disagreement about what the "mission" of Lonely Planet actually was. His MBA training suggested that it was important for these things to be clear, that they should not be vague—his notes from Strategic Management reminded him that "clarity and constancy of purpose was critical." And yet, many people in Lonely Planet argued that more definition would just limit things, and that it was better if people had their own feeling about what the purpose of Lonely Planet was and why people bought their books. What surprised Steve was how well this vague, informal approach seemed to work.

The dilemma he faced regarding the mission statement was a specific example of the broader sense of unease he felt about what seemed to be a trade-off between a disciplined and systematic approach and the costs and, in some ways, constraints that this more professional approach entailed. A management information system and regular reporting cost money; job descriptions limited what people did.

Richard Ivey School of Business
The University of Western Ontario

This case was prepared by Geoffrey Lewis. It is based on an earlier case developed by students at Melbourne Business School. The assistance of Claude Calleja, MBA 1993, in preparing an earlier draft is gratefully acknowledged.

When Steve first arrived at Lonely Planet, he had made the mistake of putting things into "MBA categories." Lonely Planet was not doing any formal market research and did not have a marketing plan. The editors and publishers just talked about "making the books nicer." He had been convinced it was a "product-driven organization." As time went on, however, Steve came to realize that the people at Lonely Planet were more in tune with their customers than any of the "customer-focused" organizations he had studied during the MBA.

figure 1   Draft Mission Statement (May 1994)

Why Are We Doing This?

Best Guess

To be the planet's best source of interesting, down-to-earth information for the independent traveller.

To operate a business which is environmentally and socially responsible, by:

- Encouraging responsible travelling practices
- Recognizing the impact of our material, and striving to ensure it has a positive impact on the places we encourage people to visit
- Making a positive contribution to the communities in which we work

We want to foster a working environment which is productive, creative, participatory, and fun. One which will attract and retain people committed to quality, and which will encourage them to grow and learn and feel positive about our role in the global community.

We must be an effective, profitable business. Profit is a prerequisite for our continuing ability to pursue the above goals.

figure 2   Draft Mission Statement (January 1995)

Aim

To be the planet's preferred choice for useful, accurate, interesting, entertaining, and down-to-earth information for the independent traveller.

To achieve this we will:

- Gather, store, filter, and communicate up-to-date information relevant to independent travellers
- Facilitate the exchange of information between independent travellers
- Encourage cross-cultural understanding and responsible travel practices; provide the information necessary for "aware" travellers to make responsible choices
- Make a positive contribution to the destinations we cover and the communities in which we work
- Develop an international organization working in an interactive and responsive partnership with an international audience
- Foster a working environment that is productive, challenging, creative, participatory, fun, and financially rewarding
- Attract and retain motivated and talented people and encourage them to grow and learn
- Operate a profitable business to enable the continued pursuit of these goals

At Lonely Planet, Steve gained some insights into what a brand franchise really meant:

> To build a brand requires real values, integrity, and consistency. Lonely Planet publishes information for travellers. Tony Wheeler is still the quintessential traveller and remains one of the best, and most prolific, authors we have.
>
> Valuable brands engender real loyalty in customers—often beyond the rational level. Lonely Planet engages the customer at every opportunity—with letter correspondence, by putting contributors' names in books, by getting into the media at every opportunity with the direct, personal style of the authors. We also engage the industry through debates, travel summits, bookstore talks, radio appearances, etc. We engage the trade with long-term loyalty, mutually supportive arrangements, sales conferences, and square dealings.
>
> We often turn down opportunities for quick profit because it would dilute the brand. We constantly decline invitations to accept advertising in books, or to endorse travel products such as backpacks, etc.
>
> Independence is required for brand building. Financial stakeholders have often required short-term rewards. We are doing stuff now that cannot be explained with a spreadsheet or in terms of cash flow, but we are maintaining and building the value of the brand, which may only be fully realized over 10–20 years or with the sale of the whole thing.
>
> Another reason independence is required relates back to the integrity argument. We have turned down very attractive offers to work with other companies to co-produce a product, because their brand conveys a different message than ours and co-branding would send confusing messages about what we stand for.
>
> You have to love what you are doing to build a brand; it's a long, hard slog.

Steve stared out of the window of his small office—one of the few in Lonely Planet—at the wintery Melbourne weather and pondered. "How much do you try to implement what you learned in the MBA? How much chaos and inefficiency do you tolerate? Particularly when people like it that way."

THE LONELY PLANET STORY

The Early Years: Lonely Planet Finds a Niche

In 1972 a young and adventurous newly married English couple, Tony and Maureen Wheeler, then 26 and 22 years old, respectively, walked, hitched, and backpacked their way to Australia across Asia from England. They arrived in Sydney on Boxing Day 1972 with precisely $0.27 in their pockets. In order to survive, Tony pawned his camera and Maureen got a job in a milk bar.

Soon the numerous "How did you do it?" inquiries from friends inspired them to write down their travel experiences. With virtually no publishing knowledge (although Tony had worked on a university newspaper in his student days), and working from a kitchen table in the basement of a Sydney flat, they converted their meticulously kept travel notes into a publication—a cut and paste job they called *Across Asia on the Cheap.*

Tony Wheeler described those early days:

> We did everything. We wrote the books, we edited them, we sold them, and we delivered them. When *Across Asia* was published, I took a day off work in Sydney to come sell it in Melbourne. I loaded up a suitcase with books, flew to Melbourne, took a bus to the city, put the books in the left luggage office at the train station, went around the book shops and sold the books, went back to the station, picked up the suitcase and then delivered them.

Across Asia on the Cheap became an instant success, with the initial print run of 1,500 copies becoming sold out in ten days. It inspired thoughts of a second trip to Asia. Encouraged by their success and driven by their love of being "on the road," they postponed their return to England and set out again for Southeast Asia.

This trip resulted in *Southeast Asia on a Shoestring*. Cobbled together in a cheap Singapore hotel between fortnightly visits to the authorities to renew their visas, *Southeast Asia on a Shoestring* was published in 1973. Fifteen thousand copies were sold in Australia, New Zealand, Britain, the United States, and Asia. Its meticulously researched information, communicated in a down-to-earth style, was to create an entirely new genre of travel-guide writing.

Tony Wheeler, reflecting on this early success, observed:

> Now I can look back and think that was a really clever idea, but at the time I didn't realize it. It was just a nice thing to do. As soon as we saw how well the first book went we thought, "Let's do another." We grew very slowly at first. It took us five years to get to ten titles.

The name "Lonely Planet" surfaced while working on their first book over pizza and red wine. They were musing about names: "It came out of a song by Joe Cocker from the album *Mad Dogs and Englishmen*. There's a line in it about a lovely planet and we just changed it to Lonely Planet."

With the success of its second publication the fledgling company expanded its title list with books on Nepal and Africa, and guides to New Zealand and Papua New Guinea. The early growth, however, was not without difficulties—financing expansion was a real problem in the early days. According to Maureen:

> Once you're in debt to the bank for a couple of million, you can borrow as much as you want. But when you're getting started and you want to borrow maybe a thousand to buy a car to get around the city to sell your books, or a two thousand dollar overdraft to pay your print bill, you can go on your hands and knees and kiss their feet but, boy, you won't get it.

The first ten years were a real struggle as Tony and Maureen tried to keep the business going. Exploring Third World countries in the region, living out of a backpack, and writing in cheap hotels for weeks and months on end became a normal way of life. Despite its promise of adventure and excitement, life "on the road" was, more often than not, a less than salubrious experience. Their obsession with detail, and their insistence on experiencing life as a traveller, often took them to regions where few Westerners had been, much less written about.

Jim Hart: A New Partner

The year 1980 was an important one for Lonely Planet. Jim Hart, a friend of the Wheelers with a mixture of travel and publishing experience, joined Lonely Planet from a major publishing house in Adelaide, South Australia. With Jim's involvement, the Wheelers' shoestring operation gradually took on more permanence, allowing them more time to travel and to undertake the intensive, year-long research effort necessary for the production of an India guide. When the first edition of *India: A Travel Survival Kit* came out in 1981, it marked a major turning point for Lonely Planet. Previously, books priced at A$3.95 had sold up to 30,000 copies; by 1981 books priced at A$14.95 sold 100,000 copies. The India guidebook provided the steady income desperately needed for the company to finance its operations.

By the time Jim joined, Tony and Maureen had already established the Lonely Planet name and set up the beginning of an international distribution system. With Jim's involvement, and with the publication of the India guide, Tony and Maureen could look forward to a period of stability.

Shortly after Jim joined the company, however, disaster struck. He became critically ill and was out of action for almost eight months. Also, during this time Maureen gave birth to her first child, which left Tony with the main responsibility of running their growing business, while supporting a new family and their sick friend in hospital.

Doing It Tough: The First Overseas Office

The Wheelers came close to throwing it in on several occasions: "There were a couple of awful times when no money was coming in and nothing was happening and you look at each other and think how long can we keep this going for."

One such time was during 1984–85, when the Wheelers set out to open an office in the United States. Originally Tony and Maureen went to the United States for a few weeks intending to arrange warehousing, but it didn't take them long to realize that they needed to spend more time there to set up a full distribution operation. Their direct involvement in the United States lasted more than a year.

Setting up the United States office turned out to be a very difficult experience. The cutthroat competitive environment in that country, coupled with a lack of appropriate personnel, looked as if they would sink Lonely Planet. Maureen reflected on the personal toll:

> It was a terrible time. The U.S. became a big hole into which we poured money for well over a year and from which we wondered if we'd ever get out. In order to try and make it work, Tony and I had to spend time there trying to run the office ourselves, which of course affected our operations in Australia, because we could not be in two places at one time. To cap it all, the Americans threw us out because of some visa technicality. The situation came close to unbearable. Tony became ill and started to suffer high blood pressure.

Internationalizing the Business

It was only after some major staff changes, numerous trips across the Pacific, and the installation of an accountant to run the United States office that things began to stabilize and improve. By 1991, Lonely Planet was in a position to open another office overseas.

The United Kingdom was the natural choice, given its status as the centre of English-language publishing in the large European market, and Lonely Planet's decision to commence publishing guides to European destinations. Lonely Planet had been represented in the United Kingdom for many years by a small specialist distributor, but there was potential to do much more. They opened a small office in London to promote the books and to handle distribution in the United Kingdom and on the continent.

Lonely Planet's expansion into Europe was another major test for the company. In Asia Lonely Planet was preeminent, but in the "Old World" such long-established guides as *Frommer's*, *Let's Go*, *Baedackers*, and *Fodor's* battled for superiority. Furthermore, Lonely Planet, which had created a name for itself by publishing guidebooks to the world's more out-of-the way places, did not have an image as a provider of travel information about the industrialized countries of the West. Lonely Planet expected to meet fierce competition in the European market, which was dominated by the big American-produced guides.

Opening the English office turned out to be much easier than the United States experience. This was in large part due to the efforts of an enthusiastic young Englishwoman who, after working for a number of years with Lonely Planet in Melbourne, was charged with the task of setting up the United Kingdom operation. The United Kingdom market had always been important to Lonely Planet, and establishing a dedicated sales and promotions office there ensured the continuation of high levels of sales (see Figure 3).

Two years later, heartened by its United Kingdom experience, Lonely Planet set up an office in France. The French office marked a significant development for the company in that, unlike its other overseas offices, its role was not limited to promotion and distribution, but included production of French translations.

The opening of Lonely Planet's French office was also significant because it marked the company's first attempt to diversify into non-English-speaking markets and at controlling the content, presentation, and marketing of its products and brand in those markets.

Until this time, Lonely Planet had considered itself to be exclusively an English-language publisher. The translation of its books into other languages had been undertaken by foreign publishers under various licensing arrangements.

Lonely Planet Comes of Age

In November 1994 Lonely Planet turned 21. The celebrations the Wheelers organized reflected the creativity and spontaneity with which they had infused the organization. What started out as a party for a few of the staff grew into a weekend bash that attracted some of the world's leading travel writers, journalists, and publishing bosses to Lonely Planet's hometown of Melbourne. Rather than waste such a pool of talent, the Wheelers organized a one-day travel summit, which was open to the public. "We

figure 3   Lonely Planet Sales by Region

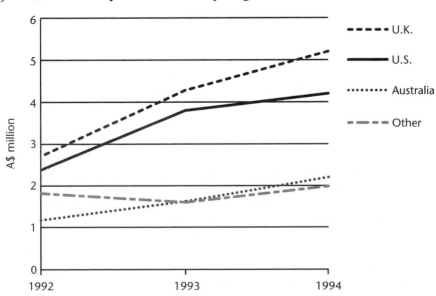

thought 'Wouldn't it be nice to get all our staff from all over the world together in one space and just have a party,'" recalled Maureen. "And then we thought of all the people who have worked with us for years—booksellers, journalists, etc.—so we began to expand it out to other people we'd like to have. And then we thought, 'We have some fantastic names coming, why don't we have a public event?'"

"Party guests" included English author Eric Newby, freelance writer Pico Iyer, travel writers from the *San Francisco Examiner*, *The Times*, *The Independent*, and *The Sunday Mail*, and bosses of some of the world's leading publishing houses. That Lonely Planet could attract such big names to the far side of the world showed the esteem in which the company was held.

On the Road Again: The Wheelers in the 1990s

While continuing to run the business, much of the Wheelers' time was still spent on the road—researching, which they described as "dawn-to-dusk hard work and not without some annoyances." Typically they travelled overseas half-a-dozen times a year, investigating new places, double-checking facts from one of their books, or simply enjoying life on the road. In 1994, for example, they went to Queensland, Tahiti, and made two trips to the United States. Tony also spent time in Britain researching Lonely Planet's first guide to that country.

In typical Wheeler fashion the United States trips were anything but ordinary. They bought a 1959 Cadillac and drove from San Francisco to Boston in April, and then flew back to the United States in July to make a return trip to San Francisco. "The car was so big it took a mile to stop and used fuel like a 747, but it was a load of fun," remembered Tony. The car was featured on the front cover of Lonely Planet's 1994 product catalogue. Tony explained the reasons for their travel:

> With Lonely Planet preparing guidebooks on each U.S. state, the trip was important to get a feel for the country.
>
> It's never really a holiday. We always travel with all the guidebooks, others' as well as our own, and are always checking facts.
>
> All trips are a potential source of new ideas. A few years ago we went outback in Australia—up the Birdsville track and then crossed the Simpson desert. It was the kids' vacation (the Wheelers have two teenage children) and we hadn't intended to make a book at all. But we came back so enthusiastic we ended up with an "Outback Australia" guide.

For the book about Britain, Tony made two trips to the country, travelling mostly on foot with a rucksack and often staying at the cheapest B&Bs he could find.

Can they ever see the time when they run out of projects or ideas? "No way," says Tony. "They keep making new countries. Every time we turn around they create a whole new country. We are doing Slovenia right now. The potential for city guides hasn't been tapped yet, either." And when it comes to their favourite destinations they are not easy to pin down. They both love Nepal and the wide-open spaces of the Australian outback. But deep down they simply enjoy being on the road. "I always love the last place I've been to," says Tony. "I always like the next place we're going to," laughs Maureen.

The primary passion of the Wheelers was always to produce good travel information. Profit was important, but mainly because it was the means to grow and do more for travellers. Until recent years, when the accountants forced change, the owners drew a salary lower than the average first-year MBA.

According to Maureen the fairy tale was a long time coming: "It took us a long, long time. It is a fairy tale existence now, but it took a lot of years of scrimping and scraping and watching other people fly way beyond us."

Maureen gives this advice to anyone starting their own business:

Find something that you love to do, so that the fact that you're not earning a lot of money for a long time, and the fact that you're working eighteen hours a day for an awful long time ... is not a hassle. If you're doing it for the money, and you're doing all the right things laid down by accountancy principles, you might do well and you might do well faster but you wouldn't have any fun.

The Wheelers planned to live in Paris during 1996—because they had always wanted to.

THE PUBLISHING INDUSTRY

Emerging Trends

During the late 1980s and early 1990s a number of important changes occurred in the book publishing industry. Dramatic worldwide rationalization saw smaller, regionally based publishers who, until this time, had operated independently in many countries around the world taken over by powerful international publishing houses. This trend was evident first in America and Europe, but soon spread to Australian publishing houses, which were seen as strategic launching pads for English-language books into the rapidly growing Asia Pacific region.

The 150 members of the Australian Book Publishers Association in 1995 represented an industry with $1.5 billion turnover. Eighty percent of members had a turnover of less than $2 million. The top five competitors dominated the industry. These large publishers had their own distribution capabilities and were often part of a larger communications conglomerate covering electronic as well as the print media.

The trends toward global consolidation of the industry appeared to be part of the large players' corporate strategies. Control of newspapers, printing works, film libraries and production, databases, book retailing and publishing, radio and television broadcasting, satellite television, and magazines began to converge in the expectation of massive economies of scale.

These global companies were also at the forefront of the implementation of new technologies that offered the possibility of increasing audience size and, hence, further leveraging the returns from their "information stores." In this climate, smaller publishers survived by catering to specialist niche markets, which the large corporates could not service economically.

In the mass-market segment of the book trade, paperbacks had to compete with a multitude of other "entertainment" products for the consumer dollar, with the result that some publishers anticipated that, by the end of the 1990s, the growth in the sale of books would become stagnant in many countries. In 1994, however, the book market was still growing (see Figure 4 on the next page).

Lonely Planet had been protected, to a large degree, from these industry trends. Its products provided readers with factual information with a specific purpose and did not have to compete solely on entertainment value. In addition, although the international recession had slowed the growth of tourist travel, there always seemed to be a demand for travel information by Lonely Planet's particular target niche, the independent traveller.

figure 4   Demand Trends for Books

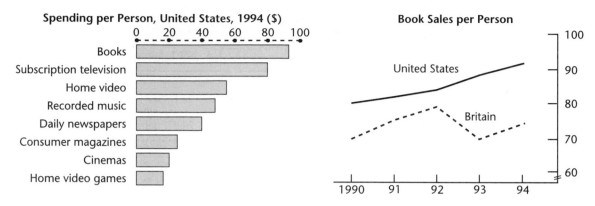

Source: *Economist*, September 30, 1995, from information supplied by Veronis, Suhler & Associates and the Publishers Association.

Book Distribution

The difficulties faced by small publishers following consolidation of the industry were exacerbated by changes in distribution channels.

In the late 1980s the owner-operators of independent bookstores numerically dominated the market. In Australia, for instance, 75–80 percent of bookstores were owner-operated stores, or small chains with two to five stores. The majority of these were not commercially aggressive, and books were generally sold at the publishers' recommended retail prices (RRP). This pricing structure was supported by a 100-year-old international publishing cartel. Book retailers competed on the basis of convenience and service rather than price. As in most markets overseas, there were few independent book wholesalers in Australia. Books were generally distributed to retailers directly by publishers or their exclusive licensees.

By the early 1990s however, bookstore chains and large department stores were becoming increasingly dominant in the book-retailing segment throughout the world. Book superstores had emerged in the United States to compete with discount stores—Wal-Mart alone had 18 percent of the United States book retail market. These stores were much more commercially oriented. They offered a wide selection of books, and their size and buying power allowed them to negotiate large margins with publishers, who often had no choice but to comply or be denied access to their readers. Lower prices were, in part, then passed on to consumers through heavy discounting of many titles. Discounting of hardback bestsellers was starting to occur in the United States.

Travel Guide Publishing

In the early 1990s the competitive environment facing Lonely Planet varied from country to country. While there were a large number of travel-guide publishers all around the world, there were only a few which operated internationally.

Rough Guides

Rough Guides is a United Kingdom–based publisher that focused initially on the British independent traveller, predominantly to European destinations and gradually to a wider readership. It was, however, expanding its subject coverage to a broader range of destinations. Certainly, Rough Guides looked as if they would pose a greater threat to Lonely Planet's position with Asian destinations, and would continue to be a strong competitor in European destinations. Rough Guides were Lonely Planet's closest competitor in terms of target customers and style of book.

The Let's Go *Series*

A United States series that targeted young budget travellers, predominantly students from the United States and Canada. It covered all the major destinations within the United States and Europe and parts of northern Africa. *Let's Go* concentrated on its specific market segment and destinations. It used student researchers to update its books annually in time for the United States summer break. *Let's Go* was owned by St. Martin's Press.

Frommer's

Frommer's is a United States publisher (owned by Prentice Hall), popular with the "traditional" North American traveller. Its books focused on middle-class, middle-aged travellers going to major destinations. While it had guides covering the emerging destinations that were Lonely Planet's stronghold, its target audience was quite different.

Fodor's

Fodor's tended to compete directly with Frommer's. It was United States–based and aimed at wealthier American travellers with limited time. It had, however, a wider international perspective than Frommer's, with good coverage of all destinations except Africa. Its 180 titles, all in a recognizable format, were updated annually. In 1992 Fodor's released a budget-conscious series called *Berkeley Guides* in an attempt to tap this growing segment, and in direct competition with *Let's Go*. Fodor's was owned by Random House.

Traditionally, travel guide publishers enjoyed regional strongholds and/or unique customer niches. Lonely Planet, for example, primarily published books about Asia for independent travellers from the English-speaking West (Europe, the United States, and Australia). By the 1990s, however, most of the popular destinations had been covered, and travel guide publishers began moving out of their traditional range of titles and into new regions formerly the exclusive domain of other publishers. As a consequence, sales were becoming less regional, and the market was becoming more global.

This globalization drove industry rationalization and alliances. For example, Rough Guides formed an alliance with "deep-pocketed" Penguin for access to technology, distribution, marketing, and financial resources. Similarly, Fodor's entered into a partnership with Worldlink, a global travel information network that could provide customers with supplemental current events and destination guides. The supplemental guide information was time-sensitive and geared to a particular customer's interests and itinerary. Fodor's expansion into new geographical and demographic markets, and its experimentation with new information technology, were a result of a very aggressive international expansion strategy.

In non-English-speaking countries, the market for travel guides was serviced by local companies publishing in their native language and competing aggressively against one another. Many of these publishers were long-established and they tailored their products to the particular needs of their local markets. Most did not publish in English.

Technological Change

In addition to industry consolidation and major changes in distribution channels that occurred in the early 1990s, the whole publishing industry was on the brink of a technological revolution. The introduction of electronic media and the convergence of communication and computer technologies, creating the "information superhighway," was reshaping the entire industry.

The basic concept of presenting prepackaged information via the printed page in book form, the primary method of communicating information since the discovery of printing, was being challenged. Publishers of travel information were frantically trying to assess the implications of new technologies, which saw an entire collection of books, weighing several kilograms, stored on one compact disk weighing no more than a few grams. The significance of this was not lost on Lonely Planet, which had been using lightweight paper in its bigger editions for several years in an effort to keep weight and volume down. Nonetheless, the practice of ripping out and discarding irrelevant sections in the company's regional guides was common among its prime backpacker market.

Further, the Internet allowed virtually free access to information from anywhere in the world and, significantly for Lonely Planet with its two-year recycle time, allowed users to gain instant access to current information. By 1990 it was possible to download current information on train timetables and weather patterns for most European cities from anywhere in the world.

Tourism Trends

By 1993 there were almost 500 million tourist arrivals worldwide. While Europe had by far the largest number, Asia had the fastest rate of growth (see Table 1).

Tourism had been booming worldwide since the 1950s (Figure 5). Tourism trends revealed that Asia was the fastest-growing destination market, with some industry observers predicting that tourist arrivals to the region would equal those to Europe by the year 2001.

Many social, political, and demographic factors contributed to the rapid worldwide growth in tourism since the early 1970s. Among the most important were:

- Greater competition among airlines, resulting in decreased real costs of international travel
- Easing of political restrictions on travel by many countries attempting to capture part of the estimated US$2 trillion (1993) worldwide travel market

table 1   World Tourism Trends

Continent	Share of Total Tourists (%)	Growth Rate (%)
Africa	5	9.6
Latin America	6	3.4
North America	11	2.6
Asia	19	12.1
Europe	57	2.7

Source: "Worldwide Travel and Tourism Review," *Economist*, 1991.

figure 5   Development of World Tourism (1950–1992)

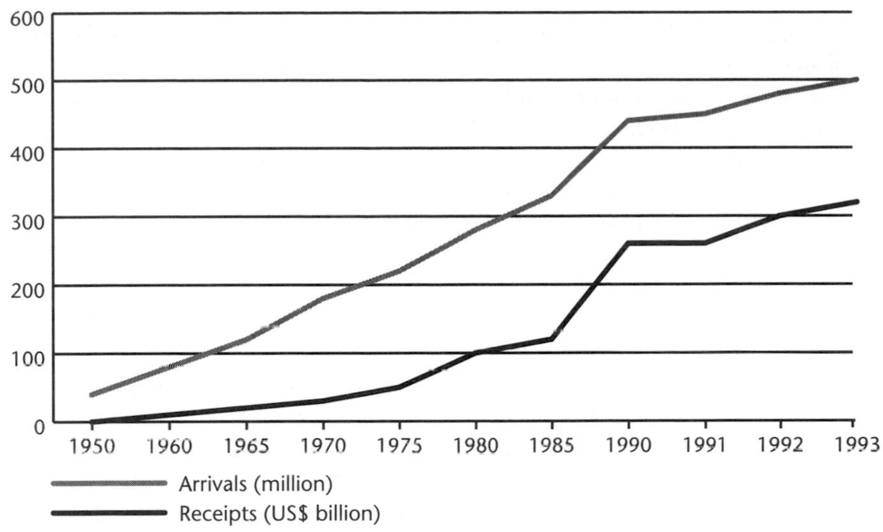

Source: WTO.

- Demographic shifts in developing countries, such as an increase in dual-income families, later marriage, and fewer children

The travel guide market could be segmented in terms of customer needs—ranging from the "armchair traveller" with a strong desire to learn, but little desire (or ability) to experience a foreign culture, to the hardened, independent traveller with a strong desire for both. In between were those travellers, more commonly referred to as tourists, who through lack of resources or personal disposition wanted to learn about and experience a foreign culture, but were less likely to travel off the beaten path. Independent travellers required very specific and detailed information of a practical nature, for example local road conditions, the nature, availability, and types of transport, and the availability and range of accommodation.

LONELY PLANET'S OPERATIONS

Lonely Planet in 1995

By 1995 Lonely Planet's publishing process had come a long way from the husband-and-wife operation working on a kitchen table. The company produced 180 titles (some of which were in their seventh edition), covering some of the most inaccessible regions in the world. It employed over 150 staff in four offices on three continents, though the largest proportion (around 80 percent) were still employed in Melbourne, where the company continued to undertake the production of all its English-language books. Lonely Planet also had 20 full-time writers, with another 80 authors who worked occasionally, and had an annual turnover in excess of A$17 million.

The financial performance of Lonely Planet was impressive by almost any measure. During the early 1990s the company enjoyed rapid growth and high profitability.

For example, in 1993 sales were up 38 percent over the previous year to $12 million, while EBIT (earnings before interest and tax) was up 50 percent to $3.1 million. Ninety-two percent of sales came from guidebooks (*Shoestring Guides* and *Travel Survival Kits*), the remainder coming from its newer lines such as *City Guides and Phrase Books.*

Lonely Planet donated approximately 1 percent of sales to charities in the countries it covered, funding small-scale projects such as cornea transplants in Nepal, as well as larger organizations like Greenpeace and Amnesty International.

In spite of the change in the nature of the organization as it grew, the books retained their chatty style and practical format, with much material being sent in from backpackers on the road.

Product Range

During the late 1980s Lonely Planet began to rapidly diversify its product lines, as well as its destination titles. Its two main travel guide series, *Shoestring Guides* and *Travel Survival Kits* remained, however, its core product lines. (See Appendix A on pages 399 and 400 for a brief description of Lonely Planet's product range.)

Lonely Planet attributed its success to a large range of titles, brand loyalty, and the best form of advertising that accompanied that loyalty—word of mouth. Inherent to its brand franchise were the integrity and consistency of the product. Lonely Planet guidebooks were thoroughly revised on average every two to three years. By contrast, most of the company's competitors updated only small sections of their books, some on a yearly basis. Each Lonely Planet book was in a constant state of revision. New editions incorporated not only the latest research by writers sent out into the field specifically for the purpose, but also comments and suggestions sent into the company by travellers using the previous version of the book. The company maintained its reliance on its far-flung readers for information and ideas, with in excess of 10,000 letters arriving at its office every year. Some argued that Lonely Planet knew as much about conditions in other countries as the Department of Foreign Affairs.

Lonely Planet's readers' letters department made sure that an acknowledgement was sent to every person who wrote to Lonely Planet, and awarded a free book to all those who supplied important updated information. Every writer to Lonely Planet was mentioned in the following edition of the relevant guide and received "Planet Talk," a free, bimonthly publication with information and experiences drawn from readers.

Editors in Melbourne kept an eye on competitors' products and made suggestions about ways the books could be enhanced. Lonely Planet believed that its consumers were primarily independent Western travellers, between the ages of 20 and 40, but market research had never been carried out to confirm this belief.

During the 1970s and 1980s, while the large publishers concentrated on the established North American or European destinations, Lonely Planet had the market for Asian titles virtually to itself. By the 1990s, however, travel guide publishing was globalizing and had become so competitive that the main guidebook publishers were looking to each others' traditional regional strongholds for both new destination titles and markets.

Although the Lonely Planet guidebook "formula" was developed with English-speaking Westerners in mind, the company has had some success in foreign translations. Lonely Planet books have been translated into nine languages including Italian, German, Japanese, and French. The company's policy was to sell translation rights to third parties for a small royalty. These publishers were then allowed to "repackage" the company's information as they liked. Translated books were not marketed under the Lonely Planet logo. Other than an acknowledgement of the source of information, which was carried inside the translated version of its books, the company did not have a translation policy. Consequently, there was a large variation in the way Lonely Planet translations reappeared in non-English versions. Some bore little resemblance to the standard format of a Lonely Planet book. Others, however, copied the format to the smallest detail, including the full-colour picture on the front cover and the hallmark banner at the top of the page, but replacing the Lonely Planet logo with their own.

The Publishing Process

Most of the research and writing for Lonely Planet was done by a small army of free-lance, experienced travellers with a proven ability to collect and present information. Lonely Planet supplied a "style guide" which described the format that writers had to follow. Most authors are not salaried, but are contracted for individual books. They are paid by flat fee and, occasionally, by a royalty on sales.

All authors are featured prominently in the front pages of each Lonely Planet book. Black-and-white photographs, often taken on the road, accompany a short tongue-in-cheek biographical paragraph describing how the writer (invariably) "dropped out" and became a writer-traveller. Some Lonely Planet writers "went feral"—they "dropped out" so seriously that they never returned from a "life on the road."

Lonely Planet prides itself on being an early adopter of new technology. Computers have long been used at Lonely Planet in all stages of production, and a "techo" group of three full-time computer experts maintains the company's computer network in Melbourne. Computer backups are made weekly, and duplicate copies of all the information in the company's system is stored off-site.

Printing and binding of finished books is mostly done in Hong Kong and Singapore. Apart from cost considerations and delivery time to major overseas markets, printers have to be able to "section sew" books. This type of binding, which prevents pages from falling out and book spines from being broken, guarantees that Lonely Planet books stand up to the hard treatment that they receive on the road.

Bulk distribution is decentralized through regional warehouses located in Melbourne, San Francisco, London, and Singapore. From these locations, books are supplied to wholesale distributors in each country except Australia and the United States, where sales and distribution to retailers is done directly by Lonely Planet.

Organization and Management

The Lonely Planet culture is often described as "funky." It has a non-commercial feel to it and is often perceived as an organization of "travellers helping travellers." Employees are generally younger people, and editors often work to the sound of their favourite music, with earphones connected to portable CD players.

Lonely Planet seems to attract creative people. Apart from writers, there are musicians, actors, and other artists, several of whom are very successful in their artistic careers outside of Lonely Planet. The people employed by Lonely Planet were, almost without exception, travellers. The people the Wheelers intentionally employed were, like themselves, their own customers.

Lonely Planet's two-storey headquarters in suburban Melbourne is an open-plan office on two floors, with just glass walls to define meeting rooms. Dress code is relaxed in the extreme. Well-loved jeans are the standard dress from the directors down. In summer, staff walk around in shorts and T-shirts and are often barefooted. Staff are encouraged to cycle to work or take public transport, and daypacks can be seen everywhere.

A door separates the office from a large warehouse, which is a hive of activity—often to the sound of the latest rock or heavy metal hit—during working hours. The warehouse doubles as a meeting place for staff "general meetings." Every Friday evening the company ships in cartons of beer and bottles of champagne and throws a party. This Friday ritual had started as a celebration of sending the latest book to the printer.

The relaxed atmosphere at Lonely Planet, which often catches visitors by surprise, belies the professionalism of the company's staff. Virtually everyone at Lonely Planet has at least one university degree, including two in 1995 who had Ph.D.s. There were, however, only two with MBAs (one of whom was Tony Wheeler, who completed an MBA at London Business School in the early seventies).

New Technology: The Internet

Lonely Planet went its own way in developing applications in response to the rapid developments in technology. In 1994, in its typical "try it first and fix it later if something goes wrong" operating style, it created a position which it called Manager, Information Systems. One of the editors in the Melbourne office was invited to take the position.

Within a short while the new manager had gathered a small group of editors and cartographers to develop applications for a Lonely Planet Internet site. None of the group had any previous programming experience. In fact, one member of the team had started at Lonely Planet a few years earlier as a packer in the warehouse. Baptising themselves "The e-Team," they had to unlearn much of what they learnt from book publishing. In a few months this group of half-a-dozen "experimenters" had developed what became one of the largest Internet sites in Australia.

While they were delighted with the result, which was generally considered to have very successfully translated Lonely Planet's youth-oriented culture to the new medium, everyone was still trying to figure out what could be done with it. As one of the directors said:

> It's fun. But what are we going to do with it? I can't see anybody using anything but books on their travels well into the future. Sometimes I wonder if we're wasting our time and money going down this path.

Tony Wheeler, it was said, just could not get himself excited about multimedia and sometimes wished the new technology would "go away." This sentiment was not shared by the younger staff, who were more comfortable, if not outright enthusiastic, with the developments resulting from the convergence of computer and communication technologies.

Lonely Planet Attracts Attention

The Wheelers' work had a pioneering quality, and the company acquired a reputation for blazing trails—where Tony and Maureen went one day (and later their writers), others were soon to follow. An industry observer commented that "Tony's books transformed the overland hippie trail to Asia and its grapevine more surely than if he'd hammered in signposts." The pathfinding skills of the young couple led, in fact, to one of the main—if scarcely logical—criticisms levelled at Lonely Planet; namely, that it had helped open up and commercialize what were previously "pristine places" known only to a deserving and adventurous few.

It didn't take long for the drawing power of Lonely Planet books to be appreciated by tourist operators in the budding tourist industry of the region. Self-titled "Lonely Planet" restaurants and touring companies began to sprout up in several developing countries from India to Kenya. And a mention of one's restaurant, hotel, or nightspot in a Lonely Planet book became a virtual guarantee of success. Because of this, Tony and Maureen were careful, when out in the field, not to reveal their identities.

The Wheelers' insistence on providing accurate information on the commercial establishments mentioned in their guides was a cornerstone on which they built Lonely Planet's reputation for unbiased, factual, down-to-earth travel information. To this day, Lonely Planet authors tend to travel incognito when they are in the field and, unlike most of its competitors, Lonely Planet continues to abhor the notion of carrying any form of advertising in its publications.

It wasn't only commercial establishments that began to take an interest in the company. As they became better known among more and more travellers, they also began to attract the attention of governments keen to capitalize on the growth in tourism. Sometimes, however, Lonely Planet's down-to-earth, no-holds-barred, somewhat irreverent writing style attracted unfavourable attention from governments. In Malawi, for instance, president-for-life Banda took a dislike to certain references to his country in *Africa on a Shoestring* and banned it. Vietnam also banned *Vietnam: a Travel Survival Kit* soon after it was published, citing as the reason a number of references, including one which informed travellers that its police force was "one of the best money could buy." Despite this action, a few weeks after it was banned, pirated copies of the book appeared for sale in government book shops with the offending passages intact.

Reaction to what Lonely Planet was saying and the way it was said was not limited to developing countries:

> The British press has hit back at an Australian tourist guide which is scathingly critical of some of London's most popular historical attractions.
>
> The latest Melbourne-compiled Lonely Planet guide, released last week, suggests the best way to aggravate the English is to tell them what they have always known—that their food is inedible, their weather an embarrassment and their beer a joke.
>
> And Auberon Waugh, an arch-conservative commentator, was oozing subtle sarcasm when he described the guide's editor thus: "It was written by an Australian originating in Bournemouth called Tony Wheeler, who wears spectacles."
>
> But Tony Wheeler naturally is delighted by all the free publicity. "I'm totally happy about it ... I expect it's going to be a very good seller for us," he said.[1]

Some of the observations in the guidebook about Britain included:

> Looking at Margate, God got so depressed she created Torremolinos.

> [Buckingham Palace] bad kitsch to tasteless opulence, like being trapped inside a chocolate box.

> Manchester ... a city so ugly it can almost be exhilarating.

Lonely Planet also attracted the attention of the corporate giants of the publishing industry. During the late 1980s, the Wheelers began to receive lucrative buyout offers

---

[1]Ed Rush, *The Advertiser*, Adelaide, March 3, 1995.

from a number of large organizations who, as Maureen explains, "after leaving us alone for all those years had finally woken up to our existence and the dynamism of our niche market." The offers kept coming. "People would drop in 'on the way somewhere' and casually ask us whether we were for sale. Everybody knows that Australia is not on the way to anywhere," laughed Maureen.

One organization which courted Lonely Planet was the software giant Microsoft, whose activity in multimedia and the "information superhighway" led it to approach Lonely Planet about joint development of multimedia travel publications. Although flattered by Microsoft's interest, Tony, Maureen, and Jim declined the offer, feeling that an association with such a large and powerful organization could compromise Lonely Planet's independence. As Tony said: "It really felt like we would be going to bed with an elephant and if it rolled over we would be crushed."

When asked why they didn't "take the money and run," Maureen said:

I don't know if I'd like to travel without a reason, and I really, really like the books we do. I always did, right from the very first book. On a day-to-day basis I really like all the people who work here, and who still enjoy working here. I suppose I just love the books.

STEVE HIBBARD JOINS LONELY PLANET

Restructuring the Organization

Steve Hibbard was completing his MBA at the Melbourne Business School in 1993. He had decided he didn't want to make a career in a large corporation. His plan was to identify a high-growth company he could join and perhaps later get some equity in.

A group case-writing assignment during the final year of the MBA introduced him to Lonely Planet. Steve described what happened:

I was intrigued by Lonely Planet—it seemed to be a great company—so I called the owner, Tony Wheeler, and said, "Remember me? I interviewed you for a business school project. Can I come and do some projects for you?"

So Tony, Jim, and I ended up sitting around a little black table. There was a long silence ... so I started to probe them about their "list of worries" and suggested I spend a week or two talking to people and then tell them where I might be able to help.

Anyway, I found lots of things were going on, but nobody was looking after them. Management information was inaccurate or unobtainable. They were licensing the Lonely Planet name for a television program, with too little control on the use of the name. The sales system and inventory system were out of date and it wasn't clear even who I should talk to about these issues. I tried to draw the organization chart. No one could agree how it should look ... the telephone list had things like "PC Guru." The organization seemed to be like this [see Figure 6].

Steve suggested to the directors that they should consider a reorganization and that he should be engaged to look after it. To his surprise "they bought it." Later, Tony and Maureen admitted to Steve that they felt, "We're big enough now that nothing you can do can damage it."

Steve recalled the first "interview" as an introduction to Tony's style:

I had to drive the meeting, that's Tony's style. He trusts people and if it's 70 percent what he thinks, he says do it your own way.

Take atlases, for example. Tony wanted to do it, but he wouldn't drive it. He would say, "Wouldn't it be a good idea to do atlases," and then waited for someone to pick it up.

figure 6   Lonely Planet's Organization Structure, 1993

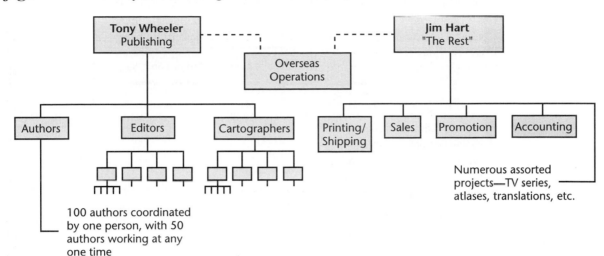

As Steve went around and talked to people he encountered a lot of sentiments such as, "It (Lonely Planet)'s not as good as it gets bigger," and "We need to preserve the good things while putting in place an information structure." As he started to understand the business better, a concept of what the organization structure should be started to emerge:

> I talked to everyone and I must have drawn the proposed structure on the whiteboard a thousand times. Gradually it got refined. There was a person looking after the authors, someone looking after the editors, and someone for the cartographers. They were in "departments" but they were getting too large and a "hands-off mentality" was starting to form. There were barriers to the process flow and the U.S. and France offices were like satellites hanging off the structure. Signs of strain from the relentless growth were everywhere.

Out of all the conversations emerged the idea of restructuring along process-flow lines (see Figure 7 on the next page). The regions Lonely Planet covered were divided between three groups, that were named Venus, Mars, and Pluto (other names had been considered, for example Itchy and Scratchy, and Laurel and Hardy). There was no management ruling on the names; they just came into common usage.

One person suggested she set up a Travel Literature section (to publish travel stories); it was something she (and Tony) had always wanted to do. The former head of editors decided he would rather be an author, and the person who was head of the cartographers took responsibility for design and ensuring consistency of "look."

The departments under Steve still had "functional heads," including Steve himself, who headed up Sales. In Steve's terms, the organization was now "a classic matrix." The other general manager, Richard Everist, had been an author and, before that, an editor. He and Steve formed a close working relationship and "made sure it all pulled in the same direction."

The objective of the restructuring was to maintain small teams while overcoming the barriers to the process flows: "It was commonsense. The MBA gets you in touch with your commonsense. You get used to laying things out on paper. Tony (Wheeler) uses his MBA more than he likes to admit—it's a way of thinking."

figure 7   Lonely Planet's New Organization Structure

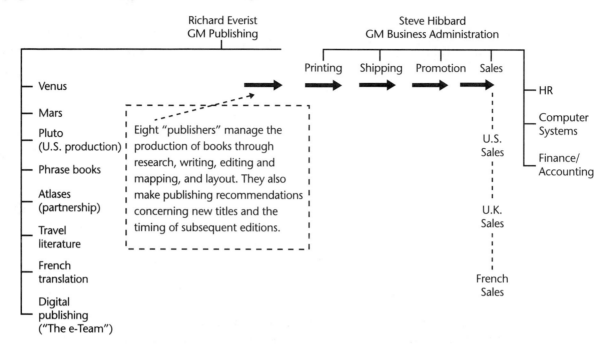

Tony, Maureen, and Jim expressed skepticism about the restructuring. Steve had to first convince them, and deal with their concerns about "too much bureaucracy and extra layers in the organization." Steve had to be careful to avoid "technical" language and to use a commonsense approach. Frequent use of the whiteboard earned him the title "The Whiteboard Kid." No whiteboards existed at Lonely Planet before Steve ordered one.

The new structure took about six months to be implemented, with a lot of consultation—too much, in Maureen's opinion. A lot of sorting out of relationships in Richard Everist's areas was done, and a new Financial Controller was employed. Steve continued to work on making his side of the organization more effective.

The new structure allowed Tony and Jim to step back from the day-to-day running of the business. Tony defined his responsibilities in terms of being an author, quality control ("trying out the books to see if they work"), the public face of the company, and visionary ("what's next").

Management control in Lonely Planet was described by Steve as being "like herding sheep; you come along after the fact and just try to shape the general direction." The United States publishing office was an example of this approach to management control. It was set up without any clear guidelines, and in the early stages experienced its share of problems, but was now up and running beyond anyone's expectations: "Sometimes it is better to get it running and fix it when it comes off the rails, than to try to plan everything."

The installation of a new accounting system to track payments, credits, etc. provided another illustration of the company's approach. Lonely Planet had been quoted $12,000 by a large accounting firm to do a needs analysis. Lonely planet decided just to buy a $20,000 software package and implement the system.

Tony's philosophy of life appeared to be "You often have to learn the hard way."

Future Challenges

One thing the MBA had taught Steve was that changing industry structures, including globalization, could turn competitive advantages into liabilities. He read about changes in the international publishing industry:

> British publishers, faced with a flat market and rising costs, have torn up their cartel. American experience suggests that the main beneficiaries will be consumers, and innovative retailers.
>
> In Britain, the market has stagnated, leading to the death of a 100-year-old price-fixing agreement.
>
> In the 1980s big media groups swooped on the industry across the English-speaking world, believing they could improve on its traditional low margins and genteel inefficiency. In an orgy of consolidation, venerable imprints were swept into big groups such as Rupert Murdoch's HarperCollins or Bertelsmann's Bantam Doubleday Dell.
>
> Not everyone is persuaded that amalgamation has achieved much. "Paradoxically, the editorial aspect of publishing works better as a cottage industry but finance and distribution are better done on a big scale," says Anthony Cheetham who founded Orion, a British house. But in America, bigger, more professionally managed publishers have combined with discount retailers to transform the economics of the industry. There, publishers now make money by selling huge quantities of books at low prices, mostly through big, specialist chains or other large retailers.[2]

Steve, along with others, was concerned that Lonely Planet was being crowded out by increasing competition, and that it was becoming increasingly difficult to "shine through" as the industry changed. Would Lonely Planet be able to continue to compete in the globalizing publishing industry without changing? Steve's dilemma was how he could change Lonely Planet to ensure it could continue to compete in the changing global industry without destroying the essence of its competitive advantage in the process.

Steve was wondering what role the mission statement might play in the change process when Tony Wheeler dropped into his office and said, "Steve, Microsoft wants to come and see us again."

appendix a   Lonely Planet's Products

Travel Guides

These fall into four categories. The main ones are the *Shoestring Guides*, which are targeted specifically at backpackers travelling on a tight budget, and *Travel Survival Kits*, which are the company's general-purpose travel guidebooks to individual countries. The company also produces a *Walking Guide* series covering some of the world's most interesting bushwalking and trekking routes. More recently, Lonely Planet began production of small pocket-sized *City Guides*. These provide in-depth travel coverage to some of the world's most exciting cities. All guides share a common format and down-to-earth writing style which have become the hallmark of the company's products and which have endeared the company to its loyal readership base.

Phrase Books and Audiopacks

Lonely Planet produces pocket-sized phrasebooks for some of the world's less-known languages (e.g., *Thai Hill Tribes Phrasebook*) as well as for some of its more common

---

[2]*Economist*, September 30, 1995.

ones. Language audiopacks (on cassette or CD) complement its phrasebook series, offering a fun and practical way of learning a foreign language.

Travel Atlases

The company recently began production of travel atlases. These are produced for some of the most remote regions in the world, regions for which good roadmaps are generally nonexistent.

Multimedia Applications

The company has recently developed a fully functioning Internet site which has quickly become one of Australia's largest sites. It is also considering other multimedia applications such as compact disc technology and fax-back services.

appendix b   Critical Acclaim, Awards, etc.

1982

- Australian Export Award
- Victorian Small Business Award
- Winner, Thomas Cook Award for Best Guidebook of the Year (*India: A Travel Survival Kit*)

1984

- Finalist, Thomas Cook Award for Best Guidebook of the Year (*Thailand: A Travel Survival Kit*)

1986

- Australian Export Award
- Runner-up, Lowell Thomas Award for Travel Journalism (*Fiji: A Travel Survival Kit*)

1991

- Finalist, Thomas Cook Award for Best Guidebook of the Year (*Vietnam, Laos, and Cambodia*)
- Grand Award Winner, Pacific Asia Travel Association Award for Best Guidebook (*Islands of Australia's Great Barrier Reef*)
- Nominated, European Book Awards (*India: A Travel Survival Kit*)
- Finalist, Ben Franklin Award USA (*Islands of Australia's Great Barrier Reef*)
- First Runner-up, SATW Lowell Thomas Award for Travel Journalism (*La Ruta Maya: Yucatán, Guatemala, and Belize*)
- Special Commendation, Reference Review Awards, Best Specialist Reference Work (*Nepal*)

1992–93

- Victorian State Winner, Australian British Chamber of Commerce Small Business Award for Export Growth, Initiative and Innovation
- Gold Medal Winner, SATW Lowell Thomas Award for Travel Journalism (*Costa Rica*)

1994

- Business Review Weekly, Top 100 Fastest-Growing Private Companies (*Lonely Planet ranked number 67*)
- Silver Medal Winner, Best Guidebook, SATW Lowell Thomas Award for Travel Journalism (*Guatemala, Belize, and Yukatán*)

1995

- Gold Award, Pacific Asia Travel Association Award for Best Guidebook (*Outback Australia*)

case 31 Jonathon Elderslie and the Board Decision

After 30 years in business—the last seven as the president of a division of a large, public company in the agribusiness field—Jonathon Elderslie had enjoyed his first summer of retirement. He played golf five times a week, did some long-needed repairs to his boathouse at the cottage, and even caught up with a reading list that had simply grown too long after so many years of doing, doing, doing.

Now, however, as the shorter, fall days arrived, Elderslie started to think about what he wanted to do over the next few years. He'd made enough to retire on: those options that had been granted at various stages during his business career had amounted to a tidy lump sum; he'd been slowly cashing in his options and diversifying his portfolio for about 10 years, and he and his wife Barbara would be comfortably off, no matter how long they lived. The kids were launched in their careers and, while he hoped that he would have a good estate to leave to them, they could also fend for themselves.

A CONVERSATION WITH A FRIEND

Several people had approached Elderslie over the last few years to ask him to sit on corporate boards. He'd never seriously considered it; after all, it took him all of his waking hours to be the president of his own division of his own company . . . how on earth others were able to combine being a chief executive officer (CEO) with being an active board member he had no idea!

Jerome Haskins, one of Elderslie's acquaintances commented,

> But it only takes a few hours every two to three months. The largest board I'm on meets for one day, seven times a year; add a few teleconferences to that, maybe a two-day retreat

Professor Jeffrey Gandz prepared this case solely to provide material for class discussion. The author does not intend to illustrate either effective or ineffective handling of a managerial situation. The author may have disguised certain names and other identifying information to protect confidentiality.

Copyright © 2002, Ivey Management Services Version: (A) 2003-09-02

every three years, an hour or so every now and then giving some advice to the CEO, and that's about it.

"But how about preparation?" Elderslie had asked. "I mean, doesn't it take forever to go through all that material?"

Haskins replied,

Not really, almost all of the boards I sit on have got really slick systems. A couple of days before the meetings, they send me out a Board-Book. The best of these are really great. All of the data and the issues are well summarized in an easy-to-digest format. I usually look at it on the trip to the meeting; it takes only an hour or so. Then there are additional presentations at the meetings, but these are usually very well put together and well rehearsed so as not to waste too much of the directors' time.

There is more work if you are on one of the committees but, with the exception of the Audit Committee, it's not very time consuming. For example, the major board on which I sit has an Environment and Safety Committee that meets three times a year, usually for a couple of hours, and a Human Resources and Compensation Committee (HRCC) that meets four times a year, also for a couple of hours.

"What happens on those committees?" asked Elderslie.

Haskins replied,

Oh, the same kind of thing. The board committee gets reports from management about things like accidents that have taken place, safety audits, accidental emissions from plants, and so on. Or, in the case of the HRCC, it is mainly to approve option grants or executive bonus arrangements.

"So, what real good is the board doing?" asked Elderslie. Haskins looked quite offended, but responded,

A great deal, knowing that they have to report to the board really gets management to think carefully about the issues on which they are reporting. They want to put their best feet forward . . . make an impression. And a good, experienced board member can look at the information provided, listen to presentations and spot any weaknesses that are there.

As he listened to Haskins, Elderslie thought about his own experiences with the board of the company from which he had just retired. His boss—the CEO—had also been the chairman. He had decided on the agenda and told all of his divisional people what he wanted to prepare for the board meetings. They had rehearsed presentations a few days before, made them, answered some pretty easy questions . . . and that had been that. Sometimes the questions had been tough, as one might expect from experienced lawyers, accountants and former CEOs. But Elderslie could not remember one occasion when he'd been asked something that was not expected and for which he was not prepared.

As he thought more, Elderslie also realized that his boss—the chairman and CEO—had also hand-picked the directors, certainly the half-dozen who had joined the board after he became chairman. Sure, there was a nominating committee, but he sensed that the CEO had a pretty strong role in selecting candidates for the nominating committee to consider.

"So, what do you get out of the experience?" he asked Haskins.

Haskins commented,

Well, it's not the money! The pay is pitiful and no one would do it for that alone. The norm for a board member is about $35,000 per year retainer and, maybe, $1,000 to $1,500 per meeting. So maybe $50,000 a year, all told.

It's more a matter of recognition and prestige. You get to mix with some pretty interesting people and it's a way of staying in touch with what's going on in a business after you're no longer involved in running it. Also, while there are restrictions on when you can trade and on not using privileged information, being a board member gives you excellent insights into a company and you should be able to benefit, perfectly legally, from owning or not owning its stock.

SOME CONCERNS

Some weeks passed before Elderslie settled down to think again about becoming a board member. He'd been collecting material on governance, and what he had did not amount to an attractive package. Enron had collapsed amid rumors of fraudulent and unethical behaviors by top management, apparently either unnoticed or approved of by a board that, by any standards, seemed to consist of outstanding business leaders; Arthur Andersen, Enron's auditor and one of the "Big 5" U.S. accounting firms had collapsed. Worldcom had admitted to several billion dollars of accounting fraud that had, once more, appeared to go unnoticed by the board.

Closer to home, the board of Hydro One had either been fired or had resigned in the wake of scandals surrounding the salary and benefits package of its CEO as well as a failed initial public offering (IPO) blocked by a court order challenging its legality. Former directors of YBM Magnex—including a provincial premier—had been ordered to appear in front of the Ontario Securities Commission to answer questions about the collapse of that company and the involvement of the Russian mafia. As well, one of the most prestigious corporate boards in Canada had come under intense criticism in the media over the bankruptcy of Dylex. Class action suits were flying around all over the place, and many of these claims would tie up directors and officers of companies in the courts and in front of regulatory agencies for years to come.

Martha Stewart's empire was teetering on the brink of collapse after her alleged (but as yet unproven) involvement in an insider trading situation. Several corporate leaders from companies such as Tyco and Adelphia Communications were being accused of looting their corporate treasuries for personal gain. All this had caused the Federal Reserve Board to state that:

> The softening in the growth of aggregate demand that emerged this spring has been prolonged in large measure by weakness in financial markets and heightened uncertainty related to problems in corporate reporting and governance.

The companies involved were not confined to the "new economy." Merrill Lynch had already settled lawsuits in New York emanating from recommendations made by its analysts to buy stocks that they considered to be "crap." Ongoing investigations in New York and elsewhere, involving firms such as Morgan Stanley, Citigroup and others, centred on conflicts of interest between investment banking and brokerage as well as those companies' involvement and complicity in schemes to assist clients with financial engineering designed to obfuscate or misrepresent the true nature of their financial states.

Legislation had been rushed through congress and the legislative branch in the United States requiring CEOs and chief financial officer (CFOs) to attest to the validity and veracity of financial results and increasing by huge amounts the penalties for corporate fraud. Canadian authorities were also toughening up standards of accounting, hoping to cut off some of the more egregious uses of discretion in corporate accounting in

Canada. Reports from regulatory agencies, stock exchanges and advisory bodies in the United States, the United Kingdom, Canada and Europe all seemed to be addressing some of the more obvious shortcomings in corporate governance. Maybe this would be a good time to get involved as a director!

Set against all of the stories coming out of the United States, and the spectacle of "perp-walks" on nightly newscasts, there were those such as Mathew Ingram (a respected columnist from the Globe and Mail), who seemed to suggest that most of this was narrowly confined to a few bad actors and was not, in any way, a condemnation of the whole system of business. But, as Elderslie thought,

> How would I even know if these bad actors were at work in a company of which I was a director? After all, the directors of Enron, Worldcom, Dylex and YBM Magna seemed to be taken by surprise. Couldn't that happen to me?

A DECISION

All of this was swirling around in Elderslie's head when the telephone rang. His friend, Jerome Haskins, wanted to know if he was interested in joining a board on which Haskins served. If so, he'd like Elderslie to get together with the CEO and chairman (different people) for lunch the following week. "Should I be interested?" thought Elderslie. "And if I were interested, what questions should I ask before agreeing to join the board?"

case 32 CCL Industries Inc.: Building and Maintaining an Effective Board

"I have to work harder to ensure stakeholders don't think of CCL as a 'controlled' company. As CEO, I am accountable for the outcome of our decisions, not the board."

Donald Lang reflected on the relationship between himself, president and chief executive officer (CEO) of CCL Industries Inc. (CCL), and the CCL board of directors. CCL had recently undertaken a major change in strategy when the planned and publicly announced sale of one of CCL's major divisions was abruptly cancelled.

"We had specific conditions and they ultimately were not met, so I decided to cancel the deal. I then had to explain the rationale to the board." Fortunately for Lang, he and the CCL board had an excellent and effective working relationship. It was not always this way. In the past, the CCL board was much less involved and less effective. Through hard work, the CEO/board team was on pace to meet its goal of being the world's premier packager of consumer products by 2005. In order to ensure this goal was attained, Lang and the board felt that there were issues that needed to be addressed to further the improvements they had made over the years.

CCL INDUSTRIES INC.

CCL was founded in 1951 by Stuart Lang Sr., his brother and Stuart's two sons, Gordon and Jim.[1] It was Gordon, however, who built CCL into the preeminent aerosol, custom manufacturing, rigid packaging and labeling business in North America. Fifty

Trevor Hunter prepared this case under the supervision of Professor Larry Tapp solely to provide material for class discussion. The authors do not intend to illustrate either effective or ineffective handling of a managerial situation. The authors may have disguised certain names and other identifying information to protect confidentiality.

Copyright © 2002, Ivey Management Services   Version: (A) 2003-01-09

[1]For a comprehensive history of CCL Industries, see D.B. Davies, *Magic in the Mist: The exciting and improbable saga of CCL Industries 1951-2001*, CCL Industries Inc., 2001.

years after its founding, sales topped (see Exhibit 1) $1.6 billion, and CCL employed 7,500 people around the world.

CCL was originally named Connecticut Chemicals Limited and originated as a joint venture with an American company. Under the leadership of Gordon Lang, Conn-Chem (as it was more widely known in the early days) eventually outgrew its American parent and repatriated the balance of the equity it didn't own.

Through a number of acquisitions, the lines of business expanded beyond aerosols. To reflect this change of direction, the company's name was further shortened to CCL Industries Inc. in 1980.

Essentially an outsourcer to major packaged goods and consumer products firms, CCL produced some of the best-known name brands in the world, yet was largely unknown to the general public. The company produced its various products in close association with its customers and was divided into four divisions:[2]

1. CCL Custom Manufacturing—was the largest contract manufacturer of outsourced consumer products in North America and the United Kingdom. Products included some of the best-known brand names in the world for personal care, household, over-the-counter (OTC) pharmaceutical, oral care and specialty food products.

2. CCL Container—provided packaging solutions to the major global consumer products manufacturers from locations in North and Central America. Products included aluminium aerosol containers, tubes and jars.

3. CCL Plastic Packaging—from operations in the United States, this division produced plastic tubes, tamper-evident closures, dispensing closures, lined closures and jars.

4. CCL Label—was the largest North American printer of identification and information labels (paper and film pressure sensitive), with plants located in the United States, Canada, Europe, Mexico and Puerto Rico.

CCL first went public in 1972. Its shares consistently performed well on the Toronto Stock Exchange (TSE) until the 1976 "ozone scare." Reports issued by the Environmental Protection Agency (EPA) and the Food and Drug Administration (FDA) had suggested that chloro-fluorocarbons (CFCs), the propellant in aerosol cans, lead to depletion of the earth's ozone layer. These reports seriously injured the global aerosol market. By this time, CCL had both diversified its product line (sufficiently that a decrease in aerosol sales did not cripple the firm) and converted away from use of CFCs (which were ultimately banned in the United States in 1978 and in Canada in 1979). Nevertheless, the "ozone scare" significantly depressed CCL's share price.

Sensing an opportunity, management repurchased all outstanding shares and took CCL private. The firm went public again in 1980 and has remained public since then.

DONALD LANG

Although he was the son of the man who built CCL, Donald Lang was not automatically given the job of president and CEO.

After graduating from the HBA program at the Richard Ivey School of Business (formerly Western Business School), Lang worked at Nabisco Canada for two years.

---

[2]This information was taken from the CCL Web site, www.cclind.com.

He knew that he wanted to eventually work at CCL, but felt it was important to gain some management experience in a larger, more formalized organization prior to joining CCL Industries.

He entered the business in a plant operations role in 1982. By 1993, he had been appointed president of CCL Custom Manufacturing and later, president and chief operating officer (COO) of CCL. Finally, he became CEO in 1999. Although by 2002 he had held the top management position in CCL for only three years, he had been involved with the corporation's governance as a member of the board of directors since 1991.

During his time as a board member, Lang had been considered a catalyst for change. He had often not agreed with the processes or extent of involvement of the CCL board. He had been only a minority voice, however, and was unable to effect change. When Lang wrote a letter that suggested he might resign from the board should change not be forthcoming, the board responded by agreeing to some initial modifications.

THE CCL BOARD

From its incorporation, CCL has had only three board chairs. The first was Gordon Lang. In discussion with the board, a succession plan was developed whereby he would step down from his position but would be recognized for his contributions with the new title, founder chairman. The chairman title and corresponding responsibilities were appointed to the then-current president and CEO, a longtime senior CCL manager. In 1999, the first independent board chair, Jon Grant, was appointed (see Exhibit 2).

In the heyday of CCL's rapid growth in the 1960s and 1980s, the board could arguably have been characterized as a rubber stamp to management. The senior management of CCL was composed of longtime employees who had been hired by Gordon Lang and had worked their way up the ladder through hard work. There was no doubt that they were exceedingly hard-working and competent, but decisions were made with the expectation that once made, they would have to be approved by the board.

A quote from Edward W. Dobson, former executive vice-president and chief administrative officer and one of the builders of CCL, illustrates this point well. "We didn't have time for regular meetings, memos, reports or a rigid management structure. We just talked about it, made a decision and did it."[3]

Donald Lang recalls:

> After we went public we were trying to make the bridge to a public structure but we still clung to our past. We brought in outside directors, but we were still only providing a rubber stamp. The firm's managers were not being held accountable for their actions. Then we had U.S. directors who were getting frustrated with the situation and pushed for a change. I was in a better position as COO and together we were able to make the necessary changes.

It was Donald Lang who ultimately instigated a formal evolution of the board, including a change in the nominating and governance committee chairman, the hiring of a search company for new directors and a succession plan for his father to retire as chairman with the long-term plan of separating the chairman and CEO roles.

---

[3]Quoted in D.B. Davies, *Magic in the Mist: The exciting and improbable saga of CCL Industries 1951–2001*, CCL Industries Inc., 2001, pg. 49.

Lang commented, "Unfortunately business performance has to get pretty bad before the board is compelled to take any action against a CEO. When I was appointed CEO, I wanted to make sure the CEO was held accountable to the board." The separation of the CEO and chairman roles was advocated by Lang, even though he was the incoming CEO.

The focus on accountability went beyond management however. In 1994, the board itself decided to bring in a consultant to assist in a board self-evaluation. The purpose of the evaluation was to improve the process and contribution the board made to the operations of CCL to ensure it was acting as more than a rubber stamp. Three annual evaluations followed until 1997, when they were stopped. Lang suggested that the evaluations were both not welcomed by the board members and had received negative feedback:

> During that time (i.e., the period between 1994 and 1997) the company's strategy lacked focus. There was a need for the board to work better together and to be more aligned. They were not interested in being evaluated when there were other issues that were considered a higher priority.

Lang was convinced that self-evaluation was critical to the success of the board as an effective group. "The intention (of the evaluations) was good, but the execution was wrong. We needed to find a better way to make them a priority and make them work," said Lang. A new evaluation process was introduced in 2000 that received more positive feedback. The addition of new directors, with differing opinions than those on the board from 1994 to 1997, helped improve the reception and effectiveness of the evaluations.

In order to give structure to CCL's governance policies, a document titled "Statement of Governance Policies of the Board of Directors of CCL Industries Inc." was prepared in 1994. This document was updated regularly and was given to every current and new director. Its purpose was to:

> Set forth the mandates and principles adopted by the board of directors of CCL Industries Inc. for the good stewardship of the company. It is intended as guidance for the board, for each director and for the committees of the board in the exercise of their respective responsibilities in the governance of the company.

The document contained policies on the following:

- The mandate of the board as a whole,
- The mandates of the audit, human resources, nominating and governance, and environment and occupational health and safety committees,
- The composition of the board,
  - Related and unrelated directors
  - The role of the chair
  - The composition of committees
- The role of a director,
  - Access to management and independent counsel
- New directors,
  - Criteria for new director selection
  - Orientation and training for new directors
- Duties of the president and CEO,
- Performance assessment procedure for the president and CEO,

- Proceedings and meetings,
  - Meeting procedures
  - Information

The following is a list of some of the specific activities undertaken by the board that Lang felt significantly improved the performance of the board after his appointment as CEO in 1999:

1. The appointment of a non-executive board chair. Aside from the skills and experience Board Chair Jon Grant brought to the position, the fact that there was independence at the top allowed for constructive challenging of the CEO and other senior executives that pushed for performance, clarity and accountability.

2. Grant, like Lang, was interested in bringing in more unrelated directors to further enhance the independence of the board. Members were selected strategically. The contribution and skill set each potential member could bring and how each prospect could help improve CCL's performance were heavily considered.

3. On average, Lang expected that directors should spend one day's worth of preparation briefing themselves on the materials the corporation sent them one week in advance of meetings for each four-hour board meeting, aside from their additional roles on the various committees.

4. Board committees were chaired by outside directors with functional executives acting as secretaries. There was thus more direct contact between board members and other senior executives. Senior executives were also required to make presentations to the board on topics of business plans. This gave the board more freedom to critique their strategies directly and assess the ability of the senior executives the CEO had hired and promoted.

5. A two-day board member retreat entirely devoted to strategic planning was instituted. Day one involved presentations from the divisional presidents that included an exchange of ideas and opinions. Day two was reserved for the board and the CEO only. The CEO was challenged and pushed, while at the same time, the experience and skills of the board members were leveraged.

6. One board meeting per year would be held at one of the manufacturing sites as an opportunity to better understand the business details.

7. One half-hour was set aside at every meeting for the board to meet without the CEO present. This time allowed for frank discussion on such issues as CEO performance, compensation, evaluation or any other sensitive topic.

8. It was usual for the board members to meet for dinner informally the night preceding the CCL board meeting with, and sometimes without, management, which offered another opportunity for directors to converse and build a stronger relationship.

9. The splitting of the CEO and chair positions was a shift from the way the roles had been conceived and institutionalized at CCL in the past. There was frequent contact between Lang and Grant, and a good working relationship was fostered. Lang was accountable to Grant, but while Lang often consulted Grant, decisions were made by Lang. As a non-executive chair, Grant was an "outsider." Although the two worked together closely, Lang ran the business.

10. Board agendas were very detailed and included:
    - Scheduled time for outside directors' discussions
    - General background information

- Consent agenda items;
  – Items that could be approved with one motion, past board minutes, for example,
- Committee reports
- Operations update

All pertinent information was included in advance briefing books, including a summary of the resolutions to be proposed.

11. The amount and type of documentation directors received was revamped. Agendas were set one month before the meeting, and materials were delivered to directors no less than one week before the meeting. If an item missed the agenda, it had to be held for the next meeting (emergencies excepted). Thus, senior executives that wanted something on the board agenda had to be sure that their timing was on schedule. Meetings were scheduled on a two-year rotating basis to ensure full attendance. There was a conscious attempt to strike a balance between providing too much detail (thus overwhelming the directors) and too little information.

These and other measures had led many of the directors to feel that the CCL board was one of the most effective on which they had served.

MOVING FORWARD

Although the CCL board and Lang had made an effective team and understood and fulfilled their roles with accountability, there were still issues that needed improvement. The latest board evaluation had resulted in some concerns that needed to be addressed.[4]

Three main areas in which the board could be strengthened emerged from the evaluation: the strategic planning process, succession planning and board composition.

Strategic Planning

While the directors noted that this process had improved over the years and that the value of the two-day retreat was clear, they felt that more of their time should be spent on reviewing strategic opportunities and risks, and the plans for execution, rather than management reports. There was concern over a lack of clarity and direction on the part of the board. While unanimity was not the goal, greater consensus was desired. Concerns as to how to reach a consensus in a timely and effective manner were raised. The directors felt that in order to effectively aid in the strategic planning process they needed to be involved in the process on a more regular basis. The content, amount and timing of the information they received regarding strategic planning needed to be reviewed. Did they need more information? Should they meet more often? Who should be at the meetings? What sort of information should they receive? These questions needed to be addressed.

Succession Planning

Nearly all the directors felt that more time needed to be spent on the issue of succession planning. Many felt that this issue was often considered secondary, which is why it had not been given its due attention. An annual discussion regarding potential

---

[4]This information is drawn from a report prepared by Patrick O'Callaghan & Associates for CCL Industries Inc.

successor candidates for all senior positions was suggested. The discussion would center on their readiness, development plans, retention risk and compensation.

Another issue of key personnel involved a lack of clarity of the role of the board's HR committee and the degree of support the committee received. The HR committee saw part of its role as challenging the CEO on whether the senior executives were not only experts in their area, but also strategic thinkers and could take work off the desk of the CEO. This followed the philosophy of CCL founder Gordon Lang who said "I hired good people and then got out of their way. I had no time to constantly look over people's shoulders or question their every decision."[5] Perhaps the content of the annual reviews needed to be changed. Perhaps the HR committee needed a broader scope for potential candidates.

A further important issue that needed attention was the development of an emergency plan in case of an accident involving the CEO or other senior executives.

Board Composition

Although the majority of board members was composed of "outside and non-related" directors, there was a concern regarding the skills and experience that were needed at the board level to assist with strategic planning in the coming years. Criteria for future directors included:

- U.S. or international background (with a concern regarding the logistics problem for international directors)
- Experience in corporate finance and mergers and acquisitions
- Information technology experience
- A current CEO of a significant-sized public corporation operating internationally
- Human resources experience

Although the board was always looking for the best candidate, there was a clear recognition of the lack of women and visible minorities at the board level. While not looking to fulfill a quota, there was a desire to break away from the "white male" stereotype characteristics of many boards.

THE CURRENT SITUATION

After the change in strategy, Lang recognized the need and potential for greater board involvement in the strategic activities of CCL. As this sort of activity could be the norm in the future, the need for flexible, nimble strategic planning, along with informed governance, would only increase in the face of competition and global uncertainty.

In 2002, CCL operated in nine countries around the world. There was a global economic slowdown and decreased consumer confidence. The effects of the terrorists' attacks on September 11 had further exacerbated the poor economic conditions. Acquisitions and divestitures, keys to CCL's growth strategy, would be difficult in the coming years, particularly in new markets around the world.

The challenge was to develop and execute strategy and appropriately develop and leverage the skills and experience of the board. Clearly, the board was working well

---

[5]Quote taken from in D.B. Davies, *Magic in the Mist: The exciting and improbable saga of CCL Industries 1951–2001*, CCL Industries Inc., 2001, Prologue.

now; however, there were issues regarding strategic planning, succession planning and composition that needed to be addressed if it was going to fulfill its role as steward in the future business environment facing CCL. Making changes to the board as an anticipatory change tended to be difficult, especially when the change affected something that was working well. What needed to be done to increase the involvement of the board? How could the board's concerns be handled? Was it time to update or overhaul CCL's governance policies? There was a fine line between governing and running the firm; and neither Lang, nor Grant, wanted to cross that line.

The Richard Ivey School of Business gratefully acknowledges the generous support of CCL Industries Inc. in the development of these learning materials.

exhibit 1   Selected Financial Data from the CCL 2001 Annual Report for Years Ending 2000 and 2001(in thousands of dollars except for per-share data)

	2001	2000
Sales	1,600,497	1,589,087
EBITDA	159,879	183,295
Depreciation, amortization of other assets	73,439	75,351
Interest	32,415	36,560
Income from operations before unusual items, income tax and goodwill amortization	54,025	71,384
Unusual item (net)	7,684	18,776
Earnings before income taxes and goodwill amortization	46,341	52,608
Income taxes	7,993	13,156
Earnings before goodwill amortization	38,348	39,452
Goodwill amortization, net of tax	13,457	12,798
Net earnings	24,891	26,654
Per class B share		
Earnings before goodwill amortization	1.08	1.04
Earnings before unusual item	0.83	1.10
Net earnings	0.70	0.70
Cash flow before unusual item	3.39	3.47
At year end		
Total assets	1,454,991	1,392,820
Net debt	435,755	486,139
Shareholders' equity	563,704	558,201
Net debt to equity ratio	0.77	0.87
Return on average equity	4.4%	4.7%
Net debt-to-total capitalization	43.6%	46.5%
Book value per share	16.52	15.22

exhibit 2   Profile of CCL Industries Inc. Board of Directors

Jon Grant – Chairman of the Board of CCL Industries Inc.

Chairman of the board of the Laurentian Bank of Canada and former chairman of Canada Lands Company Limited and a director of CCL since 1994. Former chairman and CEO of the Quaker Oats Company of Canada Limited, former chairman of Scott Paper Limited and former chairman of the board of governors of Trent University. Mr. Grant is also a director of AXA Pacific Insurance Company. He is currently chairman of the Ontario Board of the Nature Conservancy of Canada.

Donald G. Lang – President and CEO, CCL Industries Inc.

CEO of CCL Industries since June 1999 in addition to his previous role as president. Mr. Lang was appointed president and chief operating officer of CCL in April 1998. Prior to his appointment as COO, he was president of the company's largest division, CCL Custom Manufacturing. Mr. Lang has served on CCL's Board of Directors since 1991. Additionally, he is a member of the Advisory Committee at the Richard Ivey School of Business. Mr. Lang holds an Honours Bachelor of Arts degree from the Richard Ivey School of Business, University of Western Ontario.

Stuart W. Lang – President of CCL Label International

Mr. Lang has held progressively senior positions throughout the Custom and Label Manufacturing divisions in Canada, Mexico and Europe since joining the company in 1982, and has served as a director of CCL Industries since 1991. Mr. Lang has a BSc in Chemical Engineering from Queen's University. Prior to this he played for the CFL's Edmonton Eskimos for eight years.

Paul J. Block

Chairman and CEO of Proteus Capital Associates. Previously, Mr. Block was chairman and president of Revlon International. Mr. Block is a board member of the China Retail Fund and the Shanghai-Syracuse University International School of Business. He is also a member of the Advisory Board of the Syracuse University School of Management. Mr. Block has served as a director of CCL since 1997.

Dermot G. Coughlan

Former chairman and chief executive officer of Derlan Industries Limited. A director of CCL Industries Inc. since 1991, Mr. Coughlan is also a director of Mackenzie Financial Corporation and chairman of a number of North American and international manufacturing companies.

Stephan J. Friedman

Senior partner with the international law firm of Debevoise & Plimpton. Mr. Friedman was previously executive vice president and general counsel of the Equitable Companies Inc. He served as commissioner of the Securities and Exchange Commission and as deputy assistant secretary of the Treasury for Capital Markets Policy. Mr. Friedman also serves on the boards of the American Ballet Theatre, the Practising Law Institute and the United Way of New York City.

Albert Gnat

Partner at Lang Michener, a Toronto law firm. A director of CCL since 1973, Mr. Gnat also serves on the boards of CamVec Corporation, GEAC Computer Corporation Limited, Leitch Technology Corporation, IKEA Limited, MDC Corporation, Rogers Communication and Vitran Corporation.

Jean-René Halde

President and chief executive officer of Irwin Toys and was president and CEO of Livgroup Investments which succeeded Livingston Group where he was president and CEO from 1995–2000. Prior to this he served as president and CEO to Culinar Inc. Mr. Halde's other directorships include the boards of Bracknell Corporation and the Institute of Corporate Directors.

Lawrence G. Tapp

Dean of the Richard Ivey School of Business since 1995. He also served as executive-in-residence and adjunct professor, Faculty of Business, University of Toronto from 1993–1995, vice chairman, president and CEO of Lawson Mardon Group Ltd. (a packaging conglomerate) from 1985–1992. He has served as a director of CCL since 1994.

Source: CCL Industries Inc. Web site, http://www.cclind.com/corp_profile_directors_bio.html.

case 33 Western Area Youth Services

Brenda Hall, executive director of Western Area Youth Services (WAYS), sat in her office pondering the case of "deja vu" she was experiencing. At its September 2000 meeting, the board of directors spent a great deal of time discussing the implications of a significant potential liability for staff salaries. A merger was identified as a possible solution, and Hall was instructed by the board to begin the process of seeking a possible merger partner for the agency. It didn't seem that long ago that Hall had been through the merger that had created WAYS, a children's mental health centre located in London, Ontario. Hall wondered how she might initiate the process on behalf of her board and what she should be looking for in a potential partner. She also wondered how a merger might benefit the agency at this point in time.

THE CMHO AND THE STATE OF CHILDREN'S MENTAL HEALTH

The Children's Mental Health Organization (CMHO) was established in 1972 as a member organization to promote the mental health and well-being of children and youth and their families in Ontario. Its member organizations served children and youth from birth to age 18. The organization's primary goals were to promote service excellence and innovation in its member organizations through accreditation, and to advocate for policies, programs and funds to improve the state of children's mental health. According to CMHO, about 500,000 children in Ontario, about 18 per cent of Ontario's children, had psychiatric disorders in 1999. It's 90 member organizations served over 120,000 children with extremely high levels of emotional disorder. Another 7,000 children were on waiting lists for services, with an average wait time of six

Mary Heisz prepared this case to provide material for class discussion. The author does not intend to illustrate either effective or ineffective handling of a managerial situation. The authors may have disguised certain names and other identifying information to protect confidentiality.

Ivey Management Services prohibits any form of reproduction, storage or transmittal without its written permission. This material is not covered under authorization from CanCopy or any reproduction rights organization. To order copies or request permission to reproduce materials, contact Ivey Publishing, Ivey Management Services, c/o Richard Ivey School of Business, The University of Western Ontario, London, Ontario, Canada, N6A 3K7; phone (519) 661-3208; fax (519) 661-3882; e-mail cases@ivey.uwo.ca.

Richard Ivey School of Business
The University of Western Ontario

months. The average annual cost of service in a children's mental health centre was Cdn$2,500 per child. In the 1995 to 2000 time period, government funding to children's mental health centres was cut by eight per cent, while the number of children served increased by 75 per cent. At the same time, children's mental health issues became more extreme; for example, the rate of youth suicide increased 400 per cent from the 1970s. CMHO believed that the treatment programs of its member organizations worked. Data collected by the organization between April 1991 and June 1995, showed that treatment in children's mental health centres was associated with a reduction in aggression, violence, opposition to authority and hyperactivity; a reduction in severe anxiety, worry, depression and low self-esteem; and a reduction in poor social relations, both at home and at school. According to CMHO, Ontario's future depended on its government making children's mental health a priority, both through its policies and its funding decisions.

WESTERN AREA YOUTH SERVICES

WAYS was formed in July 1996, as a result of the amalgamation of three agencies—Belton House, Hardy Geddes House and Mission Services of London's Teen Girl's Home. WAYS was incorporated under the Canada Corporations Act as a not-for-profit organization and was a registered charity under the Canadian Income Tax Act. It was also a member of CMHO. Brenda Hall was the executive director of Belton House at the time of the amalgamation, and she recalled that the process of merging the three agencies was a difficult and, at times, acrimonious process for board members and staff alike. In July 1995, the chairperson of each agency's board of directors received a letter from their primary funder, the Ontario Ministry of Community and Social Services (MCSS), notifying them that as a result of recent community planning, it was MCSS's intent to be "working with one administrative structure for the services" provided by their agencies before the end of the next fiscal year, March 31, 1996. Hall recalled the frustration felt by her board members at the ambiguity of the direction and MCSS's unwillingness to provide any further direction other than its intent to reduce the budgets of each of the three agencies by 10 to 15 per cent for the next fiscal year. Shortly after receiving the letter, the three agencies, each represented by the executive director, the board chairperson and one other board member, began meeting on a weekly basis to plan. The chairperson of the meeting was rotated weekly from among the executive directors of the three agencies. It quickly became clear that each board had a different interpretation of the funder's direction. One agency believed that MCSS was looking for a more collaborative effort but separate agencies. Another agency believed that MCSS was looking for a new administrative agency overseeing the existing three agencies. The third agency believed that MCSS was looking for a complete merger of the existing agencies. What became even clearer, however, was the significant amount of difference in the three organization's cultures and philosophies.

Belton House, Hardy Geddes House and Mission Services of London's Teen Girl's Home program were all established in the early 1970s, with their main purpose to provide residential services to adolescents in the community. Each agency was managed by an executive director who reported to a volunteer board of directors. Belton House provided services to young women aged 12 through 18. Its programs were strictly voluntary, and the agency was highly regarded in the community for its innovativeness and willingness to work with other community service providers. Hardy Geddes House provided services to young men aged 12 through 18. Its programs were also strictly voluntary, but were often seen in the community as rather selective. Mission Services of London was a large social service agency in London with a Christian focus that pervaded its mission statement, philosophies and operations. Teen Girl's Home was only one of Mission Service's many, varied programs. Teen Girl's Home provided services to young women as well, but focused primarily on a younger age group than did Belton House. Its programs were similar to Belton House but were carried out with a Christian influence. Other programs run by Mission Services included shelters for homeless men and women, addiction support programs and a second-hand clothing store.

The months of July and August 1995 were marked with little progress and significant tension for the committee. Heated debates took place in the group over the necessity of and funding for a facilitator. One group announced its wish to "take over" the other two agencies. The individual boards refused to fund any expenditures relating to the efforts of the committee. Finally, a facilitator was agreed upon, and Dr. William Avison, a well-known and highly respected expert in children's services, was hired, with Cdn$10,000 in funding provided by MCSS. Dr. Avison's strategy was to focus the group on the selection of an administrative structure, and he suggested five possibilities, including: maintaining the status quo; absorption by a fourth, outside agency; merging two of the agencies into the third; amalgamating the three agencies to form a new agency; and forming a consortium for administrative purposes only, while maintaining separate programs and boards. The committee members quickly eliminated the first two possibilities as unacceptable to their funder and to the group, respectively. Left with three options, each agency selected a different one as most acceptable. Once again, heated debate, negotiations and side deals took place as Dr. Avison attempted to move the group towards a common choice. Eventually, two of the agencies teamed up and supported the consortium model. The third agency, which was in favor of the amalgamation model, was thereby "out-voted" and in October 1995, the agencies reluctantly presented a signed letter of agreement to MCSS indicating their willingness to move towards a consortium arrangement for administrative services. Two months later MCSS formally responded to the agencies and indicated that the consortium model was not acceptable and that the three agencies were to be fully amalgamated by the summer of 1996. If the boards did not choose to amalgamate, the services provided by the agencies would be tendered out to other community agencies. The boards were given two weeks to consider MCSS's directive, and on December 31, 1995, each board responded in the affirmative and agreed to proceed with an amalgamation.

Once again a committee was struck, the amalgamation steering committee. Two board representatives from each agency were selected, as well as two independent community representatives. MCSS assigned one of its program supervisors to the committee as well as provided funding for a facilitator. This time, executive directors were not included on the committee, as the first tasks handled by the committee involved the selection of an executive director for the amalgamated agency and the consideration of potential severance liabilities for the unsuccessful candidates. After much heated deliberation and community input, Hall, the executive director of Belton House, was chosen to manage the new agency. A new agency name was selected following an employee contest. New corporate bylaws were agreed to, stipulating that the new board would consist of two members from each of the existing agencies and six members chosen from the community. By June 1996, the Public Trustee of Ontario had issued its consent to the amalgamation, and on July 16, 1996, the first board meeting of Western Area Youth Services took place. Hall began the onerous task of integrating three very distinct cultures, employee groups and board members into one agency.

In keeping with its mission statement, WAYS provided residential programs and community services to adolescents and their families in London and the surrounding communities. Though the mental health services provided by WAYS were governed by The Child and Family Services Act (CFSA), they were not considered mandated services and, as a result, were subject to more volatile government (i.e., MCSS) funding. As well, historically, funding for adolescents was viewed by MCSS as less crucial than funding for young children. The primary residential program at WAYS comprised 26 beds in three London locations for male and female adolescents between the ages of 14 and 18. The goal of this program was to provide safe, supported and structured 24-hour residence living. Counselling in this program focused on life skills, social skills and job training. Only a limited amount of psychiatric counselling was provided to youths, due to funding constraints. WAYS also had two four-bed transition homes for youths between the ages of 16 and 24. The transition program's goal was to provide a semi-structured living experience for youth and to assist them in developing skills necessary to live successfully and independently in the community. The program focused on the teaching of social skills, coping skills, life skills and employment-related skills. Finally, the most recent addition to WAYS residential programs was the provision of an eight-bed, fee-for-service program for males aged 12 to 16 under the care of the Children's Aid Society (CAS). These beds were specifically contracted with and paid for by CAS as a result of recent expansions in the number of children requiring care from the CAS. This program's goals were similar to those of the WAYS primary residential program. WAYS community programs focused on prevention by working with youth and their families before, during and after residence. Through its community programs, WAYS assisted youth in accessing other community programs, transitioning to new living environments and improving life skills. Services included therapeutic groups, individual counselling, an after-care program and a follow-up program.

Hall recognized that, although adolescents voluntarily entered the WAYS programs, they were a very difficult and demanding group to work with. Although WAYS did not receive any funding under the Young Offenders Act, 50 per cent of the residents at WAYS were convicted young offenders and were part of the WAYS programs as a result of a legal "order to reside" or a requirement of their probation. Typical WAYS residents had many of the following characteristics: emotional and relationship problems in the home, community and school; oppositional or defiant; aggressive and destructive; problems with depression; witness of violence in their home; alcohol or drug abuse; psychotropic medication user; underachiever at school; diagnosed learning problems.

WAYS was governed by a community-based, volunteer board consisting of 12 directors, some of whom were founding members from the predecessor agencies. Like many volunteer agencies, WAYS often had difficulty filling the available board positions with qualified, dedicated individuals. The day-to-day affairs of the organization were managed by Hall and approximately 85 staff members, 30 of whom were full-time employees. Hall was well respected in the community and by her staff. She was active in several community planning committees and was viewed as an excellent manager. The majority of the staff were college-educated child and youth-care workers (CYCW). Staff-to-client ratios were dictated by government legislation, leaving WAYS with very little flexibility in its spending on wages. The staff group was not unionized and was compensated at a level comparative to other non-union social service organizations in the area. Hall believed that the staff group had very little interest in becoming unionized at this point. Staff safety and burnout were key issues, due to the intense needs of the adolescents served. The management group was relatively small and consisted of two program managers and an administrative officer, all of whom had worked at the agency for several years. Due to the small size of the agency, there was little opportunity for promotion or staff development within the agency. In addition to the board, WAYS had a well-established fundraising committee, which competed with other social service agencies in the community for donors and their dollars. WAYS recently established a charitable foundation to concentrate on fundraising activities; however, the foundation was not very active. Select financial and client statistics for WAYS are presented in Exhibit 1.

MERGER THOUGHTS AT *WAYS*

Hall's thoughts returned to the recent board meeting and the discussion of the potential salary liability. The Pay Equity Act was made law in Ontario on January 1, 1988, to narrow the wage gap that existed between the relative wages earned by women and men. In Ontario, female workers received, on average, 26 per cent less in wages than male workers did. This law intended to address this inequity and to ensure equal pay for work of equal or comparable value. The law required, among other things, comparing the value of jobs traditionally done by women to the value of different jobs traditionally done by men. It then required that compensation (i.e., wages and benefits) be at least the same for jobs performed mainly by women that were equal or comparable in value to jobs performed mainly by men, even if the jobs were quite different.

This legislation had a tremendous impact on the salaries of primarily female organizations such as Belton House, one of the amalgamating agencies in WAYS. Belton House's board was forced to approve a pay equity plan that resulted in its non-unionized employees being paid at rates comparable to those paid by a sizable, unionized London area hospital. On amalgamation, WAYS not only inherited the Belton House pay equity plan but, in order to ensure equitable salaries across the organization, was forced to extend the plan to the entire agency. Although government funding was originally provided to agencies such as WAYS to cover the increased salary expenditures, by 1995, this funding was discontinued, putting agencies such as WAYS in a conundrum. Though WAYS was legally required to enact pay equity, it was not provided with the funding to cover the added expense. As a result, the WAYS board estimated that the organization's unfunded liability for pay equity-related salaries would grow over the next 10 years to almost Cdn$1 million—an amount that would surely bankrupt the agency. WAYS problem was not an exclusive one. Several government-funded social service agencies were in very similar positions and were struggling with how to fund the liability. Different strategies developed. Some agencies chose to ignore pay equity entirely on the premise that the government was essentially ignoring it by refusing to fund it. Other agencies were funding their pay equity liability through their operating budgets, resulting in decreased service provided to the community.

At WAYS, an ad hoc planning committee was struck by the board to address its long-term strategic plan, including the financial issues the agency faced due to pay equity. The committee identified a merger or amalgamation as appealing for two reasons. First, the committee believed that by becoming a larger agency through merger, WAYS would have a stronger political position for advocacy and future negotiations with MCSS. Second, the committee hoped that by merging with a larger agency with higher existing pay scales, the WAYS pay equity plan could be abandoned. However, the committee recognized that this would not be easy to do and would require the agreement of the potential merger partner's union. In considering a merger, the committee believed that there were two possibilities—traditional and non-traditional. A traditional merger was one with an agency that provided similar services to those of WAYS and had similar funding sources. A non-traditional merger was one with an agency that operated in an entirely different business and, as a result, had different funding sources. The committee turned to Hall to more fully develop the pros and cons of a merger and to identify potential partners, both traditional and non-traditional.

Potential Partners

Hall first turned to the task of potential merger partners. Having spent her career working in children's mental health in the London area, Hall was well aware of the other agencies in the area and their executive directors and the culture in which they operated their agency. She made a summary list for the board of what she believed would be viable partners. Included in Hall's list were Madame Vanier Children's Services, The Children's Aid Society of London and Middlesex, The Memorial Boys and Girls Club of London, Anago Resources and Community Homes.

Madame Vanier Children's Services

Madame Vanier Children's Services (Vanier's) received its charter as a children's mental health centre in 1965 and was the first centre to be licensed in 1968 under the Children's Mental Health Act. The centre was a leader in children's services in the Ontario and was accredited by CMHO. Similar to WAYS, the majority of Vanier's funding came from MCSS. Vanier's, operating under the guidance of its mission statement, promoted the emotional and social health of children and their families; provided effective help for complex emotional and behavioral problems; and built on child, family and community strengths. Vanier's offered a full range of programs to children from birth to 16 years of age and their families living in the London area (and the surrounding area for residential services). In September 1999, Vanier's reorganized its system of care in response to an MCSS direction. As a result of this reorganization, more of the agency's resources were focused on fewer, higher needs children. While all children were seen immediately by the agency, those children not considered high risk were diverted to other community agencies.

The agency's services included community-based assessments, counselling and treatment for children and families, early intervention programs for children of preschool to kindergarten age, short- and long-term residential programs and day programs, both at Vanier's and in community schools. Treatment programs included family therapy, parent counselling, individual art and play therapy, group programs and individual counselling. Vanier's had 17 residential treatment beds and seven-day treatment classrooms. In many cases, clients of Vanier's were serviced in their later years by WAYS. Vanier's had a long history of community collaboration and was involved in several joint programs with WAYS, including staff training and client intake and crisis services. Similar to WAYS, Vanier's operated a six-bed, fee-for-service program under contract with CAS.

Vanier's was governed by a 12-member community board and an executive director, Dr. Barrie Evans, and had approximately 90 multidisciplinary staff, composed of child and youth workers, social workers, psychologists, psychiatrists and other professional and support staff. Dr. Evans was particularly well known in the province for his work in advocating for children's mental health and was active in the community as well as with the provincial association, the CMHO. The majority of the staff members were part of the Ontario Public Service Employee Union (OPSEU). Many of Vanier's relief staff were also relief staff at WAYS. Selected financial and client statistics are summarized in Exhibit 2. Hall was very familiar with Vanier's, having worked there herself in her early career, and she knew that the idea of amalgamation was quite appealing to Dr. Evans.

The Children's Aid Society of London and Middlesex

The Children's Aid Society of London and Middlesex was formed in 1893 and was a member of the Ontario Association of Children's Aid Societies (OACAS). The CAS, under the direction of its executive director, John Liston, had a wide variety of programs, including the investigation of allegations of child abuse or neglect; provision of temporary and long-term care through foster homes, group homes and institutions; residential programs; individual and family counselling; family supervision; and adoption. Approximately 95 per cent of the programs offered by CAS were considered mandated programs under the CFSA. For example, child protective services were mandated by the Act and were required by law to be provided at all times; however, certain counselling programs were not mandated under the Act. Similar to WAYS, the CAS received the majority of its funding from MCSS. Mandated services were perceived to have more secure funding (see Exhibit 3). Significant financial pressure due to increased caseloads had recently caused CAS to review its balance of mandated and non-mandated services. CAS estimated that there was a 42 per cent increase in admissions over the 1995 to 2000 period. It was also estimated that 58 per cent of CAS admissions were children under the age of 13, and that these children had greater needs than ever before. Eighty-two per cent of Crown wards (i.e., children the courts have removed from parental custody) had an external diagnosis of special needs; 92 per cent of the children in care were victims of maltreatment such as sexual, physical or emotional abuse or neglect. As a result of increasing caseloads and decreasing resources, CAS was forced to look to outside agencies for additional services. In the year 2000, CAS estimated a 76 per cent increase in the number of children in outside, contracted foster or group homes. WAYS already operated one such contracted group home for adolescent males and was in negotiations with CAS to contract a second group home, this one for adolescent females. CAS was also in the process of contracting out a group home for younger children requiring highly structured care as well as a 12- to 16-bed receiving home for emergency placements. In total, CAS estimated that it contracted 140 beds with outside providers. While Hall understood the pressures that had led CAS to look for contracted group home beds, she also recalled that the same community planning that recommended the merger of smaller agencies such as Belton House had also recommended that CAS discontinue its direct provision of group home services. Hall was also certain that it was less expensive for CAS to purchase rather than provide group home beds from agencies such as WAYS, given the unionized wage rates of CAS. She also knew that CAS offices across Ontario were being pressured to reduce the number of children in group homes and increase the number of children in foster care. They were also being pressured to focus more fully on their basic mandated services, such as child protection and investigation. Hall knew that the board would expect her to consider CAS as a potential merger partner and that there were benefits to WAYS merging with a powerful community agency like the CAS. She also understood that there would be some significant benefits to CAS of an amalgamation and the opportunity to more fully combine child treatment services like WAYS with CAS's own child welfare services. However, Hall was concerned about the long-term implications of combining WAYS non-mandated services with CAS services and CAS's future ability to provide both types of services.

The Memorial Boys and Girls Club of London

The Memorial Boys and Girls Club of London was part of a national organization, Boys and Girls Clubs of Canada, which was founded more than 100 years ago. The national organization had over 100 clubs located in over 150 communities across Canada and served more than 130,000 children and youth. The Clubs boasted safe and caring environments and stimulating programs based on their board's four "cornerstones of healthy development": personal growth and empowerment; learning; community service; and health and safety. Programs such as group homes and emergency shelters, family and parent support and youth-at-risk support were part of the community service tenet of the national organization. Substance abuse programs, suicide prevention and street-proofing were part of the health and safety tenet. Clubs across Canada varied greatly in the types of services provided, and Hall believed that the London-based club did not provide any group home programs and focused on services for children and youth from lower-income families. Boys and Girls Clubs received some funding from governmental agencies such as Health Canada; however, they relied heavily on donations from the United Way, individuals and corporations for survival. The staff at the Boys and Girls Club was not unionized.

Although the board's planning committee had identified the Boys and Girls Club of London as a very attractive potential merger partner, Hall had some concerns about an amalgamation with this agency. In response to her request for information, the executive director, Donald Donner, referred Hall to the national organization's Web site and was unwilling to provide any specific financial or program information for the London-based club. Donner also hinted at his concerns about the stigma attached to children's mental health programs and the effect on his agency's existing programs. He was concerned that his current clientele and funders would discontinue their support of the agency if they believed that the programs were directed to youth with mental health issues. Finally, he indicated that though he would not support an amalgamation with WAYS, he would support the takeover of WAYS and some other children's mental health centres in the community by his agency.

Anago Resources and Community Homes

Hall thought that Anago Resources and Community Homes might also be viable merger partners. Anago Resources provided "closed custody" group homes for youth under the age of 16, while Community Homes provided "open custody" group homes for youth of the same age. Closed custody beds were used by youth who had been charged with a criminal offence and needed to be detained, but who had not yet been through the court system. Closed custody beds were also used by youths under 16 who had been convicted of a criminal offence and ordered by the court to a closed custody facility. In contrast, open custody beds were used by youth under 16 who had been convicted of a criminal offence and ordered by the courts to an open custody facility. Unlike jail and closed custody facilities, residents in open custody facilities could receive temporary passes to leave the residence. Anago Resources and Community Homes services were provided under contract with MCSS and were funded under the Young Offenders Act. Anago Resources also provided residential services to developmentally challenged youth. Similar to WAYS, Community Homes had recently contracted with CAS to provide an eight-bed receiving home to be used for emergency placements by CAS and 12 foster care beds. Hall was certain that both Anago Resources and Community Homes would not be willing to amalgamate with WAYS but would be willing to take over the services provided by WAYS.

Hall turned to the task of assessing the pros and cons of an amalgamation. She frequently followed the financial news and understood that for-profit companies often merged in order to gain market share through reduced competition and to reduce administrative spending, but Hall wasn't sure whether these concepts applied in the non-profit sector as well. Certainly the previous amalgamation that she had been through had reduced competition, but Hall wasn't convinced that reduced competition was necessarily a good result for the community. The previous amalgamation had also reduced administrative spending somewhat, but Hall recognized that administration in a small social service agency was often quite limited and that significant savings were unlikely. There must be other pros and cons for her list! As she looked at the list of potential partners she had assembled for the board, Hall also knew that each possibility had its own pros and cons.

exhibit 1   Western Area Youth Services Select Financial and Program Statistics

	2001	2000
Financial Highlights		
Revenues	$2,751,717	$2,705,602
Wages and benefits	1,959,783	1,886,378
Other expenditures	722,244	699,901
Surplus	69,690	119,323
Total Assets	764,730	1,368,049
Sources of Revenues		
MCSS	$1,819,383	$1,805,221
CAS	670,609	574,364
Donations/fundraising	40,760	52,734
Other	220,965	173,283
Client Statistics		
Total no. of children served – all programs	351	385
No. of children intensive residential programs	67	81
No. of children in family preservation programs (Community Programs)	247	233
No. of children in day treatment programs	37	38
Transitional Housing Program		
No. of children on waiting list for Intensive Residential	39	32

exhibit 2   Madame Vanier Children's Services Select Financial and Program Statistics

	2001	2000
Financial Highlights		
Revenues	$4,655,000	$3,959,000
Wages and benefits	3,872,000	3,346,000
Other expenditures	774,000	576,000
Surplus	9,000	37,000
Total Assets	1,781,000	1,626,000
Sources of Revenues		
MCSS	$3,577,000	$3,387,000
CAS	591,000	429,000
Donations/fundraising	39,000	15,000
Other	448,000	128,000
Client Statistics		
Total no. of children served – all programs	541	1,273
No. of children in residential programs	98	78
No. of children in family preservation programs	102	84
No. of children in day treatment programs	121	97

exhibit 3   The Children's Aid Society of London and Middlesex Select Financial and Program Statistics

	2001	2000
Financial Highlights		
Revenues	$35,446,032	$28,492,077
Wages and benefits	13,494,503	11,200,533
Other expenditures	21,884,545	16,943,645
Surplus/Deficit	66,984	347,899
Total Assets	9,471,900	10,401,275
Sources of Revenues		
MCSS	$33,642,813	$27,332,691
Other	1,800,219	1,159,386
Client Statistics		
Total no. of children served – all programs	4,080	3,026

case 34 Maple Leaf Consumer Foods— Fixing Hot Dogs (A)

Kelly Gervin hardly had the chance to get things straightened around in her new office. It was June 5, 2001, and Gervin had been the senior marketing director of the packaged meats group in the consumer foods division of Maple Leaf Foods (MLF) for all of four hours. She was still unpacking boxes in her office when the division's vice-president of marketing, Pat Jacobs, came flying in. He tossed a pile of papers on her desk (see Exhibits 2 to 7).

> Kelly . . . these reports I received this morning are scary. We have a serious problem in our hot dog business. Of our nine hot dog brands, five are losing significant market share and another one is down marginally. We've lost as much as 45 per cent relative to last year in one category . . . and that's just the start of it! Kelly, I need you to figure out what is going on and solve this problem, and I need you to do it quickly.

MAPLE LEAF FOODS

The MLF brand had been around in Canada for over 100 years. The organization had grown and evolved out of a number of mergers and amalgamations, but its origins could be traced as far back as 1836 when Grantham Mills opened a flour production and distribution facility in St. Catharines, Ontario. In 1991, U.K.-based Hillsdown Holdings PLC amalgamated with MLF through the purchase and merger of Canada Packers and Maple Leaf Mills. In 1995, McCain Capital Corporation and the Ontario Teachers' Pension Plan Board came together to acquire controlling interest of MLF. Between 1995 and 2001, new systems were introduced, operations streamlined, and several new acquisitions were completed.

IVEY

Richard Ivey School of Business
The University of Western Ontario

By 2001, MLF was Canada's largest and most dominant food processor, generating nearly $4.8 billion in annual sales. The MLF organization and its products were also gaining significant momentum on the international scene. The company's operations focused on three core areas of business: bakery products, meat products and agribusiness. Each core business was composed of several independent operating companies (IOCs) and each IOC was run by a president who controlled the overall profitability and competitive strategy of the business. Under the direction of MLF chief executive officer (CEO), Michael McCain, IOCs were encouraged to follow a common set of values and strategic principles that emphasized the importance of brand equity, operating efficiencies, market leadership and continuous improvement (see Exhibit 1).

The meat products group was by far the largest of the company's core groups, with 2000 sales of nearly $2.5 billion and EBITDA (earnings before interest, taxes, depreciation and amortization) of $26.5 million. The group consisted of all the company's meat and meat-related businesses and included four distinct IOCs: Maple Leaf Pork, Maple Leaf Poultry, Maple Leaf International and Maple Leaf Consumer Foods. While each IOC operated independently, efforts were under way in 2001 to optimize the vertical co-ordination of IOCs within the broader MLF organization.

The packaged meats division, in which Kelly Gervin worked, was part of the Consumer Foods IOC. Consumer Foods had full responsibility for the production and distribution of all branded and value-added prepared meat products. This included bacon, ham, hot dogs, cottage rolls, a wide variety of delicatessen products, prepared turkey products, sliced meats, cooked sausage products, frozen entrees, lard and canned meats. In 2000, Consumer Foods generated in excess of half a billion dollars in sales, representing over 10 per cent of MLF's overall revenues.

Excluding commodities, the MLF hot dog portfolio of products was by far the largest meat category at MLF Consumer Foods, with over twice the dollar sales of any other MLF branded, value-added or prepared meat category within the IOC. The MLF organization had been acquiring expertise in the production and distribution of hot dogs for nearly 75 years. The organization first entered the hot dog business when Canada Packers began producing hot dogs in 1927. At that time, hot dog and sausage production was seen as a financially viable method to dispose of beef, pork and chicken trimmings. It was this profitable opportunity to use up raw material—in combination with the increasing momentum the hot dog was gaining as a cultural icon in the marketplace—that traditionally drove the business.

In 2000, total MLF hot dog sales were approximately $50 million. Industry professionals used both dollar sales and volume by weight to measure sales performance, and these sales correlated with a total of approximately 10.5 million kilograms of hot dogs sold. In the preceding year, total MLF hot dog sales were also approximately $50 million, but volume by weight had actually been approximately 11.2 million kilograms. In Gervin's words, "Our average price per kilo was going up, but there was no question we were selling less. We were losing market share and this became our primary concern."

THE HOT DOG INDUSTRY

A good deal of disagreement exists over the origin of the hot dog. People in Frankfurt, Germany, claim they discovered the hot dog in 1487. Others argue that it was Johan Georghehner, a butcher from Coburg who travelled to Frankfurt to promote this product—which he called the "dachshund" because of its shape—in the late

1600s. Others in Vienna point to the name "wiener" as evidence of the product's Austrian roots.

In the United States, the origins of the hot dog industry can be traced to the arrival of a German immigrant by the name of Charles Feltman who opened up the first Coney Island hot dog stand in 1871. In 1893, Chris Ahe, the owner of the St. Louis Browns baseball team, started selling hot dogs in his ball park. This laid the groundwork for what would become an inseparable connection between hot dogs and the game of baseball.

The actual phrase "hot dog" was coined in 1901. It all started on a cold April day in New York City when concessionaire Harry Stevens became frustrated with losing money selling ice cream and soda. He ordered his assistant to go out and buy all the long, skinny sausages he could find and to sell them from portable hot-water tanks while yelling "get your red hot dachshund while they last!" Sports cartoonist Ted Dorgan became quite amused with the scene, and did a cartoon strip on it. When he had trouble spelling "dachshund," he substituted the term "dog," and the rest, as they say, is history.

THE INDUSTRY TODAY

At the aggregate level, per capita demand for hot dogs was slightly higher in the United States than in Canada. In 2000, consumers in the United States spent nearly $1.7 billion on hot dogs in retail outlets. The average U.S. household purchased 7.65 pounds of hot dogs annually, which translated into about 65 hot dogs per person per year. In 2000, total Canadian hot dog market sales were just over $220 million, which represented approximately 52.5 million kilograms of hot dogs. This translated into an annual consumption rate of about 52 hot dogs per person in Canada. Sixty-four per cent of hot dogs sold in Canada were pork and meat combinations, 24 per cent were all-beef hot dogs, and 12 per cent were made from poultry.

Demand for hot dogs was consistently strongest during the summer months. Since the turn of the century, hot dogs in buns at baseball games, summer picnics, backyard barbecues and roadside diners had become a tradition in North American culture. Hot dog sales from May to August represented more than 44 per cent of the annual total, with July—National Hot Dog Month in the United States—leading the pack. In both Canada and the United States, hot dogs were popular at barbecues and entertainment events. Four hot dogs were consumed for every 10 baseball tickets sold, so it was projected that there would be more than 26 million hot dogs consumed in major league ballparks in 2001.

Hot dog consumption preferences were subject to significant regional differences in Canada. Western Canadian consumers had the strongest demand in Canada for beef hot dogs. The Quebec market was partial to hot dogs in a specific (lower) price segment—due to the influence of "steamies" or "toasties"—hot dogs that were prepared using unique cooking methods. (In this market, lower-priced hot dogs were considered adequate since any hot dog could be prepared in the preferred manner.) Atlantic Canada had the largest per capita consumer of low-fat hot dogs, due in part to the higher average age of the population versus other parts of Canada.

Hot dog consumption was consistently uniform throughout all income levels. Wealthy and low-income Canadians appeared to consume approximately the same volume of hot dogs on an annual basis. Larger families with five or more members tended to eat larger numbers of hot dogs, as did younger families where heads of households were under the age of 35. Children were heavy influencers in hot dog purchase decisions.

Despite their broad consumption, hot dogs had always been subject to considerable consumer scrutiny concerning their content and manufacture. For some time, consumers had been concerned about the presence of "mystery" meat in hot dogs. Both the Canadian and U.S. Departments of Agriculture required by law that meats used in hot dogs include only muscle meat. In addition to meeting this requirement, there was a movement in the industry to introduce all-meat, byproduct-free hot dogs.

COMPETITIVE LANDSCAPE

In 2001, the competitive landscape of the hot dog industry in Canada was dominated by two organizations: MLF and Schneider Foods (JMS). Each had over 20 per cent share of the national market (see Exhibit 2). Other competitors were relatively small (less than one-quarter the size of MLF and JMS) and were regionally focused.

Based in Kitchener, Ontario, JMS had over 110 years of experience in producing and distributing meat products throughout the Canadian marketplace. JMS also had a reputation as a tough competitor; it fought for every inch of shelf space and was tactically reactive and retaliatory. It also knew the hot dog business well and had loyal employees.

In June of 2001, JMS led the industry, possessing over 28 per cent of the dollar share of the hot dog market in Canada. The company was not only the largest hot dog producer in Canada, it was the fastest growing. Between mid-2000 and mid-2001, JMS's dollar sales increased by nearly three per cent; in contrast, MLF's overall sales declined by just over two per cent. JMS had strong national brands that it supported with consistently effective promotional campaigns. It was also very aggressive on pricing. While MLF raised hot dog prices in both 2000 and 2001, JMS held firm to is prices and picked up market share.

In assessing JMS's performance in the Canadian hot dog market, one MLF insider commented:

> Schneider has done a great job of managing its product line from a quality perspective and overall consistency. It has done very little to its hot dog product line over the years. It has not proliferated sub-brands as we did. It did not change packaging on a regular basis as we did. It has also had great consistency in its sales and marketing staff—as we did not. Also, Schneider has done a great job managing its trade relations.
>
> Consumers consistently tell us that JMS means quality, heritage and great-tasting products. This is something that Consumer Foods has to overcome!

HOT DOG SEGMENTATION

For marketing purposes, MLF segmented the hot dog market in two ways: 1) by target consumer (adult or family), and 2) by price (premium, mainstream and value/economy). While there were plenty of small niche players, both JMS and MLF competed in all major hot dog markets in Canada.

Target Segment

The adult segment consisted of franks and sausages. Franks had a larger diameter, slightly more coarse emulsion (meat blend), larger particle definition and more spices than wieners. Also, franks were at least six inches long and by weight were usually about six per pound (2.5 ounces each). Sausages were curved and by weight were three to five per pound (three to five ounces each). Unlike franks, which were always sold pre-cooked, sausages could be sold either uncooked or pre-cooked. In 2001, the adult segment was growing at a rate of about 11 per cent industrywide, but this segment still represented approximately only 16 per cent of the total hot dog industry. In the adult segment, MLF's brands included *ML 100s, Overlander* and *Shopsy's Original Recipe*. JMS's primary adult segment hot dog was *Juicy Jumbos*.

Products targeted towards the family segment were called wieners and represented 84 per cent of overall industry sales. Wieners were also six inches long, but had a finer emulsion than franks and by weight were generally about 12 per pound (1.3 ounces each). Across the industry, the family segment was growing at a rate of about two per cent per year. Industry observers believed that, increasingly, consumers were trading up towards adult categories. In the family segment, JMS offered *Red Hots* (in Ontario) and an identical product simply called *Wieners* for the rest of Canada. MLF's brands in the family segment included *Top Dogs* (Regular and BBQ), *Lean 'n Lite* (Regular and all-Beef), *Beef Dogs* and *Shopsy's Beef*.

Price Segment

Premium hot dogs sold at a price point greater than $3.50 per pound and contained franks and sausages. In addition, Maple Leaf competed in this segment with *Top Dogs Singles*, which were premium priced to reflect the quality of their ingredients and high packaging and high labor costs. Mainstream hot dogs were the largest price segment and included all hot dogs priced between $2.50 and $3.50. MLF's *Top Dogs, Lean 'n Lite, Beef Dogs* and *Shopsy's Beef* fit into this segment. Hot dogs in the value segment sold for between $1.89 and $2.50 per pound. MLF's products in this segment included *Maple Leaf Original* (Regular and Beef), *Burns* (Regular, Beef, and 6+6), *Hygrade* (Regular and Beef), and *Shopsy's* (Regular and BBQ). Wieners in the economy segment were priced under $1.89 per pound; MLF produced several retail brands in this segment including *No-Name* and *Smart Choice*. JMS's *Red Hots* and *Wieners* were both considered mainstream hot dogs. However, during 2001, both products were heavily discounted (to $1.99), which gave them about a 10 per cent to 20 per cent price advantage over MLF's value-price products.

MLF'S CURRENT BRAND STRATEGY

In mid-2001, MLF had nine different brands competing in the Canadian marketplace. Exhibit 3 summarizes the positioning of each of the Maple Leaf hot dog brands. While MLF had strong regional brands, none of the company's brands had a strong national presence. Instead, *Shopsy's* brands were sold only in Ontario, *Burns* and *Overlander* brands competed only in Western Canada, and *Hygrade* was distributed only in Quebec.

For some time, MLF had emphasized different brands for different geographic regions within Canada. This development had resulted in strong brand equity in each of Canada's major regions. The *Burns* brand was strong in Western Canada. In the late 1990s, *Burns* lost substantial market share due to a cost-plus pricing structure which drove prices substantially higher than key competitors. MLF had recently fixed the pricing formula and had moved to reduce production costs, thereby stabilizing the brand. The *Hygrade* brand was a leader in the Quebec hot dog marketplace, possessing a 25 per cent share in that province (eight per cent nationally). The *Shopsy's* brand boasted an eight per cent market share in Ontario (two per cent nationally). All MLF hot dog products were produced at the company's manufacturing facility in Stoney Creek, Ontario. Despite brand distinctions and minor taste differences, there were essentially no major differences in the hot dog products within each price segment. At MLF, the senior marketing director did not have direct authority over, or responsibility for manufacturing.

When interviewing for her current position, Gervin had asked about the origins of regional hot dog branding at MLF. To her surprise, no one in MLF could fully explain why the company had so many regional brands. Some believed it was the result of the company's numerous mergers and acquisitions and the desire to preserve the strength in each new brand that was acquired. Others felt the brand differences could be traced to the different consumer preferences in each region. Notwithstanding these explanations, one of the first things that Gervin noticed about the MLF hot dog portfolio was that often as many as six different MLF brands competed for shelf space in any given retail outlet at the same time.

In 1994, MLF launched *Lean 'n Lite* brand hot dogs. The product was introduced in an effort to meet increasing consumer demands for low-fat food products. The initial launch was very successful and produced strong profit margins for the company. However, sales for *Lean 'n Lite* peaked in 1997, and between 1998 and 2001, sales dropped every year. Many at MLF believed that the decline was the result of growing consumer unwillingness to compromise taste for low fat. However, this belief had not been substantiated with market research. Furthermore, the company was familiar with national consumer research that showed that 70 per cent of consumers were interested in low-fat products with acceptable taste.

In 1999, MLF introduced *Top Dogs* as a national hot dog. The launch was in response to consumer trends that seemed to emphasize healthy and natural food products and ingredients. The all-meat product was designed to appeal to both children and parents, and was initially launched with vitamins and protein added. *Top Dogs* were the first—and only—hot dogs sold in North America that were nutritionally enhanced. The product was launched with a value price of $1.99 per package, and initial consumer demand was strong. However, in the summer of 2000, the price was increased to $2.49, and sales declined noticeably. The perception was that the new price alienated many price-sensitive shoppers. Also, during this period, the formulation for *Top Dogs* was altered several times in an attempt to lower per-unit costs. The result was a product that was priced too high and that, in the minds of many consumers, lacked good taste. By June 2001, *Top Dogs* had captured just 2.8 per cent of the national market (4.6 per cent in Western Canada, 2.6 per cent in Ontario, 2.3 per cent in the Maritimes and 1.7 per cent in Quebec).

Based on the initial success of *Top Dogs*, MLF launched *Beef Dogs* in 2000. The launch was designed to replace the company's existing beef hot dog product called *Maple Leaf All Beef Hot Dogs*. *Beef Dogs* were fortified with calcium and iron. Initial taste tests were positive. However, the product's formulation came under the scrutiny of the Canadian Food Inspection Agency (CFIA), which raised concerns over the sourcing of calcium for *Beef Dogs*. *Beef Dogs* were then reformulated to incorporate a new source of calcium. Several internal taste panels concluded that the newly reformulated *Beef Dogs* tasted chalky and somewhat artificial. By June 2001, *Beef Dog* sales were down seven per cent from 2000 levels.

Kelly Gervin

Kelly Gervin had a solid professional marketing management background. Prior to joining the MLF organization, Gervin had been North American director of marketing for Moulinex, a French appliance manufacturer. She had joined Moulinex after graduating from the University of Toronto with a bachelor of science degree in microbiology. She decided to leave Moulinex after it became apparent that her opportunities for professional growth were stagnating.

Gervin first applied for a job with MLF in 1996 in response to a newspaper advertisement. Always one to embrace a challenge, she jumped at the opportunity to join an organization she could grow with. She initially accepted the position of category manager within Consumer Foods and then spent five years in sales and 18 months in purchasing, where she was presented with the opportunity to take over her current position as senior marketing director. Reporting directly to the vice-president of marketing, Gervin had responsibility for overseeing all marketing decisions (product, price,[1] promotions, packaging and marketing communications strategies) for Maple Leaf's lines of hot dogs, sliced meats and meat snack products. While success in all categories was critical, hot dogs represented by far the largest portion of the portfolio of products over which Gervin was responsible.

Recent Developments

From 1995 through 1999, MLF went through a period of reorganization of the meats business, refocusing on vertically co-ordinating both its pork and poultry protein value chains. By 2000, Consumer Foods had a new president and vice-president of marketing. The president, Rick Young, had built a very successful career in sales and general management while working within the Maple Leaf Companies. The vice-president, Pat Jacobs, had just arrived at Maple Leaf Consumer Foods, having built a marketing career in the packaged goods industry. During 2000, Young focused on strengthening the management team, while Jacobs concentrated on organizing a strong marketing team. As 2001 approached, it was becoming clear to Young that the team was not coming together, and he began to pay increasing attention to the marketing operations. In 2001, Young came to the conclusion that marketing needed additional changes in leadership. It was through this decision that Gervin arrived in her new role.

In Gervin's mind, the market-share reports that had come to Jacobs' attention unquestionably reflected the lack of stability in the packaged meats group. Although she knew MLF's hot dog business was struggling, she was hoping that additional market analysis and customer survey data would provide her with the information needed to make appropriate decisions. On her first morning as the new marketing director, she was troubled to find many of the data she needed were simply not available. During the late 1990s, considerable research had been carried out on brands culminating with the introduction of *Top Dogs*. But the individual who conducted this research had since been promoted and transferred out of the IOC. The data were now a couple of years old and had not been updated. In addition, there was essentially no consumer research relating to what drove consumers to buy MLF's hot dog products.

In addition to segment sales numbers and market-share data referred to by Jacobs, Gervin found two notes of interest. One was written by the previous marketing director,

---

[1] Pricing responsibility also fell under Category Management, which set price in consultation with Gervin.

suggesting that his group had been working diligently to become the low-cost producer in the value segment. On this matter, Gervin did a couple of quick calculations and realized that they weren't even close to achieving this goal. The second document of interest was a hand-written note from an unidentified source that indicated growing concerns over recent losses in market share in the adult segment. That was it.

To complicate matters, the group did not seem to have a business plan. Being new to the team, Gervin was unsure of the backgrounds, skills and commitments of her direct reports. Also, she could sense that morale was low—not surprising, given the recent declines in market share and changes in staff. Beyond the organizational concerns, MLF hot dogs were having real problems in the marketplace. Earlier in the morning, Gervin had placed a call to a major grocery retailer to get a sense of what that customer thought of MLF's hot dog products. The retailer was surprisingly cool to Gervin and offered the following observation: "MLF has an uncompetitive product portfolio. Quite frankly, some of your hot dogs taste lousy." Gervin had no idea whether these sentiments were shared across all of MLF's retail customers, whether this retailer was dissatisfied for other reasons, or whether the retailer was, in fact, satisfied but was playing games with her to win later concessions on price or service.

In organizing a business plan, Gervin knew that she would have to work within the constraints of the broader Consumer Foods organization. As senior marketing director, she had full profit and loss accountability for hot dogs. But, others in the organization were also responsible for various determinants of profit. For example, the sales team in the field—account managers, directors, and the vice-president of sales for the IOC—were in part measured by hot dog profits. Manufacturing also had a stake in the game. So, while she was responsible for profits, people outside her direct control impacted how far she could go and whether her overall approach would succeed.

Decisions

As soon as Jacobs left her office, Gervin closed the door and put her phone on voice mail. She needed time to think. There was clearly good news and bad news in what she had learned on her first day on the job. The bad news was MLF's hot dog business was a mess in almost every sense of the word, and if not handled deftly, the business could go from bad to worse. The good news was that Gervin felt the business could be turned around and that it had huge up-side potential for growth and profitability. She knew this, and she believed that Jacobs and Young also believed in the huge up-side potential in hot dogs. Reversing the negative trends and moving MLF to a leadership position in the marketplace would have positive spill-over effects on the entire Consumer Foods product line and would almost certainly capture the attention of the broader MLF organization.

As the challenges of turning the hot dog business around were becoming more and more apparent, Gervin recognized the need for short-term "fixes" and a clear strategy for the future. She pulled out a pen and scratched down two questions: (1) Which hot dog segments do we most want to be in? and (2) How are we going to grow the business in these segments?

While these were simple questions, the answers would be much more difficult. As Gervin contemplated her next steps, additional questions came to mind. Should MLF even "make" hot dogs? Gervin was aware that an increasing number of companies like Nike, IBM and Matsushita were contracting all or part of their manufacturing over to others. Should hot dogs be any different? She also wondered whether the fact that MLF was Canada's largest supplier of pork and poultry products should influence a decision on the composition of hot dogs and their overall positioning in the marketplace. Gervin was also uncertain how the positioning of hot dogs might influence other products manufactured and sold by Consumer Foods. For example, how might an emphasis on the value segment affect the sales of branded lunch meats? Finally, she wondered what role brands should play in growing hot dog sales in a chosen segment? Should she emphasize a national brand or brands, and if so, what impact might national branding have on existing regional brands?

The more Gervin thought about the challenges she faced, the more questions came to her mind. She had no idea how to answer them, but she knew that a number of senior executives were waiting to hear what she had to say.

exhibit 1   Maple Leaf Foods Core 7 Principles

Maple Leaf Foods' broad strategic direction is shaped by the Core 7 strategic principles. Continuously evolving, these seven principles are strongly grounded in the Maple Leaf culture and provide the guiding framework for the planning and execution of the company's corporate and competitive strategies.

1. Build high potential leadership.
2. Focus on markets and categories where we can lead.
3. Develop brand equity.
4. Create customer value with Six Sigma processes and products.
5. Be the lowest-cost producer.
6. Execute with precision and continuous improvement.
7. Think global.

Source: Company files.

exhibit 2   Canadian Market Share Analysis (as at June 5, 2001)

	Latest 52 Weeks			
Company	Share in Weight	Share Point Change in weight	$ Share	Share Point Change in $
MLF	19.3	−1.6	22.9	−2.1
Hub Larsen	5.0	−0.1	4.0	0.0
JM Schneider	22.6	2.7	28.2	2.9
Fleetwood	1.4	0.2	2.2	0.3
Freybe	0.8	0.2	1.5	0.3
Grimms	0.6	0.0	1.2	−0.1
Harvest	1.0	0.2	1.4	0.2
Fletchers	1.7	0.0	2.1	0.0
Lafleur	3.6	0.0	3.4	0.1
Lesters	0.4	−0.2	0.4	−0.1
Lilydale	0.2	−0.2	0.4	−0.1
Maple Lodge	4.2	−1.5	2.7	−0.7
Mitchells	3.9	0.8	5.0	1.1
Olymel	1.3	−0.2	1.3	−0.2
Control Label	32.3	−0.3	22.9	−0.2

Source: Company files.

exhibit 3   Maple Leaf Foods Hot Dog Product Line (segmentation)

	Family (Wieners)	Adult (Franks & Sausages)
Premium (>$3.50)	● Top Dogs Singles (450g)	
Mainstream ($2.50 to $3.50)	● Top Dogs (Reg. & BBQ) ● Lean 'n Lite (Reg. & Beef) ● Beef Dogs ● Shopsy's Beef	● Maple Leaf 100's ● Overlander ● Shopsy's Original Recipe
Value ($1.89 to $2.50)	● Maple Leaf Original (& BBQ) ● Burns (Reg., Beef, & 6+6) ● Hygrade (Reg. & Beef) ● Shopsy's (Reg. & BBQ)	
Economy (<$1.89)	● Control Label	

Source: Company files.

exhibit 4   Canadian Hot Dog Market Review (as of June 5, 2001)

	Total	Family	Adult
Last 52 Weeks	Category: +2.5% ML: −5.0% JMS: +18.2%	Category: +0.7% ML: +0.7% JMS: +14.5%	Category: +11.2% ML: −44.8% JMS: +35%
Last 12 Weeks	Category: +3.2% ML: −8.8% JMS: +9.6%	Category: +2.6% ML: −4.9% JMS: +10.0%	Category: +1.0% ML: −38.4% JMS: +15.5%
Last 4 Weeks	Category: +4.0% ML: −9.3% JMS: +10.6%	Category: +3.1% ML: −6.5% JMS: +10.4%	Category: −1.0% ML: −30.5% JMS: +16.4%

Source: Company files.

exhibit 5   Current Brand Share (as of June 5, 2001)

	1998 Volume	Share	1999 Volume	Volume Variance To PY	National Share	Share Variance To PY	2000 Volume	Volume Variance To PY	National Share	Share Variance To PY	2001 LE Volume	Volume Variance To PY	National Share*	Regional Share	National Share Variance To PY
Burns	1,071,903	1.7	1,033,266	−4%	1.5	−0.2	810,295	−22%	1.1	(0.4)	711,491	(0.1)	0.9	3.8	−28%
Hygrade	2,065,039	4.6	2,171,784	5%	4.6	0	2,449,504	13%	5.1	0.5	2,630,840	0.1	5.0	22.5	16%
Lean 'n Lite	588,071	1.1	597,365	2%	1.2	0.1	448,795	−25%	0.9	(0.3)	328,384	(0.3)	0.6		−24%
ML Reg./ BBQ	2,917,099	4.9	2,512,953	−14%	3.8	−1.1	2,087,457	−17%	3.7	(0.1)	2,291,438	0.1	3.9		−1%
ML Beef	932,830	1.7	868,634	−7%	1.3	−0.4	798,928	−8%	1.5	0.2	687,283	(0.1)	1.2		−7%
Top Dogs		0	1,467,889		2.6	2.6	1,199,268	−18%	2.6	–	1,243,616	0.0	2.2		−6%
ML 100's	1,019,974	2.4	1,139,581	12%	2.4	0	710,382	−38%	1.5	(0.9)	600,205	(0.2)	1.0		−45%
Top Dogs Singles		0			0		123,572		0.2	0.2	215,655	0.8	0.3		N/A
Overlander	394,373	0.9	470,076	19%	1	0.1	416,278	−11%	0.8	(0.2)	365,957	(0.1)	0.6	2.9	−28%
Shopsys	2,058,655	3.7	2,230,319	8%	3.5	−0.2	2,154,001	−3%	3.7	0.2	2,255,999	0.1	3.5	9.2	6%
TOTAL	11,047,944	21.4	12,491,867	13%	22.1	0.7	11,198,480	−10%	20.9	(0.8)	11,330,868	0.0	19.3		−5%

Source: Latest 52 weeks, June 2001.

exhibit 6   Maple Leaf Consumer Foods: Hot Dog Margins

	Projected 2001	Actual 2000
Hot Dog Margins by Category		
Regular	$0.44	$0.56
Adult	0.16	0.37
Beef	0.24	0.27
Better for You	0.60	0.75
Total	0.38	0.59
Hot Dog Margins by Brand		
Maple Leaf Regular	$0.71	$0.92
Maple Leaf 100%'s	0.31	0.47
Maple Leaf Beef Dogs	0.10	0.27
Lean 'n Lite	0.35	0.33
Top Dogs	0.60	0.78
Overlander	(0.14)	0.20
Hygrade	0.23	0.20
Burns	(0.14)	0.23
Shopsy's	0.43	0.50
Total	0.39	0.49

GP – = Gross Profit

exhibit 7   TL Wieners—National Tonnage Trends

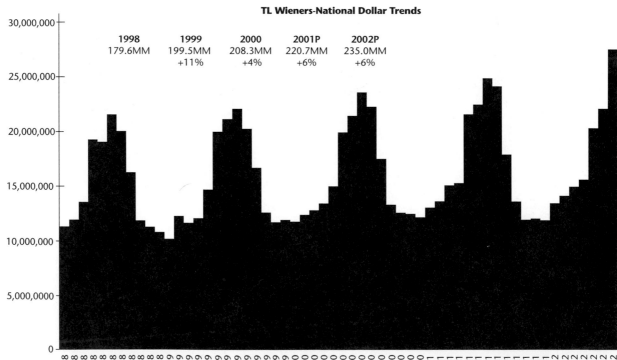

TL Wieners-National Dollar Trends

1998	1999	2000	2001P	2002P
179.6MM	199.5MM	208.3MM	220.7MM	235.0MM
	+11%	+4%	+6%	+6%

Source: Company files.

case 35 Globalization and the Canadian Publishing Industry

George Spaulding, owner and president of Spaulding Books Canada, wanted to retire.[1] After 30 years in the publishing business, he had built a small but viable publishing company that had launched dozens of young Canadian authors on their writing careers. In the 1970s, Spaulding was one of a handful of young Canadian nationalists who believed in the necessity of building a national publishing industry that could provide new Canadian writers with a voice. He threw himself into the task of building his company with unflagging zest and enthusiasm, and many of the authors his company had supported developed into renowned celebrities with international followings. But at age 65, he no longer enjoyed the 14-hour days he was accustomed to putting in at Spaulding. He wanted some time to spend with his family and a well-deserved rest.

Spaulding could not retire, however, because there was no one to succeed him. None of his children was interested in taking over the business, so there was no heir apparent to whom he could pass the company reins. No one wanted to buy his company because his profit margins, hovering around the generally low industry average of two per cent, did not make it an attractive acquisition. Like other Canadian publishing companies, Spaulding Books relied on subsidies from the federal government, and without them, the company probably would have gone under long ago. The low profit rates and limited capacity for expanding business in the Canadian market also meant it was difficult to attract investors, and the company was undercapitalized. A comparable firm in the United States could probably count on being acquired by one of the huge international media conglomerates that dominated the U.S. publishing industry. However,

Barbara Jenkins prepared this case under the supervision of Professor Gerry Keim solely to provide material for class discussion. The authors do not intend to illustrate either effective or ineffective handling of a managerial situation. The authors may have disguised certain names and other identifying information to protect confidentiality.

IVEY

Richard Ivey School of Business
The University of Western Ontario

[1]This scenario, the owner's name and the company name are fictitious.

foreign ownership restrictions in the Canadian industry meant that, except for special circumstances, only 25 per cent of a Canadian publishing company could be acquired by a foreign firm. Limits on foreign ownership had been established to protect small Canadian firms like Spaulding Books from foreign competition. Ironically, this further diminished the potential sale price of Spaulding's firm: without competition from foreign buyers, it was unlikely he would be able to recoup the personal investment he had made in his company. Spaulding had benefited from government assistance to the industry for decades, but it seemed that government measures designed to build up the Canadian publishing industry had also brought the value of his individual investment down.

The next day, Spaulding would join a group of Canadian publishers who would lobby Canadian Heritage Minister Sheila Copps for tax incentives that would encourage investment in the publishing industry and increase its profitability. Given that Canadian publishing houses produced cultural products that were part of Canada's vibrant cultural community, publishers believed that their investors should receive a tax write-off for their contributions, just as a donor to a theatre company or national orchestra would. They also wanted a tax credit for investors buying shares in publishing companies, similar to the benefits received by investors in the high-risk oil and gas industry. With new infusions of investment, Spaulding and others could make some of the technological changes necessary to compete in the new global publishing environment. Eventually, Spaulding hoped the investment incentives would attract enough money to wean his company off the government subsidies it relied on.

With a reputation as Canada's "cultural Joan of Arc," Canadian Heritage Minister Sheila Copps would probably be sympathetic to the publishers' predicament. Unfortunately, the decision to assist the publishing industry was not entirely in her hands. Tax credits and incentives were expensive, and further assistance to the already subsidized publishing industry would not be popular with some other members of the cabinet. Furthermore, the Department of Finance could object to giving special tax treatment to a specific industry, and there was also the question of whether privately owned, for-profit companies deserved the same kind of tax benefits not-for-profit institutions such as theatres did. More importantly, Canadian cultural subsidies and protection were under growing international scrutiny. In 1999, Copps's attempt to protect the Canadian magazine industry through Bill C-55 sparked a major trade war with the United States. The United States was waging an ongoing campaign in the World Trade Organization (WTO) to eliminate special treatment for cultural subsidies and protection. Until cultural protection was eliminated, the United States argued that if governments did assist cultural producers, aid should be in the form of subsidies rather than tax preferences. Subsidies are easier for the United States to monitor, and thus are considered more "transparent" than tax measures are.

Another option Copps could consider would be to remove the foreign ownership restrictions in the book publishing industry. The long-term cultural impact of such a move could be very negative, however. In November 1998, Canadian publishers were the first to complain when the German media giant Bertelsmann wanted to merge its newly acquired Canadian subsidiaries to create the largest trade book publishing company in Canada. The newly merged firm, with sales greater than the five largest Canadian publishers combined, soon dominated the Canadian trade publishing business. Also in 1998, the thriving Canadian book publisher Little Brown was promptly shut down after being acquired by the U.S. media conglomerate Time-Warner because it did not fit into the American firm's global investment strategy. Without continued protection, how could Canadian publishers compete against international giants like Bertelsmann or AOL/Time Warner? Internationally, the publishing industry is dominated by a global oligopoly of huge media companies that dwarf most Canadian book publishers (see Exhibit 1). Exhibit 2 illustrates that Canadian-owned presses tend to be much smaller than foreign-owned publishers in Canada, and that they are minuscule compared to the conglomerates listed in Exhibit 1. Without protection, small Canadian publishers would surely disappear. And if the Canadian book publishing industry fell apart, who would be around to publish Canadian authors or foster new Canadian writing talent? After 30 years of building up the Canadian publishing industry, opening it up to foreign competition could bring it down in one fell swoop.

Copps and Spaulding shared a similar interest—enhancing the profitability and viability of the Canadian publishing industry. The question was, how was this goal best achieved?

CANADIAN CULTURAL POLICY AND THE BOOK PUBLISHING INDUSTRY

Canada has a long history of subsidizing and protecting its cultural industries. The main reason for this is Canada's openness to foreign cultural products. The Canadian market is inundated with them: over 80 per cent of English language magazines sold in Canada are foreign, 70 per cent of books sold, 70 per cent of radio and 64 per cent of English language television, and 96 per cent of screen time for film.[2] Of course, the vast majority of these imported cultural commodities come from the United States, raising the spectre of U.S. cultural imperialism and concern for the survival of Canadian culture in the face of American cultural influence. Fear of American encroachment on Canadian cultural territory has been a longstanding Canadian preoccupation, dating back to the first comprehensive cultural policy review, known as the Massey Report of 1951. The authors warned:

> It cannot be denied, . . . that a vast and disproportionate amount of material coming from a single alien source may stifle rather than stimulate our own creative effort; and, passively accepted without any standard of comparison, this may weaken critical faculties. We are now spending millions to maintain a national independence which would be nothing but an empty shell without a vigourous and distinctive cultural life. We have seen that we have its elements in our traditions and in our history; we have made important progress, often aided by American generosity. We must not be blind, however, to the very present danger of dependence.[3]

To rectify this situation and to encourage Canadian cultural productivity, Canada developed various policies and institutions that subsidized and protected its cultural industries. Assistance to cultural industries in Canada has taken three basic forms: 1. subsidies and tax measures, 2. protection from foreign takeovers and, 3. Canadian content regulations. Aid to the book-publishing industry is focused on the first two of these measures.

The book-publishing industry has benefited greatly from government assistance. At the federal level, the three main funding instruments are the Book Publishing Industry

---

[2]Keith Acheson and Christopher Maule, "You Can't Have it Both Ways," in *Canadian Foreign Policy*, 4:3 (Winter 1997), p. 66.

[3]Joanne Boucher, *Funding Culture: Current Arguments on the Economic Importance of the Arts and Culture*, Current Issue Paper 158, Government of Ontario, March 1995, p. 4.

Development Program (BPIDP) administered by Copps's Department of Canadian Heritage (DCH), the Block Grants Program provided by the Canada Council, and the Aid to Scholarly Publishing Program administered by the Social Sciences and Humanities Research Council of Canada. The most substantial of these programs, BPIDP, in turn provides four different kinds of funding initiatives: aid to publishers, aid to industry and associations, distribution assistance and international marketing assistance. The federal government also sponsors a loan program in collaboration with the Royal Bank that offers up to $20 million in loans to small and medium-size publishers who have difficulty obtaining bank financing.[4] Aside from the subsidies provided to individual authors by the Canada Council, the industry as a whole receives about $18 million a year for production subsidies. It receives an additional $30 million per year in industrial and marketing support. To protect Canadian publishers from foreign competition, the government also forbids more than 25 per cent ownership of a publishing company unless it is okayed by the investment review agency, Investment Canada, as well as by the DCH. One of the considerations for approving more than 25 per cent control is the overall impact on the publishing industry as a whole. If the impact is deemed negative, more than 25 per cent foreign ownership cannot be approved.

Without these subsidies and protection from foreign competition, it is doubtful that Canadian publishers could survive. Exhibit 3 shows that none of the Canadian publishing companies who received BPIDP grants between 1994 and 1999 would have been profitable without them. In 1999, for example, earnings before taxes (EBT) including grants were $12.7 million. When grants were excluded, EBT dropped to –$21.3 million.

There are numerous reasons for the lack of profitability of Canadian publishing companies. One of the key factors influencing costs in the industry is the importance of economies of scale. Although confidentiality issues mean that no precise data exist on changes in unit costs as production runs increase, there is evidence that longer print runs decrease costs. Larger firms with longer print runs have lower costs and smaller losses. For example, pre-tax losses (excluding grants) as a percentage of total revenues (excluding grants) decline as firm size increases. Also, total operating costs as a percentage of total revenues (excluding grants) decrease as firms get larger (see Exhibit 4).

The relatively small size of the Canadian market means that Canadian firms cannot benefit from the same economies of scale as their main price competitors in the United States do. For example, in the United States, about 70,000 trade books are printed every year, with an average printing run of 50,000 to 100,000 copies. In Canada, approximately 7,000 books are published annually with a run of 2,500 to 3,000 copies. Exhibit 5 shows that the U.S. market is almost three times larger than the next largest market of Germany. Thus, U.S. producers can spread their production costs and research and development (R&D) costs (including authors' advances, editorial and design work, typesetting and other one-time expenses) over a much larger customer base. They can afford to invest in new technologies such as digital on-demand printing, while Canadian companies cannot. Firms with on-demand technology store books in a digital library, then print them as they are ordered by retailers. This eliminates inventories and reduces the economies-of-scale issue dramatically.

---

[4]Arthur Donner Consultants Inc. and Lazar and Associates, *The Competitive Challenges Facing Book Publishers in Canada*, May 2000, pp. 22-23.

Because U.S. book sellers have free access to the Canadian market through their Canadian subsidiaries, however, they set the book prices Canadian publishers must compete with. Consequently, Canadian companies face higher production costs due to a lack of economies of scale, combined with a price ceiling because of U.S. price competition. The downward pressure on prices is further exacerbated by changes in the way books are sold. The sale of books on the Internet by companies such as Amazon.com and Chapters.ca means that customers are used to receiving 40 per cent to 50 per cent discounts from the prices charged in bookstores. The growing concentration amongst Canadian book retailers puts even more pressure on publishers, as large retailers such as Chapters and Indigo use their massive buying power to demand price discounts of up to 50 per cent from publishing houses.

Canadian publishers have scrambled to adapt to these changing conditions. For example, Spaulding Books attempted to mitigate the economies-of-scale problem by increasing exports in order to expand sales beyond the Canadian market. The company had been fairly successful in doing so—Spaulding Books increased its exports to the U.S. market by 300 per cent over the past 10 years. The fact that Spaulding produced books with a Canadian focus severely limited its market in the United States, however. In addition, the agents of many of the individual fiction writers Spaulding published generally sold the out-of-Canada rights of their authors' books to publishers in foreign markets. Canadian authors benefited significantly from this practice, but it limited the export potential of their Canadian publishers.

Spaulding's second strategy was to reorient the kind of books he published from literary works to books with a more commercial appeal, hoping this would increase production runs for individual books. He was forced to adopt this tactic when the DCH cut grants to Canadian publishers by 50 per cent in 1995, and it helped to some degree.[5] The problem was that this meant abandoning what Spaulding believed was the true vocation of his company: printing new Canadian authors. The DCH was unhappy about this change in focus as well. A central goal of their funding strategy was to ensure the survival of small, regional presses that would print less-popular authors who were just starting out.

DCH's funding formula reflected this goal by favoring small presses. Funding for Canadian publishers is based on eligible sales of book titles. DCH multiplies a publisher's initial $400,000 of sales of Canadian-authored titles by three to compensate small publishers for the greater expenses of publishing with fewer sales. Grants are limited to $750,000 per firm, which means that companies with larger sales hit a grant ceiling and are not entitled to further funds. The result of this funding formula is that small presses receive proportionately more funding, creating a disincentive to grow larger, or for smaller firms to consolidate.[6]

Although this system encourages an usually large number of small companies, supporters say that the benefit is a generally healthy "ecosystem" for Canadian literature. Because of the system of grants supporting small presses and new writers, Canada has gained worldwide literary visibility far beyond what its population size might warrant. Canadian writers regularly win international prizes such as the Booker, the Pulitzer and the Prix Goncourt, and are read around the globe. Although foreign-owned companies publish many Canadian authors, they tend to be more interested in

---

[5]Some of these grants have been reinstated by the Department of Canadian Heritage, but they are still not back to pre-1995 levels.

[6]Donner and Lazar, *The Competitive Challenges Facing Book Publishers in Canada*, p. 30.

established talent rather than more experimental younger writers. About 85 per cent of Canadian-authored titles are published by Canadian-owned publishers. Although that percentage is declining due to the attractiveness of Canadian authors such as Margaret Atwood and Michael Ondaatje to international publishers, the danger is that larger companies could "skim the cream" of the most-profitable authors by offering them large royalties and advances, making it more difficult for smaller Canadian companies to survive or grow and for less-known Canadian authors to get published. Michael Harrison, president of the Association of Canadian Publishers (ACP), makes the analogy to the NHL farm-team system. He argues that without the small companies to nurture new Canadian writers the same way that farm teams train hockey players for the NHL, there would be no "stars" to play in the big leagues. Consequently, he maintains, protection for small Canadian firms is integral to the overall welfare of the industry, including the international conglomerates.

CULTURAL POLICY AND INTERNATIONAL TRADE

Aid to the book-publishing industry has definitely created a vibrant literary environment in Canada. But subsidizing and protecting national industries in the context of the more-open trading systems of the 21st century is a complicated matter. Originally, provisions for aiding and protecting cultural industries were considered matters of domestic policy. As Canada's trade-dependent economy became more open through the Canada-U.S. Free Trade Agreement (CUSTA), the North American Free Trade Agreement (NAFTA) and the increasingly stringent requirements of the WTO, and as the federal government paid more attention to raising Canada's visibility on the international stage, Canadian cultural policies began to come under intense scrutiny.

In 1993, the Department of Foreign Affairs and International Trade (DFAIT) began an intensive review of its foreign policy objectives. The report that emerged from this review, entitled *Canada in the World*, listed culture as one of the three key objectives of Canadian foreign policy. Known as the "Third Pillar," the projection of Canadian values and culture became an integral component of Canadian foreign policy. The reasons for the increased focus on culture within the context of Canadian foreign policy were twofold: first, as a small country whose focus is more on "soft power" as opposed to the "hard power" politics of the United States, culture provides status and visibility for Canada on the international stage, portraying it as a vital, culturally prosperous nation. DFAIT argued that the stronger Canada's cultural image was, the greater Canada's capacity for effective and independent action in foreign affairs would be.

Second, culture plays an increasingly important economic role—globally, the entertainment industry earns approximately $150 billion per year, with an annual growth rate of 15 per cent. In Canada, about 660,000 jobs exist as a result of the arts and cultural industries. In terms of international trade, foreign demand for Canadian cultural goods increased by 83 per cent between 1990 and 1995, accounting for $3 billion in export sales and supporting approximately 50,000 jobs that are directly connected to overseas cultural sales. Cultural exports, therefore, contribute to Canada's overall trade balance, and securing access to foreign markets for these products is important.

From this perspective, it is in Canada's interest to encourage an open and uninhibited trade environment for Canadian cultural products. Ensuring free trade in cultural goods means more secure market access for Canadian cultural commodities abroad. Promoting an open trade environment also fulfils Canada's obligations as a member of the WTO and NAFTA and generally portrays the image that Canada is "open for business." On the other hand, it is questionable whether there would be any cultural commodities for Canada to sell if cultural industries were ruled entirely by market forces. As noted above, Canada's small internal market does not allow the economies of scale necessary to operate profitably and compete with larger American firms. In many cultural industries, government assistance has always been necessary to ensure the viability of smaller Canadian cultural producers in the face of foreign competition. From this perspective, therefore, the subsidization of culture seems essential. In the words of one Canadian Heritage official, culture "is not something to be left to the market. It is not something that should only be considered as entertainment. The market does not necessarily deliver on choice, and access and diversity—and cultural rights and human rights. The market is not democratization."[7]

Culturally, therefore, Canada is obviously faced with a conundrum: Canadian cultural producers need exports to foreign markets to achieve economies of scale and gain important export earnings. Encouraging free trade in cultural products would enhance access to these markets and provide greater economic security. On the other hand, opening up cultural industries completely to market forces would probably result in the inundation of the Canadian market with foreign goods, potentially wiping out Canada's cultural industries.

Canada's approach to this problem has been to continue participation in international trade agreements while seeking international allies for its attempt to exempt culture from international trade rules. France, Belgium and newly industrializing countries such as Malaysia also have been in the forefront of efforts to exempt culture from international trade agreements. All these countries are major consumers of American cultural products whose native industries would collapse under free competition with the United States. They have consistently argued in trade negotiations that cultural goods cannot be separated from the broader cultural context or way of life that they represent, and thus should not be included in trade agreements as if they were "just any commodity." On the basis of this argument, Canada maintained that cultural industries, narrowly defined as books, magazines, periodicals, newspapers, film, music and radio communications, should be exempt from both CUSFTA and NAFTA. Canada has also negotiated absolute exemptions for culture from bilateral free-trade agreements with Chile and Israel, and through Foreign Investment Protection Agreements with at least 21 other countries. Along with other cultural industries, the ACP has supported these efforts by calling for the creation of an international cultural trade instrument that would recognize that cultural industries should be exempt from international trade agreements in order to protect cultural diversity.[8]

For the United States, whose large trade surplus in cultural goods contrasts with its overall trade deficit (entertainment is second only to the aerospace industry in terms of generating export incomes), countering these demands for cultural protectionism is essential. The United States Trade Representative (USTR) argues that cultural commodities are not "culture" but "entertainment," in an attempt to sidestep the more emotional issue of including goods that affect cultural identity in free-trade

---

[7]Quoted in Charissa McIntosh, "Exploring Dynamics of Culture within Canadian Foreign Policy: A Salient Issue for 1990's Canada," *MA Research Essay*, Carleton University, 1999, p. 33.

[8]Association of Canadian Publishers, *Pre-Budget Submission to the Standing Committee on Finance*, September 1999, p. 9.

agreements. In response to Canada's demand that culture be excluded from NAFTA, the United States insisted on a provision that any party could respond to cultural protectionism with an equivalent commercial response, meaning that tariffs could be levied on other products in retaliation for cultural protectionism. This provision led Canadian cultural critics to charge that the cultural exemption from NAFTA was a hollow one. As one commentator noted, it basically means that "if a party is ready to pay the price it can maintain cultural measures that are incompatible" with NAFTA.[9]

The United States does maintain cultural policies that subsidize cultural producers, but in the book-publishing industry, there are no specific measures prohibiting foreign ownership or stipulating domestic content. Currently, only three major publishing houses, AOL/Time-Warner, William Morrow and Simon and Schuster, remained U.S.-owned. As a spokesman for the outspoken "America First" proponent Senator Ernest Hollings noted, "Americans tend not to be concerned about their culture. But by the same token, I don't think you are ever going to see a Seagram buying CBS."[10] From a U.S. perspective, unless national security is affected, its thriving culture industries do not need protection. A side effect of these foreign acquisitions is the growing concentration of the book-publishing industry. Currently, 20 publishers control 90 per cent of the U.S. book market. Three foreign firms control 90 per cent of the U.S. market for specialized technical, scientific and medical books.[11]

The result is a situation that is causing growing concern in the United States. Andre Schriffin, the owner and founder of the American publishing house New Press, is vocal about the long-term cultural implications of letting huge foreign conglomerates take over the U.S. publishing industry. Because these conglomerates will not settle for the smaller profits publishing houses make, Schriffin argues, the inevitable outcome will be to spend less money trying out more difficult or more experimental literature. Instead, the tendency will be to publish simplistic products with a broad appeal that will increase sales and thus profits, leading to an overall demise in the quality of American literature. "Canadians," Schriffin argues, "because of their proximity to the United States, have learned ways of maintaining an independent culture. Americans have been too insular and too proud to do that."[12]

The ACP hopes to build on the obvious coincidence of interests between smaller U.S. presses and Canadian publishers in its quest for cultural protection. The ACP's Harrison notes,

> Canadians tend to think in terms of Canada versus the United States. I think it's important for us to recognize that our friends to the south are an acutely diverse society, and we need to find allies there as well. If you're a small university press, or a small trade house, or a children's house, or a poetry press, you may find that similar companies in the United States face the same problems. In many ways, their competition is our competition—it's Time Warner, Disney and so on that are a concern. It's big versus little, really, and I think we're foolish not to make some attempt to try and find allies in the States.[13]

In the meantime, however, high profile cultural-trade disputes between Canada and the United States are still a matter of concern.

---

[9]Professor Ivan Bernier, as quoted in Dennis Browne, editor, *The Culture/Trade Quandry: Canada's Policy Options,* Ottawa: Centre for Trade Policy and Law, 1998, p. 12.

[10]*Financial Post*, June 6/8, 1998, p. 10.

[11]*National Post*, November 5, 1998, p. C5.

[12]Quoted in *The Globe and Mail*, November 27, 2000, p. R1.

[13] Interview with ACP President Michael Harrison in *Quill and Quire*, February 2000, p. 20.

CANADA-U.S. TRADE DISPUTES IN CULTURE: SPLIT-RUN MAGAZINES

Schriffin's admiration for Canadian cultural policies is not shared by the U.S. Trade Representative. The dispute between Canada and the United States over split-run magazines, ongoing for over 35 years, illustrates how acrimonious the battle over Canadian cultural policies can become. The term "split-run" refers to U.S. magazines that slightly alter their editorial content for distribution in the Canadian market, selling space to Canadian advertisers at discount rates and thereby siphoning advertising revenues from Canadian magazines. This means that the original version is typeset in the United States, a few Canadian articles are inserted, and a new "Canadian Edition" is ready for the market. Split-runs are highly profitable ventures for American magazines, since their production costs have already been covered by sales in the U.S. market. Magazines such as *Time* and *Reader's Digest* have been doing this since the 1940s with enormous success—by the mid-1950s, four out of five magazines read by Canadians were American.

In response to the domination of U.S. magazines in the Canadian market and the failure of several large Canadian magazines in the face of this competition, the federal government tried a variety of measures to support the Canadian magazine industry. Since 1965, it has made numerous attempts to prevent foreign periodicals with advertising directed at the Canadian market from entering the country.[14] It was *Sports Illustrated*'s decision to run a Canadian edition in 1993, however, that really heated up the trade war over split-runs. In January of that year, the magazine's owner, Time Warner, announced its plan to issue six special Canadian issues featuring expanded coverage of Canadian sports. With most of the editorial content of these issues already accounted for in its U.S. issues, *Sports Illustrated* would beam the information electronically across the border where Canadian content would be added before sending it to a printer in Richmond Hill, Ontario. Because most of its editorial costs were already covered by sales in the U.S. markets, the magazine could offer lucrative prices to Canadian companies who wanted to advertise in these issues. For example, it offered a full-page, four-color advertisement for $6,250, approximately one-half of what it would cost for the same ad in a U.S. regional edition of the magazine with similar circulation.[15] The cost of a comparable ad in the Canadian magazine *Maclean's* would be about $25, 400.[16]

In response to intense lobbying by the Canadian magazine industry, which claimed that the industry stood to lose about 37 per cent of its advertising revenue if split-runs were allowed to continue, the Canadian government announced its intentions in 1993 to reaffirm its "commitment to protect the economic foundations of the Canadian periodical industry . . . [and] discourage the establishment of split-run or 'Canadian' regional editions."[17] Under intense lobbying pressure from its own magazine industry,

---

[14]The Pearson government passed a bill in 1965 directed at limiting the damage inflicted by split-runs. The bill disallowed tax deductions of advertising costs when ads were placed in foreign periodicals aimed at the Canadian market, and amended the Customs Tariff to prevent entry into Canada of split-runs with advertising directed at the Canadian market. A follow-up bill implemented in 1976 defined a periodical as Canadian provided it was 75 per cent Canadian-owned. Canadian periodicals had to be edited, typeset and printed in Canada, and their content had to be 80 per cent different from a non-Canadian periodical.

[15]Government of Canada, *A Question of Balance: Report of the Task Force on the Canadian Magazine Industry*, Ottawa: Minister of Supply and Services Canada, 1994, pp. 44-45.

[16]Israel, *Final Editions*, p. 8.

[17]*Ibid.*, p. 11.

the U.S. government launched a WTO challenge of Canadian measures in the magazine industry in December 1995. In 1997, the WTO ruled conclusively against Canada on all issues, and the United States demanded that all measures be rescinded. Victorious, U.S. Trade Representative Charlene Barshefsky declared that the split-run decision was only the thin edge of the wedge, and that the WTO ruling could be used to unravel all of Canada's cultural policies.[18]

Undaunted, Heritage Minister Copps and International Trade Minister Sergio Marchi looked for different angles to protect the Canadian magazine industry. Copps hosted an international meeting of culture ministers, looking for allies in her quest for a genuine cultural exemption from the WTO. The United States was not invited. When asked why, Copps replied, "They don't have a Minister of Culture." For his part, Marchi announced at the WTO that it was time to consider the specificity of culture in international trade agreements. In October 1998, Copps introduced Bill C-55 which made it illegal for Canadian companies to advertise in split-run magazines. U.S. magazines that defied the decree could be fined up to $250,000.

The U.S. reaction was swift and vociferous. Trade Representative Barshefsky argued that Bill C-55 was not a cultural issue, but had more to do with powerful publishing interests in Canada. She threatened $1 billion in trade sanctions against the Canadian steel, lumber, textiles, plastics and wood industries if the bill was not withdrawn. She received the full support of the U.S. Congress in this respect—both Democrats and Republicans on the House Ways and Means Committee and the Senate Finance Committee said the United States would not accept the passage of a law that exposed U.S. magazine publishers to "criminal penalties" and strongly supported the Barshefsky ultimatum.[19]

The battle that ensued over split-run magazines was high profile and acrimonious, a war of nerves that became front-page news. After negotiations broke down in May 1999, the Canadian Ministry of International Trade intervened to come up with a last-ditch solution. The Canadian government would agree to allow foreign magazines to carry up to 12 per cent Canadian advertising immediately, increasing that to 15 per cent in 18 months and 18 per cent in 36 months, without having to provide any editorial content unique to Canada. Foreigners would be able to acquire up to 49 per cent of a Canadian publisher, increased from 25 per cent previously, or could own 100 per cent of their own startups in Canada. Tax rules would be changed to allow full deductibility for advertising bought in any magazine with a least 80 per cent original or Canadian content, or half deductibility in certain other circumstances. Canadian content was defined as content original to the Canadian market or that has been produced by a Canadian or a permanent resident of Canada. To make up for the advertising revenue Canadian magazines would lose under this agreement, Ottawa announced intentions to provide subsidies amounting to at least $100 million to Canadian magazine publishers. Although Copps's plan maintained special treatment for the Canadian magazine industry, the fact that the assistance came in the more-transparent form of subsidies made it more palatable to USTR than forbidding foreign ownership in the industry outright.

---

[18]Browne ed., *The Culture Trade Quandry*, p. 3.
[19]*Canadian Press Newswire*, February 25, 1999.

FOREIGN COMPETITION IN THE CANADIAN BOOK PUBLISHING INDUSTRY

Foreign firms were also creating waves in the book publishing industry. In November 1998, the huge German media conglomerate Bertelsmann acquired the American company Random House International, the largest trade-book publisher in the world.[20] In doing so, it also acquired Random House's Canadian subsidiary, Random House Canada, as well as the publisher Alfred A. Knopf Canada. Bertelsmann had already acquired the U.S. publishing company Bantam Doubleday Dell, and held a minority share in Doubleday Canada. In order to simplify its structure in Canada, Bertelsmann wanted to merge Random House Canada with Doubleday Canada, making it one of the largest trade-book publishers in Canada. Investment Canada had to approve the merger since it meant Random House would be increasing its minority share in Doubleday to a majority foreign-owned share.

The ACP was alarmed by this prospect, claiming that the merger would give the company a 40 per cent share of the trade-book market in Canada. As Paul Davidson, former executive director of the ACP noted, Ottawa had spent 30 years fostering the indigenous publishing industry so that Canadians could tell their own stories and express their own ideas. "But now these policies are being undermined, and we're concerned that we could lose control of our culture and publishing industry."[21] According to Random House, the 40 per cent market share estimate was a vast exaggeration, with the company's own figures giving it slightly less than 20 per cent of the Canadian trade-book market. The company denied that foreign acquisition would make it less representative of Canadian literature, noting that company policy was dedicated to local input and was determined to continue representing Canadian authors. In the end, Investment Canada allowed the merger on the basis of a loophole.

George Spaulding had opposed the Doubleday-Random House merger as vociferously as any other member of the ACP, but he had to admit that his own company would be a lot easier to sell if a large conglomerate like Bertelsmann could purchase a 100 per cent share in his company. Spaulding was not alone in his dilemma. When real estate magnate Avie Bennett, also the owner and president of the large Canadian publishing company McClelland and Stewart (M&S), wanted to retire, he faced a situation identical to George Spaulding's. None of his children was interested in the company, and given the lack of foreign buyers and the relative undercapitalization of his firm, Bennett could not possibly recoup the $2.5 million annual investment he had personally made in the firm. Bennett's solution was to sell 25 per cent of his company to the newly merged Random House, and donate the other 75 per cent to the University of Toronto. The $15 million tax receipt he got for this donation was written off against his real estate income, recouping some of his initial investment in M&S in this form.

Spaulding didn't have any other income against which to write off a tax receipt, so donating his company was not an option. In any case, along with other industry members, he was somewhat critical of what Bennett had done. Bennett argued that selling the 25 per cent share to Random House was necessary to ensure the future viability of

---

[20]Bertelsmann owns 40 publishers worldwide, as well as several European television stations and three major record companies.

[21]Quoted in the *Catholic New Times*, October 17, 1999, p. 12.

the company. By selling to Random House, he ensured Canadian authors international marketing of their books, the ability to digitize books cheaply and sell them on the Internet, and sufficient capitalization of the company. Other Canadian publishers felt that Bennett had simply passed off a huge percentage of Canadian authors to a foreign firm, and questioned why he didn't sell that share to one of them. Jack Stoddard of Stoddard Publishing argued that when Bennett broke up McClelland and Stewart, he doomed Stoddard to selling to a foreign firm as well, because there was no other Canadian company large enough to acquire his company. He wished Bennett had sold to him or to another Canadian publisher.[22]

To be entirely honest, Spaulding could afford to be critical of selling out to a foreign company because he knew that his own firm was unlikely to be an attractive purchase for even the largest media conglomerate. Aside from low profits, the company was highly leveraged and had difficulty attracting investor capital of any sort to expand or to implement technological improvements. Exhibit 6 shows the ratio of total shareholders equity to total assets by size of firm, indicating that many of the firms in the industry are highly leveraged.

Spaulding needed to find some way to make his business more profitable in order to sell it, and he thought an equity tax credit might be a way to attract investors and interest in his company. The ACP proposed a model where the rate of the tax credit would be set as a percentage of the investment involved and would be paid out over three years. The investor would be required to retain equity in the proposed firm for at least three years and would be required to submit a three-year business plan to obtain the investment tax credit. The ACP estimated the plan would cost about $10 million per year.[23]

Spaulding believed an equity tax credit would be the impetus the industry needed to become more competitive. It would attract new investors to the publishing industry along with new ideas and experience. It could spur new alliances with other industries such as television and new media. If successful, it might eventually make his company profitable so that it would no longer need government subsidies. He realized, however, that the Department of Canadian Heritage would question giving more handouts to an industry that already benefited significantly from government largesse. The Department of Finance would oppose giving the publishing industry special tax treatment. He also knew that Heritage was under increasing international fire for the assistance it gave Canadian cultural industries and that the U.S. government would object strongly to tax incentives as opposed to subsidies. Yet without further assistance, Spaulding feared the Canadian industry would soon be non-existent or completely foreign-owned. He hoped that the federal government and the publishing industry could find a solution somewhere in between.

---

[22]*The Globe and Mail*, November 27, 2000, p. R-4.

[23]ACP, Pre-budget Submission, p. 7.

exhibit 1   The Global Publishing Industry: Who Owns Whom?

Company	Sales (billions)	Publishers Owned
Bertelsmann AG (Germany)	$5.5	Random House, Bantam Doubleday Dell, Alfred Knopf, Crown, Villard, Ballantine, Fawcett, Times Books, Modern Library, Delacorte, William Heinemann, Methuen, Mandarin and Minerva
Pearson PLC (U.K.)	$3.7	Penguin, Putnam, Addison Wesley Longman, Recoletos, Simon and Schuster
Wolters Kluwer NV (Netherlands)	$2.7	CCH and Lippincott
Thomson Corp. (Canada)	$2.4	West Publishing Co., Jane's Publishing Co., Carswell Co., Gale Research Co., Wadsworth Inc. and Clark Boardman Co.
Reed Elsevier NV (Netherlands & U.K.)	$1.4	R.R. Bowker and Matthew Bender & Co.
Time Warner Inc. (U.S.)	$1.1	Little Brown & Co., Grosset and Dunlap, Time Life Books and Warner Books

Source: Financial Post, November 5, 1998, p. C5.

exhibit 2   Selected Indicators for English Book Publishers in Canada 1996–97

	English Foreign-Owned	English Canadian-Owned
Number of Firms	29	204
Titles Published 1996-97	1,340	6,738
Revenues per Firm	$22.7 million	$2.7 million

Source: Derived from Statistics Canada Data cited in *Competitive Challenges Facing Book Publishers in Canada*, prepared by Arthur Donner Consultants Inc. and Lazar and Associates, May 2000, Table 1, p. 14.

exhibit 3   Selected Financial Indicators ($ millions) for Firms Receiving Government Grants

	1994–95	1995–96	1996–97	1997–98	1998–99
Total Revenues	$525.8	$542.9	$525.8	$540.3	$569.9
EBT*	$ 25.8	$ 29.6	$ 11.0	$ 1.0	$ 12.2
EBT (excluding grants)	–$ 13.6	–$ 15.2	–$ 26.5	–$ 30.3	–$ 21.3

*EBT = earnings before taxes

Source: Competitive Challenges Facing Book Publishers in Canada, prepared by Arthur Donner Consultants Inc. and Lazar and Associates, May 2000. Data derived from Table 9, p. 25.

exhibit 4   Operating Costs and Pre-tax Losses as Percentage of Revenues (5-year average 1994–1999, by size of firm sales)

	<$200K	$200–500K	$0.5m–$1m	$1–5m	$5m+
Operating Costs as % of Total Revenues*	83.9%	82.3%	65.9%	50.9%	35.9%
Pre-tax Losses* as % of Total Revenues*	−36.4%	−34.4%	−19.0%	−9.4%	−3.3%

*Excluding Grants

Source: *Competitive Challenges Facing Book Publishers in Canada*, prepared by Arthur Donner Consultants Inc. and Lazar and Associates, May 2000. Data derived from Table 24, p. 46.

exhibit 5   Book Sales in Major Markets, 1996 (US$ Millions)

	Sales
United States	$26,127
Germany	9,773
Japan	9,126
United Kingdom	4,772
France	3,306
Spain	2,981
South Korea	2,742
Brazil	2,678
Italy	2,500
China	1,867
Canada	1,296

Source: Open Book Publishing, *The Subtext 1998 Perspectives on Book Publishing*, 1998, Table 6.4.

exhibit 6   Ratio of Shareholders' Equity to Total Assets by Firm Size

	<$200k	$200k–$500k	$500k–$1m	$1m–$5
Shareholders' Equity to Total Assets Ratio	33%	54%	37%	45%

Source: *Competitive Challenges Facing Book Publishers in Canada,* prepared by Arthur Donner Consultants Inc. and Lazar and Associates, May 2000, p. 27.

case 36 Swatch and the Global Watch Industry[1]

In early June 1999, the management of the Swatch Group could be satisfied with the company's accomplishments over the last 15 years. Thanks to its 14 brands and unusual approach to marketing, and with 116 million finished watches and movements produced in 1997, the Swatch Group had helped resuscitate the Swiss watch industry and become, in value terms, the world's largest watch manufacturer. Despite an enviable track record, there was a growing sense of anxiety over the future of the company in an industry that seemed to be in a perpetual state of change.

EARLY HISTORY

Until 1957, all watches were mechanical. The aesthetics of the exterior visible elements (dials, hands and case) as well as the reliability and accuracy of a traditional timepiece depended on the meticulous care and precision that had been dedicated to its manufacturing and assembling processes. Mechanical watches consisted of between 100 and 130 components that were to be fitted together in the ébauche (winding stem, gear train) and regulating parts (mainspring, escapement, balance wheel). Most expensive watches contained at least 15 jewels (very hard stones such as synthetic sapphires or rubies that had been drilled, chamfered and polished), which were inserted in places that were most subject to metal wear. The tiny dimensions of a watch case did not leave much room for approximation, and watchmakers were required

Cyril Bouquet prepared this case under the supervision of Associate Professor Allen Morrison solely to provide material for class discussion. The authors do not intend to illustrate either effective or ineffective handling of a managerial situation. The authors may have disguised certain names and other identifying information to protect confidentiality.

IVEY

Richard Ivey School of Business
The University of Western Ontario

---

[1]This case has been written on the basis of published sources only. Consequently, the interpretation and perspectives presented in this case are not necessarily those of the Swatch Group or any of its employees.

to have a great deal of micro-mechanical engineering expertise, craftsmanship spirit, patience, experience and ingenuity.

By most accounts, the first reliable pocket watch was invented in 1510 by Peter Henlein, a locksmith from Nuremburg, but the promising art of watchmaking in Germany was rapidly killed by the Thirty Years War (1618 to 1648). Starting in the late 1500s, the development of the watchmaking industry in Europe traced its roots to the flight of protestant Huguenots who were driven out of France by a series of religious persecutions. The Huguenots found refuge in Geneva, bringing with them skills in numerous handicrafts. For centuries, Geneva had been a centre of ornate jewelry making, but it was left with little industry after John Calvin's famous *Sittenmandate* edicts against luxury and pleasure had progressively put an end to the goldsmiths' activities in the city. Looking for a new source of income, and with their knowledge of metals, skills in jewelry making and artistic flair, many Genevan goldsmiths embraced the watchmakers' profession.

As they were becoming more and more numerous, watchmakers decided to regulate their activities, and incorporated into a guild in 1601. The development of the industry in Geneva and the surrounding Jura mountains was rapid. By 1686, there were 100 masters in Geneva; 165 in 1716; and 800 in 1766, employing some 3,000 people. By 1790, Geneva exported more than 60,000 watches throughout Europe. Many of the Genevese moved north along the French frontier in the Vallée de Joux, Neuchatel and La Chaux-de-Fonds (see Exhibit 1).

The emergence of the watch industry in Switzerland was a blessing for the local farmers who could extract only modest agricultural revenues from their mountainous terrain. In fact, many families—who had been educated through a close-knit system of community schools—were looking for an additional source of income, particularly during the long and snow-filled winters. Thanks to advances in new machine-powered watchmaking tools, individual Swiss families began to specialize, some in the production of single components, others in assembly. The small size of watches and watch components allowed for relatively easy transportation from mountain farms and villages to commercial centres.

Swiss watches were sold exclusively through jewelry and up-scale department stores, which were also fully responsible for repair and aftersales services. Watches were purchased as lifetime investments and were often handed down from generation to generation. Swiss watches found ready acceptance throughout Europe and later in the U.S., in part because of their promotion by jewellers who saw them as a source of ongoing revenues through their repair services.

In the 18th and 19th centuries, English competitors were a constant challenge for the Swiss, who undertook serious efforts to overcome early British supremacy. First, the Swiss invested in education and training, establishing several watchmaking academies at home and watch-repair schools in major foreign markets. Second, and to strengthen their image internationally, they created a "Swiss made" label, which would become by 1920, an important symbol of quality, style and prestige. Third, the Swiss significantly improved process technology, setting up the world's first mechanized watch factory in 1839. British watchmakers made no attempt to mass-manufacture watches until much later. Seeing mass-production techniques as a threat to their craft, they persuaded Parliament to pass a law barring the use of specialty production tools in the British watch industry, and devoted themselves to the production of very expensive marine chronometers. As a result, the British watch industry steadily declined during the 19th century, while the Swiss industry was on its way to achieving world dominance, thanks to significant advances in design,

exhibit 1   Watch Production in Switzerland

Source: FH, Federation of the Swiss Watch Industry

features, standardization, interchangeability of parts and productivity. In 1842, Adrien Philippe introduced complicated watches featuring perpetual calendars, flyback hands and/or chronographs. Other early Swiss names included Beaume & Mercier (1830), Longines (1832), Piaget (1874), Omega (1848), Movado (1881) and Rolex (1908).

The U.S. watch industry appeared in the middle of the 19th century. Local production consisted of high-volume, standardized products manufactured in machine-driven factories. U.S. watches—such as the US$1 *Turnip* pocket watch introduced under the Ingersoll brand name by the Waterbury Clock Company—were cheap but also of very poor quality. Anyone who wanted a "real" watch bought Swiss.

In the early 20th century, the hard economic times (collapsing sales and soaring unemployment) following the First World War, led to a profound reorganization of the Swiss watch industry. Almost 2,500 distinct watchmaking firms grouped together into three associations, namely the Federation of the Swiss Watch Industry (FH) in 1924, the Ebauches SA in 1926, and the group Union des Branches Annexes de l'Horlogerie (UBAH) in 1926. The associations agreed to co-ordinate activities (for example, watch components had to be bought from members of the associations only) and maintain high prices. The Swiss Laboratory for Watchmaking Research (CEH) was also founded in 1924, with the objective of strengthening the country's technological advantage. Finally, and in response to the world depression at the time, the Swiss government pushed several important watch assembly firms to form a holding company, ASUAG, in 1931.

POSTWAR COMPETITIVE CHANGES (1945 TO 1970)

By 1945, the Swiss accounted for 80 per cent of the world's total watch production, and 99 per cent of all U.S. watch imports. Swiss watch production was divided among nearly 2,500 distinct companies, 90 per cent of which employed fewer than 50 people. Despite the 200-year dominance of Swiss watchmaking companies, much would change in a short period of time.

U.S. Competitors

The main source of competition for the Swiss arose from two American watchmakers, Timex and Bulova. Using a combination of automation, precision tooling and simpler design than that of higher-priced Swiss watches, U.S. Time Corporation introduced in 1951 a line of inexpensive (US$6.95 to US$7.95), disposable, yet stylized and highly durable Timex watches, whose movements had new hard alloy bearings instead of traditional and more expensive jewels. Hard alloy metals allowed for the creation of durable watches at lower costs than jewelled lever timepieces. They also allowed U.S. Time to more effectively automate its production lines, further lowering costs.

Traditional jewellers were very reluctant to carry the brand for a variety of reasons. Its prices and margins were slim compared to those offered by the Swiss, while the watches' riveted cases could not be opened, thereby eliminating the possibility for jewellers to generate aftersales repair revenues. Locked out of jewelry stores, Timex had no choice but to innovate in its marketing and distribution strategy. Their first extensive worldwide advertising campaign on television, "Took a licking and kept on ticking," was to become a legend in marketing history. Consumer demand soared after John Cameron Swazey, a famous U.S. news commentator, was featured in live "torture tests" commercials emphasizing the watch's low cost and incredible durability. The disposable aspect of Timex watches (no local repair involved) pushed the company to develop new distribution channels, including drugstores, discount houses, department stores, catalogue showrooms, military bases and sporting goods outlets. By 1970, Timex (having changed its name from U.S. Time) had established a manufacturing and/or marketing presence in over 30 countries and become the world's largest watch manufacturer in terms of units sold.

Bulova was the leading U.S. manufacturer of quality, jewelled-lever watches. Integrating the highly accurate tuning fork technology bought from a Swiss engineer in 1959, after the main Swiss companies had turned down the technology, Bulova introduced *Accutron* in 1962. Five years later, *Accutron* was the best-selling watch over $100 in the U.S. Bulova also formed a partnership with Japan's Citizen Watch Company to produce the movements for the *Caravelle* line, designed to meet the low-cost/high-quality challenge imposed by Timex. By 1970, Bulova had expanded its international presence all around the world, and become the largest seller of watches, in revenue terms, in both the United States and the world overall.

Japanese Competitors

Like the U.S. industry, the Japanese watch industry was highly concentrated. In 1950, three main competitors, K. Hattori (which marketed the Seiko brand), Citizen and Orient accounted for 50 per cent, 30 per cent, and 20 per cent of the Japanese market respectively. Their positions were protected by the 70 per cent tariff and tax sales imposed on all imported watches by the Japanese government.

As the Japanese market became saturated in the 1960s, Hattori and Citizen moved aggressively into other Asia Pacific countries. After first exporting from Japan, Hattori and Citizen established component and assembly operations in low-cost Hong Kong, Singapore and Malaysia. With hundreds of millions of unserved consumers, the region was also a highly attractive market. From a position of strength in Asia, the Japanese watch companies began in earnest to push into Europe and North America.

The Swiss response to the growing power of U.S. and Japanese competitors was limited. In 1962, the Swiss FH and ASUAG created a research organization, the Centre Electronique Horloger (CEH) to develop a competitive alternative to the tuning fork technology patented by Bulova. These efforts were unsuccessful, in part because of only lukewarm support from member companies. A rising worldwide demand for watches did little to slow the steady decline in the Swiss share of the world market (from 80 per cent in 1946 to 42 per cent in 1970).

CHANGING TECHNOLOGIES (1970 TO 1990)

The advent of light-emitting diodes (LED) and liquid crystal display (LCD) watches constituted a true revolution in the world of watchmaking, as they allowed the digital display of time. In 1970, Hattori Seiko became the first to develop and commercialize a quartz watch named *Astron*, based on LED technology.

Despite their novelty, LED watches had many flaws. A button had to be pushed to activate the display of LED watches, a process that consumed a lot of electrical energy and wore out batteries quickly. Additionally, most people felt that LEDs were distracting and inconvenient to use. In 1973, Seiko introduced the world's first LCD quartz watch with six-digit display, and by the late 1970s, LCDs dominated the digital segment. However, digital watches remained largely plagued by quality problems, and consumers never fully embraced the style. Quartz analogue watches, which involved a more delicate manufacturing, and conserved—with their hands and gear train—the traditional appearance of mechanical timepieces, increasingly gained consumers' acceptance. By 1984, over 75 per cent of all watches sold around the world were based on quartz technology, versus only three per cent in 1975. The large majority of quartz watches were analogue.

Quartz watches used an integrated circuit, made up of numerous electronic components grouped together on the basis of a few square millimetres. Extremely accurate, thanks to their high frequency of vibrations (32 kHz), they were accurate to less than one second per day. Generally more sophisticated—in terms of functions—than their mechanical counterparts, they were also far less expensive to manufacture. The average production cost of a standard quartz watch fell from US$200 in 1972 to about US$0.50 in 1984, the cost of components being constantly driven down by the main U.S. chipmakers such as National Semiconductor and Texas Instruments.

Faced with soaring international competition, the Swiss abolished all internal regulations in 1981, and the industry began to consolidate. Many firms merged in an attempt to leverage their marketing and/or manufacturing capabilities. The largest operation resulted in the creation of the Société Suisse pour L'Industrie Horlogère (SSIH), which controlled brands such as Omega and Tissot, among others.

THE JAPANESE INDUSTRY

Convinced that technologically sophisticated watches could allow Swiss prices at Timex costs, Hattori Seiko and Citizen made important efforts to promote the new quartz technology. Large investments were made in plant and equipment for fully automated high-volume production of integrated circuits, batteries and LCD panels. Hattori's production lines were designed to produce up to 1,000,000 watches per year per product line. Manufacturing/assembly facilities were set up all around the world (Japan, the United States, western Europe, Australia, Brazil, Hong Kong, Korea, Mexico). To ease the transition, employees were retrained, relations with distributors were reinforced, and advertising budgets were increased.

By 1979, Hattori produced about 22 million watches annually and became the world's largest watch company in terms of revenues, with sales approaching US$1.2 billion, versus only US$503 million for the Swiss ASUAG. Citizen launched the world's first wristwatch movement with a thickness of less than one millimetre in 1978, and became the global leader in both movement and finished wristwatch production volumes in 1986.

Casio entered the watch market in 1974 with a digital model priced at US$39.95. Its subsequent low-cost, multifunction digital plastic watches were rapidly fitted with gadgetry such as timers and calculators. By 1980, the company had captured 10 per cent of the Japanese digital watch market, and became the world's second most important player in the under US$50 world watch market, behind Timex.

Hattori, Casio and Citizen were largely integrated companies. Most operations, from the production of movements and components to the assembly and distribution of finished watches, were carried out through wholly owned subsidiaries and/or majority joint ventures. In 1980, Japan produced about 67.5 million watches, up from 12.2 million in 1970.

THE U.S. INDUSTRY

U.S. competitors were relatively slow to get on the electronic bandwagon. Neither Bulova nor Timex's facilities easily allowed the production of quartz crystal or integrated circuits. In fact, they were rapidly becoming obsolete in light of those new technologies sweeping the industry. In addition, Timex was struggling with management problems, as Mr. Lehmkuhl—who had run the business for almost 30 years with no clear successor—fell ill and could no longer work. Nevertheless, both companies finally entered the quartz watch market in the mid-1970s, sourcing their quartz components from a variety of suppliers and backing their product lines with full-scale advertising and promotion campaigns. The Timex model was priced at US$125, which was 60 per cent below Seiko's least expensive watch on the market at that time.

About 100 semiconductor firms such as National Semiconductor, Texas Instruments (TI), and Litronix, were also attracted to the promising market for digital watches and circuits for electronic movements in the mid-1970s. Most started as suppliers of quartz movements and components, then invested in high-volume, fully automated watch-manufacturing plants. The belief was that their huge existing distribution channels for consumer electronics products would give them a strong competitive advantage. Watches were introduced at very aggressive prices (TI's retailed at $19.95 in 1976 and $9.99 in 1977). In 1978, TI's digital watch sales reached $100 million, for a pretax profit of US$28 million. However, stagnant demand coupled with continuous price wars and numerous distribution problems led all semiconductor firms to exit the market one by one. In the end, most customers felt uncomfortable buying watches in electronic stores where the semiconductor firms had a distribution advantage.

The price wars following the arrival of these semiconductor firms were also largely detrimental to the main U.S. watchmaking companies. Although it was constantly underpriced by Texas Instruments, Timex turned down a number of propositions to form manufacturing partnerships with several chipmakers. Some observers argued that Timex was probably too proud to accept the idea of co-operation. Timex lost US$10 million in 1980, being surpassed by Seiko as the world's largest watch manufacturer company (both in units and total sales), while its share of the U.S. market fell to under 33 per cent. The two other U.S. players remaining in the industry were not in a much better situation. Bulova experienced three years of significant losses before being purchased by Loews Corporation; Hamilton lost $15 million in 1970 and went bankrupt in 1978: the Pulsar rights were bought by Seiko and the remaining assets purchased by SSIH.

WATCHMAKING ACTIVITIES IN HONG KONG AND KOREA

By the end of the 1970s, Hong Kong had become the highest volume producer of timepieces in the world. Japanese, American and European watchmakers had all established assembly plants (mechanical, digital and quartz analogue watches) in the city to take advantage of highly skilled, cheap labor and favorable tax conditions. Numerous local semiconductor firms had also engaged in the production of low-cost digital quartz watches that were then distributed through local retail chains and department stores, or exported, mainly to mainland China.

The timepiece industry in Korea also experienced considerable growth in the 1970s. By 1988, the country's total watch exports amounted to US$39 million, along with a rising reputation in the eyes of the world for quality assembling capabilities.

The Hong Kong and Korean watch industries benefited from their flexible manufacturing systems, capable of handling small quantity orders in different styles. However, downward pressures on prices and low profit margins discouraged local watch producers from investing in technology and branding.

THE SWISS INDUSTRY RESPONDS SLOWLY

Although the Swiss pioneered quartz technology, they were particularly reluctant to adopt the new technology. Contrary to the Japanese, their industry structure was very fragmented and, therefore, not adapted to high-volume mass-production procedures. Besides, electronic watches were regarded as being unreliable, unsophisticated, and not up to Swiss quality standards. Consequently, digital and analogue quartz watches were regarded as just a passing fad, and in 1974, accounted for only 1.7 per cent of the 84.4 million watches exported from Switzerland. Instead, the Swiss focused on the high-end, mechanical segment of the industry, where traditional craftsmanship remained the deciding factor.

As SSIH and ASUAG regularly increased prices to maintain profitability, foreign competition rapidly established a strong foothold in the low- and middle-price ranges where the Swiss were forced to abandon their leadership, virtually without a fight. Compounding the problems faced by the Swiss, the U.S. dollar more than halved its value against the Swiss franc during the 1970s. The appreciating Swiss franc effectively raised the export prices of Swiss watches (see Exhibit 2).

The Swiss industry experienced a severe crisis in the late 1970s and early 1980s. Its exports of watches and movements decreased from 94 million in 1974 to 43 million in 1983, while its world market share slid from 43 per cent to less than 15 per cent during that same period. Employment fell from 90,000 (1970) to 47,000 (1980) to 34,000 (1984), and bankruptcies reduced the number of firms from 1,618 to 860 to 630 respectively. These competitive changes resulted mainly from the seeming inability of the Swiss to adapt to the rapid emergence of new watch technologies.

Near-Death Experience

In the early 1980s, Swiss watch production hit an all-time low. SSIH and ASUAG faced liquidation, and a profound restructuring of the Swiss industry became necessary. The Swiss government provided financial assistance and initiated the "electronic watch" program in 1978 to promote new technologies as well as the production of electronic watch components in Switzerland. But this initiative was not sufficient, and in 1981 SSIH reported a loss of SFr142 million, giving the company a negative net worth of SFr27.4 million. The Swiss creditor banks—which had just taken over the country's two largest watchmaking groups—were getting ready to sell prestigious brand names, such as Omega, Tissot or Longines to the Japanese. But Nicolas Hayek, the already well-known founder and CEO of Hayek Engineering, a consulting firm based in Zurich, was convinced he could revive the Swiss industry and regain lost market share, primarily in the lower-end segment. He invested $102 million—mostly his own money—and led a group of 16 investors in buying back the two groups, before orchestrating their merger in 1983.

SMH and Swatch

Hayek teamed with Dr. Ernst Thomke to head the new group, Société Micromécanique et Horlogère (SMH). After the merger, SMH owned many of the country's famous watchmaking names, such as Omega, Tissot, Longines and Rado. Five years later, the group had become the world's largest watchmaking company. Its first product initiative, Swatch, was to become an enormous commercial success, as well as the main instrument behind the revitalization of the entire Swiss industry.

The Swatch mania marked the 1980s for the Swiss industry. The Swatch (contraction of "Swiss" and "watch") was conceived as an inexpensive, SFr50 (US$40), yet good-quality watch, with quartz accuracy, water and shock resistance, as well as a one-year guarantee. The concept was challenging. Particular efforts were needed to reduce production costs down to Asian levels. Watch engineers slashed the number of

exhibit 2   Exchange Rate to the U.S. Dollar (Annual Average)

	1950-1970	1971	1972	1974	1976	1978	1980
Swiss Franc	4.37	4.15	4.15	3.58	2.89	2.24	2.18

Source: International Monetary Fund Yearbook of Statistics.

individual parts required in the production of a watch from 91 to 51, and housed them in a standardized plastic case that could be produced on a fully automated assembly line. For the first time ever, it became possible to produce cheap watches in high-cost Switzerland. By 1985, production costs were decreased to under SFr10 per unit, and only 130 people were needed to assemble the first eight million Swatch models. By comparison, 350 people were still required to assemble 700,000 Omega watches.

Swatch was an immediate success. Within two years of its 1983 launch, sales were averaging 100,000 units a months, for a cumulative total of 13 million sold. In 1985, Swatch accounted for over 80 per cent of SMH's total unit sales, and by 1989, just six years after its debut, the company had placed 70 million Swatches on customers' wrists.

Marketing was key to the watch's success. Franz Sprecher, an independent consultant, and Max Imgrüth, a graduate of New York's Fashion Institute of Technology, helped SMH position the watch as a lifestyle symbol and fashion accessory, not as a traditional timekeeping instrument. With their trendy and colorful designs, models were created for every occasion.

Initially, the media appeared to be mesmerized by Hayek's charismatic style and unusual approach to marketing. This resulted in lots of free media coverage and publicity. The company also spent liberally on special events and public relations activities. SMH budgeted about SFr5 million per Swatch product line per year in promotional money, and used celebrity endorsements extensively. Swatches were sold through nonconventional channels of distribution such as discount houses and department stores, where variety and low prices constituted the main selling points. Swatch made a few attempts to diversify, but its line of accessories (casual clothing and footwear, umbrellas, sunglasses, and cigarette lighters) experienced mixed success and was discontinued in 1988.

COMPETING IN REAL TIME (1990s)

Global watch production grew steadily in the 1990s, at a rate of about four per cent per annum, and reached 1.3 billion watches in 1998, equivalent to 22 per cent of the world's population (see Exhibit 3). The production of mechanical watches (and to a lesser extent, that of digital watches) gradually decreased over the years, while that

exhibit 3   Global Watch Production—1984 to 1998

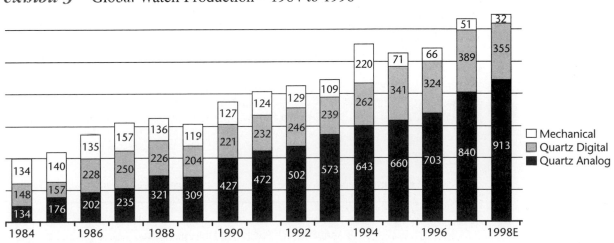

Source: FH, Federation of the Swiss Watch Industry, and Japan Clock and Watch Association

of analogue quartz watches rose 11 per cent per year on average. In 1998, quartz watches—digital and analogue—accounted for about 97 per cent of the worldwide industry's production in volume. On average, annual watch purchases were about one unit per person in North America, and 0.6 unit per person in Europe and Japan. Together these three regions—which accounted for 14 per cent of the world's population—generated about 56 per cent of global watch demand (see Exhibit 4).

Industry Restructuring

The global watch industry experienced downward profit pressures in the 1990s, as many watchmakers incessantly cut prices—driven in part by a push for economies of scale. Overcapacity and tough head-to-head competition led prices of basic watch movements to be slashed by over 30 per cent in 1998 alone. By the end of the decade, consolidation had reduced the number of watch movement manufacturers from 30 to just three (the Swatch Group—having changed its name from SMH—as well as Seiko and Citizen). The achievement of a critical mass was becoming a necessity to compete globally in all segments of the industry.

Several types of internal reorganizations allowed companies to realize economies of scale and/or maintain profitability. These included:

Restructuring Initiatives

Many watchmaking companies reacted to declining prices in their core business by increasing productivity and shifting manufacturing overseas. With the exception of the Swatch Group, most watch companies manufactured in Southeast Asia exclusively.

Pursuing Acquisitions

In tune with its strategy to reinforce its position in the luxury or prestige brands, the Swatch Group acquired Blancpain in 1992, thereby also taking control of Frederic

exhibit 4   Per Capita GNP and Annual Watch Purchases, by Region

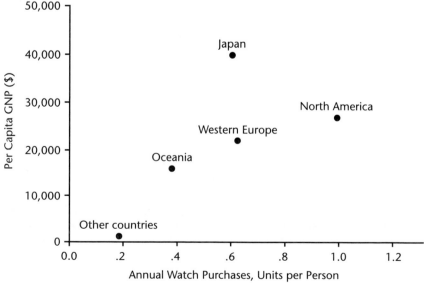

Source: Japan Clock and Watch Association, United Nations Demographic Yearbook, The World Bank.

Piguet, a company admired for its complex, high-quality mechanical movements. In January 1999, the Swatch Group purchased the total shares of Favre and Perret, the highly reputed producer of quality Swiss watchcases. As another example, Gucci, the luxury Italian company, acquired Severin Montres, its 23-year Swiss watch manufacturer, for $150 million in November 1997. The following year, Gucci's watch sales increased by 160 per cent to $60.1 million. "There is no question that Gucci is destined to become more than a shoe and bag business," said De Boisgelin, an equity analyst with Merrill Lynch in London.[2]

Accessing New Distribution Channels

Watchmakers traditionally used independent agents to sell products around the world. However, increasing difficulties controlling the merchandising and pricing policies used by local retailers led many of them to alter their strategies. In 1997, the Swatch Group opened 61 new free-standing Swatch stores (mostly operated as franchises), bringing the total to 120 (including five megastores) in more than 20 countries. Despite the risks involved, the strategy was promising: sales at New York's Swatch Time Shop boutiques approached 100,000 units in 1998, up 32 per cent over 1997. By taking over 85 per cent of its distribution network, Tag Heuer increased its gross margins from 45 per cent to 65 per cent, which more than offset the cost of running local subsidiaries. According to CEO Christian Viros, the move allowed "greater control of our destiny, better control of the implementation of our marketing programs, better understanding of local issues, and greater reactiveness to new developments."[3]

Creating New Niche Products

Despite ongoing consolidation, there was a viable place for niche companies with clearly defined brands and images. By the late 1990s, Switzerland had about 600 watchmaking companies, employing 34,000 employees, in addition to the big four (The Swatch Group, The Vendôme Luxury Group, Rolex and Tag Heuer), which together accounted for 75 per cent to 80 per cent of Swiss industry turnover. As examples of niche players, St. John Timepieces entered the industry in 1997 with a collection of Swiss watches specifically designed for sophisticated women, retailing from $450 to $18,000. Breitling scarcely deviated from the aerial image it established in 1884. In 1999, it equipped Breitling Orbiter 3's pilots, Bertrand Piccard and Brian Jones, with wristwatches for their successful, first nonstop 26,602 miles balloon flight around the world.

Increasing Advertising

The overabundance of supply in the industry implied that watchmakers had to find ways to distinguish their offerings from those of their competitors. Advertising expenditures reached unprecedented levels. In the 1990s, 40 per cent of the value of all Swiss advertisements in international media promoted wristwatches, not banking institutions. Seiko's 1998 *Electricity* campaign was backed with a 60 per cent increase in media spending, while Timex allocated about US$8 million in 1999 to market its *Turn 'n' Pull* Alarm watches.

Huge advertising budgets were not, per se, a guarantee of success. The campaigns also needed to be creative in order to get consumers' attention. Companies turned down

---

[2]*Women's Wear Daily*, March 20, 1998.

[3]*Chief Executive*, 1998.

conservative ads in favor of eye-popping, humorous, and thought-provoking messages that obtained an emotional reaction from viewers. For example, Bulgari formed a one-year partnership with Alitalia, Italy's national airline, to have a personalized Boeing 747 fly around the world with a three-dimensional image of its latest cutting-edge aluminum timepiece painted on the fuselage. Audemars Piguet's ad crusade, "Who is behind an Audemars Piguet Watch?" featured mysterious men and women showing off their watch faces while their own faces remain obscured. Other watchmakers tried to get exposure in action-packed movies such as Men in Black and Lethal Weapon 4 (Hamilton), James Bond (Omega), or Armageddon (Tag Heuer). Strong marketing muscle was also put behind sports partnerships. For example, Tag Heuer and Hugo Boss had long been associated with Formula One auto racing, and Spanish-based Festina with cycling events such as the Tour de France.

Emphasizing Quality

Faced with strong competition from independent, low-cost Asian producers, many European and U.S. watchmakers chose to gradually reposition their brands in the upper market, and proposed increasingly expensive and sophisticated watches. According to the Federation of the Swiss Watch Industry, the average price of a Swiss wristwatch, taking account of all materials, rose from US$132 in 1996 to US$157 in 1997. A growing number of customers was becoming aware of quality and increasingly wanted a watch with lasting value.

Emphasizing Technology

The end of the 1990s looked promising in terms of technological breakthroughs. Bulova's *Vibra Alarm* watch featured dual sound and vibrating alarms. In Seiko's *Kinetic*, an oscillating weight was set in motion by the slightest movements of the wearer's arm ("If you're going to create electricity, use it!"). Timex's *DataLink* pioneered the utilization of wristwatches as wearable information devices. Following Timex's lead, various watch manufacturers introduced multifunctional watches that could be interfaced with personal computers. Other manufacturers designed watches with built-in global positioning systems (Casio, Timex), or offered fast, customized and reliable access to Internet services.

Accentuating Fashion

Another noticeable trend was the entry of fashion-house designers. By 1999, and partly thanks to the Swatch revolution, people increasingly believed that they were judged by what they wore on their wrists. Fashion designers strove to create new watch brands to meet every one of their possible fashion needs. Some decided to put their signatures on stylized watches produced in co-operation with major specialist manufacturers. Examples included Emporio Armani (Fossil), Calvin Klein (The Swatch Group), Guess (Timex) and Yves St Laurent (Citizen). Others, such as Bulgari, Hermes, and Dior set up their own in-house manufacturing operations. "We have very high expectations for this side of the business," said Guillaume de Seynes, director of Hermes Montres. "Watches are already our fourth biggest product in sales terms after leather, silk, and ready-to-wear. We've made a significant investment in the new factory because we expect even faster growth in the future."[4]

---

[4]*Financial Times*, April 24/25, 1999.

DEVELOPMENTS IN THE HONG KONG AND JAPANESE INDUSTRIES

In the late 1990s, Hong Kong was the world's dominant centre for watch assembly. In 1998, about 80 per cent of all watches produced worldwide were assembled in the city (see Exhibit 5).

Japanese watch manufacturers saw their combined domestic and overseas watch production rise about 14 per cent per year in the 1990s. Particularly strong in the sports watch segment, the Japanese offered an impressive range of multifunction chronographs for virtually any type of outdoor activity, including diving, mountain climbing and flying. However, sales and profitability deteriorated between 1993 and 1996 due to a rapid appreciation of the yen. In addition, the average unit price of analogue quartz movements fell by nearly 50 per cent to ¥234 in the first half of the decade, and by over 30 per cent in 1998, as major companies boosted production. This collapse severely shook the industry, and many manufacturers, such as Orient Watch, had to exit the market. Throughout the last half of the 1990s, Seiko and Citizen began cutting production in order to hold prices firm.

Citizen maintained its world's volume leadership, with 2,500 new models released every year and 311 million timepieces produced in 1997 (about 25 per cent of the world's total and 36 per cent of the global market for analogue quartz watches). Sales were mainly dependent upon Japan (38 per cent), Asia (32 per cent), America (15 per cent) and Europe (14 per cent). Two new collections—the light-powered *Eco-Drive* watches and the affordable luxury *Elegance Signature* dress watches—marked the company's desire to move from traditional sports watches towards more sophisticated or expensive timepieces.

Seiko introduced a few technological marvels in the early 1990s, such as the *Perpetual Calendar* watch, with the first built-in millennium plus (1,100 years) calendar, *the Scubamaster,* with the first integrated computerized dive table, and the *Receptor MessageWatch,* with paging functions and built-in antenna that allowed access to

exhibit 5   World Production of Finished Watches: 500 Million Pieces (1997)

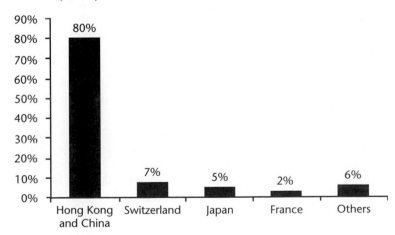

Source: Federation of the Swiss Watch Industry

specialized information services and incoming alphanumeric messages. In 1995, Seiko introduced the *Kinetic* series, backed with a $20 million advertising campaign. The futuristic line became the driving force behind the company's growth in the late 1990s, accounting for 25 per cent of Seiko's $3 billion global sales. Great hopes were also placed on *Kinetic's* lower-cost cousin, the $200 *Pulsar* solar-powered quartz watch, which was launched at the end of 1996.

Casio enjoyed a significant expansion of its wristwatch division, thanks to the successful launches of the *G-shock* and *Baby-G* product lines. The company was particularly strong in the U.S. (second largest market share after Timex), but also heavily dependent on domestic Japanese sales, which made up two-thirds of total *G-shock* and *Baby-G* sales. A depressed Japanese economy in the late 1990s had a profound negative effect on the company's profits, which were estimated to drop from ¥38 billion in 1998 to ¥19 billion in 1999.[5]

THE U.S. INDUSTRY

The biggest single watch market in the world was also the one with the largest trade deficit. In 1991, exports amounted to $73.4 million, compared to an import total of $1.84 billion. Thanks to a factory in Little Rock, Arkansas, Timex was the only U.S. watch company with any domestic production in the late 1990s.

Timex

From sports watches and classic styles to watches featuring *Star Trek* and Walt Disney characters, Timex offerings strove to address a variety of consumer trends in the 1990s. The production of watches for Guess, Timberland, Nautica, and Reebok further emphasized Timex's willingness to reach a mass audience. Two innovations distinguished the company. The first was the durable, multi-function *Ironman Triathlon* watch, named after the gruelling annual Hawaiian sports event. Initially positioned as an instrument for serious athletes, the watch rapidly appealed to a wider audience of pedestrian customers. By the late 1990s, it was the world's best-selling sports watch, with more than 25 million units sold since its 1986 introduction. The second was *Indiglo*, a patented luminescent dial technology launched in 1992, and credited with more than doubling the company's sales by 1994. *Indiglo* received considerable attention in 1993 after a group of people trapped in the World Trade Center bombing had been led to safety by an *Indiglo* owner, who guided them down 34 flights of pitch-black stairs through the glow of his Timex watch. Other technological innovations rapidly followed, with Timex *DataLink*, a $139 wristwatch allowing wireless transfer to and from a desktop PC, and *Beepwear*, a $160 alphanumeric pager wristwatch developed and commercialized in partnership with Motorola.

Timex's annual sales exceeded $600 million in the late 1990s, one-quarter of which came from the U.S. market, where the company remained the top-selling watch company, far ahead of its main competitors. By 1999, with a 30 per cent market share in its hands, Timex had sold more watches in the U.S. than the next five competitors combined (see Exhibit 6). However, the huge majority of these watches were manufactured in Asia.

---

[5]In June 1999 US$1 = ¥119

exhibit 6   Share of Purchasers by Brand in the U.S. Market—1999

Timex	30.6%	Gitano	2.0%
Casio	7.8%	Gucci	1.9%
Seiko	7.4%	Swatch	1.6%
Guess (Timex)	5.0%	Rolex	1.1%
Armitron (Gluck)	4.5%	Movado	1.0%
Citizen	4.0%	Tag Heuer	0.8%
Fossil	3.5%	Hamilton (Swatch)	0.7%
Pulsar (Seiko)	3.1%	Tissot (Swatch)	0.7%
Lorus (Seiko)	2.5%	Omega (Swatch)	0.5%
Bulova	2.2%	Rado (Swatch)	0.2%

Source: Euromonitor

NEW ENTRANTS IN THE 1990s

By the early 1990s, mainland China and India had emerged among the fastest-growing watch markets in the world. With a combined population of 2.1 billion people, these markets could not be ignored, especially after a series of government decisions to liberalize trade and investment in those countries. A number of reputable watchmaking companies had established a presence in India and mainland China, despite the threat of counterfeiting (about 50 per cent of wristwatches sold in those markets were either counterfeited or smuggled in). Most came in via the trading route, appointing local distributors such as Dream Time Watches in India. This strategy was ideal for the Swiss, who could capitalize on the well-appreciated label "Swiss made." Others such as Timex, Seiko and Citizen established their own production facilities, often in co-operation with key local partners.

Titan Industries was probably one of the most remarkable industry success stories of the 1990s. The group was established in 1987, with a greenfield investment of $130 million from giant Indian conglomerate Tata Group and the government of Tamil Nadu state, where Titan built one of the world's biggest integrated watch factories, near India's technological centre Bangalore. Constantly scanning the world for best practices, Titan sourced designs and technology from France, Switzerland and Germany, watch-straps from Austria, and cases from Japan. This world-class strategy created a remarkably successful company. During its first year of operation, 750,000 high-quality finished timepieces were produced and, in 1997, the company enjoyed a dominant 60 per cent share of the organized Indian watch market, with pretax profits amounting to US$7.5 million on turnover of US$96 million. Titan's management believed the company had little choice but to internationalize, partly to defend its own domestic position. Mr. Desai, Titan's vice-chairman and managing director, commented on the need to globalize: "India is being globalized and the whole world is now turning up in India. So the kind of protection we've enjoyed will go. It's going to get very crowded."[6] By 1997, the company exported over 600,000 watches annually and had established offices in Dubai, London, New York and Singapore. However, by the end of the 1990s, and despite the company's recent $20 million advertising campaign, it was difficult to predict international success. Seducing consumers into buying $120 to $700 Indian-made wristwatches was challenging, given the country's reputation for the poor quality of its exports.

[6]*Financial Times London Edition. Financial Times.* September 10, 1997; 43.

THE SWISS INDUSTRY IN THE LATE 1990s

In the late 1990s, watch production in Switzerland was the country's third most important industry behind the chemical-pharmaceutical and electronic industries. In 1998, 34 million timepieces were produced in Switzerland for a total value of SFr8.2 billion.[7] Of those, 90 per cent were exported, positioning the country as the world's leading exporter—in value—of finished watches (see Exhibit 7).

The Swiss industry had the ability to provide consumers with a comprehensive choice of products in all market segments. Whatever their needs and preferences (mechanical versus quartz technologies; diamond set watch of precious metals versus stainless steel, plastic or ceramic; classic appearance versus trendy design), consumers could always find a "Swiss-made" solution when shopping for their wristwatches. Of course, the Swiss industry stood apart in the upper market range, where its watches had gained an unequalled reputation for quality, styling, reliability and accuracy. In 1998, the average price of watches exported by Switzerland was SFr235, four times higher than the average of the world industry (see Exhibits 8 and 9). The "Swiss-made" label remained one the oldest examples of a registered and fiercely protected national branding name, which could be used only on watches and clocks containing at least 50 per cent Swiss-manufactured components by value.

The Vendôme Luxury Group accounted for about 20 per cent of Swiss industry turnover, privately held Rolex for 15 per cent, and Tag Heuer—which sold over 673,000 units in 1997, for seven per cent. The Swatch Group was the main player, with a third of industry turnover. Thanks to its 14 brands (Blancpain, Omega, Rado, Longines, Tissot, Calvin Klein, Certina, Mido, Hamilton, Pierre Balmain, Swatch, Flick Flack, Lanco, and Endura), the group had gained a presence in all price and market categories.

Swiss watches were sold all around the world. Exports to the United States increased by more than 10 per cent in 1998 for the third consecutive year. Sales in Europe were also on the rise, especially in Spain (+41.3 per cent), Italy (+18 per cent) and France (+16 per cent). In Asia, the ongoing economic crisis depressed demand and put downward pressures on prices (the demand in Hong Kong, Singapore, Thailand and Taiwan dropped by 23 per cent or SFr500 million in 1998). In 1997, Tag Heuer saw

exhibit 7   World Production of Finished Watches in Value Terms: 16 Billion Swiss Francs (1997)

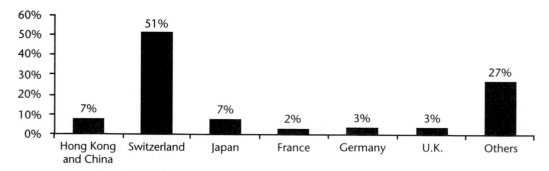

Source: Federation of the Swiss Watch Industry

---

[7]In June 1999, SF 1 = US$0.66.

exhibit 8   Luxury, Prestige and Top Range: Global Market Players (1998)

	Turnover in SFr. Million	Market Share
Rolex	2,200	28%
Vendôme*	1,540	20%
Swatch Group**	1,000-1,100	14%
Gucci	620	8%
TAG Heuer	470	6%
Patek Philippe	250	3%
Bulgari	215	3%
Chopard	195	3%
Jaeger LeCoultre	180	2%
Audemars Piguet	120	2%
Other (Ebel, IWC, Breguet,…)	910	12%
Total	7,750	100%

*(Cartier, Piaget, Vacheron and Constantin, Beaume & Mercier)
**(Blancpain, Omega, Rado, Longines)
Source: Bank Leu estimates, Vendôme Group Data

exhibit 9   Average Price of Watches in 1998 (in Swiss francs)*

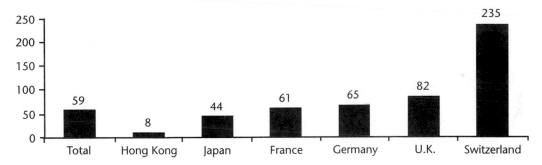

*estimate
Source: Federation of the Swiss Watch Industry

Asian sales drop by 21.4 per cent, from SFr130 million to SFr102.9 million, accounting for the brand's overall 5.4 per cent decrease.

The Swatch Group

In value terms, the Swatch Group was the world's leading manufacturer of watches (14 per cent share of the world market). In 1998, the Swatch Group increased its gross sales and net profits by 7.1 per cent and 7.5 per cent respectively. With a growth averaging 15 per cent to 25 per cent per year, Omega had been a major profit driver for the group (see Exhibit 12 on page 471), thanks to a successful repositioning strategy initiated in the early 1990s. To rejuvenate the brand, cheaper, silver-plated gold was used to replace more expensive metals (platinum, titanium, solid gold and special steel alloys). The company also streamlined its models from 2,500 to 130, representing four distinct product lines. Other major initiatives consisted of integrating distribution and launching a new advertising campaign (with Cindy Crawford, Michael Schumacher, Martina Hingis and Pierce Brosnan as high-profile "ambassadors"). The strategy was quite successful and, with an average price point 50 per cent lower than its main competitor, Rolex, Omega seemed to have plenty of room to grow.

Despite the success of the Omega brand, the Swatch Group was facing several issues. Management problems were plaguing the organization. Key figures such as Klaus Schwab, a professor at the University of Geneva and founder of the World Economic Forum in Davos, Drs. Stephan Schmidheiny, Pierre Arnold and Walter Frehner all stepped down from the board of directors in the mid-1990s. Several managing directors also left the group in the last two years. Hayek's management style was resulting in growing criticism in the company. Dr. Ernst Thomke, a former partner, had less-than-flattering comments about Hayek: "He has to be the big boss alone, and can never share opinions. He was a consultant all his life and he wanted to become a marketer and product developer. But he never learned that job."[8]

The Swatch Group was also experiencing persistent difficulties in establishing a strong foothold in the U.S. market, where it faced stiff competition from Timex, Casio, Seiko and Citizen. Even the Swatch Group's role as the official timekeeper of the 1996 Summer Olympic Games in Atlanta failed to significantly boost interest in the company's offerings. Although the group generated about 19 per cent of its sales in the U.S., its market share in the basic and middle-priced segments was particularly weak (see Exhibit 6 on page 465 and Exhibit 10 on page 469). Finally, its highly successful and emblematic Swatch brand appeared to be at a crucial crossroads.

The brand had sold a total of 200 million watches since its introduction in 1983. A Collectors' Club (100,000 members worldwide) was founded in 1990 to create an international link between fans around the world. Limited-edition watches, special events, and the quarterly *Swatch World* journal also contributed to reinforce the value of the brand. Demand rapidly exceeded supply for a number of special launches and collectors started to compare the rarity of their collections, to trade and to speculate around Swatches during auction sales. In the early 1990s, it looked as if Swatch's expansion had no limit. So great was management's confidence that the group even decided to actively contribute to the development and market introduction of the small, ecological smart car.

Despite the growing interest of many, Swatch sales had plateaued at 18 million to 20 million units a year. In 1998, sales and profit margins were well below the levels achieved in the early 1990s, as Swatch was facing increased competition from the likes of Fossil and Guess. One concern was whether there were too many Swatch products on the market. Another concern centred on the product mix. Many young Swatch fans of the past wanted more expensive and sophisticated watches as their incomes increased. A proliferation of products also led to a growing problem with Swatch distributors. Many retailers were dropping Swatch from their shelves. The number of stores selling the trendy watch decreased from 3,000 in the early 1990s to 1,200 in 1998. Steven Rosdal, co-owner of Hyde Park Jewelers, expressed the views of some retailers: "Swatch came out with more products than the market could bear,

---

[8]*Time*, March 28, 1994.

exhibit 10   U.S. Market and Swatch Group's Market Share—1999

	Units	%	Value	%	Swatch market share
Mass (under $50)	124,653	78%	2,056	34%	9%
Middle market ($50-299)	31,840	20%	2,219	37%	4%
Upper/Luxury ($300)	2,705	2%	1,771	29%	21%
Total	159,198	100%	6,046	100%	11%

Source: Dresdner Kleinwort Benson estimates

and the consumers seemed to back off. I guess if you use the word 'fad' for anything, it could be used for Swatch."[9]

The group was undertaking several steps to revamp and differentiate the brand. First, Swatch was trying to reposition itself from a low margin, high-volume business involved in day-to-day fashion watches to a high-margin, high-volume enterprise focusing on watches fitted with state-of-the-art electronic gadgetry. As an example of its repositioning efforts, it launched the *Access* watch in 1995, which could be programmed to function as a pass to access ski lifts, hotel chains, public transport and numerous other applications. Although the watch had yet to achieve its commercial potential, there were promising signals: Swatch equipped the Lisbon universal exhibition with one million units and about 200 ski resorts in some 17 countries. Also, with assistance from German Electronics giant Siemens, Swatch developed *Swatch Talk*, a Dick Tracy-type wristwatch with an integrated mobile telephone. Finally, Swatch created the *Swatch Beat*, as a completely new global concept of time, as well as a whole new area of market potential. With *Swatch Beat*, time was the same all over the world "No Time Zones, No Geographical Borders." People using the same clock could agree to a phone call at "500," without time-zone arithmetic required. The day was divided into 1,000 units (each one being the equivalent of one minute and 26.4 seconds) with a new BMT meridian created in Bienne, home of the Swatch Group.

As a second initiative, Swatch launched a new advertising campaign ("Time is what you make of it") designed to reinforce the brand's primary message ("Innovation, provocation, fun. Forever.") Sponsorship was primarily focused on new and youth-oriented sports or events with an offbeat lifestyle, such as snowboarding, mountain biking, bungee jumping, and rock climbing.

However, in October 1998, Swatch sold its minority 19 per cent shareholding of Micro Compact Car, the vehicle producer, to manufacturing partner Daimler-Benz. Although the group was still looking for key partners to develop the hybrid electric *Swatchmobile*, management made it clear that its core business remained the watch industry and microelectronics.

STRATEGIC DECISIONS

In early June 1999, Hayek was under growing pressure to clarify the company's strategy. Many observers and shareholders were wondering whether the original management philosophy that shaped the company's success remained viable.

---

[9]Jewellers' Circular-Keystone, December 1998

Conventional wisdom suggested that all watch companies should locate manufacturing activities in countries that offered low-cost production solutions. The Swatch Group had always remained committed to its Swiss home base, leaving the bulk of its technology, people and manufacturing in the isolated villages surrounding the Jura Mountains. Those places possessed hundreds of years of experience in the art of watchmaking. Employees had spent generations in the factories controlled by the Swatch Group, where they developed a special feel and touch for this business, along with a true sense of organizational commitment. However, the company's junior secretaries in Switzerland earned more than senior engineers at competitors in Thailand, Malaysia, China or India. Maybe it was time to move on and stop building watches in one of the most expensive countries in the world. But which, if any, of the value-added chain activities should be moved (see Exhibit 11)?

With its huge domestic demand and low-cost labor, India offered interesting sourcing opportunities. Many industry analysts believed that Titan Industries was looking for key foreign partners, after the demise of an early alliance with Timex. Would a partnership with a company like Titan make sense, or, if and when the company were to move, should it go it alone?

Another trend management had to address was the movement of many watch companies into ever-more narrow or differentiated market niches. The Swatch Group was present in all market segments and price categories, but its performance depended mainly on four brands names, Omega, Swatch, Tissot and Rado, which together accounted for 82 per cent of total sales and 88 per cent of operating profit in 1998 (see Exhibit 12). Perhaps it was time to reorganize the company's portfolio. Advertising budgets had already been reallocated towards the luxury and high-tech markets, where the company was also constantly looking for key partners and acquisition targets. However, for many industry observers, this product market strategy (luxury-high tech and/or globalization) was becoming too complex for the company's internal capabilities, as indicated by the failure of the smart car project.

exhibit 11   Watch Production and Value Added Chain

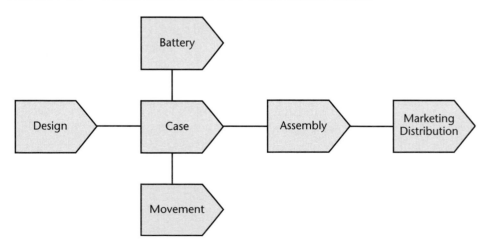

exhibit 12 The Swatch Group's Turnover and Margin Estimates for 1998

	Units in thou.	Average price in SFr*	Turnover in SFr. million	% of total	EBIT in SFr. million	% of total	Margin in %
Omega	550	1,200	670	28%	147	47%	22%
Swatch	26,000	36	925	38%	79	25%	9%
Tissot	1,600	100-150	210	9%	20	6%	10%
Rado	300	570	170	7%	31	10%	18%
Longines	550	270	150	6%	23	7%	15%
Calvin Klein	600	130	75	3%	4	1%	5%
Blancpain	10	6,500	65	3%	6	2%	9%
Other	1,500	80	145	6%	3	1%	2%
Total	31,110	80	2,410	100%	312	100%	13.0%

* Factory gate price

Source: Bank Leu estimates

ANNOTATED INSTRUCTOR'S EDITION

From Master Student to Master Employee

Houghton Mifflin Company   Boston   New York

...sher: Patricia Coryell
...r Sponsoring Editor: Mary Finch
...lopment Editor: Shani B. Fisher
...rial Associate: Andrew Sylvester
...r Project Editor: Cathy Labresh Brooks
...rial Assistant: Neil Reynolds
...ufacturing Manager: Karen Banks
...and Design Coordinator: Jill Haber
...nposition Buyer: Sarah Ambrose
...rketing Manager: Elinor Gregory
...rketing Assistant: Evelyn Yang

...ver credit: Cover image © Robert Schoen Photography

...llege Survival
...75 Foxfield Drive
... Charles, IL 60174

...800-528-8323
...llegesurvival@hmco.com

...oto and illustration credits appear on page 354.

...ted in the U.S.A.

...ry of Congress Control Number: 2004113719

...nt Edition ISBN: 0-618-49325-5
...ated Instructor's Edition ISBN: 0-618-49327-1

...4 5 6 7 8 9 — WC — 08 07 06 05

annotated instructor's edition
contents

 Chapter annotations

Please note: Chapter annotations can be found on an insert
that appears before the beginning of each of the main text
chapters, starting with the Introduction.

Get the most out of
the Annotated Instructor's Edition

Get familiar with the Annotated Instructor's Edition. The Annotated Instructor's Edition of *From Master Student to Master Employee* will help guide you through using this textbook. This annotated textbook contains materials to support your course as you work to introduce students to higher education and help them to make connections from the classroom to the workplace. These resources are available at the front of the core text, in pages prior to each chapter, and at the back of the book. Each chapter is preceded by four pages that highlight special features within the chapter and include suggested exercises and ideas for in-class discussion, teaching tips, and information about additional resources. The Master Student Resource Guide highlights all of the tools available from Houghton Mifflin Company to support each chapter as you develop and teach your course. Icons indicate instructor supplements including the *Course Manual*, the HM ClassPrep CD (with PowerPoint slides), and a Web site. All of the pages in this Annotated Instructor's Edition have a different numbering system (AIE Chapter One, AIE Chapter Two, etc.), so that the textbook pages are numbered the same as the student edition of the text. This allows you to stay on the same page as your students when assigning readings and exercises.

Do a textbook reconnaissance. As the exercise to the right suggests, you can start becoming a master instructor this moment. Do a textbook reconnaissance by reviewing the big picture of *From Master Student to Master Employee*. Look for fresh ideas you can use to support your course objectives. Explore the different features, such as Career Applications, short case studies that will help your students begin to apply classroom strategies to scenarios they may encounter in the workplace.

Get to know your College Survival consultant. For the past 20 years, College Survival has provided consultation and training for the design and implementation of student success and first-year courses. Our team of consultants has extensive experience in teaching and administering the first-year course and in facilitating training sessions and conferences. Get to know your consultant today by calling 1-800-528-8323. Or visit us online at **collegesurvival.hmco.com**. Be sure to ask your consultant how you can attend a conference or workshop—for free!

Preview each chapter to find your way. If you have used previous editions of *Becoming a Master Student*, you may be familiar with some of the tried and true features, like the Discovery Wheel, Discovery and Intention Journal Entry system, Power Processes, and Master Student Profiles. *From Master Student to Master Employee* offers new features, including *Thinking Critically in the Classroom* and *Thinking Critically in the Workplace* exercises, *From the Desk of…*, words of encouragement from master students who have become master employees, and *Career Applications*.

Rewrite this book. If there are sections of the book that don't apply to your course at all, skip them. Later, see if you can help your students gain value from these sections anyway. When you are committed to getting the most out of this book, your students will take note. If an idea doesn't work for you, rewrite it. Change the exercises to fit your needs. Create a new technique by combining several others. Create a technique out of thin air! As you dig into the following chapters, think about what you would say if you could add your voice to this book. Drop us a line at **collegesurvival@hmco.com** to share your comments.

Model the concepts. Action makes this book work. You are your students' best role model. Completing the exercises along with your students will enable you to stay involved and speak from experience when you discuss each chapter in class. The exercises and readings will help you write, touch, feel, move, see, search, ponder, speak, listen, recall, choose, commit, and create. You might even sing and dance. Learning often works best when it involves action.

Discover a new way to teach learning styles with the Master Student Map. The Master Student Map (**M**etacognitive **A**pplication **P**rocess) guides students toward maximum learning by asking the four basic questions—*Why? What? How?* and *What if?*—that correlate to the Learning Style Inventory as explained in Chapter One. By becoming aware of their preferred learning style and by using the Master Student Map, students will be better able to explore new styles. Read more about the Master Student

Map and how it works on page AIE-xii. After you and your students have had a chance to read the chapter content, close your lesson with the new Learning Styles Application at the end of each chapter, which invites students to "cycle" through the four styles, or modes, of learning. In answering the four questions posed in each Learning Styles Application, students explore the different modes and apply their new knowledge.

Navigate the textbook. The icons and key visuals in this book carry special meanings.

The *Master Student* logo is a tangram, an ancient Chinese puzzle consisting of a square cut into seven sections. Hundreds of images can be devised and new relationships and possibilities discovered by rearranging these basic geometric shapes in different patterns. An

icon for the Journal Entries uses a tangram to show a student writing. You'll notice that the chapter exercises and Thinking Critically in the Classroom and the Workplace exercises also have icons using a tangram. Can you tell what the images represent? Just as working with tangrams encourages creative thinking, many students learn by putting together pieces of knowledge in as many ways as they can.

From Master Student to Master Employee provides the basic building blocks with which a creative and active mind can succeed—in the classroom and in the workplace.

A toolbar signals when each chapter is coming to an end, with its Power Process article, Career Application, Quiz, Learning Styles Application, and Master Student Profile. Flip to the back of one of the chapters now!

Link to the Web. Throughout this book, look for reminders to visit the Web site for *From Master Student to Master Employee*: **masterstudent.college.hmco.com**.

You'll find articles, online exercises, and links to other useful Web sites with support for both students and instructors. ◪

TEXTBOOK RECONNAISSANCE

Start becoming a master instructor this moment by doing a 15-minute "textbook reconnaissance." Here's how.

First, read the table of contents. Do it in three minutes or less. Next, look at every page in the book. Move quickly. Scan headlines. Look at pictures. Notice forms, charts, and diagrams. Don't forget the Annotated Instructor's Edition pages before each chapter, which include tips for teaching each chapter and using the resources available to you from Houghton Mifflin Company.

A textbook reconnaissance shows you where a textbook is going. It gives you the big picture. That's useful because brains work best when going from the general to the specific. Getting the big picture before you start makes it easier to recall and understand details later on.

Your textbook reconnaissance will work even better if, as you scan, you look for ideas you can use for your course. When you find one, write the page number and a short description of it in the space below. If you run out of room, just continue your list on a separate sheet of paper. Or use Post-it Notes to flag the pages that look useful. You could even use notes of different colors to signal priority, such as green for ideas you want to use right away and yellow for those to apply later.

The idea behind this technique is simple: It's easier to teach a course when you're excited, and it's easier to get excited if you know the content is going to be useful, interesting, or fun—for both you and your students.

Remember, look at every page, and do it quickly. And here's another useful tip for the master instructor: Do it now.

Page number   *Description*

_____

_____

_____

_____

_____

_____

_____

_____

Finding the master instructor in you

Teaching a student success course for the first time might seem a bit intimidating. Most of us teach classes only in our primary area of expertise, so teaching a course outside our field can be challenging on many levels.

Here are some helpful suggestions I received from Dave Ellis and College Survival consultants when I first started teaching the student success course at my college some 19 years ago.

Model the behavior you want to see in your students. If you want your students to be organized, be organized in your class. If you want your students to show up on time, always be punctual yourself. See the next suggestion for an invaluable resource!

The textbook is for you, too. I have been able to apply many of the tools in this textbook to my professional and personal life. This resource has helped me sharpen my memory, manage my time, and improve my relationships. Use the Table of Contents and the Index to find strategies that can help you model the kind of behavior you want to see in your students.

Remember, this book contains dozens of success strategies—it would be unrealistic to try to perform all of them. Once when I was conducting a teacher training workshop, a dedicated instructor asked, "How can I model and teach promptness if I'm always late to class?" I told him that as teacher, I build on my strengths, not my weaknesses. If I cannot model a certain behavior, I let the textbook

cover that. Instead, I focus on the positive traits that I can successfully model in class.

Be inquisitive. There are many resources for you to use in the process of developing lesson plans for your student success course. In addition to this Annotated Instructor's Edition, with its suggestions located at the front of the book, in pages preceding each chapter, and at the back of the book, explore these additional resources to help you create and improve lesson plans and organize all aspects of your course:

- **HM ClassPrep CD**—provides specific tools to use while teaching your course, including video clips, PowerPoint slides, sample syllabi, chapter-by-chapter lecture outlines, teaching tips, exercises, quizzes, Web links, suggestions for service-learning activities, and more. The HM ClassPrep CD is compatible for both PC and MAC users, and you can edit the files to tailor them for your course.

- **Videos**—perfect for supplementing your lecture, videos can be used as a "guest speaker" in your course. For a complete listing of available videos, and for information about new Power Process videos, review the Master Instructor Resources at the end of this book.

- **Master Student Web site**—check out the online exercises and resources for students and instructors by visiting **masterstudent. college.hmco.com.**

- **College Survival consultants**—available by toll-free phone (1-800-528-8323) and e-mail (**collegesurvival@hmco.com**), your consultant can assist you with planning, class activities, research, and implementing a course on your campus. Ask about a customized on-campus training session, or attend the College Survival conferences and workshops.

- **Faculty members on your campus**—invite a respected colleague to lunch to find out how she solves grading, attendance, logistic, and student problems. Share ideas and learn from each other.

Take it one step at a time. Creating the perfect course won't happen overnight. This textbook explains tools and techniques so clearly that you don't need to try to cover all of them in class. Start by identifying one or two topics in each chapter that you have personally found valuable. Look for activities or lecture ideas on the ClassPrep CD or in this Annotated Instructor's Edition, and build your lesson plans around those topics that you want to emphasize. Use videos and guest speakers from your campus to augment your class meetings. Reinforce concepts by conducting review sessions and giving weekly quizzes. For additional lesson planning strategies, see the article "Creating an engaging classroom" on page AIE-x.

—*Dean Mancina, Instructor, Golden West College, CA*

DEAN MANCINA

'm sure most of us remember the college professors who had the most influence on our lives. I do. Though I was majoring in Business Administration, it was, surprisingly, my Folklore and Mythology professor and my Introduction to Sociology instructor who helped me see things in a different way. Back then, I dreamed that someday I might have a similar, profound influence on others. Teaching student success classes has given me the opportunity to be one of those influential, memorable teachers. It's an honor when a student tells me that this is the best class she's taken in college, or that it has changed her life.

In 1985, I attended a workshop presented by Dave Ellis, hoping to learn new ways to help the students at my community college succeed. By the end of that workshop, I knew that Dave had the answer I was looking for. I returned to Southern California, and, with Dave's and College Survival's help, I developed a course for Golden West College that has become one of my institution's most popular classes.

Many students come to my college and to my class with low self-expectations. They aren't sure if they are "college material." They think they might be too old or not smart enough. They wonder if they have the motivation to do the work or the means to attend college. Most students leave my class with renewed enthusiasm about themselves and their dream of completing an educational program. Many of them get involved in student government and receive scholarships and awards. Two of my former students who became college educators have developed similar courses on their campuses for the students they now teach.

By modeling this book's concepts both in and outside the classroom, I've enjoyed the added side benefit of being happier in my personal life. I've changed my habits, attitudes, and approaches to problem solving. I've gained confidence as a teacher and member of my campus community. By creating and implementing a course that has been popular and successful, I've earned respect from my colleagues. Over the last 10 years I've had the wonderful opportunity to help other colleges and universities design and update their courses, and to teach their instructors how to present this course material. And,

more recently, I've helped shape the updated editions of this book so that it continues to be current and relevant to students who read it.

Additionally, by learning more about learning style theory as presented in Chapter One, I have become a better teacher. Like most instructors, I prefer to teach the way that I prefer to learn. I just wasn't aware that I was teaching this way, and that there are equally effective ways of perceiving and processing information. Using the Learning Style Inventory and exercises in my classroom not only has helped my students develop understanding, tolerance, and skills to adjust to different teaching styles, but also has helped me understand and reach out to students who prefer to learn differently than I do.

I see myself as a facilitator in the classroom. This book is so well written that I just need to follow it, support it, and provide an environment in my classroom that is safe and inviting so that students are encouraged to reach for their dreams.

My suggestions throughout this Annotated Instructor's Edition are just that—suggestions. As you find your own voice in this material, you will develop your own way of teaching it to your students. Please change, adapt, alter, and re-create my ideas so they will work for you and your students. ⊠

ELDON MCMURRAY

I **recently discovered this quote** from German poet, dramatist, novelist, and scientist Johann Wolfgang von Goethe, in which he stresses the importance of pushing students toward their potential: "Treat people as they are and they remain that way. Treat them as though they already are what they can be, and they can become what they are capable of becoming." My teaching philosophy includes helping ensure that students take significant steps to discover their genius and become their own best teachers in whatever subject or discipline they study so they can achieve their educational goals and dreams. For the last eight years I have used the dynamic wisdom encapsulated in *From Master Student to Master Employee* as the pivotal guide to assist students in achieving those aspirations.

Many entering students begin their college studies inadequately prepared. They have clear intellect but do not have the vocabulary or literacy skills requisite to reason successfully on the college level. They might have had too little experience, knowledge, or training in preparing for college-level assignments. In the past, these students would have been considered remedial at best or simply not "college material." I am convinced that such students have the potential to succeed. The Discovery and Intention Journal system is a reasoning system that will have an immediate and a positive impact on the critical thinking skills and decision-making consciousness of these students.

Students need concerned, caring teachers as adult mentors to help them understand their learning styles and develop a powerful sense of self-awareness. As the instructor, you will play a pivotal role in this process. Also needed is a textbook system that includes a set of essential, cognitive reasoning steps to move students' knowledge to comprehensive levels that they refer back to during the development of their enhanced learning system. Once students have developed a study system, they can implement the Power Processes in each chapter. When realized, these concepts will make their college experience more productive and manageable. I believe the early development of these systematic skills and attitudes can significantly increase students' chances for success throughout their entire academic experiences; in fact, with these tools they can become lifelong learners. *From Master Student to Master Employee* helps students refine this systematic way of thinking and also provides examples of how the book has worked for others.

I am convinced that when students understand what is required of college learners, most can make successful adjustments. They must realize that successful college students are self-motivators who are expected to do things that might at first seem "beyond the call of duty" compared to the requirements they experienced in the high school culture. They need to complete reading assignments before attending class, form their own study groups, and seek tutorial help. This textbook addresses each of the areas that research suggests students need to gain an understanding and awareness of in order to survive the transition to and succeed in higher education. Its encyclopedic, magazine format increases its readability. I have taught for 20 years, and in that time I have never found a book that includes as significant an outcome design as the pre- and post-Discovery Wheel exercises. This documents their new skills and translates into the academic confidence they need to succeed at the college level.

Well-adjusted students are in charge of their own learning whether they like it or not and, therefore, will often be involved in self-teaching situations. This is, perhaps, the greatest single lesson college students learn—that they are capable of teaching themselves. This powerful textbook holds the keys to help each of them, as the title implies, become a master student. ⬟

College Survival: committed to student success

Houghton Mifflin's College Survival Consulting Group is dedicated to providing educators with proven instructional strategies and tools that lead to student success. For the past 20 years, our team of consultants has provided guidance and training for the design and implementation of student success and first-year courses.

The College Survival consulting team is available to assist with any stage of student success program development, including:

- Designing course curriculums
- Developing student retention strategies
- Implementing student success courses
- Training faculty members
- Engaging students as active learners
- Transforming the learning environment
- National conferences
- Regional workshops

Our team

Our team of consultants has extensive experience in teaching and administering the first-year course and in facilitating trainings at national education conferences throughout the year. We provide full-time support to help educators establish and maintain effective student success programs.

Web site

Visit our Web site at **collegesurvival.hmco.com** for additional resources and more information about College Survival:

- Get the latest industry information
- Read our quarterly newsletter
- Find out about our student scholarship

Conferences/workshops

College Survival conferences and workshops offer highly interactive and informative sessions designed to equip you with ideas and activities that you can apply immediately in your classroom. All educators involved in enhancing instruction and improving students' motivation and performance are encouraged to attend.

About our national conferences. Our two- to three-day conferences provide informative, interactive sessions on a wide range of topics, such as adult learners, learning styles, student retention, motivation, technology, and much more. Presenters include nationally known authors, student success instructors, and College Survival consultants who offer invaluable instructional strategies based on their experience teaching the first-year course. This forum for learning and sharing with colleagues will furnish you with activities and ideas to implement immediately in your course.

About our regional workshops. Led by College Survival consultants, our regional workshops are smaller, one-day events designed for hands-on group interaction. These workshops, which focus on the most current issues in student success, will equip you with ideas and activities to enliven the teaching and learning experience. We offer general student success workshops as well as workshops for instructors who use or are considering using *From Master Student to Master Employee*.

To see a current schedule of conferences and workshops, or to register, visit

collegesurvival.hmco.com

Who should attend? If you are an educator, new or experienced, who is dedicated to promoting student success in career schools, community colleges, or four-year colleges and universities, these events are for you! Those who will benefit from these workshops include:

- Academic and student affairs administrators
- Student success and freshman seminar coordinators
- Faculty members (full-time and adjunct instructors)
- Retention/enrollment management directors
- Counselors and orientation directors

Workshop topics. Topics presented at the workshops might include the following:

- Using learning styles in the classroom
- Offering student success courses online
- Strategies for reaching resistant students
- Developing a comprehensive student success course
- Student success across the curriculum
- Creative and critical thinking skills
- Integrating e-mail and the Internet into your course
- Student success strategies for ESL students
- Preparing a faculty development workshop for your campus ⊠

Creating an engaging classroom

Using an involving course model as a framework can provide an opportunity to engage students as active participants and partners in the learning process. The concept planning ideas are structured in this format for easier application to both the planning and teaching process. The objective is to use varying modes of instruction in order to facilitate a course that accesses and maximizes each student's method of learning. Consider this seven-part course model:

Lectures	20%
Exercises	20%
Sharing	20%
Guest Speakers	20%
Evaluation Preview/Review Assignments	} 20%

While this structure consists of seven parts, it will not always be possible to include all parts in every class period. Each of the seven parts can usually be included at least once a week. Ideally, over the entire term 20 percent of class time is recommended for lectures, 20 percent for exercises, 20 percent for conversations and sharing, 20 percent for guest speakers, and the remaining 20 percent for previewing/reviewing, quizzes and evaluations, and giving assignments.

 A complete overview of this course model is available in the *Course Manual*.

My class meets once a week for three hours and 10 minutes. Using this seven-part course model can be a challenge and in some ways might seem like more work than just lecturing for three hours. My attitude is that while it might take more effort to prepare these lessons, when the work is done, I get to have fun along with my students. Once the students get used to the unusual format, they enjoy the variety and report to me that the class goes by much faster than their other classes.

Below is a sample lesson plan for my 190-minute, once-a-week student success course. If your course meets twice a week, you could do the first half during the first meeting each week, and the second half during the second meeting.

CHAPTER 3—Memory
Collect homework (:05)
Preview the class agenda (:05)
Tutorial learning center—guest speakers (:15)
Review Chapter 3 (:30)
Lecture—mnemonic devices (:20)
–break– (:20)
Activity—loci system (:20)
Sharing successful memory experiences in groups (:20)
Activity—"Be here now" (:30)
Quiz on Chapter 3 (:20)
Assignment—read/do pages XX–XX (Chapter 4) (:05)

Collect homework I collect homework at the beginning of the class to encourage students to arrive on time. If they are late, they don't get any points for their homework. Suggestions regarding homework assignments and collecting and grading them are available on your HM ClassPrep CD.

Preview I preview the class agenda by writing it on poster paper and taping it to the wall. The agenda can be used as a framework for note taking and helps explain the organization of the work we will do in class.

Guest speaker Each week I invite guest speakers from support programs to make brief presentations on their services. This helps students learn what kinds of assistance are available at our college.

Review I randomly assign students to groups of four to conduct a review of the material they have read prior to coming to class. I provide poster paper and colored pens, and show them how to make a mind map. The students write their first names at the tops of posters and tape them to the walls using removable tape. Staying in their groups, they walk around to view the other mind maps, confirming what they have created and noticing what other groups included that they did not. Because they are having a quiz at the end of class, students stay motivated, focused, and on task for this activity.

Lecture Lecturing on only a portion of the text encourages students to learn from the textbook and provides variety during the class meeting. It's challenging to lecture on just one or two topics from the assigned reading. When I first started teaching, I selected topics I was most familiar with and felt I could add to. As I became more confident about the content of the book, I began to focus on articles that students had greater difficulty understanding.

Activity While activities take time, they are often more effective than other methods in teaching skills that students retain. The HM ClassPrep CD has many activities listed by chapter. Scan them, pick a few that fit your teaching style and time constraints, and then try them with your class.

Sharing Most of the time my students are in groups during class. Over the course of the semester, they get to know each other and usually form a few close friendships. Studies have shown that forming friendships on campus significantly reduces the likelihood that students will drop out of college. Participating in a sharing period allows students to talk candidly with their peers about their concerns, questions, and frustrations, both at college and at home. I give them a topic for discussion and sometimes, depending on the topic, will ask for group sharing at the end of this segment.

Evaluation Each week I give a short quiz to my students at the end of the class. Doing so ensures that they read the textbook material, remain focused during class, and stay until the end of the session, because they lose points if they miss the quiz. See page AIE-xxxiii for suggestions on using the three-part forms for administering quizzes in your class.

Assignments Each week I assign specific pages as a reading assignment, even if I want students to read the entire chapter. I call it "read/do" since I require that all Journal Entries, Discovery/Intention Statements, and Practicing Critical Thinking exercises between the pages of the assignment be completed. This seven-part course model is a proven strategy for organizing, planning, and revitalizing lesson plans. Whether you're a novice or a veteran teacher of student success courses, I encourage you to try it.

A Master Student Map (**M**etacognitive **A**pplication **P**rocess) is located on the title page of each chapter. The Master Student Map is a reasoning model based on the Learning Style Inventory. Even the most inexperienced students can quickly begin to apply this simple, systematic process to monitor their thinking and learning. What makes this model so effective is that by utilizing the strengths of each learning style, students can implement the monitoring aspect of metacognition as soon as they achieve awareness.

Each category of the Master Student Map begins with a basic question designed to engage students' interest and lead to the important ideas presented in the chapter. A closer look at the design and formatting of each question in the Master Student Map will reveal the logic behind this innovative approach to introducing chapter topics.

why this chapter matters . . . The role of this question is to encourage personal interest and a "need to know" in the learner. Initiating the Master Student Map with this type of question leads Mode 1 learners toward a deeper metacognitive understanding of their thinking, allowing them to call on principles within their prior knowledge that help structure the ideas in the chapter.

what is included . . . This question is followed by a list of specific, thought-provoking article titles from the chapter. This helps Mode 2 learners probe and analyze the factual and conceptual ideas presented in the chapter and become more aware of what will be expected of them.

how you can use this chapter . . . Mode 3 students will experience the impact of acclaimed features of *From Master Student to Master Employee,* such as the Discovery and Intention Journal Entry system, Power Processes, and Master Student Profiles, which uplift and inspire students to make personal commitments and set goals to accomplish. By consciously choosing their attitude about a chapter topic before they begin to study, students gain confidence in their own ability to initiate action and synthesize solutions to pressing problems. In this stage, have students go through the list of articles and mark the ones they predict they will know something about. The articles they do not mark indicate topics they are least familiar with. Having been made aware of knowledge gaps, they will have a better idea of what they need to study for tests.

as you read, ask yourself what if . . . Taking advantage of the action-oriented strength of Mode 4 learners, *What if?* questions lead to more lateral thinking and thus better-quality decisions. Specific skills do not necessarily transfer from one mental schema to another. Asking provocative *What if?* questions triggers the students' imagination to transfer skills and create new schema for developing skills in their other classes and in the workplace. Students are intrigued by inquiry rather than pat answers. *What if?* questions stimulate discussion and further the transfer of skills in situations outside the classroom as well.

Based on the latest theories of brain-active learning, the Master Student Map feature helps students activate relevant memories with regard to the subject matter in the chapter. Since all learning is dependent on prior knowledge, beginning each chapter with this reasoning model helps students in several ways. First, distractions can be reduced or eliminated, as the model allows students to study the most interesting or important topics first. Next, it helps increase the speed of students' learning by organizing the ideas in the beginning pages. Finally, it links all of the ideas in the entire textbook to the learning style of each student in a simple but powerful way.

Another important benefit of the Master Student Map is that it provides the instructor with a clear outline of what is going to be investigated in each chapter and a framework for guiding the discussion.

The four basic questions not only help instructors better understand what the students need to know but also serve as a catalyst for both pre- and post-assessment in the students' minds.

In a pilot study using this model, instructors at Utah Valley State College found these questions to be very helpful as teaching tools, primarily because it gave them a place to begin instruction and a final destination.

Instructors who were more adept at viewing the curriculum in a holistic fashion were able to use this feature of overarching guiding questions to help them convey to students the big picture of the chapter in an efficient and a meaningful way. Those instructors who were more linear in their thinking leaned toward the *What?* category of guiding questions and allowed their students to discover how the other questions fit in during the course of the discussion. This flexibility instilled confidence in the instructors to teach the magazine format of this textbook in their own preferred style and enabled them to be more comfortable with the teaching process. Consequently, students reported high satisfaction with both the course instructor and the material. ◪

Helping your students become master students and master employees

The new **chapter opener** design includes a **Master Student Map** to help students preview chapter concepts and chart their course to success. With this map, your students can begin to address each of the four modes of learning right from the start.

A focus on **Mastering Work,** Chapter Ten, will help your students take the skills they have learned in college and apply them to job searches, interviews, and to the workplace environment.

10

Mastering Work

Passion for what you do is an important ingredient for success, and if you don't love what you do, it's not worth the time and energy.

CARLY FIORINA

By concentrating on a few key efforts such as sharing credit, showing grace under pressure, and promoting your ambition in appropriate ways, your day job can lead to the career of your dreams.

STEPHEN VISCUSI

MASTER STUDENT MAP

why
this chapter matters . . .

You can gain strategies to succeed as you transition from master student to master employee.

what
is included . . .

The Master Employee
Use power tools for finding work
Tell everyone you know: The art of networking
Write a résumé that gets noticed
Sell your résumé with an effective cover letter
Creating and using portfolios
Use interviews to hire yourself an employer
Learning on the job
Join a diverse workplace
Decoding corporate culture
Dealing with sexism and sexual harassment
Strategies for working with a mentor
We are all leaders
Loving your next job
Define your values, align your actions
One set of values
Power Process: "Be it"
Master Student Profile: Craig Kielburger

how
you can use this chapter . . .

Learn effective strategies for job hunting.
Create résumés that lead to job interviews.
Go into job interviews fully prepared.
Build satisfying relationships with coworkers.

As you read, ask yourself
what if . . .

I could find work that expresses my core values and connects daily with my passions?

The master employee

The title of this book—*From Master Student to Master Employee*—implies that these two types of mastery have something in common. To some people, this idea sounds half-baked. They separate life into two distinct domains: work and school. One is the "real" world. The other is the place where you attend classes to prepare for the real world.

Consider another point of view—the idea that success in higher education promotes success on the job.

There's some pretty hard-nosed evidence for this idea. One factor is that higher levels of education are correlated with higher levels of income. Another is that mastery in school and in work seem to rest on a common set of transferable skills.

In this book you've seen several references to the Secretary's Commission on Achieving Necessary Skills (SCANS) issued by the U.S. Department of Labor. According to this document, one crucial skill for the workplace is a personal quality called responsibility. This is demonstrated by any employee who:

- "Exerts a high level of effort and perseverance toward goal attainment.

- "Works hard to become excellent at doing tasks by setting high standards, paying attention to details, working well, and displaying a high level of concentration even when assigned an unpleasant task.

- "Displays high standards of attendance, punctuality, enthusiasm, vitality, and optimism in approaching and completing tasks."

A better definition of mastery would be hard to find. And if you've ever exerted a high level of effort to complete an assignment, paid attention to the details of a lecture, or displayed a high level of concentration while reading a tough textbook, then you've already demonstrated some key aspects of self-responsibility and mastery.

When you graduate from school, you don't leave your capacity for mastery locked inside a classroom. Excellence in one setting paves the way for excellence in other settings.

For example, a student who knows how to show up for class on time is ready to show up for work on time. The student who knows how to focus attention during a lecture is ready to focus attention during a training session at work. And a student who's worked cooperatively in a study group brings a lot of skills to the table when joining a workplace team. You can multiply this list by reflecting on each of the skills explained in this book.

journal entry 30

Discovery/Intention Statement

Reflect on all the jobs you've held in your life. What aspect of working would you most like to change? Answers might include job hunting with less frustration, resolving conflicts with coworkers, building a better relationship with your boss, or coping with office politics. Describe the change that would make the biggest positive difference in your job satisfaction over the long run.

I discovered that I . . .

_____

_____

_____

Now preview this chapter for ideas that could help you make the positive change you just described. List three to five suggestions below, along with the page numbers where you can read more about them.

Strategy   *Page number*

_____

_____

_____

A master employee embraces change, takes risks, and looks for chances to lead others while contributing to the quality of their lives. A master employee completes tasks efficiently, communicates openly and respectfully, and commits to lifelong learning. In developing a mastery of higher education, you'll do all this and more. *Master student* and *master employee* are names for qualities that already exist in you, waiting to be expressed as you embrace new ideas and experiment with new behaviors. ✂

Chapter Ten MASTERING WORK **311**

A **Journal Entry** icon reminds students that the Discovery and Intention Statements are a means to interact with the chapter content, declare their goals, and commit to taking action.

Action makes this book work. Student **exercises** encourage active learning and help develop critical thinking.

USE Q-CARDS TO REINFORCE MEMORY

One memory strategy you might find useful involves a special kind of flash card. It's called a *Question Card*, or *Q-Card* for short.

To create a standard flash card, you write a question on one side of a 3x5 card and its answer on the other side. Q-Cards have a question on *both* sides. Here's the trick: The question on each side of the card contains the answer to the question on the other side.

The questions you write on Q-Cards can draw on both lower- and higher-order thinking skills. Writing these questions forces you to encode material in different ways. You activate more areas of your brain and burn the concepts even deeper into your memory.

For example, say that you want to remember the subject of the 18th Amendment to the United States Constitution, the one that prohibited the sale of alcohol. On one side of a 3x5 card, write *What amendment prohibited the sale of alcohol?* Turn the card over and write *What did the 18th Amendment do?*

To get the most from Q-Cards:

- Add a picture to each side of the card. This helps you learn concepts faster and develop a more visual learning style.

- Read the questions and recite the answers out loud. Two keys to memory are repetition and novelty, so use a different voice whenever you read and recite. Whisper the first time you go through your cards, then shout or sing the next time. Doing this develops an auditory learning style.

- Carry Q-Cards with you and pull them out during waiting times. To develop a kinesthetic learning style, handle your cards often.

- Create a Q-Card for each new and important concept within 24 hours after attending a class or completing an assignment. This is your *active stock* of cards. Keep answering the questions on these cards until you learn each new concept.

- Review all of the cards from the term for a certain subject on one day each week. For example, on Monday, review all cards from biology; on Tuesday, review all cards from history. These cards make up your *review stacks*.

How do living organisms obtain ENERGY?

Why do living things need METABOLISM?

What is the formula for factoring the difference of squares?

$a^2-b^2=(a+b)(a-b)$

Sidebars highlight key information and concepts.

Sustaining business relationships

Many workplace relationships are time limited. Teams meet regularly to accomplish an objective—and then disband. Even though you may feel intensely connected to coworkers for a while, you can easily lose touch with them over the years.

The people you meet in a work context get to know you in a different way than do family or friends. Coworkers observe your work performance directly. They can give an objective view of your skills and honest feedback that stands the test of time. They can also help you keep failures in perspective and celebrate your workplace success. You can do the following to enjoy the benefits of sustained business relationships.

Rank your business relationships. Take a quick inventory of people you've worked with in the jobs you've held to date. List the people who served as career mentors, models, or coaches. Add anyone else whose presence creates value in your professional life. These are your key business relationships.

Keep track of people. Start with your Rolodex or address book. Once a year, review and update the entries. Make sure that you've got current addresses, phone numbers, and e-mail addresses for the people who rank high on your list of business relationships.

Stay in contact. Remember the time-management technique of distinguishing between tasks that are urgent and those that are important. Sustaining business relationships may not be an urgent task today. Yet it can be one of the most important things you do over the long run. Make time for staying in contact.

Keep boundaries in mind. Business relationships differ from personal relationships. Among friends and family members, you are on equal footing, and your relationships are based on strong emotional ties. In the workplace, you might stay in contact with people who are not your equals in an organizational setting—a former boss, a person you used to supervise, or a coworker who moves to a competing company. While these people can become close friends over time, they may expect to retain certain limits on emotional intimacy and physical contact. Respect those boundaries.

Put the relationship first. Sustaining business relationships goes beyond networking. Your network consists largely of "contacts"—people who could help you find a new job or change careers someday. Although long-term business relationships can often help you in these ways, the people involved are often more than contacts. These are people whom you value for themselves, beyond any favors that they can do. Let them know how important they are to you.

From the desk of . . . allow current readers to learn about their peers' first-hand experiences using strategies they learned in the classroom, with an explanation of how they carry over to the workplace.

from the desk of . . .

KIMANI JONES, PARENT AND STUDENT:

With three children and having not been to school in 10 years, it has been a real challenge for me. I require that my children spend a certain amount of time each evening studying as well as doing chores. I cook several meals on the weekend for the week. The time they spend studying, I study with them. I find that it encourages them to study when they see me do it with them. It helps me because when I don't study, my 14 year old will peak in my room and say, "Ahhhhh, do you have all A's? Don't you think it's a good time to be studying?" When hear your own words come back to you, what can you say?

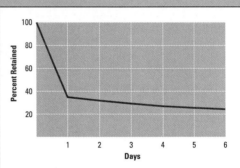

To study the process of memory and forgetting, Hermann Ebbinghaus devised a method for testing memory. The results, shown here in what has come to be known as the Ebbinghaus forgetting curve, demonstrate that forgetting occurs most rapidly shortly after learning and then gradually declines over time.

Charts, tables, and graphs help students practice the skills needed for comprehending college-level texts.

PLANNING CRITICALLY IN THE WORKPLACE

If you did Exercise #30 on page 286, you created a rough draft of your career plan. (If you skipped that exercise, please go back and do it now.) Take the time now to review what you wrote and think critically about your plan. Answer the following questions:

Did you consider the possibility of having several different careers within your lifetime?

Did you list the skills you need for each career that you want—and include a way to develop each skill?

Did you include a way to document the value that you create for an employer—such as new products or services you can develop, sales goals that you can meet, or savings that you can create?

Did you include a way to monitor developments in your career field—especially those that could affect your ability to find employment or meet your income goals?

Did you name the specific jobs that you would like to have?

Did you name specific organizations that you would like to work for, their location, and people at those organizations who could hire you?

In the space below, summarize your answers to these questions. Note any specific changes to make in your career plan.

Thinking Critically in the Classroom and **Thinking Critically in the Workplace** exercises reinforce concepts learned in each chapter through problem solving, creative thinking, and decision making.

A **toolbar** highlights the features that will help students navigate through the end-of-chapter materials.

power process

Ideas are tools

There are many ideas in this book. When you first encounter them, don't believe any of them. Instead, think of them as tools.

For example, you use a hammer for a purpose—to drive a nail. When you use a new hammer, you might notice its shape, its weight, its balance. You don't try to figure out whether the hammer is "right." You just use it. If it works, you use it again. If it doesn't work, you get a different hammer.

This is not the attitude most people adopt when they encounter new ideas. The first thing most people do with new ideas is to measure them against old ones. If a new idea conflicts with an old one, the new one is likely to be rejected.

People have plenty of room in their lives for different kinds of hammers, but they tend to limit their capacity for different kinds of ideas. A new idea, at some level, is a threat to their very being—unlike a new hammer, which is simply a new hammer.

Most of us have a built-in desire to be right. Our ideas, we often think, represent ourselves. And when we identify with our ideas, they assume new importance in our lives. We put them on our mantels. We hang them on our walls. We wear them on our T-shirts and display them on our bumpers. We join associations of people who share our most beloved ideas. We make up rituals about them, compose songs about them, and write stories about them. We declare ourselves dedicated to these ideas.

Some ideas are worth dying for. But please note: This book does not contain any of those ideas. The ideas on these pages are strictly "hammers."

Imagine someone defending a hammer. Picture this person holding up a hammer and declaring, "I hold this hammer to be self-evident. Give me this hammer or give me death. Those other hammers are flawed. There are only two kinds of people in this world: people who believe in this hammer and people who don't."

That ridiculous picture makes a point. This book is not a manifesto. It's a toolbox, and tools are meant to be used. This viewpoint is much like one advocated by psychologist and philosopher William James. His approach to philosophy, which he called "pragmatism," emphasized the usefulness of ideas as a criterion of truth." James liked to talk about the "cash value" of an idea—whether it leads to new actions and new results.

If you read about a tool in this book that doesn't sound "right" or one that sounds a little goofy, remember that the ideas here are for using, not necessarily for believing. Suspend your judgment. Test the idea for yourself.

Ask: What if it's true?

When presented with a new idea, some of us take pride in being critical thinkers. We look for problems. We probe for weaknesses. We continue to doubt the idea until there's clear proof. Our main question seems to be "What's wrong with this idea?"

This approach can be useful when it is vital to expose flaws in ideas or reasoning. On the other hand, when we constantly look for what's wrong with new ideas, we might not recognize their value. A different and potentially more powerful approach is to ask yourself: What if that idea is true? This opens up all sorts of new possibilities and variations. Rather than looking for what's wrong, we can look for what's potentially valuable. Faced with a new idea, we can stay in the inquiry, look deeper, and go further.

Keep looking for answers

The light bulb, the airplane, the computer chip, the notion of the unconscious—these and many other tools became possible when their inventors practiced the art of continually looking for additional answers.

Another way to expand your toolbox is to keep on looking for answers. Much of your education will be about finding answers to questions. Every subject you study—from algebra to history to philosophy—poses a unique set of questions. Some of the most interesting questions are those that admit many answers: How can we create a just society? How can we transmit our values to the next generation? What are the purposes of higher education? How can we prevent an environmental crisis?

Other questions are ...

career shall I choose? Shall I get married? Where shall I live and how shall I spend my leisure time? What shall I have, do, and be during my time on earth?

Perhaps you already have answers to these questions. Answers are wonderful, especially when they relate to our most persistent and deeply felt questions. Answers can also get in the way. Once we're convinced that we have the "right" answer, it's easy to stop looking for more answers. We then stop learning. Our range of possible actions becomes limited.

This book is not a manifesto. It's a toolbox and tools are meant to be used.

Instead of latching on to one answer, we can look for more. Instead of being content with the first or easiest options that come to mind, we can keep searching. Even when we're convinced that we've finally handled a problem, we can brainstorm until we find five more solutions. Brainstorming can lead to creative thinking—a transferable skill that can help you to make new connections between seemingly unrelated ideas and to reveal new possibilities.

When we keep looking for answers, we uncover fresh possibilities for thinking, feeling, and behaving. Like children learning to walk, we experience the joy of discovery.

A caution

A word of caution: Any tool—whether it's a hammer, a computer program, or a study technique—is designed to do a specific job. A master mechanic carries a variety of tools because no single tool works for all jobs. If you throw a tool away because it doesn't work in one situation you might not be able to pull it out later when it's just what you need. So if an idea doesn't work for you and you are satisfied that you gave it a fair chance, don't throw it away. File it away instead. The idea might come in handy sooner than you think.

And remember, this book is not about figuring out the "right" way. Even the "ideas are tools" approach is not "right."

It's a hammer . . . (or maybe a saw).

Chapter One SELF-DISCOVERY 55

Each chapter has a **Power Process,** a unique motivational article that empowers success through the application of strategies that relate to a wide variety of circumstances, issues, and problems. Look for **"Discover what you want,"** a Power Process in the Introduction that helps students define their goals and move from discovery to action.

career application

Shortly after graduating with an A.A. degree in Business Administration, Sylvia Lopez was thrilled to land job as a staff accountant at a market research firm. After one week, she wanted to quit. She didn't think she would ever learn to deal with her coworkers. Their personalities just seemed too different.

For example, there was the account coordinator, Ed Washington. He spent hours a day on the phone calling prospective customers who responded to the corporate Web site. Since Ed's office door was always open and he had a loud voice, people inevitably overheard his calls. It seemed to Sylvia that he spent a lot of time socializing with clients—asking about their hobbies and family lives. Even though Ed was regarded as a skilled salesperson, Sylvia wondered when he actually got any work done.

Sylvia also felt uncomfortable with Linda Martinez, the firm's accounting analyst and her direct supervisor. Linda kept her office door closed most of the time. In contrast to Ed, Linda hardly ever stopped to chat informally. Instead of taking lunch breaks, she typically packed a bag lunch and ate it while checking e-mail or updating the company databases. Linda had a reputation as a top-notch employee. Yet the only time people saw her was at scheduled staff meetings. Linda led those meetings and distributed a detailed agenda in advance. And while Ed was on a first-name basis with everyone in the office, Linda made it clear that she wished to be addressed as "Ms. Martinez."

After worrying for several days about how to deal with the differences between her coworkers, Sylvia scheduled times to meet with Ed and Linda individually about her concerns. Before each meeting, she carefully prepared her opening remarks, writing them out beforehand. For Ed, her notes included this comment: "Since I'm new on the job and feel pressed for time, I'd prefer to keep our meetings short and get down to business right away." And for Linda she wrote: "I'd like to make sure my performance is up to par, but I don't see you very often. Is there any way I can get regular feedback from you about how I'm doing?"

Reflect on this scenario:

1. How would you describe Ed's working style? How about Linda's?

2. Referring to the SCANS skills on page 8, list two transferable skills that Sylvia demonstrates in this scenario.

3. Using the same SCANS chart, identify two more skills that would be useful to Sylvia in this situation. Explain why you chose those two.

4. List two strategies from this chapter that would be useful to Sylvia in this situation. Briefly describe how she could apply each one.

56 Chapter One SELF-DISCOVERY

The **Career Application** reinforces the transferability of skills by encouraging students to think critically about how concepts and techniques they are learning in school might apply to workplace applications.

AIE-xv

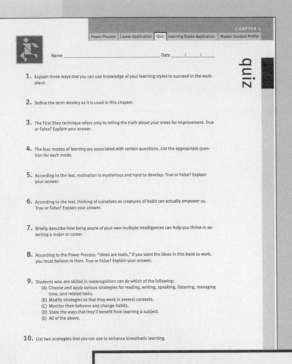

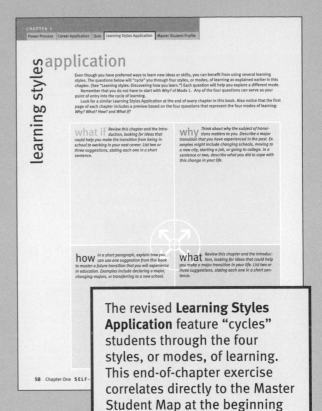

The end-of-chapter **quiz** allows students to assess their comprehension of the materials covered in each chapter.

The revised **Learning Styles Application** feature "cycles" students through the four styles, or modes, of learning. This end-of-chapter exercise correlates directly to the Master Student Map at the beginning of the chapter, asking the same four questions that represent the four modes of learning: *Why? What? How?* and *What if?*

Each **Master Student Profile** highlights a person who embodies the qualities of a master student. This edition features Mike Lazidiris, Christopher Reeve, Ruth Handler, and Craig Kielburger.

masterstudent.college.hmco.com   Log on to the *From Master Student to Master Employee* **Web site** to tap into additional resources, identified in the textbook with this icon, that support student success. Find connections to in-text articles and exercises, ACE practice quizzes, interactive exercises, "Remembering cultural differences" articles, and flashcards. Visit the **Master Student Hall of Fame** to access biographical information about past and present Master Student Profiles.

From Master Student to Master Employee

Doug Toft
Contributing Editor

Houghton Mifflin Company   Boston   New York

Publisher: Patricia A. Coryell
Senior Sponsoring Editor: Mary Finch
Development Editor: Shani B. Fisher
Editorial Associate: Andrew Sylvester
Senior Project Editor: Cathy Labresh Brooks
Editorial Assistant: Neil Reynolds
Composition Buyer: Sarah Ambrose
Art and Design Manager: Jill Haber
Manufacturing Manager: Karen Banks
Marketing Manager: Elinor Gregory
Marketing Assistant: Evelyn Yang

Cover credit: Cover image © Robert Schoen Photography

College Survival
2075 Foxfield Drive, Suite 100
St. Charles, IL 60174
1-800-528-8323
collegesurvival@hmco.com

Photo and illustration credits appear on page 354.

Printed in the U.S.A.

Library of Congress Control Number: 2004113719

Student Edition ISBN: 0-618-49325-5
Annotated Instructor's Edition ISBN: 0-618-49327-1

1 2 3 4 5 6 7 8 9 – WC – 08 07 06 05

As part of Houghton Mifflin's ongoing
commitment to the environment, this text
has been printed on recycled paper.

advisory board

reviewers

brief table of contents

table of contents

Link to the Work World

1 Self-Discovery

4 Reading

5 Notes

6   Tests

7   Thinking

8 Communicating

9 Career Planning

From Master Student to Master Employee

INTRODUCTION
Link to the World of Work

Many institutions of higher education have become more and more conscious of the need to specify and promote the ways in which their curricula better prepare students to enter the workforce. *From Master Student to Master Employee* sets the stage for students entering the culture of higher education (whether it be straight from high school, attending college for the first time as an adult learner, or returning to college after a long absence being in the workforce) and is created to help your students connect to their new surroundings. *Link to the World of Work* helps students to identify their transferable skills by identifying the Labor Department Secretary's Commission on Achieving Necessary Skills (SCANS).

Students using *From Master Student to Master Employee* will learn how to acquire learning strategies that will help them to make a smooth and successful transition to the world of higher education, and will help them to succeed in both college and in the workplace.

Master Student Map

The Master Student Map, as explained on page AIE-xii, provides students with a critical thinking tool that is found at the start of each chapter to preview content. Begin using the Master Student Map right from the start of *From Master Student to Master Employee*. If you have ever had trouble convincing your students to read the introduction to their textbook, this simply formatted framework will help them grasp the value of this book right away. Use the Master Student Map (**M**etacognitive **A**pplication **P**rocess) as a jumping-off point for sparking classroom discussion. Then teach your students how they can begin to use this model to preview chapter content in this textbook. Take it another step further and show your students how creating a similar schema for textbooks in other courses can help activate background knowledge and provide a "hook" to get them ready for the material within the chapter. Start now by asking your students the following questions. Consider writing them on your whiteboard, posting them to your discussion board in an online course, or creating a PowerPoint presentation with them.

why? Why is it important to read the Introduction?

what? What kind of information does an Introduction provide for the reader? What information does the Introduction to *From Master Student to Master Employee* provide?

how? Rate your level of effectiveness with the information presented in the Introduction now. (How much do you already know about the topics presented? How will this book help you become a better student?) Ask yourself: "How can I get more value from my textbook by reading the Introduction?"

what if? What if you skipped the Introduction? Ask yourself: "What if I could use this Introduction right now to become a better student?"

Page 1
EXERCISE #1: "Textbook reconnaissance"

Even though your students may not have purchased their textbook before the first day of class, preview this exercise with your students. The textbook reconnaissance shows students the big picture before they begin the course and will help them to identify resources they may want to skip ahead to before it is assigned in class. Have a discussion during your second class where students share what they discovered in their textbook reconnaissance that they plan to use right away. This will help generate long-term interest in your course—and the textbook.

Exercise #2: "Commitment":

After my students have read this chapter and hopefully completed this exercise, at the following class meeting I ask them to open their books to this exercise, so that they can review what they wrote while I comment on it. I point out that, contrary to a popular student myth, just because something is easy doesn't mean it is not powerful, too! This simple exercise, which takes less than five minutes to complete, helps students confirm their commitment to this course and, indirectly, to their entire college experience. To reinforce this exercise and remind students of it throughout the semester, I have them write in large letters on a sheet of paper the level of commitment they have chosen, and then have them sign their name at the bottom. I ask them to put this paper in the very front of their three-ring binder for this course, so that every time they open their binder, they'll be reminded of their commitment to this textbook.

—DEAN MANCINA,

GOLDEN WEST COLLEGE, CA

Page 2
This book is worthless . . . if you just read it

This first article helps you "sell" this course to resistant students. Whether your student success course at your college is required or not, review the seven pitches, even if your students have not read the article or purchased the text. Show students how *taking action* makes this book work.

Page 6
Jumpstart your education with transferable skills

This article acts as an introduction to the U.S. Department of Labor's report created by the Secretary's Commission on Necessary Skills (SCANS). Defining and discussing transferable skills, and their value in the classroom and the workplace, will help all students gain their footing in the culture of higher education. Have students use the list of twenty-five transferable skills in the sidebar on page 7 and create their own personal list based on their experiences. When your students have questions like, "How will learning this help me in the real world?" this article will provide you with a point of reference.

Page 8
Use the SCANS report to discover your skills

Your students have the unique opportunity of participating in a course that will help them to develop the SCANS competencies and skills—and help them to succeed in the job market, and in all of their courses. These skills are highlighted throughout the text, and are available for easy reference on the inside front cover of this text, to help students gain self-confidence in discussing their development and mastery of skills as they begin their school and professional careers.

Page 10
The Discovery and Intention Journal Entry system

The Discovery and Intention Journal Entry system allows students to begin the reflective critical thinking process they will need to grasp the concepts and develop the skills studied in this student success course, and to transfer those skills to their other classes. This simple yet powerful system is one of the foundations of the textbook. As students read the book, they are often asked to write Discovery Statements about what they are learning and Intention Statements about what they plan to do, based on the new information they are assimilating. In addition to assigning the many Discovery and Intention Statements in the book, ask students to write statements in-class after activities such as guest speakers, videos, lectures, etc.

Page 14
Making the transition to higher education

Have your students partner up and review the list of expectations in this article. Ask them to predict the two transition ideas from the article that would cause students the most trouble and to discuss why. Then they should reason out some possible solutions for students who might be facing these problems. To help them connect to the article on a personal level, ask students to decide which of the items listed in the article present a challenge.

Page 21
POWER PROCESS: "Discover what you want"

Begin using the idea presented by the Master Student Map to think critically about the new Power Process in the Introduction. Explain the purpose of each Power Process to your students: The Power Process will change the way you think, or change your consciousness, because it is your consciousness that determines your behavior.

Syllabus building

During the first class, I ask my students to pre-view the text, paying particular attention to the table of contents. I then give students my course syllabus, which lists a suggested schedule of top-ics for the semester. The students' first assign-ment is to look at the Table of Contents and rearrange the schedule of topics in a way that fits their needs. (Another way to do this is by using students' completed Discovery Wheels—see Chapter One.) During the second class meeting, we list the topics on a flip chart and vote on the order of the chapters. Then we rearrange the syllabus according to the prefer-ences of the students. This method helps me design the course to meet students' immediate needs. Since the course is mandatory, some of the students have negative feelings when they come to class. Allowing them input on the order of the topics sparks interest and gives them ownership of the course.

—DR. JENNIFER HURD

Ask your students to consider: (1) **Why** this Power Process might matter to them (or their children, family, coworkers, etc.); (2) **What** goal setting means with regard to this Power Process; (3) **How** will they begin to make the transition to college work for them, to get what they want; and (4) **What** they risk by not getting started with this transition now.

In addition, ask your students, "What do you want?" Have them write down their response. Then, be more specific by asking, "What do you want out of this course?" and "What do you want out of college?" Begin to align these answers with the statements on the SCANS report. Have students identify those SCANS skills that they want to master. A second textbook recon-naissance can help students quickly highlight how they will accomplish mastering these skills.

The *What Do You Want?* videotape is a perfect 10-minute "guest speaker"—especially for the first day of class. Showing the videotape encourages students to think about what they want to get out of college and about their long-term goals. Consider these follow-up discussion questions:

- One of the students interviewed on this videotape says, "I create the A. I create the F. Whatever the grade is, I create it." For the moment, accept this idea as true—whether or not you agree with it. Then ask yourself: "If this statement is true, what do I stand to gain from this course?"

- Answer the question posed to the people in this videotape: What do you want?

Remember, this videotape is available free of charge. Additional exercises to accompany *What Do You Want?* are available on the HM ClassPrep CD.

→ Organize for success

The HM ClassPrep CD for *From Master Student to Master Employee* includes a valuable tool for master students: a place to organize key information to have "at their fin-gertips" throughout their college experience. You can find this information sheet with the materials for the Introduction. Distribute this to students on the first day of class. Have your students fill in their information while they wait for you to begin class, or leave a few minutes at the end of your first meeting.

Take this idea to other courses. Illustrate how stu-dents can immediately apply this new strategy to their other courses. While not every textbook has a place to record information on the inside cover, students can use the inside front and back covers as quick references—for personal information, key facts, such as formulas or Web site addresses, and any other idea they will need to frequently refer to.

Make a new contact. Encourage your students to iden-tify a student in each class who seems responsible and dependable. Have them exchange e-mail addresses and phone numbers and record it. Suggest to students that if they know they won't be in class, they can contact this student ahead of time to ask them to pick up extra copies of handouts and request to copy their notes.

Invite your students to your office. Take this oppor-tunity to invite your students to visit you during office hours. Provide your e-mail, phone, and office location to your students.

Master Instructor Resource Guide

Introduction: Link to the World of Work

Course Manual

Refer to the *Course Manual* for guidance as you work with your students throughout the semester. The *Course Manual* covers essentials for planning and instruction that are helpful as you and your students work through each and every chapter. Newcomers to this discipline should consider this manual a reference of topics related to teaching courses for first-year students.

Start off your semester by doing a textbook reconnaissance of the *Course Manual* to find out about

✔ Classroom management and troubleshooting

✔ Ideas for in class conversations and sharing

✔ Grading, quizzes, exercises, journal entries, and other evaluations

✔ Lesson planning tools

✔ Icebreaker activities

✔ Tips for teaching large groups

✔ Suggestions for ways to increase diversity awareness throughout your course

✔ Suggestions for ways to increase student retention on your campus

✔ Information about evaluating your course

HM ClassPrep CD

The Houghton Mifflin ClassPrep CD is a resource that provides information to guide you through using the content in *From Master Student to Master Employee*. This CD is compatible with both PC and MAC computers. The value of this electronic resource is that materials can be viewed by either chapter (1, 2, 3...) or by asset (Lecture Topics, Quiz Answers, PowerPoint Slides, etc.). Use this CD to get help in preparing your lesson plans, creating classroom discussion topics, generating test questions, suggestions for guest speakers, using videotapes, and teaching tips. Customize these documents to meet the specific needs of your course.

PowerPoint for the Introduction features a dynamic visual model for the Discovery and Intention Journal Entry system.

Warm-up activities will help get you started off on the right foot.

Building relationships activities will allow your students to begin making connections with their classmates.

Journal writing may be new to you and your students. Find tips on assigning these to your students and how to best assess their progress.

Prompts for conversations and sharing offer inspirational quotes and ideas for getting conversations started in your classroom.

Set the stages for your course by showing the **What Do You Want? video** in your first class meeting. Get your students to think about what they want out of your course and set the stage for further conversations about goal setting.

Students can assess their understanding of key concepts in the text by taking an **ACE quiz** on the Student Web site.

For more ways to integrate diversity into your course, have your students read the **Remembering Cultural Differences articles** on the Web site.

Instructors can **join a discussion group** to talk about questions or problems they are facing at throughout the semester on the Instructor Web site.

Additional Resources

Videos: Videos can be used to provide variety to your course, provide stimulation to a variety of learning styles, emphasize important concepts, and expose students to other voices. They are also a great way to invite a "guest speaker" into your classroom.

(masterstudent.college.hmco.com) **Web site:** Using the web site to accompany *From Master Student to Master Employee* is a great way to invite your students to get comfortable with using technology and explore additional exercises, articles, and resources related to your course. As an instructor, you will have additional resources available to you on the Web site, including the College Survival quarterly newsletter, sample syllabi, and discussion groups.

INTRODUCTION
Link to the Work World

Learning how to learn is life's most important skill.
MICHAEL GELB AND TONY BUZAN

The human ability to learn and remember is virtually limitless.
SHEILA OSTRANDER AND LYNN SCHROEDER

why
the Introduction matters . . .

You will acquire learning strategies that will help you make a smooth and successful transition to the world of higher education, and will help you succeed in both college and the workplace.

what
is included . . .

From master student to master employee

This book is worthless—if you just read it

Get the most out of this book

Jumpstart your education with transferable skills

Use the SCANS reports to discover your skills

The value of higher education

The Discovery and Intention Journal Entry system

Discovery and Intention Statement guidelines

Making the transition to higher education

The art of re-entry: Going back to school as an adult learner

Connect to school resources

Power Process: "Discover what you want"

how
you can use this Introduction . . .

Use writing to translate personal discoveries into new behaviors.

Discover—in the concept of transferable skills—a tool to promote your success in school and in your career.

As you read, ask yourself
what if . . .

I could use the strategies that help me succeed in college to also succeed in the workplace?

From master student to master employee

Once upon a time, people thought of education as an enterprise set apart from the business of daily life. The halls of colleges, universities, and other schools were described as ivory towers—places where scholars retreated from the world of work to pursue knowledge.

Today, a different point of view prevails. The boundaries between classroom, office, and factory floor are fluid and flexible. Some people earn a high-school diploma, enter the work force, and then enroll in higher education to expand their career options. Other people continue directly from high school to college. Even so, their learning includes practicums, internships, work-study assignments, and other career-related experiences. Many students work full-time while attending classes.

Instead of competing, workplaces and classrooms can now complement each other. This development mirrors some key discoveries in the psychology of learning: that we learn by immersing ourselves in concrete experiences, reflecting on them, constructing theories, and then testing those theories in action.

Pioneers of both liberal education and modern work methods would agree. In his classic book *The Idea of a University,* John Henry Newman wrote that "all Knowledge is a whole and the separate Sciences parts of one"—leaving no room to divorce theory from practice or knowledge from application. And even though he completed only eight years of formal schooling.[1] Henry Ford said, "The only real security that a person can have in this world is a reserve of knowledge, experience, and ability. Without these qualities, money is practically useless."[2]

The purpose of this book is to build two kinds of bridges between your classroom experiences and your career. One is the bridge of skills—your ability to perform tasks that are valued by employers. Second is the bridge of learning—the ability to update your skills and acquire new ones any time you choose.

As a student, you are now involved in a multimillion-dollar enterprise called higher education. By focusing on the skills you acquire and the results you create, you can move between the role of employee and role of student as easily as you change clothes. As a student, you are also at work, performing in ways that produce measurable results. This is natural, since both roles draw on a common set of skills. The phrases *master student* and *master employee* are terms for qualities that live inside you, waiting only to be discovered.

exercise 1

TEXTBOOK RECONNAISSANCE

Start becoming a master student this moment by doing a 15-minute "textbook reconnaissance." Here's how.

First, read the table of contents. Do it in three minutes or less. Next, look at every page in the book. Move quickly. Scan headlines. Look at pictures. Notice forms, charts, and diagrams. Don't forget the last few pages in back, which include extra copies of planning forms that you might find useful.

A textbook reconnaissance shows you where a course is going. It gives you the big picture. That's useful because brains work best when going from the general to the specific. Getting the big picture before you start makes it easier to recall and understand details later on.

Your textbook reconnaissance will work even better if, as you scan, you look for ideas you can use. When you find one, write the page number and a short description of it in the space below. If you run out of room, just continue your list on a separate sheet of paper. Or use Post-it Notes to flag the pages that look useful. You could even use notes of different colors to signal priority, such as green for ideas to use right away and yellow for those to apply later. The idea behind this technique is simple: It's easier to learn when you're excited, and it's easier to get excited about a course if you know it's going to be useful, interesting, or fun.

Remember, look at every page, and do it quickly. And here's another useful tip for the master student: Do it now.

Description	Page number

This book is worthless
—if you just read it

The first edition of *Becoming a Master Student* began with the sentence *This book is worthless.* Many students thought this was a trick to get their attention. It wasn't. Others thought it was reverse psychology. It wasn't that, either. Still others thought it meant that the book was worthless if they didn't read it. It's more than that.

From Master Student to Master Employee is worthless *even if you read it*—if reading is all you do. What was true of that first edition is true of this one. Until you take action and use the ideas in it, *From Master Student to Master Employee* really is worthless.

The purpose of this book is to help you make successful transitions to higher education and to your chosen career by setting up a pattern of success that will last the rest of your life. You probably won't take action and use the ideas in this book until you are convinced that you have something to gain. That's one reason for this Introduction—to persuade you to use this book actively.

Before you stiffen up and resist this sales pitch, remember that you have already bought the book. Now you can get something for your money by committing yourself to take action—in other words, by committing yourself to becoming a master student. Here's what's in it for you.

Pitch #1: You can save money now and make more later. Start with money. Your college education is one of the most expensive things you will ever buy. Typically, it costs students $30 to $70 an hour to sit in class. Unfortunately, many students think their classes aren't worth even 50 cents an hour.

As you discover what works, you will develop a unique style of learning that you can use for the rest of your life.

As a master student, you control the value you get out of your education, and that value can be considerable. The joy of learning aside, college graduates make more money during their lifetimes than their nondegreed peers. According to the U.S. Department of Labor, the median income for people with a high school degree in 2001 was $29,200. People with an associate degree had a median income of $36,400. For those with a bachelor's degree, the median income was $47,000.[3] Multiply those differences by the number of years you expect to work. The income advantage you gain through higher education could total over half a million dollars. It pays to be a master student.

Pitch #2: You can rediscover the natural learner in you. Joy is important, too. As you become a master student, you will learn to gain knowledge in the most effective way possible by discovering the joyful, natural learner within you.

Children are great natural students. They quickly master complex skills, such as language, and they have fun doing it. For them, learning is a high-energy process involving experimentation, discovery, and sometimes broken dishes. Then comes school. For some students, drill and drudgery replace discovery and dish breaking. Learning can become a drag. You can use this book to reverse that process and rediscover what you knew as a child—that laughter and learning go hand in hand.

Sometimes learning does take effort, especially in higher education. As you become a master student, you will learn many ways to get the most out of that effort.

Pitch #3: You can choose from hundreds of techniques. This book is packed with hundreds of practical, nuts-and-bolts techniques. And you can begin using them immediately. For example, during the textbook reconnaissance on page 1, you can practice three powerful learning techniques in one 15-minute exercise. Even if you doze in lectures, drift during tests, or dawdle on term papers, you'll find ideas in this book that you can use to become a more effective student.

Not all of these ideas will work for you. That's why there are so many of them in this book. You can experiment with the techniques. As you discover what works, you will develop a unique style of learning that you can use for the rest of your life.

Pitch #4: You get the best suggestions from thousands of students.

The concepts and techniques in this book are here not because learning theorists, educators, and psychologists say they work. They are here because tens of thousands of students from all kinds of backgrounds have tried them and say that they work. These are people who dreaded giving speeches, couldn't read their own notes, and fell behind in their course work. Then they figured out how to solve these problems. Now you can use their ideas.

Pitch #5: You can learn about you.

The process of self-discovery is an important theme throughout this book. You can use Discovery and Intention Statements explained in this chapter for everything from organizing your desk to choosing long-term goals. Studying for an organic chemistry quiz is a lot easier with a clean desk and a clear idea of the course's importance to you.

→ ## This book is worth $1,000

Houghton Mifflin Student Success is proud to present three students each year with a $1,000 scholarship for tuition reimbursement. Any post-secondary school in the United States and Canada can nominate one student for the scholarship. To be considered, students must write an essay that answers the question "How do you define success?"

For more details, go to

masterstudent.college.hmco.com

Pitch #6: You can use a proven product.

Becoming a Master Student has proved successful for hundreds of thousands of students. In schools where it was widely used, the dropout rate decreased as much as 25 percent, and in some cases, 50 percent. Student feedback has been positive. In particular, students with successful histories have praised these techniques that are now included in this book.

Pitch #7: You can learn the secret of student success.

If this sales pitch still hasn't persuaded you to use this book actively, maybe it's time to reveal the secret of student success.

(Provide your own drum roll here.) The secret is—that there are no secrets. Perhaps the ultimate formula is to give up formulas and keep inventing.

The strategies and tactics that successful students use are well known. You have hundreds of them at your fingertips right now, in this book. Use them. Modify them. Invent new ones. You're the authority on what works for you.

However, what makes any technique work is commitment—and action. Without them, the pages of *From Master Student to Master Employee* are just 2.1 pounds of expensive mulch. Add your participation to the mulch, and these pages are priceless. ◼

desk of . . .

from the

STUART SHOSTAK,
STRUCTURED FINANCE ANALYST:

The first and most important thing college does is it shifts all the responsibility for getting ahead to you. If you don't want to do your homework or class work or even show up to class, you fail. End of story. You don't get called into the principal's office. College is like the minor leagues for the corporate world. Obviously you gain the knowledge and skills you need; you also gain this intangible social quality that allows you to interact with your corworkers and bosses on the proper level.

Get the most out of this book

1. Rip em out. The pages of this book are perforated because some of the information here is too important to leave in the book and some your instructor might want to see. For example, Journal Entry #2 asks you to list some important things you want to get out of your education. To keep yourself focused, you could rip that page out and post it on your bathroom mirror or some other place where you'll see it several times a day.

You can reinsert the page later by sticking it into the spine of the book. A piece of tape will hold it in place.

2. Skip around. You can use this book in several different ways. Read it straight through. Or pick it up, turn to any page, and find an idea you can use. Look for ideas you can use right now. For example, if you are about to choose a major, skip directly to the articles on this topic in Chapter Two.

3. If it works, use it. If it doesn't, lose it. If there are sections of the book that don't apply to you at all, skip them—unless, of course, they are assigned. Then see if you can gain value from these sections anyway. When you are committed to getting value from this book, even an idea that seems irrelevant or ineffective at first can turn out to be a powerful tool.

4. Put yourself into the book. As you read about techniques in this book, create your own scenarios, starring yourself in the title role. For example, when reading through Exercise #1: "Textbook reconnaissance," picture yourself using this technique on your world history textbook.

5. Listen to your peers. Throughout this book you will find elements titled From the Desk of . . . . These short features contain quotations from people who provide models of success. As you dig into the following chapters, think about what you would say if you could add your voice to theirs. Look for tools and techniques that can make a huge difference in your life.

6. Own this book. Right now, put your name, address, and related information on the inside cover of this book, and don't stop there. Determine what you want to get out of school and create a record of how you intend to

get it by reading the Power Process and completing the Journal Entries in this Introduction. Every time your pen touches a page, you move closer to mastery of learning.

7. Do the exercises. Action makes this book work. To get the most out of an exercise, read the instructions carefully before you begin. To get the most out of this book, do most of the exercises. More important, avoid feeling guilty if you skip some. And by the way, it's never too late to go back and do the ones you skipped.

These exercises invite you to write, touch, feel, move, see, search, ponder, speak, listen, recall, choose, commit, and create. You might even sing and dance. Learning often works best when it involves action.

8. Practice critical thinking. Throughout this book are exercises titled Thinking Critically in the Workplace and Thinking Critically in the Classroom. Their purpose is to reinforce contemplation, creativity, and problem solving. Note that other elements of this text, including other exercises and the Journal Entries, also promote critical thinking.

9. Learn about learning styles. Check out the Learning Styles Application in each chapter. These exercises are included to increase your awareness of your preferred learning styles and to help you explore new styles. Each application will guide you through experiencing four specific modes of learning as applied to the content of the chapter. The modes can be accessed by asking four basic questions: *Why? What? How?* and *What if?* You'll find more details in the Learning Style Inventory in Chapter One.

10. Navigate through learning experiences with the Master Student Map. You can orient yourself for maximum learning every time you open this book by asking those same four questions. That's the idea behind the Master Student Map included on the first page of each chapter. Eventually, you'll be able to use the four-part structure of this map to guide yourself in effectively learning anything.

11. Link to the Web. Throughout this book, you'll notice reminders to visit the Web site for *From Master Student to Master Employee:*

masterstudent.college.hmco.com

Check regularly for articles, online exercises, and links to other useful Web sites.

12. Sweat the small stuff. Look for sidebars—short bursts of words and pictures placed between longer articles—throughout this book. These short pieces might offer an insight that transforms your experience of higher education. Remember this related point: Shorter chapters in this book are just as important as longer chapters.

13. Take it to work now. You can apply nearly all of the techniques in this book to your current job or next career. Look for highlighted information about *transferable skills* in the articles throughout this book, and begin to identify skills you already have and uncover ways to develop new ones. To stimulate your thinking, see the Career Application at the end of each chapter. Use these case studies to plan for seamless transitions from success in school to success on the job.

14. Get used to a new look and tone. This book looks different from traditional textbooks. Each chapter presents major ideas in magazine-style articles. You will discover lots of lists, blurbs, one-liners, pictures, charts, graphs, illustrations, and even a joke or two.

Even though this book is loaded with special features, you'll find some core elements. For example, the two pages that open each chapter include a "lead" article and an introductory Journal Entry. And at the end of each chapter you'll find a Power Process, Career Application, chapter quiz, Learning Styles Application, and Master Student Profile—all noted in a toolbar at the top of the page.

Note: As a strategy for avoiding sexist language, this book alternates the use of feminine and masculine pronouns.

COMMITMENT

This book is worthless unless you actively participate in its activities and exercises. One powerful way to begin taking action is to make a commitment. Conversely, without commitment, sustained action is unlikely, and the result is again a worthless book. Therefore, in the interest of saving your valuable time and energy, this exercise gives you a chance to declare your level of involvement up front. From the choices below, choose the sentence that best reflects your commitment to using this book. Write the number in the space provided at the end of the list.

1. "Well, I'm reading this book right now, aren't I?"
2. "I will skim the book and read the interesting parts."
3. "I will read the book and think about how some of the techniques might apply to me."
4. "I will read the book, think about it, and do the exercises that look interesting."
5. "I will read the book, do some exercises, and complete some of the Journal Entries."
6. "I will read the book, do some exercises and Journal Entries, and use some of the techniques."
7. "I will read the book, do most of the exercises and Journal Entries, and use some of the techniques."
8. "I will study this book, do most of the exercises and Journal Entries, and use some of the techniques."
9. "I will study this book, do most of the exercises and Journal Entries, and experiment vigorously with most of the suggestions in order to discover what works best for me."
10. "I promise myself to get value from this book, beginning with Exercise #1: 'Textbook reconnaissance,' even if I have to rewrite the sections I don't like and invent new techniques of my own."

Enter your commitment level and today's date here:

Commitment level _____   Date _____

If you selected commitment level 1 or 2, you might consider passing this book on to a friend. If your commitment level is 9 or 10, you are on your way to terrific success in school. If your level is somewhere in between, experiment with the techniques and learning strategies in this book. If you find that they work, consider returning to this exercise and raising your level of commitment.

Jumpstart your education with transferable skills

When meeting with an academic advisor, some students say, "I've just been taking general education and liberal arts courses. I haven't got any marketable skills."

Think again.

Few words are as widely misunderstood as *skill*. Defining it carefully can have an immediate and positive impact on your career planning.

Two kinds of skills

One dictionary defines *skill* as "the ability to do something well, usually gained by training or experience." Some skills—such as the ability to repair fiber-optic cables or do brain surgery—are acquired through formal schooling, on-the-job training, or both. These abilities are called *work-content skills.* People with such skills have mastered a specialized body of knowledge needed to do a specific kind of work.

However, we develop another category of skills through experiences both inside and outside the classroom. We may never receive formal training to develop these abilities. Yet they are key to success in the workplace. These are *transferable skills.* Transferable skills are the kind of abilities that help people thrive in any job—no matter what work-content skills they have. Perhaps you've heard someone described this way: "She's really smart and knows what she's doing, but she's got lousy people skills." People skills—such as *listening* and *negotiating*—are prime examples of transferable skills. Other examples are listed in the sidebar to this article.

Succeeding in many situations

Transferable skills are often invisible to us. The problem begins when we assume that a given skill can only be used in one context, such as being in school or working at a particular job. Thinking in this way places an artificial limit on our possibilities.

As an alternative, think about the things you routinely do to succeed in school. Analyze your activities to isolate specific skills. Then brainstorm a list of jobs where you could use the same skills.

Consider the task of writing a research paper. This calls for skills such as the following:

- *Planning*—setting goals for completing your outline, first draft, second draft, and final draft.

- *Managing time* to meet your writing goals.

- *Interviewing* people who know a lot about the topic of your paper.

- *Researching* using the Internet and campus library to discover key facts and ideas to include in your paper.

- *Writing* to present those facts and ideas in an original way.

- *Editing* your drafts for clarity and correctness.

Now consider the kinds of jobs that draw on these skills. For example, you could transfer your skill at writing papers to a possible career in journalism, technical writing, or advertising copywriting. You could use your editing skills to work in the field of publishing as a magazine or book editor. Interviewing and research skills could help you enter the field of market research. And the abilities to plan, manage time, and meet deadlines will help you succeed in all the jobs mentioned so far.

Use the same kind of analysis to think about transferring skills from one job to another job. Say that you work part-time as an administrative assistant at a computer dealer that sells a variety of hardware and software. You take phone calls from potential customers, help current customers solve problems using their computers, and attend meetings where your coworkers plan ways to market new products. You are developing skills at *selling, serving customers,* and *working on teams* that could help you land a job as a sales representative for a computer manufacturer or software developer.

The basic idea is to take a cue from the word *transferable.* Almost any skill you use to succeed in one situation can *transfer* to success in another situation.

The concept of transferable skills creates a powerful link between higher education and the work world. Skills are the core elements of any job. While taking any course, list the specific skills you are developing and how you can transfer them to the work world. Almost everything you do in school can be applied to your career—if you consistently pursue this line of thought.

Ask four questions

To experiment further with this concept of transferable skills, ask and answer four questions derived from the Master Student Map.

Why *identify my transferable skills?* Getting past the "I-don't-have-any-skills" syndrome means that you can approach job hunting with more confidence. As you uncover these hidden assets, your list of qualifications will grow as if by magic. You won't be padding your résumé. You'll simply be using action words to tell the full truth about what you can do.

Identifying your transferable skills takes a little time. And the payoffs are numerous. A complete and accurate list of transferable skills can help you land jobs that involve more responsibility, more variety, more freedom to structure your time, and more money.

Transferable skills also help you thrive in the midst of constant change. Technology will continue to upgrade. Ongoing discoveries in many fields could render current knowledge obsolete. Jobs that exist today may disappear in a few years, to be replaced by entirely new ones. Your keys to prospering in this environment are transferable skills—those that you can carry from one career to another.

What *are my transferable skills?* Discover your transferable skills by reflecting on key experiences. Recall a time when you performed at the peak of your ability, overcame obstacles, won an award, gained a high grade, or met a significant goal. List the skills you used to create those successes.

In each case, remember that the word *skill* applies to something that you *do*. In your list of transferable skills, start each item with an action verb such as *budget* or *coach* or *consult*. Or use a closely related part of speech—*budgeting* or *coaching*.

For a more complete picture of your transferable skills, describe the object of your action. For instance, if one of the skills on your list is *organizing*, this action verb could refer to organizing ideas, organizing people, or organizing objects in a room. Specify the kind of organizing that you like to do.

How *do I perform these skills?* You can bring your transferable skills into even sharper focus by adding adverbs—words that describe *how* you take action. You

might say that you edit *accurately* or learn *quickly*.

In summary, you can use a three-column chart to list your transferable skills. For example:

Verb	Object	Adverb
Organizing	Records	Effectively
Serving	Customers	Courteously
Coordinating	Special events	Efficiently

Add a specific example of each skill to your list, and you're well on the way to an engaging résumé and a winning job interview.

As you list your transferable skills, focus on the skills that you enjoy using the most. Then look for careers and jobs that directly involve those skills.

What *if I could expand my transferable skills?* In addition to thinking about the skills you already have, consider the skills you'd like to acquire. Describe them in detail and list experiences that can help you develop them. Possibilities include extracurricular activities, group memberships, internships, volunteer positions, work-study assignments, and other part-time jobs. As you read this book, pay attention to articles that highlight the transferable skills you can build in the classroom and in your current job. Let your list of transferable skills grow and develop as you do. ▨

→ Twenty-five transferable skills

Use the following list of transferable skills as a starting point for making an inventory of your abilities. There are literally hundreds of transferable skills, so expand this list based on your own experiences.

Analyzing	Planning
Budgeting	Reading
Coaching	Researching
Consulting	Problem solving
Decision making	Selling
Editing	Serving customers
Evaluating	Speaking
Interviewing	Supervising
Learning	Thinking critically
Listening	Training
Managing time	Writing
Negotiating	Working on teams
Organizing	

Use the SCANS reports to discover your skills

The U.S. Department of Labor has issued a series of reports created by the Secretary's Commission on Achieving Necessary Skills (SCANS). This influential series of documents lists essential skills for workers in the twenty-first century. You might find this list helpful in assessing your current skills and planning to develop new ones. Refer to the articles throughout this book for help in uncovering transferable skills that will help you achieve success in the classroom and the workplace.

Basic skills

- Reading to locate, understand, and interpret written information
- Writing to communicate ideas and information
- Using mathematics to perform basic computations and solve problems
- Listening to interpret and respond to verbal messages and other cues
- Speaking clearly and making organized presentations

Thinking skills

- Creative thinking to generate new ideas
- Decision making to set and meet goals
- Problem solving to identify challenges and implement action plans
- Seeing things in the mind's eye to interpret and create symbols, pictures, graphs, and other visual tools
- Knowing how to learn
- Reasoning to discover underlying principles and apply them when solving a problem

Personal qualities

- Responsibility to exert high effort and persist in meeting goals
- Self-esteem to maintain a positive view of your abilities
- Social skills that demonstrate adaptability and empathy
- Self-management to assess yourself accurately, set personal goals, and monitor personal progress
- Integrity to choose ethical behaviors

Skills in using resources

- Allocating time for goal-relevant activities
- Allocating money to prepare budgets and meet them
- Allocating materials and facilities
- Allocating human resources to assign tasks effectively and provide others with feedback

Interpersonal skills

- Participating as a member of a team
- Teaching others
- Serving clients and customers
- Exercising leadership
- Negotiating to reach agreements
- Working well with people from diverse backgrounds

Skills in working with information

- Acquiring and evaluating information
- Organizing and maintaining information
- Interpreting and communicating information in oral, written, and visual forms
- Using computers to process information

Skills in working with complex interrelationships

- Understanding social, organizational, and technological systems and operating within them
- Monitoring and correcting performance
- Improving or designing systems

Skills in working with technology

- Selecting appropriate technology
- Applying technology to tasks
- Maintaining and troubleshooting equipment[4]

The value of higher education

When you're waist-deep in reading assignments, writing papers, and studying for tests, you might well ask yourself: Is all this effort going to pay off someday?

That's a fair question. And it addresses a core issue—the value of getting an education beyond high school.

Be reassured. The potential benefits of higher education are enormous.

Gain a broad vision. One benefit of studying the liberal arts is the chance to gain a broad vision. People with a liberal arts background are aware of the various kinds of problems tackled in psychology and theology, philosophy and physics, literature and mathematics. They understand how people in all of these fields arrive at conclusions and how these fields relate to each other.

Master the liberal arts. The word *liberal* comes from the Latin verb *libero,* which means "to free." Liberal arts are those that promote critical thinking. Studying them can free us from irrational ideas, half-truths, racism, and prejudice. The liberal arts grant us freedom to explore alternatives and create a system of personal values. These benefits are priceless, the very basis of personal fulfillment and political freedom.

Discover your values. We do not spend all of our waking hours at our jobs. That leaves us with a decision that affects the quality of our lives: how to spend leisure time. By cultivating our interest in the arts and community affairs, the liberal arts provide us with many options for activities outside of work. These studies add a dimension to life that goes beyond having a job and paying the bills.

Discover new interests. Taking a broad range of courses has the potential to change your direction in life. A student previously committed to a career in science might try out a drawing class and eventually switch to a degree in studio arts. Or a person who swears that she has no aptitude for technical subjects might change her major to computer science after taking an introductory computer course. To make effective choices about your long-term goals, base those choices on a variety of academic and personal experiences.

Hang out with the great. Today we enjoy a huge legacy from our ancestors. The creative minds of our species have given us great works of art, systems of science, and technological advances that defy the imagination. Through higher education we can gain firsthand knowledge of humanity's greatest creations. The poet Ezra Pound defined literature as "news that stays news."[5] Most of the writing in newspapers and magazines becomes dated quickly. In contrast, many of the books you read in higher education have passed the hardest test of all—time. Such works have created value for people for decades, sometimes for centuries. These creations are inexhaustible. We can return to them time after time and gain new insights. These are the works we can justifiably deem great. Hanging out with them transforms us. Getting to know them exercises our minds, just as running exercises our bodies.

Join the conversation. The world's finest scientists and artists have joined voices in a conversation that spans centuries and crosses cultures. This is a conversation about the nature of truth and beauty, knowledge and compassion, good and evil—ideas that form the very basis of human society. Robert Hutchins, former president of the University of Chicago, called this the "great conversation."[6] By studying this conversation, we take on the most basic human challenges: coping with death and suffering, helping create a just global society, living with meaning and purpose. Our greatest thinkers have left behind tangible records. You'll find them in libraries, concert halls, museums, and scientific laboratories across the world. Through higher education, you gain a front-row seat for the great conversation—and an opportunity to add your own voice. ◪

The Discovery and Intention Journal Entry system

AIRPORT

One way to become a better student is to grit your teeth and try harder. There is another way. Using familiar tools and easily learned processes, the Discovery and Intention Journal Entry system can help increase your effectiveness by showing you how to focus your energy.

The Discovery and Intention Journal Entry system is a little like flying a plane. Airplanes are seldom exactly on course. Human and automatic pilots are always checking positions and making corrections. The resulting flight path looks like a zigzag. The plane is almost always flying in the wrong direction, but because of constant observation and course correction, it arrives at the right destination.

A similar system can be used by students. Most Journal Entries throughout this book are labeled as either Discovery Statements or Intention Statements—some are Discovery/Intention Statements. Each Journal Entry will contain a short set of suggestions that involve writing.

Through Discovery Statements, you can assess "where you are." These statements are a record of what you are learning about yourself as a student—both strengths and weaknesses. Discovery Statements can also be declarations of your goals, descriptions of your attitudes, statements of your feelings, transcripts of your thoughts, and chronicles of your behavior.

Sometimes Discovery Statements chronicle an "aha!" moment—a flash of insight that results when a new idea connects with your prior experiences, preferred styles of learning, or both. Perhaps a solution to a long-standing problem suddenly occurs to you, or a life-changing insight wells up from the deepest recesses of your mind. Don't let such moments disappear. Capture them in Discovery Statements.

Intention Statements can be used to alter your course. They are statements of your commitment to do a specific task or take a certain action. An intention arises out of your choice to direct your energy toward a particular goal. While Discovery Statements promote awareness, Intention Statements are blueprints for action. The two processes reinforce each other.

The purpose of this system is not to get you pumped up and excited to go out there and try harder. Rather, Discovery and Intention Statements are intended to help you focus on what you want to accomplish and how you plan to achieve your goals. You can start using this system while you're in school—and then take it with you for the rest of

GOAL

Some books should be preserved in pristine condition. This isn't one of them.

Something happens when you interact with your book by writing in it. This book is about learning, and learning is an active pursuit, not a passive one. When you make notes in the margin, you can hear yourself talking with the author. When you doodle and underline, you can see the author's ideas taking shape. You can even argue with the author and come up with your own theories and explanations. In all of these ways, you become a coauthor of this book. You rewrite it to make it yours.

While you're at it, you can create symbols or codes that will help when reviewing the text later on, such as "Q" for questions or exclamation points for important ideas. You can also circle words to look up in a dictionary.

Remember, if any idea in this book doesn't work for you, you can rewrite it. Change the exercises to fit your needs. Create a new technique by combining several others. Create a technique out of thin air!

Find something you agree or disagree with and write a short note in the margin about it. Or draw a diagram. Better yet, do both. Let creativity be your guide. Have fun.

Begin rewriting now.

come immediately. Do not be concerned. Stay with the cycle. Use Discovery Statements to get a clear view of your world and what you want out of it. Then use Intention Statements to direct your actions. When you notice progress, record it.

The following statement might strike you as improbable, but it is true: It often takes the same amount of energy to get what you want in school as it takes to get what you *don't* want. Sometimes getting what you don't want takes even more effort. An airplane burns the same amount of fuel flying away from its destination as it does flying toward it. It pays to stay on course.

You can use the Discovery and Intention Journal Entry system to stay on your own course and get what you want out of school. Consider the guidelines for Discovery and Intention Statements that follow, and then develop your own style. Once you get the hang of it, you might discover you can fly. ✖

your life. Journaling is a transferable skill. In the workplace, you can use it to monitor your skill development and maintain your career direction.

The Journal Entry process is a cycle. First, you write Discovery Statements about where you are now and where you want to be. Next, you write Intention Statements about the specific steps you will take to get there. Then you follow up with Discovery Statements about whether you completed those steps and what you learned in the process, followed by more Intention Statements, and so on. Sometimes a statement will be long and detailed. Usually, it will be short—maybe just a line or two. With practice, the cycle will become automatic.

Don't panic when you fail to complete an intended task. Straying off course is normal. Simply make the necessary corrections. Miraculous progress might not

desk of...

Discovery and Intention Statement guidelines

Discovery Statements

1 Record the specifics about your thoughts, feelings, and behavior. Thoughts include inner voices. We talk to ourselves constantly in our heads. When internal chatter gets in the way, write down what you are telling yourself. If this seems difficult at first, just start writing. The act of writing can trigger a flood of thoughts.

Thoughts also include mental pictures. These are especially powerful. Picturing yourself flunking a test is like a rehearsal to do just that. One way to take away the power of negative images is to describe them in detail.

Also notice how you feel when you function well. Use Discovery Statements to pinpoint exactly where and when you learn most effectively.

In addition, observe your actions and record the facts. If you spent 90 minutes chatting online with a favorite cousin instead of reading your anatomy text, write about it and include the details, such as when you did it, where you did it, and how it felt. Record your observations quickly, as soon as you make them.

2 Use discomfort as a signal. When you approach a daunting task, such as a difficult accounting problem, notice your physical sensations—a churning stomach, perhaps, or shallow breathing or yawning. Feeling uncomfortable, bored, or tired might be a signal that you're about to do valuable work. Stick with it. Tell yourself you can handle the discomfort just a little bit longer. You will be rewarded.

You can experience those rewards at any time. Just think of a problem that poses the biggest potential barrier to your success in school. Choose a problem that you face right now, today. (Hint: It might be the thing that's distracting you from reading this article.) If you have a lot of emotion tied up in this problem, that's even better. Write a Discovery Statement about it.

3 Suspend judgment. When you are discovering yourself, be gentle. Suspend self-judgment. If you continually judge your behaviors as "bad" or "stupid" or "galactically imbecilic," sooner or later your mind will revolt. Rather than put up with the abuse, it will quit making discoveries. For your own benefit, be kind.

4 Tell the truth. Suspending judgment helps you tell the truth about yourself. "The truth will set you free" is a saying that endures for a reason. The closer you get to the truth, the more powerful your Discovery Statements will be. And if you notice that you are avoiding the truth, don't blame yourself. Just tell the truth about it.

Intention Statements

1 Make intentions positive. The purpose of writing intentions is to focus on what you want rather than what you don't want. Instead of writing "I will not fall asleep while studying accounting," write "I intend to stay awake when studying accounting."

Also avoid the word *try*. Trying is not doing. When we hedge our bets with *try*, we can always tell ourselves, "Well, I *tried* to stay awake." We end up fooling ourselves into thinking we succeeded.

2 Make intentions observable. Experiment with an idea from educational trainer Robert Mager, who suggests that goals be defined through behaviors that can be observed and measured.[7] Rather than writing "I intend to work harder on my history assignments," write "I intend to review my class notes, and I intend to make summary sheets of my reading." Then, when you review your progress, you can determine more precisely whether you have accomplished what you intended.

3 Make intentions small and keepable. Give yourself opportunities to succeed by setting goals you can meet. Break large goals into small, specific tasks that can be accomplished quickly. If you want to get an A in biology, ask yourself: "What can I do today?" You might choose to study biology for an extra hour. Make that your intention.

When setting your goals, anticipate self-sabotage. Be aware of what you might do, consciously or unconsciously, to undermine your best intentions. If you intend to study differential equations at 9 p.m., notice when you sit down to watch a two-hour movie that starts at 8 p.m.

Also, be careful of intentions that depend on others. If you write that you intend for your study group to complete an assignment by Monday, then your success depends on the other students in the group.

4 Set timelines that include rewards. Timelines can focus your attention. For example, if you are assigned to write a paper, break the assignment into small tasks and set a precise due date for each one. You might write "I intend to select a topic for my paper by 9 a.m. Wednesday."

Timelines are especially useful when your intention is to experiment with a technique suggested in this book. The sooner you act on a new idea, the better. Consider practicing a new behavior within four hours after you first learn about it.

Remember that you create timelines for your own benefit, not to set yourself up to feel guilty. And you can always change the timeline.

When you meet your goal on time, reward yourself. Rewards that are an integral part of a goal are powerful. For example, your reward for earning a degree might be the career you've always dreamed of. External rewards, such as a movie or an afternoon in the park, are valuable, too. These rewards work best when you're willing to withhold them. If you plan to take a nap on Sunday afternoon whether or not you've finished your English assignment, the nap is not an effective reward.

Another way to reward yourself is to sit quietly after you have finished your task and savor the feeling. One reason why success breeds success is that it feels good. ✖

journal entry 1

Discovery Statement

Welcome to the first Journal Entry in this book. You'll find Journal Entries in every chapter, all with a similar design that allow space for you to write.

In the space below, write a description of a time in your life when you learned or did something well. This experience does not need to be related to school. Describe the details of the situation, including the place, time, and people involved. Describe how you felt about it, how it looked to you, how it sounded. Describe the physical sensations you associate with the event. Also describe your emotions.

I discovered that . . .

_____

_____

_____

_____

_____

_____

_____

_____

_____

_____

_____

_____

You share one thing in common with other students at your vocational school, college, or university: Entering higher education represents a major change in your life. You've joined a new culture with its own set of rules, both spoken and unspoken.

Making the transition to higher education

Whether they've just graduated from high school or have been out of the classroom for decades, students new to higher education immediately face many differences between secondary and post-secondary education. The sooner you understand such differences, the sooner you can deal with them. Some examples include:

- *New academic standards.* Often there are fewer tests in higher education than in high school, and the grading might be tougher. You'll probably find that teachers expect you to study more. At the same time, your instructors might give you less guidance about what or how to study, and less feedback about how you are doing.

- *Differences in teaching styles.* Instructors at colleges, universities, and vocational schools are often steeped in their subject matter. Many did not take courses on how to teach and might not be as interesting as some of your previous teachers. And some professors might seem more focused on research than on teaching.

- *A larger playing field.* The institution you've just joined might seem immense, impersonal, and even frightening. The sheer size of the campus, the variety of courses offered, the large number of departments—all of these can add up to a confusing array of options.

- *More students and more diversity.* The school you're attending right now might enroll thousands of students. And the range of diversity among these students might surprise you.

There's an opportunity that comes with all of these changes: a greater degree of freedom. Higher education presents you with a new world of choices. You are now responsible for deciding what classes to take, how to structure your time, and with whom to associate. Perhaps more than ever before, you'll find that your education is your own creation. When making decisions that lead to the future of your dreams, keep the following in mind.

Decrease the unknowns. Before classes begin, get a map of the school property and walk through your first day's schedule, perhaps with a classmate or friend. Visit your instructors in their offices and introduce yourself. Anything you can do to get familiar with the new routine will help.

Admit your feelings—whatever they are. Higher education can be an intimidating experience for new students. People of diverse cultures, adult learners, commuters, and people with disabilities can feel excluded. Anyone can feel anxious, isolated, homesick, or worried about doing well academically.

Those emotions are common among new students, and there's nothing wrong with them. Simply admitting the truth about how you feel—to yourself and to someone else—can help you cope. And you can almost always do something constructive, no matter how you feel.

If your feelings about this transition make it hard for you to carry out the activities of daily life—going to class, working, studying, and relating to people—then get professional help. Start with a counselor at the student health service on your campus. The mere act of seeking help can make a difference.

Access resources. A supercharger increases the air supply to an internal combustion engine. The resulting difference in power can be dramatic. You can make just as powerful a difference in your education by using all of the resources available to students. In this case, your "air supply" includes people, campus clubs and organizations, and school and community services.

Of all resources, people are the most important. You can isolate yourself, study hard, and get a good education. When you make the effort to establish relationships with teachers, staff members, fellow students, and employers, you can get a *great* education.

Meet with your academic advisor.
One person in particular can help you access resources and make the transition to higher education—your academic advisor. Meet with this person regularly. Advisors generally have a big picture of course requirements, options for declaring majors, and the resources available at your school. Peer advisory programs might also be available.

When you work with an advisor, remember that you're a paying customer and have a right to be satisfied with the service you get. Don't be afraid to change advisors when that seems appropriate.

Learn the language of higher education. Terms such as *grade point average (GPA), prerequisite, accreditation, matriculation, tenure,* and *syllabus* might be new to you. Ease your transition to higher education by checking your school catalog for definitions of these words and others that you don't understand. Also ask your academic advisor for clarification.

Attend class. In higher education, teachers generally don't take attendance. Yet you'll find that attending class is essential to your success. The amount that you pay in tuition and fees makes a powerful argument for going to classes regularly and getting your money's worth. In large part, the material that you're tested on comes from events that take place in class.

"Showing up" for class occurs on two levels. The most visible level is being physically present in the classroom. Even more important is showing up mentally. This includes taking detailed notes, asking questions, and contributing to class discussions.

Don't assume that you already know how to study.
You can cope with increased workloads and higher academic expectations by putting all of your study habits on the table and evaluating them. Keep the habits that serve you, drop those that hold you back, and adopt new ones to promote your success. On every page of this book, you'll find helpful suggestions.

Become a self-regulated learner. Psychologists use the term *self-regulation* to describe people who set specific goals, monitor their progress toward those goals, and regularly change their behavior to produce the desired results. These people have a clear idea of their objectives and their capabilities.

This book promotes self-regulation through the ongoing cycle of discovery, intention, and action. Write Discovery Statements to monitor yourself and evaluate the results you're currently creating in life. Create Intention Statements to determine exactly what you want. And use the exercises throughout the book to experience the power of putting your ideas into practice.

Take the initiative in meeting new people. Promise yourself to meet one new person each week, then write an Intention Statement describing specific ways to do this. Introduce yourself to classmates. Just before or after class is a good time to do so. Realize that most of the people in this new world of higher education are waiting to be welcomed. You can help them and help yourself at the same time. ✖

> *Perhaps more than ever before, you'll find that your education is your own creation.*

→ Mastering transitions

To be in transition means to be moving between two worlds. The world of your immediate past is still familiar, though becoming more distant. Yet the new world you've entered can seem alien—frightening, even. The ability to move successfully between these two worlds is the art of making transitions.

During your lifetime, you'll get many chances to master the art of transitions. The transition to higher education is just one example. Use the following strategies to deal with any transition that comes your way.

Remember earlier transitions. Recall times in the past when you coped with a major change. Write about those experiences in detail. Describe how you felt and list any strategies you used to make those transitions effectively. You've weathered major change before. You can do it again.

Learn optimism. Martin Seligman, author of *Learned Optimism,* states that the key difference between optimists and pessimists is *explanatory style*—the way that they talk about events such as making transitions.[8] Pessimists might describe the transition to higher education in ways that are:

- *Permanent*: "I'll never be able to handle college-level classes."

- *Pervasive*: "Whenever I get involved in a new situation, I always make a lot of mistakes."

- *Personal*: "I'm just no good at making transitions."

In contrast, optimists tend to make statements that can be described as:

- *Temporary*: "I'm feeling anxious about starting school, and that's normal at first."

- *Specific* : "While this transition might be hard for me, on the whole I can learn to handle change well."

- *External*: "My circumstances have changed a lot, so it's natural to find that I have a lot of new feelings."

The key point is that *over time you can learn to change your explanatory style.* Doing so can make a difference in how you think and feel about any transition. Notice when you talk about difficult events in terms that are permanent, pervasive, or personal. Make a point to speak in ways that are temporary, specific, or external.

Seek stability zones. Any kind of transition can bring a kind of culture shock—and the thought "I don't know who I am anymore." To deal with this, remember that not every part of your life has to change at the same time. Balance change in one area with stability in another. While in school, keep in contact with family members and old friends. Maintain long-term relationships, including relationships with key places, such as your childhood home. Postpone other major changes for now.

Balance work and school schedules. As you coordinate your work and study schedules, consider the limits on your energy and time. To create balance in your life, experiment with options such as these:

- Register for fewer classes during a term when you expect heavier demands at your job.

- Avoid loading your schedule with classes that require unusually heavy amounts of reading or writing.

- Create "buffer zones" in your schedule—pockets of unplanned time that you can use for unforeseen events.

Stay in the present moment. Anxiety can arise when we allow our thoughts to dwell on how long it might take to adjust to new circumstances. Return to the present moment, and such worries start to fade. Ask what you can do right here, right now to ease your transition. Take it one day at a time, even one hour at a time. Handle each task as it arises, and the future will take care of itself.

If you're returning to school after a long break from the classroom, there's no reason to feel out of place. Returning adults and other nontraditional students are already a majority in some schools.

The art of re-entry
Going back to school as an adult learner

Being an adult learner puts you on strong footing. With a rich store of life experience on which to draw, you can ask meaningful questions and more easily make connections between course work and daily life. Many instructors will especially enjoy working with you.

Following are some suggestions for returning adult students. Even if you don't fit into this category, you can look for ways to apply these ideas.

Ease into it. If you're new to higher education, consider easing into it. You can choose to attend school part-time before making a full-time commitment.

Plan your week. Many adult learners report that their number one problem is time. One solution is to plan your week. By planning ahead a week at a time, you get a bigger picture of your multiple roles as a student, an employee, and a family member. For more suggestions on managing time, see Chapter Two: Planning.

Add 15 minutes to your day. If you're pressed for time, plan to get up 15 minutes earlier or stay up 15 minutes later. Chances are, the lost sleep won't affect your alertness during the day. You can use the extra time to scan a reading assignment or outline a paper. Stretching each day by just 15 minutes yields 91 extra hours in a year. That's time you can use to promote your success in school.

Delegate tasks. Consider hiring others to do some of your household work or errands. Yes, this costs money.

It's also an investment in your education and future earning power.

If you have children, delegate some of the chores to them. Or start a meal co-op in your neighborhood. Cook dinner for yourself and someone else one night each week. In return, ask that person to furnish you with a meal on another night. A similar strategy can apply to childcare and other household tasks.

Get to know younger students. You share a central goal with younger students: succeeding in school. It's easier to get past the generation gap when you remember this. Consider pooling resources with younger students. Share notes, form study groups, or edit each other's term papers.

Get to know other returning students. Introduce yourself to other adult learners. Being in the same classroom gives you an immediate bond. You can exchange work, home, or cell phone numbers and build a network of mutual support. Some students adopt a buddy system, pairing up with another student in each class to complete assignments and prepare for tests.

Find common ground with instructors. Many of your teachers might be juggling academic careers, work schedules, and family lives, too. Finding common ground gives you one more way to break the ice with instructors.

Enlist your employer's support. Employers often promote continuing education. Further education can increase your skills in a specific field while enhancing your ability to work with people. That makes you a more valuable employee or consultant.

Let your employer in on your educational plans. Point out how the skills you gain in class will help you meet work objectives. Offer informal "seminars" at work to share what you're learning in school.

Get extra mileage out of your current tasks.
You can look for specific ways to merge your work and school lives. Some schools will offer academic credit for work and life experience. Your company might reimburse its employees for some tuition costs or even grant time off to attend classes.

Experiment with combining tasks. For example, when you're assigned a research paper, choose a topic that relates to your current job tasks.

Look for childcare.
For some students, returning to class means looking for childcare outside the home. Many schools offer childcare facilities at reduced rates for students.

Review your subjects before you start classes.
Say that you're registered for trigonometry and you haven't taken a math class since high school. Consider brushing up on the subject before classes begin. Also talk with future instructors about ways to prepare for their classes.

Prepare for an academic environment.
If you're used to an efficient corporate setting, school life might present some frustrations. A lack of advanced computer systems might slow down your class registration. Faculty members might take a little longer to return your calls or respond to letters, especially during holiday and summer breaks. Knowing the rhythm of academic life can help you plan around these possibilities.

Be willing to adopt new study habits.
Rather than returning to study habits from previous school experiences, many adult learners find it more effective to treat their school assignments exactly as they would treat a project at work. They use the same tactics in the library as they do on the job, which often helps them learn more actively.

Integrate class work with daily experiences.
According to psychologist Malcolm Knowles, adult learners in particular look for ways to connect classroom experience with the rest of their lives.[9] This approach can promote success in school for students of any age. You can start by remembering two words: *why* and *how. Why* prompts you to look for a purpose and benefit in what you're learning. Say that your psychology teacher lectures about Abraham Maslow's ideas on the hierarchy of human needs. Maslow stated that the need for self-actualization is just as important as the need for safety, security, or love.[10]

As you learn what Maslow meant by *self-actualization,* ask yourself why this concept would make a difference in your life. Perhaps your reason for entering higher education is connected to your own quest for self-actualization, that is, for maximizing your fulfillment in life and living up to your highest potential. The theory of self-actualization could clarify your goals and help you get the most out of school.

How means looking for immediate application. Invent ways to use and test concepts in your daily life—the sooner, the better. For example, how could you restructure your life for greater self-actualization? What would you do differently on a daily basis? What would you have that you don't have now? And how would you be different in your moment-to-moment relationships with people?

"Publish" your schedule.
After you plan your study and class sessions for the week, hang your schedule in a place where others who live with you will see it. You could make it look like an "official" document. Laminate a daily calendar, fill in your schedule with a magic marker, and post this in a high-traffic area in your house. Designate open slots in your schedule where others can sign up for "appointments" to see you. If you use an online calendar, print out copies to put in your school binder or on your refrigerator door, bathroom mirror, or kitchen cupboard.

Share your educational plans.
The fact that you're in school will affect the key relationships in your life. Attending classes and doing homework will mean less time to spend with others. You can prepare family members and help prevent problems by discussing these issues ahead of time. You can also involve your spouse, partner, children, or close friends actively in your schooling. Offer to give them a tour of the campus, introduce them to your instructors and classmates, and encourage them to attend social events at school with you.

Take this a step further and ask the key people in your life for help. Ask them to think of ways that they can support your success in school and to commit to those actions. Make your own education a joint mission that benefits everyone. ⬛

More resources are available for adult learners at masterstudent.college.hmco.com

Connect to school resources

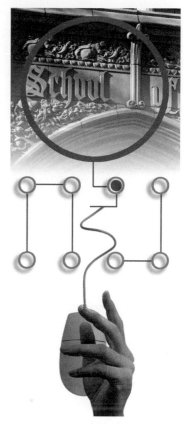

When you entered higher education, you also signed up for a world of student services. Any of them can help you succeed in school. Many of them are free.

Following are a few examples of school resources. Check your school catalog, newspaper, and Web site for the specific resources available to you. Your school fees pay for them. Now use them.

Academic advisors can help you with selecting courses, choosing majors, planning your career, and adjusting in general to the culture of higher education.

Alumni publications and alumni themselves can be good sources of information about the benefits and potential pitfalls of being a student at your school.

Arts resources can include museums, galleries, special libraries, and music and film recording and editing equipment.

Athletic centers and *gymnasiums* often open weight rooms, swimming pools, indoor tracks, basketball courts, and racquet-sport courts to all students.

Car-pooling maps provide information on getting across town or across the country.

Chapels are usually open to students of any religion.

Childcare is sometimes made available to students at a reasonable cost through the early childhood education department.

Computer labs where students can go 24 hours a day to work on projects and access the Internet are usually free.

Counseling centers help students deal with the emotional pressures of school life, usually for free or at low cost.

The *financial aid office* assists students with loans, scholarships, and grants.

Job placement offices can help you find part-time employment while you are in school and a job after you graduate.

The *registrar* handles information about transcripts, grades, changing majors, transferring credits, and dropping or adding classes.

The *school catalog* lists course descriptions and tuition fees, requirements for graduation, and information on everything from the school's history to its grading practices.

The *school newspaper* provides information about activities, services, and policies.

School security agencies can provide information about parking, bicycle regulations, and traffic rules. Some offer safe escorts at night for female students.

Student government can help you develop skills in leadership and teamwork.

Student health clinics often provide free or inexpensive treatment for minor problems. Many offer information about alcohol and drug abuse and addiction.

Student organizations present an opportunity to explore fraternities, sororities, service clubs, veterans' organizations, religious groups, sports clubs, political groups, and programs for special populations.

Student unions are hubs for social activities, special programs, and free entertainment.

Tutoring can help, even if you think you are hopelessly stuck in a course. It is usually free and is available through academic departments or counseling centers.

Community resources can also help you in higher education. For more details, go to

masterstudent.college.hmco.com

journal entry 2

Discovery Statement

Success is a choice—your choice. To *get* what you want, it helps to *know* what you want. That is the purpose of this Journal Entry, which has two parts.

You can begin choosing success right now by setting a date, time, and place to complete this Journal Entry. Write your choices here, then block out the time on your calendar.

Date: _____

Time: _____

Place: _____

Part 1

Select a time and place when you know you will not be disturbed for at least 20 minutes. (The library is a good place to do this.) Relax for two or three minutes, clearing your mind. Next, complete the following sentences—and then keep writing.

When you run out of things to write, stick with it just a bit longer. Be willing to experience a little discomfort. Keep writing. What you discover might be well worth the extra effort.

What I want from my education is . . .

_____

_____

_____

_____

When I complete my education, I want to be able to . . .

_____

_____

_____

_____

I also want . . .

_____

_____

_____

_____

Part 2

After completing Part 1, take a short break. Reward yourself by doing something that you enjoy. Then come back to this Journal Entry.

Now, review the list of things that you want from your education. See if you can summarize them in a one-sentence, polished statement. This will become a statement of your purpose for taking part in higher education.

Allow yourself to write many drafts of this mission statement, and review it periodically as you continue your education. With each draft, see if you can capture the essence of what you want from higher education and from your life. State it in a vivid way—a short sentence that you can easily memorize, one that sparks your enthusiasm and makes you want to get up in the morning.

You might find it difficult to express your purpose statement in one sentence. If so, write a paragraph or more. Then look for the sentence that seems most charged with energy for you.

Following are some sample purpose statements:

- My purpose for being in school is to gain skills that I can use to contribute to others.

- My purpose for being in school is to live an abundant life that is filled with happiness, health, love, and wealth.

- My purpose for being in school is to enjoy myself by making lasting friendships and following the lead of my interests.

Write at least one draft of your purpose statement below:

_____

_____

_____

_____

_____

_____

_____

_____

power process

Discover what you want

Imagine a person who walks up to a counter at the airport to buy a plane ticket for his next vacation. "Just give me a ticket," he says to the reservation agent. "Anywhere will do."

The agent stares back at him in disbelief. "I'm sorry, sir," he replies. "I'll need some more details. Just minor things—such as the name of your destination city and your arrival and departure dates."

"Oh, I'm not fussy," says the would-be vacationer. "I just want to get away. You choose for me."

Compare this with another traveler who walks up to the counter and says, "I'd like a ticket to Ixtapa, Mexico, departing on Saturday, March 23, and returning Sunday, April 7. Please give me a window seat, first class, with vegetarian meals."

Now, ask yourself which traveler is more likely to end up with a vacation that he'll enjoy.

The same principle applies in any area of life. Knowing where we want to go increases the probability that we will arrive at our destination. Discovering what we want makes it more likely that we'll attain it. Once our goals are defined precisely, our brains reorient our thinking and behavior to align with those goals—and we're well on the way there.

There's power in precision

The example about the traveler with no destination seems far-fetched. Before you dismiss it, do an informal experiment: Ask three other students what they want to get out of their education. Be prepared for hemming and hawing, vague generalities, and maybe even a helping of pie-in-the-sky à la mode.

That's amazing, considering the stakes involved. Our hypothetical vacationer is about to invest a couple weeks of his time and hundreds of dollars—all with no destination in mind. Students routinely invest years of their lives and thousands of dollars with an equally hazy idea of their destination in life.

Suppose that you ask someone what she wants from her education and you get this answer: "I plan to get a degree in journalism with double minors in earth science and Portuguese so that I can work as a reporter covering the environment in Brazil." Chances are you've found a master student. The precision of a person's vision offers a clue to mastery.

Put it in writing

For maximum precision, write down what you want. Goals that reside strictly in your head can remain fuzzy. Writing them down brings them into sharper focus.

As you write about what you want, expand your imagination to many different time frames. Define what you want to be, do, and have next week, next month, and next year. Write about what you want five years from now—and five minutes from now.

It's important to approach this process with a sense of adventure and play. As you write, be willing to put any option on the table. List any goal—including those that might look outrageous in writing.

You might want to travel to India, start a consulting business, or open a library in every disadvantaged neighborhood. Write those goals down.

You might want to own a ranch in a beautiful valley, become a painter, or visit all of the hot springs in the world. Write those down, too.

Perhaps you want to restore the integrity of the ozone layer or eliminate racism through international law. Or perhaps you simply want to be more physically fit, more funny, or more loving. Whatever you want, write it down.

One way to determine what you want in detail is to prompt yourself with questions. For starters, ask the "four W's":

- *What* do I want?
- *Who* do I want to be with in the future?
- *Where* do I want to be in the future?
- *When* can I make my desired future occur?

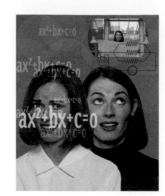

Stay open to possibility

While asking these questions, people sometimes stop themselves with a single line of thought: "Who am I kidding anyway? There's no way I'll ever be able to get what I really want. My goals are just too impractical."

Statements like these can sink us back into the status quo and stop us from painting a bold vision of the future. These are thoughts that erase dreams from the drawing board.

If this happens to you, remember that many goals—from the invention of the airplane to the lunar landing to the development of the computer chip—appeared ridiculous or unworkable when they were first proposed. These remarkable ideas came to life because their creators kept lifting their eyes to the horizon and holding fast to a sense of possibility.

When determining what you want, you can also think big. Write down any goal that comes to mind—even those that seem impossible to fulfill. You might discover ways to satisfy even the boldest, most "impractical" desires. And even if you don't achieve *all* your goals, you can achieve *many* of them, including those that radically affect the quality of your life.

Later, if you want, you can let go of some goals. But first live with them for a while. Goals that sound outlandish right now might seem more realistic in a few weeks, months, or years. Time often brings a more balanced perspective, along with an expanded sense of possibility.

Imagine that time and money are no problem

One way to keep worries about practicality from cramping your creativity is to play with the several scenarios.

To begin, imagine that you've just won a lottery with a

When you follow the path of getting what you truly want, you can enjoy yourself even if the path is uphill.

jackpot of $5 million. You now have all the money needed to sustain yourself for a lifetime. You have a steady stream of income extending decades into the future—enough to support any career you want. Once you've created this mental picture, describe what you want to be, do, and have during the rest of your life.

Or pretend that a philanthropist will pay you $500,000 per year to do whatever project you think will benefit your community most. What would you do?

Another scenario is to imagine that a philanthropist will provide funds for you and 30 people you supervise to do something of value for the entire planet. You have a budget of $1 billion and 30 years to accomplish your project. Again, what would you do?

Expand your goals by asking *how?*

Once you've opened up your imagination and gained some clarity about *what* you want, you can add depth to your dreams by asking *how?* This question helps you to develop action plans—specific steps that will lead to achieving your goals.

When asking *how?* avoid answers that lead to prescriptions—the idea that there is only *one* way to accomplish any goal. In reality, you can create several detailed action plans for getting anything you want. Most goals can be reached through multiple pathways.

For example, you might determine that you want to earn $100,000 per year while working from your home as a freelance consultant. To meet that income goal, you could choose from several strategies. One is to charge $50 per hour and work 40 hours per week for 50 weeks per year. Another is to charge $100 per hour and work only 20 hours per week for the same number of weeks per year. You could also consider working more hours during the winter months so that you could take summers off and still earn $100,000 yearly. These are just a few examples.

Discover the benefits

Discovering what you want greatly enhances your odds of succeeding in higher education. Many students quit school simply because they are unsure of their goals. With well-defined objectives in mind, you can constantly look for connections between what you want and what you study. The more connections you discover, the more likely you'll stay in school—and the more likely you'll benefit from higher education.

Having a clear idea of your goals makes many decisions easier. Knowing what you want from your education helps you choose the school you'll attend, the courses you'll take, the major you'll declare, and the next career you'll pursue.

Discovering what you want also enhances your study skills. An example is memorizing. A skydiver will not become bored learning how to pack her parachute. Her reward for learning the skill is too important. Likewise, when information helps you get something you want, it becomes easier to remember.

You can have more energy when your daily activities lead to what you want. If you're bogged down in quadratic equations, stand back for a minute. Think about how that math course ties in with your goal of becoming an electrical engineer, how your philosophy course relates to your aim of becoming a minister, or how your English course can help you become a better teacher.

Succeeding in higher education takes effort. When you follow the path of getting what you truly want, you can enjoy yourself even if the path is uphill. You can expend great energy and still feel fresh and eager to learn. When you take on courses that you care about and prepare for a career that you look forward to, you can play full out. You can work even to the point of exhaustion at times, and do it happily.

That's one purpose of discovering what you want. Your vision is not meant to be followed blindly—it's meant to pull you forward.

Move from discovery to action

Discovering what you want can be heady fun. And it can quickly become an interesting but irrelevant exercise unless you take action to get what you want. Most discoveries come bundled with hints to *do* something—perhaps to change a habit, contact someone, travel, get educated, or acquire a new skill. Dreams that are not followed with action tend to die on paper. On the other hand, dreams that lead to new behaviors can lead to new results in your life.

To move into action, use this book. It's filled with places to state what you want to accomplish and how you intend to go about it. Every Journal Entry and exercise exists for this purpose. Fill up those pages. Take action and watch your dreams evolve from fuzzy ideals into working principles.

Your action plans can include strategies and techniques, including the hundreds of suggestions presented in these pages. However, remember that strategies and techniques are not guarantees. They're just means to an end—moving you into action. Your clarity about what you want and your commitment to get it can be far more powerful than any plan or technique.

With your dreams and new behaviors in hand, you might find that events fall into place almost magically. Start telling people about what you want, and you'll eventually find some who are willing to help. They might offer an idea or two or suggest a person to call or an organization to contact. They might even offer their time or money. The sooner you discover what you want, the sooner you can create the conditions that transform your life.[11] ❌

→ Extracurricular activities: Reap the benefits

Participation in extracurricular activities can ease the transition to higher education and help you to discover what you want. Through student organizations you can develop new skills, explore possible careers, build contacts for jobs, and add experience to your resumé. Use these suggestions to get started.

■ **Make conscious choices** about how to divide your time between schoolwork and extracurricular activities. Decide up front how many hours each week or month you can devote to a student organization. Leave room in your schedule for relaxing and for unplanned events.

■ **Look to the future** when making commitments. Write down three or four goals you'd like to achieve. Then choose extracurricular activities that directly support those goals.

■ **Recognize reluctance** to do activities that fail to create value for you. Avoid joining groups only because you feel guilty or obligated to do so.

■ **Check out the rules** before joining any student organization. Ask about dues and attendance requirements.

■ **Do a trial run** by attending one or two meetings of an organization. Explain that you want to find out what the group is about before making a commitment.

■ **Learn new skills** in managing your time. Many students reap the benefits of extracurricular activities while staying on course with their academic workload. Chapter Two is teeming with ideas.

CHAPTER 1
Self-Discovery

Many students taking a student success course start out the semester with a high level of enthusiasm and energy, and that's good, because there's a lot of meaty and important foundation material in the Introduction and in Chapters One and Two. Chapter One is about self-discovery and taking first steps towards achieving goals. Visual measures of success—such as top grades and résumés filled with accomplishments—start with an invisible asset: the willingness to discover who you are and what you want. Use the Master Student Map on the chapter opener page to inspire your students, stimulate class discussion, and preview the chapter topics.

Page 24
Master Student Map

Begin each of your chapters with a brain-active learning exercise, using the learning styles reasoning model to create interest in the chapter for all of the learning styles and to energize the prior knowledge students have with the content in the chapter. Use these questions as a discussion guide in your class:

why? Why is self-discovery important?

what? Read through the list of articles and pick three that look interesting. What interests you about these three articles?

how? How would you rate your level of effectiveness with the idea covered in this chapter now? (How much do you already know about learning styles, multiple intelligences, and motivation?)

what if? What if the secret to your personal success in college and life are in this chapter?

Page 28
EXERCISE #4: The Discovery Wheel

The Discovery Wheel is an opportunity for students to take a First Step in telling the truth about the kind of student they are and the kind of student they want to become. This is not a test, but an opportunity to change. Students complete the Discovery Wheel in Chapter One and then again in Chapter Ten. This provides them with a chance to measure their progress. Results from the Discovery Wheel exercises can be used in your course in a variety of ways. Consider the following suggestions:

- Ask students to list their intentions or commitments for improving particular skills during the term. At the end of the term, they can assess their progress in those areas by using the Discovery Wheel in Chapter Ten.

- Create an assignment requiring students to contact people on campus or in the community who could assist them in enhancing particular skills. For example, the reading center could provide specific strategies for improving comprehension, word attack skills, and concentration.

- Allow the Discovery Wheel exercises to help shape course content. You can use the results to plan future lessons or to determine what students want to learn or accomplish during the course as a result of their self-assessments.

- Ask students to form small groups and coach each other. Coaching could include how to capitalize on and share talents and how to strengthen areas for growth. If you choose to do this, let students know your reasons for forming small groups. For many, self-assessment is personal and sharing the results might seem risky. Ask students to coach themselves. They can imagine that the self-assessment is for someone special whose success in school and life is important to them. Ask students to take their best suggestions and implement them.

■ Create a resource network. Using the titles of each section of the Discovery Wheel (Self-Discovery, Time, Memory, and so on), list one title per piece of paper. Ask a particular section to sign their names to that piece of paper if they are willing to assist others in enhancing their skills in this area. Then distribute the lists to the class or post them on your course Web site.

Pages LSI-1–LSI-8
The Learning Style Inventory

Being aware of learning styles is an important strategy for success because it helps students understand differences in the ways people like to perceive and process new information. Your students will learn about their own preferred style of learning and how this tool can help them observe and ascertain the preferred teaching styles of their professors.

The Learning Style Inventory (LSI) is a unifying theme woven skillfully throughout *From Master Student to Master Employee*. Activities are crafted to engage students not only in the strengths of their own learning preference, but in the strengths of other styles as well. The Master Student Map at the beginning of each chapter and the Learning Styles Application at the end can help students internalize the strategies taught in each chapter. Study skills do not transfer from a student success class to other courses accidentally. It takes a talented and prepared instructor to help students build other schema and develop the confidence that is necessary to transfer new strategies to different learning settings. Teaching this might seem intimidating for first-time instructors. Remember, when you teach with *From Master Student to Master Employee,* you are not alone. We want you to become a master instructor. Your support materials include a talented team of College Survival consultants. Call (1-800-528-8323) or e-mail (collegesurvival@hmco.com) your consultant today!

Additional resources to help guide you in administering the LSI and applying the Master Student Map and Learning Styles Application are in the *Course Manual* and on the HM ClassPrep CD. A video for instructors is also available on VHS and on your HM ClassPrep CD.

Page 33
Learning by seeing, hearing, and moving: The VAK system

Learning by seeing (visual learning), hearing (auditory learning), and moving (kinesthetic learning) allows students to perceive information through their senses. Engage your students by asking them to take the informal inventory. Have your students submit Discovery Statements to highlight the new strategies they have discovered and Intention Statements to describe the new options for learning that they intend to implement.

Page 39
Adapting to styles in the workplace

From Master Student to Master Employee focuses on helping students prepare for the workplace—whether it is a part-time job a student is holding while they are attending college or a full-time job they will have after college. Ask your students in class to talk about experiences they have had working with others in positions they have held in the past. What are pros and cons of working with a manager or coworker who has a similar style to you? What if their style is different? Brainstorm techniques for addressing these differences by asking for student volunteers to provide real-world examples.

voices

advisory board member

The Learning Styles Inventory is unique and relevant to success in the classroom and the workplace. It is the most comprehensive coverage of learning styles I have encountered. The examples featured in the "Cycle of learning" provide immediate application of how the learning cycle works. The chart in "Balancing your preferences" allows the student to see the strengths and tendencies which can result from too much or too little of a mode. This is amazing, and such helpful information for coping with oneself as well as others! "Adapting to styles in the workplace" is on target with the options of be able to recognize and accommodate differences in the workplace.

—DEBRA WATSON,
MISSISSIPPI GULF
COAST COMMUNITY COLLEGE

Page 41
Claim your multiple intelligences

Howard Gardner's (Harvard University) theory of several types of intelligence complements the discussion in this chapter on different learning styles: both recognize that there are alternative ways for people to learn and assimilate knowledge. This expanded article provides students with concepts for exploring additional methods to achieve success in school, work, and relationships. A new chart on pages 42–43 presents an overview of the characteristics of each intelligence and possible learning strategies, and links these with possible careers. Have your students further explore these career choices as they consider different majors or areas of focused study.

Page 46
Discovering mastery

Use this article to help your students to articulate the characteristics of a successful student and employee. Reinforce the concept of mastery by dividing your class into small groups (3-4 students). Have half of your class select what their group feels are the five most important master student qualities. Have the other half of your class select the five most important master employee qualities. Invite each group to write their top five lists on a whiteboard or flip chart and bring the whole class together to discuss the similarities between master student qualities and master employee qualities.

This article is also a way to introduce the Master Student Profiles that appear at the end of each chapter. These profiles highlight a person who embodies several qualities of a master student. Invite your students to look for timeless qualities in the people they read about. Use this article as a "guest speaker" in your course. Start now by having your students read and identify the master student qualities demonstrated by Master Student Mike Lazaridis (see page 59).

Page 51
Ways to change a habit

After your students have reviewed this article, consider holding a brainstorming session in class to discuss habits your students would like to start, stop, or change. Dean Mancina, an instructor at Golden West College, CA, has his students select one habit that his students would like to complete successfully within the next 16 weeks of his course. He has students write down their habit on a two-part note paper (available from College Survival free to adopters of this textbook). One part is placed in an envelope addressed to each student. The copy is kept by the student as a reference and reminder of their habit change plan. Then, Dean sends the addressed envelopes to his students several months later (after the course has been completed) as an incentive for students to keep working on their habit change.

Page 56
Career Application

Each chapter in *From Master Student to Master Employee* includes a culminating exercise called the Career Application. In each of these case studies, the reader is introduced to a workplace situation that is related to the material covered within the chapter. Following the scenario, students are asked a series of four questions. The questions often ask students to identify SCANS skills. This will allow students to connect to the Career Application even when their particular area of interest or study is not highlighted. For example, in Chapter One, the Career Application features Sylvia Lopez, a staff accountant at a market research firm. The scenario talks about styles in the workplace, and focuses on interpersonal skills valuable to any job. Students can apply the learning styles information that they have learned in this chapter to the workplace scenario presented here.

Page 57
Quiz

Eldon McMurray, instructor at Utah Valley State College, saves class time for instruction and discussion by administering the quiz in a unique way. He informs his students that he is going to select only one 10-point question for the quiz (from the questions listed in the textbook). He places the question on an overhead projector in class and asks student to respond using the three-part quiz forms (available from College Survival). When they have answered the question and written their name on the paper, he has students tear off the white sheet and hand it in. Then, students compare answers with their neighbor and seek insight from each other. If a student does not have the answer, Eldon offers a way to "make up" the points. Students can return their pink sheet of three-part paper with the answers to all ten questions for 7/10 points.

Page 59
Learning Styles Application

The updated Learning Styles Application (LSA) exercises will help your students discover their new abilities and put them into action. Do the first LSA as a discussion exercise in class. With the help of feedback, students quickly grasp this powerful idea. They gain confidence in their own learning style and, by answering different questions, learn to develop the skills of the other learning styles.

Course Manual

 Learning Style Inventory
Dr. David Kolb of Case Western Reserve University in Cleveland, OH, developed the Learning Style Inventory used in this text. Materials in the *Course Manual* will help you to

✔ Find out more about *perception* and *process*

✔ Gain confidence in administering the Learning Style Inventory with step-by-step instruction

✔ Help your students use the LSI to improve learning and problem solving

✔ Learn how to create lesson plans around the cycle of learning

✔ Find information on additional resources, references, and Web sites related to learning styles

HM ClassPrep CD

 PowerPoint for Chapter One features information to support your administration of the Learning Style Inventory and supports claiming multiple intelligences and the VAK system.

Warm-up activities inspire creative and critical thinking.

Houghton Mifflin scholarship essay contest guidelines and suggestions for assigning it in class are provided. Your students have a chance to win one of three $1,000 scholarships.

Chapter One **quiz answers** are available, as are **Test Bank** questions.

Articles features in the Web-based **Career Resource Center** that are related to the materials in this chapter are listed. These additional reading materials can be used to facilitate further discussion with the Career Application at the end of the chapter.

If you are interested in having your students **create a portfolio** of their student success course materials, information is available to help guide you and your students.

Watch short **video clips** to help motivate you before you administer the Learning Style Inventory to your students.

Additional Resources

 Set the stage for your course by showing the *What Do You Want?* video in your first class meeting. Get your students to think about what they want out of your course and encourage further conversations about goal setting.

 masterstudent.college.hmco.com Have your students complete their **Discovery Wheel** on the *From Master Student to Master Employee* Web site and submit their Journal Entry questions electronically.

The **HM Assessment and Portfolio Builder** (available for packaging with your textbook) is a personal assessment tool that will help students take the First Step in being successful both throughout college and as they enter the workplace. Students will create a portfolio by responding to questions in the Personal, Interpersonal, Career, and Community modules, and by reflecting on their skills, attitudes, values, and behaviors. An Accomplishments Report will help students analyze their responses and will provide them with suggestions for building a résumé and preparing for interviews. Contact your sales representative or College Survival consultant for a preview of this product.

Equipped with the information from their Accomplishments Report, students can explore Houghton Mifflin's Web-based **Career Resource Center** for articles, exercises, and ideas to help them succeed on their journey from college to career. Visit **masterstudent.college. hmco.com**. Log in as follows:

> *Username:* careercenter
> *Password:* exploration

1

Self-Discovery

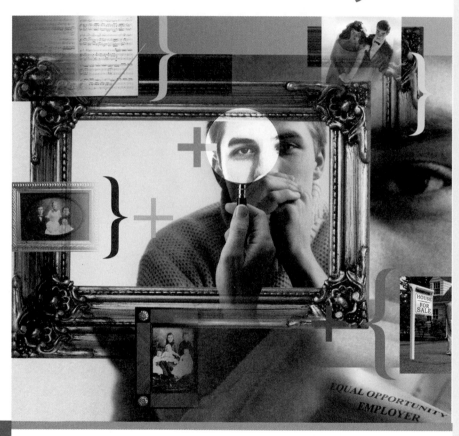

Once we have identified our special talents it doesn't matter whether or not we find immediate success in them, what does matter is that we take a step each day towards our intended goal!

JOSH HINDS

Be patient with yourself. Self-growth is tender; it's holy ground. There's no greater investment.

STEPHEN R. COVEY

why
this chapter matters . . .

Visible measures of success—such as top grades and résumés filled with accomplishments—start with the willingness to discover who you are and what you want.

what
is included . . .

First Step: Truth is a key to mastery
If you skipped the Introduction . . .
The Discovery Wheel
Learning by seeing, hearing, and moving: The VAK system
Learning styles: Discovering how you learn
Using your learning style profile to succeed in school
Adapting to styles in the workplace
Claim your multiple intelligences
Developing self-esteem
Discovering mastery
Motivation
Ways to change a habit
Power Process: "Ideas are tools"
Master Student Profile: Mike Lazaridis

how
you can use this chapter . . .

Experience the power of telling the truth about your current skills.
Discover your preferred learning styles and develop new ones.
Define what you want from your education and your career.

As you read, ask yourself
what if . . .

I could discover my interests, skills, and passions—and build a successful education and career on them?

First Step: Truth is a key to mastery

The First Step technique is simple: Discover the truth about who you are and what you want. End of discussion. Now proceed to Chapter Two. Well, it's not *quite* that simple.

The First Step is one of the most valuable tools in this book. It magnifies the power of all the other techniques. It is a key to becoming a master student and master employee. Unfortunately, a First Step is easier to explain than it is to do. Discovering the truth sounds like pie-in-the-sky moralizing, but there is nothing pie-in-the-sky or moralizing about a First Step. It is a practical, down-to-earth way to change our behavior. No technique in this book has been field-tested more often or more successfully— or under tougher circumstances.

This First Step and the exercises that follow will help you to develop the transferable skill of self-management—accurately assessing your knowledge and abilities. Success starts with discovering what *is working*— and what *isn't*—in our lives right now. When we discover our strengths, we gain an accurate picture of what we can accomplish. When we discover that we have a problem, we free up energy to find a solution. Ignoring the truth, on the other hand, can lead to problems that stick around for decades.

The principle of discovering the truth—and openly admitting it— is applied universally by people who want to turn their lives around. For members of Alcoholics Anonymous, the First Step is acknowledging that they are powerless over alcohol. For people who join Weight Watchers, the First Step is admitting how much they weigh. This discovery reinforces the personal qualities of self-esteem, integrity, and honesty—transferable skills that you can use right away.

It's not easy to discover the truth about ourselves. And for some of us, it's even harder to recognize our strengths. Maybe we don't want to brag. Maybe we're attached to a poor self-image. The reasons don't matter. The point is that using the First Step technique means discovering the truth about our positive qualities, too.

Many of us approach a frank evaluation of ourselves about as enthusiastically as we'd anticipate an audit by the IRS. There is another way to think about self-evaluations. If we could see them as opportunities to solve problems and take charge of our lives, we might welcome them. Believe it or not, we can begin working with our list of weaknesses by celebrating them.

Consider the most accomplished, "together" people you know. If they were totally candid with you, you'd

journal entry 3

Discovery/Intention Statement

Take five minutes to skim the Discovery Wheel exercise starting on page 28. Find one statement that describes a skill you already possess—a personal strength that will promote your success in school, in your career, or both. Write that statement here:

_____

_____

_____

_____

The Discovery Wheel might also prompt some thoughts about skills that you can use in the classroom and apply to the workplace. Describe one of those skills by completing the following sentence:

I discovered that . . .

_____

_____

_____

_____

_____

Now, skim the appropriate chapter in this book for at least three articles that could help you develop this skill. For example, if you want to take more effective notes, turn to Chapter Five. List the names of your chosen articles here and a time when you will read them in more detail.

I intend to . . .

_____

_____

_____

_____

_____

soon hear about their mistakes and regrets. The more successful people are, the more willing they are to discover their flaws.

It might seem natural to judge our own shortcomings and feel bad about them. Some people believe that such feelings are necessary in order to bring about change. Others think that a healthy dose of shame can turn negatives into positives. There is an alternative. We can discover a way to gain skill without feeling rotten about the past. By taking a First Step, we can change the way things *are* without having to be upset about the way things *have been*. We can learn to see shame or blame as excess baggage and just set it aside. It might also help to remember that weaknesses are often strengths taken to an extreme. The student who carefully revises her writing can make significant improvements in a term paper. If she hands in the paper late, though, her grade might suffer. Any success strategy carried too far can backfire.

Whether written or verbal, First Steps are more powerful when they are specific. For example, if you want to improve your note-taking skills, you might write, "I am an awful note taker." It would be more effective to phrase this self-discovery as, "I can't read 80 percent of the notes I took in Introduction to Psychology last week, and I have no idea what was important in that class." When you discover what you want to achieve, be just as specific. You might declare, "I want to take legible notes that help me predict what questions will be on the final exam."

Complete the exercises in this chapter, and your courage will be rewarded. The Discovery Wheel exercise and the rest of the activities in this book can help you tap resources you never knew you had. They're all First Steps—no kidding. It's just that simple. The truth has power. ▨

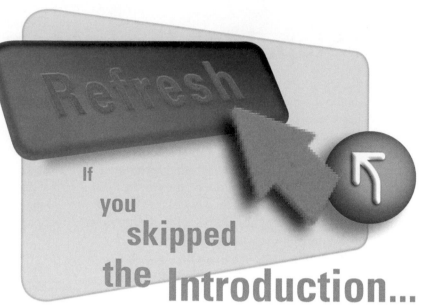

If you skipped the Introduction...

Some people think introductions have little to offer and are a waste of time. The Introduction to this book is important. It suggests ways to get your money's worth out of these chapters—and out of your education.

Here are some of the informative articles that await you:

- Get the most out of this book
- Jumpstart your education with transferable skills
- Use the SCANS reports to discover your skills
- The value of higher education
- The Discovery and Intention Journal Entry system
- Making the transition to higher education
- The art of re-entry: Going back to school as an adult learner
- Connect to school resources
- Extracurricular activities: Reap the benefits
- Connect to community resources
- Power Process: Discover what you want

Please go back and read the Introduction now. ▨

desk of . . .

from the

SHARI MESULAM, PUBLICIST:

My internship was a first step into the workplace. The experiences I had as an intern taught me how important a role everyone in the office plays. I also was able to develop skills that have been valuable in other jobs I have taken since: how to work with people and taking responsibility.

TAKING THE FIRST STEP

 The purpose of this exercise is to give you a chance to discover and acknowledge your own strengths, as well as areas for improvement. For many people, this is the most difficult exercise in the book. To make the exercise worthwhile, do it with courage.

Some people suggest that looking at areas for improvement means focusing on personal weaknesses. They view it as a negative approach that runs counter to positive thinking. Well, perhaps. Positive thinking is a great technique. So is telling the truth, especially when we see the whole picture—the negative aspects as well as the positive ones.

If you admit that you can't add or subtract and that's the truth, then you have taken a strong, positive First Step toward learning basic math. On the other hand, if you say that you are a terrible math student and that's not the truth, then you are programming yourself to accept unnecessary failure.

The point is to tell the truth. This exercise is similar to the Discovery Statements that appear in every chapter. The difference is that in this case, for reasons of confidentiality, you won't write down your discoveries in the book.

Be brave. If you approach this exercise with courage, you are likely to disclose some things about yourself that you wouldn't want others to read. You might even write down some truths that could get you into trouble. Do this exercise on separate sheets of paper, then hide or destroy them. Protect your privacy.

To make this exercise work, follow these suggestions:

Be specific. It is not effective to write "I can improve my communication skills." Of course you can. Instead, write down precisely what you can *do* to improve your communication skills, for example, "I can spend more time really listening while the other person is talking, instead of thinking about what I'm going to say next."

Look beyond the classroom. What goes on outside school often has the greatest impact on your ability to be an effective student.

Be courageous. This exercise is a waste of time if it is done half-heartedly. Be willing to take risks. You might open a door that reveals a part of yourself that you didn't want to admit was there. The power of this technique is that once you know what is there, you can do something about it.

Part 1

Time yourself, and for 10 minutes write as fast as you can, completing each of the following sentences at least 10 times with anything that comes to mind. If you get stuck, don't stop. Just write something—even if it seems crazy.

> I never succeed when I . . .
>
> I'm not very good at . . .
>
> Something I'd like to change about myself is . . .

Part 2

When you have completed the first part of the exercise, review what you have written, crossing off things that don't make any sense. The sentences that remain suggest possible goals for uncovering mastery.

Part 3

Here's the tough part. Time yourself, and for 10 minutes write as fast as you can, completing the following sentences with anything that comes to mind. As in Part 1, complete each sentence at least 10 times. Just keep writing, even if it sounds silly.

> I always succeed when I . . .
>
> I am very good at . . .
>
> Something I like about myself is . . .

Part 4

Review what you have written and circle the things that you can fully celebrate. This is a good list to keep for those times when you question your own value and worth.

THE DISCOVERY WHEEL

The Discovery Wheel is another opportunity to tell the truth about the kind of student you are and the kind of student you want to become. It will also preview the topics that are covered throughout this text and help you begin to think about the transferable skills you will be able to master at school and at work.

This is not a test. There are no trick questions, and the answers will have meaning only for yourself.

Here are two suggestions to make this exercise more effective. First, think of it as the beginning of an opportunity to change. There is another Discovery Wheel at the end of this book. You will have a chance to measure your progress, so be honest about where you are now. Second, lighten up. A little laughter can make self-evaluations a lot more effective.

Here's how the Discovery Wheel works. By the end of this exercise, you will have filled in a circle similar to the one on this page. The Discovery Wheel circle is a picture of how you see yourself. The closer the shading comes to the outer edge of the circle, the higher the evaluation of a specific skill. In the example to the right, the student has rated her reading skills low and her note-taking skills high.

The terms "high" and "low" are not meant to reflect a negative judgment. The Discovery Wheel is not a permanent picture of who you are. It is a picture of how you view your strengths and weaknesses as a student today. To begin this exercise, read the following statements and award yourself points for each one, using the point system described below. Then add up your point total for each section and shade the Discovery Wheel on page 31 to the appropriate level.

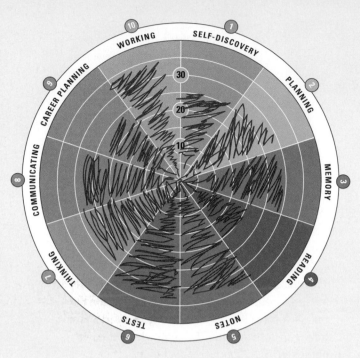

Do this exercise online at ⟨ masterstudent.college.hmco.com ⟩

5 points
This statement is always or almost always true of me.

4 points
This statement is often true of me.

3 points
This statement is true of me about half the time.

2 points
This statement is seldom true of me.

1 point
This statement is never or almost never true of me.

1. _____ I enjoy learning.

2. _____ I understand and apply the concept of multiple intelligences.

3. _____ I connect my courses to my purpose for being in school and the benefits I intend to get from my education.

4. _____ I regularly assess my personal strengths and areas for improvement.

5. _____ I am satisfied with how I am progressing toward achieving my goals.

6. _____ I use my knowledge of learning styles to support my success in school and at work.

7. _____ I am willing to consider any idea that can help me succeed in school—even if I initially disagree with that idea.

8. _____ I monitor my habits and change them in ways that support my success.

_____ Total score (1) *Self-Discovery*

1. _____ I set long-term goals and periodically review them.
2. _____ I set midterm and short-term goals to support my long-term goals.
3. _____ I write a plan for each day and each week.
4. _____ I assign priorities to what I choose to do each day.
5. _____ I plan regular recreation time.
6. _____ I adjust my study time to meet the demands of individual courses.
7. _____ I have adequate time each day to accomplish what I plan.
8. _____ I effectively plan projects and manage time in work settings.

_____ Total score (2) *Planning*

1. _____ I am confident of my ability to remember.
2. _____ I can remember people's names.
3. _____ At the end of a presentation, I can summarize what was presented.
4. _____ I apply techniques that enhance my memory skills.
5. _____ I can recall information when I'm under pressure.
6. _____ I remember important information clearly and easily.
7. _____ I can jog my memory when I have difficulty recalling.
8. _____ I can relate new information to what I've already learned.

_____ Total score (3) *Memory*

1. _____ I preview and review reading materials.
2. _____ When reading, I ask myself questions about the material.
3. _____ I underline or highlight important passages when reading.
4. _____ When I read textbooks or reports, I am alert and awake.
5. _____ I relate what I read to my life.
6. _____ I select a reading strategy to fit the type of material I'm reading.

7. _____ I take effective notes when I read.
8. _____ When I don't understand what I'm reading, I note my questions and find answers.

_____ Total score (4) *Reading*

1. _____ When I am in class, I focus my attention.
2. _____ I take notes in class and during meetings.
3. _____ I am aware of various methods for taking notes and choose those that work best for me.
4. _____ I distinguish major ideas from examples and other supporting material.
5. _____ I copy down material that the presenter writes on the board or overhead projector.
6. _____ I can put important concepts into my own words.
7. _____ My notes are valuable for review.
8. _____ I review notes within 24 hours.

_____ Total score (5) *Notes*

1. _____ I feel confident and calm during an exam.
2. _____ I manage my time during exams and am able to complete them.
3. _____ I am able to predict test questions.
4. _____ I adapt my test-taking strategy to the kind of test I'm taking.
5. _____ I create value from any type of evaluation, including performance reviews.
6. _____ I start reviewing for tests at the beginning of the term and continue reviewing throughout the term.
7. _____ I manage stress and maintain my health even when I feel under pressure.
8. _____ My sense of personal worth is independent of my test scores.

_____ Total score (6) *Tests*

1. _____ I have flashes of insight and often think of solutions to problems at unusual times.
2. _____ I use brainstorming to generate solutions to a variety of problems.

3. _____ When I get stuck on a creative project, I use specific methods to get unstuck.

4. _____ I see problems and tough decisions as opportunities for learning and personal growth.

5. _____ I am open to different points of view and diverse cultural perspectives.

6. _____ I can support my points of view with sound logic and evidence.

7. _____ I use critical thinking to resolve ethical dilemmas.

8. _____ As I share my viewpoints with others, I am open to their feedback.

_____ Total score (7) *Thinking*

1. _____ I am candid with others about who I am, what I feel, and what I want.

2. _____ Other people tell me that I am a good listener.

3. _____ I can communicate my upset and resolve conflict without blaming others.

4. _____ I work effectively as a member of a project team.

5. _____ I am learning ways to thrive with diversity—attitudes and behaviors that will support my career success.

6. _____ I can effectively plan, research, draft, and revise a large writing assignment.

7. _____ I learn effectively from materials and activities that are posted online.

8. _____ I prepare and deliver effective speeches and presentations.

_____ Total score (8) *Communicating*

1. _____ I relate school to what I plan to do for the rest of my life.

2. _____ I connect my attitudes, interests, and skills to career possibilities.

3. _____ I use the library, the Internet, and other resources to monitor developments in the job market.

4. _____ I use the career planning and job placement services offered by my school.

5. _____ In work settings, I look for models of success and cultivate mentors.

6. _____ I manage my income and expenses to fund my education and meet other financial goals.

7. _____ I have a written career plan and update it regularly.

8. _____ I use internships and other work experiences to refine my career plans.

_____ Total score (9) *Career Planning*

1. _____ My work contributes something worthwhile to the world.

2. _____ My work creates value for my employer.

3. _____ I see working as a way to pursue my interests, expand my skills, and develop mastery.

4. _____ I support other people in their career planning and job hunting—and am willing to accept their support.

5. _____ I can function effectively in corporate cultures and cope positively with office politics.

6. _____ I create résumés and cover letters that distinguish me from other job applicants.

7. _____ I can accurately predict and prepare responses to questions asked by job interviewers.

8. _____ I see learning as a lifelong process that includes experiences inside and outside the classroom.

_____ Total score (10) *Working*

Filling in your Discovery Wheel

Using the total score from each category, shade in each section of the Discovery Wheel. Use different colors, if you want. For example, you could use green to denote areas you want to work on. When you have finished, complete the Journal Entry on p. 32.

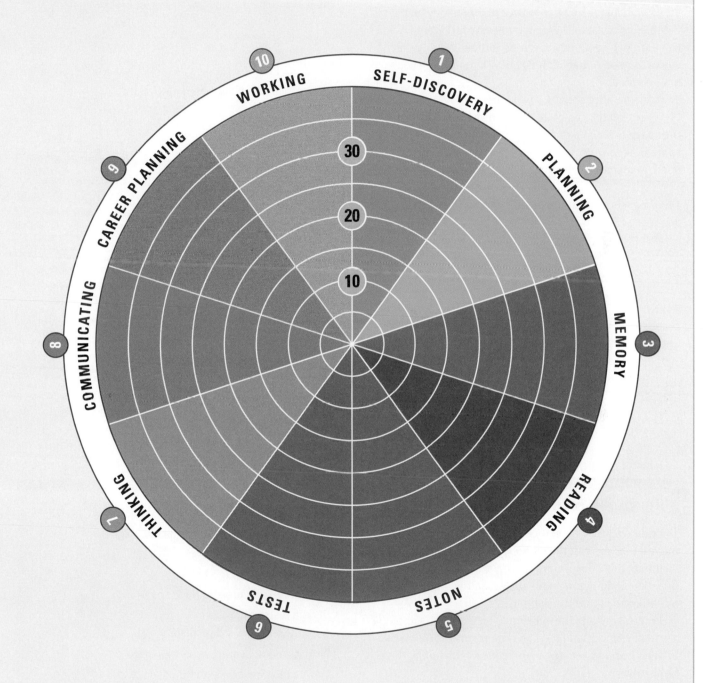

journal entry 4

Discovery/Intention Statement

Now that you have completed your Discovery Wheel, spend a few minutes with it. Get a sense of its weight, shape, and balance. Can you imagine running your hands around it? If you could lift it, would it feel light or heavy? How would it sound if it rolled down a hill? Would it roll very far? Would it wobble? Make your observations without judging the wheel as good or bad. Simply be with the picture you have created.

After you have spent a few minutes studying your Discovery Wheel, complete the following sentences in the space below. Don't worry if you can't think of something to write. Just put down whatever comes to mind. Remember, this is not a test.

This wheel is an accurate picture of my ability as a student because . . .

_____

_____

This wheel is an accurate picture of my workplace skills because . . .

_____

_____

My self-evaluation surprises me because . . .

_____

_____

The two areas in which I am strongest are . . .

_____

_____

The areas in which I want to improve are . . .

_____

_____

I want to concentrate on improving these areas because . . .

_____

_____

Now, select one of your discoveries and describe how you intend to benefit from it. Complete the statement below.

To gain some practical value from this discovery, I will . . .

_____

_____

Textbook reconnaissance, take two

The first chapter of a textbook usually includes key material—ideas that the author wants you to have up front. Likewise, this book is packed with articles that could benefit you right now. There just wasn't enough room to put them all in the first chapter.

While skimming the book for Exercise #1: "Textbook reconnaissance," you might have spotted the following articles in later chapters. If not, consider sampling them right now.

The seven-day antiprocrastination plan, page 80

More ways to stop procrastination, page 81

25 ways to get the most out of now, page 82

20 memory techniques, page 104

Muscle Reading, page 125

The note-taking process flows, page 147

Disarm tests, page 171

Gaining skill at decision making, page 210

Writing and delivering speeches, page 259

Communicating across cultures, page 243

Becoming an online learner, page 264

Career planning: Begin the process now, page 281

Learning by seeing, hearing, and moving:

The VAK system

You can approach the topic of learning styles with a simple and powerful system—one that focuses on just three ways of perceiving through your senses:

- Seeing, or *visual* learning

- Hearing, or *auditory* learning

- Movement, or *kinesthetic* learning

To recall this system, remember the letters *VAK*, which stand for **v**isual, **a**uditory, and **k**inesthetic. The theory is that each of us prefers to learn through one of these sense channels. And we can enrich our learning with activities that draw on the other channels. Understanding learning styles can help you learn how to learn—a key transferable skill.

To reflect on your VAK preferences, answer the following questions. Each question has three possible answers. Circle the answer that best describes how you would respond in the stated situation. This is not a formal inventory—just a way to prompt some self-discovery.

When you have problems spelling a word, you prefer to:
1. *Look it up in the dictionary.*
2. *Say the word out loud several times before you write it down.*
3. *Write out the word with several different spellings and choose one.*

You enjoy presentations the most when you get to:
1. *View slides, overhead transparencies, videos, and readings with plenty of charts, tables, and illustrations.*
2. *Ask questions, engage in small-group discussions, and listen to guest speakers.*
3. *Take field trips, participate in lab sessions, or apply the new material while working as a volunteer or intern.*

When giving someone directions on how to drive to a destination, you prefer to:
1. *Pull out a piece of paper and sketch a map.*
2. *Give verbal instructions.*
3. *Say, "I'm driving to a place near there, so just follow me."*

When planning an extended vacation to a new destination, you prefer to:
1. *Read colorful, illustrated brochures or articles about that place.*
2. *Talk directly to someone who's been there.*
3. *Spend a day or two at that destination on a work-related trip before taking a vacation there.*

You've made a commitment to learn to play the guitar. The first thing you do is:
1. *Go to a library or music store and find an instruction book with plenty of diagrams and chord charts.*
2. *Pull out your favorite CDs, listen closely to the guitar solos, and see if you can sing along with them.*
3. *Buy or borrow a guitar, pluck the strings, and ask someone to show you how to play a few chords.*

You've saved up enough money to lease a car. When choosing from among several new models, the most important factor in your decision is:
1. *The car's appearance.*
2. *The information you get by talking to people who own the cars you're considering.*

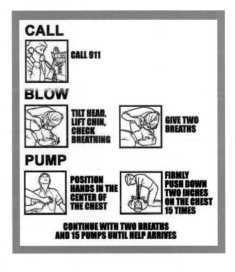

3. *The overall impression you get by taking each car on a test drive.*

You've just bought a new computer system—monitor, central processing unit, keyboard, CD burner, cable modem, and external speakers. When setting up the system, the first thing you do is:
1. *Skim through the printed instructions that come with the equipment.*
2. *Call up someone with a similar system and ask her for directions.*
3. *Assemble the components as best as you can, see if everything works, and consult the instructions only as a last resort.*

Your boss has asked you to travel to a conference next month in another country where Spanish is the most widely spoken language. To learn as much Spanish as you can before you depart, you:

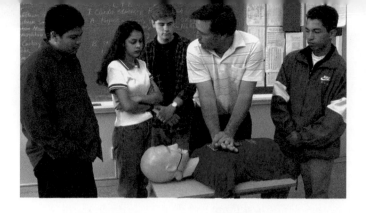

1. *Buy a video-based language course that's recorded on a DVD.*
2. *Set up tutoring sessions with a friend who's fluent in Spanish.*
3. *Sign up for a short immersion course in an environment in which you speak only Spanish, starting with the first class.*

Now take a few minutes to reflect on the meaning of your responses. All of the answers numbered "1" are examples of visual learning. The "2's" refer to auditory learning, and the "3's" illustrate kinesthetic learning. Finding a consistent pattern in your answers indicates that you prefer learning through one sense channel more than the others. Or you might find that your preferences are fairly balanced.

Listed below are suggestions for learning through each sense channel. Experiment with these examples and create more techniques of your own. Use them to build on your current preferences and develop new options for learning.

To enhance *visual* learning:

- Preview reading assignments by looking for elements that are highlighted visually—bold headlines, charts, graphs, illustrations, and photographs.

- When taking notes, leave plenty of room to add your own charts, diagrams, tables, and other visuals later.

- Whenever a presenter writes information on the board or overhead projector, copy it exactly in your notes. Request a copy of PowerPoint slides from a presenter to provide you with visual cues to remember key concepts and supplement your notes.

- Transfer your handwritten notes to your computer. Use word processing software that allows you to format your notes in lists, add headings in different fonts, and create visuals in color.

- Before you begin an exam, quickly sketch a diagram on scratch paper. Use this diagram to summarize the key formulas or facts you want to remember.

- During tests, see if you can visualize pages from your handwritten notes or images from your computer-based notes.

To enhance *auditory* learning:

- Reinforce memory of your notes and readings by talking about them. When studying, stop often to recite key points and examples in your own words.

- After doing several verbal summaries, record your favorite version or write it out.

- Read difficult passages slowly and out loud.

- Converse with your coworkers or join study groups to discuss relevant topics and issues.

- Visit your instructors during office hours to ask questions.

- Set a time to meet your boss or academic advisor to clarify answers to important questions.

To enhance *kinesthetic* learning:

- Look for ways to translate new material into three-dimensional models that you can build. While studying biology, for example, create a model of a human cell using different colors of clay.

- Supplement lectures with trips to museums, field observations, lab sessions, tutorials, and other hands-on activities.

- Recite key concepts from your courses or meetings while you walk or exercise.

- Intentionally set up situations in which you can learn by trial and error.

- Create a practice test and write out the answers in the room where you will actually take the exam. ☒

learning styles

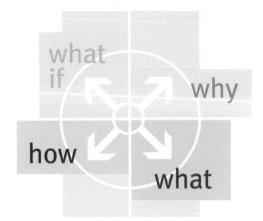

what if · why · how · what

Discovering
how you learn

When we learn, two things initially happen. First, we notice new information. We *perceive* and take in what's before us. Second, we make sense of the information. We *process* it in a way that helps us understand what's going on and makes the information our own. *Learning styles* is a term that takes into account differences in how people prefer to perceive and process information.

Knowing your preferred learning style helps you understand why some courses or work assignments appeal to you while others seem dull or boring. Figuring out when to use your preferences—and when it might be helpful to include another style of learning—can help you create value from your experiences and function successfully as a student in many different settings.

Perceiving information. The ways that people perceive information typically range from a preference for concrete experience (CE) to a preference for abstract conceptualization (AC):

■ People who favor perceiving by *concrete experience* like to absorb information through their five senses. They learn by getting directly involved in new experiences. When solving problems, they rely on their intuition as much as their intellect. These people typically function

well in unstructured learning classes that allow them to take the initiative.

■ People who favor perceiving by *abstract conceptualization* take in information best when they can think about it as a subject separate from themselves. They analyze, intellectualize, and create theories. Often these people take a scientific approach to problem solving and excel in traditional classrooms.

Processing information. The ways that people process information typically range from a preference for active experimentation (AE) to a preference for reflective observation (RO):

■ People who favor processing information by *active experimentation* prefer to jump in and start doing things immediately. They do not mind taking risks as they attempt to make sense of things, because this helps them learn. They are results-oriented and look for practical ways to apply what they have learned.

■ People who favor processing information by *reflective observation* prefer to stand back, watch what is going on, and think about it. Often they consider several points of view as they attempt to make sense of things and can generate many ideas about how something happens. They value patience, good judgment, and a thorough approach to understanding information.

According to David Kolb, a psychologist who developed the theory of experiential learning, learners have natural preferences for how they perceive and process information.[1] Yet they benefit most fully if they allow themselves to participate in all four points of the continuums described above. Successful learners:

1. involve themselves fully, openly, and without bias in new experiences (CE);

2. observe and reflect on these experiences from many points of view (RO);

3. integrate these observations into logically sound theories (AC) that include predictions about the consequences of new behaviors; and

4. use these theories to make decisions, solve problems, and take effective action (AE). This view of learning is quite flexible. You can start learning at any one of the four points listed above and cycle through the rest. In any case, the power of your learning derives from testing theories in your daily life—and in changing those theories based on the feedback you get from concrete experiences.

You can use Kolb's ideas to increase your skills at learning anything. First, start by understanding your natural preferences. Then balance them with activities that you consciously choose to support your learning.

Taking Your Learning Style Inventory

To help you become more aware of what you currently do to support your learning, David Kolb has developed the Learning Style Inventory (LSI), which is included on the next few pages. Completing this inventory will help you discover more about how you learn.

Step 1 Keep in mind that this is not a test. There are no right or wrong answers. Your goal is to develop a profile of your learning. Take the inventory quickly. There's no need to agonize over your responses. Recalling a recent situation in which you learned something new at school,

at work, or in your life might make it easier for you to focus and answer the questions.

Step 2 Remove the sheet of paper following page LSI-2. When you're ready to write on the inventory, press firmly so that your answers will show up on the page underneath the questions.

Step 3 Note that the LSI consists of 12 sentences, each with four different endings. You will read each sentence, then write a "4" next to the ending that best describes the way you currently learn. Then you will continue ranking the other endings with a "3," "2," or "1." This is a forced choice inventory, so you must rank each ending; no items can be left out. *Look at the example provided at the top of page LSI-1 before you begin.*

When you understand the example, you're ready to respond to the 12 sentences of the LSI:

- After you answer item #1, check to be sure that you wrote one "1," one "2," one "3," and one "4."

- Also check to make sure that your markings are showing through onto the scoring page (LSI-3).

- After you have responded to the 12 items, go to page LSI-3, which has instructions for computing your results. ⊠

→ **A note about learning styles**

This chapter introduces several approaches to learning styles: the Learning Style Inventory, multiple intelligences, and the VAK system. That's a lot of information to absorb. Remember that each approach presents an option, not the final word on learning styles. Above all, look for ideas from any of these methods that you can put to immediate use, both inside and outside the classroom. When you write Intention Statements, keep these questions in mind: How can I use this idea to be more successful in school and at work? What will I do differently as a result of reading about learning styles? If I develop new learning styles, what skill will I have that I don't have now?

Learning Style Inventory

Fill in the following blanks like this example:

A. When I learn: _2_ I am happy.   _3_ I am fast.   _4_ I am logical.   _1_ I am careful.

Remember: **4** = Most like you   **3** = Second most like you   **2** = Third most like you   **1** = Least like you

---

Remove the sheet of paper following this page. Press firmly while writing.

1. **When I learn:** _____ I like to deal with my feelings. _____ I like to think about ideas. _____ I like to be doing things. _____ I like to watch and listen.

2. **I learn best when:** _____ I listen and watch carefully. _____ I rely on logical thinking. _____ I trust my hunches and feelings. _____ I work hard to get things done.

3. **When I am learning:** _____ I tend to reason things out. _____ I am responsible about things. _____ I am quiet and reserved. _____ I have strong feelings and reactions.

4. **I learn by:** _____ feeling. _____ doing. _____ watching. _____ thinking.

5. **When I learn:** _____ I am open to new experiences. _____ I look at all sides of issues. _____ I like to analyze things, break them down into their parts. _____ I like to try things out.

6. **When I am learning:** _____ I am an observing person. _____ I am an active person. _____ I am an intuitive person. _____ I am a logical person.

7. **I learn best from:** _____ observation. _____ personal relationships. _____ rational theories. _____ a chance to try out and practice.

8. **When I learn:** _____ I like to see results from my work. _____ I like ideas and theories. _____ I take my time before acting. _____ I feel personally involved in things.

9. **I learn best when:** _____ I rely on my observations. _____ I rely on my feelings. _____ I can try things out for myself. _____ I rely on my ideas.

10. **When I am learning:** _____ I am a reserved person. _____ I am an accepting person. _____ I am a responsible person. _____ I am a rational person.

11. **When I learn:** _____ I get involved. _____ I like to observe. _____ I evaluate things. _____ I like to be active.

12. **I learn best when:** _____ I analyze ideas. _____ I am receptive and open-minded. _____ I am careful. _____ I am practical.

LSI-1

Interpreting your Learning Style Graph

NOTE: Before you read this page, score your inventory by following the directions on page LSI-3. Then complete the Learning Style Graph on page LSI-5. The following information appears on this page so that you can more easily compare your completed graph to the samples below. You will make this comparison *after* you remove page LSI-3.

Four modes of learning

When we're learning well, we tend to search out the answers to four key questions: *Why? What? How?* and *What if?* Each of these questions represents a different *mode of learning*. The modes of learning are patterns of behavior—unique combinations of concrete experience, reflective observation, abstract conceptualization, and active experimentation. When you are in a learning situation, you might find that you continually ask yourself one of these key questions more than the others. Or you might routinely ask several of these questions. Read the descriptions below to get a better idea of how you approach learning.

Mode 1: Why? Some of us question why we are learning things. We seek a purpose for information and a personal connection with the content. We want to know a rationale for what we're learning—why the course content matters and how it challenges or fits in with what we already know.

Mode 2: What? Some of us crave information. When learning something, we want to know critical facts. We seek a theory or model to explain what's happening and follow up to see what experts have to say on the topic. We break a subject down into its key components or steps and master each one.

Mode 3: How? Some of us hunger for an opportunity to try out what we're studying. We ask ourselves: Does this idea make sense? Will it work, and, if so, *how* does it work? How can I make use of this information? We want to apply and test theories and models. We excel at taking the parts or key steps of a subject and assembling them into a meaningful sequence.

Mode 4: What if? Some of us get excited about going beyond classroom assignments. We aim to adapt what we're learning to another course or to a situation at work or at home. By applying our knowledge, we want to make a difference in some area that we care about. We ask ourselves: What if we tried . . .? or What if we combined . . .?

Your preferred learning mode

When you examine your completed Learning Style Graph on page LSI-5, you will notice that your learning style profile (the "kite" that you drew) might be located primarily in one part of the graph. This will give you an idea of your preferred mode of learning, that is, the kind of behaviors that feel most comfortable and familiar to you when you are learning something. Using the descriptions below and the sample graphs, identify your preferred learning mode.

Mode 1: Why? If the majority of your learning style profile is in the upper right-hand corner of the Learning Style Graph, you probably prefer Mode 1 learning. You like to consider a situation from many different points of view and determine why it is important to learn a new idea or technique.

Mode 2: What? If your learning style profile is mostly in the lower right-hand corner of the Learning Style Graph, you probably prefer Mode 2 learning. You are interested in knowing what ideas or techniques are important. You enjoy learning lots of facts and then arranging these facts in a logical and concise manner.

Mode 3: How? If most of your learning style profile is in the lower left-hand corner of the Learning Style Graph, you probably prefer Mode 3 learning. You get involved with new knowledge by testing it out. You investigate how ideas and techniques work, and you put into practice what you learn.

Mode 4: What if? If most of your learning style profile is in the upper left-hand corner of the Learning Style Graph, you probably prefer Mode 4 learning. You like to take what you have practiced and find other uses for it. You seek ways to apply this newly gained skill or information at your workplace or in your personal relationships.

Combinations. Some learning style profiles combine all four modes. The profile to the right reflects a learner who is focused primarily on gathering information—*lots* of information! People with this profile tend to ask for additional facts from an instructor, or they want to know where they can go to discover more about a subject.

The profile to the right applies to learners who focus more on understanding what they learn and less on gathering lots of information. People with this profile prefer smaller chunks of data with plenty of time to process it. Long lectures can be difficult for these learners.

The profile to the right indicates a learner whose preferences are fairly well balanced. People with this profile can be highly adaptable and tend to excel no matter what the instructor does in the classroom. These people enjoy learning in general and do well in school. ◪

Remove this sheet before completing the Learning Style Inventory.

This page is inserted to ensure that the other writing you do in this book doesn't show through on page LSI-3.

Remove this sheet before completing the Learning Style Inventory.

This page is inserted to ensure that the other writing you do in this book doesn't show through on page LSI-3.

Scoring your Inventory

1 First, add up all of the numbers you gave to the items marked with brown **F** letters. Then write down that total to the right in the blank next to "**Brown F**." Next, add up all of the numbers for "**Teal W**," "**Purple T**," and "**Orange D**," and also write down those totals in the blanks to the right.

2 Add the four totals to arrive at a GRAND TOTAL and write down that figure in the blank to the right. (*Note:* The grand total should equal 120. If you have a different amount, go back and re-add the colored letters; it was probably just an addition error.) Now remove this page and continue with Step 3 on page LSI-5.

scorecard

Brown **F** total _____

Teal **W** total _____

Purple **T** total _____

Orange **D** total _____

GRAND TOTAL _____

F	T	D	W
W	T	F	D
T	D	W	F
F	D	W	T
F	W	T	D
W	D	F	T
W	F	T	D
D	T	W	F
W	F	D	T
W	F	D	T
F	W	T	D
T	F	W	D

Remove this page after you have completed Steps 1 and 2 on page LSI-3. Then continue with Step 3 on page LSI-5.

Once you have completed Step 3, discard this page so that you can more easily compare your completed Learning Style Graph with the examples on page LSI-2.

Learning Style Graph

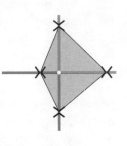

3 Remove the piece of paper that follows this page and then transfer your totals from Step 2 on page LSI-3 to the lines on the Learning Style Graph below. On the brown (F) line, find the number that corresponds to your "**Brown F**" total from page LSI-3. Then write an X on this number. Do the same for your "**Teal W**," "**Purple T**," and "**Orange D**" totals.

4 Now, pressing firmly, draw four straight lines to connect the four X's and shade in the area to form a "kite." This is your learning style profile. Each X that you placed on these lines indicates your preference for a different aspect of learning:

Concrete experience ("Feeling"). The number where you put your X on this line indicates your preference for learning things that have personal meaning. The higher your score on this line, the more you like to learn things that you feel are important and relevant to yourself.

Reflective observation ("Watching"). Your number on this line indicates how important it is for you to reflect on the things you are learning. If your score is high on this line, you probably find it important to watch others as they learn about an assignment and then report on it to the class. You probably like to plan things out and take the time to make sure that you fully understand a topic.

Abstract conceptualization ("Thinking"). Your number on this line indicates your preference for learning ideas, facts, and figures. If your score is high on this line, you probably like to absorb many concepts and gather lots of information on a new topic.

Active experimentation ("Doing"). Your number on this line indicates your preference for applying ideas, using trial and error, and practicing what you learn. If your score is high on this line, you probably enjoy hands-on activities that allow you to test out ideas to see what works.

5 Read page LSI-2 to understand further your preferences for learning.

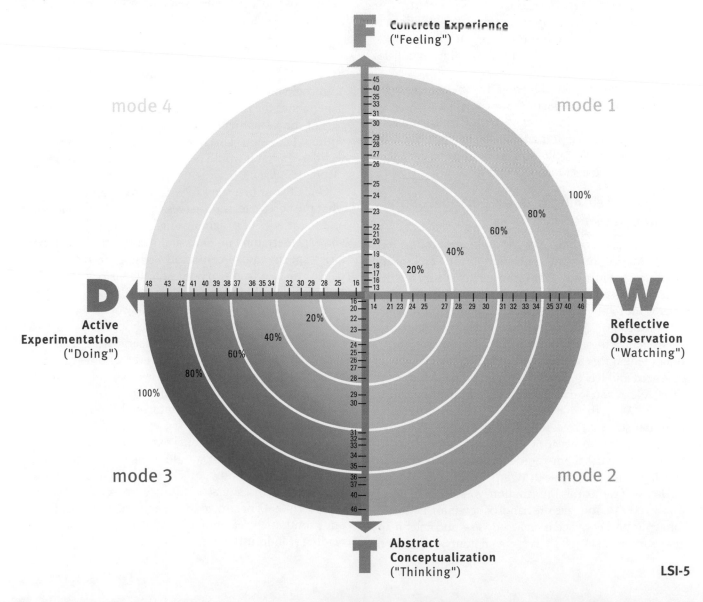

LSI-5

Cycle of learning

These examples show how the learning cycle works. You're interested in something (Mode 1), so you gather information about it (Mode 2). You try out what you're learning (Mode 3), then you integrate it into your day-to-day life (Mode 4). You go through this cycle many times as one learning experience generates another.

Example 1 Learning about a historical issue

You're required to take an elective in history, and you decide to take a course on the history of immigration in the United States. Your great-grandparents came to this country as immigrants, and immigration is still taking place today. You conclude that this topic is interesting—in part, because of your family background (Mode 1: *Why?*).

Soon you're in class, and you learn that from the early years of the country's history, many Americans have had misconceptions and fears about immigration that persist to the present day (Mode 2: *What?*).

You find yourself re-evaluating your own beliefs and assumptions. You wonder whether new immigrants in your city are experiencing some of the same stereotyping that was commonplace in earlier times. You decide to become more active in a community organization that deals firsthand with the impact of immigration policies (Mode 3: *How?*).

You also start to consider what it would be like to become an attorney and devote your career to creating a system that treats all immigrants with fairness and respect. You realize that you want to make a positive difference in the lives of people who are coming to live in the United States today (Mode 4: *What if?*).

Example 2 Learning to use a personal digital assistant (PDA)

Learning begins with developing an interest in this technology. Maybe you want to manage your to-do lists and appointments in a way that is more efficient than writing notes to yourself on random bits of paper. Maybe you never want to buy another pocket calendar. Or maybe you want to store your planning information digitally and exchange files with your personal computer. You conclude that this technology could help you finally get organized and feel on top of your schedule (Mode 1: *Why?*). Next, you learn as much as you can about the different PDAs on the market. You visit Web sites, go to a computer store, and ask for a demonstration. You also talk to friends who swear by PDAs—and those who swear never to use them—and weigh their advice and differing opinions (Mode 2: *What?*).

After you gather this information, you decide to buy your own PDA. You take the handwritten information from your pocket calendar and to-do lists and enter it all into your new PDA. This takes several hours, including the time spent learning to write with a stylus (Mode 3: *How?*).

Once you've conquered the mechanics of using a PDA, you begin to use it on a daily basis—and encounter some unexpected hassles. For one thing, writing with the stylus requires you to form individual letters in a special way. Also, your friends who stick with paper-based planning can simply open up their pocket calendars and quickly pencil in appointments. Meanwhile, you have to turn on your PDA and wait for it to boot up before you can use it. Instead of feeling more organized, you end up feeling behind. You wonder what it would be like to switch back to paper-based planning. After your experiences with a PDA, you decide to do just that. This time, however, you introduce a change in your behavior. Instead of recording your to-do items on any scrap of paper that is lying around, you put a pen and some 3x5 index cards in your pocket and carry them with you at all times. Whenever you want to make a note to yourself, you simply pull out a card and jot down your thoughts. Cards are easy to store and sort. This new system, while it seems so simple and so "low-tech," finally helps you achieve that sense of organization you've been craving (Mode 4: *What if?*).

Example 3 Thinking about the effects of television

Your sociology instructor asks you to write a 2,000-word paper about the impact of television on our society. As part of the assignment, you're asked to envision a society without television. This interests you, since you've often wondered what it would be like to give up television (Mode 1: *Why?*).

One of your first steps in writing this paper is to ask what purposes television serves. You conclude that, based on the varieties of programming, several purposes are involved: entertainment, news and information, documentaries, sports, and, of course, advertising. To research the paper, you also read two books on the history of American television (Mode 2: *What?*).

Still wondering how your own life would change if you were to give up television, you choose to do so on a trial basis—for two weeks—and observe the effects. This change in your behavior frees up several hours each week, which you use for reading newspapers and magazines. You find that you don't miss television news and that reading leaves you better informed about the world (Mode 3: *How?*).

As a result of your personal experiment with television, you wonder what it would be like to give up television news permanently. You choose to do this for at least six more months. You also volunteer for a local literacy campaign that encourages people to go television-free for one month each year and devote the time they save to reading (Mode 4: *What if?*). ✖

Remove this sheet before completing the Learning Style Graph.

This page is inserted to ensure that the other writing you do in this book doesn't show through on page LSI-7.

Remove this sheet before completing the Learning Style Graph.

This page is inserted to ensure that the other writing you do in this book doesn't show through on page LSI-7.

Name _____ Date _____/_____/_____

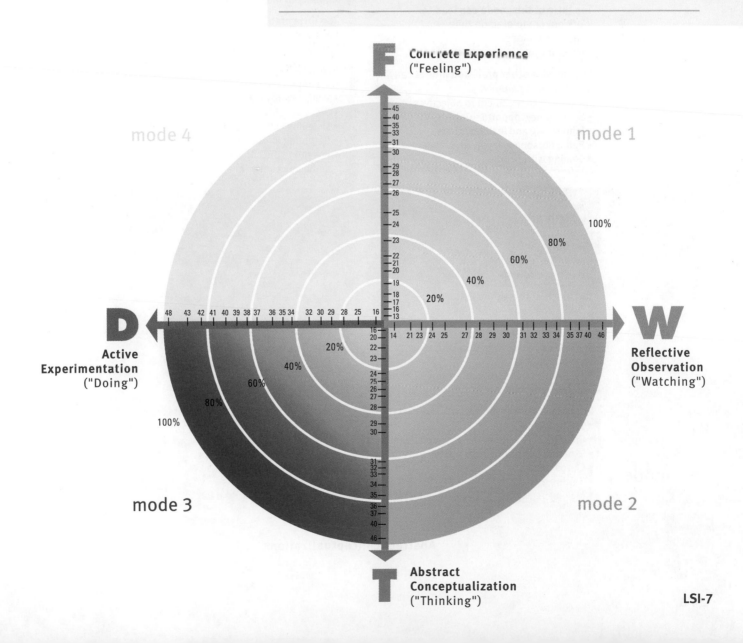

journal entry 5

Discovery/Intention Statement

Note: After completing your Learning Style Inventory (page LSI-1) and filling in the Learning Style Graph (page LSI-5), be sure to read the sections titled "Interpreting Your Learning Style Graph" (page LSI-2) and "Cycle of Learning" (page LSI-6). Then complete the following Journal Entry.

To make this concept of the learning cycle more useful, start applying it right away. You can begin with the content of this book. For example, as you read the Master Student Profiles, ask questions based on each mode of learning: *Why* is this person considered a master student? *What* attitudes or behaviors helped to create her mastery? *How* can I develop those qualities? *What if* I could use her example to create significant new results in my own life? (Or, *What if* I ignore the lessons to be learned from this Master Student Profile and experience significant costs as a result?) Also see the Master Student Map at the beginning of each chapter for sample answers to *Why? What? How?* and *What if?* questions.

Regarding my preferences for learning, I discovered that...

_____

Given my preferences for learning, I intend to...

_____

F Concrete Experience ("Feeling")

mode 4

mode 1

— 45
— 40
— 35
— 33
— 31
— 30

— 29
— 28
— 27
— 26

— 25
— 24

— 23

100%
80%
60%
40%
20%

— 22
— 21
— 20
— 19
— 18
— 17
— 16
— 13

D ← 48 43 42 41 40 39 38 37 36 35 34 32 30 29 28 25 16 — 16 — 13

16 —
20 — 14 21 23 24 25   27 28 29 30   31 32 33 34   35 37 40 46   → **W**

Active Experimentation ("Doing")

20%
40%
60%
80%
100%

— 22
— 23

— 24
— 25
— 26
— 27
— 28

— 29
— 30

Reflective Observation ("Watching")

— 31
— 32
— 33
— 34
— 35
— 36
— 37
— 40
— 46

mode 3

mode 2

T Abstract Conceptualization ("Thinking")

Balancing your preferences

The chart below identifies some of the natural talents as well as challenges for people who have a strong preference for any one mode of learning. For example, if most of your "kite" is in Mode 2 of the Learning Style Graph, then look at the lower right-hand corner of the following chart to see if this is an accurate description of yourself.

After reviewing the description of your preferred learning mode, read all of the sections that start with the words "People with other preferred modes." These sections explain what actions you can take to become a more balanced learner.

Concrete Experience

mode 4

Strengths:
Getting things done
Leadership
Risk taking

Too much of this mode can lead to:
Trivial improvements
Meaningless activity

Too little of this mode can lead to:
Work not completed on time
Impractical plans
Lack of motivation to achieve goals

People with other preferred modes can develop Mode 4 by:
• Making a commitment to objectives
• Seeking new opportunities
• Influencing and leading others
• Being personally involved
• Dealing with people

mode 1

Strengths:
Imaginative ability
Understanding people
Recognizing problems
Brainstorming

Too much of this mode can lead to:
Feeling paralyzed by alternatives
Inability to make decisions

Too little of this mode can lead to:
Lack of ideas
Not recognizing problems and opportunities

People with other preferred modes can develop Mode 1 by:
• Being aware of other people's feelings
• Being sensitive to values
• Listening with an open mind
• Gathering information
• Imagining the implications of ambiguous situations

Active Experimentation

Reflective Observation

Strengths:
Problem solving
Decision making
Deductive reasoning
Defining problems

Too much of this mode can lead to:
Solving the wrong problem
Hasty decision making

Too little of this mode can lead to:
Lack of focus
Reluctance to consider alternatives
Scattered thoughts

People with other preferred modes can develop Mode 3 by:
• Creating new ways of thinking and doing
• Experimenting with fresh ideas
• Choosing the best solution
• Setting goals
• Making decisions

mode 3

Strengths:
Planning
Creating models
Defining problems
Developing theories

Too much of this mode can lead to:
Vague ideals ("castles in the air")
Lack of practical application

Too little of this mode can lead to:
Inability to learn from mistakes
No sound basis for work
No systematic approach

People with other preferred modes can develop Mode 2 by:
• Organizing information
• Building conceptual models
• Testing theories and ideas
• Designing experiments
• Analyzing quantitative data

mode 2

Abstract Conceptualization

Using your learning style profile
to succeed in school

what
if
why
how
what

To get the most value from knowing your learning style profile, look for ways to apply this knowledge in school and at work. Consider the suggestions that follow.

Tolerate discomfort. Discomfort is a natural part of the learning process. As you participate in modes of learning that do not energize you, allow yourself to notice your struggle with a task or your lack of interest in completing it. Realize that you are balancing your learning preferences. Resist the temptation to skip a mode of learning or move too quickly through it. By tolerating discomfort and using all of the modes, you increase your chances for success.

Match activities to your learning style profile. You might want to examine your learning style profile when choosing your major and planning your career. You could focus on courses or jobs that suit your preferred modes of learning. Consulting with people who have different learning preferences can also be beneficial when you approach course work or other learning situations.

Ask for what you want. You might find that the way an instructor teaches is not the way you prefer to learn, and that teachers don't always promote all four modes of learning. Once you know your learning preferences, you can take a more active role in ensuring that your learning needs are met.

- *If you have a strong preference for Mode 1,* you are likely to spend time observing others and planning out your course of action. You probably also enjoy working with other students. To assist yourself in school, ask questions that help you understand why it is important for you to learn about a specific topic. You might also want to form a study group.

- *If you have a strong preference for Mode 2,* you are skilled in understanding theories and concepts.

When in learning situations, you are likely to enjoy lectures and individual class assignments. Chances are that you also enjoy solitary time and are not fond of working in groups. To assist yourself in school, ask questions that help you gather enough information to understand what you are learning. You might also increase your effectiveness by

---

➡ When learning styles conflict, you have options

When they experience difficulty in school, some students say: "The classroom is not conducive to the way I learn." Or "This teacher creates tests that are too hard for me." Or "In class, we never have time for questions." Or "The instructor doesn't teach to my learning style."

Such statements can become mental crutches—a set of beliefs that prevent you from taking responsibility for your education. To stay in charge of your learning, consider adopting attitudes such as the following:

I will discover the value in learning this information.

I will find out more details and facts about this information.

I will discover how I can experiment with this information.

I will discover new ways to use this information in my life.

I will study this information with modes of learning that are not my preferred style.

Note that you can base your behaviors on such statements even if you don't fully agree with them. One way to change your attitudes is to adopt new behaviors and watch for new results in your life.

choosing not to concentrate equally on all of the material in a chapter, focusing primarily on specific parts of the text.

- *If you have a strong preference for Mode 3,* you probably excel at working with your hands and at laboratory stations. When in a learning situation, you are interested in knowing how things work. In addition, you probably enjoy working alone or with a small group. To assist yourself in school, ask questions that help you understand how something works and how you can experiment with these new ideas. Also allow time to practice and apply what you learn. You can conduct experiments, create presentations, tabulate findings, or even write a rap song that summarizes key concepts. Such activities provide an opportunity to internalize your learning through hands-on practice.

- *If you have a strong preference for Mode 4,* you are skilled at teaching others what you have learned and helping them see the importance of these concepts. Whether in a learning situation or in everyday life, you like to apply facts and theories. You probably enjoy carrying out plans and having new and challenging experiences. You also prefer working with others and are likely to have a large social circle. To assist yourself in school, ask questions that help you determine where else in your life you can apply what you have just learned. Also seek opportunities to demonstrate your understanding. You could coach a classmate about what you have learned, present findings from your research, explain how your project works, or perform a rap song that someone else might have written.

Associate with students who have different learning style profiles. If your instructor asks your class to form groups to complete an assignment, avoid joining a group in which everyone shares your preferred modes of learning. Get together with people who both complement and challenge you. This is one way you can develop skills in all four learning modes and become a more well-rounded student.

Use this book with the modes of learning in mind. The four modes of learning are part of a natural cycle. Master students learn in all four ways. If you strongly prefer one mode, then experiment with the others. This book can help. It is designed to move you through all four modes of learning.

- At the beginning of each chapter, you are asked to complete a Journal Entry designed to stimulate your thinking and connect the chapter content to your current life experience—to help you see why learning this material is beneficial (a Mode 1 activity).

- Next, you read articles that are filled with ideas, information, and suggestions that can help you succeed in school (a Mode 2 activity).

- You are also asked to practice new skills with exercises provided throughout each chapter (a Mode 3 activity).

- Finally, at the end of each chapter Discovery and Intention Statements and Learning Styles Applications help you tie all of this information together and suggest ways that you can use it in your future (a Mode 4 activity).

This article and the previous one were written following the same four-mode learning cycle. The previous article, "Learning styles: Discovering how you learn," first reviewed the value of knowing about learning styles (Mode 1). Then facts and theories about learning styles were discussed (Mode 2). Next, you took action and did the Learning Style Inventory (Mode 3). Finally, this article invites you to apply your newfound knowledge of learning styles in your daily life (Mode 4). ✖

from the desk of...

KATE USDIN,
FINANCIAL SERVICES ANALYST:

I was a business major in college. Most of the classes I took involved doing group projects. I think at the time it is hard to realize how valuable those experiences are. I rarely work on my own on the job. In class, you are in groups with people who have very different working habits than you, and it can get frustrating. However, the same exact thing happens on the job. You have to change your style at times to accommodate that of others.

Adapting to styles in the workplace

As the workplace becomes more diverse and technology creates a global marketplace, you'll meet people who differ from you in profound ways. Your coworkers will behave in ways that express a variety of preferences for learning, completing tasks, and building relationships. Those preferences add up to a working style that's unique to each person.

Sometimes styles clash. When that happens, we have several options. One is to throw up our hands and resign ourselves to "personality conflicts." Another option is to recognize differences, accept them, and respect them as complementary ways to meet common goals. The more you can adapt to differences in style, the more likely you are to enjoy your job, forge positive work relationships, and meet your career goals. Develop your sociability, a transferable skill that will serve to help you adapt to other people in different types of group settings.

Notice learning styles

You can learn a lot about other people's styles simply by observing them during the workday. For example, some people process new information by sitting quietly and reading or writing. When learning to use a new computer, they'll read the manual first. Others will skip the manual, unpack all the boxes, and start setting up equipment. And others might ask a more experienced colleague to guide them in person, step by step.

Other clues to learning style come with word choice. Some people like to process information visually. You might hear them say, "I'll look into that" or "Give me the big picture first." Others like to solve problems verbally: "Let's talk through this problem" or "I hear you!" In contrast, some people focus on body sensations ("This

product feels great") or action ("Let's run with this idea and see what happens").

Accommodate learning styles

Once you've discovered differences in styles, look for ways to accommodate them. As you collaborate on projects with coworkers, encourage them to answer all four learning style questions. The benefit is that you complete the cycle of learning, draw more powerful lessons from your experience, and work successfully with people who have a variety of styles.

Asking *Why?* means defining the purpose and desired outcomes of a project. Before moving into action, help participants answer the questions *What's in this for our organization?*—and *What's in this for me?*

Asking *What?* means assigning major tasks, setting due dates for each task, and generating commitment to action. As you answer this question, allow for coworkers who excel at reflecting on experience and making predictions based on theories. When appropriate, provide handouts or give presentations that include visuals, bulleted lists, and step-by-step instructions. Visual learners and people who like organized information will appreciate it. Also schedule periods for questions and answers, which will draw in auditory learners.

Asking *How?* means carrying out assigned tasks, discussing what's working well, and brainstorming ways to improve performance. Here you can allow time for active experimentation and concrete experience. Offer people a chance to try out a new product or process for themselves—to literally "get the feel of it."

Asking *What if?* means discussing what the team has learned from the project and ways to apply that learning to the larger organization. Other project teams can avoid any mistakes you made and build on your successes.

Notice relationship styles

In addition to learning on the job and completing projects, people are constantly defining their workplace relationships. To get a sense of this, notice how often coworkers or classmates make eye contact with you. Observe how close they sit or stand next to you. Also notice their gestures, the volume and tone of their voice, and the pace of their speech. These are all clues to the kind of relationship your coworkers want to have with you. If you miss or misinterpret these signals, you could find your workplace relationships deteriorating—and have no idea why.

Authors Barry Reece and Rhonda Brandt suggest that you prepare for several kinds of relationship styles in the workplace.[2]

People with an **emotive style** use vigorous gestures, talk rapidly, and behave spontaneously. These people are often described as "extroverted" and "upbeat." They like to be informal and will probably call you by your first name.

In contrast, people with a **director** style may come across as formal, even detached. Their gestures and tone of voice project determination, power, and a desire to control outcomes.

Other people operate with a **reflective** style. One clue to this style is a desk that's organized and neat. These people often take an orderly approach to information as well. At meetings, they prefer a precise agenda distributed in advance. They focus on details and take their time in making decisions. When reflecting on a problem, they may appear to be lost in thought.

You may also meet people with a **supportive** style. They excel at listening. Instead of ascending to positions of power in an organization, they like to function as your equal. They are warm, friendly, and naturally persuasive.

Accommodate relationship styles

Recognizing relationship styles allows you to literally get "in sync" with your coworkers. By understanding and responding to their preferences, you can gain their trust and enhance your credibility.

Relationship style	Ways to respond
Emotive	• Allow some time for socializing as well as taking care of business. • Focus on main points rather than details. • Allow conversations to be fast-paced and cover a wide range of topics.
Director	• Begin and end meetings on time. • Get down to business right away, keeping written and oral presentations brief and to the point. • Make eye contact and express yourself with confidence. • When presenting a proposal, anticipate possible questions and objections—and be prepared to answer them.
Reflective	• Organize ideas carefully. • Offer plenty of details about your proposal, in both written and verbal form. • Allow for slow-paced, systematic conversations and time to cover all major topics.
Supportive	• Find areas of common interest and identify mutual acquaintances. • Listen carefully to find out how this person feels about a project and wants to gain from it. • Focus on building a "win-win" relationship.

Deepen your experience of styles

Beyond noticing and accommodating styles is another dimension—learning to value individual differences and thrive on them.

Introduce a conversation about styles. Attend a workshop on styles and share what you learn. Or bring such training directly to your workplace.

When collaborating on projects, look for ways to complement each other's styles. If you're skilled at planning, find someone who excels at doing. Also seek people who can reflect on and interpret the team's experience. Pooling different styles allows you to pool everyone's strengths and draw more powerful lessons from your collective experience.

Let people expand their styles. Style is both stable and dynamic. People gravitate toward the kinds of tasks and relationships that they've succeeded at in the past. They can also broaden their styles by acquiring new behaviors. As people change, let your opinions about them change as well.

Of course, no list of ideas can tell you exactly how to succeed with each of your coworkers. Use the above suggestions as starting points for developing your own strategies. The point is to expect differences in style—and to make conscious choices about working with them. ◼

Claim your multiple intelligences

People often think that being smart means the same thing as having a high IQ, and that having a high IQ automatically leads to success. However, psychologists are finding that IQ scores do not always foretell which students will do well in academic settings—or after they graduate.

Howard Gardner of Harvard University believes that no single measure of intelligence can tell us how smart we are. Instead, Gardner identifies many types of intelligence, as described below.[3] Gardner's theory of several types of intelligence complements the discussion in this chapter on different learning styles. Both recognize that there are alternative ways for people to learn and assimilate knowledge. You can use Gardner's concepts to explore additional methods for achieving success in school, work, and relationships.

People using **verbal/linguistic intelligence** are adept at language skills and learn best by speaking, writing, reading, and listening. They are likely to enjoy activities such as telling stories and doing crossword puzzles.

Those using **mathematical/logical intelligence** are good with numbers, logic, problem solving, patterns, relationships, and categories. They are generally precise and methodical, and are likely to enjoy science.

When people learn visually and by organizing things spatially, they display **visual/spatial intelligence.** They think in images and pictures, and understand best by seeing the subject. They enjoy charts, graphs, maps, mazes, tables, illustrations, art, models, puzzles, and costumes.

People using **bodily/kinesthetic intelligence** prefer physical activity. They enjoy activities such as building things, woodworking, dancing, skiing, sewing, and crafts. They generally are coordinated and athletic, and would rather participate in games than just watch.

Those using **musical/rhythmic intelligence** enjoy musical expression through songs, rhythms, and musical instruments. They are responsive to various kinds of sounds, remember melodies easily, and might enjoy drumming, humming, and whistling.

People using **intrapersonal intelligence** are exceptionally aware of their own feelings and values. They are generally reserved, self-motivated, and intuitive.

Evidence of **interpersonal intelligence** is seen in outgoing people. They do well with cooperative learning and are sensitive to the feelings, intentions, and motivations of others. They often make good leaders.

Those using **naturalist intelligence** love the outdoors and recognize details in plants, animals, rocks, clouds, and other natural formations. These people excel in observing fine distinctions among similar items. Each of us has all of these intelligences to some degree. And each of us can learn to enhance them.

Experiment with learning in ways that draw on a variety of intelligences—including those that might be less familiar. When we acknowledge all of our intelligences, we can constantly explore new ways of being smart. The following chart summarizes the multiple intelligences discussed in this article and suggests ways to apply them. This is not an exhaustive list or a formal inventory, so take what you find merely as points of departure. You can invent strategies of your own to cultivate different intelligences. ✖

Type of intelligence	Possible characteristics	Possible learning strategies	Possible careers
Verbal/linguistic	• You enjoy writing letters, stories, and papers. • You prefer to write directions rather than draw maps. • You take excellent notes from textbooks and lectures. • You enjoy reading, telling stories, and listening to them.	• Highlight, underline, and write other notes in your textbooks. • Recite new ideas in your own words. • Rewrite and edit your class notes. • Talk to other people often about what you're studying.	Librarian, lawyer, editor, journalist, English teacher, radio or television announcer
Mathematical/logical	• You enjoy solving puzzles. • You prefer math or science class over English class. • You want to know how and why things work. • You make careful step-by-step plans.	• Analyze tasks into a sequence of steps. • Group concepts into categories and look for underlying patterns. • Convert text into tables, charts, and graphs. • Look for ways to quantify ideas—to express them in numerical terms.	Accountant, auditor, tax preparer, mathematician, computer programmer, statistician, economist, math or science teacher
Visual/spatial	• You draw pictures to give an example or clarify an explanation. • You understand maps and illustrations more readily than text. • You assemble things from illustrated instructions. • You especially enjoy books that have a lot of illustrations.	• When taking notes, create concept maps, mind maps, and other visuals (see Chapter Five). • Code your notes by using different colors to highlight main topics, major points, and key details. • When your attention wanders, bring it into focus by sketching or drawing. • Before you try a new task, visualize yourself doing it well.	Architect, commercial artist, fine artist, graphic designer, photographer, interior decorator, engineer, cartographer
Bodily/kinesthetic	• You enjoy physical exercise. • You tend to avoid sitting still for long periods of time. • You enjoy working with your hands. • You use a lot of gestures when talking.	• Be active in ways that support concentration; for example, pace as you recite, read while standing up, and create flash cards. • Carry materials with you and practice studying in several different locations. • Create hands-on activities related to key concepts; for example, create a game based on course content. • Notice the sensations involved with learning something well.	Physical education teacher, athlete, athletic coach, physical therapist, chiropractor, massage therapist, yoga teacher, dancer, choreographer, actor

(continued)

Type of intelligence	Possible characteristics	Possible learning strategies	Possible careers
Musical/rhythmic	• You often sing in the car or shower. • You tap your foot to the beat of a song. • You play a musical instrument. • You feel most engaged and productive when music is playing.	• During a study break, play music or dance to restore energy. • Put on background music that enhances your concentration while studying. • Relate key concepts to songs you know. • Write your own songs based on course content.	Professional musician, music teacher, music therapist, choral director, musical instrument sales representative, musical instrument maker, piano tuner
Intrapersonal	• You enjoy writing in a journal and being alone with your thoughts. • You think a lot about what you want in the future. • You prefer to work on individual projects over group projects. • You take time to think things through before talking or taking action.	• Connect course content to your personal values and goals. • Study a topic alone before attending a study group. • Connect readings and lectures to a strong feeling or significant past experience. • Keep a journal that relates your course work to events in your daily life.	Minister, priest, rabbi, professor of philosophy or religion, counseling psychologist, creator of a home-based or small business
Interpersonal	• You prefer group work over working alone. • You have plenty of friends and regularly spend time with them. • You enjoy talking and listening more than reading or writing. • You thrive in positions of leadership.	• Form and conduct study groups early in a term. • Create flash cards and use them to quiz study partners. • Volunteer to give a speech or to lead group presentations on course topics. • Teach the topic you're studying to someone else.	Manager, school administrator, salesperson, teacher, counseling psychologist, arbitrator, police officer, nurse, travel agent, public relations specialist, creator of a mid-size to large business
Naturalist	• As a child, you enjoyed collecting insects, leaves, or other natural objects. • You enjoy being outdoors. • You find that important insights occur during times you spend in natural surroundings. • You read books and magazines on nature-related topics.	• During study breaks, take walks outside. • Post pictures of outdoor scenes where you study and play recordings of outdoor sounds while you read. • Invite classmates to discuss course work while taking a hike or going on a camping trip. • Focus on careers that hold the potential for working outdoors.	Environmental activist, park ranger, recreation supervisor, historian, museum curator, biologist, criminologist, mechanic, woodworker, construction worker, construction contractor or estimator

The magic of metacognition

It's pronounced "me-ta-cog-ni-shun." *Meta* means *beyond* or *above*, and *cognition* refers to everything that goes on inside your brain—thinking, perceiving, and learning. *Metacognition* is thinking about thinking, learning about learning. It's your ability to stand "above" your mental processes—to observe them and to take conscious control of them.

Metacognition is one of the main benefits of higher education. Mastering this skill allows you to learn anything you want, any time. Among other things, metacognition includes:

- *Planning*—the ability to determine your purpose, choose from alternative behaviors, predict their consequences, and monitor your progress in meeting your goals

- *Analysis*—the ability to separate a whole subject into its parts

- *Synthesis*—the ability to combine parts to form a meaningful whole

- *Application*—the ability to transfer new concepts and skills from one life situation to another

Each aspect of metacognition dovetails nicely with a mode of learning. Mode 1 involves planning—connecting the content of a course to your personal interests and goals. In Mode 2, you analyze by taking key ideas apart, separating skills into their component steps, and learning each step in turn. In Mode 3, you synthesize—that is, combine all of the separate ideas, facts, and skills you learned to see how they work in a real-life situation. And in Mode 4, you take what you have learned in one course and apply it in other courses and outside the classroom.

Students who master metacognition can do things such as:

- state the ways that they'll benefit from learning a subject;

- describe their preferred learning styles and develop new ones;

- make accurate statements about their current abilities;

- monitor their behavior and change their habits;

- choose and apply various strategies for reading, writing, speaking, listening, managing time, and related tasks; and

- modify strategies so that they work in several contexts.

Remember that the teachers and the managers in your life will come and go. Some are more skilled than others. None of them are perfect. With metacognition, you can view any course as one step along the path to learning what you want to learn—in the way that *you* prefer to learn it. The magic of metacognition is that you become your own best teacher.

journal entry 6

Discovery/Intention Statement

Think of a conflict you're experiencing with a coworker or other significant person in your life. Consider whether the conflict may spring from a difference in style. If so, describe that difference in a sentence or two:

I discovered that . . .

_____

_____

_____

_____

Next, list one action you can take to accommodate the other person's style. Think of something you can do to gain a mutually beneficial result.

I intend to . . .

_____

_____

_____

_____

_____

Developing self-esteem

The challenge of higher education often puts self-esteem at risk. The rigors of class work, financial pressures, and new social settings can test our ability to adapt and change.

During the past 30 years, psychologists have produced several key studies about self-efficacy. This term refers to your belief in your ability to determine the outcomes of events—especially outcomes that are strongly influenced by your own behavior. While self-esteem refers to an overall impression of your abilities, self-efficacy is more exact, pointing to specific factors that influence the ways you think, feel, and act. A strong sense of self-efficacy allows you to tackle problems with confidence, set long-term goals, and see difficult tasks as creative challenges rather than potential disasters.

The field of self-efficacy research is closely associated with psychologist Albert Bandura of Stanford University.[4] According to Bandura, self-efficacy has several sources. You can use specific strategies to strengthen them.

Set up situations in which you can win. Start by planning scenarios in which you can succeed. Bandura calls these "mastery situations." For example, set yourself up for success by breaking a big project down into small, doable tasks. Then tackle and complete the first task. This accomplishment can help you move on to the next task with higher self-efficacy. Success breeds more success.

Set goals with care. If you want to boost self-efficacy, also be picky about your goals. According to the research, goals that you find easy to meet will not boost your self-efficacy. Instead, set goals that call on you to overcome obstacles, make persistent effort, and even fail occasionally.

At the same time, it's important to avoid situations in which you are *often* likely to fail. Setting goals that you have little chance to meet can undermine your self-efficacy. Ideal goals are both challenging *and* achievable.

Adopt a model. In self-efficacy research, the word *model* has a special definition. This term refers to someone who is similar to you in key ways, and who

succeeds in the kinds of situations in which you want to succeed. To find a model, gather with people who share your interests. Look for people with whom you have a lot in common—and who have mastered the skills that you want to acquire. Besides demonstrating strategies and techniques for you to use, these people hold out a real possibility of success for you.

Change the conversation about yourself. People with a strong sense of self-efficacy attribute their failures to skills that they currently lack—and that they can acquire in the future. This is much different than discussing failures in terms of permanent, personal defects. Rather than saying "I just don't have what it takes to become a skilled test taker," say "I can adopt techniques to help me remember key facts even when I feel stressed."

Interpret stress in a new way. The way you interpret stress as you become aware of it can make a big difference in your sense of self-efficacy. Remember that the experience of stress has two major elements—thoughts and physical sensations. Thoughts can include mental pictures of yourself making mistakes, and statements such as *This situation is terrible.* Sensations can include feeling short of breath, dry mouth, knots in your stomach, tingling sensations, headaches, and other forms of discomfort.

In situations where you want to do well, you may rely on your stream of thoughts and sensations to judge your performance. Rather than attaching negative interpretations to your experience of stress, simply notice your thoughts and sensations. Instead of trying to resist them, simply notice those thoughts and sensations and let them go.

Remember that the physical sensations associated with stress are often similar to those associated with excitement. Instead of viewing these sensations as signs of impending doom, see them as a boost of energy that you can channel into performing well. ⬟

In 1482, **Leonardo da Vinci** wrote a letter to a wealthy baron, applying for work. In excerpted form, he wrote,

"I can contrive various and endless means of offense and defense. . . . I have all sorts of extremely light and strong bridges adapted to be most easily carried. . . . I have methods for destroying every turret or fortress. . . . I will make covered chariots, safe and unassailable. . . . In case of need I will make big guns, mortars, and light ordnance of fine and useful forms out of the common type." And then he added, almost as an afterthought, *"In times of peace I believe I can give perfect satisfaction and to the equal of any other in architecture . . . can carry out sculpture . . . and also I can do in painting whatever may be done."*

The **Mona Lisa,** for example.

Discovering Mastery

This book is about something that cannot be taught. It's about mastery.

A master is a person who has attained a level of skill that goes beyond technique. For a master, methods and procedures are automatic responses to the needs of the task. Work is effortless; struggle evaporates. The master carpenter is so familiar with her tools, they are part of her. To a master chef, utensils are old friends. Because these masters don't have to think about the details of the process, they bring more of themselves to their work.

Mastery can lead to flashy results—an incredible painting, for example, or a gem of a short story. In basketball, mastery might result in an unbelievable shot at the buzzer. For a musician, it might be the performance of a lifetime, the moment when everything comes

together. For the entrepreneur, it might be a business plan that attracts investors or a product that corners the market.

Often the result of mastery is a sense of profound satisfaction, well-being, and timelessness. Work seems self-propelled. The master is *in* control by being *out* of control. He lets go and allows the creative process to take over. That's why after a spectacular performance, it is often said of an athlete or a performer, "He was playing out of his mind."

Likewise, the master student is one who "learns out of her mind." And the master employee is one who creates value for her organization in ways that defy analysis.

Of course, these statements make no sense. Mastery, in fact, doesn't make sense. It cannot be captured with words. Mastery cannot be taught, only learned and experienced.

Examine the following list of characteristics of mastery in light of your own experience. The list is not complete. It merely points in a direction. Look in that direction, and you'll begin to see endless diversity. People who demonstrate mastery are old and young, male and female. They exist in every period of history. They are students, business people, educators, inventors, and artists. They work and learn in every kind of setting. And they come from every culture, race, and ethnic group.

Also remember to look to yourself. No one can teach us mastery; we are born with this capacity. We are natural learners by design. We are born to love and to work—to care deeply about people and contribute to the world. In the classroom and in the workplace, we can discover that every day.

Following are some aspects of mastery.

Inquisitive.   The person who discovers mastery is curious about everything. By posing questions she can generate interest in the most mundane, humdrum situations. When she is bored during a biology lecture, she thinks to herself, "I always get bored when I listen to this instructor. Why is that? Maybe it's because he reminds me of my boring Uncle Ralph, who always tells those endless fishing stories. He even looks like Uncle Ralph. Amazing! Boredom is certainly interesting." Then she asks herself, "What can I do to get value out of this lecture, even though it seems boring?" And she finds an answer.

Able to focus attention.   Watch a 2-year-old at play. Pay attention to his eyes. The wide-eyed look reveals an energy and a capacity for amazement that keep his attention absolutely focused in the here and now. With mastery comes focused attention that has a childlike quality. The world, to a child, is always new. Because the person who discovers mastery can focus attention, to him the world is also new

Willing to change.   As we discover mastery, the unknown does not frighten us. In fact, we welcome it—even the unknown in ourselves. We all have pictures of who we think we are, and these pictures can be useful. They also can prevent learning and growth. In discovering mastery, we remain open to changes in our environment and in ourselves.

Able to organize and sort.   Mastery enables us to take a large body of information and sift through it to discover relationships. We can play with information, organizing data by size, color, function, timeliness, and hundreds of other categories.

Competent.   Skills are key to mastery. When we learn mathematical formulas, we study them until they become second nature. We practice until we know them cold, then put in a few extra minutes. We also are able to apply what we learn to new and different situations.

Joyful.   More often than not, the person who discovers mastery is seen with a smile on his face—sometimes a smile at nothing in particular other than amazement at the world and his experience of it.

Able to suspend judgment.   In the state of mastery, we have opinions and positions, and we are able to let go of them when appropriate. We realize that we are more than our thoughts. We can quiet our internal dialogue and listen to an opposing viewpoint. We don't let judgment get in the way of learning. Rather than approaching discussions with a "Prove it to me and then I'll believe it" attitude, we ask, What if this is true? and explore the possibilities.

Energetic.   Notice the student or employee with a spring in his step, the one who is enthusiastic and involved. When he reads, he often sits on the very edge of his chair, and he plays with the same intensity. He has discovered mastery.

Well.   Health is important to mastery, though not necessarily in the sense of being free of illness. Rather, mastery means valuing your body and treating it with respect. You tend to your emotional and spiritual health, as well as your physical health.

Self-aware.   With mastery comes the willingness to evaluate ourselves and our behavior. We regularly tell the truth about our strengths and those aspects of ourselves that could be improved.

Responsible.   There is a difference between responsibility and blame. As a person discovers mastery, she is willing to take responsibility for everything in her life—even for events that most people would blame on others.

For example, if a master student is served cold eggs in the cafeteria, she chooses to take responsibility for getting cold eggs. This is not the same as blaming herself for cold eggs. Rather, she looks for ways to change the situation and get what she wants. She could choose to eat breakfast earlier, or she might tell someone in the kitchen that the eggs are cold and request a change. The cold eggs might continue. Even then, the master student takes responsibility and gives herself the power to choose her response to the situation.

Willing to take risks.   The master student or master employee often takes on projects with no guarantee of success. He participates in dialogues at the risk of looking foolish. He tackles difficult subjects in term papers. He promises results and then delivers. He welcomes the risk of a new challenge.

Willing to participate.   Don't look for the master student or employee on the sidelines. She's in the game. She is a player who can be counted on. She is willing to make a commitment and to follow through on it.

A generalist.   Master students and master employees are interested in everything around them. They have a broad base of knowledge in many fields and can apply their specialties.

Willing to accept paradox. The word *paradox* comes from two Greek words, *para* (beyond) and *doxen* (opinion). A paradox is something that is beyond opinion or, more accurately, something that might seem contradictory or absurd yet might actually have meaning.

For example, mastery means that we are committed to managing money and reaching our financial goals. At the same time, we can be totally detached from money, knowing that our real worth is independent of how much money we have. We recognize the limitations of the mind and feel at home with paradox. We can accept ambiguity.

Courageous. In a state of mastery, we admit fear and fully experience it. For example, we will approach a tough exam or job interview as an opportunity to explore feelings of anxiety and tension related to the pressure to perform. We do not deny fear; we embrace it.

Self-directed. Rewards or punishments provided by others do not motivate the master student or master employee. Her motivation to learn comes from within.

Spontaneous. Mastery means entering the here and now. We are able to respond to the moment in fresh, surprising, and unplanned ways.

Relaxed about grades. Grades make the master student neither depressed nor euphoric. She recognizes that grades are important, and grades are not the only reason she studies. She does not measure her worth as a human being by the grades she receives.

Intuitive. Mastery taps into sources of knowledge that cannot be explained by logic. We learn to trust our feelings, and we open up to insights that come from beyond the rational mind.

Creative. Where others see dull details and trivia, the master student or master employee sees opportunities to create and innovate. She can gather pieces of knowledge from a wide range of subjects and put them together in new ways. Mastery brings creativity in every aspect of her life.

Willing to be uncomfortable. In the state of mastery, we do not place comfort first. When discomfort is necessary to reach a goal, we are willing to experience it. We can endure personal hardships and can look at unpleasant things with detachment.

Accepting. The master student or master employee accepts herself, the people around her, and the challenges that life offers.

Willing to laugh. Mastery brings the ability to laugh at any moment, and our sense of humor includes the ability to laugh at ourselves.

Going to school or launching a new career is a big investment. The stakes are high. It's OK to be serious about all this, but you don't have to go to school or work on the deferred-fun program. In the state of mastery, we celebrate learning, and one of the best ways to do that is to have a laugh now and then.

Hungry. Human beings begin life with a natural appetite for knowledge and skills. In some people it soon gets dulled. The master student has tapped that hunger, and it gives her a desire to learn for the sake of learning.

Willing to work. Once inspired, the master student or master employee is willing to follow through with sweat. He knows that genius and creativity are the result of persistence and work. When in high gear, he works with the intensity of a child at play.

Caring. In discovering mastery, we uncover a passion for ideas. We also care about people and appreciate learning from others. We flourish in a community that values "win-win" outcomes, cooperation, and love.

Discover mastery in you. Mastery exists in all of us. By design, human beings are learning machines. We have an innate ability to learn, to love, and to do work that leaves a legacy.

For anyone who wants to gain skills through education and develop them in the workplace, it is important to understand the difference between learning and being taught. Human beings can resist being taught anything. Carl Rogers goes so far as to say that anything that can be taught to a human being is either inconsequential or just plain harmful. What matters, Rogers asserts, is *learning*. And everyone has the ability to learn.[5]

Unfortunately, people also learn to hide that ability. As they experience the pain that sometimes accompanies learning, they shut down. If a child experiences embarrassment in front of a group of people, he could learn to avoid similar situations. In doing so, he restricts his possibilities.

Some children "learn" that they are slow learners. If they learn it well enough, their behavior comes to match that label.

As people grow older, they sometimes accumulate a growing list of ideas to defend, a catalog of familiar experiences that discourages them from learning anything new.

Still, the capacity for mastery survives. To tap that resource, you don't need to acquire anything. You already have everything you need. Every day you can rediscover mastery within you. ✖

Motivation

In large part, this chapter is about discovering who you are and what you want. Self-discovery can fuel your motivation to succeed in school, in the workplace, and in any other aspect of your life. And a First Step in creating motivation is to define it accurately.

The terms *self-discipline, willpower,* and *motivation* are often used to describe something missing in ourselves. Time after time we invoke these words to explain another person's success—or our own shortcomings: "If I were more motivated, I'd get more involved in school." "Of course she got an A. She has self-discipline." "If I had more motivation, I'd get out of this dead-end job." It seems that certain people are born with lots of motivation, while others miss out on it.

An alternative is to stop assuming that motivation is mysterious, determined at birth, or hard to come by. Perhaps what we call *motivation* is something that you already possess—or simply a habit that you can develop with practice. Take this opportunity to commit to developing the transferable skill of self-responsibility—setting high standards, motivating yourself toward attaining goals, and functioning as a "self-starter." The following suggestions offer ways to do that.

Promise it. Motivation can come simply from being clear about your goals and acting on them. Say that you want to start a study group. You can commit yourself to inviting people and setting a time and place to meet. Promise your classmates that you'll do this, and ask them to hold you accountable. Self-discipline, willpower, motivation—none of these mysterious characteristics needs to get in your way. Just make a promise and keep your word.

Befriend your discomfort. Sometimes keeping your word means doing a task you'd rather put off. The mere thought of asking for a raise or revising your résumé can lead to discomfort. In the face of such discomfort, we can procrastinate. Or we can use this barrier as a means to get the job done.

Begin by investigating the discomfort. Notice the thoughts running through your head and speak them out loud: "I'd rather walk on a bed of coals than do this."

"This is the last thing I want to do right now."

Also observe what's happening with your body. For example, are you breathing faster or slower than usual? Is your breathing shallow or deep? Are your shoulders tight? Do you feel any tension in your stomach?

Once you're in contact with your mind and body, stay with the discomfort a few minutes longer. Don't judge it as good or bad. Accepting the thoughts and body sensations robs them of power. They might still be there, but in time they can stop being a barrier for you.

Discomfort can be a gift—an opportunity to do valuable work on yourself. On the other side of discomfort lies mastery.

Change your mind—and your body. You can also get past discomfort by planting new thoughts in your mind or changing your physical stance. For example, instead of slumping in a chair, sit up straight or stand up. You can also get physically active by taking a short walk. Notice what happens to your discomfort.

Work with thoughts, also. Replace "I can't stand this" with "I'll feel great when this is done" or "Doing this will help me get something I want."

Sweeten the task. Sometimes it's just one aspect of a task that holds us back. We can stop procrastinating merely by changing that aspect. If distaste for our physical environment keeps us from studying, we can change that environment. Reading about social psychology might seem like a yawner when we're alone in a dark corner of the house. Moving to a cheery, well-lit library can sweeten the task.

Talk about how bad it is. One way to get past negative attitudes is to take them to an extreme. When faced with an unpleasant task, launch into a no-holds-barred gripe session. Pull out all the stops: "There's no way I can start my income taxes now. This is terrible beyond words, an absolute disaster. This is a catastrophe of global proportions!" Griping taken this far can restore perspective. It shows how self-talk can turn inconveniences into crises.

Turn up the pressure. Sometimes motivation is a luxury. Pretend that the due date for your project has been moved up one month, one week, or one day. Raising the stress level slightly can spur you into action. Then the issue of motivation seems beside the point, and meeting the due date moves to the forefront.

Turn down the pressure. The mere thought of starting a huge task can induce anxiety. To get past this feeling, turn down the pressure by taking "baby steps." Divide a large project into small tasks. In 30 minutes or less, you could respond to a backlog of e-mail messages or create a rough outline for a presentation. Careful planning can help you discover many such steps to make a big job doable.

Ask for support. Other people can become your allies in overcoming procrastination. For example, form a support group and declare what you intend to accomplish before each meeting. Then ask members to hold you accountable. If you want to begin exercising regularly, ask another person to walk with you three times weekly. People in support groups ranging from Alcoholics Anonymous to Weight Watchers know the power of this strategy.

Adopt a model. One strategy for succeeding at any task is to hang around the masters. Find someone you consider successful and spend time with her. Observe this person and use her as a model for your own behavior. You can "try on" this person's actions and attitudes. Look for tools that feel right for you. This person can become a mentor for you.

Compare the payoffs to the costs. Behaviors such as cramming for exams or showing up late for work have payoffs. Cramming might give us more time that's free of commitments. Coming to work later can give us more time to sleep.

Motivation can come simply from being clear about your goals and acting on them.

One way to let go of such unwanted behaviors is first to celebrate them—even embrace them. We can openly acknowledge the payoffs.

Celebration can be especially powerful when we follow it up with the next step—determining the costs. For example, putting off some work-related reading can give you time to go to the movies. However, you might be unprepared for the next day's meeting and have twice as much to read the following week.

Maybe there is another way to get the payoff (going to the movies) without paying the cost (skipping the reading). With some thoughtful weekly planning, you might choose to give up a few hours of television and end up with enough time to read *and* go to the movies.

Comparing the costs and benefits of any behavior can fuel our motivation. We can choose new behaviors because they align with what we want most.

Do it later. At times, it's effective to save a task for later. For example, writing a résumé can wait until you've taken the time to analyze your job skills and map out your career goals. This is not a lack of motivation—it's planning.

When you do choose to do a task later, turn this decision into a promise. Estimate how long the task will take and schedule a specific date and time for it on your calendar.

Heed the message. Sometimes lack of motivation carries a message that's worth heeding. An example is the student who majors in accounting but seizes every chance to be with children. His chronic reluctance to read accounting textbooks might not be a problem. Instead, it might reveal his desire to major in elementary education. His original career choice might have come from the belief that "real men don't teach kindergarten." In such cases, an apparent lack of motivation signals a deeper wisdom trying to get through. ✖

Ways to change a habit

  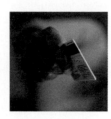

Thinking about ourselves as creatures of habit actually gives us power. Then we are not faced with the monumental task of changing our very nature. Rather, we can take on the doable job of changing our habits. One change in behavior that seems insignificant at first can have effects that ripple throughout your life.

After interviewing hundreds of people, psychologists James Prochaska, John Norcross, and Carlo DiClemente identified stages that people typically go through when adopting a new behavior.[6] These stages take people from *contemplating* a change and making a clear *determination* to change to taking *action* and *maintaining* the new behavior. Following are ways to help yourself move successfully through each stage.

Consider a new way to think about the word *habit*. Imagine for a moment that many of our most troublesome problems and even our most basic traits are just habits.

That expanding waistline that is being blamed on a spouse's cooking—maybe that's just a habit called overeating.

That fit of rage that an employee blames on his boss—maybe that's just the employee's habit of closing the door to new ideas.

Procrastination, stress, and money shortages might just be names that we give to collections of habits—scores of simple, small, repeated behaviors that combine to create a huge result. The same goes for health, wealth, love, and many of the other things that we want from life.

One way of thinking about success is to focus on habits. Behaviors such as failing to complete reading assignments or skipping class might be habits leading to an outcome that "couldn't" be avoided—dropping out of school.

When you confront a behavior that undermines your goals or creates a circumstance that you don't want, consider a new attitude: It's just a habit. And it can be changed.

Tell the truth

Telling the truth about any habit—from chewing our fingernails to cheating on tests—frees us. Without taking this step, our efforts to change might be as ineffective as rearranging the deck chairs on the Titanic. Telling the truth allows us to see what's actually sinking the ship.

When we admit what's really going on in our lives, our defenses are down. We're open to accepting help from others. The support we need to change the habit has an opportunity to make an impact.

Choose and commit to a new behavior

It often helps to choose a new habit to replace an old one. First, make a commitment to practice the new habit. Tell key people in your life about your decision to change. Set up a plan for when and how. Answer questions such as these: When will I apply the new habit? Where will I be? Who will be with me? What will I be seeing, hearing, touching, saying, or doing? Exactly how will I think, speak, or act differently?

Take the student who always snacks when he studies. Each time he sits down to read, he positions a bag of potato chips within easy reach. For him, opening a book is a cue to start chewing. Snacking is especially easy, given the place he chooses to study: the kitchen. He decides to change this habit by studying at a desk in his bedroom instead of at the kitchen table. And every time he feels the urge to bite into a potato chip, he drinks from a glass of water instead.

Affirm your intention

You can pave the way for a new behavior by clearing a mental path for it. Before you apply the new behavior, rehearse it in your mind. Mentally picture what actions you will take and in what order.

Say that you plan to improve your handwriting when taking notes. Imagine yourself with a blank notebook poised before you. See yourself taking up a finely crafted pen. Notice how comfortable it feels in your hand. See yourself writing clearly and legibly. You can even picture how you will make individual letters—the *e*'s, *i*'s, and *r*'s. Then, when class is over, see yourself reviewing your notes and taking pleasure in how easy they are to read.

Such scenes are more vivid if you include all of your senses. Round out your mental picture by adding sounds, textures, and colors.

You can act as if your intention is already a reality, as if the new habit is already a part of you. Be the change you want to see—today. In some cases, this might be enough to change the old habit completely.

Start with a small change

You can sometimes rearrange a whole pattern of behaviors by changing one small habit. If you have a habit of always being late for meetings, and if you want to change that habit, then be on time for one meeting. As soon as you change the old pattern by getting ready and going on time to one meeting, you'll likely find yourself arriving at all of your meetings on time. You might even start arriving everywhere else on time.

Likewise, if you know that you are usually nervous before tests, you don't have to change how you react in all situations at all times. Just change your nervous behavior in one test situation. Like magic, you might watch the rest of your nervousness lessen or even disappear. The joy of this process is watching one small change of habit ripple through your whole life.

Get feedback and support

This is a crucial step and a point at which many plans for change break down. It's easy to practice your new behavior with great enthusiasm for a few days. After the initial rush of excitement, however, things can get a little tougher. We begin to find excuses for slipping back into old habits: "One more cigarette won't hurt." "I can get back to my diet tomorrow." "It's been a tough day. I deserve this beer."

One way to get feedback is to bring other people into the picture. Ask others to remind you that you are changing your habit. If you want to stop an old behavior, such as cramming for tests, then it often works to tell everyone you know that you intend to stop. When you want to start a new behavior, though, consider telling only a few people—those who truly support your efforts. Starting new habits might call for the more focused, long-lasting support that close friends or family members can give.

Support from others can be as simple as a quick phone call: "Hi. Have you started that outline for your research paper yet?" Or it can be as formal as a support group that meets once weekly to review everyone's goals and action plans.

You are probably the most effective source for your own support and feedback. You know yourself better than anyone else does and can design a system to monitor your behavior. You can create your own charts or diagrams to track your behavior or you can write about your progress in your journal. Figure out a way to monitor your progress.

Practice, practice, practice—without self-judgment

Psychologists such as B. F. Skinner define learning as a stable change in behavior that comes as a result of practice.[7] This idea is key to changing habits. Act on your intention. If you fail or forget, let go of any self-judgment. Just keep practicing the new habit and allow whatever time it takes to make a change.

Accept the feelings of discomfort that might come with a new habit. Keep practicing the new behavior, even if it feels unnatural. Trust the process. You will grow into the new behavior. Keep practicing until it becomes as natural as breathing. However, if this new habit doesn't work, simply note what happened (without guilt or blame), select a new behavior, and begin this cycle of steps over again.

Making mistakes as you practice doesn't mean that you've failed. Even when you don't get the results you want from a new behavior, you learn something valuable in the process. Once you understand ways to change one habit, you understand ways to change almost any habit—and you're well on your way to mastering another transferable skill: self-management. ▨

THINKING CRITICALLY IN THE CLASSROOM

Review the article "Discovering mastery" in this chapter. Then skim the profiles on the last page of each chapter throughout this book. Finally, choose one of the people profiled and describe in the space below how this person demonstrates mastery.

_____
_____
_____
_____
_____
_____
_____
_____
_____
_____
_____
_____

The critical thinking exercises that appear throughout this book incorporate ideas from Peter Facione, Dean of the College of Arts and Sciences, Santa Clara University, and creator of the California Critical Thinking Disposition Inventory. Mr. Facione provided substantial suggestions for these exercises and edited them. He can be contacted through the California Academic Press on the World Wide Web at **http://www.insightassessment.com/about.html.**

Adapted with permission from Critical Thinking: What It Is and Why It Counts *by Peter Facione (Millbrae, CA: The California Academic Press, 1996).*

→ Master Student Profiles

In each chapter of this text there is an example of a person who embodies several qualities of a master student. As you read about these people and others like them, ask yourself: How can I apply this? Look for the timeless qualities in the people you read about. Many of the strategies used by master students from another time or place are tools that you can use today.

The master students in this book were chosen because they demonstrate unusual and effective ways to learn.

Remember that these are just 10 examples of master students (one for each chapter). You can read more about them in the Master Student Hall of Fame at **masterstudent.college.hmco.com.** Also reflect on other master students you've read about or know personally. As you meet new people, look for those who excel at learning. The master student is not a vague or remote ideal. Rather, master students move freely among us.

In fact, there's one living inside your skin.

| Power Process | Career Application | Quiz | Learning Styles Application | Master Student Profile |

power process

Ideas are tools

There are many ideas in this book. When you first encounter them, don't believe any of them. Instead, think of them as tools.

For example, you use a hammer for a purpose—to drive a nail. When you use a new hammer, you might notice its shape, its weight, and its balance. You don't try to figure out whether the hammer is "right." You just use it. If it works, you use it again. If it doesn't work, you get a different hammer.

This is not the attitude most people adopt when they encounter new ideas. The first thing most people do with new ideas is to measure them against old ones. If a new idea conflicts with an old one, the new one is likely to be rejected.

People have plenty of room in their lives for different kinds of hammers, but they tend to limit their capacity for different kinds of ideas. A new idea, at some level, is a threat to their very being—unlike a new hammer, which is simply a new hammer.

Most of us have a built-in desire to be right. Our ideas, we often think, represent ourselves. And when we identify with our ideas, they assume new importance in our lives. We put them on our mantels. We hang them on our walls. We wear them on our T-shirts and display them on our bumpers. We join associations of people who share our most beloved ideas. We make up rituals about them, compose songs about them, and write stories about them. We declare ourselves dedicated to these ideas.

Some ideas are worth dying for. But please note: This book does not contain any of those ideas. The ideas on these pages are strictly "hammers."

Imagine someone defending a hammer. Picture this person holding up a hammer and declaring, "I hold this hammer to be self-evident. Give me this hammer or give me death. Those other hammers are flawed. There are only two kinds of people in this world: people who believe in this hammer and people who don't."

That ridiculous picture makes a point. This book is not a manifesto. It's a toolbox, and tools are meant to be used. This viewpoint is much like one advocated by psychologist and philosopher William James. His approach to philosophy, which he called "pragmatism," emphasized the usefulness of ideas as a criterion of truth.[8] James liked to talk about the "cash value" of an idea—whether it leads to new actions and new results.

If you read about a tool in this book that doesn't sound "right" or one that sounds a little goofy, remember that the ideas here are for using, not necessarily for believing. Suspend your judgment. Test the idea for yourself.

If it works, use it. If it doesn't, don't.

Ask: What if it's true?

When presented with a new idea, some of us take pride in being critical thinkers. We look for problems. We probe for weaknesses. We continue to doubt the idea until there's clear proof. Our main question seems to be "What's wrong with this idea?"

This approach can be useful when it is vital to expose flaws in ideas or reasoning. On the other hand, when we constantly look for what's wrong with new ideas, we might not recognize their value. A different and potentially more powerful approach is to ask yourself: What if that idea is true? This opens up all sorts of new possibilities and variations. Rather than looking for what's wrong, we can look for what's potentially valuable. Faced with a new idea, we can stay in the inquiry, look deeper, and go further.

Keep looking for answers

The light bulb, the airplane, the computer chip, the notion of the unconscious—these and many other tools became possible when their inventors practiced the art of continually looking for additional answers.

Another way to expand your toolbox is to keep on looking for answers. Much of your education will be about finding answers to questions. Every subject you study—from algebra to history to philosophy—poses a unique set of questions. Some of the most interesting questions are those that admit many answers: How can we create a just society? How can we transmit our values to the next generation? What are the purposes of higher education? How can we prevent an environmental crisis?

Other questions are more personal: What career shall I choose? Shall I get married? Where shall I live and how shall I spend my leisure time? What shall I have, do, and be during my time on earth?

Perhaps you already have answers to these questions. Answers are wonderful, especially when they relate to our most persistent and deeply felt questions. Answers can also get in the way. Once we're convinced that we have the "right" answer, it's easy to stop looking for more answers. We then stop learning. Our range of possible actions becomes limited.

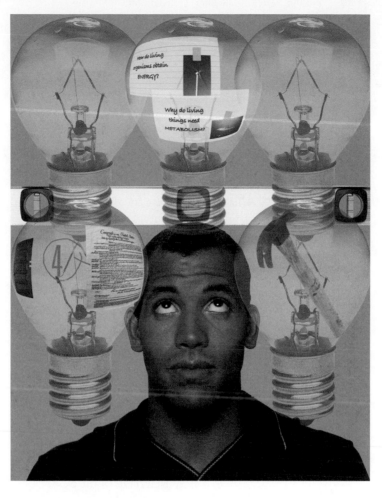

This book is not a manifesto. It's a toolbox, and tools are meant to be used.

Instead of latching on to one answer, we can look for more. Instead of being content with the first or easiest options that come to mind, we can keep searching. Even when we're convinced that we've finally handled a problem, we can brainstorm until we find five more solutions. Brainstorming can lead to creative thinking— a transferable skill that can help you to make new connections between seemingly unrelated ideas and to reveal new possibilities.

When we keep looking for answers, we uncover fresh possibilities for thinking, feeling, and behaving. Like children learning to walk, we experience the joy of discovery.

A caution

A word of caution: Any tool—whether it's a hammer, a computer program, or a study technique—is designed to do a specific job. A master mechanic carries a variety of tools because no single tool works for all jobs. If you throw a tool away because it doesn't work in one situation, you won't be able to pull it out later when it's just what you need. So if an idea doesn't work for you and you are satisfied that you gave it a fair chance, don't throw it away. File it away instead. The idea might come in handy sooner than you think.

And remember, this book is not about figuring out the "right" way. Even the "ideas are tools" approach is not "right."

It's a hammer . . . (or maybe a saw). ⊠

career application

Shortly after graduating with an A.A. degree in Business Administration, Sylvia Lopez was thrilled to land job as a staff accountant at a market research firm. After one week, she wanted to quit. She didn't think she would ever learn to deal with her coworkers. Their personalities just seemed too different.

For example, there was the account coordinator, Ed Washington. He spent hours a day on the phone calling prospective customers who responded to the corporate Web site. Since Ed's office door was always open and he had a loud voice, people inevitably overheard his calls. It seemed to Sylvia that he spent a lot of time socializing with clients—asking about their hobbies and family lives. Even though Ed was regarded as a skilled salesperson, Sylvia wondered when he actually got any work done.

Sylvia also felt uncomfortable with Linda Martinez, the firm's accounting analyst and her direct supervisor. Linda kept her office door closed most of the time. In contrast to Ed, Linda hardly ever stopped to chat informally. Instead of taking lunch breaks, she typically packed a bag lunch and ate it while checking e-mail or updating the company databases. Linda had a reputation as a top-notch employee. Yet the only time people saw her was at scheduled staff meetings. Linda led those meetings and distributed a detailed agenda in advance. And while Ed was on a first-name basis with everyone in the office, Linda made it clear that she wished to be addressed as "Ms. Martinez."

After worrying for several days about how to deal with the differences between her coworkers, Sylvia scheduled times to meet with Ed and Linda individually about her concerns. Before each meeting, she carefully prepared her opening remarks, writing them out beforehand. For Ed, her notes included this comment: "Since I'm new on the job and feel pressed for time, I'd prefer to keep our meetings short and get down to business right away." And for Linda she wrote: "I'd like to make sure my performance is up to par, but I don't see you very often. Is there any way I can get regular feedback from you about how I'm doing?" ☒

Reflect on this scenario:

1. How would you describe Ed's working style? How about Linda's?

   _____

   _____

   _____

2. Referring to the SCANS skills on page 8, list two transferable skills that Sylvia demonstrates in this scenario.

   _____

   _____

   _____

3. Using the same SCANS chart, identify two more skills that would be useful to Sylvia in this situation. Explain why you chose those two.

   _____

   _____

   _____

4. List two strategies from this chapter that would be useful to Sylvia in this situation. Briefly describe how she could apply each one.

   _____

   _____

   _____

Name _____ Date _____/_____/_____

quiz

1. Explain three ways that you can use knowledge of your learning styles to succeed in the workplace.

2. Define the term *mastery* as it is used in this chapter.

3. The First Step technique refers only to telling the truth about your areas for improvement. True or False? Explain your answer.

4. The four modes of learning are associated with certain questions. List the appropriate question for each mode.

5. According to the text, motivation is mysterious and hard to develop. True or False? Explain your answer.

6. According to the text, thinking of ourselves as creatures of habit can actually empower us. True or False? Explain your answer.

7. Briefly describe how being aware of your own multiple intelligences can help you thrive in selecting a major or career.

8. According to the Power Process: "Ideas are tools," if you want the ideas in this book to work, you must believe in them. True or False? Explain your answer.

9. Students who are skilled in metacognition can do which of the following:
  (A) Choose and apply various strategies for reading, writing, speaking, listening, managing time, and related tasks.
  (B) Modify strategies so that they work in several contexts.
  (C) Monitor their behavior and change habits.
  (D) State the ways that they'll benefit from learning a subject.
  (E) All of the above.

10. List two strategies that you can use to enhance kinesthetic learning.

learning styles application

Even though you have preferred ways to learn new ideas or skills, you can benefit from using several learning styles. The questions below will "cycle" you through four styles, or modes, of learning as explained earlier in this chapter. (See "Learning styles: Discovering how you learn.") Each question will help you explore a different mode.

Remember that you do not have to start with *Why?* of Mode 1. Any of the four questions can serve as your point of entry into the cycle of learning.

Look for a similar Learning Styles Application at the end of every chapter in this book. Also notice that the first page of each chapter includes a preview based on the four questions that represent the four modes of learning: *Why? What? How?* and *What if?*

what if
Review this chapter and the Introduction, looking for ideas that could help you make the transition from being in school to working in your next career. List two or three suggestions, stating each one in a short sentence.

why
Think about why the subject of transitions matters to you. Describe a major transition that you have experienced in the past. Examples might include changing schools, moving to a new city, starting a job, or going to college. In a sentence or two, describe what you did to cope with this change in your life.

how
In a short paragraph, explain how you can use one suggestion from this book to master a future transition that you will experience in education. Examples include declaring a major, changing majors, or transferring to a new school.

what
Review this chapter and the Introduction, looking for ideas that could help you make a major transition in your life. List two or three suggestions, stating each one in a short sentence.

master student

profile

MIKE LAZARIDIS

CEO of Research in Motion and father of the Blackberry

I*f we someday drive* floating cars without wheels, or sprint to neighboring solar systems, it may be because physicists have learned to manipulate gravity, or reconciled the contradictions between Einstein's relativity and quantum theory, and linked the atom to the black hole.

Mr. Lazaridis says it may take a half-century to produce a major breakthrough. By then, he will be 91. He's prepared to be patient.

His company, though hardly immune to the technology-sector meltdown, is a rare creation—a tech firm that invented something people can actually name. His brainchild, the result of a white paper he wrote in three hours on his basement computer in 1997, has changed the way users talk and work and move their thumbs.

The Blackberry caught on first with stockbrokers;[today] its name is becoming as ubiquitous as Kleenex.

Slightly larger than a credit card, with a keyboard that requires thumb type, the Blackberry has spawned new slang: "Berry me," addicts say, even on Parliament Hill. Back at the Research in Motion headquarters in

Waterloo, however, everybody—including the boss they call Mike—still uses the more traditional, "Send me an e-mail."

"His curiosity is beyond bounds," says Ray Laflamme, an associate physicist at the Perimeter. "He wants to know the little details of how things work and the big pictures of where things are going. And he wants to connect the dots in between."

In high school, he juggled shop classes with the academic courses required for college. He spent hours tinkering with the equipment that a wealthy benefactor had donated to the school—an example he follows with local schools today—and it was there that he and Mr. Fregin met John Micsinszki, the electronics shop teacher. Mr. Micsinszki let the boys use the lab during the summer, and would take Mr. Lazaridis to ham-radio swap meets, where he could buy parts on the cheap.

Mr. Lazaridis is generous in his credit for all his teachers, but it was Mr. Micsinszki who once said to him: "Don't get too hooked on computers. Someday the person who puts wireless and computers together is really going to make something."

Mr. Lazaridis sat in his basement at midnight and e-mailed to his office the white paper titled "Success Lies in Paradox." When, he asked, is a tiny keyboard more efficient than a large one? When you use your thumbs.

That became the blueprint for the Blackberry, and the engineers in "the pit" went to work finding ways to keep the power demands small and the capacity big on a device then the size of a hamburger. "Have you saved a milliwatt today?" became the company's unofficial in-house slogan.

Indeed, pushing Canadians to understand the value of investing in education and basic research has become Mr. Lazaridis's self-appointed mission. He believes most of us take them for granted. Canada is too small to be good at everything, he argues, but could be world-class at many things, including raising the most educated population on earth.

A wooden model of the Avro Arrow sits on his desk at RIM—a reminder, he says, of the country's "great engineering capabilities" and the danger of missed opportunities. "We need to focus," he says. "You can't solve problems without knowledge. It's logic. If we're expecting to make the right decision, we need to be properly educated." ▣

Reprinted with permission of *The Globe and Mail.*

For more biographical information on Mike Lazaridis, visit the Master Student Hall of Fame on the *Becoming a Master Student* Web site at

masterstudent.college.hmco.com

CHAPTER 2
Planning

The second chapter of *From Master Student to Master Employee* is all about planning. Planning is an important concept for first-year students. Whether they are traditional students attending college right out of high school or returning students attending college for the first time after an absence from formal education, your students each have only 168 hours per week to allocate their many priorities. Students preparing to demonstrate SCANS skills to employers will need to practice using their resources for allocating time for goal-related activities. The articles and exercises in this chapter will help your students to get started on the right foot.

In previewing this chapter with your students, remind students that time is an equal opportunity resource: All people, regardless of race, gender, creed, or national origin, have exactly the same number of hours per week. As your help your students with setting goals, prioritizing tasks and overcoming procrastination, remind them that planning increases their options. Planning offers all of us the freedom to act in response to our intentions, rather than to our moods. And planning vastly increases the odds of getting what we want.

Page 60
Master Student Map

Now that your students have completed their Learning Style Inventory in the previous chapter, they will find the framework for the Master Student Map easier to use as you begin your discussion of Chapter Two. Consider writing these questions on the chalkboard or whiteboard. Post them to your online course discussion board. Tap into all the different learning styles of your students by asking these questions in class:

why? Why does *From Master Student to Master Employee* cover the topic of planning?

what? What is planning? Read through the list of articles in this chapter and pick three that look interesting. What interests you about these three articles?

how? How would you rate your level of success with the ideas covered in this chapter? (How much do you already know about prioritizing your time or setting goals?)

what if? What if you start to apply these strategies to your life right now? And what if you don't?

Page 62
EXERCISE #5: "The Time Monitor/Time Plan process"

The Time Monitor/Time Plan requires some advance preparation. Ask your students to begin monitoring their time a week before you plan on teaching this chapter. When students complete the exercise prior to reading the chapter, they will be more motivated to learn the new strategies to help them make the most of their 168 hours per week. Get involved and show your students your commitment to this course by completing your own Time Monitor/Time Plan. When students bring their Time Monitor/Time Plan to class, ask them to talk about what they have discovered about their time management skills, and what they intend to do differently. What actions will they take to change their ways?

Page 67
Setting and achieving goals

Your student success course has specific goals for first year students. Most courses have a great emphasis on helping students with planning. Use your course goals to begin your discussion on goals in the classroom. Help your student to create a written plan (see Exercise #6 on page 69) for achieving personal and professional goals. One way to jumpstart this lesson plan is to have students complete an online exercise, *Create a Lifeline* on the *From Master Student to Master Employee* Web site (**masterstudent.college. hmco.com**). This exercise asks students to note milestones that they have already completed, and plan for those that they would like to complete in the future. This type of long-range planning helps students to make choices based on their plans and create their own experiences.

When students are creating effective goals, have them add a rating of priority (see "The ABC daily to-do list" on pages 70–71) and a timeline (or due date) for each goal. Remind students of the Power Process in Chapter One, "Discover what you want."

Page 70
The ABC daily to-do list

Many students have had prior experience with to-do lists. Their testimonials in class can help convince students who have not yet tried making to-do lists to experiment with them. The ABC priority aspect is usually a new concept for all students. Learning this technique helps them make better decisions about *what* to do and *when* to do it.

Page 72
Organizing time and tasks in the workplace

Use the diversity of experience in your class to have students talk about their experiences with managing time and tasks in the workplace. Multitasking has become a buzz-word around many busy offices. Ask your students to describe how macro-organizing and micro-organizing can help address the frustrations associated with multitasking.

voices

advisory board member

I am excited about the concepts of getting the big picture and macro-organizing [in the article "Organizing time and tasks in the workplace"]! The focus on micro-organizing is also excellent. I have found that many of my students in the past have trouble in both areas and I think making the distinction is essential and very needed in the presentation of time management.

—DR. JUDY BRANDON, CLOVIS COMMUNITY COLLEGE

Page 76
"But I don't know what I want to do"

First year college students are frequently asked, "What's your major?" Whether your students have declared a major upon entering college, or are not required to determine a major until after first semester, a majors discussion is important for all students. Help students make the connection between majors and careers by talking about short-term goals (selecting a major) and long-term goals (what they will do after graduation). For many students, this type of goal setting strikes fear into their hearts. Remind your students that they have the tools to help them to succeed. If your students need a jumpstart, refer them back to the charts with the article "Claiming your multiple intelligences" on pages 41–43.

Pages 80–81
The seven-day antiprocrastination plan *and* More ways to stop procrastination

Allocating time is a skill students will want to master in the classroom and in the workplace. Many students report that procrastination is their number one obstacle to success in school, work, and in their personal lives. Preview memory strategies and mnemonics by introducing

voices

consultant

Time-management discussion

When covering the ABC daily to-do's in Chapter Two, I ask my students to respond to a series of statements, such as "Think about the most important relationships in your life" and "Think about what you would do if you knew you had only one year left to live." I allow my students 5 to 10 minutes to write down whatever comes to mind. The goal is to get them thinking more about the big picture rather than having them catalog long lists of things to do. I ask them to organize—in outline form, pictorially, or in a few sentences—what they have written. Then, before we have a class discussion about their responses, I ask them to label these priorities A, B, or C. This experience allows students who do not really like to-do lists still to use the ABC priorities.

— MIKE ROBINSON

the seven-day antiprocrastination plan to your students. Have your students create a list of common reasons for procrastinating and then brainstorm solutions using the antiprocrastination strategies. Devise a class list of new strategies and consider posting it to your course Web site or typing it up and distributing it to your students for additional reference.

Page 82
25 ways to get the most out of now
Twenty-five may seem like too large of a number for students to master. Remind them that ideas are tools. Have your students select just 5 tools that they are interested in testing out and write an Intention Statement about how they plan to use these tools. After about a week, ask your students to report back on what they have discovered. Which of the tools will go to their toolboxes for later use? Which will they continue to apply? First-hand experience stories can be real motivational tools for the more reluctant students in your class.

Page 88
EXERCISE #9: "Master monthly calendar"
The words *planning* and *time management* strike terror in every student's heart. This is the number one skill research tells us that students need. Students cannot control time, but they *can* control the way they respond to it. They cannot control the past, but they *can* have an impact on their future by planning the semester. The master monthly calendar is an opportunity for you to work with your students to plan out an entire semester. Using the blank monthly calendar in the textbook (with additional sheets at the back of the text or available on the Master Student Web site), have students create their master plan based on the course syllabi from all of their classes. Transfer key dates for tests and papers and ask them to plug in interim deadlines, such as "Write draft of English paper." Some students have success with developing a master plan if during this exercise they also create a timeline for each of the bigger projects. An example of such a timeline is available on the HM ClassPrep CD.

Page 96
Career Application
Advisory Board member Kathy Scholljegerdes, Director of Career Services at Bethel College, suggests adding a question to the Career Application to help students to connect more deeply with the situation. "I would ask them to put themselves into Steve's place. 'If you were Steve, what would you do? Look at your goals [exercise] and decide how this situation would impact the goals you have set for yourself. Think of a couple of ways that you might handle the situation.'"

Page 99
Master Student Profile: Barbara Jordan
Ask your students to write a brief response paper after they read about the student success strategies Barbara Jordan used, as identified in this article. What strategy did Jordan use to help her to succeed in college? Some students focus on the study groups, while others point out that Jordan used the library as a quiet place for studying. Ask students to try one of these strategies and write about this as part of their response.

Page 102
POWER PROCESS: "Be here now"
Students often bring up the challenge of concentrating in class, and this simple yet powerful tool can help them focus their attention, whether it is in class, at work, or at play. I use an in-class exercise that asks students to "pay attention to their attention." Have students pair up and stand, facing each other, with their hands held up, palms facing their partner, but not touching. Students take turns as the leader, moving their hands around while their partners try to keep their hands aligned. Have your students vary their hand movements—up, down, forward, backward, and in random patterns—to provide an opportunity for their partners to practice "being here now."

MASTER Student

Course Manual

Planning is key to your success as an instructor of your course. Find **essentials for planning and instruction** in your *Course Manual*. Learn about the **values-based education** system integrated in *From Master Student to Master Employee* to understand the foundation of the study skills, life skills, and activities presented in the text. As you plan your course, create a **course purpose**. Get help determining which materials to cover when you're having difficulty picking and choosing. And if you are having trouble keeping your students on task, refer to the **classroom management and troubleshooting** techniques.

HM ClassPrep CD

PowerPoint for Chapter Two features information to help you assist students with planning.

Lecture ideas provide you with tools to promote planning as a tool that will set you free.

Applying skills provides ways to encourage your students to use the new information they have learned in this chapter.

Chapter Two **quiz answers** are available, as are **Test Bank** questions.

Chapter Two begins a discussion on goal setting that continues throughout the textbook. The HM ClassPrep CD will guide you on beginning this discussion, and help you to plan to carry this important topic throughout the term. Look for handouts related to goal setting, including a list of questions to help stimulate student's thinking about personal goals, additional exercises, and examples of SMART goals.

Additional Resources

masterstudent.college.hmco.com Integrate technology into your course. "The interactive time chart" and "Create a lifeline" exercises are interactive Web-based activities that will get the attention of your students no matter what their learning style is.

Find more biographical information about Master Student Barbara Jordan in our online **Master Student Hall of Fame**.

Use the **HM Assessment and Portfolio Builder** (available for packaging with your textbook) to guide your students toward their goals and use planning to expand their Accomplishments Report.

Begin discussions about **career planning** in your course, incorporating ideas students generate for their long-term goals, and connect with the Web-based **Career Resource Center** to begin planning.

2

Planning

Even if you are on the right track,
you'll get run over if you just sit there.

WILL ROGERS

When we are motivated by goals that have deep meaning,
by dreams that need completion, by pure love that needs
expressing, then we truly live life.

GREG ANDERSON

why
this chapter matters . . .

Your ability to manage time is a major
predictor of your success in school
and in the work world.

what
is included . . .

You've got the time
Setting and achieving goals
The ABC daily to-do list
Organizing time and tasks at work
Planning sets you free
"But I don't know what I want to do":
   Choosing a major
The seven-day antiprocrastination
   plan
25 ways to get the most out of now
Time management for right-brained
   people
Gearing up: Using a long-term planner
Strategies for even *longer*-term
   planning
Power Process: "Be here now"
Master Student Profile: Barbara Jordan

how
you can use this chapter . . .

Know exactly what you want to
   accomplish today, this month, this
   year—and beyond.
Eliminate stress due to poor planning
   and procrastination.
Gain the ability to focus your attention
   whenever you choose.

As you read, ask yourself
what if . . .

I could have more than enough time
   to accomplish whatever I choose?

You've got the time

The words *planning* and *time management* can call forth images of restriction and control. You might visualize a prune-faced Scrooge hunched over your shoulder, stopwatch in hand, telling you what to do every minute. Bad news. Good news: You do have enough time for the things you want to do. All it takes is learning to plan.

Planning is about time, and time is an equal opportunity resource. All of us, regardless of gender, race, creed, or national origin, have exactly the same number of hours in a week. No matter how newsworthy we are, no matter how rich or poor, we get 168 hours to spend each week—no more, no less.

Time is also an unusual commodity. It cannot be saved. You can't stockpile time like wood for the stove or food for the winter. It can't be seen, felt, touched, tasted, or smelled. You can't sense time directly. Even scientists and philosophers find it hard to describe. Because time is so elusive, it is easy to ignore. That doesn't bother time at all. Time is perfectly content to remain hidden until you are nearly out of it. And when you are out of it, you are out of it.

Time is a nonrenewable resource. If you're out of wood, you can chop some more. If you're out of money, you can earn a little extra. If you're out of love, there is still hope. If you're out of health, it can often be restored. But when you're out of time, that's it. When this minute is gone, it's gone. Time seems to pass at varying speeds. Sometimes it crawls and sometimes it's faster than a speeding bullet. On Friday afternoons, classroom clocks can creep. After you've worked a 10-hour day, reading the last few pages of an economics assignment can turn minutes into hours. A year in school can stretch out to an eternity. At the other end of the spectrum, time flies. There are moments when you are so absorbed in what you're doing that hours disappear like magic.

You can manage this commodity so you won't waste it or feel regretful about how you spent it. Approach time as if you are in control. Sometimes it seems that your friends control your time, that your boss controls your time, that your teachers or your parents or your kids or somebody else controls your time. Maybe that is not true. When you say you don't have enough time, you might really be saying that you are not spending the time you *do* have in the way that you want.

Planning involves determining what you want to achieve and how you intend to go about it. You can state your wants as written goals. Then use your time-management skills to schedule activities that will help you meet those goals. As you plan, be willing to include all areas of your life. In addition to setting academic goals, write down goals relating to your career, family life, social life, or anything else that matters to you.

Planning gives you a chance to spend your most valuable resource in the way you choose. Start by observing how you use time. The next exercise gives you this opportunity. ◼

journal entry 7

Discovery/Intention Statement

Completing this exercise will help you develop transferable skills associated with self-management—allocating time and paying attention to details. Think back to a time during the past year when you rushed to finish a project or when you did not find time for an activity that was important to you. List one thing you might have done to create this outcome.

I discovered that I . . .

_____

_____

_____

Take a few minutes to skim this chapter. Find three to five articles that might help you avoid such outcomes in the future and list them below.

Title   *Page number*

_____

_____

_____

_____

If you don't have time to read these articles in depth right now, schedule a time to do so.

I intend to . . .

_____

_____

_____

THE TIME MONITOR/TIME PLAN PROCESS

The purpose of this exercise is to transform time into a knowable and predictable resource. You can do this by repeating a two-phase cycle of monitoring and planning.

This exercise takes place over two weeks. During the first week, you can monitor your activities to get a detailed picture of how you spend your time. Then you can plan the second week thoughtfully. Monitor your time during the second week, compare it to your plan, and discover what changes you want to make in the following week's plan.

Monitor your time in 15-minute intervals, 24 hours a day, for seven days. Record how much time you spend sleeping, eating, studying, attending lectures, traveling to and from class, working, watching television, listening to music, taking care of the kids, running errands—everything.

If this sounds crazy, hang on for a minute. This exercise is not about keeping track of the rest of your life in 15-minute intervals. It is an opportunity to become conscious of how you spend your time, your life. Use the Time Monitor/Time Plan process only for as long as it is helpful to do so.

When you know how your time is spent, you can find ways to adjust and manage it so that you spend your life doing the things that are most important to you. Monitoring your time is a critical first step toward putting you in control of your life.

Some students choose to keep track of their time on 3x5 cards, calendars, campus planners, or software designed for this purpose. You might even develop your own form for monitoring your time.

1. Get to know the Time Monitor/Time Plan.
Look at the Time Monitor/Time Plan on pages 65–66. Note that each day has two columns, one labeled "monitor" and the other labeled "plan." During the first week, use only the "monitor" column. After that, use both columns simultaneously to continue the monitor-plan process.

To become familiar with the form, look at the example on page 63. When you begin an activity, write it down next to the time you begin and put a line just above that spot. Round off to the nearest 15 minutes. If, for example, you begin

Do this exercise online at

masterstudent.college.hmco.com

eating at 8:06, enter your starting time as 8:00. Over time, it will probably even out. In any case, you will be close enough to realize the benefits of this exercise. (Note that you can use the blank spaces in the "monitor" and "plan" columns to cover most of the day.)

On Monday, the student in this example got up at 6:45 a.m., showered, and got dressed. He finished this activity and began breakfast at 7:15. He put this new activity in at the time he began and drew a line just above it. He ate from 7:15 to 7:45. It took him 15 minutes to walk to class (7:45 to 8:00), and he attended classes from 8:00 to 11:00.

Keep your Time Monitor/Time Plan with you every minute you are awake for one week. Take a few moments every two or three hours to record what you've done. Or enter a note each time you change activities.

Here's an eye opener for many students. If you think you already have a good idea of how you manage time, predict how many hours you will spend in a week on each category of activity listed in the form on page 64. (Four categories are already provided; you can add more at any time.) Do this before your first week of monitoring. Write your predictions in the margin to the left of each category. After monitoring your time for one week, see how accurate your predictions were.

2. Remember to use your Time Monitor/Time Plan.
It might be easy to forget to fill out your Time Monitor/Time Plan. One way to remember is to create a visual reminder for yourself. You can use this technique for any activity you want to remember.

Relax for a moment, close your eyes, and imagine that you see your Time Monitor/Time Plan. Imagine that it has arms and legs and is as big as a person. Picture the form sitting at your desk at home, in your car, in one of your classrooms, or in your favorite chair. Visualize it sitting wherever you're likely to sit. When you sit down, the Time Monitor/Time Plan will get squashed.

You can make this image more effective by adding sound effects. The Time Monitor/Time Plan might scream, "Get off me!" Or since time can be related to money, you might associate the Time Monitor/Time Plan with the sound of an old-fashioned cash register. Imagine that every time you sit down, a cash register rings.

MONDAY 9 / 12

Monitor	Plan
Get up	
Shower	
7:00 ————	7:00
7:15 Breakfast	
7:30 ⊥	
7:45 Walk to	
8:00 class	8:00
8:15	
8:30 Econ 1	
8:45	
9:00	9:00
9:15	
9:30	
9:45	
10:00 Bio 1	10:00
10:15	
10:30	
10:45	
11:00	11:00
11:15 Study	
11:30	
11:45	
12:00	12:00
12:15 Lunch	
12:30	
12:45	
1:00	1:00
1:15 Eng. Lit	
1:30	
1:45	
2:00	2:00
2:15 Coffeehouse	
2:30	
2:45	
3:00	3:00
3:15	
3:30	
3:45	
4:00	4:00
4:15 Study	
4:30	
4:45	
5:00	5:00
5:15 Dinner	
5:30	
5:45	
6:00	6:00
6:15	
6:30 Work at restaurant	
6:45	
7:00	7:00

TUESDAY 9 / 13

Monitor	Plan
Sleep	
7:00	7:00
7:15	
7:30	
7:45 Shower	
8:00 Dress	8:00
8:15 Eat	
8:30	
8:45	
9:00 Art	9:00
9:15 Apprec.	
9:30 Project	
9:45	
10:00	10:00
10:15	
10:30	
10:45	
11:00 Data	11:00
11:15 process	
11:30	
11:45	
12:00	12:00
12:15	
12:30	
12:45	
1:00	1:00
1:15 Lunch	
1:30	
1:45	
2:00 Work	2:00
2:15 on book	
2:30 report	
2:45	
3:00 Art	3:00
3:15 Apprec.	
3:30	
3:45	
4:00	4:00
4:15	
4:30	
4:45	
5:00 Dinner	5:00
5:15	
5:30	
5:45	
6:00 Letter to	6:00
6:15 Uncle Jim	
6:30	
6:45	
7:00	7:00

3. Evaluate the Time Monitor/Time Plan.

After you've monitored your time for one week, group your activities together by categories. The form on page 64 lists the categories "sleep," "class," "study," and "work." Think of other categories you could add. "Grooming" might include showering, putting on makeup, brushing teeth, and getting dressed. "Travel" can include walking, driving, taking the bus, and riding your bike. Other categories might be "exercise," "entertainment," "meals," "television," "domestic," and "children."

Write in the categories that work for you, and then add up how much time you spent in each of your categories. Put the totals in the "monitored" column on page 64. Make sure that the grand total of all categories is 168 hours.

Now take a minute and let these numbers sink in. Compare your totals to your predictions and notice your reactions. You might be surprised. You might feel disappointed or even angry about where your time goes. Use those feelings as motivation to plan your time differently. Go to the "planned" column and decide how much time you want to spend on various daily activities. As you do so, allow yourself to have fun. Approach planning in the spirit of adventure. Think of yourself as an artist who's creating a new life.

In several months you might want to take another detailed look at how you spend your life. You can expand the two-phase cycle of monitoring and planning to include a third phase: evaluating. Combine this with planning your time, following the suggestions in this chapter. You can use a continuous cycle: monitor, evaluate, plan; monitor, evaluate, plan. When you make it a habit, this cycle can help you get the full benefits of time management for the rest of your life. Then time management becomes more than a technique. It's transformed into a habit, a constant awareness of how you spend your lifetime.

Planning is a broad word that refers to all aspects of creating a vision for your future. Goal setting, time management, budgeting—all are tools that allow you to maximize your freedom and live a full life. Few architects propose a building project without a blueprint. Few entrepreneurs get venture capital without a sound business plan. And few film producers begin shooting a movie without a script. In each case, the rationale is to avoid actions that waste time, money, effort, and talent. In this light, it's amazing that so many people lack a plan for something as important as their own lives.

Planning and motivation are mutually reinforcing. When your goals connect to your deepest desires, you discover new reserves of energy. Moving into action becomes almost effortless. When you clearly define a goal, your mind and body start to operate more consistently in ways to achieve your dreams. As you meet goals and cross them off your list, you experience the satisfaction of success.

Look for extra copies of the Time Monitor/Time Plan at the back of this book.

WEEK OF ___ / ___ / ___ /		
Category	**Monitored**	**Planned**
Sleep		
Class		
Study		
Work		

MONDAY __ / __ / __ /	
Monitor	**Plan**
7:00	7:00
7:15	
7:30	
7:45	
8:00	8:00
8:15	
8:30	
8:45	
9:00	9:00
9:15	
9:30	
9:45	
10:00	10:00
10:15	
10:30	
10:45	
11:00	11:00
11:15	
11:30	
11:45	
12:00	12:00
12:15	
12:30	
12:45	
1:00	1:00
1:15	
1:30	
1:45	
2:00	2:00
2:15	
2:30	
2:45	
3:00	3:00
3:15	
3:30	
3:45	
4:00	4:00
4:15	
4:30	
4:45	
5:00	5:00
5:15	
5:30	
5:45	
6:00	6:00
6:15	
6:30	
6:45	
7:00	7:00
7:15	
7:30	
7:45	
8:00	8:00
8:15	
8:30	
8:45	
9:00	9:00
9:15	
9:30	
9:45	
10:00	10:00
10:15	
10:30	
10:45	
11:00	11:00
11:15	
11:30	
11:45	
12:00	12:00

TUESDAY __ / __ / __ /	
Monitor	**Plan**
7:00	7:00
7:15	
7:30	
7:45	
8:00	8:00
8:15	
8:30	
8:45	
9:00	9:00
9:15	
9:30	
9:45	
10:00	10:00
10:15	
10:30	
10:45	
11:00	11:00
11:15	
11:30	
11:45	
12:00	12:00
12:15	
12:30	
12:45	
1:00	1:00
1:15	
1:30	
1:45	
2:00	2:00
2:15	
2:30	
2:45	
3:00	3:00
3:15	
3:30	
3:45	
4:00	4:00
4:15	
4:30	
4:45	
5:00	5:00
5:15	
5:30	
5:45	
6:00	6:00
6:15	
6:30	
6:45	
7:00	7:00
7:15	
7:30	
7:45	
8:00	8:00
8:15	
8:30	
8:45	
9:00	9:00
9:15	
9:30	
9:45	
10:00	10:00
10:15	
10:30	
10:45	
11:00	11:00
11:15	
11:30	
11:45	
12:00	12:00

WEDNESDAY __ / __ / __ /	
Monitor	**Plan**
7:00	7:00
7:15	
7:30	
7:45	
8:00	8:00
8:15	
8:30	
8:45	
9:00	9:00
9:15	
9:30	
9:45	
10:00	10:00
10:15	
10:30	
10:45	
11:00	11:00
11:15	
11:30	
11:45	
12:00	12:00
12:15	
12:30	
12:45	
1:00	1:00
1:15	
1:30	
1:45	
2:00	2:00
2:15	
2:30	
2:45	
3:00	3:00
3:15	
3:30	
3:45	
4:00	4:00
4:15	
4:30	
4:45	
5:00	5:00
5:15	
5:30	
5:45	
6:00	6:00
6:15	
6:30	
6:45	
7:00	7:00
7:15	
7:30	
7:45	
8:00	8:00
8:15	
8:30	
8:45	
9:00	9:00
9:15	
9:30	
9:45	
10:00	10:00
10:15	
10:30	
10:45	
11:00	11:00
11:15	
11:30	
11:45	
12:00	12:00

THURSDAY ___ / ___ / ___ /		FRIDAY ___ / ___ / ___ /		SATURDAY ___ / ___ / ___ /	
Monitor	Plan	Monitor	Plan	Monitor	Plan
7:00	7:00	7:00	7:00		
7:15		7:15			
7:30		7:30			
7:45		7:45			
8:00	8:00	8:00	8:00		
8:15		8:15			
8:30		8:30			
8:45		8:45			
9:00	9:00	9:00	9:00		
9:15		9:15			
9:30		9:30			
9:45		9:45			
10:00	10:00	10:00	10:00		
10:15		10:15			
10:30		10:30			
10:45		10:45			
11:00	11:00	11:00	11:00		
11:15		11:15			
11:30		11:30			
11:45		11:45			
12:00	12:00	12:00	12:00		
12:15		12:15			
12:30		12:30			
12:45		12:45			
1:00	1:00	1:00	1:00		
1:15		1:15			
1:30		1:30			
1:45		1:45			
2:00	2:00	2:00	2:00		
2:15		2:15			
2:30		2:30			
2:45		2:45			
3:00	3:00	3:00	3:00		
3:15		3:15			
3:30		3:30			
3:45		3:45			
4:00	4:00	4:00	4:00		

SUNDAY ___ / ___ / ___ /	
Monitor	Plan

THURSDAY (cont.)		FRIDAY (cont.)	
4:15		4:15	
4:30		4:30	
4:45		4:45	
5:00	5:00	5:00	5:00
5:15		5:15	
5:30		5:30	
5:45		5:45	
6:00	6:00	6:00	6:00
6:15		6:15	
6:30		6:30	
6:45		6:45	
7:00	7:00	7:00	7:00
7:15		7:15	
7:30		7:30	
7:45		7:45	
8:00	8:00	8:00	8:00
8:15		8:15	
8:30		8:30	
8:45		8:45	
9:00	9:00	9:00	9:00
9:15		9:15	
9:30		9:30	
9:45		9:45	
10:00	10:00	10:00	10:00
10:15		10:15	
10:30		10:30	
10:45		10:45	
11:00	11:00	11:00	11:00
11:15		11:15	
11:30		11:30	
11:45		11:45	
12:00	12:00	12:00	12:00

Discovery Statement

After one week of monitoring my time, I discovered that . . .

_____

_____

_____

_____

_____

I want to spend more time on . . .

_____

_____

_____

I want to spend less time on . . .

_____

_____

_____

_____

I was surprised that I spent so much time on . . .

_____

_____

_____

_____

I was surprised that I spent so little time on . . .

_____

_____

_____

I had strong feelings about my use of time when (describe the feeling and the situation) . . .

_____

_____

_____

_____

Setting and achieving goals

Many of us have vague, idealized notions of what we want out of life. These notions float among the clouds in our heads. They are wonderful, fuzzy, safe thoughts such as "I want to be a good person," "I want to be financially secure," or "I want to be happy."

If you really want to meet a goal, translate it into specific, concrete behaviors. Find out what that goal looks like. Listen to what it sounds like. Pick it up and feel how heavy that goal is. Inspect the switches, valves, joints, cogs, and fastenings of the goal. Make your goal as real as a chain saw. There is nothing vague or fuzzy about chain saws. You can see them, feel them, and hear them. They have a clear function. Goals can be every bit as real and useful. And the ability to set and achieve goals enhances several transferable skills—allocating time and monitoring and correcting your performance.

If you really want to meet a goal, translate it into specific, concrete behaviors.

Writing down your goals exponentially increases your chances of meeting them. Writing exposes undefined terms, unrealistic time frames, and other symptoms of fuzzy thinking. If you've been completing Intention Statements as explained in the Introduction to this book, then you've already had experience writing goals. Goals and Intention Statements both address changes you want to make in your behavior, your values, your circumstances—or all of these. To keep track of your goals, write each one on a separate 3x5 card or key them all into a word processing file on your computer.

There are many useful methods for setting goals. Following is one of them. In this method, the key words to remember are _specific, time, areas,_ and _reflect._ Combine the first letter of each word and you get the acronym _STAR._ Use this acronym to remember the suggestions that follow.

Write specific goals. Suppose that one of your goals is to become a better student by studying harder. You're headed in a powerful direction; now go for the specifics. Translate that goal into a concrete action, such as "I will study two hours for every hour I'm in class." Specific goals make clear what actions are needed or what results are expected. Consider these examples:

Vague goal	Specific goal
Get a good education.	Graduate with an AA degree in medical assistance, with honors, by 2009.
Enhance my spiritual life.	Meditate for 15 minutes daily.
Improve my appearance.	Lose six pounds during the next six months.

When stated specifically, a goal might look different to you. If you examine it closely, a goal you once thought you wanted might not be something you want after all. Or you might discover that you want to choose a new path to achieve a goal that you are sure you want.

Write goals in several time frames. To get a comprehensive vision of your future, write down:

- *Long-term goals.* Long-term goals represent major targets in your life. These goals can take 5 to 20 years to achieve. In some cases, they will take a lifetime.

- *Mid-term goals.* Mid-term goals are objectives you can accomplish in one to five years. They include goals such as completing a course of education, paying off a car loan, or achieving a specific career level. These goals usually support your long-term goals.

- *Short-term goals.* Short-term goals are the ones you can accomplish in a year or less. These goals are specific achievements, such as completing a particular course or group of courses, hiking down the Appalachian Trail, or organizing a family reunion.

Write goals in several areas of life. People who set goals in only one area of life—such as their career—can find that their personal growth becomes one-sided. To avoid this outcome, set goals in a variety of categories. Consider what you want to experience in your:

- education
- career
- financial life
- family life
- social life
- spiritual life
- level of health.

Add goals in other areas as they occur to you.

Reflect on your goals. Each week, take a few minutes to think about your goals. You can perform the following "spot checks":

- *Check in with your feelings.* Think about how the process of setting your goals felt. Consider the satisfaction you'll gain in attaining your objectives. If you don't feel a significant emotional connection with a written goal, consider letting it go or filing it away to review later.

- *Check for alignment.* Look for connections between your goals. Do your short-term goals align with your mid-term goals? Will your mid-term goals help you achieve your long-term goals?

- *Check for obstacles.* All kinds of things can come between you and your goals, such as constraints on time and money. Anticipate obstacles and start looking now for workable solutions.

- *Check for immediate steps.* Here's a way to link goal setting to time management. Decide on a list of small, achievable steps you can take right away to accomplish each of your short-term goals. Write these small steps down on a daily to-do list. If you want to accomplish some of them by a certain date, enter them in a calendar that you consult daily. Then, over the coming weeks, review your to-do list and calendar. Take note of your progress and celebrate your successes. ◪

GET REAL WITH YOUR GOALS

One way to make goals effective is to examine them up close. That's what this exercise is about. Using a process of brainstorming and evaluation, you can break a long-term goal into smaller segments until you have taken it completely apart. When you analyze a goal to this level of detail, you're well on the way to meeting it.

For this exercise, you will use a pen, extra paper, and a watch with a second hand. (A digital watch with a built-in stopwatch is even better.) Timing is an important part of the brainstorming process, so follow the stated time limits. This entire exercise takes about an hour. Use it to set and meet any goal related to your education, career, or personal life.

Part one: Long-term goals

Brainstorm. Begin with an eight-minute brainstorm. For eight minutes write down everything you think you want in your life. Write as fast as you can and write whatever comes into your head. Leave no thought out. Don't worry about accuracy. The object of a brainstorm is to generate as many ideas as possible. Use a separate sheet of paper for this part of the exercise.

Evaluate. After you have finished brainstorming, spend the next six minutes looking over your list. Analyze what you wrote. Read the list out loud. If something is missing, add it. Look for common themes or relationships between goals. Then select three long-term goals that are important to you—goals that will take many years to achieve. Write these goals below in the space provided.

_____

_____

_____

Before you continue, take a minute to reflect on the process you've used so far. What criteria did you use to select your top three goals? For example, list some of the core values (such as love, wealth, or happiness) underlying these goals.

Part two: Mid-term goals

Brainstorm. Read out loud the three long-term goals you selected in Part One. Choose one of them. Then brainstorm a list of goals you might achieve in the next one to five years that would lead to the accomplishment of that

Do this exercise online at

masterstudent.college.hmco.com

one long-term goal. These are mid-term goals. Spend eight minutes on this brainstorm. Remember, neatness doesn't count. Go for quantity.

Evaluate. Analyze your brainstorm of mid-term goals. Then select three that you determine to be important in meeting the long-term goal you picked. Allow yourself six minutes for this part of the exercise. Write your selections below in the space provided.

_____

_____

_____

Again, pause for reflection before going on to the next part of this exercise. Why do you see these three goals as more important than the other mid-term goals you generated? Write about your reasons for selecting these three goals.

Part three: Short-term goals

Brainstorm. Review your list of mid-term goals and select one. In another eight-minute brainstorm, generate a list of short-term goals—those you can accomplish in a year or less that will lead to the attainment of that mid-term goal. Write down everything that comes to mind. Do not evaluate or judge these ideas yet. For now, the more ideas you write down, the better.

Evaluate. Analyze your list of short-term goals. The most effective brainstorms are conducted by suspending judgment, so you might find some bizarre ideas on your list. That's fine. Now is the time to cross them out. Next evaluate your remaining short-term goals and select three that you are willing and able to accomplish. Allow yourself six minutes for this part of the exercise, then write your selections below in the space provided.

_____

_____

_____

The more you practice, the more effective you can be at choosing goals that have meaning for you. You can repeat this exercise, employing the other long-term goals you generated or creating new ones. By using this brainstorm and evaluation process, you can make goals come to life in the here and now.

One of the most effective ways to stay on track and actually get things done is to use a daily to-do list. While the Time Monitor/Time Plan gives you a general picture of the week, your daily to-do list itemizes specific tasks you want to complete within the next 24 hours.

The ABC daily to-do list

One advantage of keeping a daily to-do list is that you don't have to remember what to do next. It's on the list. A typical day in the life of a student is full of separate, often unrelated tasks—reading, attending lectures, reviewing notes, working at a job, writing papers, researching special projects, running errands. It's easy to forget an important task on a busy day. When that task is written down, you don't have to rely on your memory.

The following steps present one method for to-do lists. Experiment with these steps, modify them as you see fit, and invent new techniques that work for you.

Step 1 Brainstorm tasks. To get started, list all of the tasks you want to get done tomorrow. Each task will become an item on a to-do list. Don't worry about putting the entries in order or sched-

uling them yet. Just list everything you want to accomplish on a sheet of paper or a planning calendar, or in a special notebook. You can also use 3x5 cards, writing one task on each card. Cards work well because you can slip them into your pocket, rearrange them, and you never have to copy to-do items from one list to another.

Step 2 Estimate time. For each task you wrote down in step 1, estimate how long it will take you to complete it. This can be tricky. If you allow too little time, you end up feeling rushed. If you allow too much time, you become less productive. For now, give it your best guess. Your estimates will improve with practice. Now pull out your calendar or Time Monitor/Time Plan. You've probably scheduled some hours for activities such as classes or work. This leaves the unscheduled hours for tackling your to-do lists.

Add up the time needed to complete all your to-do items. Also add up the number of unscheduled hours in your day. Then compare the two totals. The power of this step is that you can spot overload in advance. If you have eight hours' worth of to-do items but only four unscheduled hours, that's a potential problem. To solve it, proceed to step 3.

Step 3 Rate each task by priority.
To prevent overscheduling, decide which to-do items are the most important given the time you have available. Learning how to create a to-do list that ranks activities in order of importance is a transferable skill with extremely high returns. One suggestion for doing this comes from the book *Take Control of Your Time and Life* by Alan Lakein: Simply label each task A, B, or C.[1]

The A's on your list are those things that are the most critical. These are assignments that are coming due or jobs that need to be done immediately. Also included are activities that lead directly to your short-term goals.

The B's on your list are important, but less so than the A's. B's might someday become A's. For the present, these tasks are not as urgent as A's. They can be postponed, if necessary, for another day.

The C's do not require immediate attention. C priorities include activities such as "shop for a new blender" and "research computer training courses on the Internet." C's are often small, easy jobs with no set timeline. These, too, can be postponed.

Once you've labeled the items on your to-do list, schedule time for all of the A's. The B's and C's can be done randomly during the day when you are in between tasks and are not yet ready to start the next A.

Step 4 Cross off tasks.
Keep your to-do list with you at all times, crossing off activities when you finish them and adding new ones when you think of them. If you're using 3x5 cards, you can toss away or recycle the cards with completed items. Crossing off tasks and releasing cards can be fun—a visible reward for your diligence. This step fosters a sense of accomplishment.

When using the ABC priority method, you might experience an ailment common to students: C fever. This is the uncontrollable urge to drop that A task and begin crossing C's off your to-do list. If your history paper is due tomorrow, you might feel compelled to vacuum the rug, call your third cousin in Tulsa, and make a trip to the store for shoelaces. The reason C fever is so common is that A tasks are usually more difficult or time-consuming to achieve, with a higher risk of failure.

If you notice symptoms of C fever, ask: Does this job really need to be done now? Do I really need to alphabetize my CD collection, or might I better use this time to study for tomorrow's data processing exam? Use your to-do list to keep yourself on task, working on your A's. Don't panic or berate yourself when you realize that in the last six hours, you have completed 11 C's and not a single A. Calmly return to the A's.

Step 5 Evaluate.
At the end of the day, evaluate your performance. Look for A priorities you didn't complete. Look for items that repeatedly turn up as B's or C's on your list and never seem to get done. Consider changing these to A's or dropping them altogether. Similarly, you might consider changing an A that didn't get done to a B or C priority. When you're done evaluating, start on tomorrow's to-do list. Be willing to admit mistakes. You might at first rank some items as A's only to realize later that they are actually C's. Some of the C's that lurk at the bottom of your list day after day might really be A's. When you keep a daily to-do list, you can adjust these priorities *before* they become problems.

The ABC system is not the only way to rank items on your to-do list. Some people prefer the "80-20" system. This is based on the idea that 80 percent of the value of any to-do list comes from only 20 percent of the tasks on that list. So on a to-do list of 10 items, find the two that will contribute most to your life, and complete those tasks without fail.

Another option is to rank items as "yes," "no," or "maybe." Do all of the tasks marked "yes." Ignore those marked "no." And put all of the "maybe's" on the shelf for later. You can come back to the "maybe's" at a future point and rank them as "yes" or "no."

Or you can develop your own style for to-do lists. You might find that grouping items by categories such as "errands" or "reading assignments" works best. Be creative.

Keep in mind the power of planning a whole week or even two weeks in advance. Planning in this way can make it easier to put activities in context and see how your daily goals relate to your long-term goals. Weekly planning can also free you from feeling that you have to polish off your whole to-do list in one day. Instead, you can spread tasks out over the whole week.

In any case, make starting your own to-do list an A priority. ✖

Organizing time and tasks at work

Getting organized and staying that way will serve you in any career you choose. Following are techniques that can help you stay on top of your workload and focus on what's important. In addition, you will develop a cluster of transferable skills related to allocating time—along with the personal qualities of responsibility and self-management. Many of these ideas can also help you manage time at school and at home.

To succeed at getting organized, think in terms of two broad strategies. First, get the big picture—what you intend to accomplish this month, this quarter, this year, and beyond. Another name for this is *macro-organizing*. (*Macro* is a prefix that means "large" or "inclusive.")

Second, set priorities for your day-to-day, hour-to-hour tasks. This process of working with shorter time intervals can be called *micro-organizing*. (*Micro* means "small.")

Macro-organizing

Get real with project due dates. The more complicated the project, the more you can benefit from getting organized. This is especially true with projects that extend well into the future.

Start by scheduling a long-term goal—the due date for the final product. Next, set interim due dates—what you'll produce at key points leading up to that final date. These interim dates function as mid-term goals. In turn, each mid-term goal can lead you to more immediate, short-term goals.

For example, say that you're a computer technician and your team plans to complete a major hardware and software upgrade for your company in one year (long-term goal). As a team, set goals for finishing major parts of this project, such as due dates for installing new computers in individual departments (mid-term goals). You could also set up meetings with each department head over the next month to update them on your plans (short-term goals).

You may end up juggling several major projects at once. To plan effectively, enter all the relevant due dates in a weekly or monthly calendar so that you can see several of them at a glance.

Think beyond the next project. As you schedule projects, take some time to lift your eyes to the horizon. Step back for a few minutes and consider your longer-range goals—what you want to accomplish at your job and in your career in the next six months, the next year, and the next five years.

Ask whether the activities you've scheduled actually contribute to those goals. If they do, great. If not, determine whether you can delete some items from your daily calendar and to-do list to free up more hours for meeting longer-term goals.

Monitor work time and tasks. Another way to get a big picture of your work life is to look for broad patterns in how you currently spend your work time. Use the Time Monitor/Time Plan explained earlier in this chapter to do this analysis. Find out which tasks burn up most of your hours on the job.

With this data in hand, you can make immediate choices to minimize downtime and boost your productivity. Start by looking for low-value activities to eliminate. Also note your peak periods of energy during the workday. Schedule your most challenging tasks for these times.

Micro-organizing

Schedule fixed blocks of time first. Start with recurring meetings, for instance. These time periods are usually determined in advance and occur at regular times each week or month. Be realistic about how much time you need for such events. Then schedule other tasks around them.

Set realistic goals. Don't set yourself up for failure by telling yourself you can do a four-hour job in two hours. There are only 40 to 50 hours in a typical full-time workweek. If you schedule 65 hours, you've lost before you begin.

This is where your Time Monitor/Time Plan can really help. Monitor your time often to obtain a realistic idea of how long it takes to complete typical tasks. This will help you in scheduling future projects.

Allow flexibility in your schedule. Recognize that unexpected things will happen, and plan for them. Leave some holes in your schedule. Build in blocks of unplanned time. Consider setting aside time each week marked "flextime" or "open time." Use these hours for emergencies, spontaneous activities, catching up, or seizing new opportunities.

Set clear starting and stopping times. Tasks often expand to fill the time we allot for them. "It always takes me two hours just to deal with my e-mails each day" might become a self-fulfilling prophecy.

Try scheduling a certain amount of time for reading and responding to e-mail. Set a timer and stick to it. People often find that they can gradually decrease such time by forcing themselves to work a little more efficiently. This can usually be done without sacrificing the quality of your work.

Feeling rushed or sacrificing quality is not the goal here. The point is to push ourselves a little and discover what our time requirements really are.

Calculate the cost of attending meetings. Meetings can eat up hours each week. If you're in a management or supervisory position, in fact, meetings can make up most of your job. The problem is that some meetings take place without a clear agenda. Or the discussion wanders off in irrelevant directions, agreements are not clarified, and the people who attend fail to take follow-up action.

To get a concrete sense of such problems, calculate what it costs you to attend meetings. On your Time Monitor/ Time Plan, add up the number of hours you spend in meetings each week. Then multiply this number by your hourly wage. The result is how much it costs you to attend those meetings. (If you receive a salary instead of an hourly wage, estimate the total number of hours you will work this year. Then take your gross annual salary and divide it by this total. This will give you an hourly "wage.")

Knowing how many dollars it costs to attend meetings can motivate you to use that time wisely. Write an Intention Statement about how you plan to get the most value out of upcoming meetings. See if you can stop attending meetings that consistently fail to produce any value.

Involve others when appropriate. Sometimes the activities we schedule depend on gaining information, assistance, or direct participation from supervisors or other coworkers. If we neglect to inform them of our plans or forget to ask for their cooperation at the outset—surprise! Our schedules can crash.

Statements such as these often follow the breakdown: "I just assumed you were free for a working lunch at 11:30 p.m. on Tuesday." Or "I'm working overtime this month and hoped that you'd lead the weekly staff meetings for a while."

When you schedule a task that depends on another person's involvement, let that person know—the sooner, the better.

Avoid the perils of multitasking. Our effectiveness often decreases when we try to do several things at once, such as talking on a cell phone while driving. When you get busy at work, you might feel tempted to multitask. Yet studies indicate that multitasking reduces metabolic activity in the brain, lowers ability to complete tasks efficiently, and increases the number of errors made in following a procedure.[2]

To avoid these problems, plan your workday as a succession of tasks, then do each task with full attention. Use the ABC priority system to weed out tasks of lower importance. This can give you more time to focus on the A's. ◪

exercise 7

CHOOSE STRATEGIES TO MANAGE TIME AND TASKS

Read the article "Organizing time and tasks at work." Then choose one technique to apply—preferably within the next 24 hours. In the space below, summarize that technique in one sentence:

_____

_____

After using the technique for at least one week and observing the results, use the space below to describe how well it worked for you:

_____

_____

If the technique worked well, consider making it a habit. If it did *not* work well, list a way to modify the strategy so that it becomes a better fit for you:

_____

_____

WIDER

TALLER

Planning
sets you free

When you plan, you can create freedom. This contradicts the common notion of planning: "Me? Plan? No way. I don't want to be uptight. I don't want to be restrained. I don't want to lose my spontaneity. I don't want to be some tense person who never gets to have any fun. I want to be free."

One freedom in planning stems from the simple fact that you set the plan. The course and direction are yours. Often, particularly at work or in school, people do not feel this way. They feel that the plan is coming from someone else—an employer, a supervisor, or a teacher.

Consider that this view is inaccurate. If we look ahead into the future, we can choose to see any circumstance as part of a plan for our whole lives. Even when we don't like aspects of a job, for example, working provides income and helps us develop useful skills for the next job. When we plan far enough in advance, a job no longer has to feel limiting.

You can change the plan

Another freedom in planning is the freedom to make changes. An effective plan is flexible, not carved in stone. Tell people that you have a 20-year plan for your career. They might ask, "Well, if the economy changes, would you consider changing your plan?" "Yes," you reply. "I change it every year." Then comes the laughter: "Well, it really isn't a 20-year plan if you change it every year. It's actually a one-year plan."

In reality, we can change our plans frequently and still preserve the advantages of long-range planning. Those advantages come from choosing our overall direction and taking charge of our lives.

You choose how to achieve the plan

Suppose you take a new job and with it comes a detailed agenda of goals to achieve in one year. You might say, "I didn't choose these goals. I guess I'll just have to put up with them." There is another point of view you can take in this situation: Even when others select the goals, you can choose whether to accept them. You can also choose your own way to achieve any goal. The outcome might be determined for you, but the way you produce that outcome can be up to you.

When there's a plan, there's a chance

Planning to meet a goal doesn't ensure accomplishment, but it does boost the odds of success. Your clearly defined goals and carefully chosen action plans increase the probability that you'll achieve what you want. You have a goal. You've laid out the necessary actions in logical sequence. And you've set a due date to perform each action. Now the goal seems possible, whereas before it might have seemed impossible.

Much of what people undertake at school, at work, in relationships, and at home is simply "digging in"—frantic action with no plan. "Sure, we might never reach the goal," they say, "but at least we're out there trying." In this statement we hear a loss of hope. Planning can replace despair with a purpose and a timeline.

Planning frees you from constant decisions

When we operate without a plan, we might change our minds often: "Hmmm. . . . That chocolate cake smells great. Maybe I'll have a piece—but maybe I shouldn't. It's a lot of calories. I don't know. . . ." That kind of debate takes up a lot of time and energy.

But suppose you plan to stop eating chocolate cake. You write down this plan. You speak about this plan to friends, even commit yourself to it in their presence. Temptation still occurs: "Gee, that cake smells great." But then you remember: "Wait. I don't have to make this decision now. I'll just follow my plan and avoid chocolate cake."

Planning makes adjustments easier

Suppose you are scheduled to give a talk in your speech class next week. Suddenly you find out there was a misprint in the course schedule. You're supposed to speak two days from now, not seven. Without a plan, you would face a lengthy mental process, a whole series of questions: What will I do now? When will I have time to get that speech done? How will this affect the rest of my schedule?

With a plan, things are different. You might say, "I don't have to worry about this. I've done my plan for the week, and I know I have free time tomorrow night between 7 and 10 p.m. I can finish the speech then."

Planning enables you to respond to crises—or opportunities. With a plan, you are free to handle unexpected change. With a plan, you can take initiative rather than merely react. When you plan, you *give* your time to things instead of allowing things to *take* your time.

Planning is about creating your own experience. When you plan, your life does not just "happen." When you plan, you are the equal of the greatest sculptor, painter, or playwright. More than creating a work of art, you are designing a life.

"But I don't know what I want to do"
Choosing a major

One decision that troubles many students in higher education is the choice of an academic major. Here is an opportunity to apply your skills of critical thinking, decision making, and problem solving. The following suggestions can guide you through this process.

Link choosing a major to getting what you want

Your choice of a major can fall into place once you determine what you want in life. Before you choose a major, back up to a bigger picture. List your core values, such as contribution to society, wealth, recognition, health, or fun. Also write goals for what you want to accomplish in 5 years, 10 years, or even 50 years from today. After doing these things, choosing a major can seem like a piece of cake.

Many students find that the prospect of getting what they want in life is what justifies all the time, money, and day-to-day effort invested in going to school. Having a major gives you a powerful incentive for attending classes, taking part in discussions, reading textbooks, writing papers, and completing other assignments. When you see a clear connection between completing school and creating the life of your dreams, then the daily tasks of higher education become charged with meaning.

Studies indicate that the biggest factor associated with finishing a degree in higher education is commitment to personal goals.[3] A choice of major is one of those goals, and selecting the appropriate

courses to complete your major is a form of planning that directly promotes your success.

Your career goals can have a big impact on your choice of major. For an overview of this topic and an immediate chance to put ideas on paper, see "Career planning: Begin the process now" in Chapter Nine.

Just choose, now

Don't delay in experiencing the benefits of choosing a major. Even if you say that you're undecided right now, you probably know a lot about what your major's going to be.

To verify this, do a short experiment. Search your school's catalog, online or in print, for a list of available majors. Read through the list two or three times. Then pretend that you have to choose a major today. Write down the first three ideas that come to mind.

Hold on to this list, which reflects your intuition or "gut wisdom," as you perform the more intellectual task of researching various majors and careers in detail. Your research may lead to a new choice of major—or it may simply confirm one of the majors on your original list.

Test your trial choice

When you've made a trial choice of major, take on the role of a scientist. Treat your choice as a hypothesis and then design a series of experiments to test it. For example, try the following:

- Study your school's list of required courses for this major, looking for a fit with your interests and long-term goals.

- Visit with instructors who teach courses in the major and ask them about required course work and career options in the field.

- Discuss your trial choice with an academic advisor or career counselor.

- Enroll in a course related to your possible major.

- Find a volunteer experience, internship, part-time job, or service learning experience related to the major.

- Meet informally with students who have declared the same major.

- Interview someone who works in a field related to the major.

If these experiences confirm your choice of major, celebrate that fact. If they result in choosing a new major, celebrate that outcome as well.

Ask other people for ideas

Other people might have valuable suggestions about a choice of major or career for you. Ask key people in your life for their ideas and listen with an open mind.

At the same time, resist any pressure from family members or friends to choose a major or career that fails to interest you. People define success in different ways. Someone else's definition might not agree with yours. If you choose a career based solely on other people's expectations, you could end up with a job you don't enjoy—and a major barrier to your life satisfaction.

Learn more about yourself

Choosing a major can be more effective when you begin from a basis of self-knowledge. As you learn about your passions and potentials, in your current job and while in school, let your choice of a major reflect that ongoing discovery.

The exercises and Journal Entries in this book are a starting place. As you complete them, look for insights that bear on your choice of major.

Another path to self-knowledge includes questionnaires or inventories that are designed to correlate your interests with specific career choices. Your academic advisor or someone at your school's career planning and job placement office can give you more details about these inventories. You might wish to take several of them and meet with an advisor to interpret the results.

Remember that no questionnaire, inventory, test, or other tool can tell you exactly what career to choose or what goals to set for the rest of your life. Likewise, no expert can make these choices for you. Inventories can help you gain self-knowledge, and other people can offer valuable perspectives. However, what you do with the knowledge you gain is entirely up to you. The only expert on your life choices is you.

Invent a major

When choosing a major, you might not need to limit yourself to those listed in your course catalog. Many schools now have flexible programs that allow for independent study. Through such programs you might be able to combine two existing majors or invent an entirely new one of your own.

Choose a complementary minor

You can add flexibility to your academic program through your choice of a minor to complement or contrast with your major. For example, the student who wants to be a minister could opt for a minor in English; all of those courses in composition can help in writing sermons. Or the student with a major in psychology might choose a minor in business administration with the idea of managing a counseling service someday. An effective choice of a minor can expand your skills and career options.

Remember that you can change your mind

Keep your choice of a major in perspective. There is probably no single "correct" choice for you. Rather, your unique collection of skills is likely to give you the basis for several majors.

The odds are that you'll change your major at least once—and that you'll change careers several times during your life. You may even pursue a career that's unrelated to your major.

Students often find that their choice of a major does not bind them to a certain job or career. Many of the majors offered in higher education can help you prepare for several different careers or for further study in graduate school. One benefit of higher education is mobility—gaining transferable skills that can help you move into a new career field at any time.

Viewing a major as a one-time choice that determines your future can raise your stress levels to artificially high levels. Instead, look at choosing a major as the start of a continuing path of discovery, intention, and action. ✖

→ Majors for the taking

The variety of majors available in higher education is staggering. Below, for example, is a list of 100 majors culled from the catalogs of several colleges.

Accounting
Actuarial Science
Advertising
Aerospace Engineering
African American and African
 Studies
Agronomy
American Indian Studies
American Studies
Anthropology
Architecture
Art
Astronomy
Biochemistry
Biology
Botany
Broadcast Engineering
Building Construction
Chemical Engineering
Chemistry
Chicano Studies
Child Psychology
Civil Engineering
Clothing Design
Computer Engineering
Construction Management
Corrections Management
Criminal Justice
Dance
Dental Hygiene
Dentistry
Dietetics
Economics
Education

Electrical Engineering
English
Environmental Sciences
Equestrian Studies
Exercise and Sport Science
Family Social Science
Fashion Design and Merchandising
Film Studies
Finance
Fisheries and Wildlife
Food Science
Forestry
Geography
Geological Engineering
Geology
Geophysics
Global Studies
Graphic Arts
History
Hospital Administration
Hospitality and Tourism Services
Human Resource Development
Industrial Psychology
Industrial Technology
Interior Design
International Relations
Jewish Studies
Journalism
Kinesiology
Labor Relations
Latin
Liberal Studies
Library Science
Linguistics

Management Information Systems
Marketing
Mass Communication
Mathematics
Mechanical Engineering
Medical Records Services
Medical Technology
Merchandising
Meteorology
Microbiology
Music
Nursing
Personnel Management
Pharmacy
Philosophy
Physical Therapy
Physics
Physiology
Political Science
Psychology
Public Relations
Religious Studies
Retail Merchandising
Scientific and Technical
 Communication
Sociology
Speech and Hearing Science
Statistics
Substance Abuse Counseling
Theatre Arts
Theology
Urban Studies
Women's Studies
Zoological Sciences

This is not an exhaustive list. You'll find additional examples in your own school catalog.

Many schools also allow for double majors, individually designed majors, interdepartmental majors, and minors in many areas. You have plenty of options for creating a course of study that matches your skills, interests, and passions.

exercise 8

MAKE A TRIAL CHOICE OF MAJOR

Read the list of majors in the sidebar "Majors for the taking." Expand this list by adding majors listed in your own school's catalog.

Next, take your expanded list and cross out all the majors that you already know are not right for you. You will probably eliminate well over half the list.

Now scan the remaining majors. Next to the ones that definitely interest you, write "yes." Next to majors that you're willing to consider but are unsure about, write "maybe."

Focus on your "yes" choices. See if you can narrow this list down to three majors. List those here.

_____

_____

_____

Finally, mark an asterisk next to the major that interests you most right now. This is your trial choice of major.

desk of . . .

from the

ANDY FISHER,
EXECUTIVE MARKETING MANAGER,
MARKET RESEARCH & DEVELOPMENT:

While the courses were important, and many apply to "technical" skills that I use every day (i.e., data analysis), the personal/social aspects of my college career were perhaps more important. It's through those aspects that I learned about time management, prioritization, project management, and people management skills.

journal entry 9

Discovery/Intention Statement

Reflect for a moment on your experience with Exercise #8. If you had already chosen a major, did it confirm that choice? Did you uncover any new or surprising possibilities for declaring a major?

I discovered that I . . .

_____

_____

_____

_____

_____

Now, list the major that is your top choice for right now. Also list publications you will find and people you will consult to gather more information about this major.

I intend to . . .

_____

_____

_____

_____

_____

_____

_____

_____

_____

Plan to repeat this Journal Entry and the preceding exercise several times. You may find yourself researching several majors and changing your mind. That's fine. The aim is to start thinking about your major now.

MONDAY	TUESDAY	WEDNESDAY	THURSDAY	FRIDAY	SATURDAY	SUNDAY
Make it meaningful.	Take it apart.	Write an intention statement.	Tell everyone.	Find a reward.	Settle it now.	Say no.

The seven-day
antiprocrastination plan

L isted here are seven strategies you can use to reduce or eliminate many sources of procrastination. The suggestions are tied to the days of the week to help you remember them. Use this list to remind yourself that each day of your life presents an opportunity to stop the cycle of procrastination.

1 Make it meaningful. What is important about the task you've been putting off? List all the benefits of completing it. Look at it in relation to your short-, mid-, or long-term goals. Be specific about the rewards for getting it done, including how you will feel when the task is completed. To remember this strategy, keep in mind that it starts with the letter *M*, like the word *Monday*.

2 Take it apart. Break big jobs into a series of small ones you can do in 15 minutes or less. If a long reading assignment intimidates you, divide it into two-page or three-page sections. Make a list of the sections and cross them off as you complete them so you can see your progress. Even the biggest projects can be broken down into a series of small tasks. This strategy starts with the letter *T*, so mentally tie it to *Tuesday*.

3 Write an intention statement. For example, if you can't get started on a term paper, you might write, "I intend to write a list of at least 10 possible topics by 9 p.m. I will reward myself with an hour of guilt-free Web surfing." Write your intention on a 3x5 card and carry it with you, or post it in your study area where you can see it often. In your memory, file the first word in this strategy—*write*—with *Wednesday*.

4 Tell everyone. Publicly announce your intention to get a task done. Tell a friend that you intend to learn 10 irregular French verbs by Saturday. Tell your spouse, roommate, parents, and children. Include anyone who will ask whether you've completed the assignment or who will suggest ways to get it done. Make the world your support group. Associate *tell* with *Thursday*.

5 Find a reward. Construct rewards to yourself carefully. Be willing to withhold them if you do not complete the task. Don't pick a movie as a reward for completing a report at work if you plan to go to the movie anyway. And when you legitimately reap your reward, notice how it feels. Remember that *Friday* is a fine day to *find* a reward. (Of course, you can find a reward on any day of the week. Rhyming Friday with fine day is just a memory trick.)

6 Settle it now. Do it now. The minute you notice yourself procrastinating, plunge into the task. Imagine yourself at a cold mountain lake, poised to dive. Gradual immersion would be slow torture. It's often less painful to leap. Then be sure to savor the feeling of having the task behind you. Link *settle* with *Saturday*.

7 Say no. When you keep pushing a task into a low-priority category, re-examine your purpose for doing it at all. If you realize that you really don't intend to do something, quit telling yourself that you will. That's procrastinating. Just say no. Then you're not procrastinating. You don't have to carry around the baggage of an undone task. *Sunday*—the last day of this seven-day plan—is a great day to finally let go and just *say* no. ⊠

→ More ways to stop procrastination

Perhaps you didn't get around to using the seven-day antiprocrastination plan. Well, there's plenty more where that plan came from. Consider seven more suggestions.

Trick yourself into getting started. Practice being a con artist—and your own unwitting target. If you have a 50-page chapter to read, grab the book and say to yourself, "I'm not really going to read this chapter right now. I'm just going to flip through the pages and scan the headings for ten minutes." If you have a paper due next week, say, "I'm not really going to outline this paper today. I'll just spend five minutes writing anything that comes into my head about the assigned topic."

Tricks like these can get you started on a task you've been dreading. Once you get started, you might find it easy to keep going.

Choose to work under pressure. Sometimes people thrive under pressure. As one writer put it, "I don't do my best work because of a tight timeline. I do my only work with a tight timeline." Used selectively, this strategy might also work for you.

Put yourself in control. You might consciously choose to work with a timeline staring you in the face. If you do, then schedule a big block of time right before your project is due. Until then, enjoy!

Take it easy. You can find shelves full of books with techniques for overcoming procrastination. Resist the temptation to use all of these techniques at once. You could feel overwhelmed, give up, and sink back into the cycle of procrastination.

Instead, make one small, simple change in behavior—today. Tomorrow, make the change again. Take it day by day until the new behavior becomes a habit. One day you might wake up and discover that procrastination is part of your past.

THINKING CRITICALLY IN THE WORKPLACE

Some thoughts fuel procrastination and keep you from experiencing success at work. Psychologists Jane Burka and Lenora Yuen list these examples:[4]

I must be perfect.
Everything I do should go easily and without effort.
It's safer to do nothing than to take a risk and fail.
If it's not done right, it's not worth doing at all.
If I do well this time, I must always do well.
If I succeed, someone will get hurt.

Choose one of these statements—or think of a similar one—and write a sentence or two about how it could promote procrastination.

_____

_____

_____
_____
_____
_____
_____
_____
_____

In the space below, create an alternative to the statement you just wrote about. Write a sentence that puts you back in charge of your time and no longer offers an excuse for procrastination. For example: "Even if I don't complete a task perfectly, I can give it my best shot and learn from my mistakes."

_____
_____
_____
_____
_____
_____

25 ways to
get the most out of **now**

The following time-management techniques are about:

- **When to study**
- **Where to study**
- **Ways to handle the rest of the world**
- **Things to ask yourself if you get stuck**

Don't feel pressured to use all of the techniques listed here or to tackle them in order. As you read, note the suggestions you think will be helpful. Pick one technique to use now. When it becomes a habit, come back to this article and select another one. Repeat this cycle and enjoy the results as they unfold in your life. Mastery of allocating time and following schedules are transferable skills that can improve your performance in the classroom and in the workplace.

When to study

1 **Study difficult (or "boring") subjects first.** If your algebra problems put you to sleep, get to them first, while you are fresh. We tend to give top priority to what we enjoy studying, yet the courses we find most difficult often require the most creative energy. Save your favorite subjects for later. If you find yourself avoiding a particular subject, get up an hour earlier to study it before breakfast. With that chore out of the way, the rest of the day can be a breeze.

Continually being late with course assignments indicates a trouble area. Further action is required. Clarify your intentions about the course by writing down your feelings in a journal, talking with an instructor, or asking for help from a friend or counselor. Consistently avoiding study tasks can also be a signal to re-examine your major or course program.

2 **Be aware of your best time of day.** Many people learn best in daylight hours. If this is true for you, schedule study time for your most difficult subjects before nightfall.

Unless you grew up on a farm, the idea of being conscious at 4 a.m. might seem ridiculous. Yet many successful business people begin the day at 5 a.m. or earlier. Athletes and yogis use this time, too. Some writers complete their best work before 9 a.m.

For others, the same benefits are experienced by staying up late. They flourish after midnight. If you aren't convinced, then experiment. When you're in a time crunch, get up early or stay up late. You might even see a sunrise.

3 Use waiting time. Five minutes waiting for a subway, 20 minutes waiting for the dentist, 10 minutes in between classes—waiting time adds up fast. Have short study tasks ready to do during these periods. For example, you can carry 3x5 cards with facts, formulas, or definitions and pull them out anywhere.

A digital voice recorder can help you use commuting time to your advantage. Make tape cassettes of yourself reading your notes. Then play these tapes in a car stereo as you drive, or listen through your headphones as you ride on the bus or subway.

Where to study

4 Use a regular study area. Your body and your mind know where you are. Using the same place to study, day after day, helps train your responses. When you arrive at that particular place, you can focus your attention more quickly.

5 Study where you'll be alert. In bed, your body gets a signal. For most students, that signal is more likely to be "Time to sleep!" than "Time to study!" Just as you train your body to be alert at your desk, you also train it to slow down near your bed. For that reason, don't study where you sleep.

Easy chairs and sofas are also dangerous places to study. Learning requires energy. Give your body a message that energy is needed. Put yourself in a situation that supports this message.

Some schools offer empty classrooms as places to study. Many students report finding themselves studying effectively in a classroom setting.

6 Use a library. Libraries are designed for learning. The lighting is perfect. The noise level is low. A wealth of material is available. Entering a library is a signal to focus the mind and get to work. Many students can get more done in a shorter time frame at the library than anywhere else. Experiment for yourself.

desk of...

from the

JONATHAN WOLF,
LIBRARY INFORMATION ASSISTANT:

Time management is the key to keeping my commitments of career and personal life separate, but focused. I have to understand what each part of my life requires of me and how much time I can dedicate to this event. Once that is calculated and prioritized I try to maximize my free time while reducing time spent on lower-level goals. This increases my choices on how to spend this time, which reduces stress and confusion.

Ways to handle the rest of the world

7 Pay attention to your attention. Breaks in concentration are often caused by internal interruptions. Your own thoughts jump in to divert you from your studies. When this happens, notice these thoughts and let them go.

Perhaps the thought of getting something else done is distracting you. One option is to handle that other task now and study later. Or you can write yourself a note about it, or schedule a specific time to do it.

8 Agree with living mates about study time. This includes roommates, spouses, and children. Make the rules clear, and be sure to follow them yourself. Explicit agreements—even written contracts—work well. One student always wears a colorful hat when he wants to study. When his wife and children see the hat, they respect his wish to be left alone.

9 Get off the phone. The telephone is the ultimate interrupter. People who wouldn't think of distracting you might call at the worst times because they can't see that you are studying. You don't have to be a telephone victim. If a simple "I can't talk, I'm studying" doesn't work, use dead silence. It's a conversation killer. Or short-circuit the whole problem: Unplug the phone. Other solutions include turning off your cell phone and studying at the library.

10 Learn to say no. This is a timesaver and a valuable life skill for everyone. Some people feel it is

rude to refuse a request. But saying no can be done effectively and courteously. Others want you to succeed as a student. When you tell them that you can't do what they ask because you are busy educating yourself, most people will understand.

11 Hang a "do not disturb" sign on your door. Many hotels will give you a free sign, for the advertising. Or you can create a sign yourself. They work. Using signs can relieve you of making a decision about cutting off each interruption—a timesaver in itself.

12 Get ready the night before. Completing a few simple tasks just before you go to bed can help you get in gear the next day. If you need to make some phone calls first thing in the morning, look up those numbers, write them on 3x5 cards, and set them near the phone. If you need to drive to a new location, make note of the address and put it next to your car keys. If you plan to spend the next afternoon writing a paper, get your materials together: dictionary, notes, outline, paper, and pencil (or disks and portable computer). Pack your lunch or gas up the car. Organize your diaper bag, briefcase, or backpack.

13 Call ahead. We often think of talking on the telephone as a prime time-waster. Used wisely, the telephone can actually help manage time. Before you go shopping, call the store to see if it carries the items you're looking for. If you're driving, call for directions to your destination. A few seconds on the phone can save hours in wasted trips and wrong turns.

14 Avoid noise distractions. To promote concentration, avoid studying in front of the television and turn off the radio. Many students insist that they study better with background noise, and this might be true. Some students report good results with carefully selected and controlled music. For many others, silence is the best form of music to study by.

At times noise levels might be out of your control. A neighbor or roommate might decide to find out how far he can turn up his boom box before the walls crumble. Meanwhile, your ability to concentrate on the principles of sociology goes down the drain. To avoid this scenario, schedule study sessions during periods when your living environment is usually quiet. If you live in a residence

hall, ask if study rooms are available. Or go somewhere else where it's quiet, such as the library. Some students have even found refuge in quiet cafés, self-service laundries, and places of worship.

15 Notice how others misuse your time. Be aware of repeat offenders. Ask yourself if there are certain friends or relatives who consistently interrupt your study time. If avoiding the interrupter is impractical, send a clear message. Sometimes others don't realize that they are breaking your concentration. You can give them a gentle yet firm reminder. If this doesn't work, there are methods to make your message more effective. For more ideas, see Chapter Eight: Communicating.

Things to ask yourself if you get stuck

16 Ask: What is one task I can accomplish toward achieving my goal? This is a helpful technique to use when faced with a big, imposing job. Pick out one small accomplishment, preferably one you can complete in about five minutes; then do it. The satisfaction of getting one thing done can spur you on to get one more thing done. Meanwhile, the job gets smaller.

> ### Keep on going?
>
> Some people keep on going, even when they get stuck or fail again and again. To such people belongs the world. Consider the hapless politician who compiled this record:
>
> - Failed in business, 1831
> - Defeated for legislature, 1832
> - Second failure in business, 1833
> - Suffered nervous breakdown, 1836
> - Defeated for Speaker, 1838
> - Defeated for Elector, 1840
> - Defeated for Congress, 1843
> - Defeated for Senate, 1855
> - Defeated for Vice President, 1856
> - Defeated for Senate, 1858
> - Elected President, 1860
>
> Who was the fool who kept on going in spite of so many failures?
>
> Answer: The fool was Abraham Lincoln.

17 **Ask: Am I being too hard on myself?** If you are feeling frustrated with a reading assignment, if your attention wanders repeatedly, or if you've fallen behind on math problems that are due tomorrow, take a minute to listen to the messages you are giving yourself. Are you scolding yourself too harshly? Lighten up. Allow yourself to feel a little foolish and then get on with the task at hand. Don't add to the problem by berating yourself.

Worrying about the future is another way people beat themselves up: How will I ever get all this done? What if every paper I'm assigned turns out to be this hard? If I can't do the simple calculations now, how will I ever pass the final? Instead of promoting learning, such questions fuel anxiety.

Labeling and generalizing weaknesses are other ways people are hard on themselves. Being objective and specific will help eliminate this form of self-punishment and will likely generate new possibilities. An alternative to saying "I'm terrible in algebra" is to say "I don't understand factoring equations." This rewording suggests a plan to improve.

18 **Ask: Is this a piano?** Carpenters who construct rough frames for buildings have a saying they use when they bend a nail or accidentally hack a chunk out of a two-by-four: "Well, this ain't no piano." It means that perfection is not necessary. Ask yourself if what you are doing needs to be perfect. Perhaps you don't have to apply the same standards of grammar to lecture notes that you would apply to a term paper. If you can complete a job 95 percent perfectly in two hours and 100 percent perfectly in four hours, ask yourself whether the additional 5 percent improvement is worth doubling the amount of time you spend.

Sometimes it *is* a piano. A tiny miscalculation can ruin an entire lab experiment. A misstep in solving a complex math problem can negate hours of work. Computers are notorious for turning little errors into nightmares. Accept lower standards only when appropriate.

A related suggestion is to weed out low-priority tasks. The to-do list for a large project can include dozens of items, not all of which are equally important. Some can be done later, while others could be skipped altogether, if time is short.

Apply this idea when you study. In a long reading assignment, look for pages you can skim or skip. When it's appropriate, read chapter summaries or article abstracts. As you review your notes, look for material that might not be covered on a test and decide whether you want to study it.

19 **Ask: Would I pay myself for what I'm doing right now?** If you were employed as a student, would you be earning your wages? Ask yourself this question when you notice that you've taken your third snack break in 30 minutes.

Or consider that students who skip class are sacrificing the tuition they've already paid for that class. If they use that time to goof off rather than work at a paid job, they are paying twice for their decision.

Most students are, in fact, employed as students. They are investing in their own productivity and paying a big price for the privilege of being a student. Sometimes they don't realize that doing a mediocre job now might result in fewer opportunities for the future.

20 **Ask: Can I do just one more thing?** Ask yourself this question at the end of a long day. Almost always you will have enough energy to do just one more short task. The overall increase in your productivity might surprise you.

21 **Ask: Am I making time for things that are important but not urgent?** If we spend most of our time putting out fires, we can feel drained and frustrated. According to Stephen R. Covey, this happens when we forget to take time for things that are not urgent but are truly important.[5] Examples include exercising regularly, reading, praying or meditating, spending quality time alone or with family members and friends, traveling, and cooking nutritious meals. Each of these can contribute directly to a long-term goal or life mission. Yet when schedules get tight, we often forgo these things, waiting for that elusive day when we'll "finally have more time."

That day won't come until we choose to make time for what's truly important. Knowing this, we can use some of the suggestions in this chapter to free up more time.

22 **Ask: Can I delegate this?** Instead of slogging through complicated tasks alone, you can draw on the talents and energy of other people. Busy executives know the value of delegating tasks to coworkers. Without delegation, many projects would flounder or die.

You can apply the same principle. Instead of doing all the housework or cooking by yourself, for example, you can assign some of the tasks to family members or roommates. Rather than making a trip to the library to look up a simple fact, you can call and ask a library assistant to research it for you. Instead of driving across town to deliver a package, you can hire a delivery service to do so. All of these tactics can free up extra hours for studying.

It's not practical to delegate certain study tasks, such as writing term papers or completing reading assignments. However, you can still draw on the ideas of others in completing such tasks. For instance, form a writing group to edit and critique papers, brainstorm topics or titles, and develop lists of sources.

If you're absent from a class, find a classmate to summarize the lecture, discussion, and any upcoming assignments. Presidents depend on briefings. You can use this technique, too.

23 Ask: How did I just waste time? Notice when time passes and you haven't accomplished what you had planned to do. Take a minute to review your actions and note the specific ways you wasted time. We tend to operate by habit, wasting time in the same ways over and over again. When you are aware of things you do that drain your time, you are more likely to catch yourself in the act next time. Observing one small quirk might save you hours. But keep this in mind: Asking you to notice how you waste time is not intended to make you feel guilty. The point is to increase your skill by getting specific information about how you use time.

24 Ask: Could I find the time if I really wanted to? The way people speak often rules out the option of finding more time. An alternative is to speak about time with more possibility.

The next time you're tempted to say, "I just don't have time," pause for a minute. Question the truth of this statement. Could you find four more hours this week for studying? Suppose that someone offered to pay you $10,000 to find those four hours. Suppose, too, that you will get paid only if you don't lose sleep, call in sick for work, or sacrifice anything important to you. Could you find the time if vast sums of money were involved?

Remember that when it comes to school, vast sums of money *are* involved.

25 Ask: Am I willing to promise it? This might be the most powerful time-management idea of all. If you want to find time for a task, promise yourself— and others—that you'll get it done.

To make this technique work, do more than say that you'll try or that you'll give it your best shot. Take an oath, as you would in court. Give it your word.

One way to accomplish big things in life is to make big promises. There's little reward in promising what's safe or predictable. No athlete promises to place seventh in the Olympic games. Chances are that if we're not making big promises, we're not stretching ourselves.

The point of making a promise is not to chain ourselves to a rigid schedule or to impossible expectations. We can also promise to reach goals without unbearable stress. We can keep schedules flexible and carry out our plans with ease, joy, and satisfaction.

At times we can go too far. Some promises are truly beyond us, and we might break them. However, failing to keep a promise is just that—failing to keep a promise. A broken promise is not the end of the world.

Promises can work magic. When our word is on the line, it's possible to discover reserves of time and energy we didn't know existed. Promises can push us to exceed our expectations. ◪

Time management for right-brained people

Ask some people about managing time, and a dreaded image appears in their minds.

(. . . or what to do if to-do lists are not your style)

They see a person with a 50-item to-do list clutching a calendar chock-full of appointments. They imagine a robot who values cold efficiency, compulsively accounts for every minute, and is too rushed to develop personal relationships. Often this image is what's behind the comment "Yeah, there are some good ideas in those time-management books, but I'll never get around to using them. Too much work."

The trick is to discover what works for you. A few basic principles can do that as well as a truckload of cold-blooded time-management techniques.

Know your values. As a thought-provoking exercise, write your own obituary. Describe the way you want to be remembered. List the contributions you intend to make during your lifetime. If this is too spooky, write a short mission statement for your life—a paragraph that describes your values and the kind of life you want to lead. Periodically during the day, stop to ask if what you're doing is contributing to those goals.

Do less. Managing time is as much about dropping worthless activities as about adding new and useful ones. The idea is to weed out those actions that deliver little reward.

Decide right now to eliminate activities with a low payoff. When you add a new item to your schedule, consider dropping a current one.

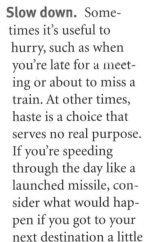

Slow down. Sometimes it's useful to hurry, such as when you're late for a meeting or about to miss a train. At other times, haste is a choice that serves no real purpose. If you're speeding through the day like a launched missile, consider what would happen if you got to your next destination a little bit later than planned. Rushing to stay a step ahead might not be worth the added strain.

Remember people. Efficiency is a concept that applies to things—not people. When it comes to maintaining and nurturing relationships, we can often benefit from loosening up our schedules. We can allow extra time for conflict management, spontaneous visits, and free-ranging conversations.

Focus on outcomes. You might feel guilty when you occasionally stray from your schedule and spend two hours napping or watching soap operas. But if you're regularly meeting your goals and leading a fulfilling life, there's probably no harm done. When managing time, the overall goal of personal effectiveness counts more than the means used to achieve it. This can be true even when your time-management style differs from that recommended by experts.

Handle it now. A backlog of unfinished tasks can result from postponing decisions or procrastinating. An alternative is to handle the task or decision immediately. Answer that letter now. Make that phone call as soon as it occurs to you. You can also save time by graciously saying no immediately to projects that you don't want to take on. Saying "I'll think about it and get back to you later" might mean that you'll have to take more time to say no later.

Buy less. Before you purchase an item, estimate how much time it will take to locate, assemble, use, repair, and maintain it. You might be able to free up hours by doing without. If the product comes with a 400-page manual or 20 hours of training, beware.

Forget about time. Schedule "downtime"—a period when you're accountable to no one else and have nothing to accomplish—into every day. This is time to do nothing, free of guilt. Even a few minutes spent in this way can yield a sense of renewal.

Take time to retreat from time. Create a sanctuary, a haven, a safe place in your life that's free from any hint of schedules, lists, or accomplishments. One of the most effective ways to manage time is periodically to forget about it. ◙

MASTER MONTHLY CALENDAR

This exercise will give you an opportunity to step back from the details of your daily schedule and get a bigger picture of your life. The more difficult it is for you to plan beyond the current day or week, the greater the benefit of this exercise.

Your basic tool is a one-month calendar. Use it to block out specific times for upcoming events, such as study group meetings, due dates for assignments, review periods before tests, and other time-sensitive tasks.

To get started, you might want to copy the blank monthly calendar on page 89 onto both sides of a sheet of paper. Or make several copies of these pages and tape them together so that you can see several months at a glance.

Also be creative. Experiment with a variety of uses for your monthly calendar. For instance, you can note day-to-day changes in your health or moods, list the places you visit while you are on vacation, or circle each day that you practice a new habit. For examples of filled-in monthly calendars, see below.

MONDAY	TUESDAY	WEDNESDAY	THURSDAY	FRIDAY	SATURDAY	SUNDAY

Name _____   Month _____

Gearing up:
Using a long-term planner

Planning a day, a week, or a month ahead is a powerful practice. Using a long-term planner—one that displays an entire quarter, semester, or year at a glance—can yield even more benefits.

With a long-term planner, you can eliminate a lot of unpleasant surprises. Long-term planning allows you to avoid scheduling conflicts—the kind that obligate you to be in two places at the same time three weeks from now. You can also anticipate busy periods, such as finals week, and start preparing for them now. Good-bye, all-night cram sessions. Hello, serenity.

Find a long-term planner, or make your own. Many office supply stores carry academic planners in paper form that cover an entire school year. Computer software for time management offers the same feature. You can also be creative and make your own long-term planner. A big roll of newsprint pinned to a bulletin board or taped to a wall will do nicely.

Enter scheduled dates that extend into the future. Use your long-term planner to list commitments that extend beyond the current month. Enter test dates, lab sessions, days that classes will be canceled, and other events that will take place over this term and next term.

Create a master assignment list. Find the syllabus for each course you're currently taking. Then, in your long-term planner, enter the due dates for all of the assignments in all of your courses. This can be a powerful reality check.

The purpose of this technique is not to make you feel overwhelmed with all the things you have to do. Rather, its aim is to help you take a First Step toward recognizing the demands on your time. Armed with the truth about how you use your time, you can make more accurate plans.

Armed with the truth about how you use your time, you can make more accurate plans.

Include nonacademic events. In addition to tracking academic commitments, you can use your long-term planner to mark significant events in your life outside of school. Include due dates for projects at work, birthdays, doctor's appointments, concert dates, credit card payment due dates, and car maintenance schedules.

Use your long-term planner to divide and conquer. Big assignments such as term papers or major presentations pose a special risk. When you have three months to do a project, you might say to yourself, "That looks like a lot of work, but I've got plenty of time. No problem." Two months, three weeks, and six days from now, it could suddenly be a problem.

For some people, life is a series of last-minute crises punctuated by periods of exhaustion. You can avoid that fate. The trick is to set due dates *before* the final due date.

When planning to write a term paper, for instance, enter the final due date in your long-term planner. Then set individual due dates for each milestone in the writing process—creating an outline, completing your research, finishing a first draft, editing the draft, and preparing the final copy. By meeting these interim due dates, you make steady progress on the assignment throughout the term. That sure beats trying to crank out all those pages at the last minute. ◙

Week of	Monday	Tuesday	Wednesday	Thursday	Friday	Saturday	Sunday
9 / 5							
9 / 12		English quiz					
9 / 19			English paper due		Speech #1		
9 / 26	Chemistry test					Skiing at the lake	
10 / 3		English quiz			Speech #2		
10 / 10				Geography project due			
10 / 17				--- No classes ---			

LONG-TERM PLANNER ___ / ___ / ___ to ___ / ___ / ___

Week of	Monday	Tuesday	Wednesday	Thursday	Friday	Saturday	Sunday
___ / ___							
___ / ___							
___ / ___							
___ / ___							
___ / ___							
___ / ___							
___ / ___							
___ / ___							
___ / ___							
___ / ___							
___ / ___							
___ / ___							
___ / ___							
___ / ___							
___ / ___							
___ / ___							
___ / ___							
___ / ___							
___ / ___							
___ / ___							
___ / ___							
___ / ___							
___ / ___							
___ / ___							
___ / ___							
___ / ___							
___ / ___							
___ / ___							
___ / ___							
___ / ___							
___ / ___							

LONG-TERM PLANNER ___ / ___ / ___ to ___ / ___ / ___

Week of	Monday	Tuesday	Wednesday	Thursday	Friday	Saturday	Sunday
___ / ___							
___ / ___							
___ / ___							
___ / ___							
___ / ___							
___ / ___							
___ / ___							
___ / ___							
___ / ___							
___ / ___							
___ / ___							
___ / ___							
___ / ___							
___ / ___							
___ / ___							
___ / ___							
___ / ___							
___ / ___							
___ / ___							
___ / ___							
___ / ___							
___ / ___							
___ / ___							
___ / ___							
___ / ___							
___ / ___							
___ / ___							
___ / ___							
___ / ___							
___ / ___							
___ / ___							

Strategies for even longer-term planning

The following suggestions can help you plan anything in your life, from getting an education or managing money to finding a job or developing new relationships. You can do all this by lifting your eyes to the horizon and thinking years—even decades—into the future.

Keep in mind that there's really no "right" way to do longer-term planning. The main thing is to immerse yourself in the process of planning. Then you can see for yourself the benefits it brings. Begin by planning to plan—setting aside time to put down your goals in writing. From there you can launch your future.

Just open your mouth and talk planning. Conversations about planning can bring our intentions into focus. We can even start talking about a plan before we really have one.

Talk to others about your dreams, wishes, fantasies, and goals. Speak of your desire to take charge of your learning, your life, and your career. Talk about where you want to be working in 5 years, 10 years, and 20 years from today. The more you speak about your longest-term goals, the more real they become. Your plan might start out as a hazy ideal. That's fine. By speaking about it with others, you can fill in the details.

Look boldly for things to change. To create new goals, open up your thinking about what aspects of your life can be changed and what cannot. Be willing to put every facet of your life on the table.

It's fascinating to note the areas that are off-limits when people set goals. Money, sex, spirituality, career, marriage, and other topics can easily fall into the category "I'll just have to live with this." When creating your future by setting goals, consider the whole range of your experience. Staying open-minded can lead to a future you never dreamed was possible.

Be willing to act—even if the plan is not complete. Many careers, successful businesses, and enduring social changes have begun with the most simple intention or sketchy plan. One African American woman, Rosa Parks, sparked the civil rights movement by refusing to sit at the back of a bus. Albert Schweitzer first considered doing medical relief work in Africa when he saw a magazine article about the needs of people in the Belgian Congo.

Complete, detailed plans are powerful. At the same time, taking action on an incomplete plan is one way to fill in the gaps. An unfinished plan is no excuse for missing a rewarding experience or for ignoring a worthy idea.

Create a vision for the ages. Think of long-term planning as "visioning." This process can include goals that we want to achieve 10, 20, or even 50 years from now. Visions that extend beyond our lives are especially powerful. Throughout history, people have created compelling projects that have inspired action over many generations. The pyramids built in ancient Egypt are an example. They were conceived by pharaohs whose vision for these structures was so stunning that their descendants chose to continue the work for decades. Another example of a multigenerational project is taking place in the Black Hills of South Dakota. In 1938, the sculptor Korczak Ziolkowski envisioned a monument to the Indian chief Crazy Horse that would be carved from a mountain larger than Mount Rushmore and would stand taller than the Washington Monument.

As Ziolkowski saw it, this monument and a related educational center would testify to the Native American way of life. Ziolkowski died in 1982. Today his work is continued by his family and other people inspired by his original vision.

Take time to create multi-generational goals. Describe your own "pyramids"—projects so important that others might be moved to continue them after you die. These projects could involve physical creations. They could also be organizations, such as Mothers Against Drunk Driving, or enterprises, such as a family farm.

Express your ideas in writing, visual art, music, or any other appropriate medium. Create a vision that could survive you for lifetimes. ◪

power process

Be here now

Being right here, right now is such a simple idea. It seems obvious. Where else can you be but where you are? When else can you be there but when you are there?

The answer is that you can be somewhere else at any time—in your head. It's common for our thoughts to distract us from where we've chosen to be. When we let this happen, we lose the benefits of focusing our attention on what's important to us in the present moment.

To "be here now" means to do what you're doing when you're doing it and to be where you are when you're there. Developing any transferable skill depends on the ability to focus your attention and sustain a high level of concentration—another term for "be here now." Students consistently report that focusing attention on the here and now is one of the most powerful tools in this book.

Leaving the here and now

We all have a voice in our head that hardly ever shuts up. If you don't believe it, conduct this experiment: Close your eyes for 10 seconds and pay attention to what is going on in your head. Please do this right now.

Notice something? Perhaps your voice was saying, "Forget it. I'm in a hurry." Another might have said, "I wonder when 10 seconds is up." Another could have been saying, "What little voice? I don't hear any little voice." That's the voice.

This voice can take you anywhere at any time—especially when you are studying. When the voice takes you away, you might appear to be studying, but your brain is at the beach.

All of us have experienced this voice, as well as the absence of it. When our inner voices are silent, time no longer seems to exist. We forget worries, aches, pains, reasons, excuses, and justifications. We fully experience the here and now. Life is magic.

There are many benefits of such a state of consciousness. It is easier to discover the world around us when we are not chattering away to ourselves about how we think it ought to be, has been, or will be. Letting go of inner voices and pictures—being totally in the moment—is a powerful tool. Do not expect to be rid of daydreams entirely. That is neither possible nor desirable. Inner voices serve a purpose. They enable us to analyze, predict, classify, and understand events out there in the "real" world.

Your stream of consciousness serves a purpose. When you are working on a term paper, your inner voices might suggest ideas. When you are listening to your sociology instructor, your inner voices can alert you to possible test questions. When you're about to jump out of an airplane, they could remind you to take a parachute. The trick is to consciously choose when to be with your inner voices and when to let them go.

Returning to the here and now

A powerful step toward returning to the here and now is to notice when we leave it. Our mind has a mind of its own, and it seems to fight back when we try to control it too much. If you doubt this, for the next 10 seconds do not, under any circumstances, think of a pink elephant. Please begin not thinking about one now.

Persistent image, isn't it? Most ideas are this insistent when we try to deny them or force them out of our consciousness.

For example, during class you might notice yourself thinking about your work schedule, a test you took the previous day, a party planned for the weekend, or the DVD player you'd like to have.

Instead of trying to force a stray thought out of your head—a futile enterprise—simply notice it. Accept it. Tell yourself, "There's that thought again." Then gently return your attention to the task at hand. That thought, or another, will come back. Your mind will drift. Simply notice again where your thoughts take you and gently bring yourself back to the here and now.

Another way to return to the here and now is to notice your physical sensations. Notice the way the room looks or smells. Notice the temperature and how the chair feels. Once you've regained control of your attention by becoming aware of your physical surroundings, you can more easily take the next step and bring your full attention back to your present task.

We can often immediately improve our effectiveness—and our enjoyment—by fully entering into each of our activities, doing one thing at a time.

For example, take something as simple as peeling and eating an orange. Carefully notice the color, shape, and texture of the orange. Hold it close to your nose and savor the pungent, sweet smell. Then slowly peel the orange and see if you can hear every subtle sound that results. Next take one piece of the orange and place it in your mouth. Notice the feel of the fruit on your tongue. Chew the piece slowly, letting the delicious juice bathe your taste buds. Take note of each individual sensation of pleasure that ripples through your body as you sample this delicious treat.

"Be here now" can turn the act of eating an orange into a rich experience. Imagine what can happen when you bring this quality of attention to almost everything that you do.

Choose when to be here now

Remember that no suggestion is absolute—including the suggestion to do one thing at a time with full, focused attention. Sometimes choosing to do two or more things at once is useful, even necessary. For example, you might study while doing laundry. You might ask your children to quiz you with flash cards while you fix dinner.

The key to this Power Process is to *choose.* When you choose, you overcome distractions and stay in charge of your attention.

Experiment with noticing your inner voices. Let go of the ones that prevent you from focusing on learning. Practice the process. Be here now, moment by moment.

To "be here now" means to do what you're doing when you're doing it and to be where you are when you're there.

The here and now in your future

You also can use this Power Process to keep yourself pointed toward your goals. In fact, one of the best ways to get what you want in the future is to realize that you do not have a future. The only time you have is right now.

The problem with this idea is that some students might think: "No future, huh? Terrific! Party time!" Being in the here and now, however, is not the same as living for today and forgetting about tomorrow.

Nor is the "be here now" idea a call to abandon goals. Goals are merely tools we create to direct our actions right now. They are useful only in the present. Goals, like our ideas of the past and future, are creations of our minds. The only time they are real is in the here and now.

The power of this idea lies in a simple but frequently overlooked fact: The only time to do anything is now. You can think about doing something next Wednesday. You can write about doing something next Wednesday. You can daydream, discuss, ruminate, speculate, and fantasize about what you will do next Wednesday.

But you can't do anything on Wednesday until it is Wednesday.

Sometimes students think of goals as things that exist in the misty future. And it's easy to postpone action on things in the misty future, especially when everyone else is going to a not-so-misty party.

However, the word *goal* comes from the Anglo-Saxon *gaelan,* which means "to hinder or impede," as in the case of a boundary. That's what a goal does. It restricts, in a positive way, our activity in the here and now. It channels our energy into actions that are more likely to get us what we really want. That's what goals are for. And they are useful only when they are directing action in the here and now.

The idea behind this Power Process is simple. When you plan for the future, plan for the future. When you listen to a lecture, listen to a lecture. When you read this book, read this book. And when you choose to daydream, daydream. Do what you're doing when you're doing it.

Be where you are when you're there. Be here now . . . and now . . . and now. ⬛

career application

S teve Carlson is a technical writer for DCS, a company that makes products for multimedia teleconferencing: digital video cameras, large-screen televisions, and software. He joined DCS two years ago, after graduating with a BA in Technical Communications. This is his first full-time, professional job.

Steve works in a five-person Documentation Department. The department creates sales brochures, user manuals, and other documents about DCS products. Working with his manager, Louise Chao, Steve helps decide which documents are needed for each DCS product. He then writes documents, edits documents written by others, and works closely with a graphic designer who oversees document production.

On a Friday afternoon, Louise knocks on the door of Steve's office. She wants Steve to handle a rush project— a new product brochure to be researched, written, designed, and printed in two weeks. Louise is on the way to another meeting and only has five minutes to talk.

Steve's schedule is already full of projects. For the last month, he has been working Saturdays to stay on top of his workload. As Louise describes the project, Steve listens without comment. When Louise is finished, Steve points to a large wallboard in his office.

This wallboard is a chart that shows all of Steve's active projects. Included is a visual timeline for each project that shows due dates for researching, outlining, drafting, and revising each document. Steve has negotiated these dates with the product development teams. Each timeline is color-coded—red for urgent projects, green for other active projects, and yellow for planned projects that are not yet active. Steve uses the wallboard to plan his day-to-day tasks and visually represent his workload.

"I estimate that it would take me at least three full days to research and write the document you're talking about," Steve says. "In addition, meetings with my designer would take up another two days. So, doing the brochure means that I'd need to free up at least one week of my time."

Steve then points to the projects shown in red on his wallboard. "Louise, I know this new product brochure is important to you," he says. "Can we schedule a time to choose which of these urgent projects I could delay for a week to meet your request?"

Reflecting on this scenario:

1. Recall the four modes of learning explained in Chapter One: *Why? What? How?* or *What if?* In this example, what was Steve's primary learning mode? Explain your reason for choosing this mode.

_____

_____

_____

2. Referring to the SCANS chart on page 8, list two transferable skills that Steve demonstrates in this scenario.

_____

_____

3. Using the same SCANS chart, identify two more skills that would be useful to Steve in this situation. Explain why you chose those two.

_____

_____

_____

4. List two planning strategies from this chapter that would be useful to Steve in this situation. Briefly describe how he could apply each one.

_____

_____

_____

Name _____ Date _____/_____/_____

1. Name three ways you can control interruptions when you are trying to concentrate.

2. It is effective to leave holes in your schedule to allow for the unexpected. True or False? Explain your answer.

3. Suppose that after you choose where to focus your attention, your mind wanders. The Power Process: "Be here now" suggests that one of the most effective ways to bring your focus back to the here and now is to:
(a) Slap your cheek and shout "Attention" as loudly as you can.
(b) Notice that your thoughts have wandered and gently bring them back.
(c) Sleep.
(d) Concentrate as hard as you can to force distracting thoughts out of your head.
(e) Ignore physical sensations.

4. What are at least 5 of the 25 ways to get the most out of now?

5. In time-management terms, what is meant by "This ain't no piano"?

6. Define "C fever" as it applies to the ABC priority method.

7. Describe at least three strategies for overcoming procrastination.

8. Summarize the difference between macro-organizing and micro-organizing as explained in this chapter.

9. Write an example of a vague goal. Then rewrite it as a specific goal.

10. List three ways to test your trial choice of major.

learning styles application

The questions below will "cycle" you through four styles, or modes, of learning as explained in the article "Learning styles: Discovering how you learn" in Chapter One. Each question will help you explore a different mode. You can answer the questions in any order.

what if *Describe exactly how you will change your behavior to free up four additional hours each week for the upcoming month. (That's a total of 16 extra hours over the next four weeks.) Choose from the techniques presented in this chapter or any that you have created yourself.*

why *Suppose that you could use the techniques in this chapter to free up four additional hours each week to do whatever you please. Describe the things you would do with this extra time and why these activities matter to you.*

how *Describe exactly how you will change your behavior to free up four additional hours in the next week. Choose from the techniques presented in this chapter or any that you have created yourself.*

what *Choose three techniques from this chapter that you could use to free up four additional hours in the next week. Summarize those techniques in a single phrase or sentence and list them here.*

master student

profile

BARBARA JORDAN

(1936–1996) the first African American to become a state senator in Texas and the first African American to enter Congress since the Reconstruction.

So I was at Boston University in this new and strange and different world, and it occurred to me that if I was going to succeed at this strange new adventure, I would have to read longer and more thoroughly than my colleagues at law school had to read. I felt that in order to compensate for what I had missed in earlier years, I would have to work harder, and study longer, than anybody else.... I did my reading not in the law library, but in a library at my graduate dorm, upstairs where it was very quiet, because apparently nobody else studied there. So I would go there at night after dinner. I would load my books under my arm and go to the library, and I would read until the wee hours of the morning and then go to bed....

I was always delighted when I would get called upon to recite in class. But the professors did not call on the "ladies" very much. There were certain favored people who always got called on, and then on some rare occasions a professor would come in and would announce: "We're going to have Ladies Day today." And he would call on the ladies. We were just tolerated. We weren't considered really top drawer when it came to the study of law.

At some time in the spring, Bill Gibson, who was dating my new roommate, Norma Walker, organized a black study group, as we blacks had to form our own. This was because we were not invited into any of the other study groups. There were six or seven in our group—Bill, and Issie, and I think Maynard Jackson—and we would just gather and talk it out and hear ourselves do that. One thing I learned was that you had to talk out the issues, the facts, the cases, the decisions, the process. You couldn't just read the cases and study alone in your library as I had been doing; and you couldn't get it all in the classroom. But once you had talked it out in the study group, it flowed more easily and made a lot more sense....

Finally I felt I was really learning things, really going to school. I felt that I was getting educated, whatever that was. I became familiar with the process of thinking. I learned to think things out and reach conclusions and defend what I had said.

In the past I had got along by spouting off. Whether you talked about debates or oratory, you dealt with speechifying. But I could no longer orate and let that pass for reasoning because there was not any demand for an orator in Boston University Law School. You had to think and read and understand and reason. I had learned at twenty-one that you couldn't just say a thing is so because it might not be so, and somebody brighter, smarter, and more thoughtful would come out and tell you it wasn't so. Then, if you still thought it was, you had to prove it. Well, that was a new thing for me. I cannot, I really cannot describe what that did to my insides and to my head. I thought: I'm being educated finally.

From *Barbara Jordan, a Self-Portrait* by Barbara Jordan and Shelby Hearon. Reprinted by permission of The Wendy Weil Agency, Inc. Copyright © 1978, 1979 by Barbara Jordan and Shelby Hearon.

For more biographical information about Barbara Jordan, visit the Master Student Hall of Fame on the *From Master Student to Master Employee* Web site at

masterstudent.college.hmco.com

CHAPTER 3
Memory

A primary objective of student success courses is to nurture the fundamental skill of memorizing key information. Memory is a complicated multidepartmental operation that does its work at many diverse brain sites, some of which have not even been located by neuroscientists. Nothing is ever learned without tapping into some component of memory. A child might be able to understand a fact, process, or concept as it is being explained or demonstrated, but without memory, none of it can be stored, retrieved, and applied. Without the collaboration of the proper memory functions, learning fails. An explanation of the steps in photosynthesis might make perfect sense to an attentive seventh grader, but if she can't properly retain at least an overview of the information, the lesson loses much of its value. It is frustrating when we can't remember something we're certain that we know, especially in a high-stakes situation, such as during a test or at a job interview.

This chapter opens with new information about the brain—how it changes physically by growing more connections between neurons. Help your students improve their memory by learning to "wire" those neural networks into place.

Page 108
Master Student Map

After your students begin to read about memory and learn to activate the connections between neurons, you will have empowered them to connect memory to the Learning Styles Application questions.

why? Why does *From Master Student to Master Employee* cover the topic of memory?

what? What is memory? Read through the list of articles in this chapter and pick three that look interesting. What interests you about these three articles?

how? How can knowing more about how your memory works improve your memory skills? How will this help you in college and in life?

what if? What if you start to apply these memory techniques to your other classes? And what if you don't?

Page 109
EXERCISE #11: "Use Q-Cards to reinforce memory"

Help your students enhance their active memory with Q-Cards. Eldon McMurray of Utah Valley State College created the concept of Q-Cards after working with a frustrated student who failed her biology exam. She had created flashcards by putting question on one side and the answer on the other side. Her review questions did not align well with the instructor's test question, so she was unable to retrieve the answer from her memory during the exam. Q-Cards have a question on *both* sides. Here's the trick: The question on each side of the card contains the answer to the question on the other side. This portable studying device helps students break information into manageable pieces and forces them to use a higher level of thinking. You can promote even further connection with materials by asking students to draw pictures to help them remember concepts. Reviewing these materials consistently before an exam will aid students' recall.

Page 112
Remembering names

A core competency from the SCANS report is information, a direct link to memory. Organizing and maintaining information can be helped by a sharp memory. Remembering names is an opportunity for discussion about a topic everyone in your class has experience with. Use the names of the students in your class to help students practice new memory techniques—and help to build community and new relationships. If you and your students are not all familiar with each others names, try some of the suggested exercises for learning them. Challenge each of your students to know each of their classmates by name.

Page 115
Notable failures

Students enjoy reading about people they "know" and how they have learned from their mistakes. This is an excellent pre-reading for the Power Process in this chapter, "Love your problems." Students can research any of these notable failures to find about more about their experiences, and link them to the SCANS skills and competencies. For extra credit, consider asking your students to create a Master Student Profile of one of the notable failures. Host your own Master Student Hall of Fame in your class and have students make presentations on the additional information they learned.

Page 118
POWER PROCESS: "Love your problems (and experience your barriers)"

One of many problem-solving tools in *From Master Student to Master Employee*, this Power Process helps students explore an alternative to avoiding problems that they encounter in college. By embracing a problem, you can diffuse its energy and find a solution. Consider bringing a word puzzle or mind game to class. Students who hate these types of puzzles get frustrated. Competitive students become anxious because each wants to be the first to solve it. Allow time for your students to try to solve the problem by loving it. Tell them to relax; to enjoy the process; to notice their frustration level, competitiveness, and anxiety; and just to love the problem. Many students are able to solve this puzzle, individually or in groups. Your HM ClassPrep CD has a sample puzzle that you can hand out to your students as part of this exercise.

Page 123
Master Student Profile: Cesar Chavez

One suggestion for discussing Master Student Profiles in your class is to use your peer leaders or teaching assistants (if you have them) or the other students in the course to deliver a message about the profile. Most students are more receptive to hearing about these profiles from their peers. It helps to break up the amount of time you spend as the instructor in front of the classroom, too. Ask your student leaders to make this presentation by talking about **why** Cesar Chavez is an example of a master student; **what** qualities Chavez had that they would like to emulate; **how** they could obtain and practice these qualities; and **what if,** like Chavez, they fought for what they believed in.

voices

advisory board member

I have always loved the 20 Memory Techniques … In my classes I stress the importance of making all techniques your own. Needless to say, the custom-made memory system is right on target! Throughout the list of techniques I especially like that with each technique there is a clear-cut example for the student. It also gives each student choices.

—MARIA PARNELL,
BREVARD COMMUNITY COLLEGE, FL

→ A purpose for listening

This story is designed for the instructor to read to the class. It should not be distributed to the students. The purpose of the story is to show how people who hear the same story remember different things about it, based on the purpose of their listening.

The instructor should give each student a slip of paper with either the words "Setting up an account in this bank" or "Robbing this bank." Students should not share with other students what is on their slip of paper. Read the story and then have students jot down things they want to remember. Ask the students to call out things they remember about the story.

THE BANK

The bank representative cordially introduced herself to the tall man dressed in casual but very nice clothes. "Hello, my name is Kendra, and I'll be giving you a tour of our bank today. I'm sure you'll be pleased with what we have to offer." As Kendra and the man walked to her desk, she continued, "I know how important bank security is to you since you'll be depositing such a large sum of money here."

Kendra went on to explain the different types of accounts available at the bank. She summarized the high interest rates the bank offered and the benefits of their free checking accounts. Then she escorted the man to the room where the bank keeps safety deposit boxes. She explained how the man would need a special PIN number to receive the key to his safety deposit box. The keys were all kept in a secure place in the bank, and only two bank employees had access to them. One of them was at the bank during all business hours. "You can be sure that your valuables will be safe with us," added Kendra. "We have safely stored many precious items for our customers here for many years. There are some very valuable collections here at our bank—rare coin collections, precious jewels, famous paintings."

Kendra further assured the man of the bank's security measures as they visited the bank's huge vault. Kendra informed him that the vault was very secure and that money was picked up regularly every Tuesday and Friday at 3:00 p.m. by an armored car. "We will also be getting a 24-hour guard soon from the most highly rated security firm in the state. He'll be starting a week from Monday," Kendra informed the man. "Even though our bank has never been robbed, we employ all possible security measures for our customers."

"It sounds like your bank has everything I need and want," complimented the man. "I'll set up a time to come back soon and take advantage of the many things your bank has to offer." After a cordial "thank you," the man said good-bye to Kendra and walked out the door.

Excerpted from *Teacher's Guide, College Transition,* by Sue Vander Hook, Houghton Mifflin Company, ©2001. Reprinted by permission.

Master Instructor Resource Guide

MASTER Student

Course Manual

 The *Course Manual* is your resource for addressing the needs of your students. Get tips on working with **adult learners, ESL students, student athletes,** and **many other specific populations.** Are you looking for **classroom strategies** to help promote student success in your classroom and across your campus? Find information in the *Course Manual* that addresses the **role of faculty** and **administrators** in supporting your course goals.

HM ClassPrep CD

PowerPoint for Chapter Three will help you set up Q-Cards with your students and talk about brain-active learning strategies. PowerPoint can help visual learners make learning connections.

Warm-up ideas include having your class start off by participating in an active learning assignment called "Scene of the crime." Thanks to the recent focus in television programs on the role of forensic medicine in solving crimes, your students will get involved from the moment they walk through the door.

Lecture ideas provide you with alternative strategies for presenting the topic of memory in your class. Help your students love their problems by embracing how they forget things—then explain how this can help them remember.

If you are having trouble remembering the names of the students in your classes, use the **resource** sheet in Chapter Three for suggested strategies to help master this technique.

Chapter Three **quiz answers** are available, as are **Test Bank** questions.

Additional Resources

masterstudent.college.hmco.com

Visit the *From Master Student to Master Employee* Web site with your class and have them do the **"Chunk of pie"** exercise. Can they memorize the number of pi beyond 3.14? Have them try out this strategy for "chunking" information into their working memory.

An interactive version of the Memory Jungle is available on the Master Student Web site as well. Visual learners will find seeing this in another way helpful to bookmarking this technique into their long-term memory.

Your students can also access a Microsoft Word version of the Master Review Schedule for updating on their computer, or a PDF file to use for additional months they want to plot out.

3

Memory

The art of true memory is the art of attention.
SAMUEL JOHNSON

Memory is the mother of imagination, reason and skill. . . .
This is the companion, this is the tutor, the poet, the
library with which you travel.
MARK VAN DOREN

why
this chapter matters . . .

Memory techniques can increase your
retention of reading materials,
notes, and other essential job skills.
Applying these strategies can boost
your test scores and help you to
perform better at work.

what
is included . . .

Take your memory out of the closet
The memory jungle
20 memory techniques
Pay attention to your attention
Set a trap for your memory
Remembering names
Mnemonic devices
Power Process: "Love your problems
(and experience your barriers)"
Master Employee Profile: Cesar Chavez

how
you can use this chapter . . .

Focus your attention.
Make conscious choices about what
to remember.
Recall facts and ideas with more ease.

As you read, ask yourself
what if . . .

I could use my memory to its full
potential?

Take your memory out of the closet

Once upon a time, people talked about human memory as if it were a closet. You stored individual memories there like old shirts and stray socks. Remembering something was a matter of rummaging through all that stuff. If you were lucky, you found what you wanted.

This view of memory creates some problems. For one thing, closets can get crowded. Things too easily disappear. Even with the biggest closet, you eventually run out of space. If you want to pack some new memories in there—well, too bad. There's no room. Brain researchers have shattered this image to bits. Memory is not a closet. It's not a place or a thing. Instead, memory is a *process*.

On a conscious level, memories appear as distinct and unconnected mental events: words, sensations, images. They can include details from the distant past—the smell of cookies baking in your grandmother's kitchen or the feel of sunlight warming your face through the window of your first-grade classroom. On a biological level, each of those memories involves millions of nerve cells, or neurons, firing chemical messages to each other. If you could observe these exchanges in real time, you'd see regions of cells all over the brain glowing with electrical charges at speeds that would put a computer to shame.

When a series of cells connects several times in a similar pattern, the result is a memory. Psychologist Donald Hebb uses the aphorism "Neurons which fire together, wire together" to describe this principle.[1]

This means that memories are not really "stored." Instead, remembering is a process in which you *encode* information as links between active neurons that fire together and *decode*, or reactivate, neurons that wired together in the past. Memory is the probability that certain patterns of brain activity will occur again in the future. In effect, you re-create a memory each time you recall it.

Whenever you learn something new, your brain changes physically by growing more connections between neurons. The more you learn, the greater the number of connections. For all practical purposes, there's no limit to how many memories your brain can encode.

There's a lot you can do to wire those neural networks into place. That's where the memory techniques described in this chapter come into play. Step out of your crowded mental closet into a world of infinite possibilities. ☒

journal entry 10

Discovery/Intention Statement

Write a sentence or two describing the way you feel when you want to remember something but have trouble doing so. Think of a specific incident in which you experienced this problem, such as trying to remember someone's name or a fact you needed during a test.

I discovered that I . . .

_____

_____

_____

Now spend five minutes skimming this chapter and find three to five memory strategies you think could be helpful. List the strategies below and note the page numbers where they are explained. Then write an Intention Statement scheduling a time to study them in more detail.

Strategy	Page number

I intend to . . .

_____

_____

_____

_____

_____

_____

The memory jungle

The more often you recall information, and the more often you put the same information into your memory, the easier it is to find.

Think of your memory as a vast, overgrown jungle. This memory jungle is thick with wild plants, exotic shrubs, twisted trees, and creeping vines. It spreads over thousands of square miles—dense, tangled, forbidding.

Imagine that the jungle is encompassed on all sides by towering mountains. There is only one entrance to the jungle, a small meadow that is reached by a narrow pass through the mountains.

In the jungle there are animals, millions of them. The animals represent all of the information in your memory. Imagine that every thought, mental picture, or perception you ever had is represented by an animal in this jungle. Every single event ever perceived by any of your five senses—sight, touch, hearing, smell, or taste—has also passed through the meadow and entered the jungle. Some of the thought animals, such as the color of your seventh-grade teacher's favorite sweater, are well hidden. Other thoughts, such as your cell phone number or the position of the reverse gear in your car, are easier to find.

There are two rules of the memory jungle. Each thought animal must pass through the meadow at the entrance to the jungle. And once an animal enters the jungle, it never leaves.

The meadow represents short-term memory. You use this kind of memory when you look up a telephone number and hold it in your memory long enough to make a call. Short-term memory appears to have a limited capacity (the meadow is small) and disappears fast (animals pass through the meadow quickly).

The jungle itself represents long-term memory. This is the kind of memory that allows you to recall information from day to day, week to week, and year to year. Remember that thought animals never leave the long-term memory jungle. The following visualizations can help you recall useful concepts about memory.

Visualization #1: A well-worn path

Imagine what happens as a thought, in this case we'll call it an elephant, bounds across short-term memory and into the jungle. The elephant leaves a trail of broken twigs and footprints that you can follow. Brain research suggests that thoughts can wear paths in the memory.[2] These paths are called *neural traces*. The more well-worn the neural trace, the easier it is to retrieve (find) the thought. In other words, the more often the elephant retraces the path, the clearer the path becomes. The more often you recall information, and the more often you put the same information into your memory, the easier it is to find. When you buy a new car, for example, the first few times you try to find reverse, you have to think for a moment. After you have found reverse gear every day for a week, the path is worn into your memory. After a year, the path is so well-worn that when you dream about driving your car backward, you even dream the correct motion for putting the gear in reverse.

Visualization #2: A herd of thoughts

The second picture you can use to your advantage is the picture of many animals gathering at a clearing—like thoughts gathering at a central location in the memory. It is easier to retrieve thoughts that are grouped together, just as it is easier to find a herd of animals than it is to find a single elephant.

Pieces of information are easier to recall if you can associate them with similar information. For example,

you can more readily remember a particular player's batting average if you can associate it with other baseball statistics.

Visualization #3: Turning your back

Imagine releasing the elephant into the jungle, turning your back, and counting to 10. When you turn around, the elephant is gone. This is exactly what happens to most of the information you receive.

Generally, we can recall only 50 percent of the material we have just read. Within 24 hours, most of us can recall only about 20 percent. This means that 80 percent of the material has not been encoded and is wandering around, lost in the memory jungle.

The remedy is simple: Review quickly. Do not take your eyes off the thought animal as it crosses the short-

term memory meadow, and review it soon after it enters the long-term memory jungle. Wear a path in your memory immediately.

Visualization #4: You are directing the animal traffic

The fourth picture is one with you in it. You are standing at the entrance to the short-term memory meadow, directing herds of thought animals as they file

through the pass, across the meadow, and into your long-term memory. You are taking an active role in the learning process. You are paying attention. You are doing more than sitting on a rock and watching the animals file past into your brain. You have become part of the process, and in doing so, you have taken control of your memory. ✉

Experience these visualizations online at masterstudent.college.hmco.com

20 memory techniques

Experiment with these techniques to develop a flexible, custom-made memory system that fits your style of learning. Applying these techniques promotes several transferable skills, including reading, speaking, note taking, and learning how to learn. The 20 techniques are divided into four categories, each of which represents a general principle for improving memory.

Briefly, the categories are:

Organize it. Organized information is easier to find.

Use your body. Learning is an active process; get all of your senses involved.

Use your brain. Work *with* your memory, not *against* it.

Recall it. This is easier when you use the other principles efficiently to notice and elaborate on incoming information.

The first three categories, which include techniques #1 through #16, are about storing information effectively. Most memory battles are won or lost here.

To get the most out of this article, first survey the following techniques by reading each heading. Then read the techniques. Next, skim them again, looking for the ones you like best. Mark those and use them.

Organize it

1 Be selective. To a large degree, the art of memory is the art of selecting what to remember in the first place.

As you dig into your textbooks and notes, make choices about what is most important to learn. Imagine that you are going to create a test on the material and consider the questions you would ask.

When reading, look for chapter previews, summaries, and review questions. Pay attention to anything printed in bold type. Also notice visual elements—tables, charts, graphs, and illustrations. All of these are clues pointing to what's important. During a presentation at work, notice what the speaker emphasizes. Anything that's presented visually—on the board, on overheads, or with slides—is probably key.

2 Make it meaningful. One way to create meaning is to learn from the general to the specific. Before you begin your next reading assignment, skim it to locate the main idea. You can use the same techniques you learned in Exercise #1: "Textbook reconnaissance" on page 1. If you're ever lost, step back and look at the big picture. The details might make more sense.

You can organize any list of items—even random ones—in a meaningful way to make them easier to remember. In his book *Information Anxiety*, Richard Saul Wurman proposes five principles for organizing any body of ideas, facts, or objects.[3]

Principle	Example
Organize by **time**	Events in history or in a novel flow in chronological order.
Organize by **location**	Addresses for a large company's regional offices are grouped by state and city.
Organize by **category**	Nonfiction library materials are organized by subject categories.
Organize by **continuum**	Products rated in *Consumers Guide* are grouped from highest in price to lowest in price, or highest in quality to lowest in quality.
Organize by **alphabet**	Entries in a book index are listed in ABC order.

3 Create associations. The data already encoded in your neural networks is arranged according to a scheme that makes sense to you. When you introduce new data, you can remember it more effectively if you associate it with similar or related data.

Think about your favorite courses. They probably relate to subjects that you already know something about.

Even when you're tackling a new subject, you can build a mental store of basic background information—the raw material for creating associations. Preview reading assignments, and complete those readings before you attend lectures. Before taking upper-level courses, master the prerequisites.

Use your body

4 Learn it once, actively. Action is a great memory enhancer. You can test this theory by studying your assignments with the same energy that you bring to the dance floor or the basketball court.

You can create those opportunities yourself. For example, your introductory psychology book probably offers some theories about how people remember information. Choose one of those theories and test it on yourself. See if you can turn that theory into a new memory technique.

Your sociology class might include a discussion about how groups of people resolve conflict. See if you can apply any of these ideas to resolving conflict in your own family.

You can use simple, direct methods to infuse your learning with action. When you sit at your desk, sit up straight. Sit on the edge of your chair, as if you were about to spring out of it and sprint across the room.

Also experiment with standing up when you are tackling a difficult task. It's harder to fall asleep in this position. Some people insist that their brains work better when they stand.

Pace back and forth and gesture as you recite material out loud. Use your hands. Get your whole body involved in your work.

5 Relax. When you're relaxed, you absorb new information quickly and recall it with greater ease and accuracy. Students who can't recall information under the stress of a final exam can often recite the same facts later when they are relaxed.

Relaxing might seem to contradict the idea of active learning as explained in technique #4, but it doesn't. Being relaxed is not the same as being drowsy, zoned out, or asleep. Relaxation is a state of alertness, free of tension, during which your mind can play with new information, roll it around, create associations with it, and apply many of the other memory techniques. You can be active *and* relaxed.

6 Create pictures. Draw diagrams. Make cartoons. Use these images to connect facts and illustrate relationships. Associations within and among abstract concepts can be "seen" and recalled more easily when they are visualized. The key is to use your imagination.

For example, Boyle's law states that at a constant temperature, the volume of a confined ideal gas varies inversely with its pressure. Simply put, cutting the volume in half doubles the pressure. To remember this concept, you might picture someone "doubled over" using a bicycle pump. As she increases the pressure in the pump by decreasing the volume in the pump cylinder, she seems to be getting angrier. By the time she has doubled the pressure (and halved the volume) she is boiling ("Boyle-ing") mad.

To visualize abstract relationships effectively, create an action-oriented image, such as the person using the pump. Make the picture vivid, too. The person's face could be bright red. And involve all of your senses. Imagine how the cold metal of the pump would feel and how the person would grunt as she struggled with it. (Most of us would have to struggle. It would take incredible strength to double the pressure in a bicycle pump, not to mention a darn sturdy pump.)

7 Recite and repeat. When you repeat something out loud, you anchor the concept in two different senses. First, you get the physical sensation in your throat, tongue, and lips when voicing the concept. Second, you hear it. The combined result is synergistic, just as it is when you create pictures. That is, the effect of using two different senses is greater than the sum of their individual effects.

The "out loud" part is important. Reciting silently in your head can be useful—in the library, for example— but it is not as effective as making noise. Your mind can trick itself into thinking it knows something when it doesn't. Your ears are harder to fool.

The repetition part is important, too. Repetition is a common memory device because it works. Repetition blazes a trail through the pathways of your brain, making the information easier to find. Repeat a concept out loud until you know it, then say it five more times.

Recitation works best when you recite concepts in your own words. For example, if you want to remember that the acceleration of a falling body due to gravity at sea level equals 32 feet per second per second, you might say, "Gravity makes an object accelerate 32 feet per second faster for each second that it's in the air at sea level." Putting it in your own words forces you to think about it.

8 Write it down. This technique is obvious, yet easy to forget. Writing a note to yourself helps you remember an idea, even if you never look at the note again.

Writing engages a different kind of memory than speaking. Writing prompts us to be more logical, coherent, and complete. Written reviews reveal gaps in knowledge that oral reviews miss, just as oral reviews reveal gaps that written reviews miss.

Finally, writing is physical. Your arm, your hand, and your fingers join in. Remember, learning is an active process—you remember what you *do*.

Use your brain

9 Engage your emotions. One powerful way to enhance your memory is to make friends with your amygdala. This is an area of your brain that lights up with extra neural activity each time you feel a strong emotion. When a topic excites love, laughter, or fear, the amygdala sends a flurry of chemical messages that say, in effect: *This information is important and useful. Don't forget it.*

You're more likely to remember course material when you relate it to a goal—whether academic, personal, or career—that you feel strongly about. This is one reason why it pays to be specific about what you want. The more goals you have and the more clearly they are defined, the more channels you create for incoming information.

You can use this strategy even when a subject seems boring at first. If you're not naturally interested in a topic, then create interest. Find a study partner in the class—if possible, someone you know and like—or form a study group. Also consider getting to know the instructor personally. Getting to know your coworkers, and your customers, can help you achieve more on the job. When you create a bridge to human relationships, you become engaged in a more emotional way.

10 Overlearn. One way to fight mental fuzziness is to learn more than you need to know about a subject simply to pass a test. You can pick a subject apart, examine it, add to it, and go over it until it becomes second nature.

This technique is especially effective for problem solving. Do the assigned problems, and then do more problems. Find another textbook and work similar problems. Then make up your own problems and solve them.

11 Escape the short-term memory trap. Short-term memory is different from the kind of memory you'll need when your boss asks you a question on the spot, or during exam week. For example, most of us can look at an unfamiliar seven-digit phone number once and remember it long enough to dial it. See if you can recall that number the next day. A quick minireview can save you hours of study time when exams roll around.

Short-term memory can fade after a few minutes, and it rarely lasts more than several hours. A short review within minutes or hours of a study session can move material from short-term memory into long-term memory. Similarly, reviewing your meeting notes for action points can help you remember your responsi-

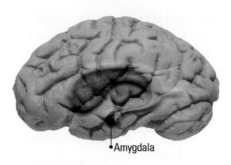

•Amygdala

The amygdala, highlighted in this illustration, is an area of your brain that sends neural messages associated with strong emotions. When you link new material to something that you feel strongly about, you activate this part of your brain. In turn, you're more likely to remember that material.

bilities long term to meet the goals of your team.

12 Use your times of peak energy. Study your most difficult subjects and conquer difficult workplace tasks during the times when your energy peaks. Many people can concentrate more effectively during daylight hours. The early morning hours can be especially productive, even for those who hate to get up with the sun. Observe the peaks and valleys in your energy flow during the day and adjust your tasks accordingly. Perhaps you will experience surges in memory power during the late afternoon or evening.

13 Distribute learning. As an alternative to marathon study sessions, experiment with shorter, spaced-out sessions. You might find that you can get far more done in three two-hour sessions than in one six-hour session.

For example, when you are studying for your American history exam, study for an hour or two and then wash the dishes. While you are washing the dishes, part of your mind will be reviewing what you studied. Return to American history for a while, then call a friend. Even when you are deep in conversation, part of your mind will be reviewing history.

You can get more done if you take regular breaks. You can even use the breaks as minirewards. After a productive study session, give yourself permission to log on and check your e-mail, listen to a song, or play 10 minutes of hide-and-seek with your kids.

By taking periodic breaks while studying, you allow information to sink in. During these breaks, your brain is taking the time to literally rewire itself by growing new connections between cells. Psychologists call this process *consolidation.*[4]

There is an exception to this idea of allowing time for consolidation. When you are so engrossed in a book that you cannot put it down, when you are consumed by an idea for a term paper and cannot think of anything else—keep going. The master student within you has taken over. Enjoy the ride.

14 Be aware of attitudes. If you think a subject is boring, remind yourself that everything is related to everything else. Look for connections that relate to your own interests.

For example, consider a person who is fanatical about cars. She can rebuild a motor in a weekend and has a good time doing so. From this apparently specialized interest, she can explore a wide realm of knowledge. She can relate the workings of an engine to principles of physics, math, and chemistry. Computerized parts in newer cars can lead her to the study of data processing. She can research how the automobile industry has changed our cities and helped create suburbs, a topic that includes urban planning, sociology, business, economics, psychology, and history.

15 **Give your "secret brain" a chance.** Sometimes the way you combine studying with other activities can affect how well you remember information. The trick is to avoid what psychologists call *retroactive inhibition*, something that happens when a new or unrelated activity interferes with previous learning. Say that you've just left your evening psychology class, which included a fascinating lecture on Sigmund Freud's theory of dreams. When you arrive home, you decide to sneak in a few pages of that mystery novel you've wanted to finish. After you find out who poisoned the butler, you settle in for a well-deserved rest. In this scenario, the key concepts of the psychology lecture are pushed aside by the gripping drama of the whodunit. Consider another scenario instead. You have arranged to car-pool with a classmate, and on the way home, you talk about the lecture. The discussion ignites into a debate as you and your friend take opposite stands on a principle of Freud's theory. Later, just before going to sleep, you mull over the conversation. While you sleep, your brain can now process the key points of the lecture—something that will come in handy for the midterm exam.

16 **Combine techniques.** All of these memory techniques work even better in combination. Choose two or three techniques to use on a particular task and experiment for yourself. For example, after you take a few minutes to get an overview of a reading assignment, you could draw a quick picture or diagram to represent the main point. Or you could overlearn a chemistry equation by singing a jingle about it all the way to work.

Recall it

17 **Remember something else.** When you are stuck and can't remember something that you're sure you know, remember something else that is related to it.

During an economics exam, if you can't remember anything about the aggregate demand curve, recall what you do know about the aggregate supply curve. If you cannot recall specific facts, remember the example that the instructor used during her lecture. Information is encoded in the same area of the brain as similar information. You can unblock your recall by stimulating that area of your memory.

You can take this technique one step further with a process that psychologists call *elaboration*.[5] The key is to ask questions that prompt you to create more associations. For example, when you meet someone new, ask yourself: What are the distinctive features of this person's face? Does she remind me of someone else?

A brainstorm is a good memory jog. If you are stumped when taking a test, start writing down lots of answers to related questions, and—pop!—the answer you need is likely to appear.

18 **Notice when you do remember.** Everyone has a different memory style. Some people are best at recalling information they've read. Others have an easier time remembering what they've heard, seen, or done.

To develop your memory, notice when you recall information easily and ask yourself what memory techniques you're using naturally. Also notice when it's difficult to recall information. Be a reporter. Get the facts and then adjust your learning techniques. And remember to congratulate yourself when you remember.

19 **Use it before you lose it.** To remember something, access it a lot. Read it, write it, speak it, listen to it, apply it—find some way to make contact with the material regularly. Each time you do so, you widen the neural pathway to the material and make it easier to recall the next time.

Another way to make contact with the material is to teach it. Teaching demands mastery. When you explain the concept of learning styles to a fellow student or coworker, you discover quickly whether you really understand it yourself.

Study groups and project teams in the workplace are especially effective because they put you on stage. The friendly pressure of knowing that you'll teach the group helps focus your attention.

20 **Adopt the attitude that you never forget.** You might not believe that an idea or a thought never leaves your memory. That's OK. In fact, it doesn't matter whether you agree with the idea or not. It can work for you anyway.

Test the concept. Instead of saying, "I don't remember," you can say, "It will come to me."

Or even "I never forget!" ☒

Pay attention to your attention

Many of the memory glitches of everyday life result from simple absent-mindedness and a failure to concentrate. Often, the results are minor inconveniences, such as misplacing an umbrella or entering a room and forgetting why. Sometimes, though, the consequences are serious—missing an important meeting, forgetting to answer key questions on a final exam, or running a stop sign and causing an accident.

When you notice your mind heading off on an unscheduled vacation, use any of the following techniques to return to the here and now.

Reduce interference. Turn down the music—or turn it off—when you are concentrating. Find a quiet place that is free from distractions. If there's a party in your office, consider finding a quite place to work, like an empty conference room. If you like to snack, don't tempt yourself by studying next to the refrigerator. Two hours of studying in front of the television might be worth 10 minutes of studying where it is quiet. If you have two hours in which to study *and* watch television, it's probably better to study for an hour and then watch television for an hour. Doing one activity at a time increases your ability to remember.

Think out loud. You can also train your attention by noticing unconscious actions and making them conscious. An example is the sequence of actions you might take before you leave home for the day—grabbing your keys, turning off lights, and locking the front door. If you go through this series in a robotic trance of semiattention, you might get to campus and wonder, Did I remember to lock the door? You can eliminate such worries by saying to yourself before you leave home, Now I am turning out the lights. . . . Now I am checking the stove. . . . Now I am turning the lock. Instead of coasting through large portions of your life on automatic pilot, you'll wake up and pay attention.

Doing one activity at a time increases your ability to remember.

Bring your attention to your body—or your body to attention. In any given moment, your mind can be in two or more places at once. Your body, however, is always parked in one spot and dwells contentedly in the present moment. To focus your attention instantly, simply return to your body. Notice simple sensations—the air passing in and out of your nostrils, or your clothes gently resting on your skin. Then redirect your attention to the task at hand. Another option is to bring your body to a state of attention. Stand erect or sit with a straight spine on the edge of your chair. Visualize yourself on a tennis court, poised to return a serve. Repeat this process whenever your mind drifts.

Use a concentration cheat sheet. Each time that your attention wanders during a class or meeting, make a tick mark in the margins of your note paper. Creating a visible record of your distractions is one way to reduce them. In addition, the physical act of writing re-engages your attention. **Note:** This technique works only if you release any self-judgment about how often your mind wanders. At first, you might end up with row after row of tick marks. That's OK. With time and consistent practice, they will decrease.

Deal with distraction. One source of distraction is an urgent task that constantly resurfaces in your mind. Perhaps there is an important phone call to make, an errand to run, or a pressing problem to solve. When time and circumstances allow, deal with the distraction by taking care of the matter now.

If that's not feasible, write a detailed Intention Statement that describes exactly what you will do to handle the distraction. With your intention safely recorded in writing, you can now zero in on studying, working, or whatever else is most important in the present moment.

Know when to get help. A condition called attention deficit/hyperactivity disorder (ADHD) interferes with the ability to concentrate. People with ADHD consistently experience negative consequences—missed due dates, low grades, poor work performance, strained relationships with friends and family, and more—as a result of being unable to focus their attention.

If you find that none of the above techniques helps you take charge of your attention, then meet with an academic advisor or counselor and ask for help. ADHD can be reliably diagnosed and treated. ✉

USE Q-CARDS TO REINFORCE MEMORY

One memory strategy you might find useful involves a special kind of flash card. It's called a *Question Card*, or *Q-Card* for short.

To create a standard flash card, you write a question on one side of a 3x5 card and its answer on the other side. Q-Cards have a question on *both* sides. Here's the trick: The question on each side of the card contains the answer to the question on the other side.

The questions you write on Q-Cards can draw on both lower- and higher-order thinking skills. Writing these questions forces you to encode material in different ways. You activate more areas of your brain and burn the concepts even deeper into your memory.

For example, say that you want to remember the subject of the 18th Amendment to the United States Constitution, the one that prohibited the sale of alcohol. On one side of a 3x5 card, write *What amendment prohibited the sale of alcohol?* Turn the card over and write *What did the 18th Amendment do?*

To get the most from Q-Cards:

- Add a picture to each side of the card. This helps you learn concepts faster and develop a more visual learning style.

- Read the questions and recite the answers out loud. Two keys to memory are repetition and novelty, so use a different voice whenever you read and recite. Whisper the first time you go through your cards, then shout or sing the next time. Doing this develops an auditory learning style.

- Carry Q-Cards with you and pull them out during waiting times. To develop a kinesthetic learning style, handle your cards often.

- Create a Q-Card for each new and important concept within 24 hours after attending a class or completing an assignment. This is your *active stack* of cards. Keep answering the questions on these cards until you learn each new concept.

- Review all of the cards from the term for a certain subject on one day each week. For example, on Monday, review all cards from biology; on Tuesday, review all cards from history. These cards make up your *review stacks*.

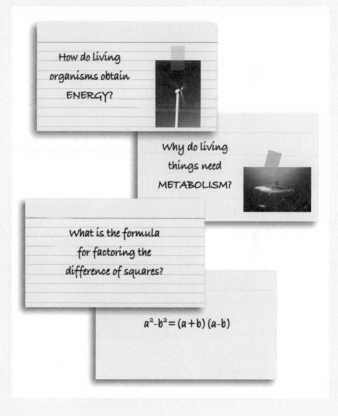

Set a trap for your memory

When you want to remind yourself to do something, link this activity to another event you know will take place. The key is to "trap" your memory by picking events that are certain to occur.

Say that you're helping a client and suddenly remember that your accounting assignment is due tomorrow. Switch your watch to the opposite wrist. Now you're "trapped." Every time you glance at your wrist and remember that you have switched your watch, it becomes a reminder that you were supposed to remember something else. (You can do the same with a ring.)

If you empty your pockets every night, put an unusual item in your pocket in the morning to remind yourself to do something before you go to bed. For example, to remember to call your younger sister on her birthday, pick an object from the playpen—a teething toy, perhaps—and put it in your pocket. When you empty your pocket that

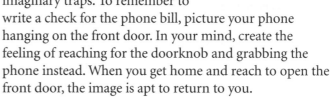

evening and find the teething toy, you're more likely to make the call.

Everyday rituals that are seldom neglected, such as feeding a pet, listening to the weather report, and unlacing shoes, provide opportunities for setting traps. For example, tie a triple knot in your shoelace as a reminder to set the alarm for your early morning study group meeting. You can even use imaginary traps. To remember to write a check for the phone bill, picture your phone hanging on the front door. In your mind, create the feeling of reaching for the doorknob and grabbing the phone instead. When you get home and reach to open the front door, the image is apt to return to you.

Link two activities together, and make the association unusual.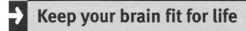

→ Keep your brain fit for life

Your brain is an organ that needs regular care and exercise. Higher education gives you plenty of chances to exercise that organ. Don't let those benefits fade after you leave school. Starting now, adopt habits to keep your brain lean and fit for life.

Seek out new experiences. If you sit at a desk most of the workday, take a dance class. If you seldom travel, start reading maps of new locations and plan a cross-country trip. Seek out museums, theaters, concerts, and other cultural events. Even after you graduate, consider learning another language or taking up a musical instrument. Your brain thrives on novelty. Build it into your life.

Shaking up your routines might involve some initial discomfort. Hang in there. Remind yourself that new experiences give your brain a workout just like sit-ups condition your abs.

Take care of your health. Exercising regularly, staying tobacco-free, and getting plenty of sleep can reduce your risk of cancer, heart disease, stroke, and other conditions

that interfere with memory. Eating well also helps. A diet rich in fruits and vegetables boosts your supply of antioxidants—natural chemicals that nourish your brain.

Drink alcohol moderately, if at all. A common definition of moderate consumption for people of legal drinking age is no more than one drink per day for women and no more than two drinks per day for men. Heavier drinking can affect memory. In fact, long-term alcoholics tend to develop conditions that impair memory. One is Korsakoff's syndrome, a disorder that causes people to forget incidents immediately after they happen.

Engage life fully. Research sponsored by the MacArthur Foundation indicates that engagement with life acts as a strong predictor of successful aging.[6] Researchers define engagement as maintaining close relationships with friends and family, and staying productive in paid or volunteer work. Both loving and working help keep your brain fit to handle a lifetime of memories.

→ Notable failures, part one

You might feel discouraged about your failure to remember information at critical moments, such as during a test. Before you despair over your test scores or grade point average, remember that history is filled with examples of people who struggled academically and then went on to achieve great things. These notable failures, some of whom are listed below, are emblazoned in our collective memory, while their detractors are long forgotten.

Einstein was four years old before he could speak and seven before he could read. **Isaac Newton** did poorly in grade school. **Beethoven**'s music teacher once said of him, "As a composer he is hopeless."

When **Thomas Edison** was a boy, his teachers told him he was too stupid to learn anything. **F. W. Woolworth** got a job in a dry goods store when he was 21, but his employers would not let him wait on customers because he "didn't have enough sense."

A newspaper editor fired **Walt Disney**, claiming that he had "no good ideas." **Caruso**'s music teacher told him,

"You can't sing. You have no voice at all." The director of the Imperial Opera in Vienna told **Madame Schumann-Heink** that she would never be a singer and advised her to buy a sewing machine. **Leo Tolstoy** flunked out of college. **Wernher von Braun** flunked ninth-grade algebra. Admiral **Richard E. Byrd** had been retired from the navy as "unfit for service" until he flew over both Poles.

Louis Pasteur was rated as "mediocre" in chemistry when he attended the Royal College. **Abraham Lincoln** entered the Black Hawk War as a captain and came out as a private. **Louisa May Alcott** was told by an editor that she could never write anything that would have popular appeal. **Fred Waring** was once rejected for high school chorus. **Winston Churchill** failed the sixth grade.

"Humbling Cases for Career Counselors," by Dr. Milton E. Larson, from *Phi Delta Kappan,* February 1973 issue, Volume LVI, no. 6, p. 374. © 1973. Reprinted by permission.

exercise 11

REMEMBERING YOUR CAR KEYS— OR ANYTHING ELSE

Pick something you frequently forget. Some people chronically lose their car keys or forget to write down checks in their check register. Others let anniversaries and birthdays slip by.

Pick an item or a task you're prone to forget. Then design a strategy for remembering it. Use any of the techniques from this chapter, research others, or make up your own from scratch. Describe your technique and the results in the space below.

_____

_____

_____

_____

In this exercise, as in most of the exercises in this book, a failure is also a success. Don't be concerned with whether your technique will work. Design it, and then find out. If it doesn't work for you this time, use another method.

journal entry 11

Discovery Statement

Take a minute to reflect on the memory techniques in this chapter. You probably use some of them already without being aware of it. In the space below, list at least three techniques you have used in the past and describe how you used them.

_____

_____

_____

_____

_____

_____

_____

_____

_____

_____

Remembering names

One powerful way to immediately practice memory techniques is to use them to remember names. Developing this skill can help you quickly develop rapport with classmates and coworkers. Remembering names is an element of sociability—a transferable skill that includes demonstrating politeness and friendliness.

Recite and repeat in conversation. When you hear a person's name, repeat it. Immediately say it to yourself several times without moving your lips. You could also repeat the name out loud in a way that does not sound forced or artificial: "I'm pleased to meet you, Maria."

Ask the other person to recite and repeat. You can let other people help you remember their names. After you've been introduced to someone, ask that person to spell the name and pronounce it correctly for you. Most people will be flattered by the effort you're making to learn their names.

Visualize. After the conversation, construct a brief visual image of the person. For a memorable image, make it unusual. Imagine the name painted in hot pink fluorescent letters on the person's forehead.

Admit you don't know. Admitting that you can't remember someone's name can actually put people at ease. Most of them will sympathize if you say, "I'm working to remember names better. Yours is right on the tip of my tongue. What is it again?" (By the way, that's exactly what psychologists call that feeling—the "tip of the tongue" phenomenon.)

Introduce yourself again. Most of the time we assume introductions are one-shot affairs. If we miss a name the first time around, our hopes for remembering it are dashed. Instead of giving up, reintroduce yourself: "Hello, again. We met earlier. I'm Jesse, and please tell me your name again."

Use associations. Link each person you meet with one characteristic that you find interesting or unusual. For example, you could make a mental note: "Vicki Cheng—long, black hair" or "James Washington—horn-rimmed glasses." To reinforce your associations, write them on 3x5 cards as soon as you can.

Limit the number of new names you learn at one time. Occasionally, we find ourselves in situations where we're introduced to many people at the same time: "Dad, these are all the people in my Boy Scout troop." "Let's take a tour so you can meet all 32 people in this department."

When meeting a group of people, concentrate on remembering just two or three names. Free yourself from feeling obligated to remember everyone. Few of the people in mass introductions expect you to remember their names. Another way to avoid memory overload is to limit yourself to learning just first names. Last names can come later.

Ask for photos. In some cases, you might be able to get photos of all the people you meet. For example, a small business where you apply for a job might have a brochure with pictures of all the employees. Ask for individual or group photos and write in the names if they're not included. You can use these photos as "flash cards" as you drill yourself on names.

Go early. Consider going early to conventions, parties, and classes. Sometimes just a few people show up on time at these occasions. That's fewer names for you to remember. And as more people arrive, you can overhear them being introduced to others—an automatic review for you.

Make it a game. In situations where many people are new to one another, consider pairing up with another person and staging a contest. Challenge each other to remember as many new names as possible. Then choose an "award"—such as a movie ticket or free meal—for the person who wins.

Intend to remember. The simple act of focusing your attention at key moments can do wonders for your memory. Test this idea for yourself. The next time you're introduced to someone, direct 100 percent of your attention to hearing that person's name. Do this consistently and see what happens to your ability to remember names.

The intention to remember can be more powerful than any single memory technique. ✖

Mnemonic devices

It's pronounced *ne-mon´-ik*. The word refers to tricks that can increase your ability to recall everything from grocery lists to speeches.

Some entertainers use mnemonic devices to perform "impossible" feats of memory, such as recalling the names of everyone in a large audience after hearing them just once. Waiters use mnemonics to take orders from several tables without the aid of pad and pencil. Using mnemonic devices, speakers can go for hours without looking at their notes. The possibilities for students are endless.

There is a catch. Mnemonic devices have three serious limitations.

First, they don't always help you understand or digest material. Instead of encouraging critical thinking skills, mnemonics rely only on rote memorization.

Second, the mnemonic device itself is sometimes complicated to learn and time-consuming to develop. It might take more energy to create such a device than to memorize something by using a more traditional memory technique, such as repetition.

Third, mnemonic devices can be forgotten. Recalling a mnemonic device might be as hard as recalling the material itself.

In spite of their limitations, mnemonic devices can be powerful. There are five general categories: new words, creative sentences, rhymes and songs, the loci system, and the peg system.

New words. Acronyms are words created from the initial letters of a series of words. Examples include NASA (**N**ational **A**eronautics and **S**pace **A**dministration), radar (**ra**dio **d**etecting **a**nd **r**anging), scuba (**s**elf-**c**ontained **u**nderwater **b**reathing **a**pparatus), and laser (**l**ight **a**mplification by **s**timulated **e**mission of **r**adiation). You can make up your own acronyms to recall series of facts. A common mnemonic acronym is Roy G. Biv, which has helped thousands of students remember the colors of the visible spectrum (**r**ed, **o**range, **y**ellow, **g**reen, **b**lue, **i**ndigo, and **v**iolet). IPMAT helps biology students remember the stages of cell division (**i**nterphase, **p**rophase, **m**etaphase, **a**naphase, and **t**elophase).

Creative sentences. Acrostics are sentences that help you remember a series of letters that stand for something. For example, the first letters of the words in the sentence "Every good boy does fine" (E, G, B, D, and F) are the music notes of the lines of the treble clef staff.

Rhymes and songs. Madison Avenue advertising executives spend billions of dollars a year on commercials designed to burn their messages into your memory. Coca-Cola's song, "It's the Real Thing," practically stands for Coca-Cola, despite the fact that the soda contains artificial ingredients.

Rhymes have been used for centuries to teach children basic facts: "In fourteen hundred and ninety-two, Columbus sailed the ocean blue" or "Thirty days hath September."

The loci system. The word *loci* is the plural of *locus*, a synonym for *place* or *location*. Use this system to create visual associations with familiar locations. Unusual associations are the easiest to remember.

Example 1
The loci system is an old one. Ancient Greek orators used it to remember long speeches. For example, if an orator's position was that road taxes must be raised to pay for school equipment, his loci visualizations might have looked like the following.

First, as he walks in the door of his house, he imagines a large *porpoise* jumping through a hoop. This reminds him to begin by telling the audience the *purpose* of his speech.

Next, he visualizes his living room floor covered with paving stones, forming a road leading into the kitchen. In the kitchen, he pictures dozens of schoolchildren sitting on the floor because they have no desks.

Now it's the day of the big speech. The Greek politician is nervous. He is perspiring, and his toga sticks to his body. He stands up to give his speech, and his mind goes blank. Then he starts thinking to himself:

> *I am so nervous that I can hardly remember my name. But no problem—I can remember the rooms in my house. Let's see, I'm walking in the front door and—wow! I see the porpoise. That reminds me to talk about the purpose of my speech. And then there's that road leading to the kitchen. Say, what are all those kids doing there on the floor? Oh, yeah, now I remember—they have no desks! We need to raise taxes on roads to pay for their desks and the other stuff they need in classrooms.*

Example 2
The loci system can also be based on parts of your body. When studying biology, for instance, use the loci system to memorize the order of structures of living things.

Start with your toes, the lowest points of your body. Associate them with the lowest structure of living things—*atoms*.

The top of your head is the highest point on your body. So associate it with the highest order of living things—*biosystems*, or groups of species.

Then associate the intermediate structures with points on your body between your head and toes.

Link *molecules* to your feet.
Link *cells* to your ankles.
Link *tissues* with your knees.
Link *organs* with your waist.
Link *organ systems* with your chest.
Link *organisms* with your neck.

The peg system. This technique employs key words that are paired with numbers. Each word forms a "peg" on which you can "hang" mental associations. To use this system effectively, learn the following peg words and their associated numbers well:

bun goes with 1
shoe goes with 2
tree goes with 3
door goes with 4
hive goes with 5
sticks goes with 6
heaven goes with 7
gate goes with 8
wine goes with 9
hen goes with 10

Believe it or not, you can use the peg system to remember the Bill of Rights (the first ten amendments to the United States Constitution). For example, amendment number *four* is about protection from unlawful search and seizure. Imagine people knocking at your *door* who are demanding to search your home. This amendment means that you do not have to open your door unless those people have a proper search warrant. ⊠

exercise 12

BE A POET

Construct your own mnemonic device for remembering some of the memory techniques in this chapter. Make up a poem, jingle, acronym, or acrostic, or use another mnemonic system. Write your mnemonic device on a separate sheet of paper. Describe it completely and then rehearse it.

desk of ...

from the

DR. GWEN RAPHAN, PEDIATRIC INTERN:
Many mnemonic devices in medicine are standardized. We refer to these mnemonics at work frequently. I can still remember the mnemonic devices I created myself while in school. By making them personally meaningful, and in my own words, I can easily access them from my long-term memory.

Notable failures, part two

Albert Einstein's parents thought he was retarded. He spoke haltingly until age nine, and after that he answered questions only after laboring in thought about them. He was advised by a teacher to drop out of high school: "You'll never amount to anything, Einstein."

Charles Darwin's father said to his son, "You will be a disgrace to yourself and all your family." (Darwin did poorly in school.)

Henry Ford barely made it through high school.

Sir Isaac Newton did poorly in school and was allowed to continue only because he failed at running the family farm.

Pablo Picasso was pulled out of school at age 10 because he was doing so poorly. A tutor hired by Pablo's father gave up on Pablo.

Giacomo Puccini's first music teacher said that Puccini had no talent for music. Later Puccini composed some of the world's greatest operas.

The machines of the world's greatest inventor, **Leonardo da Vinci**, were never built, and many wouldn't have worked anyway.

Clarence Darrow became a legend in the courtroom as he lost case after case.

Edwin Land's attempts at instant movies (Polarvision) failed completely. He described his efforts as trying to use an impossible chemistry and a nonexistent technology to make an unmanufacturable product for which there was no discernible demand.

After the success of the show *South Pacific,* composer **Oscar Hammerstein** put an ad in *Variety* that listed over a dozen of his failures. At the bottom of the ad, he repeated the credo of show business, "I did it before, and I can do it again."

Asked about how he felt when his team lost a game, **Joe Paterno,** coach of the Penn State University football team, once replied that losing was probably good for them since that was how the players learned what they were doing wrong.

R. Buckminster Fuller built his geodesic domes by starting with a deliberately failed dome and making it "a little stronger and a little stronger . . . a little piece of wood here and a little piece of wood there, and suddenly it stood up."

Igor Stravinsky said, "I have learned throughout my life as a composer chiefly through my mistakes and pursuits of false assumptions, not by my exposure to the founts of wisdom and knowledge."

Charles Goodyear bungled an experiment and discovered vulcanized rubber.

Before gaining an international reputation as a painter, **Paul Gauguin** was a failed stockbroker.

The game Monopoly was developed by **Charles Darrow**, an unemployed heating engineer. Darrow presented his first version of the game to a toy company in 1935. That company originally rejected the game for containing 52 "fundamental errors." Today the game is so successful that its publisher, Parker Brothers, prints more than $40 billion of Monopoly money each year. That's twice the amount of real money printed annually by the U.S. Treasury.

Robert Pirsig's best-selling book, *Zen and the Art of Motorcycle Maintenance*, was rejected by 121 publishers.

Spike Lee applied for graduate study at the top film schools in the country, including the University of Southern California and the University of California at Los Angeles. Due to his scores on the Graduate Record Exam, both schools turned Lee down.

Jaime Escalante is a nationally known educator and the subject of the film *Stand and Deliver*. When he first tried to get a teaching job in California, the state refused to accept his teaching credentials from Bolivia.

Before **Alan Page** became the first African American to sit on the Minnesota Supreme Court, he played in the American Football League. Seeking a career change, he entered law school. After three weeks he dropped out and did not enroll again for another eight years.

Before the career-planning book *What Color Is Your Parachute?* became a perennial best-seller, author **Richard Nelson Bolles** got laid off from a job and ended up broke. One Friday in 1971, his cash reserves included only the $5.18 in his pocket. Bolles sold two copies of his book that day and was able to survive through the weekend. Today, *What Color Is Your Parachute?* sells nearly 20,000 copies every month.

Reprinted with permission by Stillpoint Publishing, Walpole, NH (USA) 03608 from the book *Diet for a New America* by John Robbins. Copyright © 1987. From *Information Anxiety* by Richard Saul Wurman, copyright © 1989 by Richard Saul Wurman. Used by permission of Doubleday, a division of Bantam Doubleday Dell Publishing Group, Inc.

THINKING CRITICALLY IN THE CLASSROOM

Take five minutes to remember a time when you enjoyed learning something. In the space below, describe that experience in a sentence or two. Then make a brief list of the things you found enjoyable about that experience.

_____

_____

_____

_____

_____

_____

_____

_____

_____

Within the next 24 hours, compare your list with those of other classmates. Look for similarities and differences in the descriptions of your learning experiences.

Based on your comparisons, form a tentative explanation about what makes learning enjoyable for people. Summarize your explanation here:

_____

_____

_____

_____

_____

_____

_____

_____

_____

_____

_____

desk of...

from the

**ZOBIDA MALHOTRA,
CUSTOMER SERVICE REPRESENTATIVE:**

At 39 years of age, I was very anxious about attending college for the first time. I haven't been in the classroom since I was in high school. I decided to return to school to learn more about computers since I need to use them in my job every day. Love my problems has helped me to understand that I do not need to fight my fears. Instead, I have accepted them. And now as an adult student, I have formed study groups with other adult students in my classes and together we have found a comfortable place to learn.

MOVE FROM PROBLEMS TO SOLUTIONS

You can promote your chances of thriving in school and in the workplace by anticipating possible barriers to your success and putting solutions in place now.

Many people find it easy to complain about problems and dwell on them. This exercise gives you an opportunity to change that habit and respond creatively to any problem you're currently experiencing.

The key is to dwell more on solutions than on problems. Do that by inventing as many solutions as possible for any given problem. Shifting the emphasis of your conversation from problems to solutions raises your sense of possibility and unleashes the master learner within you.

In the space below, describe at least three problems that could interfere with your success in school or at work. The problems can be related to courses, teachers, personal relationships, finances, or anything else that might get in the way of your success.

My problem is that . . .

_____

_____

_____

_____

My problem is that . . .

_____

_____

_____

_____

My problem is that . . .

_____

_____

_____

_____

Next, brainstorm at least five possible solutions to each of those problems. Ten is even better. You might find it hard to come up with that many ideas. That's OK. Stick with it. Stay in the inquiry, give yourself time, and ask other people for ideas.

I could solve my problem by . . .

_____

_____

_____

_____

_____

I could solve my problem by . . .

_____

_____

_____

_____

I could solve my problem by . . .

_____

_____

_____

_____

Now go online to (masterstudent.college.hmco.com)

Look for links to discussion groups with other students and share your responses to this exercise. By reviewing other students' postings, you could discover many more possible solutions to your own problems. While you're there, offer some possible solutions to the problems that others have posted.

power process

Love your problems

(and experience your barriers)

We all have problems and barriers that block our progress or prevent us from moving into new areas. Often, the way we respond to our problems puts boundaries on our experiences. We place limitations on what we allow ourselves to be, do, and have.

Our problems might include fear of speaking in front of a group, anxiety about math problems, or reluctance to sound ridiculous when learning a foreign language. We might have a barrier about looking silly when doing something new at work. Some of us even have anxiety about being successful.

Problems often work like barriers. When we bump up against one of our problems, we usually turn away and start walking along a different path. And all of a sudden—bump!—we've struck another barrier. And we turn away again. As we continue to bump into problems and turn away from them, our lives stay inside the same old boundaries. Inside these boundaries, we are unlikely to have new adventures. We are unlikely to improve or to make much progress.

The word *problem* is a wonderful word coming from the ancient Greek word *proballein,* which means "to throw forward." In other words, problems are there to provide an opportunity for us to gain new skills. If we respond to problems by loving them instead of resisting them, we can expand the boundaries in which we live our lives. The willingness to recognize that a problem exists is a transferable skill. When approached with acceptance, and even love, the problem can "throw" us forward.

Three ways to handle a barrier

It's natural to have barriers, but sometimes they limit our experience so much that we get bored, angry, or frustrated with life. When this happens, consider the following three ways of dealing with a barrier. One way is to pretend it doesn't exist. Avoid it, deny it, lie about it. It's like turning your head the other way, putting on a fake grin, and saying, "See, there's really no problem at all. Everything is fine. Oh, that problem. That's not a problem—it's not really there."

In addition to making us look foolish, this approach leaves the barrier intact, and we keep bumping into it. We deny the barrier and might not even be aware that we're bumping into it. For example, a student who has a barrier about math might subconsciously avoid enriching experiences that include math.

A second approach is to fight the barrier, to struggle against it. This usually makes the barrier grow. It increases the barrier's magnitude. A person who is obsessed with weight might constantly worry about being fat. She might struggle with it every day, trying diet after diet. And the more she struggles, the bigger the problem gets.

The third alternative is to love the barrier. Accept it. Totally experience it. Tell the truth about it. Describe it in detail. When you do this, the barrier loses its power. You can literally love it to death.

The word *love* might sound like an overstatement. In this Power Process, the word means to accept your problems, to allow and permit them. When we fight a problem, it grows bigger. The more we struggle against it, the stronger it seems to become. When we accept the fact that we have a problem, we are more likely to find effective ways to deal with it.

Suppose one of your barriers is being afraid of speaking in front of a group. You can use any of these three approaches.

First, you can get up in front of the group and pretend that you're not afraid. You can fake a smile, not admitting to yourself or the group that you have any concerns about speaking—even though your legs have turned to rubber bands and your mind to jelly. The problem is that everyone in the room, including you, will know you're scared when your hands start shaking, your voice cracks, and you forget what you were going to say.

The second way to approach this barrier is to fight it. You can tell yourself, "I'm not going to be scared," and then try to keep your knees from knocking. Generally, this doesn't work. In fact, your knee-knocking might get worse.

The third approach is to go to the front of the room, look out into the audience, and say to yourself, "I am scared. I notice that my knees are shaking and my mouth feels dry, and I'm having a rush of thoughts about what might happen if I say the wrong thing. Yup, I'm scared, and that's OK. As a matter of fact, it's just part of me, so I accept it and I'm not going to try to fight it. I'm going to make this presentation even though I'm scared." You might not actually eliminate the fear; however, your barrier about the fear—which is what inhibits you—might disappear. And you might discover that if you examine the fear, love it, accept it, and totally experience it, the fear itself also disappears.

Applying this process

Applying this process is easier if you remember three ideas. First, loving a problem is not necessarily the same as enjoying it. Love in this sense means total and unconditional acceptance.

This can work even with problems as thorny as physical pain. When we totally experience pain, it often diminishes and sometimes it disappears. This strategy can work with emotions and even with physical pain. Make it your aim to love the pain, that is, to fully accept the pain and know all the details about it. Most pain has a wavelike quality. It rises, reaches a peak of intensity, and then subsides for a while. See if you can watch the waves as they come and go.

Second, unconditional acceptance is not the same as unconditional surrender. Accepting a problem does not mean escaping from it or giving up on finding a solution. Rather, this process involves freeing ourselves from the

When we accept the fact that we have a problem, we are more likely to find effective ways to deal with it.

grip of the problem by diving *into* the problem headfirst and getting to know it in detail.

Third, love and laughter are allies. It's hard to resist a problem while you are laughing at it. Sure, that incident when you noticed the spinach in your teeth only *after* you got home from a first date was a bummer. But with the passage of time, you can admit that it was kind of funny. You don't have to wait weeks to gain that perspective. As long as you're going to laugh anyway, why wait? The sooner you can see the humor in your problems, the sooner you can face them.

When people first hear about loving their problems, they sometimes think it means being resigned to problems. Actually, loving a problem does not need to stop us from solving it. In fact, fully accepting and admitting the problem usually helps us take effective action—which can free us of the problem once and for all. ◈

career application

Debbie Jones is a sales representative for a medical supplies company. She joined the company six months ago. This is her first job after graduating with a BA in marketing.

A key part of Debbie's job is quickly learning the names of her customers—purchasing agents at hospitals and medical clinics. Debbie wants to establish long-term relationships with these customers. She enjoys chatting with them informally for a few minutes after taking care of business. In addition to recalling customer names, she wants to remember something unique about them—perhaps their hobbies or the names of their children.

Debbie has a solid foundation for meeting this goal. During her senior year in college, she networked extensively and developed a list of job contacts that she updated monthly. She also joined the student chapter of a professional association for people majoring in marketing. Debbie was on a first-name basis with her chapter's 20 members. After a meeting in which members stated their five-year career goals, she was able to recall each person's goal for months afterward.

Debbie's company is now phasing in new contact management software for all its sales representatives to use. That way, they can share contact information such as customer names, billing addresses, and recent orders.

Debbie acknowledges the value of this software. Yet she's struggling to learn it and is embarrassed to admit this fact. The software is just so different from anything she's used before. She has trouble remembering keyboard commands. Her customer files are incomplete, and she's taken to writing information on 3x5 cards instead of using the computer.

While in college, Debbie gained her computer skills by watching classmates demonstrate software and then trying it out herself while asking questions. At her job, however, she fears that this will take too much time and make her appear unprofessional. ⊠

Reflecting on this scenario:

1. How would you describe Debbie's learning style?

_____

_____

_____

2. List two transferable skills that Debbie demonstrates in this scenario.

_____

_____

_____

3. Referring to the SCANS chart listed on page 8, identify two skills that would be useful for Debbie to develop.

_____

_____

_____

4. List two strategies from this chapter that would be useful to Debbie. Briefly describe how she could apply each one.

_____

_____

_____

Name _____ Date _____/_____/_____

quiz

1. Explain how the "recite and repeat" memory technique leads to synergy.

2. Give a specific example of "setting a trap" for your memory.

3. Describe a visualization that can help you remember Boyle's law.

4. Define *acronym* and give an example.

5. Memorization on a deep level can take place if you:
   (A) Repeat the idea.
   (B) Repeat the idea.
   (C) Repeat the idea.
   (D) All of the above.

6. Mnemonic devices are tricks that can increase your ability to:
   (A) Manage your time.
   (B) Understand or digest material.
   (C) Recall information that you already understand.

7. Briefly describe at least three memory techniques.

8. There are five general categories of mnemonic devices given in the text. Explain two of them.

9. Briefly describe two ideas that can help you unconditionally accept a problem you're having right now.

10. Explain a strategy that can help transfer information from your short-term memory into your long-term memory.

learning styles application

The questions below will "cycle" you through four styles, or modes, of learning as explained in the article "Learning styles: Discovering how you learn" in Chapter One. Each question will help you explore a different mode. You can answer the questions in any order.

what if Describe how you intend to use a technique from this chapter in a situation outside school where memory skills are important.

why List some important situations in which you could be more effective by improving your memory skills.

how Describe how you intend to use a technique from this chapter in a class where memory skills are important.

what List the three most useful memory techniques you learned from this chapter.

master student

profile

CESAR CHAVEZ

(1927–1993) leader of the United Farm Workers (UFW), organized strikes, boycotts, and fasts to improve conditions for migrant workers.

A **few men and women have** engraved their names in the annals of change through nonviolence, but none have experienced the grinding childhood poverty that Chavez did after the Depression-struck family farm on the Gila River was foreclosed in 1937. Chavez was 10. His parents and the five children took to the picking fields as migrant workers.

Chavez's faith sustained him, but it is likely that it was both knowing and witnessing poverty and the sheer drudgery and helplessness of the migrant life that drove him.

He never lost the outreach that he had learned from his mother, who, despite the family's poverty, told her children to invite any hungry people in the area home to share what rice, beans and tortillas the family had.

He left school to work. He attended 65 elementary schools but never graduated from high school . . . .

It was in the fields, in the 1950s, that Chavez met his wife, Helen. The couple and their eight children gave much to "La Huelga," the strike call that became the UFW trademark, from their eventual permanent home near Bakersfield. Chavez did not own

the home . . . but paid rent out of his $900 a month as a union official.

Yet, in the fields in the 1930s, something happened that changed Chavez's life. He was 12 when a Congress of Industrial Organizations union began organizing dried-fruit industry workers, including his father and uncle. The young boy learned about strikes, pickets and organizing.

For two years during World War II, Chavez served in the U.S. Navy; then it was back to the fields and organizing. There were other movements gaining strength in the United States during those years, including community organizing.

From 1952 to 1962, Chavez was active outside the fields, in voter registration drives and in challenging police and immigration abuse of Mexicans and Mexican-Americans.

At first, in the 1960s, only one movement had a noticeable symbol: the peace movement. By the time the decade ended, the United Farm Workers, originally established as the National Farm Workers Association, gave history a second flag: the black Aztec eagle on the red background.

In eight years, a migrant worker son of migrants helped change a nation's perception through non-violent resistance. It took courage, imagination, and the ability to withstand physical and other abuse.

The facts are well-known now. During the 1968 grape boycott, farmers and growers fought him, but

Chavez stood firm. Shoppers hesitated, then pushed their carts past grape counters without buying. The growers were forced to negotiate.

The UFW as a Mexican-American civil rights movement in time might outweigh the achievements of the UFW as a labor movement, for Chavez also represented something equally powerful to urban Mexican-Americans and immigrants—a nonviolent leader who had achieved great change from the most humble beginnings.

Yet, through the UFW, Chavez and his colleagues brought Americans face-to-face with the true costs, the human costs, of the food on their tables and brought Mexican-Americans into the political arena and helped keep them there. . . .

Word of Chavez's death spread to the union halls decorated with the Virgin of Guadalupe and UFW flag, to the fields, to the small towns and larger cities. And stories about the short, compact man with the ready smile, the iron determination, the genuine humility and the deep faith were being told amid the tears. ◪

Reprinted by permission of the *National Catholic Reporter*, Kansas City, MO 64111.

For more biographical information about Cesar Chavez, visit the Master Student Hall of Fame on the *From Master Student to Master Employee* Web site at

masterstudent.college.hmco.com

CHAPTER 4
Reading

Much of this chapter is a review of what students might have learned in grade school. Relearning these skills as an adult is important. Our motivation, maturity, and life experiences all contribute to valuing the skills of reading comprehension and reading speed more than we might have as children. Accelerate your students' ability to learn new material by helping them activate relevant prior knowledge. Encourage your students to use the information they have learned about the brain in the memory chapter to enhance their skill at reading. Consider the Master Student Map at the beginning of the chapter as a stepping-stone.

Page 124
Master Student Map

Now that your students have practiced using the Master Student Map in previous chapters, see if they can generate their own questions before you present yours to the class.

why? Why does *From Master Student to Master Employee* include a chapter on reading?

what? Read through the list of articles and select three that you believe will enhance your reading skills.

how? can you be more successful in college with these additional strategies for successful reading? How will these strategies help you in your intended career?

what if? What if you apply these reading strategies to your coursework for other classes? And what if you begin to use these strategies in the workplace?

Page 125
Muscle Reading

Muscle Reading is designed as a balanced literacy approach, incorporating the three aspects of a metacognitive reading system. This means that it presents specific strategies for students to use before, during, and after the reading. Presenting the many steps using these three principles will help those students who feel that this process has too many "steps" be more at ease. Consider demonstrating the steps with your class. An easy way to do this is to use one of the chapters in *From Master Student to Master Employee*. Try the different steps using Chapter Five: Notes.

Remind students that Muscle Reading is an example of a mnemonic device in action. Chances are if they find success using this process they may be further encouraged to try creating their own devices in the future.

SCANS highlights reading skills under several different auspices. Basic skills (reading to locate, understand, and interpret written information), thinking skills (seeing things in the mind's eye to interpret and create symbols, pictures, graphs, and other visual tools), and information competencies (acquiring and evaluating; organizing and maintaining; and, interpreting and communicating) are integral to success in college and in the workplace. Have your students align the steps of Muscle Reading to the SCANS skills that are mentioned above. Your students will quickly see how important each of the Muscle Reading skills are important as a whole.

Eldon McMurray, instructor at Utah Valley State College, divides his students into three groups when discussing Muscle Reading: before, during, and after. He has each group prepare a 10-minute presentation on the three steps within their given area, aiming for a memorable lesson that provides examples of their strategies. As a concluding project, each group comes up with a sample test question to help determine how the rest of the class understood their presentation.

Page 131
Reading fast

The objective of this technique is to increase reading speed without sacrificing comprehension. The tools presented in this article can be practiced on the Master Student Web site (**masterstudent.college.hmco.com**) in an exercise titled "Timed reading." Twenty-four different articles on a variety of topics (from the communication styles of men and women to Pablo Picasso) are available for this exercise. Students click a button to begin the timed reading exercise and a "finished" button when they are done. Their reading rate for that passage is then displayed. Next, students answer multiple choice comprehension questions to ensure that they understand what they have read.

Page 136
Reading with children underfoot

Returning students and single parents feel validated by the inclusion of this article in the book. The practical and useful strategies presented here were reviewed by students who are currently raising children while pursuing their degrees.

Parents can join in the discussion group on the Master Student Web site to share their experiences and read about new ideas for balancing school and family responsibilities.

Page 138
Exercise #16: Revisit your goals

One powerful way to achieve any goal is to assess periodically your progress in meeting it. This exercise provides you and your students an opportunity to reflect on the materials that have been covered to date. Students are asked to reflect on their goals set in Chapter Two and make adjustments to their plan. While discussing this exercise with your students, suggest that they look back at their Discovery Wheel in Chapter One and review their progress to date. Students will be given a formal post-course Discovery Wheel in Chapter 10.

Page 152
POWER PROCESS: "Notice your pictures and let them go"

Dean Mancina, instructor at Golden West College, approaches this Power Process as a problem-solving technique. When students feel frustrated because reality does not match their expectations, "notice your pictures"

helps them let go of those expectations and experience what their reality *does* have to offer. In class, Dean has his students individually brainstorm "pictures" that interfere with their success in college. Examples include "I'm not smart enough to get a college degree" or "I'll never graduate—I can't stick with anything for four years." Then the students select one picture to "let go." They rewrite it on a small piece of paper and fold it up. As a class, Dean takes his students outside and put these negative pictures in the dumpster—literally letting them go! When the students return to class, they briefly write about a new, positive picture to replace the negative one they have let go.

The *Power Up: Four-in-one Power Process* video has a section related to this Power Process. Use the video as a "guest speaker" for your class and let the classroom and workplace examples that are demonstrated teach the lesson for you!

Page 143
Career Application

After your students work through the case study for Chapter Four, they may be interested in some new approaches to reading materials for the workplace. Consider sharing some of these ideas. Remind students that they *read with a purpose*. At work, understanding the purpose of reading each document in order to achieve the desired outcome is important. In today's workplace, students will face full e-mail in-boxes. Suggest students *print e-mails for reading offline*. Talking about what you read is a powerful way to transform data into insight. Encourage students to *discuss what they read with coworkers*.

Page 145
Master Student Profile: Ruth Handler

Ruth Handler's profile provides students with an example of someone who displayed the master student qualities discussed in the Power Process "Notice your pictures and let them go." When Handler wanted to attend college, and marry her high school sweetheart, she didn't let anything get in her way. Her focus and awareness of her pictures provided her with strength throughout her lifetime. In 1970, Handler was diagnosed with breast cancer and had to undergo a mastectomy. While she didn't have pictures of what people with a mastectomy looked like, she overcame her depression by finding a solution to her problem. When she didn't find a prosthesis that fit comfortably, she began a new venture and began a new company, Nearly Me, which she ran until 1991 when it was sold to Spenco, a subsidiary of Kimberly Clark. Begin a discussion with your students about how you can change your pictures based on extreme need by adding this information to Handler's story. Have your students use the additional biographical information about Handler located in the Master Student Hall of Fame on the *From Master Student to Master Employee* Web site to have further basis for conversation.

masterstudent.college.hmco.com

Guest speaker idea

One suggestion for inviting guest speakers to class while you discuss the topic of reading is to invite instructors from a variety of disciplines to talk about reading strategies appropriate to their course content. Prior to their visiting your class, ask them to come prepared to answer the following questions for your students:

why? Why is the reading material in your discipline area unique?

what? What strategies would work best to tackle the reading material in your discipline area? Suggest your discipline expert bring a sample passage for students (as a handout) that they can use this new strategy to read with.

how? How can students improve their reading comprehension in your discipline area using these strategies?

what if? What if the students are still having trouble with reading in this discipline? What resources do you suggest (on-campus labs, ancillary textbooks, Web sites, etc.)?

Practicing critical thinking in the classroom

Developing critical thinking strategies throughout the semester will help your students master their college-level reading. Use this exercise to help students further develop their skills. This works best as either an extra credit assignment or as homework.

One of the suggested strategies for understanding difficult reading material is to read another publication on the same subject. This is one example of critical thinking skills—explaining and assessing alternative views on an issue.

Apply this strategy now. Ask your students to find and read a newspaper or magazine article that's relevant to one of their current reading assignments. Have your students summarize and compare the viewpoints on the subject presented by both authors. Ask them to list the major questions addressed along with the answers that are offered and have them highlight points of disagreement and agreement.

Finally, have your students consider the methods the authors use to reach their conclusion and evidence they present. Have students determine if one author's viewpoint is more reasonable, given all of the suitable evidence, by writing their response in a paragraph that supports their conclusion.

If you assign this for extra credit or homework, be sure to clarify for your students exactly which materials they should submit. Consider asking them to submit their articles or a bibliography page. If you are trying to encourage students to get familiar with technology, ask them to forward you the materials in an e-mail attachment or post to your online course management system.

Additional resources for ESL students

English as a second language (ESL) students working towards mastering higher education and a new language may benefit from additional resources for student success. The *From Master Student to Master Employee* Web site (**masterstudent.college.hmco.com**) connects with XPRESLINK from Houghton Mifflin's English as a Second Language textbook list.

XPRESLINK is an Internet activity designed to help students develop language skills from authentic Web sites. Sites organized by topics—with questions at low, middle, and high language levels—are provided to stimulate student discussion and writing.

Course Manual

As you are teaching the chapter on reading, you might be uncertain if your students are actually completing the reading for *this* course. The *Course Manual* provides information about ways to encourage reading:

✔ Testing on the reading

✔ Collecting the quizzes, exercises, and Journal Entries

✔ Allowing students to do the teaching

✔ Tailoring the textbook to your class

Strategies for encouraging students to purchase the textbook are also provided in the *Course Manual*.

HM ClassPrep CD

PowerPoint for Chapter Four walks students through the Muscle Reading strategies. Highlight for your students the three short sentences that will help them recall the different steps:

✔ Pry out questions.

✔ Root up answers.

✔ Recite, review, and review again.

In-class exercises that will help your students improve their reading comprehension can be found on the HM ClassPrep CD accompanying this chapter. Try the techniques discussed in "Reading comprehension" and "Drawing conclusions."

Additional Resources

The *Power Up: Four-in-One Power Process* video features a segment about "Notice your pictures and let them go." Examples of how to apply this process in higher education and in the workplace are provided. Exercises to accompany this are available on the HM ClassPrep CD.

Invite your students to test their vocabulary with **100 words** that every high school student should know. The words were selected by the editors of the *American Heritage Dictionary*.

Articles on **timed reading** are available to help students improve their reading speed without sacrificing comprehension.

Did your students understand the materials in this chapter? Have them complete the ACE Practice test to see how they measure up.

4

Reading

Let us read with method, and propose to ourselves an end to which our studies may point. The use of reading is to aid us in thinking.

EDWARD GIBBON

There would seem to be almost no limit to what people can and will misunderstand when they are not doing their utmost to get at a writer's meaning.

EZRA POUND

why
this chapter matters . . .

Success in the workplace and in higher education requires extensive reading that results in comprehension of facts, figures, and concepts.

what
is included . . .

Muscle Reading
How Muscle Reading works
Phase one: Before you read
Phase two: While you read
Phase three: After you read
Building your vocabulary
Reading fast
When reading is tough
English as a second language
Reading with children underfoot
Power Process: "Notice your pictures and let them go"
Master Student Profile: Ruth Handler

how
you can use this chapter . . .

Analyze what effective readers do and experiment with new techniques.
Increase your vocabulary and adjust your reading speed for different types of material.
Comprehend difficult content with more ease.

As you read, ask yourself
what if . . .

I could finish my reading with time to spare and easily recall the key points?

Muscle Reading

Picture yourself sitting at a desk, a book in your hands. Your eyes are open, and it looks as if you're reading. Suddenly your head jerks up. You blink. You realize your eyes have been scanning the page for 10 minutes, and you can't remember a single thing you have read.

Or picture this: You've had a hard day. You were up at 6 a.m. to get the kids ready for school. A coworker called in sick, and you missed your lunch trying to do his job as well as your own. You picked up the kids, then had to shop for dinner. Dinner was late, of course, and the kids were grumpy.

Finally, you get to your books at 8 p.m. You begin a reading assignment on something called "the equity method of accounting for common stock investments." "I am preparing for the future," you tell yourself, as you plod through two paragraphs and begin the third. Suddenly, everything in the room looks different. Your head is resting on your elbow, which is resting on the equity method of accounting. The clock reads 11:00 p.m. Say good-bye to three hours.

Sometimes the only difference between a sleeping pill and a textbook is that the textbook doesn't have a warning on the label about operating heavy machinery.

Muscle Reading is a technique you can use to avoid mental minivacations and reduce the number of unscheduled naps during study time, even after a hard day. More than that, this technique is a way to decrease effort and struggle by increasing energy and skill. The ability to find information, locate main ideas, and identify relevant details are all transferable skills that can be further developed and practiced through Muscle Reading. Once you learn this technique, you can actually spend less time on your reading and get more out of it.

This is not to say that Muscle Reading will make your education or job a breeze. Muscle Reading might even look like more work at first. Effective reading is an active, energy-consuming, sit-on-the-edge-of-your-seat business. That's why this strategy is called Muscle Reading. ✖

journal entry 12

Discovery/Intention Statement

Recall a time when you encountered problems with reading, such as words you didn't understand or paragraphs you paused to reread more than once. Sum up the experience and how you felt about it by completing the following statement.

I discovered that I . . .

_____

_____

_____

_____

_____

Now list three to five specific reading skills you want to gain from this chapter.

I intend to . . .

_____

_____

_____

_____

_____

_____

_____

_____

_____

How Muscle Reading works

Muscle Reading is a three-phase technique you can use to extract the ideas and information you want.

Phase one includes steps to take *before* you read. Phase two includes steps to take *while* you read. Phase three includes steps to take *after* you read.

Each phase has three steps.

PHASE ONE
Before you read

Step 1   Preview
Step 2   Outline
Step 3   Question

PHASE TWO
While you read

Step 4   Read
Step 5   Underline
Step 6   Answer

PHASE THREE
After you read

Step 7   Recite
Step 8   Review
Step 9   Review again

A nine-step reading strategy might seem cumbersome and unnecessary for a two-page reading assignment. It is. Use the steps appropriately. Choose which ones to apply as you read.

To assist your recall of Muscle Reading strategies, memorize three short sentences:

Pry Out Questions.
Root Up Answers.
Recite, Review, and Review again.

These three sentences correspond to the three phases of the Muscle Reading technique.

Each sentence is an acrostic. The first letter of each word stands for one of the nine steps listed above.

Take a moment to invent images for each of those sentences. For *phase one*, visualize or feel yourself prying out questions from a text. These are questions you want answered based on a brief survey of the assignment. Make a mental picture of yourself scanning the material, spotting a question, and reaching into the text to pry it out. Hear yourself saying, "I've got it. Here's my question." Then for *phase two*, get your muscles involved. Feel the tips of your fingers digging into the text as you root up the answers to your questions. Finally, you enter *phase three*. Hear your voice reciting what you have learned. Listen to yourself making a speech or singing a song about the material as you review it.

To jog your memory, write the first letters of the Muscle Reading acrostic in a margin or at the top of your notes. Then check off the steps you intend to follow. Or write the Muscle Reading steps on 3x5 cards and then use them for bookmarks. Keep in mind that these steps apply to all kinds of reading beyond textbooks. Use Muscle Reading to get what you want from work-related reading materials as well: reports, brochures, trade journals, meeting minutes, e-mails, and Web pages.

Muscle Reading could take a little time to learn. At first you might feel it's slowing you down. That's natural when you're gaining a new skill. Mastery comes with time and practice.

PHASE ONE
Before you read

Step 1 Preview

Before you start reading, preview the material. You don't have to memorize what you preview to get value from this step. Previewing sets the stage for incoming information by warming up a space in your mental storage area.

If you are starting a new book, look over the table of contents and flip through the text page by page. If you're going to read one chapter, flip through the pages of that chapter. Even if you plan to only read a few pages in a book, you can benefit from a brief preview of the table of contents.

Keep the preview short. If your entire reading session will take less than an hour, your preview might take five minutes. Previewing is also a way to get yourself started when material looks too big to handle. It is an easy way to step into the reading.

Keep an eye out for summary statements. If the assignment is long or complex, read the summary first. Many books and articles have summaries in the introduction or in the closing paragraph.

Read all headings and subheadings. Like the headlines in a newspaper, these are usually printed in large, bold type. Often headings are brief summaries in themselves.

When previewing, seek out familiar concepts, facts, or ideas. These items can help increase comprehension by linking new information to previously learned material. Look for ideas that spark your imagination or curiosity. Inspect drawings, diagrams, charts, tables, graphs, and photographs. Imagine what kinds of questions will show up on a test. Previewing helps to clarify your purpose for reading. Ask yourself what you will do with this material and how it can relate to your long-term goals. Are you reading just to get the main points? Key supporting details? Additional details? All of the above? Your answers will guide what you do with each step that follows.

Step 2 Outline

With complex material, take time to understand the structure of what you are about to read. Outlining actively organizes your thoughts about the assignment and can help make complex information easier to understand.

If your book, article, or other document provides an outline, spend some time studying it. When an outline is not provided, sketch a brief one in the margin of the page or at the beginning of your notes on a separate sheet of paper. Later, as you read and take notes, you can add to your outline.

Headings in the text can serve as major and minor entries in your outline. For example, the heading for this article is "Phase one: Before you read," and the subheadings list the three steps in this phase. When you outline, feel free to rewrite headings so that they are more meaningful to you.

The amount of time you spend on this step will vary. For some assignments, a 10-second mental outline is all you might need. For other assignments (fiction and poetry, for example), you can skip this step altogether.

Step 3 Question

Before you begin a careful reading, determine what you want. Write down a list of questions to answer, including any that resulted from your preview of the material.

Another useful technique is to turn headings and subheadings into questions. For example, if a heading is "Transference and suggestion," you can ask yourself, "What are *transference* and *suggestion*? How does *transference* relate to *suggestion*?" Make up a quiz as if you were teaching this subject to your classmates. If there are no headings, look for key sentences and turn these into questions. These sentences usually show up at the beginnings or ends of paragraphs and sections.

Have fun with this technique. Make the questions playful or creative. You don't need to answer every question that you ask. The purpose of making up questions is to get your brain involved in the assignment. Take your unanswered questions to class, where they can be springboards for class discussion.

Demand your money's worth from your textbooks. Aim to create value from anything you read at work and home. If you do not understand a concept, write specific questions about it. The more detailed your questions, the more powerful this technique becomes.

PHASE ONE
BEFORE YOU READ

STEP 1 PREVIEW   STEP 2 OUTLINE   STEP 3 QUESTION

PHASE TWO
WHILE YOU READ

STEP 4
STEP 5
UNDERLINE
STEP 6
ANSWER

PHASE TWO

While you read

Step 4 **Read** At last! You have previewed the assignment, organized it in your mind, and formulated questions. Now you are ready to begin reading.

Before you dive into the first paragraph, take a few moments to reflect on what you already know about this subject. Do this even if you think you know nothing. This technique prepares your brain to accept the information that follows.

As you read, stay focused. Avoid marathon reading sessions. Schedule breaks, and set a reasonable goal for the entire session. Then reward yourself with an enjoyable activity for 5 or 10 minutes every hour or two. For difficult reading, set more limited goals. Read for a half-hour and then take a break.

You can use several techniques to stay focused as you read. First, visualize the material. Form mental pictures of the concepts as they are presented. If you read that a voucher system can help control cash disbursements, picture a voucher handing out dollar bills. Also read the material out loud, especially if it is complicated. Remember that a goal of your reading is to answer the questions you listed during phase one. After you've identified the key questions, predict how the author will answer them. Then read to find out if your predictions were accurate.

Step 5 **Underline** Underlining can save lots of time when you are studying for tests. When you read with a pen or pencil in your hand, you involve your kinesthetic senses of touch and motion.

Avoid underlining too soon. Wait until you complete a chapter or section to make sure you know the key points. Then mark up the text. Sometimes, underlining after you read each paragraph works best.

Underline sparingly, usually less than 10 percent of the text. If you mark up too much on a page, you defeat the purpose—to flag the most important material for review.

Step 6 **Answer** As you read, seek out the answers to your questions and write them down. You are a detective, watching for every clue, sitting erect in your straight-back chair, demanding that the material you are reading gives you what you want—the answers.

→ Five smart ways to highlight a text

Read carefully first. Read an entire chapter or section at least once before you begin highlighting. Don't be in a hurry to mark up your book. Get to know the text first. Make two or three passes through difficult sections before you highlight.

Make choices up front about what to highlight. When you highlight, remember to look for passages that directly answer the questions you posed during step 3 of Muscle Reading. Within these passages, highlight individual words, phrases, or sentences rather than whole paragraphs.

Recite first. You might want to apply step 7 of Muscle Reading before you highlight. Talking about what you read—to yourself or with other people—can help you grasp the essence of a text. Recite first, then go back and highlight. You'll probably highlight more selectively.

Underline, then highlight. Underline key passages lightly in pencil. Then close your text and come back to it later. Assess your underlining. Perhaps you can highlight less than you underlined and still capture the key points.

Use highlighting to monitor your comprehension. Stop reading periodically and look back over the sentences you've highlighted. See if you are making accurate distinctions between main points and supporting material.

In addition to underlining and highlighting, there are more strategies for marking up your text available online at

masterstudent.college.hmco.com

PHASE THREE
After you read

PHASE THREE
AFTER YOU READ
STEP 7 RECITE   STEP 8   STEP 9 REVIEW AGAIN

Step 7

Recite Talk to yourself about what you've read. Or talk to someone else. When you're finished with a reading assignment, make a speech about it. A classic study suggests that you can profitably devote up to 80 percent of your study time to active reciting.[1]

One way to get yourself to recite is to look at each underlined point. Note what you marked, then put the book down and start talking out loud. Explain as much as you can about that particular point. To make this technique more effective, do it in front of a mirror. It might seem silly, but the benefits can be enormous. Reap them at exam time. Classmates are even better than mirrors. Form a group and practice teaching each other what you have read. One of the best ways to learn anything is to teach it to someone else.

Talking about your reading reinforces a valuable skill—the ability to summarize. To practice this skill, use the "topic-point" method. Pick one chapter (or one section of one chapter) from any book. State the main topic covered in this chapter. Then state the main points that the author makes about this topic. Practicing this technique can prepare you for summarizing reports or meeting notes for your boss or your coworkers. For example, the main topic up to this point in this chapter is Muscle Reading. The main point about this topic is that Muscle Reading includes three phases—steps to take before you read, while you read, and after you read. For a more detailed summary, you could name each of the nine steps.

Step 8

Review Plan to do your first complete review within 24 hours of reading the material. If you read it on Wednesday, review it on Thursday. During this review, look over your notes and clear up anything you don't understand. Recite some of the main points again. This review can be short. You might spend as little as 15 minutes reviewing a difficult two-hour reading assignment. Investing that time now can save you hours later—especially when studying for exams.

Step 9

Review again The final step in Muscle Reading is the weekly or monthly review. This step can be very short—perhaps only four or five minutes per assignment. Simply go over your notes. Read the highlighted parts of your text. Recite one or two of the more complicated points. Reviewing meeting notes in this way can help keep you focused on the big picture in the workplace. The purpose of these reviews is to keep the neural pathways to the information open and to make them more distinct. That way, the information can be easier to recall. You can accomplish these short reviews anytime, anywhere, if you are prepared.

Decades ago, psychologists identified the primacy-recency effect, which suggests that we most easily remember the first and last items in any presentation.[2] Previewing and reviewing your reading can put this theory to work for you. ✖

> ## ➜ Muscle Reading—a leaner approach
>
> Keep in mind that Muscle Reading is an overall approach, not a rigid, step-by-step procedure. Here's a shorter variation that students have found helpful. Practice it with any chapter in this book:
>
> - ***Preview and question.*** Flip through the pages, looking at anything that catches your eye—headings, subheadings, illustrations, photographs. Turn the title of each article into a question. For example, "How Muscle Reading works" can become "How does Muscle Reading work?" List your questions on a separate sheet of paper, or write each question on a 3x5 card.
>
> - ***Read to answer your questions.*** Read each article, then go back over the text and underline or highlight answers to the appropriate questions on your list.
>
> - ***Recite and review.*** When you're done with the chapter, close the book. Recite by reading each question—and answering it—out loud. Review the chapter by looking up the answers to your questions. (It's easy—they're already highlighted.) Review again by quizzing yourself one more time with your list of questions.

Building your vocabulary

A large vocabulary makes reading more enjoyable and increases the range of materials you can read. In addition, building your vocabulary gives you more options for self-expression when speaking or writing. When you can choose from a larger pool of words, you increase the precision and power of your thinking. One strategy for success in the workplace is quickly mastering the specialized vocabulary that people in your career field use. Building vocabulary also helps to develop the transferable skills related to reading, strengthening your ability to infer or locate the meaning of unknown terms.

Keep a dictionary handy

One potent ally in building your vocabulary is a dictionary. Print dictionaries come in many shapes and sizes and media: pocket dictionary, desk dictionary, and unabridged (the heftiest and most complete).

Don't forget digital dictionaries. You can buy dictionary software to use on your computer. Also search for dictionary sites on the World Wide Web. To find them, go to your favorite search site and use the keywords *dictionary* or *reference*.

Put your dictionaries to active use. When you find an unfamiliar word, write it down on an index card. Copy the sentence in which it occurred below the word. You can look up each word immediately or accumulate a stack of these cards and look them up later. Write definitions on the back of the cards.

Consider using a computer to create a specialized glossary for each of your courses. As you complete assigned readings and review your class notes, underline key terms. Use a word-processing program to catalog these words and their definitions into an electronic file. Revise definitions and add new terms as the course proceeds. Then print your glossaries to study for tests.

Look for context clues

You can often deduce the meaning of an unfamiliar word simply by paying attention to context—the surrounding words or images. Later you can confirm your trial definition of the word by consulting a dictionary.

Context clues include:

- *Definitions.* A key word may be defined right in the text. Look for phrases such as *the definition is* or *in other words*.

- *Examples.* Authors often provide examples to clarify a word meaning. If the word is not explicitly defined, then study the examples. They're often preceded by the phrases *for example, for instance,* or *such as*.

- *Lists.* When a word is listed in a series, pay attention to the other items in the series. They may, in effect, define the unfamiliar word.

- *Comparisons.* You may find a new word surrounded by synonyms—words with a similar meaning. Look for synonyms after words such as *like* and *as*.

- *Contrasts.* A writer may juxtapose a word with its antonym—a word or phrase with the opposite meaning. Look for phrases such as *on the contrary* and *on the other hand*.

Distinguish between word parts

Words consist of discrete elements that can be combined in limitless ways.

Roots are "home base," a word's core meaning. A single word can have more than one root. *Bibliophile*, for example, has two roots: *biblio* (book) and *phile* (love). A *bibliophile* is a book lover.

Prefixes come at the beginning of a word and often modify the meaning of the word root. In English, a common prefix is the single letter *a*, which often means *not*. Added to *typical*, for example, this prefix results in the word *atypical*, which means "not typical."

Suffixes come at the end of a word. Like prefixes, they can alter or expand the meaning of the root. For instance, the suffix *ant* means "one who." Thus, an *assistant* is "one who assists."

See an unabridged dictionary for more word parts. The time you spend is an investment in your word power. ◪

Learn strategies for further enhancing your vocabulary with a dictionary on the *From Master Student to Master Employee* Web site at

masterstudent.college.hmco.com

One way to read faster is to read faster. This might sound like double talk, but it is a serious suggestion. The fact is, you can probably read faster—without any loss in comprehension—simply by making a conscious effort to do so. Your comprehension might even improve.

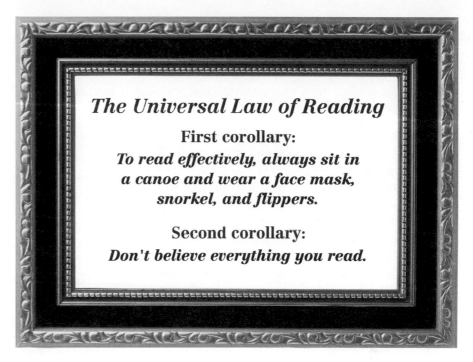

The Universal Law of Reading

First corollary:
To read effectively, always sit in a canoe and wear a face mask, snorkel, and flippers.

Second corollary:
Don't believe everything you read.

Reading fast

Experiment with the "just do it" method right now. Read the rest of this article as fast as you can. After you finish, come back and reread the same paragraphs at your usual rate. Note how much you remember from your first sprint through the text. You might be surprised to find out how well you comprehend material even at dramatically increased speeds. Build on that success by experimenting with the following guidelines.

Get your body ready. Gear up for reading faster. Get off the couch. Sit up straight at a desk or table, on the edge of your chair, with your feet flat on the floor. If you're feeling adventurous, read standing up.

Set a time limit. When you read, use a clock or a digital watch with a built-in stopwatch to time yourself. You are not aiming to set speed records, so be realistic. For example, set a goal to read two or three sections of a chapter in an hour, using all of the Muscle Reading steps. If that works, set a goal of 50 minutes for reading the same number of sections. Test your limits. The idea is to give yourself a gentle push, increasing your reading speed without sacrificing comprehension.

The idea is to give yourself a gentle push, increasing your reading speed without sacrificing comprehension.

Relax. It's not only possible to read fast when you're relaxed, it's easier. Relaxation promotes concentration. And remember, relaxation is not the same as sleep. You can be relaxed *and* alert at the same time.

Move your eyes faster. When we read, our eyes leap across the page in short bursts called *saccades* (pronounced *să-käds´*). A saccade is also a sharp jerk on the reins of a horse—a violent pull to stop the animal quickly. Our eyes stop like that, too, in pauses called *fixations.*

Although we experience the illusion of continuously scanning each line, our eyes actually take in groups of words, usually about three at a time. For more than 90 percent of reading time, our eyes are at a dead stop, in those fixations.

One way to decrease saccades is to follow your finger as you read. The faster your finger moves, the faster your eyes move. You can also use a pen, pencil, or 3x5 card as a guide.

Your eyes can move faster if they take in more words with each burst—for example, six instead of three. To practice taking in more words between fixations, find a newspaper with narrow columns. Then read down one column at a time and fixate only once per line.

In addition to using the above techniques, simply make a conscious effort to fixate less. You might feel a little uncomfortable at first. That's normal. Just practice often, for short periods of time.

Notice and release ineffective habits. Our eyes make regressions, that is, they back up and reread words. You can reduce regressions by paying attention to them. Use the handy 3x5 card to cover words and lines that you have just read. You can then note how often you stop and move the card back to reread the text. Don't be discouraged if you stop often at first. Being aware of it helps you regress less frequently.

Also notice vocalizing. You are more likely to read faster if you don't read out loud or move your lips. You can also increase your speed if you don't subvocalize— that is, if you don't mentally "hear" the words as you read them. To stop doing it, just be aware of it.

Another habit to release is reading letter by letter. When we first learn to read, we do it one letter at a time. By now you have memorized many words by their shape, so you don't have to focus on the letters at all. Read this example: "Rasrhcers at Cbmrigae Uivnretisy funod taht eprxert raeedrs dno't eevn look at the lteters." You get the point. Skilled readers recognize many words and phrases in this way, taking them in at a single glance.

When you first attempt to release these habits, choose simpler reading material. That way, you can pay closer attention to your reading technique. Gradually work your way up to more complex material.

If you're pressed for time, skim. When you're in a hurry, experiment by skimming a document instead of reading the whole thing. Read the headings, subheadings, lists, charts, graphs, and summary paragraphs. Summaries are especially important. They are usually found at the beginning or end of a chapter or section.

Stay flexible. Remember that speed isn't everything. Skillful readers vary their reading rate according to their purpose and the nature of the material. An advanced text in analytic geometry usually calls for a different reading rate than the Sunday comics.

You also can use different reading rates on the same material. For example, you might first sprint through an article for the key words and ideas, then return to the difficult parts for a slower and more thorough reading.

Explore more resources. You can find many books about speed-reading. Using them can be a lot of fun. For more possibilities, including courses and workshops, go to your favorite search engine on the Internet and key in the word *speed-reading*.

In your research, you might discover people who offer to take you beyond speed-reading. According to some teachers, you can learn to flip through a book and "mentally photograph" each page—hundreds or even thousands of words at once. To prepare for this feat, you first do relaxation exercises to release tension while remaining alert. In this state, you can theoretically process vast quantities of information at a level other than your conscious mind.

You might find these ideas controversial. Approach them in the spirit of the Power Process: "Ideas are tools." Also remember that you can use more conventional reading techniques at any time.

One word of caution: Courses and workshops range from free to expensive. Before you lay out any money, check the instructor's credentials and talk to people who've taken the course. Also find out whether the instructor offers free "sampler sessions" and whether you can cancel at some point in the course for a full refund.

Finally, remember the first rule of reading fast: Just do it! ◪

exercise 14

RELAX

Eye strain can be the result of continuous stress. Take a break from your reading and use this exercise to release tension.

1. Sit on a chair or lie down and take a few moments to breathe deeply.

2. Close your eyes, place your palms over your eyes, and visualize a perfect field of black.

3. Continue to be aware of the blackness for two or three minutes while you breathe deeply.

4. Now remove your hands from your eyes and open your eyes slowly.

5. Relax for a minute more, then continue reading.

When reading is tough

Sometimes ordinary reading methods are not enough. Many students get bogged down in a murky reading assignment. If you are ever up to your neck in textbook alligators, you can use the following techniques to drain the swamp.

Read it again. Difficult material—such as the technical writing in science, math, or specialized subjects—is often easier the second time around. If you read a document and feel completely lost, do not despair. Admit your confusion. Sleep on it. When you return to the text, regard it with fresh eyes.

Look for essential words. If you are stuck on a paragraph, mentally cross out all of the adjectives and adverbs and read the sentence without them. Find the important words. These will usually be verbs and nouns.

Hold a minireview. Pause briefly to summarize—either verbally or in writing—what you've read so far. Stop at the end of a paragraph and recite, in your own words, what you have just read. Jot down some notes or create a short outline or summary.

Read it out loud. Make noise. Read a passage out loud several times, each time using a different inflection and emphasizing a different part of the sentence. Be creative. Imagine that you are the author talking.

Talk it over. Admit when you are stuck and make an appointment with your instructor. For work-related reading, pose questions to your supervisor or a knowledgeable coworker. Most teachers welcome the opportunity to work individually with students. In the workplace, people may be flattered you asked for the benefit of their wisdom. Be specific about your confusion. Point out the paragraph that you found toughest to understand.

Stand up. Changing positions periodically can combat fatigue. Experiment with standing as you read, especially if you get stuck on a tough passage and decide to read it out loud.

Skip around. Jump immediately to the end of the article or chapter. You might have lost the big picture. Sometimes simply seeing the conclusion or summary is all you need to put the details in context. Retrace the steps in a chain of ideas and look for examples. Absorb facts and ideas in whatever order works for you—which may be different from the author's presentation.

Find a tutor. Many schools provide free tutoring services. If tutoring services are not provided by your school, other students who have completed the course can assist you.

Read related material. Find a similar text in the library. Sometimes a concept is easier to understand if it is expressed another way. Children's books, especially children's encyclopedias, can provide useful overviews of baffling subjects.

Pretend you understand, then explain it. We often understand more than we think we do. Pretend that the material is clear as a bell and explain it to another person, or even yourself. Write down your explanation. You might be amazed by what you know.

Ask: "What's going on here?" When you feel stuck, stop reading for a moment and diagnose what's happening. At these stop points, mark your place in the margin of the page with a penciled "S" for "Stuck." A pattern to your marks over several pages might indicate a question you want to answer before going further. Or you might discover a reading habit you'd like to change.

Stop reading. When none of the above suggestions work, do not despair. Admit your confusion and then take a break. Catch a movie, go for a walk, study another subject, or sleep on it. The concepts you've already absorbed might come together at a subconscious level as you move on to other activities. Allow some time for that process. When you return to the reading material, see it with fresh eyes. ▨

desk of ...

from the

TATYANA LUKANOV, LEGAL SECRETARY:

As a recently hired legal secretary, I am responsible for transcribing correspondence, legal pleadings, and memoranda for the staff attorneys I work for. While handling these documents, I frequently encounter vocabulary that I am unfamiliar with. I keep a legal dictionary handy at my desk, and I use the Internet to research any information I need further explanation on.

journal entry 13

Discovery Statement

Now that you've read about Muscle Reading, review your assessment of your reading skills in the Discovery Wheel on page 28. Do you still think your evaluation was accurate? What new insights do you have about the way you read? Are you a more effective reader than you thought you were? Less effective? Record your observations below.

_____

_____

_____

_____

_____

_____

_____

_____

_____

_____

_____

_____

_____

_____

_____

_____

_____

_____

_____

_____

_____

_____

_____

_____

English as a second language

If you grew up speaking a language other than English, you're probably called a student of English as a Second Language (ESL). This term might not do full justice to your experience. Your cultural background as a whole might differ greatly from many of your fellow students. You might also speak several languages in addition to English.

Knowing a language other than English offers advantages. You can think thoughts that are not possible in English and see the world in ways that are unique to people who speak your native language.

If you are having difficulties mastering English, experiment with the following suggestions to learn English with more success.

Celebrate mistakes

English is a complex language. Whenever you extend your vocabulary and range of expression, the likelihood of making mistakes increases. The person who wants to master English yet seldom makes mistakes is probably being too careful. Do not look upon mistakes as a sign of weakness. Mistakes can be your best teachers—if you are willing to learn from them.

Analyze mistakes

To learn from your mistakes, first make a list of them. Ask an instructor or an English-speaking friend to help you.

Analyze the list and note your most common errors in English vocabulary, grammar, and usage. Write down several examples of these mistakes. For each example, write a corresponding sentence in your native language. Then write the examples correctly in English. Comparing the sets of examples will help you understand how the languages differ and can help you discover the source of your errors.

Learn by speaking and listening

You probably started your English studies by using textbooks. Writing and reading in English are important. To gain greater fluency, also make it your goal to hear and speak English.

For example, listen to radio talk shows. Imitate the speaker's pronunciation by repeating phrases and sentences that you hear. During conversations, also notice the facial expressions and gestures that accompany certain English words and phrases.

If you speak English with an accent, do not be concerned. Many people speak clear, accented English. Work on your accent only if you can't be easily understood.

When in doubt, use expressions you understand

Native speakers of English use many informal expressions that are called *slang*. You are more likely to find slang in conversations than in written English.

Native speakers also use *idioms*—colorful expressions with meanings that are not always obvious. Idioms can often be misunderstood. For instance, a "fork in the road" does not refer to an eating utensil discarded on a street.

Learning how to use slang and idioms is part of gaining fluency in English. However, these elements of the language are tricky. If you mispronounce a key word or leave one out, you can create a misunderstanding. In important situations—such as applying for a job or meeting with a teacher—use expressions you fully understand.

Create a community of English learners

Learning as part of a community can increase your mastery. For example, when completing a writing assignment in English, get together with other people who are learning the language. Read each other's papers and suggest revisions. Plan on revising your paper a number of times based on feedback from your peers. This strategy also applies in the workplace. Building community with your peers is a transferable skill that will help you to develop essential relationships and help you to improve your exchange of job-related information.

You might feel awkward about sharing your writing with other people. Accept that feeling—and then remind yourself of everything you have to gain by learning from a group. In addition to learning English more quickly, you can raise your grades and make new friends.

Native speakers of English might be willing to assist your group. Ask your instructors to suggest someone. This person can benefit from the exchange of ideas and the chance to learn about other cultures.

Celebrate your gains

Every time you analyze and correct an error in English, you make a small gain. Celebrate those gains. Taken together over time, they add up to major progress in mastering English as a second language. ◪

Reading with children underfoot

It is possible to combine effective study time *and* quality time with children. The following suggestions come mostly from students who are also parents. The specific strategies you use will depend on your schedule and the ages of your children.

Attend to your children first. When you first come home from school, keep your books out of sight. Spend 10 minutes with your children before you settle in to study. Give them hugs and ask about their day. Then explain that you have some work to do. Your children might reward you with 30 minutes of quiet time. A short time of full, focused attention from a parent can be more satisfying than longer periods of partial attention.

Of course, this suggestion won't work with the youngest children. If your children are infants or toddlers, schedule sessions of concentrated study for when they are asleep.

Use "pockets" of time. See if you can arrange study time at school or work before you come home. If you arrive at school 15 minutes earlier and stay 15 minutes later, you can squeeze in an extra half-hour of study time that day. Also look for opportunities to study in between classes.

Before you shuttle children to soccer games or dance classes, throw a book in the car. While your children are warming up for the game or changing clothes, steal another 15 minutes to read.

Plan special activities for your child. Find a regular playmate for your child. Some children can pair off with close friends and safely retreat to their rooms for hours of private play. You can check on them occasionally and still get lots of reading done.

Another option is to take your children to a public playground. While they swing, slide, and dig in the sand, you can dig into your textbooks. Lots of physical activity will tire out your children in constructive ways. If they go to bed a little early, that's extra time for you to read.

After you set up appropriate activities for your children, don't attend to them every second, even if you're nearby as they play. Obviously, you want to break up fights, stop unsafe activity, and handle emergencies. Short of such incidents, you're free to read.

Use television responsibly. Another option is to use television as a baby sitter—when you can control the programming. Rent a videotape for your child to watch as you study. If you're concerned about your child becoming a "couch potato," select educational programs that keep his mind active and engaged.

See if your child can use headphones while watching television. That way, the house stays quiet while you study.

Allow for interruptions. It's possible that you'll be interrupted even if you set up special activities for your child in advance. If so, schedule the kind of studying that can be interrupted. For instance, you could write out or review flash cards with key terms and definitions. Save the tasks that require sustained attention for other times.

Plan study breaks with children. Another option is to spend 10 minutes with your children for every 50 minutes that you study. View this not as an interruption but as a study break.

Or schedule time to be with your children when you've finished studying. Let your children in on the plan: "I'll be done reading at 7:30. That gives us a whole hour to play before you go to bed."

Many children love visible reminders that "their time" is approaching. An oven timer works well for this purpose. Set it for 15 minutes of quiet time. Follow that with five minutes of show-and-tell, storybooks, or another activity with your child. Then set the timer for another 15 minutes of studying, another break, and so on.

Develop a routine. Many young children love routines. They often feel more comfortable and secure when they know what to expect. You can use this to your benefit. One option is to develop a regular time for studying and let your child know this schedule: "I have to do my homework between 4 p.m. and 5 p.m. every day." Then enforce it.

Bargain with children. Reward them for respecting your schedule. In return for quiet time, give your child an extra allowance or a special treat. Children might enjoy gaining "credits" for this purpose. Each time they give you an hour of quiet time for studying, make an entry on a chart, put a star on their bulletin board, or give them a "coupon." After they've accumulated a certain number of entries, stars, or coupons, they can cash them in for a big reward—a movie or a trip to the zoo.

Ask other adults for help. This suggestion for studying with children is a message repeated throughout the book: Enlist other people to help support your success.

Getting help can be as simple as asking your spouse, partner, neighbor, or a fellow student to take care of the children while you study. Offer to trade childcare with a neighbor: You will take his kids and yours for two hours on Thursday night if he'll take them for two hours on Saturday morning. Some parents start blockwide baby-sitting co-ops based on the same idea.

Find community activities and services. Ask if your school or place of employment provides a day care service. In some cases, these services are available to students at a reduced cost. Community agencies such as the YMCA might offer similar programs.

You can also find special events that appeal to children. Storytelling hours at the library are one example. While your child is being entertained or supervised, you can stay close by. Use the time in this quiet setting to read a chapter or review class notes.

Make it a game. Reading a chemistry textbook with a 3-year-old in the same room is not as preposterous as it sounds. The secret is to involve your child. For instance, use this time to recite. Make funny faces as you say the properties of the transition elements in the periodic table. Talk in a weird voice as you repeat Faraday's laws. Draw pictures and make up an exciting story about the process of titration.

Read out loud to your children, or use them as an audience for a speech. If you invent rhymes, poems, or songs to help you remember formulas or dates, teach them to your children. Be playful. Kids are attracted to energy and enthusiasm.

Whenever possible, involve family members in tasks related to reading. Older children can help you with research tasks—finding books at the library, looking up news articles, even helping with typing.

When you can't read everything, just read something. One objection to reading with children nearby is "I just can't concentrate. There's no way I can get it all done while children are around."

That's OK. Even if you can't absorb an entire chapter while the kids are running past your desk, you can skim the chapter. Or you could just read the introduction and summary. When you can't get it *all* done, just get *something* done.

Caution: If you always read this way, your education might be compromised. Supplement this strategy with others so that you can get all of your reading done. ⊠

Discover more ways to study with children underfoot at (masterstudent.college.hmco.com)

desk of . . .

from the

KIMANI JONES, PARENT AND STUDENT:

With three children and having not been to school in 10 years, it has been a real challenge for me. I require that my children spend a certain amount of time each evening studying as well as doing chores. I cook several meals on the weekend for the week. The time they spend studying, I study with them. I find that it encourages them to study when they see me do it with them. It helps me because when I don't study, my 14 year old will peak in my room and say, "Ahhhhh, do you have all A's? Don't you think it's a good time to be studying?" When hear your own words come back to you, what can you say?

REVISIT YOUR GOALS

One powerful way to achieve any goal is to assess periodically your progress in meeting it. This is especially important with long-term goals—those that can take years to achieve.

When you did Exercise #6: "Get real with your goals" on page 69, you focused on one long-term goal and planned a detailed way to achieve it. This involved setting mid-term and short-term goals that will lead to achieving your long-term goal. Take a minute to review that exercise and revisit the goals you set. Then complete the following steps.

1. Take your long-term goal from Exercise #6 and rewrite it in the space below. If you can think of a more precise way to state it, feel free to change the wording.

_____

_____

_____

2. Next, check in with yourself. How do you feel about this goal? Does it still excite your interest and enthusiasm? On a scale of 1 to 10, how committed are you to achieving this goal? Write down your level of commitment in the space below.

_____

3. If your level of commitment is five or less, you might want to drop the goal and replace it with a new one. To set a new goal, just turn back to Exercise #6 and do it again. And release any self-judgment about dropping your original long-term goal. Letting go of one goal creates space in your life to set and achieve a new one.

4. If you're committed to the goal you listed in step 1 of this exercise, consider whether you're still on track to achieve it. Have you met any of the short-term goals related to this long-term goal? If so, list your completed goals in the space below.

_____

_____

_____

_____

Before going on to the next step, take a minute to congratulate yourself and celebrate your success.

5. Finally, consider any adjustments you'd like to make to your plan. For example, write additional short-term or mid-term goals that will take you closer to your long-term goal. Or cross out any goals that you no longer deem necessary. Make a copy of your current plan in the space below.

Long-term goal (to achieve within your lifetime):

_____

_____

Supporting mid-term goals (to achieve in one to five years):

_____

_____

_____

_____

_____

Supporting short-term goals (to achieve within the coming year):

_____

_____

_____

_____

_____

_____

THINKING CRITICALLY IN THE CLASSROOM

Read an editorial in a newspaper or magazine. Analyze this editorial by taking notes in the three-column format below. Use the first column for listing major points, the second for supporting points, and the third for key facts or statistics that support the major or minor points. For example:

Major point

The "female condom" has not yet been proved effective as a method of birth control.

Supporting point

Few studies exist on this method.

Key fact

One of the few studies showed a 26 percent failure rate for the female condom.

Major point	*Supporting point*	*Key fact*

Ask another student to do this exercise with you. Then compare and discuss your notes. See if you identified the same main points.

power process

Notice your pictures and let them go

One of the brain's primary jobs is to manufacture images. We use mental pictures to make predictions about the world, and we base much of our behavior on those predictions.

When a cook adds chopped onions, mushrooms, and garlic to a spaghetti sauce, he has a picture of how the sauce will taste and measures each ingredient according to that picture. When an artist is creating a painting or sculpture, she has a mental picture of the finished piece. Novelists often have mental images of the characters that they're about to bring to life. Many parents have a picture about what they want their children to become.

These kinds of pictures and many more have a profound influence on us. Our pictures direct our thinking, our conversations, and our actions—all of which help create our immediate circumstances. That's amazing, considering that we often operate with little, if any, conscious knowledge of our pictures.

Just about any time we feel a need, we conjure up a picture of what will satisfy that need. A baby feels hunger pangs and starts to cry. Within seconds, his mother appears and he is satisfied. The baby stores a mental picture of his mother feeding him. He connects that picture with stopping the hunger pangs. Voilà! Now he knows how to solve the hunger problem. The picture goes on file.

According to psychologist William Glasser, our minds function like a huge photo album.[3] Its pages include pictures of all the ways we've satisfied needs in the past. Whenever we feel dissatisfied, we mentally search the album for a picture of how to make the dissatisfaction go away. With that picture firmly in mind, we act in ways to make the world outside our heads match the pictures inside.

Remember that pictures are not strictly visual images. They can involve any of the senses. When you buy a CD, you have a picture of how it will sound. When you buy a sweater, you have a picture of how it will feel.

A problem with pictures

The pictures we make in our heads are survival mechanisms. Without them, we couldn't get from one end of town to the other. We couldn't feed or clothe ourselves. Without a picture of a socket, we couldn't screw in a light bulb.

Pictures can also get in our way. Take the case of a student who plans to attend a school he hasn't visited. He chose this school for its strong curriculum and good academic standing, but his brain didn't stop there. In his mind, the campus has historic buildings with ivy-covered walls and tree-lined avenues. The instructors, he imagines, will be as articulate as Bill Moyers and as entertaining as Oprah Winfrey. The cafeteria will be a cozy nook serving delicate quiche and fragrant teas. He will gather there with fellow students for hours of stimulating, intellectual conversation. The library will have every book, while the computer lab will boast the newest technology.

The school turns out to be four gray buildings downtown, next to the bus station. The first class he attends is taught by an overweight, balding instructor, who is wearing a purple-and-orange bird of paradise tie and has a bad case of the sniffles. The cafeteria is a nondescript hall with machine-dispensed food. This hypothetical student gets depressed. He begins to think about dropping out of school.

The problem with pictures is that they can prevent us from seeing what is really there. That happened to the student in this story. His pictures prevented him from noticing that his school is in the heart of a culturally vital city—close to theaters, museums, government offices, clubs, and all kinds of stores. The instructor with the weird tie is not only an expert in his field, but is also a superior teacher. The school cafeteria is skimpy because it can't compete with the variety of inexpensive restaurants in the area. In addition, the school has a thriving career planning and job placement center that connects students with nearby companies for paid internships and professional mentoring.

Anger and disappointment are often the results of our pictures. We set up expectations of events before they occur, which can lead to disappointment. Sometimes we don't even realize that we have these expectations. The next time you discover you are angry, disappointed, or frustrated, look to see which of your pictures aren't being fulfilled.

Take charge of your pictures

Having pictures is unavoidable. Letting these pictures control our lives *is* avoidable. Some techniques for dealing with pictures are so simple and effortless, they might seem silly.

One way to deal with pictures is to be aware of them. Open up your mental photo album and notice how the pictures there influence your thoughts, feelings, and actions. Just becoming aware of your pictures—and how they affect you—can help you take a huge step toward dealing with them effectively.

Our pictures direct our thinking, our conversations, and our actions—all of which help create our immediate circumstances.

When you notice that pictures are getting in your way, then, in the most gentle manner possible, let your pictures go. Let them drift away like wisps of smoke picked up by a gentle wind.

Pictures are persistent. They come back over and over. Notice them again and let them go again. At first, a picture might return repeatedly and insistently. Pictures are like independent beings. They want to live. If you can see the picture as a thought independent from you, you will likely find it easier to let it go.

You are more than your pictures. Many images and words will pop into your head in the course of a lifetime. You do not have to identify with these pictures. You can let pictures go without giving up yourself.

If your pictures are interfering with your performance at work or in the classroom, visualize them scurrying around inside your head. See yourself tying them to a brightly colored helium balloon and letting them go. Let them float away again and again.

Sometimes we can let go of old pictures and replace them with new ones. We stored all of those pictures in the first place. We can replace them. Our student's new picture of a great education can include the skimpy cafeteria and the professor with the weird tie.

We can take charge of the images that float through our minds. We don't have to be ruled by an album of outdated pictures. We can stay aware of our pictures and keep looking for new ones. And when *those* new pictures no longer serve us, we can also let them go. ✖

career application

Sachin Aggarwal worked as a bank teller during the summers while he was in school. After earning an Associate in Science degree in Marketing, he was promoted and gained a new job title: personal banker. When bank customers want to open a new account or take out a car loan, Sachin is the first person they see.

His career plan is to stay at this job for two years and then transfer his degree to a college where he can earn a four-year degree. While working as a teller, Sachin gained a reputation as a "quick study." When the bank installed a new computer system, he completed the online tutorials and stayed on top of the software updates. Within a few weeks, Sachin was training new tellers to use the system.

In addition, he often fielded questions from some of the bank's older employees who described themselves as "computer challenged." Sachin's most recent performance review acknowledged his patience and ability to adapt his explanations to people with various levels of computer experience.

Right now, Sachin's biggest challenge is job-related reading. He never anticipated the number of documents—both printed and online—that would cross his desk after he got promoted. His supervisor has asked him to read technical manuals for each of the bank's services and account plans. He's also taking a customer service course with a 400-page textbook. In addition, he gets about 10 e-mail messages each day, some of them several screens long.

Within the first week after his promotion, Sachin often asked himself, "Why am I being bombarded with all this material? Most of it doesn't seem relevant to my job." Even so, he decided to put these reactions on hold and just dig in to his reading stack. He figures the best way to proceed is start with any document at random and read it straight through before starting another one. Eventually, he hopes, he'll see a use for it all. ☒

Reflecting on this scenario:

1. Based on his initial response to his reading load, how would you describe Sachin's learning style?

_____

_____

_____

2. Referring to the SCANS chart on page 8, list a transferable skill that Sachin demonstrates in this scenario.

_____

_____

_____

3. Using the same SCANS chart, identify another skill that would be useful to Sachin in this situation. Explain why you chose this skill.

_____

_____

_____

4. List three strategies from this chapter that would be useful to Sachin. Briefly describe how he could apply each one.

_____

_____

_____

Name _____ Date _____/_____/_____

quiz

1. Name the acrostic that can help you remember the steps of Muscle Reading.

2. You must complete all nine steps of Muscle Reading to get the most out of any reading assignment. True or False? Explain your answer.

3. Describe at least three strategies you can use to preview a reading assignment.

4. What is one benefit of outlining a reading assignment?

5. Define the terms *prefix* and *suffix,* and explain how they can assist you in learning the meanings of new words.

6. To get the most benefit from marking a book, underline at least 25 percent of the text. True or False? Explain your answer.

7. Explain at least three techniques you can use when reading is tough.

8. According to the Power Process in this chapter, mental pictures are strictly visual images. True or False? Explain your answer.

9. Define the "topic-point" method of summarizing.

10. List at least three techniques for increasing your reading speed.

learning styles application

The questions below will "cycle" you through four styles, or modes, of learning as explained in the article "Learning styles: Discovering how you learn" in Chapter One. Each question will help you explore a different mode. You can answer the questions in any order.

what if
Consider how you might adapt or modify Muscle Reading to make it more useful. List any steps that you would add, subtract, or change.

why
List current reading assignments that you could use to practice Muscle Reading.

how
Briefly describe how you will approach reading assignments differently after studying this chapter.

what
List the three most useful suggestions for reading that you gained from this chapter.

master student profile

RUTH HANDLER

As a cofounder of Mattel, she invented the Barbie doll in 1959. After being diagnosed with breast cancer and undergoing a mastectomy, she designed a prosthetic breast that was later patented as Nearly Me.

When Ruth Handler first proposed the idea of a grown-up doll to the toy designers at Mattel—the company she and her husband ran—the designers thought she was crazy. Little girls want to pretend to be mommies, she was told.

No, said Handler. Little girls want to pretend to be bigger girls. And she knew this because she spent a lot of time observing one little girl in particular—her daughter, Barbara, nicknamed "Barbie."

All her life, Ruth has considered the word "no" just another challenge.

When Ruth graduated from East Denver High School and announced her intention to attend college, her family didn't give her a lot of encouragement. Marrying her high-school sweetheart—a broke-but-talented artist named Elliot Handler—was more traditional than going to college. But she ended up at the University of Denver. And she married Elliot anyway. When she took two semesters of business education at the University of California at Los Angeles, she was the only married woman in her class. And she became the first woman to complete the program.

Ruth fell in love with Southern California and was hired as a stenographer at Paramount Studios in Hollywood. The year was 1937. Ruth worked at Paramount until 1941, when she became pregnant with Barbara, and stayed home until after the birth of her son, Ken, in 1944. Staying home made Ruth restless; she wanted to help [her husband] Elliot run his giftware and costume jewelry business. "You make something; I'll sell it," she told him.

In 1944, while the United States was embroiled in World War II, Elliot designed a new style of picture frame made out of the then-revolutionary new plastics. His partner, Harold "Matt" Matson, built samples and Ruth took the frames to a chain of photography studios and got a large order. The three celebrated, calling their new business "Mattel" after MATT and ELliot.

Soon after, plastic was needed for the war effort and became unavailable for civilian use. Fortunately, Elliot came up with the idea of making frames out of scrap wood. Ruth took the samples back to the photography studio and got an even bigger order. Mattel could continue operating. The leftover wood from the picture frames led to a thriving business making doll house furniture.

Worldwide, Mattel sold millions of Ruth Handler's Barbie dolls, boosting the company's sales to $18 million. Within ten years, customers had bought $500 million worth of Barbie products.

Over the years, Ruth moved up from cofounder of the company to executive vice president to president to cochairman of the board of directors. These titles were practically unheard of for women in the 1960s.

Handler remembers one episode that occurred despite her executive status. A brokerage house was holding a meeting with the investment community at a private club, and Handler was to be the keynote speaker. When she arrived at the club, the program planners ushered her into the club through the alley and kitchen. Later, she discovered that she was sneaked into the building because the club didn't allow women. ◼

From Ethlie Ann Vare and Greg Placek, *Women Inventors and Their Discoveries.* Copyright ©1993. Reprinted by permission of The Oliver Press.

For more biographical information on Ruth Handler, visit the Master Student Hall of Fame at the *From Master Student to Master Employee* Web site at

masterstudent.college.hmco.com

CHAPTER 5
Notes

Introducing note taking as a three-part process asks students to understand **why** it is important to capture the context of **what** they are taking notes on. This chapter will help your students identify **what** effective note-taking strategies consist of: observing, recording, and reviewing. Each part of the process is essential and depends on the others. After your students learn new ways to take notes, ask them **how** they will begin to apply these techniques to their other courses and how note-taking will be useful in their intended career. Practice is important in note taking. Encourage your students to test out the new methods over a period of time before they evaluate the effectiveness of a particular method.

Page 146
Master Student Map

Students can begin practicing new note-taking techniques immediately after reading this chapter. As your students begin to transfer and apply what they learn in this course to their other courses, more aha! moments will begin to occur.

why? Why learn about new methods of note taking?

what? What is the Cornell format? What is mind mapping?

how? How can reviewing your notes help you be more successful in school? How can reviewing your notes in the workplace help you be more successful on the job?

what if? What if you observe, record, and review your notes in a new way in all of your classes?

Page 148
Observe

Consider using this strategy to help students become better observers in class. Ask your students to select three of their other courses where they would like to try their advanced note-taking system. By being asked to apply the note-taking concepts to their other courses, students begin to realize the power of the ideas presented in the text. Students are encouraged to develop their own customized way of taking notes. To give them a head start and to help them to understand the idea of setting the stage, I have them prepare their class notes by outlining the textbook reading that the professor's lecture will cover that day.

One strategy for observing more intently is to "Be here now." Students can review this article for strategies that can help them pay closer attention to meetings or classroom experiences. Eldon McMurray, an instructor at Utah Valley State College, has his students designate the upper right-hand corner of their class notes pages as their "be here now" corner. When they catch their mind wandering, they can jot down a note and then bring their attention back to the speaker. Practicing this helps students to stay focused and pay attention to when (and why) their mind wanders.

Page 157
What to do when you miss class

This new sidebar reminds students of the importance of being in class. Encourage students to be sure to record your office hours and contact information, and exchange e-mail addresses and phone numbers with one of their classmates. Take this opportunity to refresh your students on other classroom etiquette or campus policies.

Page 151
Record

After your students have read through the variety of note-taking strategies, have each of your students select one strategy to try while you give a short lecture. The lecture you provide can be on a topic of interest to your students. Consider talking about the importance of note-taking in different career choices. Or invite a guest speaker to administer a brief lecture on a topic of interest specific to your student body. While this lecture is given, students should practice the note-taking strategy they have selected. After the lecture, have students form groups with students who used alternative note-taking strategies so that they can compare differences. As a whole class, discuss the strengths and weaknesses of the different techniques. This in-class practice helps convince students to try something new in their other courses.

Page 156
Review

For many students, 24 hours is too long to wait before reviewing and processing their notes into long-term memory. For difficult classes or upper-division theory-based courses, ask your students to answer the questions using the strengths of each mode in the Learning Styles Application or Master Student Map exercises. Students can summarize their notes during their review by answering these key questions: **Why** is this idea important? **What** are the details I need to know? **How** will I remember and prepare to be tested on this material? **What if** the test is multiple choice? What if the test is an essay question?

Page 158
Observe, record, and review at meetings

Many people are resigned to writing illegibly for the rest of their lives. They feel that they have no control over their handwriting. If your students feel that their handwriting could hold them back—in the workplace or in the classroom—share some techniques for improvement. Appreciate the value of legible writing in your students' work. Suggest that they focus their attention ("Be here now") on the tip of the pen, where it meets the paper.

This provides the brain with something to do, and allows the body to do the writing. Have your students practice their best handwriting by submitting their work to you as clearly as they can. Clean and neat work makes a long and lasting impression.

Page 164
POWER PROCESS: "I create it all"
Ask your students to recall a recent situation at college, work, or home and ask them to write a brief summary of this situation in their notes. Then ask them to identify six ways that they created that successful situation. After they have completed this exercise, ask for volunteers to share these stories.

Then repeat this exercise asking students to recall a recent situation that did *not* work out well. Students will find this harder to complete. Have volunteers share these stories with other members of the class.

Page 166
Career Application
The application in this case study focuses on how the importance of note taking might come into play in any type of career. This also addresses SCANS skills related to understanding systems, applying technology to tasks, and maintaining and troubleshooting technology. Hanae also must practice interpersonal skills by participating as a member of a team, teaching others, serving internal clients and customers, and exercising leadership. This is an opportunity to put these skills into practice. Ask students in your class to share stories where they have had to take notes, and bring information back from one source to share with team members. What are some strategies that worked? Which ones did not work?

Page 169
Master Student Profile: Faye Wattleton
Ask your students to further research one idea mentioned in Wattleton's profile. Write down one fact or piece of information that is new and interesting. This is an opportunity to practice acquiring and evaluating information. Have students share this information during your next class meeting and teach the other students in your class about what they learned. Some suggested outside topics for this article include information about Planned Parenthood or the Center for the Advancement of Women.

Master Instructor Resource Guide

MASTER
Student

Course Manual

 Take this opportunity to review information in the *Course Manual* article **"An involving course model."** Let your students know when you are taking time to preview and especially *review* material in your course, emphasizing how this can help them be more successful note takers. As you preview, set the stage for learning and application. State questions for students to consider during lectures. Remind students to make sure that they know the answers to these questions before they leave class—especially if a quiz or an evaluation is scheduled for the following class meeting.

HM ClassPrep CD

 PowerPoint for Chapter Five provides additional examples of note-taking strategies to share with your students.

The HM ClassPrep CD has ideas to help you encourage class participation, using a technique called SLANT.

Invite a guest speaker to your class to lecture on a new topic, so students can practice their new note-taking techniques in a comfortable learning environment.

Invite other guest speakers from across the disciplines to speak about effective note-taking strategies for their own subject areas.

Additional Resources

 The *I Create It All* video highlights key concepts from this Power Process. Use it to augment your in-class discussion, and follow up with the exercise mentioned in AIE Chapter Five. Exercises to use with your students after viewing the videotape are available on the HM ClassPrep CD.

masterstudent.college.hmco.com Additional examples of **sample concept maps** for selected articles in the textbook can be found on the *From Master Student to Master Employee* Web site. Ask your students to create a concept map for one of the articles in the next chapter, so they can begin to transfer the strategies from one chapter to the next.

The Web site also includes ideas on how to take notes while reading materials or attending lectures online. Have your students review these ideas and then provide you with a summary or a concept map of what they have learned.

5

Notes

Rather than try to gauge your note-taking skill by quantity, think in this way: am I simply doing clerk's work or am I assimilating new knowledge and putting down my own thoughts? To put down your own thoughts you must put down your own words. . . . If the note taken shows signs of having passed through a mind, it is a good test of its relevance and adequacy.

JACQUES BARZUN AND HENRY GRAFF

why
this chapter matters . . .

Note taking makes you an active learner, enhances memory, and influences how well you do on tests and other types of evaluations.

what
is included . . .

The note-taking process flows
Observe
Record
Review
Observe, record, and review at meetings
Taking notes while reading
Create your instructor
When a speaker talks fast
Power Process: "I create it all"
Master Student Profile: Faye Wattleton

how
you can use this chapter . . .

Experiment with several formats for note taking.
Create a note-taking format that works especially well for you.
Take effective notes in special situations—while reading, when speakers talk fast, and during meetings.

As you read, ask yourself
what if . . .

I could take notes that remain informative and useful for weeks, months, or even years to come?

The note-taking process flows

One way to understand note taking is to realize that taking notes is just one part of the process. Effective note taking consists of three parts: observing, recording, and reviewing. First, you observe an "event"—a statement by an instructor, a lab experiment, a slide show of an artist's works, a meeting, or a chapter of required reading. Then you record your observations of that event—that is, you "take notes." Finally, you review what you have recorded.

Each part of the process is essential, and each depends on the others. Your observations determine what you record. What you record determines what you review. And the quality of your review can determine how effective your next observations will be. For example, if you review your notes on the Sino-Japanese War of 1894, the next day's lecture on the Boxer Rebellion of 1900 will make more sense.

Legible and speedy handwriting is also useful in taking notes. A knowledge of outlining is handy, too. A nifty pen, a new notebook, and a laptop computer are all great note-taking devices. And they're all worthless—unless you participate as an energetic observer *in* class and regularly review your notes *after* class. If you take those two steps, you can turn even the most disorganized chicken scratches into a powerful tool.

Sometimes note taking looks like a passive affair, especially when a large group is meeting. One person at the front of the room does most of the talking. Everyone else is seated and silent, taking notes. The lecturer seems to be doing all of the work.

Don't be deceived. Observe more closely, and you'll see some people taking notes in a way that radiates energy. They're awake and alert, poised on the edge of their seats. They're writing, a physical activity that expresses mental engagement. These participants listen for levels of ideas and information, make choices about what to record, and compile materials to review.

In higher education, you might spend hundreds of hours taking notes. Making them more effective is a direct investment in your success. Think of your notes as a textbook that *you* create—one that's more current and more in tune with your learning preferences than any textbook you could buy. ⊠

journal entry 14

Discovery/Intention Statement

Think about the possible benefits of improving your skills at note taking. Recall a recent incident in which you had difficulty taking notes. Perhaps you were listening to a speaker who talked fast, or you got confused and stopped taking notes altogether. Describe the incident in the space below.

_____

_____

_____

_____

_____

Now preview this chapter to find at least five strategies that you can use right away to help you take better notes. Sum up each of those strategies in a few words and note page numbers where you can find out more about each suggestion.

Strategy   *Page number*

_____

_____

_____

_____

_____

Reflect on your intention to experiment actively with this chapter. Describe a specific situation in which you might apply the strategies you listed above. If possible, choose a situation that will occur within the next 24 hours.

I intend to . . .

_____

_____

_____

_____

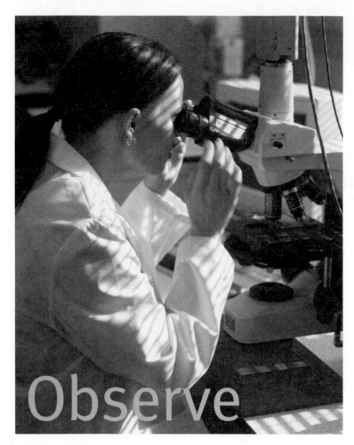

Observe

The note-taking process flows

Sherlock Holmes, a fictional master detective and student of the obvious, could track down a villain by observing the fold of his scarf and the mud on his shoes. In real life, a doctor can save a life by observing a mole—one a patient has always had—that undergoes a rapid change.

An accountant can save a client thousands of dollars by observing the details of a spreadsheet. A student can save hours of study time by observing that she gets twice as much done at a particular time of day.

Keen observers see facts and relationships. They know ways to focus their attention on the details, then tap their creative energy to discover patterns. To sharpen your classroom observation skills, experiment with the following techniques and continue to use those that you find most valuable.

Note: Remember that the following techniques can assist you in the classroom (at a lecture) and in the workplace (during meetings or presentations). Developing the skill of active observation is a transferable skill that will serve you at every step in your career.

Set the stage

Complete outside assignments. Nothing is more discouraging (or boring) than sitting through a lecture about the relationship of Le Chatelier's principle to the principle of kinetics if you've never heard of Henri Louis Le Chatelier or kinetics. Instructors usually assume that students complete assignments, and they construct their lectures accordingly. The more familiar you are with a subject, the more easily you can absorb important information during class lectures.

Bring the right materials. A good pen does not make you a good observer, but the lack of a pen or a notebook can be distracting enough to take the fine edge off your concentration. Make sure you have a pen, pencil, notebook, and any other materials you will need. Bring your textbook to class, especially if the lectures relate closely to the text.

If you are consistently unprepared, that might be a message about your intentions concerning a course or a meeting. Find out if it is. The next time you're in a frantic scramble to borrow pen and paper 37 seconds before the start of the presentation, notice the cost. Use the borrowed pen and paper to write a Discovery Statement about your lack of preparation. Consider whether you intend to be successful—in the course or at your job.

Sit front and center. Students who get as close as possible to the front and center of the classroom often do better on tests for several reasons. The closer you sit to the lecturer, the harder it is to fall asleep. The closer you sit to the front, the fewer interesting, or distracting, classmates are situated between you and the instructor. Material on the board is easier to read from up front. Also, the instructor can see you more easily when you have a question.

Instructors are usually not trained to perform. While some can project their energy to a large audience, some cannot. A professor who sounds boring from the back of the room might sound more interesting up close.

Sitting up front enables you to become a constructive force in the classroom. By returning the positive energy that an engaged teacher gives out, you can reinforce the teacher's enthusiasm and enhance your experience of the class.

In addition, sound waves from the human voice begin to degrade at a distance of 8 to 12 feet. If you sit more than 15 feet from the speaker, your ability to hear and take effective notes might be compromised. Get close to the source of the sound. Get close to the energy.

Sitting close to the front is a way to commit yourself to getting what you want out of school. One reason students gravitate to the back of the classroom is that they think the instructor is less likely to call on them. Sitting in back can signal a lack of commitment. When you sit up front, you are declaring your willingness to take a risk and participate.

Conduct a short preclass review. Arrive early, then put your brain in gear by reviewing your notes from the previous class. Scan your reading assignment. Look at the sections you have underlined. Review assigned problems and exercises. Note questions you intend to ask.

"Be here now"

Accept your wandering mind. Listening can be defined as the process of overcoming distraction. And distraction is a constant factor in human interaction.

In the classroom or during a meeting at work, you may have to deal with external distractions—noises from the next room, people who have side conversations, a lecturer who speaks softly, or audiovisual equipment that malfunctions. Internal distractions can be even more potent. These might include memories about last Saturday night's party, daydreams about what you'll do after work, or feelings of stress.

When the problem is an external distraction, you'll often know what to do about it. You may need to move closer to the front of the room, ask the presenter to speak up, or politely ask people to keep quiet.

Internal distractions can be more tricky. The techniques in the Power Process: "Be here now" can be especially useful when your head soars into the clouds. Don't fight daydreaming. When you notice your mind wandering during class, look at this as an opportunity to refocus your attention. If thermodynamics is losing out to beach parties, let go of the beach.

Notice your writing. When you discover yourself slipping into a fantasyland, feel the weight of your pen in your hand. Notice how your notes look. Paying attention to the act of writing can bring you back to the here and now.

You also can use writing in a more direct way to clear your mind of distracting thoughts. Pause for a few seconds and write those thoughts down. If you're distracted by thoughts of errands you need to run after class, list them on a 3x5 card and stick it in your pocket. Or simply put a symbol, such as an arrow or asterisk, in your notes to mark the places where your mind started to

wander. Once your distractions are out of your mind and safely stored on paper, you can gently return your attention to taking notes.

Be with the speaker. In your mind, put yourself right up front with the speaker. Imagine that you and the speaker are the only ones in the room and that the lecture is a personal conversation between the two of you. Pay attention to the instructor's body language and facial expressions. Look the speaker in the eye.

Notice your environment. When you become aware of yourself daydreaming, bring yourself back to class by paying attention to the temperature in the room, the feel of your chair, or the quality of light coming through the window. Run your hand along the surface of your desk. Listen to the chalk on the blackboard or the sound of the teacher's voice. Be in that environment. Once your attention is back in the room, you can focus on what's happening in class.

Participate in activities. Volunteer for demonstrations. Join in class discussions. If you're at a workshop that includes a group activity, participate fully. Be willing to take a risk or look foolish, if that's what it takes for you to learn. Also ask questions about anything that confuses you. Chances are, the question you think is "dumb" is also on the minds of the people around you.

Relate the class to your goals. If you have trouble staying awake in a particular class, write at the top of your notes how that class relates to a specific goal. Identify the reward or payoff for reaching that goal.

Sharpen your listening skills

Listening, a transferable skill, means interpreting verbal messages as well as body language. Begin to sharpen your listening skills by looking for ways to master both.

Distinguish between main points and supporting material. Most human speaking—and most published material—is based on the interplay between generals and particulars. General statements are key points, the major ideas, the "bottom line" or "take-away" messages. To illustrate and support these statements, speakers offer examples, facts, statistics, quotations, anecdotes, stories, and other details.

As you take notes, graphically emphasize the general statements. Underline them, write them in all uppercase letters, write them in a different color of ink, or go over them with a highlighter after the lecture. In your notes, record only the most vivid examples and details used to support each main point.

Postpone debate. When you hear something you disagree with, note your disagreement and let it go. Don't allow your internal dialogue to drown out subsequent material. If your disagreement is persistent and strong, make note of this and then move on. Internal debate can prevent you from absorbing new information. It is OK to absorb information you don't agree with. Just absorb it with the mental tag "The speaker has indicated . . . , and I don't agree with this."

Let go of judgments about lecture styles. Human beings are judgment machines. We evaluate everything, especially other people. If another person's eyebrows are too close together (or too far apart), if she walks a certain way or speaks with an unusual accent, we instantly make up a story about her. We do this so quickly that the process is usually not a conscious one.

Don't let your attitude about a speaker's lecture style, habits, or appearance get in the way of your education or success at work. You can decrease the power of your judgments if you pay attention to them and let them go.

You can even let go of judgments about rambling, unorganized lectures. Turn them to your advantage. Take the initiative and organize the material yourself. While taking notes, separate the key points from the examples and supporting evidence. Note the places where you got confused and make a list of questions to ask.

Think critically about what you hear. This might seem contrary to the previously mentioned technique "Postpone debate." It's not. You might choose not to think critically about a speaker's ideas during the presentation. That's fine. Do it later, as you review and edit your notes. This is a time to list questions or write down your agreements and disagreements.

Watch for clues

Be alert to repetition. When an instructor repeats a phrase or an idea, make a note of it. Repetition is a signal that the instructor thinks the information is important.

Listen for introductory, concluding, and transition words and phrases. When reading, you are constantly responding to clues about the levels of ideas in a text. Newspapers and magazines include headlines and photographs with captions to grab your attention and direct you to key points. Textbooks usually include tables of contents, headings, subheadings, illustrations,

summaries, and other devices that alert you to what's important.

When you're listening, these visual clues are often absent. However, speakers usually provide verbal clues, and you can learn to spot them. These include phrases such as "the following three factors," "in conclusion," "the most important consideration," "in addition to," and "on the other hand." Phrases such as these signal relationships, definitions, new subjects, conclusions, cause and effect, and examples. They reveal the structure of the lecture.

You can use these phrases to organize your notes. For example, use numbered lists to record the sequence of events. When you want to indicate a series of events that take place in time, number each event in chronological order. This device applies naturally to subjects such as history. During training sessions at work, use numbers for procedures that call for performing tasks in a certain order.

Listen for comparisons and contrasts. Speakers signal comparison with phrases such as "In comparison . . . ," "Compare this to . . . ," "Contrast this with . . . ," "Instead of . . . ," "In contrast . . . ," and "On the other hand. . . ." See if you can create a chart to visually summarize comparisons and contrasts. If the lecturer is comparing two topics, create a two-column chart. List the main points about the first topic in one column; use the other column to record the main points about the second topic. Structure your chart so that similarities and differences between the topics become clear. If this is too hard to do during class, then go back to your notes and do it later.

Watch the board or overhead projector. If an instructor takes the time to write something down, consider the material to be important. Copy all diagrams and drawings, equations, names, places, dates, statistics, and definitions.

Watch the speaker's eyes. If an instructor glances at her notes and then makes a point, it is probably a signal that the information is especially important. Anything she reads from her notes is a potential test question.

Highlight the obvious clues. Instructors will often tell students point-blank that certain information is likely to appear on an exam. Make stars or other special marks in your notes next to this information. Instructors are not trying to hide what's important.

Notice the instructor's interest level. If the instructor is excited about a topic, it is more likely to appear on an exam. Pay attention when she seems more animated than usual. ✖

Record

The note-taking process flows

According to the SCANS report, note taking is a formal strategy associated with the transferable skill of knowing how to learn. Included in this skill is the ability to record information in both words and images. The following techniques can improve the effectiveness of your notes.

General techniques for note taking

Use key words. An easy way to sort the extraneous material from the important points is to take notes using key words. Key words or phrases contain the essence of communication. They include technical terms, names, numbers, equations, and words of degree: *most, least, faster,* etc.

One key word can initiate the recall of a whole cluster of ideas. A few key words can form a chain from which you can reconstruct an entire lecture.

To see how key words work, take yourself to an imaginary classroom. You are now in the middle of an anatomy lecture. Picture what the room looks like, what it feels like, how it smells. You hear the instructor say:

OK, what happens when we look directly over our heads and see a piano falling out of the sky? How do we take that signal and translate it into the action of getting out of the way? The first thing that happens is that a stimulus is generated in the neurons—receptor neurons—of the eye. Light reflected from the piano reaches our eyes. In other words, we see the piano. The receptor neurons in the eye transmit that sensory signal, the sight of the piano, to the body's nervous system. That's all they can do, pass on information. So we've got a sensory signal coming into the nervous

system. But the neurons that initiate movement in our legs are effector neurons. The information from the sensory neurons must be transmitted to effector neurons or we will get squashed by the piano. There must be some kind of interconnection between receptor and effector neurons. What happens between the two? What is the connection?

Key words you might note in this example include *stimulus, generated, receptor neurons, transmit, sensory signals, nervous system, effector neurons,* and *connection.* You could reduce the instructor's 163 words to these 12 key words. With a few transitional words, your notes might look like this:

> Stimulus (piano) generated in receptor neurons (eye).
> Sensory signals transmitted by nervous system to effector neurons (legs).
> What connects receptor to effector?

Note the last key word of the lecture above—*connection.* This word is part of the instructor's question and leads to the next point in the lecture. Be on the lookout for questions like this. They can help you organize your notes and are often clues for test questions.

Use pictures and diagrams. Make relationships visual. Copy all diagrams from the board and invent your own. A drawing of a piano falling on someone who is looking up, for example, might be used to demonstrate the relationship of receptor neurons to effector neurons. Label the eyes "receptor" and the feet "effector." This picture implies that the sight of the piano must be translated into a motor response. By connecting the explanation of the process with the unusual picture of the piano falling, you can link the elements of the process together.

Write notes in paragraphs. When it is difficult to follow the organization of a lecture or to put information into outline form, create a series of informal paragraphs. These paragraphs will contain few complete sentences. Reserve complete sentences for precise definitions, direct quotations, and important points that the instructor emphasizes by repetition or other signals—such as the phrase "This is an important point." For other material, apply the suggestions in this article for using key words.

Copy material from the board. Record all formulas, diagrams, and problems that the teacher writes down. Copy dates, numbers, names, places, and other facts. If it's on the board, put it in your notes. You can even use your own signal or code to flag that material. If it appears on the board, it can appear on a test.

Use a three-ring binder. Three-ring binders have several advantages over other kinds of notebooks. First, pages can be removed and spread out when you review. This way, you can get the whole picture of a lecture. Second, the three-ring binder format allows you to insert handouts right into your notes. Third, you can insert your own out-of-class notes in the correct order. Fourth, you can easily make additions, corrections, and revisions.

Use only one side of a piece of paper. When you use one side of a page, you can review and organize all your notes by spreading them out side by side. Most students find the benefit well worth the cost of the paper. Perhaps you're concerned about the environmental impact of consuming more paper. If so, you can use the blank side of old notes and use recycled paper.

Keep your own thoughts separate. For the most part, avoid making editorial comments in your lecture notes. The danger is that when you return to your notes, you might mistake your own idea for that of the instructor. If you want to make a comment—either a question to ask later or a strong disagreement—clearly label it as your own. Pick a symbol or code and use it in every class.

Use an "I'm lost" signal. No matter how attentive and alert you are, you might get lost and confused in a lecture. If it is inappropriate to ask a question, record in your notes that you were lost. Invent your own signal— for example, a circled question mark. When you write down your code for "I'm lost," leave space for the explanation or clarification that you will get later. The space will also be a signal that you missed something. Later, you can speak to your instructor or ask to see a fellow student's notes. As long as you are honest with yourself when you don't understand, you can stay on top of the course.

Label, number, and date all notes. Develop the habit of labeling and dating your notes at the beginning of each class. Number the page, too. Sometimes the sequence of material in a lecture is important. Write your name and phone number in each notebook in case you lose it. Class notes become more and more valuable as a term or semester progresses.

Use standard abbreviations. Be consistent with your abbreviations. If you make up your own abbreviations or symbols, write a key explaining them in your notes. Avoid vague abbreviations. When you use an abbreviation such as *comm.* for *committee,* you run the risk of not being able to remember whether you meant *committee, commission, common, commit, community, communicate,* or *communist.*

One way to abbreviate is to leave out vowels. For example, *talk* becomes *tlk, said* becomes *sd, American* becomes *Amrcn.*

If you use inconsistent or vague abbreviations, there will be a price to pay in confusion later on. One way to avoid that is to write out abbreviated terms during pauses in a lecture, when the meaning of your notes is still fresh in your short-term memory.

Leave blank space. Notes tightly crammed into every corner of the page are hard to read and difficult to use for review. Give your eyes a break by leaving plenty of space.

Later, when you review, you can use the blank spaces in your notes to clarify points, write questions, or add other material. Instructors often return to material covered earlier in the lecture.

Take notes in different colors. You can use colors as highly visible organizers. For example, you can signal important points with red. Or use one color of ink for notes about the text and another color for lecture notes. Notes that are visually pleasing can be easier to review.

Use graphic signals. The following ideas can be used with any note-taking format.

- Use brackets, parentheses, circles, and squares to group information that belongs together.
- Use stars, arrows, and underlining to indicate important points. Flag the most important points with double stars, double arrows, or double underlines.
- Use arrows and connecting lines to link related groups and to replace words such as *leads to, becomes,* and *produces.*
- Use equal signs and greater- and less-than signs to indicate compared quantities.
- Use question marks for their obvious purpose. Double question marks can signal tough questions or especially confusing points.

To avoid creating confusion with graphic symbols, use them carefully and consistently. Write a "dictionary" of your symbols in the front of your notebooks, such as the one shown below.

Use voice recorders effectively. When you record a lecture, there is a strong temptation to daydream. After all, you can always listen to the lecture again later on. Unfortunately, if you let the recorder do all of the work, you are skipping a valuable part of the learning process. Actively participating in class can turn a lecture into a valuable study session.

There are more potential problems. Listening to recorded lectures can take a lot of time—more time than reviewing written notes. Recorders can't answer the questions you didn't ask in class. Also, recording devices malfunction. In fact, the unscientific Hypothesis of Recording Glitches states that the tendency of recorders to malfunction is directly proportional to the importance of the material.

With those warnings in mind, some students use a recorder effectively. For example, you can use recordings as backups to written notes. (Check with your instructor first, since some prefer not to be recorded.) Turn the recorder on, then take notes as if it weren't there. Recordings can be especially useful if an instructor speaks fast.

You could also record yourself after class, reading your written notes. Teaching the class to yourself is a powerful review tool. Instead of recording all of your notes, for example, you might record only the key facts or concepts.

The Cornell format

A note-taking system that has worked for students around the world is the *Cornell format*.[1] Originally developed by Walter Pauk at Cornell University during the 1950s, this approach continues to be taught across the United States and in other countries as well.

The cornerstone of this system is what Pauk calls the *cue column*—a wide margin on the left-hand side of the paper. The cue column is the key to the Cornell format's many benefits. Here's a way to use the Cornell format.

Format your paper. On each sheet of your note paper, draw a vertical line, top to bottom, about two inches from the left edge of the paper. This line creates the cue column—the space to the left of the line.

Take notes, leaving the cue column blank. As you read an assignment or listen to a speaker, take notes on the right-hand side of the paper. Fill up this column with sentences, paragraphs, outlines, charts, or drawings. Do not write in the cue column. You'll use this space later, as you do the next steps.

Condense your notes in the cue column. Think of the notes you took on the right-hand side of the paper as a set of answers. In the cue column, list potential test questions that correspond to your notes. Write one question for each major term or point.

As an alternative to questions, you can list key words from your notes. Yet another option is to pretend that your notes are a series of articles on different topics. In the cue column, write a newspaper-style headline for each "article." In any case, be brief. If you cram the cue column full of words, you defeat its purpose—to reduce the number and length of your notes.

Write a summary. Pauk recommends that you reduce your notes even more by writing a brief summary at the bottom of each page. This step offers you another way to engage actively with the material. It can also make your notes easier to review for tests.

Use the cue column to recite. Cover the right-hand side of your notes with a blank sheet of paper. Leave only

Cue column	Notes
What are some key changes in U.S. health over the last 50 years?	Over the past 50 years in the U.S.: — The number of smokers decreased. — Infant mortality dropped to a record low. — Life expectancy hit a record high—about 77 years.
Who announced these changes?	Source: Health, United States 2002, Centers for Disease Control. Health and Human Services Secretary Tommy Thompson announced this report.

Summary
Changes in American health over the last 50 years include fewer smokers, lower infant mortality, and record life expectancy.

the cue column showing. Then look at each item you wrote in the cue column and talk about it. If you wrote questions, answer each question. If you wrote key words, define each word and talk about why it's important. If you wrote headlines in the cue column, explain what each one means and offer supporting details. After reciting, uncover your notes and look for any important points you missed. Repeat this cycle of reciting and checking until you've mastered the material.

Mind mapping

This system, developed by Tony Buzan,[2] can be used in conjunction with the Cornell format. In some circumstances, you might want to use mind maps exclusively.

To understand mind maps, first review the features of traditional note taking. Outlines (explained in the next section) divide major topics into minor topics, which, in turn, are subdivided further. They organize information in a sequential, linear way.

This kind of organization doesn't reflect certain aspects of brain function, a point that has been made in discussions about "left brain" and "right brain" activities. People often use the term *right brain* when referring to creative, pattern-making, visual, intuitive brain activity. They use the term *left brain* when talking about orderly, logical, step-by-step characteristics of thought. Writing teacher Gabrielle Rico uses another metaphor. She refers to the left-brain mode as our "sign mind" (concerned with words) and the right-brain mode as our "design mind" (concerned with visuals).[3]

A mind map uses both kinds of brain functions. Mind maps can contain lists and sequences and show relationships. They can also provide a picture of a subject. Mind maps are visual patterns that can serve as a framework for recalling information. They work on both verbal and nonverbal levels.

One benefit of mind maps is that they quickly, vividly, and accurately show the relationships between ideas. Also, mind mapping helps you think from general to specific. By choosing a main topic, you focus first on the big picture, then zero in on subordinate details. And by using only key words, you can condense a large subject into a small area on a mind map. You can review more quickly by looking at the key words on a mind map than by reading notes word for word. The following guidelines can assist you in creating mind maps.

Give yourself plenty of room. Use blank paper that measures at least 11 by 17 inches. If that's not available, turn regular notebook paper on its side so that you can take notes in a horizontal (instead of vertical) format. Another option is to find software that allows you to draw flow charts or diagrams. Then you can generate mind maps on a computer.

Determine the main concept of the lecture. Write that concept in the center of the paper and circle it, underline it, or highlight it with color. You can also write the concept in large letters. Record concepts related to the main concept on lines that radiate outward from the center. An alternative is to circle these concepts.

Use key words only. Whenever possible, reduce each concept to a single word per line or circle in your mind map. Though this might seem awkward at first, it prompts you to summarize and to condense ideas to their essence. That means fewer words for you to write now and fewer to review when it's time to prepare for tests. (Using shorthand symbols and abbreviations can help.) Key words are usually nouns and verbs that communicate the bulk of the speaker's ideas. Choose words that are rich in associations and that can help you re-create the lecture.

Jazz it up. Use color to organize your mind map. If there are three main subjects covered in the lecture, you can record each subject in a different color. Add symbols and other images as well.

Create links. One mind map doesn't have to include all of the ideas in a book or an article. Instead, you can link mind maps. For example, draw a mind map that sums up the five key points in a chapter, and then make a separate, more detailed mind map for each of those key points. Within each mind map, include references to the other mind maps. This helps explain and reinforce the relationships among many ideas. Some students pin several mind maps next to each other on a bulletin board or tape them to a wall. This allows for a dramatic—and effective—look at the big picture.

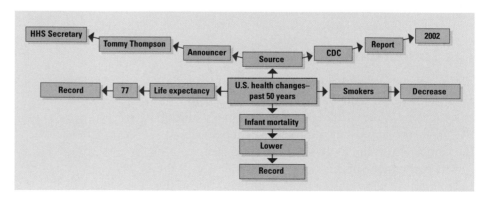

Outlining

An outline shows the relationship between major points and supporting ideas. One benefit of taking notes in the outline format is that doing so can totally occupy your attention. You are recording ideas and also organizing them. This can be an advantage if the material has been presented in a disorganized way. Perhaps you've had negative experiences with outlining in the past. Teachers might have required you to use complex, rigid outlining formats based exclusively on Roman numerals or on some unfamiliar system. By playing with variations, you can discover the power of outlining to reveal relationships between ideas. Technically, each word, phrase, or sentence that appears in an outline is called a *heading*. These are arranged in different levels:

- In the first or "top" level of headings, note the major topics that are presented in a lecture or reading assignment.

- In the second level of headings, record the key points that relate to each topic in the first-level headings.

- In the third level of headings, record specific facts and details that support or explain each of your second-level headings. Each additional level of subordinate heading supports the ideas in the previous level of heading.

Roman numerals offer one way to illustrate the difference between levels of headings. See the following example.

First-level heading

I. Health and Human Services Secretary Tommy G. Thompson reports that Americans' health changed over the past 50 years.

Second-level heading
    A. Thompson: "When you take the long view, you see clearly how far we've come in combating diseases, making workplaces safer, and avoiding risks such as smoking."
    B. Thompson referred to *Health, United States, 2002*, a report from the Centers for Disease Control and Prevention (CDC).

II. By 2000, infant morality dropped to a record low and life expectancy hit a record high.
    A. Death rates among children up to age 24 were cut in half.
    B. Americans enjoyed the longest life expectancy in U.S. history.

III. Among working-age adults, fewer are dying from unintentional injuries, heart disease, stroke, and AIDS.

Third-level heading
    A. After 1995, deaths from AIDS dropped.
        1. Powerful new drugs contributed to this result.
        2. Other drugs are now in development.
    B. A decline in smoking contributed to the decline in heart disease.
        1. More than 40 percent of adults were smokers in 1965.
        2. In 2000, just 23 percent smoked.

You can also use other heading styles, as illustrated here.

Distinguish levels with indentations only:

First-level heading
    Second-level heading
        Third-level heading
            Fourth-level heading

Distinguish levels with bullets and dashes:

FIRST–LEVEL HEADING
    • Second-level heading
        – Third-level heading

Distinguish headings by size:

FIRST–LEVEL HEADING
Second-level heading
Third-level heading

Combining formats

Feel free to use different note-taking systems for different subjects and to combine formats. Do what works for you.

For example, combine mind maps along with the Cornell format. You can modify the Cornell format by dividing your note paper in half, reserving one half for mind maps and the other for linear information, such as lists, graphs, and outlines, as well as equations, long explanations, and word-for-word definitions. You can incorporate a mind map into your paragraph-style notes whenever you feel one is appropriate. Mind maps are also useful for summarizing notes taken in the Cornell format.

John Sperry, a teacher at Utah Valley State College, developed a note-taking system that can include all of the formats discussed in this article:

- Fill up a three-ring binder with fresh paper. Open your notebook so that you see two blank pages—one on the left and one on the right. Plan to take notes across this entire two-page spread.

- During class or while reading, write your notes only on the left-hand page. Place a large dash next to each main topic or point. If your instructor skips a step or switches topics unexpectedly, just keep writing.

- Later, use the right-hand page to review and elaborate on the notes that you took earlier. This page is for anything you want. For example, add visuals such as mind maps. Write review questions, headlines, possible test questions, summaries, outlines, mnemonics, or analogies that link new concepts to your current knowledge.

- To keep ideas in sequence, place appropriate numbers on top of the dashes in your notes on the left-hand page. Even if concepts are presented out of order during class, they'll still be numbered correctly in your notes. ⊠

Review

The note-taking process flows

Think of reviewing as an integral part of note taking rather than as an added task. To make new information useful, encode it in a way that connects to your long-term memory. The key is reviewing.

Review within 24 hours. The sooner you review your notes, the better, especially if the class was difficult. In fact, you can start reviewing during class. When your instructor pauses to set up the overhead projector or erase the board, scan your notes. Dot the i's, cross the t's, and write out unclear abbreviations. Another way to use this technique is to get to your next class as quickly as you can. Then use the four or five minutes before the lecture begins to review the notes you just took in the previous class. If you do not get to your notes immediately after class, you can still benefit by reviewing later in the day. A review right before you go to sleep can also be valuable.

Think of the day's unreviewed notes as leaky faucets, constantly dripping, losing precious information until you shut them off with a quick review. Remember, it's possible to forget up to 80 percent of the material within 24 hours—unless you review.

Edit notes. During your first review, fix words that are illegible. Write out abbreviated words that might be unclear to you later. Make sure you can read everything. If you can't read something or don't understand something you *can* read, mark it, and make a note to ask your instructor or another student. Check to see that your notes are labeled with the date and class and that the pages are numbered. You can edit with a different colored pen or pencil if you want to distinguish between what you wrote in class and what you filled in later.

Fill in key words in the left-hand column. This task is important if you are to get the full benefit of using the Cornell format. Using the key word principles described earlier in this chapter, go through your notes and write key words or phrases in the left-hand column.

These key words will speed up the review process later. As you read your notes and focus on extracting important concepts, your understanding of the lecture is further reinforced.

Use your key words as cues to recite. With a blank sheet of paper, cover your notes, leaving only the key words in the left-hand margin showing. Take each key word in order and recite as much as you can about the point. Then uncover your notes and look for any important points you missed.

Conduct short weekly review periods. Once a week, review all of your notes again. The review sessions don't need to take a lot of time. Even a 20-minute weekly review period is valuable. Some students find that a weekend review, say, on Sunday afternoon, helps them stay in continuous touch with the material. Scheduling regular review sessions on your calendar helps develop the habit.

As you review, step back to see the larger picture. In addition to reciting or repeating the material to yourself, ask questions about it: "Does this relate to my goals? How does this compare to information I already know, in this field or another? Will I be tested on this material? What will I do with this material? How can I associate it with something that deeply interests me? Am I unclear

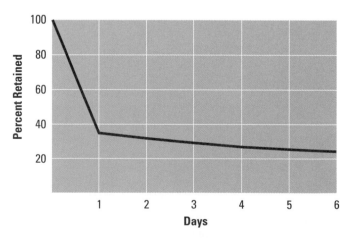

To study the process of memory and forgetting, Hermann Ebbinghaus devised a method for testing memory. The results, shown here in what has come to be known as the Ebbinghaus forgetting curve, demonstrate that forgetting occurs most rapidly shortly after learning and then gradually declines over time.

on any points? If so, what exactly is the question I want to ask?"

Consider typing up your notes. Some students type up their handwritten notes using a computer. The argument for doing so is threefold. First, typed notes are easier to read. Second, they take up less space. Third, the process of typing them forces you to review the material.

Another alternative is to bypass handwriting altogether and take notes in class on a laptop computer. This solution has drawbacks: Laptops are more expensive than PCs, and computer errors can wipe out your notes, leaving you with no handwritten backup.

Experiment with typing notes and see what works for you. For example, you might type up only key portions of notes, such as summaries or outlines.

Create mind map summaries. Mind mapping is an excellent way to make summary sheets. After drawing your map, look at your original notes and fill in anything you missed. This system is fun to use. It's quick, and it gives your brain a hook on which to fasten the material. ✖

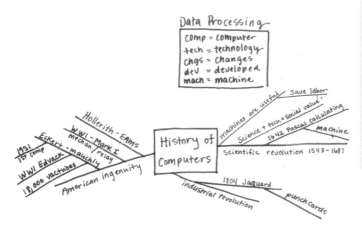

journal entry 15

Discovery Statement

Think about the way you have conducted reviews of your notes in the past. Respond to the following statements by checking "Always," "Often," "Sometimes," "Seldom," or "Never" after each.

I review my notes immediately after class.
___Always   ___Often   ___Sometimes
___Seldom   ___Never

I conduct weekly reviews of my notes.
___Always   ___Often   ___Sometimes
___Seldom   ___Never

I make summary sheets of my notes.
___Always   ___Often   ___Sometimes
___Seldom   ___Never

I edit my notes within 24 hours.
___Always   ___Often   ___Sometimes
___Seldom   ___Never

Before class, I conduct a brief review of the notes I took in the previous class.
___Always   ___Often   ___Sometimes
___Seldom   ___Never

What to do when you miss a class

For most courses, you'll benefit by attending every class session. If you miss a class, try to catch up as quickly as possible.

Clarify policies on missed classes. On the first day of classes, find out about your instructors' policies on absences. See if you can make up assignments, quizzes, and tests. Also inquire about doing extra-credit assignments.

Contact a classmate. Early in the semester, identify a student in each class who seems responsible and dependable. Exchange e-mail addresses and phone numbers. If you know you won't be in class, contact this student ahead of time. When you notice that your classmate is absent, pick up extra copies of handouts, make assignments lists, and offer copies of your notes.

Contact your instructor. If you miss a class, e-mail, phone, or fax your instructor, or put a note in her mailbox. Ask if she has another section of the same course that you could attend so you won't miss the lecture information. Also ask about getting handouts you might need before the next class meeting.

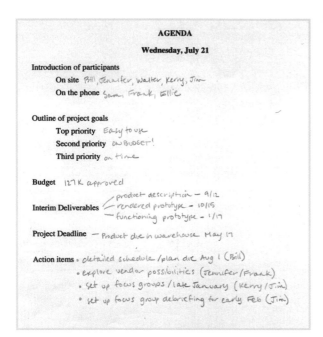

AGENDA
Wednesday, July 21

Introduction of participants
  On site Bill, Jennifer, Walter, Kerry, Jim
  On the phone Sam, Frank, Ellie

Outline of project goals
  Top priority Easy to use
  Second priority on Budget!
  Third priority on time

Budget 127K approved
Interim Deliverables — product description — 9/12
  — rendered prototype — 10/15
  — functioning prototype — 1/17
Project Deadline — Product due in warehouse May 17

Action items • detailed schedule/plan due Aug 1 (Bill)
  • explore vendor possibilities (Jennifer/Frank)
  • set up focus groups/late January (Kerry/Jim)
  • set up focus group debriefing for early Feb (Jim)

Observe, record, and review at meetings

In the workplace, notes matter. During meetings, people are hired, fired, and promoted. Problems are tackled. Negotiations take place. Decisions are made. Your job might depend on what you observe during meetings, what you record, and how you respond.

Meetings offer a prime chance to apply many of the transferable skills covered in this book—listening, memory, writing, and critical thinking. Developing the ability to take clear and concise meeting notes is one way to make yourself valuable to an employer. It might even help you get promoted.

To get the most from meeting notes, experiment with several formats explained in this chapter—Cornell format, mind maps, concept maps, and more. Feel free to add boldface headings, charts, tables, graphs, and other visuals that make the main ideas stand out. If you're taking notes to distribute to coworkers, they will appreciate it if you get to the point and keep paragraphs short.

Your employer may have specific guidelines for taking meeting notes. Ask your supervisor about this. Note that in some cases—such as minutes taken during a board of directors meeting—notes may function as legal documents reviewed by the IRS or another independent auditor. Keeping this fact in mind can help you take better notes. Also consider adding the following topics to your notes.

Attendance. Start by observing who shows up. In many organizations, people expect meeting notes to include a list of attendees.

Agenda. One path to more powerful meeting notes is observing the agenda. Think of it as a road map—a way to keep the discussion on track. Skilled planners often put an agenda in writing and distribute it in advance. Record this agenda and use it to organize your notes. Listen carefully for items that are added to the agenda—and for agenda items that are shelved for discussion at another meeting.

Agreements. During meetings, people can easily digress from the agenda. Following the thread of the discussion can be tricky, particularly when lots of new topics come up. Remember that you usually don't have to record everything that's said during a meeting. Rather, your job is to summarize and hit the main points.

Listen especially for the agreements that people reach. Record these carefully. And if a question is raised but not answered, ask for clarification.

Actions. Even brilliant meetings can fade into misty obscurity when people forget to carry through on their agreements. After each meeting, promptly review your notes. Ask whether any of the points you noted call for follow-up action on your part—perhaps a phone call to make, a fact to find, or another task to complete. Highlight such items in your notes. Then add them to your calendar or to-do list. ⊠

desk of ...

from the

**TASHIANA CLARKE,
ADMINISTRATIVE ASSISTANT:**

Note-taking is a skill that plays a significant role in my daily responsibilities. I attend every meeting with my supervisor and take notes for his files. As administrative assistant for the managing director, I am also responsible for taking notes at the biweekly companywide meetings and distributing them to the entire staff. Because the employees value my detailed notes, they are willing to slow down or repeat information if it is requested.

Get to the bones of your book with concept maps

Concept mapping, pioneered by Joseph Novak and D. Bob Gowin, is a tool to make the main ideas in a book leap off the page.[4] In creating a concept map, you reduce an author's message to its essence—its bare bones. Concept maps can also be used to display the organization underlying lectures, discussions, and other reading materials.

Concept maps also promote critical thinking. Creating a concept map can alert you to gaps in your understanding—missing concepts or concepts with illogical links.

Concept maps and mind maps are both visual forms of note taking. However, there are significant differences between these techniques. If you find that mind maps are too unstructured or messy for your tastes, try your hand at concept mapping.

To create a concept map, use the following four steps:

1. List the key concepts in the text. Aim to express each concept in three words or less. Most concept words are nouns, including terms and proper names. At this point, you can list the concepts in any order. For ease in ranking the concepts later, write each one on a single 3x5 card.

2. Rank the concepts so that they flow from general to specific. On a large sheet of paper, write the main concept at the top of the page. Place the most specific concepts near the bottom. Arrange the rest of the concepts in appropriate positions throughout the middle of the page. Circle each concept.

3. Draw lines that connect the concepts. On these connecting lines, add words that describe the relationship

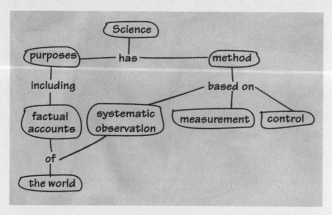

between the concepts. Again, limit yourself to the fewest words needed to make an accurate link—three words or less. Linking words are often verbs, verb phrases, or prepositions.

4. Finally, review your map. Look for any concepts that are repeated in several places on the map. You can avoid these repetitions by adding more links between concepts. Also look for accurate linking words and missing concepts.

As you gain facility with concept maps, you might wish to create them on a computer. Use any software with drawing capabilities. For example, the software program Inspiration, a visual thinking and learning tool, is specifically designed to create concept maps.

Sample concept maps based on selected articles in this book are available online at masterstudent.college.hmco.com

journal entry 16

Discovery/Intention Statement

Think back on the last few lectures you have attended. How do you currently observe (and record) lectures? What specific behaviors do you have as you sit and listen? Briefly describe your responses in the space below.

I discovered that I . . .

_____

_____

_____

Now write an Intention Statement about any changes you want to make in the way you respond to lectures.

I intend to . . .

_____

_____

_____

_____

Taking notes while reading

There are two kinds of notes that apply to reading: review notes and research notes.

Review notes. These will look like the notes you take in class. Sometimes you will want more extensive notes than writing in the margin of your text allows. You can't underline or make notes in library books, so these sources will require separate notes, too.

Mind map summaries of textbook materials are particularly useful for review. You can also use outlining or take notes in paragraph form. Single out a particularly difficult section of a text and make separate notes. Or make mind map summaries of overlapping lecture and textbook materials. Use the left-hand column for key words and questions, just as you do in your class notes.

When you read scientific or other technical materials, copy important formulas or equations and write down data that you will need to remember or that might appear on an exam. Re-create important diagrams and draw your own visual representations of concepts.

Research notes. Research notes—those used for papers, in-class speeches, and workplace presentations—follow a different format. Use the mighty 3x5 card. There are two kinds of research cards: source cards and information cards. Source cards identify where you found the information contained in your paper or speech. For example, a source card for a book will show the author, title, date and place of publication, and publisher. Source cards are also written for magazine articles, interviews, dissertations, tapes, or any other research materials.

When you write source cards, give each source a code—the initials of the author, a number, or a combination of numbers and letters. A key advantage of using source cards is that you are creating your bibliography as you do the research. When you are done, simply alphabetize the cards by author and—voilà!—instant bibliography.

Write the actual research notes on information cards. At the top of each information card, write the code for the source from which you got the information. Also include the page numbers your notes are based on. Most important, write only one piece of information on each information card. You can then sort the cards and use them to construct an outline of your paper or speech.

Another option is to take notes using a computer. This offers the same advantage as 3x5 cards—ease of rearranging text and pictures—while enabling you to print out copies to exchange with other students.

Online material. You can print out anything that appears on a computer screen. This includes online course materials, articles, books, manuscripts, e-mail messages, chat room sessions, and more. One potential problem: You might skip taking notes on this material altogether. ("I can just print out everything!") Doing this may cause you to miss the chance to internalize a new idea by restating it in your own words—a principal benefit of note taking. Result: Material passes from computer to printer without ever intersecting with your brain.

To prevent this problem, find ways to engage actively with online materials. Take review notes in Cornell, mind map, concept map, or outline format. Write Discovery and Intention Statements to capture key insights from the materials and to state ways you intend to apply them. Also talk about what you're learning. Recite key points out loud and discuss what you read online.

Of course, it's fine to print out online material. If you do, treat your printouts like a textbook and apply the steps of Muscle Reading explained in Chapter Four.

A key advantage of using source cards is that you are creating your bibliography as you do the research.

Thinking about notes. Whenever you take notes, use your own words as much as possible. When you do so, you are thinking about what you are reading. If you do quote your source word for word, put that material within quotation marks.

Close the book after reading an assignment and quickly jot down a summary of the material. This writing can be loose, without any structure or format. The important thing is to do it right away, while the material is still fresh in your mind. Restating concepts in this way helps you remember them. ◪

Create your instructor

There are as many definitions of a "poor" instructor as there are students. For some students, "poor" means "boring," "rude," or "insensitive." Or maybe it's an instructor who never remembers what day it is, blows her nose every five minutes, and wears a cologne that could kill a hamster at 30 paces. Even when you don't like an instructor, you can take responsibility for your education.

Notice and release judgments. Maybe your instructor reminds you of someone you don't like—your annoying aunt Edna, a rude store clerk, the fifth-grade teacher who kept you after school, or the boss who made you work weekends. Your attitudes are in your own head and beyond the instructor's control. Remember, you don't have to like an instructor to learn from one.

An instructor's beliefs about politics, religion, or feminism are not related to teaching ability. Likewise, using a formal or informal lecture style does not indicate knowledge of subject matter. Being aware of such things can help you let go of negative judgments.

Get to know the instructor better. You might be missing the strong points of an instructor you don't like. Meet with your instructor during office hours. Ask questions that weren't answered in class. Teachers who seem boring in class can be fascinating in person.

Open up to diversity. Sometimes students can create their instructors by letting go of pictures about different races and ethnic groups. According to one picture, a Hispanic person cannot teach English literature. According to other pictures, a white teacher cannot have anything valid to say about African music, a teacher in a wheelchair cannot command the attention of 100 people in a lecture hall, and a male instructor cannot speak credibly about feminism. All of those pictures can clash with reality. Releasing them can open up new opportunities for understanding and appreciation.

Form your own opinion about each instructor. You might hear conflicting reports about teachers from other students. The same instructor could be described as a riveting speaker or as completely lacking in charisma. Decide for yourself.

Avoid excuses. Instructors know them all. Most teachers can see a snow job coming before the first flake hits the ground. Accept responsibility for your own mistakes, and avoid thinking that you can fool the teacher. When you treat instructors honestly, you are more likely to be treated as a responsible adult in return.

Submit professional work. Prepare papers and projects as if you were submitting them to an employer. Pay attention to form. Imagine that a promotion and raise will be determined by your work. Instructors often grade hundreds of papers during a term. Your neat, orderly, well organized paper can lift a teacher's spirits after a long night of deciphering gibberish.

Use conference time effectively. Instructors are usually happy to answer questions about class content. To get the most out of conference time, be prepared to ask those questions. Bring your notes, text, and any other materials you might need. During this session you can also address more difficult subjects, such as grades, attendance policies, lecture styles, term papers, or personality conflicts.

Use course evaluations. In many classes you'll have an opportunity to evaluate the instructor. When you're asked to do so, respond honestly. Write about the aspects of the class that did not work well for you. Offer specific ideas for improvement. Also note what *did* work well.

Take further steps, if appropriate. Sometimes severe conflict develops between students and instructors. Feedback from students might not be enough to reach a resolution. In such cases, you might decide to file a complaint or ask for help from a third party, such as an administrator.

If you do, be prepared to document your case in writing. When talking about the instructor, offer details. Describe specific actions that created problems for the class. Stick to the facts—events that other class members can verify. Your school might have a set of established grievance procedures to use in these cases. Before you act, understand what the policies are. You are a consumer of education. You have a right and a responsibility to complain if you think you have been treated unfairly. ◪

When a speaker *talks fast*

Take more time to prepare. Familiarity with a subject increases your ability to pick up on key points. If an instructor lectures quickly or is difficult to understand, conduct a thorough preview of the material to be covered. If an agenda or program is distributed before a meeting, be sure to review the content and materials.

Be willing to make choices. When a presenter talks too fast, focus your attention on key points. Instead of trying to write everything down, choose what you think is important. Occasionally, you will make a wrong choice and neglect an important point. Worse things could happen. Stay with the speaker, write down key words, and revise your notes immediately.

Exchange photocopies of notes. Other listeners might write down something you missed. At the same time, your notes might help them. Exchanging photocopies can fill in the gaps.

Leave large empty spaces in your notes. Leave plenty of room for filling in information you missed. Use a symbol that signals you've missed something, so you can remember to come back to it.

Follow up with questions. Take your class notes with you and show the instructor what you missed. After a presentation at work, go up to the speaker and ask questions about what confused you.

Use a recorder. Recording a lecture or other presentation gives you a chance to hear it again whenever you choose.

Before class, take notes on your reading assignment. You can take detailed notes on the text before class. Leave plenty of blank space. Take these notes with you to class and simply add your lecture notes to them.

Go to the lecture again. Many classes are taught in multiple sections. That gives you the chance to hear a lecture at least twice—once in your regular class and again in another section of the class.

Learn shorthand. Some note-taking systems, known as shorthand, are specifically designed for getting ideas down fast. Books and courses are available to help you learn these systems. You can also devise your own shorthand method by inventing one- or two-letter symbols for common words and phrases.

Ask questions—even if you're totally lost. There might be times when you feel so lost that you can't even formulate a question. That's OK. One option is to report this fact to the speaker. She can often guide you to a clear question. Another option is to ask a related question. This might lead you to the question you really wanted to ask.

Ask the speaker to slow down. This is the most obvious solution. If asking the speaker to slow down doesn't work, ask her to repeat what you missed. ◪

exercise 16

TELEVISION NOTE TAKING

You can use evening news broadcasts to practice listening for key words, writing quickly, focusing your attention, and reviewing. As with other skills, the more you practice note taking, the better you become.

The next time you watch the news, use pen and paper to jot down key words and information. During the commercials, review and revise your notes. At the end of the broadcast, spend five minutes reviewing all of your notes. Create a mind map of a few news stories, then sum up the news of the day for a friend.

This exercise will help you develop an ear for key words. Since you can't ask questions or request that the speaker slow down, you train yourself to stay totally in the moment. If you get behind, relax, leave a space, and return your attention to the broadcast.

Don't be discouraged if you miss a lot the first time around. Do this exercise several times and observe how your mind works.

If you find it too difficult to take notes during a fast-paced television news show, check your local broadcast schedule for a news documentary. These are often slower paced. Another option is to tape a program and then take notes. You can stop the tape at any point to review your notes.

You can also ask a classmate to do the same exercise, and then compare notes the next day.

Use a concept map as a tool to interpret and evaluate a piece of writing. First, list the key concepts from a chapter (or section of a chapter) in a textbook you're reading. Then connect these concepts with linking words, using the format described in the sidebar "Get to the bones of your book with concept maps." Create your concept map in the space below or on a separate sheet of paper, if you need more room.

Now take a few minutes to assess the author's presentation as reflected in your concept map. Pay special attention to the links between concepts. Are they accurate? Do they reveal false assumptions or lack of evidence? Write your evaluation in the following space.

_____

_____

_____

_____

_____

_____

journal entry 17

Discovery/Intention Statement

Choose a set of notes that you've taken in class recently. Next to it, place notes that you took during a meeting at work.

Now compare the two sets of notes. Look past their content and consider their format. What visual differences do you see between the notes from work and the notes from class?

I discovered that . . .

_____

_____

_____

Also think about the *process* of taking notes in these two settings. Did you find it easier or more difficult to take notes at work than in class?

I discovered that . . .

_____

_____

After comparing these two sets of notes, reflect on what you can do differently in the future to take more effective notes at work.

I intend to . . .

_____

_____

power process

I create it all

This is a powerful tool in times of trouble. In a crisis, "I create it all" can lead the way to solutions. "I create it all" means treating experiences, events, and circumstances in your life as if you created them.

When your dog tracks fresh tar on the white carpet, when your political science teacher is a crushing bore, when your spouse dents the car, when your test on Latin American literature focuses on an author you've never read—it's time for a Power Process. Tell yourself, "I created it all."

"Baloney!" you shout. "I didn't let the dog in, that teacher really is a bore, I wasn't even in the car, and nobody told me to read Gabriel García Márquez. I didn't create these disasters."

Good points. Obviously, "I create it all" is one of the most unusual and bizarre suggestions in this book. It certainly is not an idea that is easily believed. In fact, believing it can get you into trouble. "I create it all" is strictly a practical idea. Use it when it works. Don't when it doesn't.

Keeping that caution in mind, consider how powerful this Power Process can be. It is really about the difference between two distinct positions in life: being a victim or being self-responsible. A victim of circumstances is controlled by outside forces. We've all felt like victims at one time or another. When tar-footed dogs tromped on the white carpets of our lives, we felt helpless. In contrast, we can take responsibility. *Responsibility* is the important word. It does not mean "blame." Far from it. Responsibility is "response-ability"—the ability to choose a response.

Practicing resignation

By not taking responsibility, we are acknowledging that the power to determine what happens in our lives is beyond our grasp. When we feel as if we don't have control over our lives, we feel resigned. The opposite of practicing "I create it all" is practicing resignation.

There is a phenomenon called *learned resignation*. An interesting experiment with dogs demonstrates how learned resignation works. A dog is put in a caged pen with a metal floor that can be electrified. When the cage door is left open and the dog is given a mild shock, she runs out of the cage to escape the discomfort. Then the dog is put back into the cage, the door is shut and locked, and a mild shock is given again. The dog runs around, looking for an escape. When she doesn't find one, she just lies down, sits, or stands there, and quits trying to find a way out. She has no control over her circumstances and is learning to be resigned.

Now, here comes the interesting part. After the dog has consistently stopped trying to escape the shock, the door is opened and the dog is led in and out several times. Then the dog is left in the cage, the door is left open, and the shock is administered once again. Amazingly, the dog doesn't even try to escape, even though the open door is right there in front of her. Instead, the dog continues to endure the shock. She has learned to be resigned.

A variety of this phenomenon can occur in human beings as well. When we consistently give control of our lives over to other people and to circumstances, we run the risk of learning to give up. We might develop the habit of being resigned, even though there is abundant opportunity all around us.

Applying this process

Many students approach grades from the position of being victims. When the student who sees the world this way gets an F, she reacts something like this:

"Oh, no!" (Slaps forehead)

"Rats!" (Slaps forehead again) (Students who get lots of F's often have flat foreheads.)

"Another F! That teacher couldn't teach her way out of a wet paper bag. She can't teach English for anything.

And that textbook—what a bore! How could I read it with a houseful of kids making noise all the time? And then I had to go to work, and . . . ."

The problem with this viewpoint is that in looking for excuses, the student is robbing herself of the power to get any grade other than an F. She's giving all of her power to a bad teacher, a boring textbook, noisy children, and work.

There is another way, called *taking responsibility*. You can recognize that you choose your grades by choosing your actions. Then you are the source, rather than the result, of the grades you get. The student who got an F could react like this:

"Another F! Oh, shoot! Well, hmmm . . . . How did I choose this F? What did I do to create it?"

Now, that's power. By asking, "How did I contribute to this outcome?" you give yourself a measure of control. You are no longer the victim. This student might continue by saying, "Well, let's see. I didn't review my notes after class. That might have done it." Or "I studied in the same room with my children while they watched TV. Then I worked a double shift the night before the test. Well, that probably helped me fulfill some of the requirements for getting an F."

The point is this: When the F is the result of your kids, your work, the book, or the teacher, you probably can't do anything about it. However, if you *chose* the F, you can choose a different grade next time. You are in charge.

Choosing our thoughts

There are times when we don't create it all. We do not create earthquakes, floods, avalanches, or monsoons. Yet if we look closely, we discover that we *do* create a larger part of our circumstances than most of us are willing to admit.

For example, we can choose our thoughts. And thoughts can control our perceptions by screening information from our senses. We can never be aware of every single thing in our environment. If we could, we'd go crazy from sensory overload. Instead, our brains filter out most sensory inputs. This filtering colors the way we think about the world.

Choosing our behaviors

Moment by moment we make choices about what we will do and where we will go. The results of these choices are

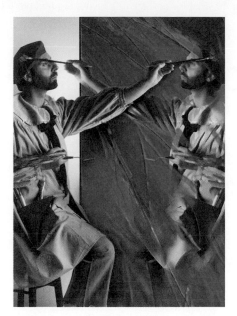

where we are in life. A whole school of psychology called *control theory* is based on this idea, and psychiatrist William Glasser has written extensively about it.[5]

All of those choices help create our current circumstances—even those circumstances that are not "our fault." After a car accident, we tell ourselves, "It just happened. That car came out of nowhere and hit me." We forget that driving five miles per hour slower and paying closer attention might have allowed us to miss the driver who was "to blame."

Some cautions

The presence of blame is a warning that this Power Process is being misused. "I create it all" is not about blaming yourself or others.

Feeling guilty is another warning signal. Guilt actually involves the same dynamic as blame. If you are feeling guilty, you have just shifted the blame from another person to yourself.

Another caution is that this Power Process is not a religion. Saying that you "create it all" does not mean that you have divine powers. It is simply a way to expand the choices you already have. This Power Process is easy to deny. Tell your friends about it, and they're likely to say, "What about world hunger? I didn't cause that. What about people who get cancer? Did they create that?"

These are good arguments—and they miss the point. Victims of rape, abuse, incest, and other forms of violence can still use "I create it all" to choose their response to the people and events that violated them.

Some people approach world hunger, imprisonment, and even cancer with this attitude: "Pretend for a moment that I am responsible for this. What will I do about it?" These people see problems in a new way, and they discover choices that other people miss.

"I create it all" is not always about disaster. It also works when life is going great. We often give credit to others for our good fortune when it's actually time to pat ourselves on the back. By choosing our behavior and thoughts, we can create A's, interesting classes, enjoyable relationships, material wealth, and ways to contribute to a better world.

Whenever tar-footed dogs are getting in the way of your education, remember this Power Process. When you use it, you instantly open up a world of choices. You give yourself power. ◪

career application

Hanae Niigata is a part-time receptionist at a large cardiovascular clinic. Her responsibilities include handling incoming calls, scheduling patient visits, maintaining medical records, and completing other tasks assigned by her office manager.

Hanae's career focus is health care. She has worked as a home health aide and is currently enrolled in school. Her goal is to complete an Associate in Science degree in nursing and work as a registered nurse.

Hanae has a reputation as a hard worker. Even in a noisy environment with frequent interruptions, she completes tasks that require attention to detail and sustained concentration. She catches errors on medical records that her coworkers tend to miss. In addition, Hanae is often the first person in the office to whom people turn when they have a problem to solve. Even in the most difficult circumstances, she can generate a list of options—including solutions that occur to no one else.

Today, the office manager asked Hanae to attend a two-hour course on a new telephone system soon to be installed in her office. She was told to take good notes so she could teach the other five receptionists. Hanae was shocked that the old system was being replaced. In her opinion, it was user-friendly.

As the training session began, Hanae diligently attempted to write down almost everything the instructor said. While doing so, she repeatedly found herself distracted by the thought that her manager was replacing a perfectly good phone system with some "sure-to-be-a-nightmare, high-tech garbage."

After completing the course, Hanae sat down with her manager to fill him in on the new system. As she thumbed through her notes, she realized they didn't make much sense to her even though she had just finished writing them. She couldn't recall much of the course from memory, either, leaving her with little information to share with her manager. ✖

Reflecting on this scenario:

1. List two or three suggestions for Hanae that could make her note taking more effective. Be specific.

_____

_____

_____

2. Refer to the SCANS chart on page 8. Identify a transferable skill that Hanae already has.

_____

_____

_____

3. What behaviors lead you to conclude that Hanae has this skill?

_____

_____

_____

4. Using the same SCANS chart, identify a skill that would be useful for Hanae to develop.

_____

_____

_____

Name _____ Date _____/_____/_____

quiz

1. What are the three major steps of effective note taking as explained in this chapter? Summarize each step in one sentence.

2. Explain what is meant in this chapter by "setting the stage" for note taking.

3. What is an advantage of sitting in the front and center at a presentation?

4. By the way they behave, instructors sometimes give clues that the material they are presenting is important. Describe at least three of these behaviors.

5. An effective method to postpone debate during a lecture is to ignore your own opinions and passively record the speaker's words. True or False? Explain your answer.

6. When using the Cornell system of note taking:
   (A) Write the main point on a line or in a box, circle, or any other shape.
   (B) Use only Roman numerals in an outline form.
   (C) Copy each new concept on a separate 3x5 card.
   (D) Remember never to combine it with mind mapping.
   (E) Draw a vertical line about two inches from the left edge of the paper.

7. Explain how key words can be used when taking notes. Then select and write down at least five key words from this chapter.

8. Explain a benefit of reviewing your notes within 24 hours after you take them.

9. Compare and contrast source cards and information cards. How are they alike? How are they different?

10. Briefly explain one of the cautions given regarding the use of the Power Process: "I create it all."

learning styles application

The questions below will "cycle" you through four styles, or modes, of learning as explained in the article "Learning styles: Discovering how you learn" in Chapter One. Each question will help you explore a different mode. You can answer the questions in any order.

what if *Create an original format for taking notes. Think about how you could modify or combine the note-taking systems discussed in this chapter. Describe your format here.*

why *Describe a situation in school or at work in which you could benefit by taking more effective notes.*

how *Of the note-taking techniques in this chapter that you like and intend to apply, choose one and describe when and where you will use it.*

what *Think back to the major note-taking systems discussed in this chapter: the Cornell format, mind mapping, outlining, concept mapping, or some combination. Choose one system that you intend to apply and briefly summarize its key features.*

master student

profile

FAYE WATTLETON

was president of Planned Parenthood Federation of America from 1978 until 1992. She is currently the founder and president of the Center for the Advancement of Women.

don't ever recall not wanting to be a nurse, or not saying I wanted to be a nurse. This was, in part, certainly my mother's influence. She wanted me to be a missionary nurse. It wasn't sufficient just to be a nurse, I had to commit to a religious cause as well. Missionary nurses work in church hospitals, in Africa and all over the world. I suspect this was suggested to me before I even understood the power of suggestion, and I always grew up saying I was going to be a nurse. I earned two degrees in nursing, but never practiced as a nurse. In the broadest sense of the word, you can say I have nursed all the time, but not in the technical sense. After undergraduate school, I taught nursing for two years. Then I went to graduate school at Columbia University and earned my master's degree. Following that I moved to Dayton, Ohio to work in a public health department. There, I was asked to join the board of the local Planned Parenthood. Two years later, I became executive director of the local chapter. Then, seven years later, I became the national president of the organization.

I'm sure the suggestion to become a nurse was colored by the limitation on women's options in those years. Women were nurses, social workers, or teachers. I don't ever remember being explicitly told, "Oh, you can't be that because you're a girl." It just was....It was never conveyed to me there were any limitations on what I could do and what my work could be, although I'm sure the idea that I be a nurse, as opposed to a doctor or something else, was due to the limitations on the role of women at that time.

Even though we lived in a working class community, there wasn't as much integration, so blacks of all economic levels lived in the black community. My father was a laborer, and my mother was a seamstress, but I went to nursery school with our doctor's son. The doctor's family lived a few blocks from us. This was before the Civil Rights movement, and before blacks moved into white or integrated neighborhoods. That experience also played a very important role in my sense of who I am ethnically, as well as what the possibilities were for me. We lived next door to professionals, as well as the housepainter who had the most beautiful house on the block because he painted and decorated it beautifully.

I try to find the best people I can in various specialties so I can learn from them. I want people who are better than me in their specialties, maybe not better than me in running the whole shebang, but better than me in the communications field or legal field. Stitching everything together to make it work as a [piece of] machinery is, for me, the challenge and the excitement.

I try very hard to listen. If there is conflict, I want to hear what the other side says.... As long as I feel there is mutual respect, it does not hurt me to listen to someone with whom I am really in conflict, to hear what they are saying even if I disagree. If it's a conflict I really want to resolve, I try to find ways we can come to mutual points of agreement. One thing I always believe is if you talk long enough you can almost always reach a resolution. Just the process of talking has a de-fanging influence. I have great faith in human beings finding ways to relate if they have enough contact with each other. ▧

Lucinda Watson, *How They Achieved: Stories of Personal Achievement and Business Success.* Copyright © 2001. Reprinted with permission of John Wiley & Sons, Inc.

For more biographical information on Faye Wattleton, visit the Master Student Hall of Fame at the *From Master Student to Master Employee* Web site at

masterstudent.college.hmco.com

CHAPTER 6
Tests

Test taking is a high-priority issue for students. Discussing this topic together in class can help students prepare more successfully before tests, while learning to manage anxiety during tests. This chapter reinforces how the strategies in *From Master Student to Master Employee* can help students reduce stress at school, work, and home. Staying healthy while pursuing higher education is an important skill all students need to master. Juggling work, college courses, and family responsibilities can be quite stressful. This chapter also provides a unique opportunity to talk about how techniques related to preparing for tests can be helpful when preparing for performance reviews or other important tasks in the workplace.

Page 170
Master Student Map

In Chapter Six, the article "Cooperative learning: Studying with people" addresses the topic of working cooperatively in group study sessions. Use the Master Student Map to begin the discussion of tests and cooperative learning. Divide your class into four groups, assigning each group one of the learning styles. Next, with their books closed, ask students to write down as many answers to their question (**why? what? how? what if?**) in relation to test taking as they can in one minute. After a minute, have each group pick their best answer and report it back to the class. Then have the students open their textbooks and compare their lists to the Master Student Map.

why? Why does this chapter appear in *From Master Student to Master Employee*?

what? What is included in this chapter?

how? How can you use this chapter?

what if? What if you use the techniques in this chapter to be better prepared for tests?

Guest speaker idea for this chapter

Consider inviting faculty members from different departments to talk to your class about their expectations regarding tests. Ask them to prepare a few suggestions for studying materials in their discipline. Suggest that they provide information on the importance of attending class, reading assigned textbook materials, and completing homework assignments. Also have students prepare questions to ask these faculty members during a question-and-answer session.

Page 172
What to do before the test

Mind maps are powerful visual review tools. This article is important to all students because so many of them cram at the last minute and have never practiced any test preparation strategies. Dean Mancina, an instructor at Golden West College, has groups of students (4) pick a chapter from the textbook and create a mind map of the chapter's content on power paper with colored markers. Start your students off by having them each write their names at the top of the page. This helps to ensure that everyone is actively participating in the group. Hang completed posters on the wall in the classroom and have students walk around with their groups to review their classmates' work. This in-class practice opportunity has students convinced that they can try this on their own outside of class, and exhibits effective cooperative learning.

Page 175
Cooperative learning

Forming study groups or committees helps students to develop critical workplace skills. Almost every job is accomplished by the combined efforts of many people. For example, manufacturing a single car calls for the contribution of designers, welders, painters, electricians, marketing executives, computer programmers, and many others. Joining study groups while students are in school can help to expand learning and working style appreciation.

One potential trap of working in teams is that one person ends up doing most of the work. This person might feel resentful and complain. Ask students to brainstorm and create a list of qualities of a master team member. Post this list in your classroom.

Page 180
The test isn't over until . . .

It is vital for students to find out what questions they missed on a test and to understand why they missed them. In college, testing is a cumulative process, and if the student is stuck on a key concept and they do not address it after the first test, the subsequent tests are going to be increasingly more difficult. Ask your students to take a test or quiz from one of their core courses and analyze the test using the list chart in the text. For "grading" this project, ask your students to submit to you a list only of the sources of the test errors they encountered, and the possible solution that is specific to the test that they have re-reviewed. One alternative is to ask students to use the learning styles questions to identify what they have done incorrectly. **Why** did I answer this question incorrectly? **What** was incorrect about it? **How** will I remember the correct answer for future tests? **What if** I studied this material differently?

Page 181
Integrity in test taking

Each campus has its own official policies for handling cheating on campus. Take this opportunity to point out to your students where they can find this policy. Consider handing out a printed version, or assign students to find and submit the policy to you in class for attendance points at your next course meeting.

Page 186
Staying healthy under pressure

For three minutes at the beginning of class, have your students brainstorm a list of things that they can do during the next month to improve the ways that they fuel, move, rest, and observe their body. Ask them to answer the question by completing the sentence, "I discovered that I . . ."

Next, have students select three ideas that they can begin to use or practice this week. Writing an Intention Statement about how and when the student intends to use these ideas will help them to commit to participating.

The health center on your campus may have a health educator or nutritionist that can visit your class as a guest speaker. Use this expert to answer medical questions. If you don't have an on-campus health center, explore community clinics or programs that might provide you with a guest speaker. Often students' attention to a visiting professional will be more focused. Be sure to allow time for a question and answer period.

Page 189
Make performance reviews work for you

Appraisals often are used to justify merit increases in the workplace and this often causes anxiety for students, and reminds them of the stress they felt prior to test taking in the classroom. Review the strategies on page 182 in the article "Let go of test anxiety" and see if students can make connections between pretest jitters and performance review anxiety.

→ What to do when you get stuck on a test question

Help your students with tips for working through difficult test questions using the following strategies. A copy of this material is available on the HM ClassPrep CD.

- **Read it again.** Eliminate the simplest sources of confusion, such as misreading the question.

- **Skip the question for now.** This advice is simple—and it works. Let your subconscious mind work on the answer while you respond to other questions. The trick is to truly let go of answering the puzzling question, for the moment. Questions that nag at the back of your mind can undermine your concentration and interfere with your recall while answering other questions.

- **Look for answers in other test questions.** A term, name, date, or other fact that escapes you might appear in another question on the test itself. Use other questions to stimulate your memory.

- **Treat intuitions with care.** In quick-answer questions (multiple choice, true/false), go with your first instinct as to which answer is correct. If you think your first answer is wrong because you misread the question, do change your answer.

- **Visualize the answer's "location."** Think of the answer to any test question as being recorded someplace in your notes or assigned reading. Close your eyes, take a deep breath, and see if you can visualize that place—its location on a page in the materials you studied for the test.

- **Rewrite the question.** See if you can put a confusing question into your own words. Doing so might release the answer.

- **Free-write.** Just start writing anything at all. On scratch paper or in the margins of your test booklet, record any response to the test question that pops into your head. Instead of just sitting there, stumped, you're doing something—a fact that can reduce anxiety. Writing might also trigger a mental association that answers the question.

- **Write a close answer.** If you simply cannot think of a direct, accurate answer to the question, give it a shot anyway. Answer the question as best as you can, even if you don't think your answer is fully correct. This technique might help you get partial credit for short-answer questions, essay questions, and problems on math or science tests.

voices

advisory board member

*One thing that I tell my students about essay tests is to write as if they were writing to someone who knows absolutely nothing about the subject. In that way they should include all the basic information that they might not otherwise think of. I also use LIBEC, which was in a College Survival newsletter several years ago. LIBEC stands for **l**egible, **i**ntroduction, **b**ody, **e**xample, and **c**onclusion. We talk about these steps and then my students (in groups) write answers to questions I make up from the reading in the chapter. With their group members they exchange answers and check to see if all the areas were covered. They enjoy working on an essay question with others and then evaluating what others have done.*

—BARBARA FOWLER,
LONGVIEW COMMUNITY COLLEGE, MO

Page 193
8 reasons to celebrate mistakes

Ask students to recall a mistake they have made at work and then write about it. In a Discovery Statement, have students describe what they did to create a result they did not want ("I discovered that I tend to underestimate the number of hours projects take"). Follow up with an Intention Statement describing something they can do differently in the future ("I intend to keep track of my actual hours on each project so that I can give more accurate estimates").

Page 194
POWER PROCESS: "Detach"

Writing good essay exam answers is something that is rarely discussed outside of the student success classroom. Review these strategies and then ask students to write an answer to the following essay question: "Fully explain the Power Process: Detach." This provides them with an opportunity to practice developing an essay and spend additional time on this important Power Process.

Course Manual	HM ClassPrep CD	Additional Resources

 Grading tests that you administer in your first-year course is different from grading tests in a traditional academic course. Revisit the *Course Manual* for ideas on effectively evaluating your students' work.

PowerPoint for Chapter Six can help you strengthen discussions of what students should do *before, during,* and *after* tests.

The HM ClassPrep CD has more tips for using 3x5 cards to help with studying, managing study time, and creating study checklists. Use these new ideas to supplement the textbook and present additional materials to help your students succeed on tests.

masterstudent.college.hmco.com   The *From Master Student to Master Employee* Web site includes **interactive flash cards** that contain the key words introduced in the article "Words to watch for in essay questions." Your students can flip through the cards and test their recall. This is great for the visual learners, who like to see the word and its definition in print, and using the computer will be a tactile stimulus for your kinesthetic learners.

Your students can also learn relaxation techniques to use before they begin their tests by visiting the Master Student Web site.

The Career Resource Center has additional resources for working in teams that can support your discussion of the importance of study groups.

Page 199
Master Student Profile: Christopher Reeve

Christopher Reeve passed away in October of 2004, nine years after he was left paralyzed from a horse-riding accident on Memorial Day 1995. His powerful story of actor and superhero turned inspirational voice for people with disabilities has touched the hearts and minds of many. In his role as an advocate, Reeve has raised money for the Christopher Reeve Paralysis Foundation (CRPF) and other organizations towards improving the quality of life for people living with disabilities.

Ask your students how they would connect Reeve's Master Student Profile with the Power Process "Surrender." Are there any other Power Processes that Reeve exhibits? Reeve wrote in his book, *Still Me*, "Just as my accident and its af-termath caused me to re-define what a hero is, I've had to take a hard look at what it means to live as fully as possible in the present." Reeve's focus on the present moment has a definite connection to the Power Process: "Be here now."

Reeve also lobbied on behalf of the National Institute of Health and worked towards increasing government funding for stem cell research. Use Reeve's story to encourage your students to take a stand or act as an advocate for something they feel strongly about. You can suggest that your students raise money for the CRPF as a service-learning exercise. Information about organizing a fundraiser is available at the foundation's Web site at **http://www.christopherreeve.org/**.

6

Tests

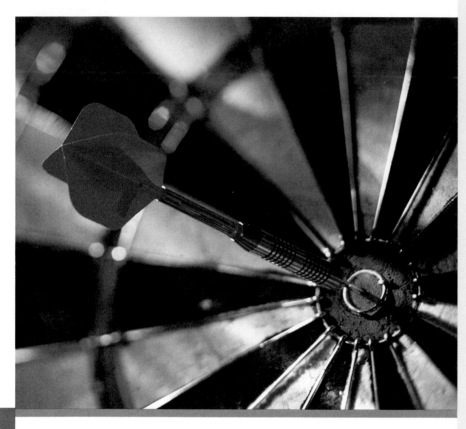

Learn from the mistakes of others—you can never live long enough to make them all yourself.

JOHN LUTHER

Keep in mind that neither success nor failure is ever final.

ROGER BABSON

why
this chapter matters . . .

Adopting a few simple techniques can make a major difference in how you feel under pressure—and improve your performance during test taking.

what
is included . . .

Disarm tests
What to do before the test
Ways to predict test questions
Cooperative learning: Working in teams
What to do during the test
The test isn't over until . . .
Integrity in test taking: The costs of cheating
Let go of test anxiety
Staying healthy under pressure
Make performance reviews work for you
Overcoming math and science anxiety
Taking math and science tests
8 reasons to celebrate mistakes
Power Process: "Detach"
Master Student Profile: Christopher Reeve

how
you can use this chapter . . .

Predict test questions and use your study time more effectively.
Harness the power of cooperative learning by studying with other people.
Learn to look on an F as *feedback* rather than *failure*.

As you read, ask yourself
what if . . .

I could let go of anxiety about tests—or anything else?

Disarm tests

On the surface, tests don't look dangerous, yet sometimes we treat them as if they were land mines. Suppose a stranger walks up to you on the street and asks, "Does a finite abelian P-group have a basis?" Will you break out in a cold sweat?

Probably not. Even if you have never heard of a finite abelian P-group, you are likely to remain coolly detached. However, if you find the same question on a test and if you have never heard of a finite abelian P-group, your hands might get clammy.

We use grades (A to F) to give power to tests. And there are lots of misconceptions about what grades are. Grades are not a measure of intelligence or creativity. They are not an indication of our ability to contribute to society. Grades are not a measure of self-worth. Grades are simply a measure of how well we do on tests. The truth is that if you do badly on a test, you are a person who did badly on a test. That's all.

Some people think that a test score measures what a student has accomplished in a course. This is false. A test score is a measure of what a student scored on a test. If you are anxious about a test and blank out, the grade cannot measure what you've learned. If you are a lucky guesser, the score won't accurately reflect what you know.

Tests come in many forms—quizzes, midterms, finals. In addition, there are certification exams taken by nurses, doctors, lawyers, accountants, and other professionals. And tests are just one form of evaluation. If you were born after 1952, your first evaluation probably took place within one minute of your birth. This was an Apgar score, named after Dr. Virginia Apgar, who developed a way to test the reflexes, heart rate, breathing rate, skin color, and muscle tone of newborns.

Evaluations usually put you under pressure. But no matter when or where you're evaluated—in school or in the workplace—you can avoid unnecessary pressure. Don't give evaluations some magical power. They are not a matter of life and death. A low score on important tests—entrance tests for college or medical school, bar exams, CPA exams—usually means only a delay. At work, a low score on a performance review usually means only that you have areas for improvement. Who doesn't?

It's like balancing on a railroad track. Many people can walk along the rail and stay balanced for long periods. Yet the task seems entirely different if the rail is placed between two buildings, 52 stories up. Deal with tests by keeping them in perspective. Keep the railroad track on the ground. ✖

journal entry 18

Discovery/Intention Statement

Mentally re-create a time when you had difficulty taking a test. Do anything that helps you re-experience this event. You could draw a picture of yourself in this situation, list some of the questions you had difficulty answering, or tell how you felt after finding out your score on the test. Briefly describe that experience in the space below.

I discovered that I . . .

_____

_____

_____

Now wipe your mental slate clean and declare your intention to replace it with a new scenario. Describe how you want your experience of test taking to change. For example, you might write: "I intend to walk into every test I take feeling well rested and thoroughly prepared."

I intend to . . .

_____

_____

_____

Preview this chapter, looking for at least five strategies that can help you accomplish your goal. List those strategies below and note the page numbers where you can find out more about them.

Strategy   *Page number*

_____

_____

_____

_____

_____

_____

_____

_____

_____

What to do before the test

One way to save hours of wasted study time is to look on each test as a performance. From this point of view, preparing for a test means *rehearsing*.

Study for a test in the way that a musician rehearses for a concert or an actor prepares for opening night—by simulating the physical and psychological conditions you'll encounter when you actually enter the exam room.

Rehearsing means doing the kind of tasks that you'll perform during a test—answering questions, solving problems, composing essays. Start this process with regular reviews of course content. Test preparation comes down to answering questions about your self-awareness (What do I know?), task awareness (What do I have to learn?), and strategy awareness (How can I close the gap between what I know and what I don't know?). Answering these questions means managing your review time, creating review tools, and planning your test-taking strategy.

Manage review time

Daily reviews. Concentrate daily reviews on two kinds of material: material you have just learned, either in class or in your reading, and material that involves simple memorization (equations, formulas, dates, definitions). Conduct short daily reviews several times throughout the day.

Begin to review on the first day of class. Most instructors outline the whole course at that time. You can start reviewing within seconds after learning. During a lull in class, go over the notes you just took. Then immediately after class, review your notes again.

Weekly reviews. Weekly reviews are longer—about an hour per subject. They are also more structured than short daily reviews. These sessions include reviews of assigned reading and lecture notes. Look over any mind map summaries or flash cards you have created. You can also practice working on sample problems.

Major reviews. Major reviews are usually conducted the week before finals or other critical exams. They help integrate concepts and deepen understanding of the material presented throughout the term. These are longer review periods—two to five hours at a stretch,

punctuated by sufficient breaks. Remember that the effectiveness of your review begins to drop after an hour or so unless you give yourself a short rest.

Scheduling reviews. If you have a monthly or weekly planner, use it to schedule specific review periods. Plan on at least two major review sessions, lasting two to five hours each, for every course. If you think you'll need extra time for review, consider rearranging tasks or changing their priority in order to free up more study time. Start reviewing key topics at least five days before you'll be tested on them. This allows plenty of time to find the answers to questions and close any gaps in your understanding.

Create review tools

Checklists, mind map summaries, and flash cards take the guesswork and much of the worry out of studying. They divide a big job into smaller parts. When you use these review tools, your confidence increases, you can sleep better at night, and you can stay focused at work.

Study checklists. A study checklist is not a review sheet; it is a to-do list. Checklists contain the briefest possible description of each item to study. Make a list for each subject. List reading assignments by chapters or page numbers. List dates of lecture notes. Write down various types of problems you will need to solve. Write down other skills you must master. Include major ideas, definitions, theories, formulas, and equations. For math and science tests, choose some problems and do them over again as a way to review for the test. Begin keeping a study checklist the very first day of class. Add to it as the term progresses. When you conduct your final review, check items off the list as you review them.

Mind map summary sheets. There are several ways to make a mind map as you study for tests. Start by creating a map totally from memory. You might be surprised by how much you already know. After you have gone as far as you can using recall alone, go over your notes and text and fill in the rest of the map.

Another way to create a mind map summary is to go through your notes and pick out key words. Then, without looking at your notes, create a mind map of everything you can recall about each key word. Finally,

Cramming creates extra work. It takes longer to learn material when you do it under pressure. You can't learn the same quantity of material in less time when you cram. You can learn *some* of the material, though with less comprehension and little or no long-term retention.

The purpose of cramming, therefore, is only to make the best of the situation. Cram to get by in a course so that you can do better next time. Keep the limitations and costs of cramming in mind as you read the following suggestions to help with last-minute studying.

Make choices. Don't try to learn it all when you cram. You can't. Instead, pick out a few of the most important elements of the course and learn those backwards, forwards, and upside down.

Make a plan. Cramming is always done when time is short. It's easy to panic and jump right in. Taking a few minutes to create a plan first can actually save you time and allow you to work faster. After you've chosen what you want to study, determine how much time you have and set timelines for yourself.

Use mind map review sheets and flash cards. Condense the material you have chosen to learn onto mind maps. Choose several elements of the mind maps to put on 3x5 flash cards. Practice re-creating the mind maps, complete with illustrations. Drill yourself with the flash cards.

Recite and recite again. The key to cramming is repetitive recitation. Recitation can burn facts into your brain like no other study method. Go over your material again and again and again. One option is to do a voice recording of yourself while you recite. Then play the recording as you fall asleep and as you get up in the morning.

---

go back to your notes and fill in material you left out. You can also start a mind map with underlined sections from your text. Make mind maps for small, detailed topics as well as for broad ones. You can mind map a whole course or a single lecture or a single point from a lecture.

Flash cards. Three-by-five flash cards are like portable test questions. Take them with you everywhere and use them anytime. On one side of the cards, write the questions. On the other, write the answers. It's that simple. Use flash cards for formulas, definitions, theories, key words from your notes, axioms, dates, foreign language phrases, hypotheses, and sample problems. Create flash cards regularly as the term progresses. Buy an inexpensive card file to keep your flash cards arranged by subject. Always carry a pack of flash cards with you, and review them whenever you have a minute to spare.

Monitoring your reviews. Each day that you prepare for a test, assess what you have learned and what you still need to learn. See how many items you've covered from your study checklist. Look at the tables of contents in your textbooks and write an X next to the sections that you've summarized. Using a monitoring system can help you gauge the thoroughness of your reviews and alert you to areas that still need attention.

Plan a test-taking strategy

Do a dry run. Write up your own questions and take this "test" several times before the actual exam. Say that the exam will include mainly true/false or short-answer questions. Brainstorm a list of such questions—a mock test—and do a dry run. You might type up this "test" so that it looks like the real thing. Meet with your teacher to go over your mock test. Ask whether your questions focus on appropriate topics and represent the kind of items you can expect to see on the actual test.

Get copies of old exams. Copies of previous exams for the class might be available from the instructor, the instructor's department, the library, or the counseling office. Old tests can help you plan a review strategy. Caution: If you rely on old tests exclusively, you might gloss over material the instructor has added since the last test. Also check your school's policy about making past tests available to students. Some might not allow it. ▨

Ways to predict test questions

Predicting test questions can do more than get you a better grade. It can also keep you focused on the purpose of a course and help you design your learning strategies. Making predictions can be fun, too—especially when they turn out to be accurate.

Ask about the nature of the test. Eliminate as much guesswork about tests as possible. Ask your instructor to describe upcoming tests. Do this early in the term so you can be alert for possible test questions throughout the course. Many instructors are happy to answer such questions directly.

Some possible questions to ask are:

- What course material will the test cover—readings, lectures, lab sessions, or a combination?

- Will the test be cumulative, or will it cover just the most recent material you've studied?

- Will the test focus on facts and details or major themes and relationships?

- Will the test call on you to solve problems or apply concepts?

- What types of questions will be on the test—true/false, multiple choice, short-answer, essay?

- Will you have choices about which questions to answer?

- Will your teacher write and score the test—or will a teaching assistant perform those tasks?

Note: In order to study appropriately for essay tests, find out how much detail the instructor wants in your answers. Ask how much time you'll be allowed for the test and how long the essay answers should be (number of pages, blue books, or word limit). Having that information before you begin studying will help you gauge the depth to which you must know the material.

Put yourself in your instructor's shoes. If you were teaching the course, what information would you want students to take away? What kinds of questions would you put on an exam? Make up practice test questions and then answer them. You can also brainstorm test questions with other students—a great activity for study groups.

Look for possible test questions in your notes. Have a separate section in your notebook labeled "Test questions." Add several questions to this section after every lecture and assignment. You can also create your own code or graphic signal—such as a *T!* in a circle—to flag possible test questions in your notes.

Look for clues to possible questions during class. During lectures you can predict test questions by observing what an instructor says and how he says it. Instructors often give clues. For example, they might repeat important points several times, write them on the board, or return to them in subsequent classes.

Certain gestures can indicate critical points. For example, your instructor might pause, look at notes, or read passages word for word.

Notice whether your teacher has any strong points of view on certain issues. Questions on those issues are likely to appear on a test. Also pay attention to questions the instructor poses to students, and note questions that other students ask.

When material from reading assignments is covered extensively in class, it is likely to be on a test. For science courses and other courses involving problem solving, work on sample problems using different variables.

Save all quizzes, papers, lab sheets, and graded materials of any kind. Quiz questions have a way of reappearing, in slightly altered form, on final exams. If copies of previous exams and other graded materials are available, use them to predict test questions.

Remember the obvious. Be on the lookout for these words: *This material will be on the test.*[1] ✉

For suggestions on how to best apply your predictions as you review, visit the *From Master Student to Master Empoyee* Web site at

(masterstudent.college.hmco.com)

Cooperative learning
Working in teams

In addition to offering camaraderie, study groups can elevate your spirits and motivate you on days when you just don't feel like studying for a test. If you skip a solo study session, no one else will know. If you declare your intention to study with others who are depending on you, your intention gains strength.

Forming study groups and joining committees develops your ability to work in teams—a key transferable skill. In the workplace, projects often combine the efforts of many people. For example, manufacturing a single car calls for the contribution of designers, welders, painters, electricians, marketing executives, computer programmers, and many others. Joining teams now, while you are in school, can help you expand your learning styles and advance in your career.

Study groups are especially important if going to school has thrown you into a new culture. Joining a study group with people you already know can help ease the transition. Promote your success in school by refusing to go it alone.

To multiply the benefits of working with study groups, seek out people of other cultures, races, and ethnic groups. You can get a whole new perspective on the world, along with some valued new friends. And you can experience what it's like to be part of a diverse team—an important asset in today's job market.

Form a study group

Look for dedicated students. Find people you are comfortable with and who share some of your academic goals. Look for students who pay attention, ask questions, and take notes during class, and invite them to join your group. Studying with friends is fine, but if your common interests are beer and jokes, beware of getting together for schoolwork. Another way to form a study group is to post a note on a bulletin board asking interested students to contact you. Or pass around a sign-up sheet before class. While these methods can reach many people, they take more time to achieve results. And you have less control over who applies to join the group.

Limit groups to four people. Research on cooperative learning indicates that four people is an ideal group size.[2] Larger ones can be unwieldy.

Hold a planning session. Ask two or three people to get together for a snack and talk about group goals, meeting times, and other logistics. You don't have to make an immediate commitment.

Do a trial run. Test the group first by planning a one-time session. If that session works, plan another. After a few successful sessions, you can schedule regular meetings.

Conduct your study group

Test each other by asking questions. Group members can agree to bring five to ten sample test questions to each meeting. Then you can all take the test made up from these questions.

Practice teaching each other. Teaching is a great way to learn something. Turn the material you're studying into a list of topics and assign a specific topic to each person, who will then teach it to the group. When you teach something, you naturally assume a teacher's attitude ("I know this"), as opposed to a student's attitude ("I still have to learn this"). The vocalization involved in teaching further reinforces the concepts.

Compare notes. Make sure that you all heard the same thing in class and that you all recorded the important information. Ask others to help explain material in your notes that is confusing to you.

Brainstorm test questions. Set aside 5 to 10 minutes of each study session to use brainstorming techniques (described in detail in Chapter Seven) to create test questions. You can add these to the "Test questions" section of your notebook.

Set an agenda for each meeting. Select activities from this article, or create other activities to do as a group. Set approximate time limits for each agenda item and determine a quitting time. Finally, end each meeting with assignments for all members.

Keep the group on task. If the discussion wanders off-topic, remind members of the time limits and agenda for the meeting.

exercise 17

REHEARSE FOR SUCCESS

Sit up in a chair, legs and arms uncrossed. Close your eyes, let go of all thoughts, and focus on your breathing for a minute or two.

Then relax various parts of your body, beginning with your feet. Relax your toes, your ankles. Move up to your calves and thighs. Relax your buttocks. Relax the muscles of your lower back, abdomen, and chest. Relax your hands, arms, and shoulders. Relax your neck, jaw, eyelids, and scalp.

When you are completely relaxed, imagine yourself in an exam room. It's the day of the test. Visualize taking the test successfully. The key is detail. See the test being handed out. Notice your surroundings. Hear the other students shift in their seats. Feel the desk, the pen in your hand, and the exam in front of you. See yourself looking over the exam calmly and confidently. You discover that you know all of the answers.

Stay with this image for a few minutes. Next, imagine yourself writing quickly. Watch yourself turn in the test with confidence. Finally, imagine receiving the test grade. It is an A. Savor the feeling.

As soon as you realize you are feeling anxious about an upcoming test, begin using this technique. The more you do this visualization, the better it can work.

An online version of this exercise is available at

(masterstudent.college.hmco.com)

journal entry 19

Intention Statement

In the space below, outline a plan to form a study group. Explain the steps you will take to get the group organized and set a first meeting date.

I intend to . . .

_____

_____

_____

Now describe the reward you anticipate for fulfilling this intention.

_____

_____

_____

Work in groups of two at a computer to review a course. One person can operate the keyboard while the other person dictates summaries of lectures and assigned readings. Together, both group members can check facts by consulting textbooks, lecture notes, and class handouts.

Create wall-sized mind maps or concept maps to summarize a textbook or series of lectures. Work on large sheets of butcher paper, or tape together pieces of construction paper. When doing a mind map, assign one branch of the mind map to each member of the study group. Use a different colored pen or marker for each branch. (For more information on concept maps and mind maps, see Chapter Five: Notes.)

Pair off to do "book reports." One person can summarize a reading assignment. The other person can act as an interviewer on a talk show, posing questions and asking for further clarification.

Ask for group support in personal areas. Other people might have insight into problems such as transportation, childcare, finances, and time scheduling. Study groups can provide personal support for getting what you want from school. ✖

Ask each member to contribute. Recognize signs that group members are not contributing in equal ways. For instance, someone in your group might consistently fail to prepare for meetings or feel that he has nothing to contribute. Other members might dominate the group discussions. As a group, brainstorm ways to get unprepared members involved. Reel in a dominating member by reminding him of the importance that everyone's voice be heard.

One potential trap of working in teams is that one person ends up doing most of the work. This person might feel resentful and complain. If you find yourself in this situation, transform your complaint into a request. Instead of scolding team members for being lazy, request help. Ask team members to take over specific tasks.

What to do during the test

As you begin

Ask the teacher or test administrator if you can use scratch paper during the test. If you have permission, use this paper to jot down memory aids, formulas, equations, facts, or other material you know you'll need and might forget. An alternative is to make quick notes in the margins of the test sheet.

Pay attention to verbal directions given as a test is distributed. Then scan the whole test immediately. Evaluate the importance of each section. Notice how many points each part of the test is worth and estimate how much time you'll need for each section, using its point value as your guide.

Read the directions slowly. Then reread them. It can be agonizing to discover that you lost points on a test merely because you failed to follow the directions. When the directions are confusing, ask to have them clarified.

Now you are ready to begin the test. Answer the easiest, shortest questions first. This gives you the experience of success. It also stimulates associations and prepares you for more difficult questions. Next answer multiple choice, true/false, and fill-in-the-blank questions. Then proceed to short-answer and essay questions. Pace yourself and watch the time. If you can't think of an answer, move on. Follow your time plan.

Multiple choice questions

Most multiple choice questions ask the student to select the "best answer." Therefore, read all of the choices in case more than one answer is correct. When you're clear about the type of answers you're looking for, keep the following steps in mind:

- *Answer each question in your head first.* Do this before you look at the possible answers. If you come up with an answer that you're confident is right, look for that answer in the list of choices.

- *Read all possible answers before selecting one.* This is essential for multiple choice questions when you must select the best answer, or more than one answer. Sometimes two answers will be similar and only one will be correct.

- *Test each possible answer.* Remember that multiple choice questions consist of two parts: the stem (an incomplete statement at the beginning) and a list of possible answers. Each answer, when combined with the stem, makes a complete statement that is either true or false. When you combine the stem with each possible answer, you are turning each multiple choice question into a small series of true/false questions. Choose the answer that makes a true statement.

- *Eliminate incorrect answers.* Sometimes you can "back in" to the correct answer by using the process of elimination. Cross off the answers that are clearly *not* correct. The answer you cannot eliminate is probably the best choice.

True/false questions

Often, true/false questions are not worth many points individually. Yet they can be tricky and turn into a source of lost points. Use the following strategies to complete these test items successfully:

- *Read the entire question.* Separate the statement into its grammatical parts—individual clauses and phrases—and then test each one. If any part is false, the entire statement is false.

- *Look for qualifiers.* These include words such as *all, most, sometimes,* or *rarely.* Absolute qualifiers such as *always* or *never* generally indicate a false statement.

- *Find the devil in the details.* Double-check each number, fact, and date in a true/false statement. Look for numbers that have been transposed or facts that have been slightly altered. These are signals of a false statement.

- *Watch for negatives.* Look for words such as *not* and *cannot.* Read the sentence without these words and see if you come up with a true or false statement. Then reinsert the negative words and see if the statement makes more sense. Watch especially for sentences with two negative words. As in math operations, two negatives cancel each other out: *We cannot say that Chekhov never succeeded at short story writing* means the same as *Chekhov succeeded at short story writing.*

- **Read it again.** Eliminate the simplest sources of confusion, such as misreading the question.

- **Skip the question for now.** This advice is simple—and it works. Let your subconscious mind work on the answer while you respond to other questions. The trick is to truly let go of answering the puzzling question, for the moment. Questions that nag at the back of your mind can undermine your concentration and interfere with your recall while answering other questions.

- **Look for answers in other test questions.** A term, name, date, or other fact that escapes you might appear in another question on the test itself. Use other questions to stimulate your memory.

- **Treat intuitions with care.** In quick-answer questions (multiple choice, true/false), go with your first instinct as to which answer is correct. If you think your first answer is wrong because you misread the question, do change your answer.

- **Visualize the answer's "location."** Think of the answer to any test question as being recorded someplace in your notes or assigned reading. Close your eyes, take a deep breath, and see if you can visualize that place—its location on a page in the materials you studied for the test.

- **Rewrite the question.** See if you can put a confusing question into your own words. Doing so might release the answer.

- **Free-write.** Just start writing anything at all. On scratch paper or in the margins of your test booklet, record any response to the test question that pops into your head. Instead of just sitting there, stumped, you're doing something—a fact that can reduce anxiety. Writing might also trigger a mental association that answers the question.

- **Write a close answer.** If you simply cannot think of a direct, accurate answer to the question, give it a shot anyway. Answer the question as best as you can, even if you don't think your answer is fully correct. This technique might help you get partial credit for short-answer questions, essay questions, and problems on math or science tests.

- *Write clearly.* Don't let your handwriting cost you points. Make a clear difference in the way you write letters such as T and F. When written hastily, they can look alike.

Open-book tests

- Carefully organize your notes, readings, and any other materials you plan to consult when writing answers.

- Write down any formulas you will need on a separate sheet of paper.

- Bookmark the table of contents and index in each of your textbooks. Place Post-it Notes and Index Flags or paper clips on other important pages of books (pages with tables, for instance). Don't waste time flipping through the pages.

- Create an informal table of contents or index for the notes you took in class.

- Predict which material will be covered on the test and highlight relevant sections in your readings and notes.

Matching tests

- Begin by reading through each column, starting with the one with fewer items. Check the number of items in each column to see if they're equal. If they're not, look for an item in one column that you can match with two or more items in the other column.

- Look for any items with similar wording and make special note of the differences between these items.

- Match words that are similar grammatically. For example, match verbs with verbs and nouns with nouns.

- When matching individual words with phrases, first read a phrase. Then look for the word that logically completes the phrase.

- Cross out items in each column when you are through with them.

Essay questions

Managing your time is crucial to answering essay questions. Note how many questions you have to answer and monitor your progress during the test period. Writing shorter answers and completing all of the questions on an essay test will probably yield a better score than leaving some questions blank.

Find out what an essay question is asking—precisely. If a question asks you to *compare* the ideas of Sigmund Freud and Karl Marx, no matter how eloquently you *explain* them, you are on a one-way trip to No Credit City.

To plan your answer, make a list of some type on scratch paper. For example, list important historical events or key steps in a process. You might also create a chart that shows similarities and differences between items in your list. You could even include the list or chart in your answer.

Before you write, make a quick outline. There are three reasons for making a quick outline. First, an outline can help speed up the writing of your detailed answer. Second, you're less likely to leave out important facts. Third, if you don't have time to finish your answer, your outline could win you some points.

Introduce your answer by getting to the point. General statements such as "There are many interesting facets to this difficult question" can cause acute irritation for teachers grading dozens of tests.

One way to get to the point is to begin your answer with part of the question. Suppose the question is "Discuss how increasing the city police budget might or might not contribute to a decrease in street crime." Your first sentence might be "An increase in police expenditures will not have a significant effect on street crime for the following reasons." Your position is clear. You are on your way to an answer.

When you expand your answer with supporting ideas and facts, start out with the most solid points. Be brief and avoid filler sentences.

Write legibly. Grading essay questions is in large part a subjective process. Sloppy, difficult-to-read handwriting might actually lower your grade.

Write on one side of the paper only. If you write on both sides of the paper, writing will show through and obscure the writing on the other side. If necessary, use the blank side to add points you missed. Leave a generous left-hand margin and plenty of space between your answers, in case you want to add to them later.

Finally, if you have time, review your answers for grammar and spelling errors, clarity, and legibility. ✉

For more suggestions on mastering tests, visit the *From Master Student to Master Employee* Web site at

masterstudent.college.hmco.com

→ Words to watch for in essay questions

The following words are commonly found in essay test questions. If you want to do well on essay tests, study this sidebar thoroughly. Know these words backward and forward. To heighten your awareness of them, underline the words when you see them in a test question.

Analyze: Break into separate parts and discuss, examine, or interpret each part. Then give your opinion.

Compare: Examine two or more items. Identify similarities and differences.

Contrast: Show differences. Set in opposition.

Criticize: Make judgments. Evaluate comparative worth. Criticism often involves analysis.

Define: Explain the exact meaning—usually, a meaning specific to the course or subject. Definitions are usually short.

Describe: Give a detailed account. Make a picture with words. List characteristics, qualities, and parts.

Discuss: Consider and debate or argue the pros and cons of an issue. Write about any conflict. Compare and contrast.

Explain: Make an idea clear. Show logically how a concept is developed. Give the reasons for an event.

Prove: Support with facts (especially facts presented in class or in the text).

Relate: Show the connections between ideas or events. Provide a larger context for seeing the big picture.

State: Explain precisely.

Summarize: Give a brief, condensed account. Include conclusions. Avoid unnecessary details.

Trace: Show the order of events or the progress of a subject or event.

If any of these terms are still unclear to you, consult your unabridged dictionary. A thorough knowledge of these words helps you answer essay questions in a way that best demonstrates your understanding of the course content.

Review these key words and other helpful vocabulary terms by using the online flash cards at

masterstudent.college.hmco.com

The test isn't over until . . .

Many students believe that a test is over as soon as they turn in the answer sheet. Consider another point of view: You're not done with a test until you know the answer to any question that you missed—and why you missed it. To get the most value from any test, take control of what you do at two critical points: the time immediately following the test, and the time when the test is returned to you.

After finishing a test, your first thought might be to nap, snack, rent a DVD, or go out with friends to celebrate. Restrain those impulses for a short while so that you can reflect on the test. The time you invest now carries the potential to raise your grades in the future.

To begin with, sit down in a quiet place and take a few minutes to write some Discovery Statements related to your experience of taking the test. Doing this while the test is still fresh in your mind increases the value of this technique. Describe how you felt about taking the test, how effective your review strategies were, and whether you accurately predicted the questions that appeared on the test. Follow up with an Intention Statement or two. State what, if anything, you will do differently to prepare for the next test. The more specific you are, the better. If the test revealed any gaps in your knowledge, list follow-up questions to ask in class.

When a returned test includes a teacher's comments, view this document as a treasure-trove of intellectual gold. First, make sure that the point totals add up correctly and double-check for any other errors in grading. Even the best teachers make an occasional mistake.

See if you can correct any answers that lost points. To do this, carefully analyze the source of your errors and find a solution. Ask yourself, what types of questions did I miss? On what material did the teacher base the test question? Can I learn anything from the instructor's comments that will help me prepare for the next tests? Consult the following chart for help. ⊠

Source of test error	Possible solutions
Study errors–studying material that was not included on the test, or spending too little time on material that *did* appear on the test	• Ask your teacher about specific topics that will be included on a test. • Practice predicting test questions. • Form a study group with class members to create mock tests.
Careless errors, such as skipping or misreading directions	• Read and follow directions more carefully–especially when tests are divided into several sections with different directions. • Set aside time during the next test to proofread your answers.
Concept errors–mistakes made when you do not understand the underlying principles needed to answer a question or solve a problem	• Look for patterns in the questions you missed. • Make sure that you complete all assigned readings, attend all lectures, and show up for laboratory sessions. • Ask your teacher for help with specific questions.
Application errors–mistakes made when you understand underlying principles but fail to apply them correctly	• Rewrite your answers correctly. • When studying, spend more time on solving sample problems. • Predict application questions that will appear in future tests and practice answering them.
Test mechanics errors–missing more questions in certain parts of the test than others, changing correct answers to incorrect ones at the last minute, leaving items blank, miscopying answers from scratch paper to the answer sheet	• Set time limits for taking each section of a test and stick to them. • Proofread your test answers carefully. • Look for patterns in the kind of answers you change at the last minute. • Change answers only if you can state a clear and compelling reason to do so.

Integrity in test taking
The costs of cheating

Cheating on tests can be a tempting choice. One benefit is that we might get a good grade without having to study.

Instead of studying, we could spend more time watching TV, partying, sleeping, or doing anything that seems like more fun. Another benefit is that we could avoid the risk of doing poorly on a test—which could happen even if we *do* study. But before you rush out to make cheating a habit, remember that it also carries costs. Here are some to consider.

We learn less. While we might think that some courses offer little or no value, it is more likely that we can create value from any course. If we look deeply enough, we can discover some idea or acquire some skill to prepare us for future courses or a career after graduation.

We lose money. Getting an education costs a lot of money. Cheating sabotages our purchase. We pay full tuition without getting full value for it.

Fear of getting caught promotes stress. When we're fully aware of our emotions about cheating, we might discover intense stress. Even if we're not fully aware of our emotions, we're likely to feel some level of discomfort about getting caught.

Violating our values promotes stress. Even if we don't get caught cheating, we can feel stress about violating our own ethical standards. Stress can compromise our physical health and overall quality of life.

Cheating on tests can make it easier to violate our integrity again. Human beings become comfortable with behaviors that they repeat. Cheating is no exception.

Think about the first time you drove a car. You might have felt excited—even a little frightened. Now driving is probably second nature, and you don't give it much thought. Repeated experience with driving creates familiarity, which lessens the intense feelings you had during your first time at the wheel.

We can experience the same process with almost any behavior. Cheating once will make it easier to cheat again. And if we become comfortable with compromising our integrity in one area of life, we might find it easier to compromise in other areas.

Handling tests with integrity helps you develop the habit of handling *any* task with integrity. In turn, this habit promotes ethical behavior in the workplace—a transferable skill that employers value.

Cheating lowers our self-concept. Whether or not we are fully aware of it, cheating sends us the message that we are not smart enough or responsible enough to make it on our own. We deny ourselves the celebration and satisfaction of authentic success.

An effective alternative to cheating is to become a master student. Ways to do this are described on every page of this book. ✉

> ## Have some FUN!
>
> Contrary to popular belief, finals week does not have to be a drag.
>
> In fact, if you have used techniques in this chapter, exam week can be fun. By planning ahead, you will have done most of your studying long before finals arrive. You can feel confident and relaxed.
>
> When you are well prepared for tests, you can even use fun as a technique to enhance your performance. The day before a final, go for a run or play a game of basketball. Take in a movie or a concert. Watch TV. A relaxed brain is a more effective brain. If you have studied for a test, your mind will continue to prepare itself even while you're at the movies.
>
> Get plenty of rest, too. There's no need to cram until 3 a.m. when you have used the techniques in this chapter.
>
> On the first day of finals, you can wake up refreshed, have a good breakfast, and walk into the exam room with a smile on your face. You can also leave with a smile on your face, knowing that you are going to have a fun week. It's your reward for studying regularly throughout the term.
>
> If this kind of exam week sounds inviting, you can begin preparing for it right now.

Let go of test anxiety

Test anxiety has two components: mental and physical. The mental component of stress includes all of your thoughts and worries about tests. The physical component includes bodily sensations and tension. The following techniques can help you deal with stress in any situation, from test anxiety to stage fright.

Dealing with thoughts

Yell "Stop!" When you notice that your mind is consumed with worries and fears, that your thoughts are spinning out of control, mentally yell "Stop!" If you're in a situation that allows it, yell it out loud. This action is likely to bring your focus back to the present moment and allow you to redirect your thoughts. Once you've broken the cycle of worry or panic, you can use any of the following techniques.

Daydream. When you fill your mind with pleasant thoughts, there is no room left for anxiety. If you notice yourself worrying about an upcoming test, replace visions of doom with images of something you like to do. Daydream about being with a special friend or walking alone in a favorite place.

Visualize success. Most of us live up—or down—to our own expectations. If we spend a lot of time mentally rehearsing what it will be like to fail a test, our chances of doing so increase. Instead, you can take time to rehearse what it will be like to succeed. Be specific. Create detailed pictures, actions, and even sounds as part of your visualization. If you are able to visit the room where you will take the test, mentally rehearse while you are actually in this room.

Focus. Focus your attention on a specific object. During an exam, take a few seconds to listen to the sounds of concentration—the squeaking of chairs, the scratching of pencils, the muted coughs. Touch the surface of your desk and notice the texture. Concentrate all of your attention on one point. Don't leave room in your mind for anxiety-related thoughts.

Praise yourself. Talk to yourself in a positive way. Many of us take the first opportunity to belittle ourselves: "Way to go, dummy! You don't even know the answer to the first question on the test." We wouldn't dream of treating a friend this way, yet we do it to ourselves. An alternative is to treat yourself as if you were your own best friend. Consider telling yourself, "I am very relaxed. I am doing a great job on this test."

Consider the worst. Rather than trying to put a stop to your worrying, consider the very worst thing that could happen. Take your fear to the limit of absurdity.

Imagine the catastrophic problems that might occur if you were to fail the test. You might say to yourself, "Well, if I fail this test, I might fail the course, lose my financial aid, and get kicked out of school. Then I won't be able to get a job, so the bank will repossess my car, and I'll start drinking." Keep going until you see the absurdity of your predictions. After you stop chuckling, you can backtrack to discover a reasonable level of concern. Your worry about failing the entire course if you fail the test might be justified. At that point ask yourself, "Can I live with that?" Unless you are taking a test in parachute packing and the final question involves jumping out of a plane, the answer

F is for feedback, not failure

Sometimes when students get an F on an assignment, they interpret that letter as a message: "You are a failure." That interpretation is not accurate.

Getting an F means only that you failed a test—not that you failed your life. From now on, imagine that the letter *F* when used as a grade represents another word: *feedback*. An F is an indication that you didn't understand the material well enough—it's a message to do something differently before the next test or assignment. If you interpret *F* as *failure*, you don't get to change anything. But if you interpret *F* as *feedback*, you can change your thinking and behavior in ways that promote your success.

TEST CHANGED TO TODAY

will almost always be yes. (If the answer is no, use another technique. In fact, use several other techniques.)

Zoom out. When you feel distressed, zoom out. Think the way film directors do when they dolly a camera out and away from an action scene. In your mind, imagine that you're floating away and viewing the situation as a detached outside observer. If you're extremely distressed, let your imagination take you even farther. See yourself rising above the scene so that your whole community, city, nation, or planet is within view. Another option is to zoom out in time. Imagine yourself one week, one month, one year, one decade, or one century from today. Assess how much the current situation will matter when that time comes.

From this larger viewpoint, ask yourself whether this situation is worth worrying about. A negative response is not a license to belittle or avoid problems; it is permission to gain some perspective.

Imagine yourself one week, one month, one year, one decade, or one century from today. Assess how much the current situation will matter when that time comes.

Dealing with the physical sensations of anxiety

Breathe. You can calm physical sensations within your body by focusing your attention on your breathing. Concentrate on the air going in and out of your lungs. Experience it as it passes through your nose and mouth. If you notice that you are taking short, shallow breaths, begin to take longer and deeper breaths.

Scan your body. Simple awareness is an effective technique to reduce the tension in your body. Sit comfortably and close your eyes. Focus your attention on the muscles in your feet and notice if they are relaxed. Tell the muscles in your feet that they can relax. Move up to your ankles and repeat the procedure. Next go to your calves and thighs and buttocks, telling each group of muscles to relax. Do the same for your lower back, diaphragm, chest, upper back, neck, shoulders, jaw, face, upper arms, lower arms, fingers, and scalp.

Tense and relax. Find a muscle that is tense and make it even more tense. If your shoulders are tense, pull them back, arch your back, and tense your shoulder muscles even more tightly. Then relax. The net result is that you can be aware of the relaxation and allow yourself to relax even more.

Use guided imagery. Relax completely and take a quick fantasy trip. Close your eyes, free your body of tension, and imagine yourself in a beautiful, peaceful, natural setting. Create as much of the scene as you can. Be specific. Use all of your senses.

For example, you might imagine yourself at a beach. Hear the surf rolling in and the sea gulls calling to each other. Feel the sun on your face and the hot sand between your toes. Smell the sea breeze. Taste the salty mist from the surf. Notice the ships on the horizon and the rolling sand dunes. Use all of your senses to create a vivid imaginary trip.

Describe it. Focus your attention on your anxiety. If you are feeling nauseated or if you have a headache, concentrate on that feeling. Describe it to yourself. Tell yourself how large it is, where it is located in your body, what color it is, what shape it is, what texture it is, how much water it might hold if it had volume, and how heavy it is. As you describe your anxiety in detail, don't resist it. When you completely experience a physical sensation, it will often disappear.

Exercise aerobically. This is one technique that won't work in the classroom or while you're taking a test. Yet it is an excellent way to reduce body tension. Exercise regularly during the days that you review for a test. See what effect this has on your ability to focus and relax *during* the test.

Get help. When these techniques don't work, when anxiety is serious, get help. If you become withdrawn, have frequent thoughts about death or suicide, get depressed and stay depressed for more than a few days, or have prolonged feelings of hopelessness, see a counselor. ⊠

from the desk of...

RAYMOND PEREZ, JR.,
HIGHWAY ENGINEER PROFESSIONAL:

I found filling out forms to secure my job as a highway engineer professional a lot like taking a test—I was so nervous the night before. As I prepared for my interview and for filling out paperwork, I was able to reduce my "test anxiety" by staying focused, getting a good night's sleep, and eating a healthy breakfast. In the end, I got the job.

exercise 18

TWENTY THINGS I LIKE TO DO

One way to relieve tension is to mentally yell "Stop!" and substitute a pleasant daydream for the stressful thoughts and emotions you are experiencing.

In order to create a supply of pleasant images to recall during times of stress, conduct an eight-minute brainstorm about things you like to do. Your goal is to generate at least 20 ideas. Time yourself and write as fast as you can in the space below.

_____
_____
_____
_____
_____
_____
_____
_____
_____
_____
_____
_____
_____
_____
_____
_____

When you have completed your list, study it. Pick out two activities that seem especially pleasant and elaborate on them by creating a mind map. Write down all of the memories you have about that activity.

You can use these images to calm yourself in stressful situations.

THINKING CRITICALLY IN THE CLASSROOM

Create a short multiple choice test on a topic in a course you're taking right now. Ask several people from the class to take this exam.

Then, as a group, discuss the answer you chose for each question. Also talk about *why* and *how* you chose each answer. The purpose is to identify the strategies that different people use when answering a multiple choice question—especially when they are unsure of the correct answer.

You might discover some test-taking strategies that you would use in the future. List those strategies in the space below.

_____
_____
_____
_____
_____

Repeat this exercise by creating and discussing tests in other formats: short-answer, true/false, and essay.

_____
_____
_____
_____
_____
_____
_____
_____

journal entry 20

Discovery/Intention Statement

Do a timed, four-minute brainstorm of all the reasons, rationalizations, justifications, and excuses you have used to avoid studying. Be creative. List your thoughts in the space below by completing the following Discovery Statement.

I discovered that I . . .

_____

_____

_____

_____

_____

_____

_____

_____

_____

_____

Next, review your list, pick the excuse that you use the most, and circle it. In the space below, write an Intention Statement about what you will do to begin eliminating your favorite excuse. Make this Intention Statement one that you can keep, with a timeline and a reward.

I intend to . . .

_____

_____

_____

_____

journal entry 21

Discovery Statement

Explore your feelings about tests. Complete the following sentences.

As exam time gets closer, one thing I notice that I do is . . .

_____

_____

When it comes to taking tests, I have trouble . . .

_____

The night before a test, I usually feel . . .

_____

_____

The morning of a test, I usually feel . . .

_____

_____

During a test, I usually feel . . .

_____

_____

After a test, I usually feel . . .

_____

_____

When I get a test score, I usually feel . . .

_____

_____

An online version of this exercise is available at [masterstudent.college.hmco.com]

Staying healthy under pressure

One key strategy for improving your performance under pressure goes beyond memory techniques or other study skills. This strategy involves taking care of your body.

Human bodies are incredible. They often continue to operate despite abuse. We run them too hard or let them sit idle for years. We pollute our bodies with junk food and expose them to illness. Yet we expect them to run flawlessly—even during stressful situations such as tests or long days at work.

If you want your body to perform at peak levels while you're in school or on the job, then fuel it with healthful food. Energize it with exercise. Rest it with sleep and stress management. Also make conscious choices about how you consume chemicals. These are transferable skills that can lengthen your life—and maybe even save it. Take care of your body, and it will take care of your mind and soul during tests or any other time when the pressure is on.

Fuel it

Despite the steady stream of fad diets with contradictory claims, there is wide agreement among nutritional scientists about how to eat well. The following guidelines are adapted from *Dietary Guidelines for Americans 2000*, fifth edition, from the U.S. Department of Agriculture and U.S. Department of Health and Human Services.

Choose a variety of fruits, vegetables, and grains daily, especially whole grains. Eating plenty of fruits, vegetables, and grains of different kinds may help protect you against many chronic diseases. Remember that whole grains provide more fiber and other nutrients than processed grains.

Keep food safe to eat. Wash hands and cooking surfaces often. Separate raw, cooked, and ready-to-eat foods while shopping, preparing, or storing. Read labels for instructions on preparing foods, and refrigerate perishable foods promptly.

Choose a diet that is low in saturated fat and cholesterol and moderate in total fat. Limit solid fats, such as butter, hard margarines, lard, and partially hydrogenated shortenings. Use vegetable oils as a substitute.

Choose beverages and foods to moderate your intake of sugars. Get most of your calories from whole grains, fruits and vegetables, low-fat or nonfat dairy products, and lean meats or meat substitutes. Don't let soft drinks or other sweets crowd out other foods you need to maintain health. Drink water often.

Choose and prepare foods with less salt. Many people can reduce their chances of developing high blood pressure by consuming less salt.

If you drink alcoholic beverages, do so in moderation. Alcoholic beverages supply calories but few nutrients. Excess alcohol alters judgment. It also raises your risk for motor vehicle crashes, other injuries, high blood pressure, stroke, violence, suicide, and certain types of cancer. If you choose to drink alcoholic beverages, consume them only in moderation—up to one drink per day for women or two drinks per day for men. Drink with meals to slow alcohol absorption.

Two risks related to alcohol use are substance abuse and addiction. Substance abuse is compulsive use of alcohol or other drugs. Some people will stop abusing a substance when the consequences get serious enough. Other people don't stop. They continue their self-defeating behaviors, no matter what the consequences for themselves, their friends, or their families. At that point the problem goes beyond abuse. It's addiction.

Many people find that they cannot treat addiction on their own. Two broad options exist for getting help. One is the growing self-help movement. The other is formal treatment. People recovering from addiction often combine the two.

If you're addicted to alcohol or another drug, consider taking a First Step: Acknowledge your lack of control over the drug once you start using it. In many self-help groups, this is called surrender. This does not mean giving up. It does mean admitting that the problem is too big for you to handle alone, and that you are willing to ask for help.

Move it

In addition to following the above guidelines for nutrition, work toward getting moderate physical activity each day—the equivalent of walking two miles in 30 minutes.

Physical activity helps to control weight, prevent heart disease, control cholesterol levels and diabetes, and slow the bone loss that comes with aging. Exercise also lowers the risk of certain cancers and helps to reduce anxiety and depression.

Do something you enjoy. You could start by walking briskly for at least 15 minutes every day. Increase that time gradually and add a little jogging or running. Other options include stair climbing, swimming, bicycling, rope jumping, and dancing. You can even burn calories by gardening, raking leaves, and working around the house.

Once you're in reasonable shape, you can stay there by doing aerobic activity on most days of the week. An hour of daily activity is ideal, but do whatever you can. Some activity is better than none. Look for exercise facilities on campus. School can be a great place to get in shape.

Before beginning any vigorous exercise program, consult a health care professional. This is critical if you are overweight, over age 60, in poor condition, or a heavy smoker, or if you have a history of health problems.

Rest it

A lack of sleep can decrease your immunity to illness and impair your performance in school and at work. Excess stress can have similar effects.

Promote sound sleep.
Lack of sleep can interfere with your memory, your concentration, and your ability to stay awake in class. The solution is a good night's sleep.

As a student, you might be tempted to cut back drastically on your sleep once in a while. All-nighters before final exams are an example. If you indulge in them, read Chapter Two for some time-management ideas. Depriving yourself of sleep is a choice you can avoid.

Sometimes, getting to sleep isn't easy, even when you feel tired. If you have trouble falling asleep, experiment with the following suggestions:

- Exercise daily. For many people, this promotes sounder sleep. However, finish exercising at least several hours before you want to go to sleep.

- Avoid naps during the daytime.

- Monitor your caffeine intake, especially in the afternoon and evening.

Manage stress. Stress has both mental and physical components. The mental components include thoughts that promote fear and sadness. The physical components include unpleasant sensations such as muscle tension. You can use three broad strategies to manage stress:

- *Deal with stressful thoughts by releasing irrational beliefs.* According to Martin Seligman and other cognitive psychologists, stress results not from events in our lives but from the way we *think* about those events.[3] If we believe that people should always behave in exactly the way we expect them to, for instance, we set ourselves up for stress. Noticing these beliefs and replacing them with more rational ones (such as "I can control my own behavior but not the behavior of others") can reduce stress significantly.

- *Deal with stressful thoughts by releasing them altogether.* Meditation offers a way to release distressing thoughts. While meditating, you simply notice your thoughts as they arise and pass—without reacting to them. Eventually, your stream of thinking slows down. You may even find that it comes to a complete stop while at the same time you remain alert and aware. This is a state of deep relaxation that may also yield life-changing insights.

- *Counter the physical element of stress.* Options include breathing exercises, relaxation techniques, yoga, and therapeutic bodywork such as massage.

- *Use this book.* It includes relaxation and breathing exercises. Many of the Power Processes and the techniques for letting go of test anxiety can also help you manage stress. This includes stress at work. Apply techniques for managing the mental and physical aspects of stress while interviewing for a job, making a presentation, doing a performance review, or carrying out any task that raises your anxiety level.

If the above techniques don't work within a few weeks, get help. See your doctor or a counselor at your student health service. ✖

For more tips on staying healthy under pressure, visit the *From Master Student to Master Employee* Web site at

[masterstudent.college.hmco.com]

desk of . . .

from the

CRISTINA BAHR, LAW SCHOOL STUDENT:

It's very important to set time aside away from work for three things: exercise, sleep, and time doing absolutely nothing (alone or with family or friends). The key to doing this is to make them as high of a priority as any professional obligation. Would you skip a meeting at work? No. Keep that same mentality when setting aside time to get to the gym or have dinner with your family.

→ Some facts . . .

In the United States, substance abuse and addiction take a heavy toll on students in higher education, especially those aged 18 to 24. In this group:

- 31 percent met criteria for a diagnosis of alcohol abuse and 6 percent for a diagnosis of alcohol dependence in the past 12 months, according to questionnaire-based self-reports about their drinking.

- About 25 percent report academic consequences of their drinking, including missing class, falling behind, doing poorly on exams or papers, and receiving lower grades overall.

- 1,400 die each year from alcohol-related unintentional injuries, including motor vehicle crashes.

- 500,000 are unintentionally injured under the influence of alcohol.

- 400,000 had unprotected sex, and more than 100,000 students report having been too intoxicated to know if they consented to having sex.

- 70,000 are victims of alcohol-related sexual assault or date rape.

For related information from the National Institute for Alcohol Abuse and Alcoholism, go online to **http://www.collegedrinkingprevention.gov**.

Sources: R. W. Hingson, T. Heeren, R. C. Zakocs, A. Kopstein, and H. Wechsler, "Magnitude of Alcohol-Related Mortality and Morbidity among U.S. College Students Ages 18–24," *Journal of Studies on Alcohol* 63, no. 2 (2002): 136–144.

H. Wechsler, J. E. Lee, M. Kuo, M. Seibring, T. F. Nelson, and H. P. Lee, "Trends in College Binge Drinking during a Period of Increased Prevention Efforts: Findings from Four Harvard School of Public Health Study Surveys, 1993–2001," *Journal of American College Health* 50, no. 5 (2002): 203–217.

J. R. Knight, H. Wechsler, M. Kuo, M. Seibring, E. R. Weitzman, and M. Schuckit, "Alcohol Abuse and Dependence among U.S. College Students," *Journal of Studies on Alcohol* 63, no. 3 (2002): 263–270.

Make performance reviews work for you

Performance reviews are opportunities to get feedback about how you're doing at work. Like tests, they are occasions where your knowledge and skills get evaluated. Unlike tests, the results can range from getting a large raise to getting fired.

Performance reviews usually take place in a meeting with your direct supervisor. Meetings follow various formats, and many organizations have their own systems for rating performance. Yet the basic idea is for you to walk away with answers to three questions: What am I doing well? What could I do better? and How can I develop the skills to improve?

You can use performance reviews as tools for taking charge of your career development. Previous articles in this chapter suggested that you apply certain strategies before a test, during a test, and after a test. The same three-part approach can also help you with performance reviews.

Before the review. Your organization may schedule performance reviews only once or twice per year. Yet effective performance review is a continuous process. For optimum results, begin this process on your first day at work.

When you start a new job, meet with your direct supervisor to define exactly what "effective performance" means for you. Here's where your skills at goal setting can be a lifesaver (see Chapter Two). Set work-related goals that you can achieve. State them in specific, measurable terms. Whenever possible, include a specific date to meet each goal. Put your goals in writing and share them with your supervisor.

You can use the Journal Entry System from this book to take a "snapshot" of your performance at any point in time. State your goals in the form of Intention Statements. Use Discovery Statements to state and assess your progress in meeting those goals. The idea is to continually monitor and improve your performance—well before it's time to meet with your supervisor.

As the date of your performance review approaches, anticipate the kind of questions your supervisor will ask. For example:

- What was your biggest accomplishment since your last performance review?
- In light of your stated goals, how did you feel about your performance?
- What prevented you from performing well or meeting any of your goals?
- What can you do to overcome those obstacles?
- What can coworkers and managers do to help you overcome those obstacles?

During the review. When you meet with your supervisor, refer to your list of goals and note which ones you met. Take time to celebrate your accomplishments and set new goals.

If you missed a goal, talk about how that happened. Instead of focusing on failure or placing blame, take a problem-solving approach. If you made a mistake, talk about what you learned from the experience and what you intend to do differently in the future. Revise the goal and create a new plan for achieving it.

Effective performance reviews include time for you to *give* feedback as well as receive it. Discuss what you like about your job and what you would like to change. If meeting your goals calls for extra resources or changes in your job description, then ask for them.

After the review. Ask for feedback on a regular basis. This process can be simple and informal. At any time you can take a few minutes to ask your supervisor or a coworker *How am I doing?* and *How can I improve?* You might find these "minireviews" to be more useful than formal performance reviews.

To multiply the value of performance reviews, use them to power your career plan. Regularly update your list of job accomplishments, along with any new skills you develop. Then add them to your résumé. Based on your current job experience, also define the next job you want. Every performance review can be one more step to the career of your dreams. ◼

Overcoming math and science an~~x~~iety

$$\sum_{n=1}^{\infty} (-1)^n \frac{|\sin(n)|}{n}$$

$$(xy) = \begin{cases} \dfrac{x \cos x}{\sin x} \\ 1 \end{cases}$$

Many schools offer courses in overcoming math and science anxiety. It can pay to check them out. The following suggestions just might start you on the road to enjoying science and mathematics.

Take a First Step about your current level of knowledge. Before you register for a math or science course, seek out the assigned texts for the class. Look at the kind of material that's covered in early chapters. If that material seems new or difficult for you, see the instructor and express any concerns you have. Ask for suggestions on ways to prepare for the course. Remember that it's OK to continue your study of math and science from your current level of ability—whatever that level might be.

Choose teachers with care. Whenever possible, find a math teacher whose approach to math matches key aspects of your learning style. One way to do this is trial and error. Simply try several teachers until you find one whom you enjoy. However, this approach takes time and could lead to needless frustration. An alternative is to ask around and discover which teachers have a gift for making math understandable.

Schedule courses from a big picture of your time. Science and math classes can be homework-heavy. Before you register for one, consider all the demands on your time. Think about the homework load you'll get from other courses. Also think about your commitments at work and at home. Choose courses in a way that promotes balance in your schedule. Make room for the hours you'll need each week to succeed in all your courses.

Whenever possible, take math courses "back to back." Think about math in the same way that you think about learning a foreign language. If you take a year off in between Spanish I and Spanish II, you won't expect to gain much fluency. To master a language, you take courses back to back. It works the same way with math—a language in itself.

Beware of short courses. Courses that you take during summer school or another shortened term are—by necessity—condensed. You can find yourself doing far more reading and homework each week than you do in longer courses. If you enjoy math, the extra intensity can provide a stimulus to learn. If math is not your favorite subject, give yourself the gift of extra course time. Enroll in courses with more calendar days.

Make your text an A priority. In a history, an English, or an economics class, the teacher might refer to some of the required readings only in passing. In contrast, math and science courses are often text-driven—that is, class activities closely follow the format and content of the book. This makes it doubly important to complete your reading assignments. Master one concept before going on to the next, and stay current with your reading. To get the most out of your text, be willing to read each sentence slowly and reread it as needed.

Read actively. Science is not only a body of knowledge, it is an activity. To get the most out of your math and science texts, read with paper and pencil in hand. Work out examples and copy diagrams, formulas, and equations. Understand each step used in solving a problem or testing a hypothesis. *Study diagrams, charts,* *and other illustrations carefully*. They are important learning tools and are often a source for test questions.

Participate actively in class. Success in math and science depends on your active involvement. Attending class regularly, completing homework assignments, speaking up when you have a question, and seeking extra help can be crucial. If you want to succeed, make daily contact with these subjects.

Use lab sessions to your advantage. Laboratory work is crucial to many science classes. To get the most out of these sessions, prepare. Know in advance what procedures you'll be doing and what materials you'll need. If possible, visit the lab before your assigned time and get to know the territory. Find out where materials are stored and where to dispose of chemicals or specimens. Bring your lab notebook and worksheets to class to record and summarize your findings.

More suggestions for overcoming math and science anxiety are available on the *From Master Student to Master Employee* Web site at

masterstudent.college.hmco.com

journal entry 22

Discovery/Intention Statement

Most of us can recall a time when learning became associated with anxiety. For many of us, this happened early with math and science.

One step toward getting past this anxiety is to write a math or science autobiography. Recall specific experiences in which you first felt stress over these subjects. Where were you? How old were you? What were you doing, thinking, and feeling? Who else was with you? What did those people say or do?

Describe one of these experiences in the space below.

_____

_____

_____

_____

Now recall any incidents in your life that gave you positive feelings about math or science. Describe one of these incidents in detail in the space below.

_____

_____

_____

_____

Now sum up the significant discoveries you made while describing these two sets of experiences.

I discovered that my biggest barrier in math or science is . . .

_____

_____

_____

I discovered that the most satisfying aspect of doing math and science is . . .

_____

_____

_____

Now prepare to take positive action. List three things you can do to overcome any anxiety you feel about math or science. Include a specific time frame for taking each action.

Action 1: I intend to . . .

_____

_____

Action 2: I intend to . . .

_____

_____

Action 3: I intend to . . .

_____

_____

Taking Math & Science Tests

Use time drills. To prepare for math and science tests, practice working problems fast. Time yourself. Exchange problems with a friend and time each other. You can also do this in a study group.

Review formulas. Right before the test, review any formulas you'll need to use. Then write them down in the margins of the test or on the back of the test paper. Check with your instructor before the day of the test to make sure he will allow you to write formulas or prompts on the test form or your answer sheet or on scratch paper.

Read the problem at least twice. Read slowly. Be sure to understand what is being asked. Let go of the expectation that you'll find the answer right away. You might make several attempts at solving the problem before you find a solution that works.

Translate problems into English. Putting problems into words aids your understanding. When you study equations and formulas, put those into words, too. Using words can help you see a variety of applications for each formula. For example, $c^2 = a^2 + b^2$ can be translated as "the square of the hypotenuse of a right triangle is equal to the sum of the squares of the other two sides."

Analyze before you compute. Set up the problem before you begin to solve it. When a problem is worth a lot of points, read it twice, slowly. Examine it carefully. When you take the time to analyze a problem, you can often discover computational shortcuts.

List what you already know and what you want to find out. Survey each problem for all of the givens. Look for what is to be proved or what is to be discovered. Consider using three columns labeled "What I already know," "What I want to find out," and "What relates the two." This last column is the place to record a formula that can help you solve the problem.

For clarity in problem solving, reduce the number of unknowns as much as you can. You might need to create a separate equation to solve each unknown.

Decide how you will solve the problem. Before you start crunching numbers or punching a calculator, take a moment to plan your approach. Choose which arithmetic operations (addition, subtraction, multiplication, division) or formulas you will use.

Estimate first. Estimating is a good way to double-check your work. Doing this first can help you notice when your computations go awry, allowing you to correct the error quickly.

Perform opposite operations. If a problem involves multiplication, check your work by division; add, then subtract; factor, then multiply; find the square root, then the square; differentiate, then integrate.

Make a picture. When you are stuck, draw a picture or a diagram. Sometimes a visual representation will clear a blocked mind. Making pictures is also an excellent study and review tool in math and science.

Play with possible solutions. There's usually not one "right" way to solve a problem. Several approaches or formulas might work, though one might be more efficient than another. Be willing to think about the problem from several angles or to proceed by trial and error. Remember that solving a math or science problem is like putting together a puzzle. You might work around the edges for a while and try many pieces before finding one that fits.

Check your work for precision and accuracy. Use common sense. Step back and ask if the solution seems reasonable at first glance. Reread the problem and remind yourself of the key question it asks. For example, if you're asked to apply a discount to an item, that item should cost less in your solution.

Keep units of measurement clear. Say that you're calculating the velocity of an object. If you're measuring distance in meters and time in seconds, the final velocity should be in meters per second.

Put your answers to the test. Plug your answer back into the original equation or problem and see if it works out correctly. ◪

8 reasons to celebrate mistakes

I learned from my mistake

Rather than fearing mistakes, we could actually celebrate them. We could revel in our redundancies, frolic in our failures, and glory in our goof-ups. We could marvel at our mistakes and bark with loud laughter when we "blow it." A creative environment is one in which failure is not fatal. Businesses, striving to be on the cutting edge of competition, desperately seek innovative changes. They know that innovation requires risk taking, despite the chance of failure. Explore this point of view by considering several solid reasons to celebrate mistakes.

1 Celebration allows us to notice the mistake. Celebrating mistakes gets them out into the open. This is the opposite of covering up mistakes or blaming others for them. Hiding mistakes takes a lot of energy—energy that could be channeled into correcting errors.

2 Mistakes are valuable feedback. A manager of a major corporation once made a mistake that cost his company $100,000. He predicted that he would be fired when his boss found out. Instead, his boss responded, "Fire you? I can't afford to do that. I just spent $100,000 training you." Mistakes are part of the learning process. Not only are mistakes usually more interesting than most successes—they're often more instructive.

3 Mistakes demonstrate that we're taking risks. People who play it safe make few mistakes. Making mistakes is evidence that we're stretching to the limit of our abilities—growing, risking, and learning. Fear of making mistakes can paralyze us into inaction. Celebrating mistakes helps us move into gear and get things done.

4 Celebrating mistakes reminds us that it's OK to make them. When we celebrate, we remind ourselves that the person who made the mistake is not bad—just human. This is not a recommendation that you purposely set out to make mistakes. Mistakes are not an end in themselves. Rather, their value lies in what we learn from them. When we make a mistake, we can admit it and correct it.

5 Celebrating mistakes includes everyone. It reminds us that the exclusive club named the Perfect Performance Society has no members. All of us make mistakes. When we notice them, we can work together. Blaming others or the system prevents the cooperative efforts that can improve our circumstances.

6 Mistakes occur only when we aim at a clear goal. We can express concern about missing a target only if the target is there in the first place. If there's no target or purpose, there's no concern about missing it. Making a mistake affirms something of great value—that we have a plan.

7 Mistakes happen only when we're committed to making things work. Systems work when people are willing to be held accountable. Openly admitting mistakes promotes accountability. Imagine a school where there's no concern about quality and effectiveness. Teachers usually come to class late. Residence halls are never cleaned, and scholarship checks are always late. The administration is in chronic debt, students seldom pay tuition on time, and no one cares. In this school, the word *mistake* would have little meaning. Mistakes become apparent only when people are committed to improving the quality of an institution.

8 Celebrating mistakes cuts the problem down to size. On top of the mistake itself, there is often a layer of regret, worry, and desperation about having made the mistake in the first place. When we celebrate mistakes, we eliminate that layer of concern. When our anxiety about making a mistake is behind us, we can get down to the business of correcting the mistake.

THINKING CRITICALLY IN THE WORKPLACE

Reflect on a mistake you made in the workplace. This can be an incident related to any job you've ever had. Now, read or review the article "8 reasons to celebrate mistakes." Can you use any of these reasons to take a new attitude toward your mistake—or to actually celebrate it? On a separate sheet of paper, first describe the incident in a few sentences. Then explain how you could celebrate your mistake.

power process

Detach

This Power Process helps you release the powerful, natural student within you. It is especially useful whenever negative emotions are getting in the way of meeting your goals at school and at work.

Attachments are addictions. When we are attached to something, we think we cannot live without it, just as a drug addict feels he cannot live without drugs. We believe our well-being depends on maintaining our attachments.

We can be attached to just about anything—expectations, ideas, objects, self-perceptions, people, results, rewards. The list is endless. One person, for example, might be so attached to his car that he takes an accident as a personal attack. Pity the poor unfortunate who backs into this person's car. He might as well back into the owner himself. Another person might be attached to his job. His identity and sense of well-being depend on it. He could become suicidally depressed if he gets fired.

We can be addicted to our emotions as well as to our thoughts. We can identify with our anger so strongly that we are unwilling to let it go. We can also be addicted to our pessimism and be reluctant to give it up. Rather than perceive these emotions as liabilities, we can see them as indications that it's time to practice detachment.

Most of us are addicted, to some extent, to our identities. We are Americans, veterans, high achievers, bowlers, loyal friends, business owners, humanitarians, devoted parents, dancers, hockey fans, or birdwatchers. If we are attached to these roles, they can dictate who we think we are.

When these identities are threatened, we might fight for them as if we were defending our lives. The more addicted we are to an identity, the harder we fight to keep it.

Ways to recognize an attachment

When we are attached and things don't go our way, we might feel irritated, angry, jealous, confused, fatigued,

The more addicted we are to an identity, the harder we fight to keep it.

bored, frightened, or resentful.

Suppose you are attached to getting an A on your physics test. You feel as though your success in life depends on getting an A. It's not just that you want an A. You *need* an A. During the exam, the thought "I must get an A" is in the back of your mind as you begin to work a problem. And the problem is difficult. The first time you read it, you have no idea how to solve it. The second time around, you aren't even sure what it's asking. The more you struggle to understand it, the more confused you get. To top it all off, this problem is worth 40 percent of your score.

As the clock ticks away, you work harder, getting more stuck, while that voice in your head gets louder: "I must get an A. I MUST get an A. I MUST GET AN A!"

At this point, your hands begin to sweat and shake. Your heart is pounding. You feel nauseated. You can't concentrate. You flail about for the answer as if you were drowning. You look up at the clock, sickened by the inexorable sweep of the second hand. You are doomed.

Now is a time to detach.

Ways to use this process

Detachment can be challenging. In times of stress, it might seem like the most difficult thing in the world to do. You can practice a variety of strategies to help you move toward detachment.

Practice observer consciousness. This is the quiet state above and beyond your usual thoughts, the place where you can be aware of being aware. It's a tranquil spot, apart from your emotions. From here, you can observe yourself objectively, as if you were someone else. Pay attention to your emotions and physical sensations. If you are confused and feeling stuck, tell yourself, "Here I am, confused and stuck." If your palms are sweaty and your stomach is one big knot, admit it. Practice detaching. The key is to let go of automatic emotional reactions when you don't get what you want.

Practice perspective. Put current circumstances into a broader perspective. View personal issues within the larger context of your community, your nation, or your planet. You will likely see them from a different point of view. Imagine the impact your present problems will have 20 or even 100 years from now.

Take a moment to consider the worst that could happen. During that physics exam, notice your attachment to getting an A. Realize that even flunking the test will not ruin your life. Seeing this helps you put the test in perspective.

Practice breathing. Calm your mind and body with breathing or relaxation techniques. It might be easiest to practice these techniques when you're not feeling strong emotions. Notice your thoughts, behaviors, and feelings during neutral activities such as watching television or taking a walk.

Rewrite the equation

To further understand this notion of detaching, we can borrow an idea from mathematics. An equation is a set of symbols joined by an equal sign (=) that forms a true statement. Examples are $2 + 2 = 4$ and $a + b = c$.

Equations also work with words. In fact, our self-image can be thought of as a collection of equations. For example, the thought "I am capable" can be written as the equation "I = capable." "My happiness depends on my car" can be written as "happiness = car." The statement "My well-being depends on my job" becomes "well-being = job." Each equation is a tip-off to an attachment. When we're upset, a closer look often reveals that one of our attachments is threatened. The person who believes that his happiness is equal to his current job will probably be devastated if his company downsizes and he's laid off.

Once we discover a hidden equation, we can rewrite it. In the process, we can watch our upsets disappear. The person who gets laid off can change his equation to "my happiness = my happiness." In other words, his happiness does not have to depend on any particular job.

People can rewrite equations under the most extreme circumstances. A man dying from lung cancer spent his last days celebrating his long life. One day his son asked him how he was feeling.

"Oh, I'm great," said the man with cancer. "Your mom and I have been having a wonderful time just rejoicing in the life that we have had together."

"Oh, I'm glad you're doing well," said the man's son. "The prednisone you have been taking must have kicked in again and helped your breathing."

Once you accept and fully experience your emotions, you can more easily move beyond them.

"Well, not exactly. Actually, my body is in terrible shape, and my breathing has been a struggle these last few days. I guess what I'm saying is that my body is not working well at all, but I'm still great."

The dying man rewrote the equation "I = my body." He knew that he had a body and that he was more than his body. This man lived this Power Process and gave his son—the author of this book—an unforgettable lesson about detachment.

Some cautions

Giving up an addiction to being an A student does not mean giving up being an A student. And giving up an addiction to a job doesn't mean getting rid of the job. It means not investing your entire well-being in the grade or the job. Keep your desires and goals alive and healthy while detaching from the compulsion to reach them.

Notice also that detachment is different from denial. Denial implies running away from whatever you find unpleasant. In contrast, detachment includes accepting your emotions and knowing the details of them—down to every last thought and physical sensation involved. It's OK to be angry or sad. Once you accept and fully experience your emotions, you can more easily move beyond them.

Being detached is not the same as being apathetic. We can be 100 percent detached and 100 percent involved at the same time. In fact, our commitment toward achieving a particular result is usually enhanced by being detached from it.

This Power Process is useful when you notice that attachments are keeping you from accomplishing your goals. Behind your attachments is a master student. By detaching, you release that master student. Detach. ⬛

career application

During his senior year of high school, Chang Lee read about the favorable job market for medical assistants.

He set a goal to enroll in a local community college and earn his A.A. degree in medical assisting. This was a logical choice for Chang. His mother worked as a psychiatric nurse, and he'd always been interested in health care. He figured that his degree would equip him with marketable skills and a way to contribute to society.

Chang's choice paid off. He excelled in classes. With his career goal in mind, he often asked himself: *How could I use this information to become a better medical assistant?*

During his second year of college, Chang landed an internship with a large medical clinic near campus. The clinic offered him a job after he graduated, and he accepted.

Chang enjoyed the day-to-day tasks of medical assisting. He helped doctors run medical tests and perform physical exams. In addition, he ordered lab work and updated medical records.

After three months on the job, Chang was on a first-name basis with many of the clinic's regular patients. No matter how busy the clinic's schedule, Chang made time for people. When they finished describing their symptoms, he frequently asked, "Is there anything else that's on your mind?" Then he listened without interrupting. Chang's ability to put people at ease made him popular with patients, who often asked specifically to see him.

The only part of his job that Chang dreaded was performance reviews, which took place twice during each year of employment. Even though he was respected by coworkers, Chang felt nervous whenever the topic of evaluating work performance came up. "It just reminds me too much of final exams during school," he said. "I like my job and I try to do it well every day. Having a performance review just raises my anxiety level and doesn't really benefit me." ▨

Reflecting on this scenario:

1. Referring to the SCANS chart on page 8, list a transferable skill that Chang demonstrates in this scenario.

_____

_____

_____

_____

2. How would you describe Chang's learning style?

_____

_____

_____

_____

3. List three strategies from this chapter that Chang could use to create value from performance reviews.

_____

_____

_____

_____

Name _____ Date _____/_____/_____

quiz

1. Choose one of the suggestions for creating or running a study group. Explain how you could apply this suggestion to a team project in the workplace.

2. When answering multiple choice questions, it is better to read all of the possible answers before selecting one. True or False? Explain your answer.

3. The presence of absolute qualifiers, such as *always* or *never*, generally indicates a false statement. True or False? Explain your answer.

4. Grades are:
   (A) A measure of creativity.
   (B) An indication of your ability to contribute to society.
   (C) A measure of intelligence.
   (D) A measure of test performance.
   (E) C and D.

5. Describe how *detachment* differs from *denial*.

6. Choose one technique for taking math and science tests and explain how it, or some variation of it, could apply to taking a test in another subject.

7. Name at least three benefits of participating in a study group.

8. Describe at least three techniques for dealing with the thoughts connected to test anxiety.

9. Describe at least three techniques for dealing with the physical feelings connected to test anxiety.

10. Take any technique for managing test anxiety and explain how you could use it during a performance review.

learning styles application

The questions below will "cycle" you through four styles, or modes, of learning as explained in the article "Learning styles: Discovering how you learn" in Chapter One. Each question will help you explore a different mode. You can answer the questions in any order.

what if *Explain how a suggestion for managing test anxiety could help you manage stress in a situation that you face outside school.*

why *Name at least one benefit you could experience—in addition to better grades— by taking tests more effectively.*

how *Of the techniques that you gained from this chapter, choose one that you will use on your next test. Describe exactly how you intend to apply the technique.*

what *List three new techniques for reviewing course material or taking tests that you gained from reading this chapter.*

master student

profile

CHRISTOPHER REEVE

(1952–2004) left paralyzed after a horseback riding accident in 1995, this on-screen Superman and real-life hero was a tireless activist who helped raise millions of dollars for spinal cord research before his death in 2004.

Soon I realized that I'd have to leave Kessler [hospital] at some point. A tentative date was set for sometime between Thanksgiving and mid-December. I thought: God, I've totally given up on breathing. So what am I going to do, stay on a ventilator for the rest of my life?...

I announced that on the first Monday of November, I was going to try again to breathe on my own. At 3:30 in the afternoon of November 2, Bill Carroll, Dr. Kirshblum, Dr. Finley, and Erica met me in the PT room. And I remember thinking: This is it. I've got to do something, I have simply got to. I don't know where it's going to come from, but I've got to produce some air from someplace.

Dr. Finley said, "We're going to take you off the ventilator. I want you to try to take ten breaths. If you can only do three, then that's the way it is, but I want you to try for ten. And I'm going to measure how much air you move with each breath, and let's just see where you are. Okay?"

And I took ten breaths. I was lying on my back on the mat. My head moved as I struggled to draw in air; I wasn't able to move my diaphragm at all, just my chest, neck, and shoulder muscles in an intense effort to bring some air into my lungs. I was only able to draw in an average of 50 cc's with each attempt. But at least it was something. I had moved the dial.

We came back the next day, and now I was really motivated. I prepared myself mentally by imagining my chest as a huge bellows that I could open and close at will. I told myself over and over again that I was going home soon and that I couldn't leave without making some real progress. Dr. Finley asked me to take another ten breaths for a comparison with yesterday's numbers. I took the ten breaths, and my average for each one was 450 cc's.

They couldn't believe it. I thought to myself: All right. Now we're getting somewhere.

At 3:30 the next day I was in place and ready to begin.... Finally I was really taking charge. When Dr. Finley arrived once again he asked me to take ten breaths. This time the average was 560 cc's per breath. A cheer broke out in the room....

After that Erica and I worked alone. Every day we would breathe. I went from seven minutes to twelve to fifteen. Just before I left Kessler on the thirteenth of December, I gave it

everything I had, and I breathed for thirty minutes.... The previous summer, still adjusting to my new circumstances, I had given up. But by November I had the motivation to go forward....

Juice had often told me, "You've been to the grave two times this year, brother. You're not going there again. You are here for a reason." He thought my injury had meaning, had a purpose. I believed, and still do, that my injury was simply an accident. But maybe Juice and I are both right, because I have the opportunity now to make sense of this accident. I believe that it's what you do after an accident that can give it meaning.

I began to face my new life. On Thanksgiving in 1995, I went home to Bedford to spend the day with my family. In the driveway, when I saw our home again, I wept. Dana held me. At the dinner table, when each of us in turn spoke a few words about what we were thankful for, Will said, "Dad." ◪

From *Still Me* by Christopher Reeve. Copyright © 1998 by Cambria Productions, Inc. Used by permission of Random House, Inc.

For more biographical information on Christopher Reeve, visit the Master Student Hall of Fame on the *From Master Student to Master Employee* Web site at

masterstudent.college.hmco.com

CHAPTER 7
Thinking

Critical thinking is an essential skill for success in the classroom and in the workplace. While critical thinking is introduced through the Master Student Map, Learning Styles Applications, chapter exercises, Journal Entries, and Critical Thinking exercises, Chapter Seven takes a more in-depth look at how students can practice the strategies presented in Chapters One through Six using higher levels of thinking. At this point, your students will have taken their first set of tests in their other courses and will have become familiar with the learning strategies provided in the earlier chapters. Now you can help them take the next step toward thinking critically in higher education.

Page 200
Master Student Map

A primary objective of the student success course is to nurture the fundamental skill of critical thinking. Using the Master Student Map as a means of thinking critically is something your students have been doing from the beginning of this text. When they ask **why?** they need this chapter, have them complete a chapter reconnaissance of **what?** new materials are in this chapter. Together you can discuss **how?** these new ideas will help them become better students. Remind your students that with these techniques they can open the door of possibility (**what if?**) to solve problems more creatively and make decisions with confidence.

Guest speaker idea for this chapter
Critical thinking is a priority for many workplace scenarios. Any police officer, attorney, or law school professor would be a great guest speaker for this chapter. These guests can provide students with a dramatic "reality check." This will help you enforce the importance of critical thinking in the real world. Have your guests prepare approximately a 10-minute discussion on the importance of critical thinking in their jobs.

Page 203
Becoming a critical thinker
Select a current, controversial article in a newspaper (consider using your school's paper if there is one) on an issue that is important to your students. Ask students to answer the first two learning styles questions (**Why?** and **What?**) based on the information in the article. Divide your students into groups of four to discuss what they have come up with. It is not likely that there will be enough information in the article to present various viewpoints on the issue at hand. This allows you to have your students continue this project outside of the classroom, using on-campus resources (such as the library and the Internet) to fully answer the additional learning styles questions. At the next class meeting, student can discuss their findings and draw their own conclusions.

Page 207
Attitudes, affirmations, and visualizations
Self-awareness is the key to self-regulation and eventually self-mastery. Affirmations are employed to help students sustain a positive self-image and develop attitudes that lead to success. The Web site to accompany *From Master Student to Master Employee* contains an affirmation certificate creator, perfect for kinesthetic students who might want to hold their affirmation in their hands.

Page 210
Gaining skill at decision making
Too often, the hectic process of registering for classes results in a schedule based on convenience rather than critical decision making. Ask your students to follow the systematic procedure described in this article to decide which classes to take next semester—even if it is before the schedule of classes has been posted. Alternatively, ask students to use the procedure to think about selecting a major, or a career that they are interested in pursuing.

Page 221
Thinking critically about career planning

Invite someone from your Career Planning Center to be the guest speaker during this class period to talk about the center's services. Have your students visit the career center to take an inventory or vocational assessment that will assist them in making choices about careers (or majors). A followup report can be written to identify what the students have discovered.

The U.S. Labor Department's Bureau of Labor Statistics (http://stats.bls.gov) is a resource for students planning their careers, especially the *Occupational Outlook Handbook*. Information from this resource was not included in this textbook because of the changing nature of the statistics. Ask your students to review this handbook for information about the program of study that they have chosen. What is the outlook? Discuss how to interpret and think critically about the materials in this report—without being reactionary and switching careers based on just one source of information.

Page 222
Making ethical decisions at work

Ethics and values are important to discuss in the student success classroom. Social responsibility can be explored through service learning projects, or further research. Suggest students learn more about the world of corporate social responsibility before they create their own personal code of ethics. One resource is the Business of Social Responsibility Web site (www.bsr.org). Additional information about service learning and linking projects to your course are available on the HM ClassPrep CD.

Page 224
Thinking about diversity

From Master Student to Master Employee values diversity as a key element to success in school, at work, and in our neighborhoods. There are many benefits to learning to understand different customs and relate to different cultures. Thinking is the foreground for discussing diversity and the impact is has on your students' lives.

When we celebrate diversity, we prosper as a people and as a nation. Consider having a celebration of diversity in your classroom. One way to share diversity is through food. Ask your students if they would like to participate in a pot luck with foods from different cultures. Students who are shy about cooking can help out by bringing in paper goods or soda.

Invite a local employer to come to your class and discuss with your students discrimination policies and diversity initiatives as they apply to businesses on a corporate level.

Page 227
Overcome stereotypes with critical thinking

To begin a conversation with your students about generalizations and way to decrease stereotyping, use the concepts presented earlier in this chapter. Remind students how attitudes and perceptions are reflected in our thinking.

Page 230
POWER PROCESS: "Find a bigger problem"

This Power Process can help students who may feel they are trapped by personal situations or learning problems that are impairing their ability to succeed. Community service projects can again be a way to help students get involved in activities that take them into the larger world. Finding a bigger problem helps students bring their own problems into perspective. One resource for service learning that you may find valuable is http://service-learningpartnership.org.

Page 235
Master Student Profile: Paul Farmer

You and your students might not be familiar with this new master student, Dr. Paul Farmer, so take this opportunity to do a little additional reading before assigning the article. Visit the Master Student Hall of Fame online at masterstudent.college.hmco.com and read about Farmer's experiences. The article and Farmer's biography will help you discuss the Power Process: "Find a bigger problem." They can also help students connect thinking critically to possible careers or real-world situations.

voices

consultant

Icebreaker for thinking

As a warm-up exercise or icebreaker for this chapter, I put my students into groups and give each group an ordinary household object (such as a napkin, candle, coaster, cup). Then I have the groups brainstorm ways to use the objects in a different fashion than the most obviously intended purpose. This helps students embrace different ways of thinking, and stretches their minds to see things in new ways.

—MICHELLE MARTIN

→ Misconceptions about thinking instruction

As a result of the historic neglect of thinking, many people harbor misconceptions about thinking instruction. The following ones are the most damaging:

That thinking can't be taught. A related misconception is that thinking can only be taught to "gifted" people. The basis of both misconceptions is the pessimistic view that intelligence is fixed and therefore cannot be increased. Formal research and the experience of innumerable thinking-skills instructors disprove this notion.

That thinking is taught automatically in certain courses. Some people reason that English courses teach thinking automatically because they deal with the expression of ideas and expression is intimately connected to thought. Others make similar claims for science because it deals with scientific method, history because it deals with the record of human thought and action, or psychology because it deals with behavior. Research has long made clear that no course content, by itself, can teach thinking; in other words, that thinking skills are developed only when students receive direct instruction in them and frequent opportunities for guided practice.

That thinking skills are necessarily subject specific. According to this view, economists use one set of thinking skills, biologists another, and anthropologists yet another; no generic thinking skills exist. Yet close examination of what thinkers do in everyday situations reveals great similarity in their patterns of thought. Moreover, the patterns of error are also remarkably similar. That is why the list of logical fallacies has remained essentially the same since the time of the ancient Greeks. Though different academic disciplines may employ certain patterns of thinking more often and in slightly different ways than others, the fundamental fact is that the human mind created the academic disciplines and is neither defined nor limited by them.

That students learn to think by being exhorted or inspired. Exhortation and inspiration can surely motivate students to learn, but these approaches have little if any teaching force, particularly where skills are involved. No one ever learned to master driving a car or playing the piccolo or dribbling a basketball by hearing a lecture. Similarly, intellectual skills are learned by doing and by receiving guidance and encouragement from knowledgeable people.

Source: Vincent Ryan Ruggiero, *Instructor's Resource Manual* to Accompany *Becoming a Critical Thinker,* Fourth Edition. Copyright ©2002 by Houghton Mifflin Company. Reprinted by permission.

→ The diversity circle

Some diversity trainers use the *diversity circle* exercise to help workers appreciate diversity and overcome misperceptions. The exercise adapts well for classroom use. Form a group of about ten students. Arrange your chairs into a circle, and put one additional chair in the center of the circle. A "diverse" group member volunteers to sit in the center chair and become the first "awareness subject." Because most people are diverse in some way, most people are eligible to occupy the center chair.

The person in the center tells the others how he or she has felt about being diverse or different and how people have reacted to his or her diversity. For example, an Inuit described how fellow workers were hesitant to ask him out for a beer, worrying whether he could handle alcohol.

An equally effective alternative to the procedure just described is for each class member to come up in front of the class to describe a significant way in which he or she is different. After each class member has presented, a discussion might be held of observations and interpretations.

What lessons did you learn about interpersonal relations from this exercise that will help you be a more effective leader?

Source: Andrew J. Dubrin, *Leadership,* Fourth Edition. Copyright ©2004 by Houghton Mifflin Company. Reprinted by permission.

Master Instructor Resource Guide

MASTER Student

Course Manual

 Thinking critically is something that instructors and facilitators of student success courses frequently call upon to answer students' questions and concerns about campus issues, personal situations, and decision making (such as majors and course selection). Use the *Course Manual* to spend time thinking critically about your **course purpose and goals.** Look for more strategies to help you manage your course or spice up your lesson plans.

"The diverse classroom" can help you with strategies for assisting multicultural students to be successful, both inside and outside of the classroom. Gather ideas from the *Course Manual* for working with **international** or **ESL students, adult learners, student athletes,** or **students with learning disabilities.**

HM ClassPrep CD

 PowerPoint for Chapter Seven can show your students how to gain mastery by using critical thinking as a survival skill.

Diversity is a topic that professors might hesitate to talk about because the conversation could become uncomfortable or out of control. Use the tips and suggestions on the HM ClassPrep CD for in-class exercises that will help you explore various topics related to diversity.

Your student success course is a great place for students to practice speaking in front of a group. Use an activity called "Critical thinking infomercials" on your HM ClassPrep CD for in-class group presentation ideas.

Additional Resources

The *Power Up: Four-in-One Power Process* video includes a segment on "Find a bigger problem." Use this video as a guest speaker in your course.

masterstudent.college.hmco.com "Qualities of a critical thinker" is an article on the *From Master Student to Master Employee* Web site that lists master student qualities similar to those introduced in Chapter One. Invite your students to read this article online and identify other qualities that they feel are important to thinking. You can also ask them to identify the qualities exemplified by this chapter's master student, Paul Farmer.

Have your students access the Career Resource Center to access articles in the Workplace diversity issues section under Skills for Your Future.

7

Thinking

I always wanted to be somebody, but I should've been more specific.

LILY TOMLIN

Creativity was in each one of us as a small child. In children it is universal. Among adults it is almost nonexistent. The great question is: What has happened to this enormous and universal human capacity?

TILLIE OLSEN

why
this chapter matters . . .

The ability to think creatively and critically helps you succeed in school and promotes many skills that transfer to the workplace—including reading, writing, and speaking.

what
is included . . .

Critical thinking: A survival skill
Becoming a critical thinker
Attitudes, affirmations, and visualizations
Gaining skill at decision making
Four ways to solve problems
Solving math and science problems
Finding "aha!": Creativity fuels critical thinking
Ways to create ideas
Uncovering assumptions
Ways to fool yourself: Six common mistakes in logic
Thinking critically about career planning
Making ethical decisions at work
Thinking about diversity
Diversity is real—and valuable
Overcome stereotypes with critical thinking
Asking questions
Power Process: "Find a bigger problem"
Master Student Profile: Paul Farmer

how
you can use this chapter . . .

Choose attitudes that promote your success.
Learn strategies to enhance your success in problem solving.
Apply thinking skills to practical decisions such as career planning and ethical choices.

As you read, ask yourself
what if . . .

I could solve problems more creatively and make decisions in every area of life with more confidence?

Critical thinking: A survival skill

Society depends on persuasion. Advertisers want us to spend money on their products. Political candidates want us to "buy" their stands on the issues. Teachers want us to agree that their classes are vital to our success. Parents want us to accept their values. Authors want us to read their books. Broadcasters want us to spend our time in front of the radio or television, consuming their programs and not those of the competition. The business of persuasion has an impact on all of us.

A typical American sees thousands of television commercials each year. And that's just one medium of communication. Add to that the writers and speakers who enter our lives through radio shows, magazines, books, billboards, brochures, Internet sites, and fundraising appeals—all with a product, service, cause, or opinion for us to embrace.

This leaves us with hundreds of choices about what to buy, where to go, and who to be. It's easy to lose our heads in the crosscurrent of competing ideas—unless we develop skills in critical thinking. When we think critically, we can make choices with open eyes.

Uses of critical thinking

Critical thinking underlies reading, writing, speaking, and listening. These are the basic elements of communication—a process that occupies most of our waking hours in the classroom or at work.

Critical thinking also plays an important part in social change. Consider that the institutions in any society—courts, governments, schools, businesses—are the products of a certain way of thinking. Any organization draws its life from certain assumptions about the way things should be done. Before the institution can change, those assumptions need to be loosened up or reinvented. In many ways, the real location of an institution is inside our heads.

In addition, critical thinking helps us uncover bias and prejudice. This is a first step toward communicating with people of other races, ethnic backgrounds, and cultures.

Crises occur when our thinking fails to keep pace with reality. An example is the world's ecological crisis, which arose when people polluted the earth, air, and water without considering the long-term consequences. Imagine how different our world would be if our leaders

journal entry 23

Discovery/Intention Statement

Think back to a time when you felt unable to choose among several different solutions to a problem or several stands on a key issue in your life. In the space below, describe this experience.

I discovered that . . .

_____

_____

_____

_____

Now scan this chapter to find useful suggestions for decision making, problem solving, and critical thinking. Note below at least four techniques that look especially promising to you.

Strategy   *Page number*

_____

_____

_____

_____

_____

_____

Finally, declare a time that you intend to explore these techniques in more detail, along with a situation coming up during this term in which you could apply them.

I intend to improve my thinking skills by . . .

_____

_____

_____

_____

_____

had thought like the first female chief of the Cherokees. Asked about the best advice her elders had given her, she replied, "Look forward. Turn what has been done into a better path. If you are a leader, think about the impact of your decision on seven generations into the future."

Novelist Ernest Hemingway once said that anyone who wants to be a great writer must have a built-in, shockproof "crap" detector.[1] That inelegant comment points to a basic truth: As critical thinkers, we are constantly on the lookout for thinking that's inaccurate, sloppy, or misleading.

Critical thinking is a skill that will never go out of style. Throughout history, half-truths, faulty assumptions, and other nonsense have at one time been commonly accepted as true. Examples include:

- Illness results from an imbalance in the four vital fluids: blood, phlegm, water, and bile.

- Caucasians are inherently more intelligent than people of other races.

- Women are incapable of voting intelligently.

- We will never invent anything smaller than a transistor. (That was before the computer chip.)

- Computer technology will usher in the age of the paperless office.

The critical thinkers of history courageously challenged such ideas. These men and women pointed out that—metaphorically speaking—the emperor had no clothes.

Critical thinking is a path to freedom from half-truths and deception. You have the right to question what you see, hear, and read. Acquiring this ability is a major goal of preparing for the workplace while attending college.

Critical thinking as thorough thinking

For some people, the term *critical thinking* has negative connotations. If you prefer, use *thorough thinking* instead. Both terms point to the same activities: sorting out conflicting claims, weighing the evidence, letting go of personal biases, and arriving at reasonable conclusions. This adds up to an ongoing conversation—a constant process, not a final product.

We live in a society that seems to value quick answers and certainty. This is often at odds with effective thinking. Thorough thinking is the ability to examine and re-examine ideas that might seem obvious. Such thinking takes time and the willingness to say three subversive words: "I don't know."

Thorough thinking is also the willingness to change our opinion as we continue to examine a problem. This calls for courage and detachment. Just ask anyone who has given up a cherished point of view in light of new evidence.

Skilled students and business people are thorough thinkers. They distinguish between opinion and fact. They ask probing questions and make detailed observations. They uncover assumptions and define their terms. They make assertions carefully, basing them on sound logic and solid evidence. Almost everything that we call *knowledge* is a result of these activities. This means that critical thinking and learning are intimately linked.

It's been said that human beings are rational creatures. Yet no one is born a thorough thinker. This is a learned skill.

Thinking provides the basis for all the study skills suggested in this book. The exercises, Master Student Maps, Learning Styles Applications, and Career Applications offer additional practice in thorough thinking. Now, use this chapter to take your critical thinking skills to the next level. Here you'll find strategies for handling some of the most complex thinking tasks in school and the workplace—decision making, problem solving, communicating, career planning, and making ethical choices. Remember, the critical thinker is one aspect of the master student who lives inside you. ▨

desk of ...

from the

KIM GARLAND, WEB SITE DESIGNER AND DEVELOPER:

When developing Web sites, I am essentially solving a client's problem. When a potential client comes to me, they believe that they have a problem and that a Web site will solve it. My job is to unearth whether the problem they think they have is in fact the real problem, and whether or not a Web site is the appropriate solution.

Becoming a Critical Thinker

According to the U.S. Department of Labor, critical thinking is one of the key transferable skills that workers will need to compete successfully for jobs. The department defines a critical thinker as a person who "uses logic to draw conclusions from available information, extracts rules or principles from a set of objects or written text" and "applies rules and principles to a new situation."[2]

Stripped to its essence, critical thinking means asking and answering questions. The four basic questions in the Learning Styles Applications in this book—*Why? What? How?* and *What if?*—are a powerful tool for thinking. As they take you through the cycle of learning, they can also guide you in becoming a critical thinker. This article offers a variety of tools for answering those questions.

1 Why am I considering this issue? Critical thinking and personal passion go together. Begin critical thinking with a question that matters to you. Seek a rationale for your learning. Understand why it is important for you to think about a specific topic. You might want to arrive at a new conclusion, make a prediction, or solve a problem. By finding a personal connection with an issue, your interest in acquiring and retaining new information increases.

2 What are various points of view on this issue? Imagine Karl Marx, Cesar Chavez, and Donald Trump assembled in one room to choose the most desirable economic system. Picture Mahatma Gandhi, Winnie Mandela, and General George Patton lecturing at a United Nations conference on conflict resolution. Visualize Fidel Castro, George W. Bush, and Mother Teresa in a discussion about distributing the world's resources equitably. When seeking out alternative points of view, let such events unfold in your mind.

Dozens of viewpoints exist on every important issue—reducing crime, ending world hunger, preventing war, educating our children, and countless other concerns. In fact, few problems allow for any single, permanent solution. Each generation produces its own answers to critical questions, based on current conditions. Our search for answers is a conversation that spans centuries. On each question, many voices are waiting to be heard.

You can take advantage of this diversity by seeking out alternative views with an open mind. When talking to another person, be willing to walk away with a new point of view—even if it's the one you brought to the table, supported with new evidence. After thinking thoroughly, you can adopt new perspectives or hold your current viewpoints in a different way.

Examining different points of view is an exercise in analysis, which you can do with the suggestions that follow.

Define terms. Imagine two people arguing about whether an employer should limit health care benefits to members of a family. To one person, the word *family* means a mother, father, and children; to the other person, the word *family* applies to any long-term, supportive relationship between people who live together. Chances are, the debate will go nowhere until these people realize that they're defining the same word in different ways.

Conflicts of opinion can often be resolved—or at least clarified—when we define our key terms up front. This is especially true with abstract, emotion-laden terms such as *freedom, peace, progress,* or *justice.* Blood has been shed over the meaning of these words. Define them with care.

Look for assertions. A speaker's or writer's key terms occur in a larger context called an assertion. An *assertion* is a complete sentence that directly answers a key question. For example, consider this sentence from the article

People are free to post anything on the Internet, and this can include outdated facts as well as intentional misinformation. Thinking critically about what you see online is a key transferable skill that will increase your value to employers. In addition to the general guidelines for critical thinking offered in this chapter, keep the following in mind.

Look for overall quality. To begin thinking critically about a Web site, step back and examine the features of that site in general. Notice the effectiveness of the text and visuals as a whole. Also note how well the site is organized and whether you can navigate the site's features with ease. Look for the date that crucial information was posted, and determine how often the site is updated.

Next, take a more detailed look at the site's content. Link between several of the site's pages and look for consistency of facts, quality of information, and competency with grammar and spelling.

Also evaluate the site's links to related Web pages. Look for links to pages of reputable organizations. Click on a few of those links. If they lead you to dead ends, this might indicate a site that's not updated often—one that's not a reliable source for late-breaking information.

Look at the source. Think about the credibility of the person or organization that posts a Web site. Look for a list of author credentials and publications.

Notice evidence of bias or special interest. Perhaps the site's sponsoring organization wants you to buy a service, a product, or a point of view. If so, determine whether this fact colors the ideas and information posted on the Web site.

The domain in the Uniform Resource Locator (URL) for a Web site can give you clues about sources of information and possible bias. For example, distinguish between information from a for-profit commercial enterprise (URL ending in .com), a nonprofit organization (.org), a government agency (.gov), and a school, college, or university (.edu). In addition, reputable sites usually include a way for you to contact the author or sponsoring organization outside the Internet, including a mailing address and phone number.

Look for documentation. When you encounter an assertion on a Web page or some other Internet resource, note the types and quality of the evidence offered. Look for credible examples, quotations from authorities in the field, documented statistics, or summaries of scientific studies. Also look for source notes, bibliographies, or another way to find the original sources of information on your own.

"Discovering Mastery" in Chapter One: "A master is a person who has attained a level of skill that goes beyond technique." This sentence is an assertion that answers an important question: How do we recognize a master?

Look for at least three viewpoints. When asking questions, let go of the temptation to settle for just a single answer. Once you have come up with an answer, say to yourself, "Yes, that is one answer. Now what's another?" Using this approach can sustain honest inquiry, fuel creativity, and lead to conceptual breakthroughs. Be prepared: The world is complicated, and critical thinking is a complex business. Some of your answers might contradict others. Resist the temptation to have all of your ideas in a neat, orderly bundle.

Practice tolerance. One path to critical thinking is tolerance for a wide range of opinions. Taking a position on important issues is natural. When we stop having an opinion on things, we've probably stopped breathing.

The problem occurs when we become so attached to our current viewpoints that we refuse to consider alternatives. Many ideas that are widely accepted in Western cultures—for example, civil liberties for people of color and the right of women to vote—were once considered dangerous. Viewpoints that seem outlandish today might become widely accepted a century, a decade, or even a year from now. Remembering this can help us practice tolerance for differing beliefs and, in doing so, make room for new ideas that might alter our lives.

3 *How* **well is each point of view supported?** Uncritical thinkers shield themselves from new information and ideas. As an alternative, you can follow the example of scientists, who constantly search for evidence that contradicts their theories. The following suggestions can help.

Look for logic and evidence. The aim of using logic is to make statements that are clear, consistent, and coherent. As you examine a speaker's or writer's assertions, you might find errors in logic—assertions that contradict each other or assumptions that are unfounded.

Also assess the evidence used to support points of view. Evidence comes in several forms, including facts, expert testimony, and examples. To think critically about evidence, ask questions such as:

- Are all or most of the relevant facts presented?

- Are the facts consistent with each other?

- Are facts presented accurately—or in a misleading way?

- Are enough examples included to make a solid case for the viewpoint?

- Are the examples typical? That is, could the author or speaker support the assertion with other examples that are similar?

Consider the source. Look again at that article on the problems of manufacturing cars powered by natural gas. It might have been written by an executive from an oil company. Check out the expert who disputes the connection between smoking and lung cancer. That "expert" might be the president of a tobacco company.

This is not to say that we should dismiss the ideas of people who have a vested interest in stating their opinions. Rather, we can take their self-interest into account as we consider their ideas.

Understand before criticizing. Polished debaters can sum up their opponents' viewpoints—often better than the people who support those viewpoints themselves. Likewise, critical thinkers take the time to understand a statement of opinion before agreeing or disagreeing with it.

Effective understanding calls for listening without judgment. Enter another person's world by expressing her viewpoint in your own words. If you're conversing with that person, keep revising your summary until she agrees that you've stated her position accurately. If you're reading an article, write a short summary of it. Then scan the article again, checking to see if your synopsis is on target.

Watch for hot spots. Many people have mental "hot spots"—topics that provoke strong opinions and feelings. Examples are abortion, homosexuality, gun control, and the death penalty.

To become more skilled at examining various points of view, notice your own particular hot spots. Make a clear intention to accept your feelings about these topics and to continue using critical thinking techniques.

One way to cool down our hot spots is to remember that we can change or even give up our current opinions without giving up ourselves. That's a key message behind the articles "Ideas are tools" and "Detach." These Power Processes remind us that human beings are much more than the sum of their current opinions.

Be willing to be uncertain. Some of the most profound thinkers have practiced the art of thinking by using a magic sentence: "I'm not sure yet."

Those are words that many people do not like to hear. Our society rewards quick answers and quotable sound bites. We're under considerable pressure to utter the truth in 10 seconds or less.

In such a society, it is courageous and unusual to take the time to pause, to look, to examine, to be thoughtful, to consider many points of view—and to be unsure. When a society adopts half-truths in a blind rush for certainty, a willingness to embrace uncertainty can move us forward.

4 *What if* **I could combine various points of view or create a new one?** Finding the truth is like painting a barn door by tossing an open can of paint at it. Few people who throw at the door miss it entirely. Yet no one can cover the whole door in a single toss.

People who express a viewpoint are seeking the truth. And no reasonable person claims to cover the whole barn door—to understand the whole truth about anything. Instead, each viewpoint can be seen as one approach among many possible alternatives. If you don't think that any one opinion is complete, combine different perspectives on the issue.

Create a critical thinking "spreadsheet." When you consult authorities with different stands on an issue, you might feel confused about how to sort out, evaluate, and combine their points of view. To overcome confusion, create a critical thinking "spreadsheet." List the authorities across the top of a page and key questions down the left side. Then indicate each authority's answer to each question, along with your own answers.

For example, the following spreadsheet clarifies different points of view on the issue of whether to outlaw boxing.

	Medical doctor	Former boxer	Sports journalist	Me
Is boxing a sport?	No	Yes	Yes	Yes
Is boxing dangerous?	Yes	Yes	Yes	Yes
Is boxing more dangerous than other sports?	Yes	No	Yes	No
Can the risk of injury be overcome by proper training?	No	No	No	Yes

Source: Vincent Ryan Ruggiero, *Becoming a Critical Thinker,* Fourth Edition. Copyright © 2002 by Houghton Mifflin Company. Reprinted with permission.

You could state your own viewpoint by combining your answers to the questions in the spreadsheet: "I favor legalized boxing. While boxing poses dangers, so do other sports. And as with other sports, the risk of injury can be reduced when boxers get proper training."

Write about it. Thoughts can move at blinding speed. Writing slows down that process. Gaps in logic that slip by us in thought or speech are often exposed when we commit the same ideas to paper. Writing down our thoughts allows us to compare, contrast, and combine points of view more clearly—and therefore to think more thoroughly.

Accept your changing perspectives. Researcher William Perry found that students in higher education move through stages of intellectual development.[3]

Students in earlier stages tend to think there is only one correct viewpoint on each issue, and they look to their instructors to reveal that truth. Later, students acknowledge a variety of opinions on issues and construct their own viewpoints.

Monitor changes in your thinking processes as you combine viewpoints. Distinguish between opinions that you accept from authorities and opinions that are based on your own use of logic and your search for evidence. Also look for opinions that result from objective procedures (such as using the *Why? What? How?* and *What if?* questions in this article) and personal sources (using intuition or "gut feelings").

Remember that the process of becoming a critical thinker will take you through a variety of stages. Give yourself time, and celebrate your growing mastery. ◪

→ Attitudes of a critical thinker

The American Philosophical Association invited a panel of 46 scholars from the United States and Canada to come up with answers to the following two questions: "What is college-level critical thinking?" and "What leads us to conclude that a person is an effective critical thinker?"[4] After two years of work, this panel concluded that critical thinkers share the attitudes summarized in the following chart.

Attitude	Sample statement
Truth-seeking	"Let's follow this idea and see where it leads, even if we feel uncomfortable with what we find out."
Open-minded	"I have a point of view on this subject, and I'm anxious to hear yours as well."
Analytical	"Taking a stand on the issue commits me to take some new action."
Systematic	"The speaker made several interesting points, and I'd like to hear some more evidence to support each one."
Self-confident	"After reading the book for the first time, I was confused. I'll be able to understand it after studying the book some more."
Inquisitive	"When I first saw that painting, I wanted to know what was going on in the artist's life when she painted it."
Mature	"I'll wait until I gather some more facts before reaching a conclusion on this issue."

Beyond promoting success in the classroom, these qualities will serve you in the workplace. Observe employees with high-level skills at making decisions, solving problems, and resolving conflict. You'll see each of these attitudes in action. Adopting them now can give you an edge in job hunting and increase your value to employers.

Attitudes, affirmations, and visualizations

"I have a bad attitude." Some of us say this as if we were talking about having the flu. An attitude is certainly as strong as the flu, but it isn't something we have to succumb to or accept.

Some of us see our attitudes the way we see our height or eye color: "I might not like it, but I might as well accept it."

Acceptance is certainly a worthwhile approach to things we cannot change. When it comes to attitudes, acceptance is not necessary—attitudes can change. We don't have to live our lives with an attitude that doesn't work.

Attitudes are powerful. They create behavior. If your attitude is that you're not very interesting at a party, then your behavior will probably match your attitude, and you might act like a bore. If your attitude is that you are fun at a party, then your behavior is more likely to be playful. Soon you are the life of the party. All that has to change is attitude.

Success in school starts with attitudes. Some attitudes will help you benefit from all the money and time you invest in higher education. Other attitudes will render your investment worthless.

The ability to monitor and choose your attitudes is a critical workplace skill. Under the stress of project deadlines and unresolved conflict, people who work together can create an interpersonal atmosphere that's polluted with negative attitudes. Some people resign themselves to this fate: "It's the way people are. You just have to live with it."

You do not have to live with it. Negative attitudes may be rampant in a classroom or workplace, but you don't have to adopt them. There are multiple ways to think about any situation, and you can choose freely among them.

You can change

your attitudes through regular practice with affirmations and visualizations.

Affirm it. An affirmation is a statement describing what you want. The most effective affirmations are personal, positive, and written in the present tense.

Affirmations have an almost magical power. They are used successfully by athletes and actors, executives and ballerinas, and thousands of people who have succeeded in their lives. Affirmations can change your attitudes and behaviors.

To use affirmations, first determine what you want, then describe yourself as if you already have it. To get what you want from your education, you could write, "I, Malika Jones, am a master student. I take full responsibility for my education. I learn with joy, and I use my experiences in each course to create the life that I want."

If you decide that you want a wonderful job, you might write, "I, Susan Webster, have a wonderful job. I respect and love my colleagues, and they feel the same way about me. I look forward to going to work each day."

Or if money is your desire, you might write, "I, John Henderson, am rich. I have more money than I can spend. I have everything I want, including a six-bedroom house, a new sports car, a 200-watt sound system, and a large-screen television with a satellite dish receiver."

What makes the affirmation work is detail. Use brand names, people's names, and your own name. Involve all of your senses—sight, sound, smell, taste, touch. Take a positive approach. Instead of saying, "I am not fat," say, "I am slender."

Once you have written the affirmation, repeat it. Practice saying it out loud several times a day. This works best if you say it at a regular time, such as just before you go to sleep or just after you wake up.

Sit in a chair in a relaxed position. Take a few deep and relaxing breaths, and then repeat your affirmation with emotion. It's also effective to look in a mirror while saying the affirmation. Keep looking and repeating until you are saying your affirmation with conviction.

Visualize it. It would be difficult to grow up in our culture without hearing the maxim that "practice makes perfect." The problem is that most of us limit what we consider to be practice. Effective practice can occur even when we are not moving a muscle.

You can improve your golf swing, tennis serve, or batting average while lying in bed. You can become a better driver, speaker, or cook while sitting silently in a chair. In line at the grocery store, you can improve your ability to type or to take tests. This is all possible through visualization—the technique of seeing yourself be successful.

The SCANS reports mentioned in the Introduction to this book describe "seeing things in the mind's eye" as a key transferable skill. For example, a skilled construction supervisor can visualize a finished building by looking at blueprints. And a skilled manager can visualize a flow of work activities after reading job descriptions for her employees.[5] Practicing visualization

can help you develop such abilities.

Here's one way to begin your practice. Decide what you want to improve, and write down what it would look like, sound like, and feel like to have that improvement in your life. If you are learning to play the piano, write down briefly what you would see, hear, and feel if you were playing skillfully. If you want to improve your relationships with coworkers, write down what you would see, hear, and feel if you were communicating with them successfully.

A powerful visualization involves other senses besides seeing. Feel the physical sensations. Hear the sounds. Note any smells, tastes, textures, or qualities of light that accompany the scene in your mind.

Once you have a sketch of what it would be like to be successful, practice it in your imagination—successfully. As

→ Attitude replacements

You can use affirmations to replace a negative attitude with a positive one. There are no limitations, other than your imagination and your willingness to practice. Here are some sample affirmations. Modify them to suit your individual hopes and dreams, and then practice them. The article "Attitudes, affirmations, and visualizations" explains ways to use these attitude replacements.

I, _____, am healthy.

I, _____, have abundant energy and vitality throughout the day.

I, _____, exercise regularly.

I, _____, work effectively with many different kinds of people.

I, _____, eat wisely.

I, _____, plan my days and use time wisely.

I, _____, have a powerful memory.

I, _____, take tests calmly and confidently.

I, _____, have a sense of self-worth that is independent of my test scores.

I, _____, am a great speller.

I, _____, fall asleep quickly and sleep soundly.

I, _____, am smart.

I, _____, learn quickly.

I, _____, am creative.

I, _____, am aware of and sensitive to other people's moods.

I, _____, have relationships that are mutually satisfying.

I, _____, work hard and contribute to other people through my job.

I, _____, am wealthy.

I, _____, know ways to play and have fun.

I, _____, am attractive.

I, _____, focus my attention easily.

I, _____, like myself.

I, _____, am liked by other people.

I, _____, am a worthwhile person even though I am _____.

I, _____, have a slim and attractive body.

I, _____, am relaxed in all situations, including _____.

I, _____, make profitable financial investments.

I, _____, have an income that far exceeds my expenses.

I, _____, live a life of abundance and prosperity.

I, _____, always live my life in positive ways for the highest good of all people.

To hear an online version of these affirmations, link to — masterstudent.college.hmco.com

you play out the scenario, include as many details as you can. Always have your practices be successes. Whenever you toss the basketball, it swishes through the net. Every time you invite someone out on a date, the person says yes. Each test the teacher hands back to you is graded an A. Practice at least once a day.

You can also use visualizations to replay errors. When you make a mistake, replay it in your imagination. After a bad golf shot, stop and imagine yourself making

I am a Loving Parent!

that same shot again, this time very successfully. If you just had a discussion with your roommate that turned into a fight, replay it successfully. Get all of your senses involved. See yourselves calmly talking things over together. Hear the words and feel the pleasure of a successful interaction. Visualizations and affirmations can restructure your attitudes and behaviors. Be clear about what you want—and then practice it.

REPROGRAM YOUR ATTITUDE

Affirmations and visualizations can be employed successfully to reprogram your attitudes and behaviors. Use this exercise to change your approach to any situation in your life.

Step 1

Pick something in your life that you would like to change. It can be related to anything—relationships, work, money, or personal skills. Below, write a brief description of what you choose to change.

_____

_____

_____

Step 2

Add more details about the change you described in Step 1. Write down how you would like the change to come about. Be outlandish. Imagine that you are about to ask your fairy godmother for a wish that you know she will grant. Be detailed in your description of your wish.

_____

_____

_____

Step 3

Here comes the fairy godmother. Use affirmations and visualizations to start yourself on the path to creating

exactly what you wrote about in Step 2. Below, write at least two affirmations that describe your dream wish. Also, briefly outline a visualization that you can use to picture your wish. Be specific, detailed, and positive.

_____

_____

_____

Step 4

Put your new attitudes to work. Set up a schedule to practice them. Let the first time be right now. Then set up at least five other times and places that you intend to practice your affirmations and visualizations.

I intend to relax and practice my affirmations and visualizations for at least five minutes on the following dates and at the times and location(s) given.

Date	Time	Location
1.		
2.		
3.		
4.		
5.		

Gaining skill at decision making

When people refuse to make decisions, they leave their lives to chance. Philosopher Walter Kaufman calls this *decidophobia*—the fear of making decisions. He defines the alternative—*autonomy*—as "making with open eyes the decisions that give shape to one's life."[6]

We make decisions all of the time, whether we realize it or not. Even avoiding decisions is a form of decision making. The student who puts off studying for a test until the last minute might really be saying, "I've decided this course is not important" or "I've decided not to give this course much time."

Decision making is a transferable skill that will serve you in any career you choose. This skill is required for many of the higher-paying jobs in the workplace, including supervisory and managerial positions. Developing your skill at making decisions can reward you with greater career satisfaction and higher income.

Decide right now to apply some of the following suggestions, and you can take your overall decision making to new heights of effectiveness.

Recognize decisions. Decisions are more than wishes or desires. There's a world of difference between "I wish I could be a better student" and "I will take more powerful notes, read with greater retention, and review my class notes daily." Decisions are specific and lead to focused action. When we decide, we narrow down. We give up actions that are inconsistent with our decision. Deciding to eat fruit for dessert instead of ice cream rules out the next trip to the ice cream store.

Establish priorities. Some decisions are trivial. No matter what the outcome, your life is not affected much. Other decisions can shape your circumstances for years. Devote more time and energy to the decisions with big outcomes.

Clarify your values. When you know specifically what you want from life, making decisions becomes easier. Saying that you value education is fine. Now give that declaration some teeth. Note that you value continuous learning as a chance to upgrade your career skills, for instance. That can make registering for next term's classes much easier.

Choose an overall strategy. Every time you make a decision, you choose a strategy—even when you're not aware of it. Effective decision makers can articulate and choose from among several strategies. Experiment with these:

- *Find all of the available options and choose one deliberately.* Save this strategy for times when you have a relatively small number of options, each of which leads to noticeably different results.

- *Find all of the available options and choose one randomly.* This strategy can be risky. Save it for times when your options are basically similar and fairness is the main issue. An example is choosing among three equally qualified applicants for a job.

- *Limit the options, then choose.* As an example, when deciding which search engine to use on the World Wide Web, visit many sites and then narrow the list down to two or three that you choose to use regularly.

- *Choose the first acceptable option that you find.* This strategy can work well when you have many options, and when thoroughly researching each option will take too much time or create too little benefit. For instance, when you're writing a paper and are pressed for time, write down the first five facts you find that directly support your thesis. You could look for more facts, but the extra investment of time might not produce enough usable results.

- *Choose to act on someone else's decision.* You use this strategy, for example, when you buy a CD based on a friend's recommendation. A more sophisticated version of this strategy is arbitration—people who are in conflict agree to act on the decision made by a third party, such as a judge, who listens to each person's case.

Use time as an ally. Sometimes we face dilemmas—situations in which any course of action leads to undesirable consequences. In such cases, consider putting a decision on hold. Wait it out. Do nothing until the circumstances change, making one alternative clearly preferable to another.

Use intuition. Some decisions seem to make themselves. A solution pops into our mind and we gain newfound clarity. Suddenly we realize what we've truly wanted all along.

Using intuition is not the same as forgetting about the decision or refusing to make it. Intuitive decisions usually arrive after we've gathered the relevant facts and faced a problem for some time.

Act on your decision. There comes a time to move from the realm of discovery and intention to the arena of action. Action is a hallmark of a true decision.

Evaluate your decision. Reflect on how well your decision worked and what you might have done differently. Look on each individual decision as a source of feedback that will improve your overall skill at decision making. ✖

Four ways to solve problems

There is a vast literature on problem-solving techniques. Much of it can be traced to American philosopher John Dewey, who defined these steps in effective problem solving:

- Perceive a "felt difficulty" and state it clearly and concisely.
- Invent possible solutions.
- Rationally test each solution by anticipating its possible consequences.
- Act on the preferred solution, evaluate the consequences, and determine whether a new solution is needed.[7]

The SCANS reports on necessary job skills define problem solving in a similar way: Skilled problem solvers first recognize a discrepancy between what *is* present in their lives and what *could* be. They identify possible reasons for the discrepancy, create a plan to resolve it, implement the plan, and monitor the results.[8]

Much of what you'll read about problem solving amounts to variations on Dewey's steps. Think of problem solving as a process with four P's: Define the *problem*, generate *possibilities*, create a *plan*, and *perform* your plan.

1 Define the problem.

To define a problem effectively, understand what a problem is—a mismatch between what you want and what you have. Problem solving is all about reducing the gap between these two factors.

Start with what you have. Tell the truth about what's present in your life right now, without shame or blame. For example: "I often get sleepy while reading technical manuals for the computer equipment that I service. Five minutes after putting a manual back on the shelf, I cannot remember what I just read."

Next, describe in detail what you want. Go for specifics: "I want to remain alert as I read the technical materials required for my work. I also want to accurately follow any instructions I read."

Remember that when we define a problem in limiting ways, our solutions merely generate new problems. As Einstein said, "The world we have made is a result of the level of thinking we have done thus far. We cannot solve problems at the same level at which we created them."[9]

This idea has many applications for success in school. An example is the student who struggles with note taking. The problem, she thinks, is that her notes are too sketchy. The logical solution, she decides, is to take *more* notes, and her new goal is to write down almost everything her instructors say. No matter how fast and furiously she writes, she cannot capture all of the instructors' comments.

Consider what happens when this student defines the problem in a new way. After more thought, she decides that her dilemma is not the *quantity* of her notes but their *quality*. She adopts a new format for taking notes, dividing her note paper into two columns. In the right-hand column she writes down only the main points of each lecture. And in the left-hand column she notes two or three supporting details for each point.

Over time, this student makes the joyous discovery that there are usually just three or four core ideas to remember from each lecture. She originally thought the solution was to take more notes. What really worked was taking notes in a new way.

2 Generate possibilities.

Now put on your creative thinking hat. Open up. Brainstorm as many possible solutions to the problem as you can. At this stage, quantity counts. As you generate possibilities, gather relevant facts. For example, when you're faced with a dilemma about what courses to take next term, get information on class times, locations, and instructors. If you haven't decided which job offer to accept, gather information on salary, benefits, and working conditions.

3 Create a plan.

After rereading your problem definition and list of possible solutions, choose the solution that seems most workable. Think about specific actions that will reduce the gap between what you have and what you want. Visualize the steps you will take to make this solution a reality and arrange them in chronological order. To make your plan even more powerful, put it in writing.

4 Perform your plan.

This step gets you off your chair and out into the world. Now you actually *do* what you have planned. Ultimately, your skill in solving problems lies in how well you perform your plan. Through the quality of your actions, you become the architect of your own success. ◪

Define the **problem**	**What** is the problem?
Generate **possibilities**	**What if** there are several possible solutions?
Create a **plan**	**How** would this possible solution work?
Perform your plan	**Why** is one solution more workable than another?

Solving math and science problems

In essence, math and science are specialized forms of problem solving. You can approach math and science problems the way rock climbers approach mountains. The first part of the process is devoted to preparations you make before you get to the rock. The second part is devoted to techniques used on the rock (or problem) itself.

To the uninitiated, rock climbing looks dangerous. For the unprepared, it is. A novice might come to a difficult place in a climb and panic. When a climber freezes, she is truly stuck. Experienced rock climbers figure out strategies in advance for as many situations as possible. With preparation and training, the sport takes on a different cast.

Sometimes students get stuck, panic, and freeze when working on problems. Use the following suggestions to avoid that. Experiment with these techniques as you work your way through textbooks in math and science. You can also use them on tests.

Before you get to the rock

1 Review. Review problems you've solved before. Look over assigned problems and more. Come up with your own variations on these problems. Work with a classmate and make up problems for each other to solve. The more problems you review, the more comfortable you're likely to feel solving new ones. Set clear goals for practice and write Intention Statements about meeting those goals. Find out if practice problems or previous tests are on file in the library.

2 Classify problems by type. Make a list of the different kinds of problems and note the elements of each. After classifying problems by type or category, you can isolate those that you find the most difficult. Practice them more often and get help if you need it.

3 Know your terminology. Mathematicians and scientists often borrow words from plain English and assign new meanings to them. For example, the word *work* is usually thought of as referring to a job. For the physicist, *work* means *force multiplied by distance*. To ensure that you understand the terminology used in a problem, see if you can restate the problem in your own words. Translate equations into English sentences. Use 3x5 flash cards to study special terms.

4 Understand formulas. Some students memorize the problems and answers discussed in class without learning the formulas or general principles behind the problems. This kind of rote learning doesn't allow for the application of principles and formulas to new problems. One approach is to practice a variety of problems to understand ways to arrive at the correct solutions.

You might be asked to memorize some formulas for convenience. If you understand the basic concepts behind these formulas, it is easier to recall them accurately. More important, you will probably be able to re-create the formulas if your recall falters. Understanding is preferable to memorization.

5 Learn the metric system. Developed in France during the 1790s, this decimal system of weights and measures is based on the meter as a unit of length and the gram as a unit of mass or weight. Long used universally in science, and now in trade and commerce as well, the metric system forms units by powers of ten. For instance, the U.S. dollar, the world's first decimal currency, consists of 100 cents. Known today as the International System of Units, the metric system is easy to learn—and it's a great example of applying a logical thought process to a problem.

6 Use summary sheets. Groups of terms and formulas can be easier to recall if you list them on a sheet of paper or put them on 3x5 cards. Mind map summary sheets allow you to see how various kinds of problems relate to one another. Creating a structure on which you can hang data helps your recall.

7 Time yourself. Sometimes speed counts. When practicing problems, notice how fast you can work them. This gives you an idea of how much time to allot for different types of problems. Remember that it is always important to practice before taking tests.

8 Use creative visualizations. Before you begin a problem-solving session, take a minute to relax, breathe deeply, and prepare yourself for the task ahead. See yourself solving problems successfully. A calm attitude is important. Visualize preparing for a test, taking the test, and solving the problems with ease.

On the rock

1 Survey the territory thoroughly. Read the problem at least twice before you begin. Read slowly. Be sure you understand what is being asked.

Let go of the expectation that you'll find the solution right away. You might make several attempts at solving the problem before you find a solution that works.

2 Sort the facts. Survey the problem for all of the givens. Determine the principles and relationships involved. Look for what is to be proved or what is to be discovered. Write these down.

3 Set up the problem. Before you begin to compute, determine the strategies you will use to arrive at solutions. When solving equations, carry out the algebra as far as you can before plugging in the actual numbers.

Remember that solving a math or science problem is like putting together a puzzle. You might work around the edges for a while and try many pieces before finding one that fits.

4 Cancel and combine. When you set up a problem logically, you can take shortcuts. For example, if the same term appears in both dividend and divisor, they will cancel each other out.

5 Draw a picture. Or make a diagram. A visual approach to math and science problems might work best for you. Pictures and diagrams help keep the facts straight. They can show relationships more effectively than words can.

To keep on track, record your facts in tables. Consider using three columns labeled "What I already know," "What I want to find out," and "What connects the two." This third column is the place to record a formula that can help you solve the problem.

6 Read the problem out loud. Sometimes the sound of your voice will jar loose the solution to a problem. Talk yourself through the solution. Read equations out loud.

7 Play with possibilities. There's usually not one "right" way to solve a problem. Several approaches or formulas might work, though one might be more efficient than another. Be willing to think about the problem from several angles or to proceed by trial and error.

8 Notice when you're in deep water. It's tempting to shy away from difficult problems. Unfortunately, the more you do this, the more difficult the problems become.

Math and science courses present wonderful opportunities to use the First Step technique explained in Chapter One. When you feel that you're beginning to get into trouble, write a precise Discovery Statement about the problem. Then write an Intention Statement about what you will do to solve the problem.

9 Check results. Work problems backward, then forward. Start at both ends and work toward the middle to check your work.

Take a minute to make sure you've kept the units of measurement clear. Say that you're calculating the velocity of an object. If you're measuring distance in meters and time in seconds, the final velocity should be in meters per second.

Another way to check your work is to estimate the answer before you compute it. Then ask yourself if your answer to the problem seems likely when compared with the estimate.

10 Savor the solution. Savor the times when you're getting correct answers to most of the problems in the textbook. Relish the times when you feel relaxed and confident as you work, or when the problems seem easy. Then remember these times if you feel math or science anxiety. ▨

Finding "aha!"
Creativity fuels critical thinking

This chapter offers you a chance to practice two types of critical thinking: convergent thinking and divergent thinking. One focuses on finding a single solution to a problem, while the other asks you to consider as many viewpoints as possible.

Convergent thinking involves a narrowing-down process. Out of all the possible viewpoints on an issue or alternative solutions to a problem, you choose the one that is the most reasonable or that provides the most logical basis for action.

Some people see convergent thinking and critical thinking as the same thing. However, there's more to critical thinking. Before you choose among viewpoints, generate as many of them as possible. Open up alternatives and consider all of your options. Define problems in different ways. Keep asking questions and looking for answers. This opening-up process is called *divergent* or *creative thinking*. Creative thinking provides the basis for convergent thinking. In other words, one path toward having good ideas is to have *lots* of ideas. Then you can pick and choose from among them, combining and refining them as you see fit.

Choose when to think creatively. The key is to make conscious choices about what kind of thinking to do in any given moment. Generally speaking, creative thinking is more appropriate in the early stages of planning and problem solving. Feel free to dwell in this domain for a while. If you narrow

down your options too soon, you run the risk of missing an exciting solution or of neglecting a novel viewpoint. Convergent thinking is essential, and you should save it until you have plenty of options on the table. Remember that creative thinking and convergent thinking take place in a continuous cycle. After you've used convergent thinking to narrow down your options, you can return to creative thinking at any time to generate new ones.

Cultivate "aha!" Central to creative thinking is something called the "aha!" experience. Nineteenth-century poet Emily Dickinson described aha! this way: "If I feel physically as if the top of my head were taken off, I know that is poetry." Aha! is the burst of creative energy heralded by the arrival of a new, original idea. It is the sudden emergence of an unfamiliar pattern, a previously undetected relationship, or an unusual combination of familiar elements. It is an exhilarating experience.

Aha! does not always result in a timeless poem or a Nobel Prize. It can be inspired by anything from playing a new riff on a guitar to figuring out why your car's fuel pump doesn't work. A nurse might notice a patient's symptom that everyone else missed. That's an aha! An accountant might discover a tax break for a client. That's an aha! A teacher might devise a way to reach a difficult student. Aha!

Follow through. The flip side of aha! is following through. Thinking is both fun *and* work. It is effortless and uncomfortable. It's the result of luck and persistence. It involves spontaneity and step-by-step procedures, planning and action, convergent and creative thinking.

Employers in all fields are desperately seeking those rare people who can find aha! and do something with it. The necessary skills include the ability to spot assumptions, weigh evidence, separate fact from opinion, organize thoughts, and avoid errors in logic. All of this can be demanding work. Just as often, it can be energizing and fun. With these creative and critical thinking skills, you'll have a combination to supercharge your success in school and at work. ✕

Tangram

A tangram is an ancient Chinese puzzle game that stimulates the "play instinct" so critical to creative thinking. The cat figure above was created by rearranging seven sections of a square. Hundreds of images can be devised in this manner. Playing with tangrams allows us to see relationships we didn't notice before.

The rules of the game are simple: Use these seven pieces to create something that wasn't there before. Be sure to use all seven. You might start by mixing up the pieces and seeing whether you can put them back together to form a square.

Make your own tangram by cutting pieces like those above out of poster board. When you come up with a pattern you like, trace around the outside edges of it and see if a friend can discover how you did it.

Ways to
create ideas

Creative thinking means using your imagination freely, combining ideas or information in new ways, making connections between seemingly unrelated ideas, and reshaping goals in ways that reveal new possibilities.

Use the following techniques to create ideas about anything, whether you're studying math problems, remodeling a house, composing a business plan, or writing a bestseller. With practice, you can set the stage for creative leaps, jump with style, and land on your feet with brand-new ideas in hand.

Conduct a brainstorm. Brainstorming is a technique for finding solutions, creating plans, and discovering new ideas. When you are stuck on a problem, brainstorming can break the logjam.

For example, if you run out of money two days before payday every week, you can brainstorm ways to make your money last longer. You can brainstorm ways to pay for your education. You can brainstorm ways to find a job.

The purpose of brainstorming is to generate as many solutions as possible. Sometimes the craziest, most outlandish ideas, while unworkable in themselves, can lead to new ways to solve problems. Use the following steps to try out the brainstorming process.

First, state the issue or problem precisely by writing it down. State it as a question. For example: "How can I take my love of film and turn it into a successful career in screenwriting?"

Next, schedule a brainstorming session to create answers. Use a clock to time it to the minute. Digital sports watches with built-in stopwatches work well. Experiment with various lengths of time. Both short and long brainstorms can produce powerful results.

Before you begin, sit quietly for a few seconds to collect your thoughts. Then start timing and write as fast as you can.

Write down everything. Accept every idea. If it pops into your head, put it down on paper. Quantity, not quality, is the goal. Avoid making judgments and evaluations during the brainstorming session.

After the session, review, evaluate, and edit. Toss out any truly nutty ideas, but not before you give them a chance.

For example, during your brainstorm on succeeding in screenwriting, you might have written "Interview the five top screenwriters working today and ask them how they got started." Impossible? Perhaps your school offers a course in screenwriting that is taught by someone working in the field. You might be able to get an internship with a film production company. You could also look for Web sites created by your favorite screenwriters and interview them via e-mail.

Brainstorms often produce solutions that look wacky at first and can later bring about surprising, life-changing results. Stay open to possibilities.

Here are some other tips for brainstorming sessions:

- *Let go of the need for a particular solution.* Brainstorming sessions can reveal new ways of thinking about old problems.

- *Relax.* Creativity is enhanced by a state of relaxed alertness. If you are tense or anxious, use some of the relaxation techniques described in this text. (Start with the article "Let go of test anxiety" in Chapter Six: Tests.)

- *Set a quota or goal for the number of solutions you want to generate.* Goals give your subconscious mind something to aim for.

- *Use 3x5 cards or a computer to record each solution.* When you review your session, you can arrange solutions in patterns to look for relationships. Or you can arrange them in order of priority.

- *Brainstorm with others.* This is a powerful technique. Group brainstorms can take on a life of their own. Ask one member of the group to write down solutions. Feed off the ideas of others, and remember to avoid evaluating or judging anyone's idea during the brainstorm.

- *Multiply brainstorms.* Pick one item from your first brainstorm and conduct another brainstorm about that idea.

- *Be wild and crazy.* If you get stuck, think of an outlandish idea and write it down. One crazy idea can unleash a flood of other, more workable solutions.

Focus and let go. Focusing and letting go are alternating parts of the same process. Intense focus taps the resources of your conscious mind. Letting go gives your subconscious mind time to work. When you focus for intense periods and then let go for a while, the conscious and subconscious parts of your brain work in harmony. In doing so, they can produce the highest-quality results.

Focusing attention means being in the here and now. To focus your attention on a project, notice when you pay attention and when your mind starts to wander. And involve all of your senses.

For example, if you are having difficulty writing a paper at a computer, practice focusing by listening to the sounds as you type. Notice the feel of the keys as you strike them. When you know the sights, sounds, and sensations you associate with being truly in focus, you'll be able to repeat the experience and return to your paper more easily.

You can use your body to focus your concentration. Some people concentrate better lying down. Others focus more easily if they stand or pace back and forth. Still others need to have something in their hands. Experiment. Notice what works for you and use it.

Be willing to recognize conflict, tension, and discomfort. Notice them and fully accept them, rather than fighting against them. Look for the specific thoughts and body sensations that make up the discomfort. Allow them to come fully into your awareness, and then let them pass.

You might not be focused all of the time. Periods of inspiration might last only seconds. Be gentle with yourself when you notice that your concentration has lapsed.

In fact, that might be a time to let go. "Letting go" means not forcing yourself to be creative.

Practice focusing for short periods at first, then give yourself a break. Phone a friend. Get up and take a walk around the room or around your block. Take a few minutes to look out your window. Listen to some music or, better yet, sing a few songs to yourself.

You also can break up periods of focused concentration with stretches, sit-ups, or pushups. Use relaxation and breathing exercises. Muscle tension and the lack of oxygen can inhibit self-expression.

Movies, music, walks in the park, and other pleasant activities stir the creative soup that's simmering in your brain.

Take a nap when you are tired. Thomas Edison took frequent naps. Then the light bulb clicked on.

Cultivate creative serendipity. The word *serendipity* was coined by the English author Horace Walpole from the title of an ancient Persian fairy tale, "The Three Princes of Serendip." The princes had a knack for making lucky discoveries. Serendipity is that knack, and it involves more than luck. It is the ability to see something valuable that you weren't looking for. History is full of serendipitous people. Country doctor Edward Jenner noticed "by accident" that milkmaids seldom got smallpox. The result was his discovery that mild cases of cowpox immunized them. Penicillin was also discovered "by accident." Scottish scientist Alexander Fleming was growing bacteria in a laboratory petri dish. A spore of *Penicillium notatum,* a kind of mold, blew in the window and landed in the dish, killing the bacteria. Fleming isolated the active ingredient. A few years later, during World War II, it saved thousands of lives. Had Fleming not been alert to the possibility, the discovery might never have been made.

You can train yourself in the art of serendipity. First, keep your eyes open. You might find a solution to an accounting problem in a Saturday morning cartoon. You might discover a topic for your term paper at the corner convenience store. Multiply your contacts with the world. Resolve to meet new people. Join a study or discussion group. Read. Go to plays, concerts, art shows, lectures, and movies. Watch television programs you normally wouldn't watch. Use idea files and play with data.

Finally, expect discoveries. One secret for success is being prepared to recognize "luck" when you see it.

Keep idea files. We all have ideas. People who are viewed as creative are those who treat their ideas with care. That means not only recognizing ideas, but also recording them and following up on them.

One way to keep track of ideas is to write them down on 3x5 cards. Invent your own categories and number the cards so you can cross-reference them. For example, if you have an idea about making a new kind of bookshelf, you might file a card under "Remodeling." A second card might also be filed under "Marketable Ideas." On the first card, you can write down your ideas, and on the second, you can write "See card #321—Remodeling." Include in your files powerful quotations, random insights, notes on your reading, and useful ideas that you encounter in class. Collect jokes, too.

Keep a journal. Journals don't have to be exclusively about your own thoughts and feelings. You can record observations about the world around you, conversations with friends, important or offbeat ideas—anything.

To fuel your creativity, read voraciously, including newspapers, Web sites, and magazines. Keep a clip file of interesting articles. Explore beyond mainstream journalism. There are hundreds of low-circulation specialty magazines and online news journals that cover almost any subject you can imagine.

Keep letter-sized file folders of important correspondence, magazine and news articles, and other material. You can also create idea files on a computer using word processing, outlining, or database software.

Safeguard your ideas, even if you're pressed for time. Jotting down four or five words is enough to capture the essence of an idea. You can write down one quotation in a minute or two. And if you carry 3x5 cards in a pocket or purse, you can record ideas while standing in line or sitting in a waiting room.

Review your files regularly. Some amusing thought that came to you in November might be the perfect solution to a problem in March.

Collect and play with data. Look from all sides at the data you collect. Switch your attention from one aspect to another. Examine each fact, and avoid getting stuck on one particular part of a problem.

Turn a problem upside down by picking a solution first and then working backward. Ask other people to look at the data. Solicit opinions.

Living with the problem invites a solution. Write down data, possible solutions, or a formulation of the problem on 3x5 cards and carry them with you. Look at them before you go to bed at night. Review them when you are waiting for the bus. Make them part of your life and think about them frequently.

Look for the obvious solutions or the obvious "truths" about the problem—then toss them out. Ask yourself: "Well, I know X is true, but if X were *not* true, what would happen?" Or ask the reverse: "If that *were* true, what would follow next?"

Put unrelated facts next to each other and invent a relationship between them, even if it seems absurd at first. In *The Act of Creation,* novelist Arthur Koestler says that finding a context in which to combine opposites is the essence of creativity.[10]

Make imaginary pictures with the data. Condense it. Categorize it. Put it in chronological order. Put it in alphabetical order. Put it in random order. Order it from most to least complex. Reverse all of those orders. Look for opposites.

It has been said that there are no new ideas—only new ways to combine old ideas. Creativity is the ability to discover those new combinations.

Create while you sleep. A part of our mind works as we sleep. You've experienced this directly if you've ever fallen asleep with a problem on your mind and awakened the next morning with a solution. For some of us, the solution appears in a dream or just before falling asleep or waking up.

You can experiment with this process. Ask yourself a question as you fall asleep. Keep pencil and paper or a recorder near your bed. The moment you wake up, begin writing or speaking and see if an answer to your question emerges.

Many of us have awakened from a dream with a great idea, only to fall asleep and lose it forever. To capture your ideas, keep a notebook by your bed at all times. Put the notebook where you can find it easily.

There is a story about how Benjamin Franklin used this suggestion. Late in the evenings, as he was becoming drowsy, he would sit in his rocking chair with a rock in his right hand and a metal bucket on the floor beneath the rock. The moment he fell asleep, the rock would fall from his grip into the bottom of the bucket, making a loud noise that awakened him. Having placed a pen and paper nearby, he immediately wrote down what he was thinking. Experience taught him that his thoughts at this moment were often insightful and creative.

Refine ideas and follow through. Many of us ignore this part of the creative process. How many great moneymaking schemes have we had that we never pursued? How many good ideas have we had for short stories that we never wrote? How many times have we said to ourselves, "You know, what they ought to do is attach two handles to one of those things, paint it orange, and sell it to police departments. They'd make a fortune." And we never realize that we are "they."

Genius resides in the follow-through—the application of perspiration to inspiration. One powerful tool you can use to follow through is the Discovery and Intention Journal Entry system. First write down your idea in a Discovery Statement, and then write what you intend to do about it in an Intention Statement. You also can explore the writing techniques discussed in Chapter Eight: Communicating as a guide for refining your ideas.

Another way to refine an idea is to simplify it. And if that doesn't work, mess it up. Make it more complex.

Finally, keep a separate file in your ideas folder for your own inspirations. Return to it regularly to see if there is anything you can use. Today's defunct term paper idea could be next year's A in speech class.

Create success strategies. Use creative thinking techniques to go beyond the pages of this book and create your own ways to succeed in school and at work. Read other books on success. Interview successful people. Reflect on any of your current behaviors that help you do well in school and think about how they will help you succeed in the workplace. Change any habits that fail to serve you.

If you have created a study group with people from one of your classes, set aside time to talk about ways to succeed in any class. Challenge each other to practice your powers of invention. Test any new strategies you create and report to the group on how well they're working for you.

Trust the process. Learn to trust the creative process—even when no answers are in sight. We are often reluctant to look at problems if no immediate solution is at hand. We grow impatient and tend to avoid frustration by giving up altogether. Most of us do this to some degree with personal problems as well. If we are having difficulty with a relationship and don't see a quick resolution, we deny that the problem exists rather than facing up to it.

Trust that a solution will show up. Frustration and a feeling of being stuck are often signals that a solution is imminent.

Sometimes solutions break through in a giant AHA! More often they come in a series of little aha!s. Be aware of what your aha!s look, feel, and sound like. That sets the stage for even more flights of creative thinking. ⊠

➔ Create on your feet

A popular trend in executive offices is the "stand-up" desk—a raised working surface at which you stand rather than sit.

Standing has advantages over sitting for long periods. You can stay more alert and creative when you're on your feet. One theory is that our problem-solving ability improves when we stand, due to increased heart rate and blood flow to the brain.

Standing is great for easing lower-back pain, too. Sitting aggravates the spine and its supporting muscles.

This is a technique with tradition. If you search the Web for stand-up desks, you'll find models based on desks used by Thomas Jefferson, Winston Churchill, and writer Virginia Woolf. Consider setting your desk up on blocks or putting a box on top of your desk so that you can stand while writing, preparing speeches, or studying. Discover whether this approach works for you.

Consider the following argument:

Orca whales mate for life.
Orca whales travel in family groups.
Science has revealed that Orca whales are intelligent.
Therefore, Orca whales should be saved from extinction.

One idea underlies this line of thought:

Any animal that displays significant human
characteristics deserves special protection.

Whether or not you agree with this argument, consider for a moment the process of making assumptions. Assumptions are assertions that guide our thinking and behavior. Often these assertions are unconscious. People can remain unaware of their most basic and far-reaching assumptions—the very ideas that shape their lives.

Spotting assumptions can be tricky, since they are usually unstated and offered without evidence. And scores of assumptions can be held at the same time. Those assumptions might even contradict each other, resulting in muddled thinking and confused behavior. This makes uncovering assumptions a feat worthy of the greatest detective.

Letting assumptions remain in our subconscious can erect barriers to our success. Take the person who says, "I don't worry about saving money for the future. I think life is meant to be enjoyed today—not later." This statement rests on at least two assumptions: *Saving money is not enjoyable*, and *we can enjoy ourselves only when we're spending money*.

It would be no surprise to find out that this person runs out of money near the end of each month and depends on cash advances from high-interest credit cards. She is shielding herself from some ideas that could erase her debt: Saving money can be a source of satisfaction, and many enjoyable activities cost nothing.

The stakes in uncovering assumptions are high. Prejudice thrives on the beliefs that certain people are inferior or dangerous due to their skin color, ethnic background, or sexual orientation. Those beliefs have led to flawed assumptions such as *mixing the blood of the races will lead to genetically inferior offspring* and *racial integration of the armed forces will lead to the destruction of morale*.

When we remain ignorant of our assumptions, we also make it easier for people with hidden agendas to do our thinking for us. Demagogues and unethical advertisers know that unchallenged assumptions are potent tools for influencing our attitudes and behavior.

Take this claim from an advertisement: "Successful business people have large vocabularies, so sign up today

Uncovering assumptions

for our seminar on word power!" Embedded in this sentence are several assumptions. One is that a cause-and-effect relationship exists between a large vocabulary and success in the workplace. Another is that a large vocabulary is the single or most important factor in that success. This claim also assumes that the advertiser's seminar is the best way to develop your vocabulary. In reality, none of these assumptions is necessarily true.

Assertions and opinions flow from our assumptions. Heated conflict and hard feelings often result when people argue on the level of opinions—forgetting that the real conflict lies at the level of their assumptions.

An example is the question about whether the government should fund public works programs that create jobs during a recession. People who advocate such programs might assume that creating such jobs is an appropriate task for the federal government. On the other hand, people who argue against such programs might assume that the government has no business interfering with the free workings of the economy. There's little hope of resolving this conflict of opinion unless we deal with something more basic: our assumptions about the proper role of government.

You can follow a three-step method for testing the validity of any viewpoint. First, look for the assumptions—the assertions implied by that viewpoint. Second, write down these assumptions. Third, see if you can find any exceptions to them. This technique helps detect many errors in logic. ☒

Ways to fool yourself

Six common mistakes in logic

Logic is a branch of philosophy that seeks to distinguish between effective and ineffective reasoning. Students of logic look for valid steps in an *argument*, or a series of assertions. The opening assertions of the argument are the *premises*, and the final assertion is the *conclusion*.

Over the last 2,500 years, specialists in logic have listed some classic land mines in the field of logic—common mistakes that are called *fallacies*. These fallacies are included in just about every logic textbook. Following are six examples. Knowing about them before you string together a bunch of assertions can help you avoid getting fooled.

1 Jump to conclusions. Jumping to conclusions is the only exercise that some lazy thinkers get. This fallacy involves drawing conclusions without sufficient evidence. Take the bank officer who hears about a student failing to pay back an education loan. After that, the officer turns down all loan applications from students. This person has formed a rigid opinion on the basis of hearsay. Jumping to conclusions—also called *hasty generalization*—is at work here.

2 Attack the person. This mistake in logic is common at election time. An example is the candidate who claims that her opponent has failed to attend church regularly during the campaign. People who indulge in personal attacks are attempting an intellectual sleight of hand to divert our attention from the truly relevant issues.

3 Appeal to authority. A professional athlete endorses a brand of breakfast cereal. A famous musician features a soft drink company's product in a rock video. The promotional brochure for

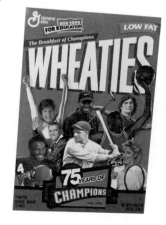

an advertising agency lists all of the large companies that have used its services.

In each case, the people involved are trying to win your confidence—and your dollars—by citing authorities. The underlying assumption is usually this: *Famous people and organizations buy our product. Therefore, you should buy it too.* Or: *You should accept this idea merely because someone who's well known says it's true.*

Appealing to authority is usually a substitute for producing real evidence. It invites sloppy thinking. When our only evidence for a viewpoint is an appeal to authority, it's time to think more thoroughly.

4 Point to a false cause. The fact that one event follows another does not necessarily mean that the two events have a cause-and-effect relationship. All we can actually say is that the events might be correlated. For example, as children's vocabularies improve, they can get more cavities. This does not mean that cavities are the result of an improved vocabulary. Instead, the increase in cavities is due to other factors, such as physical maturation and changes in diet or personal care.

5 Think in all-or-nothing terms. Consider these statements: *Doctors are greedy.... You can't trust politicians.... Students these days are in school just to get high-paying jobs; they lack idealism.... Homeless people don't want to work.*

These opinions imply the word *all.* They gloss over individual differences, claiming that all members of a group are exactly alike. They also ignore key facts, for instance, that some doctors volunteer their time at free medical clinics and that many homeless people are children who are too young to work. All-or-nothing thinking is one of the most common errors in logic.

6 Base arguments on emotion. The politician who ends every campaign speech with flag waving and slides of her mother eating apple pie is staking her future on appeals to emotion. So is the candidate who paints a grim scenario of the disaster and ruination that will transpire unless she is elected. Get past the fluff and histrionics to see if you can uncover any worthwhile ideas. ⊠

Thinking critically about career planning

One practical way to develop your transferable skills in critical thinking is to apply them to career planning.

Some people approach this activity with beliefs such as the following:

1. Career planning is complicated, and there is no clear place to start.

2. The best way to plan a career is to enter a field that is in high demand.

3. With all of my current commitments, I don't have the energy or time for career planning.

4. I already know what I want to do, so career planning would just waste my time.

5. I'm in school now, so I don't have to worry about career planning until the future.

These beliefs, even when we are not aware of them, can color our actions. Given such attitudes, it's no wonder that people find career planning as enjoyable as chickenpox.

To generate new possibilities for career planning, consider some alternatives. Take the beliefs listed above and state their opposites. Then collect evidence for the ideas you've just created. Like most of the important challenges in life, this calls for an open mind and a willingness to experiment with new behaviors.

Listed below are the opposites of the ideas stated above—statements that are reworded in a positive, proactive way. Consider ways that they could apply to your life.

1 I can use this book to start career planning. There is no "right" way to begin career planning. This is a many faceted, open-ended process that will help you learn more about yourself and the world. Use this book to access strategies that can help you do both.

Success in career planning does not depend on following specific steps in a certain order. Nor does it depend on specialized knowledge or training. Rather, career planning rests on a commitment to learn, plan, and take action.

You can begin now with the concept of transferable skills. Read each chapter of this book with two questions in mind: "What skills will I need to create the career of my dreams?" and "How can I use this article, exercise, or journal entry to gain those skills?" Right now, review the article about the SCANS report in the Introduction. Refer often to this list of skills as a blueprint for choosing your courses, declaring a major, and finding work that you love.

2 I can plan a career in a field I enjoy—even if it's not in demand. When planning a career, we may gravitate toward fields with the most job openings. This could work against our long-term goals.

Even in fields that are highly competitive, there are often openings for qualified people. And the jobs that are "hot" today may be "cool" by the time you've completed your education. In the face of accelerating change in the job market, following your own interests and values can be just as reliable as chasing current trends.

3 I can begin planning my career now, even if I'm busy. When it comes to career planning, sooner is more effective than later. A little planning now can help you avoid months or years in a job that fails to match your skills and interests. Also, career planning includes many tasks that you can complete in short periods of time. Start with Chapter Nine of this book. Even spending five minutes a day on an exercise or journal entry included there can make a difference.

4 Even if I know what I want to do, career planning still offers benefits. Career planning can reinforce choices that you've already made, helping you approach the future with more confidence. And if you do it with an open mind, career planning can unleash new possibilities.

One way to approach career planning is to pretend that you have no idea what you want to do and then see what happens. Planning from a blank slate can introduce you to possibilities you overlooked and options you did not fully consider.

5 Being in school offers me an opportunity to plan my career. Everything you do in higher education can help you to create a compelling future. A course in French suddenly takes on a new meaning when your goal is to work in a foreign embassy. A required writing course becomes a step toward a career as a magazine editor or news reporter. When you relate your current activities to a career goal that you care about, you tap a limitless source of energy.

Making ethical decisions at work

As the twenty-first century began, reports about accounting fraud, insider trading, conflicts of interest, and other unethical practices dominated the business news. Photos of impeccably dressed executives being led to jail reminded us that a single dishonest act can end a career, cheat stockholders, or cause entire companies to collapse.

Today, ethical decision making is not only a moral thing for organizations to do—it's essential to guarding the bottom line. Corporate ethics programs can detect ethical lapses before they generate lurid headlines and hefty fines.

Every day that you attend classes or go to work, you make choices that either reinforce or violate your core values. One of the most important transferable skills you can develop is ethical decision making and acting with integrity. Your employers and coworkers want to know that they can trust you. It pays to think through potential issues now.

Dilemmas present tough choices

Some workplace behaviors are widely acknowledged to be unethical. Examples are submitting false expense reports, operating machinery while intoxicated, stealing from a cash drawer, diverting corporate funds for personal uses, or using work time to download explicit sexual images from the Internet.

However, the ethical dilemmas you're likely to encounter in the workplace don't always involve clear choices. Instead, you may find yourself in gray areas, where no option seems clearly right or wrong. For instance, consider the following scenarios:

- You visit with a potential customer who says he wants one of your company's services but can't afford it. You know that a competitor offers the same service for a lower price. Do you reveal what you know?
- You're a supervisor who's been asked to lay off one of your long-term employees next quarter. Before you get a chance to meet with her, she tells you that she's been diagnosed with cancer and plans to pay

out of pocket for alternative treatments that are not covered by insurance. Do you tell her about her job fate now?
- Due to conflicts with a verbally abusive supervisor, you're planning to quit your job as soon as you can find a new one. However, your supervisor is in the process of hiring another person for your department. She asks you to meet with job applicants to talk about your experiences with the company. Do you tell these potential coworkers the truth about your plans?

Heed the signs of trouble

Under the stress of deadlines or fear of rejection by peers, even people who are normally trustworthy can let down their ethical guard and make decisions they later regret. One key to avoiding this situation is staying alert to signs of impending ethical problems. You might find it easier to stop unethical behavior in its early stages—before it becomes habitual or widespread.

According to *Setting the Standard*, published by the Office of Ethics and Business Conduct at Lockheed Martin Corporation, you're probably walking on thin ethical ice when you hear the following statements as justifications for taking a certain action:

- "It doesn't matter how it gets done as long as it gets done."
- "Everyone does it."
- "Shred that document."
- "We can hide it."
- "No one will get hurt."
- "This will destroy the competition."
- "We didn't have this conversation."[11]

Consider three classic ethical theories

Philosophers and religious teachers have been debating ethical issues for several thousand years. These thinkers don't always agree. Some say that right and wrong choices are determined by universal rules that apply to all people at all times. Others hold that a given behavior might be ethical in some situations but unethical in others. This debate has focused on three elements of behavior:

Intention. Suppose that a consultant plans to take one of her clients out for dinner and drinks with the intention of seducing him afterward. The client cancels at the last minute, so the supervisor never gets a chance to act on her plan. According to some theorists, the consultant is ethically at fault for her goal even though she never had the opportunity to achieve it. This argument rests on the idea that our intentions shape our character as much as our behaviors.

Consequences. According to another theory, the most ethical decision is the one that benefits the most people. Using this criteria, a supervisor might argue that he can ethically lay off two people in his department without two weeks' notice—if doing so lowers costs enough to save the jobs of four people across the company as a whole during a financial crisis. This is sometimes called "the greatest good for the greatest number" school of ethics.

Action. Some ethicists deny that either intentions or consequences are a reliable guide to making ethical decisions. We can seldom be sure of another person's intentions, and often we cannot accurately predict the consequences of an action. For this reason, some ethicists focus on the action itself. These people argue that ethical behavior is consistent with enduring, universal principles for behavior. An example is the "Golden Rule": Do unto others as you would have them do unto you.

You can reduce these three perspectives on ethical decision making to three key questions:

- In taking this action, what is my intention and how does it compare to the probable results?
- If I take this action, who will be helped and who will be harmed?
- Does my spiritual tradition or life philosophy offer any guidelines for action in this situation?

Create a ongoing conversation about ethics

Many organizations create committees to write a corporate code of ethics. You might hear objections to these codes, such as "Nobody reads them" or "They're too general to be useful in real life."

In some cases, companies overcome these problems by including ethics in their training programs and revising their codes frequently based on employee feedback.

→ **Create an ethics checklist**

You don't have to be a philosopher in order to make sound ethical decisions. Start with a working definition of ethics as using moral standards to guide your behavior. Next, turn your personal moral standards into a checklist of pointed questions that you can use to make choices in daily life. Though there is no formula for making ethical decisions, you can gain clarity with questions that can be answered yes or no. Following is a sample checklist:

Is this action legal?	❏ Yes	❏ No
Is this action consistent with my organization's mission, goals, and policies?	❏ Yes	❏ No
Is this action consistent with my personal values?	❏ Yes	❏ No
If I continue to make choices such as this, will I be happy with the kind of person I become?	❏ Yes	❏ No
Will this action stand the test of time? Will I be able to defend this action tomorrow, next month, and next year?	❏ Yes	❏ No
In taking this action, am I setting an example that I wish others to follow?	❏ Yes	❏ No
Am I willing to make this decision public—to share it wholeheartedly with my boss, my family, and my friends? Would I feel confident if an article about my decision was published in tomorrow's newspaper?	❏ Yes	❏ No
Has everyone who will be affected by this decision had the chance to voice their concerns?	❏ Yes	❏ No

Perhaps a code is most effective when it's used to create a continuous conversation about ethics. Having this conversation helps organizations to create an atmosphere of honesty and openness—qualities that promote more effective teams and higher productivity.

When presented with any code of ethics, ask whether it's useful to you personally. Think of the toughest ethical decision you've faced on the job. Then ask if the code would have helped. If it doesn't, make a suggestion for improvement. Your ideas—and your personal example—can make a difference. ▨

exercise 20

CREATE A PERSONAL CODE OF ETHICS

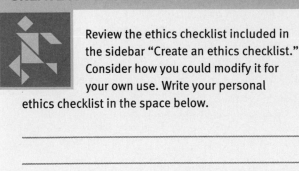

Review the ethics checklist included in the sidebar "Create an ethics checklist." Consider how you could modify it for your own use. Write your personal ethics checklist in the space below.

_____

_____

_____

_____

_____

_____

_____

_____

_____

_____

from the desk of...

**MARIANNA SARCLETTI,
FIELD SALES REPRESENTATIVE:**

I have often been asked to attend industry conferences where I communicate with people from around the world. At first this was intimidating to me, especially if I had trouble communicating with someone as a result of language barriers. As a student, it was helpful to learn how to embrace our differences and our similarities. Over time I became more open to learning about the people I was meeting with and this has helped to build more solid relationships at work and in my personal life.

Thinking about diversity

Those of us who can study, work, and live with people from other cultures, economic classes, and races can enjoy more success at school, on the job, and in our neighborhoods.

Sharing in this success means learning new ways to think, speak, and act. Learning about diversity opens up a myriad of possibilities—an education in itself. At first, this can seem frightening, frustrating, or even painful. It can also be exciting, enriching, and affirming.

The people called "minorities" in this country are already a numerical majority across the world. According to the world population profile from the U.S. Census Bureau, China and India account for almost two of every five people on earth. The more developed countries make up only 20 percent of the world's population, and the population of the United States makes up less than 5 percent of our global village. In the United States, white people of non-Hispanic origin could make up just 53 percent of the population by 2050—down from the current level of 69 percent.[12] The cultures of the world meet daily. Several forces are shrinking our globe. One is the growth of a world economy. Another is the "electronic village" forged across nations by newspapers, radios, televisions, telephones, fax machines, and computers.

We have an opportunity to benefit from this change instead of merely reacting to it. At one time, only sociologists and futurists talked about the meeting of cultures. Now all of us can enter this conversation. We can value cultural differences and learn how to thrive with them. It starts with the way we think about diversity.

There are no quick, easy answers to overcoming the long history of prejudice and the need to embrace diversity. Continue to experiment and see what works for you. As you read, ask yourself a question to promote critical and creative thinking about diversity: "How can I use this material to live and work more effectively in a multicultural world?" The answers could change your life. ◪

Diversity is real—and valuable

We have always lived with people of different races and cultures. Many of us come from families who immigrated to the United States or Canada just two or three generations ago. The things we eat, the tools we use, and the words we speak are a cultural tapestry woven by many different peoples.

Think about a common daily routine. A typical American citizen awakens in a bed (an invention from the Near East). After dressing in clothes (often designed in Italy), she slices a banana (grown in Honduras) in her bowl (made in China) of cereal, and brews coffee (shipped from Nicaragua). After breakfast, she reads the morning newspaper (printed by a process invented in Germany on paper, which was first made in China). Then she flips on a CD player (made in Japan) and listens to music (possibly performed by a band from Cuba). Multiculturalism refers to racial and ethnic diversity—and many other kinds of diversity as well. As anthropologist Dorothy Lee reminds us, culture is simply one society's solutions to perennial human problems, such as how to worship, celebrate, resolve conflict, work, think, and learn.[13] Culture is a set of learned behaviors—a broader concept than race, which refers to the biological makeup of people. From this standpoint, we can speak of the culture of large corporations or the culture of the fine arts. There are the cultures of men and women; heterosexual, homosexual, and bisexual people; and older and younger people. There are differences between urban and rural dwellers, between able-bodied people and those with disabilities, and between people from two-parent families and people from single-parent families. There are social classes based on differences in standards of living. And diversity in religion is a factor, too. This can be especially difficult to accept, since many people identify strongly with their religious faith. In some respects, culture can be compared to an iceberg. Only parts of any given culture—such as language patterns or distinctive apparel—exist on a visible level. Just as most of an iceberg lies under water and out of sight, many aspects of culture lie beneath our conscious awareness. This invisible realm includes assumptions about the meanings of beauty and friendship, the concepts of sin and justice, approaches to problem solving, interpretations of eye contact and body language, and patterns of supervisor and employee relationships.

People can differ in countless ways—race, gender, ethnic group, sexual orientation, and more. The following suggestions can help you respond effectively to the many kinds of diversity you'll encounter. Higher education can help reinforce an attitude of tolerance, open-mindedness, and respect for individual differences.

Discrimination is also real. The ability to live with diversity is now more critical than ever. Racism, homophobia, and other forms of discrimination still exist, even in higher education. According to the FBI, a total of 7,462 hate crimes took place in the United States during 2002. About 49 percent of those crimes were based on race, and nearly 17 percent were based on sexual orientation. Almost 11 percent of all hate crimes took place in college and other school settings.[14]

Of course, discrimination can be far more subtle than hate crimes. Consider how you would respond to the following situations:

- As a marketing major, you regularly take part in focus groups that are designed to determine consumer attitudes toward new products. During one group, the leader calls on a person from a reservation and says, "Tell us. Do you think Native Americans would buy this?" Here one person is being typecast as a spokesperson for her entire ethnic group.

Multiculturalism refers to racial and ethnic diversity—and many other kinds of diversity as well.

■ Students in a mass media communications class are learning to think critically about television programs. They're talking about a situation comedy set in an urban high-rise apartment building with mostly African American residents. "Man, they really whitewashed that show," says one student. "It's mostly about inner-city black people, but they didn't show anybody on welfare, doing drugs, or joining gangs." The student's comment perpetuates common racial stereotypes.

■ On the first day of the term, students taking English composition enter a class taught by a professor from Puerto Rico. One of the students asks the professor, "Am I in the right class? Maybe there's been a mistake. I thought this was supposed to be an English class, not a Spanish class." The student assumed that only Caucasian people are qualified to teach English courses.

Forrest Toms of Training Research and Development defines racism as "prejudice plus power"—the power to define reality, to enshrine one set of biases. The operating assumption behind racism is that differences mean deficits.[15]

When racism lives, we all lose—even those groups with social and political power. We lose the ability to make friends and to function effectively on teams. We crush human potential. People without the skills to bridge cultures are already at a disadvantage.

Higher education offers a chance to change this. Academic environments can become cultural laboratories—places where people of diverse races and cultures can meet in an atmosphere of tolerance. Students who create alliances outside their immediate group are preparing to succeed in both school and work.

Diversity is valuable. Synergy is the idea that the whole is more than the sum of its parts. Consider some examples: A symphony orchestra consists of many different instruments; when played together, their effect is multiplied many times. A football team has members with different specialties; when their talents are combined, they can win a league championship.

Diversity in a society offers another example of synergy. It takes no more energy to believe that differences enrich us than it does to believe that differences endanger us. Embracing diversity adds value to any organization and can be far more exciting than just meeting the minimum requirements for affirmative action.

Today we are waking up not only to the *fact* of diversity but also to the *value* of diversity. Biologists tell us that diversity of animal species benefits our ecology. The same idea applies to the human species. Through education our goal can be to see that we are all part of a complex world—that our own culture is different from, not better than, others. Knowing this, we can stop saying, "This is the way to work, learn, relate to others, and view the world." Instead, we can say, "Here is the way I have been doing it. I would also like to see your way."

The fact of diversity also represents opportunity in the workplace. Understanding cultural differences—internationally and domestically—will help you to embrace others' viewpoints that lead to profitable solutions. Organizations that are attuned to diversity are more likely to prosper in the global marketplace.

Accepting diversity does not mean ignoring the differences among cultures so that we all become part of a faceless "melting pot." Instead, we can become more like a mosaic—a piece of art in which each element maintains its individuality and blends with others to form a harmonious whole.

Learning to live with diversity is a process of returning to "beginner's mind"—a place where we question our biases and assumptions. This is a magical place, a place of new beginnings and options. It takes courage to dwell in beginner's mind—courage to go outside the confines of our own culture and world-view. It can feel uncomfortable at first. Yet there are lasting rewards to gain.

As you expand your thinking and embrace diversity, look at yourself. All the transferable skills presented in this book depend on self-awareness—the ability to look at your current beliefs and behaviors and evaluate them objectively. With awareness of your own biases, you can go beyond them. ⊠

> *Higher education can help reinforce an attitude of tolerance, open-mindedness, and respect for individual differences.*

Overcome stereotypes with critical thinking

Consider assertions such as "College students like to drink heavily," "People who speak English as a second language are hard to understand," and "Americans who criticize the President are unpatriotic."

These are examples of stereotyping—generalizing about a group of people based on the behavior of isolated group members. Stereotypes are a potent source of intellectual error. They are signals to expand our transferable skills in critical thinking—to demand evidence, examine logic, and insist on accurate information. Using these tools to release stereotypes will in turn help you develop another essential skill for the workplace—the ability to work with people of many racial and ethnic backgrounds.

Stereotypes infiltrate every dimension of human individuality. People are stereotyped on the basis of their race, ethnic group, religion, political affiliation, geographic location, job, age, gender, IQ, height, or hobby. We stereotype people based on everything from the color of their hair to the year of their car.

Mentally sorting people, events, and objects into groups allows us to make sense of the world. But when we consciously or unconsciously make generalizations that rigidly divide the people of the world into "us" versus "them," we create stereotypes and put on the blinders of prejudice.

You can take several steps to free yourself from stereotypes.

Look for errors in thinking. Some of the most common errors are:

- *Selective perception.* If we assume that homeless people are lazy, for instance, we might notice only the examples that support our opinion.

- *Self-fulfilling prophecy.* For example, when people of color were denied access to higher education based on stereotypes about their intelligence, they were deprived of opportunities to demonstrate their intellectual gifts.

- *Self-justification.* An unemployed white male might believe that affirmative action programs are making it impossible for him to get a job—even as he overlooks his own lack of experience or qualifications.

Create categories in a more flexible way. Stereotyping has been described as a case of "hardening of the categories." Avoid this problem by making your categories broader. Instead of seeing people based on

their skin color, for example, you could look at them on the basis of their heredity. People of all races share most of the same genes.

Test your generalizations about people through action. Inaccurate pictures tend to die when people from different cultures study together, work together, and live together. Consider joining a school or community organization that will put you in contact with people of other cultures. Your rewards will include a more global perspective and an ability to thrive in a multicultural world.

Be willing to see your own stereotypes. The Power Process: "Notice your pictures and let them go" can help. One belief about ourselves that many of us can shed is *I have no pictures about people from other cultures.* Even people with the best of intentions can harbor subtle biases. Every time that we notice an inaccurate picture buried in our mind and let it go, we take a personal step toward embracing diversity. ◼

exercise 21

EXAMINE ASSUMPTIONS ABOUT DIVERSITY

Write down the first words that come to mind when you hear the terms listed below. Do this now.

homeless people

_____

football players

_____

computer programmers

_____

disabled person

_____

retired person

_____

Next, exchange your responses to this exercise with a friend. Did you discover stereotypes or other examples of bias?

Asking questions

Thinking is born of questions. Questions open up options that might otherwise remain unexplored. Questions wake up people and lead them to investigate more closely issues and assumptions that had previously gone unchallenged. Questions promote curiosity, create new distinctions, and multiply possibilities.

Asking questions is also a great way to improve relationships. When you ask a question, you offer a huge gift to people—an opportunity for them to speak their brilliance and for you to listen to their answers.

Students often say, "I don't know what to ask." If you have ever been at a loss for what to ask, here are some ways to construct powerful questions about any subject you study in school, or about any area of your life that you choose to examine.

Let your pen start moving. Sometimes you can access a deeper level of knowledge by taking out your pen, putting it on a piece of paper, and writing down questions—even before you know *what* to write. Don't think. Just watch the paper and notice what appears. The results might be surprising.

Ask about what's missing. Another way to invent useful questions is to notice what's missing from your life and then ask how to supply it. For example, if you want to take better notes, you can write, "What's missing is skill in note taking. How can I gain more skill in taking notes?" Or "What's missing is time. How do I create enough time in my day to actually do the things that I say I want to do?"

Pretend to be someone else. Another way to invent questions is first to think of someone you greatly respect. Then pretend you're that person and ask the questions you think *she* would ask.

Begin a general question, then brainstorm endings. By starting with a general question and then brainstorming a long list of endings, you can invent a question that you've never asked before. For example:

What can I do when ...? What can I do when an instructor calls on me in class and I have no idea what to say? What can I do when I feel overwhelmed with the responsibilities of work, family, and school? What can I do if I get laid off my job?

How can I ...? How can I get just the kind of courses that I want? How can I expand my career options? How can I resolve a long-standing conflict with my boss? How can I get a promotion at work?

When do I ...? When do I decide on a major? When do I transfer to another school? When do I meet with an instructor to discuss an upcoming term paper?

Ask what else you want to know. Many times you can quickly generate questions by simply asking yourself, "What else do I want to know?" Ask this question immediately after you read a paragraph in a book or listen to someone speak.

Start from the assumption that you are brilliant, and begin asking questions that can help you unlock your brilliance. ◙

desk of ...

from the

HAKIM WALKER,
ACCOUNTING ASSOCIATE:

Critical thinking is the most essential skill I use on the job every day. When there are problems to resolve for our clients, my supervisors count on me to brainstorm solutions based on previous experiences I've had in the workplace. I take these past practices into account and apply the best strategies for executing resolutions.

THINKING CRITICALLY IN THE CLASSROOM

The art of asking questions is just as important to critical thinking as answering them. One eye-opening way to create questions is to write something you're sure of and simply put a question mark after it. (You might need to rephrase the question for grammatical sense.) The question you create can lead to others.

For example, someone might say, "I would never take a philosophy course." This person can write "I would never take a philosophy course?" That suggests other questions: "In what ways would taking a philosophy course serve my success in school?" "Could taking a philosophy course help me become a better writer?"

In the space below, write three statements that you accept with certainty. Then rephrase each statement as a question.

exercise 22

TRANSLATING GOALS INTO ACTION

Goal setting is an exercise in decision making and problem solving. Choose one long-range goal such as a personal project or a social change you'd like to help bring about. Examples include learning to scuba dive, eating a more healthful diet, studying to be an astronaut, improving health care for chronically ill children, inventing energy-saving technology, increasing the effectiveness of American schools, and becoming a better parent. List your goal here.

_____

Next, ask yourself: "What specific actions are needed in the short term to meet my long-range goal?" List those actions, focusing on those you could complete in less than one hour or could start in the next 24 hours.

_____
_____
_____
_____
_____

Statement #1:

_____
_____
_____
_____

Question #1:

_____
_____
_____
_____

Statement #2:

_____
_____
_____

Question #2:

_____
_____
_____
_____

Statement #3:

_____
_____
_____

Question #3:

_____
_____
_____
_____

power process

Find a bigger problem

Most of the time we view problems as barriers. They are a source of inconvenience and annoyance. They get in our way and prevent us from having happy and productive lives. When we see problems in this way, our goal becomes to eliminate problems.

This point of view might be flawed. For one thing, it is impossible to live a life without problems. Besides, they serve a purpose. They are opportunities to participate in life. Problems stimulate us and pull us forward.

Seen from this perspective, the goal becomes not to eliminate problems, but to find problems that are worthy of us. Worthy problems are those that draw on our talents, move us toward our purpose, and increase our skills. The challenge is to tackle those problems that provide the greatest benefits for others and ourselves. Viewed in this way, problems give meaning to our lives.

Problems fill the available space

Problems seem to follow the same law of physics that gases do: They expand to fill whatever space is available. If your only problem is to write a follow-up letter to a job interview, you can spend the entire day thinking about what you're going to say, writing the letter, finding a stamp, going to the

One way to handle little problems is to find bigger ones.

post office—and then thinking about all of the things you forgot to say. If, on that same day, you also need to go food shopping, the problem of the letter shrinks to make room for a trip to the grocery store. If you want to buy a car, too, it's amazing how quickly and easily the letter and the grocery shopping tasks are finished. One way to handle little problems is to find bigger ones. Remember that the smaller problems still need to be solved. The goal is to do it with less time and energy.

Bigger problems are plentiful

Bigger problems are not in short supply. Consider world hunger. Every minute of every day, people die because they don't have enough to eat. Also consider nuclear war, which threatens to end life on the planet. Child abuse, environmental pollution, terrorism, human rights violations, drug abuse, street crime, energy shortages, poverty, and wars throughout the world await your attention and involvement. You can make a contribution.

can experience efficiency and enthusiasm as natural parts of our daily routines. Energy and vitality can accompany most of our activities.

When we take on a bigger problem, we play full out. We do justice to our potentials. We then love what we do and do what we love. We're awake, alert, and engaged. Playing full out means living our lives as if our lives depended on it.

You can make a difference

Perhaps a little voice in your mind is saying, "That's crazy. I can't do anything about global problems" or "Everyone knows that hunger has always been around and always will be, and there is nothing anyone can do about it." These thoughts might prevent you from taking on bigger problems.

Realize that you *can* make a difference. Your thoughts and actions can change the quality of life on the planet.

This is your life. It's your school, your city, your country, and your world. Own it. Inhabit it. Treat it with the same care that you would a prized possession.

One way to find problems that are worthy of your talents and energies is to take on bigger ones. Take responsibility for problems that are bigger than you are sure you can handle. Then notice how your other problems dwindle in importance—or even vanish.

Playing full out means living our lives as if our lives depended on it.

Play full out

Considering bigger problems does not have to be depressing. In fact, it can be energizing—a reason for getting up in the morning. Taking on a huge project can provide a means to channel your passion and purpose.

Some people spend vast amounts of time in activities they consider boring: their jobs, their hobbies, their relationships. They find themselves going through the motions, doing the same walk-on part day after day without passion or intensity. American author Henry David Thoreau described this kind of existence as "lives of quiet desperation."

Playing full out suggests another possibility: We can spend much of our time fully focused and involved. We

exercise 23

FIX-THE-WORLD BRAINSTORM

This exercise works well with four to six people. Pick a major world problem such as hunger, nuclear proliferation, poverty, terrorism, overpopulation, or pollution. Then conduct a 10-minute brainstorm about the steps an individual could take to contribute to solving the problem.

Use the brainstorming techniques explained earlier in this chapter. Remember not to evaluate or judge the solutions during the process. The purpose of a brainstorm is to generate a flow of ideas and record them all.

After the brainstorming session, discuss the process and the solutions that it generated. Did you feel any energy from the group? Was a long list of ideas generated? Are several of them worth pursuing?

career application

Maria Sanchez graduated with an associate's degree in legal assistance and has been working for two years as a paralegal at a large law firm.

Maria's work is supervised by an attorney who is ultimately responsible for the documents she produces. As a paralegal, she cannot set legal fees, give legal advice, or present cases in court. Outside of these restrictions, however, she does many of the same things that lawyers do. Maria's current job centers on legal research—identifying laws, judicial decisions, legal articles, and other materials that are relevant to her assigned cases.

Maria is one of three paralegals who work with her supervising attorney. Recently she applied for a new paralegal job that's opened up in the firm. In addition to legal research, this job involves drafting legal arguments and motions to be filed in court. Getting this job would mean a promotion and raise for Maria.

Maria has formally applied for the job and expressed strong interest in it. She believes that her chances are excellent. One of the paralegals she works with is not interested in the job, and she knows that the other one plans to announce next month that she's quitting the firm to attend law school.

One day, Maria finds the first draft of an e-mail that her supervisor has printed out and accidentally placed in a stack of legal documents for Maria to file. The e-mail is a note of congratulations that offers the new paralegal job to the person who plans to quit. ⊠

Reflecting on this scenario:

1. Does Maria face an ethical dilemma in this situation? Explain your answer.

_____

_____

_____

_____

2. Review the guidelines for decision making given in this chapter—particularly the suggestions for ethical decision making. Choose one and explain how Maria could apply it.

_____

_____

_____

_____

3. In this chapter, Exercise #20: "Create a personal code of ethics" encourages you to list your own criteria for ethical decision making. If you have not done this exercise, complete it now. Does your personal code of ethics offer any guidelines for Maria? If so, explain.

_____

_____

_____

_____

quiz

Name _____ Date _____/_____/_____

1. List four questions that can guide you on your path to becoming a critical thinker.

2. Explain what is meant in this chapter by *aha!*

3. Define *serendipity* and give an example.

4. List and briefly describe three ways to create ideas.

5. List three questions you could ask yourself when making an ethical decision at work.

6. According to the text, *critical thinking* and *thorough thinking* are two distinct and different activities. True or False? Explain your answer.

7. Define *all-or-nothing thinking* and give an example.

8. Explain the suggestion "watch for hot spots" and describe its connection to critical thinking.

9. Name at least one fallacy involved in this statement: "Everyone who's ever visited this school has agreed that it's the best in the state."

10. List the four suggested steps for problem solving and give an example of each step.

learning styles application

The questions below will "cycle" you through four styles, or modes, of learning as explained in the article "Learning styles: Discovering how you learn" in Chapter One. Each question will help you explore a different mode. You can answer the questions in any order.

what if Explain how you would modify a technique from this chapter to make it a more effective tool for decision making—or describe an original technique of your own.

why Think of a major decision you face right now and put it into the form of a question. Possible examples are: "What major will I declare?" or "What is my top priority goal for this year?"

how Briefly describe how you will use a technique from this chapter to make a major decision.

what List a technique from this chapter that could help you make a major decision you face right now (such as the decision you list under Why?).

master student

profile

PAUL FARMER

a Harvard professor, renowned infectious-disease specialist, and the recipient of a MacArthur Foundation "genius" award. In medical school, found his life's calling—to diagnose and cure infectious diseases and to bring the lifesaving tools of modern medicine to those who need them most.

Dr. Farmer does not have anywhere near the name recognition of, say, Albert Schweitzer or Mother Teresa. But if any one person can be given credit for transforming the medical establishment's thinking about health care for the destitute, it is Paul Farmer.

Through the charity that Dr. Farmer helped found, Partners in Health, the health system, Zanmi Lasante (Creole for Partners in Health), not only cares for hundreds of thousands of peasants, but has also built schools and sanitation and water systems, vaccinated all the children, reduced the rate of H.I.V. transmission from mothers to babies, and successfully treated patients suffering from complicated drug-resistant strains of tuberculosis.

How has he done it? Dr. Farmer simply refuses to accept any excuse—no matter how reasonable—for not treating the poor. No doctors? We'll train them. High drug prices? We'll get the pharmaceutical companies to lower them. Misguided policies? We'll change them.

Working locally and globally simultaneously means pushing himself to extremes. He has a punishing schedule and rarely sees his Haitian-born wife, Didi, and daughter.

"The problem is, if I don't work this hard, someone will die who doesn't have to," he confesses in a rare moment of frustration. Dr. Farmer [was] pushed to branch out from Haiti after his colleague and kindred spirit, Jim Yong Kim, discover[ed] puzzling cases of lethal and drug-resistant strains of TB in the slums of Peru. Peru had an excellent TB control program. But in one of the horribly twisted ironies that tend to afflict the poor, the very medicine that was saving lives was also—through repeated treatments—breeding mutant strains resistant to conventional drugs.

Getting the medical establishment in Peru and at W.H.O., [World Health Organization] a United Nations agency, to change the prescribed regimen for TB drugs was formidable. Health experts dismissed the idea that complex diseases like drug-resistant TB or AIDS could even be treated in poor areas. In the end, Dr. Farmer and Dr. Kim prevailed, helping to lower the price of drugs and changing W.H.O.'s treatment guidelines. What's more, they had challenged the philosophy and the accuracy of cost-effectiveness analysis that ruled public health-care decisions at the highest level.

Near the end of [*Mountains Beyond Mountains*, author Tracy] Kidder details the wrenching efforts of some Partners in Health workers to help a 12-year-old Haitian boy suffering from a rare cancer. They hire a medevac helicopter for nearly $19,000 to bring the deathly ill boy to Boston for treatment. When he arrives the doctors learn the cancer has infiltrated his wasted body. He [died] three weeks later. To some it was an exercise in futility and excessive heroics. After all, how many other children could have been fed with that money?

But as Mr. Kidder explains, that kind of cost-benefit analysis is what Dr. Farmer has been fighting his whole life. If it were you, if it were your child and there was a chance to save him, would you think it was too much? Why, Dr. Farmer wants to know, don't people question why a young American doctor earns "five times what it cost to try to save a boy's life?" ◼

For more biographical information on Paul Farmer, visit the Master Student Hall of Fame on the *From Master Student to Master Employee* Web site at

masterstudent.college.hmco.com

CHAPTER 8
Communicating

Communicating effectively is discussed indirectly in many chapters of *From Master Student to Master Employee*. Taking a closer look in this chapter, you can help your students become proficient in the related skills of *speaking, listening,* and *writing,* now that they have the necessary foundations to work toward mastery. The Communicating chapter provides an opportunity to discuss conflict resolution, public speaking (including communication apprehension), and plagiarism. These communication abilities are essential workplace skills that can be practiced and mastered in the college setting. Use this Annotated Instructor's Edition and other resources available to you to highlight and discuss key concepts in class and to devise assignments that allow students to practice communication skills outside of the classroom. And consider this: Developing relationships through effective communication is essential for first-year student success and retention at your college.

Page 236
Master Student Map

This chapter is certainly one that your students will be energized to talk about. It will be especially easy for them to create schema using their prior knowledge of the subject before learning new information. Spend time focusing on the **what if?** in this chapter. Ask students **what if?** they use the ideas presented in this chapter to help them succeed in the workplace. Ask your students to consider the importance of communication to the major they have chosen (connecting back to Chapter Two) or to their future career choice (looking ahead to Chapter Nine).

Page 241
Five ways to say "I"

Students who have not taken an interpersonal communication course generally do not know how to create "I" statements. Putting students into groups and having them practice writing and speaking "I" statements helps them understand how to do so. Building relationships and teamwork works well to help students to gauge their effectiveness in communicating and works towards helping them find success in getting their message across.

Page 247
Create high-performing teams

Student success courses are perfect for helping students become accustomed to working in teams. As students work together with their peers, they have an opportunity to practice leadership roles, and another key communication skill—listening. Effective leaders exhibit the ability to listen carefully and respond appropriately. Students must take responsibility as part of a team. They embrace diversity by seeking out different viewpoints that lead to solid decision making. Your class may have completed an earlier exercise of creating a list of qualities of a master team member (in Chapter Six). Consider revisiting that list or starting one now if you did not do this activity before. Command that your classroom respects these qualities as they work in groups—in your class and with others at your college.

Page 248
Sustaining business relationships

Workplace relationships—and even relationships in higher education—are changing due to technological innovation and change. Communicating in the online and wireless workplace has different pros and cons. Engage your students in a discussion of sustaining relationships and communicating using technology. What are the benefits of technology in regard to building relationships in higher education and in the workplace? Which learning styles might benefit from technology?

Page 262
Three phases of effective writing

Are you looking for an assignment that can help your students practice their writing *and* provide them with an opportunity to win a $1,000 scholarship? This is a perfect place to announce the Houghton Mifflin Scholarship Essay Contest. Host a contest on your campus, select the best essay (that answers the scholarship essay question, posted on the *From Master Student to Master Employee* Web site, **masterstudent.college.hmco.com**), and submit this winning essay to the national contest. Remind your students that they have the formula for writing a successful essay in their hands! Previous winning essays are available on the Web site for reflection.

Writing well pays. Writing effectively can help students to express themselves powerfully and persuasively. Writing helps to organize information and adapt ideas to different audiences. It can also help to give clear instructions—a task that occupies much of our waking time. By becoming a skilled writer, your students can become better thinkers, speakers, readers, and listeners.

Good writing is a marketable skill. To verify this, have your students flip through the Help Wanted section in a large Sunday newspaper or do a quick search for writing skills at an online job listing Web site (like **http://www. monster.com**). Have them note how many job descriptions call for good writing skills. Consider also having students write out their own "ad" for the writing skills necessary for their intended career. What specific skills would be necessary?

Remind students that when they write, they not only gather information; they also assess it. You sift through the data, play with it, and sort it out. You look for relationships among facts and choose ideas that are useful to you. Through writing, you turn data into insight—a key transferable skill applicable to ALL jobs.

Page 256
Library—the buried treasure

Many students suffer from some form of "library-phobia." Either they never learned how to use a library, or they have been away from one for so long that they no longer remember how to look up information. Additionally, technological advances have changed the way information is accessed in a library, with some libraries posting their entire collections on the Internet, allowing students to conduct online searches.

One solution for overcoming "library-phobia" is to in-

voices

consultant

Using writing to combat math anxiety

Math classes, especially developmental math, seem to be inhabited by a fair number of students suffering from math anxiety. Math teachers tend to have their students communicate the way they were taught to communicate: by solving problems using a myriad of math symbols that only heightens the students' anxiety. These same students may enjoy writing and, in many cases, are better than average writers. If we were to intersect these two characteristics by having anxious math students communicate math through writing, it would place the student into a more relaxed communication domain that would in turn lessen their anxiety.

Two ways that I have required writing in math class is through in-class prompts and by rewriting instructions to problems.

Examples of writing prompts could include:

- *If someone were absent from class today, how would you explain what was covered?*

- *List as many jobs that you can think of that require a knowledge of math.*

- *Explain how old you would be if you lived for one million seconds.*

Instead of the traditional instructions "Solve $4x + 8 = 0$ for x," you can ask "How do you know that the solution to $4x + 8 = 0$ is a negative number?" Or, "Identify which of the following numbers are integers and which are rational," becomes, "Explain how integers and rational numbers are similar and how they are different."

These writing experiences will not only lower students' level of math anxiety but will strengthen their writing skills at the same time.

—DR. MIKE HAMM

vite a librarian as a guest speaker to teach your students how to locate information at the library at your college. If your library has a classroom, hold class in the library. Have students walk through the initial stages of doing a research paper by using the library as a resource to pick a topic, narrow it down, and then develop a thesis statement. (It is not necessary to have the students actually *write* the paper in your class, but instead just have them walk through this initial process. Encourage students to use a real assignment from one of their core courses for this assignment.) If students are stuck on selecting a topic, encourage them to select a topic related to their major or intended career, or a topic that is covered already in *From Master Student to Master Employee* that they'd like to take a closer look at.

Page 259
Writing and delivering speeches
Participating in class is an excellent way for students to practice speaking in public. Many students experience communication apprehension when they are called upon in class or to speak before a group. Ask your students to write a Discovery Statement about a time they remember about this type of situation. Have them describe their physical sensations, the effectiveness of their presentation, feedback from the audience, and so forth.

Ask your students to write an Intention Statement concerning how they intend to participate in class in order to experience talking to a group of people. Ask them to be specific about which class they intend to speak in, how they will set up the opportunity to speak (e.g., having questions ready, sitting in front, asking to give a presentation, etc.), and how they intend to record their observations of the experience. Connect this lesson with "Risk being a fool" and you have a practical application of the Power Process.

Have your students prepare a short speech and present it in your class. A "process speech" about how to do or make something is a topic that students feel fairly comfortable with. Review the criteria for an effective presentation with your class. Challenge your students to include visuals with their presentation. If you have a classroom with the necessary technology, ask students to create a PowerPoint presentation to accompany their speech. Use a peer grading system asking the students in the audience to provide a score for the presentation. Was the speech organized? Was there a clear introduction, body, and conclusion? Did the speaker deliver the content well and within the allotted time?

Page 264
Becoming an online learner
Consider holding one of your class meetings in a computer lab so that students will have an opportunity to use unfamiliar technology in a nonthreatening environment. If your school offers online courses, this would allow an opportunity to give your students an orientation session to using the course management system (like BlackBoard or WebCT). Or your students could take part in an orientation session provided by your campus information technology department. Grant extra credit to students who attend one of these sessions and complete Discovery and Intention statements that illustrate what they have learned. Have these students report back to your class about their experiences.

If your students need additional information to support learning online, suggest the *E-Learning Companion* by Watkins and Corry ©2005 (Houghton Mifflin Company). Visit the Web site for this text with your students and walk through the online tutorials (they're free!). You can access them at **studentsuccess.college.hmco.com**.

Page 270
POWER PROCESS: "Employ your word"
To help illustrate the effectiveness of this Power Process, have your students individually think about it and then write two promises: one to themselves, and one to a significant person in their life. This helps demonstrate how to use the ideas in the article. Remind your students that this promise they are making is, culturally, the highest level of commitment we make to each other.

Page 275
Master Student Profile: Ron Brown
Remind students that Master Student Profiles can be a source of inspiration. You can also use the Master Student Profiles to discuss the topics covered in the article. Ask your students why they think that Ron Brown was selected in connection with the Communication chapter. You can assign additional reading or research related to this article. Have your students begin with the biographical information and links that are provided on the *From Master Student to Master Employee* Web site.

Master Instructor Resource Guide

Course Manual

 Engaging students in your classroom to communicate through conversations is a valuable experience for both you and your students. Take this time to revisit your *Course Manual* for new ideas on conversations and sharing. When you introduce this chapter, review "Practice listening for what's really going on" in the *Course Manual* with your students.

Whether technology is an integral part of your student success course or just a component, ancillary materials related to *From Master Student to Master Employee* are available to you. The *Course Manual* includes a section entitled **Creating and Teaching an Online Course.** You can also get tips on using and assigning the *From Master Student to Master Employee* Web site in your classroom.

HM ClassPrep CD

 PowerPoint for Chapter Eight can help your visual learners understand concepts more easily. "The communication loop" is a powerful visual explanation of the processes surrounding effective communication.

Evaluating Web sites is crucial for student success and might not be taught to your students in any of their other courses. Use the checklist on the **HM ClassPrep CD** to help your students evaluate any type of site they visit. Consider collecting useful sites that have been evaluated by your students and posting them to your class Web site.

"Writing and delivering speeches" is an important article in this chapter. On the HM ClassPrep CD you will find tools for helping students plan an effective speech, sample speech grading forms, and suggestions for integrating this topic into your course.

Use an Assertiveness Inventory to help your students determine how they relate to people. The materials include exercises for follow-up and discussion to raise awareness in your classroom.

Additional Resources

One way to talk about the importance of communicating is to discuss the transferability of these skills from higher education to the workplace. A new 30-minute videotape, *The Interviewing Process: Strategies for Making the Right Impression,* takes students through the interviewing process from start to finish, and also covers preparing interview questions and answers. Accompanying exercises are available on the HM ClassPrep CD and on the Instructor's Web site at **masterstudent.college.hmco.com.**

Have your students listen to the Power Process audio files on the *Becoming a Master Student* Web site to practice their listening skills. Encourage them to read along with the print version in their textbook or to review it after they listen.

masterstudent.college.hmco.com — As you focus on technology integration, you and your students can stay up-to-date with technology by bookmarking the *From Master Student to Master Employee* Web site, and the Web site for the **Career Resource Center**. Check back frequently for updates. Have you signed up for the online newsletter for instructors?

8

Communicating

Listening means trying to see the problem the way the speaker sees it—which means not sympathy, which is feeling for him, but empathy, which is feeling with him.

S. I. HAYAKAWA

You have two ears and one mouth. Remember to use them in more or less that proportion.

PAULA BERN

why

this chapter matters . . .

Your communication abilities are as important to your success in the workplace as your technical skills.

what

is included . . .

how

you can use this chapter . . .

Listen, speak, and write more effectively.

Prevent and resolve conflict with other people.

Experience more satisfying relationships in all areas of your life.

As you read, ask yourself

what if . . .

I could communicate in specific ways to increase my success at work and satisfaction in personal relationships?

The communication loop

Communication is often garbled when we try to send and receive messages at the same time.

One effective way to improve your ability to communicate is to be aware of when you are the receiver and when you are the sender. If you are receiving (listening), just receive. Avoid switching into the sending (talking) mode. When you are sending, stick with it until you are finished.

If the other person is trying to send a message when you want to be the sender, you have at least three choices: Stop sending and be the receiver, stop sending and leave, or ask the other person to stop sending so that you can send. It is ineffective to try to send and receive at the same time.

This becomes clear when we look at what happens in a conversation. When we talk, we put thoughts into words. Words are a code for what we experience. This is called *encoding*. The person who receives the message takes our words and translates them into his own experience. This is called *decoding*.

A conversation between two people is like a communication between two telegraph operators. One encodes a message and sends it over the wire. The operator at the other end receives the coded signal, decodes it, evaluates it, and sends back another coded message. The first operator decodes this message and sends another. The cycle continues. The messages look like this:

1 ..—..—.-.-   3 —.—..— OPERATOR 1

2 —.-..-..   4 -..- —...-. OPERATOR 2

This encoding-decoding loop is most effective when we continually switch roles. One minute we send, the next we receive. If both operators send at the same time, neither knows what the other one sent. Neither can reply. Communication works best when each of us has plenty of time to receive what others send—that is, to *listen*—and the opportunity to send a complete message when it's our turn. ⊠

journal entry 24

Discovery/Intention Statement

Think of a time when you experienced an emotionally charged conflict with another person. Were you able to resolve this dispute effectively? If so, list below the strategies you used. If not, describe what you could have done differently.

I discovered that I . . .

_____

_____

_____

Now scan this chapter for ideas that can help you get your feelings across more skillfully in similar situations. List at least four ideas here, along with the page numbers where you can read more about them.

Strategy   *Page number*

_____

_____

_____

_____

_____

_____

Describe an upcoming situation in which you intend to apply these techniques. If possible, choose a situation that will occur within the next week.

I intend to . . .

_____

_____

_____

_____

_____

_____

THE COMMUNICATION LOOP
Listening

You observe a person in a conversation who is not talking. Is he listening? Maybe. Maybe not. He might be preparing his response or daydreaming.

Listening is not easy. Doing it effectively requires concentration and energy.

It's worth it. Listening well promotes success in school: more powerful notes, more productive study groups, and better relationships with students and instructors. Through skilled listening, you gain more than respect. You gain insight into other people. You learn about the world and about yourself. A skilled listener is appreciated by friends, family, and colleagues. The best salespeople, consultants, and customer service representatives are the best listeners. So are the best teachers, health care providers, and managers. In any work setting, people love a good listener.

To be a good listener, choose to listen. Once you've made this choice, you can use the following techniques to be a more effective listener. These ideas are especially useful in times of high emotional tension.

Through skilled listening, you gain more than respect. You gain insight into other people. You learn about the world and about yourself.

Nonverbal listening

Much of listening is nonverbal. Here are five guidelines for effective nonverbal listening.

Be quiet. Silence is more than staying quiet while someone is speaking. Allowing several seconds to pass before you begin to talk gives the speaker time to catch his breath and gather his thoughts. He might want to continue. Someone who talks nonstop might fear he will lose the floor if he pauses.

If the message being sent is complete, this short break gives you time to form your response and helps you avoid the biggest barrier to listening—listening with your answer running. If you make up a response before the person is finished, you might miss the end of the message—which is often the main point.

In some circumstances, pausing for several seconds might be inappropriate. Ignore this suggestion completely when someone asks in a panic where to find the nearest phone to call the fire department.

Maintain eye contact. Look at the other person while he speaks. Doing so demonstrates your attentiveness and helps keep your mind from wandering. Your eyes also let you "listen" to body language and behavior. When some of us avoid eye contact, not only do we fail to see—we fail to listen.

This idea is not an absolute. While maintaining eye contact is important in some cultures, people from other cultures are uncomfortable with sustained eye contact. Some individuals learn primarily by hearing; they can listen more effectively by turning off the visual input once in a while. Keep in mind the differences among people.

Display openness. You can communicate openness by means of your facial expression and body position. Uncross your arms and legs. Sit up straight. Face the other person and remove any physical barriers between you, such as a pile of books.

Listen without response. This doesn't mean that you should never respond. It means that you should wait for an appropriate moment to respond. When listening to another person, we often interrupt with our own stories, opinions, suggestions, and comments, as in the following dialogue:

"Oh, I'm so excited. I just found out that I've been nominated to be in *Who's Who in American Musicians*."

"Yeah, that's neat. My Uncle Elmer got into *Who's Who in American Veterinarians*. He sure has an interesting job. One time I went along when he was treating a cow."

Watch your nonverbal responses, too. A look of "Good grief!" from you can deter the other person from finishing his message.

Send acknowledgments. It is important to let the speaker know periodically that you are still there. Words and nonverbal gestures of acknowledgment convey to the speaker that you are interested and that you are receiving his message. These include "Umhum," "OK," "Yes," and head nods.

These acknowledgments do not imply your agreement. When people tell you what they don't like about you, your head nod doesn't mean that you agree. It just indicates that you are listening.

Verbal listening

Sometimes speaking promotes listening. Below are suggestions for effective verbal listening.

Feed back meaning. Paraphrase the communication. This does not mean parroting what another person says. Instead, briefly summarize. Feed back what you see as the essence of that person's message: "Let me see if I understood what you said . . ." or "What I'm hearing you say is. . . ." (Psychotherapist Carl Rogers referred to this technique as *reflection*.)[1] Often, the other person will say, "No, that's not what I meant. What I said was. . . ."

There will be no doubt when you get it right. The sender will say, "Yeah, that's it," and either continue with another message or stop sending when he knows you understand.

If you don't understand the message, be persistent. Also be concise. This is not a time to stop the other person by talking on and on about what you think you heard.

Listen beyond words. Be aware of nonverbal messages and behavior. You might point out that the speaker's body language seems to be the exact opposite of his words. For example: "I noticed you said you are excited, but you look bored."

Keep in mind that the same nonverbal behavior can have different meanings, depending on the listener's cultural background. Someone who looks bored might simply be listening in a different way.

The idea is to listen not only to the words but also to the emotion behind the words. Sometimes that emotional message is more important than the verbal content.

Take care of yourself. People seek good listeners, and there are times when you don't want to listen. You might be distracted with your own concerns. Be honest. Don't pretend to listen. You can say, "What you're telling me is important, and I'm pressed for time right now. Can we set aside another time to talk about this?" It's OK *not* to listen.

Listen for requests and intentions. "This class is a waste of my time." "Our instructor talks too fast." An effective way to listen to such complaints is to look for the request hidden in them.

"This class is a waste of my time" can be heard as "Please tell me what I'll gain if I participate actively in class." "The instructor talks too fast" might be asking "What strategies can I use to take notes when the instructor covers material rapidly?" We can even transform complaints into intentions. Take this complaint: "The parking lot by the office is so dark at night that I'm afraid to go to my car." This complaint can result in having a light installed in the parking lot.

Viewing complaints as requests gives us more choices. Rather than responding with defensiveness ("What does he know anyway?"), resignation ("It's always been this way and always will be"), or indifference ("It's not my job"), we can decide whether to grant the request (do what will alleviate the other's difficulty) or help the person translate his own complaint into an action plan.

THE COMMUNICATION LOOP
Sending

We have been talking with people for years, and we usually manage to get our messages across. There are times, though, when we don't. Often, these times are emotionally charged.

Sometimes we feel wonderful or rotten or sad or scared, and we want to express it. Emotions can get in the way of the message. Described below are four techniques for delivering a message through tears, laughter, fist pounding, or hugging.

Replace "You" messages with "I" messages. It can be difficult to disagree with someone without his becoming angry or your becoming upset. When conflict occurs, we often make statements about the other person, or "You" messages:

"You are rude."
"You make me mad."
"You must be crazy."
"You don't love me anymore."

This kind of communication results in defensiveness. The responses might be:

"I am not rude."
"I don't care."
"No, *you* are crazy."
"No, *you* don't love *me*!"

"You" messages are hard to listen to. They label, judge, blame, and assume things that might or might not be true. They demand rebuttal. Even praise can sometimes be an ineffective "You" message. "You" messages don't work.

When communication is emotionally charged, psychologist Thomas Gordon suggests that you consider limiting your statements to descriptions about yourself.[2] Replace "You" messages with "I" messages.

"You are rude" might become "I feel upset."
"You make me mad" could be "I feel angry."
"You must be crazy" can be "I don't understand."
"You don't love me anymore" could become "I'm afraid we're drifting apart."

Suppose a friend asks you to pick him up at the airport. You drive 20 miles and wait for the plane. No friend. You decide your friend missed his plane, so you wait three hours for the next flight. No friend. Perplexed and worried, you drive home. The next day, you see your friend downtown.

"What happened?" you ask.
"Oh, I caught an earlier flight."
"You are a rude person," you reply.

Look for the facts, the observable behavior. Everyone will agree that your friend asked you to pick him up, that he did take an earlier flight, and that you did not receive a call from him. But the idea that he is rude is not a fact—it's a judgment.

He might go on to say, "I called your home and no one answered. My mom had a stroke and was rushed to Valley View. I caught the earliest flight I could get." Your judgment no longer fits.

When you saw your friend, you might have said, "I waited and waited at the airport. I was worried about you. I didn't get a call. I feel angry and hurt. I don't want to waste my time. Next time, you can call me when your flight arrives, and I'll be happy to pick you up."

"I" messages don't judge, blame, criticize, or insult. They don't invite the other person to counterattack with more of the same. "I" messages are also more accurate. They report our own thoughts and feelings.

At first, "I" messages might feel uncomfortable or seem forced. That's OK. Use the five ways to say "I" explained on the next page.

Remember that questions are not always questions.
You've heard these "questions" before. A parent asks, "Don't you want to look nice?" Translation: "I wish you'd cut your hair, lose the blue jeans, and put on a tie." Or how about this question from a spouse: "Honey, wouldn't you love to go to an exciting hockey game tonight?" Translation: "I've already bought tickets."

We use questions that aren't questions to sneak our opinions and requests into conversations. "Doesn't it upset you?" means "It upsets me," and "Shouldn't we hang the picture over here?" means "I want to hang the picture over here."

Communication improves when we say, "I'm upset" and "Let's hang the picture over here."

Choose nonverbal messages. How you say something can be more important than what you say. Your tone of voice and gestures add up to a silent message that you send. This message can support, modify, or contradict your words. Your posture, the way you dress, how often you shower, and even the poster hanging on your wall can negate your words before you say them. Most nonverbal behavior is unconscious. We can learn to be aware of it and choose our nonverbal messages. The key is to be clear about our intention and purpose. When we know what we want to say and are committed to getting it across, our inflections, gestures, and words work together and send a unified message.

> *Most nonverbal behavior is unconscious. We can learn to be aware of it and choose our nonverbal messages.*

Notice barriers to sending messages. Sometimes fear stops us from sending messages. We are afraid of other people's reactions, sometimes justifiably. Being truthful doesn't mean being insensitive to the impact that our messages have on others. Tact is a virtue; letting fear prevent communication is not.

Assumptions can also be used as excuses for not sending messages. "He already knows this," we tell ourselves.

Predictions of failure can be barriers to sending, too. "He won't listen," we assure ourselves. That statement might be inaccurate. Perhaps the other person senses that we're angry and listens in a guarded way. Or perhaps he is listening and sending nonverbal messages we don't understand.

Or we might predict, "He'll never do anything about it, even if I tell him." Again, making assumptions can defeat your message before you send it.

It's easy to make excuses for not communicating. If you have fear or some other concern about sending a message, be aware of it. Don't expect the concern to go away. Realize that you can communicate even with your concerns. You can choose to make them a part of the message: "I am going to tell you how I feel, and I'm afraid that you will think it's stupid."

Talking to someone when you don't want to could be a matter of educational survival. A short talk with an advisor, a teacher, or a coworker might solve a problem that could jeopardize your education or your job. The more you advance in your chosen career, the more your success will depend on getting your message across. ◼

→ Five ways to say "I"

An "I" message can include any or all of the following five elements. Be careful when including the last two, since they can contain hidden judgments or threats.

Observations. Describe the facts—the indisputable, observable realities. Talk about what you—or anyone else—can see, hear, smell, taste, or touch. Avoid judgments, interpretations, or opinions. Instead of saying, "You're a slob," say, "Last night's lasagna pan was still on the stove this morning."

Feelings. Describe your own feelings. It is easier to listen to "I feel frustrated" than to "You never help me." Stating how you feel about another's actions can be valuable feedback for that person.

Wants. You are far more likely to get what you want if you say what you want. If someone doesn't know what you want, he doesn't have a chance to help you get it. Ask clearly. Avoid demanding or using the word *need*. Most people like to feel helpful, not obligated. Instead of saying, "Do the dishes when it's your turn, or else!" say, "I want to divide the housework fairly."

Thoughts. Communicate your thoughts, and use caution. Beginning your statement with the word "I" doesn't make it an "I" message. "I think you are a slob" is a "You" judgment in disguise. Instead, say, "I'd have more time to study if I didn't have to clean up so often."

Intentions. The last part of an "I" message is a statement about what you intend to do. Have a plan that doesn't depend on the other person. For example, instead of "From now on we're going to split the dishwashing evenly," you could say, "I intend to do my share of the housework and leave the rest."

journal entry 25

Discovery/Intention Statement

Think about one of your relationships for a few minutes. It can involve a parent, sibling, spouse, child, friend, coworker, hairdresser, or anyone else. In the space below, write down some things that are not working in the relationship. What bugs you? What do you find irritating or unsatisfying?

I discovered that . . .

_____

_____

_____

_____

_____

_____

_____

Now think for a moment about what you want from this relationship. More attention? Less nagging? More openness, trust, financial security, or freedom? Choose a suggestion from this chapter and describe how you could use it to make the relationship work.

I intend to . . .

_____

_____

_____

_____

_____

_____

_____

_____

Communicating
across cultures

With the desire to communicate and gain knowledge of other cultures, you can develop specific skills on three levels.

The first is personal—becoming aware of your own biases. The second is interpersonal—forming alliances with people of other races and cultures. The third is institutional—pointing out the discrimination and racism that you observe in organizations. Be an advocate for change.

It's ineffective to assume that these skills will come to you merely by sharing the same classroom with people from other races and ethnic groups. It's not the responsibility of others to raise your cultural awareness.

Look for common ground. Some goals cross culture lines. Most people want health, physical safety, economic security, and education. Most students want to succeed in school and prepare for a career. They often share the same teachers. They have access to many of the same resources at school. They meet in the classroom, on the athletic field, and at cultural events. To promote cultural understanding, we can become aware of and celebrate our differences. We can also return to our common ground.

Practice looking for common ground. You can cultivate friends from other cultures. Do this through volunteering, serving on committees, or joining study groups—any activity in which people from other cultures are also involved. Then your understanding of other people unfolds in a natural, spontaneous way.

Assume differences in meaning. After first speaking to someone from another culture, don't assume that you've been understood or that you fully understand the other person. The same action can have different meanings at different times, even for members of the same culture. Listen to see if what you spoke is what the other person received.

If you're speaking to someone who doesn't understand English well, keep the following ideas in mind:

- Speak slowly and distinctly.

- To clarify your statement, don't repeat individual words over and over again. Restate your entire message in simple, direct language. Avoid slang.

- Use gestures to accompany your words.

- Since English courses for non-native speakers often emphasize written English, write down what you're saying. Print your message in capitalized block letters.

- Stay calm and avoid sending nonverbal messages that you're frustrated.

Get inside another culture. You might find yourself fascinated by one particular culture. Consider learning as much about it as possible. Immerse yourself in that culture. Read novels, see plays, go to concerts, listen to music, look at art, take courses, learn the language. Find opportunities to speak with members of that culture. Your quest for knowledge will be an opening to new conversations.

Celebrate your own culture. Learning about other cultures does not mean abandoning your own. You could gain new appreciation for it. You might even find out that members of your ethnic group have suffered discrimination. In the process of celebrating your own culture, you can gain valuable insights into the experiences of other people.

Find a translator, mediator, or model. People who move with ease in two or more cultures can help us greatly. Diane de Anda, a professor at the University of California, Los Angeles, speaks of three kinds of people who can communicate across cultures. She calls them *translators, mediators,* and *models.*[3]

A *translator* is someone who is truly bicultural—a person who relates skillfully to people in a mainstream culture and people from a contrasting culture. This person can share her own experiences in overcoming discrimination, learning another language or dialect, and coping with stress. She can point out differences in meaning between cultures and help resolve conflict.

Mediators are people who belong to the dominant or mainstream culture. Unlike translators, they might not be bicultural. However, mediators value diversity and are committed to cultural understanding. Often they are teachers, counselors, tutors, mentors, or social workers.

Models are members of a culture who are positive examples. Models include students from any racial or cultural group who participate in class and demonstrate effective study habits. Models can also include entertainers, athletes, and community leaders.

Your school or your workplace might have people who serve these functions, even if they're not labeled translators, mediators, or models. Some schools have mentor or "bridge" programs that pair new students with teachers of the same race or culture. Students in these programs get coaching in study skills and life skills; they also develop friendships with possible role models. Ask your student counseling service about such programs.

Develop support systems. Students with strong support systems—such as families, friends, churches, self-help groups, and mentors—are using a powerful strategy for success in school. As an exercise, list the support systems that you rely on right now. Also list new support systems you could develop. Support systems can help you bridge culture gaps. With a strong base of support in your own group, you can feel more confident in meeting people outside that group.

Ask for help. If you're unsure about how well you're communicating, ask questions: "I don't know how to make this idea clear for you. How might I communicate better?" "When you look away from me during our conversation, I feel uneasy. Is there something else we need to talk about?" "When you don't ask questions, I wonder if I am being clear. Do you want any more explanation?" Questions such as these can get cultural differences out in the open in a constructive way.

Remember diversity when managing conflict. Keep the following suggestions in mind:

■ *Keep your temper in check.* People from other cultures might shrink from displays of sudden, negative emotion—for example, shouting or pointing.

■ *Deliver your criticisms in private.* People in many Asian and Middle Eastern cultures place value on "saving face" in public.

■ *Give the other person space.* Standing too close can be seen as a gesture of intimidation.

■ *Address people as equals.* For example, don't offer the other person a chair so that she can sit while you stand and talk.

■ *Stick to the point.* When feeling angry or afraid, you might talk more than usual. A person from another culture—especially one who's learning your language—might find it hard to take in everything you're saying. Pause from time to time so that others can ask clarifying questions.

■ *Focus on actions, not personalities.* People are less likely to feel personally attacked when you request specific changes in behavior. "Please show up for work right at 9 a.m." is often more effective than "You're irresponsible."

■ *Be patient.* This guideline applies especially when you're a manager or supervisor. People from other cultures might find it difficult to speak candidly with someone they view as an authority figure. Encourage others to speak. Allowing periods of silence might help.

■ *Take time to comment when others do well.* However, avoid excessive compliments. People from other cultures might be uncomfortable with public praise and even question your sincerity.

Change the institution. As a student, you might see people of color ignored in class. You might see people of a certain ethnic group passed over in job hiring or underrepresented in school organizations. And you might see gay and lesbian students ridiculed or even threatened with violence. One way to stop these actions is to point them out.

Federal civil rights laws, as well as the written policies of most schools, ban racial and ethnic discrimination. If your school receives federal aid, it must set up procedures that protect students against such discrimination. Find out what those procedures are and use them, if necessary.

Throughout recent history, much social change has been fueled by students. When it comes to ending discrimination, you are in an environment where you can make a difference. Run for student government. Write for school publications. Speak at rallies. Express your viewpoint. This is training for citizenship in a multicultural world. ⊠

For more suggestions on
communicating across
cultures, visit

masterstudent.college.hmco.com

The fine art of conflict management

Conflict management is one of the most transferable skills you'll ever learn. Whenever human beings associate, there is the potential for conflict. Following are several strategies that can help. To bring these ideas to life, think of ways to apply them to a current conflict in your education, work, or family life.

State the problem openly. Using "I" messages as explained earlier in this chapter, state the problem. Tell people what you observe, feel, think, want, and intend to do. We can move toward agreement more quickly by laying all of our cards on the table. People are often reluctant to communicate all of their concerns. This very reluctance holds some problems in place.

An alternative is to simply "empty our buckets"— to let the words and the feelings flow spontaneously. In this case, we don't worry about making a perfect "I" statement. We just say the first things that come to mind. This is one way to get all of our cards on the table.

Understand all points of view. If you want to defuse tension or defensiveness, set aside your opinions for a moment. Take the time to understand the other points of view. Sum up those viewpoints in words that the other parties can accept. When people feel that they've been heard, they're often more willing to listen.

Step back from the conflict. Instead of trading personal attacks during a conflict, step back. Defuse the situation by approaching it in a neutral way. Define the conflict as a problem to be solved, not as a contest to be won. Detach. Let go of being "right" and aim for being effective instead.

Let it get worse before it gets better. Sometimes a conflict needs to escalate so that everyone is truly aware of it. Many of us are reluctant to allow this to happen. That's understandable—and it can prevent us from getting to the bottom of the problem.

Commit to the relationship. Begin by affirming your commitment to the other person: "I care about you, and I want this relationship to last. So I'm willing to do whatever it takes to resolve this problem." Also ask the other person for a similar commitment.

You might be unsure of your commitment to the relationship. If so, postpone any further communication for now.

Back up to common ground. List all of the points on which you are *not* in conflict: "I know that we disagree about how much to spend on a new car, but we do agree that the old one needs to be replaced." Often, such comments put the problem in perspective and pave the way for a solution.

Slow down the communication. In times of great conflict, people often talk all at once. Words fly like speeding bullets and no one is really listening. When this happens, choose either to listen or to talk—not both at the same time. Just send your message. Or just receive the other person's message. Usually, this slows down the pace, clears the smoke, and allows everyone to become more levelheaded.

To slow down the communication even more, take a break. Depending upon the level of conflict, that might mean anything from a few minutes to a few days.

Be a complete listener. Listening completely includes asking for more discussion. People will often stop short of their true message. Encourage them to continue by asking for it: "Anything else that you want to say about that? Is something more on your mind right now?"

Get to the point—then elaborate. Making your listener wait in suspense while you build your case can lead to problems. During the interval, the listener might become impatient and more irritable. Or he could imagine something far worse than what you actually intend to say. As an alternative, get to your point right away. When that's done, there is usually the opportunity to provide supporting details.

Recap your message. As we send messages in times of conflict, we might talk for a long time. Sometimes people under emotional stress can't take it all in. And even if they get our whole message, they might not understand which of our points is most important. Before you yield the floor to someone else, review your main messages and repeat your key requests.

Use a mediator. Even an untrained mediator—someone who's not a party to the conflict—can do much to decrease tension. Mediators can help all those involved get their points of view across. In this case, the mediator's role is not to give advice but to keep the discussion on track and moving toward a solution.

Apologize or ask for forgiveness. Conflict often arises from our own errors. We usually don't do these things on purpose. They're just mistakes.

Others might move quickly to end the conflict when we acknowledge this fact, apologize, and ask for forgiveness. This is "spending face"—an alternative to the age-old habit of "saving face." We can simply admit that we are less than perfect by owning up to our mistakes.

Write a letter and send it. What can be difficult to say to another person face to face might be effectively communicated in writing. Letter writing is a way to slow down the communication and ensure that only one person at a time is sending a message.

It's possible for people to misunderstand what you say in a letter. To avoid further problems, make clear what you are *not* saying: "I am saying that I want to be alone for a few days. I am *not* saying that I want you to stay away forever." Saying what you are *not* saying is often useful in face-to-face communication as well.

Write a letter and don't send it. Consider a way to get the problem off your chest and the upset out of your system without beating up the other person: Write the nastiest, meanest letter you can imagine. Let all of your frustration, anger, and venom flow onto the page. Be as mean and blaming as possible. Then take the letter and destroy it. Your writing has served its purpose. Chances are that you've calmed down and are ready to engage in skillful conflict management.

Note: If you're composing the letter while using e-mail software, do not insert the complete address of the recipient. This will prevent you from accidentally sending the letter.

Permit the emotion. Crying is OK. Being upset is all right. Feeling angry is often appropriate. Allowing other people to see the strength of our feelings can go a long way toward clearing up the conflict. Emotion is part of life and an important part of any communication. Just allow the full range of your feelings. Often what's on the far side of

WRITE AN "I" MESSAGE

First, pick something about school that irritates you. Then pretend that you are talking to the person who is associated with this irritation. In the space below, write down what you would say to this person as a "You" message.

_____

_____

_____

Now write the same complaint as an "I" message. Include at least the first three elements suggested in "Five ways to say 'I.'"

_____

_____

_____

anger is love. When we clear out the resentment and hostility, we might find genuine compassion in its place.

Agree to disagree. Sometimes we say all we have to say. We do all of the problem solving we can do. We get all points of view across. And the conflict still remains, staring us right in the face. What's left is to recognize that honest disagreement is a fact of life. We can peacefully coexist with other people—and respect them—even though we don't agree on fundamental issues. Conflict can be accepted even when it is not resolved.

Do nothing. Sometimes we worsen a conflict by insisting that it be solved immediately. An alternative is to sit tight and wait things out. Some conflicts resolve themselves with the passage of time.

See the conflict within you. When we're angry or upset, we can take a minute to look inside. Perhaps we were ready to take offense, waiting to pounce on something the other person said. Perhaps, without realizing it, we did something to create the conflict. Or maybe the other person is simply saying what we don't want to admit is true. When these things happen, we can shine a light on our own thinking. A simple spot check might help the conflict disappear—right before our eyes. ▨

For more ways to resolve conflict, visit   (masterstudent.college.hmco.com)

Create high-performing teams

Working in teams helps you to develop several transferable skills. One is sociability—taking an interest in people, valuing what they think, and understanding how they feel. Another is understanding social systems in organizations and operating effectively in them. Teamwork also gives you a chance to practice all the communication skills explored in this chapter.

In the workplace, teams abound. To research their book *When Teams Work Best,* Frank LaFasto and Carl Larson studied 600 teams. These ranged from the Mount Everest climbing team to the teams that produced the Boeing 747 airplane—the world's largest aircraft and a product of 75,000 blueprints.[4]

LaFasto and Larson found that empowered teams set their own goals, plan their own schedule, and make decisions democratically. They also design their work-space and choose their own members.

You might wonder how to make all this happen. One answer is to take your cue from the word *empowered* and review the Power Processes included throughout this book. Following are ways you can use several of them to supercharge your next team project.

Discover what you want

When forming a team, look for a fit between individual goals and the team's mission. Team members might want formal recognition for taking part in the project and meeting its objectives. People naturally ask, "What's in this for me?" Provide answers to that question. Emphasize the chance to develop marketable skills by joining the team.

Equally important is ensuring that the organization knows what it wants from the team. To promote effective results, ask your company's executives to explain the team's purpose, its expected results, and how it will be held accountable. Also ask for enough support—in terms of time, money, and other resources—for the team to produce those results.

Ideas are tools

Teams tend to fizzle when they create new ideas that meet with immediate skepticism or outright rejection. After proposing changes to a company's existing policies and procedures, team members might face resistance: "This suggestion will never work." "That's just not the way we do things around here." "We can't break with tradition."

Managers can prevent this outcome by asking pointed questions before a team convenes its first meeting: Are we truly interested in change? Are we willing to act on what the team recommends? Or are we just looking for a team to reinforce our current practices?

People who want a team to succeed will treat its ideas as tools. Instead of automatically looking for what's wrong with a proposal, look for potential applications. Even a proposal that seems outlandish at first might become workable with a few modifications. In an empowered team, all ideas are welcome, problems are freely admitted, and any item is open for discussion.

Be here now

Concentration and focused attention are attributes of effective students—and effective teams. When a team tries to tackle too many problems or achieve too many goals, it gets distracted. Members can forget the team's purpose and lose their enthusiasm for the project. You can help restore focus by asking: "What is the single most important goal that our team can meet?" and "What is the single most important thing we can do *now* to meet that goal?"

Another source of team distraction is a member who doesn't perform—someone who comes to meetings unprepared, consistently fails to complete individual assignments, or attacks new ideas. Effective teams have a leader who focuses the group on its agenda and tactfully asks nonperforming members to change their behavior.

from the

ERICA VOLINI, CONSULTING MANAGER:

Consulting is equivalent to problem solving: the ability to take a complex issue and break it into easy-to-manage parts. Consulting projects are almost always executed in teams. The teams are often made up of professionals with varying skill sets, roles, and accountabilities. Being able to work within that team to accomplish a set of tasks is key. Without the appropriate level of teamwork, it would not be possible to get the job done. A great team player is able to leverage every individual's capabilities to maximize the team's performance.

Love your problems

Many teams develop problems—lack of clarity about their mission, missed goals, personality conflicts, and more. Team members can learn to love each problem as a stimulus for learning.

As you create team projects, make time for mileposts in the learning cycle. Cycle through the following steps several times during the life of your team:

- *Reflecting*—setting goals, assigning tasks to individual team members, and meeting regularly to discuss what's working well about the team and what can be improved.

- *Doing*—carrying out assigned tasks and meeting due dates specified in the work plan.

- *Experiencing*—observing the results of the team's actions, remaining sensitive to the feelings of coworkers and customers.

→ Sustaining business relationships

Many workplace relationships are time limited. Teams meet regularly to accomplish an objective—and then disband. Even though you may feel intensely connected to coworkers for a while, you can easily lose touch with them over the years.

The people you meet in a work context get to know you in a different way than do family or friends. Coworkers observe your work performance directly. They can give an objective view of your skills and honest feedback that stands the test of time. They can also help you keep failures in perspective and celebrate your workplace success. You can do the following to enjoy the benefits of sustained business relationships.

Rank your business relationships. Take a quick inventory of people you've worked with in the jobs you've held to date. List the people who served as career mentors, models, or coaches. Add anyone else whose presence creates value in your professional life. These are your key business relationships.

Keep track of people. Start with your Rolodex or address book. Once a year, review and update the entries. Make sure that you've got current addresses, phone numbers, and e-mail addresses for the people who rank high on your list of business relationships.

Stay in contact. Remember the time-management technique of distinguishing between tasks that are urgent and those that are important. Sustaining business relationships may not be an urgent task today. Yet it can be one of the most important things you do over the long run. Make time for staying in contact.

Keep boundaries in mind. Business relationships differ from personal relationships. Among friends and family members, you are on equal footing, and your relationships are based on strong emotional ties. In the workplace, you might stay in contact with people who are not your equals in an organizational setting—a former boss, a person you used to supervise, or a coworker who moves to a competing company. While these people can become close friends over time, they may expect to retain certain limits on emotional intimacy and physical contact. Respect those boundaries.

Put the relationship first. Sustaining business relationships goes beyond networking. Your network consists largely of "contacts"—people who could help you find a new job or change careers someday. Although long-term business relationships can often help you in these ways, the people involved are often more than contacts. These are people whom you value for themselves, beyond any favors that they can do. Let them know how important they are to you.

- *Thinking*—abstracting core insights from the team's experience and looking for ways to apply those insights to the whole organization.

To promote team success, combine the learning styles of individual members in complementary ways. If you're skilled at reflecting, for example, find someone who excels at doing. Also seek people who can reflect on the team's experience and think in more abstract ways. Pooling different styles allows you to draw on everyone's strengths.

Notice your pictures

During much of the previous century, many large businesses and nonprofit organizations were organized as hierarchies with multiple layers—executives, middle-level managers, supervisors, and employees. People who worked for such a company had jobs with clearly defined and limited responsibilities. Collaborations among employees in different departments were rare.

Teams present a different picture of how to operate a workplace. And old pictures die hard. Companies may give lip service to the idea of teams and yet fall back into traditional practices. Managers might set up teams but offer little training to help people function in this new working environment.

You can prepare for this situation now. While you are in school, seize opportunities to work collaboratively. Form study groups. Enroll in classes that include group projects. Show up for your next job with teamwork skills. At the same time, remember that some of your coworkers may not share your assumptions about the value of teams. By demonstrating your abilities, you help them to form new pictures. ▨

desk of...

from the

ROSS JACKSON, HELP DESK TECHNICIAN:

Getting involved on campus in extracurricular activities helped to prepare me for working with people and forming sustaining relationships. I've transferred these practices to the workplace. As treasurer of one of the organizations I belonged to, I learned how to work in groups to accomplish goals, and I was able to practice taking charge of different types of situations.

journal entry 26

Discovery/Intention Statement

There are things we think about telling people, but don't. Examine your relationships and complete the following statements.

I discovered that I am not communicating about . . .

_____

_____

with . . .

_____

_____

I discovered that I am not communicating about . . .

_____

_____

with . . .

_____

_____

I discovered that I am not communicating about . . .

_____

_____

with . . .

_____

_____

Now choose one idea from this chapter that can open communication with these people in these areas. Describe below how you will use this idea.

I intend to . . .

_____

_____

_____

_____

V.I.P.'S (VERY IMPORTANT PERSONS)

Step 1 Under the column below titled "Name," write the names of at least seven people who have positively influenced your life. They might be relatives, friends, teachers, coworkers, or perhaps persons you have never met. (Complete each step before moving on.)

Step 2 In the next column, rate your gratitude for this person's influence (from 1 to 5, with 1 being a little grateful and 5 being extremely grateful).

Step 3 In the third column, rate how fully you have communicated your appreciation to this person (again, 1 to 5, with 1 being not communicated and 5 being fully communicated).

Step 4 In the final column, put a U to indicate the persons with whom you have unfinished business (such as an important communication that you have not yet sent).

	Name	Grateful (1–5)	Communicated (1–5)	U
1.				
2.				
3.				
4.				
5.				
6.				
7.				

Step 5 Now select two persons with U's beside their names and write them a letter. Express the love, tenderness, and joy you feel toward them. Tell them exactly how they have helped change your life and how glad you are that they did.

Step 6 You also have an impact on others. Make a list of people whose lives you have influenced. Consider sharing with these people why you enjoy being a part of their lives.

_____

_____

_____

_____

_____

_____

_____

_____

Three phases of effective writing

Writing helps you organize information, adapt your ideas to different audiences, and persuade other people to accept your suggestions. Writing well also enhances your other language abilities—thinking, speaking, listening, and reading. These are highly transferable skills that can help you advance in any career. Use this three-phase process for writing any paper, presentation, or speech.

PHASE ONE
Getting ready to write

Refine initial ideas

Select a topic and working title. It's easy to put off writing if you have a hard time choosing a topic. However, it is almost impossible to make a wrong choice at this stage. Just choose any subject. You can choose again later.

If you are preparing materials for a course, use your instructor's guidelines for the paper or speech. Write down a list of topics that interest you. List as many of these as you can think of in two minutes. Then choose one. If you can't decide, then pick one at random. To avoid getting stuck on this step, set a precise timeline: "I will choose a topic by 4 p.m. on Wednesday."

The most common pitfall is selecting a topic that's too broad. "Harriet Tubman" is not a useful topic for your American history paper. Instead, consider "Harriet Tubman's activities as a Union spy during the Civil War." Your topic statement can function as a working title.

Write a thesis statement. Clarify what you want to say by summarizing it in one concise sentence. This sentence, called a thesis statement, refines your working title. It also helps in making a preliminary outline.

You might write a thesis statement such as "Harriet Tubman's activities with the Underground Railroad led to a relationship with the Union army during the Civil War." A statement that's clear and to the point can make your paper easier to write. Remember, you can always rewrite your thesis statement as you learn more about your topic.

A thesis statement differs from a topic statement. Like newspaper headlines, a thesis statement makes an assertion or describes an action. It is expressed in a complete sentence, including a verb. "Diversity" is a topic. "Cultural diversity in the workplace is valuable" is a thesis statement.

Note: Narrowing your topic and writing a thesis statement are not skills that you're meant to use in school and then forget. These skills also apply to any formal writing or speaking you do on the job. In a business setting you may only have a few minutes of meeting time to get your point across. Workers who ascend to jobs with higher salaries and prestige are those who use language efficiently, with precision and power.

Pretend that you are a sales representative and that you have only 30 seconds to sell a potential customer on your idea. State your topic and write your thesis with that time limit in mind.

Consider your purpose

Effective writing flows from a purpose. It may help to discuss the purpose of your assignment with your instructor or your supervisor at work. Also think about how you'd like your reader or listener to respond after considering your ideas. Do you want him to think differently, to feel differently, or to take a certain action? Do you need to persuade management of the need for new resources or funding for a product or service?

Your writing strategy is greatly affected by how you answer these questions. If you want someone to think differently, make your writing clear and logical. Support your assertions with evidence. If you want someone to feel differently, consider crafting a story. Write about a character your audience can empathize with, and tell how he resolves a problem that they can relate to. And if your purpose is to move the reader into action, explain exactly what steps to take and offer solid benefits for doing so.

To clarify your purpose, state it in one sentence. For example, "The purpose of this paper is to define the term *success* in such a clear and convincing way that I win a scholarship from Houghton Mifflin."

Do initial research

At this stage, the objective of your research is not to uncover specific facts about your topic. That comes later. For now, just discover the structure of your topic—its major divisions and branches. Also list sources of ideas and information for your paper, including published material, interviews with experts, and your personal experience.

Outline

An outline keeps you from wandering off the topic. To start an outline, gather a stack of 3x5 cards and brainstorm ideas you want to include in your paper. Write one phrase or sentence per card. Then experiment with the cards. Group them into separate stacks, each stack representing one major category. After that, arrange the stacks in order. Finally, arrange the cards within each stack in a logical order. Rearrange them until you discover an organization that you like. If you write on a computer, consider using outlining software.

Do in-depth research

Now it's time to take detailed notes on your key sources. See Chapter Five: Notes—especially "Taking notes while reading."

A common mistake that beginning writers make is to hold their noses, close their eyes, and jump into the writing process with both feet first—and few facts. Avoid this temptation by gathering more information than you think you can use.

Also remember that you can begin writing even before your research is complete. The act of writing creates ideas and reveals areas where more research is needed. You might instead get a strong sense of how to write just one small section of your paper or speech. When this happens, write.

FIRST DRAFT

PHASE TWO
Writing a first draft

To create your draft, gather your notes and arrange them to follow your outline. Then write about the ideas in your notes.

Write in paragraphs, one idea per paragraph. If you have organized your notes logically, related facts will appear close to each other. As you complete this task, keep the following suggestions in mind.

Remember that the first draft is not for keeps. You can save quality for later, when you revise. Your goal at this point is simply to generate lots of material. Don't worry about grammar, punctuation, or spelling as you write your first draft. Write as if you were explaining the subject to a friend. Let the words flow. The very act of writing will release creative energy. It's perfectly all right to crank out a draft that you heavily rewrite or even throw away.

Write freely. Many writers prefer to get their first draft down quickly. Their advice is just to keep writing, much as in free writing. You can pause occasionally to glance at your notes and outline. The idea is to avoid stopping to edit your work. You can save that for the next step.

Sometimes you can write a first draft without referring back to your notes and outline. If you've immersed yourself in the topic, chances are that much of the information is already bubbling up near the surface of your mind anyway. Later, when you edit, you can go back to your notes and correct any errors.

Be yourself. Let go of the urge to sound "official" or "scholarly," and write in a natural voice instead. Address your thoughts not to the teacher but to an intelligent student or coworker. Visualize this person and choose the three or four most important things you'd say to him about the topic. This helps you avoid the temptation to write merely to impress.

Let your inner writer take over. There might be times when ideas come to you spontaneously—when thoughts flow from your head to your hand without conscious effort. These are moments of pure joy. Often, those moments come just after a period of feeling stuck.

Ease into it. Some people find that it works well to forget the word *writing*. Instead, they ease into the task with activities that help generate ideas. You can free-associate, cluster, meditate, daydream, doodle, draw diagrams, visualize the event you want to describe, talk into a voice recorder—anything that gets you started.

Get physical. Writing is physical, like jogging or playing tennis. You can move your body in ways that are in tune with the flow of your ideas. While working on the first draft, take breaks. Go for a walk. Speak or sing your ideas out loud. From time to time, practice relaxation techniques and breathe deeply.

Hide it in your drawer for a while. Schedule time for rewrites before you begin, and schedule at least one day in between revisions so that you can let the material sit. On Tuesday night, you might think your writing sings the song of beautiful language. On Wednesday, you will see that those same words, such as the phrase "sings the song of beautiful language," belong in the trash basket.

Ideally, a writer will revise a document two or three times, make a clean copy of those revisions, then let the last revised draft sit for at least three or four days. The brain needs that much time to disengage itself from the project. Obvious grammatical mistakes, awkward constructions, and lapses in logic are hidden from us when we are in the middle of the creative process. Give yourself time to step back, and then go over your writing one last time before starting the third phase of the writing process.

PHASE THREE
Revising your draft

People who rewrite care. They care about the reader. They care about precise language and careful thinking. And they care about themselves. They know that the act of rewriting teaches them more about the topic than almost any other step in the process.

There's a difference in pace between writing a first draft and revising it. Keep in mind the saying "Write in haste, revise at leisure." When you edit and revise, slow down and take a microscope to your work. One guideline is to allow 50 percent of writing time for planning,

research, and writing the first draft. Then give the remaining 50 percent to revising.

An effective way to revise your writing is to read it out loud. The eyes tend to fill in the blanks in our own writing. The combination of voice and ears forces us to pay attention to the details.

Another technique is to have a friend look over your document. Remember, when other people criticize or review your work, they're not attacking you. They're just commenting on your paper.

For efficient revision, cycle through the following steps.

Cut

Cut passages that don't contribute to your purpose. It might not pay to polish individual words, phrases, and sentences right now—especially if you end up deleting them later. To save time, focus instead on deciding which words you want to keep and which ones you want to let go.

Look for excess baggage. Avoid at all costs and at all times the really, really terrible mistake of using way too many unnecessary words, a mistake that some student writers often make when they sit down to write papers for the various courses in which they participate at the fine institutions of higher learning that they are fortunate enough to attend. (Example: The previous sentence could be edited to "Avoid unnecessary words.")

Note: For maximum efficiency, make the larger cuts first—sections, chapters, pages. Then go for the smaller cuts—paragraphs, sentences, phrases, words.

Keep in mind that cutting a passage means just for now, for this paper, for this assignment. You might want to keep a file of deleted writings to save for future use.

Paste

In deleting passages, you've probably removed some of the original transitions and connecting ideas from your draft. The next task is to rearrange what's left of your paper or speech so that it flows logically. Look for consistency within paragraphs and for transitions from paragraph to paragraph and section to section.

If your draft doesn't hang together, reorder your ideas. Imagine yourself with a pair of scissors and glue, cutting the paper into scraps—one scrap for each point. Then paste these points down in a new, more logical order.

Fix

Now it's time to look at individual words and phrases.

In general, rely on nouns and verbs. Using too many adjectives and adverbs weakens your message and adds

☐ Avoid ~~at all costs and at all times the really, really terrible mistake of~~ using ~~way too many~~ unnecessary words. ~~a mistake that some student writers often make when they sit down to write papers for the various courses in which they participate at the fine institutions of higher learning which they are fortunate to attend.~~

unnecessary bulk to your writing. Write about the details and be specific. Use active verbs. Whenever possible, describe people *doing* something.

Also, define any terms that the reader might not know, putting them in plain English whenever you can.

Prepare

In a sense, any paper is a sales effort. If you hand in a document with wrinkled jeans, its hair tangled and unwashed and its shoes untied, the intended reader is less likely to buy it. To avoid this situation, format your paper following accepted standards for margin widths, endnotes, title pages, and other details.

When writing in school, ask your instructor for specific instructions on how to cite the sources used in writing your paper. You can find useful guidelines in the *MLA Handbook for Writers of Research Papers,* a book from the Modern Language Association. Also visit the MLA Web site at **http://www.mla.org/style_faq**.

In the workplace, ask your supervisor about a recommended format for written documents. Many organizations publish their own style guides. Others follow recommendations from a well-known guide such as *The Chicago Manual of Style, The Associated Press Stylebook and Libel Manual,* or the *APA (American Psychological Association) Publication Manual.*

If you "cut and paste" material from a Web page directly into your paper, be sure to place that material in quotation marks and cite the source. And before referencing an e-mail message, verify the sender's identity. Remember that anyone sending e-mail can pretend to be someone else.

Use quality paper for your final version. For an even more professional appearance, bind your paper with a paper or plastic cover.

Proof

As you ease down the homestretch, read your revised paper one more time. This time, go for the big picture and look for:

- A clear thesis statement.

- Sentences that introduce your topic, guide the reader through the major sections of your paper, and summarize your conclusions.

- Details—such as quotations, examples, and statistics—that support your conclusions.

- Lean sentences that have been purged of needless words.

- Plenty of action verbs and concrete, specific nouns.

Finally, look over your paper with an eye for spelling and grammar mistakes.

When you're through proofreading, take a minute to savor the result. You've just witnessed something of a miracle—the mind attaining clarity and resolution. That's the aha! in writing. ◪

journal entry 27

Discovery Statement

This Journal Entry is for people who avoid writing. As with any anxiety, you can approach writing anxiety by accepting it fully. Realize that it's OK to feel anxious about writing. Others have shared this feeling, and many people have worked with it successfully.

Begin by telling the truth. Describe exactly what happens when you start to write. What thoughts or images run through your mind? Do you feel any tension or discomfort in your body? Where? Let the thoughts and images come to the surface without resistance. Complete the following statement.

When I begin to write, I discover that I . . .

_____

_____

_____

_____

_____

Giving credit where credit is due

Avoiding the high cost of PLAGIARISM

There's a branch of law known as *intellectual property.* This field is based on the idea that original works—such as speeches, publications, and works of art—are not free for the taking. Anyone who borrows from these works is obligated to acknowledge the work's creator. This is the purpose behind copyrights, patents, and trademarks.

Using another person's words or pictures without giving proper credit is called *plagiarism.* This is a real concern for anyone who writes, including students. Plagiarism amounts to stealing someone else's work and claiming it as your own—the equivalent of cheating on a test.

People who plagiarize are making an ethical decision with negative consequences. Higher education consists of a community of scholars who trust each other to speak and write with integrity. Plagiarism undermines this trust. The consequences can range from a failing grade to expulsion from school. In the workplace, plagiarism can lead to lawsuits, the loss of a job, and a loss of reputation.

There are several ways to avoid plagiarism when writing. If your writing includes a passage, identifiable phrase, sequence of ideas, or visual image created by another person, be sure to acknowledge this fact.

Also be careful as you take notes. Clearly distinguish your own ideas from the ideas of others. If you use a direct quote from another writer or speaker, put that person's words in quotation marks. Also note details about the source of the quotation: author, publication title, publisher, date, and page number. Many instructors will require you to add endnotes to your paper with this information, so include it with each quotation in your notes. Ask your instructor for examples of the format to use for endnotes.

If you do research online, you might find yourself copying sentences or paragraphs from a Web page and pasting them directly into your notes. This is the same as taking direct quotes from your source. To avoid plagiarism, identify such passages in an obvious way. Besides enclosing them in quotation marks, you could format them in a different font or color. Also capture relevant information about the Web page where the passages originally appeared: author, title, sponsoring organization, URL, publication date, revision date, and date that you accessed that page. For more information crediting Internet sources, go online to the Modern Language Association's Web site at **http://www.mla.org/ publications/style/style_faq/style_faq4**.

Instead of using a direct quote, you might choose to paraphrase an author's words. Paraphrasing means restating the original passage in different words, usually making it shorter and simpler. Paraphrase with care. Students who copy a passage word for word and then just rearrange or delete a few phrases are running a serious risk of plagiarism. Consider this paragraph:

Higher education also offers you the chance to learn how to learn. In fact, that's the subject of this book. Employers value the person who is a "quick study" when it comes to learning a new job. That makes your ability to learn a marketable skill.

Following is an improper paraphrase of that passage:

With higher education comes the chance to learn how to learn. Employers value the person who is a "quick study" when it comes to learning a new job. Your ability to learn is a marketable skill.

A better paraphrase of the same passage would be:

The author notes that when we learn how to learn, we gain a skill that is valued by employers.

Be sure to credit paraphrases in the same way that you credit direct quotes.

When you use the same sequence of ideas as one of your sources—even if you haven't summarized, para- phrased, or quoted—cite that source.

Finally, submit only your own original work, not materials that have been written or revised by someone else.

Out of a concern for avoiding plagiarism, some students go overboard in crediting their sources. You do not need to credit wording that's wholly your own. Nor do you need to credit general ideas. For example, the suggestion that people use a to-do list to plan their time is a general idea. When you use your own words to describe to-do lists, there's no need to credit a source. But if you borrow someone else's words or images to explain this idea, do give credit. ✖

Library
the buried treasure

Getting familiar with the resources and services at campus and community libraries will help you succeed in school. Knowing ways to unearth a library's treasures can enhance your writing, boost your presentation skills, help you plan your career, and enable you to continue learning for the rest of your life.

Remember the best library resource. Libraries give you access to one resource that goes beyond the pages of a book or a site on the Web. That resource is a living person called a librarian.

Librarians have different specialties. Start with a reference librarian, who can usually tell you whether the library has the material that you want. This person might suggest a different library or direct you to another source, such as a business, community agency, or government office.

Librarians are trained explorers who can guide you on your expedition into the information jungle. Asking them for help can save you hours.

Take a tour. Before you start your next research project, take some time to investigate your campus or community library. Start with a library orientation session or tour. Step into each room and ask about what's available there. Find out whether the library houses any special collections or provides access to primary sources that are related to your major.

Search the catalog. A library's catalog lists the materials available in its collections. These listings used to be kept on index cards. Today, libraries catalog their materials on computers; some even include listings for several libraries. To find materials in a library's collections, do a key word search—much like using a search engine on the Internet.

The catalog is an alphabetical listing that is cross-referenced by subject, author, and title. Each listing carries the author's name, the title, the publisher, the date of publication, the number of pages and illustrations, the Library of Congress or Dewey decimal system number (for locating materials), and sometimes a brief description of the material.

Inspect the collection. When inspecting a library's collections, look for materials such as the following:

- *Encyclopedias*—Leading print encyclopedias like *Encyclopaedia Britannica*. Specialized encyclopedias cover many fields and include, for example, *Encyclopedia of Psychology, Encyclopedia of the Biological Sciences, Encyclopedia of Asian History,* and *McGraw-Hill Encyclopedia of Science and Technology.*

- *Biographies*—Read accounts of people's lives in biographical works such as *Who's Who, Dictionary of American Biography,* and *Biography Index: A Cumulative Index to Biographical Material in Books and Magazines.*

- *Critical works*—Read what scholars have to say about works of art and literature in *Oxford Companion* volumes (such as *Oxford Companion to Art* and *Oxford Companion to African American Literature*).

- *Statistics and government documents*—Among many useful sources are *Statistical Abstract of the United States, Current Index to Statistics, Handbook of Labor Statistics, Occupational Outlook Handbook,* U.S. Census publications, and *Digest of Educational Statistics.*

- *Almanacs, atlases, and gazetteers*—For population statistics and boundary changes, see *The World Almanac, Countries of the World,* or *Information Please.*

- *Dictionaries*—Consult *American Heritage Dictionary of the English Language, Oxford English Dictionary, Facts on File* specialized dictionaries, and other specialized dictionaries such as *Dictionary of Literary Terms and Literary Theory* and *Dictionary of the Social Sciences*.

- *Indexes and databases*—Databases contain publication information and an abstract, or sometimes the full text, of an article, available for downloading or printing from your computer. Your library houses print and CD-ROM databases and subscribes to some online databases; others are accessible through online library catalogs or Web links.

- *Reference works in specific subject areas*—These cover a vast range. Examples include the *Oxford Companion to Art, Encyclopedia of the Biological Sciences,* and *Concise Oxford Companion to Classical Literature*. Ask a librarian for more.

- *Periodical articles*—Find articles in periodicals (works issued periodically, such as scholarly journals, magazines, and newspapers) by using a periodical index. Use electronic indexes for recent works, print indexes for earlier works—especially for works written before 1980. Indexes might provide abstracts; some, such as Lexis-Nexis Academic Universe, Infotrac, OCLC FirstSearch, and New York Times Ondisc, provide the full text of articles.

Access computer resources. Many libraries offer computers with Internet access. These computers are often available on a first-come, first-served basis, for free or for a nominal cost.

Also remember that the Web gives you access to the online resources of many libraries. Some useful sites are Library of Congress (**http://lcweb.loc.gov**), Smithsonian Institution Libraries (**http://www.sil.si.edu/**), New York Public Library (**http://www.nypl.org/**), Internet Public Library (**http://www.ipl.org**), and WWW Virtual Library (**http://www.vlib.org**).[5]

Gain information literacy. *Information literacy* is the ability to locate, evaluate, interpret, and document sources of ideas and facts. Improving your ability to access information efficiently will help promote your success in school and beyond. The SCANS report from the U.S. Department of Labor specifically mentions acquiring and evaluating information as necessary skills for the workplace.

Start with the distinction between primary and secondary sources. *Primary sources* are often the researcher's dream. These are firsthand materials such as personal journals, letters, speeches, reports of scientific research, scholarly articles, field observations, archeological digs, and original works of art.

Secondary sources explain and comment on primary sources. Examples are nationally circulated newspapers such as the *Washington Post, New York Times*, and *Los Angeles Times*. Magazines with wide circulation but substantial treatment of current issues—such as the *Atlantic Monthly* and *Scientific American*—are secondary sources. So are general reference works such as the *Encyclopedia Britannica*.

Secondary sources are useful places to start your research by getting an overview of your topic. They might even be all you need for informal research. Other research projects in higher education—major papers, presentations, theses, or manuscripts you want to publish—will call on you to find primary sources.

Once you find the sources you want, inspect each one. With print sources, look at the preface, publication data, table of contents, bibliography, glossary, endnotes, and index. (Nonprint materials, including online documents, often include similar types of information.) Also scan any headings, subheadings, and summaries. If you have time, read a chapter or section. Then evaluate sources according to their:

- *Relevance*—Look for sources that deal directly with your research questions. If you're in doubt about the relevance of a particular source, ask yourself: "Will this material help me achieve the purpose of my research and support my thesis?"

- *Currentness*—Notice the published date of your source material (usually found in the front matter on the copyright page). If your topic is time-sensitive, set some guidelines about how current you want your sources to be.

- *Credibility*—Scan the source for biographical information about the author. Look for education, training, and work experience that qualifies this person to publish on the topic. Also notice any possible sources of bias, such as political affiliations or funding sources that might color the author's point of view.

Keen researchers see facts and relationships. They focus their attention on the details, then discover unifying patterns. Far from being a mere academic exercise, library research can evolve into a path of continual discovery. ◪

Finding what you want on the Internet

Go to:
:-) forward >
search keyword
.com
< back WWW .http:/
:-)

Imagine a library with millions of books—a place where anyone can bring in materials and place them on any shelf or even toss them randomly on the floor. That's something like the way information accumulates on the Internet. Finding your way through this maze can be a challenge. But it's worth it.

As online publishing and research expand, your ability to locate information efficiently can help you save time at work and stay up-to-date in your career field.

Experiment with different search sites. When searching the Internet—especially the World Wide Web—you can use several tools:

- *Directories* such as Yahoo.com offer extensive lists of Web pages, all grouped by topic. You might find it helpful to use directories when starting your research. Since these sites are organized by subject, you can often get results that are relevant to your purpose. Go to a search engine later in your research, when you've narrowed down your topic.

- *Search engines* are more like indexes. These tools send out "spiders"—computer programs that "crawl" the Web and other parts of the Internet to find sites that relate to a specific topic.

- *Meta search engines* draw on the capabilities of several search engines at once. Examples of meta search engines include Dogpile.com and Metacrawler.com. These tools can be useful when directories and conventional search engines come up with disappointing results.

Each search site has different features. Some, such as Google.com, combine aspects of directories and search engines. Look for links on each search site that explain how to use advanced search capabilities. In any case, find a few search sites you like and use them consistently. That way you get to know each one well and capitalize on its strengths.

Treat searches as dialogues with your computer. When doing research, start with a question you want to answer, such as "What mutual funds invest in bonds issued by the U.S. Treasury?" Write the question out as precisely as you can.

Next, identify the key words in this question—for example, *mutual funds, bonds,* and *U.S. Treasury.* Type these words into the blank box that appears on your search site's main page. Be sure you spell your key words correctly. Hit the return key or "Search" button on the screen and wait for your computer to answer with a "hit list" of relevant Web pages.

Check three to five of these pages to see if they include answers to your original question. If not, rephrase your question and search again with different key words.

Use Boolean operators. Boolean operators include the words *AND, OR,* and *NOT.* For example, if you type *portfolios AND résumés,* you'll get a list of Web sites that refer to both portfolios and résumés. *Portfolios OR résumés* will give you sites that refer to either topic. *Portfolios NOT résumés* will give you sites that relate only to portfolios. With some search tools, a plus sign (+) functions like the term *AND.* A minus sign (−) functions in the same way as the term *NOT.*

Dig into the "invisible Web." As you use the Web for research, remember that some pages elude conventional search engines. Examples are pages that are searchable only *within* a particular Web site—for example, databases that you can access exclusively from the U.S. Census Bureau site. A popular name for this group of "hidden" pages is the *invisible Web.*

Over time, the size of the invisible Web will shrink as more sophisticated search engines appear. For now, check out search sites that mine all of those hard-to-find pages—for example, *Invisible-Web.net* (**www.invisible-web.net**) and *The Invisible Web* (**www.invisibleweb.net**). ✖

exercise 26

EVALUATE SEARCH SITES

Use a computer to access several popular search sites on the Web. Possibilities include:

Alta Vista	www.altavista.com
Ask Jeeves	www.ask.com
Dogpile	www.dogpile.com
Excite	www.excite.com
Google	www.google.com
HotBot	www.hotbot.com
Yahoo	www.yahoo.com

Choose a specific topic that you'd like to research—preferably one related to a paper or other assignment that you will complete this term. Identify key words for this topic and enter them in several search sites. (Open up a different window in your browser for each site.) Be sure to use the same key words each time that you search.

Next, evaluate the search sites by comparing the results that you got and the following factors:

- Simplicity of the site's design and use.
- Number of results you got.
- Presence of duplicate results.
- Quality of results—that is, their relevance to your topic.
- Number of sponsored results (links to the search site's advertisers or paid sponsors) and how clearly these results are identified.
- Number of results that are "dead" links (leading you to inactive Web sites).
- Options for doing advanced searches and the ease of using those options.

Based on your evaluation, list your favorite search sites here:

_____

_____

_____

_____

_____

_____

Writing and delivering speeches

J ust think of all the times you have listened to instructors, lecturers, politicians, and others. Remember all the wonderful daydreams you have had during their speeches.

Your audiences are like you. The way you plan and present your speech can determine the number of audience members who will stay with you until the end. Polishing your speaking and presentation skills can also help you think on your feet and communicate clearly. These are skills that you can use in any career you choose. The SCANS report on necessary workplace skills (see page 8) specifically lists speaking. In addition, speaking is essential to other key skills, including:

- Participating as a member of a team.
- Teaching others.
- Serving clients and customers.
- Exercising leadership.
- Negotiating to reach agreements.

Organize your presentation

To make an effective speech, be precise about your purpose and main point, or thesis. Speeches can inform, persuade, motivate, or entertain. Choose what you want to do, let your audience know what your intention is, and state your thesis early on.

Consider the length of your presentation. Plan on delivering about 100 words per minute. This is only a general guideline, however, so time yourself as you practice your presentation. Aim for a lean presentation—enough words to make your point but not so many as to make your audience restless. Be brief, be seated, and leave your listeners wanting more.

Writing a speech is similar to writing a paper. Speeches are usually organized in three main parts: the introduction, the main body, and the conclusion.

Write the introduction. Rambling speeches with no clear point or organization put audiences to sleep. Solve this problem with your introduction. The following introduction, for example, reveals the thesis and exactly what's coming. The speech will have three distinct parts, each in logical order:

Dog fighting is a cruel sport. I intend to describe exactly what happens to the animals, tell you who is doing this, and show you how you can stop this inhumane practice.

Whenever possible, talk about things that hold your interest. Include your personal experiences and start with a bang! Consider this introduction to a speech on the subject of world hunger:

I'm very honored to be here with you today. I intend to talk about malnutrition and starvation. First, I want to outline the extent of these problems, then I will discuss some basic assumptions concerning world hunger, and finally I will propose some solutions.

You can almost hear the snores from the audience. Following is a rewrite:

More people have died from hunger in the past five years than have been killed in all of the wars, revolutions, and murders in the past 150 years. Yet there is enough food to go around. I'm honored to be here with you today to discuss solutions to this problem.

Write the main body. The main body of your speech is the content, which accounts for 70 to 90 percent of most speeches. In the main body, you develop your ideas in much the same way that you develop a written paper.

In speeches, transitions are especially important. Give your audience a signal when you change points, using meaningful pauses and verbal emphasis as well as transitional phrases: "On the other hand, until the public realizes what is happening to children in these countries . . ." or "The second reason hunger persists is. . . ."

In long speeches, recap from time to time and preview what's to come. Use facts, descriptions, expert opinions, and statistics to hold your audience's attention.

Write the conclusion. At the end of the speech, summarize your points and draw your conclusion. You started with a bang; now finish with drama. The first and last parts of a speech are the most important. Make it

---

➜ Making the grade in group presentations

When preparing group presentations, you can use three strategies for making a memorable impression.

Get organized. As soon as you get the assignment, select a group leader and exchange contact information. Schedule specific times and places for planning, researching, writing, and practicing your presentation.

At your first meeting, write a to-do list including all of the tasks involved in completing the assignment. Distribute tasks fairly, paying attention to the strengths of individuals in your group. For example, some people excel at brainstorming while others prefer researching.

As you get organized, remember how your presentation will be evaluated. If the instructor doesn't give grading criteria, create your own.

One powerful way to get started is to define clearly the topic and thesis, or main point, of your presentation. Then support your thesis by looking for the most powerful facts, quotations, and anecdotes you can find.

Get coordinated. Coordinate your presentation so that you have transitions between individual speakers. Practice making those transitions smooth.

Also practice using visuals such as flipboards, posters, DVDs, videotapes, or slides. To give visuals their full impact, make them appropriate for the room where you will present. Make sure that text is large enough to be seen from the back of the room. For bigger rooms, consider using presentation software or making overhead transparencies.

Get cooperation. Presentations that get top scores take teamwork and planning—not egos. Communicate with group members in an open and sensitive way. Contribute your ideas and be responsive to the viewpoints of other members. When you do, your group is on the way to scoring well.

clear to your audience when you've reached the end. Avoid endings such as "This is the end of my speech." A simple standby is "So in conclusion, I want to reiterate three points: First. . . ." When you are finished, stop talking.

Create speaking notes. Some professional speakers recommend writing out your speech in full, then putting key words or main points on a few 3x5 cards. Number the cards so that if you drop them, you can quickly put them in order again. As you finish the information on each card, move it to the back of the pile. Write information clearly and in letters large enough to be seen from a distance.

Some speakers prefer to use standard outlined notes. Another option is mind mapping. Even an hour-long speech can be mapped on one sheet of paper. You can also use memory techniques to memorize the outline of your speech.

Practice your presentation

Use your "speaker's voice." When you practice, do so in a loud voice. Your voice sounds different when you talk loudly, and this can be unnerving. Get used to it early on.

Practice in the room in which you will deliver your speech. Hear what your voice sounds like over a sound system. If you can't practice your speech in the actual room, at least visit the site ahead of time. Also make sure that the materials you will need for your speech, such as an overhead projector and screen, will be available when you want them.

Listen for repeated phrases. Examples include *you know, kind of, really,* plus any little *uh*'s, *umm*'s, and *ah*'s. To get rid of these, tell yourself that you intend to notice every time they pop up in your daily speech. When you hear them, remind yourself that you don't use those words anymore.

Keep practicing until you know your material inside and out. Avoid speaking word for word, as if you were reading a script. When you know your material well, you can deliver it in a natural way. Practice your presentation until you could deliver it in your sleep, then run through it a few more times.

Deliver your presentation

Before you begin, get the audience's attention. If people are still filing into the room or adjusting their seats, they're not ready to listen. When all eyes are on you, then begin.

Maintain eye contact. When you look at people, they become less frightening. Remember, too, that it is easier for the audience to listen to someone when that person is

---

→ Make effective presentations with visuals

In the workplace, you might make full-length presentations rather than short speeches. Presentations often include visuals such as overhead transparencies, flip charts, or "slides" created with presentation software such as PowerPoint. Visuals can reinforce your main points and help your audience understand how your presentation is organized. In addition, visuals can serve as your speaking notes.

Use visuals to *complement* rather than *replace* your speaking. If you use too many visuals—or visuals that are too complex—your audience might focus on them and forget about you. To avoid this fate, do the following:

- Limit the amount of text on each visual. Stick to key words presented in short sentences and bulleted or numbered lists. Use a consistent set of plain fonts that are large enough for all audience members to see.

- Stick with a simple, coherent color scheme. Use light-colored text on a dark background, or dark text on a light background.

- Use consistent terminology in your speaking, your handouts, and your visuals. Inconsistency can lead people to feel lost or to question your credibility.

- Proofread your visuals for spelling and other mechanical errors.

---

looking at them. Find a few friendly faces around the room and imagine that you are talking to each person individually.

Notice your nonverbal communication. Only a fraction of our communication is verbal. Be aware of what your body is telling your audience. Contrived or staged gestures will look dishonest. Be natural. If you don't know what to do with your hands, notice that. Then don't do anything with them.

Notice the time. You can increase the impact of your words by keeping track of the time during your speech. Better to end early than run late. The conclusion of your speech is what is likely to be remembered, and you might lose this opportunity if people are looking at the clock.

Have fun. One way to feel at ease while speaking is to look at your audience and imagine everyone dressed as clowns. Chances are that if you lighten up and enjoy your presentation, so will they. ⊠

If you feel nervous before you make a presentation, then you're normal. When asked to list their favorite activities, few people would place public speaking at the top.

Even so, consider the benefits of public speaking. This is a highly transferable skill—one that you can develop in school and use to enhance any job you take. As you gain work experience and become more active in professional associations or your community, you're more likely to get speaking invitations. Handling these assignments well can help you advance in your career.

One powerful strategy for preventing and reducing fear of public speaking is to prepare thoroughly. Knowing your topic inside and out can create a baseline of confidence. Also look for opportunities to speak briefly and frequently in public. In addition, experiment with the following suggestions.

Overcoming fear of public speaking

Accept your physical sensations. You've probably experienced physical sensations that are commonly associated with stage fright: dry mouth, a pounding heart, sweaty hands, muscle jitters, shortness of breath, and a shaky voice.

One immediate way to deal with sensations like these is to simply notice them. Tell yourself, "Yes, my hands are clammy. Yes, my stomach is upset. Also, my face feels numb." Trying to deny or ignore such facts can increase your fear. When you fully accept sensations, however, they create less suffering.

A Power Process to apply is "Be here now." Be totally in the present moment. Notice how the room looks. Notice the temperature and lighting. Make eye contact with the people in the audience and release any judgments about them. Fear is often associated with racing thoughts. One way to quiet them down is to focus your attention on neutral sights and sounds.

Change your mind. Fear begins in your mind. You can deal with it by using your mind in new ways.

One strategy is to relax and visualize success: Sit or lie down in a comfortable position. Breathe deeply and slowly. Let your mind clear. Then visualize yourself speaking in public. Imagine yourself being introduced to the audience, seeing if you can stay relaxed at the same time. When you can, add more visual images. See yourself delivering the opening lines of your speech. Some psychologists use this technique with clients. Ask a speech teacher or counselor at your student health service for more information.

Also consider that fear is caused not by external events but by the way you *interpret* those events. If you feel jittery before you begin a speech, one possible interpretation is, "Uh-oh. I'm getting nervous. I'm going to blow this speech." Another valid interpretation is, "Wow, I feel jittery. I'm really psyched up to give a great speech." The first interpretation is likely to increase your fear. The second one can reduce it.

The idea is to get your irrational beliefs out in the open and replace them with more rational beliefs.

Again, ask a counselor for help with this technique.

Focus on content, not delivery. Michael Motley, a professor at the University of California—Davis, distinguishes between two orientations to speaking. People with a *performance orientation* believe that the speakers must captivate their audiences by using formal techniques that differ from normal conversation. In contrast, speakers with a *communication orientation* see public speaking simply as an extension of one-to-one conversation. The goal is not to perform but to communicate your ideas to an audience in the same ways that you would explain them to a friend.[6]

Adopting a communication orientation can reduce your fear of public speaking. Instead of thinking about yourself, focus on your message. Your audiences are more interested in *what* you have to say than *how* you say it. Give them valuable ideas and information that they can use right away. They'll thank you afterward—even if you're not a professional speaker. ✖

Connect to
cyberspace @ school

You can take two paths to accessing information technology in higher education. One is through the resources offered by your school. The other is through your own technology resources, including a personal computer.

Many campuses have computer labs with equipment that's available to students for free. These labs can get crowded, especially during finals week or when other major assignments are due in large courses. To maintain your access to computers, find several sources of public computers on campus and check their availability.

With some creative thinking, you might find even more possibilities. A library on campus or in your community might offer public access. Some students get permission to use computers at their workplace after hours. Perhaps a friend or family member would be willing to loan you a computer or offer you computer time at his home. If you choose one of these options, be realistic about the number of hours that the computer will be available to you.

You might find that it's more convenient to buy your own computer and peripheral equipment. Find out whether your campus bookstore or another outlet on campus sells computer hardware at a student discount. Also ask about getting an extended warranty with technical support. Other options include leasing a computer or buying a used one.

To make an informed purchase, take your time. Start by contacting an admissions counselor or academic advisor at your school and asking the following questions.

Should I get a laptop computer or a desktop computer?
Laptop computers have the obvious advantage of portability. They also take up less space—a key consideration if you live in a dorm room. Yet laptops tend to be more fragile and more expensive than desktop computers. Also, the portability of laptop computers makes them easy targets for thieves. If you get one, keep it in a secure place or always carry it with you in public.

What hardware specifications should my computer meet?
To find a personal computer that supports your academic success, think about technical specifications. These are the requirements that computers must meet in order to connect to the campus network and run software applications commonly used by students. In particular ask about requirements for your computer's:

- *Operating system*, the built-in software that keeps track of computer files and allows you to run software applications. Be sure to keep the CDs that contain backup of files of your operating system software and upgrades.

- *Processor*, the piece of hardware that actually carries out the operating system's commands. Processor speed is measured in megahertz (MHz) or gigahertz (GHz). The higher this rating, the faster your computer will run.

- *Random Access Memory (RAM)*, a temporary storage area for data that you're actively using, such as word processing or database files. RAM is measured in megabytes (MB). Get as much RAM as you can afford. The extra memory helps your computer run faster and allows you to open up more software applications at once.

- *Hard drive*, which stores the operating system along with all of the other files you save and use. Space on a hard drive is measured in gigabytes (GB). Again, the more, the better.

- *Ethernet card*, sometimes called a network adapter or network interface card (NIC). This allows you to connect your computer to campus networks and the Internet. Find out what kind of card is recommended for your campus.

- *Optical drive*, which allows you to read and write data to compact discs (CDs), digital video discs (DVDs), or both. You can use optical drives to make backup copies of all your working files. Another option is to use an Iomega Zip drive and Zip disks to create backups.

What software do I need to successfully complete coursework?
Many students find that a package—including a word processor as well as spreadsheet, database, and presentation software—meets their needs. Find out what's recommended for your campus. Also ask whether your school provides software to access the Internet (e-mail and Web browsers) and to protect your computer from viruses. ◼

Course management software creates virtual classrooms—sites on the World Wide Web where a teacher can post a syllabus, readings, announcements, tests, grades, and a digital "drop box" for student assignments. Digital discussions and debates can also take place via computer bulletin boards, chat rooms, and two-way audio and visual connections. The term *online learning* refers to all of these tools.

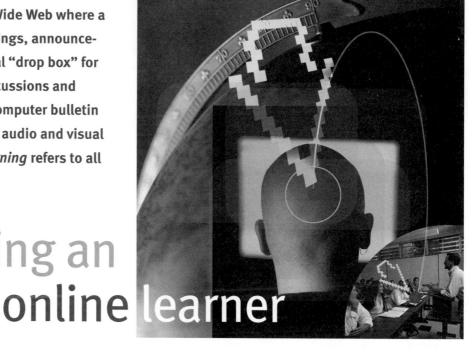

Becoming an
online learner

You can use your online learning experiences to develop technology skills that are valued in the workplace:

- Using computers to acquire, organize, analyze, and communicate information.
- Judging which computers and programs will produce the results you want to achieve.
- Using computers to store records in a systematic way.

Take a First Step about technology. Before you begin your next experience with online learning, practice telling the truth about your current skills in this area. The *From Master Student to Master Employee* Web site has a special tool for this purpose. Go online to **masterstudent.college.hmco.com** and look for a link to the E-Learning Readiness Self-Assessment.

Check out the technology requirements for your courses. Contact instructors before courses begin. Ask about the specifications your computer will need to meet and the applications you'll be expected to use. Your instructors might also assume that students have a certain amount of experience with online learning, so ask about that as well.

If you're planning to use a computer lab on campus, find one with hardware and software that meets course requirements. Whenever possible, choose a single computer for online coursework—one that's available

when you need it, complete with the specifications that you want.

Do a trial run with course technology. Most online courses have been created using WebCT or Blackboard software programs. You do not need to install this software to access the online course, but you will need to know the procedure, access code, and password to get into the online course site, Web pages, and materials. Get the details and then verify your access to course Web sites, including online tutorials, presentations, readings, quizzes, tests, assignments, and links to other sites. Also see if you can log on to course-based bulletin boards and chat rooms. Work out any bugs well before the first assignment is due.

Locate support services. If you feel intimidated by technology, remember that there are living, breathing human beings who can help. Possibilities include instructors, people who staff computer labs, librarians, and on-campus technical support services. Computer dealers or manufacturers might offer similar resources, including online help and toll-free numbers for customer service.

Develop a contingency plan. Murphy's Law of Computer Crashes states that technology tends to break down at the moment of greatest inconvenience. You might not find this piece of folklore to be true, but it's still wise to prepare for it in advance:

- Identify several on-campus computer labs with the technology you need.

- Find a technology buddy in each of your classes—someone who can update you on assignments and contact the instructor if you lose Internet access.

- Set up a backup e-mail account in case your Internet service provider goes offline. Many Web sites offer this service for free.

- Get complete contact information—address and office phone and fax numbers—for your instructors in case you lose e-mail service.

- Keep extra printer supplies—paper and toner or ink cartridges—always on hand. Don't run out of either on the day that a paper is due.

Set up files. Before classes meet, create a separate folder for each class on your computer's hard disk. Give each folder a meaningful name, such as *biology-spring2008*. Place all files related to a course in the appropriate folder. Doing this can save you from one of the main technology-related time-wasters—searching for lost files.

Also name individual files with care. Avoid changing extensions that identify different types of files, such as .ppt for PowerPoint presentations or .pdf for files in the Adobe Reader portable document format. If you change extensions, you could have problems finding files later or sharing them with other users.

The earlier you clarify expectations for online coursework, the greater your opportunities to succeed.

Manage your time. Some students act as if they have all the time in the world to complete their online assignments. The temptation to procrastinate can be strongest with courses that take place mostly or totally online. To succeed at online learning, front-load your efforts. Early in the term, create a detailed timeline with a due date for each assignment. Break big assignments into smaller steps and schedule a due date for each step.

The earlier you clarify expectations for online coursework, the greater your opportunities to succeed. When you receive an online assignment, e-mail questions immediately. If you want to meet with an instructor in person, request an appointment several days in advance. In addition, download or print out online course materials as soon as they're posted on the class Web site. These materials might not be available later in the term.

Consider scheduling times in your daily or weekly calendar to complete online coursework. Give these scheduled sessions the same priority as regular classroom meetings. At these times, check for announcements relating to assignments, tests, and other course events.

Ask for feedback. To get the most from online learning, request feedback from your instructor via e-mail. When appropriate, ask for conferences by phone or in person as well. Be sure to check with your instructor to see how he wants e-mail messages from online course students to be addressed. Many teachers use a standard subject area format so that e-mails from online students can be quickly and easily recognized.

Contact other students. Make personal contact with at least one other student in each of your classes—especially those that involve lots of online coursework. Meet with this person to share notes, quiz each other, critique papers, and do other cooperative learning tasks. This source of support can help you keep current with online work and promote your success.

Create course glossaries. You can integrate information technology with daily study tasks in a variety of ways. For example, create and maintain a glossary of key terms for each of your courses. Every time you encounter a key word or technical term in your course notes or textbooks, key that word into a word processing or database file. Create a separate file for each of your courses. For each term, write a definition and a sentence using the word in context. Sort the terms in alphabetical order. Your glossary will come in handy as you review for tests.

Capture your notes on disk. Software offers many possibilities for organizing and reviewing the notes you take when listening to lectures or studying textbooks. For example, take lecture notes directly on a laptop, or take handwritten notes and key them into your computer after class. Divide your notes into sections, then write a heading to capture the main point of each section. For greater depth of detail, use several levels of headings ranging from major to minor. To save time when you review, display the headings and scan them as you would scan the headlines in a newspaper. Also use drawing and painting tools to create maps, charts, diagrams, and other visuals that enhance your notes. Look for personal digital assistants that can convert your handwritten notes into text that can be uploaded to your personal computer.

Use computers for cooperative learning. You can turn any study group into an active online community. Experiment with e-mail, bulletin boards, chat rooms, and instant messaging software. These technologies can be lifesavers when your group finds it too difficult to meet in person. ✉

For more suggestions on becoming a successful online learner, visit

masterstudent.college.hmco.com

Write e-mail that gets results

According to a study from the University of California at Berkeley, e-mail ranks second only to the telephone as a source of information flow.

Across the world, about 31 billion e-mails are sent each day—a number that will double within a few years.[7] Plan to master this form of digital communication, no matter what career you choose.

Target your audience. Be conscious of the amount of e-mail that busy people receive. Send e-mail messages only to the people who need them, and only when necessary.

Write an informative subject line. Rather than writing a generic description, include a capsule summary of your message. "Biology 100 Report due next Tuesday" packs more information than "Report." If your message is urgent, include that word in the subject line as well. Your teachers might require a specific format for the subject line of e-mail messages you send to them. Follow those instructions.

Think short. Keep your subject line short, your paragraphs short, and your message as a whole short. Most people don't want to read long documents on a computer screen.

Put the point first. To make sure your point gets across, put it at the top of the first paragraph. If your message will take up more than one screen's worth of text, break it up into short sections and add a heading for each section.

Consider how long your message might be stored. Your message could dwell in a recipient's in-basket for weeks or months. Think carefully about the impact of your message, both in the short term and the long term. Edit messages written in the heat of a strong emotion—messages that you might regret later. Also remember that it's easy to send a message to the wrong person. Don't include a statement in any e-mail that would embarrass you if this should happen.

Review your message. Every message you send—even the shortest, most informal message—says something about your attention to detail. Put your best electronic foot forward. If you plan to send a long message, draft it in a word processing program first so that you can take advantage of spelling checkers and other editing devices. Then copy the text and paste it into the body of an e-mail message.

Use text formatting carefully. Boldface, italics, underlining, smart quotes, and other formatting options might not transfer well across e-mail programs. If your message will be widely circulated, use generic characters that any computer can read.

Test attachments. If you plan to send an attachment, do a dry run first. You might find that it takes a couple of tries to send attachments in a format that your recipient can read. For instructions on how to prepare files as attachments, see the help feature in your e-mail program.

Note: Attachments sometimes come with computer viruses that can damage your hard disk. Open attachments only from people you know, and use antivirus software. Forward attachments with extreme care.

Reply promptly and consciously. Provide context. If you're responding to a question from a previous e-mail, include that question in your response.

Be aware of everyone who will receive your reply. If you hit the "reply to all" button, your response will go to all of the people who received the original message—including those on the "cc" (carbon copy) line. Instead, you might want to reply to just one or two of these people.

Forward messages selectively. Think twice before forwarding generic messages from other sources—cartoons, joke files, political diatribes, and "inspirational" readings. Your recipients might already have an in-basket overflowing with e-mail. Such forwarded messages might be viewed as irritating clutter.

Protect your privacy. Any competent hacker can intercept a private message. Treat all online communication as public communication. Include only content that you're willing to circulate widely. Share personal data with caution. Before sending, ask yourself: "What would be the costs if this information were made public?" ✉

"Netiquette"

Being kind while you're online

Certain kinds of exchanges can send the tone of online communications into the gutter. To promote a cordial online community, abide by the following guidelines.

Respect others' time. Write concise messages. Adopt the habit of getting to your point, sticking to it, and getting to the end.

Avoid typing passages in ALL UPPERCASE LETTERS. This is the online equivalent of shouting.

Design your messages for fast retrieval. Avoid graphics and attachments that take a long time to download, tying up your recipient's computer.

Don't dish out spam. *Spam* refers to unsolicited messages, often meant to advertise a product or service, that are sent indiscriminately to large numbers of computer users.

Can the sarcasm. Use humor—especially sarcasm—with caution. A joke that's funny when you tell it in person might fall flat or even offend someone when you put it in writing and send it down the computer wires.

Put out flames. *Flaming* takes place when someone sends an online message tinged with sarcasm or outright hostility. To create positive relationships when you're online, avoid sending such messages. If you get one, do not respond in kind.

Remember that the message is missing the emotion. When you communicate online, the people who receive your e-mail will miss out on voice inflection and nonverbal cues that are present in face-to-face communication. Without these cues, words can be easily misinterpreted. Reread your message before sending it to be sure you have clarified what you want to say and how you feel.

Remember common courtesy. The idea of Netiquette extends to the way that you use any piece of technology. For instance, a cell phone that rings in class offends teachers and irritates almost everyone else in the room. Turn off your cell phone and check voice mail messages after class. The cornerstone of Netiquette is to remember that the recipient on the other end is a human being. Whenever you're at the keyboard typing up messages, ask yourself one question: "Would I say this to the person's face?" ✉

Whenever you're at the keyboard typing up messages, ask yourself one question: "Would I say this to the person's face?"

from the desk of...

JESSICA BONDELL,
BANK BRANCH SECRETARY:

Many of my e-mails go out to the entire region and senior management. Therefore, it is very important (to me and my superiors) that my writing is grammatically correct and concise. I always try to represent myself as an authority figure, which to me means demonstrating proficiency in communicating.

ANDREW ROHR, PUBLIC RELATIONS
SENIOR ACCOUNT EXECUTIVE:

As a public relations practitioner, your clients are looking to you to perform [as a writer]. Also, with the advent of e-mail, I have to send out dozen or so memos every day to clients and maintain correspondence with key reporters. To establish and maintain credibility I have to be able to write in a clear and concise manner.

Joining online communities

Online communities come in many varieties. You can find them in three basic formats: e-mail lists, newsgroups, and chat rooms.

Listservs

Listservs consist of e-mail addresses for groups of people who want to automatically receive messages on a certain topic. To get the messages, you have to subscribe to the list.

Your instructors might use listservs to communicate with members of a class, especially when large numbers of students are involved.

When you subscribe to a listserv, you can send a message to a posting address at any time. Everyone who subscribes to the list will receive your message. Likewise, you will receive e-mails that other subscribers send to the posting address. Some lists are highly active, generating dozens of messages daily.

Newsgroups

Newsgroups—also called *Usenet groups, Web forums, bulletin boards,* and *discussion boards*—allow members to post and read e-mail messages. Usually, there is some type of subscribing process, which is often free. Once you subscribe to a group, you can choose whether you want to receive new e-mail messages as they appear, daily summaries of messages, or no e-mail messages at all. In the last case, you just view messages at the group's Web site at your convenience.

Newsgroups usually focus on a particular topic—anything from astronomy to Zen Buddhism. Some groups are moderated by a person or group that screens messages. Other groups are a free-for-all, open to any message from any person. Again, instructors might set up newsgroups for members of a class.

To access a newsgroup, you'll need special software. Today that software is often bundled into a Web browser such as Internet Explorer or an e-mail program.

Chat rooms

Chat rooms—sometimes called MUDs (multi-user domains) or MOOs (multi-user domains, object oriented)—allow you to send and receive messages live, in real time. This is as close to a live conversation as most computer users get while they're online. To join in, you'll need to download instant messaging software or use a similar application bundled with your Web browser.

Some chat rooms are set up for specific audiences and special purposes. Rooms might be ongoing or planned to last only for a limited time. For example, newspapers and magazines might create chat rooms that allow readers to discuss feature articles. Your teachers might also set up chat rooms where you and your classmates can take part in digital exchanges for the duration of a course. You might even do group exercises and role playing via chat rooms.

Consider the following suggestions for mastering online communities.

Learn the ground rules. Online communities have written policies about what kinds of messages are permitted. Often you'll receive these rules when you join. Look for a frequently asked questions (FAQ) file that explains the policies.

Stick to the topic. To make an effective contribution to the discussion, write courteous messages that are brief, informative, and relevant to the topic.

Review before you post. By observing what people write and what they don't, you'll learn the unwritten rules for that group. If you include statistics or quote material from someone else, cite the source. Avoid slang, jargon, and sarcasm, especially in class-related discussions. ✖

For more information on mastering online communities, visit

(masterstudent.college.hmco.com)

THINKING CRITICALLY IN THE WORKPLACE

The purpose of this exercise is to use your skills in critical thinking and writing to help resolve a conflict in the workplace. Perhaps you are currently in conflict with a coworker, manager, or supervisor. For the purpose of this exercise, that is ideal. Keep this situation in mind as you proceed. If you have no workplace conflict at this moment, then think of a conflict you've experienced in the past.

Write your responses in the spaces provided. Use additional paper as needed, or open up a computer file to complete this exercise.

1. Summarize the conflict in writing as accurately as possible. Instead of describing the personalities of anyone involved ("My boss is rigid and inflexible"), state the core issue as a question ("Shall I get promoted to the new position that's opened up in my department?"). Note that in this step you are practicing a key conflict resolution skill—focusing on problems rather personalities.

_____

_____

_____

_____

_____

2. Now answer this question as if you were the other person in this conflict. If more than one person is involved, then choose the person you disagree with most. Make your "opponent's" case as clearly and powerfully as you can. Include a direct answer to the question you posed in step 1 and the most compelling fact or example you can think of to support that answer.

This step asks you to directly apply a critical thinking skill—considering more than one point of view on an issue. If you feel any resistance to doing so, simply notice it and keep writing.

_____

_____

_____

_____

_____

_____

3. Next, state *your* answer to the question you posed in step 1, along with a supporting fact or example.

_____

_____

_____

_____

_____

_____

4. Finally, reflect on the results of the writing you've just done. Has it affected the way you feel about the conflict? Can you now approach the conflict with more clarity and calm? Has writing suggested an additional point of view or a potential solution to the conflict? If so, summarize that solution below and consider presenting it in writing to the other person involved in this conflict.

_____

_____

_____

_____

_____

_____

power process

Employ your word

When you speak and give your word, you are creating—literally. Your speaking brings life to your values. In large part, others know who you are by the words you speak and the agreements you make. You can learn who you are by observing which commitments you choose to make and which ones you choose to avoid.

Your word makes things happen. Circumstances, events, and attitudes fall into place. The resources needed to accomplish whatever was promised become available. When you give your word, all this comes about.

The person you are right now is, for the most part, a result of the choices and agreements you've made in your life up to this point. Your future is determined largely by the choices and agreements you will make from this point on. By making and keeping agreements, you employ your word to create your future.

The world works by agreement

There are over six billion people on planet Earth. We live on different continents and in different nations, and communicate in different languages. We have diverse political ideologies and subscribe to various social and moral codes.

This complex planetary network is held together by people keeping their word. Agreements minimize confusion, prevent social turmoil, and keep order. Projects are finished, goods are exchanged, and treaties are made. People, organizations, and nations know what to expect when agreements are kept. When people keep their word, the world works. Agreements are the foundation of many things that we often take for granted. Language, our basic tool of communication, works only because we agree about the meanings of words. A pencil is a pencil only because everyone agrees to call a thin, wood-covered column of graphite a pencil. We could just as easily call them ziddles. Then you might hear someone say, "Do you have an extra ziddle? I forgot mine."

Money exists only by agreement. If we leave a $100 Monopoly bill (play money) on a park bench next to a real $100 bill (backed by the United States Treasury), one is more likely to disappear than the other. The only important difference between the two pieces of paper is that everyone agrees that one can be exchanged for goods and services and the other cannot. Shopkeepers will sell merchandise for the "real" $100 bill because they trust a continuing agreement.

Relationships work by agreement

Relationships are built on agreements. They begin with our most intimate personal contacts and move through all levels of families, organizations, communities, and nations.

When we break a promise to be faithful to a spouse, to help a friend move to a new apartment, or to pay a bill on time, relationships are strained and the consequences can be painful. When we keep our word, relationships are more likely to be satisfying and harmonious. Expectations of trust and accountability develop. Others are more likely to keep their promises to us.

Perhaps our most important relationship is the one we have with ourselves. Trusting ourselves to keep our word is enlivening. As we experience success, our self-confidence increases.

When we commit to complete a class assignment and then keep our word, our understanding of the subject improves. So does our grade. We experience satisfaction and success. If we break our word, we create a gap in our learning, a lower grade, and possibly negative feelings.

Ways to make and keep agreements

Being cautious about making agreements can improve the quality of our lives. Making only those promises that we fully intend to keep improves the likelihood of reaching our goals. We can ask ourselves what level of commitment we have to a particular promise.

At the same time, if we are willing to take risks, we can open new doors and increase our possibilities for success. The only way to ensure that we keep all of our agreements is either to make none or to make only those that are absolutely guaranteed. In either case, we are probably cheating ourselves. Some of the most powerful promises we can make are those that we have no idea how to keep. We can stretch ourselves and set goals that are both high and realistic.

If we break an agreement, we can choose to be gentle with ourselves. We can be courageous, quickly admit our mistake to the people involved, and consider ways to deal with the consequences.

Examining our agreements can improve our effectiveness. Perhaps we took on too much—or too little. Perhaps we did not use all the resources that were available to us—or we used too many. Perhaps we did not fully understand what we were promising. When we learn from both our mistakes and our successes, we can become more effective at employing our word.

Move up the ladder of powerful speaking

The words used to talk about whether or not something will happen fall into several different levels. We can think of each level as one rung on a ladder—the ladder of powerful speaking. As we move up the ladder, our speaking becomes more effective.

Obligation. The lowest rung on the ladder is *obligation*. Words used at this level include *I should, he ought to,*

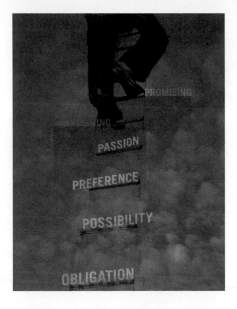

By making and keeping agreements, you employ your word to create your future.

someone better, they need to, I must, and *I had to*. Speaking this way implies that people and circumstances other than ourselves are in control of our lives. When we live at the level of obligation, we often feel passive and helpless to change anything.

Note: When we move to the next rung, we leave behind obligation and advance to self-responsibility. All of the rungs work together to reinforce this characteristic.

Possibility. The next rung up is *possibility*. At this level, we examine new options. We play with new ideas, possible solutions, and alternative courses of action. As we do, we learn that we can make choices that dramatically affect the quality of our lives. We are not the victims of circumstance. Phrases that signal this level include *I might, I could, I'll consider, I hope to,* and *maybe*.

Preference. From possibility we can move up to *preference*. Here we begin the process of choice. The words *I prefer* signal that we're moving toward one set of possibilities over another, perhaps setting the stage for eventual action.

Passion. Above preference is a rung called *passion*. Again, certain words signal this level: *I want to, I'm really excited to do that, I can't wait.* Possibility and passion are both exciting places to be. Even at these levels, though, we're still far from action. Many of us want to achieve lots of things and have no specific plan for doing so.

Planning. Action comes with the next rung—*planning*. When people use phrases such as *I intend to, my goal is to, I plan to,* and *I'll try like mad to*, they're at the level of planning. The Intention Statements you write in this book are examples of planning.

Promising. The highest rung on the ladder is *promising*. This is where the power of your word really comes into play. At this level, it's common to use phrases such as these: *I will, I promise to, I am committed, you can count on it.* This is where we bridge from possibility and planning to action. Promising brings with it all of the rewards of employing your word. ⊠

career application

After Mark Hyland earned his associate degree in dental hygiene, he applied to work with his family's dentist. He got the job the day after he graduated.

M ark welcomed the chance to apply the skills he'd gained in school. He examined patients' teeth and gums. He removed stains and plaque. Mark asked if he could expand his job duties to include taking and developing dental x-rays. The dentist who hired him agreed.

Everyone in the dental office admitted that Mark's technical skills were superb. His communication skills were another matter. Several long-term patients complained that Mark's manner was condescending—even harsh at times.

One day, the dentist who hired Mark overheard him talking to a patient.

"You can't expect to have white teeth if you drink coffee," Mark told the patient.

The patient tried to make light of the situation. "Oh well," she said, "we all have our vices, and. . . ."

"Yeah, but it's your teeth we're talking about here," Mark said, interrupting her. "Tea is just as bad, and hot chocolate is even worse. On top of that, you've got a lot of plaque on your upper teeth. Do you *ever* floss?"

The dentist winced. He feared he was about to lose a valued patient. On the other hand, he'd known Mark for years and counted his parents as friends. He wanted to meet with Mark and give him feedback about his "chair side manner." Yet the dentist knew that this conversation would be awkward for both of them. He found this meeting an easy thing to put off. ✉

Reflecting on this scenario:

1. Review the suggestions given in this chapter for creating "I" messages. Then write an "I" message that the dentist could use to express his concerns with Mark.

_____

_____

_____

2. List at least two other suggestions for sending or receiving messages that the dentist could use.

_____

_____

_____

3. List at least two suggestions for Mark to use when communicating with patients.

_____

_____

_____

4. Review the list of SCANS skills on page 8 and list three that could benefit Mark and the dentist in this scenario.

_____

_____

_____

Name _____ Date _____/_____/_____

quiz

1. What is the difference between *encoding* and *decoding* as explained in this chapter?

2. In communicating across cultures, the primary role of a translator is to overcome differences in language. True or False? Explain your answer.

3. The suggested techniques for verbal listening include which of the following?
   (A) Parrot exactly what another person says.
   (B) Pay attention to the speaker's words and not the emotions behind the words.
   (C) Always put your own concerns aside in order to listen attentively.
   (D) Look for the requests hidden in complaints.

4. Reword the following complaint as a request: "You always interrupt when I talk!"

5. List the five parts of an "I" message (the five ways to say "I").

6. The fact that a disagreement is getting worse means that there's little hope for conflict resolution. True or False? Explain your answer.

7. Which of the following is an effective thesis statement? Explain your answer.
   (A) Two types of thinking.
   (B) Critical thinking and creative thinking go hand in hand.
   (C) The relationship between critical thinking and creative thinking.

8. Define *plagiarism* and explain ways to avoid it.

9. List three techniques for overcoming fear of public speaking.

10. What characteristic distinguishes the top five rungs of the ladder of powerful speaking from the bottom rung?

learning styles application

The questions below will "cycle" you through four styles, or modes, of learning as explained in the article "Learning styles: Discovering how you learn" in Chapter One. Each question will help you explore a different mode. You can answer the questions in any order.

what if
After reading this chapter, will you generally approach conflict management in a different way? Briefly explain your answer.

why
Think of a conflict you are experiencing right now with an important person in your life. (If you cannot think of one, recall a conflict you've experienced in the past.) Do you think that any of the suggestions in this chapter could help you resolve this conflict? Briefly explain your answer.

how
Describe when and where you plan to use a suggestion from this chapter to resolve a conflict with another person.

what
Choose a specific suggestion from this chapter that could help you resolve a conflict you are experiencing right now with another person.

master student profile

RON BROWN

(1941–1996) first African American secretary of commerce and first African American chairman of the Democratic National Committee. Died in a plane crash in Bosnia while on a diplomatic mission.

Ron Brown was born in Washington, D.C., to William and Gloria Brown, both graduates of Howard University. The family moved to New York City when he was relatively young. His father managed the legendary Hotel Theresa in Harlem. Here, Ron encountered the social, artistic, political, and powerful elite of the African-American community. He encountered people who ran the race of life brilliantly, daring to be first in what they did. They were people like Jackie Robinson, the first African American to play professional baseball; W. E. B. Du Bois, one of the first African Americans to receive a Ph.D. from Harvard; Duke Ellington, one of the first African Americans to own and lead an internationally acclaimed big band; Ralph Ellison, one of the first widely successful African-American writers; Adam Clayton Powell, the first African-American congressman from Harlem. . . . Often as he peered out of the twelfth floor window of the Hotel Theresa, and observed the hustle and bustle of 125th St. below, he realized how easy it was to get lost in the superficial crowd of everyday life. He realized that the view from the top was a little better than the view from the bottom and that the Hotel Theresa with its legendary reputation and world famous clientele was simply his personal tutoring ground, training him to see above and beyond the crowded streets of New York City.

From the many heated discussions that Ron was involved in at the Hotel Theresa, Ron developed an agile mind and a disciplined tongue. He became almost invincible in his ability to present sound and convincing arguments. In this black cultural Mecca, he studied how creative, artistic, and powerful African-American people behaved. He learned early that hard work, commitment, and perseverance characterized people of position and power. He learned the importance of appearance, preparation, and personal influence in the race called life as he listened intensely to guests' lively stories and daring escapades of world travel.

With this strong sense of self and the willingness to seek different academic and cultural experiences, he got himself accepted by Middlebury College in rural Vermont. This was significant, in that Middlebury was the first college known to have graduated an African American (Alexander L. Twight, in 1823). At Middlebury, far from the blacktop boulevards and the high-rise tenements of Harlem, Ron really began to excel. He was the first black initiated into the Middlebury chapter of the national, all-white fraternity Sigma Phi Epsilon, which eventually lost its national charter because of his induction. . . .

Paramount in Ronald Harmon Brown's strategies for success was knowing how to solicit trust from himself. He learned early to accept himself for who he was and what he could or couldn't do. Knowing his own strengths and weaknesses, he never shortchanged himself. He learned self-reliance by preparing for every area of his life. He was confident in his ability to lead, orchestrate, mediate, and guide. He knew the importance of building lasting relationships. . . .

Ron Brown's life shouts to each of us, "Be your own best cheerleader. Root for a winner. Be that winner yourself." ✶

Osborne Robinson, Jr., *African American Master Student Profiles.* Copyright © 1998 by Houghton Mifflin Company. Reprinted with permission.

For more biographical information on Ron Brown, visit the Master Student Hall of Fame on the *From Master Student to Master Employee* Web site at

masterstudent.college.hmco.com

CHAPTER 9
Career Planning

This chapter invites students to begin planning their career. Higher education presents students with many choices—where to attend school, how to manage time effectively, what to study, and with whom to associate. These experiences are valuable practice as students make the move from college to career. Making a commitment to college is good practice for making the transition to career. Use this chapter to help students take charge of planning their career—and getting ready to step into the shoes of a master employee.

Page 277
Master Student Map

The Career Planning chapter of *From Master Student to Master Employee* focuses on the transfer of knowledge best displayed by mode 4 learners who ask **what if?** Your students will have practice using the metacognitive map for a whole semester. Now you can challenge them to think of their own questions. **What if?** they apply the skills they learned in this course to planning their career? **What if?** they use these skills in the workplace. **What if?** they select one major and then want to change majors because they have changed career goals? This is a great time to continue to reinforce the transferable skills discussed throughout this book.

Page 278
You've got a world of choices

Some of the choices presented to students may feel overwhelming. By discovering what students *can* do through their development of transferable skills in college, they can multiply their skills to apply to different subjects and career options. Start by asking students to link skills to achievements. All of your students have completed a difficult or challenging task that required their best efforts. Remembering achievements can help students become more aware of their skills. Ask your students to list as many achievements as they can recall. Then, have students write the skills that were used in accomplishing one. For example, they may have been hired for a part-time job. For this they used speaking skills and persuading skills (in an interview) and writing skills (in creating a résumé or completing a job application). Have your students refer back to the list of transferable skills in the Introduction on page 7 if they are having trouble making connections.

Page 279
Explore vocational assessments

The career center on your campus may offer the administration of one or more of these assessments (for a fee or they may be included in tuition fees). Collect this information for your students to inform them of what is available. Assign students to complete one assessment and analyze the results as a source of information for making decisions.

Page 281
Career planning: Begin the process now

Have your students prepare for an evolving job market by listing 20 skills that they think will be valued in the workplace 20 years from now. Then have them write one action that they can take to increase their proficiency at each skill they have listed. Setting a due date for taking each action will help students create specific and measurable goals they can achieve.

Page 285
Ways to learn about careers

Students can learn more about their interests and career options by studying materials that they are familiar with already. Ask students to spend 15 minutes glancing through a magazine or newspaper of their choice. Review the articles, people in photographs, and illustrations. As they do this, ask them to keep several questions in mind. What are the people described as or depicted doing? What goods or services are being provided? What careers are described or shown? Have students list the ideas that they gained from this resource for thinking about careers.

Page 286
EXERCISE #32: Create your career plan—now

Getting started with the process of career planning, even if your students are not sure where to begin, is a first step. This is another opportunity for your students to practice their writing skills, and apply information of self-discovery they have learned throughout the course of the semester. As your students complete this exercise, remind them to think about the experiences that they have had in their past that can help them succeed in their intended career. What transferable skills can they apply to this career choice? These skills should appear in their answers to the questions in the textbook. At this point, students should also begin to identify if their educational goals and their career goals are in line. This is a good time to encourage students to talk with their academic advisor, career counselor, or other staff on campus if they have questions related to their educational and career goals.

Your right-brained students may be interested in creating career plans using different formats. Suggest students make a timeline that marks dates for major career events in the future. Or, have your student create a mind map that links personal values to desired skills that could be used in multiple careers. Career goals can also be listed according to priority (using the ABC method as described in Chapter Two or another method created by the student).

Page 287
Test the waters—jump into the job market

Your students may be interested in the idea of informational interviews. They may also have trouble preparing for this type of task. Networking is a first step to finding resources for informational interviews. As the instructor, consider tapping into your personal network and inviting several contacts of yours to participate in informational interviews in your classroom. Have your students create a list of questions that they would like to ask, using the list of questions in the textbook as a stepping-stone. Discuss preparing for the informational interview as a class, and then evaluate the interview at the end. What was the best part? What would you do differently the next time? If you have several informational interviewers come to your class, consider having them on different dates so that your class can work to improve on their first interview and feel how much easier it is to participate in the second interview. This may eliminate some interviewing jitters.

The Interviewing Process: Strategies for Making the Right Impression is a free resource from Houghton Mifflin Student Success that provides valuable insight to interviewing if you can't find a speaker to come to your class. A section on the videotape focuses on informational interviews (in Segment Two). Materials on the Web site and HM ClassPrep CD for instructors provide activities and assessment for you to use with your students. Request a copy of the videotape from your sales representative or your College Survival Consultant.

Page 289
EXERCISE #33: Revisit your goals, take two

While students have created their career plan in this chapter, they should have reviewed their goal-setting exercises from Chapter Two. This exercise provides a formal opportunity to reevaluate and assess their accomplishments during the semester and set future goals. Students can also restate their commitment level.

Page 290
Financial planning

Help your students to think critically about financial planning by reviewing ideas from Chapter Two. Strategies that apply to time management and goal setting can be helpful in setting specific plans for your finances. The students are introduced to a solution for managing their finances: increase your income, decrease your expenses, or do both. But how? Ask your students to consider which of these goals they are willing to adopt. Then have them plan to meet the goal by taking a specific action. For example, they could decrease their expenses by finding a cheaper place to live or spending less on entertainment. Have students state their financial goal and list at least two ways that they plan to meet this goal.

An online exercise helps students to carefully observe how money flows into an out of their lives. Have students monitor their money by downloading the Microsoft Excel spreadsheet from the *From Master Student to Master Employee* Web site, or you can print the monitor from your HM ClassPrep CD and hand it out to students.

Page 295
EXERCISE #34: Education by the hour
Talking about finances in your class may not be something students want to discuss amongst each other—but most are interested in learning how to get more for their money. When students in your class have computed their total in this exercise, have them write their figure anonymously on a 3x5 card and then arrange the cards on the chalkboard tray in your classroom in order from lowest to highest. Initiate a discussion about how the amount on the card is the amount of money students are throwing away each time they miss a class meeting during the term—in your class and any other.

Page 296
Using technology to manage time and money
Time management will likely be on your student's minds as they work toward balancing busy schedules: demands at school, family responsibilities, and workplace tasks. Demonstrating that studying technology can help solve personal problems might trigger an aha! moment for your students. This article can be a stepping-stone to conversations about using technology to conquer other tasks. Challenge your students to think of ways that technology can help them with note taking, reading, memory, and test taking. Demonstrate online flash cards on the *From Master Student to Master Employee* Web site. Ask a colleague to show you a Web site for a textbook assigned in another class, or use the Houghton Mifflin College Division homepage (**college.hmco.com**) to find additional textbook resources. This will show students that using technology to support their textbook reading can help them be more successful in all of their academic courses.

Page 297
Choose your conversations
Raise your students' "conversation consciousness" by asking them to reflect on the quality of the conversations they take part in daily. These conversations might include class meetings, course lectures, social events, reading materials, and television. Students can describe a publication they read regularly (in print or online), pointing out the conversations and insights they gain from this material. Invite your students to write Discovery and Intention Statements highlighting the amount of time they currently spend talking about the past, present, and future, and stating how they intend to change their conversations. A central thesis of *From Master Student to Master Employee* is that education works when it is value driven. We can choose to engage in value-driven conversations—those that move us toward our goals and affirm our intentions.

Page 304
POWER PROCESS: "Risk being a fool"
Consider beginning your discussion of this Power Process by asking students "What percent of the shots you never take in a basketball game will you miss?" (0 percent is the answer.) "Will you ever win a game?" (The answer, of course, is no). It often helps students to connect to this Power Process by thinking about the risks they are taking—or not taking. Ask your students to identify **what?** they have to understand in order to practice "Risk being a fool." **How?** might this apply to selecting a career or accepting a job offer?

Page 309
Master Student Profile: Fred Smith
Technology is a driving force in the Federal Express empire created by Fred Smith. This Master Student Profile provides an occasion to talk about technology in the

Master Instructor Resource Guide

Course Manual

 Preparing your students for their destination—the workplace—was likely part of your course purpose. Teaching this course is a process, full of growth and learning. Take a moment to review your course purpose and begin to think about measuring its effectiveness. Take note of which topics are discussed most in your classroom and make note of them in your *Course Manual* or in the back of the Annotated Instructor's Edition so that you can easily access them next semester.

Begin to review the materials provided in the *Course Manual* to evaluate your course so that you are ready to administer an evaluation tool by the time students complete Chapter Ten. Discuss strategies with other professors teaching student success courses on your campus, or consider talking with your College Survival Consultant to brainstorm ideas.

HM ClassPrep CD

PowerPoint for Chapter Nine includes resources to discuss the article "Choose your conversations" and the Power Process: "Risk being a fool."

Help your students to carefully observe how money flows into and out of their lives. Use the budgeting exercises as an opportunity to discuss money management. Have your students monitor their money by connecting to the *From Master Student to Master Employee* Web site to download the Microsoft Excel spreadsheet, or use the materials provided on the HM ClassPrep CD.

Materials to help you administer and discuss the value of the HM Assessment and Portfolio Builder are available on the HM ClassPrep CD. Additional suggested articles for students to access from the Career Resource Center are also listed here. Have your students read additional case studies online and submit their answers to the Questions for Critical Thought for credit.

Additional Resources

Supplement your lecture with a free video, *Money and Finances*. Resources for using this video in your class can be downloaded on the *From Master Student to Master Employee* Web site and on the HM ClassPrep CD. Compliment your lesson with "Where does all the money go?" This online exercise asks students to complete a money monitor (either by printing it out and writing in the data, or by entering it electronically using Microsoft Excel). A monthly budget and long-term budget are also available online.

masterstudent.college.hmco.com Find more biographical information about Master Student Fred Smith in our **Master Student Hall of Fame.**

Use the HM Assessment and Portfolio Builder (available for packaging with your textbook) to guide your students towards their goals and have a conversation about planning their Accomplishments Report.

Articles on the **Career Resource Center** further support long-term planning goals, short-term goals and career planning. Log on and explore the wealth of materials available to you.

---

workplace and the impact technology has had on different work environments. Have your students access the Federal Express Web site at **http://www.fedex.com**. Then ask them to brainstorm ways in which they would improve or change the home page to make it more user friendly. Encourage them to send their feedback to Fed Ex.

In reviewing Smith's biographical information posted on the *From Master Student to Master Employee* Web site, your students will find that after graduating from Yale,

Smith joined the Marines. He first served in Vietnam as a platoon leader and then trained as a pilot. During his four years of service in the Marines, he flew more than 200 ground-support missions in Vietnam and was awarded the Bronze and Silver Stars. Have your students discuss how Smith's experience as a pilot might have influenced his planning for Federal Express. What transferable skills did Smith obtain in the Marines that he applies to the workplace today?

9

Career Planning

We are meant to work in ways that suit us, drawing on our natural talents and abilities as a way to express ourselves and contribute to others. This work, when we find it and do it—even if only as a hobby at first—is a key to our happiness and self-expression.

MARSHA SINETAR

Freedom is the confidence that you can live within the means of something you're passionate about.

PO BRONSON

why
this chapter matters . . .

By discovering your passions and skills, you can plan for a successful career.

what
is included . . .

Choosing who you want to be
You've got a world of choices
Explore vocational assessments
Career planning: Begin the process now
Ways to learn about careers
Test the waters—jump into the job market
Gaining experience as an intern
Financial planning: Meeting your money goals
Take charge of your credit card
Using technology to manage time and money
Choose your conversations
Contributing: The art of selfishness
Keep your career plan alive
Power Process: "Risk being a fool"
Master Student Profile: Fred Smith

how
you can use this chapter . . .

Expand your career options.
Discover a career that aligns with your interests, skills, and values.
Find your place in the world of work through concrete experiences—informational interviews, internships, and more.
Meet your financial goals while contributing to other people.

As you read, ask yourself
what if . . .

I could create the career of my dreams—starting today?

Choosing who you want to be

When people ask about your choice of career, they often pose this question: What do you want to be?

One response is to name a job. "I want to be a computer technician." "I want to be a recording engineer." "I want to be a chef." These answers really suggest what we want to *do*.

Another response is to describe a certain income level or lifestyle. "I want to be rich, with all the free time in the world." "I want to sell all my belongings, move to Hawaii, and live on the beach." These statements are actually about what we'd like to *have*.

Yet another option is to describe what you want your life to stand for—the kind of person you want to become. You could talk about being trustworthy, fun-loving, compassionate, creative, honest, productive, and accountable. These are just a few examples of the core values you can bring to any job or lifestyle that you choose.

Career planning does not begin with grinding out résumés, churning out cover letters, poring over want ads, saving for an MBA, or completing a 100-question vocation interest assessment. Any of those steps can become important or even essential—later. And they can be useless until you take time to exercise your imagination and consider what you want most of all. Career planning starts with dreaming about who you want to *be*.

Dreaming makes sense in a hard-nosed, practical way. Consider people who change careers in midlife. Many of these people have been in the work force for several decades. They've raised families, received promotions, acquired possessions. They've spent a lifetime being "practical." These people are looking for more than just another job. They want a career that pays the bills *and* excites their passions.

There's no need to wait 10, 20, or 30 years to discover your passions. You can start now by reading and completing the exercises in this chapter.

Bring up the subject of career planning and someone might say, "Well, just remember that even if you hate your job, you can always do what you want in your free time." Consider that *all* your time is free time. You give your time freely to your employers or clients, and you do this for your own purposes. All of us are "self-employed," even if we work full-time for someone else.

In this chapter you'll find many suggestions for career planning. Remember that there's more to this process than listing job titles, describing the preferred state of your bank account, or checking off a list of the possessions that you desire. Those are valid concerns—and the foundation for them includes your core values and driving desires. Through career planning, you translate these into transferable skills that are valued by employers. Once you make this translation, your career choices can fall into place like magic.

If you want to be practical, then dream about who you want to be. ◪

journal entry 28

Discovery/Intention Statement

Recall a time when you felt powerful, competent, and fulfilled. Examples might include writing a paper when the words flowed effortlessly, skillfully leading a bar mitzvah service, or working in a restaurant and creating a new dish that won rave reviews. Mentally re-create this experience and the feelings that came with it.

Now, reflect on this experience. Briefly describe the skills that you were using at that moment, the values you were demonstrating, or both.

I discovered that I . . .

_____

_____

Next, review what you just wrote for an intention that can guide your overall career plan. For example, you might write, "I intend, no matter what job I have, to be an effective leader." Or "I intend to create a career that gives free expression to my creativity."

I intend to . . .

_____

_____

Now scan this chapter for ideas that can help you act on your intention. List at least four ideas here, along with the page numbers where you can read more about them.

Strategy   *Page number*

_____

_____

_____

_____

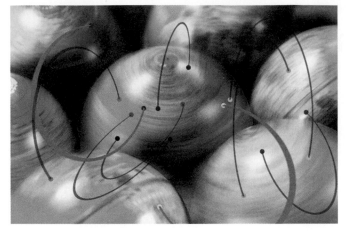

You've got a world of choices

Our society offers a limitless array of careers. You no longer have to confine yourself to a handful of traditional categories, such as business, education, government, or manufacturing.

People are constantly creating new products and services to meet emerging demands. The number of job titles is expanding so rapidly that we can barely track them.

In addition, people are constantly creating new goods and services to meet emerging needs. For instance, there are people who work as *ritual consultants*, helping people to plan weddings, anniversaries, graduations, and other ceremonies. *Space planners* help individuals and organizations to arrange furniture and equipment efficiently. *Auto brokers* will visit dealers, shop around, and buy a car for you. *Professional organizers* will walk into your home or office and advise you on managing time and paperwork. *Pet psychologists* will help you raise a happy and healthy animal. And *life coaches* will assist you to set and achieve goals relating to your career or anything else.

The global marketplace creates even more options for you. Through Internet connections and communication satellites that bounce phone calls across the planet, you can exchange messages with almost anyone, anywhere. Your customers or clients could be located in Colorado or China, Pennsylvania or Panama. You can track packages worldwide in real time and stay on top of investment opportunities as they emerge. Your skills in thinking globally could help you create a new product or service for a new market—and perhaps a career that does not even exist today.

In addition to choosing the *content* of your career, you have many options for integrating work into the context of your life. You can work full-time. You can work part-time. You can commute to a cubicle in a major corporation. Or you can work at home and take the one-minute commute from your bedroom to your desk. You can join a thriving business—or create one of your own.

If the idea of self-employment seems far-fetched, consider that as a student you already *are* self-employed. You are setting your own goals, structuring your time, making your own financial decisions, and monitoring your performance. These are all transferable skills that you could use to become your own boss.

Reading and doing this chapter will help you start gathering information on possible careers. Just remember that there is no reason to limit your choices too soon. You've got the world to choose from. ▧

exercise 27

DIG OUT THE "LIFE STORY" OF A PRODUCT

All the goods and services in our society result from work done by people. Pondering this fact may give you new possibilities for career planning.

For example, pick up any object near the place where you sit or stand right now—perhaps a computer, notebook, pen, pencil, CD, DVD, or piece of clothing. If possible, choose something that holds a special interest for you.

Next, reflect for a moment on the path that this product took from its creator into your hands. See if you can list the job title of every person who helped to plan, produce, distribute, and sell this item. If you're not sure, just brainstorm answers. After doing this exercise, you can do some research to confirm your answers.

Create your list of job titles in the space below.

_____

_____

_____

_____

Finally, scan this list for any jobs that interest you. To find out more about them, use the resources listed in the article "Ways to learn about careers."

Explore vocational assessments

Vocational assessments can be a helpful resource for self-discovery and career planning. These assessments might also be called vocational aptitude tests, skill inventories, or interest assessments. They provide useful information about personality, comfort with technology, and work preferences.

Your school's career planning, counseling, or job placement center may offer one or more of these assessments. Ask if there is a cost and if anyone will review the results with you.

The following are some better-known vocational assessments. Bear in mind that they are not tests. There are no right or wrong answers to the questions they ask. Take several of these assessments and compare the results. And what you do with the results is always a personal choice. No assessment can dictate your career direction. The choice is always yours.

No assessment can dictate your career direction. The choice is always yours.

California Psychological Inventory. The California Psychological Inventory provides a view of your professional and personal style by measuring a range of individual differences: interpersonal skills, social skills, values, achievement-seeking needs, and stylistic modes. The inventory also measures managerial potential and creative temperament.

Career Ability Placement Survey (CAPS). CAPS provides you with information about your abilities. It helps you understand your potential, and your strengths and weaknesses, and gives you a prediction of success in various types of occupations.

Career Thoughts Inventory. This vocational assessment can help you uncover negative thoughts that may impede effective, successful career planning. The inventory provides suggestions about how to change negative thoughts to positive ones required for good career choices.

Eureka Skills Inventory. This is a card-sorting skills assessment that includes the skills you normally use at work or for daily activities. You select the skills you enjoy using into categories: very satisfying, moderately satisfying, or somewhat satisfying. Your choices are mapped by a computer to show the ways you would prefer to spend your time on the job and types of occupations that use the skills you have selected in the assessment.

Hall Occupational Orientation Inventory (HOOI). This values inventory is designed to help you rank personal factors that are important aspects of choosing your career. The HOOI gives you information about your interests, abilities, needs, and values.

Myers-Briggs Type Indicator® (MBTI) Instrument. The MBTI provides insight about yourself and how someone like you fits into the world of work, working with others of similar and different profiles. Results provide personal awareness and help you identify careers and work environments where you are most likely to thrive and feel fulfilled.

Personal Career Development Profile (PCDP). The PCDP shows you how your personality relates to your career plans and potential job performance. The profile provides you with insights into your choices and preferences, emphasizing your personal strengths, including an analysis of your approach to problem solving and stress management.

The Self-Directed Search (SDS). The SDS asks you to answer a questionnaire about your interests and abilities. Upon completion, you receive a computerized report that provides you with a personality summary code. The report then lists occupations and fields of study that correlate with your personality code. You can begin career exploration with a list of occupations at your fingertips.

Strong Interest Inventory. This inventory helps you identify your interests and matches them with possible occupations. It measures interests rather than abilities and compares your likes and dislikes to those of people who are satisfied in specific careers.

Vocational Preference Inventory (VPI). This inventory is a brief personality test based on the theory that occupations can be based on personality traits. It is especially useful to people who've had ambiguous results on other vocational assessments.

USE INFORMAL WAYS TO DISCOVER YOURSELF

Vocational assessments offer one path to self-discovery. Another option is to explore your interests in a more informal and playful way. The results can be revealing and useful.

Answer the following questions by writing the first ideas that come to mind. Use additional paper as needed or create a computer file for your writing. Have fun and stay open to new insights.

Imagine that you're at a party and you're having a fascinating conversation with someone you just met. What does this person do for a living? What is your conversation about?

_____

_____

_____

_____

_____

What do you enjoy doing most with your unscheduled time? List any hobby or other activity that you do not currently define as "work."

_____

_____

_____

_____

Think about the kinds of books, newspaper and magazine articles, and television shows that are most likely to capture your attention. What subjects or situations do they involve?

_____

_____

_____

_____

If you bookmark Web sites in your Internet browser, review that list. What interests does it reveal?

_____

_____

_____

_____

_____

_____

What kind of problems do you most enjoy solving—those that involve ideas, people, or products? Give an example.

_____

_____

_____

_____

_____

_____

_____

Finally, reread your answers to the above questions. List three to five interests that are critical to your choice of career.

_____

_____

_____

_____

_____

_____

_____

Career planning

Begin the process now

When you clearly define both your career goal and path to reaching that goal, you can plan your education effectively.

Career planning is an adventure that involves continuous exploration. There are dozens of effective ways to plan your career. You can begin your career-planning adventure now by remembering the following ideas.

Acknowledge what you already know

When people learn study skills and life skills, they usually start with finding out things they don't know. That means discovering new strategies for taking notes, reading, writing, managing time, and the other subjects covered in this book.

Career planning is different. You can begin by realizing how much you know right now. You've already made many decisions about your career. This is true for young people who say, "I don't have any idea what I want to be when I grow up." It's also true for midlife career changers.

Consider the student who can't decide if he wants to be a cost accountant or a tax accountant and then jumps to the conclusion that he is totally lost when it comes to career planning. It's the same with the student who doesn't know if he wants to be a veterinary assistant or a nurse.

These people forget that they already know a lot about their career choices. The person who couldn't decide between veterinary assistance and nursing had already ruled out becoming a lawyer, computer programmer, or teacher. He just didn't know yet whether he had the right bedside manner for horses or for people. The person who was debating tax accounting versus cost accounting already knew he didn't want to be a doctor, playwright, or taxicab driver. He did know he liked working with numbers and balancing books.

In each case, these people have already narrowed their list of career choices to a number of jobs in the same field—jobs that draw on the same core skills. In general, they already know what they want to be when they grow up.

Demonstrate this for yourself. Find a long list of occupations. (One source is the *Occupational Outlook Handbook*, published by the U.S. Department of Labor and available online at **http://www.bls.gov/oco/oco1001.htm**.) Using a stack of 3x5 cards, write down about 100 randomly selected job titles, one title per card. Sort through the cards and divide them into two piles. Label one pile "Careers I've Definitely Ruled Out for Now." Label the other pile "Possibilities I'm Willing to Consider."

It's common for people to go through a stack of 100 such cards and end up with 95 in the "definitely ruled out" pile and five in the "possibilities" pile. This demonstrates that they already have a career in mind.

See your career as your creation

Many people approach career planning as if they were panning for gold. They keep sifting through the dirt, clearing the dust, and throwing out the rocks. They are hoping to strike it rich and discover the perfect career.

Other people believe that they'll wake up one morning, see the heavens part, and suddenly know what they're supposed to do. Many of them are still waiting for that magical day to dawn.

We can approach career planning in a different way. Career planning can be the bridge between our dreams and the reality of our future. Instead of seeing a career as something we discover, we can see it as something we choose. We don't find the right career. We create it.

There's a big difference between these two approaches. Thinking that there's only one "correct" choice for your career can lead to a lot of anxiety: "Did I choose the right one?" "What if I made a mistake?"

Viewing your career as your creation helps you relax. Instead of anguishing over finding the right career, you can stay open to possibilities. You can choose one career today, knowing that you can choose again later.

Suppose that you've narrowed your list of possible careers to five, and you still can't decide. Then just choose one. Any one. You might have several careers during your lifetime. You might be able to do any one of these careers next. The important thing is to choose.

One caution is in order. Choosing your career is not something to do in an information vacuum. Rather, choose after you've done a lot of research. That includes research into yourself—your skills and interests— and a thorough knowledge of what careers are available.

After all of the data has been gathered, there's only one person who can choose your career: you. This choice does not have to be a weighty one. In fact, it can be like going into your favorite restaurant and choosing from a menu that includes all of your favorite dishes. At this point, it's difficult to make a mistake. Whatever your choice, you know you'll enjoy it.

Career planning can be the bridge between our dreams and the reality of our future.

Prepare for an evolving job market

According to one traditional model of career success, the path to prosperity was to do your job well, gradually acquire new skills through training provided by your company, and get along with your coworkers. As long as you met those primary goals, you could expect a long-term relationship with a single employer, along with a stream of promotions and salary raises.

That model is history. In the job market of the twenty-first century, you can get laid off from a job even if you perform well and bond closely with colleagues. When companies merge or acquire their competitors, decisions about hiring and firing are often made on the basis of costs, not employee competence. Evolving technology will render some jobs obsolete. In addition, employers may decide to change their focus or shed certain lines of business. Corporate downsizing and reorganization could take away your job with little, if any, warning.[1]

Even when faced with these realities, you can still take charge of your career with the following strategies:

- Plan for the possibility of several careers within your lifetime—perhaps across several fields.

- Direct your own professional development by listing the transferable skills you want to acquire, creating a specific plan to develop them, and periodically assessing your progress.

- Anticipate changes in your career field and consciously choose your response to those trends.

- Define specifically how your skills contribute to an employer—and carefully document the value you add to an organization.

At any point in your career, ask: "Will my current job exist in five years? If not, what else can I do that aligns with my interests, skills, and values? And even if my job will continue, what can I do to ensure that I'm still enjoying my life's work and meeting my income goals five years from today?" That will give you time to develop new skills and expertise—or even to create a new career.

Plan by naming names

One key to making your career plan real and to ensuring that you can act on it is naming. When you create your career plan, see that you include specific names whenever they're called for:

- *Name your job.* Take the skills you enjoy using and find out which jobs use them. What are those jobs called? List them. Note that the same job might have different names.

- *Name your company—the agency or organization you want to work for.* If you want to be self-employed or start your own business, name the product or service you'd sell. Also list some possible names for your business. If you plan to work for others, name the organizations or agencies that are high on your list.

- *Name your contacts.* Take the list of organizations you just compiled. What people in these organizations are responsible for hiring? List those people and contact them directly. If you choose self-employment, list the names of possible customers or clients. All of these people are job contacts.

Expand your list of contacts by brainstorming with your family and friends. Come up with a list of names—anyone who can help you with career planning and job hunting. Write each of these names on a 3x5 card or Rolodex card. You can also use a spiral-bound notebook or a computer.

Next, call the key people on your list. After you speak with them, make brief notes about what you discussed. Also jot down any actions you agreed to take, such as a follow-up call.

Consider everyone you meet a potential member of your job network, and be prepared to talk about what you do. Develop a "pitch"—a short statement of your career goal that you can easily share with your contacts. For example: "After I graduate, I plan to work in the travel business. I'm looking for an internship in a travel agency for next summer. Do you know of any agencies that take interns?"

- *Name your location.* Ask if your career choices are consistent with your preferences about where to live and work. For example, someone who wants to make a living as a studio musician might consider living in a large city such as New York or Toronto. This contrasts with the freelance graphic artist who conducts his business mainly by phone, fax, and e-mail. He might be able to live anywhere and still pursue his career.

Remember your purpose

While digging deep into the details of career planning, take some time to back up to the big picture. Listing skills, researching jobs, writing résumés—all of this is necessary and useful. At the same time, attending to these tasks can obscure our broadest goals. To get perspective, we can go back to the basics—a life purpose.

Your deepest desire might be to see that hungry children are fed, to make sure that beautiful music keeps getting heard, or to help alcoholics become sober. When such a large purpose is clear, smaller decisions about what to do are often easier.

A life purpose makes a career plan simpler and more powerful. It cuts through the stacks of job data and employment figures. Your life purpose is like the guidance system for a rocket. It keeps the plan on target while revealing a path for soaring to the heights.

Test your career choice—and be willing to change

Career-planning materials and counselors can help you on both counts. Read books about careers and search for career-planning Web sites. Ask career counselors about skills assessments that can help you discover more about your skills and identify jobs that call for those skills. Take career-planning courses and workshops sponsored by your school. Visit the career-planning and job placement offices on campus.

Once you have a possible career choice in mind, run some informal tests to see if it will work for you. For example:

Your life purpose is like the guidance system for a rocket. It keeps the plan on target while revealing a path for soaring to the heights.

- Contact people who are actually doing the job you're researching and ask them what it's like (an *informational interview*).

- Choose an internship or volunteer position in a field that interests you.

- Get a part-time or summer job in your career field.

The people you meet through these experiences are possible sources of recommendations, referrals, and employment in the future.

Career planning is not a once-and-for-all proposition. Rather, career plans are made to be changed and refined as you gain new information about yourself and the world. Career planning never ends. If your present career no longer feels right, you can choose again—no matter what stage of life you're in. The process is the same, whether you're choosing your first career or your fifth.[2] 🖾

For more career planning strategies, visit the Houghton Mifflin Career Resource Center at

masterstudent.college.hmco.com

INVENTORY YOUR SKILLS

This exercise about discovering your skills includes three steps. Before you begin, gather at least 100 3x5 cards and a pen or pencil. Allow about one hour to complete the exercise.

Step 1

Recall your activities during the past week or month. To refresh your memory, review your responses to Exercise #5: "The Time Monitor/Time Plan process" in Chapter Two. (You might even benefit from doing that exercise again.)

Write down as many activities as you can, listing each one on a separate 3x5 card. Include work-related activities, school activities, and hobbies. Some of your cards might read "washed dishes," "tuned up my car," or "tutored a French class."

In addition to daily activities, recall any rewards you've received or recognition of your achievements during the past year. Examples include scholarship awards, athletic awards, or recognitions for volunteer work. Again, list the activities that were involved.

Spend 20 minutes on this step, listing all of the activities you can recall.

Step 2

Next, look over your activity cards. Then take another 20 minutes to list any specialized knowledge or procedures needed to complete those activities. These are your *content skills*. For example, tutoring a French class requires a working knowledge of that language. Tuning a car requires knowing how to adjust a car's timing and replace spark plugs. You could list several content skills for any one activity. Write each skill on a separate card and label it "Content."

Step 3

Go over your activity cards one more time. Look for examples of *transferable skills*. For instance, giving a speech or working as a salesperson in a computer store requires the ability to persuade people. That's a transferable skill. Tuning a car means that you can attend to details and troubleshoot. Tutoring in French requires teaching, listening, and speaking skills.

Write each of your transferable skills on a separate card.

Congratulations—you now have a detailed picture of your skills. Keep your lists of content and transferable skills on hand when writing your résumé, preparing for job interviews, and other career-planning tasks. As you think of new skills, add them to the lists.

journal entry 29

Discovery/Intention Statement

Now that you have a detailed picture of your skills, think about your intended career choice. Take a minute to reflect on the skills that you already have in relation to your career plan.

I discovered that I . . .

_____

_____

_____

Now list three specific transferable skills you want to continue to develop in school that will help you prepare for the workplace.

I intend to . . .

_____

_____

_____

Ways to learn about careers

To discover the full range of jobs that exist in our society, you can turn to many sources. These include friends, family members, teachers, classmates, coworkers—and anyone else who's ever held a job. Also check out the following sources of career information. They can lead you to more.

Publications. Visit the career planning and job hunting sections in bookstores and libraries. Look for books, magazines, videos, and other nonprint materials related to career planning. Libraries may subscribe to trade journals and industry newsletters.

Career counseling. Your school may offer career counseling as well as links to similar services in the off-campus community. Private consultants and companies offer career counseling for a fee. Ask around to find someone who's seen a career counselor and get some recommendations.

Before you pay for career counseling, find out exactly what kind of help you'll get and how much it will cost. Read contracts carefully before you sign. Talk directly to a career counselor rather than a salesperson, and see if you can get permission to contact some of the counselor's former clients.

Group sessions led by career counselors are valuable because you get to hear about the problems that other people are facing and work together to create solutions.

The Internet. Through your own searching and suggestions from others, you can find useful Web sites devoted to job hunting and career planning. One place to start is JobHuntersBible.com, which includes links to sites screened by Richard Bolles, author of *What Color Is Your Parachute?* It's online at **http://www.jobhuntersbible.com**. Bolles organizes this site around five ways that the Internet can be used in career planning and job hunting:

- To search for job openings ("want ads") posted online
- To post your résumé online
- To get career counseling
- To research potential careers and places that you might like to work
- To make contacts with people who can provide information or help you get a job interview

Also visit the Occupational Information Network (O*NET) site posted by the U.S. Department of Labor at **http://online.onetcenter.org**. Here you'll find information on hundreds of jobs that you can search by using keywords or browsing a complete list. You'll also find Skills Search, an online tool that helps you list your skills and then matches the list with potential jobs.

Another site that may interest you is CareerOneStop at **http://www.careeronestop.org**. It includes America's Job Bank (where you can search job openings and post your résumé), America's Career InfoNet (information on wages and employment trends), and America's Service Locator (a way to find career planning and job hunting services in your local area).

Of course, your searching may turn up hundreds of other sites. Evaluate them carefully.

Organizations. Professional associations exist for people in almost any career—from the American Institute of Certified Public Accountants to the American Association of Zookeepers. One function of these associations is to publicize career options and job openings of interest to their members. Search the Internet with the key words *professional associations* and follow the links that interest you. Consider joining organizations that interest you. Many offer student rates.

Government agencies at all levels—from local employment agencies to the U.S. Department of Labor—can assist you with learning about the world of work. Search the government listings in your local Yellow Pages under *employment* and *job placement*.

Trade unions, chambers of commerce, and branches of the armed forces are additional sources of information.

Elected representatives. One duty of your congressional representatives, senators, and city council members and school board members is to help create a thriving work force. Contact these people for career planning and job hunting services in your community.

CREATE YOUR CAREER PLAN—NOW

Write your career plan. Now. Get started with the process of career planning, even if you're not sure where to begin. Your response to this exercise can be just a rough draft of your plan, which you can revise and rewrite many times. The point is to start getting your ideas in writing.

Ultimately, the format of your plan is up to you. You could include many details, such as the next job title you'd like to have, the courses required for your major, and other training that you want to complete. You could list companies to research and people that could hire you. You could also include target dates to complete each of these tasks. Another option is to represent your plan visually through flow charts, timelines, mind maps, or drawings.

For now, experiment with career planning by completing the following sentences. Use the space below and continue on additional paper as needed:

The career I choose for now is . . .

_____

_____

_____

_____

_____

_____

_____

_____

The three major steps that will guide me to this career are . . .

1. _____

_____

_____

_____

_____

2. _____

_____

_____

_____

_____

_____

3. _____

_____

_____

_____

_____

_____

The three immediate steps I will take to pursue this career are . . .

1. _____

_____

_____

_____

_____

2. _____

_____

_____

_____

_____

3. _____

_____

_____

_____

_____

Test the waters—jump into the job market

Do informational interviews. Talk to people who actually do the kind of work that you'd like to do. Schedule an informational interview to ask them about their work. With their permission, go to their job sites. Spend time with them during a workday. Hang around. Ask questions.

To get the most out of an informational interview, first research the career field you've chosen and the particular business or organization you're going to visit. For example, before you interview a mutual fund manager, be sure you know what a mutual fund is. Also find some basic information about the manager's company, such as its general investment policies and recent financial history.

When scheduling an informational interview, make it clear that your purpose is not job hunting but career research. If you set up an informational interview and then use the occasion to ask for a job, you send mixed messages and risk making a negative impression.

Before your interview, prepare a list of questions, such as:

- How did you enter this line of work?
- What are your major tasks and responsibilities?
- What kind of problems and decisions do you regularly face?
- What do you like most—and least—about your job?
- What changes are occurring in this field?
- What are the salary ranges and opportunities for employment and promotion?
- How can I effectively prepare to work in this field?

While informational interviews are often one-time events, they can also involve multiple visits to several people at the same work site. You might even spend several days or weeks following people on the job. Such extended experience is sometimes referred to as *job-shadowing* or an *externship*.

Volunteer. Volunteering offers another path to work experience that you can list on your résumé. To gain the most from this experience, research and choose volunteer positions as carefully as you would a full-time, salaried job. Identify organizations that are doing the kind of work that excites you. Contact them and ask for the person who supervises volunteers. Then schedule a face-to-face meeting to find out more.

Work. To find out more about working, go to work. Beyond gaining experience, you'll get insights that can change your life. A short-term job assignment can help you define your current skills, develop new ones, refine your career plan, develop contacts, and even lead to doing work that you love.

Cooperative education programs offer one option. These programs combine specific classroom assignments with carefully supervised work experience. In addition to getting academic credit, most "co-op" students get paid and function as productive employees.

Other options include freelancing and "temping." Rather than becoming an employee, a freelancer works for organizations on specific projects. Rates of payment, due dates, and other details are specified by contract. Freelancers typically work "off site" at their own office. A temporary worker ("temp") also works on a contract basis but reports to an organization's work site.

Share the process with others. Consider forming a career planning group. Working in groups allows you to give and receive career coaching. Group members can brainstorm options for each other's careers, research the work world, share information of mutual interest, trade contacts, and pair up for informational interviews. This is one way to raise your energy level for career planning.

Taking part in a group can open you up to your dream career. Others can point out ideas and information you've overlooked. They may alert you to opportunities you never considered or skills you were not aware you had. Working with such a group gives you a firm foundation for networking—building relationships that can lead directly to a job offer. For more ideas on networking, see Chapter Ten. ✖

Gaining experience as an intern

One way to start your career path is an internship. Internships blend classroom learning with on-the-job experience and let you put your transferable skills into action. As an intern, you work in a job that relates directly to your career interests. Internships often offer academic credit. Some involve paid positions, while other internships are volunteer opportunities. Interns usually prepare for their assignments by completing courses in a specific field.

Note that internships may be called by other names. You might talk to people who use the terms *co-op experience, practicum, externship, field experience,* and *internship* synonymously. The key is to find a program that fits with your courses, your career interests, and your schedule.

Develop job skills now. Through an internship you develop skills specific to your field—as well as transferable skills that you can apply to other jobs in the same field (or even a different field). For instance, you might perform administrative duties that give you professional experience in fielding phone calls, writing correspondence, and serving customers.

Internships are also ways to learn about organizational culture, hone your skills at coping with office politics, and add contacts to your job-hunting network. These are key aspects of the work world that you experience by getting outside the classroom.

Find internships. To find an internship, make an appointment with someone at the career planning and job placement office on your campus. There you can connect with employers in your area who are looking for interns. You will likely submit a résumé and cover letter explaining your career interests. This is valuable in itself as experience in applying for jobs.

You can also locate organizations that interest you and contact them directly about internships. Even companies that do not have formal internship programs may accept applications.

Other suggestions to keep in mind:

- *Start early.* Think two or three terms ahead. During a fall semester, for example, start searching for internships for the spring or summer.
- *Network.* Talk to your friends, parents, family, neighbors, and instructors to discover if they know about internships for you. Mention your career interests and ask for suggestions.
- *Surf the Net.* Use Internet search engines to find employment or internship listings. Research organizations that interest you and contact them via e-mail.
- *Use the library.* Ask a reference librarian to help you find internship guides. Some look like college catalogs, listing popular positions with key contacts, due dates for applications, and information about getting paid.

Cultivate contacts. If the internship offers an experience aligned with your career goals and skills, your role as an intern may help lead to permanent job offers following graduation. Keep in touch with the people you meet through internships. They may be working at another company when you graduate and offer help to get your foot in the door.

Reflect on your internship. After you have completed your internship, review your experience. Write Discovery Statements about what worked well and what you would like to improve. Referring to the SCANS skills on page 8, list the transferable skills that you used and additional skills you want to gain.

Internships offer a great way to test a career choice—even if you find out that you don't like a particular field or job. Discovering what you do *not* want in a career can be just as valuable as gaining any type of work experience. You can benefit from ruling out an inappropriate career choice early on—especially if it involves a major with a lot of required courses.

Even if you find that the workplace setting or tasks involved in your internship did not meet your expectations, you can create a list of criteria that you want your next work experience to include. Be sure to incorporate the skills and experiences from any internship on your résumé—no matter what career field or job you eventually choose.

REVIST YOUR GOALS, TAKE TWO

One powerful way to achieve any goal is to assess periodically your progress in meeting it. This is especially important with long-term goals—those that can take years to achieve.

When you did Exercise #6: "Get real with your goals" on page 69, you focused on one long-term goal and planned a detailed way to achieve it. This involved setting mid-term and short-term goals that will lead to achieving your long-term goal. Take a minute to review that exercise and revisit the goals you set.

Take your long-term goal from Exercise #6 and rewrite it in the space below. If you can think of a more precise way to state it, feel free to change the wording.

I intend to . . .

_____

_____

_____

Next, check in with yourself. How do you feel about this goal? Does it still excite your interest and enthusiasm? On a scale of 1 to 10, how committed are you to achieving this goal? Describe your level of commitment in the space below.

I discovered that I . . .

_____

_____

_____

If your level of commitment is 5 or less, you might want to drop the goal and replace it with a new one. To set a new goal, just turn back to Exercise #6 and do it again. And release any self-judgment about dropping your original long-term goal. Letting go of one goal creates space in your life to set and achieve a new one.

If you're committed to the goal you just listed, consider whether you're still on track to achieve it. Have you met any of the short-term goals related to this long-term goal? If so, list your completed goals in the space below.

_____

_____

_____

Before going on, take a minute to congratulate yourself and celebrate your success.

Finally, consider any adjustments you'd like to make to your plan. For example, write additional short-term or mid-term goals that will take you closer to your long-term goal. Or cross out any goals that you no longer deem necessary. Make a copy of your current plan in the space below.

Long-term goal (to achieve within your lifetime):

_____

_____

_____

Supporting mid-term goals (to achieve in one to five years):

_____

_____

_____

Supporting short-term goals (to achieve within the coming year):

_____

_____

_____

Financial planning

Meeting your money goals

Some people shy away from setting financial goals. They think that money is a complicated subject.

Yet most money problems result from spending more than is available. It's that simple, even though often we do everything we can to make the problem much more complicated.

The solution also is simple: *Don't spend more than you have.* If you are spending more money than you have, increase your income, decrease your spending, or do both. This idea has never won a Nobel Prize in economics, but you won't go broke applying it.

Starting today, you can take three simple steps to financial independence:

- Tell the truth about how much money you have and how much you spend.

- Make a commitment to spend no more than you have.

- Begin saving money.

If you do these three things consistently, you could meet your monetary goals and even experience financial independence. This does not necessarily mean having all of the money you could ever desire. Rather, you can be free from money worries by living within your means. Soon you will control money instead of letting money control you.

Increase money in

For many of us, making more money is the most appealing way to fix a broken budget. This approach is reasonable—and it has a potential problem: When our income increases, most of us continue to spend more than we make. Our money problems persist, even at higher incomes. You can avoid this dilemma by managing your expenses no matter how much money you make.

There are several ways to increase your income while you go to school. One of the most obvious ways is to get a job. You could also apply for scholarships and grants. You might borrow money, inherit it, or receive it as a gift. You could sell property, collect income from investments, or use your savings. Other options—such as lotteries and gambling casinos—pose obvious risks. Stick to making money the old-fashioned way: Earn it.

If you work while you go to school, you can earn more than money. Working helps you gain experience, establish references, and expand your contacts in the community. Doing well at a work-study position or an internship while you're in school can also help you land a good job after you graduate.

Regular income, even at a lower wage scale, can make a big difference. Look at your monthly budget to see how it would be affected if you worked just 15 hours a week (times 4 weeks a month) for $8 an hour.

If you are currently looking for a job, make a list of several places that you would like to work. Include places that have advertised job openings and those that haven't. Then go to each place on your list and tell someone that you would like a job. This will yield more results than depending on the want ads alone.

The people you speak to might say that there isn't a job available, or that the job is filled. That's OK. Ask to see the person in charge of hiring and tell him that you want to be considered for future job openings. Then ask when you can check back.

Keep your job in perspective. If your current job relates to your major or your career field, great. If it is meaningful and contributes to society, great. If it involves working with people you love and respect, fantastic. If not—well, remember that almost any job can help you reach your career goals. Any job offers a chance to develop a skill that you can transfer to the next career of your choice.

Decrease money out

To control your expenses, you do not have to live like a miser, pinching pennies and saving used dental floss. There are many ways to decrease the amount of money you spend and still enjoy life. Consider the ideas that follow.

Look to the big-ticket items. Your choices about which school to attend, what car to buy, and where to live can save you tens of thousands of dollars. When you look for places to cut expenses, start with the items that cost the most. For example, there are several ways to keep your housing costs reasonable. Sometimes a place a little farther from your school or a smaller house will be much less expensive. You

can cut your housing costs in half by finding a roommate. Also look for opportunities to house-sit rather than paying rent. Some homeowners will even pay a responsible person to live in their house when they are away.

Look to the small-ticket items. Decreasing the money you spend on small purchases can help you balance your budget. A three-dollar cappuccino tastes good, but the amount that some people spend on such treats over the course of a year could give anyone the jitters.

Monitor money out. Each month, review your checkbook, receipts, and other financial records. Sort your expenditures into major categories such as school expenses, housing, personal debt, groceries, eating out, and entertainment. At the end of the month, total up how much you spend in each category. You might be surprised. Once you discover the truth, it might be easier to decrease unnecessary spending.

Create a budget. When you have a budget and stick to it, you don't have to worry about whether you can pay your bills on time. The basic idea is to project how much money is coming in and how much is going out and to make sure that those two amounts balance.

Creating two kinds of budgets is even more useful. A monthly budget includes regularly recurring income and expense items such as paychecks, food costs, and housing. A long-range budget includes unusual monetary transactions such as annual dividends, grants, and tuition payments that occur only a few times a year. With an eye to the future, you can make realistic choices about money today.

Do comparison shopping. Prices vary dramatically on just about anything you want to buy. You can clip coupons and wait for sales or shop around at secondhand stores, mill outlets, or garage sales. When you first go shopping, leave your checkbook and credit cards at home, a sure way to control impulse buying. Look at all of the possibilities, then make your decision later when you don't feel pressured. To save time, money, and gas, you can also search the Internet for sites that compare prices on items.

Use public transportation or car pools. Aside from tuition, a car can be the biggest financial burden in a student's budget. The purchase price is often only the tip of the iceberg. Be sure to consider the cost of parking, insurance, repairs, gas, maintenance, and tires. When you add up all of those items, you might find it makes more sense to car-pool or to take the bus or a cab instead.

Notice what you spend on "fun." Blowing your money on fun is fun. It is also a quick way to ruin your budget. When you spend money on entertainment, ask yourself what the benefits will be and whether you could get the same benefits for less money. You can read or borrow magazines for free at the library. Most libraries also loan CDs, DVDs, and videotapes at no cost. Student councils often sponsor activities, such as dances and music performances, for which there is no fee. Schools with sports facilities set aside times when students can use them for free. Meeting your friends for a pick-up basketball game at the gym can be more fun than meeting at a bar, where there is a cover charge.

Free entertainment is everywhere. However, it usually isn't advertised, so you'll have to search it out. Start with your school bulletin boards and local newspapers.

Redefine money. Think of money as what you accept in exchange for the time and energy that you put into working. When you take this view of money, you might naturally find yourself being more selective about how often you spend it and what you spend it on. It's not just cash you're putting on the line—it's your life energy.

Remember that education is worth it . . .

A college degree is one of the safest and most worthwhile investments you can make. Money invested in land, gold, oil, or stocks can be lost, but your education will last a lifetime. It can't rust, corrode, break down, or wear out. Once you have an education, it becomes a permanent part of you.

Think about all of the services and resources that your tuition money buys: academic advising; access to the student health center and counseling services; career planning and job placement offices; athletic, arts, and entertainment events; and a student center where you can meet people and socialize. If you live on campus, you get a place to stay with meals provided. By the way, you also get to attend classes.

In the long run, education pays off in increased income, job promotions, career satisfaction, and more creative use of your leisure time. These are benefits that you can sustain for a lifetime.

. . . And you can pay for it

Most students can afford higher education. If you demonstrate financial need, you can usually get financial aid. In general, financial need equals the cost of your schooling minus the amount that you can reasonably be expected to pay. Receiving financial assistance has little to do with "being poor." Your prospects for aid depend greatly on the costs of the school you attend.

Financial aid includes money you don't pay back (grants and scholarships), money you do pay back (low-interest loans), and work-study programs that land you a job while you're in school. Most students receive aid awards that include several of these elements. Visit the financial aid office on campus to find out what's available.

In applying for financial aid, you'll need to fill out a form called the Free Application for Federal Student Aid (FAFSA). You can access it on the World Wide Web at **http://www.fafsa.ed.gov**. For links to a wealth of information about financial aid in general, access **http://www.students.gov**. Create a master plan—a long-term budget listing how much you need to complete your education and where you plan to get the money. Having a plan for paying for your entire education makes completing your degree work a more realistic possibility.

Once you've lined up financial aid, keep it flowing. Find out the requirements for renewing your loans, grants, and scholarships.

Create money for the future

You don't have to wait until you finish school to begin saving and investing. You can start now, even if you are in debt and living on a diet of macaroni.

Start saving. Saving is one of the most effective ways to reach your money goals. Aim to save at least 10 percent of your monthly take-home pay. If you can save more, that's even better.

One possible goal is to have savings equal to at least six months of living expenses. Build this nest egg first as a cushion for financial emergencies. Then save for major, long-term expenses.

Put your money into insured savings accounts, money market funds, savings bonds, or certificates of deposit. These are low-risk options that you can immediately turn into cash. Even a small amount of money set aside each month can grow rapidly. The sooner you begin to save, the more opportunity your money has to grow. Time allows you to take advantage of the power of compound interest.

Invest after you have a cushion. Remember that investing is risky. Invest only money that you can afford to lose. Consider something safe, such as Treasury securities (bills, notes, and bonds backed by the federal government), bonds, no-load mutual funds, or blue chip stocks.

Avoid taking a friend's advice on how to invest your hard-earned money. Be wary, too, of advice from someone who has something to sell, such as a stockbroker or a realtor. See your banker or an independent certified financial planner instead.

Save on insurance. Once you have insured your health or your life, it's usually possible to stay insured, even if you develop a major illness. For that reason, insuring yourself now is a wise investment for the future.

Shop around for insurance. Benefits, premiums, exclusions, and terms vary considerably from policy to policy, so study each one carefully. Buy health, auto, and life insurance with high deductibles to save on premiums. Also ask about safe driver, nonsmoker, or good student discounts.

Be careful with contracts. Before you sign anything, read the fine print. If you are confused, ask questions and keep asking until you are no longer confused. After you sign a contract, policy, or lease, read the entire document again. If you think you have signed something that you will regret, back out quickly and get your release in writing. Purchase contracts in many states are breakable if you act quickly.

Use credit wisely. If you don't already have one, you can begin to establish a credit rating now. Borrow a small amount of money and pay it back on time. Also pay your bills on time. Avoid the temptation to let big companies wait for their money. Develop a good credit rating so that you can borrow large amounts of money if you need to.

Before you take out a loan to buy a big-ticket item, find out what that item will be worth *after* you buy it. A brand-new $20,000 car might be worth only $15,000 the minute you drive it off the lot. To maintain your net worth, don't borrow any more than $15,000 to buy the car.

If you're in trouble. If you find yourself in over your financial head, get specific data about your present situation. Find out exactly how much money you owe, earn, and spend on a monthly basis. If you can't pay your bills in full, be honest with creditors. Many will allow you to pay off a large debt in small installments. Also consider credit counseling with professional advisors who can help you straighten out your financial problems. You can locate these people through your campus or community phone directories. ✖

→ Places to find money for school

- Grants: Pell Grants, Supplemental Educational Opportunity Grants, state government grants

- Scholarships from federal, state, and private organizations

- Loan programs: Perkins Loans, Stafford Loans, Supplemental Loans, Consolidation Loans, Ford Direct Student Loans, and PLUS (Parent Loans for Undergraduate Students)

- Part-time or full-time jobs, including work-study programs

- Military programs: funds from the Veterans Administration and financial aid programs for active military personnel

- Programs to train the unemployed, such as JTPA (Job Training Partnership Act) and WIN (Work Incentive)

- Company assistance programs

- Social security payments

- Relatives

- Personal savings

- Selling a personal possession, such as a car, boat, piano, or house

Note: Programs change constantly. In some cases, money is limited and application deadlines are critical. Be sure to get the most current information from the financial aid office at your school.

desk of . . .

from the

MICHAEL TUCKER,
CONSTRUCTION FOREMAN:

Raising a family, holding a full-time job, and attending college part-time was initially a financial burden on my household. My academic advisor suggested I meet with a counselor from the financial aid office. Since that time, I have created a budget that is manageable, and I've even been able to put away some money for my children's education.

Take charge
of your
credit card

7389 9267 8473 9572

A credit card is compact and convenient. That piece of plastic seems to promise peace of mind. Low on cash this month? Just whip out your card, slide it across the counter, and relax. Your worries are over—that is, until you get the bill.

Credit cards often come with a hefty interest rate, sometimes as high as 27 percent. That can be over one-fifth of your credit card bill. Imagine working five days a week and getting paid for only four: You'd lose one-fifth of your income. Likewise, when people rely on high-interest credit cards to get by from month to month, they lose one-fifth of their monthly payments to interest charges. In a 2000 survey by Nellie Mae, a student loan corporation, 78 percent of undergraduate students had credit cards. Their average credit card debt was $2,748. Suppose that a student with this debt used a card with an annual percentage rate of 18 percent. Also suppose that he pays only the minimum balance due each month. He'll be making payments for 15

years and will pay an additional $2,748 in interest fees.

Credit cards do offer potential benefits. Getting a card is one way to establish a credit record. Many cards offer rewards, such as frequent flier miles and car rental discounts. Your monthly statement also offers a way to keep track of your expenses.

Used wisely, credit cards can help us become conscious of what we spend. Used unwisely, they can leave us with a load of debt that takes decades to repay. That load can seriously delay other goals—paying off student loans, financing a new car, buying a home, or saving for retirement.

Use the following three steps to take control of your credit cards before they take control of you. Write these steps on a 3x5 card and don't leave home without it.

Do a First Step about money. See your credit card usage as an opportunity to take a financial First Step. If you rely on credit cards to make ends meet every month, tell the truth about that. If you typically charge up to the maximum limit and pay just the minimum balance due each month, tell the truth about that, too.

Write Discovery Statements focusing on what doesn't work—and what does work—about the way you use credit cards. Follow up with Intention Statements regarding steps you can take to use your cards differently. Then take action. Your bank account will directly benefit.

Scrutinize credit card offers. Beware of cards offering low interest rates. These rates are often only temporary. After a few months, they could double or triple. Also look for annual fees and other charges buried in the fine print.

To simplify your financial life and take charge of your credit, consider using only one card. Choose one with no annual fee and the lowest interest rate. Don't be swayed by offers of free T-shirts or coffee mugs. Consider the bottom line and be selective.

Pay off the balance each month. Keep track of how much you spend with credit cards each month. Then save an equal amount in cash. That way, you can pay off the card balance each month and avoid interest charges. Following this suggestion alone might transform your financial life.

If you do accumulate a large credit card balance, ask your bank about a "bill-payer" loan with a lower interest rate. You can use this loan to pay off your credit cards. Then promise yourself never to accumulate credit card debt again. ✍

---

desk of...

from the

TOMÁS RAMOS,
PHARMACY TECHNICIAN:

Education by the hour is one of the exercises that opened my eyes to getting the most out of my education. Each hour that I am at school or studying is also time away from the workplace where I could be earning money. I discovered that not attending class just to be with my friends was a real mistake. I intend to be in class on time and pay full attention to get the most out of my education.

EDUCATION BY THE HOUR

Determine exactly what it costs you to go to school. Fill in the blanks below using totals for a semester, quarter, or whatever term system your school uses.

Note: Include only the costs that relate directly to going to school. For example, under "Transportation," list only the amount that you pay for gas to drive back and forth to school—not the total amount you spend on gas for a semester.

Tuition	$_____
Books	$_____
Fees	$_____
Transportation	$_____
Clothing	$_____
Food	$_____
Housing	$_____
Entertainment	$_____
Other (such as insurance, medical, childcare)	$_____
Subtotal	$_____
Salary you could earn per term if you weren't in school	$_____
Total (A)	$_____

Now figure out how many classes you attend in one term. This is the number of your scheduled class periods per week multiplied by the number of weeks in your school term. Put that figure below:

Total (B) _____

Divide the **Total (B)** into the **Total (A)** and put that amount here:

$_____

This is what it costs you to go to one class one time.

On a separate sheet of paper, describe your responses to discovering this figure. Also list anything you will do differently as a result of knowing the hourly cost of your education.

Using technology to manage time and money

When it comes to managing your time and financial resources, your computer can become as valuable as your calendar and your checkbook. In addition, gaining experience with time management, project planning, and financial software now—while you are in school—can give you additional skills to list on your résumé. Get started with the following options.

Set and meet goals. Review your responses to the goal-setting exercises in Chapter Two of this book. Take your written goals—long-term, mid-term, and short-term—and key them into a word processing file or database file. Open up this file every day to review your goals and track your progress toward meeting them.

Since success hinges on keeping goals fresh in your memory, print out a copy of your goals file each time you update it. You might wish to post your printout in a visible place, such as in your study area, on your refrigerator, or even next to a bathroom mirror.

Save yourself a trip or phone call. The Web offers sites that allow you to manage your bank account, get stock quotes, place classified ads for items you want to sell, book airline reservations, and buy almost anything. Use these sites to reduce shopping time, eliminate errands, and get discounts on purchases.

Also employ technology to decrease phone time and avoid long-distance charges. Use e-mail and real time online chatting software to stay in contact with friends, family members, classmates, and teachers.

Manage calendars, contacts, and projects. Software can help you create and edit calendars and to-do lists on your computer. Typically, these applications also allow you to store contact information—mailing addresses, phone numbers, and e-mail addresses—for the key people in your life. To find such products, search the Web using the keywords *contact management, project management, time management,* and *software.*

Also use your computer to prevent the snafus that can result when you want to coordinate your calendar with those of several other people. This is often a necessity in completing group projects. Consider creating an area on the Web where group members can post messages, share files, and access an online calendar that shows scheduled events. One option is the *calendar* link at **www.yahoo.com**.

Crunch numbers and manage money. Many students can benefit from crunching numbers on a computer with spreadsheets such as Excel. This type of computer software allows you to create and alter budgets of any size. By plugging in numbers based on assumptions about the future, you can quickly create many scenarios for future income and expenses. Quicken and similar products include spreadsheets and other features that can help you manage personal and organizational finances.

Employ a personal digital assistant (PDA). These devices—also called *palmtops* or *pocket PCs*—are handheld computers designed to replace paper-based calendars and planning systems. Many PDAs are small enough to fit in a pocket or purse. You can use them to list appointments and view your schedule in a daily, weekly, or monthly format. If you have a recurring event, such as a meeting that takes place at the same time every week, you can just enter it once and watch it show up automatically on your PDA.

Using a PDA, you can also take notes, create contact lists, manage to-do lists, and keep track of personal expenses. Capabilities for connecting to the Internet and sending e-mail are becoming standard features as well. In addition, PDAs come with software for exchanging files with a personal computer. This allows you to store essential information—such as appointments, to-do lists, and contacts—in a form that's even more portable than a laptop computer. ⊠

Choose your conversations

From Master Student to Master Employee invites you to take part in a conversation about success in higher education and the workplace.

This chapter, in particular, aims to engage you in a conversation about career planning. By doing the exercises and journal entries in this chapter and discussing the articles in class, you choose to make this conversation come alive.

The idea of referring to a book as a *conversation* might seem strange to you. If so, consider that conversations can exist in many forms. One involves people talking out loud to each other. At other times, the conversation takes place inside our own heads, and we call it thinking. In this sense, we are even having a conversation when we read a magazine or a book, watch television or a movie, or write a letter or a report. These observations have three implications that wind their way through every aspect of our lives.

Conversations exercise incredible power over what we think, feel, and do. We become our conversations. They shape our attitudes, our decisions, our opinions, our emotions, and our actions. Each of these is primarily the result of what we say over and over again, to ourselves and to others. If you want clues as to what a person will be like tomorrow, listen to what she's talking about today.

Conversation is constant

Given that conversations are so powerful, it's amazing that few people act on this fact. Most of us swim in a constant sea of conversations, almost none of which we carefully and thoughtfully choose.

Consider how this works. It begins when we pick up the morning paper. The articles on the front page invite us to a conversation about current events. The advertisements start up a conversation about fantastic products for us to buy. They talk about hundreds of ways for us to part with our money.

That's not all. If we flip on the radio or television, or if we surf the Web, millions of other conversations await us. Thanks to modern digital technology, many of these conversations take place in surround sound, high-resolution images, and living color 24 hours each day.

Something happens when we tune in to conversation in any of its forms. We give someone else permission to dramatically influence our thoughts—the conversation in our heads. It's possible to let this happen dozens of times each day without realizing it.

You have a choice

We can choose our conversations. Certain conversations create real value for us. They give us fuel for reaching our goals. Others distract us from what we want. They might even create lasting unhappiness and frustration.

We can choose more of the conversations that exhilarate and sustain us. Sometimes we can't control the outward circumstances of our lives. Yet no matter what happens, we can retain the right to choose our conversations.

If you want clues as to what a person will be like tomorrow, listen to what she's talking about today.

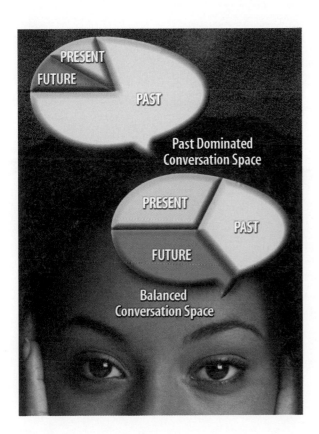

PRESENT
FUTURE
PAST

Past Dominated Conversation Space

PRESENT
PAST
FUTURE

Balanced Conversation Space

Suppose that you meet with your supervisor at work to ask for help in writing an e-mail that will go out to members of a project team. She launches into a tirade about your writing skills. This presents you with several options. One is to talk about what a jerk the supervisor is and give up on the idea of learning to write well. Another option is to refocus the conversation on what you can do to improve your writing skills, such as working with a writing coach or taking a class in writing for the workplace. These two sets of conversations will have vastly different consequences for your success.

The conversations you have are dramatically influenced by the people you associate with. If you want to change your attitudes about almost anything—prejudice, politics, religion, humor—choose your conversations by choosing your community. Spend time with people who speak about and live consistently with the attitudes you value. Use conversations to change habits. Use conversations to create new options in your life.

Consider choosing *not* to participate in certain conversations. Sometimes we find ourselves in conversations that are not empowering—gripe sessions, gossip, and the like. That's a time for us to switch the conversation channel. It can be as simple as changing the topic, politely offering a new point of view, or excusing ourselves and walking away.

Conversations promote success

When we choose our conversations, we discover a tool of unsurpassed power. Career planning is simply a sustained conversation about creating your life's work—and the life of your dreams. Conversation has the capacity to remake our thoughts—and thus our lives. It's as simple as choosing the next article you read or the next topic you discuss with a friend.

Start choosing your conversations and watch what happens. ❖

CREATE A SUPPORT TEAM

To fuel your energy for career planning, create your own support team.

Begin by listing the names of at least five people with whom you can share your frustrations and successes in career planning and job hunting. These can be friends, family members, coworkers, or classmates. Include each person's name, telephone number, and e-mail address. Begin your list in the space below.

_____

_____

_____

_____

_____

_____

_____

_____

_____

_____

_____

_____

_____

_____

_____

_____

_____

From this list, recruit people to be on your support team. Tell each team member your goals and intended actions. Ask them to help in holding you accountable to your plan. Keep touching base with each member of your team and support them in return.

Keep adding to your support team. Post the most current list of members in a conspicuous place. Then use it.

Contributing: The art of selfishness

This book is about contributing to yourself—about taking care of yourself, being selfish, and fulfilling your own needs. The techniques and suggestions in these pages focus on ways to get what you want out of school and out of life.

One of the results of all this successful selfishness is the capacity for contributing, for giving to others. Contributing is what's left to do when you're satisfied, when your needs are fulfilled—and it completes the process.

People who are satisfied with life can share that satisfaction with others. It is not easy to contribute to another person's joy until you experience joy yourself. The same is true for love. When people are filled with love, they can more easily contribute love to others.

One way to transform your conversation about career planning is to look at work as a form of contribution. Through your skills and effort, you offer something to the world. You help to create a product or service that can generate value for other people. The work that you do can contribute in some way to reducing human suffering and helping people to create happiness, health, love, and wealth.

Our interdependence calls for contributing. Every day we depend on contributing. We stake our lives on the compassion of other people. When we drive, we depend on others for our lives. If a driver in an oncoming lane should cross into our own lane, we might die. We also depend upon the sensibilities of world leaders for our safety. People everywhere are growing more interdependent. A plunge in the U.S. stock market reverberates in markets across the planet. A decrease in oil prices gives businesses everywhere a shot in the arm. A nuclear war would ignore national boundaries and devastate life on the planet. Successful arms negotiations allow all people to sleep a little easier.

In this interdependent world, there is no such thing as win/lose. If others lose, their loss directly affects us. If we lose, it is more difficult to contribute to others.

The only way to win and to get what we want in life is for others to win, also.

A caution. The idea of contributing is not the same as knowing what is best for other people. We can't know. There are people, of course, who go around "fixing" others: "I know what you need. Here, do it my way." That is not contributing. It often causes more harm than good and can result in dependence on the part of the person we are "helping."

True contributing occurs only after you find out what another person wants or needs and then determine that you can lovingly support his having it.

How you can begin contributing. The world will welcome your gifts of time, money, and talent. The advantages of contributing are clear. When we contribute, the whole human family benefits in a tangible way. Close to home, contributing often means getting involved with other people. This is one way to "break the ice" in a new community and meet people with interests similar to your own.

When you've made the decision to contribute, the next step is knowing how. There are ways to contribute in your immediate surroundings. Visit a neighbor, take a family member to a movie, or offer to tutor a roommate. Look for ways you can contribute by volunteering. An additional benefit of volunteer work is that it offers a way to explore possible career choices. Consider the following organizations, for starters.

Sierra Club, Greenpeace, Audubon Society, World Wildlife Fund, and similar organizations are dedicated to protecting the environment and endangered species.

Amnesty International investigates human rights violations. It assists people who are imprisoned or tortured for peacefully expressing their points of view. You can participate in letter-writing campaigns.

Museums and art galleries need interested people to conduct tours and provide supervision. Performing arts organizations, such as local theater groups or ballet companies, are always in need of volunteers for everything from set decoration to ticket sales.

Hospitals and hospice programs often depend on volunteer help to supplement patient care provided by the professional staff. Nursing homes welcome visitors who are willing to spend time listening to and talking with residents. Most communities have volunteer-based programs for people living with HIV infection or AIDS that provide daily hot meals to men, women, and children too ill to cook for themselves. Political parties, candidates, and special interest groups need volunteers to stuff envelopes, gather petition signatures, and distribute

It is not easy to contribute to another person's joy until you experience joy yourself.

literature. The American Red Cross provides disaster relief. Local community care centers use volunteers to help feed homeless people.

Service organizations such as Jaycees, Kiwanis, Lions, American Association of University Women, Business and Professional Women, and Rotary want members who are willing to serve others.

Tutoring centers offer opportunities for competent students to help non-English-speaking people, grade school and high school students, and illiterate adults. Churches of all denominations want volunteers to assist with projects for the community and beyond. World hunger groups want you to help feed starving people and to inform all of us about the problems of malnutrition, food spoilage, and starvation. These groups include Oxfam America, CARE, and The Hunger Project.

Considering the full scope of our international problems reminds us that there are plenty of opportunities for contributing. For instance, there are still enough nuclear warheads on the planet to end human life. And according to the *Human Development Report 2003*, commissioned by the United Nations, 1,242 million people in the world live on less than one dollar per day.[3]

If they remain unused, the techniques and strategies in this book make no difference in all this. However, *you* can make a difference. By using these techniques to work with others, you can choose a new future for our planet. ✖

from the desk of…

MELISSA SILVESTRI, SPECIAL EVENTS ASSOCIATE:
I had participated in a charity bike ride that benefited my organization. After working on fundraising for this event, I realized nonprofit work was a field I was interested in. Two years later a position opened, and I had a foot in the door due to my past contact. I was able to get an interview and score the job.

If you did Exercise #30 on page 286, you created a rough draft of your career plan. (If you skipped that exercise, please go back and do it now.) Take the time now to review what you wrote and think critically about your plan. Answer the following questions:

Did you consider the possibility of having several different careers within your lifetime?

_____

_____

Did you list the skills you need for each career that you want—and include a way to develop each skill?

_____

_____

Did you include a way to document the value that you create for an employer—such as new products or services you can develop, sales goals that you can meet, or savings that you can create?

_____

_____

_____

Did you include a way to monitor developments in your career field—especially those that could affect your ability to find employment or meet your income goals?

_____

_____

_____

Did you name the specific jobs that you would like to have?

_____

_____

Did you name specific organizations that you would like to work for, their location, and people at those organizations who could hire you?

_____

_____

_____

In the space below, summarize your answers to these questions. Note any specific changes to make in your career plan.

_____

_____

_____

Keep your career plan alive

You can use a variety of means to remember your goals and continue creating your future, including your career. Following are some suggestions.

Display your goals. Without reminders, even skilled planners can forget their goals. One solution is to post written goals in prominent locations—the bathroom, bedroom, hall mirror, or office door. Also write goals on 3x5 cards and tape them to walls or store them next to your bed. Review the cards every morning and night.

You can make goals even more visible. Create an elaborate poster or collage that displays your life purpose. Use frames, color, graphics, and other visual devices to rivet your attention on your goals.

Add to your plan. Goals might pop into your mind at the oddest moments—while you're waiting in line, riding the bus, or stuck in rush-hour traffic. With a little preparation, you can capture those fleeting goals. Carry around a few 3x5 cards and a pen in your pocket or purse.

As the advertisement said, don't leave home without them. Or pack a small voice recorder with you. Speak your goals and preserve them for the ages.

Schedule time for career planning. Schedule a regular time and place to set and review career goals. This is an important appointment with yourself. Treat it as seriously as an appointment with your doctor.

Remember that planning does not have to take a lot of time. In just one minute you can do the following:

- Reread your life purpose statement.
- Review your career plan.
- Jot down a goal or two.
- Visualize yourself meeting a goal.
- Repeat an affirmation related to your goals.

Advertise your career plan. When it comes to achieving your goals, everyone you know is a potential ally. Take a tip from Madison Avenue and advertise. Tell friends and family members about what you plan to be, do, or have. Make your career plan public.

Enlist support. People might criticize your goals: "You want to promote world peace *and* become a millionaire? That's crazy." Remember that there are ways to deal with resistance.

One is to ask directly for support. Explain how much your goal means to you and what you'll do to achieve it. Mention that you're willing to revise your goal as circumstances change. Also *keep* talking about your vision. Goals that sound outlandish at first can become easier to accept over time.

Get coaching. You can hire a personal life coach to assist with goal setting and achievement. The principle is the same as hiring a personal trainer to set and meet fitness goals. A life coach engages you in a conversation about goals for all areas of your life—work, family, finances, education, spirituality, and more. To find such a person, key the words *life coach* into your favorite search site on the Web. National organizations for life coaches have their own sites, which can link you with resources in your own area.

Teach career planning. There's a saying: We teach what we most want to learn. You can turn this idea into an incentive for creating your future. Explain the process of career planning to friends and family. Volunteer to lead an informal seminar or workshop on this topic. If you have children, help them to set and meet goals.

Enjoy the rewards. Break large, long-term career goals into small tasks that you can finish in one hour or less.

Savor the feeling that comes with crossing items off a to-do list. Experience accomplishment often.

At least once each year, list the career goals that you achieved and celebrate. Do the same with goals in all areas of your life. Let the thrill of meeting one goal lead you to setting more. ◙

exercise 34

TRANSLATE CAREER GOALS INTO ACTION

1. Choose one goal from your career plan. List that goal here:

_____

_____

_____

_____

_____

2. Next, list some follow-up actions. Ask yourself: What will it really take for me to meet this goal? List at least five ideas below:

_____

_____

_____

_____

_____

_____

_____

_____

_____

_____

3. Finally, translate any action you just listed into immediate steps—the kind of items that you would include on a daily to-do list. Think of tasks that you could complete in less than one hour, or start within the next 24 hours.

_____

_____

_____

_____

_____

_____

_____

_____

_____

_____

You can apply this three-step technique to any goal for your career or the rest of your life. The point is to move from ideas into action.

power process

Risk being a fool

A powerful person has the courage to take risks. And taking risks means being willing to fail sometimes—even to be a fool. This idea can work for you because you already are a fool.

Don't be upset. All of us are fools at one time or another. There are no exceptions. If you doubt it, think back to that stupid thing you did just a few days ago. You know the one. Yes . . . *that* one. It was embarrassing and you tried to hide it. You pretended you weren't a fool. This happens to everyone.

People who insist that they have never been fools are perhaps the biggest fools of all. We are all fallible human beings. Most of us, however, spend too much time and energy trying to hide our fool-hood. No one is really tricked by this—not even ourselves. And whenever we pretend to be something we're not, we miss part of life.

For example, many of us never dance because we don't want to risk looking ridiculous. We're not wrong. We probably would look ridiculous. That's the secret of risking being a fool.

It's OK to look ridiculous while dancing. It's all right to sound silly when singing to your kids. Sometimes it's OK to be absurd. It comes with taking risks.

Taking risks is not being foolhardy

Sometimes it's not OK to be absurd. This Power Process comes with a warning label: Taking risks does *not* mean escaping responsibility for our actions. "Risk being a fool" is not a suggestion to get drunk at a party and make a fool of yourself. It is not a suggestion to act the fool by disrupting class. It is not a suggestion to be foolhardy or to "fool around."

"Risk being a fool" means recognizing that foolishness—along with dignity, courage, cowardice, grace, clumsiness, and other qualities—is a human characteristic. We all share it. You might as well risk being a fool because you already are one, and nothing in the world can change that. Why not enjoy it once in a while? Consider the case of the person who won't dance because he's afraid he'll look foolish. This same person will spend an afternoon tripping over his feet on a basketball court. If you say that his jump shot from the top of the key looks like a circus accident, he might even agree.

"So what?" he might say. "I'm no Michael Jordan." He's right. On the basketball court, he is willing to risk looking like a fool in order to enjoy the game.

He is no Fred Astaire, either. For some reason, that bothers him. The result is that he misses the fun of dancing. (Dancing badly is as much fun as shooting baskets badly—and maybe a lot more fun.)

There's one sure-fire way to avoid any risk of being a fool, and that's to avoid life. The writer who never finishes a book will never have to worry about getting negative reviews. The center fielder who sits out every game is safe from making any errors. And the comedian who never performs in front of an audience is certain to avoid telling jokes that fall flat. The possibility of succeeding at any venture increases when we're comfortable with making mistakes—that is, with the risk of being a fool.

Look at courage in a new way

Again, remember the warning label. This Power Process does not suggest that the way to be happy in life is to do

The possibility of succeeding at any venture increases when we're comfortable with making mistakes—that is, with the risk of being a fool.

things badly. Courage involves the willingness to face danger and risk failure. Mediocrity is not the goal. The point is that mastery in most activities calls for the willingness to do something new, to fail, to make corrections, to fail again, and so on. On the way to becoming a good writer, be willing to be a bad writer.

Consider these revised clichés: Anything worth doing is worth doing badly at first. Practice makes improvement. If at first you don't fail, try again.

Most artists and athletes have learned the secret of being foolish. Comedians are especially well versed in this art. All of us know how it feels to tell a joke and get complete silence. We truly look and feel like fools. Professional comedians risk feeling that way for a living. Being funny is not enough for success in the comedy business. A comedian must have the courage to face failure.

Courage is an old-fashioned word for an old-fashioned virtue. Traditionally, people have reserved that word for illustrious acts of exceptional people—the campaigns of generals and the missions of heroes.

This concept of courage is fine. At the same time, it can be limiting and can prevent us from seeing courage in everyday actions. Courage is the kindergartner who, with heart pounding, waves good-bye to his parents and boards the bus for his first day of school. Courage is the 40-year-old who registers for college courses after being away from the classroom for 20 years.

For a student, the willingness to take risks means the willingness to experiment with new skills, to achieve personal growth, and sometimes to fail. The rewards of risk taking include expanded creativity, more satisfying self-expression, and more joy.

An experiment for you

Here's an experiment you can conduct to experience the joys of risk taking. The next time you take a risk and end up doing something silly or stupid, allow yourself to be totally aware of your reaction. Don't deny it. Don't cover it up. Notice everything about the feeling, including the physical sensations and thoughts that come with it. Acknowledge the foolishness. Be exactly who you are. Explore all of the emotions, images, and sensations surrounding your experience.

Also remember that we can act independently of our feelings. Courage is not the absence of fear but the willingness to take risks even when we feel fear. We can be keenly homesick and still register for classes. We can tremble at the thought of speaking in public yet still walk up to the microphone.

When we fully experience it, the fear of taking risks loses its power. Then we have the freedom to expand and grow. ⬛

from the desk of . . .

HEATHER HOLDREDGE, TEACHER:

I worked in the banking sector post graduation, but did not enjoy it. I quit my job after two years and traveled through Europe for seven weeks by myself. After I returned, I was asked by a relative to volunteer at the local middle school for a computer project. After a month, the principal asked if I wanted to try teaching for the rest of the year. I thought I had nothing to lose. I was hooked by the end of the school year.

career application

Tiana Kabiri earned her BA in computer science and found a job in her field within a month after she graduated.

She now works as a systems programmer for a large bank with seven local branches. Tiana was the first person in her family to gain a college degree. Her friends and relatives are thrilled with her accomplishments.

While in school, Tiana took part in several workshops on career planning. However, she never did many of the suggested exercises and largely downplayed the concept of career planning. Defining her interests, thinking about the skills she most wanted to develop, and researching employment trends just seemed like too much work.

Besides, according to the National Association of Colleges and Employers, starting salary offers for graduates with a bachelor's degree in computer programming averaged $45,558 a year in 2003. When Tiana heard this, she figured that was all the information she needed in order to choose her career.

One day at work, Tiana received an e-mail from a friend who was still in school—a student majoring in computer science and actively engaged in career planning. The message included these quotations from the online version of the *Occupational Outlook Handbook* published by the U.S. Department of Labor:

Employment of programmers is expected to grow about as fast as the average for all occupations through 2012. . . . Employment of programmers, however, is expected to grow much more slowly than that of other computer specialists. With the rapid gains in technology, sophisticated computer software now has the capability to write basic code, eliminating the need for more programmers to do this routine work. . . . Furthermore, as the level of technological innovation and sophistication increases, programmers are likely to face increasing competition from programming businesses overseas, to which much routine work can be contracted out at a lower cost.

Tiana read this and felt a wave of panic. As an entry-level programmer, she was now worried about her long-term job security. She was happy with her salary and her job seemed secure for the near future. But she worried that her skills would eventually become obsolete or that her job would be "outsourced" and eliminated. ◪

Reflecting on this scenario:

1. Imagine that you are a career counselor and that Tiana has scheduled an appointment with you. You have one hour to give her a crash course on career planning. What are two or three of the major points you would make?

_____

_____

_____

2. Access the online *Occupational Outlook Handbook* at **http://www.bls.gov/oco/ocos110.htm#outlook**. Search the term *computer and mathematical occupations*. Based on the kinds of jobs listed there, what computer skills could you recommend that Tiana develop in order to enhance her long-term job security?

_____

_____

_____

3. Looking beyond Tiana's skills in programming, list five transferable skills that you would recommend Tiana to develop that will help her in the future.

_____

_____

_____

Name _____ Date _____/_____/_____

1. Aside from looking for a specific position on the Internet, name two useful ways to use the Web as a tool for career planning.

2. The text suggests that you add specifics to your career plan by "naming names." List three examples of these specifics.

3. Define the traditional model of career success and give one reason why it is changing.

4. Describe two reasons why internships are valuable experiences as you create your career plan.

5. The best way to get useful information from a vocational assessment is to take one and make it a blueprint for choosing your career. True or False? Explain your answer.

6. List three questions that you could ask during an informational interview.

7. List the three steps recommended in this chapter for achieving financial independence.

8. Explain how career planning can be a process of choosing instead of a process of discovery.

9. Contributing to others does *not* involve:
   (A) Telling people what is best for them.
   (B) Finding out what people want or need.
   (C) Determining if you can help people get what they want.
   (D) Giving your time, talent, or money.
   (E) Making sure that you experience satisfaction, also.

10. List three options for decreasing spending.

learning styles application

The questions below will "cycle" you through four styles, or modes, of learning as explained in the article "Learning styles: Discovering how you learn" in Chapter One. Each question will help you explore a different mode. You can answer the questions in any order.

what if *Imagine that you will do no career planning. After reading this chapter, do you see any advantages to this approach? How about any disadvantages? Summarize your thoughts in the space below.*

why *Supposed that another student in one of your classes says, "Career planning is irrelevant to me. Besides being in school, I work full-time and have a family. I don't have time to plan a career." In a brief paragraph, sum up your response to this statement.*

how *Name a job you would like to have in the next 3 to 10 years. Then, list the five most important skills you will need to have in order to do that job.*

what *Do a very brief career plan by naming the job titles you would like to hold in 3 years, 5 years, and 10 years from today.*

master student

FRED SMITH

a graduate of Yale and the founder and CEO of Federal Express Corporation.

Frederick W. Smith may have a common last name, but he is a most uncommon man. What other American business leader of today had a revolutionary idea and converted it into a company that, starting from scratch and with heavy early losses, passed the $500 million revenue mark and had a 10 percent net profit margin in a few years?

What other American business leader with so brilliant an idea first wrote it out in a college paper that was graded C? Or says that the people with the greatest impact on him have been a poorly educated sergeant whom he led in combat and a science professor who liked to buzz a university stadium in a fighter plane?

Fred Smith is chairman and chief executive officer of Memphis-based Federal Express Corporation, an air cargo firm that specializes in overnight delivery door-to-door, using its own planes.

To put it another way, Fred Smith is Federal Express.

Smith got his revolutionary idea in the 60's while majoring in economics and political science at Yale. Technological change had opened a radically new transportation market, he decided. . . .

"Steamboats and trains were the logistics arm of the Industrial Revolution's first stage," he says. "Trucks became a good logistics arm later—and still are because of their flexibility. But moving the parts and pieces to support the Electronics Age requires very fast transportation over long distances. I became convinced that a different type of system was going to be a major part of the national economy. . . ."

Smith spelled it out in an overdue economics paper. To cut cost and time, packages from all over the country would be flown to a central point, there to be distributed and flown out again to their destinations—a hub-and-spokes pattern, his company calls it today. The flying would be late at night when air lanes were empty. Equipment and documents from anywhere in the U.S. could be delivered anywhere in the U.S. the next day. . . .

For the benefit of business history, it would be nice to have that college paper today. But who saves college papers, particularly those done in one night and branded mediocre?

He says one reason he was no scholastic superstar was that many courses he had to take didn't interest him. Other things did. He and two faculty members resurrected a long-dormant flying club at Yale. One of his cohorts was Professor Norwood Russell Hansen.

"Russ taught the psychology of science—how science was developed," Smith says. "I was a friend of his, not one of his students. He had a big impact on me because of his outlook on life. He was a great singer and a pianist of virtual concert talent. He rode a motorcycle, and he had a World War II fighter plane that he flew all over the place. He buzzed Yale Bowl from time to time. He marched to the beat of a different drummer. . . ."

Will Smith be successful in future undertakings? Says Arthur C. Bass, vice chairman: "A few years ago, some of us used to let off steam in the afternoon playing basketball on a court behind an apartment house. It was amazing—no matter who had the ball and no matter where Fred was on the court, if Fred's side needed to score to win, he would get the ball and make the winning basket. That's the way he is in the business world." ⌧

"A Business Visionary Who Really Delivered" by Henry Altman, from *Nation's Business,* November 1981. Reprinted by permission of *Nation's Business,* November 1981. Copyright ©1981, U.S. Chamber of Commerce.

For more biographical information on Fred Smith, visit the Master Student Hall of Fame on the *Becoming a Master Student* Web site at:

> masterstudent.college.hmco.com

CHAPTER 10
Mastering Work

Chapter Ten is about helping students succeed as they begin to make transitions from master student to master employee. This includes preparing them for sending out résumés and going on interviews. The lead article helps students continue to make the connection between school and the workplace. Success in higher education promotes success in the workplace. Use these culminating ideas to promote success in gaining employment and applying the skills from this course to the workplace.

Chapter Ten provides so much reflection and closure that it's essential to plan your course out carefully so students will have time to read and complete the activities in this final chapter. Dean Mancina, an instructor at Golden West College, has this students reread the Introduction during the final week of class. He reports that his students find the materials take on a new meaning because students understand them better. Dean also encourages his students to make a commitment to review the chapters of the textbook in the following semester, one per week, to keep the concepts and strategies fresh in their minds. Rereading the Introduction demonstrates the benefits of a second reading of the text.

Page 310
Master Student Map

Students can use this chapter to answer important questions you've likely been discussing all semester: **how?** can I effectively use the strategies I learned in this class for job hunting; **how?** can I be fully prepared for job interviews? Students should be able to freely talk about transferable skills and answer **what if?** questions: **what if?** I apply the skills from this course to assist me in meeting my goals in higher education?

Page 316
Write a résumé that gets noticed

The materials provided in *From Master Student to Master Employee* related to résumé building should be considered a preliminary guideline. This is a tool to help students get started and perhaps gain employment while they are in school. If your students are not yet ready to create their own résumés, consider having them create a résumé that answers a specific Help Wanted ad that they pull from the newspaper or a Web site with job listings. This mock résumé can be used as a goal-setting tool. What skills do you want to be able to write on your résumé? How can you successfully practice these skills in higher education, or at an internship?

Page 320
Sell your résumé with an effective cover letter

Have your students follow up their work on their résumés by writing a cover letter that addresses their accomplishments and skills, aligning them to a position they are applying for (building on the previous article's exercise). This is another opportunity for students to practice their writing skills. Use the examples in the text as models. Have your students do peer editing in the classroom. More information on peer editing techniques is available on the HM ClassPrep CD.

The HM Assessment and Portfolio Builder tool can be used in guiding students to create effective résumés. Have your students complete the assessment and fill in their Accomplishments Report. This report can be used to populate their résumé and will help students focus on their accomplishments. The report will also show students where they need continue to build skills through community services, campus activities, or internships.

Page 326
Use interviews to hire yourself an employer

Set up a day of mock interviews with your students. Have students prepare to answer key interviewing questions. Instruct each student to write one interviewing question on a 3x5 card. Collect these cards and use them at your mock interviews to ask students key questions. Encourage your students to dress as they would for an interview. Invite upperclassmen to be the interviewees, or pair students up with their peers in class.

Alternatively, a free video, *The Interviewing Process: Strategies for Making the Right Impression*, is available for you to use in your course. Taking students through the interviewing process from start to finish, this video provides strategies to be successful in a job search, and has tips from Career Counselor Susan Loffredo. Simulated interviewing scenarios conducted by actual professionals and managers will allow your students to have a bird's eye view of what a real interview looks like. To enhance this video, accompanying activities and discussion questions to help students better understand the strategies for successful interviewing are available on your HM Class Prep CD and on the Instructor's Web site.

Page 343
EXERCISE #37: "The Discovery Wheel—coming full circle"

Begin this in-class assignment by having your students complete the post-Discovery Wheel in this final chapter. Ask them to compare the scores they have just given themselves to the scores from the pre-Discovery Wheel they completed in Chapter One. Then have students subtract their pre-Discovery Wheel scores from their post-Discovery Wheel scores. This difference can be insightful. Some students like to divide the pre-Wheel by the post-Wheel and note the percentage difference in their scores. They describe the result as a percentage increase in their academic awareness.

The total difference represents the change in their self-confidence. Many students see dramatic improvements. This is a powerful tool—the Discovery Wheel reveals the truth about students to themselves. **Note:** Occasionally you will have a student whose scores go down. This is an important example of the power of telling the truth and how the truth can change.

Page 348
POWER PROCESS: "Be it"

Now that this course is completed, it's exciting for students to reflect on their educational and career goals one last time before exiting the class. Once they learn to use the tools and strategies presented in *From Master Student to Master Employee*, many of my students raise their level of expectation to include additional educational and career achievements. They know now how easy it can be for them to pursue goals they would never have considered before. In class, ask them to brainstorm individually a list of their hopes, dreams, and goals. Have them answer the following questions on a sheet of paper: What do you want to be? What do you want to do? What do you want to have? For example, they might write:

> I want to be a poet.
> I want to go to Stanford University.
> I want to have a career in which I travel throughout the world.

Then ask the students to sit in a large circle. Ask them to change WANTs to BEs. In the example above, the changes might look like this:

> I am a poet.
> I am a Stanford University student.
> I am in a career in which I travel throughout the world.

Ask them to look at their paper and read it to themselves silently. How does it feel to see this on paper? It's as if the future is happening in the present! Ask students to read their affirmation statements out loud to their classmates. It's an opportunity to proclaim their goals. It's a First Step of the Power Process: "Be it."

→ Conveying the relevance of portfolios

Your first-year experience course is a perfect place for students to practice collecting their work in a way that reflects their academic development and accomplishments. Encourage students to personalize their portfolios using the following portfolio exercise suggestions to help students reflect on their growth over time. A portfolio is a work in progress. Each of your student's portfolios will be uniquely different from each other's at the conclusion of the course. Consider having a sharing day and end-of-semester celebration at the end of your course where students can review and reflect on each other's portfolios.

- **Create a personal profile.** Personal profiles help to catalog your student's background, education, employment, activities, hobbies, and college skills. It can be used as a resource for learning more about your students. A sample personal profile form is available for download and distribution to your students from the HM ClassPrep CD. Consider customizing the profile to your liking, and to your campus. Consider allowing students to omit sensitive items if they prefer not to answer them (especially if you are requiring that they submit it for a grade).

- **Discover learning preferences.** After your students complete their Discovery Wheel in Chapter One, have them include their wheel and Journal Entry in their portfolio. At the end of the course they can use their portfolio to compare their discoveries from the first week of class, to those discoveries they have in the post-course Discovery Wheel in Chapter Ten.

  The Learning Style Inventory is another item that should be cataloged for future reflection. Students can pursue other inventories available on your campus (like the MBTI, Strong Interest Inventory). These tools can help students to prepare for their future courses and career choices.

- **Review goal-setting exercises.** *From Master Student to Master Employee* provides students with many opportunities for setting goals. Beginning with Exercise 6 (page 69) students can begin to plan long-term goals, mid-term goals and short-term goals. Periodically they are encouraged to revisit these goals and make updates. Filing this material in a portfolio provides them with the ability to easily measure their growth and note their changes throughout their semester, and college experience.

  The HM Assessment and Portfolio Builder provides students with another opportunity for self-reflection and future planning. The Assessment and Portfolio builder is an online tool that you can use in your classroom to reinforce goal setting, accomplishments, attitudes, and values to your students. Have you students assess the skills that they come to college with, and work with your students to plan for accomplishments throughout their college experience and their future in the workplace.

- **Prepare for the future.** As students assess their major and career interest, their portfolio can be a place to keep track of their education plan, lists of courses they need to complete in order to graduate, and other program requirements. Help your students also to consider what types of materials may be relevant work to share with their perspective employers. For example, if a student writes for a publication on your campus, their published articles could be inserted into their portfolio and shared during an interview. If a student participates in campus organizations or service-learning projects, photographs and documented activities would also be relevant portfolio additions.

Some ideas for this sidebar were collected from the work of Eve Evans Walden, *Portfolio to Accompany Becoming a Master Student,* Ninth Edition. Copyright ©2001 by Houghton Mifflin Company. Reprinted by permission.

Page 353
Master Student Profile: Craig Kielburger

The final Master Student Profile, Craig Kielburger, provides your students an example of a person who encapsulates the Power Process: "Be it." Ask your students to identify how Kielburger used master student qualities in a leadership role. This is also a good place to have a discussion about values, as they were introduced earlier and are shown in action in this profile.

Master Instructor Resource Guide

MASTER
Student

Course Manual

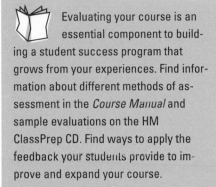 Evaluating your course is an essential component to building a student success program that grows from your experiences. Find information about different methods of assessment in the *Course Manual* and sample evaluations on the HM ClassPrep CD. Find ways to apply the feedback your students provide to improve and expand your course.

HM ClassPrep CD

PowerPoint for Chapter Ten features information on transfer logic, mastering transferable skills, and SCANS.

Have you considered a **final exam portfolio?** Ask your students to collect the materials they have completed in this class for assessment purposes. Refer to the HM ClassPrep CD for details.

Additional resources for talking about diversity in your classroom and its importance in the workplace are available on the HM ClassPrep CD.

Tools for facilitating the HM Assessment and Portfolio Builder with your students are available on the HM ClassPrep CD. Have your students use their Accomplishments Report to work on their résumés and prepare for interviews.

Additional Resources

Supplement your discussions on career planning with a video titled *The Interviewing Process: Strategies for Making the Right Impression.* This new 30-minute video takes students through the interviewing process from start to finish, providing students with strategies for success. From preparing for the interview to suggestions for questions and answers to think about, these real-life scenarios provide students with examples of the actual interview process. Exercises are available on the HM ClassPrep CD and the Instructor's Web site.

A great way to end your class and show students their growth over time is to have your students complete their **Discovery Wheel** online.

The **HM Assessment and Portfolio Builder** (available for packaging with your textbook) is a personal assessment tool that will help students take a First Step toward being successful throughout college and as they enter the workplace. The **Accomplishments Report** will help students analyze their responses and will provide them with suggestions for building a résumé and preparing for interviews.

Equipped with the information from their Accomplishments Report, students can explore Houghton Mifflin's Web-based **Career Resource Center** for articles, exercises, and ideas that can help them succeed on their journey from college to career. Visit

    masterstudent.college.hmco.com

and log in as follows:

Username: careercenter
Password: exploration

Note: The username and password are case sensitive.

10

Mastering Work

Passion for what you do is an important ingredient for success, and if you don't love what you do, it's not worth the time and energy.

CARLY FIORINA

By concentrating on a few key efforts such as sharing credit, showing grace under pressure, and promoting your ambition in appropriate ways, your day job can lead to the career of your dreams.

STEPHEN VISCUSI

why
this chapter matters . . .

You can gain strategies to succeed as you transition from master student to master employee.

what
is included . . .

The Master Employee
Use power tools for finding work
Tell everyone you know: The art of networking
Write a résumé that gets noticed
Sell your résumé with an effective cover letter
Creating and using portfolios
Use interviews to hire yourself an employer
Learning on the job
Join a diverse workplace
Decoding corporate culture
Dealing with sexism and sexual harassment
Strategies for working with a mentor
We are all leaders
Loving your next job
Define your values, align your actions
One set of values
Power Process: "Be it"
Master Student Profile: Craig Kielburger

how
you can use this chapter . . .

Learn effective strategies for job hunting.
Create résumés that lead to job interviews.
Go into job interviews fully prepared.
Build satisfying relationships with coworkers.

As you read, ask yourself
what if ...

I could find work that expresses my core values and connects daily with my passions?

The master employee

The title of this book—*From Master Student to Master Employee*—implies that these two types of mastery have something in common. To some people, this idea sounds half-baked. They separate life into two distinct domains: work and school. One is the "real" world. The other is the place where you attend classes to prepare for the real world.

Consider another point of view—the idea that success in higher education promotes success on the job.

There's some pretty hard-nosed evidence for this idea. One factor is that higher levels of education are correlated with higher levels of income. Another is that mastery in school and in work seem to rest on a common set of transferable skills.

In this book you've seen several references to the Secretary's Commission on Achieving Necessary Skills (SCANS) issued by the U.S. Department of Labor. According to this document, one crucial skill for the workplace is a personal quality called responsibility. This is demonstrated by any employee who:

- "Exerts a high level of effort and perseverance toward goal attainment.

- "Works hard to become excellent at doing tasks by setting high standards, paying attention to details, working well, and displaying a high level of concentration even when assigned an unpleasant task.

- "Displays high standards of attendance, punctuality, enthusiasm, vitality, and optimism in approaching and completing tasks."

A better definition of mastery would be hard to find. And if you've ever exerted a high level of effort to complete an assignment, paid attention to the details of a lecture, or displayed a high level of concentration while reading a tough textbook, then you've already demonstrated some key aspects of self-responsibility and mastery.

When you graduate from school, you don't leave your capacity for mastery locked inside a classroom. Excellence in one setting paves the way for excellence in other settings.

For example, a student who knows how to show up for class on time is ready to show up for work on time. The student who knows how to focus attention during a lecture is ready to focus attention during a training session at work. And a student who's worked cooperatively in a study group brings a lot of skills to the table when joining a workplace team. You can multiply this list by reflecting on each of the skills explained in this book.

journal entry 30

Discovery/Intention Statement

Reflect on all the jobs you've held in your life. What aspect of working would you most like to change? Answers might include job hunting with less frustration, resolving conflicts with coworkers, building a better relationship with your boss, or coping with office politics. Describe the change that would make the biggest positive difference in your job satisfaction over the long run.

I discovered that I . . .

_____

_____

_____

_____

_____

Now preview this chapter for ideas that could help you make the positive change you just described. List three to five suggestions below, along with the page numbers where you can read more about them.

Strategy   *Page number*

_____

_____

_____

_____

_____

A master employee embraces change, takes risks, and looks for chances to lead others while contributing to the quality of their lives. A master employee completes tasks efficiently, communicates openly and respectfully, and commits to lifelong learning. In developing a mastery of higher education, you'll do all this and more. *Master student* and *master employee* are names for qualities that already exist in you, waiting to be expressed as you embrace new ideas and experiment with new behaviors.

Use power tools for finding work

Tool #1: Upgrade your strategies

When applied to finding work, not all strategies are equal. People often find job searches less effective when they do the following things:

- Rely exclusively on want ads when looking for a job.
- Mail out a stack of résumés and cover letters and simply wait for a reply.
- Wait for a job to open up before contacting potential employers.
- Work only with employment agencies and human resources departments in large companies.
- Rely on a job interview as their only source of information about an employer.

These methods are not all useless. Rather, problems arise when we rely on just one strategy and exclude others.

As an alternative, consider the following ideas. They can greatly increase your chances of finding the work you want:

- Make direct contact with a person who can hire you.
- Make such contacts even when the job you want is not yet open or even conceived.
- Cultivate a list of contacts, join professional associations, and meet people in your field.
- Do thorough research on a company before approaching someone for a job there. Do part of this research via informational interviews.
- Approach a potential employer with a way to solve a problem or achieve a company goal. Talk about what's in it for her—the benefits to the company if you are hired.
- Follow up a résumé with letters and well-timed phone calls.
- Write thank-you notes after an interview.
- Present yourself impeccably—everything from error-free résumés to well-polished shoes.

Tool #2: Consider more than one career

As you begin career planning and job hunting, consider ways to increase your options and stay flexible over the long term. Avoid specializing in a certain field too soon, or becoming so specialized that it's difficult to find work as the market changes.

You can benefit from keeping an overall perspective. Use your education to learn transferable skills and then relate them to several potential careers and jobs. Look for the common threads that unite your courses and your career options.

Tool #3: Develop outside interests

You might find it refreshing to learn about yourself outside the context of your career choices. To do this, break out of ruts. Be creative and open to new activities. Take a course that has nothing to do with your major. Volunteer. Find new ways to invest time and energy in the lives of others.

These kinds of activities promote creative thinking by disrupting old habits and infusing our lives with new possibilities. The potential payoffs include new skills and added career options.

Tool #4: Use spare minutes

The time you spend waiting in line at a grocery store or gas station never needs to be wasted again. Thinking about finding work gives you a way to create value in any spare moment. Many career planning and job hunting tasks can be done in one hour or less.

In fact, there's a lot you can do in a few spare minutes. One option is to take a five-minute career-planning break. Fill that break with "micro-tasks." Do an exercise or journal entry from this book. Visit the Web site for a company that interests you. Or call one person to set up an informational interview.

Tool #5: Create your own job

Lists of job openings never include positions that are waiting to be created. With a little imagination and analysis, you can create a job or career where none exists.

Students have a long history of creating self-employment and small businesses to help pay the bills. Some examples are:

- Word processing for papers and theses
- Computer consulting
- Baby sitting and childcare
- Gardening and lawn care
- Doing minor house repairs and odd jobs
- Sewing and mending clothes
- Offering a delivery and errand service
- Pet care and dog walking
- House painting
- Taking photographs or producing videos of weddings and parties
- Working as a singing messenger
- Providing live or recorded music for parties and weddings
- Writing, editing, and proofreading on a freelance basis

You might use creative thinking to create a lifelong career. All it takes is looking for an unmet need that you can respond to with a new product or service.

Another option is to redesign a job you already have. Sometimes companies allow employees to create new positions or businesses "within" a business. Companies may also allow job-sharing, converting a full-time job to a contract position, or working from home.

Tool #6: Attend to the details

The whole process of finding work may hang on details such as getting to appointments on time, respecting an interviewer's schedule, and staying no longer than agreed. Thanking people for their time, dressing appropriately for an interview, and sending follow-up notes can also be crucial.

To make your job search more effective, sweat the small stuff. Ask yourself: "What is one more thing I can do to make my job research more complete or my presentation effective?" Keep taking that next step, however small. Each one takes you closer to finding the work you love.

Tool #7: Use technology to power your job search

Modern technology is creating new ways for you to plan your career and find jobs in the future. On the World Wide Web, you can research companies you'd like to work for, read lists of job openings, and post your résumé and a digital recording of yourself. Through faxes, overnight deliveries, mobile phones, and e-mail, you can stay in continual contact with potential employers. Widespread availability of high-speed Internet access has increased the number of long-distance job interviews being conducted via video conference or in a real time chat room, and has increased the possibility of sending an electronic portfolio attachment with a résumé.

According to one estimate, about two million people go online every month to hunt for jobs. That's a testament to the potential power of the digital medium and to some of its pitfalls as well. When you're looking for a job, the strength of the Internet—the sheer density of data—can also lead to frustration:

- The haphazard organization of the Internet makes it hard for potential employers to find your résumé when you post it online. The organizations you most want to work for might avoid using the Internet to find job applicants.

- Job openings listed on the Internet can be heavily skewed to certain fields, such as jobs for computer professionals or people in other technical fields.

- Across all fields, the majority of job openings are not listed on the Internet (or in newspaper want ads, for that matter).

This is not meant to disparage the Internet as a tool for job hunters and career planners. The point is that posting a résumé on a Web site will not automatically lead to an e-mail in-basket that's bursting to its digital seams with job offers. For an effective job search, view the Internet as just one resource. ⬥

REHEARSE YOUR JOB SEARCH

Imagine that you've completed your education as of today. Your next task is to find a job in a field of interest to you. The following questions will help you rehearse this job hunt.

If you are unsure of an answer, write down your best guess. For now, the process of considering the question is more valuable than any particular answer.

Write your answers in the space below each question. Use separate paper as needed.

1. What kind of job will you apply for? If you choose self-employment, what product or service will you offer?

_____

_____

_____

_____

2. Where will you go to find a job? Will you approach an existing company or choose self-employment? If you opt for self-employment, how will you find potential customers or clients?

_____

_____

_____

_____

3. What kind of training, education, and experience is required for the kind of work that you want?

_____

_____

_____

_____

4. If you plan to apply for an existing job, how will you find out who's in charge of hiring?

_____

_____

_____

_____

_____

5. Next, visualize your job interview. Who will interview you? What questions will this person ask? What questions will you ask the interviewer?

_____

_____

_____

_____

6. Will this job be your "dream job"? If not, how long will take you to find that ideal job?

_____

_____

_____

_____

Finally, review what you've just written. Does any of it suggest changes to make in your current course work or major? If so, describe the specific changes you intend to make.

_____

_____

_____

_____

Tell everyone you know
The art of networking

Networking means staying in touch with people to share career planning ideas and track job openings. It's possible that more jobs are filled through networking than through any other method.

When done with persistence over a period of time, networking can lead you effortlessly from one contact to another.

Following are ideas that can help you create a powerful network.

Start by listing people you already know

Start your list of contacts with names of family members and friends who could help you define your career or land a job. List each person's name, phone number, and e-mail address on a separate 3x5 card or Rolodex card. Another option is to keep your list on a computer, using word processing or contact management software.

Whenever you speak to someone on your contact list, make brief notes about what you discussed. Also jot down any further actions you'll take to follow up on your discussion.

Be open to making contacts

Consider everyone you meet to be a potential friend—and a networking partner. Look for things you have in common. If you're both planning a career or looking for a job, that's plenty.

Craft your "pitch"

Develop a short statement of your career goal that you can easily share with people. For example: "After I graduate, I plan to work in the travel business. I'm looking for an internship in a travel agency that helps business people arrange international trips. Do you know of any agencies that take interns?"

Get past the fear of competition

When told about networking, some people feel intimidated. They fear that others will steal or conceal job openings. *Why should I share this information with anybody?* goes the objection. *After all, we're competing with each other for the same jobs.*

In response, remember that few people in any network are actually going after the same jobs. Students majoring in broadcasting, for example, have many different job goals. Some want to be newscasters. Others want to work as video editors or scriptwriters. And even people interested in the same jobs may be looking for positions with different duties or in different parts of the country.

Also, any "competitor" could turn into a friend. Suppose someone in your network lands a job before you. Send a note of congratulations to this person along with your phone number and e-mail address. This person might be in a position to recommend you for another job opening—or even to hire you.

Follow up

Networking uncovers "leads"—companies with job openings and people with the power to hire. Keeping a live list of leads takes action. You might benefit from sending a letter and résumé or making a five-minute call. Any of these steps could bring your name in front of a person who's ready to hire you. ✉

Write a résumé that gets noticed

Your résumé is a living document that distills an essential part of your overall life plan. The attention you give to your résumé can pay you back hundreds of time over. Use a résumé to find a job that you love and a salary that matches your skills.

Writing an effective résumé creates value in many ways. For one, a résumé can help you discover and express your skills by writing them down. It can serve as a calling card for you to leave with employers. It can remind you of key points to make in a job interview. A résumé can also refresh a potential employer's memory after the interview. If you're applying for a job that's miles away from home, a résumé is essential.

A résumé is a piece of persuasive writing, not a laundry list of previous jobs or dry recitation of facts. This document has a purpose—to get you to the next step in the hiring process, usually an interview. What follows are suggestions for résumés that win attention.

Avoid getting weeded out

Your résumé could be the most important document that you ever write. Yet many résumés fail. They get tossed. They get set aside, lost, or shuffled into oblivion. One goal in résumé writing is to get past the first cut. Several techniques can help you meet this goal.

Start with presentation. Neatness, organization, and correct grammar and punctuation are essential.

Next, leave out irrelevant information that could possibly eliminate you from the hiring process and send your résumé hurtling into the circular file. Some items to delete or question are these:

- Boilerplate language—stock wording from job descriptions or résumé writing services.
- The date you're available to start a new job.
- Salary information, including what you've earned in the past and want to earn now.
- Details about jobs you held over 10 years ago.
- Reasons for leaving previous jobs.

Note that employers cannot legally discriminate against job applicants based on personal information such as age, national origin, race, religion, disability, and pregnancy status. Including this kind of information on your résumé might even hurt your job prospects. To learn more about types of job discrimination, access the U.S. Equal Employment Opportunity Commission (EEOC) at **http://www.eeoc.gov/types/index.html**. This Web site also explains how to file a charge of discrimination.

Consider a standard format

There is no formula for a perfect résumé, and people have different preferences for what they want to see in one. However, following is one common résumé format.

Begin with contact information—your name, mailing address, e-mail address, and phone number.

Next, you might choose to name your desired job, often called an *objective* or *goal*. This is an optional feature, and not all résumé experts agree on the value of including it.

Follow with the body of your résumé—major headings such as *skills*, *experience*, and *education* with key details. Put those headings in bold print or in the left margin of the page. Whenever possible, use phrases that start with an active verb: "*Supervised* three people." "*Generated* leads for sales calls." "*Wrote* speeches and *edited* annual reports." These verbs refer directly to your skills. Make them relevant to the job you're seeking.

Finish on a strong note. You might end your résumé with an intriguing statement ("I enjoy turning around departments with low morale") or a favorable quote from a coworker ("Julio regularly exceeded the requirements of his job").

Sell your skills as solutions

Every organization has problems to solve—coping with employee turnover, beating the competition, increasing market share and revenues. Do research to discover the typical problems faced by organizations in your career field—and the specific problems faced by individual employers.

In the body of your résumé, show that you know about these problems. Offer your skills as solutions. Give evidence that you've solved similar problems in the past, offering credible numbers whenever possible: "Created a program that reduced training time by 25 percent."

Remember to give a full picture of your skills. This includes content skills—specialized knowledge and abilities that qualify you to do a specific job—along with transferable skills that can help you in *any* job.

Make it easy to skim

Knowing that employers are pressed for time when reading résumés, design yours accordingly. Write your résumé so that key facts leap off the page. Use short paragraphs and short sentences. Use bulleted lists for key points. Also avoid filling the page with ink. Instead, leave some blank space between the major sections of your résumé.

Make it unusual

Sometimes an offbeat approach will attract an employer's attention. If you're applying for a job in public relations, you could write your résumé as a press release formatted to be read by a news announcer. If you're applying for work as an administrator at an art museum, you could design your résumé as a collage.

Before you use such a gimmick, however, carefully consider the ways that it could backfire. When it doubt, stick to a conventional résumé.

Get feedback

Ask friends and family members if your résumé is persuasive and easy to understand. Also get feedback from someone at your school's career planning and job placement office. Revise your résumé based on their comments. Then revise some more. Create sparkling prose that will intrigue a potential employer enough to call you for an interview.

Combine your résumé with other strategies

Do not view a résumé as the core of your job search. Employers might get hundreds of résumés for a single job opening. And interviewers might spend only a few seconds on each résumé. These figures have nothing to do with your skills. They just reflect the constant pressures on people with jobs to fill.

To get the most from your résumé, use it to supplement other job-hunting strategies. Research companies and do informational interviews. Take part in internships and other work experiences in your chosen field. Create a support group and find a mentor. More strategies are listed throughout this chapter and in Chapter Nine.

Go ahead and contact potential employers directly—even if they don't have a job opening at the moment. Use your job contacts to find people within that organization with the power to hire. Then use every job contact you have to introduce yourself to those people and schedule an interview. If you just send out résumés and neglect to make personal contacts, you'll be disappointed.

→ Keys to scannable résumés

Many companies use a computerized scanning program to catalog résumés and fill positions by using keyword searches. Human resources associates can quickly retrieve and route résumés to fill positions by matching their specifications with your qualifications. Including appropriate keywords on your résumé will help you stand out from others. Review job postings to find buzzwords that employers are searching for in your field of interest to include on your résumé. Get recognized by including specific positions and leadership roles you have held, related work experience, and degrees or certifications you have completed. Remember to also include your skills and core competencies.

Some specific things to keep in mind:

- Use enough keywords to define your skills, education, experience, professional affiliations, and so on.

- Describe your experience with concrete terms. For example: "manager of mechanical engineering team" instead of "responsible for managing professionals."

- When in doubt, spell it out. Some systems are programmed with basic abbreviations like BA, MS, Ph.D. But the general rule is if you are not sure, spell it out. You can assume employers will search for standard abbreviations for terms in your field.

- Use common headings such as: Objective, Experience, Education, Professional, Affiliations, and Certifications.

- Remember to describe your interpersonal traits and attitudes. For example: communication skills, leadership, time management, high energy.

Print your scannable résumé on one side of an $8\frac{1}{2} \times 11"$ sheet of plain white paper with an easy-to-read font and layout. If your résumé is more than one page in length, be sure your name and contact information appear on both sheets of paper. Avoid using italics, boldface, or underlining and other special text formatting. Do not staple or fold the résumé. It is best when hand delivered or sent in an oversized envelope.

Each time you meet with someone, leave your résumé behind. Then stay in touch. Periodically remind a potential employer of your existence. Send a short personal note: "Here's an updated résumé to put in my file." If the company doesn't have a file on you yet, chances are that somebody will start one. At that point, your name will start to stand out from the crowd. Your résumé is doing its job. ◪

Sample résumés

Susan Chang
susangeorgia276@aol.com
2500 North Highland Avenue, Atlanta, GA 30306
770-899-8707

Work Experience:	**LAND Enterprises, Inc., Atlanta, GA**
	Administrative Assistant—January 2004–present
	• Responsible for supporting national sales manager and three district managers in creating reports for nationwide sales staff.
	• Create, prepare, and maintain Excel spreadsheets with weekly sales data.
	• Manage sales representative calendar of events in Lotus Notes database.
	Peachtree Bank, Alpharetta, GA
	Teller—May 2001–December 2003
	• Responsible for receiving cash/checks for deposits, processing withdrawals, and accepting loan payments.
	• Communicated with customers and provided account balance and savings and loan information.
	• Provided friendly and prompt customer service.
Education:	**Macon State Community College, Macon, GA**
	AA—Communications and Information Technology; May 2003
	Overall GPA–3.0.
Volunteer:	**Macon Chamber of Commerce**
	Holiday Events Coordinator 2000–2003
	• Maintained budget from Chamber of Commerce for annual holiday parties.
	• Solicited donations from local businesses to support monthly events.
Computer Skills:	Microsoft Word, Microsoft Excel, Microsoft Access, Lotus Notes, Powerpoint.
Personal:	Interested in writing poetry, playing team sports, and traveling.
References:	Available upon request.

Lamont Jackson
2250 First Avenue, #3 • New York, NY 10029 • (212) 222-5555
Lamont_Jackson44@hotmail.com

Objective

To obtain a position as a public relations associate that allows me to utilize
my writing and communication skills.

Education

Rutgers University, New Brunswick, NJ
BA in English, Minor in Business Communication; May 2004
Major GPA — 3.2; Minor GPA — 3.3

Experience

The Medium, Rutgers University, New Brunswick, NJ
Contributing Writer, August 2003–May 2004
• Developed feature articles pertaining to faculty and student issues on
campus and community issues.
• Responsible for writing weekly sidebar featuring community service on
and off campus.

Shandwick Public Relations, New York, NY
Intern, Summer 2003
• Coordinated mass mailings of press releases to medical community biweekly.
• Conducted health surveys focusing on nutrition habits of senior citizens in the
tristate area; organized all retrieved data of 1000 respondents.
• Handled telephone inquiries efficiently from clients and corporations
represented by firm.

Activities

• Intramural Soccer Team, Spring 2003
• Habitat for Humanity, *Treasurer*, Fall 2003–Spring 2004
• Rutgers University Orientation Leader, Summer 2002

Skills

• Ability to perform on both PC and Macintosh platforms.
• Software knowledge that includes: Windows NT, Microsoft Office, Lotus Notes,
Lotus 1-2-3, Quark, and beginning HTML.
• Fluency in Spanish — oral and written competency.

Honors

Rutgers University Dean's List, Fall 1999, Spring 2004

Sell your résumé with an effective cover letter

An effective cover letter can leave a prospective employer waiting with bated breath to read your résumé. An ineffective letter can propel your résumé to that nefarious stack of papers to be read "later." In some cases, a well-written letter alone can land you an interview.

Many cover letters are little more than a list of stock phrases. In essence, they say: "I want that job you listed. Here's my résumé. Read it."

You can write a more interesting letter that practically demands a response. Remember the primary question in an employer's mind: What do you have to offer us? Using a three-part structure can help you answer this question.

1 In your first sentence, address the person who can hire you and grab that person's attention. Make a statement that appeals directly to her self-interest. Write something that moves potential employer to say, "We can't afford to pass this person up. Call him right away to set up an appointment."

To come up with ideas for your opening, complete the following sentence: "The main benefits that I can bring to your organization are. . . ."

2 Next, build interest. Add a fact or two to back up your opening paragraph. Briefly refer to your experience and highlight one or two key achievements. If you're applying for a specific job opening, state this. If you're not, then offer an idea that will intrigue the employer enough to respond anyway.

3 Finally, take care of business. Refer the reader to your résumé. Then mention that you'll call at a specific point to set up an interview.

Write several drafts of your cover letter. Taking your cue from the Master Student Map at the beginning of each chapter in this book, see if you can answer several key questions on a potential employer's mind:

- *Why* should we be interested in this person?
- *What* value can this person add to our organization?
- *How* would we be better off after hiring this person?
- *What if* hiring this person could create the opportunity to expand into new markets or expand the range of services that we offer?

Keep your letter short—two or three paragraphs. Employers are busy people. Reading cover letters is probably not high on their list of fun things to do. Make it easy on them. ⊠

→ Correspondence quick tips

Use these additional suggestions for making your cover letter a "must read."

- Address your letter to a specific individual. Make sure to use the correct title and mailing address. Mistakes in such details could detract from your credibility.

- Use a simple typeface that is easy to read.

- Tailor each letter you write to the specific company and position you are applying for.

- Be honest. During an interview, an employer may choose to ask you questions about information you present in your résumé or cover letter. Be prepared to expand upon and support your statements. The ability to do this enhances your reputation as an ethical employee.

- Thank your reader for her time and consideration.

- Check for typographical, grammatical, and word usage errors. Do not rely on your computer to spell check.

- Ask someone to read over your letter before you send it out. An extra pair of eyes may help you uncover errors.

- Use high-quality paper stock for your hard copy letters.

- When sending cover letters via e-mail, use a meaningful subject header and a professional tone. Do not use emoticons like :-). Be sure to include your phone number in case the contact prefers to follow up with you via phone.

- When faxing a cover letter and résumé, indicate the total number of pages in the transmission.

Sample cover letters

Example 1

My name is Michael Romano and I recently moved to this area. I have worked in the auto industry for the last seventeen years, and I am interested in continuing in that industry as a worker for DWC Radiators. I worked for Angelo's Auto Supplies in Lansing, MI, before moving to Minnesota.

My background is in the repairs department. I played a key role on the team that serviced imported radiators. I have excellent references from my former employer.

I will stop by your office next Wednesday afternoon to fill out a formal application. If you could take a few minutes to see me at that time, I would be very grateful. I will give you a call on Tuesday to see if this can be arranged.

Example 2

As a recent college graduate, I am the perfect candidate for your entry-level position as an editorial assistant for *Seventeen* magazine. During my studies, I have held three positions at my college's magazine, including Features Editor, Campus Correspondent, and Senior Copyeditor. In my senior year, I initiated a new section in our magazine, *Style File*, featuring local clothing and accessories stores. A similar *Style File* in your magazine from different cities across the nation would be an intriguing section for your readers.

I am proficient in using both PC and MAC platforms, and have skills using programs in Microsoft Office Suite and Quark. The enclosed résumé explains how my past positions and other qualifications are a perfect fit for your opening. I will call you in a few days to schedule a time when we can talk in more detail. I would also like the opportunity to share with you my writing portfolio.

Example 3

The flyer announcing the position of Program Coordinator caught my attention immediately. This position interests me because I have the skills required to work on a diverse team. I am fluent in Spanish, French, and English and have had a long-standing interest in working with people from many cultures. My experience as a vendor in an Argentina zoo and my current job as unit manager at the UN Communications Center are two examples of the unique and relevant background I would bring to the position of Program Coordinator at the UC International House.

As a member of the International House, I also have a firsthand understanding about how residents feel about the activities and special events hosted by the office throughout the year. Because of this, I am in an excellent position to help plan a variety of activities residents will appreciate.

As directed in the job announcement, I am requesting an appointment for an interview on March 28, between 2 p.m. and 6 p.m., at a time convenient for you. Please contact me if another time is more appropriate. Thank you very much for your time and consideration.

Example 4

As a recent recipient of an Associates Degree in medical assisting, I am the perfect candidate for the position of team leader for the medical assistant group at Health First Wellness Associates. My experience as a receptionist in the North Shore Medical Center before returning to college has been supplemented by my recent employment in the billing department, where I became proficient using MediSoft.

After you have reviewed my enclosed résumé, I would appreciate the opportunity to discuss with you further my qualifications and explain how I could help create solutions for success with the newly formed MA Team. I can be reached by phone or e-mail as noted above.

Example 5

Your Chief Financial Officer, Elena Perez, told me recently that you were looking for an MIS director. Because of my background, she encouraged me to contact you directly. I am very impressed with the growth your company made in the last two years. With that kind of expansion, I can understand your need to create a separate MIS department.

This position relates well to my current experience at Murphy and Sons, LLP, as you will see from my enclosed résumé. I possess a diversified background that would enable me to serve your organization's MIS needs efficiently. I am a creative and highly motivated individual with good communication and interpersonal skills. I am confident that these qualifications coupled with my work ethic and enthusiasm would allow me to make a positive contribution to your company.

I welcome the opportunity to meet with you to discuss how my qualifications may best meet your needs. Thank you in advance for your time and consideration.

Example 6

When posting your résumé online, include a cover memo such as the example below. Include key information from your résumé and explain your job objective in detail.

Subject: Seeking advertising account position

I am interested in finding a position with a major advertising firm. I have worked in advertising for four years. As a junior advertising assistant, my duties include contract negotiation, lead liaison, and creative development. My present account assignments include Intel, Cisco, Coca-Cola, and Ford.

My attached résumé includes information about my work history, including related internship experiences in advertising. Please e-mail me at mraj212@mindspring.com.

Attached: MRAJ Resume.doc

Creating and using
portfolios

The word *portfolio* derives from two Latin terms: *port,* which means "to move," and *folio,* which means "papers" or "artifacts." True to these ancient meanings, portfolios are movable collections of papers and artifacts.

Portfolios differ from résumés. A résumé lists facts, including your interests, skills, work history, and accomplishments. Although a portfolio might include these facts, it also includes tangible objects to verify the facts—anything from transcripts of your grades to a videotape that you produced. Résumés offer facts; portfolios provide artifacts.

Photographers, contractors, and designers regularly show portfolios filled with samples of their work. Today, employers and educators increasingly see the portfolio as a tool that's useful for everyone. Some schools require students to create them, and some employers expect to see a portfolio before they'll hire a job applicant.

Enjoy the benefits—academic, professional, and personal

A well-done portfolio benefits its intended audience. To an instructor, your portfolio gives a rich, detailed picture of what you did to create value from a class. To a potential employer, your portfolio gives observable evidence of your skills and achievements. In both cases, a portfolio also documents something more intangible—

In medieval times, artisans who wished to join a guild presented samples of their work. Furniture makers showed cabinets and chairs to their potential mentors. Painters presented samples of their sketches and portraits. Centuries later, people still value a purposeful collection of work samples. It is called a portfolio.

you think about the skills you want to develop and ways to showcase those skills. And when you're applying for work, creating a portfolio prepares you for job interviews. Your portfolio can stand out from stacks of letters and résumés and distinguish you from other applicants.

By creating and using portfolios, you also position yourself for the workplace of the future. People such as William Bridges, author of *Jobshift,* have predicted a "jobless economy."[1] In such an economy, work will be done by teams assembled for specific projects instead of by employees in permanent positions. Workers will move from team to team, company to company, and career to career far more often than they do today. If these changes take place on a wide scale, listing your job titles on a résumé will be less useful than documenting your skills in a vivid, detailed way. Creating and using portfolios is a wonderful way to provide that documentation.

In a more general sense, creating a portfolio helps you reflect on your life as a whole. When selecting artifacts to include in your portfolio, you celebrate your levels of energy, passion, and creativity.

Portfolios benefit you in specific ways. When you create a portfolio to document what you learned during a class, you review the content of the entire course. When you're creating a portfolio related to your career,

→ Artifacts for your portfolio

When looking for items to include in a portfolio, start with the following checklist. Then brainstorm your own list of added possibilities.

❏ Brochures describing a product or service you've created, or workshops you've attended

❏ Certificates, licenses, and awards

❏ Computer disks with sample publications, databases, or computer programs you've created

❏ Course descriptions and syllabuses of classes you've taken or taught

❏ Formal evaluations of your work

❏ Job descriptions of positions you've held

❏ Letters of recommendation

❏ Lists of grants, scholarships, clients, customers, and organizations you've joined

❏ Newspaper and magazine articles about projects you've participated in

❏ Objects you've created or received—anything from badges to jewelry

❏ Plans—lists of personal and professional values, goals, action plans, completed tasks, project timelines, and lifelines

❏ Printouts of e-mail and Web pages (including your personal Web page)

❏ Programs from artistic performances or exhibitions

❏ Recordings (digital or voice), compact discs, or CD-ROMs

❏ Résumés or a curriculum vitae

❏ Sheet music or scores

❏ Transcripts of grades, test scores, vocational aptitude tests, or learning style inventories

❏ Visual art, including drawings, photographs, collages, and computer graphics

❏ Writing samples, such as class reports, workplace memos, proposals, policy and mission statements, bids, manuscripts for articles and books, and published pieces or bibliographies of published writing

accomplishments. You discover key themes in your experience. You clarify what's important to you and create goals for the future. Portfolios promote the cycle of discovery, intention, and action presented in the journal entries and exercises throughout this text. To create a portfolio, experiment with a four-step process:

1. Collect and catalog artifacts.

2. Plan your portfolio.

3. Assemble your portfolio.

4. Present your portfolio.

Collect and catalog artifacts

An artifact is any object that's important to you and that reveals something about yourself. Examples include photographs, awards, recommendation letters, job descriptions for positions you've held, newspaper articles about projects you've done, lists of grants or scholarships you've received, programs from performances you've given, transcripts of your grades, or models you've constructed.

Taken together, your artifacts form a large and visible "database" that gives a picture of you—what you value, what you've done, and what skills you have. You can add to this database during every year of your life. From this constantly evolving collection of artifacts, you can create many portfolios for different purposes and different audiences.

Start collecting now. Write down the kinds of artifacts you'd like to save. Think about what will be most useful to you in creating portfolios for your courses and your job search. In some cases, collecting artifacts requires follow-up. You might call former instructors or employers to request letters of recommendation. Or you might track down newspaper articles about a service-learning project you did. Your responses to the journal entries and exercises in this book can also become part of your portfolio. To save hours when you create your next portfolio, start documenting your artifacts. On a 3x5 card, record the "five W's" about each artifact: *who* was involved with it, *what* you did with it, *when* it was created, *where* it was created, and *why* the artifact is important to you. File these cards and update them as you collect new artifacts. Another option is to manage this information with a computer, using word processing or database software.

Plan your portfolio

When you're ready to create a portfolio for a specific audience, allow some time for planning. Begin with your purpose for creating the portfolio—for example, to demonstrate your learning or to document your work experience as you prepare for a job interview.

Also list some specifics about your audience. Write a description of anyone who will see your portfolio. List what each person already knows about you and predict what else these people will want to know. Answer their questions in your portfolio.

Being aware of your purpose and audience will serve you at every step of creating a portfolio. Screen artifacts with these two factors in mind. If a beautiful artifact fails to meet your purpose or fit your audience, leave it out for now. Save the artifact for a future portfolio.

When you plan your portfolio, also think about how to order and arrange your artifacts. One basic option is a chronological organization. For example, start with work samples from your earliest jobs and work up to the present.

Another option is to structure your portfolio around key themes, such as your values or work skills. When preparing this type of portfolio, you can define *work* to include any time you used a job-related skill, whether or not you got paid.

Assemble your portfolio

With a collection of artifacts and a written plan, you're ready to assemble your portfolio. Arranging artifacts according to your design is a big part of this process. Also include elements to orient your audience members and guide them through your portfolio. Such elements can include:

- A table of contents.
- An overview or summary of the portfolio.
- Titles and captions for each artifact.
- An index to your artifacts.

Although many portfolios take their final form as a collection of papers, remember that this is just one possibility. You can also create a bulletin board, a display, or a case that contains your artifacts. You could even create a recording or a digital portfolio in the form of a personal Web site.

You might find it useful to combine your résumé and portfolio into one document. In other cases, you can mention in your résumé that a separate portfolio is available on request.

Present your portfolio

Your audience might ask you to present your portfolio as part of an interview or oral exam. If that's the case,

desk of...

from the

**SHERRI MARGULIES,
POSTPRODUCTION EDITOR:**

My portfolio is actually a reel of some of the spots and videos I have edited. I use the portfolio as a constant reevaluation of my talent, past and present, and it is constantly evolving.

**WEI H. LEE,
MARKETING COMMUNICATIONS:**

Since I have graduated from college, I have collected all of the marketing promotional pieces I have written at various jobs in a portfolio. I have used this portfolio to monitor my own growth and experiances, and I have used it as a tool to document accomplishments. This is very helpful when you are up for a promotion or even during review time.

JAN ANDREWS, BIOLOGIST:

I learned early in my career to keep an up-to-date portfolio. Much of my work depends on the acceptance of grant proposals that I write. I am constantly applying for grants to keep my work going. My field is competitive, and my work is the only thing I have to distinguish me from other applicants.

rehearse your portfolio presentation the way you would rehearse a speech. Write down questions that people might ask about your portfolio. Prepare some answers, then do a dry run. Present your portfolio to friends and people in your career field, and request their feedback.

That feedback will give you plenty of ideas about ways to revise your portfolio. Any portfolio is a living document. Update it as you acquire new perspectives and skills. ✖

**For more ideas on portfolios,
go online to**

masterstudent.college.hmco.com

Use interviews to hire yourself an employer

The young man's palms are sweating, his heart pounding. His hands are shaking so much that it's hard to button his coat. He fumbles for his keys. Locking the door to his apartment, he anticipates returning there later after a disastrous interview. Huddled against the cold, he slouches out the door, eyes cast downward, walking with short, clipped steps. He's got to hurry. Being late for this appointment could dash his already meager chances.

This is the way that some experience their last moments before a job interview. Instead of sensing opportunity, they're acting like they're about to be sentenced for a crime.

Job interviews don't have to be this way. In fact, they can be exhilarating. They offer a way to meet people. They give you a chance to present your skills. They can expand your network of contacts.

If you've written a career plan, developed a network of job contacts, and prepared a résumé, you've already done much of your preparation for a successful interview. You probably have specific ideas about *what* job skills you want to use and *where* you want to use them. By the time you get to a job interview, you'll be able to see if the job is something that you really want. An interview is a chance for you to assess a potential job and work environment. By interviewing, you're "hiring" yourself an employer.

Many of the suggestions for writing résumés also apply to preparing for a job interview. For example, learn everything you can about the organization. Also be able to list your skills and explain how they can benefit the employer. Following are additional ways to get the most out of an interview.

Start on a positive note and stay there

Many interviewers make their decision about an applicant early on. This can happen during the first five minutes of the interview.

With this in mind, start on a strong note. Do everything you can to create a positive impression early in the interview. Even if you're nervous, you can be outgoing and attentive. Explain how your research led you to the company. Focus on how you can contribute to the employer. Talk about skills or experiences that make you stand out from the crowd of other applicants.

One way to create a favorable first impression is through the way you look. Be well groomed. Wear clothing that's appropriate for the work environment.

Also monitor your nonverbal language. Give a firm handshake and make eye contact (without looking like a zombie). Sit in a way that says you're at ease with people and have a high energy level. During the interview, seize opportunities to smile or even tell an amusing story, as long as it's relevant and positive.

As the interview gets rolling, search for common ground. Finding out that you share an interest with an interviewer can make the conversation sail—and put you closer to a job offer. You can demonstrate interest through focused attention. Listen carefully to everything interviewers say. Few of them will mind if you take notes. This might even impress them.

As the interviewer speaks, listen for challenges that the company faces. Then paint yourself as someone who can help meet those challenges. Explain how you've solved similar problems in the past—and what you can do for the employer right now. To support your claims, mention a detail or two about your accomplishments and refer the interviewer to your résumé for more.

Once you hit a positive note, do everything possible to stay there. When speaking about other people, for example, be courteous. If you find it hard to say something positive about a previous coworker or supervisor, shift the focus back to the interviewer's questions.

Show that you know the value of time. If your interview is scheduled to end soon, mention this to the interviewer. Allow this person the option to end the conversation or extend the interview time.

Ask open-ended questions and listen

Come with your own list of questions for the interviewer. Skilled interviewers will leave time for these. Through your questions, find out:

- What qualifications the job requires—and whether your skills and experience offer a match.
- Whether the job meshes with your career plan.
- Whether the job involves contact with people you'd enjoy.

After you ask a question, give the interviewer plenty of time to talk. Listen at least 50 percent of the time.

Keep the key facts at your command

Remembering essential information during an interview can help things go smoothly. Learn everything you can about each organization that interests you. Get a feel for its strong points and know about its successes in the marketplace. Also find out what challenges the organization faces.

As in a résumé, use interviews to present your skills as unique solutions for those challenges. To jog your memory, keep vital information handy. Examples are a list of references, your social security number, and a summary of your work history. To this, add the main points you'd like to get across during the interview.

You can also bring a list of the SCANS skills (see page 8) as a reminder to mention the key abilities that you will bring to the job. Explain these skills in ways that any potential employer can understand—including those who have never heard of the SCANS report.

You can enter this information in a computer file and print it out on a single sheet of paper. Consider printing extra copies and giving one to the interviewer. After each interview, revise and update the information.

When appropriate, take the initiative

The interviewer might be uncomfortable with her role. Few people have training in this skill. Interviewers may dominate the conversation, interrupt you, or forget what they want to ask.

When things like this happen, take the initiative. Ask for time to get your questions answered. Sum up your qualifications, and ask for a detailed job description.

Some employers do structured interviews. In this case, a group of people meet with each job candidate and ask similar questions each time. The idea behind this technique is to make sure that all job candidates get a hearing and have an equal chance of getting hired.

When done poorly, structured interviews can be artificial or limiting. If you feel this way, remember the key points you want to make about yourself. Seize every opportunity to weave these points into your answers.

Give yourself a raise before you start work

Effective salary discussion can make a huge difference to your financial well-being. Consider the long-term impact of making just an extra $1,000 per year. Over the next decade, that's an extra $10,000 dollars in pretax income, even if you get no other raises.

It's possible to discuss salary too early in the interview. Let the interviewer bring up this topic. In many cases, an ideal time to talk about salary is when the interviewer is ready to offer you a job. At this point, the employer might be willing to part with more money.

Many interviewers use a standard negotiating strategy. They come to the interview with a salary range in mind. Then they offer a starting salary at the lower end of that range.

This strategy holds an important message for you: Salaries are often flexible, especially for upper-level jobs. You usually do not have to accept the first salary offer.

When you finally get down to money, be prepared. Begin by knowing the salary range that you want. First, figure out how much money you need to maintain your desired standard of living. Then add some margin for comfort. If you're working a job that's comparable to the one you're applying for, consider adding 10 percent to your current salary. Also take into account the value of any benefits the employer provides. Consider stating a desired salary range at first rather than a fixed figure.

Sometimes you can look up standard salary ranges for certain jobs. Reference materials such as the *Occupational Outlook Handbook* (available online at **http://www.bls.gov/oco/**) include this information. Also ask friends who work in your field, and review notes from your informational interviews. Another option is the obvious one—asking interviewers what salary range they have in mind.

Once you know that range, aim high. Name a figure toward the upper end and see how the interviewer responds. Starting high gives you some room to negotiate. See if you can get a raise now rather than later.

Use each *no* to come closer to *yes*

Almost everyone who's ever applied for a job knows the lines: "We have no job openings right now." "We'll keep

PRACTICE ANSWERING AND ASKING QUESTIONS

Job interviewers ask many questions. Most of them boil down to a few major concerns:

- Would we be comfortable working with you?

- How did you find out about us?

- How can you help us?

- Will you learn to do this job quickly?

- What makes you different from other applicants?

- Will you work for a salary we can afford?

You can prepare your answers to these questions by focusing on key words from the four learning styles questions explained in Chapter One. In other words, your job during an interview is to explain *why* you are an ideal candidate for the job, *what* skills and experience you bring to the company, *how* well you will get along with other employees, and *what* specific benefits an employer can expect to gain *if* she hires you.

Before your next job interview, also set up situations where you can practice answering common interview questions. Enroll a friend to play the part of an interviewer and ask you the questions listed above or variations of them.

During your practice interview, keep your speaking brief and to the point. See if you can respond to each question in two minutes or less. Also be alert to any inconsistencies in your answers. For example, if you say that you're a "team player" but prefer to work independently, be prepared to explain. When you're done, ask your friend for feedback.

Also list the three most important things that *you* want to find out about a potential job. Phrase these as questions to ask during the interview and write them in the space below.

_____

_____

_____

_____

_____

_____

your résumé on file." "There were many qualified applicants for this position." "Even though you did not get the job, thanks for applying." "Best of luck to you as you pursue other career opportunities."

Each of those statements is a different way of saying no. And they can hurt.

However, *no* does not have to be the final word. Focus on the future. If you're turned down for one job, consider ways to turn that *no* into a *yes* next time. Could you present yourself differently during the interview? Could you do more thorough research? Can you fine-tune your career goals? You might even ask the interviewer for suggestions. Also ask for referrals to other companies that might be hiring.

Think about what a job rejection really means. It's not an eternal judgment of your character. It only reflects what happened between you and one potential employer, often over just a few hours or even a few minutes. It means no for right now, for this job, for today—not for every job, forever. Every interview is a source of feedback about what works—and what doesn't work—in meeting

with employers. Use that feedback to interview more effectively next time.

Eventually an employer or client will hire you. It's just a matter of time before the inevitable *yes*. When you're turned down for a job, that is just one more *no* that's out of the way.

Follow up

Within 24 hours, send a thank-you note to the person who interviewed you. To personalize your note, mention a detail from your conversation. Also send thank-you's to anyone else who assisted you with the interview— receptionists, assistants, or contacts within the organization. Prompt follow-up can make you stand out in an interviewer's mind. That could make a difference when the next job opens up.[2]

For more interviewing strategies, go online to (masterstudent.college.hmco.com)

Sample thank-you notes

A thank-you note can be as important as the interview itself—especially if an employer uses your letter as a deciding factor. Include information in your note that will help remind the employer of your conversation. Follow up with any thoughts you had after your interview. Hand-written or word-processed notes are acceptable.

Remember to send thank-you letters to each person who has interviewed you, and highlight specific references to your meeting. This will help them recall your dialogue. After emphasizing your continued interest, be sure to thank the interviewer for her time.

Thank you for the opportunity to interview for the open paralegal position at Robinson, Muñoz, and Martinez. Learning about the day-to-day aspects of the paralegal cohort at your firm has increased my interest in the position with your firm. Thank you also for inviting the paralegal supervisor to speak with me.

I am attaching my references per your request. I hope you will consider contacting my internship coordinator to learn more about how my skills align with your needs. I look forward to hearing from you soon.

Thank you for taking the time to meet with me on Monday. After learning more about EnviroTechnologies and the role of the IT group, I am very excited about the opportunity to work for your company.

As I mentioned in the interview, I would be very interested in the IT Helpdesk position and feel that I could be an asset to your team because of my experience with crystal reports and Microsoft Access.

Thank you for your consideration. I look forward to hearing your decision.

It was very helpful to speak with you and Mr. Qian last Thursday, and I want to thank you for taking the time to show me around your facilities and providing information about Metropolitan Enterprises, Inc. My previous experience as a Marketing Associate at Southwest Communications has prepared me for the role of Account Manager at your company.

I reviewed the internal Web site that you provided me access to; I was impressed with the development that was done to keep your employees informed of company information. I have some ideas for increasing traffic to this Intranet site that I would like to discuss with you. Let me know when would be a good time for us to meet again. I can be available on Tuesday at 10 a.m. or Wednesday at 1 p.m. If these times do not work with your schedule, please suggest another time.

If you have any questions about my résumé, please call me at (617) 662-1234, or e-mail me at jsmarshall@comcast.com.

Learning on the job

Besides a paycheck, the workplace offers constant opportunities for learning. Employers value the person who is a "quick study"—someone who can get up to speed at a new job in minimum time.

In addition, some of the information you acquired in school might become quickly outdated. Learning how to learn—a key transferable skill—is a necessity if you want to survive in the job market and advance in your career.

Let go of old ideas about learning. Educational literature is full of distinctions such as "theory versus application" and "beginning versus advanced." These distinctions are useful. But if you want to learn on the job, you can often benefit by letting them go. In workplace-based learning, for example:

- There is no "finish" line such as a graduation ceremony. Rather, you learn continuously, taking periodic progress checks to assess your current skills.

- Outside of formal training programs, there are no course divisions. A new job might call on you to integrate knowledge of several subjects at once.

- There is no syllabus for learning a subject with assignments carefully laid out in planned sequence. You might learn concepts in an "illogical" order as dictated by the day-to-day demands of a job.

If all this sounds like a prescription for chaos, consider that it reflects the ways you've always learned outside the classroom. Teaching yourself anything from a new golf swing to a new song on the guitar has a lot in common with the way you teach yourself on the job.

Seize informal opportunities to learn. At work, your learning may take place in unplanned, informal ways. Look for opportunities to:

- Do self-directed reading on topics related to new job tasks.

- Observe people who demonstrate a skill that you would like to develop.

- Ask questions on the spot.

- Attend trade shows for new products or services offered by your company's competitors.

- Join professional organizations in your field that offer workshops and seminars.

- Make yourself into the company expert on a new product or procedure by digging into brochures, Web sites, professional journals, technical manuals, and other sources of information that your coworkers may have overlooked.

Create a development plan. Some organizations require their employees to create a professional development plan. If your employer does not require such a plan, create one anyway. You can do this by answering several "W questions":

- **What** skill or specialized base of knowledge is most essential for you to acquire now in order to do your job more effectively?

- **Who** has acquired this knowledge or demonstrated this skill and would be willing to share their expertise? Perhaps one of these people would be willing to mentor you.

- If learning your desired knowledge or skill requires experiences outside your work environment, **where** will you go to pursue those experiences? Answers might include a night class at a local business school or a company-sponsored training session.

- **When** would you like to demonstrate mastery of your new knowledge or skill? Give yourself a due date for meeting each professional development goal.

- In addition, ask **how** you will know that you've mastered the new knowledge or skill. List specifically what you will say or do differently as a result of your development.

- Finally, consider **what if**—what if the job promotions and other career possibilities that you gain help you to meet the goals in your development plan?

As you answer these questions, keep focused. If you try to develop too many skills at once, you might end with few gains over the long run. Consider setting and achieving one major development goal each year.

Act on your plan every day. Remember that the word *learning* is often defined as an enduring change in behavior. Focus on a new work-related behavior—such as creating a to-do list or overcoming procrastination—that will make a significant, positive, and immediate difference in your performance. Then do it. Every day, implement one new behavior or practice one new habit. In the workplace, learning means doing. ✖

In its *Report on the American Workforce 2001*, the U.S. Department of Labor concluded that "the United States likely will continue to be a nation in which increasing racial and ethnic diversity is the rule, not the exception."[3] Translation: Your next boss or coworker could be a person whose life experience and view of the world differ radically from yours.

Join a diverse workplace

People of all races, ethnicities, and cultures can use several strategies to reach common ground.

Expect differences

To begin, remember an obvious fact: People differ. Obvious as it is, this fact is easy to forget. Most of us unconsciously judge others by a single set of standards—our own. That can lead to communication breakdown. Consider some examples:

- A man in Costa Rica works for a multinational company. He turns down a promotion that would take his family to California. This choice mystifies the company's executives. Yet the man has grand-parents who are in ill health, and leaving them behind would be taboo in his country.

- A Native American woman avoids eye contact with her superiors. Her coworkers see her as aloof. However, she comes from a culture where people seldom make eye contact with their superiors.

- A Caucasian woman from Ohio travels to Mexico City on business. She shows up promptly for a 9 a.m. meeting and finds that it starts 30 minutes late and goes an hour beyond its scheduled ending time. She's entered a culture with a flexible sense of time.

- An American executive schedules a meeting over dinner with people from his company's office in Italy. As soon as the group orders food, the executive launches into a discussion of his agenda items. He notices that his coworkers from Italy seem unusually silent, and he wonders if they feel offended. He forgets that they come from a culture where people phase in to business discussions slowly—only after building a relationship through "small talk."

To prevent misunderstandings, remember that culture touches every aspect of human behavior, ranging from the ways people greet one another to the ways they resolve conflict. Differences in culture could affect any encounter you have with another person. Expecting differences up front helps you keep an open mind and lays the groundwork for all the strategies that follow.

Use language with care

Even people who speak the same language sometimes use simple words that can be confused with each other. For instance, giving someone a "mickey" can mean pulling a practical joke—or slipping a drug into someone's drink. We can find it tough to communicate simple observations, let alone abstract concepts.

You can help by communicating simply and directly. When meeting with people who speak English as a second language, think twice before using figures of speech or slang expressions. Stick to standard English and enunciate clearly.

Also remember that nonverbal language differs across cultures. For example, people from India may shake their head from side to side to indicate agreement, not disagreement. And the hand signal that signifies *OK* to many Americans—thumb and index finger forming a circle—is considered obscene in Brazil.

Put messages in context

When speaking to people of another culture, you might find that words carry only part of an intended message. In many countries, strong networks of shared assumptions form a context for communication.

As an example, people from some Asian and Arabic countries might not include every detail of an agreement in a written contract. These people often place a high value on keeping verbal promises. Spelling out all the details in writing might be considered an insult.

Knowing such facts can help you prevent and resolve conflicts in the workplace.

Test for understanding

To promote cross-cultural understanding, look for signs that your message got through clearly. Ask questions without talking down to your audience: *Am I making myself clear? Is there anything that doesn't make sense?* Watch for nonverbal cues of understanding, such as a nod or smile.

Relate to individuals—not "cultures"

When we see people as faceless representatives of a race or ethnic group, we gloss over important differences. One powerful way to overcome stereotypes is to treat each person as an individual. Remember that the members of any culture can differ widely in beliefs and behaviors.

Discover what you share

The word *communicate* is closely related to *commune* and *common*. This fact points to a useful strategy: When relating to people of another culture, search for what you have in common.

You can start on the job. People from different cultures can share many values related to working: the desire to make more money, to be recognized for achievements, and to win promotions. Cultures often overlap at the level of basic human values—desires for safety, health, and economic security.

Learn about another culture

You can also promote cross-cultural understanding through the path of knowledge. Consider learning everything you can about another culture. Read about that culture and take related classes. Cultivate friends from that culture and take part in their community events. Get a feel for the customs, music, and art that members of the group share. If appropriate, travel abroad to learn more. Also ask about foreign language training your company may offer to the staff.[4]

Follow up with action at work. Join project teams with diverse members. Experiencing diversity firsthand can be a positive experience when you're working with others to meet a common goal.

Expand networks

People with narrow circles of relationships can be at a disadvantage when trying to change jobs or enter a new field. For maximum flexibility in your career path, stay connected to people of your own culture—*and* cultivate contacts with people of other cultures.

Counter bias and discrimination

In the United States, laws dating back to the Equal Pay Act of 1963 and Title VII of the Civil Rights Act of 1964 ban discrimination in virtually all aspects of the work world, from hiring and firing to transfers and promotions. Congress set up the Equal Employment Opportunity Commission (EEOC) to enforce these laws. You can get more information through the EEOC Web site at **http://www.eeoc.gov**.

If you think that you've been the subject of discrimination, take time to examine the facts. Before filing a lawsuit, exhaust other options. Start by bringing the problem to your supervisor, your company's equal employment officer, or someone from the EEOC.

Stereotypes based on race, ethnic group, gender, and disability are likely to fade as the workplace becomes more diverse. As they do, disprove stereotypes through your behavior. Set high standards for yourself and meet them. Seek out key projects that make you visible in the organization, and then perform effectively. These are useful success strategies for anyone in the workplace.

Also keep records of your performance. Log your achievements. Ask for copies of your performance evaluations and make sure they're accurate. Having a stack of favorable evaluations can help you make your case when bringing a complaint or resolving conflict.

Be willing to bridge gaps

Simply being *willing* to bridge culture gaps can be just as crucial as knowing about another group's customs or learning their language. People from other cultures might sense your attitude and be willing to reach out to you.

Begin by displaying some key attributes of a critical thinker. Be open-minded and willing to suspend judgment. Notice when you make assumptions based on another person's accent, race, religion, or gender. Become willing to discover your own biases, listen fully to people with other points of view, enter new cultural territory, and even feel uncomfortable at times.

It's worth it. Bridging to people of other cultures means that you gain new chances to learn, make contacts, increase your career options, and expand your friendships. The ability to work with people of many cultures is a marketable skill—and a way to enlarge your world. ▨

Every organization, large or small, develops its own culture. One way to succeed in the workplace is to "decode" corporate cultures—the basic assumptions and shared values that shape human behavior in the workplace every day.

You can use this knowledge to prevent misunderstanding, resolve conflict, and forge lasting relationships.

Decoding corporate culture

Start by observing

Being culturally savvy starts with discovering "the way we do things around here"—the beliefs and behaviors that are widely shared by your coworkers. In terms of the cycle of learning explained in Chapter One, this means that your efforts to decode corporate culture begin with the stage of reflective observation.

In other words, keep your eyes open. See what kind of actions are rewarded and which are punished. Observe what people do and say to gain credibility in your organization.

You may disagree with what you see and find yourself making negative judgments about your coworkers. Start by noticing those judgments and letting them go. You cannot fully observe behaviors and judge them at the same time. Play the role of a social scientist and collect facts impartially.

Create theories about unwritten rules

Next, create theories about how people succeed in your organization. In terms of the learning cycle, this is the stage of abstract conceptualization. In particular, notice the unwritten "rules" that govern your workplace. Your coworkers may behave on the basis of beliefs such as:

- Never make the boss look bad.
- Some commitments are not meant to be kept.
- If you want to get promoted, then be visible.
- Everyone is expected to work some overtime.

Once you understand the norms and standards of your company, you can consciously choose to accept them. Or you can challenge them by actively experimenting with new behaviors and immersing yourself in new experiences. In any case, changing any organization begins with a first step—telling the truth about how it works right now.

Cope with office politics

The unspoken rules for getting recognized and rewarded are usually what people mean when they talk about *office politics*. One way to deal with office politics is to pretend they don't exist. The downfall of this strategy is that politics are a fact of life.

Another option is to be politically savvy—*and* still hold fast to your values. You can move through the echelons of power and meet ethical career goals at the same time. More specifically:

- **Be visible**. To gain credibility in your organization, get involved in a high-profile project that you believe in. Then perform well. Go beyond the minimum standards. Meet the project goals—and deliver even more.

- **Grow "industry-smart."** Read trade journals and newsletters related to your field. Keep up with current developments. Speak the language shared by the decision makers in your organization.

- **Promote your boss.** During your first year with an organization, the single most important person in your work life could be your boss. This is the person who most closely monitors your performance. This is also the person who can become your biggest advocate. Find out what this person needs and wants. Learn about her goals and then assist her to meet them.

- **Get close to the power centers**. People who advance to top positions are often those who know the language of sales, marketing, accounting, and information technology. These departments are power centers. They directly affect the bottom line. However, you can enhance your company's profitability no matter what position you hold. Look for ways to save money and time. Suggest workable ways to streamline procedures or reduce costs. Focus on solutions to problems, no matter how small, and you'll play the ultimate political game—making a contribution. ⊠

Dealing with sexism and sexual harassment

Sexism and sexual harassment are real. These are events that occur throughout the year at schools and workplaces. Nearly all of these incidents are illegal or violate organizational policies.

Until the early nineteenth century, women in the United States were banned from attending colleges and universities. Today they make up the majority of first-year students in higher education, yet they still encounter bias based on gender.

This bias can take many forms. For example, instructors might gloss over the contributions of women. Students in philosophy class might never hear of a woman named Hypatia, an ancient Greek philosopher and mathematician. Those majoring in computer science might never learn about Rear Admiral Grace Murray Hopper, who pioneered the development of a computer language named COBOL. And your art history textbook might not mention the Mexican painter Frida Kahlo or the American painter Georgia O'Keeffe.

Though men can be subjects of sexism and sexual harassment, women are more likely to experience this form of discrimination. Even the most well-intentioned people might behave in ways that hurt or discount women. Sexism is a factor when:

- Instructors use only masculine pronouns—*he, his,* and *him*—to refer to both men and women.
- Career counselors hint that careers in mathematics and science are not appropriate majors or career fields for women.
- Students pay more attention to feedback from a male teacher than from a female teacher.
- Women are not called on in class, their comments during meetings in the workplace are ignored, or they are overly praised for answering the simplest questions.
- Examples given in a textbook or lecture assign women only to traditionally "female" roles, such as wife, mother, day care provider, elementary school teacher, or nurse.
- People assume that middle-aged women who return to school or the workplace have too many family commitments to study adequately or do well in their jobs.

Many kinds of behavior—both verbal and physical—can be categorized as sexual harassment. This kind of discrimination involves unwelcome sexual conduct. Examples of such conduct in a school setting are:

- Sexual touching or advances.
- Any other unwanted touch.
- Unwanted verbal intimacy.
- Sexual graffiti.
- Displaying or distributing sexually explicit materials.
- Sexual gestures or jokes.
- Pressure for sexual favors.
- Talking about personal sexual activity.
- Spreading rumors about someone's sexual activity or rating someone's sexual performance.

Sexual Harassment: It's Not Academic, a pamphlet from the U.S. Department of Education, quotes a woman who experienced sexual harassment in higher education: "The financial officer made it clear that I could get the money I needed if I slept with him."

That's an example of *quid pro quo harassment.* This legal term applies when students believe that an educational decision depends on submitting to unwelcome sexual conduct. *Hostile environment harassment* takes place when such incidents are severe, persistent, or pervasive.

The feminist movement has raised awareness about discrimination against women. We can now respond to sexism and sexual harassment in the places we live, work, and go to school. Specific strategies follow.

Point out sexist language and behavior. When you see examples of sexism, point them out. Your message can be more effective if you use "I" messages instead of personal attacks, as explained in Chapter Eight: Communicating. Indicate the specific statements and behaviors that you consider sexist.

For example, you could rephrase a sexist comment so that it targets another group, such as Jews or African Americans. People might spot anti-Semitism or racism more readily than sexism.

Keep in mind that men can also be subjected to sexism, ranging from antagonistic humor to exclusion from jobs that have traditionally been done by women.

Observe your own language and behavior.
Looking for sexist behavior in others is effective. Detecting it in yourself can be just as powerful. Write a Discovery Statement about specific comments that could be interpreted as sexist. Then notice if you say any of these things. Also ask people you know to point out occasions when you use similar statements. Follow up with an Intention Statement that describes how you plan to change your speaking or behavior.

You can also write Discovery Statements about the current level of intimacy (physical and verbal) in any of your relationships at home, work, or school. Be sure that any increase in the level of intimacy is mutually agreed upon.

Encourage support for women.
Through networks, women can work to overcome the effects of sexism. Strategies include study groups for women, women's job networks, and professional organizations, such as Women in Communications. Other examples are counseling services and health centers for women, family planning agencies, and rape prevention centers. Check your school catalog and library to see if any of these services are available at your school.

If your school does not have the women's networks you want, you can help form them. Sponsor a one-day or one-week conference on women's issues. Create a discussion or reading group for the women in your class, department, residence hall, union, or neighborhood.

Set limits.
Women, value yourselves. Recognize your right to an education without the distraction of inappropriate and invasive behavior. Trust your judgment about when your privacy or your rights are being violated. Decide now what kind of sexual comments and actions you're uncomfortable with—and refuse to put up with them.

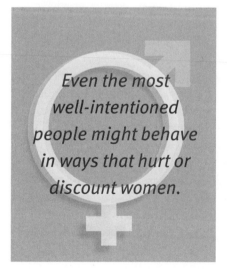

Even the most well-intentioned people might behave in ways that hurt or discount women.

Take action.
If you are sexually harassed, take action. Some key federal legislation protects the rights of women. One is Title VII of the Civil Rights Act of 1964. Guidelines for interpreting this law offer the following definition of harassment. *Unwelcome sexual advances, requests for sexual favors, and other verbal or physical conduct of a sexual nature constitute sexual harassment when:*

1. *Submission to this conduct becomes a condition of employment.*

2. *Women's response to such conduct is used as a basis for employment decisions.*

3. *This conduct interferes with work performance or creates an offensive work environment.*[5]

The law also states that schools must take action to prevent sexual harassment.

Another relevant law is Title IX of the Education Amendments of 1972. This act bans discrimination against students and employees on the basis of gender. It applies to any educational program receiving federal funds.

If you believe that you've been sexually harassed, report the incident to a school official. This person can be a teacher, administrator, or campus security officer. Check to see if your school has someone specially designated to handle your complaint, such as an affirmative action officer or Title IX coordinator.

You can also file a complaint with the Office for Civil Rights (OCR), a federal agency that makes sure schools and workplaces comply with Title IX. In your complaint, include your name, address, and daytime phone number, along with the date of the incident and a description of it. Do this within 180 days of the incident. You can contact the OCR at 1-800-421-3481 or go to the agency's Web site at **http://bcol01.ed.gov/CFAPPS/OCR/contactus.cfm**. Your community might also offer resources to protect against sexual discrimination. Examples are public interest law firms, legal aid societies, and unions that employ lawyers. People with these organizations can also advise you about when and how to take action for sexual harass-ment in the workplace to enforce these laws. You can get more information through the Equal Employment Opportunity Commission (EEOC) at **http://www. eeoc.gov**.

Strategies for working with a mentor

One strategy for planning your career and succeeding in the workplace is to find a mentor— a partner in your professional and personal development. Many people will be flattered to take on such a role in your life.

Start with a development plan.
Before you ask someone to mentor you, reflect on your goals for this relationship. Begin with *what* you want to gain rather than *who* to ask for mentoring. List the specific skills that you want to develop with a mentor's involvement. Over time you might work with several mentors, each with different expertise, to develop a variety of skills.

For maximum clarity, put your development plan in writing. Consider using the Discovery and Intention Journal Entry System. Write Discovery Statements to list your current skills, recent examples of how you've used them, and insights from your mentor.

Whenever possible, create a way to measure your progress. For example, you could note the number of times you practice a new habit. Or you could summarize ratings from your performance reviews at work. Include these measurements in your Discovery Statements and share them with your mentor.

Follow up with Intention Statements that describe exactly what new behaviors you want to implement, along with ongoing updates to your development plan.

In your Intention Statements, include a timeline. Use your goal-setting skills to set due dates for acquiring new skills or producing new outcomes in your life. Also state when you want to begin and end the mentoring sessions. Keep in mind that many mentoring relationships are short-term, taking place over weeks or months rather than years.

Approach potential mentors.
Identify several people who have demonstrated competence in the skills you want to gain, along with the energy and desire to take on a mentee—that is, you. If you can find someone at work who has a positive reputation and influence in your organization, that's an added plus.

Next, contact each person on your list and mention that you're seeking a mentor. Summarize your development plan and timetable. Also suggest ways that you can create value for a mentor, such as helping that person complete a project or achieve one of *his* development goals. The more you give to the mentor relationship, the more you'll get out of it.

If a potential mentor is too busy to work with you right now, ask if she can refer you to someone else. After meeting with several people, choose one person to work with.

Accept your mentor's feedback.
Remember that a mentor is not a boss, parent, or taskmaster. Instead, you're looking for coaching. A coach helps you clarify your goals and then offers nonjudgmental observations of your behavior along with suggestions for improvement. However, the responsibility for your day-to-day performance and long-term development lies with you.

Schedule regular meetings with your mentor. During these meetings, put all your listening skills to work. Resist the temptation to debate, argue, or justify your behavior. Simply receive what your mentor has to say. Ask questions to clarify anything you don't understand.

Remember that when you asked for mentoring, you signed on for objective feedback and suggestions—including ideas you may have resisted in the past. A commitment to change implies the willingness to think, speak, and act in new ways. Stay open to suggestion.

Beyond listening, move into action. When your mentor offers an insight, look for an immediate way to apply it. Experiment with a new behavior every day.

Seek closure—and continue.
When you've come to the end of a mentoring relationship, offer your thanks and celebrate your accomplishments. Solidify your learning by listing the top five insights or skills you gained.

In addition, choose your next step. List upcoming opportunities to practice your newly acquired skills. Also consider the benefits of working with a mentor again in the future. This is a development tool that you can use for the rest of your life. ◪

We are all leaders

Many people mistakenly think that leaders are only those with formal titles such as *supervisor* or *manager*. In fact, some leaders have no such titles. Some have never supervised others. Like Mahatma Gandhi, some people change the face of the world without ever reaching a formal leadership position.

While many of us will never become so well known, we all have the capacity to make significant changes in the world around us. Through our actions and words we constantly influence what happens in our classrooms, offices, communities, and families. We are all conscious leaders, even if sometimes we are unconscious of that fact.

Own your leadership

Let go of the reluctance that many of us feel toward assuming leadership. It's impossible to escape leadership. Every time you speak, you lead others in some small or large way. Every time you take action, you lead others through your example. Every time you ask someone to do something, you are in essence leading that person. Leadership becomes more effective when it is consciously applied.

Take on big projects

Leaders make promises. And effective leaders make big promises. These words—"I will do it. You can count on me"—distinguish a leader.

Look around your world to see what needs to be done and then take it on. Consider taking on the biggest project you can think of—ending world hunger, eliminating nuclear weapons, wiping out poverty, promoting universal literacy. Think about how you'd spend your life if you knew that you could make a difference regarding these overwhelming problems. Then take the actions you considered. See what a difference they can make for you and for others.

Tackle projects that stretch you to your limits—projects that are worthy of your time and talents.

Provide feedback

An effective leader is a mirror to others. Share what you see. Talk with others about what they are doing effectively—*and* what they are doing ineffectively.

Keep in mind that people might not enjoy your feedback. Some would probably rather not hear it at all.

Two things can help. One is to let people know up front that if they sign on to work with you, they can expect feedback. Also give your feedback with skill. Use "I" messages as explained in Chapter Eight: Communicating. Back up any criticisms with specific observations and facts. And when people complete a task with exceptional skill, point that out, too.

Model your values

"Be the change you want to see" is a useful motto for leaders. Perhaps you want to see integrity, focused attention, and productivity in the people around you. Begin by modeling these qualities yourself.

It's easy to excite others about a goal when you are enthusiastic about it yourself. Having fun while being productive is contagious. If you bring these qualities to a project, others might follow suit.

Make requests—lots of them

An effective leader is a request machine. Making requests—both large and small—is an act of respect. When we ask a lot from others, we demonstrate our respect for them and our confidence in their abilities.

At first, some people might get angry when we make requests of them. Over time, many will see that requests are compliments, opportunities to expand their skills. Ask a lot from others, and they might appreciate you for it.

Focus on the problem, not the person

Sometimes projects do not go as planned. Big mistakes occur. If this happens, focus on the project and the mistakes—not the personal faults of your colleagues. People do not make mistakes on purpose. If they did, we would call them "on-purposes," not mistakes. Most people will join you in solving a problem if your focus is on the problem, not on what they did wrong.

Share credit

As a leader, constantly give away the praise and acknowledgment that you receive. When you're congratulated for your performance, pass it on to others. Share the credit with the group.

When you're a leader, the results you achieve depend on the efforts of many others. Acknowledging that fact often is more than telling the truth—it's essential if you want to continue to count on their support in the future.

Delegate

Ask a coworker or classmate to take on a job that you'd like to see done. Ask the same of your family or friends. Delegate tasks to the mayor of your town, the governor of your state, and the leaders of your country.

Take on projects that are important to you. Then find people who can lead the effort. You can do this even when you have no formal role as a leader.

We often see delegation as a tool that's available only to those above us in the chain of command. Actually, delegating up or across an organization can be just as effective. Consider delegating a project to your boss. That is, ask her to take on a job that you'd like to see accomplished. This might be a job that you cannot do, given your position in the company.

Paint a vision

Help others see the big picture, the ultimate purpose of a project. Speak a lot about the end result and the potential value of what you're doing.

There's a biblical saying: "Without vision, the people perish." Long-term goals usually involve many intermediate steps. Unless we're reminded of the purpose for those day-to-day actions, our work can feel like a grind. Leadership is the art of helping others lift their eyes to the horizon—keeping them in touch with the ultimate value and purpose of a project. Keeping the vision alive helps spirits soar again. ◩

Loving your next job

Job disappointment has countless symptoms, including statements such as "My boss is a jerk," "I'm so bored," and "This is too hard."

Faced with such sentiments, there's a tempting short-term solution: "I quit." Sometimes that is a reasonable option. In many cases of job dissatisfaction, however, there are solutions that do less damage to your immediate income and your long-term job prospects.

Manage your expectations

Instead of changing jobs, consider changing the way you think. Perhaps you never expected to run the company within six months after joining it. Yet your expectations for your current job might still be unrealistic.

This suggestion can be especially useful if you've just graduated from school and find yourself working in an entry-level position in your field. Students who are used to stimulating class discussions and teachers with a passion for their subject might be shocked by the realities of the workplace: people who hide behind a cubicle and avoid human contact; managers with technical skills but no people skills; coworkers who get promoted on the basis of political favors rather than demonstrated skills.

If you're unhappy at work, review the Power Process: "Notice your pictures and let them go." Then ask which of your work-related pictures might be related to your upset. Perhaps you're operating on the basis of unrealistic "shoulds" such as:

- My first job after graduating *should* draw on all the skills I developed in school.
- Everyone I meet on a job *should* be interesting, competent, and kind.
- Every task that I perform at work *should* be enjoyable.
- My work environment *should* be problem-free.

See if you can replace the should in such statements with *can* or *could*. For example: "Even though I'm not using all my skills, I *can* use this job to learn about corporate culture and coping with office politics." Or "I *could* use this job to develop at least one skill that I can transfer to my next job."

Practice problem solving

Sometimes you can benefit by adjusting more than your attitude. Apply your transferable skills at problem solving. Write Discovery Statements about:

- How you felt when you started the job.
- When you started feeling unhappy with the job.
- Any specific events that triggered your dissatisfaction.

This writing can help you pinpoint the sources of job dissatisfaction. Possibilities include conflict with coworkers, a mismatch between your skills and the job requirements, or a mismatch between your personal values and the values promoted in the workplace.

No matter what the source, you can brainstorm solutions. Ask friends and family members for help. If you're bored with work, propose a project that will create value for your boss and offer to lead it. If your supervisor seems unhappy with your performance, ask for coaching to do it better. If you feel stressed, review the stress-management techniques in Chapter Six: Tests, and choose at least one to use on a daily basis. If you're in conflict with a coworker, apply strategies for resolving conflict presented in Chapter Eight: Communicating.

Moving into action to solve the problem offers a reminder that you—not your boss or coworkers—are in charge of the quality of your life.

Focus on process

You can also take a cue from the term *Power Process*. Shift your focus from the content of your job to the process you use—from *what* you do to *how* you do it. Even if a task seems boring or beneath you, see if you can do it impeccably and with total attention. As you do, project a professional image in everything from the way you dress to the way you speak. One strategy for handling a dead-end job is to do it so well that you get noticed—and promoted to a new job. ⬥

journal entry 31

Discovery/Intention Statement

You can use this journal entry any time that you feel unhappy at work. Complete the following sentences, using additional paper as needed.

I discovered that:

- If I could change one thing about this job, I would . . .

_____

_____

_____

_____

- Something I *do* like about this job is . . .

_____

_____

_____

_____

- The transferable skills I am learning on this job include . . .

_____

_____

_____

_____

- I intend to make this job—or my next job—more satisfying by . . .

_____

_____

_____

_____

Define your values, align your actions

One key way to choose what's next in your life is to define your values. Values are the things in life that you want for their own sake. Values influence and guide your choices, including your moment-by-moment choices of what to do and what to have. Your values define who you are and who you want to be.

Some people are guided by values that they automatically adopt from others or by values that remain largely unconscious. These people could be missing the opportunity to live a life that's truly of their own choosing.

Investing time and energy to define your values is a pivotal suggestion in this book. In fact, *From Master Student to Master Employee* is based on a particular value system that underlies suggestions given throughout the book. This system includes the values of:

- Focused attention
- Self-responsibility
- Integrity
- Risk-taking
- Contributing

You'll find these values and related ones directly stated in the Power Processes throughout the text. For instance:

Discover what you want is about the importance of living a purpose-based life.

Ideas are tools points to the benefits of being willing to experiment with new ideas.

Be here now expresses the value of focused attention.

Love your problems (and experience your barriers) is about seeing difficulties as opportunities to develop new skills.

Notice your pictures and let them go is about adopting an attitude of open-mindedness.

I create it all is about taking responsibility for our beliefs and behaviors.

Detach reminds us that our core identity and value as a person does not depend on our possessions, our circumstances, or even our accomplishments.

Find a bigger problem is about offering our lives by contributing to others.

Employ your word expresses the value of making and keeping agreements.

Risk being a fool is about courage—the willingness to take risks for the sake of learning something new.

In addition, most of the study skills and workplace skills you read about in these pages have their source in values. The Time Monitor/Time Plan exercise, for example, calls for focused attention. Even the simple act of sharing your notes with a student who missed a class is an example of contributing.

As you begin to define your values, consider those who have gone before you. In creeds, scriptures, philosophies, myths, and sacred stories, the human race has left a vast and varied record of values. Be willing to look everywhere, including sources that are close to home. The creed of your local church or temple might eloquently describe some of your values—so might the mission statement of your school, company, or club. Another way to define your values is to describe the qualities of people you admire.

Also translate your values into behavior. Though defining your values is powerful, it doesn't guarantee any results. To achieve your goals, take actions that align with your values. ◪

One set of values

Following is a sample list of values. Don't read it with the idea that it is the "right" set of values for you. Instead, use this list as a point of departure in creating your own list.

Value: **Be accountable**

This means being:

- Honest
- Reliable
- Trustworthy
- Operating with integrity
- Dependable
- Responsible
- Making and keeping agreements

Value: **Be loving**

This means being:

- Affectionate
- Devoted
- Accepting
- Considerate
- Respectful
- Inclusive
- Ethical
- Dedicated
- Equitable
- Gentle
- Forgiving
- Friendly
- Fair

Value: **Be promotive**

This means being:

- Nurturing
- Contributing—charitable; thrifty; generous with time, money, and possessions
- Frugal—achieving the best results with the fewest possible dollars
- Helpful
- Encouraging
- Reasonable
- Judicious
- Cooperative—working as a member of a team or a community
- Appreciative

Value: **Be candid**

This means being:

- Honest
- Genuine
- Frank
- Spontaneous
- Free of deceit
- Able to avoid false modesty without arrogance
- Self-disclosing
- Open about strengths and weaknesses
- Authentic
- Self-expressed
- Outspoken
- Sincere

Value: **Be detached**

This means being:

- Impartial
- Experimental
- Open-minded
- Adaptable
- Trusting
- Joyful
- Unbiased
- Satisfied
- Patient (not resigned)
- Without distress
- Tolerant
- Willing to surrender

Value: **Be aware of the possible**

This means being:

- Creative
- Resourceful
- Foresighted
- Visionary
- Audacious
- Imaginative
- Inventive
- Holistic
- Inquisitive
- Exploring

DISCOVERY WHEEL—COMING FULL CIRCLE

Do this exercise online at masterstudent.college.hmco.com

This book doesn't work. It is worthless. Only you can work. Only you can make a difference and use this book to become more effective at transferring skills from the classroom to the workplace.

The purpose of this book is to give you the opportunity to change your behavior. The fact that something seems like a good idea doesn't necessarily mean that you will put it into practice. This exercise gives you a chance to see what behaviors you have changed on your journey toward mastery.

Answer each question quickly and honestly. Record your results on the Discovery Wheel on this page and then compare it with the one you completed in Chapter One.

The scores on this Discovery Wheel indicate your current strengths and weaknesses. The journal entry that follows this exercise provides an opportunity to write about how you intend to change. As you complete this self-evaluation, keep in mind that your commitment to change allows you to become a master student and a master employee.

Your scores might be lower here than on your earlier Discovery Wheel. That's OK. Lower scores might result from increased self-awareness and honesty, and other valuable assets.

Note: The online version of this exercise does not include number ratings, so the results will be formatted differently than described here. If you did your previous Discovery Wheel online, do it online again. This will help you compare your two sets of responses more accurately.

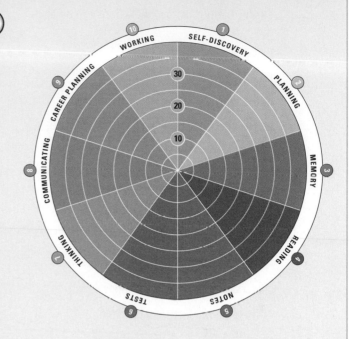

5 points
This statement is always or almost always true of me.

4 points
This statement is often true of me.

3 points
This statement is true of me about half the time.

2 points
This statement is seldom true of me.

1 point
This statement is never or almost never true of me.

1. _____ I enjoy learning.

2. _____ I understand and apply the concept of multiple intelligences.

3. _____ I connect my courses to my purpose for being in school and the benefits I intend to get from my education.

4. _____ I regularly assess my personal strengths and areas for improvement.

5. _____ I am satisfied with how I am progressing toward achieving my goals.

6. _____ I use my knowledge of learning styles to support my success in school and at work.

7. _____ I am willing to consider any idea that can help me succeed in school—even if I initially disagree with that idea.

8. _____ I monitor my habits and change them in ways that support my success.

_____ ***Total score (1) Self-Discovery***

1. _____ I set long-term goals and periodically review them.

2. _____ I set mid-term and short-term goals to support my long-term goals.

3. _____ I write a plan for each day and each week.

4. _____ I assign priorities to what I choose to do each day.

5. _____ I plan regular recreation time.

6. _____ I adjust my study time to meet the demands of individual courses.

7. _____ I have adequate time each day to accomplish what I plan.

8. _____ I effectively plan projects and manage time in work settings.

_____ *Total score (2) Planning*

1. _____ I am confident of my ability to remember.

2. _____ I can remember people's names.

3. _____ At the end of a lecture, I can summarize what was presented.

4. _____ I apply techniques that enhance my memory skills.

5. _____ I can recall information when I'm under pressure.

6. _____ I remember important information clearly and easily.

7. _____ I can jog my memory when I have difficulty recalling.

8. _____ I can relate new information to what I've already learned.

_____ *Total score (3) Memory*

1. _____ I preview and review reading assignments.

2. _____ When reading, I ask myself questions about the material.

3. _____ I underline or highlight important passages when reading.

4. _____ When I read textbooks, I am alert and awake.

5. _____ I relate what I read to my life.

6. _____ I select a reading strategy to fit the type of material I'm reading.

7. _____ I take effective notes when I read.

8. _____ When I don't understand what I'm reading, I note my questions and find answers.

_____ *Total score (4) Reading*

1. _____ When I am in class, I focus my attention.

2. _____ I take notes in class and during meetings.

3. _____ I am aware of various methods for taking notes and choose those that work best for me.

4. _____ I distinguish major ideas from examples and other supporting material.

5. _____ I copy down material that the presenter writes on the chalkboard or overhead projector.

6. _____ I can put important concepts into my own words.

7. _____ My notes are valuable for review.

8. _____ I review notes within 24 hours.

_____ *Total score (5) Notes*

1. _____ I feel confident and calm during an exam.

2. _____ I manage my time during exams and am able to complete them.

3. _____ I am able to predict test questions.

4. _____ I adapt my test-taking strategy to the kind of test I'm taking.

5. _____ I create value from any type of evaluation, including performance reviews.

6. _____ I start reviewing for tests at the beginning of the term and continue reviewing throughout the term.

7. _____ I manage stress and maintain my health even when I feel under pressure.

8. _____ My sense of personal worth is independent of my test scores.

_____ *Total score (6) Tests*

1. _____ I have flashes of insight and often think of solutions to problems at unusual times.

2. _____ I use brainstorming to generate solutions to a variety of problems.

3. _____ When I get stuck on a creative project, I use specific methods to get unstuck.

4. _____ I see problems and tough decisions as opportunities for learning and personal growth.

5. _____ I am open to different points of view and diverse cultural perspectives.

6. _____ I can support my points of view with sound logic and evidence.

7. _____ I use critical thinking to resolve ethical dilemmas.

8. _____ As I share my viewpoints with others, I am open to their feedback.

_____ **Total score (7) Thinking**

1. _____ I am candid with others about who I am, what I feel, and what I want.

2. _____ Other people tell me that I am a good listener.

3. _____ I can communicate my upset and resolve conflict without blaming others.

4. _____ I work effectively as a member of a project team.

5. _____ I am learning ways to thrive with diversity—attitudes and behaviors that will support my career success.

6. _____ I can effectively plan, research, draft, and revise a large writing assignment.

7. _____ I learn effectively from course materials and activities that are posted online.

8. _____ I prepare and deliver effective speeches and presentations.

_____ **Total score (8) Communicating**

1. _____ I relate school to what I plan to do for the rest of my life.

2. _____ I connect my attitudes, interests, and skills to career possibilities.

3. _____ I use the library, the Internet, and other resources to monitor developments in the job market.

4. _____ I use the career planning and job placement services offered by my school.

5. _____ In work settings, I look for models of success and cultivate mentors.

6. _____ I manage my income and expenses to fund my education and meet other financial goals.

7. _____ I have a written career plan and update it regularly.

8. _____ I use internships and other work experiences to refine my career plans.

_____ **Total score (9) Career Planning**

1. _____ My work contributes something worthwhile to the world.

2. _____ My work creates value for my employer.

3. _____ I see working as a way to pursue my interests, expand my skills, and develop mastery.

4. _____ I support other people in their career planning and job hunting—and am willing to accept their support.

5. _____ I can function effectively in corporate cultures and cope positively with office politics.

6. _____ I create résumés and cover letters that distinguish me from other job applicants.

7. _____ I can accurately predict and prepare responses to questions asked by job interviewers.

8. _____ I see learning as a lifelong process that includes experiences inside and outside the classroom.

_____ **Total score (10) Working**

Filling in your Discovery Wheel

Using the total score from each category, shade in each section of the Discovery Wheel on page 343. Use different colors, if you want. For example, you could use green to denote areas you want to work on. When you have finished, complete the following Journal Entry.

journal entry 32

Discovery/Intention Statement

The purpose of this journal entry is to (1) review both of the Discovery Wheels you completed in this book, (2) summarize your insights from doing them, and (3) declare how you will use these insights to promote your continued success in the classroom and in the workplace.

Again, a lower score on the second Discovery Wheel does not necessarily indicate decreased personal effectiveness. Instead, the lower score could result from increased honesty and greater self-awareness.

	Chapter 1	Chapter 12
Self-discovery	_____	_____
Planning	_____	_____
Memory	_____	_____
Reading	_____	_____
Notes	_____	_____
Tests	_____	_____
Thinking	_____	_____
Communicating	_____	_____
Career Planning	_____	_____
Working	_____	_____

Comparing the Discovery Wheel in this chapter with the Discovery Wheel in Chapter One, I discovered that I . . .

_____

_____

_____

_____

_____

_____

In the next six months, I intend to review the following articles from this book for additional suggestions I could use in the classroom:

_____

_____

_____

_____

_____

_____

_____

_____

_____

_____

In the next six months, I also intend to review the following articles for additional suggestions I could use in the workplace:

_____

_____

_____

_____

_____

_____

_____

_____

_____

_____

THINKING CRITICALLY IN THE WORKPLACE

In this exercise you will apply a higher-order thinking skill called *synthesis*—detecting key relationships between ideas and looking for broad patterns in your experiences. You'll also practice a technique for creative thinking. The focus is your experience of job hunting and the assumptions that shape your behaviors.

Recall all the jobs you've had in your life—full-time or part-time, permanent or temporary, contract or freelance. Think about the strategies you typically used to find these jobs. In the space below, list three strategies that you've depended on. Examples might include checking want ads in a newspaper and looking for job openings online.

_____

_____

_____

Next, try some new assumptions on for size. See if you can state three job-hunting strategies that contrast greatly with—or even contradict—the three strategies you just listed. Be willing to think creatively and play with new possibilities, even if you feel resistance to a new idea. If you've depended on want ads, for instance, you might write: "Instead of sending my résumé in response to want ads, I could send a résumé only after meeting face to face with people who can hire me."

List your three new strategies below.

_____

_____

_____

Finally, take the most "outrageous" strategy you just listed and list three potential benefits of using it.

_____

_____

_____

journal entry 33

Discovery/Intention Statement

You've done a lot of writing during this course. To retain your key insights from this experience, review your responses to the exercises and journal entries in this book. Writing in the space below, summarize your key discoveries. List any intentions that call for further action. Write any new Discovery Statements or Intention Statements that seem appropriate.

_____

_____

_____

_____

_____

_____

_____

_____

_____

_____

_____

_____

_____

_____

_____

_____

_____

_____

_____

_____

_____

_____

_____

_____

_____

_____

_____

_____

power process

Be it

All of the techniques in this book are enhanced by this Power Process.

To tap into its full benefits, consider that most of our choices in life fall into three categories. We can:

- Increase our material wealth (what we have).

- Improve our skills (what we do).

- Develop our "being" (who we are).

Many people devote their entire lifetime to the first two categories. They act as if they are "human havings" instead of human beings. For them, the quality of life hinges on what they have. They devote most of their waking hours to getting more—more clothes, more cars, more relationships, more degrees, more trophies. "Human havings" define themselves by looking at the circumstances in their lives—what they have.

Some people escape this materialist trap by adding another dimension to their identities. In addition to living as "human havings," they also live as "human doings." They thrive on working hard and doing everything well. They define themselves by how efficiently they do their jobs, how effectively they raise their children, and how actively they participate in clubs and organizations. Their thoughts are constantly about methods, techniques, and skills.

Look beyond doing and having

In addition to focusing on what we have and what we do, we can also focus on our being. While it is impossible to live our lives without having things and doing things, this Power Process suggests that we balance our experience by giving lots of attention to who we are—an aspect of our lives that goes beyond having and doing. Call it soul, passion, purpose, or values. Call it *being*. This word describes how we see ourselves—our deepest commitments, the ground from which our actions spring.

The realm of being is profound and subtle. It is also difficult to capture in words, though philosophers have tried for centuries. Christian theologian Paul Tillich described this realm when he defined faith as "ultimate commitment" and the "ground of being." In the New Testament, Jesus talked about being when he asked his followers to love God with all of their heart, soul, and mind. An ancient Hindu text also touches on being: "You are what your deep, driving desire is."

If all this seems far removed from taking notes or answering test questions, read on. Consider an example of how "Be it" can assist in career choices. In a letter to her father, a young woman wrote:

We just went to see the Dance Theatre of Harlem. It was great! After the last number, I decided that I want to dance more than anything. I have a great passion to do it, more than anything else I can think or dream of. Dancing is what will make me happy and feel like I can leave this earth when my time comes. It is what I must do. I think that if I never fulfill this passion, I will never feel complete or satisfied with what I have done with my life.

In her heart, this person *is* a dancer now, even before her formal training is complete. From her passion, desire, commitment, and self-image (her *being*) comes her willingness to take classes and rehearse (*doing*). And from her doing she might eventually *have* a job with a professional dance company.

Picture the result as you begin

The example of the dancer illustrates that once you have a clear picture of what you want to *be,* the things you *do* and *have* fall more naturally into place.

The idea is this: Getting where you want to be by what you do or by what you have is like swimming against the current. Have → do → be is a tough journey. It's much easier to go in the other direction: be → do → have.

Usually, we work against nature by trying to have something or do something before being it. That's hard. All of your deeds (what you do) might not get you where you want to be. Getting all of the right things (what you have) might not get you there either.

Take the person who values athletics and wants to master tennis. He buys an expensive racket and a stylish tennis wardrobe. Yet he still can't return a serve. Merely having the right things doesn't deliver what he values.

Suppose that this person takes a year's worth of tennis lessons. Week after week, he practices doing everything "right." Still, his game doesn't quite make it.

What goes wrong is hard to detect. "He lost the match even though he played a good game," people say. "Something seemed to be wrong. His technique was fine, but each swing was just a little off." Perhaps the source of his problem is that he cannot see himself as ever mastering the game. What he has and what he does are at war with his mental picture of himself.

You can see this happen in other areas of life. Two people tell the same joke in what seems to be the same way. Yet one person brings a smile, while the other person has you laughing so hard your muscles hurt. The difference in how they do the joke is imperceptible. When the successful comedian tells a joke, he does it from his experience of already being funny.

To have and do what you want, be it. Picture the result as you begin. If you can first visualize where you want to

Change the way you see yourself, and watch your actions and results shift as if by magic.

be, if you can go there in your imagination, if you can be it today, you set yourself up to succeed.

Demonstrate mastery now

Now relate this Power Process to succeeding in school and at work. All of the techniques in this book can be worthless if you operate with the idea that you are basically ineffective. You might do almost everything this book suggests and still never achieve the success that you desire.

For example, if you believe that you are stupid in math, you are likely to fail at math. If you believe that you are not skilled at remembering, all of the memory techniques in the world might not help you remember the names of coworkers or people in your job-hunting network. Generally, we don't outperform our self-concept.

If you value success, then demonstrate mastery right now. Prepare papers and projects as if you were submitting them to an employer. Imagine that a promotion and raise will be determined by the way that you complete assignments and participate in class. While you are in higher education, reflect and reinforce the view that you are a professional.

Also demonstrate mastery in the work world. If you value a fulfilling career, picture yourself as already being on a path to a job you love. Use affirmations and visualizations to plant this idea firmly in your mind.

While you're at it, remember that "Be it" is not positive thinking or mental cheerleading. This Power Process works well when you take a First Step—when you tell the truth about your current abilities. The very act of accepting who you are and what you can do right now unleashes a powerful force for personal change.

Flow with the natural current of be → do → have. Then watch your circumstances change.

If you want it, be it. ◪

career application

Duane Bigeagle earned his BA in Elementary Education and found a job teaching kindergarten in an urban public school.

To his surprise, the hardest thing about the job was not interacting with students—whom he enjoyed greatly—but interacting with his coworkers. Though Duane had heard of office politics, he did not expect them to be so strong in an educational setting.

Duane's greatest concern was a colleague named Reneé, a teacher with 25 years of experience. During weekly staff meetings, the school's principal asked teachers to share any problems they were experiencing with students and collectively brainstorm solutions. Reneé smiled a lot, offered suggestions, and freely offered praise for anyone who was willing to share a problem. During informal conversations with Duane before or after school, however, Reneé complained bitterly about other teachers on staff—including those whom she'd just praised during staff meetings.

Being new to the school and a first-year teacher, Duane decided that he wanted to avoid making enemies. His goal in relating to staff members was simply to learn everything he could from them. With that goal in mind, Duane adopted the habits of carefully observing the classroom strategies used by other teachers and listening without judgment to any coaching they offered him.

Reneé talked with Duane every day and, after gossiping about other teachers, freely offered her advice for managing his classroom. By the end of the school year, Duane had enough of this. He worried that Reneé was taking on the role of a self-appointed mentor to him, and he disagreed with many of her ideas about teaching. He also worried that other teachers would perceive he and Reneé as a "team," and that her reputation for "backstabbing" would reflect negatively on him as well. ▨

Reflecting on this scenario:

1. Refer to the list of SCANS skills on page 8. Identify a transferable skill that Duane demonstrates.

_____

_____

_____

2. What behaviors lead you to conclude that Duane has this skill?

_____

_____

_____

3. Using the same SCANS list, identify a skill that would be useful for Duane to develop.

_____

_____

_____

4. List two or three suggestions for Duane that could help him cope with office politics and solve his problem with Reneé.

_____

_____

_____

Name _____ Date _____/_____/_____

quiz

1. List three examples of unwritten rules that may be part of a corporate culture.

2. Explain the meaning of the suggestion to "promote your boss."

3. List three examples of sexual harassment in a work setting.

4. According to the text, the most important function of a leader is to prevent huge mistakes. True or False? Explain your answer.

5. Choose one Power Process from this text and briefly explain how it can help you love your next job.

6. List three strategies for keeping your career plan alive.

7. According to the text, you can delegate a job to your boss. True or False? Explain your answer.

8. Explain the suggestion to "give yourself a raise before you start work."

9. Using the Power Process: "Be it" eliminates the need to take action. True or False? Explain your answer.

10. If your scores are lower on the Discovery Wheel the second time you complete it, that means your study skills have not improved. True or False? Explain your answer.

learning styles application

The questions below will "cycle" you through four styles, or modes, of learning as explained in the article "Learning styles: Discovering how you learn" in Chapter One. Each question will help you explore a different mode. You can answer the questions in any order.

what if
Consider this statement: "You are on the edge of a universe so miraculous and full of wonder that your imagination at its most creative moment cannot encompass it. Paths are open to lead you to worlds beyond your wildest dreams." If you adopted this statement as a working principle, what would you do differently on a daily basis?

why
Consider your experience with this book and your student success class. Which of your attitudes or actions changed as a result of this experience?

how
List one suggestion from this book that you would like to apply but have not yet acted upon. Describe exactly how you will implement this suggestion.

what
List five suggestions from this book that you've already applied. Rate each suggestion for its effectiveness on a scale of 1 to 5 (1 is most effective, 5 is least effective).

master student profile

CRAIG KIELBURGER

In 1995, at age 12, Craig Kielburger founded Free the Children International, an organization of children helping children who are the victims of poverty and exploitation. He has also served as an ambassador to the Children's Embassy in Sarajevo and was named a Global Leader of Tomorrow at the 1998 World Economic Forum.

picked up the Toronto Star **and** put it on the table. But I didn't make it past the front page. Staring back at me was the headline, "BATTLED CHILD LABOUR, BOY, 12, MURDERED." It was a jolt. Twelve, the same age as I was. My eyes fixed on the picture of a boy in a bright-red vest. He had a broad smile, his arm raised straight in the air, a fist clenched....

Riding the bus to school later that morning, I could think of nothing but the article I had read on the front page. What kind of parents would sell their children into slavery at four years of age? And who would ever chain a child to a carpet loom?

Throughout the day I was consumed by Iqbal's story. In my Grade Seven class we had studied the American Civil War, and Abraham Lincoln, and how some of the slaves in the United States had escaped into Canada. But that was history from centuries ago. Surely slavery had been abolished throughout the world by now. If it wasn't, why had I never heard about it?

The school library was no help. After a thorough search I still hadn't found a scrap of information. After school, I decided to make the trek to the public library.

The librarian knew me from my previous visits. Luckily, she had read the same article that morning and was just as intrigued. Together, we searched out more information on child labour. We found a few newspaper and magazine articles, and made copies.

By the time I returned home, images of child labour had imbedded themselves in my mind: children younger than me forced to make carpets for endless hours in dimly lit rooms; others toiling in underground pits, struggling to get coal to the surface; others maimed or killed by explosions raging through fireworks factories. I was angry at the world for letting these things happen to children. Why was nothing being done to stop such cruelty?...

At lunchtime that day, some of us got together and talked about what we could do. I was amazed at how enthusiastic they all were. I told them about the youth fair on Friday.

"Do you think we could put together a display?" I asked. "We haven't got much time."

"Sure. Let's do it."

"We can all meet at my house," I said.

That night, twelve of us got together. It was a very tight deadline, with just two days to prepare. We found an old science fair board, and we covered it with coloured paper, pasting on all the information I had found on child labour in the library, then drawing pictures to illustrate it.

We had determined that our first objective should be to inform people of the plight of child labourers. Armed with such knowledge, they might be willing to help. We decided to draw up a petition to present to the government, and called on the expertise of a couple of human rights groups to refine the wording for us.

But we were still without a name for our group. For more than an hour we struggled to come up with something suitable. We flipped through the newspaper clippings for inspiration. One of them reported on a demonstration in Delhi, India, where 250 children had marched through the streets with placards, chanting, "We want an education," "We want freedom," "Free the children!"

"That's it!" someone shouted. "Free the Children." ◪

From *Free the Children* by Craig Kielburger with Kevin Major. Copyright © 1998 by Craig Kielburger. Reprinted by permission of HarperCollins Publishers, Inc.

For more biographical information on Craig Kielburger, visit the Master Student Hall of Fame on the *From Master Student to Master Employee* **Web site at**

masterstudent.college.hmco.com

photo and illustration credits

endnotes

Introduction

1. John Henry Newman, *Newman Reader*, "Discourse 5. Knowledge Its Own End," http://www.newmanreader.org/works/idea/discourse5.html (accessed May 3, 2004).
2. Fordcarz.com, "Quotations from Henry Ford," http://www.fordcarz.com/henry_ford_quotes.htm (accessed May 3, 2004).
3. U.S. Department of Labor, Bureau of Labor Statistics, "Education Pays . . . ," August 7, 2003, http://www.bls.gov/emp/emptab7.htm (accessed May 3, 2004).
4. Adapted from U.S. Department of Labor, *Skills and Tasks for Jobs: A SCANS Report for America 2000*. Access it online at http://wdr.doleta.gov/opr/fulltext/document.cfm?docn=6140.
5. Ezra Pound, *The ABC of Reading* (New York: New Directions, 1934), p. 29.
6. Robert Hutchins, "The Great Conversation: The Substance of a Liberal Education," *Great Books of the Western World, vol. 1* (Chicago: Encyclopædia Britannica, 1952), p. xi.
7. Robert Mager, *Preparing Instructional Objectives* (Belmont, CA: Fearon, 1975), p. 23.
8. Martin E. P. Seligman, *Learned Optimism* (New York: Pocket Books, 1998).
9. Malcolm Knowles, *Andragogy in Action* (San Francisco: Jossey-Bass, 1984).
10. Abraham Maslow, *The Further Reaches of Human Nature* (New York: Viking, 1971), p. 300.
11. Excerpts from *Creating Your Future*. Copyright © 1998 by Dave Ellis. Reprinted by permission of Houghton Mifflin Company. All rights reserved. Excerpts from *Human Being: A Manual for Happiness, Health, Love, and Wealth* by Dave Ellis and Stan Lankowitz. Reprinted by permission of Breakthrough Enterprises.

Chapter 1

1. David A. Kolb, *Experiential Learning: Experience as the Source of Learning and Development* (Englewood Cliffs, NJ: Prentice-Hall, 1984).
2. Barry Reece and Rhonda Brandt, *Effective Human Relations: Personal and Organizational Applications* (Boston: Houghton Mifflin, 2002), pp. 65–85.
3. Howard Gardner, *Frames of Mind: The Theory of Multiple Intelligences* (New York: Basic Books, 1993).
4. Albert Bandura, "Self-efficacy," in *Encyclopedia of Mental Health*, ed. H. Friedman (San Diego: Academic Press, 1998).
5. Carl Rogers, *Freedom to Learn* (Columbus, OH: Merrill, 1969).
6. James O. Prochaska, John C. Norcross, and Carlo C. DiClemente, *Changing for Good* (New York: Avon, 1994).

7. B. F. Skinner, *Science and Human Behavior* (Boston: Free Press, 1965).
8. William James, *Pragmatism and Other Essays* (New York: Washington Square, 1963).

Chapter 2

1. Alan Lakein, *Take Control of Your Time and Life* (New York: New American Library, 1973), p. 28.
2. M. A. Just, A. Carpenter, T. A. Keller, et al., "Interdependence of Non-overlapping Cortical Systems in Dual Cognitive Tasks," *NeuroImage* 14 (2001): 417–426.
3. Joe Cuseo, "Academic-Support Strategies for Promoting Student Retention and Achievement During the First Year of College," University of Ulster, *Student Transition and Retention*, http://www.ulst.ac.uk/star/data/cuseoretention.htm#peestud (accessed September 4, 2003).
4. Jane B. Burka and Lenora R. Yuen, *Procrastination: Why You Do It, What to Do About It* (Reading, MA: Addison-Wesley, 1983).
5. Stephen R. Covey, *The Seven Habits of Highly Effective People: Restoring the Character Ethic* (New York: Simon & Schuster, 1989), p. 152.
6. Dorothy Lee, *Freedom and Culture* (Englewood Cliffs, NJ: Prentice-Hall, 1959).

Chapter 3

1. Donald Hebb, quoted in D. J. Siegel, "Memory: An Overview," *Journal of the American Academy of Child and Adolescent Psychiatry* 40, no. 9 (2001): 997–1011.
2. Ibid.
3. Richard Saul Wurman, *Information Anxiety* (New York: Doubleday, 1989), p. 59.
4. D. J. Siegel, "Memory: An Overview," *Journal of the American Academy of Child and Adolescent Psychiatry* 40, no. 9 (2001): 997–1011.
5. Daniel L. Schacter, *The Seven Sins of Memory: How the Mind Forgets and Remembers* (Boston: Houghton Mifflin, 2001), p. 34.
6. John W. Rowe and Robert L. Kahn, *Successful Aging* (New York: Pantheon, 1998).

Chapter 4

1. G. S. Gates, "Recitation as a Factor in Memorizing," *Archives of Psychology* 40 (1917).
2. R. Rosnow and E. Robinson, eds., *Experiments in Persuasion* (New York: Academic Press, 1967).
3. William Glasser, *Take Effective Control of Your Life* (New York: Harper & Row, 1984).

Chapter 5

1. Walter Pauk, *How to Study in College* (Boston: Houghton Mifflin, 2001), pp. 236–241.
2. Tony Buzan, *Use Both Sides of Your Brain* (New York: Dutton, 1991).
3. Gabrielle Rico, *Writing the Natural Way* (Los Angeles: J. P. Tarcher, 1983).
4. Joseph Novak and D. Bob Gowin, *Learning How to Learn* (New York: Cambridge University Press, 1984).
5. William Glasser, *Take Effective Control of Your Life* (New York: Harper & Row, 1984).

Chapter 6

1. Linda Wong, *Essential Study Skills*, Fourth Edition. Copyright © 2003 by Houghton Mifflin Company. Reprinted with permission.
2. Joe Cuseo, "Academic-Support Strategies for Promoting Student Retention and Achievement During the First-Year of College," University of Ulster, *Student Transition and Retention*, http://www.ulst.ac.uk/star/data/cuseoretention.htm#peestud (accessed September 4, 2003).
3. Martin E. P. Seligman, *Learned Optimism* (New York: Pocket Books, 1998).

Chapter 7

1. Quoted in Theodore Cheney, *Getting the Words Right: How to Revise, Edit and Rewrite* (Cincinnati, OH: Writer's Digest, 1983).
2. U.S. Department of Labor, "What Work Requires of Schools: A SCANS Report for America 2000—The Secretary's Commission on Achieving Necessary Skills," June 1991, http://wdr.doleta.gov/SCANS/whatwork/whatwork.html (accessed June 2, 2004).
3. William Perry, *Forms of Intellectual and Ethical Development in the College Years* (New York: Holt, Rinehart and Winston, 1970).
4. Peter Facione, "Critical Thinking: What It Is and Why It Counts," California Academic Press, 1998, http://www.insightassessment.com/articles.html (accessed June 2, 2004).
5. U.S. Department of Labor, "What Work Requires of Schools: A SCANS Report for America 2000."
6. Walter J. Kaufman, *From Decidophobia to Autonomy: Without Guilt and Justice* (New York: Delta, 1975).
7. John Dewey, *How We Think* (Toronto, Ontario: Dover, 1997).
8. U.S. Department of Labor, "What Work Requires of Schools: A Scans Report for America 2000."
9. Quoted in Alice Calaprice, ed., *The Expanded Quotable Einstein* (Princeton, NJ: Princeton University Press, 2000).
10. Arthur Koestler, *The Act of Creation* (New York: Dell, 1964).
11. *Setting the Standard*, Office of Ethics and Business Conduct, Lockheed Martin Corporation, 2003, http://www.lockheed-martin.com (accessed June 2, 2004).
12. U.S. Census Bureau, "Current Population Reports: Population Projections of the U.S. by Age, Sex, Race and Hispanic Origin, 1995–2050," www.census.gov/prod/1/pop/p25-1130/, February 1996 (accessed January 5, 2003).

13. Dorothy Lee, *Freedom and Culture* (Englewood Cliffs, NJ: Prentice-Hall, 1959).
14. Federal Bureau of Investigation, "Uniform Crime Reports," 2003, http://www.fbi.gov/ucr/ucr.htm (accessed January 12, 2004).
15. Quoted in a personal communication from James Anderson with the author, 1990.

Chapter 8

1. Carl Rogers, *On Becoming a Person* (Boston: Houghton Mifflin, 1961).
2. Thomas Gordon, *Parent Effectiveness Training: The Tested New Way to Raise Responsible Children* (New York: New American Library, 1975).
3. Diane de Anda, *Bicultural Socialization: Factors Affecting the Minority Experience* (Washington, DC: National Association of Social Workers, 1984).
4. Frank M. J. LaFasto and Carl E. Larson, *When Teams Work Best: 6,000 Team Members and Leaders Tell What It Takes to Succeed* (Thousand Oaks, CA: Sage, 2001).
5. From Ann Raimes, *Universal Keys for Writers*. Copyright © 2005 by Houghton Mifflin Company. Reprinted with permission.
6. Michael Motely, *Overcoming Your Fear of Public Speaking: A Proven Method* (Boston: Houghton Mifflin, 2003).
7. University of California—Berkeley, School of Information Management and Systems, "How Much Information? 2003," http://www.sims.berkeley.edu/research/projects/how-much-info-2003/execsum.htm#int (accessed June 2, 2004).

Chapter 9

1. Lawrence Mishel, Jared Bernstein, and Heather Boushey, *The State of Working America 2002–03* (Ithaca, NY: Cornell University Press, 2003).
2. Dave Ellis, Stan Lankowitz, Ed Stupka, and Doug Toff, *Career Planning*, Third Edition. Copyright © 2003 by Houghton Mifflin Company. Reprinted by permission.
3. United Nations Development Programme, *Human Development Report* (New York: Oxford University Press, 2003).

Chapter 10

1. William Bridges, *Jobshift: How to Prosper in a Workplace Without Jobs* (New York: Perseus, 1995).
2. Dave Ellis, Stan Lankowitz, Ed Stupka, and Doug Toff, *Career Planning*, Third Edition. Copyright © 2003 by Houghton Mifflin Company. Reprinted by permission.
3. U.S. Department of Labor, *Report on the American Workforce 2001*, http://www.bls.gov/opub/rtaw/rtawhome.htm (accessed June 21, 2004).
4. Kathryn Tyler, "I Say Potato, You Say Patata." *HR Magazine*, January 2004, pp. 85–87.
5. U.S. Equal Employment Opportunity Commission, "Sexual Harassment," http://www.eeoc.gov/types/sexual_harassment.html, January 6, 2004 (accessed June 21, 2004).

additional reading

Adler, Mortimer, and Charles Van Doren. *How to Read a Book*. New York: Touchstone, 1972.

Anthony, Jason, and Karl Cluck. *Debt-Free by 30*. New York: Plume, 2001.

Bolles, Richard N. *What Color is Your Parachute? A Practical Manual for Job-Hunters and Career-Changers*. Berkeley, CA: Ten Speed, 2004.

Bronson, Po. *What Should I Do with My Life? The True Story of People Who Answered the Ultimate Question*. New York: Random House, 2003.

Brown, Alan C. *Maximizing Memory Power*. New York: Wiley, 1986.

Buzan, Tony. *Make the Most of Your Mind*. New York: Simon & Schuster, 1977.

Chaffee, John. *Thinking Critically*. Boston: Houghton Mifflin, 2003.

Conlin, Mary Lou, ed. *The Working Reader*. Boston: Houghton Mifflin, 2001.

Covey, Stephen R. *First Things First*. New York: Simon & Schuster, 1994.

Ellis, Dave. *Creating Your Future: Five Steps to the Life of Your Dreams*. Boston: Houghton Mifflin, 1998.

Ellis, Dave, and Stan Lankowitz. *Human Being: A Manual for Happiness, Health, Love and Wealth*. Rapid City, SD: Breakthrough Enterprises, 1995.

Ellis, Dave, Stan Lankowitz, Ed Stupka, and Doug Toft. *Career Planning*. Boston: Houghton Mifflin, 2003.

Engleberg, Isa N. and Dianna R. Wynn. *Working in Groups: Communication Principles and Strategies*. Boston: Houghton Mifflin, 2003.

Facione, Peter. *Critical Thinking: What It Is and Why It Counts*. Millbrae, CA: California Academic Press, 1996.

Ferrell, O.C., John Fraedrich, and Linda Ferrell. *Business Ethics: Ethical Decision Making and Cases*. Boston: Houghton Mifflin, 2005.

Fletcher, Anne. *Sober for Good*. Boston: Houghton Mifflin, 2001.

Gawain, Shakti. *Creative Visualization*. New York: New World Library, 1998.

Germer, Fawn. *Hard Won Wisdom: More Than 50 Extraordinary Women Mentor You to Find Self-Awareness, Perspective, and Balance*. New York: Perigree, 2001.

Gibaldi, Joseph. *MLA Handbook for Writers of Research Papers*. New York: Modern Language Association, 1999.

Golas, Thaddeus. *The Lazy Man's Guide to Enlightenment*. Layton, UT: Gibbs Smith, 1997.

Greene, Susan D., and Melanie C. L. Martel. *The Ultimate Job Hunter's Guidebook*. Boston: Houghton Mifflin, 2004.

Gross, Kim Johnson, and Jeff Stone. *Dress Smart Women: Wardrobes the Win in the New Workplace*. New York: Warner Books, 2002.

Higbee, Kenneth L. *Your Memory: How It Works and How to Improve It*. Englewood Cliffs, NJ: Prentice-Hall, 1996.

Hill, Napolean. *Think and Grow Rich*. New York: Fawcett, 1996.

Hurtado, Sylvia, et al. *Enacting Diverse Learning Environments: Improving the Climate for Racial/Ethnic Diversity in Higher Education*. Ashe-Eric Higher Education Reports, 1999.

Kaminsky, Howard, and Alexandra Penney. *Magic Words @ Work: Powerful phrases to help you conquer the working world*. New York: Broadway Books, 2004.

Kolb, David A. *Experiential Learning: Experience as the Source of Learning and Development*. Englewood Cliffs: Prentice-Hall, 1984.

Kreitner, Robert. *Management*. Boston: Houghton Mifflin, 2004.

Lathrop, Richard. *Who's Hiring Who?* Berkeley, CA: Ten Speed, 1989.

Light, Richard J. *Making the Most of College: Students Speak Their Minds*. Cambridge, MA: Harvard University Press, 2001.

Mallow, Jeffry V. *Science Anxiety: Fear of Science and How to Overcome It*. New York: Thomond, 1986.

Manning, Robert. *Credit Card Nation: The Consequences of America's Addiction to Credit*. New York: Basic Books, 2000.

Metcalf, Allan. *Predicting New Words: The Secrets of Their Success*. Boston: Houghton Mifflin, 2002.

Nolting, Paul D. *Math Study Skills Workbook*. 2nd ed. Boston: Houghton Mifflin, 2005.

Ober, Scott. *Contemporary Business English*. Boston: Houghton Mifflin, 2005.

Orman, Suze. *The Road to Wealth*. New York: Riverhead, 2001.

Pauk, Walter and Ross J.Q. Owens. *How to Study in College*. 8th ed. Boston: Houghton Mifflin, 2005.

Peddy, Shirley, Ph.D. *The Art of Mentoring: Lead, Follow and Get Out of the Way*. Houston, TX: Bullion Books, 2001.

Pirsig, Robert. *Zen and the Art of Motorcycle Maintenance*. New York: Perennial Classics, 2000.

Raimes, Anne. *Universal Keys for Writers*. Boston: Houghton Mifflin, 2004.

Robbins, John. *Diet for a New America: How Your Food Choices Affect Your Health, Happiness and the Future of Life on Earth*. New York: H J Kramer, 1998.

Rothwell, J. Dan. *In Mixed Company: Communicating in Small Groups and Teams*. Belmont, CA: Wadsworth, 2004.

Ruggiero, Vincent Ryan. *Becoming a Critical Thinker*. 5th ed. Boston: Houghton Mifflin, 2006.

Schacter, Daniel L. *Searching for Memory: The Brain, the Mind, and the Past*. New York: HarperCollins, 1997.

Schlosser, Eric. *Fast Food Nation*. Boston: Houghton Mifflin, 2001.

Semler, Ricardo. *The Seven-Day Weekend*. New York: Penguin, 2003.

Strunk, William, Jr., and E. B. White. *The Elements of Style*. New York: Macmillan, 1979.

The American Heritage Dictionary, 4th Edition.

Tobias, Sheila. *Succeed with Math: Every Student's Guide to Conquering Math Anxiety*. New York: College Board, 1995.

Ueland, Brenda. *If You Want to Write: A Book About Art, Independence and Spirit*. St. Paul, MN: Graywolf, 1987.

U.S. Department of Education. *The Student Guide*. Published yearly. (Federal Student Aid Information Center, 1-800-4-FED-AID). Available online at http://studentaid.ed.gov/students/publications/student_guide/2004_2005/english/index.htm.

Watkins, Ryan, and Michael Corry. *E-learning Companion: A Student's Guide to Online Success*. Boston: Houghton Mifflin, 2005.

Weil, Andrew. *Natural Health, Natural Medicine*. Boston: Houghton Mifflin, 1998.

Welch, David. *Decisions, Decisions: The Art of Effective Decision Making*. Amherst, NY: Prometheus, 2002.

Wurman, Richard Saul. *Information Anxiety*. New York: Doubleday, 1989.

Wurman, Richard Saul. *Information Anxiety 2*. Indianapolis: QUE, 2001.

index

MONDAY ___ / ___ / ___ /		
Monitor	**Plan**	
7:00	7:00	
7:15		
7:30		
7:45		
8:00	8:00	
8:15		
8:30		
8:45		
9:00	9:00	
9:15		
9:30		
9:45		
10:00	10:00	
10:15		
10:30		
10:45		
11:00	11:00	
11:15		
11:30		
11:45		
12:00	12:00	
12:15		
12:30		
12:45		
1:00	1:00	
1:15		
1:30		
1:45		
2:00	2:00	
2:15		
2:30		
2:45		
3:00	3:00	
3:15		
3:30		
3:45		
4:00	4:00	
4:15		
4:30		
4:45		
5:00	5:00	
5:15		
5:30		
5:45		
6:00	6:00	
6:15		
6:30		
6:45		
7:00	7:00	
7:15		
7:30		
7:45		
8:00	8:00	
8:15		
8:30		
8:45		
9:00	9:00	
9:15		
9:30		
9:45		
10:00	10:00	
10:15		
10:30		
10:45		
11:00	11:00	
11:15		
11:30		
11:45		
12:00	12:00	

TUESDAY ___ / ___ / ___ /		
Monitor	**Plan**	
7:00	7:00	
7:15		
7:30		
7:45		
8:00	8:00	
8:15		
8:30		
8:45		
9:00	9:00	
9:15		
9:30		
9:45		
10:00	10:00	
10:15		
10:30		
10:45		
11:00	11:00	
11:15		
11:30		
11:45		
12:00	12:00	
12:15		
12:30		
12:45		
1:00	1:00	
1:15		
1:30		
1:45		
2:00	2:00	
2:15		
2:30		
2:45		
3:00	3:00	
3:15		
3:30		
3:45		
4:00	4:00	
4:15		
4:30		
4:45		
5:00	5:00	
5:15		
5:30		
5:45		
6:00	6:00	
6:15		
6:30		
6:45		
7:00	7:00	
7:15		
7:30		
7:45		
8:00	8:00	
8:15		
8:30		
8:45		
9:00	9:00	
9:15		
9:30		
9:45		
10:00	10:00	
10:15		
10:30		
10:45		
11:00	11:00	
11:15		
11:30		
11:45		
12:00	12:00	

WEDNESDAY ___ / ___ / ___ /		
Monitor	**Plan**	
7:00	7:00	
7:15		
7:30		
7:45		
8:00	8:00	
8:15		
8:30		
8:45		
9:00	9:00	
9:15		
9:30		
9:45		
10:00	10:00	
10:15		
10:30		
10:45		
11:00	11:00	
11:15		
11:30		
11:45		
12:00	12:00	
12:15		
12:30		
12:45		
1:00	1:00	
1:15		
1:30		
1:45		
2:00	2:00	
2:15		
2:30		
2:45		
3:00	3:00	
3:15		
3:30		
3:45		
4:00	4:00	
4:15		
4:30		
4:45		
5:00	5:00	
5:15		
5:30		
5:45		
6:00	6:00	
6:15		
6:30		
6:45		
7:00	7:00	
7:15		
7:30		
7:45		
8:00	8:00	
8:15		
8:30		
8:45		
9:00	9:00	
9:15		
9:30		
9:45		
10:00	10:00	
10:15		
10:30		
10:45		
11:00	11:00	
11:15		
11:30		
11:45		
12:00	12:00	

THURSDAY ___ / ___ / ___ /		FRIDAY ___ / ___ / ___ /		SATURDAY ___ / ___ / ___ /	
Monitor	Plan	Monitor	Plan	Monitor	Plan
7:00	7:00	7:00	7:00		
7:15		7:15			
7:30		7:30			
7:45		7:45			
8:00	8:00	8:00	8:00		
8:15		8:15			
8:30		8:30			
8:45		8:45			
9:00	9:00	9:00	9:00		
9:15		9:15			
9:30		9:30			
9:45		9:45			
10:00	10:00	10:00	10:00		
10:15		10:15			
10:30		10:30			
10:45		10:45			
11:00	11:00	11:00	11:00		
11:15		11:15			
11:30		11:30			
11:45		11:45			
12:00	12:00	12:00	12:00		
12:15		12:15			
12:30		12:30			
12:45		12:45			
1:00	1:00	1:00	1:00		
1:15		1:15			
1:30		1:30			
1:45		1:45			
2:00	2:00	2:00	2:00		
2:15		2:15			
2:30		2:30			
2:45		2:45			
3:00	3:00	3:00	3:00		
3:15		3:15		SUNDAY ___ / ___ / ___ /	
3:30		3:30			
3:45		3:45		Monitor	Plan
4:00	4:00	4:00	4:00		
4:15		4:15			
4:30		4:30			
4:45		4:45			
5:00	5:00	5:00	5:00		
5:15		5:15			
5:30		5:30			
5:45		5:45			
6:00	6:00	6:00	6:00		
6:15		6:15			
6:30		6:30			
6:45		6:45			
7:00	7:00	7:00	7:00		
7:15		7:15			
7:30		7:30			
7:45		7:45			
8:00	8:00	8:00	8:00		
8:15		8:15			
8:30		8:30			
8:45		8:45			
9:00	9:00	9:00	9:00		
9:15		9:15			
9:30		9:30			
9:45		9:45			
10:00	10:00	10:00	10:00		
10:15		10:15			
10:30		10:30			
10:45		10:45			
11:00	11:00	11:00	11:00		
11:15		11:15			
11:30		11:30			
11:45		11:45			
12:00	12:00	12:00	12:00		

MONDAY	TUESDAY	WEDNESDAY	THURSDAY	FRIDAY	SATURDAY	SUNDAY

Name _____

Month _____

MONDAY	TUESDAY	WEDNESDAY	THURSDAY	FRIDAY	SATURDAY	SUNDAY

Name _____   Month _____

Name _____

LONG-TERM PLANNER ___ / ___ / ___ to ___ / ___ / ___

Week of	Monday	Tuesday	Wednesday	Thursday	Friday	Saturday	Sunday
___ / ___							
___ / ___							
___ / ___							
___ / ___							
___ / ___							
___ / ___							
___ / ___							
___ / ___							
___ / ___							
___ / ___							
___ / ___							
___ / ___							
___ / ___							
___ / ___							
___ / ___							
___ / ___							
___ / ___							
___ / ___							
___ / ___							
___ / ___							
___ / ___							
___ / ___							
___ / ___							
___ / ___							
___ / ___							
___ / ___							
___ / ___							
___ / ___							
___ / ___							

Name _____

LONG-TERM PLANNER ___ / ___ / ___ to ___ / ___ / ___

Week of	Monday	Tuesday	Wednesday	Thursday	Friday	Saturday	Sunday
___ / ___							
___ / ___							
___ / ___							
___ / ___							
___ / ___							
___ / ___							
___ / ___							
___ / ___							
___ / ___							
___ / ___							
___ / ___							
___ / ___							
___ / ___							
___ / ___							
___ / ___							
___ / ___							
___ / ___							
___ / ___							
___ / ___							
___ / ___							
___ / ___							
___ / ___							
___ / ___							
___ / ___							
___ / ___							
___ / ___							
___ / ___							
___ / ___							
___ / ___							
___ / ___							
___ / ___							
___ / ___							

A guide for instructors using the SCANS report to emphasize transferable skills

The foundations and themes highlighted for student success in *Becoming a Master Student* have been used by millions of students. *From Master Student to Master Employee* has been shaped by input from Advisory Board members and instructors whose inspirations and suggestions have helped to create a textbook that helps students to understand the value of developing *transferable skills* in the classroom that can be utilized in the workplace. With increased emphasis on discovering what you want, goal setting, career planning, and mastering key skills, *From Master Student to Master Employee* will provide your students with a new framework for success.

The U.S. Department of Labor issued a series of reports created by the Secretary's Commission on Achieving Necessary Skills (SCANS) identifying essential skills for workers in the twenty-first century. *From Master Student to Master Employee* addresses each of these skills throughout the text. At the start of the semester, ask your students to identify those skills they have already mastered. They can do this by referring to the easy-to-access copy of the SCANS information located on the inside cover of this textbook. Your students will be ready to set and achieve goals by highlighting those skills that they would like to expand to be prepared to enter today's workforce.

The following is the SCANS list with a notation to indicate the chapter that covers materials related to the particular skills. A detailed list of articles and exercises that will help students to develop the SCANS competencies is available on your HM ClassPrep CD to accompany this textbook.

Basic skills

- Reading to locate, understand, and interpret written information (Chapter 3: Memory; Chapter 4: Reading)

- Writing to communicate ideas and information (Chapter 8: Communicating)

- Using mathematics to perform basic computations and solve problems (Chapter 6: Tests)

- Listening to interpret and respond to verbal messages and other cues (Chapter 5: Notes)

- Speaking clearly and making organized presentations (Chapter 8: Communicating)

Thinking skills

- Creative thinking to generate new ideas (Chapter 7: Thinking)

- Decision making to set and meet goals (Chapter 2: Planning; Chapter 7: Thinking)

- Problem solving to identify challenges and implement action plans (Chapter 2: Planning, Chapter 7: Thinking)

- Seeing things in the mind's eye to interpret and create symbols, pictures, graphs, and other visual tools (Chapter 5: Notes)

- Knowing how to learn (Chapter 1: Self-Discovery)

- Reasoning to discover underlying principles and apply them when solving a problem (Chapter 7: Thinking)

Personal qualities

- Responsibility to exert high effort and persist in meeting goals (Chapter 1: Self-Discovery; Chapter 2: Planning)

- Self-esteem to maintain a positive view of your abilities (Chapter 1: Self-Discovery)

- Social skills that demonstrate adaptability and empathy (Introduction: Link to the World of Work; Chapter 1: Self-Discovery; Chapter 8: Communicating; Chapter 10: Mastering Work)

- Self-management to assess yourself accurately, set personal goals, and monitor personal progress (Chapter 2: Planning; Chapter 9: Career Planning)

- Integrity to choose ethical behaviors (Chapter 7: Thinking)

Skills in using resources

- Allocating time for goal-relevant activities (Chapter 2: Planning)

- Allocating money to prepare budgets and meet them (Chapter 9: Career Planning)

- Allocating materials and facilities (Chapter 1: Self-Discovery; Chapter 2: Planning)

- Allocating human resources to assign tasks effectively and provide others with feedback (Chapter 6: Tests; Chapter 8: Communicating; Chapter 9: Career Planning; Chapter 10: Mastering Work)

Interpersonal skills

- Participating as a member of a team (Chapter 6: Tests; Chapter 8: Communicating; Chapter 9: Career Planning)

- Teaching others (Chapter 6: Tests)

- Serving clients and customers (Chapter 8: Communicating; Chapter 10: Mastering Work)

- Exercising leadership (Chapter 10: Mastering Work)

- Negotiating to reach agreements (Chapter 8: Communicating)

- Working well with people from diverse backgrounds (Chapter 7: Thinking; Chapter 10: Mastering Work)

Skills in working with information

- Acquiring and evaluating information (Chapter 5: Reading; Chapter 7: Thinking)

- Organizing and maintaining information (Chapter 4: Reading; Chapter 5: Notes; Chapter 8: Communicating)

- Interpreting and communicating information in oral, written, and visual forms (Chapter 8: Communicating)

- Using computers to process information (Chapter 8: Communicating; Chapter 9: Career Planning)

Skills in working with complex interrelationships

- Understanding social, organizational, and technological systems and operating within them (Introduction: Link to the World of Work; Chapter 1: Self-Discovery; Chapter 10: Mastering Work)

- Monitoring and correcting performance (Chapter 2: Planning; Chapter 9: Career Planning; (Chapter 10: Mastering Work)

- Improving or designing systems (Chapter 5: Notes; Chapter 7: Thinking)

Skills in working with technology

- Selecting appropriate technology (Chapter 8: Communicating)

- Applying technology to tasks (Chapter 9: Career Planning)

- Maintaining and troubleshooting equipment (Chapter 7: Thinking) ❇

Setting up your syllabus

From *Master Student to Master Employee* can serve any first-year-student community, whether the majority of students are attending college straight out of high school or the students are adult learners returning to college after a long absence. This book was designed to help students to reflect on their past experiences and prepare to be successful in the future. By using this *Annotated Instructor's Edition*, the *Course Manual*, and the HM ClassPrep CD, you can select material that is most appropriate for both your students and your course purpose. Specific resources for **"Writing your course purpose"** and **"Creating a course philosophy"** are available in the *Course Manual* and on your HM ClassPrep CD.

In customizing your course and addressing the issues that face the first-year students at your college, you will likely discuss the following topics.

- **Discovering what you want** encourages students to make the initial connection between the classroom and the workplace. Materials in the Introduction and Chapter One provide a place for students to assess their current skills and areas for potential growth. This allows students to begin the practice of reflection through self-knowledge. These first steps may be accompanied by orientation to resources on campus as students make the transition to the world of higher education. Planning in Chapter Two helps students to continue to think about achieving their long-term and short-term goals—in higher education and in the future. Chapter Nine encourages students to expand their career options, discover careers that align with their interests and skills, and begin to plan for becoming a master employee.

- **Academic skills,** including memory, reading, note taking, and test taking, provide students with the knowledge and opportunity to improve their scholastic achievement and develop techniques necessary for success in their core curriculum courses.

- The *Career Application* feature at the end of each chapter will help your students using critical thinking skills to make connections between the classroom and the workplace using real-world scenarios.

- **Workplace skills** are developed throughout the text, and emphasized through the introduction of key life skills: thinking, communicating, diversity, technology, managing money, networking, and leadership. Chapters Nine and Ten will help transition students from master students to master employees, whether they are planning for part-time employment during college or full-time employment after they have completed their degree.

As you look at the primary themes of your student success course and review the materials in *From Master Student to Master Employee*, you will begin to understand how critical thinking, personal responsibility, ethics, and integrity are all incorporated into each of these areas. Create your syllabus to emphasize both the short-term and long term goals of your course, seminar, or workshop. And remember, you don't have to assign every article and every exercise to your students.

Consider including some of the following standard information in your course syllabus:

- Instructor's name and contact information, including office hours.

- The course title and catalog description.

- A statement of purpose for your course and a list of objectives.

- Time and location of course meetings.

- Authors and titles of required texts and supplementary materials, including videos, CDs, frequently used Web sites, etc.

- The schedule for readings and assignments. You might want to include major tests, assignments, and activities that will be graded, and quizzes.

- Your expectations for student behavior, including attendance and promptness.

- A description of lengthy or complex assignments and a schedule for completion.

- Your grading policy, including the percentages for assignments, tests, class participation, etc., that make up the total grade.

- A statement of academic honesty.

 Sample syllabi to use in different course structures are available on the HM ClassPrep CD that accompanies *From Master Student to Master Employee.* ✖

Could your students use an extra $1,000?

Houghton Mifflin Student Success is proud to present three students each year with a $1,000 scholarship for tuition reimbursement. Any postsecondary school in the United States and Canada that offers a student success course is welcome to nominate one student for the scholarship. In order to be considered, students must write an essay that answers the question "How do you define success?"

Here's how you can get your students to participate.

Host a school-wide competition for students enrolled in a first-year student success or study skills course. Consider having students participate by including the competition in your syllabus as a goal-setting or writing assignment. In your local contest, ask all of your students to write an essay on the topic "How do you define success?" The essay should not exceed 750 words.

Materials to advertise the scholarship competition are available on the HM ClassPrep CD. Download flyers for posting on bulletin boards around campus, or post to online bulletin boards on your course Web site or in your course management system. The way you select the winner to represent your college is up to you. One school allows students to be the final judges. This is a great opportunity to practice peer review in your course.

Once you have selected a winner to represent your school, send the winning essay and a completed entry form (available on the *From Master Student to Master Employee* Web site) to Houghton Mifflin Company. Each campus may submit only one entry. Entries are due each year on December 15. The winners are announced in the following spring on the Web site. Invite your students to read the winning essays of previous entrants, also available on the Web site.

Completed entries can be e-mailed to **collegesurvival@hmco.com** or mailed to Houghton Mifflin College Survival, 2075 Foxfield Road, St. Charles, IL 60174.

→ Gaining support

Student success courses and first-year seminar programs help students learn to be more effective in school, thereby improving their academic performance and increasing their level of commitment.

Gaining approval and support from administrators is important to the success of your course and requires preparation and communication. This backing is necessary to sustain the course long enough to establish both its effectiveness and its value. Below are suggestions to help establish that base of support.

Write a statement of purpose for your course. One possibility is "The purpose of our student success course is to improve students' academic performance and increase their level of commitment to our college."

Refer to your statement of purpose often. When negotiating any aspect of your course, be sure to avoid compromises that would sabotage its purpose from either the institution's or the students' perspective. For example, it would be a mistake to settle for too few course contact hours.

Seek grassroots support. The more people who have a vested interest in your proposal, the more likely it is to be accepted. Ask for assistance from the top of the administrative hierarchy. Draw a political road map encompassing crucial factors for gaining support and identifying key individuals. Include those who have behind-the-scenes influence.

Become a retention expert on your campus. Familiarize yourself with all the data, research, and institutional studies related to student performance and retention at your school. Explore options your institution might use to improve student performance and reduce attrition.

More suggestions for gaining support are available on the HM ClassPrep CD and on the *From Master Student to Master Employee* Web site.

 masterstudent.college.hmco.com

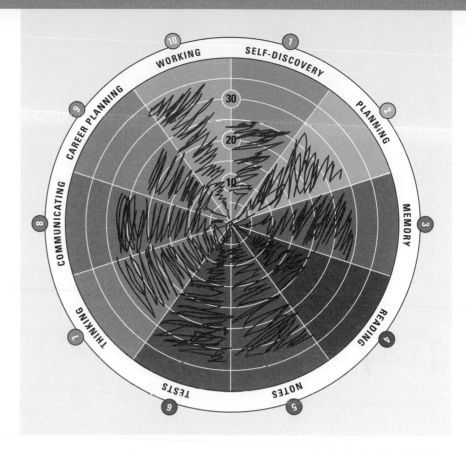

The Discovery Wheel

The Discovery Wheel is an opportunity for students to think about the kind of student they are and the kind of student they want to become. This exercise is assigned at the outset of the course to help students assess their current strengths and weaknesses in different areas of student success. Students answer a series of questions and then plot their scores on their Discovery Wheel—a graphic illustration of their skill levels—the twelve sections of which correspond to the twelve chapters in the text. This exercise is also available for students to complete on the *From Master Student to Master Employee* Web site.

masterstudent.college.hmco.com

At the end of Chapter Ten is an identical Discovery Wheel. By repeating the exercise at the completion of the course, students can trace their progress in acquiring skills and techniques that can ensure their success in school and later in life.

The purpose of this exercise is to give students the opportunity to change their behavior. Retaking the Discovery Wheel exercise allows students to see what behav-

iors they have changed on their journey to becoming a master student.

Having your students complete the Journal Entry that follows this second Discovery Wheel provides them with another opportunity to state how they intend to change. Encourage them to reconsider tools that they did not think they could use the first time they encountered them in the text.

Note: Student scores might be lower on the second Discovery Wheel. That's OK. Lower scores might result from increased self-awareness and honesty, valuable assets in themselves.

Dean Mancina, instructor at Golden West College, talks about using the Discovery Wheel in his classroom:

Most of my students have not yet purchased the text when they come to the first class meeting of my student success course. I know some students are still shopping for courses and are not fully convinced that this class is going to be useful to them. So I like to take a portion of the first class meeting to sell them on the course and the textbook.

I hold up the book and show them the Discovery Wheel, explaining that this is an example of one of the useful exercises in the book. I point out that in this course, the textbook drives the class, and that it is absolutely essential to complete all of the reading assignments and related exercises before coming to each class meeting. I also use the PowerPoint slides for Chapter One to show students the Discovery Wheel in detail.

As I do so, I say, "This picture illustrates the author's philosophy of student success. There are some topics, such as planning and tests, that one would expect to be part of a study skills course. But in the holistic approach that this course takes, we see that health, diversity, technology, and many other topics are all given equal importance in achieving student success, as reflected by the sec-tions of the pie being of equal size. When you complete this exercise, you will see, visually, your relative strengths and weaknesses in the ten areas of student success identified by this book.

"Each chapter focuses on one of these ten areas. At the end of the term, when you have completed the course, you'll see that one of the last exercises in the book is the post-Discovery Wheel. By completing this exercise and comparing it to your first Discovery Wheel, you'll have a picture of the progress you've made in this course. Of course, this can only happen if you do the first Discovery Wheel *now*. Make a commitment to get the book and do the exercises and assigned readings, especially the Discovery Wheel, so you'll be able to fully use the feedback you'll get at the end of this course." ⊠

→ If the Discovery Wheel did not convince them . . .

If your students haven't been convinced that your course will be of value to them after they complete their Discovery Wheel, consider these ideas.

Ask students to "buy" the course because it works. The following testimonials are from students who have taken the course. You might read a few of these aloud or use comments that you have collected from previous course evaluations.

- I really thought I wouldn't get anything out of this class, but through this class and what I have learned, I have been able to pass quizzes in my other classes that I've never been able to pass before.

- I have learned some effective study skills so now I can learn more in less time.

- I learned how to communicate better and not [to make] people defensive when we argue. I learned that I have a lot to learn. I learned countless ways to improve my ways of doing things, budgeting time and money.

- I would recommend this course to anyone just starting out in school. I got over several real fears I had about college and coming back to school.

- I was responsible for keeping me in college. For example, I had trouble understanding and keeping up with my history instructor. Not only did I get very good advice on how to deal with my problem, but I found that there were other students having the same problem.

- I have learned more about my goals and what I want out of life.

- I really follow the idea of "Be here now." That helps me a great deal, 24 hours a day.

- I've learned to experience a lot more of life and not to be so afraid to do it. I have overcome some of my test anxiety, and I have learned to listen, ask questions, talk, understand, and answer people better.

- I have tried some of the concepts presented in the book, and they really do help.

- This class helps me recall things much more effectively during tests or quizzes.

- I found out I wasn't shy anymore. I could speak up in a crowd, without my heart beating fast.

- I have learned more about how to study and cope with college life. I have also learned more about understanding other people and the problems and frustrations they face.

- I asked all through my high school years for people to teach me how to study, and nobody could find the right techniques. The book used in the seminar gave me something I had been asking for all along.

Invite guest speakers to class—from last semester's roster. You might also consider inviting students who have completed the course to be guest speakers in your class. They can give live and spontaneous testimonials.

Use this type of guest speaker as you review your course syllabus and review the purpose, content, and format of the class. Have students ask you questions about the syllabus, and have the student guest speaker confirm and add to your answers.

Teaching learning styles in your classroom

From *Master Student to Master Employee* introduces several approaches to learning styles: the Learning Style Inventory, multiple intelligences, and the VAK (**v**isual, **a**uditory, and **k**inesthetic) system. That's a lot of information to absorb. It is important to recognize that each approach presents a valid option and is not the final word on learning styles. Encourage your students to look for ideas from any of these methods that they can put to immediate use. When they write Intention Statements, have your students keep these questions in mind: How can I use this idea to *be* more successful in school? What will I *do* differently as a result of reading about learning styles? If I develop new learning styles, what skill will I *have* that I don't have now?

The Learning Style Inventory (LSI).

People are fascinated by why they do what they do—and students are no exception. Taking the Learning Style Inventory (LSI) in Chapter One gives students a chance to increase their self-awareness as learners. The LSI helps students make sense of what they're experiencing in college.

Developed by Dr. David Kolb at Case Western Reserve University in Cleveland, Ohio, the LSI measures a learner's preferences for *perceiving* information (taking it in) and *processing* information (making sense of what they take in). When these preferences are plotted on two continuums, four unique modes of learning are formed. Students find that while every individual is capable of employing all four modes, each person has a "preferred" way of learning.

The Master Student Map highlights these four modes to help students become more effective learners through an understanding of their own learning style preferences. More importantly, the Master Student Map can help increase students' effectiveness by encouraging them to use those modes that they have previously underutilized. At the end of each chapter, students can apply all four modes to the chapter's topic by cycling through the questions in the Learning Styles Application.

Detailed information about administering the Learning Style Inventory appears on the next page. Support materials are also available on the HM ClassPrep CD.

Multiple intelligences.

Howard Gardner of Harvard University believes that no single measure of intelligence can tell us how smart we are. Instead, Gardner identifies many types of intelligence, described in *From Master Student to Master Employee* on page 37. By applying Gardner's concepts, students can explore additional methods for achieving success in school, work, and relationships. *From Master Student to Master Employee* is designed to help students develop these different intelligences. Charts accompany the definitions of Gardner's multiple intelligences in the text, highlighting the characteristics of each intelligence, the learning strategies that are preferred by people with this type of intelligence, and the careers that might interest them. Have your students apply this information to their core courses. For example, a student with musical/rhythmic intelligence could write songs using lyrics based on class notes and could experiment with various kinds of background music while studying.

When students begin to acknowledge and trust all of their intelligences, they can understand and appreciate themselves more.

The VAK system.

The VAK system is a simple and powerful technique that focuses on perception through three sense channels: seeing, or *visual* learning; hearing, or *auditory* learning; and movement, or *kinesthetic* learning. Invite your students to discover their VAK preferences by taking the informal inventory included in the text.

Strategies in the text highlight ways students can build on their current learning preferences and develop new options by utilizing their other sense channels.

It is important that you teach students to take in information efficiently through their preferred learning style, but it is equally important that you teach them to study and learn information efficiently through a variety of other learning styles. As their instructor, you can set an example by using a mix of strategies to teach them ways to learn the largest amount of material in the least amount of time.

 Additional ideas for implementing variety in your teaching strategies can be found on the HM ClassPrep CD. ✖

Administering the Learning Style Inventory

The Learning Style Inventory (LSI) is an important tool to help your students discover their preferred mode of learning. Yet many instructors have found that students can feel overwhelmed when they are left on their own to take the LSI, score it, and interpret the results. Consider the following suggestions.

Begin by introducing the LSI to your students. The article "Learning styles: Discovering how you learn" will help you set the stage. Page 36 highlights the step-by-step directions for completing the LSI, which begins on LSI-1. Review the directions with your students. The design for the inventory will make filling out the answers easy for your students. If you are assigning the LSI as homework, consider walking students through the scoring process in class first. Or ask them to hold off scoring the inventory until they're in class with you. Refer to page LSI-2 to help your students interpret their results. Guide them in using the interpretive material—help your students connect it with their own experience. Doing so will pay big dividends. Not only will your students begin to understand why they make the choices they do, but they'll be better partners in the learning process.

Be sure to review the Cycle of Learning with your students. These three examples will be easily identifiable to all of your students and will encourage them to put the information they have discovered about themselves into practice right away. Begin your discussion by asking students about their preferred way to learn historical information or new technology. Once you have your students in the proper mindset to think about their learning style, they will be better prepared to read the Master Student Map at the beginning of each chapter and will understand the value of completing the Learning Styles Application at the end of each chapter.

Beginning on page 37, the article "Using your learning style profile to succeed in school" will have your students participating in a Mode 4 activity. In the Career Application feature at the end of Chapter One, your students will be invited to think specifically about learning styles and their application in the workplace.

Students can use their understanding of learning styles to make choices that support their academic progress. Ask them to consider these questions:

- **"Why** should I involve myself in this learning situation?"

- **"What** will I need to do in order to understand the concept?"

- **"How** is this learning meaningful to me?"

- **"What if** I apply this strategy to my other courses or to my life?"

Integrating knowledge of learning styles into the curriculum can help teachers design a course that promotes success for all students. As we choose our teaching methods to address various preferences at different points in the course, we meet different students' needs. Students in your classes typically represent all four modes of learning, so some students will sometimes find a good fit with what we're doing, while at other times they'll need to stretch beyond their preferences. Acknowledging different learning styles allows instructors to shift their energy from lecturing to facilitating. Rather than just focusing on the transfer of knowledge, use feedback about your students' learning to inform your teaching. Students come to realize that their interactions shape what happens in the classroom, and they become active participants in constructing their learning experience. Working together, instructors and students create an environment that promotes success.

The article "Adapting to styles in the workplace" will also provide you with an initial opportunity to discuss the value of understanding learning styles, and appreciating differences as they apply beyond the classroom.

More suggestions for creating lesson plans that support all four modes of learning are available on the HM ClassPrep CD. In addition, video clips from the *Learning Style Inventory* video—an overview of the LSI and its application, available free to adopters—are available on the HM ClassPrep CD. ▨

Icebreakers

Some ideas for first-day-of-class activities

Creating a sense of community in your classroom starts during your first class meeting. Icebreakers can help both you and your students create a comfortable environment that supports self-discovery and honest reflection—two processes that will help your students achieve success. Use these suggested exercises to get you started, and refer to the HM ClassPrep CD for more activities related to specific chapters that can be used at any time throughout your course.

Master Student–themed exercises

From Master Student to Master Employee has many unique messages in the beginning of the text. These messages are helpful for instructors to remember and highlight when starting the course.

"This book is worthless." How many books start out with this statement? All books are worthless unless read, so this book is useless unless students strive to adapt and adopt methods to attain personal and academic success. Students often complain about the cost of their textbooks. Yet the cost is even higher when they are paying for a text but are not actively reading it and implementing its strategies to promote their success. Ask your students to vow that they will get the most out of their investment by delving into their textbooks for hidden treasures. These exercises are pure gold: "Textbook reconnaissance," "The Discovery Wheel," "Learning Style Inventory."

What is a Master Student? Student success courses are offered at colleges and universities nationwide. Students often exhibit less resistance to taking this course when they realize that their school is not the only one requiring it. The qualities of a successful student are also the qualities of successful employees. This course can help students define the characteristics that promote excellence in their studies, and relationships, and preparation for the world of work. Have your students review the article "Discovering Mastery" in Chapter One. Divide them into groups of three and ask them to list the qualities of people they admire (family members, celebrities, or friends). When each group has named 10 characteristics, create a combined list of 20 for the entire class. Ask students to rank in order the qualities that might contribute to success in school, work, and life.

Ask your students to consider these qualities of success and then write an essay entitled "How do I define success?" Submit the best essay to the Houghton Mifflin Student Success scholarship competition (see complete details on page AIE-xx).

From the desk of . . . *From Master Student to Master Employee* includes a unique feature called "From the desk of . . ." These are real voices from the workplace providing students with insight on how they might apply the strategies for success in the classroom to their future careers. Your students can start adding their voice to this textbook right away. Many of your students may have experiences in the workplace, as a full-time employee, a part-time employee, during a summer job, or even volunteer work. Adult learners who might be returning to the classroom from raising a family also have valuable voices to share. Ask your students to contribute their insights and ideas from their experiences, or predict those skills that will help them in their intended career choice. Your students can share their ideas by submitting their "student voice" on our Web site:

masterstudent.college.hmco.com

(or by e-mailing directly to **collegesurvival@hmco.com**). Here they can share information about any article or exercise that they have found to be most valuable to their growth during the course—and why. Ask your students to suggest ways in which *From Master Student to Master Employee* could be valuable to next year's first-year students.

"What do you want?" Research indicates that more than 60 percent of first-year college and university students are not yet sure of their career choice, even if they have declared a major. A student might choose a major because of parental pressure or the institution's policy rather than because of a passionate commitment to that field of study or career. This lack of clarity about her destination could negatively affect a student's level of dedication and involvement. She might experience a lack of desire or frustration when she encounters difficulties because she does not sense that current distresses might result in long-term benefits.

When they are asked "What do you want?" students can begin to find answers to what they hope to accomplish in the course, in the term, and in the academic year. Consider having your students share their answers in class, in small groups. A free seven-minute video, *What*

Do You Want? is available for you to use in your class to help students write about their goals.

Mastering new stuff

Trying new techniques, changing habits, and practicing new behaviors can be uncomfortable at first. However, these activities make up much of what a student success course is about. When describing the benefits of the course, it is wise to be honest about the challenges students face, while expressing confidence in their ability to succeed. Some techniques to help you make this point: Ask students to write their names with their nondominant hands, to introduce themselves to one another by shaking their left hands, or to cross their arms in reverse of the way they normally do. With practice, any of these uncomfortable activities will begin to feel natural.

➤ Encourage students to participate

Your student success course will benefit from class participation that motivates students to contribute and share. As you create a sense of community in your classroom, use these suggestions for increasing overall participation.

Plan participation activities. Break your students into small groups (2–3 students) to review articles from the textbook or assignments that may have been completed outside of class. Provide some guidelines and post them so all students can see them (on a white board, overhead projector, etc.). Suggest the number of minutes that students should talk about each question you have assigned. For example, you may ask your students to do the following: *Identify the time management strategy that was most interesting to you and describe how you plan to use it in the upcoming week (2 minutes per person).*

After your students have discussed this with their group, bring the discussion back to the classroom as a whole. Create a tally to show which strategy was the most popular. Consider discussing why some of the less popular strategies are beneficial and challenge your students to try the one they selected, and then one of the less popular strategies. As the instructor, also commit to planning to practice these new strategies and collectively report back on results during the next class period. Sharing enthusiasm with students is a master instructor quality that will help to increase positive feedback and results in your course.

Call on students rather than waiting for them to volunteer. Allow all of your students to think about questions that you are asking, permitting time for reflection and contemplation. Suggest that your students who frequently get called on first write down their answers while everyone in the class has time to think. Break the ice by selecting one of your eager students. Select students who have not had a chance to share. Remind students that participating in class is a great way to connect with the instructor, and that a student success class is a perfect classroom for practicing their public speaking skills. Challenge your students to participate in their other courses as much as they participate in this class—it's engaging!

Provide a question box. This can be just like a "suggestion box" you might find in a restaurant or store. Encourage your students to write down their questions on 3x5 cards and submit them to a box or place in your classroom. Spend a few minutes at the beginning of class or the end of class answering questions. These may spark new conversations or support lessons you have already planned about campus policies, places to seek out resources for help, and other issues that many of your students may be experiencing. Consider addressing the questions as "case studies" by asking students, "What would you tell this student to do?"

Embracing diversity

Research indicates that while successful students benefit from having a relationship with a caring and competent adult, they are most likely to excel if they receive positive support from a peer group. The information here will help you foster that sense of belonging and assist students of all backgrounds in sharing with each other their discoveries and insights about higher education.

Teachers and students are currently using a Master Student textbook in the United States, Canada, and many other countries. However, a variety of cultural and life experiences will most likely be represented by the students in your class. They will come from many places with varied experiences.

Additional activities in the Diversity chapter of the HM ClassPrep CD-ROM offer ways to encourage communication among students of different races, ethnicity, ages, countries of origin, and levels of familiarity with the American language and American customs.

The video *Embracing Diversity* highlights a group of students representing diverse cultures, ages, races, and religious and ethnic backgrounds. They share their personal experiences and illustrate by example effective means of communicating across cultures. Attitudes, stereotypes, and biases are examined.

One of the major goals of diversity awareness is to understand how each person fits into the lives and world of others. For some of your students, college might be their first experience with someone different from themselves. Keep in mind as you prepare for your course that some kinds of diversity can be less obvious, though just as profound, as others. To the student from rural America, a classmate from New York or Chicago might seem nearly as strange as one from Finland or Zimbabwe, and vice versa.

International students will have additional adjustment issues beyond those of the other students in your class. They are far from home in an unfamiliar culture. Keep in mind that some statements, activities, or attitudes that seem perfectly natural in our society might seem curious or even offensive to students from other countries. Familiarize yourself with cultural differences and issues that could baffle or frustrate these students and work to overcome them before they become obstacles to learning.

Finding common ground can be an important learning experience in the classroom. Routinely pairing students from different backgrounds and circumstances when assigning group projects and activities can provide students with the opportunity to encounter ideas, attitudes, and experiences different from their own. Throughout the semester, schedule activities or exercises that accentuate the similarities among your students and also celebrate the differences.

School strategies

Promote participation. Involving students in school activities challenges them and stimulates their interest. Promote the benefits of participating by placing "ads" in school newsletters and putting notes on bulletin boards. Design and display posters. Ask other teachers to announce school activities in their classrooms. Brainstorm ways to get more students involved. Don't overlook asking students for their ideas!

Provide tutors. Encourage students to take advantage of tutors. Maintaining or improving one's performance level and gaining confidence in academic ability help ensure student success.

Structure opportunities for friendships. Having friends is widely accepted as a critical component of making a healthy adjustment to college life and achieving academic success. Friendships can be expanded beyond immediate peer groups to include faculty members, administrative staff, counselors, role models, peers from home environments, community members, or graduate students. Organize icebreakers and get-acquainted exercises during orientation and at other school happenings. Encourage the use of name tags at these events. Sponsor social activities that include faculty and staff as well as students. Encourage broad participation in all social, academic, cultural, and extracurricular events.

Examine policies and procedures. Review policies and procedures, looking for any subtle (or blatant) messages of racism or other forms of discrimination. If there is no clear disciplinary procedure for infractions of any policy, implement one.

Promote resources. New students who are unfamiliar with the resources at your school won't use them. Asking the administrators and staff who are responsible for these resources to describe their services during student orientation is only the beginning of what's possible.

Ask administrators and directors of service programs to speak in your class. Suggest that clubs and organizations offering services to diverse students sponsor programs to familiarize students with the resources at your school. Write articles about resources for the school newsletter. An open house at which refreshments are served will encourage students to get to know the facilities and the services that are available. Ask students who have benefited from the resources to give testimonials. Create contests and games that require students to visit various offices, facilities, and services personnel.

Promote the resources at your school in such a way that they attract and serve students. Have tutors and counselors introduce themselves and make short presentations in class. Ask the student advisory board for help.

Make school inviting. Students who feel comfortable are more likely to experience success in school. Do the residence halls offer quiet places to study? Are exercise facilities available at convenient times? Are the needs for student transportation and day care facilities met? Are computers and software programs up-to-date? How long do students have to wait for assistance in the financial aid and other student services offices? What is the quality of the food service? How can registration procedures be more efficient? Do instructors post office hours and keep them? What do admissions representatives say would attract more students?

Hire from different backgrounds. Whenever possible, hiring both men and women from a variety of backgrounds will provide role models for students. Whether they are faculty, staff, or administrators, they should be knowledgeable about diversity issues and committed to being involved with students on campus.

Evaluate faculty. Conduct regular student and peer evaluations of all instructors. Include the criteria of being sensitive to the needs of students and being responsive to the learning styles of all students.

Encourage leadership. Students from diverse backgrounds who are in leadership positions help promote acceptance and inclusion of all students in all areas of school life. Sponsor leadership training programs. Encourage students with leadership potential to consider running for student offices.

Sponsor panel discussions. Invite students from a variety of populations to participate in panel discussions on a wide range of topics. Each panel member can introduce himself (including a description of what it's like to be a member of his particular population on your campus, if appropriate) and then state his point of view about the topic. The discussion can then be opened for questions and answers.

Conduct workshops. Invite faculty and staff to attend workshops on the diverse backgrounds, circumstances, and cultural differences of students at your institution.

Classroom strategies

Help ensure success. You can individualize your instruction and structure your course so that students experience success. Total success in school is achieved by taking a series of small, successful steps. Set high and realistic expectations. If your course is too easy, students will lose interest. If it is too difficult, students might become discouraged. By continually evaluating students, monitoring their progress, and getting feedback from them, you can plan your classes in ways that help ensure student success.

Provide opportunities to talk. Invite students to speak about their perspectives. Suggest that students talk to others to share their concerns, celebrations, compliments, and complaints. Use small group discussions and exercises. Promote the idea of visiting with counselors and forming peer support groups. The suggestions for conversations and sharing on the HM ClassPrep CD include many ideas for stimulating discussions.

Acknowledge and appreciate cultural differences. We can learn from each other and from exploring values that are different from our own. When we exchange ideas, we can expand our perceptions and examine our values. Use conversations and sharing seeds, publications, and special events to recognize and celebrate diversity.

Communicate the advantages of being bicultural. Learning new ways of speaking and behaving does not mean denying or letting go of our traditional languages or customs. Adding alternatives does not eliminate anything. Expanding our options increases our ability to operate effectively in a variety of situations and improves our chances of success.

Discuss how the school environment is similar to, and different from, students' home environments. Then discuss ways to make effective transitions back and forth from one to the other. Explore how the expectations of one environment can be assets or liabilities in another.

Recognize that a strength in one culture might be a disadvantage in another. Tennis rackets are great on a tennis court, but they don't work very well in a game of golf. How can a student adapt so as to be successful in both environments?

Recognize different beliefs regarding time, competitiveness, and respect for authority. In some cultures, punctuality is a plus. In others, time is not measured in hours, minutes, and seconds; instead, it is measured by the movement of the sun, the changing of the seasons, and an intuitive sense of community readiness. In some cultures, competitiveness is a common incentive toward achievement. In others, it is considered antisocial and insulting. Eye contact during conversations is considered respectful in some cultures and disrespectful in others.

You can acknowledge a wide range of beliefs and, at the same time, communicate the expectations of your institution. An advantage to being bicultural is the ability to adopt behaviors that promote success in a specific environment.

Encourage exposure to different backgrounds. Encourage students to break out of old patterns and habits by associating with people from different backgrounds, as well as with those whose backgrounds are similar to their own. They could choose new lab partners, form groups with people they don't know for in-class exercises, sit in new areas in the student union, or attend events that are likely to draw crowds different from those with whom they are comfortable. Invite your class to brainstorm ways to gain exposure to people with different backgrounds.

Survey student needs. Evaluate frequently. When you become aware that a student is struggling in a certain area, make an appointment with that student to formulate an action plan.

Individualize feedback. Students appreciate getting specific feedback about their individual performance. Write relevant comments on papers you return. Send messages and comments to students through the school mail. Thank a student who has actively participated as he leaves the classroom.

Set clear expectations. Communicate expectations clearly. State them several times in several different ways. Use examples to illustrate both what is acceptable and what isn't. Invite students to ask questions in class or to contact you during your office hours if they have any questions or concerns.

Be a mediator. As an instructor of a student success course, you can facilitate communication between students and administrators. Pass students' complaints and compliments on to the people who are most directly involved. Ask for responses from those people and report back to the students. Follow up on all communications until the matter is resolved.

Include other cultural experiences. Use speakers, textbooks, classroom materials, activities, and media presentations that incorporate diverse cultural experiences. Ask students, colleagues, administrators, and community members for recommendations.

Use a critical thinking approach. Ask students to decide what they think about relevant issues and why they think it. Then ask them to seek other views and gather evidence to support the various viewpoints. Discuss which view or views are the most reasonable. When discussing issues, you can apply the strategies outlined in the articles on critical thinking in the text to recognize any errors in thinking.

Encourage proaction. When students face uncomfortable, unfamiliar, and difficult situations, they sometimes choose avoidance. They might feel powerless or resentful and choose to withdraw rather than risk embarrassment. Help students consider the long-term costs of giving up. Help them see the benefits of a positive, healthy, and proactive approach. Suggest a variety of alternatives for dealing with the problems they face. Rather than giving up, students can garner support and find or create forums to discuss and resolve their issues.

Allow personal expression. Invite students to translate material into their own words. Ask them how certain techniques, or variations of those techniques, might be applied in their own culture.

Acknowledge student expertise. Ask students to communicate course content from their unique cultural perspective. Experiencing a concept from a different cultural perspective reinforces it. Give an assignment requiring students to combine a student success strategy with some cultural event, personality, tradition, or value. For example, they could create original music and lyrics or describe what role a particular success strategy might have played in how a cultural hero changed history.

Use guest speakers. Invite guest speakers to your class who represent successful role models. Ask them to share struggles they have experienced and successes they have achieved. Be sure to include time for a question-and-answer period.

Personal strategies

Avoid generalizations. All generalizations are suspect—even this one. Avoid tendencies to lump together all people of one race or culture. Consider speaking up when you hear generalizations being made.

Examine your own prejudices. If you have painful memories that contribute to your prejudices, judgments, and generalizations, examine them. Tell the truth about the costs and benefits of holding on to them. Look at how your history encouraged you to be prejudiced in certain ways. Talk about your prejudices and formulate a plan to heal and grow.

Examine your assumptions about students. Where do you imagine that your students go during their vacations? How would you expect them to spend extra money? What type of music do they enjoy? Who are their heroes? Which holidays do they celebrate? Listen for how often your assumptions direct your teaching and your conversations with students. How would your teaching and your conversations be different if you assumed nothing about your students?

Find a translator. Taking a First Step by admitting that we are unfamiliar or uncomfortable with students from other cultures helps us bridge the gap. Ask around to find someone who can act as a translator. In this sense, a translator is someone from the students' ethnic or cultural background who has successfully adapted to the mainstream environment. Ask students if they are willing to have this person present when you discuss various issues.

Increase your sensitivity to society's exclusions and inclusions. When we become aware of what to look for, we can see many examples of how one cultural or ethnic group excludes or includes others. Watch advertising and television shows. Listen to speeches. Examine the policies and notice the membership demographics of schools, business organizations, neighborhoods, religious institutions, athletic clubs, and social groups. Look for blatant, formal structures as well as subtle or hidden messages of exclusion and inclusion.

Reach out to students. Be sure students know your office hours. Send written invitations to each student in your class to come visit you during those hours. Talk in class about what students might gain if they schedule an appointment to see you or if they just drop in. Write your reactions to what students have written on papers before you return them. Maintain accurate records about attendance and call students when they miss a class. Use whatever appropriate methods you can think of to let individual students know that you are personally interested in their success. Be a person with whom students can form a supportive, interpersonal relationship.

Give specific feedback. Feedback promotes student success. Be especially sensitive to the unspoken expectations of the environment at your school and in your community. When feedback is given with a sincere desire to promote success, it is likely to be appreciated. ✖

Critical thinking
It's all over this book

As thinking skills are necessary from the first day of the semester, tools throughout the text are designed to prepare students for the more in-depth coverage provided in Chapter Seven: Thinking.

A first-year experience course can help students develop higher-level thinking and learning skills through self-awareness, self-regulation, and self-instruction. *From Master Student to Master Employee* offers many opportunities for critical thinking through the introduction of self-awareness tools, strategies for successful studying, and opportunities for connection with other students, faculty, and campus resources.

Self-discovery is encouraged in Chapter One through the Discovery Wheel, the Learning Style Inventory, and other learning styles models. The self-awareness that students gain through using these tools provides them with a foundation for honestly assessing their experiences for the rest of their lives. By completing the Discovery Wheel at the end of the text, students can evaluate the work they have accomplished in the semester.

Time management and financial planning are crucial skills for students to develop. The exercises in Chapter Two help students take a First Step in learning how to manage their time and think critically about their resources.

As students develop effective thinking and study skills, mastering memory, reading, note taking, and test taking, encourage them to begin to transfer these concepts to their core courses. The application of the skills requires a higher level of thinking and promotes their overall success in college.

Once students reach the Thinking chapter, they have experienced the rigors of higher education and are ready to engage in *thorough thinking*. Master students use thorough thinking to select a major, choose courses for second semester, and plan for their future. They also have experience actively employing decision making skills and are ready to transition to the next step of solving problems more creatively and confidently. They will exhibit a certain attitude towards success that is highlighted in the way they ask questions, make decisions and solve problems.

The development of more advanced thinking skills helps them transition to later chapters, where students broaden their scope to consider the impact of decisions and experiences in higher education on areas in diversity, communication, health, their careers, and life beyond.

Throughout the text, students are encouraged to participate actively in developing and implementing concepts. The ideas in the text are not a list of instructions, but tools that students can try, and then decide what works best for them.

The Master Student Map on the first page of each chapter encourages students to ask questions related to the four modes of learning identified in the Learning Style Inventory in Chapter One. These questions promote curiosity and invite students to explore and investigate new materials.

Discovery and Intention Journal Entries, which appear throughout the text, promote a form of decision-making that requires students to make declarations that lead to focused action.

Exercises and Critical Thinking in the Classroom and Critical Thinking in the Workplace activities promote the application of strategies and allow students to practice problem solving. Students develop thinking techniques and chart their own course.

Career Application exercises provide students with the chance to begin making connections to their future, and think critically about the application of the skills they learn in college to the workplace. Endorse this type of thinking by asking students to create their own scenarios that apply the skills they are learning in this course to the careers they are considering.

The tools that *From Master Student to Master Employee* provide are a foundation for this success, and as the instructor, you have the ability to foster the attitudes of a critical thinker in your classroom. Ask your students *how* they will apply these skills. Advertise how these strategies work by suggesting that students ask *what if* questions. *What if* I apply these test-taking strategies to prepare for exams in my biology course? And *what if* I do not?

 For more ideas and suggestions for integrating *thinking* into your course, see the HM ClassPrep CD. ✖

Master Instructor
Resources

The Master Instructor Resource Guides in this Annotated Instructor's Edition of *From Master Student to Master Employee* highlight many chapter-specific resource materials that are available to you through Houghton Mifflin Company. Take advantage of these valuable tools to assist you in your course. Remember to call your College Survival consultant if you have any questions about acquiring materials or integrating them into your course, or if you have a suggestion you would like to see implemented in the future.

Master Student Course Manual. The *Course Manual* provides you with further support for planning your course using the philosophy of *From Master Student to Master Employee*. It includes additional information about learning styles, lecture ideas, tips for creating lesson plans, and suggestions for teaching to a wide range of students and needs (including racial and ethnic diversity, international and ESL students, students with disabilities, and returning adults). Materials to help you evaluate and measure your course success are also included in the *Course Manual*.

HM ClassPrep CD-ROM. With chapter-by-chapter resources, lecture ideas, exercises, and quiz answers, the goal of the HM ClassPrep CD is to provide you with instructional resources that you can use in electronic form. Each resource is provided in the file format we think will be most useful to you: Word files for documents you might want to edit, video files for presentation, and PDF files for handouts. Most resources can be customized so they match exactly the way you teach your class. PowerPoint slides to enhance your lecture presentations are available on the CD as well as for download on the *From Master Student to Master Employee* Web site.

You can access the files on the HM ClassPrep CD directly through the HM ClassPrep interface. This interface organizes resources for you by chapter or by asset type. Using the HM ClassPrep interface, you can open files in their appropriate applications, use them as they are, or modify them and save them to your hard drive.

From *Master Student to Master Employee* Web site. This Web site is easily accessible for students and instructors. It is complete with new activities and resources for students, including interactive exercises, discussion groups, Internet resources, and a Master Student Hall of Fame, featuring Master Student Profiles and biographical information about the master students profiled in this book.

masterstudent.college.hmco.com

Resources for instructors on the *From Master Student to Master Employee* Web site include sample syllabi, downloadable PowerPoint slides, exercises for use with student success video programs, Internet resources, and discussion groups.

New Power Process videotape. Show your students how to put the *power* into Power Processes with this all-new video of four Power Processes: *I Create It All, Notice Your Pictures and Let Them Go, Find a Bigger Problem,* and *Risk Being a Fool*. This segmented video will enhance your lecture by bringing to life the concepts and metaphors in the text, while speaking to the auditory and visual learners in your class.

You may order this Power Process video free to adopters, closed captioned, ISBN: 0-618-56263-X, approx. 30 min.) and other videotapes by calling Houghton Mifflin Faculty Services at 800-733-1717.

Additional videos. A new 30-minute video, *The Interviewing Process: Strategies for Making the Right Impression*, takes students through the interviewing process from start to finish, providing them with strategies for successful interviews. The video covers preparation for the interview with instruction on what to wear, questions and answers to think about, and research on the company. Real-life interviewing scenarios on the video provide students with examples of the actual interview process. Also covered is what to do after the interview, including evaluating how it went, seeing what you can learn, and following up.

A financial management video, *Money and Finances*, discusses strategies to help students gain control of their finances and overcome the money problems they might currently be experiencing. Students will hear advice from financial advisor Ann Egan on income and expenses, will examine the general principles of budgeting and cash flow, and will hear a discussion on financial aid. Through real-world money challenges, including the pitfalls of credit card spending, presented by real students, this video will teach your students to develop the skills of good money management.

Each of the above videos is accompanied by a program overview to guide instructors through its contents, as well as suggestions for classroom activities. These additional aids can be found on the HM ClassPrep CD or on the *From Master Student to Master Employee* Web site.

Two free videotapes are available to instructors using *From Master Student to Master Employee*. One, for use as a guest speaker on the first day of class, includes a critical reflection exercise and is titled *What Do You Want?* This videotape, which serves as a course introduction, has a running time of seven minutes. The second tape prepares instructors to administer the Learning Style Inventory (LSI). This videotape has a running time of 23 minutes.

PowerPoint slides. For each chapter of *From Master Student to Master Employee*, PowerPoint slides can be downloaded from the *From Master Student to Master Employee* Web site. The PowerPoint slides are also available on your HM ClassPrep CD-ROM.

Online Master Student course cartridge. Course cartridge materials are available in BlackBoard and WebCT platforms. This allows you to customize your course using a course management system and provides additional materials, including Power Process Case Studies, Discussion Group prompts, and Learning Reflection journals that relate to Case Studies. Visit the Web site for more information and for an interactive demo.

HM Assessment and Portfolio Builder. The HM Assessment and Portfolio Builder tool is available for packaging with your text. This student tool is a personal assessment tool to help students learn more about themselves and prepare for success in college and career. Students will build their portfolio by responding to questions in the modules **Personal, Interpersonal, Career,** and **Community**, and by reflecting on their skills, attitudes, values, and behaviors. The **Accomplishments Report** will summarize the results of students' responses in a format that is perfect for creating a résumé or preparing for interviews. More information about this resource begins on page AIE-xxxv.

3x5 cards. Provided at no charge to teachers who purchase *from Master Student to Master Employee*, 3x5 cards facilitate classroom participation. The text and the HM ClassPrep CD suggest a variety of uses for 3x5 cards. Instructors and students often report becoming obsessed with them. They find them lurking in closets, hiding under their beds, stuck on their mirrors, pinned to bulletin boards, tucked into pockets, slipped into their notes, marking their places in books, resting next to their telephones, even replacing their address and recipe books. Some instructors ask students to carry 3x5 cards with them for a few days and jot down how they use their time. By doing so, students can monitor what they are doing and the amount of time they spend doing it.

Another way to use 3x5 cards is for attendance. Have students write their names and a question on a 3x5 card. Then have students bring their cards to class each day to hand in as their admission tickets to class. Their questions can then be used to stimulate classroom discussions.

Two-part exercise sheets. Two-part exercise sheets (up to five per book ordered) provide a way to encourage students to participate in class. The final step in any classroom exercise can be for students to write Journal Entries on two-part sheets. If you collect the original, letting students keep a copy for their own use, you can read some of the student discoveries and insights anonymously to the rest of the class. Students are interested in what their peers think. Collecting two-part sheets can also be a convenient way to take attendance.

Three-part quiz sheets. To take a more active role in learning, students can participate in grading their own quizzes by using three-part quiz sheets (up to 10 per book ordered). Here's how the process works. Put the quiz questions on a transparency, whiteboard, or separate sheet of paper. Ask students to write their answers on the three-part sheet. After students complete the quiz, have them turn in the original white copy. Now ask students to look up the answers and to correct and grade their own work. (On the test form, you can indicate the number of the text page where each answer can be found and the date of the lecture, so students can refer to their notes.) Students then turn in one of the corrected copies and keep the other one for their own use. Students get immediate feedback, and you save time by not having to grade and return individual quizzes. ◰

Using your HM ClassPrep CD

Why

the HM Class Prep CD is important to your classroom . . .

Resources to support your instruction have been collected from educators whose previous experiences in the classroom have been met with success.

Access to instructional materials, provided in electronic format, allows you to easily customize and then print, e-mail or post materials to a Web site or course-management system.

What

is included . . .

Pre- and post-test retention study materials

Teaching tips

Lecture ideas

Warm-up exercises

Guest speaker ideas

Relationship building exercises

Applying skills activities

Closure exercises

Prompts for conversation and sharing exercises

Technology integration suggestions

Video discussion questions

Chapter tests

Answer keys

Final exam suggestions

PowerPoint slideshows

Video clips

Bibliography

Information on College Survival consulting services

Resources for gaining support for your first-year experience course

Information on supplementary resources

How

you can use this resource . . .

Evaluate resources while planning your course to determine in-class assignments and exercises you will use throughout the semester.

Invite guest speakers to your course at the start of the term.

Practice using technology resources.

As you review the Annotated Instructor's Edition, ask yourself

What if . . .

I need help teaching a certain skill or concept to my students?

Please note: Technical Support is available if you have difficulty using your HM ClassPrep CD by calling Houghton Mifflin Software Support at 1-800-732-3223 (Monday through Thursday, 9 a.m. to 8 p.m. Eastern time, Friday 9 a.m. to 5 p.m. Eastern) or sending an e-mail to **support@hmco.com.**

Connecting the HM Assessment
Portfolio Builder to your course

The *HM Assessment and Portfolio Builder* is a personal assessment tool that engages students in self-assessment, critical thinking, and goal setting activities to prepare them for college and the workplace.

Students build a portfolio by responding to questions about their *skills, attitudes, values, and behaviors* in four key life areas: **Personal, Interpersonal, Career,** and **Community**. The **Accomplishments Report** summarizes the results of their responses, and asks students to provide supporting evidence for response in which they rated themselves as highly proficient. This provides great practice for honing critical thinking skills as well as preparing for creating a résumé or preparing for interviews. Using the HM Assessment and Portfolio Builder will help students further highlight and develop their transferable skills.

Using this tool with *From Master Student to Master Employee* will help students to gain early insight into their long term goals and help them to create plans for improving and enhancing their skills during their time in college.

Once students have completed the assessment and begin to work on their Accomplishments Report, they may need additional support materials to build their proficiency in certain areas. Students can link to Houghton Mifflin's Career Resource Center, which offers articles, exercises, and ideas to help students succeed on their journey from college to career. **The Bridge from College to Career** lets students practice new skills acquired in college that can be applied as they enter the job market. **Finding the Perfect Job** helps student find-tune their résumé writing and interviewing skills. And **Skills for your Future** provides strategies for problem solving and decision making to help students learn to work with others and communicate on the job.

**You can view an interactive demo
of this product on the
From Master Student to Master Employee Web site.**

masterstudent.college.hmco.com

Contact your sales representative or your College Survival consultant about ordering a desk copy or shrinkwrapping this product with *From Master Student to Master Employee.*

A walkthrough of the features

Demo this product via our Web site. Visit each of the areas as described below and try it yourself.

- Each module (Personal, Interpersonal, Career or Community) has a series of statements. Students assess their response to each statement by selecting from four choices. Feedback is provided for each response to help guide students to making the most appropriate selection. Participate in the HM Assessment and Portfolio Builder by selecting the suitable response to each of the statements in the four sections. Those items that you have marked as *usually and consistently* will be carried over to the Accomplishments Report, the fifth module.

- Once the assessment portion has been completed, students are ready to enter evidence into their Accomplishments Report. This is the section in which they will provide supporting evidence for statements that were rated as *usually and consistently* most like their skills, attitudes, values and behaviors.

- The evidence is saved and a portfolio of accomplishments is generated from these entries. Students can view and update their portfolios throughout the semester, and print a hard copy to bring to class or as a reference during an interview.

- After an Accomplishments Report is generated, students will see which areas still need documentation and can explore information and resources for gaining experiences in college using the Career Resource Center. Students can access tips, exercises, articles, and additional Internet links to help them succeed in college and in the workplace. Suggestions for using the HM Assessment and Portfolio Builder to create a résumé and prepare for interviews are also available in the Career Resource Center.

Integrating the HM Assessment and Portfolio Builder into your syllabus

From Master Student to Master Employee offers students with many places for discovery and reflection. The HM

Assessment and Portfolio Builder is an additional resource to further support your students' goals for growth during their experience in higher education. While some instructors may be inclined to assign students to complete their Assessment during the first week of class, you may want to consider waiting until students are settled into their routines and have read or previewed through Chapter Two. Materials in the introduction and Chapter One of *From Master Student to Master Employee* will set the stage for discussions of self-discovery and getting oriented to higher education. Chapter Two will begin a dialogue about planning and goal setting. Consider assigning the Assessment at the end of your lessons on these topics.

After the assessment is completed, students should take a preliminary look at the responses that have been tallied in the Accomplishments Report and begin to fill in evidence in response to as many of the statements as they can. Ask your students to write Discovery and Intention Statements after they have completed this first step. What did they discover from this exercise? What do they intend to do to continue to expand on their Accomplishments Report?

This can also be used as a goal-setting exercise. The long-term goal is to have a completed Accomplishments Report, with evidence for as many areas as possible. Students can also write Discovery and Intention Statements to outline their plan for building more experiences to support their accomplishments. For example, students could write a goal to participate in a community fundraising event to support a statement from their Community module.

Consider asking students to have at least two pieces of evidence in support of their statements for each of the four modules (Personal, Interpersonal, Career, and Community). Then, throughout the semester, encourage your students to return to their assessment and update their responses based on their growing experiences. This could be assigned as a midterm project or as part of a final project.

While the Accomplishments Report is not a substitution for a résumé, or something students would distribute to an interviewer, it is a resource to help students document their transferable skills and accomplishments. As students prepare to write their résumés in Chapter 10, they can look back at their Accomplishments Report as a reminder of skills, attitudes, values and behaviors they have exhibited during their college experience and jobs they have previously held, they will be further prepared to discuss (with evidence) how they have arrived at these accomplishments.

If your students need further support in any of the areas highlighted in the assessment, they can access the Career Resource Center for further study. You can assign readings and exercises (Questions for Critical Thought and Case Studies) for completion outside of class. Suggested assignments aligned with chapter topics for *From Master Student to Master Employee* are available on the HM Class Prep CD to accompany this textbook. Additional research on specific topic areas can also be assigned; students can begin with the related links posted on the Career Resource Center.

Master students learn best from instructors who practice the master student qualities as they teach. Take the time to complete the Assessment and Portfolio Builder yourself. Encourage your students to be active participants in their future. Hold up your Accomplishments Report and even read several of your statements aloud. Discovering mastery can be fun!